CW01665597

CHAMBERS & PARTNERS
LEGAL PUBLISHERS

Chambers Student UK

CAREERS IN THE LAW

2011

Published by Chambers and Partners Publishing
(a division of Orbach & Chambers Ltd)
39-41 Parker Street, London, WC2B 5PQ
Tel: (020) 7606 8844 Fax: (020) 7831 5662
email: info@ChambersandPartners.co.uk
www.ChambersandPartners.com

Our thanks to the many students, trainees, pupils, solicitors, barristers and graduate recruitment personnel who assisted us in our research. Also to the researchers of *Chambers UK 2011* from which all firm rankings are drawn.

ISBN: 978-0-85514-313-8

Publisher: Michael Chambers
Editor: Anna Williams
Deputy Editor: Richard Simmons
Writers: Alex Hocking, Alexis Gibbs, Amie McFadzean, Emily Lauffer, Katharine Critchlow, Kathryn Bromwich, Kira Gilmore, Lauren Long, Leila Lemghalef, Phil Roe, Sam Morris, Will Martin
A-Z Co-ordinator: Gemma Buckle
Production: Jasper John, John Osborne, Paul Cummings, Pete Polanyk, Robert Howe
Business Development Manager: Brad D. Sirott
Business Development Team: Bianca Maio, Lennie Sarkis, Liz Brennan, Neil Murphy, Richard Ramsay
Proofreaders: John Bradley, Nicholas Widdows, Sally McGonigal
Printed by: Butler Tanner & Dennis

So you want to be a lawyer...

Welcome to the 2011 edition of the *Chambers Student Guide* to careers in the law. We've written this book to give you the information, tools and confidence to help you make a sound career decision.

This guide is the only publication to offer these key ingredients:

- The True Picture: an insight into the training schemes at 125 law firms, based on in-depth interviews with hundreds of trainees. The trainees were selected by us, not by their law firms, and they spoke to us freely and frankly under the protection of anonymity.
- Chambers Reports: a look at life inside 23 barristers chambers. These reports were written after visits to each of the sets and interviews with pupils, barristers and clerks.
- Law School reviews: compiled after feedback from students who have completed courses at each of the schools, plus interviews with course directors.
- Additional online advice and information in key areas including: details of the recruitment procedures at the top firms including tips from trainees and recruiters; and in-depth interviews with managing partners and training partners detailing their firms' strategies for the future.

Chambers and Partners publishes guides to the legal professions around the world. You will benefit enormously from using our *Chambers UK* guide to refine your search for a law firm or chambers to train with. The best performing firms and sets in over 65 areas of practice are identified by way of league tables in *Chambers UK*, and you can get all this information online, for free, by visiting www.chambersandpartners.com.

All the guides we publish have one thing in common – they are independent. In a market flooded with publications for law students we take great pride in this fact. No one's money influences what we say about them.

The *Chambers Student Guide* could be the most useful thing you read this year, so get stuck in and we wish you great success for your future career.

The Student Guide team
September 2010

Contents

• This guide, if used properly, can greatly ease the process of pursuing a career in the law

1: Becoming a Lawyer

Calendar of events and deadlines 9
Avoid missing law fairs and crucial application deadlines for training contracts and vacation schemes

What kind of lawyer do you want to be? 14
- Do you want to become a solicitor or a barrister?
- Learn about the different types of law firms
- What is a training contract?
- Trends affecting the recruitment market
- Some other career options
- What do recruiters really want?

Useful work experience 33
- Pro bono activities and volunteering
- Vacation schemes and the firms that offer them

Applications and selection 40
- How to make successful applications
- How to succeed at interviews and assessment days
- How to manage job offers

2: Law School

Solicitors' and barristers' timetables 46

The Graduate Diploma in Law (GDL/CPE) 48
- How non-law graduates become law students
- Our table of course providers

The Legal Practice Course (LPC) 52
- The lowdown on the LPC
- Our table of course providers
- Reports on all LPC providers

The Bar Professional Training Course (BPTC) 70
- The lowdown on the BPTC
- Our table of course providers
- Reports on all BTPC providers

How to fund law school 77
- How to pay those huge course fees and survive

An A-Z of universities and law schools 81

3: Solicitors' Practice Areas

Summaries of the main areas of legal practice. 89
Including what lawyers do in each, realities of the job and current trends and issues

• Use this book in conjunction with www.chambersandpartners.com to find your perfect traineeship or pupillage

4: The True Picture

What is the True Picture and how do we do our research? 134

Jargonbuster 136
All those confusing legal terms explained

Table of firms 138
Listed by size of firm, number of trainees and location

The True Picture reports 141
Trainees lift the lid on life inside 125 law firms. If you thought all firms were the same then think again

5: Refine Your Search

The application and selection methods of the top firms 519

Our table of salaries and law school sponsorships 525

Picking a firm for its overseas opportunities 535

6: A-Z of Solicitors

The phone numbers, addresses and e-mails you need to make your applications, plus loads of really useful facts and figures on the top law firms. All in simple, easy-to-follow A-Z format 539

7: The Bar

Barcode 678
Unfamiliar terminology explained

A career at the Bar 679
An overview of a career at the Bar and tips for applying

The Inns of Court 684

Practice areas at the Bar 686
Summaries of the main areas of practice at the Bar

Chambers Reports 694
What's it really like to train at some of the country's leading sets? Our reports will help you find the right match

An A-Z of barristers chambers 745

Useful contacts 768

Becoming a Lawyer

Calendar of events and deadlines	9
What kind of lawyer do you want to be?	14
What is a training contract?	18
Trends affecting the recruitment market	19
Some other career options	22
How suitable are you and what do recruiters want?	30
Pro bono and volunteering	33
Vacation schemes	34
Applications and selection	40

- **Procrastination is the thief of time:** Plan well ahead to ensure against missing deadlines for vacation scheme and training contract applications. These deadlines are strictly applied, and one minute late is usually too late.

top tip no. 1

Calendar of events 2010

Law Fairs

October 2010

13	Queen Mary, London; University of Kent
14	Northumbria University
20	University of Nottingham
27	City University, London; University of Liverpool; University of Cambridge (Solicitors)

November 2010

1	University of Leeds
2	University of Leeds; Cardiff University
3	University of East Anglia; University of Exeter; University of Hull; University of Reading; Queen's University Belfast
4	University of Exeter; University of York
9	University of Leicester; University of Sussex
10	LSE
11	LSE
13	University of Oxford
15	UCL; University of Newcastle; University of Warwick
16	UCL; University of Manchester
17	SOAS; University of Birmingham; University of Bristol
18	University of Southampton; University of Bristol
22	University of Durham
23	University of Durham
24	University of Essex; University of Sheffield
30	King's College London, University of Portsmouth

December 2010

1	King's College, London

- **Law fair strategies:**

1. Be passive and blend into the crowd: the most you'll get out of the experience is a few pens, bags and chocolate bars.

2. Pick up all the literature: you'll have sore arms and a mountain of material to plough through at a later date... if you ever get around to it.

3. Work out which firms fulfil your basic criteria and scout them out. You'll have less weight to haul home and you'll probably make a couple of worthwhile contacts. Shortlist your top picks by identifying the attending firms in advance and knowing which ones work in the geographical areas you're interested in.

4. The connoisseur's approach: know which of the attending firms work in your preferred geographical region and which specialise in the areas of law that most interest you. Ideally you'll have a couple of intelligent questions pre-prepared.

top tip no. 2

Vacation Scheme Deadlines

October 2010

31
Allen & Overy (for Winter – non-law)
Jones Day (for Winter – non-law)
Norton Rose (for Winter)

November 2010

7 Stephenson Harwood (for Winter)

15 Cleary Gottlieb Steen & Hamilton (for Winter)

December 2010

31 Latham & Watkins (for Easter)

January 2011

12 Skadden

January 2011

15 Freshfields

16 Allen & Overy (for summer – law)

28
Cleary Gottlieb Steen & Hamilton
Covington & Burling

30
Dundas & Wilson
McGrigors

31
Addleshaw Goddard
Ashurst
Baker & McKenzie
Barlow Lyde & Gilbert
Berwin Leighton Paisner
Clyde & Co
CMS Cameron McKenna
Dechert
Dewey & LeBoeuf
Dickinson Dees
DLA Piper
Eversheds
Farrer & Co
Government Legal Service
Hammonds
Hill Dickinson
Ince & Co
Jones Day (law)
Kennedys
Kirkland & Ellis
Latham & Watkins
Lawrence Graham
Lewis Silkin
Macfarlanes
Mills & Reeve
Mishcon de Reya
Nabarro
Norton Rose
Olswang
O'Melveny & Myers
Pinsent Masons
PricewaterhouseCoopers
SJ Berwin
Stephenson Harwood
Stevens & Bolton
Travers Smith
Walker Morris
Watson, Farley & Williams
Weil, Gotshal & Manges
White & Case
Withers

- **Better the applicant you know:** "If you have two candidates who look equally good but one has done the vac scheme, you'd take the vac schemer."

top tip no. 3

Vacation Scheme Deadlines

February 2011

4	Speechly Bircham
11	HBJ Gateley Wareing
13	Cobbetts, Field Fisher Waterhouse
15	Manches
17	Bates Wells & Braithwaite
25	Arnold & Porter, Capsticks, Muckle
28	Michelmores, Paul Hastings, Shoosmiths, Vinson & Elkins, Ward Hadaway, Wedlake Bell

March 2011

1	Beachcroft, Dawsons, Trowers & Hamlins
31	Bevan Brittan, Coffin Mew, Lester Aldridge, Penningtons

April 2011

9	Bond Pearce
30	Foot Anstey, Howes Percival, Pannone

July 2011

1	Brabners Chaffe Street

- **Behave appropiately on a vac scheme:** "Play it right, be professional, wear a suit as that way you may get taken along to client meetings. Remember that it's a two-week interview – don't let your guard down or get sucked into office banter."

top tip no. 4

Training Contract Deadlines

January 2011

- **16** Allen & Overy (non-law)
- **23** Bristows (February interviews)
- **31** Clifford Chance (non-law)

March 2011

- **31** Baker & McKenzie (non-law); SNR Denton (non-law)

May 2011

- **31** Bird & Bird; BP Collins (for 2012)

June 2011

- **30** DWF (graduates); Finers Stephens Innocent; Shearman & Sterling; Veale Wasbrough Vizards

• **Personality matters:** "You have to fit into the firm; you can't just go anywhere."

top tip no. 5

July 2011

- **1** Brabners Chaffe Street; Maxwell Winward; Michelmores
- **3** Foot Anstey
- **8** Salans
- **14** Bates Wells & Braithwaite
- **15** Freeth Cartwright
- **24** Bristows (August interviews)
- **29** Arnold & Porter; Government Legal Service; Trethowans
- **30** McGrigors
- **31** Addleshaw Goddard; Allen & Overy (law); Ashurst; Baker & McKenzie (law); Berwin Leighton Paisner; Bevan Brittan; Bingham McCutchen; Bircham Dyson Bell; Bond Pearce; Browne Jacobson; Burges Salmon; Charles Russell; Cleary Gottlieb; Clifford Chance (law); Clyde & Co; CMS Cameron McKenna; Cobbetts; Coffin Mew; Covington & Burling; Cripps Harries Hall; Davenport Lyons; Dawsons; Dechert; Dewey & LeBoeuf; Dickinson Dees; DLA Piper; Dundas & Wilson; DWF (undergraduates); Edwards Angell; Farrer & Co; Field Fisher Waterhouse; Forbes; Freshfields; Hammonds; Harbottle & Lewis; HBJ Gateley Wareing; Henmans; Herbert Smith; Hill Dickinson; Hogan Lovells; Howes Percival; Ince & Co; Irwin Mitchell; Jones Day; K&L Gates; Kennedys

Training Contract Deadlines

July 2011

31

Kirkland & Ellis
Latham & Watkins
Lawrence Graham
Macfarlanes
Manches
Martineau
Mayer Brown
McDermott Will & Emery
Memery Crystal
Mills & Reeve
Mishcon de Reya
Muckle
Nabarro
Norton Rose
Olswang
O'Melveny & Myers
Orrick
Osborne Clarke
Pannone
Paul Hastings
Penningtons
Pinsent Masons
PricewaterhouseCoopers
Pritchard Englefield
Reed Smith
Reynolds Porter Chamberlain
Sheridans
Sidley Austin
Simmons & Simmons
SJ Berwin
Skadden
SNR Denton (law)
Speechly Bircham
Stephenson Harwood
Taylor Wessing
Thomas Cooper
Thomas Eggar
TLT Solicitors
Travers Smith
Walker Morris
Ward Hadaway
Warner Goodman
Watson, Farley & Williams
Wedlake Bell
Weil, Gotshal & Manges
White & Case
Wiggin
Wilsons Solictors (for 2012/13)
Winckworth Sherwood
Withers

August 2011

1
Beachcroft
Gordons
Trowers & Hamlins

12
Capsticks

18
Higgs & Sons

31
Barlow Lyde & Gilbert
Hewitsons
Vinson & Elkins

September 2011

Maclay Murray & Spens
(check firm's website for date)

- **Be yourself:** Communicate like a natural human being. And don't try and be some-one you're not, as you may not be who the firm is looking for at all.

top tip no. 6

What kind of lawyer do you want to be?

Let's start with one of the most basic questions – do you want to be a barrister or a solicitor? Here we give a simple description of each.

Barrister

Ask a solicitor about the key difference between the two sides of the profession and they'll probably tell you it comes down to one thing: ego. At first glance the role of a barrister certainly looks a lot cooler than that of a solicitor. You know the deal – it's all about striding into courtrooms, robes flowing; tense moments waiting for missing witnesses and razor-sharp cross-examinations. Glamorous? It's downright sexy! The truth, of course, is that there's a great deal more to it than looking good in a wig…

Essentially barristers do three things:

- appear in court to represent others
- give specialised legal advice in person or in writing
- draft court documents

The proportion of time spent on each depends on the type of law the barrister practises. Criminal barristers are in court most of the time, often with only an hour or two's notice of the details of their cases. By contrast, commercial barristers spend most of their time on more academic pursuits in chambers, writing tricky opinions and advising in conference on complicated legal points.

Barristers must display the skill and clarity to make complex or arcane legal arguments accessible to lay clients, juries and the judiciary. Their style of argument must be clear and persuasive, both in court and on paper. It has been some time since barristers have had exclusive rights of audience in the courts, though. Solicitors can train to become accredited advocates in even the higher courts. This encroachment hasn't been an utter disaster for the Bar, although solicitor advocates are handling a lot more of the most straightforward cases. When it comes to more complicated and lengthy matters, barristers are usually still briefed to do the advocacy, not least because this is often the most cost-effective way of managing a case. As a point of interest, solicitor advocates do not wear the wig and gown and are referred to as 'my friend' rather than 'my learned friend'.

Solicitors value barristers' detailed knowledge of the litigation process and their ability to assess and advise on the merits and demerits of a case. A solicitor will pay good money for 'counsel's opinion'. Certainly in the area of commercial law, a barrister must understand the client's perspective and use their legal knowledge to develop solutions that make business or common sense as well as legal sense. If you were hoping a career as a barrister would allow you to rise above the rigours and scraping of modern-day capitalism, think again.

Of the UK's 15,300 or so barristers, over 12,000 are self-employed. This is why you hear the expression 'the independent Bar'. The remainder are employed by companies, public bodies or law firms, and they make up 'the employed Bar'. To prevent independence from turning into isolation, barristers, like badgers, work in groups called sets, sharing premises and professional managers, etc. Barristers do not work for their sets, just at their premises, and as 'tenants' they contribute to the upkeep of their chambers. A percentage of their earnings also goes to pay their clerks and administrators. Unlike employed barristers and solicitors, those at the independent Bar get no sickness pay, holiday pay, maternity leave or monthly salary. What they do get is a good accountant.

To enter practice, LLB grads need to complete the Bar Professional Training Course (BPTC) before starting a much sought-after year of 'pupillage'. Non-law grads need to first complete the Graduate Diploma in Law (GDL) before taking the BPTC. Hopefully, the set you're with will then take you on as a tenant, though you may have to look elsewhere. Once tenancy is established, you're home free (well, except for the gruelling schedule, high pressure, concerns over how much you'll earn, dedicated wig maintenance…).

Being a barrister is a great job, and the fact that this is no secret means competition is truly fierce. If your appetite has been whetted you will find much more information in the final section of this book, where we have detailed the recruitment process and laid bare some of the more obscure practices and terminology. We have also tried to give a fair assessment of some of the difficulties that aspiring barristers may encounter. The main difficulty is that there are many more aspiring barristers than can possibly achieve a career at the Bar. The **Chambers Reports** give invaluable insight into the lives of pupils and junior barristers at some of the best sets. The Bar's professional body is the Bar Council, and it is regulated by the Bar Standards Board.

Solicitor

Most lawyers qualify as solicitors: in fact, there are almost eight times as many solicitors as barristers in the UK. Their role is to provide legal services directly to lay clients, who could be individuals, companies (private or public) or other bodies. In short, clients come to solicitors for guidance on how to deal with their business or personal proposals and problems. These could be anything from drafting a will to defending a murder charge or buying a multibillion-pound business. The solicitor advises on the steps needed to proceed and then manages the case or the deal for the client until its conclusion. They will bring in a barrister if and when a second opinion or specialist advocacy is needed. The solicitor's role is much more like that of a project manager than the barrister's. There are over 115,000 solicitors in England and Wales, with practising certificates issued annually by the Solicitors Regulation Authority (SRA). The majority of them are in 'private practice' in solicitors' firms, though many thousands work in-house for companies, charities or public authorities.

Most readers will be well aware that after an undergraduate degree, law school beckons. Law grads need to take the Legal Practice Course (LPC). Non-law grads must first complete the Graduate Diploma in Law (GDL) before being eligible for the LPC. Next comes the practical training. The most common way of qualifying is by undertaking a two-year training contract with a firm of solicitors, Law Centre, in-house legal team or public body. Much of the rest of this book deals with the nature of training contracts at different firms and how to procure one. The SRA's website gives all the fine detail you could wish for as to the requirements for training.

However, there are changes afoot. A new scheme could make it possible to qualify as a solicitor without a traditional training contract, instead clocking up relevant work-based experiences. A pilot programme started in September 2008 with a small number of firms, full details of which can be found on the SRA's website at www.sra.org.uk/students/work-based-learning.page. The idea is that this alternative qualification route could dovetail with a relatively new option to take the LPC in two parts, perhaps blending study and work. From the limited feedback we've received, the pilot has prompted mixed responses within the profession. The work-based learning model has its fans, but it also has its detractors who question whether it is an appropriate way of introducing new lawyers to the profession. Should it be rolled out, it is unlikely to provide an easier route to qualification. More on the LPC changes later in this guide.

Upon satisfactory completion of their training contract and the mandatory Professional Skills Course (PSC), a person can be admitted to the roll of those eligible to practise as a solicitor. They are then fully qualified. There are even enrolment ceremonies for anyone who fancies that graduation experience for the umpteenth time!

Where people often trip up is not being fully aware of when they should apply for a training contract. This will depend on the kind of firm you hope to join. If you are studying for a law degree and you want to work in a commercial firm, the crucial time for research and applications is early on during your penultimate year at uni. If you are a non-law student intending to proceed straight to a GDL 'conversion course' before going to a commercial firm, you'll have to juggle exams and career considerations in your final year. Students wanting to enter high-street practice or many of the smaller firms usually don't need to worry about training contract applications quite so early. Unlike commercial firms, which generally offer contracts two years in advance of the start date, smaller firms often recruit closer to the start date, and possibly after a trial period of working as a paralegal.

Larger commercial firms more often than not cover the cost when it comes to their future trainees' law school fees and other basic expenses. Public sector organisations, eg the Government Legal Service, may also come up with some cash. Students hoping to practise in smaller firms soon learn that financial assistance is far from likely and this can make law school a costly and uncertain endeavour.

Needless to say, your choice of firm will shape the path of your career. A firm's clients, its work and its reputation will determine not only the experience you gain but probably also your future marketability as a lawyer. At Chambers and Partners, we've made it our business to know who does what, how well they do it and what it might be like working at a particular firm. Our parent publication *Chambers UK* will also be an incredibly useful resource for you. Its league tables show which firms command greatest respect from clients and other professionals in different areas of practice right across the country. You can search the entire thing for free at www.chambersandpartners.com and use it to help create a shortlist of firms to apply to.

In the **True Picture** section of this guide we've profiled 125 firms in England and Wales. Our goal is to help you understand what kind of firm might suit you and the kind of work you can expect to undertake when you get there. It is the product of many hundreds of interviews with trainees and we think you'll really benefit from making it your regular bedtime reading. You should also use our website www.chambersstudent.co.uk as we've also interviewed recruiters, training partners and managing partners to give you the lowdown on firms' business models, plans for the future and recruitment strategies. You should also read through the **Solicitors' Practice Areas** section of this guide to gain an understanding of what's involved in different fields of practice.

It will help if you understand the extent and nature of the solicitor's profession by grouping law firms into the following categories, starting with the biggest.

London: magic circle

The membership of this most exclusive of clubs traditionally extends to Allen & Overy, Clifford Chance, Freshfields Bruckhaus Deringer, Linklaters, and Slaughter and May. To those for whom bigger is better (bigger deals, bigger money, bigger staff numbers), this is the place to be. Corporate and finance work dominates these firms, as do international big-bucks business clients. By organising their training on a massive scale, these firms can offer seemingly unlimited office facilities, great perks, overseas postings and excellent formal training sessions. Although these five giants top many lists, not least for revenue and partner profits, consider carefully whether they'd top yours. Training in a magic circle firm is CV gold but not suited to everyone. One factor to consider is the requirement to work really long hours to keep profits fat and international clients happy. A great camaraderie develops among trainees, but be prepared to not see your other friends too often...

London: large commercial

The top ten City of London firms (including the magic circle) offer over 800 traineeships between them each year, representing approximately 15% of all new training contracts registered with the SRA. In terms of day-to-day trainee experiences, there's not such a huge difference between the magic circle and the so-called 'silver circle' firms such as Herbert Smith, CMS Cameron McKenna, Hogan Lovells and a few others. Training contracts at these chasing-pack firms are strongly flavoured with corporate and finance deals and, again, international work. The salaries match those paid by the magic circle, which is only fair given that many of the lawyers work equally hard.

London: American firms

Since the mid-1990s, there has been a steady stream of firms crossing the Atlantic to take their place in the UK market. Currently around 40 of them offer training contracts to would-be UK solicitors, with new schemes popping up all the time. We'd suggest staying eagle-eyed if you've a thing for stars and stripes. At the risk of over-generalising, these firms are characterised by international work (usually corporate or finance-led), smaller offices, more intimate training programmes and rather long hours. On the other hand they usually give trainees a good amount of responsibility and, famously, many of them pay phenomenally high salaries. Lawyers at the hotshot US firms frequently work opposite magic circle lawyers on deals; indeed many of them were previously magic circle and top-ten firm partners or associates. The arrival of the US firms has had a knock-on effect on City law, not least on City salaries, which soared over the past decade before stalling when the recession hit.

London: mid-sized commercial

Just like their bigger cousins, these firms are mostly dedicated to business law and business clients. Generally, they don't require trainees to spend quite so many hours in the office; however, some of the most successful mid-sizers – eg Macfarlanes and Travers Smith – give the big boys a run for their money in terms of profitability. Ostensibly, the size of deals and cases in these firms means trainees can do much more than just administrative tasks. The atmosphere is generally a bit more intimate than at the giants of the City, with the greater likelihood of working for partners directly and, arguably, more scope to stand out within the trainee group. You shouldn't expect such an international emphasis to all the work.

London: smaller commercial

For those who don't mind taking home a slightly more modest pay cheque in exchange for better hours, these firms are a great choice. After all, money isn't everything (note: those of you subscribing to Gordon Gekko's 'greed is good' credo see above and read no further). Usually these firms will be 'full-service', although some may have developed on the back of one or two particularly strong practice areas or via a reputation in certain industries. Real estate is commonly a big deal at these firms. Along with commercial work, a good number of these smaller firms offer private client services to wealthier people. At firms like these you usually get great exposure to partners and there's less risk of losing contact with the outside world.

Niche firms

London is awash with firms specialising in areas as diverse as aviation, media, insurance litigation, shipping, family, intellectual property, sport... you name it, there's a firm for it. Niche firms have also sprouted in areas of the country with high demand for a particular service. How about equine law in Newmarket? If you are absolutely certain that you want to specialise in a particular field – especially if you have already worked in a relevant industry – a niche firm is an excellent choice. You need to be able to back up your passion with hard evidence of your commitment, however. Many of these firms also cover other practice areas, but if any try to woo you by talking at length about their other areas of work, ask some searching questions.

Regional firms

Many of you will agree that there is more to life than the Big Smoke. There are some very fine regional firms acting for top-notch clients on cases and deals the City firms would snap up in a heartbeat. There is also international work going on outside the capital. The race for training contracts in the biggest of these firms is just as competitive as in the City. Some regional firms are even more discerning than their London counterparts in that applicants may have to demonstrate a long-term commitment to living in the area. Understandable, as they hardly want to shell out for training only to see their qualifiers flit off to the capital. Smaller regional firms tend to focus on the needs of regional clients and would therefore suit anyone who wants to become an integral part of their local business community. Salaries are lower outside London, in some cases significantly so, but so is the cost of living. There's a perception that working outside London means a chummier atmosphere and more time for the gym/pub/family of an evening, but do bear in mind that the biggest and most ambitious regional players will expect hours that aren't so dissimilar to firms with an EC postcode.

National and multi-site firms

Multi-site firms are necessarily massive operations, some of them with office networks spanning the length and breadth of the country and overseas. To give you just two examples, Eversheds has nine branches in England and Wales plus many overseas; DLA Piper has six in England and many more overseas. These firms attract students who want to do bigger-ticket work outside London – a sometimes unwelcome consequence of which is that they do London levels of work for a lower salary. Some of the multi-site firms allow trainees to stay in one office, whereas others expect them to move offices. Make sure you know the firm's policy or you could end up having a long-distance relationship with friends, family and your significant other while you move to a new town for a few months or are saddled with a punishing commute. The work on offer is mostly commercial, although some private client experience may be available.

General practice/high street

These range from substantial, long-established firms in town centres to sole practitioners working above shops in the suburbs. They act for legally aided clients, individuals funding themselves and local businesses. Staple work includes landlord and tenant problems, conveyancing, personal injury, employment, family, wills and probate, and crime. Given the changes to Legal Aid funding, these firms now need to take on more privately paying and commercial clients just to stay afloat. Be prepared to earn considerably less than your peers in commercial practice, and don't expect there to be an abundance of amenities or resources in the office. Excessively long hours are unlikely unless you're on a rota for police station duty, in which case you'll be paid extra for that. If you want to grow up fast as a lawyer and see how the law actually affects individuals and the community in which you practise, then this is the kind of firm to go for. Larger firms may take up to half a dozen or so trainees a year; the smallest will recruit on an occasional basis. It is in this part of the profession where salaries are the lowest, often the minimum required or recommended for trainees by the SRA.

As of 1 August 2010:

- Minimum salary Central London = £18,590 pa
- Recommended salary Central London = £19,040 pa
- Minimum salary elsewhere = £16,650 pa
- Recommended salary elsewhere = £16,940 pa

Anyone thinking of entering the Legal Aid sector should be aware that dramatic changes are affecting the public funding of legal services. We discuss this in considerable detail on www.chambersstudent.co.uk.

What is a training contract?

Basically, a training contract is the step between your academic life and your life as a fully qualified solicitor.

Most training contracts are full-time and last two years. Part-time options are much rarer: they last three years and allow you to take the LPC (or GDL) while training part-time. There is also a part-time option for those who have already completed their LPC. It involves working a minimum of two and a half days per week for up to four years.

Training contracts must comply with SRA guidelines. The most important of these are:

- It's a *training* contract not an *employment* contract: this means it is nearly impossible for you to be sacked. For a training contract to be terminated there must be mutual agreement between the firm and trainee, a cancellation clause (like failing the GDL or LPC), or a formal application to the SRA when issues cannot be resolved internally. Instances of trainees being fired are extremely rare: one was that of actor Gerard Butler, who was rumoured to have been fired the week before qualification because he was always drunk and miserable.
- Trainees must gain experience in at least three areas of English law and experience both contentious and non-contentious practice. Some firms send trainees on litigation courses that allow the fulfillment of the contentious requirement without them having to do a full contentious seat.
- Trainees must complete the Professional Skills Course.

The norm is to spend time in four departments over the two years (six months in each). Each stint is called a seat. At some firms you'll find yourself doing six four-month seats or some other more bespoke arrangement. At very small firms it's likely that your training won't be as structured. Repeating a seat is common, more so during six-seat schemes.

Besides the SRA's requirements, some firms may demand that you do a seat in one or more particular departments over the course of your training. For the other seats, firms usually ask you to identify your preferred departments and try to best accommodate your wishes. However, the most common gripe we hear from trainees is over the fairness of seat allocation – keep in mind that you can't always get what you want.

You will be allocated a supervisor in each seat who will be responsible for giving you assignments and helping out with any questions. Supervisors are typically mid-level to senior associates or partners. Usually you will share an office or sit near to them in an open-plan setting. You may also spend a seat seconded to one of your firm's clients or in one of its overseas offices. Appraisals are important and most firms will arrange a formal meeting between trainee and supervisor/HR at the end of each seat and probably also midway through.

What the experience entails:

- Long hours are a given; however, they are more likely when you work at a large, international or corporate/finance-focused firm. They are less likely at litigation-led firms and smaller domestic advisory or boutique firms.
- There is a hierarchical structure to law firms, and while this is felt more strongly at some firms than others, be prepared to start at the bottom.
- Luckily, you will have the rest of your trainee intake as back up. Trainees tend to be close-knit and most firms provide some sort of budget for trainee socialising. Larger firms with more trainees tend to have more active social scenes.
- You're not guaranteed a job at the end. If you've done well, the firm will retain you on qualification, finding you a job in a department that you've come to love... or in a department that needs new junior lawyers. The firm that trained you is not obligated to keep you: your contract is for the period of your training only. Our research shows that about 76% of qualifying trainees stayed at their firms in 2010, the other 24% either elected to look elsewhere or were forced to. You should regard your training contract as a two-year job interview.

The main thing to remember is that the purpose of training is to learn about several areas of practice and find your spot in the profession. One training partner put it perfectly when he said: "*Trainees should view the training contract as an opportunity to be a sponge and soak up all the right ways to be the lawyer they want to be. Keeping an open mind and soaking up the most idiosyncratic things can really put you ahead.*"

Trends affecting the recruitment market

You're probably already aware that this is a tough time to try and break into the legal profession. Your prospects of finding a training contract, pupillage or indeed any other kind of job were far better three years ago.

In the following feature we'll examine just how this situation has arisen – a genuinely important thing to know. We'll try and make it clear just what you're up against. But we'll also try to give you some advice to help you succeed despite the obstacles.

The recession and its effect on the legal profession

You'll be aware that the credit crunch of 2008 was followed by recession. Exactly how and why it came about need not detain us here. Subprime mortgage crisis, toxic debt, bankers bad, et cetera, et cetera. You know the drill – and if you don't, you need to go away and do some serious catching up if you really have aspirations to be a lawyer. Check in with us online, we'll discuss what you need to know there.

The effect of the recession on commercial law firms has been severe. Some were hit worse than others, of course. Those with large property departments suffered as deals dried up. M&A and finance-related transactions also slowed from a torrent to a trickle, although some firms were able to beef up their insolvency practices and swear blind they'd been 'financial restructuring' lawyers all along. The collapse of major institutions such as Lehman Brothers automatically resulted in a slew of legal work, and the top British and American firms have raked in millions of pounds in fees on big restructuring and insolvency proceedings. Meanwhile, those firms that had always focused less on transactional work and more on litigation have held up reasonably well.

One ray of light in an otherwise slow legal market is the increased emphasis being placed on regulation. The credit crisis revealed fundamental weaknesses in the financial services sector – and some others – and this has led policymakers to question the wisdom of the light-touch regulation that characterised the boom years of the noughties. Greater regulation means more work for lawyers. Certain other areas of business are also cause for optimism, among them IP, life sciences and renewable energy.

None of this should disguise the fact that, in general, commercial lawyers have had less work to do and have been forced to spend many hours comparing meerkats, browsing stupid YouTube videos or checking the Test Match score on the BBC website while waiting for a deal to come through. That's if they're lucky. If they're unlucky, they will have been made redundant. It's hard to find any accurate figures for exactly how many lawyers have lost their jobs – for obvious reasons firms like to keep redundancies quiet if they can. An article in *The Lawyer* magazine said 4,263 lawyers were ditched at the UK top 200 between autumn 2007 and spring 2010, but we can't say how accurate this is. Whatever the actual figure, it's definitely a lot.

The recession has exposed just how fragile the finances of some firms are. The obvious example to cite is that of Halliwells, a 'swashbuckling' Manchester-headquartered firm that collapsed in the summer of 2010. Ill-advised over-optimism contributed to its downfall: the downturn exposed the weaknesses at its heart. Halliwells was a large firm bringing in millions of pounds in revenue. A logical and reasonable question to ask is: Will every firm that is featured in this year's **True Picture** still exist in a year's time? Answer: Probably, but no one gives guarantees these days. If you're wondering what happened to the current and future trainees at Halliwells, the answer is that other firms stepped into the breach. Bristol firm Burges Salmon deserves particular mention for having set up a 'clearing pool'.

We've talked about the effect of the recession on commercial firms. The world of private law has not been so badly affected, although firms working in this area have their own problems to face. They must now confront 'Tesco law' and/or major changes being made to how the UK's Legal Aid system works. You can read about Legal Aid in much more detail on our website.

Longer-term consequences

As we write in September 2010, the worldwide recession is by no means over. Even the experts can't decide whether the 'green shoots' of recovery will flourish or wither here in the UK. It's an undeniable fact that whichever brand of government we ended up with after the general election would have had to make major cuts to public spending. The significance of the coalition government's approach to cuts is going to be massive. In March 2010, the OECD estimated that the public sector accounted for 53.4% of gross domestic product, compared to 40% when Labour came to power in 1997. The intention of the coalition government seems to be a re-engineering of the UK economy from one that is quite so heavily state managed to one that is more private sector led. While the transition itself may gift some law firms new business, it may also take it from others, unless those firms themselves re-engineer their service lines. Of course the very process of reining in public spending during a fragile economy could actually push the UK into the dreaded 'double-dip' recession scenario. Only the passage of time will tell. It might turn out well, especially for the likes of private equity and hedge funds and the lawyers who advise them.

We've spoken to dozens of managing partners and other senior lawyers in the course of our research this year and none of them are sticking their heads in the sand. They know the UK and world economies will deliver real challenges. However, they have an even more immediate concern: clients have seen the light on the level of fees law firms have been charging. With tighter budgets, clients are now demanding greater value for money. Law firms are being forced into a re-examination of their business models and many are discovering there are more efficient ways of providing their services. As a first measure, they are exploring alternative billing models: for example, charging one fixed fee for a job, rather than by the hour. But that's just the start...

The spinning jenny did for cotton workers, offset lithography decimated the print trade, video killed the radio star and new technology may well end the need for firms to employ legions of trainee solicitors. An increasing number of the functions performed by lawyers are now capable of being performed by legal software packages. Of course, there are tasks where human beings are still required, but paying a newly qualified solicitor £50,000 (or even a paralegal £20,000) is often not the most economical way of getting them done. As one senior partner of a major national law firm told us, clients will be happy to continue to pay lawyers for their legal expertise but not for processes that can be done by cheaper non-qualified staff. Globalisation means firms can easily outsource low-level tasks, such as document review, to countries like India or South Africa, where they can be completed by equally bright staff for much less. Several firms are already doing this: Eversheds is the prime example, but several top City outfits and other national firms are also outsourcing to a greater or lesser extent or sending work to cheaper parts of the UK.

The Legal Services Act

The Legal Services Act was introduced in 2007 to much controversy within the profession because of its radical new ideas: the Act permits non-lawyers to invest in and operate law firms. The reforms have been phased in slowly to allow the profession time to adjust, but change is almost certainly on its way. From March 2009 solicitors were permitted to form partnerships with non-solicitors such as barristers, legal executives or other professionals including HR and IT personnel. These Legal or Multi Disciplinary Partnerships (L/MDPs) mark a liberalisation of the partnership model. Nevertheless, a stake in a law firm is still only available via the holy grail of partnership, and under MDPs and LDPs at least 75% of partners still have to be lawyers.

The second wave of reform (set to take effect on 6 October 2011) is more radical still. Alternative Business Structures (ABS) could split the legal services market wide open. Lawyers will be able to team up with other professionals to offer a range of services to clients; insurance or estate agency, for instance. A high-street practice could find a house, secure mortgage arrangements and handle the conveyancing – all under one roof. ABSs will also be able to seek external investment. It's early days, but there are indications that a few firms are considering this option. Those with expansionist instincts should be able to tap into reserves of private capital to fund lateral hires, office renovations or additional branches. ABSs also open the door to the possibility of law firms floating on the stock market. 'Going public' is probably best suited to firms whose legal services are 'commoditised', that is, non-complex services such as personal injury, wills and probate and conveyancing that can be standardised though investment in technology and processes. Australian PI, family and probate specialist Slater & Gordon was the first to take the plunge when it floated on the Australian Stock Exchange in 2007. Its profits have soared and its enhanced war chest has enabled it to acquire smaller firms across Oz.

While the potential benefits of external investment are clear, the main concerns focus on the influence investors could wield over the management of firms and the potential ethical consequences. After all, investors will want a good return on their money. Furthermore, welcoming outside investment means surrendering some executive decision making. This marks a hugely significant cultural shift in the profession.

Mr Justice Darling commented 90 years ago that 'the law courts of England are open to all men like the doors of the Ritz Hotel'. Arguably this observation still rings true today. The Act aims to redress this issue by making legal services as accessible as the obligingly open doors of your local supermarket – quite literally – by allowing almost any company to offer legal services. In the future it may be possible to write your will at a bank or buy divorce services alongside your weekly shop. The prospect of so-called 'Tesco law' is still a way off, although The AA and Halifax are among the organisations that already offer limited legal services, generally related to their existing sectors. The AA focuses on personal injury, while Halifax handles conveyancing; wills and probate; and inheritance tax issues. It currently outsources its work to a panel of law firms but may eventually employ its own legal staff. That, of course, might mean less work for 'real' firms that offer the same type of services.

All these changes are being introduced in the name of increased efficiency and greater competition, each designed to benefit consumers. And yet recent surveys suggest that many members of the public and the profession remain unsure as to the wisdom of Tesco law. So, while high-street practices may find themselves competing against well-known companies that can take advantage of economies of scale, consumers may decide they still prefer tried-and-tested local firms. The key issue may turn out to be the pricing of services, which in turn could affect the demand for lawyers and the salaries they command.

In conclusion: law firms have had to re-evaluate what they do, where, for whom, and at what price. They need to be leaner and meaner. As a general rule (though there are exceptions) they are cutting back on their recruitment of junior lawyers. And all at a time when law schools are working overtime to churn out more and more GDL, BPTC and LPC students, many of whom have paid for a qualification they will never use.

So should you give up on a legal career?

Well, no, not just yet. We make no apologies for painting such an uncertain picture of the future, but of course the world will always need lawyers. You should, however, consider your options very carefully before parting with hard-earned cash to pay for law school. See our feature on **How suitable are you and what do recruiters want?** on page 30 to assess your chances. Briefly, though, the best and the brightest graduates will always attract attention from firms.

When speaking to recruiters a couple of years ago, all the chat was about widening access to the profession. Firms were keen to boast about how many university law fairs they attended, and about what diverse backgrounds their trainees came from. Many still do this, but this year we noticed a number of recruiters bluntly stating that they are now looking at a handful of 'key' universities that have served them well in the past. Essentially, with less of a budget to go out recruiting with, there has been a flight to perceived 'quality' universities. Great, if you're at Oxford, Cambridge, Durham, Bristol, Edinburgh et al, but not so encouraging if you attend a less prestigious institution. We don't know if this trend will intensify or fade away as the economic conditions play out.

If you're serious about getting a training contract or pupillage, there are things you can do to improve your chances. Firstly, work your socks off at university. A 2:2 degree is less and less likely to get you anywhere in a professional career. Yes, there are always exceptions, but they are just that – exceptions. Secondly, common sense suggests that if you apply to 100 firms, you are more likely to get a training contract interview than if you apply to ten. In this case, common sense is misleading. Recruiters are incredibly adept at spotting copy-and-paste applications. You will almost certainly meet with more success by targeting a dozen or so firms that you really want to work at, researching them properly and spending a great deal of time perfecting your application to them. Quickly dashing off as many application forms as you can and changing the firm name on each identical cover letter is a waste of your time. We bang on about this again in our feature on **Making successful applications**. Thirdly, get as much legal experience as you can as soon as possible to demonstrate your commitment to the profession. By as soon as possible, we mean NOW.

Pay and prospects

Lawyers' pay remains excellent for now. While some firms made salary freezes or cuts in 2009, many of them seem to be getting back on track. One US firm became the first in the City to pay its NQs £100,000 a year, but there's no suggestion that a pay boom is coming. Minimum trainee salaries are set by the Solicitors Regulation Authority: in 2010 they were not increased beyond 2009 levels – £18,590 in Central London and £16,650 elsewhere. However, the average starting salary for a trainee in Central London is much higher: £34,148 according to the last Law Society report in 2009. The lowest average starting salary is in Wales, where it's £17,790.

Finally, those who do manage to get a training contract should be well placed for the future. Over 82% of qualifiers at our **True Picture** firms were retained in 2008: the highest NQ retention rate we've ever recorded. In 2009, many firms announced qualification jobs much later, and the retention figure dropped to 74%. That's the lowest we've ever recorded – but still not nearly as bad as some of the dire predictions we were hearing earlier in 2009. In 2010 we found that at least as many firms had delayed their NQ job decisions, some until just a week or two before qualifiers completed their training contracts. This year our data shows that 76% of qualifiers were retained by our True Picture firms – a marginal improvement on 2009, but by no means back to '08 levels. You can go to our website for further analysis and retention stats for every firm we've ever covered in the True Picture since 2000.

Some other career options

There are a number of different roles and organisations to look at other than becoming a solicitor or barrister in private practice. Here are a few of the main ones.

Working in-house for a company

The commercial sector employs around 15,000 in-house lawyers; for example, there are many in the banking, utilities, telecommunications and entertainment industries. In England and Wales, some 48 companies offer in-house training contracts, including Sainsbury's, EDF Energy and Vodafone. The Commerce & Industry Group has recently made promoting in-house training contracts to aspiring lawyers one of its priorities. It has produced a list of companies which offer in-house training, which you can find on our website. Aspiring solicitors are welcome to contact the group (www.cigroup.org.uk) for more information, while aspiring barristers should contact the Bar Council. It's also worth keeping an eye on the legal press and in *The Times* on Thursdays to see who is recruiting.

We spoke to one junior solicitor who had trained in-house with a major international company. She started working with the company as a legal secretary and then "*when it was discovered I had a law degree, I was encouraged to go to law school.*" The company paid for her LPC and she was asked to help find out how the organisation could become an accredited training contract provider. Four years later our source is a content in-house lawyer: "*You get such a mixed bag of work; I will start the day doing contracts and end on regulatory work.*" Flexibility and good time management are important: "*All day people will turn up at your desk and ask for five minutes of your time.*" You do have to be a jack-of-all trades rather than specialising in one area: "*We are the GPs of the legal world: we are not the master of anything but cover a wide area.*" In-house lawyers retain a strong network of contacts across the industry. Finding out which companies offer training is also "*all about networking and making contracts: the C&I Group has a mentoring system and dinners which you can attend.*"

Unless an organisation publicises vacancies, usually its trainees will be recruited after having already worked there in some other capacity – often as a paralegal or equivalent. Even then they will have needed to exercise discretion when trying to obtain a contract. A softly-softly approach more in line with the tortoise than the hare usually works best.

Most in-house lawyers will have started out working for a law firm, switching to the role some time after qualification. The perception is that this career path offers good remuneration and better hours than available in private practice. In-house lawyers don't lose touch with private practice; indeed part of the job involves selecting and instructing law firms to provide specialist advice. This part of the job will keep you knee-deep in invites to parties, lunches and sporting events as different law firms curry favour.

Law Centres

From its roots in North Kensington in 1970, the network of UK Law Centres now stands at 56. Law Centres are not-for-profit legal practices with local management committees and a remit to 'help people to stay in their homes, keep their families together and get into employment and education.' Advice and representation is provided without charge to the public, with funding coming from local authorities, the Legal Services Commission and some of the major charities, such as the Big Lottery fund. Many have received additional funding from the Equality and Human Rights Commission. Community care, all types of discrimination, education, employment, housing, immigration, asylum and public law form the caseload. The legal problems handled may vary from one Centre to another, but all who work in the sector can be described as social welfare law specialists.

Law Centres' horizons tend to be broader than those of the Citizens Advice Bureaux, and they tend to take on cases with a wider social impact. A client with a consumer dispute is less likely to be helped than someone who is affected by, say, a local authority's decision on rent arrears. Law Centres identify trends and then use individual cases as a springboard for changing the big picture, perhaps by way of a test case that makes it to the highest courts and the broadsheets. Law Centres are also eager to involve the communities they operate within, providing legal training and education. As a Law Centre employee you might even find yourself at a local comprehensive imparting your legal know-how to teenagers.

Recent reforms to the provision of Legal Aid have required Law Centres to become more target-oriented, but there is still a strong campaigning angle to the sector. Recent highlights include the Hammersmith and Fulham Law Centre winning asylum status for a former child slave, the Cumbria Law Centre saving a homeless trucker's life, and the Hackney Law Centre saving a vulnerable pensioner from homelessness.

Most Law Centres employ 10-15 lawyers and, if you're attracted to working with colleagues who share your ideals and social conscience, you may want to investigate a career in the sector. Routes to a career are as varied as the work. Newly qualified solicitors with relevant experience in private practice are taken on; so too are those who have worked as paralegals for non-profit agencies and gained supervisor-level status. A career may also begin at a Law Centre itself. Mirroring a training contract in private practice, schemes expose trainees to different fields of law and allow them to learn from specialists in each area. Law Centres often liaise closely with local firms to ensure that trainees gain wide experience.

Salaries can be less competitive than in the private sector: without wishing to sound trite, those who take up positions generally feel there is more to being enriched than being rich. Law Centres operate along different lines to private practices: there's typically less hierarchy and more of an equal say for staff at all levels (some even operate as collectives with all staff drawing the same salary). Terms and conditions at work emulate those in local government and, as such, pension and holiday provisions, etc, are good, while flexible and part-time working is common. Law Centres are keen equality and diversity employers and encourage trainees from their local community. You will need to be flexible and willing to accept new challenges. It is an exciting environment and many lawyers have gone on to take up influential roles outside of the movement.

Candidates will only be considered if they respond to an advertisement. Look for these in *The Guardian* (Wednesdays), local newspapers and a monthly publication called *Legal Action* and on the Law Centres Federation website (www.lawcentres.org.uk – updated daily). To enhance your prospects you should be able to demonstrate your interest in social justice. Earn some stripes on committees or with community groups. Working in a local authority will also give you a taste of the fields Law Centres plough. While at law school take advantage of any schemes that bring you closer to working for social justice.

Some volunteers are accepted by Law Centres to help with administration and (if accredited) translation work. Volunteers usually come via other non-profit agencies so don't expect to just walk into a Law Centre and be accepted. A voluntary role with a Citizens Advice Bureau may be easier to get hold of and would prepare you well for the type of clients served by Law Centres.

Government Legal Service

The GLS ostensibly has only one client – the Queen. In practice 'the client' includes the policymakers and managers within government departments. Lawyers include full-time litigators and those who draft new legislation and advise ministers how best to legally put policy into practice. Despite government budget cuts, the GLS will still be recruiting in 2011. Before you apply, you need to know you'll be happy to work at the interface of law and politics and deal with matters that directly impact on UK society. If the idea appeals, read our **True Picture** and **Chambers Reports** features.

Local government

There are around 3,500 solicitors, as well as a host of paralegals, legal executives and barristers employed in the local government sector. Local government lawyers advise elected council members and senior officers on a wide variety of topics including commercial/contracts, conveyancing/property, employment issues, information management, administrative law and governance. Additional work will depend on the type of local authority involved – litigation/prosecution, social care, children, consumer protection, environmental, highways and planning, education and housing to name but a few. Lawyers tend to have broader practices in smaller authorities, while those in larger ones usually specialise in an area like housing, planning, highways, education or social services. Duties include keeping councils on the straight and narrow, making sure they don't spend their money unlawfully and advising councillors on the legal implications of their actions. The typical salary for a local authority solicitor is between £30,000 and £40,000.

Trainees usually follow the same seat system as trainees in private practice but have rights of audience in courts and tribunals that outstrip those of their peers. Trainees shadow solicitors and gradually build up their own caseload. If you want a sneak preview of what it's really like then most authorities offer summer placements, some of which are paid. Contact the head of legal services at a local authority to ask for further information – the more experience you can get the better.

Be prepared to wade through the bureaucratic bog, and at times be driven to distraction by the slow machinations of local government. However, the benefits of a great training contract, variety in your day-to-day work, flexible hours and a sense of serving the community generally outweigh the downsides. A common way to climb the ladder is by hopping from one authority to another. Many local authority chief executives trained as solicitors and we are told the glass ceiling is not so prevalent in local government as it is in City law firms. Training in local government can also open doors to careers in private practice, the Crown Prosecution Service and the GLS.

Each of the more than 400 authorities in England and Wales acts as a separate employer; some offer training contracts but there's no central list of vacancies and no single recruitment office. Finding out about training contract opportunities is a challenge in itself, as is finding out which councils offer sponsorship for the GDL and/or LPC. A good starting point for research is www.lgcareers.com. Click on 'Careers A-Z' and then head for 'supporting your community'. The number of training contracts available annually currently stands at around 150. Our sources told us that although government cuts and job freezes would doubtlessly affect recruitment, a good number of councils are expected to continue recruiting trainees. Most authorities advertise vacancies on their own website and in the *Law Gazette* and *The Lawyer*. Localgovernmentlawyer.co.uk and www.lgjobs.com have good job-search functions and Solicitors in Local Government (www.slgov.org.uk) provides tons of information including testimonies from qualified solicitors and trainees. You can also try the law and public service job ads in *The Times*, *The Guardian* and *The Independent*, or even approach local authorities directly.

Crown Prosecution Service

The Crown Prosecution Service is the government department responsible for bringing prosecutions against people who have been charged with a criminal offence in England and Wales. The CPS handles all stages of the process, from advising the police on the possibility of prosecution, right through to the delivery of advocacy in the courtroom.

The CPS employs over 2,700 lawyers to handle more than 1.2 million cases in the magistrates' and Crown Courts. Its prosecutors review and prosecute criminal cases following investigation by the police. They also advise the police on matters of criminal law and evidence, some working from Criminal Justice Units that operate within police stations to combat the problem of failed prosecutions. Lawyers here advise the police on the appropriate charge for the crime, spending one day in the office preparing cases and the next in the magistrates' court dealing with administrative matters. Lawyers in the Trials Unit handle Crown Court cases, including murder, rape and robbery.

We heard glum tones from CPS staff when we spoke to them in mid-2010, as the service's training programme, which we covered quite comprehensively in last year's guide, was set to suffer as part of the spending review in October 2010. Our best advice is to keep up to date with developments on the service's website (www.cps.gov.uk). The recruitment programme is almost certainly going to be suspended for a year, but the recruitment team is confident that demand and necessity will see its return. When we hear anything, you'll see it on our website.

The armed forces

As you can imagine, the army always needs lawyers, and in good army no-nonsense fashion, it knows how to sell the position: 'No billing, no timesheets, no rat race – a job worth doing,' declares the website. Fully qualified barristers and solicitors with a good understanding of army activities and preferably some work experience under their belt can join the Army Legal Services (ALS) and expect to see all sorts of work from court-martials to international cases. You should be physically fit and aged between 24 and 32.

Potential applicants should look out for ads in the national press or send their CVs to the service. Suitable candidates are called for interview, then attend the Army Officer Selection Board at Westbury in Wiltshire. Succesful applicants are offered a Short Service Commission in ALS (initial period: four years, 210 days). Six months' training will lead on to your first legal appointment, either at home or in either Germany or Cyprus. NATO and the UN are also worth bearing in mind as future job prospects. See www.army.mod.uk/agc/9935.aspx for more details.

The Royal Air Force employs both barristers and solicitors to deal with criminal cases and prosecutions, both home and abroad. The Air Force's legal department is small but the work sounds rather interesting – areas of law covered include Air Force law, the law of armed conflict, new legislation and the host of civil issues that affect RAF personnel. A clear career progression can see you rise to the position of Squadron Leader after four years and Wing Commander after a further six. The starting salary is £37,170 and recruitment is by need rather than to an annual deadline. Visit the Directorate of Legal Services to find out more: www.raf.mod.uk/legalservices.

The Navy doesn't have such a clear recruitment path, though there might be legal opportunities available after you've signed on the dotted line and joined the Senior Service.

The police

Only Sherlock Holmes can operate for and outside of the law and get away with it. All other members of the police force are as accountable as everyone else and therefore need good legal representation when their own conduct is called into question. This is where police lawyers step in, and they can find themselves working in all sorts of areas, which aside from the aforementioned civil actions include: corporate governance; employment law and discrimination; personal injury; and safer neighbourhoods (ASBOs, Sexual Offences Protection Orders, etc.).

We spoke with the Metropolitan Police force to find out about career opportunities for law grads. Sadly, government cuts in spending have meant that this is one area that is unlikely to be recruiting at entry level for the foreseeable future. However, for those that have a passionate interest in police work, our recruiter contacts recommend voluntary positions as special constable. This is often a route taken by lawyers eager to gain experience of the law being enacted at street level, rather than in the courts. If this sounds like your sort of gig, or if you want any further information about possible vacancies, check online with your local police force.

Legal executive

If you haven't found a training contract or are thinking about moving sideways into a legal career, you could consider the Institute of Legal Executives (ILEX) course. Those who complete it become qualified in what is sometimes known as the 'third branch' of the profession. Their day-to-day work is similar to that of a solicitor, although legal executives often deal with lower-value, high-volume cases such as residential conveyancing and personal injury claims. That said, it is possible to progress to more bespoke and complex work with experience.

Over 80,000 individuals have already qualified as fellows since the creation of ILEX, and there are currently over 22,000 legal executives and trainee legal executives across England and Wales. No prior legal training is required to enrol on the course, and it is open to those holding GCSEs, A levels or degrees. This makes it suitable for school leavers, new graduates or those already engaged in a career and looking to branch out. It can be taken on a part-time basis, giving students an opportunity to combine study with practical experience.

For those with no prior legal training, the ILEX Level 3 Professional Diploma in Law and Practice is the first stage of the academic training. It usually takes about two years of part-time study and costs around £3,000 for tuition and all exam and registration fees. On completion, students become Associate members of ILEX. Associate members are entitled to use the designatory letters A.Inst.L.Ex after their name, but are required to undertake eight hours of Continuing Professional Development (CPD) each year.

The second stage is ILEX Level 6 Professional Higher Diploma in Law and Practice, which is assessed at honours degree level, again typically taking two years to complete at a cost of up to £3,200. On completion, students become Graduate Members of ILEX. Graduate members are entitled to use the designatory letters G.Inst.L.Ex after their name, and are required to undertake 12 hours of CPD.

For those with a qualifying law degree obtained within the last seven years, ILEX now offers a Graduate 'Fast-Track' Diploma. Students need to choose two subjects from the range of ILEX Level 6 Practice units (one of which must relate to the subjects studied within the law degree), and take the ILEX Level 6 Client Care Skills unit to complete their academic studies. The qualification takes around nine months to complete part-time and costs around £1,900 (including ILEX fees), depending on where you choose to study.

With both the full ILEX route or the Fast-Track for law graduates, to become a fully qualified legal Executive lawyer (ILEX Fellow) it is necessary to gain five years of qualifying experience in a legal background (at least two after completing the ILEX Level 6 or Fast Track exams). Timescales for all ILEX courses are flexible, according to personal needs, and study can be fitted around a job. There is no set time to complete the exams, so people can work at their own pace. The qualifications can be studied at a local accredited centre or via distance learning.

Once qualified, ILEX graduates end up in employment across the full spectrum of legal services from private practice to government departments and the in-house legal teams of major companies. ILEX Fellows can continue studying to become ILEX Advocates. They can now also become partners in law firms alongside solicitors and even apply for judicial appointments. Being a legal executive can be a rewarding career in its own right. For those who still want to become a solicitor, ILEX can provide a useful route to qualifying as one, even if it is by no means the quickest. Most people can seek exemptions from much of the GDL (having already covered its core subjects). Crucially, they are also usually exempted from the two-year training contract, provided that they are already a qualified legal executive before completing the LPC. A full list of institutions offering the ILEX course (including the distance learning option) is available at www.ilexcareers.org.uk.

Paralegal

If you have time to fill before starting your training contract or are yet to decide whether you want to spend time and money on law school, paralegal work can provide a useful introduction to legal practice. There is no single job description: some experienced paralegals may run their own cases; others with little to offer by way of experience may end up doing very dull document management tasks for months on end. Experiences do vary widely depending on the firm. Employers view time spent paralegalling favourably as it demonstrates commitment to the profession and enables candidates to gain valuable experience and commercial or sector insight. It is a good idea to take into account factors such as the size of the firm and the number of trainees – a smaller trainee intake may mean that you get to see much better quality work. One paralegal told us: "*A major factor in getting my training contract was the fact that I could talk about my responsibilities: attending court, going to client meetings, drafting documents. I was able to show enthusiasm for the legal process and through showing enthusiasm for my current position I was able to demonstrate that I would be a committed and enthusiastic future trainee.*" Some firms and companies – though not all – offer traineeships to the most impressive of their own paralegals, but you should always keep in mind that the job is a valuable position in its own right.

The paralegal market is massively competitive, especially since the recession, so those with no legal qualifications or practical experience will find it hard to secure a position. Usually large commercial firms require all paralegal applicants to have completed the LPC or BPTC and have at least six months of prior experience. If you can get a foot in the door, you might find yourself completing a number of short-term contracts until one firm decides it wants you on a longer-term basis. Some smaller firms insist that prospective trainee solicitors complete a trial period of paralegalling before offering them a contract. Understandably, this does sometimes lead to allegations of firms exploiting paralegals. Be careful to read the small print, looking for things such as whether you get paid for overtime or not. This can make all the difference, especially if you are handed a BlackBerry and called in on weekends. Should you find yourself in a compromising position, a good organisation to contact is the Junior Lawyers Division of the Law Society.

An occasional complaint among paralegals is that they don't always feel part of the firm. As one explained: "*Sometimes the paralegals are not invited to department events. The secretaries go for drinks, the trainees meet for dinner, etc. but a paralegal is neither one nor the other. This doesn't matter in a large firm, where there are large groups of paralegals and the partners and associates organise events for their teams. In a smaller firm, however, it can be a bit depressing. The best thing to do is find another paralegal and stick with them.*"

Experienced paralegals with specialist skills can make a decent living. If you're thinking about becoming a career paralegal you should take a look at the National Association of Licensed Paralegals' website at www.nationalparalegals.com. For information on current vacancies, find out if your law school's careers office has contacts, check the legal press, register with a specialist recruitment agency and trawl law firms' own websites. It's even worth firing off a speculative letter or two as some firms will recruit this way.

Her Majesty's Court Service

Her Majesty's Court Service is the executive agency of the Ministry of Justice responsible for the daily business of the civil, family and criminal courts in England and Wales. Its stated aim is 'to ensure that access [to justice] is provided as quickly as possible and at the lowest cost consistent with open justice, and that citizens have greater confidence in, and respect for, the system of justice.' HMCS looks after the management of over 1,200 properties and court buildings. It deals with the timetabling and management of hearings, as well as lighter matters like making courts available as filming locations.

Many HMCS jobs are administrative in nature; however, three times a year the service recruits Judicial Assistants (JAs) who are assigned to one of the Court of Appeal's senior judges for a period of between three and 12 months. Duties include legal research, advice and providing assistance in drafting judgements. JAs may also help define the shape and nature of appeals in less well-presented cases. There are usually ten positions available at any one time. Applicants must be lawyers who have completed or are about to complete pupillage or traineeship; have at least a 2:1; and have the ability to work under pressure in a team. Positions are advertised according to need in *The Times* and the *Law Gazette*, as well as on the HMCS website: www.hmcourts-service.gov.uk.

Long-term careers are available for administrative officers, bailiffs, and county and Crown Court ushers or clerks. Court clerks do not have a legal advisory role and do not need legal qualifications. Their responsibilities include maintaining the records of a court and administering oaths to witnesses and jurors. Magistrates' clerks do give legal advice to lay magistrates on issues like self-defence, identification of suspects and inferences from the silence of defendants after arrest as well as points of procedure. All court clerks need to be able to think on their feet and deal confidently with people. Clerks are present at most court sessions (of which there are nine or ten a week) and also issue summonses on behalf of magistrates. One clerk we spoke to mentioned describing his role to someone from continental Europe: "*They replied that in Poland, they would call someone with that level of responsibility a judge!*"

Unfortunately, at the time of going to press HMCS had stopped recruiting trainee magistrates' court clerks. In June 2010, the coalition government announced plans to close 103 magistrates' courts across the country, as part of a programme to save over £2bn at the Ministry of Justice. This will doubtless mean fewer jobs in the sector;

however, aspiring court clerks should keep checking the jobs pages of www.hmcourts-service.gov.uk for any opportunities as well as other information on HMCS.

The Law Commission

Many laws are the product of centuries of precedent; others arise from little more than political expediency. Constant reform is needed to ensure that the law is fit for purpose in the modern age; however; the government is not always best placed to see where reforms could be made. The Law Commission, an advisory non-departmental public body sponsored by the Ministry of Justice, was set up by Parliament in 1965 to review the laws of England and Wales and propose reform where necessary. The Commission is engaged in about 20 projects at any one time. Among the topics it set out to examine in its most recent reform programme were the extremely complex laws controlling the UK's railway level crossings; the status of the insanity defence; the possible abolition of the common law offence of public nuisance; and treason – an area where the criminal law could be simplified and pruned.

It is not just a case of repealing laws that are clearly archaic; it's equally important not to accidentally remove the legal basis for someone's rights. The Commission employs around 12-15 researchers every year to help it fulfil its remit, and as a researcher you would analyse many different areas of law, identifying defects in the current system and examining foreign law models to see how they deal with similar problems. You may also help to draft consultation papers, instructions to Parliamentary Counsel and final reports.

Researchers are normally law graduates and postgraduates, those who have completed the LPC or BPTC, or people who have spent time in legal practice but are looking for a change. The job of research assistant involves some fascinating (and less fascinating) subjects and is intellectually challenging. Candidates should have a First or high 2:1, along with a keen interest in current affairs and the workings of the law. The job suits those with an analytical mind and a hatred of waffle. They must also love research because there's a lot of it, be it devising questionnaires and analysing the responses, studying statistics or examining court files. So far, more than two-thirds of the Commission's recommendations have been implemented by government.

When we last spoke to the recruitment team at the Commission, it was still awaiting news (due late October 2010) on whether a hiring freeze would affect its researcher recruitment. Keep up to speed at www.lawcom.gov.uk.

Legal Services Commission

The LSC was created by the Access to Justice Act 1999 and replaced the Legal Aid Board in 2000. In addition to its HQ in London, it has operated from 15 offices across England and Wales, helping over two million people a year by managing the distribution of public funds for both civil legal services and criminal defence services. The work of the LSC is essentially divided into the Community Legal Service (CLS) and the Criminal Defence Service (CDS).

The role of the CLS is to ensure people can get information and advice about their legal rights and help with enforcing them: this tends to be in the areas of family breakdown, debt and housing. CLS caseworkers assess the merits of applications for legal funding and means test applicants. The CLS works with Legal Aid solicitors, Citizens Advice Bureaux, Law Centres, local authority services and other organisations. Recent reforms have seen the CLS working with local authorities to create Community Legal Advice Centres in a bid to provide a more integrated service in relation to social welfare law.

The CDS manages the supply of legal advice to those under police investigation or facing criminal charges, using local solicitors accredited by the service. It also performs an audit role in relation to authorised providers of criminal legal advice. Part of the CDS's work is the Public Defender Service (PDS). Its four offices, set up in 2001, advise members of the public 24/7 in what the LSC believes to be a more cost-effective and efficient way. They are located in Cheltenham, Darlington, Pontypridd and Swansea.

There has been a recruitment freeze at the LSC. Until last year it employed nearly 1,700 staff, but it is gradually reducing the numbers with the aim of having 1,100 by 2012. The commission is undergoing a great deal of change and will be transforming from a non-departmental public body into an executive agency in the future. Keep up to date at www.legalservices.gov.uk. It's worth keeping an eye out for the work experience placements that have occasionally cropped up, which are unpaid and tend to last about six weeks.

Patent attorney

Around 1,700 patent attorneys are registered in the UK, usually in private practice firms, large companies and government departments. Their job is to obtain, protect and enforce intellectual property rights for their owners. The website for the Chartered Institute of Patent Attorneys (CIPA) is www.cipa.org.uk and it has a useful careers section and job vacancy listings. In summary, it takes four or five years to become a UK Chartered Patent Agent and/or a European Patent Attorney. All candidates must have a scientific or technical background (usually a relevant degree) and the aptitude for learning the relevant law. Attention to detail, good drafting skills and a very logical, analytical mind are crucial and, increasingly, a knowledge of French or German is seen as key due to the international dimension to the work. The traditional route is to work and study for professional exams simultaneously. It is also an option to take the Certificate or Master's courses in intellectual property. Once qualified, there is the opportunity to obtain a further qualification to become a Patent Attorney Litigator, entitled to conduct litigation in the High Court, although all patent attorneys have the right to conduct litigation and to appear as advocate in the specialist Patents County Court. In order to become a European Patent Attorney, candidates must complete another set of examinations.

Trade mark attorney

A trade mark is a form of intellectual property used to distinguish a manufacturer or trader's particular brand from its competitors. It can be anything – a logo, a picture, a name or even a smell (apparently a Dutch perfume company uses their trade-marked 'freshly cut grass smell' to give tennis balls their aroma). Trade mark attorneys provide advice on the suitability of a word or logo as a trade mark, on the action needed to safeguard a protected trade mark, and on how to deal with any infringements by another party. There are about 530 fully qualified trade mark attorneys in the UK, all registered with the Institute of Trade Mark Attorneys (ITMA). Most work for large companies or at firms of patent and trade mark attorneys. Good communication and drafting skills are required, but a degree is not a prerequisite to qualification. The minimum educational requirements are five GCSEs (grade A-C) and two A level passes in approved subjects. The road to qualification involves passing the exams set for ITMA, and it is common for aspiring practitioners to study while learning on the job as a trainee. Candidates with certain degrees, such as law, may be exempt from some foundation papers. There is no central admissions procedure, so students need to approach firms or in-house trade mark departments directly. Check out www.itma.org.uk for its helpful careers page.

Compliance officer or analyst

Banks and other financial services companies recruit law and non-law grads into their compliance units, which take on the vital role of advising senior management on how to comply with the laws, regulations and rules that govern the sector. They also ensure that the banks' own corporate procedures and policies are followed. Other functions relate to the handling of complex regulatory and internal investigations and examinations. In essence, through compliance risk management, banks improve their ability to control the risks of emerging issues, thus helping to protect the organisation's reputation and safeguard its interests. Due to the proliferation of financial regulation, the importance of compliance departments has grown enormously so that in larger banks they are often equivalent in size to in-house legal teams and offer equally solid career prospects.

The role of compliance officer or analyst requires astute advice, clear guidance, reliable professional judgement and the ability to work in a team. Attention to detail and a determination to see the consistent application of compliance policies and practices are essential. Regular exposure to senior management commonly occurs much earlier for trainees in this area than for trainee solicitors at law firms. A minimum 2:1 degree is standard for successful applicants, and salaries are typically comparable with other graduate trainees in the City. With some compliance teams numbering more than 100 staff, there is plenty of scope for career development. Several banks run a two-year compliance analyst training scheme, over the course of which a trainee will gain a broad base of business knowledge and technical experience. It is not usually necessary to have completed the GDL, LPC or even a law degree before undertaking a graduate scheme, although those with a mind to move across to an in-house legal role later in their career would need to find the time to qualify as a lawyer. Being legally qualified opens up the door to general counsel work and it is not uncommon for a bank's head of legal to also lead the compliance team.

The road less travelled

So perhaps things haven't gone exactly according to plan, and this year's round of training contract offers has failed to recognise your potential. Or perhaps you didn't graduate in law with the objective of going into legal practice in the first place, as you just wanted the degree as a platform for taking you into other areas. Whatever the case, there are various valuable ways to bide your time until the next round and/or pursue alternative routes that will keep your hand in while beefing up your CV.

The harsh truth is that a cold winter of legal recruitment is fast closing in, especially in the (quasi-)public sector and the policy/regulatory world. That's not to say that all organisations will have frozen recruiting altogether (though many have), but the onus is on you to dig a little deeper.

The policy route was described by one source as a "*magical world,*" and once you've got your foot in the door numerous others should then open for you – as long as you're prepared to be dynamic. But how to make that first step? The feedback we have received suggests that knowing the right people who might champion your cause certainly doesn't hurt (start networking early on, folks) and that luck occasionally has its part to play. Otherwise, it will be a question of researching the various government departments and regulators that might interest you and, if needs be, contacting them directly to see what their current recruitment status is. This is no conveyor belt career path, so you do have to feel your way a little, but the rewards off the beaten track are there to be found. This kind of highly malleable experience can propel you towards your preferred original career of barrister/solicitor or take you into "*other realms,*" as they were so romantically described to us. More prosaically, this means that policy work "*is a profession, but it spans all industries.*"

For ideas, try typing 'policy' into the *Guardian* jobs website search engine every so often, as well as checking regularly on the websites of organisations such as the Judicial Appointments Commission and Queen's Council Appointments. The Law Society, Solicitors Regulatory Authority, Bar Council and Bar Standards Board websites are all worth looking at for vacancies, as are various industry ombudsmen (check out www.bioa.org.uk). And then there are the heavyweight regulators such as the Financial Services Authority, which runs a graduate training scheme of its own. See www.fsagraduates.com.

Legal Secretary

"*Being a legal secretary is a good way to get your foot in the door,*" explained one of our lawyer contacts. They would know: it's exactly how they started their career. For anyone unsure of whether they want the full-bore pressure of working as a solicitor, this route could be perfect; "*the major pro being that you're working in law without the more intense responsibility of being a lawyer.*" It's also a smart way to spend a few years if you're struggling to get your finances back on track and can't yet contemplate law school. According to the Institute of Legal Secretaries and PAs (ILSPA), taking a legal secretarial role is suitable for anyone with an interest in law or a background in administrative work. That said, it's important to know that the market is pretty full right now and there's a lot of competition for jobs. As such, ILSPA recommends completing a course. For more details visit: www.institutelegalsecretaries.com.

People can take on legal secretarial positions at any stage of life, be it instead of university, after a degree or as a complete career change. Whenever you take this step, you'll need to be certain that you have the right qualities and temperament: you need to work well under pressure, have a lot of patience, pay attention to detail and be articulate. You must also get to know your boss quickly, think for them and organise them. One downside is that some people will regard your role as relatively lowly and show precious little respect for your talents. One legal secretary-turned-lawyer confirmed that it can be a challenge working for people who do what you actually want to be doing. For more on the reality of the job see www.legalsecretaryjournal.com.

A legal secretary can be employed as a shared resource for a whole department or just a few lawyers, or they may be more of a personal assistant to just one lawyer. Typical administrative tasks include typing correspondence, filing, arranging meetings and diary management. The salary range is wide and can go up to £40,000 or so a year, though it varies depending on where in the country you work. The most money is to be made in London or other big cities. As in any career, you'll need to start at the bottom of the ladder – especially if it's your first job – although our ILSPA contact reckons that law school grads may be able to start a rung or two up and definitely have scope for climbing higher.

Check recruitment sites and agencies for as many options as you can find and apply for any job for which you feel you could be suitable. Look up the law firms in your area, call them and send your CV. Junior positions are often filled via word of mouth or by speculative applicants.

How suitable are you and what do recruiters want?

The road to success is smoother for some, but a few nips and tucks to a CV and a healthy dose of self-confidence can improve anyone's prospects.

How impressive is your degree?

So you've not got a law degree. So what? From the top sets at the Bar to the little-known solicitors' firms on the high street, non-law graduates are just as able to secure training positions as their LLB peers. In the few cases where employers prefer law grads they will specify this, so unless you hear differently conversion route applicants may proceed with confidence. Many recruiters tell us just how highly they regard staff with language skills and scientific or technical degrees, particularly where their clients' businesses will benefit. Humanities degrees require many of the same research and analytical skills needed by lawyers, and believe it or not, being able to discuss literary criticism with your clients could come in handy, since clients – just like lawyers – are people too.

It's a fact of life that many solicitors' firms and barristers' chambers subscribe to the idea of a pecking order of universities; at some the bias is undeniably evident. In this tough economy, we sense something of a flight to perceived 'quality' universities by many recruiters. If you worry that your university isn't one of the best regarded then you should make sure you get the best degree result possible and work on enriching your CV in other ways.

Your degree result is going to be one of the most important things on your CV. Net a First and you'll impress all and sundry (at least on paper); walk away with a 2:1 and your path to employment will be made smoother; end up with a 2:2 and you're going to have a tough time. In exceptional circumstances the effect of a poor degree result may be softened by a letter from your tutor stipulating the reason why you underachieved, but this is only going to work when the circumstances are actually exceptional. It's rarely relevant that you just missed a 2:1 by a percentage point or two; on the other hand, if you were a star student who suffered a serious accident or illness as finals loomed, confirmation of this (perhaps also by way of a doctor's letter) might assist. Having spoken to a number of trainees and a couple of pupil barristers who left university with a 2:2, we would never presume to discourage anyone from applying for a training position, but these people all had other very impressive qualities and/or CV-enhancing experiences. Some only presented themselves as candidates once they already had other career experience under their belt. If you find yourself at the back of the job queue, think hard about what you can do to overcome that 2:2 – a year or more in a relevant job, a further degree, a commitment to voluntary work perhaps. Of course none of these factors are a guaranteed fix.

Possibly unaware that they could be applying for training contracts and vacation schemes in their second year, many new undergraduates are lulled into a false sense of security concerning their academic performance in the first year. If the only marks you have to show recruiters are thirds or 2:2s, you'll not get far. As obvious as it may sound, working for good results throughout your degree is crucial.

Get involved

Resist the urge to become an expert on daytime telly. *Jeremy Kyle*, the *Loose Women* and – much as it pains us to say it – Dick van Dyke in the role of Dr Mark Sloan have nothing to offer you. Instead, take advantage of your freedom and the practically unlimited opportunities on offer. Almost every university has a wide range of societies, meeting groups and sports clubs. Pursuing your interests will give an extra dimension to both your university experience and, crucially, your CV.

Some kind of legal experience, whether it's involvement with the student law magazine or shadowing your aunt's neighbour's lawyer friend, is pretty crucial since you need to convince prospective employers that you're serious about the profession. You can acquire experience later on through open days and vacation schemes, but it's never too early to start, not least because vac schemes and open days are now devilishly hard to get. Non-legal extra-curriculars can be just as useful to show that you play well with others. It also gives you something to write about when an application form asks 'Discuss a time when you worked with a group to achieve a common goal'. Relevant work experience is vital to almost every successful job application, so search hard for suitable positions and use them to test your own ideas of what you would like to do. Many universities run law-specific career seminars in association with solicitors' firms or barristers' chambers. Be savvy, go along and find out as much as you can by talking to trainee solicitors and recruiters. Networking is a key tactic you should be employing. Go to our website for further advice.

Many graduates adopt a scattergun approach, applying to as many firms as possible and hoping for the best. Simply sending the same covering letter to 50 firms will not make you look good. Recruiters can tell very easily which applicants have a genuine interest in their firm and which have put in minimal effort. It's all about the three Rs: research, research and research. Demonstrating your understanding of what the firm is about, what the work will entail and being able to explain honestly and realistically why you want to do it will be among the most important things to get across. Advice on how to do this can be found in the section of this guide that deals with **making applications** and on our website in the **Way in** features for every firm, and our feature on **How to research firms properly**.

Be in the know

If you want to become a commercial lawyer you'll need this thing they call commercial awareness. We're not suggesting you must become a mini Robert Peston, rather that you should gain a sense of what's going on in the commercial world. Unless you've been living in a box in a cave on Mars, you'll be aware that the recession has pummelled most of the world economies and the UK's legal sector. Be prepared to talk reasonably knowledgeably about the main themes should you be invited for an interview. But what other topics should you be aware of? How about gaining some understanding of the attraction of the BRIC economies and now Africa; the basic issues involved in UK public spending cuts; the greater emphasis placed on regulation in the financial services sector; and perhaps something from an industry sector to which you are drawn. To give just a few examples, there's a lot going on in relation to energy and natural resources; technology; aviation and travel; and private equity and funds. If you have zero interest in all this stuff, what on earth makes you think commercial law is a suitable career? Why not read the *Financial Times* or *The Economist* (it has great podcasts too) now and again, or make friends with the BBC website's business section? BBC Radio 4's *Today* programme also puts out a good daily business podcast. The *Student Guide* has a Facebook page with links to stories that will broaden your knowledge of the business world and major changes affecting private client law. Whichever method suits you best, keep up to date and make sure you're not oblivious to the events going on around you at national and international level.

It's also important to understand the role of a lawyer as a service provider. Much like a plumber or an accountant, you will be providing a service to a client and your attitude should reflect this. Lawyers must be able to relate to their clients and know something about their businesses. If the firms you apply to have certain specialisms or target certain industry sectors you'll do yourself a massive favour by finding out about those sectors.

Students looking to go into criminal law should be aware of recent legislation and current issues. Future family lawyers should be able to discuss the major cases that have hit the headlines. Needless to say, anyone interested in administrative and public law issues will have a full-time job keeping up to date with all the various developments. Radio 4's *Law in Action* podcasts are going to be a real help. Hopeful crime, family and human rights lawyers should also be aware of important current issues relating to Legal Aid provision. Why not go to our website to get started?

Time out

If you've itchy feet then let them wander – the career can wait. As well as giving you more confidence, navigating your way around a foreign country will develop your organisational and problem-solving skills and it will give you fertile ground for conversation. Recruiters do appreciate that not everyone has the desire or, more importantly, the money to swan off on a gap year. If travel is the last thing on your agenda, don't stress about it or feel you're going to be marked down for being a stay-at-home. Think about how else you can stand out.

With the advent of new legislation, an employer discriminating against candidates on the grounds of age is officially a thing of the past. Nevertheless, some mature applicants still worry that their years will disadvantage them. Remember (if you still can), with age comes experience and probably an impressive set of transferable skills. You already know how to work, your people/client-handling skills are doubtless better developed, and you may even have relevant industry knowledge. We've chatted with successful barristers and solicitors who've done everything from secretarial work, professional football, journalism, forensic science, physiotherapy and music production to accountancy, policing and soldiering. But when is old too old? If you're still in your 20s, get over yourself – you're still a kid. If you're in your 30s, ask what it is you can offer a law firm that will make your application stand out. And if you're older still? Never say never. Over the years we have run into a small number of 40-something trainees, all of whom were glad to have made the career change. These much older trainees tended to have one thing in common: they brought advantageous industry experience to their firm. Given that each year after qualification a certain percentage of the UK's lawyers move firms or even drop out of the profession for good, the argument that employers expect 30 years of service from new recruits simply doesn't hold water. Of greater relevance is the adage concerning old dogs and new tricks, so if your coat is greying, consider carefully how you'd cope with being trained and disciplined like a puppy.

Dealing with disability

Despite the legal profession now being more diverse, for students with mental or physical disabilities things are not straightforward. In the experience of the Group for Solicitors with Disabilities (GSD), many applicants with disabilities have great difficulty in securing work placements and training contracts. There are sources of advice and assistance available, and the GSD has been actively involved in approaching law firms to set up designated work placement schemes for disabled students. The group also provides a forum in which students and practitioners can meet in order to share experiences and provide one another with guidance and support. The group will run a careers guidance conference for students at the Law Society on Chancery Lane on 27 October 2010. The GSD's website is www.lawsoc.org.uk/lawyerswithdisabilities. Would-be barristers should refer to the Disability Sub-Group of the Bar Council's Equality and Diversity Committee.

Diversity matters

Long gone are the days of firms and chambers populated exclusively by white men smoking fat cigars. Not only has the smoking ban put paid to the Cubans but women and ethnic minorities are now firmly ensconced in the profession. In the course of our research this year more than 125 firms provided us with lists identifying their trainees. In most, the girls outnumber the boys – something we would expect to see given that more women have gone into the profession than men for well over a decade. The gender balance among new trainees is around 62% female. The names on most of these lists also reflect a healthy spread of ethnic backgrounds. It is worth mentioning, however, that female and non-white trainees still have too few senior role models and there are always a small number of legal sector sex or race discrimination claims going through the employment tribunals. On the subject of sexual orientation, we know scores of gay and lesbian lawyers for whom their sexuality is entirely a non-career matter. Some firms are definitely more gay-friendly than others, but happily we do not tend to hear complaints from our sources about how their employers and colleagues view their sexuality. The Lesbian and Gay Lawyers Association (LAGLA) meets monthly and welcomes student members. You can join up for free online: www.lagla.org.uk. Go to our website if you'd like to read more about LGBT issues.

A number of diversity-related organisations have sprung up and you may see evidence of them at your university. Without doubt anything that encourages genuine diversity in the workplace is to be commended, but before signing on the dotted line with any intermediary – especially if you are asked to hand over any money for their services – make sure you know you are dealing with a respected organisation. Ask if they are affiliated with particular law firms and, if so, how. The topic of diversity covers more than just gender, sexual orientation, religion and ethnicity. If you think your accent or upbringing or a disability could stand in your way then find out if there is anything these organisations can do for you. Addressing the UK's social mobility issues and the dreaded 'glass ceiling' in the legal profession is hot, both in the press and in society generally.

Likewise, if you know your university gets less attention from law firms than, say, Oxford or Durham, then a diversity-related organisation may well be just what you need to get your foot in the door. One reputable organisation is the City Solicitors' Educational Trust (CSET), which runs summer schools designed to help students not studying at one of the top UK universities, or who might not have excelled in their A Levels. More information is available at www.cset.org.uk and we've looked at this and some of the other schemes on our website.

Home or away?

London attracts professionals from all over the world, so you can skip this bit if you're a Brit intending to work in the capital. If you hold an EU passport or have a pre-existing right to live and work in the UK and you are following the appropriate path to qualification, you should also proceed with optimism. Applicants who tick none of these boxes may find doors are easier to push open if they apply to firms with business interests in the country or region from which they come. In all cases, excellent written and spoken English is essential, and you will need a convincing reason why you have chosen to commence your career in the UK. Get up to speed on the latest changes in immigration rules: one of the most recent concerns for firms that recruit non-EU candidates is the UK Border Agency's more restrictive approach to issuing visas.

Regional employers are often more comfortable recruiting candidates with a local connection. Quite simply, they want to know that whoever they take on will be committed to a long-term career with them. The picture across the UK is a variable one: some firms clearly state their preferences for local lads and lasses; others tell us that most of their applicants do have links with the region but that they are happy to consider anyone.

Use your time wisely

What with studying hard, keeping up with business and professional news, helping out at the CAB, captaining the university rugby and netball teams, debating, acting as student law society president and attending all the careers events that crop up, you'll hardly have time for a pint. Ultimately it's all about finding a good balance. Your years at university are supposed to be fun, but don't waste valuable time that could be spent CV building.

Pro bono and volunteering

Deriving from the Latin *pro bono publico*, meaning 'for the public good', the idea of providing free legal advice has been ingrained in the legal profession for centuries.

In 1594 the Lord Chief Justice explained to newly qualified barristers that the "*two tongues*" of linen hanging from counsel's shirt collars in court "*signifie that as you should have one tongue for the rich for your fee... so should you also have another tongue as ready without reward to defend the poor and oppressed.*" Traditionally done in a very British, understated way in the UK, the past decade has seen the rise of structured pro bono programmes at law firms and barristers' chambers, law schools and universities. Bringing these all together, ProBonoUK.net was started in 2003 and is the most comprehensive resource on pro bono activities in the UK. It announced in March 2010 that it was soon to provide an international pro bono database for those looking to extend their work beyond British borders. 2010's National Pro Bono week will run from the 8th – 12th November.

Why participate?

Involvement in some form of pro bono or volunteering work is becoming increasingly important, not just because there are people out there who need your help, but because pro bono experience is a clear winner with recruiters, and if you have something to put on your CV it will help take you closer to the front of the queue for training contracts and pupillages. It's not just prospective trainees and pupils who benefit: 2009's LawWorks Choices scheme for unemployed lawyers saw £700,000 of free advice offered by over 600 lawyers in its inaugural year. Participants have been able to continue to practise as lawyers by helping their communities, and this should assist them in their job search. Experience suggests that those who have been most active have found it much easier to land job interviews.

Law schools make a particular effort to introduce students to pro bono. As Laura Gerrard, Pro Bono Clinic Manager at BPP, told us: "*Pro bono remains extremely important in the current economic climate, particularly in housing and employment law, two areas in which our students are very active. Shelter and employment are fundamental needs and can be the first under threat in a financial crisis. Our students' efforts assist those most in need by bridging the gap between publicly funded Legal Aid and those fortunate enough to afford legal representation whilst providing our students with real experience in a legal setting.*"

Many firms now have formal pro bono relationships with organisations such as community legal advice centres. Arguably the increased scope and visibility of pro bono work is in part due to the greater importance placed on pro bono activities by the influx of US law firms into the UK market. Certainly more home-grown law firms now recognise the business case for doing this kind of work, not least because of the PR benefits of telling the world what caring organisations they are.

Real life

Getting involved couldn't be easier when you're at law school as most now offer extensive programmes. Cardiff Law School has an Innocence Project, for example, which deals with long-term prisoners who maintain their innocence and have exhausted the initial appeals process. The pro bono unit there has also developed a niche in assisting elderly and infirm clients, many of whom need to ascertain whether their care is categorised as nursing or social care in order to determine who should foot the bill. The University of Sheffield also has an Innocence Project, as well as providing students with the opportunity to get involved in the Pro Uno centre, which researches social welfare law issues. The University of Westminster's LPC course has a clinical law elective, during which students work on a pro bono basis for the CAB and submit a project at the end of the elective. And as if you needed a greater incentive than a warm glow in the pit of your belly, there are various national prizes on offer for students who excel in this field, including the Law Society's annual Young Lawyer Pro Bono Award.

At university level, student pro bono opportunities have been more limited, largely because it's too risky for inexperienced undergrads to provide real-life legal advice. This is changing as undergraduates are receiving more support. You can go to www.studentprobono.net for the most up-to-date information on what each institution is doing.

If you hope to go to the Bar or become a solicitor specialising in any contentious area of law then you should seriously consider becoming a ratified member of The Free Representation Unit (FRU), a charity founded in 1972 to provide legal advice, case preparation and advocacy for people who aren't able to claim Legal Aid.

If this has gone any way towards whetting your appetite then you should check out our more detailed online listing of pro bono and volunteering activities with which you can get involved.

Vacation schemes

In an ever-more competitive market, vacation scheme experience is a key piece of weaponry in the battle to secure a training contract.

In times past, having done one or two vacation schemes or periods of work experience in a legal services supplier was seen as a bonus. These days, it is much more important. Why? Quite simply, firms want to be sure of your commitment to the profession and they have also cottoned on to the fact that you can find out a lot more about a person when they are sitting at a desk next to you for two weeks than you can in a half-hour interview, or even a half-day assessment centre.

With certain firms, if you haven't done a vac scheme there, your chances of getting a training contract with them are minimal. The prime example is City firm Nabarro, which took 100% of its trainees from people it saw on its vac scheme in 2010. This is still the exception rather than the rule, but we spoke to a number of recruiters this year who were hoping to significantly increase the percentage of trainees they recruited via their vac scheme.

As well as helping you get a foot in the door, vacation schemes are one of the best ways to find out what being a lawyer is actually like, to get a sniff of the truth behind the Denny Crane and Ally McBeal fictions.

How do you get on one?

No secret here: our handy-dandy table on page 36 tells you what places are available with the firms covered by this guide and when to apply. Timing your application is important: certain schemes are targeted at penultimate-year law grads or final-year non-law grads, which can leave other students frustrated. Suffice it to say, law undergrads need to start thinking about their application campaign as early as the summer after the first year at university. The application deadlines for the majority of vac schemes come in January and February, but some firms run schemes in the Christmas and Easter holidays and the deadlines for applying to those can be as early as October. Don't miss out. You'll generally find full details of exactly how to make your application on firms' recruitment websites.

As competition for training contracts gets more intense, it's no surprise that competition for vac scheme places is equally so. Obvious conclusion: you'll need to put as much effort into vac scheme applications as you do into training contract applications. For some tips on how to do this refer to our feature on **How to make successful applications**. On our website we also have detailed advice on the application procedures for each of the firms covered in the True Picture. The strongest applicants always manage to secure a clutch of offers, but don't despair if you can't secure a place – it doesn't necessarily mean you'll never get a training contract. Try and build your CV up in other ways – say with voluntary work or other legal or commercial experience – and then have another stab at vac scheme applications.

Even if you navigate the vac scheme obstacle course perfectly, don't get complacent. You'll usually still need to prepare well for a training contract interview.

What will I get to do?

Vac schemes differ as much as the firms themselves. In some cases, your time will be structured down to the minute with talks about the firm and its training contract, followed by tasks and social engagements. At others you might find you have to hunt and gather work. For detailed information on the structure of each firm's vacation scheme, go to our website.

What should I look out for?

When on a vac scheme, become an anthropologist. Observe your environment and its inhabitants; figure out the social structures, the hierarchies, the shared values that bond people (if indeed there are any). Watch how the trainees fit in with all of this. Eavesdrop. You've got to be on your guard though because people will be conscious you're there, and some of our sources did end up concluding: *"It can be an artificial exercise – you see what they want you to see."* Your aim is to peer beyond the mask at the living, breathing, sweating entity behind it.

Try also to get a feel for how different departments work by reading as much as you can. A starting point would be our **Solicitors' practice area** features. It'll help you figure out what sort of work might suit you best and will enable you to ask intelligent questions of your supervisors. Intelligent questions pave the road to success, so lay as many down as possible without becoming annoying.

How will I be assessed?

Vac schemers are often given research to do as a way of evaluating their abilities; expect to be given some specifics to look into before reporting back to solicitors with your findings. You might be asked to shadow someone, helping them out with their workload. This is an excellent opportunity for you to find more out about the firm while proving yourself at the same time. You might even get to go to client meetings or visit court. Last, but certainly not least, are the mini-assessment tasks designed to test your ability to present, argue and work as a team. "*Don't be over-assertive, but don't fade into the background either. Remember to ask other people what their opinions are – you have to look like a team player.*" Some tasks we heard about involved advertising pitches to faux-potential clients, mini-transactions and business scenarios.

How should I act?

While you're busy watching everyone else, don't forget that they're watching you, watching them, watching you. This recruitment lark is a delicate dance, so attune yourself to the characters around you and follow their lead. More than anything else, people will be trying to see if you 'share the firm's core values'. Ultimately, 'professionalism' should be your watchword. This is a job interview, even when you're eating lunch in the canteen. Don't be late for work. Switch off your mobile phone when in the office. Don't bitch or send stupid e-mails. Thinking about browsing Facebook in a slack moment? Why take the risk?

Okay, so don't be an idiot. That much is obvious. But how can you impress? As one recruiter says, it's all about "*marketing yourself well.*" Does that sound a little intimidating? It's really not. After all, you marketed yourself well on paper when you sent your application form in, now you are just doing it in person. Asking well-timed questions and showing an interest is an easy way of doing this. Just remember, "*seeking out work and raising your profile without pestering people is a fine line to walk.*" A trainee confirmed that you have to strike the right balance, telling us that on the last vac scheme he was involved with, "*there were a couple of people who were too enthusiastic!*"

Coming for a quick drink? Bankers, lawyers, doctors and even priests all know how effective alcohol can be when it comes to greasing the wheels. But the trick is to drink the right amount or none at all. Even when firms take vac schemers out to snazzy clubs, recruiters' mental notepads will still be out. So gauge the situation: is the firm boozy or abstemious?

At the end of the day, a law firm is just like any other office workplace and you'll find all sorts of characters. You'll also find variety within any group of vac schemers. "*You get the quiet ones, the loud ones, the ones who say inappropriate things, the ones who're always smiling.*" Obviously, you're being assessed on how good a lawyer you're likely to be, but don't underestimate how far a normal, attractive personality will get you.

And finally...

There's a lot more to say about vacation schemes, and our website is the place to find it. For every firm we've covered in this book, you'll find an extra feature about its application process and vacation scheme.

Vacation Schemes

Firm name	Vacancies	Duration	Remuneration	Deadline
Addleshaw Goddard	90 Easter & summer	1, 2 or 3 weeks	Not known	31 January 2011
Allen & Overy	65 – winter (non-law); summer (law)	Not known	Not known	Winter: 31 Oct 2010 summer: 16 Jan 2011
Arnold & Porter	Up to 8 summer	2 weeks	Not known	25 February 2011
Ashurst	Easter (grads & final year non-law); summer (penult-year law)	Easter: 2 weeks summer: 3 weeks	£275 p.w.	31 January 2011
Baker & McKenzie	London: 35 international: 3-5	London: 3 weeks international: 8-12 weeks	£270 p.w.	31 January 2011
Barlow Lyde & Gilbert	Yes + open days and drop-in sessions	Not known	Not known	31 January 2011
Bates Wells & Braithwaite	18	1 week	Not known	17 February 2011
Beachcroft	Summer	Not known	Not known	1 March 2011
Berwin Leighton Paisner	Easter & summer	Easter: 1 week summer: 2 weeks	Not known	31 January 2011
Bevan Brittan	Yes	Not known	Not known	31 March 2011
Bird & Bird	Summer	Not known	Not known	Not known
Bond Pearce	Summer	2 weeks	Not known	9 April 2011
Boodle Hatfield	10	2 weeks	Not known	Not known
Brabners Chaffe Street	Summer	Not known	Not known	31 July 2011
Bristows	Spring, summer, winter	Not known	Not known	Not known
Browne Jacobson	Open day in spring	Not known	Not known	17 March 2011
Burges Salmon	40 + open days	2 weeks	£250 p.w.	Not known
Capsticks	Summer	2 weeks	Not known	25 February 2011
Cleary Gottlieb Steen & Hamilton	5 in winter, 10 in spring & 20 in summer	Not known	Not known	Winter: 15th November 2010 spring/summer: 28 January 2011
Clifford Chance	Summer + winter and spring workshops	Summer: 4 weeks	Not known	Not known
Clyde & Co	20 summer	2 weeks	Not known	31 January 2011
CMS Cameron McKenna	60 spring & summer	2 weeks	£250 p.w.	31 January 2011
Cobbetts	Easter & summer	2 weeks	Not known	13 February 2011
Coffin Mew	Open week in July	1 week	Not known	31 March 2011
Covington & Burling	24 summer	Not known	Not known	28 January 2011
Davenport Lyons	Summer	Not known	£250 p.w.	Not known
Dawsons	Easter & summer	1 week	Not known	1 March 2011
Dechert	Easter & summer (aimed at penultimate-year law)	Not known	Not known	31 January 2011

Vacation Schemes

Firm name	Vacancies	Duration	Remuneration	Deadline
Dewey & LeBoeuf	12	Spring: 1 week summer: 2 weeks	£400 p.w.	31 January 2011
Dickinson Dees	40 Easter & summer	1 week	£200 p.w.	31 January 2011
DLA Piper	170 Summer	2 weeks	Not known	31 January 2011
Dundas & Wilson	Summer	3 weeks	Not known	30 January 2011
DWF	Yes	Not known	Not known	Not known
Edwards Angell Palmer & Dodge	8-10 summer + open days	2 weeks	Not known	Not known
Eversheds	Summer	2 weeks	Not known	31 January 2011
Farrer & Co	30 Easter & summer	2 weeks	£275 p.w.	31 January 2011
Field Fisher Waterhouse	Easter & summer	2 weeks	Not known	13 February 2011
Foot Anstey	Summer	Not known	Not known	30 April 2011
Freshfields Bruckhaus Deringer	Summer (aimed at penultimate-year undergrads)	Not known	Not known	15 January 2011 (earlier apps recommended)
Government Legal Service	60	2-3 weeks	£200-250 p.w.	Late January/early February 2011
Hammonds	25 summer	2 weeks	£230 p.w. (London) £180 p.w. (regions)	31 January 2011
HBJ Gateley Wareing	Summer	2 weeks	Not known	11 February 2011
Herbert Smith	Winter, spring & summer	2 weeks	Not known	Not known
Hewitsons	Yes	1 week	Not known	Not known
Hill Dickinson	40	1 week	Not known	31 January 2011
Howes Percival	Summer	Not known	Not known	30 April 2011
Ince & Co	15	2 weeks	£250 p.w.	31 January 2011
Irwin Mitchell	Yes	Not known	Not known	Not known
Jones Day	Winter: non-law spring: non-law summer: law	2 weeks	£400 p.w.	Winter: 31 Oct 2010 spring/summer: 31 Jan 2011
K&L Gates	Yes	Not known	Not known	Not known
Kennedys	Summer	Not known	Not known	31 January 2011
Kirkland & Ellis	Up to 14	2 weeks	£350 p.w.	31 January 2011
Latham & Watkins	Yes: Easter & summer	2 weeks	£300 p.w.	Easter: 31 December 2010 summer: 31 January 2011
Lawrence Graham	Summer	2 weeks	£300 p.w.	31 January 2011
Lester Aldridge	Summer	2 weeks	Not known	Usually 31 March 2011
Lewis Silkin	Vac scheme in summer + open days in spring	2 weeks	Not known	End January 2011

Vacation Schemes

Firm name	Vacancies	Duration	Remuneration	Deadline
Linklaters	Winter: (non-law) summer (penult-year law)	Winter: 2 weeks summer: 4 weeks	Not known	Not known
Macfarlanes	55	2 weeks	£250 p.w.	31 January 2011
Manches	Approx 20	1 week	£200 (under review)	15 February 2011
Mayer Brown	Easter & summer	Easter: 2 weeks summer: 3 weeks	Not known	Not known
McGrigors	Summer	Not known	Not known	30 January 2011
Michelmores	Summer	1 week	Not known	28 February 2011
Mills & Reeve	Summer	2 weeks	Not known	31 January 2011
Mishcon de Reya	15+	2 weeks	£250 p.w.	31 January 2011
Muckle	Yes	Not known	Not known	25 February 2011
Nabarro	Summer: 65	3 weeks	Not known	31 January 2011
Norton Rose	20 winter 40 summer plus 5 open days	Winter: 2 weeks summer: 4 weeks	£250 p.w.	Winter: 31 October 2010 summer: 31 January 2011
Olswang	17	2 weeks	£275 p.w.	31 January 2011
O'Melveny & Myers	Summer	2 weeks	Not known	31 January 2011
Orrick	Open days	Not known	Not known	Not known
Osborne Clarke	Summer	2 weeks	Not known	Not known
Pannone	88	1 week	None	30 April 2011
Paul Hastings	6	2 weeks	£350 p.w.	28 February 2011
Penningtons Solicitors	Summer + information days	Not known	Not known	31 March 2011
Pinsent Masons	100	2 weeks	Not known	31 January 2011
PricewaterhouseCoopers Legal	Summer	3 weeks	Paid	31 January 2011
Reed Smith	20	Not known	Not known	Not known
Reynolds Porter Chamberlain	12	2 weeks	Not known	Not known
Shoosmiths	Summer	2 weeks	Not known	28 February 2011
Simmons & Simmons	Spring & summer; workshops + open days all year round	3 weeks	Not known	Not known
SJ Berwin	Easter & summer	Not known	Not known	31 January 2011
Skadden	Easter & summer (penult-year law + non law)	2 weeks	Paid	12 January 2011
Slaughter and May	Easter, summer & Christmas	1 or 2 weeks	Not known	Not known
SNR Denton	Summer (law) + open days (non-law + first-year law)	Summer: 1 week	Not known	Not known

Vacation Schemes

Firm name	Vacancies	Duration	Remuneration	Deadline
Speechly Bircham	Summer	3 weeks	Not known	4 February 2011
Stephenson Harwood	40 summer, Christmas & Easter	Christmas: 1 week Easter & summer: 2 weeks	£260 p.w.	Christmas: 7 November 2010 Easter & summer: 31 Jan 2011
Stevens & Bolton	Summer	1 week	Not known	31 January 2011
Taylor Wessing	Yes	2 weeks	Not known	Not known
Thomas Eggar	Summer	1 week	Travel expenses	Not known
TLT Solicitors	Yes	1 week	Not known	Not known
Travers Smith	15 Christmas 45 summer	2 weeks	£250	31 January 2011
Trowers & Hamlins	Yes	2 weeks	Not known	1 March 2011
Veale Wasbrough Vizards	Summer	1 week	Unpaid	Not known
Vinson & Elkins	Yes	Not known	Not known	28 February 2011
Walker Morris	48	1 week	£250 p.w.	31 January 2011
Ward Hadaway	Spring & summer	1 week	Not known	28 February 2011
Watson, Farley & Williams	30	2 weeks	£250 p.w.	31 January 2011
Wedlake Bell	8 summer	3 weeks	£250 p.w.	End February 2011
Weil, Gotshal & Manges	15 summer	Not known	Not known	31 January 2011
White & Case	12-15 Easter 40-50 summer	2 weeks	£350 p.w.	31 January 2011
Wilsons Solicitors	Summer	1 week	Not known	Not known
Withers	Easter & summer	2 weeks	Not known	31 January 2011

How to make successful applications

Making training applications is both an art and a science. In the current ultra-competitive market, the sooner you develop the right techniques the better.

Here's Cliff Fluet, grad recruitment partner at Lewis Silkin, on the subject of applications: "*I've seen too many copy-and-paste ones. If you can't be bothered filling in a form properly, then your chances of getting a £30k-plus job are severely limited.*" What he says is incontrovertible. In all our conversations with recruiters, they never fail to mention this fundamental error. Don't ever be generic in your applications; tailor them to each firm or set of chambers – recruiters can spot a mail merge from a mile away.

We know it's tempting to send off a generic application to as many firms as you can. It's quicker, but you mustn't believe the old adage that if you throw enough mud some of it will stick. In this more difficult market, we come across fewer and fewer people who have succeeded in getting a training contract this way. The people who are more likely to succeed will target a list of specific firms and take more time perfecting their applications.

Note that we are not saying that it's a bad thing to send off piles of applications. As we have repeatedly mentioned, this is a competitive business and even some good candidates may have to turn out 15, 20 or more, but the more care you take with each, the sooner you will get an offer.

Do your research

Choosing a firm because it's got a cool name and recruitment literature isn't the best policy; neither is random selection. Before you apply, try to work out which firms would best suit you. If you're a 'live to work' type, find an organisation that will give you what you crave. Likewise, if you just have to catch *Hollyoaks* at half six, make sure you seek out firms with shorter hours. If you want to do a certain type of law, apply to the places that specialise in the area. Carefully select your targets – they need to suit your personality and interests, otherwise you'll have a hard time persuading them to hire you, and if you do get hired you might regret it.

- Use the *Student Guide* – it's the best thing we've ever read. The **True Picture**, the **Chambers Reports**, the **Solicitors' Practice Areas** and **Practice Areas at the Bar**, the comparison charts, the bonus features on the website – all good, all useful.
- Only marginally less brilliant, our parent publication *Chambers UK* identifies and ranks all the best firms in over 60 areas of practice. It can be read online, for free, at www.chambersandpartners.com.
- Make use of as many other sources as possible. From legal gossip websites through to *The Lawyer*, *Legal Week* and *The Law Gazette*: all can be of value.
- Check the firm's requirements. Check your qualifications and abilities. Do they match? The **Applications and selections** table on page 519 and our website should help with this, as will our detailed online recruitment features for each firm.

Stay organised

- Know the deadlines and diarise the important ones. The calendar at the front of this book should help. Most commercial firms recruit two years in advance, but it might be even earlier.
- Application forms take far, far longer to complete than you'd expect, especially when they're done well. Submitting one two minutes late is too late.
- Some barristers' chambers use the Pupillage Portal, some don't. Make sure you know which is which. Check their websites. The Bar section of this guide discusses the Pupillage Portal in more detail.
- If you have to handwrite something, practise on a rough version first. If your handwriting is so atrocious that the reader will need a cipher, you'll need to improve it.
- Answer the questions directly – no cutting and pasting or repetition.
- Usually you will be told how much you can write for each question. If you are well under, don't just waffle, keep thinking.
- Keep copies of everything you send out because before an interview or assessment day you will need to remind yourself of what you wrote.
- Increasingly firms are making application forms available only to those who perform well enough in online tests, sometimes verbal reasoning, sometimes numerical. There are books and websites with sample tests and helpful hints on how to perform well. Get in some practice ahead of time.

Good form

Here are a few tips on completing application forms and CVs:

- Avoid chronological gaps in your experience. If you've taken time off, put it down and be prepared to explain why.
- Ignore all the fancy stuff and get to the details. Don't waste time with photos or unusual fonts.
- Bullet points and bold text can make things more eye-catching.
- Don't just say what you did at uni – mention sports teams, work experience and volunteering. Show that you've not simply gone to uni and gone through the process.
- A mistake on a CV can be damning. Technology is there to serve us and make things easier. You have spellcheck: use it. Ask a friend to check your CV as well because there are some areas in which us feeble humans still come up trumps.
- Don't use glossy terms or jargon. Give concise details, expanding where appropriate – not reams and reams though. Recruiters don't want an essay. A CV should be three pages max, ideally just two.
- Don't just say things; back them up. You can't just claim to be obsessed with debt and equity capital markets; you're going to have to prove your passion with examples. Speak to lawyers whenever you can – it all helps to show that you understand the reality of practice. Likewise, make sure you demonstrate your qualities rather than just stating them.
- You can use any kind of work to prove you have commercial awareness. Even if it was in a pub you can still talk about being aware of costs, budgeting and the marketing the pub did. Think about the simple things you can extrapolate from.
- As well as commercial awareness and a love of the law, applications should demonstrate teamwork and problem-solving skills.

Don't undersell yourself

If you looked at the training contract applications of a handful of different students you'd see that some include more information about their achievements than others. Usually those with less content have omitted to include things because they simply don't appreciate their significance.

- Qualifications, gap-year experiences, 17 A*s at A level, endless vac schemes – these things are obvious essentials. Applications should demonstrate teamwork and problem-solving skills as well as a commercial outlook and commitment to becoming a lawyer.
- Explain to the reader what you learned from your experiences rather than just listing them.
- Write a list of all the jobs you've ever had and consider the list as a whole. You may be able to demonstrate that you're a real grafter who's managed to help pay their way through uni. It won't always be appropriate to list all your part-time employment so you might need to group some jobs into a more general category. Unless the list is extensive, indicate the key aspects of your role in each position but make sure it doesn't appear daunting for the reader as they plough through many forms or CVs in one sitting.
- If you studied a musical instrument to a high level then say so. It shows you can commit to something and work diligently to achieve it. The same goes for other pastimes or pursuits – eg life-guarding, scuba diving, artistic endeavours.
- Sports are great application form/CV fodder. Again, the commitment factor will come through, and if it's a team sport you play then what better confirmation is there of your being a team player?
- Were you ever selected, or better still elected, to a position of responsibility? To be chosen by your peers as a student representative, for example, suggests that people admire you and have confidence in your abilities. It also shows you are naturally the sort of person who likes to take on a challenge. As to how far back in time you reach for such nuggets of gold, well, this depends on your current situation. If you are still at university, or have very recently graduated, then something from your later school days should still be suitable. If it was some time since you left uni then you need to find some more recent examples. Never forget to mention if you were a (deputy) head boy or girl, the captain of a sport team or held a position of responsibility in a society or club.

Unless otherwise stated, always include a covering letter with your CV. It's a golden opportunity to show off your writing skills, explain your motives, wax lyrical about your qualities and show how suited you are to your target firm or set. A good covering letter will highlight the best aspects of your application. If you have any weaknesses (say a poorer than anticipated degree result), it's a place to mention extenuating circumstances.

And finally...

If all this advice seems totally obvious, that's because it is. You wouldn't think anyone makes elementary mistakes any more, but every year recruiters still find themselves reading CVs that look like they've been written by Mr Bean. Poor layout, atrocious grammar, banal comments… all this from university graduates. Just think: by the simple act of not making any stupid errors, you're blowing a significant number of your potential competitors out of the water. Conversely, if you accidentally write down *it's* when you meant *its* or *there* when you mean *their* – even just the one time – then no matter what your other qualities, in the eyes of recruiters you've just lumped yourself in with all the other Beans.

How to succeed at interviews and assessment days

Interviews and assessment days are to be celebrated not dreaded. You'll send out dozens of application forms and get blanked by most firms – maybe even all of them – so when you do get an interview, give it your all.

Interviews

The biggest error that can be made while hunting the Lesser Spotted Training Contract is to confuse getting an interview with getting a job. You've worked really hard so far, but it's time to ratchet things up another notch. Turn on the charm, adopt a good posture and be thorough with your homework. It's time for a classic aphorism: 'If you fail to prepare, then you prepare to fail'. As one recruiter acknowledged: "*It's a bit David Brent, but it's true.*"

Before any interview:

Read and think about your application form. Interviewers will pick up on what you wrote and question you on it. A lot of the time, they'll discuss your application form as an icebreaker. It's your chance to speak about things that interest you and to build up rapport. Chat, be expansive, maybe even flash the pearly whites. If you fibbed on your application form, make sure you've got an extensive cover story sketched out to back up your claim or else you'll be found out. Better yet: don't lie or over-exaggerate in the first place.

Research the firm. A stock question is 'Why this firm in particular?' Recruiters tell us this is where many people trip up. Make sure you've got something good, innovative and non-generic to say. Read the **True Picture** reports and find out about the firm's strengths, its history and what is being said about it in the legal press. Ideally you will find a topic or two that can be developed into a reason why you and the firm are a perfect match.

Research the people who are interviewing you, if possible. 'Knowledge is power' and 'know your enemy', as they say. Practice area, precedent-setting cases they've won, previous firms they've worked at, their favourite colour/pet/sport – all of this is gold and law firm websites often contain such details. Don't quote it all back at them though… it's creepy.

Have a finger on the pulse of legal news and current affairs. *The Lawyer*, *Legal Week*, *Solicitors Journal* and *Law Gazette* are all very good, as is Thursday's Law supplement in *The Times*. And have you signed up for the *Student Guide*'s newsletter or Facebook updates? Be ready to see the connections between law and the real world of politics, society and business. Try to demonstrate that you're commercially aware.

Practise answers, but not too much. It's not that difficult to guess what sort of questions you're going to get; something along the lines of 'Why do you want to be a lawyer?' is a bona fide cert. It is wise to rehearse a little to collect your thoughts, but as great comedians will tell you, you've got to be ready to deviate from the script as the mood takes you. Speaking off the cuff makes you sound more interesting and often a classic question will be slightly altered and you need to be ready to adapt.

Historically, us Brits are modest folk and talking about cash is often judged to be vulgar, but a good number of our sources did say that it was a factor. Don't be scared about mentioning that the excellent financial rewards are a factor in choosing to be a lawyer. You're among friends. Just make sure you give some other, more wholesome, reasons too.

The default setting when going into an interview is to want to be liked and accepted, but remember that the interview is a crucial opportunity for you to figure out what you like about the firm. You can become the questioner; indeed you should have a couple of questions prepared for the end of the interview. There are so many things you might ask and it's best to pick something that isn't already covered in the firm's own literature. You could find out what your interviewers like about the firm or ask them about when they trained. You could ask them what the firm is doing in reaction to [insert your preferred relevant current affair here]. Be confident and use this opportunity to improve the rapport with your interviewers.

The usual interview tips apply:

- Arrive early. Have a contact number ready in case some cruel act of divine vengeance makes you late.
- Dress appropriately. Make 'ordinary' your goal.
- Be polite to EVERYONE.
- Shake hands firmly (not so they lose their balance – that's too much) and make eye contact. Smile non-menacingly.

- Speak to everyone on the panel, ensuring you make eye contact with all present.
- Don't fidget or sit awkwardly. Don't allow your body to tense.
- Do mock interviews beforehand and get feedback from whoever tests you. Even family members and friends can be surprisingly good at this if you explain what sort of questions you want them to ask. They may identify an annoying verbal tic. Do what you can to eradicate any rogue erms and umms.
- Listen carefully to questions so you can establish what it is the interviewer seeks. Don't just shoehorn in pre-packaged answers.

Assessment days

Even though you might have an LPC distinction, a First-class degree, three As at A level, 29 GCSEs, a gold star from Mrs Haslem's nursery class and many other great qualities besides, some firms still want to see you in action and test you out with their own assessments. In their arsenal, firms have written and negotiation exercises, personality profiling, research tasks and group tasks. On our website we detail the different hoops you'll need to leap through at each of our profiled firms.

Recruiters are all keen to see whether you can work as part of a team. Advertising pitches to faux-clients and pretend mini-transactions are two common exercises, but these things are always changing and different firms have different methods (and want to see different traits). One we know of even asks applicants to take part in a debate in front of the entire firm. So, always bear in mind what kind of organisation it is and what type of person they're looking for. Be careful not to dominate group tasks too much or fade into the background.

There are several types of psychometric test and law firms like to throw a mixture at applicants. Some test verbal or numerical reasoning skills, others test your judgement when confronted by certain scenarios and some aim to tap into personality traits even you didn't know you had. Although the companies that produce these tests try to keep their secrets safe, the internet is a great place to read up on them. Personality tests aim to find out whether you are a leader or a follower, a planner or impulsive, etc. In theory, there are no right or wrong answers and the standard advice is to be yourself, but before you expose your soul to recruiters, it is worth thinking about why they have set this test and what they are looking for. The general format varies between selecting adjectives that best or least describe you, to choosing a response to a given scenario. Many of the questions on this year's Clifford Chance situational judgement test, for example, began *"your supervisor is extremely busy..."* Obvious attempts to throw the test may be picked up by recruiters; however, profiling yourself as an indecisive, emotional control freak isn't going to help you. Although some people swear that these tests accurately determine an applicant's personality, others still denounce them.

Numerical and, in particular, verbal reasoning tests are the most important ones and, thankfully, they are tests you can prepare for. Look into the methodologies of the main ones (start on Wikipedia) and ask your careers service for examples. Some firms might post out samples in advance, so take advantage: it is really important to be in the right frame of mind for these. Two common ones are the Watson Glaser and SHL tests. They're usually comprised of multiple-choice, reasoning-based questions that look for intellectual rigour and some business awareness. Applicants must typically decide whether a statement is true, false, or impossible to determine given the information available. Accuracy is imperative, as is mental agility, so if your brain cells are as agile as an arthritic grandmother, get practising – they'll need to resemble a Russian gymnast come test day.

Numerical reasoning tests assess your ability to process data contained in graphs and tables. Questions ask you to find percentage changes and calculate quantities from percentages. Some tests deliberately contain too many questions, as they're designed to assess your speed under pressure. Make sure you know if you're sitting one of these and, whatever the test, try to use your time effectively.

Don't relax too much if there's a social event as these can be just as important when it comes to making a good impression. Some firms have lunches where you sit round with three or four partners and a handful of other applicants and make small talk over the duck à l'orange. Who will your prospective supervisor want to hire? The girl who kept her eyes on the plate for the entire meal and whispered unintelligible answers to every question? The chap who drank too much of the Bourgogne Pinot Noir and spent most of the meal calling him buddy? Or the nice young man who made some pertinent observations on the rise of the Gulf economies and showed an interest in his taxidermy hobby? Similarly, a drink with the firm's trainees is an opportunity to strike up a rapport with them, not to start making comments about how your vac scheme at Norton Rose was *so* much better.

And finally...

The sad fact is that for very many people it could take a while to succeed. Don't let rejection bring you down. Treat a failed interview like the end of a relationship: convince yourself it wasn't really anyone's fault and that you just weren't really suitable for the firm. Ask recruiters what led to the rejection and try and learn from it. Chin up, champ: plenty of fish left in the sea. Badmouthing a firm afterwards is optional (and cathartic) but best done privately. Go to our website for advice from applicants who failed to gain a training contract on their first attempt but then aced the process second time around.

Managing job offers

After all the hard work involved in securing a training contract offer, you'll need to know what to do when you actually land one.

The Solicitors Regulation Authority publishes a 'voluntary code to good practice in the recruitment of trainee solicitors' at www.sra.org.uk/documents/students/training-contract/voluntarycode.pdf.

Read through these guidelines if at any stage you are in doubt as to what you should do. They address the conduct of both recruiters and students. Law firms are not obliged to follow these guidelines, though most will.

On offers, the guidelines say:

- If you're still an undergrad, a training contract offer should not be made before 1 September in your final undergraduate year. If you've impressed a firm during a vacation scheme or period of work experience, it must wait until this date before making you an offer.
- At an interview, you will be told if there is a further stage to the selection process. You should also be told within two weeks of reaching the end of the process whether or not you have been successful.
- Offers should be made in writing. If you receive an offer by phone you don't need to say yes or no: you can ask the firm to send a formal offer in writing for you to consider.

On deadlines, the guidelines say:

- No deadline should expire earlier than four weeks from the date of an offer. If you need more time to mull over an offer, firms are supposed to consider your request 'sympathetically', provided you have a good reason. No definition of 'good reason' is given in the guidelines.
- If a firm is going to pay your law school fees it should set out the terms and conditions of the arrangement in the training contract offer letter. A firm's willingness to provide financial assistance should not affect the time limit for accepting the contract.
- If you feel you need more time, you will have to enter into diplomatic discussions with the law firm, telling them how much longer you need. Ask for written confirmation of any extension to the deadline so both parties are clear what has been decided.

You may want to hang on to an offer from one firm while you pursue applications with others. This is okay, but you must bear in mind the following:

- You should not hold more than two (as yet unaccepted or declined) offers at any one time.
- Students are supposed to respond promptly to a firm that's made an offer, either by accepting or rejecting it. The word 'promptly' is not defined in the code.
- Because offers can and will be made with time limits for acceptance, do guard against allowing a deadline to elapse. The stupidity tax you may otherwise pay doesn't bear thinking about.
- Once you have accepted your preferred offer in writing, you must then confirm to everyone else that you are withdrawing your application. This is only fair to busy recruiters and other applicants who may suffer if you clog up a shortlist.

The guidelines are silent on the issue of what happens if a student changes their mind after accepting an offer. It's a rare firm that will be particularly sympathetic to a post-acceptance withdrawal but, on occasions, these things do happen. We can give no general advice on this subject, as each individual case will have its own merits. What we can say is that the smooth running of the whole trainee recruitment market relies on most parties playing by the above 'rules'. So what if a law firm puts pressure on you to accept an offer earlier than the guidelines say they should? Again, there is no simple answer as the SRA's code of conduct is voluntary. If this situation arises you will have to enter into delicate negotiations with the law firm. You could also discuss the problem with your university or college careers adviser and ask if they can recommend a course of action.

Law School

Solicitors' timetable 46
Barristers' timetable 47
The Graduate Diploma in Law (GDL) 48
The Legal Practice Course (LPC) 52
LPC provider reports 56
The Bar Professional Training Course (BPTC) 70
BPTC provider reports 73
How to fund law school 77

Solicitors' Timetable

<table>
<tr><th></th><th>Law students • Penultimate undergraduate year/ Law graduates</th><th>Non-law students • Final year/ Non-law graduates</th></tr>
<tr><td>Oct/Nov 2010</td><td colspan="2">Compile info on law firms, attend law fairs and careers events – continue for 6 months</td></tr>
<tr><td></td><td colspan="2">Apply for Christmas vacation schemes</td></tr>
<tr><td>Christmas vacation</td><td colspan="2">Vacation scheme, if possible
Apply for Easter vacation schemes.</td></tr>
<tr><td>Jan 2011</td><td></td><td>Apply for GDL; initial selection round, deadline 1 February. Late applications considered in second round.</td></tr>
<tr><td>Feb</td><td colspan="2">Some training contract deadlines
Apply for summer vacation schemes</td></tr>
<tr><td>Easter vacation</td><td colspan="2">Vacation scheme, if possible</td></tr>
<tr><td>May
June
Summer vacation</td><td colspan="2">Apply for contracts and attend interviews. Vacation scheme, if possible</td></tr>
<tr><td>Sept 2011</td><td>Start final year of degree</td><td>Start GDL course</td></tr>
<tr><td>Oct/Nov 2011</td><td colspan="2">Apply for LPC place through Lawcabs. Deadline 1 December</td></tr>
<tr><td>Sept 2012</td><td colspan="2">Start LPC course</td></tr>
<tr><td>Aug/Sept 2013/March 2014</td><td colspan="2">Start training contract</td></tr>
<tr><td>Aug/Sept 2015/March 2016</td><td colspan="2">Qualify!</td></tr>
<tr><td>2046</td><td colspan="2">Become senior partner</td></tr>
</table>

Notes

1 It is important to check application closing dates for each firm as these will vary.

2 Some firms will only accept applications for vacation schemes from penultimate-year students, whether law or non-law. See A-Z pages for further information.

3 Some firms require very early applications from non-law graduates. See A-Z pages for further information.

4 The timetable refers primarily to those firms that recruit two years in advance. Smaller firms often recruit just one year in advance or for immediate vacancies.

5 This timetable assumes students will progress straight through from university to law school and a training contract. This is not necessarily the most appropriate or achievable course of action for all students.

Barristers' Timetable

<table>
<tr><th></th><th>Law students • Penultimate undergraduate year</th><th>Non-law students • Final year</th></tr>
<tr><td>Throughout the year</td><td colspan="2">Start thinking about getting some relevant work experience. Do plenty of research into chambers/mini-pupillages</td></tr>
<tr><td>By the end of January 2011</td><td></td><td>Apply for the GDL</td></tr>
<tr><td>By the end of April</td><td colspan="2">Apply for a pupillage under the year early scheme on Pupillage Portal</td></tr>
<tr><td>April</td><td></td><td>Apply for a GDL scholarship from an Inn of Court. If successful, join that Inn</td></tr>
<tr><td>June to September</td><td></td><td>Do pre-GDL mini-pupillages</td></tr>
<tr><td>September/October 2011</td><td>Start final year of degree</td><td>Start GDL</td></tr>
<tr><td>November</td><td colspan="2">Apply online for BPTC by early January deadline. Apply to an Inn of Court for a scholarship</td></tr>
<tr><td>During final year/GDL</td><td colspan="2">Apply for pupillage to non-Pupillage Portal sets. Do mini-pupillages</td></tr>
<tr><td>March/April</td><td colspan="2">Apply for pupillage through Pupillage Portal by late April deadline</td></tr>
<tr><td>May</td><td colspan="2">Apply for Inn membership by 31 May deadline</td></tr>
<tr><td>September 2012</td><td colspan="2">Start the BPTC. Pupillage applications to non-Pupillage Portal sets</td></tr>
<tr><td>March/April</td><td colspan="2">If unsuccessful last year, apply for pupillage before late April deadline</td></tr>
<tr><td>June</td><td colspan="2">Finish BPTC</td></tr>
<tr><td>October 2013</td><td colspan="2">Start pupillage</td></tr>
<tr><td>Summer</td><td colspan="2">Be offered tenancy at your pupillage chambers or apply for tenancy or a 3rd six elsewhere</td></tr>
<tr><td>October 2013</td><td colspan="2">Start tenancy</td></tr>
<tr><td>2044</td><td colspan="2">Be appointed to the High Court Bench</td></tr>
<tr><td>2054</td><td colspan="2">Get slapped on the wrist by Ministry of Justice for falling asleep in court</td></tr>
</table>

Note

This timetable assumes students will progress straight through from university to law school and a pupillage. This is not necessarily the most appropriate or achievable course of action for students.

The Graduate Diploma in Law (GDL)

Whether you opted to spend your undergrad years reading great authors, or divining the inner workings of the human body, you can still come to the law via a one-year conversion course known as the Graduate Diploma in Law.

Because skills like textual analysis, research, logical argument, and written and oral presentation can be acquired in a whole range of disciplines, from English literature to zoology, legal employers tend not to make a distinction between applicants with an LLB and those who take the GDL route. The GDL is essentially a crash law degree, designed to bring you up to the required standard in seven core legal subjects that would typically be taught in the first two years of an LLB. So that's two years of study crammed into one – not exactly a walk in the park. Taken full-time it lasts a minimum of 36 weeks and can demand up to 45 hours of lectures, tutorials and personal study each week. It is possible to take the course part-time over two years and you will find that course providers offer a surprisingly wide range of flexible study options, from distance learning to weekends or evening-only classes.

The standard requirement for admission is a degree from a university in the UK or Republic of Ireland. It is possible for non-graduates to get onto a course if they've shown the requisite drive and determination, and have exceptional ability in some other field. Such candidates – and those with a degree from an overseas university – must obtain a Certificate of Academic Standing from the Bar Standards Board or Solicitors Regulation Authority before enrolling on the GDL.

Assessment tends to be by written exams taken at the end of the academic year. These will make up the bulk of your final grade, so make sure you are adequately prepared. Most GDL providers offer their students the opportunity to take mock exams throughout the year, and while these are generally optional, it's probably a good idea to get as many as you can under your belt. Other assessments and essays completed during the year can count for up to 30% of your final grade so do not underestimate their importance. Depending on the institution, there will be more or less emphasis on academic essays, written problem questions or practical preparation for classroom debates. Because the institutions that offer the GDL vary in perceived quality, their approach and the composition of their student bodies, it is well worth doing your research before you apply. City University and Nottingham are renowned for offering more academic courses, thought to be ideally suited to students headed to the Bar. In London, BPP and the College of Law, for example, are packed with plenty of City types and place special emphasis on helping you gain practical legal skills. Be aware that an increasing number of City firms are appointing a particular law school as their preferred provider. If you have your heart set on doing your training contract with a particular law firm, do your research and find out whether they have a preferred provider before you apply to the schools.

There's a huge amount to take in so you need to be disciplined: work out a study timetable early on, and stick to it. Don't count on being able to catch up. You're there to learn a set curriculum, not to think outside the box. Probably the best use of your creativity is to come up with amusing ways of remembering case names. Attend classes: some law schools will report on attendance, if asked by your future employer.

Land law

This module will teach you everything you need to know about the ownership of land, starting with the startling realisation that all of it ultimately belongs to the Crown. Many students may find the subject off-putting because it uses archaic jargon and calls on concepts such as overreaching, flying freeholds, which defy any sense of logic. Give it some time and everything should fall into place. You'll find the topic has practical implications for everyday life, including tips on how to handle a dispute with your landlord or arrange your first mortgage. The course takes you through the basics of conveyancing and how to acquire interests in land before going through the detail of how those interests operate. The subject is formalistic and particularly statute-heavy. In addition to remembering loads of cases, you will be required to memorise countless statutory provisions on the creation and registration of interests in land. Don't wait to familiarise yourself with the most important sections of the Law of Property Act: start creating flowcharts and checklists early on and you will laugh your way through the exam. As with most topics on the GDL, you will need to gain a good overall understanding of land law to be able to deal with specific matters, so don't bet on revising selected subjects for the exam as there can be important overlap between them.

EU

EU law now affects our lives in many ways. This course should dispel a few misconceptions about the British membership of the European Union – it touches on far more than the way in which EU bureaucrats regulate the shape and size of bananas. You'll learn that the European Court of Justice (ECJ) is effectively the highest court of appeal for all the member states, and that EU law plays a central role in the creation of rights against discrimination on grounds of age, disability, race, religion or sexual orientation, for example. Students become familiar with the institutional framework, foundations and underlying principles of the European Union before going on to explore certain areas of substantive EU law. Big subjects include the free movement of goods and workers, competition law and the freedom of establishment, as well as the incorporation of the European Convention on Human Rights into our national law. For Euro-philes, this course will provide a fascinating mix of politics, history, economics and comparative jurisprudence, but its case law contains some of the longest and most tongue-twisting names you're likely to see.

Equity and trusts

This course is an introduction to the fundamental principles of equity, an intriguing area of law which calls upon the idea of conscience to remedy injustices brought about by the application of black letter law. It also deals with the concept of trust, which is the legal arrangement whereby one person holds property for the benefit of another. Some assume the subject is the preserve of future Chancery barristers and private client specialists. While this is partially true, equity and trusts form a particularly dynamic area of law, and you'll not only learn about the creation of gifts and trusts in the family context, you'll also see that the concept has many uses in the commercial world, particularly where tax evasion or the tracing of misappropriated funds is concerned. The topic is mostly precedent-based, meaning that you'll have to learn a huge number of cases. On the bright side, these can be amusing and memorable. You'll hear about adulterous husbands trying to set up secret trusts for their mistresses and illegitimate children or wealthy eccentrics attempting to set up a pension for a beloved pet. Be aware that the concept of equity pervades the GDL course, so what you've learned here will also be relevant to your land law and contract modules.

Contract

As a practising lawyer, you will apply your knowledge of contract law on a daily basis because it underpins nearly every single legal relationship. You'll start by studying the rules that determine when an agreement becomes legally binding and enforceable and which formalities are required to create a contract. You'll then move on to study what terms are permissible and find out what happens when you omit to read the small print. You'll hear about the doctrine of misrepresentation, mistake and duress, and you'll find out what your remedy is when an art dealer has neglected to tell you the Jackson Pollock you've just bought is actually the product of his son's finger painting. Armed with your knowledge of the Sale of Goods Act, you may be tempted to bring any number of small claims against the high-street retailers whose products fall apart the minute you get them home.

Crime

Studying criminal law will allow you to discover the reality behind the storylines of all those legal dramas you watch. The syllabus will take you through assault, battery, sexual offences, criminal damage, theft, fraud and homicide. Also covered are the liability of accomplices, attempted offences and the defences available to those accused of committing criminal acts. Whether your interest is in policy or the gruesome things that people do to one another, the crime course should provide plenty to engage and surprise. Overall, the subject follows a logical pattern and doesn't hide many difficult philosophical concepts. You will find out early on that you always need to identify the actus reus (the guilty act) and the mens rea (the guilty mind) in order to establish an offence. Follow this structure religiously and you can't go wrong. By the end of the course you'll also be in a better position to explain why killing someone is not necessarily unlawful or why you could be guilty of theft without actually making off with somebody else's property.

Tort

The law of tort is concerned with remedying wrongs committed by one individual against another via the civil rather than the criminal courts. Beyond this very sensible definition hides one of the most intellectually stimulating courses on the GDL. The law of negligence is the big subject in tort and you will devote the best part of the year to getting your head around it and applying it to specific situations such as clinical negligence. The course will also cover wrongs ranging from defamation to private nuisance. This is the field which fuels the so-called compensation culture and gives 'ambulance-chasing' lawyers a bad name. You will hear about the fate of victims of gruesome work or road traffic accidents and catastrophic events such as the Hillsborough disaster. You will also come across downright comical stories, including a prolific prankster playing a lavatory joke on a colleague or a case of compensation for scratchy underwear.

Public law

This course includes the study of constitutional law, human rights and administrative law. If you have no interest in politics, you may find the whole subject a little obscure, but 12 years on since the passing of the Human Rights Act, and with several constitutional reforms in the works, now is arguably the best of times to study this fascinating subject. The course will normally kick off with an analysis of the UK's constitutional arrangements. This part is largely academic and will cover the doctrines of Parliamentary sovereignty, the Rule of Law, the Royal Prerogative and Responsible Government. Those with politics degrees will hit the ground running. You're likely to enjoy the constitutional bit of the subject if you're a history or philosophy buff. If you do not fit the description, why not Google 'Dicey' and see where that takes you. You'll also be taught about the Human Rights Act, with particular emphasis being given to the concepts of freedom of speech, privacy, the right to a fair trial and the nitty-gritty of exactly how much force the police can use when they throw you in the back of their van. After the academic bit is over, much of the rest of the course is devoted to judicial review, the process by which individuals can challenge the decisions of public authorities.

How to apply

Certain GDL providers, particularly those with a City slant, also offer a range of optional classes designed to ease your passage into the corporate world. These extras may include additional lectures or seminars on things like company law, intellectual property and international law. Most schools also organise mooting competitions and pro bono work. These should give you an early opportunity to try your counselling and advocacy skills and find out if the career you had in mind is really for you, particularly if you're headed for the Bar. Some GDL providers have degree-awarding powers and allow you to upgrade your qualification to an LLB, either upon successful completion of your GDL and LPC or via a summer course after the GDL (for an additional fee). Unlike the GDL, the LLB gives you an internationally recognised accreditation.

Applications are made online through the Central Applications Board (www.lawcabs.ac.uk). It's worth getting your application in as early as possible if you have your heart set on a particular institution, particularly as Lawcabs need your referee to respond to them before your application is passed on to the schools you're interested in. First-round applications for the 2010/11 course can be made between 1 November 2010 and 1 February 2011. The institutions will consider these and make offers from 7 March 2011; students must accept a first-round offer by 15 April 2011. Applications made later than 1 February will be considered after 15 April. The later you apply the more flexible you may have to be about where you study. Applications for part-time courses should be made directly to the providers. If you intend to do an LPC or BVC at a popular institution you might stand a better chance if you choose it for your GDL as many providers guarantee places to their GDL graduates. The GDL is now offered at around 39 different universities and law schools across England and Wales. Our website has a table detailing course providers' fees and loads of other useful information.

The GDL Providers
University of Birmingham (ft)
Birmingham City University (ft/pt)
Bournemouth University (ft/pt)
BPP Law School, Leeds (ft/pt)
BPP Law School, London (ft/pt)
BPP Law School, Manchester (ft/pt)
University of Bradford (ft/pt)
University of Brighton (ft/pt)
Bristol Institute of Legal Practice (ft/pt)
Brunel University (ft)
Buckinghamshire New University (ft)
University of Central Lancashire (ft/pt)
The City Law School (ft)
College of Law, Birmingham (ft/pt)
College of Law, Bristol (ft/pt)
College of Law, Chester (ft/pt)
College of Law, Guildford (ft/pt)
College of Law, London (ft/pt)
College of Law, Manchester (ft/pt)
College of Law, York (ft/pt)
De Montfort University (ft/pt)
University of East Anglia (ft)
University of Glamorgan (ft/pt)
University of Hertfordshire (ft/pt)
University of Huddersfield (ft/pt)
Kaplan Law School (ft)
Keele University (ft/pt)
Kingston University (ft/pt)
Leeds Metropolitan University (ft/pt)
University of Lincoln (ft)
Liverpool John Moores University (ft)
London Metropolitan University (ft/pt)
London South Bank University (ft/pt)
Manchester Metropolitan University (ft/pt)
Middlesex University (ft/pt)
Northumbria University Law School (ft/pt)
Nottingham Law School (ft/pt)
Oxford Brookes University (ft/pt)
University of Plymouth (ft)
Sheffield Hallam University (ft/pt)
Staffordshire University (ft/pt)
University of Sussex (ft)
Swansea University (ft)
Thames Valley University (ft/pt)
University of Westminster (ft/pt)
Worcester College of Technology (pt)
University of Wolverhampton (ft/pt)

Gender and the law

1922 first woman solicitor Carrie Morrison admitted

63% of law graduates are women

69% of self-employed and **54%** of employed barristers are men

62% of trainees are women

One of the 12 Justices of the supreme Court is female

45% of solicitors on the Roll are women

7.4% the gender pay gap among trainee solicitors

On average **20%** of magic circle partners are women*

Rose Heilbron and Helena Normanton were appointed as the first female silks in 1949

One **fifth** of women solicitors are partners, compared to two fifths of men

52% of those called to the Bar in 2009 were women

90% of Queen's Counsel are men

16 High Court Justices are women

Four of the 38 Lords Justices of Appeal are women

All figures from the Law Society and Bar Council in 2009

*Figures from Law Society report of 2007

The Legal Practice Course (LPC)

As the necessary step between an LLB or GDL and a hallowed training contract, the decision to study this vocational course should not be taken lightly. It can be taken full time in a year or less, or part time over two or more years.

The big picture

In 2009, a report by social mobility czar Alan Milburn condemned the legal profession as a closed shop. It begs the question: are efforts to make law an accessible career choice succeeding? Enter the LPC3.

Reflecting the Solicitors Regulation Authority's (SRA) commitment to widen access to the profession, the new-style LPC represents the biggest shake-up to the course since its inception in 1993. The course is now split into two separate stages. Stage One delivers the compulsory subjects of Business Law & Practice (BLP), Litigation (civil and criminal), and Property Law & Practice (PLP), as well as skills such as drafting, interviewing and practical legal research. Stage Two covers elective subjects, of which three must be chosen. Students can opt to study Stage One at one provider, and either complete the electives at the same provider, another provider, two at one provider and one at another, or even all three at different providers. That's without even taking account of the part-time options. Students could do Stage One full time and Stage Two electives part time.

The new-look LPC also allows providers greater freedom and flexibility to tailor the course. Several have re-engineered the compulsory subjects to reflect the interests and future destinations of their students. Theoretically at least, the option is there to build your very own bespoke LPC. Pretty much anything goes so long as the LPC is completed within five years. Feedback from course providers, however, indicates that most students will continue to complete the LPC at a sole provider.

While the SRA's reforms allow more people to train, alas – and it's a major alas – the number of available training contracts has not kept pace with the growing number of LPCers. The simple fact is that each year more LPC grads enter a job market that offers too few training contracts to allow everyone to convert the on-paper qualification into an in-practice career. Some 7,759 students completed the course in the 2008/09 academic year, with only 5,809 training contracts registered during the same period (down 7.8% on the previous year), leaving many students out of luck and presumably out of pocket. Let's not forget that the figures don't take account of those LPC graduates from previous years who still haven't got training contracts. Many whose sole reward is a bunch of new letters to stick after their name and many thousands of pounds of debt must look back with regret at their decision to take the course. In the past year, the situation has only become worse. The SRA claims that it has no power to cap the number of places that institutions are validated for, so effectively there's a practically open invite, even though the dance floor is already full.

The Law Society is considering the introduction of an aptitude test for entry on to the LPC (the Bar Standards Board is currently trialling exactly that for the BPTC), but until such a scheme is brought in – and even afterwards – you need to try and work out whether you're one of those potential applicants who should be deterred, or whether you're someone with decent prospects. This self-analysis is important because there's a lot of money at stake.

Money, money, money

Unless you've been hooked up by a generous commercial law firm that's sponsoring you, it's time to dig deep. LPC fees range from £5,900 for the cheapest two-year part-time course, to £12,500 at the top end. Then you must also factor in living expenses. For a comprehensive comparison of course fees look at the **LPC Providers Table** on our website. We also have advice on funding on page 77.

Though law-firm funded LPC students may make their peers green with envy, it's important to remember that there's no such thing as a free lunch. With each passing year the conditions imposed upon sponsored students become more and more stringent. A current trend is law school/law firm tie-ups. A handful of providers are signing exclusive deals with firms to have their future trainees taught together, in the process becoming well versed with the firm's style and precedents.

Although the number of available training contracts may be falling, the number of LPC places is ever increasing. The two biggest providers in the market are BPP and the College of Law (COL). Though both are adamant that they just focus on what they're doing, it seems to be that where one goes, the other follows. Tête-à-tête in Manchester, London, Bristol and Birmingham, neither is slowing down. For the economists among you, you might expect that an increased number of places would drive the cost of the course down. While that's certainly not true of the big providers, smaller ones have taken a look at how the course is costed, making adjustments accordingly. In Bristol for example, BILP at UWE has cut its fees to cope with the September 2010 invasion of BPP and COL.

Get real

With course providers believing that it's too paternalistic to limit the number of LPC places, and the SRA claiming not to have the power to restrict the providers, who's going to make sure your money isn't wasted? You. Before signing up to the LPC, it's time to get serious. While a 2:2 degree will pretty much guarantee you a place on a course, finding a firm that will want to train you is an entirely different proposition: blind optimism won't cut it in the solicitor's world. Do make sure you have read all the advice in the previous section of this guide and be realistic about your chances. If you worry that you are not a strong candidate then take steps to improve your market appeal.

The nuts and bolts of the LPC

It's important to remember that the LPC is not an academic course – it's vocational. Treat it like the first year of your professional life. The LPC requires good time management and organisation. "*Do be well prepared for your sessions, otherwise there's not much point in attending,*" advises one LPC survivor. Write up your notes as you go along and pay attention to the outcomes of every class (as these are likely exam questions). Some providers have open-book exams, but beware: sitting at your desk with an exam paper in front of you and a leaning tower of textbooks at your side will not help. Keep on top of things as the course progresses, and perhaps even think about sharing the revision workload with classmates.

Many students complain that the "*learn and churn*" approach of the LPC isn't as stimulating as an undergraduate degree. It's not supposed to be stimulating; it's meant to get you ready to start a training contract. The days of theorising are gone. LLB and GDL essays transform into letters of advice, terms and conditions and points about tax. Forget about that dissertation on Hegelian dialectics or Foucault's contribution to post-structuralism – the LPC strips everyone back to basics. With classes on semicolons and spelling, it can feel like you've reversed back to school, but you'll pick up plenty of tricks and tips along the way, including:

- How to conduct an interview (usually utilising a strong handshake accompanied by the offer of a beverage);
- How to sign off a letter – not 'lots of love' or 'peace', as a rule;
- How to minimise tax exposure – it's about avoidance not evasion;
- How many directors it takes to make a board meeting – this isn't a bad joke;
- When litigation documents must be served on the other side – you will curse the day bank holidays were invented;
- Whether you or your landlord is responsible when the roof leaks; and
- Why it's never a good idea to dabble with clients' money.

Make the right choice

The elasticity of the LPC3 makes it more important than ever to think about which provider is right for you. With so many to choose from, it's easy to get swamped. Don't stress. Look at the law firms you want to apply to. You don't want to end up on a high-street focused LPC if you're yearning for a career with a City giant. Equally, it's important to look at what extra-curricular activities are on offer for some CV-boosting.

Arm yourself well – read prospectuses, attend open days, chat to representatives visiting your university, talk to current students and ascertain your priorities. And don't forget to read our **Provider Reports**. If you have a training contract, the choice of provider might be taken out of your hands, but if you don't, here are a few issues to take into consideration.

Career path: Even if a future employer doesn't specify where you must study, they may still be able to offer advice. If you don't yet have a training contract, look into the range of extra-curricular activities, clubs and societies on offer that may bolster your CV. Also think about the quality of careers advice available at each institution. Will they help to organise placements for you? Will they support you after you have finished the course, and if so for how long?

Electives: If you have the freedom to choose your electives then find out which providers offer the most suitable ones for the type of practice you want to move into, or at least which ones appeal to you the most. Although most providers offer a pretty standard package, some do throw in the odd wildcard such as E-Commerce or Charity Law. For a full list see the **LPC Providers Table** on our website.

Assessment grades and pass rates: Pass rates are published on the SRA's website each autumn; however, be aware that direct comparisons are difficult as each provider examines and marks independently of the others. The SRA also visits and inspects each provider and then publishes a report online.

When and how: Timetables can vary wildly between providers, with some only requiring attendance for two days a week and others scheduling face-to-face time on four days, either mornings or afternoons. Term dates can also vary substantially, and with the onset of the LPC3 so can the length of the whole course. Think realistically about what timetable structure will fit most easily into your life. Also think about whether or not you will need a job during the course. While all providers are reluctant to acknowledge that students will be able to fit in a part-time job, they have an increasing understanding of the economic realities and some timetables are more accommodating than others. If working during the course is unavoidable you may want to consider studying part-time.

The use of e-learning resources has become an increasingly popular method of delivering the LPC. COL, for example, no longer incorporates lectures into its LPC, so instead of sitting in large theatres with 200-odd other students being taught in real time by real people, you'll assimilate the lecture information via online i-tutorials. These are backed up and built upon in face-to-face, small-group workshops. Meanwhile, the use of online learning is becoming even more pervasive at BPP, which is rolling out an entirely remote learning LPC thus rendering physical attendance entirely unnecessary. Lectures are still available to those that want them, as are face-to-face small-group sessions. Some students thrive on electronic learning methods, and part-time students in particular appreciate being able to fit the work around their already busy lives. However, working from home does require a degree of dedication and self-discipline, so think carefully about what mode of teaching will suit you best before you sign up.

Assessments: The vast majority of providers examine their students using open-book exams and written assessments. A notable minority have stuck with the closed-book approach. Think carefully about what method will suit you best. It is easy to feel drawn to the open-book approach, but the time frames are such that you have very little time to check your books in the exam room and so having a leaning tower of Pisa built of resource materials on your desk is not as advantageous as it might seem.

Facilities: For every provider at which students must search plaintively for a quiet study corner, there is another where they can spread out in blessed peace in their own 'office'. Take the LPC course at a university and you'll belong to a proper law faculty; elsewhere, leather sofas and acres of plate glass might make you think you've strayed into the offices of a City firm. Given the importance of IT to the LPC course, you should consider whether the institution offers endless vistas of the latest flat screens or a few dusty computers in a basement.

Atmosphere and direction: A large institution may appeal to students keen to chug anonymously through the system. Conversely, the intimacy of fewer students and easily accessible tutors may tip the scales in favour of a smaller provider. Some places are known to attract Oxbridge types destined to be City high-flyers; others cultivate the talents of those headed for regional practice. Still others purport to offer a mix of students, so the commercially minded can mingle with future high-street practitioners. These distinctions are likely to become increasingly pronounced when the LPC3 gets into full flow, so do consider which flavour of LPC you're after.

Money and location: Fees vary and so do the providers' policies on the inclusion of the cost of textbooks and Law Society membership, etc. Even if you have sponsorship, living expenses still need to be taken into account. The cost of living in London can be an especially nasty shock. Plenty of students find that tight finances restrict their choice of provider. Living with parents will save you a packet of course, but if you are striking out on your own (or you haven't lived with The Olds for some time), it's worth considering what you like or don't like about your university or GDL provider and whether you want to prolong your undergraduate experience or escape it. Be aware that certain LPC providers are dominated by graduates of local universities. When weighing up providers in large cities, find out whether the campus is in the city centre or out on a ring road.

Extra qualifications: A trend among providers is the offer of a top-up LLM, with students using their LPC credits to count towards a Master's in legal practice. The COL is now offering the chance to study for the JD on completion of the LPC. Students will be eligible for a 22-week study programme, where successful candidates will be awarded the JD and then be eligible for the New York Bar exam. Though the COL acknowledges that the stats for unemployed lawyers in New York are just as depressing as in the UK, it nevertheless believes that such a qualification would give students an extra dimension to their CV. Not everyone is convinced.

Social mix and social life: Studenty cities such as Nottingham and Bristol are always a lot of fun, but the bright lights of the capital may be irresistible. Experience tells us that compared to those in other cities many students in London tend to slink off the moment classes end.

Making applications

The Central Applications Board (www.lawcabs.ac.uk) administers all applications for full-time LPCs. The application form is available from 1 October 2010. Those applications for 2011/12 full-time courses received by 1 December 2010 go into the first round and offers are made from 1 February 2011. Later applications are processed in a second round with offers made from 14 March 2011. Any applications made after that date are processed as and when received. Obviously later applicants' chances of securing a place at a popular provider are reduced, but it should be remembered that there are more validated places than enrolled students on both full-time and part-time courses. Some of the most popular institutions must be placed first on the LawCabs application form: see the **LPC Providers Table** on our website. Check also whether your university, GDL provider or future law firm has a useful agreement or relationship with a provider. Applications for part-time courses should be made directly to the individual provider.

The LPC Providers
Aberystwyth University (ft)
Anglia Ruskin University (ft/pt)
Birmingham City University (ft/pt)
Bournemouth University (ft/pt)
BPP Law School, Birmingham (ft/pt)
BPP Law School, Bristol (ft/pt)
BPP Law School, Leeds (ft/pt)
BPP Law School, London (ft/pt)
BPP Law School, Manchester (ft/pt)
Bristol Institute of Legal Practice at UWE (ft/pt)
Cardiff Law School (ft/pt)
University of Central Lancashire (ft/pt)
The City Law School (ft)
College of Law, Birmingham (ft/pt)
College of Law, Bristol (ft/pt)
College of Law, Chester (ft/pt)
College of Law, Guildford (ft/pt)
College of Law, London (ft/pt)
College of Law, Manchester (ft)
College of Law, York (ft/pt)
De Montfort University (ft/pt)
University of Glamorgan (ft/pt)
University of Hertfordshire (ft)
University of Huddersfield (ft/pt)
Kaplan Law School (ft)
Leeds Metropolitan University (ft/pt)
Liverpool John Moores University (ft/pt)
London Metropolitan University (ft/pt)
Manchester Metropolitan University (ft/pt)
National College of Legal Training (distance learning)
Northumbria University Law School (ft/pt)
Nottingham Law School (ft/pt)
Oxford Institute of Legal Practice (ft/pt)
University of Plymouth (ft)
University of Sheffield (ft/pt)
Staffordshire University (ft/pt)
Swansea University (ft)
Thames Valley University (ft/pt)
University of Westminster (ft/pt)
University of Wolverhampton (ft/pt)

LPC provider reports

Our website has a table detailing all the providers and allowing a comparison of their fees, student numbers, available option subjects and useful tips for applicants. Use the following provider reports to make your selections. These reports were compiled after speaking to past students and course leaders.

Aberystwyth University

Number of places: 50 full-time

The majority of this provider's LPC students were undergrads in Aberystwyth, which was once voted the UK's favourite university town for its sense of community and facilities. The course does attract international students, too, notably from Trinidad and Tobago. The school introduced its new LPC3 course in September 2010 and is hoping to also offer a top-up LLM. All teaching staff are former solicitors or barristers, and the school believes in face-to-face teaching. Students are taught mostly in small groups of up to 15 and normally have one day off per week. They can choose between morning and afternoon study. Careers advice starts in the foundation week, with sessions on how to seek training contracts, fill in applications and ace interviews. Students can also complete filmed mock interviews.

Students can apply for a variety of work placements, including at high street firms, local authorities and the Welsh Assembly. New from 2010 are placements within the university itself. A local judge is a former Aber student, and he offers students the chance to sit beside him for a day's marshalling. Working pro bono alongside charities such as Women's Aid, Mind and Age Concern enables students to demonstrate to potential employers that they have held positions of trust and responsibility.

Anglia Ruskin University

Number of places: 140 full-time, 60 part-time

It's all change from 2010 at Anglia Ruskin, with students choosing between three breeds of LPC – part-time, full-time and full-time equivalent. The Chelmsford branch continues to deliver the full-time LPC on four days a week between 10am and 4pm. The new full-time equivalent (FTE) course is taught in Cambridge, along with the part-time course. Taught over two days a week – Tuesday and Thursday – plus four hours of distance learning, the FTE was introduced in response to student feedback. Part-time students attend one day a week.

Around 90% of lectures are web-based, with workshop numbers capped at 20 to retain the *"individual ethos where everyone knows everyone."* Tutors are practising solicitors, and the centre has guest and visiting lecturers. In addition to the assessed subjects, the school has teamed up with local firms to develop three virtual-reality learning programmes: Wills and Administration of Trusts; Career and Professional Development and Billing; and File Management and Commercial Skills. Most LPC students come from East Anglia, and those who gain training tend to go on to regional firms. Students at the Cambridge branch can take advantage of a mentoring scheme with junior lawyers from the Cambridge Law Society. All students are encouraged to get involved in the National Interviewing Competition, which the school has won six times.

Birmingham City University

Number of places: 55 full-time, 25 part-time

A more flexible three-day, Monday-to-Wednesday timetable for full-time BCU students allows them to combine their studies with legal work experience opportunities. While online lectures supplement the compulsory Stage One subjects, the school places an emphasis on face-to-face teaching and models itself as a small-provider, keeping numbers low to deliver a good-quality, practical course. In addition to online lectures, the school also has a virtual solicitors' office, complete with a practice manager and receptionist, where students work on practice-based case studies. Part-timers attend two evenings a week.

Around a third of students come from either the LLB or GDL at BCU, with smaller numbers from other universities in the West Midlands or across the UK. The course takes on a few international students too. As well as the social benefits that BCU offers, students can also access the university's careers service, even though there are dedicated career advisers in the law school. A mentoring scheme pairs students with local solicitors and a guest speaker programme provides careers advice and tips on networking and time management. Most students who gain training contracts tend to go on to high street or Midlands firms. Currently there is no top-up LLM on offer, though this is under review.

Bournemouth University

Number of places: 85 full-time equivalent

LPCers are now taught in new premises in the executive business centre on the Talbot campus, complete with catering and multimedia 'technobooths' for learning and seminar preparation. The university has recently introduced a new part-time course with these students attending classes on two or three days each week alongside their full-time colleagues. As of 2011, there will be an option for those who have completed the LPC to undertake a LLM in legal practice.

While the surroundings are modern, the course is structured in a more traditional fashion, with lectures – comprising around 60 students – supported by more intimate seminars. "*Remote learning might suit some students, but the message we get is that students think the smaller, interactive small-group sessions are absolutely essential,*" said one lecturer. That said, the university acknowledges the value of online learning to a degree: specific lectures are posted online, "*like accounts, so that students can replay points.*" Students can choose from electives in Employment, Private Client, Commercial, Family, Commercial Property, Advanced Litigation and 'The Client in the Community', which deals with housing, benefits, children and juvenile crime.

Students tend to either have local links or will have attended a South Coast university. Bournemouth and Southampton unis are well represented. For those who go on to training contracts, the majority work in the region, often going into high-street practice. Some go to bigger provincial firms with corporate and commercial practices.

BPP

Number of places: see below

Flexibility is the name of the game at BPP, with the provider boasting more than 30 ways of studying the LPC. Just like arch-rival COL, it has been granted degree-awarding powers and seems intent on national domination of legal education. Its branches touch all parts of England, with new centres opening in Bristol and Birmingham in September 2010. BPP became a part of the Apollo group (a US education business) in 2009, which brings all the BPP schools together. This should bode well for any future expansion – BPP could offer the LPC at centres where it is already established for accounting or actuarial studies, for example – as was the case in Bristol.

BPP has done well to establish itself as a frontrunner in the firm-specific LPC market. Among the long list of firms that require their future trainees to attend BPP are Simmons & Simmons, Freshfields, SJ Berwin and Travers Smith. Accordingly, the emphasis is very much on commercial and City practice, and indeed in London the Business Law & Practice element of the compulsory part of the course is even more City-focused than before. New to 2010, however, is a voluntary 'high street extra' involving a case study (relating to the compulsory subjects) with a high-street slant.

The LPC3 has changed the way the course is taught at BPP. Students destined for certain firms now take a fast-tracked seven-month course, either from August to February or from March to September. This schedule fits in with their firm's spring and autumn trainee intakes. The remaining full-timers continue to take the course over the usual nine months beginning in September. From 2011, however, a January start is available to all students at London, Leeds and Manchester.

Students can opt to either attend live lectures or watch them online. Reports suggest that lecture attendance is good for core subjects but that by the time it comes to electives students are more interested in the virtual learning environment. They can take classes either in the mornings or afternoons, and over four, three or even two days a week. Reflecting its commitment to flexibility, BPP has introduced 'blended learning', where students from across the UK – and perhaps beyond – can study the course entirely remotely. With a minimum number of face-to-face hours, students join real-time small group sessions led online by a BPP tutor.

Students like the fact that "*BPP sells itself as being the start of your professional career rather than a continuation of student life,*" though when it comes to exams, it's perhaps a little less popular. BPP is certainly in the minority in its closed-book exam policy that allows students to only take 'permitted materials' (primary sources such as legislation handbooks and BPP handbooks but not students' notes) into the hall. While students might not be so keen, BPP claims this better prepares them for practice. It has also suffered in the past from negative publicity over its annotation policy for permitted materials. The policy is now clear but some students still feel that "*being able to take your notes in is more reflective of a professional situation,*" adding that with open-book exams, "*the stress might also be less.*" Having listened to it all, our tip is to understand the annotation rules right at the start of the year and then to work in a way that fits in with them.

As for pastoral care, students have personal tutors as well as open-door access to their module tutors. A mentoring scheme gives the student the opportunity to ask for guidance in any area they wish to develop, such as commercial awareness. BPP also offers an LLM programme, which can be taken either full-time over the summer or part-time over a longer period.

BPP Law School, Birmingham

Number of places: 150 full-time equivalent
Open from 2010. Look online for updated commentary.

BPP Law School, Bristol

Number of places: 80 full-time equivalent
Open from 2010. Look online for updated commentary.

BPP Law School, Leeds

Number of places: 454 full-time equivalent

As one former student told us: *"It's a great environment to study in because it's not too big or too small – it's a nice size."* The centre is located just five minutes from the train station, which makes it accessible to students who need to commute from a distance. Facilities include *"a big library, lots of computers and a good study area."* We heard positive comments about the quality of teaching and careers support was also highly praised. *"The service was exceptionally good: they were really approachable and do a lot of work to help you prepare for assessment centres."* BPP's Leeds branch runs several pro bono activities.

BPP Law School, London

Number of Holborn places – 1,588 full-time, 302 part-time

Number of Waterloo places – 265 full-time, 57 part-time

BPP is based in two locations in London. Most LPC students study at the Holborn headquarters, although late applicants are often placed at the Waterloo branch. The facilities are impressive and visitors could be forgiven for thinking that they had walked into the offices of a City law firm rather than an education provider. *"It's open quite late too, which is good."* Students rather like studying in BPP's swanky environment, not least because they can see what their money is buying; for example, a rather flashy screen at the Holborn branch informs students where to find available computers in the building. While all BPP's branches are at the expensive end of the scale, the London ones trump them all. The majority of our sources were happy with their experience: *"They did exactly what they set out to do and made studying the LPC straightforward."*

The teaching is praised by students, who say: *"The tutors are really keen and they want you to do well, not just alright."* Even so, students admit that the course materials are often a touch uninspiring. In the view of one past student, *"a lot of it is really dry, so it's amazing that the teachers can stay enthusiastic."* Another highlighted *"the systematic nature of the course, which felt too much like a conveyor belt at the time."* There is also no doubting the type of student BPP London attracts and, for some people, *"at times it can seem quite overbearingly corporate"* and *"there are loads of very driven and competitive City types... to the exclusion of others."* Whatever their career goals, students can get involved with a host of pro bono opportunities including an environmental law clinic and projects enabling students with foreign language skills to provide legal translation services.

BPP Law School, Manchester

Number of places: 278 full-time, 113 part-time

When COL opened up in the city in 2009, BPP took a hit. Student numbers dropped and several staff were made redundant. Nevertheless, the centre is confident that it will be back on track with numbers in the 2010/11 year. Applicants come in significant numbers from Manchester, Chester, Bangor, Keele, Liverpool, Lancaster and Salford universities, some of which have guaranteed-place deals with BPP. Students who gain training contracts go on to work everywhere from the high street to mid-sized firms. A full selection of electives is offered, the most popular being Employment, IP, Advanced Commercial Litigation, Advanced Property, Immigration and Media. The school added an Insurance elective for 2010.

With the school located within a large, older building just next to the Palace Theatre and across from the arty Cornerhouse foreign film theatre, students are just minutes from the city centre. They enjoy *"being out of London for another year – the BPP experience is just the same up here as it is down there,"* and praised the library for having *"all the books you need."* The tutors are *"great,"* while the careers service *"is very active and really helped with interviews."* BPP stresses its links to firms and that its professional advisory panel includes senior HR staff from major local players. Of the three LPC providers in Manchester, this one stands out for its gentle hubbub, primary school-esque parquet flooring and cheery communal areas, one of which has a pool table for that proper common room feel. Socials include quizzes,

Wii-mbledon tournaments, charity cake bakes and nights out at Dukes 92 and Love Train.

Bristol Institute of Legal Practice at UWE

Number of places: 200 full-time, 80 part-time

Since the introduction of the LPC3 in 2009, students describe the "*well-run*" course as "*buzzing.*" BILP took the opportunity to integrate online support into the course, but still places the emphasis on face-to-face interaction. It's this conviction in the merit of interpersonal contact that the institute believes will set it apart from BPP and the College of Law, which moved into its territory in 2010. This, and a hefty slashing of the course fees. The discount should certainly help with the bus fares – UWE's Frenchay campus is located well away from the city centre, and it's advisable to live on the bus route if you don't have a car. Alternatively, you can get a train to Bristol Parkway.

After a refurb in 2009, classrooms are bright and airy with egalitarian round tables and walls adorned with artwork donated from local law firms. As well as mock courtrooms, students can unleash their inner banker in the business school's Reuters Financial Trading Room, where students look at shares in real time in the banking elective. There are plans to expand use of the room to the core Business Law & Practice subject and commercial awareness sessions. Full-timers attend either two or three days per week, depending on whether they choose to go to live lectures or watch them online. In workshops of 16, students 'work' for four firms and switch between groups to encourage intermingling and emulate practice. Teaching staff are employed to only preach the subject they actually practise and they also design the course materials, which ensures that the content can be immediately updated. Staff nurture links with law firms, and several of them design and deliver bespoke training sessions to Bristol firms. Skills teaching pervades the LPC, and students build a (non-examinable) portfolio to track and reflect on their performance.

BILP's LPC is kept broad to reflect the variety of firms to which students proceed. The school monitors how many students obtain training contracts, and in 2008/09, more than 50% left with secure offers. Generally around 90-95% are in legal employment by the time of the graduation ceremony in November. BILP places emphasis on careers and pastoral support, and students can liaise with personal tutors as soon as they accept a place on the course. They also enjoy a couple of buffet lunches with tutors during the year. Commercial awareness materials are included in summer reading, which helps prep for training contract interviews. A dedicated careers adviser organises a range of events, including a speaker programme and interview speed-dating.

Cardiff Law School

Number of places: 220 full-time equivalent

Not just the official capital of Wales, Cardiff is a popular university city. Its Law School's highly rated course offers a variety of electives and sees its students go on to a variety of firms, from big commercial operations to smaller family and criminal outfits. Around half of its LPC students are Cardiff Uni grads, with the remainder coming from all corners of the UK.

Cardiff introduced the LPC3 in 2009 and now offers a part-time course too. While there are occasional online lectures, the focus remains squarely on face-to-face teaching. Lectures are delivered live to the whole cohort, and recorded and uploaded online for part-timers to watch. Teaching continues with small-group sessions of between 16 to 18 people. Being part of a university has its advantages, and students can use any campus libraries, study areas and computers, along with the legal practice library area which has practitioner texts, study space and computers. A work placement scheme helps students without training contracts, while a host of pro bono opportunities are available. Working with major Welsh firm Hugh James, the civil pro bono unit deals with NHS continuing care cases, challenging decisions by local authorities that refuse financial support. Students can also get involved with the Innocence Project, which helps convicted criminals who maintain their innocence and want a review of their case.

College of Law

Total number of places: 4,750 full-time, 2,000 part-time

"*We like to think we've got the nation covered,*" commented a COL spokesperson. With two London branches, city sites in Birmingham and Manchester, more suburban locations in Chester, York and Guildford, and a new Bristol centre since September 2010, they are not mistaken. In 2006, COL was given degree-awarding powers and so students who complete its GDL and LPC are able to receive an LLB. Though critics say this undermines the value of the LLB qualification and that law firms don't particularly care whether an applicant has an LLB or not, some students evidently derive pleasure from adding these letters after their name. In some circumstances, an LLB qualification will have measurable value: for example, you need one if you want to take the New York Bar exam. Possibly of more relevance is the opportunity for LPC students to top up their qualification with either an LLM in Professional Legal Practice or International Legal Practice, or even a JD (Juris Doctor, the standard post-grad legal qualification in the USA). From September 2010, students who have completed the LPC will be eligible for a 22-week study programme leading to the JD. This will make them eligible for the NY Bar exam. Though the COL acknowledges that the state of the market for new lawyers in the USA is as depressing as in the UK, it nevertheless believes that such a qualification would give students an extra dimension to their CV.

Like BPP and Kaplan, COL has been enormously successful in its bid to sign up exclusive LPC-provision deals with larger law firms. Future trainees of Allen & Overy, Clifford Chance and Linklaters, for example, take 'firm-specific' LPCs at the shiny Moorgate branch, and are taught using materials suited to their firms. From January 2011, Linklaters' future starters will take a new accelerated course, which shortens the LPC from the traditional one academic year to a mere seven months. Other firms such as Baker & McKenzie and Pannone have opted for the 'LPC+', where each firm's students are mixed with others for Stage One tuition and then form discrete groups for the electives in Stage Two. Certainly COL attracts a great variety of students, in part because of the range of LPCs offered. Students can choose between a corporate route, a commercial and private route, or a Legal Aid route.

Also key to the college's ethos is flexibility. There are a range of part-time options – day, evening or weekend – and new to 2010 is an accelerated part-time course which can be completed in 16 months instead of the usual two years. Also new from February 2011 is an 'S' mode part-time LPC. S stands for supervision, and instead of attending workshops like other part-timers, students access their work online and submit two tasks per fortnight to their supervisor, who will then send back one-on-one feedback. These students attend a four-day induction and two skills weekends.

After making significant changes to its LPC in 2004, the introduction of the LPC3 in 2009/10 meant little new change. COL has led the way in the provision of online teaching, and for the past two years it has provided all lecture-format teaching via 'i-tutorials', which students stream directly from ELITE (an online resource page which carries all the course materials as well as links to online resources such as LexisNexis and Westlaw). I-tutorials are used in conjunction with textbook study and online multiple-choice 'Test & Feedback' exercises as compulsory preparation for small-group workshops. Students seem to like i-tutorials and feel that the added responsibility of managing their own study is a good thing. "*The emphasis is on the individual, which is good because it's more like the training contract – nobody's there to hold your hand.*" Workshops take up around ten hours a week and are usually spread over four days. Students can opt for concentrated timetabling, however, packing four workshops into two days instead of four. This is popular at the Birmingham, York and Chester centres, where a number of students travel some distance to attend. Underlying COL's teaching philosophy is the pervasion of skills throughout the course. To achieve this integration, students are examined on their writing, and drafting skills are assessed in the core practice assessments and separate examinations.

The careers service is "*very helpful*" and students are able to log into a database containing a list of up-to-date UK-wide training contract and paralegal vacancies. There are around 25 careers advisers nationally, and students have access to all the same information and opportunities, regardless of which centre they study at. For students hoping to boost their CV, COL has ample opportunities in the form of mooting, debating and pro bono activities.

College of Law, Birmingham

A location in the historic Jewellery Quarter of the city means students can easily enjoy Birmingham's lively social life and many amenities. They speak of making long-lasting friendships. The pro bono schemes at the COL's Birmingham branch are particularly well respected. The Brum pro bono centre was shortlisted for a Birmingham Law Society Award in 2010, and one of COL's partner programmes – the Birmingham Legal Advice Clinic – won a LawWorks Award 2010 in the Best Partnership category. Other extra-curricular activities include BERAL – the Birmingham Employment Rights Advice Line – and the Refugee Council. There is also a legal French exchange with Ecole d'Avocat in Lyon and COL students can also take advantage of a "*very helpful mentoring scheme with local firms.*"

College of Law, Bristol

September 2010 sees COL and BPP going head to head for a share of the Bristol market. COL has snatched BILP's LPC director, Kerry James, and has made exclusive tie-ups with Bristol-based TLT Solicitors, Beachcroft and Osborne Clarke. The school is located just ten minutes from Temple Meads station and is a 20-minute walk from the student-popular Clifton area.

College of Law, Chester

Chester is one of COL's more rural sites, so if you're looking for the buzz of a city, this isn't for you. Still, it's a fantastic place to study. As students confirm: "*The campus was really quite stunning; it was all trees and lawns.*" Importantly, it's "*very close to a pub.*" After Richard Haggett departed to head up the Manchester centre, Carol Draycott now leads the Chester branch. "*The teaching is good,*" students enthuse, and there's also the chance to get involved in plenty of extra-curricular activites, such as training as a Mackenzie Friend to support victims of domestic violence or participation in a witness support scheme.

College of Law, Guildford

"*The Manor House is a lovely building and it's great doing your exams overlooking the fields,*" students told us. The location is incredibly popular with those who want to avoid London living but still have relatively easy access to the capital. Lots of sports are played here, not least "*out on the croquet lawn,*" and you might even "*spot some deer while coming out of the library in the evening.*" Teachers are praised for "*bringing issues back to real practice,*" and for being "*really supportive in terms of careers advice.*" The location attracts individuals with a range of legal aspirations, both those clinging to their final year out of the fast lane and those preparing for a career in the Home Counties.

College of Law, London (Bloomsbury & Moorgate)

COL is one of the cheaper providers in London and easily undercuts its closest rivals, BPP, City and Kaplan. It is also seen as one of the "*obvious choices,*" and many students come here without having really thought too much about their options. Few are greatly disappointed by their experience, whether they are stationed at the "*more studenty*" Bloomsbury branch or in the "*quite swanky and corporate*" premises opposite Slaughter and May's office at Moorgate.

The Bloomsbury branch operates out of two buildings on Store Street, just off Tottenham Court Road. The location is popular, thanks to its proximity to the night spots of Covent Garden and Soho, and the swanky bars and restaurants of nearby Charlotte Street. Despite an abundance of choice, students commonly end up in the next door College Arms, which frequently tempts them in with student discounts and other irresistible offers. COL has an in-house cyber café, in which students can while away the hours between classes. It has to be said that the layout of this branch is far from perfect, with regular complaints directed at "*lack of windows*" in several classrooms. Get past niggles regarding the facilities and the teaching is great, with students praising the "*thorough preparation*" that they receive for exams. The teachers are also on call to deal with any last-minute panics, thanks to a hotline that operates in the run-up to exams. Bloomsbury students can choose any one of the commercial, private or Legal Aid routes, resulting in "*probably a wider mix of students, unlike Moorgate where people tend to go to magic circle and City firms.*"

Moorgate is less than two miles from Store Street and yet it is a world apart in terms of facilities. The lobby sets the tone, with its broad glass façade and angular leather sofas. Venture further inside and there are wide, shiny lifts to all floors and a library with row upon row of available PCs. Should students grow tired of this monochrome visage, there is a fantastic view onto the green outfields and perfectly maintained wickets of Bunhill Fields. Moorgate students all take corporate route LPCs, and most will be heading to the City firms that surround this prime location. Local bar Parker McMillan "*offers cheap drinks and a funky ambience,*" but if you want some fresh air, try the nearby Rack & Tenter or All Bar One.

College of Law, Manchester

The Manchester centre is making its mark since opening its doors in September 2009. Centre head Richard Haggett (formerly of the Chester centre) wants COL to storm the local market, and we could see from our visit just how much effort had gone into making the Manchester centre a great place to study. By our reckoning, this is the slickest of the three providers in the city and the premises have an extremely open and airy feel to them. Students aspire to enter all parts of the profession, and links with the larger firms in the area, the judiciary, the Coroners Court and the Employment Tribunal all help bring them closer to practice. Pro bono opportunities range from a Streetlaw programme to employment law and personal injury advice lines. Towering above Piccadilly Gardens, the centre has popular Kro Bar and Krispy Kreme on its doorstep, while the lure of the trendy Northern Quarter is just a few minutes away.

College of Law, York

"*The teaching is first class,*" students in York assure us, adding that "*a good group of lecturers is always willing to help you through things.*" York is another of the COL's campus-based locations, and its rugby pitches and tennis courts mean there's a full range of sporting activities. A social committee is behind the "*good social scene*" and it organises everything from a pantomime to ski trips. There's an abundance of CV-enhancing activities on offer, including shadowing advocates and advising asylum seekers.

City Law School

Number of places: 420 full-time equivalent

With small class sizes and an emphasis on face-to-face teaching, City Law School (formerly Inns of Court School of Law) is known for its personal-touch LPC. Split between three buildings at the edge of Gray's Inn, LPCers mingle with BPTCers, which bodes well for the social calendar. The introduction of the LPC3 in 2010 did not bring any major changes, though it did allow the school to review and enhance the course. The school is committed to making the LPC as reflective of practice as possible, and has an advisory board of firms to keep the course current.

Full-time students can opt for morning or afternoon classes, four days a week, with part-timers attending once a week. Students have one large-group session for every two workshops, and skills sessions are delivered to pools of six to eight people. Though online quizzes and discussion boards supplement learning, the school has no intention to go down the online lecture route, maintaining that interpersonal interaction is more reflective of practice. "*There was a lot of one-on-one time and interaction with tutors,*" a former student advises us. "*It was a small intake and the level of contact was really good.*" The open-book exam format continues the theme of 'mirroring practice'.

Students can liaise with staff for CV and application advice as soon as they accept a place on the course, while a former law firm recruitment partner runs TCAS – the Training Contract Advisory Service – where students can undergo mock interviews. As part of City University, students can also attend commercial awareness and practitioner lectures at CASS Business School. City attracts a mix of students, and this is reflected in their future destinations, with people going on to high street firms, commercial firms, City firms and the public sector. There are plenty of pro bono opportunities, including a community employment clinic, Amnesty International, the London Innocence project and volunteering as police station advisors. Students can also top up the LPC with an LLM in Professional Legal Practice.

De Montfort University

Number of places: 80 full-time, 80 part-time

September 2010 saw the start of a "*substantially different*" LPC at DMU. The school has just moved into a brand new £35m energy-efficient building, complete with state-of-the-art classrooms, a dedicated LPC library and common room, mock courtrooms and interview rooms. As for the new-look course, Business Law & Practice now takes less of the limelight in the compulsories than previously, and the face-to-face interactions have been condensed to free up time for CV-enhancing activities. Compulsory days for full-timers are Monday and Tuesday, with optional live lectures on a Wednesday. They can also be viewed online. The structure has changed for part-time students too: teaching is restricted to the weekend to make it easier for people to maintain full-time jobs.

With a potential three free days for full-timers, students can all take advantage of the pro bono and careers services available. They can volunteer as a caseworker for Reunite – an international child abduction charity – as well as improving their research and presentation skills with the Streetlaw initiative, where students talk on a legally related topic to a lay audience. The school also has links with the CAB and Leicester County Council's legal department. A careers tutor organises a programme of events, including talks from in-house and private practice solicitors. At social events, students can network with practitioners and trainees. Students can also take part in a mentoring scheme with local solicitors, and some have successfully gone on to secure training contracts with their mentors' organisations. Those still hungry for CV fodder can top up their LPC with an LLM, consisting of a short legal research module followed by a 25,000-word dissertation.

University of Glamorgan

Number of places: 90 full-time, 40 part-time

With more than 20 years' experience of delivering professional legal education, Glamorgan introduced the LPC3 in 2009, and students can opt for either full-time or part-time study. Working 9am till 5pm, usually four days a week, full-timers are taught in one-hour 'briefing sessions' with the whole cohort together, and in smaller 'practice sessions' taken by classes of up to 15 people. Part-timers come in one day per week. Online support takes the form of podcasts, though the school is piloting some online lectures in the 2010/11 course. New electives have also been added to the 2010 course. A work-placement programme allows students to network with local firms: they can either work on a weekly basis or for a block of time with a firm. Being part of the university also allows students to take advantage of its careers services.

University of Hertfordshire

Number of places: 80 full-time

In April 2011 the law school is relocating to a brand new £10m building on its de Havilland campus. It's also a new era for the LPC: Hertfordshire's course has been turned upside down to bring it into line with new SRA regulations. Now a full-time course, the LPC is a blend of distance and campus-based learning. Classes take place on a Wednesday between 9am and 5pm (9am and 7pm for the electives), with the rest of the work and preparation done via the school's intranet. A wireless laptop computer is provided to all students (for keeps!) and the library is open 24/7. After Stage One finishes in March, students can choose from any of the 11 electives, or opt for a 'specialism,' whereby they select three subjects from either the corporate finance, commercial law, private client or dispute resolution categories.

As well as a new Law Clinic run by students under the supervision of practitioners, the new building will house a Mediation Centre, which will be the hub for training mediators in the area. It will also have a state-of-the-art courtroom with public gallery. Students can get involved in various activities from debating and mooting, to Streetlaw presentations on relevant legal topics to groups such as the YMCA and women's refuges. A public lecture series brings talks from MPs and Law Lords, followed by further discussions at local restaurant The Cock. Once completed, the LPC can be used as credit towards an LLM, with extra credit being attainable via a work placement.

University of Huddersfield

Number of places: 40 full-time, 35 part-time

Huddersfield is one of the four institutions that offer an exempting law degree. By combining LLB studies with the LPC, students are not required to complete the professional course separately. The university also offers a standalone course, and the LPC3 has brought a greater flexibility to its study. Students can opt to do one or even two electives alongside the compulsories in Stage One (subject to demand and staff availability). Alternatively, because teaching takes place on Mondays and Tuesdays, from 1.15pm to 8.15pm, with three weekdays free, LPCers can use the time to find work experience or a part-time job. Part-timers come in one day a week: Mondays for year one, Tuesdays for year two. The school is proud of its face-to-face and open-door approach, and deliberately limits the number of places on the course to allow for better pastoral care. In 2010 the business school moved into a brand spanking new building, so LPC students can expect top-notch facilities. A dedicated careers liaison counsellor in the law school offers CV and application advice, while a mentoring scheme places students with local practitioners.

Kaplan Law School

Number of places: 300 full-time

Kaplan has added to its list of law firm tie-ups and now a total of 12 City firms require their future trainees to study at the school. They include Ince & Co, Mayer Brown and Nabarro. Unlike some other providers who separate students destined for their exclusive firms, Kaplan mixes everyone together. The school maintains that students have a range of career aspirations, from the high street to commercial firms and the public sector. Those without training contracts can be confident of a supportive careers service – each student has tailored personal sessions for assistance with applications and interview prep, as well as selecting jobs and training contracts that suit their interests and skills. Kaplan introduced the LPC3 in 2009, putting skills-focused training at the forefront and shaking up the Stage One subjects of Business Law & Practice (BLP) and Criminal Law. To reflect the reality of commercial practice, BLP introduces students to public companies, while criminal law focuses on white-collar crime. Insurance and Commercial Contracts have also been added to the list of electives.

Students have personal tutors and this is reflective of the school's face-to-face teaching philosophy. On four days a week, from 9am till 5pm, students attend large-group sessions, followed by small groups for between 16 and 18 people. The course is supported by 'blended' materials, available online. There's plenty of opportunity to boost CVs with pro bono evenings twice a week, at which students can either deal directly with the public or watch and learn from a qualified solicitor. Recent experiences include representing individuals at the County Court and magistrates' court. The careers service invites practitioners to meet with students, while the new Kaplan Commercial Awareness Forum (KCAF) arranges for lawyers and other City players to talk on current issues. Borough market is on the doorstep and social interaction is aided by 'Ning' – the school's answer to Facebook. A sports and social committee arranges events, and being a part of the Nottingham Law School means that students can attend its annual law ball. Book-ending the LPC is a River Thames boat trip during the induction and a graduation ceremony in nearby Southwark Cathedral.

University of Central Lancashire

Number of places: 80 full-time, 45 part-time

After introducing the LPC3 in 2009, full-time students are timetabled from Monday to Thursday from 10am till 4pm, except on a Wednesday when students have their large-group sessions in the morning. As employees of virtual law firm Preston Harris, every day is different for students at UCLan. Monday is litigation day; on Tuesday it's Wills, Probate and Administration of Trusts; and Business Law & Practice and Property Law & Practice are on Thursdays. Along with lectures, students are taught in small groups of between 12 and 16 people, though in Stage Two there are no lectures and the timetable is reduced to two days per week. Closed-book short questions and an open-book longer paper examine compulsory subjects, while elective assessments are all open book. There's also a drafting assessment, where students use an online package to draft a legal document. Firms in the North West contact the school to advertise training contracts and paralegal vacancies, and the school organises careers talks from training partners and trainees.

Leeds Metropolitan University

Number of places: 105 full-time, 45 part-time

The introduction of the LPC3 has shaken up the course at Leeds Metropolitan, where three-hour seminars have replaced the old lecture-and-workshop format. Full-timers come in four days a week, while part-timers have one day of tuition, either between 9am and 3pm or 1pm and 8pm. Though there is some online preparation by way of podcasts and videos, the school places an emphasis on face-to-face teaching, with a maximum of 16 in seminars and eight in skills sessions. Another important focus for the school is students' professional growth. The new 'Professional and Career Development' programme aims to help them build a portfolio of competencies to give them a competitive edge in the job market. External speakers come in to present on a number of topics, including CV advice from law firms Keeble Hawson and DWF. Other recent speakers have come from Eversheds, the CPS, Leeds Law Society and local recruitment consultants. There are also plenty of law firm-sponsored competitions for students to enter, such as a mediation comp in which winners can bag a summer placement. A district judge has visited to give advocacy lessons, and there has also been a *Dragons' Den*-style competition. Students are also assigned a local solicitor as part of the school's professional mentor scheme. The facilities at Leeds Met include a mock courtroom, video suites and laptops for hire. The building is fully Wifi enabled. For another CV boost, students can top up their LPC with a dissertation to obtain an LLM, though this was under review at the time of going to press.

Liverpool John Moores University

Number of places: 72 full-time, 72 part-time

2010 heralded the start of the LPC3 at LJMU. While the course has not dramatically changed, the university has taken the decision to concentrate more on litigation in the compulsory subjects. It's also managed to squeeze the course into a three-day week – Monday to Wednesday – replacing the previous five-day slog. Part-timers stick to the same regime of either two evenings a week or day release (on a Tuesday for year one students, and a Wednesday for year two). The majority of lectures are now delivered online, with students taught in small groups of up to 20. The school has a mix of students – many are local to the North West, with contingents also coming from Ireland and the Isle of Man. The firms they go on to are just as mixed: those who obtain training or paralegal work go to everywhere from big commercial firms to high street ones. A dedicated law adviser within the Graduate Development Centre arranges careers sessions to assist with CVs, applications and mock interviews. A mentoring scheme has more than 50 lawyers on its books, and students can spend up to a week work shadowing. The school match-makes according to subject area preferences and locality. The law clinic elective will boost the CVs of those looking to improve their advisory skills. It was set up primarily to help small business start-ups. Students can also continue their studies after the LPC to work towards an LLM.

London Metropolitan University

Number of places: 99 full-time, 50 part-time

Sitting in the shadows of the iconic Gherkin, students at LMU can kit themselves out in all the solicitor's gear they need at a nearby East End market – shirts and 'Rolexes' aplenty! The introduction of the LPC3 in September 2010 has altered the course at LMU, with a realignment of compulsory subject concentrations to reflect student feedback. Litigation now takes up 50%, with Business Law & Practice and Property Law & Practice sharing the remainder. Full-time students can expect to be in for three or four days a week, with part-timers in either one day a week or two evenings. If there's space on the part-time course, full-timers can do the full-time course over two days a week. Classes are taught in three-hour blocks: one hour teacher-led, two hours student-led. There's a small staff-to-student ratio, so teachers aren't presenting the same material over and over again, and classes are supplemented with online tests and revision lectures and materials.

The university is committed to widening access to the profession, and this is reflected by the formative assessment in legal writing at the start of the LPC. Weaker candidates are referred to an 'English for the LPC' evening class. Candidates predominantly come from new universities, many taking advantage of fee discounts. The faculty advises students to be proactive in their career search, to keep a profile recording their competencies and to use both the university and law school careers advisors. There's also a mentoring scheme. LMU has links with Simmons & Simmons, Fisher Meredith, Thompsons, Russell-Cooke and Baxter Brown McArthur – and there are always more places available than students. Replacing the pro bono clinic, the Clinical Legal Education Unit offers students a chance to improve their CVs with volunteering experience.

Manchester Metropolitan University

Number of places: 168 full-time, 72 part-time

2009 saw the College of Law enter the legal education market in Manchester, with BPP having arrived the previous year. For MMU, however, it's business as usual. A key attraction must be the level of fees, which are substantially cheaper than either of its rivals in the city. The school introduced the LPC3 in 2009, and it didn't bring in any particular major changes, although it is now validated to offer an LLM. The workshop-based course is taught to groups of 16 to 20 students, with classes spanning three hours and backed up by online tutorials. Stage One takes up two days a week for full-timers, and up to three days in Stage Two, depending on elective choices. Part-time students come in one day a week. The school is proud that it produces its own materials, which are constantly reviewed and updated. All teaching staff have been practitioners, with some still in practice and coming from all types of firms – from Linklaters and Addleshaw Goddard, to high street and in-house teams. As for students, the majority come from the North West and Northern Ireland, a number being MMU students taking advantage of the 10% fee discount on offer. Around 10% of students come from Trinidad and Tobago, and they tend to complete their LPC and then return to practise at home.

In addition to dedicated LPC facilities, students enjoy the benefits of being part of a university. Leavers go on to a range of firms and there's a dedicated adviser to help them along the way. Monthly e-mails detailing law-firm vacancies, CV clinics and careers talks all help good students to gain a coveted training contract. There's also a mentoring scheme and practitioners come in to give talks. Housing elective students can boost their CVs through a work-experience week, either at the CAB or in local government. There's also a chance to get involved in pro bono, including POPs, a charity that helps the partners of prisoners; the personal support unit at the Manchester Civil Justice Centre; and the Manchester Mediation Service for those keen to learn more about ADR.

National College of Legal Training

Number of places: 100 part-time across four study centres

New to the LPC market in 2009, NCLT offers one of the most flexible and cheapest courses around. Spanning nine face-to-face weekends each year for two years, students attend one of the study centres – Coventry University, Manchester Metropolitan University, Southampton Solent University or the University of Westminster. This provider has "*more centres in the pipeline*" and is also adding a February start from 2011. With a price tag of £2,950 per year, the course is the cheapest on the market and can be paid for by 19 monthly instalments. But this is no easy ride: students must be truly committed to the course and are advised to do at least 15 hours of independent study per week. The NCLT was formed when Central Legal Training and the University of the West of England joined forces, and its students follow the UWE LPC, using the same materials. New students have a three-day induction weekend in September, and cover Business Law & Practice, Probate and Administration of Estates, Taxation, and an introduction to the core skills in year one. After a summer break, year two commences with Litigation, Property Law & Practice, the remaining skills, and the electives. As soon as students accept a place on the course, they are designated a pre-course tutor to advise them on personal and academic issues, as well as careers advice. Once the course begins, a supervising principal liaises with students on a regular basis and is always available via Blackboard. From 2011, the provider is hoping to offer a top-up LLM and work placements, after first building links with firms.

Northumbria University Law School

Number of places: 150 full-time, 100 part-time

Since the introduction of the LPC3 in 2009, students at Northumbria can choose between two Stage One routes – general or commercial. Full-timers attend four days a week, with one lecture, two workshops and one small-group session per subject. The school places an emphasis on face-to-face teaching, with workshops and small groups accommodating around 18 students. There's a good selection of general practice and commercial electives, with guest lecturers from local firms holding sessions on a regular basis. The Student Law Office (SLO) choice is an ever-popular elective, through which students hand in a portfolio of real work experiences at the end of the course. "*You get real mini-office experience, taking client queries, covering the basics of a case and doing file management.*" Students advising SLO clients find themselves drafting court documents, briefing barristers and generally experiencing all aspects of a case. Those who don't want to use up an elective on the SLO can get involved in Streetlaw, working in conjunction with law firm Eversheds. It's possible to top up the LPC with an LLM, and the school has careers advice on offer from both a dedicated LPC adviser and the university's careers team.

Northumbria has long been known as a good place to take an exempting degree that incorporates LPC teaching into an undergraduate law course. This gives a very practical emphasis to the study of law, and those trainees who've spoken to us about the course have rated it highly.

Nottingham Law School

Number of places: 650 full-time, 100 part-time

Underpinning Nottingham Law School's philosophy is flexibility, innovation and dynamism. The introduction of the LPC3 in 2009 certainly gave the school its chance to reveal these traits. In Stage One, students choose either the corporate or general LPC. For those sure of a corporate career, the course includes a brand new course on regulatory crime, while the general LPC is better suited to those students aiming for the high street or smaller firms. Another tier of tailoring is introduced via the skills pathways: commercial; public legal services; and a third 'hybrid' option. Each drafting, interviewing, and research skills exercise is thereafter based on the particular pathway the student has chosen. Teaching is delivered in a cocktail of large-group and small-group sessions, and the new 'blended' learning approach, which mixes face-to-face teaching, online group work, video simulations and independent online learning. The school is hoping to expand on this in the 2010/11 course. Full-timers tend to be off on a Friday, while part-timers have large and small group sessions at the weekend. With lectures available online within a few minutes of their live delivery, the course is becoming ever more flexible.

Students enthuse about Nottingham, saying that "*it offers more than providers in London and you get a more cohesive group.*" The different course concentrations and pathways help students tailor their CVs towards the firms they apply to and, indeed, the school places a huge emphasis on employment. It monitors the numbers who go on to obtain legal employment within six months of completing the course. In 2007, the figure stood at 95%, reducing to 83% in the poorer market in 2009. This is a very high proportion. Students go on to a range of firms – from City, American, regional and commercial players, to local authorities, the CPS and central government. "*The teaching is excellent,*" and there are three dedicated careers advisers in the law school. Each student is assigned one to help with applications, CVs and interviews. Events and seminars are organised with practitioners, and there is also a mentoring scheme in place with local law firms. Students can get heavily involved in pro bono – a new suite opened in 2010 – and the school has an employment tribunal representation unit running in connection with the Free Representation Unit (the first unit to run outside London). There's also an Innocence project, the opportunity to train at the CAB over the summer, and a mooting team that won the 2010 International Commercial Mediation Competition in Paris. Having completed the LPC, students can dissertate to achieve an LLM.

Oxford Institute of Legal Practice

Number of places: 150 full-time, 30 part-time

Located in the "*stunning*" Headington Hill Hall (once the home of media tycoon Robert Maxwell) and part of Oxford Brookes, OXILP has waited until September 2010 to introduce the LPC3. Changes include a weekly part-time course and tie-ups with firms such as Manches and Clarke Wilmott. The elective term has been shortened by a few weeks, so there is more focus on Stage One compulsory subjects. Business Law & Practice has been pared down so that all the compulsories have the same weighting, while Wills and Administration of Estates and Taxation have also been added to the mix. The new addition is in response to feedback from the profession that there is a lacuna in many LPC graduates' knowledge of these subjects. Interviewing skills will also begin at the start of the year, while the introduction of a commercial-awareness programme will involve lectures from the course director, talks from practitioners about marketing and finance in a law firm, and an online business game.

The majority of teaching is spread over five days, though full-timers can request a four-day week if they have good reason. Part-timers have two options: to attend 11 weekends per year – either from a Friday to Sunday, or Saturday to Monday – or during the week with the full-timers. The school concentrates on face-to-face teaching, and staff now only teach what they've practised. The majority of classes are for groups of 16, and lectures are recorded and put online. One event to look forward to is a full mock trial at the old Oxford Crown Court. Several firms sponsor the electives, with prizes for the best students in each. Dedicated careers tutors can offer practical advice on applications and interviews. With OXILP only relatively recently divested from Oxford University, students can still use its facilities, including its unsurprisingly impressive careers service, which has a comprehensive law firm data bank and a series of talks with big firms throughout the year. "*There are lots of social things too,*" adds a student. "*You're within the collegial atmosphere of Oxford; we were in the Oxford football league and had a darts team.*" For those who feel that their CV is on the light side, another addition to the 2010 course is a top-up LLM in Legal Practice.

University of Plymouth

Number of places: 80 full-time

Central to Plymouth University's LPC ethos is striking the balance between reflective and thoughtful practitioners and practical and efficient lawyers. Twinned with this is the aim to offer a flexible course, and the introduction of the LPC3 in September 2009 gave the school the opportunity to do so. Students now have working weeks of either two or three days, between 10am and 4pm, and they attend small-group sessions supplemented by podcasts. Students now have one day less of contact time; however, lectures are still given for more technical parts of the LPC, such as accounts. Small is beautiful at Plymouth, and the face-to-face time that students do have is shared among no more than 15 students and a minimum of six. The LPC has been running here since 2006, when it transferred from the University of Exeter, where it had been running since 1994. With the move came a number of relationships with firms, and the school tries to keep up with its alumni and find out where they have gone. Such contacts help with the work-placement scheme. The university's focus is on providing trainees for regional firms, predominantly in the South West, and the work placement certainly benefits students. More than 50% of them leave Plymouth with a training contract. There are also seven LPC tutors dedicated to pastoral support, including advising on CVs and applications. Students can apply for the Saltram scholarship, which knocks £2,000 off the LPC.

University of Sheffield

Number of places: 180 full-time, 35 part-time

Highlighting the flexibility of the LPC3, its introduction to Sheffield has allowed the university to adapt what students study and how they study. LPCers choose either a high street or a commercially focused Stage One, or a combination of the two. There's also a new part-time course on a Friday, while full-timers have the choice of classes either in the morning (10am till 1pm) or the afternoon (1.30pm till 4pm) from Monday to Thursday. Workshops each take in around 18 students and are supplemented by online lectures, multiple-choice questions and short-answer quizzes. Though the majority of lectures have shifted to on-screen streaming, there are still some for students to attend, including careers sessions. The school has a dedicated careers adviser who offers one-on-one help with CVs and applications. Students can undergo a mock interview with a practitioner, which is filmed and later picked apart by the student and the careers adviser. The law school prides itself as being small and friendly and it takes the majority of its students from the university's various undergrad courses. Other CV-boosting opportunities include pro bono work for the Innocence project, and Pro Uno – a drop-in legal help clinic that deals with things like housing, matrimonial and employment problems and debt. Dedicated students who achieve a commendation or distinction on the LPC can top up to an MA in Legal Practice.

Staffordshire University

Number of places: 150 full-time equivalent

Staffordshire offers the LPC course on both full and part-time schedules, and now has a new 'blended learning' course. Ninety percent of the course is conducted through remote online learning; the rest is comprised of a three-day foundation course and nine blocks of two-day learning sessions held over weekends throughout the year. This increased flexibility is bound to make the University even more popular with students who need to live at home and study locally for financial reasons. Additionally, following the completion of the LPC, students can supersize their qualification to a LLM in Legal Practice with a bit more time, work and cash.

There's a decent mix of 11 electives ranging from Corporate Finance & Acquisitions to Private Client. Staffs has great facilities, including mock courtrooms, a simulated solicitors' office, a dedicated law library and general IT kit. The careers department runs a practitioner mentoring programme that connects students with local solicitors and encourages pro bono participation in schemes like Streetlaw. Look out for open days held throughout the year.

Swansea University

Number of places: 100 full-time

With views of Swansea Bay to the front, and parkland and rolling hills to the rear, Swansea reckons it is one of the most idyllic places to study in the UK. Indeed in 1956, the Countryside Agency chose its patch – The Gower – as the first designated area of outstanding natural beauty under the new National Parks legislation. It's not surprising then that the majority of LPC students come from the university's undergraduate law course, having chosen to stay in these beautiful surroundings.

Swansea started its LPC is 2009. It remains committed to face-to-face learning, priding itself on its pastoral care and close personal contact. Classes are delivered between 9am and 5pm from Monday to Thursday in Stage One, and Tuesday to Thursday in Stage Two. After large-group sessions in the morning, students face smaller tutorials in the afternoon, and lessons are supplemented with online materials. Thanks to days free of contact hours, students have ample time for work experience. The university runs a scheme that places students with firms in the south of Wales. Instead of just a two-week stint, students work at one firm on their free days, building up their contacts. It sometimes leads to the offer of a paralegal position or even a training contract. Students can also network at a pro bono clinic run by practitioners in the area, and can take part in Streetlaw activities. Careers advice is on hand, with regular sessions available to students wanting assistance with their CVs and applications.

Thames Valley University

Number of places: 60 full-time equivalent

With the return of the part-time course and the beginning of a top-up LLM, the introduction of the LPC3 in September 2010 heralded a new era at TVU. The Business Law & Practice module has been cut back to concentrate more on Criminal Litigation and Property Law & Practice. The realignment is to better reflect the destination of TVU's successful students. They join firms and organisations handling everything from social welfare and Legal Aid, to property and high street practice. Most students come from the undergraduate course or GDL at the university, taking advantage of a 15% fee discount, although there are a good number of international students too. In workshops lasting two hours, students are taught in groups of 20 to 25, with fewer in the elective groups. Full-timers can expect to be in for two and a half days a week – Tuesday, Thursday and part of Wednesday, while those on the part-time course attend one day per week, with an additional evening in year two. A mini-careers module on the LPC ensures that students' CVs, applications and interview skills are up to scratch. They can also take advantage of a mentoring and work-experience scheme. The school has contacts with the Middlesex Law Society, where students can attend lectures, and there are regular talks from practitioners and organisations such as the Land Registry. TVU runs a community advice programme in conjunction with Ealing Racial Equality Council, where students can get involved with fortnightly surgeries.

University of Westminster

Number of places: 120 full-time, 64 part-time

Westminster introduced the LPC3 in 2009, and it resulted in a change to the weekly timetable from three days to four. Full-timers are taught in small groups of 15 to 18 in the morning, and either continue with further tuition in the afternoon or have large-group sessions. Online lectures were new to the 2009 course, but the emphasis is still on live lectures – it tends to be the more technical aspects of courses that are delivered online, such as tax. There's a bounty of electives, both private client and commercially oriented, and there's also a clinical elective that sees students undertake practical work with the CAB. They are then assessed on a project completed during the year. Students undertaking this elective are also given the opportunity to complete Level 1 of the Immigration Accreditation Scheme. For those who would rather not dedicate an elective choice to Legal Aid, the pro bono centre sits just beside the law school, and students can get involved in a variety of issues from the Land Registry matters to immigration. All this helps towards building a weighty CV, and a dedicated LPC member of staff trawls through training contract vacancies before advertising them to students. They also arrange careers workshops and law firm representatives visit to offer advice on applications. The law school at Westminster is spread over six floors, including an LPC suite that houses a library and computer room (it lends out laptops). Students have access to the main law school library and a mock courtroom. The school's Oxford Street location lends itself to a host of social activities, and the school organises drinks events in its foundation week, at Christmas and at the end of the course.

University of Wolverhampton

Number of places: 60 full-time, 30 part-time

Located on a business park just outside of town, Wolverhampton's Professional Legal Studies Centre views the LPC itself as the first year of professional practice: if students can't come to class, they're expected to ring the centre and explain why. While the majority of students completed undergraduate studies at the university, there's also a Caribbean contingent. As is the case with Manchester Met and Aberystwyth, the school has grown in popularity with students coming from Trinidad especially. After introducing the LPC3 in 2009, the full-time course is now timetabled over three days – lectures on a Monday; workshops on a Tuesday and Wednesday. Part-timers come in two evenings a week. Each workshop includes no more than 15 students and online materials support studying. This includes 'Wulfruns'– a virtual law firm where the staff are 'partners' and the students are 'trainees'.

The school is active in its careers support. There's a dedicated LPC careers adviser and a mentoring programme involving local firms. Most students aim for local high street firms, and the school pins up two lists – the New Practitioners Forum, made up of newly qualified solicitors; and the Solicitors Liaison Committee, composed of partners in local firms – to whom students can send their CVs to apply for work shadowing. The school also arranges the 'LPC Plus', a series of five talks throughout the academic year from various practitioners, including the CPS and commercial firms. A group of LPC students recently set up a legal advice clinic, supported by senior partners from Talbots Solicitors. For those in search of more CV padding, there's also the opportunity to top up the LPC with an LLM.

- **Start early:** Some kind of legal experience, whether it's involvement with a student law magazine or shadowing your friend's lawyer father, is pretty crucial since you need to convince potential employers that you're serious about the profession, not just following an adolescent fantasy. Always keep your ears open for useful opportunities so you can test your ideas about what it might be like to work in the law.

The Bar Professional Training Course (BPTC)

The BPTC is the sandwich filler between either an LLB or GDL and pupillage for would-be barristers. Eight law schools are authorised by the Bar Standards Board (BSB) to teach and examine the course at locations in London, Bristol, Cardiff, Nottingham, Manchester, Leeds and Newcastle. The full-time course lasts a year; the part-time option is spread over two.

Statistical paralysis

'What fine places of slow torture they are! … The waiting – the hope – the disappointment – the fear – the misery – the poverty…' While Dickens' portrayal of the poor pupil in *The Pickwick Papers* might not fit so well with pupillage in the 21st century, these words are arguably a fair account of the journey getting there. Simply, the road is expensive, it's hard work, and there's no guarantee of pupillage at the end. Figures from the BSB show that 1,330 students successfully completed the BPTC in 2008/09. In the same year, only 463 candidates secured pupillage. Those 463 will include people who left law school in earlier years and waited a long time to secure pupillage.

With the cost of the BPTC course ranging from £10,000 to £15,000, signing on the dotted line is a costly gamble for most students. The BSB is acutely mindful of the mismatch between the number of students on the course and the number of available pupillages.

A pilot scheme for an aptitude test is due to launch in September 2011: the BSB's first step towards protecting wide-eyed students from handing over thousands of pounds and then realising a year or two later that they've no chance of a career at the Bar. As one of the key recommendations from *The Wood Report* (interesting, do read it: www.barstandardsboard.org.uk/news/latest/220.html), the test will involve logic and reasoning questions, and will compare test results with students' final BPTC results in order to establish whether an aptitude test can provide a true reflection of a student's prospects. All students will have to sit the test, irrespective of their background (although in 2011 they will not need to pass it). The rationale is to maintain and strengthen the quality of the Bar, and if an aptitude test was to be adopted on a permanent basis, students would be able to resit it as many times as required. While the introduction of a test risks making the student body less diverse than it currently is, this brave step forward seems unlikely to alter the makeup of the Bar itself. Its likely effect is to protect certain misguided students from the burden of heavy debt unnecessarily incurred. The big question is just how high will the fence be set?

Failure to launch

Another way in which the number of disappointed and disaffected post-BPTC students can, and will, be reduced is through the actions of the course providers. The BSB's minimum requirement for admission onto the courses is a 2:2 on an LLB or non-law degree, and a pass on the GDL (where taken). Several providers have chosen to up the ante. Kaplan Law School, for example, requires all of its shortlisted applicants to attend a selection event, where they undertake a written advocacy exercise, an oral advocacy exercise and an interview. Bristol Institute of Legal Practice at UWE also runs a system relying on 'admissions points'. Most providers actually require their students to have a 2:1 at degree level.

Though BSB and some BPTC providers are taking clear steps to protect students' interests, you shouldn't expect them to do all the hard work for you. First of all, take a good hard look at your CV. Comparing it to those of the new tenants at the sets you're aiming for can be quite a humbling experience, but you have to be realistic. Though a First isn't a prerequisite for success, almost one in three pupils will have one. One course leader went so far as to say: "*Students with a 2:2 have more chance of going to Mars than securing pupillage.*" Invariably, the 2:2ers who do make it have exceptionally good CVs in other ways and/or a first career under their belt.

You do need much more than just good academics to succeed. It's difficult to get a firm grasp of the odds of getting pupillage, but estimates range from between one in four to one in eight. There are a couple of things worth bearing in mind. Firstly, unsuccessful pupillage applicants will, more often than not, reapply the following year. Some applicants will have completed the BPTC more than a year previous – remember that the BPTC has a lifespan of five years. That means in any given year there will be many more applicants for pupillage than students who successfully pass the BPTC. However, that trend is tempered to a certain extent by those individuals who have decided that the Bar is simply not for them, and by the significant number (estimates put it at between 20 and 23% of all BPTC students) of international students who return home rather than seeking pupillage in England and Wales.

The advice from one BPTC provider on how to improve your prospects? "*Advocacy, advocacy, advocacy.*" Most providers want to assess an applicant's commitment to practice through public speaking experience, such as mooting and debating, plus mini-pupillages and marshalling, etc. and it's no different for the sets offering pupillage.

In addition to academics and extra-curriculars, a candidate's English language skills are also considered. Currently the BSB requires all students whose first language is not English or Welsh to demonstrate that they have a minimum 7.5 IELTS standard. Over the past few years we've heard rumbling criticisms that some students' English just isn't up to par, resulting in a degradation of the classroom environment. This hasn't gone under the radar of the providers, and many believe that the problem could be solved by requiring all students to take the IELTS test in the future. In the summer of 2010, the BSB requested permission from the Legal Services Board to demand this.

From V to PT

The BPTC replaced its predecessor, the BVC, in September 2010, but with the exception of an extra consonant, the focus remains largely the same, namely to ensure that wannabe barristers acquire the skills, knowledge, attitudes and competencies needed for practice. Cue: developing students' advocacy, drafting, opinion writing, conferencing, case analysis and legal research skills. As for knowledge, students are schooled in civil litigation and remedies; criminal litigation and sentencing; evidence; and professional ethics. In the final term, students select two option subjects in areas they are targeting for practice. Most teaching is delivered to groups of 12, with skills taught in groups of six students or fewer. Teaching methods vary slightly between providers, but learning is commonly by way of case studies that track the litigation process.

Largely, the emphasis is very much on face-to-face teaching across the BPTC providers. Still, many use computers in lectures to make learning more stimulating, and writing-skills classes often involve the use of whiteboards. Oral skills classes make increasing use of video-recording equipment in role-plays. The skills acquired are then examined using a variety of assessments in the second and third terms. Written skills are tested through a mix of unseen and take-home tests, while professional actors are drafted in to take part in oral assessments. One change that the BPTC brings is the replacement of the old negotiation-skills course with something called 'Resolution of Disputes Out of Court'– this modification acknowledges that negotiation isn't the only fruit on the Alternative Dispute Resolution (ADR) tree.

Though skills assessments will continue to be set and marked by the individual providers, the future of testing knowledge could be different. The BSB had plans to set standardised exams for civil litigation, criminal litigation and ethics from 2010, to ensure confidence in the parity between course providers. After realising that central examinations entail more than just drafting one paper and picking a day for everyone to sit it, the introduction of standardised examinations has been pushed back to 2011. Indeed, on the periphery of examinations lies a minefield of grey – one provider's response to a student who is unable to sit an exam may be different to another's. When we spoke to the course leaders, some also expressed concern that it would be a challenge for the BSB to set exams without inherently prejudicing students at certain providers over others – the providers don't all use the same study texts. Like the aptitude test pilot, the examination system will require careful thought. Despite the delayed introduction of the centrally set examinations, all providers will be examining students on the same day, to get some practice in before the 2011/12 course.

Get on top

Course directors tell us that the BPTC is "*a very demanding, intensive and rigorous course,*" and students agree that it's a "*slog.*" The timetable is described as "*undulating*" – "*intense in parts and boring in others*" – and often the course is "*front loaded.*" But don't use the quieter times to relax. This is your chance to improve your pupillage prospects. As one student advises: "*Organise dining with the Inns, mooting, debating, pro bono, mini-pupillages, marshalling and the like*" to give your CV "*a fighting chance of reaching interview stage.*" It's therefore essential to look carefully at the extra-curricular opportunities offered at each of the providers and throw yourself into everything you can.

How to apply through BPTC online

An application for the BPTC costs £40, and the process is all done online. There is no cap on the number of providers you may apply to, although during the first phase of the process only your top-three choices will look at your application.

- Monday 18 October 2010 – System opens (9.00am)
- Thursday 13 January 2011 – Closes for first-round applications (2.00pm)
- Thursday 10 February – Reopens for clearing applications (2.00pm)
- Tuesday 8 March 2011 – Offers made from first-round applications (2.00pm)
- Thursday 7 April 2011 – Acceptance deadline for first round offers (2.00pm)
- Monday 11 April 2011 – Clearing pool opens to Providers (2.00pm)
- Tuesday 31 May 2011 – Closing date for application to an Inn of Court*. You must join an Inn before commencing the BPTC
- Wednesday 31 August 2011 – Clearing round closes (2.00pm)
- Wednesday 14 September 2011 – System closes (2.00pm)

* See page 684 for information on the different Inns.

Forecast your float

With the course fees at around £15,000 in London and no less than £10,000 elsewhere, it's an expensive undertaking, and that's before taking living costs into account. Most will find the course intensive – at least during some phases – and this leaves them little scope for a part-time job so it's essential to consider how you will manage your finances. The Inns of Court offer a range of scholarships and bursaries, but be sure to find out about them well in advance. The closing date for award applications is usually in the November of the year before the course begins. Other funding options include career development loans, bank loans, and for the most fortunate, the Bank of Mum & Dad. Read more on **Funding** on page 77.

How to pick a provider

The fight for pupillage is a truly testing one, so choose your course provider carefully. Pick one that's going to give you the best skills and opportunites possible. Read through prospectuses and websites, attend open days, try to speak to current or former students. Read our provider reports. Consider the following criteria:

Cost: Some providers and locations are significantly cheaper than others. London is the priciest but even here there is variation. If you're an international student, look at the differential in price. Part-timers should note whether fees increase in the second year.

The BPTC Providers
BPP Law School, Leeds (ft/pt)
BPP Law School, London (ft/pt)
Bristol Institute of Legal Practice at UWE (ft/pt)
Cardiff Law School (ft)
The City Law School (ft/pt)
College of Law, Birmingham (ft)
College of Law, London (ft/pt)
Kaplan Law School, London (ft)
Manchester Metropolitan University (ft/pt)
Northumbria University Law School (ft/pt)
Nottingham Law School (ft)

Location: Regional providers may be the best option for those looking for pupillage on the regional circuits, not least because of their stronger links and networking opportunities with the local Bar. London students benefit from proximity to the Inns of Court and more easy access for London pupillage interviews; however, through compulsory dining and advocacy training courses in the Inns, regional students are able to maintain their links with the capital's beating legal heart.

Size: Smaller providers pride themselves on offering a more intimate and collegiate environment. Student feedback indicates that this does make a positive difference to the experience, and the friends you make on the BPTC should be a source of support during the search for pupillage and beyond. There's definitely a different feel to those providers that are within universities and those that aren't.

Facilities: Students can tap into a far wider range of support services, sports and social activities by taking the BPTC at a university. Library and IT resources vary from one provider to the next, as does the level of technology used in teaching. Some providers make technology a key feature of the course.

Option subjects: Available option subjects vary. For example, although judicial review and immigration are popular, they are not offered everywhere. **The Table of BPTC Providers** on our website sets out what's on offer at each one. This table also compares fees and offers provider-specific application tips.

Pro Bono: Opportunities range from minimal to superb across the nine providers.

BPTC provider reports

Which of the law schools teaching the BPTC will be right for you? Remember, any references to the BVC relate to the very similar course that immediately predated the BPTC. All quotes come from course directors or other official sources at the providers.

BPP Law School, London

Number of places: 264 full-time, 96 part-time

Now a subsidiary of specialist US education corporation Apollo, BPP became the first privately owned, publicly traded company in the UK to be granted the right to award degrees in 2007. In 2009, BPP had its knuckles rapped for taking too many students onto its BVC, but the company assured us that this resulted from higher than normal take-up of offers by students. In 2010 it enlisted the help of a statistician to avoid repeating the mistake.

With barristers no longer holding the monopoly on higher rights of audience, BPP aims to ready students for an increasingly competitive market and the course offers around 30% more advocacy than BSB requirements stipulate. Advocacy is interwoven through knowledge classes: if summary judgment is taught in civil litigation, for example, that will then be the subject of the advocacy class. Students receive written feedback after every class. The tutors are all qualified practitioners – the majority barristers, a few solicitors – and they rotate around classes to give students a variety of perspectives.

Part-timers attend school one weekend per month over two years, and although they have the same skills programme as full-timers, more self-study is required for the knowledge elements. With a Friday free for course preparation, full-timers can commit to pro bono activities. Students must complete a minimum of five hours of pro bono and there are opportunities with Streetlaw and the Innocence project, as well as the Environmental Law Unit and the Legal Translation Service.

Mock pupillage interviews and appointments with careers advisers help those still seeking pupillage, and students can continue to use the service for a year after leaving. A programme of seminars with chambers, commercial awareness workshops and themed panel discussions with local barristers all bring networking opportunities. Former students act as buddies, while a wealth of mooting and mock trial competitions provide ample opportunity to develop advocacy skills. Those who complete the course can undergo further study to obtain an LLM.

BPP Law School, Leeds

Number of places: 48 full-time, 48 part-time

Students can expect the same course as their peers in London, albeit in a more intimate atmosphere. As with other regional providers, students can network with members of the local Bar, and BPP helps facilitate this with meet-and-greet sessions. There's plenty of scope for pro bono activities, for example a legal advice clinic and human rights unit, while a speaker programme covers a range of issues. Those who complete the BPTC can undergo additional study in the months after the course to obtain an LLM. Students who choose Leeds pay significantly lower fees than their peers in London, which has encouraged a high volume of applicants so consider putting it down as your first-choice provider.

Bristol Institute of Legal Practice at UWE

Number of places: 108 full-time, 36 part-time

BILP at UWE is now facing stiff competition in the LPC market from COL and BPP, yet it remains the only BPTC provider in the South West. Added competition led BILP to drop its LPC prices, and it hopes to get its BPTC fees down to the £9,000 mark for 2011/12. UWE's Frenchay campus is located on the outskirts of the city, and while the positives of the course seem to outweigh this negative, some students find the travelling annoying. At least the course fee cut will more than cover the bus fare. Students have seven-days-a-week access to their own base rooms in a newly refurbished department.

While the Bristol location is great for anyone keen to pursue a career on the Western Circuit, students *"come from all over and go all over."* Places are awarded on an admission points basis, which recognises academics, extra-curriculars and other achievements. Essentially, BILP wants students with a chance of actually gaining pupillage. For those whose CVs need a boost, the school has plenty to offer. "*CV-enhancing extras*" is the name of the game: prison visits to talk to inmates about rehabilitation, the Innocence Project, the Community Legal Advice and Representation Service, and an upcoming clinic to aid victims of forced marriages are all available. After the course, students can train as accredited mediators at no extra cost.

A number of new elective subjects have been added, including competition, and refugee and asylum law. The teaching staff includes former barristers, district judges, door tenants and a couple of solicitors. Each must spend a week per year linked to practice to keep up with developments. In addition the school has an advisory committee comprised of a silk, a judge and two senior juniors from the Bristol Bar. Students can get involved with mock trials, and there are three advocacy competitions sponsored by local chambers. In addition to a dedicated careers adviser, personal tutors are always on hand, not least during biannual buffet lunches for staff and students.

Cardiff Law School

Number of places: 72 full-time

Cardiff's reputation as an exciting and vibrant city grows, so it's no surprise that a significant number of its undergraduates stay on to take the law school's popular BPTC. The course receives twice as many first-choice applications as there are places, so put it down as your first choice or not at all.

The school is committed to delivering the course content to small groups, so there are a limited amount of large-group sessions and some skills are taught to groups of just four people. A teacher observes each individual's oral skills, for example, rather than circulating around the class; they also provide oral and written feedback. Students have many opportunities to practise advocacy: the BSB recommends a minimum of 12 classes; Cardiff runs more than 30. Teaching staff come from practice, and the school has course consultants and an advisory board that includes local practitioners and judges.

A two-week placement scheme enables students to spend a week marshalling a judge at circuit level or above, half of the following week on a mini-pupillage and the remainder marshalling with a district judge. The school monitors the number of students attaining pupillage: 25% secure one at a UK set. A top-up LLM should be offered from 2011, as well as additional electives in Commercial Litigation, Chancery and International Trade. At the end of the course, students can elect to study one or two extra electives at no additional charge.

It's an exciting time for pro bono at Cardiff: it is helping to set up a Personal Support Unit to assist litigants in person negotiate court procedure, and has been reviewing all the pro bono opportunities in Wales to expand its portfolio.

City Law School, London

Number of places: 420 full-time, 60 part-time

City Law School (formerly Inns of Court School of Law) has a long history of educating barristers. Once the monopoly Bar course provider, it has a wealth of famous alumni including Tony Blair and Gandhi, whose portrait graces the student common room. Primarily an "*advocacy school,*" City recognises that its students must be academically strong due to the Bar's increasing role as a referral advisory service. The school accordingly considers applicants' academic prowess and commitment to practice – mooting, debating and mini-pupillages – to select those with a realistic chance of coping with the course and securing pupillage. Students come from "*every continent except for Antarctica,*" and the school has enjoyed a great reputation across the Commonwealth, although this has led to criticism of some students' English language abilities. City told us that it deliberately recruits fewer students than it is authorised to teach: 330 full-time and 36 part-time.

Teaching emulates real-life practice as far as possible, and skills training is integrated with knowledge delivery. For example, when learning how to apply for an interim injunction, students will first watch a demonstration of how to do it and then attend small-group sessions and lectures involving case analysis and skeletons. Only then will they perform the exercise themselves. One-on-one advocacy sessions also boost students' skills. Some 22 members of the teaching staff have written legal texts and the team includes barristers and some solicitors. Students have access to careers advisers at City University (of which the law school is a part) as well as a dedicated pupillage advisory team that "*puts students through their paces*" in mock interviews. A speaker programme welcomes personalities such as Michael Mansfield QC, and a mooting and mock trial competition is useful for boosting CVs. Cross-examining trainee police officers adds a more realistic dimension to mock trials. Elective options with FRU and the National Coalition against Domestic Violence also help boost CVs. Supplementing the Inns' awards, scholarships are granted based on performance, and the school is considering awarding these to students at the end of the BPTC year.

The College of Law, London

Number of places: 240 full-time, 48 part-time

COL is validated to offer the course at its London (Bloomsbury) and Birmingham branches. Those who complete its GDL and BPTC obtain an LLB, and students can also opt to study for a top-up LLM after the course. Offering both full-time and part-time weekend study options, the London branch is less flashy than its Moorgate sibling, although there is a new IT room and revamped cybercafé. Teaching is delivered via small-group (from two to 12 people) sessions lasting three and a half hours. Full-timers attend four days a week, opting for either morning or afternoon classes.

Key at COL is the integration of skills and knowledge, with classes following the litigation process. In criminal litigation, for example, students begin by learning about an offender's rights in the police station and how to make a bail application. Later, they can unleash their inner QC in a mock trial at the Inner London Crown Court or Blackfriars Crown Court. Practitioners play the judges, while trainee police officers make the experience even more realistic. Although the BSB no longer requires compulsory court visits, COL has retained them, obviously seeing their value. It has also introduced more multi-media resources such as podcasts and video-recordings to supplement learning.

Students come from a variety of universities, and the most successful go on to a variety of pupillages. Applicants be aware: COL has its own scoring system, so it's important to rank it first if its your top pick. Its careers service – one of the largest in the country – offers the usual CV and application advice plus mock interviews, career workshops, a mentoring scheme with practitioners and a speaker programme. Students can also seek help from staff. All are from practice, including some solicitors and solicitor advocates, part-time judges and door tenants. Some full-time teaching staff practise over the summer months. A host of pro bono opportunities include FRU and the National Coalition against Domestic Violence. There are several mooting and mock trial sessions and competitions, while those on the Mediation elective can contend in the 'Plea and Mediation Competition'. If students have any time left, there are plenty of sports and social events.

The College of Law, Birmingham

Number of places: 96 full-time

Located in the historic jewellery quarter, students at COL's Birmingham branch find themselves in a smaller cohort than their peers in London. COL is the only BPTC provider in the West Midlands, and since its opening in 2007, the centre has gone from strength to strength. A new wing has been added and the library extended. As with London, there are great extra-curriculars, including assisting with the Birmingham Employment Rights Advice Line, The Refugee Council, the Trades Union Congress and Leasehold Valuation Tribunal service.

Kaplan Law School, London

Number of places: 60 full-time

Kaplan entered the LPC legal market in 2007 and is now making its bid for recognition in the BPTC market: it welcomed its first Bar students in September 2010. The course is the same as Nottingham Law School's and predominantly uses only primary sources – *Archibold* and the *White Book* – rather than school texts. The aim is to replicate real-life practice. Kaplan students can be confident that they're among *"a bright cohort."* Unlike other providers, all short-listed applicants must attend a selection event, where they are interviewed and take written and oral advocacy assessments. The rationale is two-fold: to ensure everyone's at the same level and to only accept those with *"a fighting chance of gaining pupillage."* The school looks for a minimum 2:1 (save for exceptional circumstances), at least three mini-pupillages and evidence of advocacy and public speaking experience.

Thanks to the selection process, students arrive already known to staff, and the school places an emphasis on face-to-face interaction, with one-on-one feedback for mock assessments. Teaching is delivered to large and small groups, and lectures are made available online for revision. New students' CVs are groomed and they can undergo mock interviews. The school had 60+ guest speakers lined up for its 2010 programme, and with Fridays free of classes, students can get involved in pro bono (eg Streetlaw and advocacy in the magistrates' court) and mooting and debating. Keen mooters can apply for a scholarship. The Master of Moots receives a 50% discount on course fees, while ten deputies also receive discounts of varying amounts.

Kaplan is one of the most expensive providers, something it attributes to an absence of economies of scale. The first year of its course has just 60 students and there are plans to grow to 90 students for 2011/12 and 120 for 2012/13. Located close to Borough Market, Kaplan has fantastic views of the City and its building is undergoing improvements, including a larger common room and two new mock courtrooms.

Manchester Metropolitan University

Number of places: 108 full-time, 48 part-time

Excellent links to practitioners make Man Met an ideal choice for those looking to pursue a career on the Northern Circuit. Experienced staff include deputy district judges, mediators, pupil supervisors and Inns' advocacy trainers. Students can also take advantage of additional advocacy classes (delivered by practitioners) and the Continuing Professional Development events hosted by the school for practitioners.

In response to student feedback, 2010 sees a new part-time evening course replacing the weekend course. Full-timers can still expect the usual four days of teaching, but what's new is the mode of teaching them civil and criminal litigation – students alternate between them week to week. Teaching focuses on knowledge at the beginning of the week, building up to the relevant skill, such as advocacy, at the end. Some lectures are available online and the school has a range of electronic supports, including podcasts. A dedicated careers adviser and a speaker programme enable students to learn about pupillage and the Bar. Pro bono opportunities include the Personal Support Unit at Manchester Civil Justice Centre, the Manchester Mediation Service, visits to Strangeways prison and Partners of Prisoners. Some students volunteer with Amicus, which offers legal representation to death row inmates.

Northumbria University Law School, Newcastle

Number of places: 100 full-time, 24 part-time

In 2007, the school moved to a new £76m campus in the heart of Newcastle. State-of-the-art facilities include WiFi throughout, several mock courtrooms and a popular student café. In addition to the usual three-year LLB, the law school also offers a four-year exempting degree. As a result, full and part-time BPTC students study alongside undergraduates. Full-timers normally work to a four-day week, with Friday designated as a research day. Day-release part-timers can attend on a Monday, Tuesday or Thursday. With the exception of those on the exempting degree, the majority of students come from the region, with some international students also thrown into the mix. Around 90% of staff are barristers, of which 80% still practise, which helps keep the course up-to-date.

The school prides itself on its pastoral care and every student is assigned a guidance tutor with whom they meet regularly. The Bar in Newcastle is not as well developed as in certain other UK cities, so there is an acute shortage of local pupillages. Still, the school's experienced careers service organises networking events with local chambers and practitioners, group marshalling and a mentoring scheme with alumni. Mock pupillage interviews and a CV workshop on the induction programme should also help.

Nottingham Law School

Number of places: 120 full-time

This enormously popular course enjoys a fantastic reputation and attracts candidates from "*all points of the compass.*" The school receives twice as many first and second-choice applications than there are places, so don't even bother ranking the school third on your application. With so many applications, the school selects only the best candidates. The effect is easy to see when you look at Nottingham's pupillage statistics: around 40% of grads secure pupillage by the March following the end of the course. A 2:1 (save for exceptional circumstances) and "*commitment to the profession*" (three mini-pupillages and advocacy and public speaking experience) are the minimum entry requirements.

The Wood Report heavily influenced the adaptation of the BVC into the new BPTC course. Nottingham had largely already been making the changes since it first began providing the BVC in the late 1990s. One good example is the BSB's decision to assess civil and criminal subjects by a mixture of multiple-choice questions and long and short answers. Nottingham has done this for years. With an emphasis on face-to-face teaching, the lion's share of the course is taught to small groups and is supplemented with some lectures and online support. With the exception of three solicitors, all teaching staff are former barristers, and some are door tenants and part-time judges. The school has dedicated careers advisers and a healthy speaker programme featuring members of the local Bar. Students can devote their Friday non-teaching day to mooting, marshalling and pro bono. Nottingham boasts the only FRU outside London. After an alumnus set up 'Bars in their Eyes', students can go on prison visits to help rehabilitate offenders. They can also perfect their advocacy skills at a mooting competition and 'plea in mitigation' competition sponsored by local sets.

How to fund law school

Training as a lawyer isn't cheap. According to various reports and surveys, you'll have already saddled yourself with between £15,000 and £30,000 of debt as an undergraduate. Now you're contemplating starting an even more expensive course, be it the GDL, LPC or BPTC.

Secure sponsorship before starting your training course

If you're interested in commercial law or want to work at one of the larger firms in the UK, there's a chance you might be able to find a firm that will sponsor you through law school. These firms tend to recruit two years in advance of the start of the training contract so you'll need to get your act together well ahead of time. Not only will such firms cover the cost of course fees (LPC and usually GDL too), they may well give you a few thousand pounds to cover living costs. Details of what solicitors' firms are offering their future trainees are given in the **Salaries and benefits** table on page 525 in the **Refine your search** section of this guide.

The luckiest of BPTC students will already have a pupillage lined up. At the better-off sets, the size of the pupillage award is now comparable with the sort of trainee/NQ salaries paid in the City. Usually a decent chunk of the pupillage award can be drawn down to cover BPTC expenses. At less affluent sets there may be no money available for the BPTC at all. Further information about funding is given in the **Bar** section of this guide.

Local authority grants

LEA grants are hard to get and very limited. It's still worth finding the contact details for your LEA at www.studentfinance.direct.gov and testing the water.

The Inns of Court

If you're training to be a barrister you can apply for a range of GDL and BPTC scholarships from the Inns of Court. Around a quarter of BPTC students get some funding and there's over £4.5m up for grabs. Check page 684 for more details.

Law school scholarships

Individual law schools have scholarship programmes too. Go to our website for details.

Where to study

Studying in London could set you back as much as double what it would elsewhere, say in Sheffield, Cardiff or Nottingham, and the quality of training isn't necessarily going to be any better. Go to our website for tables comparing the prices of all the law schools' courses.

Career Development Loans

First of all, if the loan isn't from Barclays or the Co-op then it isn't really a Career Development Loan (CDL), it's just a bank claiming there will be no repayments to make while you study. Though that may be the case, it doesn't mean there is no interest accruing – it could just be piling

Benefits, benefactors, begging...

So bunking up with Ma and Pa during your course isn't a dream come true, yet sometimes needs must. Forget ideas of declaring bankruptcy to evade student debt; consider other creative ways to ease the burden.

- A student card will get you low-cost travel, discount haircuts, cinema tickets and even drinks in some places. If nothing else, it'll make you feel young.
- Websites such as www.studentbeans.com have discounts and deals for meals, entertainment and more.
- Law books are pricey so don't get overzealous before term starts. College libraries will have the core texts and you're sure to find former students hawking books. Check out notice boards and online for second-hand tomes.
- A number of law schools, chambers and solicitors firms run competitions. Do a Google search to find them. Winning may bring kudos as well as cash.
- Market research focus groups will pay decent money for an hour or two of your time.

Surf the internet for scholarships

Here are some of the funds we found:

- The Law Society Bursary Scheme is open to GDL or LPC students.
- The Law Society Diversity Access Scheme supports talented people who face obstacles to qualification.
- Inderpal Rahal Memorial Trust supports women from an immigrant or refugee background. Contact irmt@gclaw.co.uk for more details.
- The Kalisher Scholarship works with each of the BPTC providers to ensure that every year one talented but financially disadvantaged student has a free place on the course. For more information: www.criminalbar.com/215/.
- The Leonard Sainer Foundation provides financial assistance in the form of interest-free loans of £7,500 each, to help fund either the LPC or BPTC. For further information go to www.dechert.com.
- The Student Disability Assistance Fund can award up to £500 for people studying on a full-time or nearly full-time basis. See www.bahshe.demon.co.uk.
- Universities and publicly funded colleges have discretionary college access funds available to assist especially hard-up students. The major LPC/BPTC providers usually have a number of scholarships to assist select students with fees, etc.
- The HM Hubbard Law Scholarship is for trainees and recently admitted solicitors who want to study the law and legal procedures in France, Spain or Canada. Up to £15,000 a year is available. See www.hubbardlawscholarship.com for more.
- The Human Rights Lawyers Association has a bursary fund of up to £6,000 from which it makes up to five awards to people wishing to undertake unpaid/poorly paid human rights work, either during their training or soon after.
- Leeds Legal runs an essay competition with a prize of £1,000 and a summer placement with a top legal firm. Visit www.leedslegal.co.uk.
- The Foreign and Commonwealth Office's Chevening Scholarships are available for overseas students wishing to study in the UK. Cuts have been made to the programme but £15.5m was still available in 2010. The figure is being revised. See www.fco.gov.uk.
- Postgrad Solutions offers a small number of £500 bursaries for LLM students. See www.llmstudy.com/editorial/llm_bursary_about/.

up, ready to swamp you once your studies finish. A true CDL allows you to borrow up to £10,000, with the interest paid by the Learning and Skills Council while you study. Because the CDL interest rate may be higher than another loan, some people recommend taking a CDL and when the interest-free honeymoon is over, paying it off using another unsecured personal loan with a lower interest rate. Unfortunately, the GDL is no longer covered by the scheme, just the LPC and BPTC.

Bank loans

There's a good chance that you've already emptied the last pennies out of your student overdraft, but never fear – you may still be eligible for more debt. Despite the credit crunch, there's still money to be had, so check the interest rates of various banks.

Check out graduate accounts because they sometimes offer slightly better overdraft terms, and be sure to mention the fact that you plan on becoming a lawyer as some of them have special packages for customers entering the legal profession. NatWest provides a Professional Trainee Loan of up to £25,000 and Lloyds TSB provides loans of up to £10,000 or two-thirds of previous salary, if in employment. Repayment is made over a maximum period of five years, starting six months after completion of the course. RBS's Law Student Loan Scheme offers £5,000 for students taking the GDL and £10,000 for the LPC (or £15,000 for the LPC if no GDL loan has been made). To be eligible, applicants must be or become RBS customers. The repayment period is up to seven years (including the study period) and there are no repayments in year one and interest-only repayments in years two and three. Whatever you do, don't make any decisions lightly: loans involve a big commitment that only continues to grow once the debt starts to accrue.

Get a job!

Law firms are increasingly interested in applicants' commercial awareness and ability to cope in a professional office environment, so what used to be an undesirable option can now be deployed in an interview as proof of your suitability for a career in law. Be sure to set yourself a manageable schedule and think long and hard whether full or part-time study is the most appropriate way forward. You'll also have to decide whether to work full or part-time.

LSC grants

The Legal Services Commission used to award grants to support individuals wanting to go into Legal Aid practice. Sadly, cuts have put paid to this programme.

- **Don't sleepwalk into law school:** The legal profession is no longer quite so eager to recruit graduates. Start career planning as early as possible because the recruitment game just got a whole tougher.

top tip no. 8

Ethnicity and the law

32% of students starting undergraduate law degrees in 2008 came from a minority ethnic background

11% of solicitors are from a minority ethnic back-ground

11% of self employed barristers are from a minority ethnic background

20% of new trainee solicitors came from a minority ethnic background in 08/09

Pupil barristers by ethnicity (08/09)
White: 81.6%
Non-white: 13.2%
Not declared: 5.2%

26% of law firm partners in private practice are from a minority ethnic back-ground

There are no minority ethnic Justices of the Supreme Court

On average, minority ethnic solicitors earn **17%** less than white solicitors

Unless otherwise stated figures are the most recent from the Law Society and Bar Standards Board.

A-Z of Universities & Law Schools

Bristol Institute of Legal Practice at UWE

Bristol Institute of Legal Practice, University of the West of England, Coldharbour Lane, Bristol BS16 1QY
Email: bilpinfo@uwe.ac.uk
Website : www.uwe.ac.uk/bilp

Contact
bilpinfo@uwe.ac.uk

Institute Profile

BILP is the leading provider of vocational legal training in Bristol with an established track record of excellence. Tutors write and deliver courses in areas of specialist expertise. Many are qualified solicitors and barristers drawing on years of practice experience, some are still in practice. The focus is on personalised delivery, treating the student as an individual. There are weekly small group, interactive classes; e-learning complements face to face teaching. BILP is large enough to provide a range and depth of quality provision, but without students feeling lost as part of a much larger enterprise. All BILP students can participate in award winning pro-bono activities.

Legal Practice Course (LPC) full-time/part-time

BILP's LPC is one of a few to repeatedly achieve an "excellent" rating from its regulator. This quality provision continues with its new and competitively priced LPC (fees of £7,860 for 2010/11) enhanced by extensive pastoral and careers support for our student cohort.

Bar Professional Training Course (BPTC) full-time/part-time

The Bristol BPTC equips you with skills to excel at the Bar and beyond, providing outstanding opportunities to develop advocacy, research, conference and mediation skills and to assist you in securing that elusive pupillage.

Graduate Diploma in Law (GDL/CPE) full-time/part-time

The GDL enables non-law graduates to progress with confidence to the LPC or BPTC. The conversion to legal study is supported by a dedicated team of tutors who understand the demands of the GDL route. GDL students share no teaching with undergraduates. The curriculum is divided into two teaching and assessment blocks.

UWE BRISTOL University of the West of England

Cardiff Law School

Cardiff Law School, Cardiff University, Museum Avenue, Cardiff CF10 3AX
Tel: (029) 2087 4941 (LPC) (029) 2087 4964 (BPTC) Fax: (029) 2087 4984
Email: law-lpc@cf.ac.uk or law-bptc@cf.ac.uk
Website: www.law.cardiff.ac.uk/cpls

University profile

Cardiff Law School is one of the most successful law schools in the UK and enjoys an international reputation for its teaching and research. The results of the 2008 Research Assessment Exercise recognise Cardiff Law School as one of the UK's leading research bodies, placing it 7th in the UK. Cardiff offers opportunities for students to pursue postgraduate study by research leading to the degrees of M.Phil and Ph.D. and a broadly based Masters (LLM) programme which is offered in full and part-time mode.

Legal Practice Course and Bar Professional Training Course

A part of the Law School, the Centre for Professional Legal Studies is the leading provider of legal training in Wales and is validated to offer both the Legal Practice Course and the Bar Professional Training Course. Students are taught by experienced solicitors and barristers who have been specifically recruited for this purpose. The Centre prides itself on its friendly and supportive teaching environment and its strong links with the legal profession. Placements with solicitors' firms or sets of Chambers are available to students pursuing the vocational courses.

In 2005 Cardiff's Legal Practice Course once again achieved the highest rating following the Law Society's assessment visit. The course has consistently been rated "Excellent" by the Law Society; one of the few providers of this course to hold the top ranking. The Law Society praised the challenging learning environment and stimulating range of activities. To accommodate differing student needs, from September 2010 Cardiff will be offering the LPC part-time in addition to the existing full-time course. Through both courses the school will continue to provide its excellent learning experience which includes a high degree of hands-on teaching. Please see the Law School website for further details.

Cardiff has delivered a high-quality and highly regarded Bar Professional Training Course since it was first introduced by the Bar Council in 1997. There is a relatively small student cohort and the course provides a highly supportive learning environment with high levels of individual tutor feedback on all live skills performances. The learning will mostly take place in small groups. There is a focus on the development of Advocacy skills, with two hour classes in groups of six or less almost every week across all three terms. The course is delivered by a small team of experienced and dedicated practitioners. Students are offered two weeks of placements giving them the opportunity to marshall with both a Circuit Judge and a District Judge in addition to undertaking a mini-pupillage.

Cardiff also has a Pro Bono Scheme which gives students an opportunity to experience the law in action, work alongside volunteer legal professionals and develop transferable skills to add to their CVs.

Facilities

The Law School has dedicated accommodation for the vocational courses which houses a practitioner library, fixed and moveable audio visual equipment for recording practitioner skills, interactive teaching equipment and extensive computer facilities. In addition, the main law library contains one of the largest collections of primary and secondary material within the UK. The Law School is housed in its own building at the heart of the campus, itself located in one of the finest civic centres in Britain and only a short walk from the main shopping area. The University has its own postgraduate centre, and a full range of sports and social facilities. Cardiff is a vibrant capital city with excellent cultural, sporting and leisure activities.

Contact
LPC: full time - Claire Shelton
part time - Lee Price
Tel: (029) 2087 4941
Email: law-lpc@cf.ac.uk
BPTC: Lucy Burns
Tel: (029) 2087 4964
Email: law-bptc@cf.ac.uk

Other postgraduate law courses:
The Postgraduate Office
Tel: (029) 2087 4351/4353
Email: law-PG@cardiff.ac.uk

CARDIFF UNIVERSITY
PRIFYSGOL CAERDYDD

The City Law School

City University London, Northampton Square, London, EC1V 0HB
Website: www.city.ac.uk/law

College profile

Located in the heart of legal London, The City Law School is one of London's major law schools and offers an impressive range of academic and professional courses. We're the first law school in London to educate students and practitioners at all stages of legal education.

The school's exceptional legal courses are fully accredited by the relevant professional bodies and are developed and delivered by its team of highly respected practitioners and academics. The school takes a personalised approach to your learning experience and aims to develop you into the professional, dynamic, highly motivated, "practice-ready" lawyers of the future.

Graduate Diploma in Law (full-time)

Started in 1976, this internationally renowned course was one of the first Common Professional Examination (CPE) programmes for non-law graduates. The course is designed to provide you with the knowledge and skills traditionally gained from an undergraduate law degree in just one year. The school teaches you the seven core legal subjects through a variety of lectures, tutorials and seminars. At The City Law School you also have the unique opportunity to convert your GDL into a full LLB degree by taking additional units.

Legal Practice Course (full-time)

The school's LPC has consistently achieved the highest possible grading by the Solicitors Regulation Authority (SRA, formerly The Law Society). The course is skills-based and replicates the demands and disciplines of practice through realistic exercises fully preparing you for professional legal life. You are taught in small groups by qualified solicitors on a wide range of specialist subjects. At The City Law School you can add value to your LPC by completing an additional research project to be awarded an LLM in Professional Legal Practice. The School also offers a two-year Graduate Entry LLB (Hons) for non-law graduates wishing to convert to law.

Bar Professional Training Course (full or part-time)

The school's BPTC delivers effective training for future barristers and equips them with the key legal skills and networking opportunities to pursue a successful career at the Bar. The core skills of advocacy, opinion writing, drafting, alternative dispute resolution and client conferencing are taught in the context of procedural and evidential knowledge in both criminal and civil practice. Pervading the course are the skills of effective legal research and case management as well as ethical professional conduct. The effective and flexible use of modern technologies on the course is designed to enhance students' learning experience. At The City Law School, you also have the opportunity to gain an LLM in Professional Legal Skills, awarded on successful completion of the BPTC and a supervised dissertation.

Masters Degrees (LLMs) (full or part-time)

The School's LLM courses give you the opportunity to develop your understanding and expertise in a number of distinct areas of law. The firm offers the following masters: LLM in EU Commercial Law; LLM in International Banking and Finance; LLM/M.Jur in International Commercial Law; LLM in International Competition Law; LLM in International Energy Litigation; LLM in Maritime Law (UK); LLM in Maritime Law (Greece); LLM in Criminal Litigation and LLM in Civil Litigation and Dispute Resolution. The School's LLMs are offered on a full and part-time basis, allowing you the freedom to fit your study in and around work, family and any other commitments you may have.

Contact

GDL
(020) 7040 8301
cpe@city.ac.uk

LPC
(020) 7404 5787
lpc@city.ac.uk

BPTC
(020) 7404 5787
bptc@city.ac.uk

Master Degrees (LLMs)
(020) 7404 5787
law@city.ac.uk

The College of Law

Admissions, Braboeuf Manor, Portsmouth Road, Guildford GU3 1HA
Freephone: 0800 289997
Email: admissions@lawcol.co.uk
Website: www.college-of-law.co.uk

College profile

At The College of Law you'll get the best possible start to your legal career. With centres in Birmingham, Bristol, Chester, Guildford, London, Manchester and York, the College is the UK's no.1 law school. Its innovative courses are designed and taught by lawyers, with a clear focus on building the practical skills, commercial awareness and independent thinking you'll need to succeed in practice. This is supported by an award-winning pro bono programme, the largest and best-resourced careers service in UK legal education and excellent tutor support.

Graduate Diploma in Law (full-time/part-time/S-mode)

Designed to build knowledge and skills that more than match a law degree – with a clear focus on preparing you for life in practice. Academic training is built around real-life examples and case studies, and you'll be given research assignments that directly reflect the way you'll work as a lawyer. Students who pass the College GDL are guaranteed a place on the College LPC, and if you go on to successfully complete your LPC or BPTC at the College, you'll graduate with an LL.B law degree without the need to study or pay for additional modules.

Legal Practice Course (full-time/part-time/S-mode)

The College LPC is rigorous and practical – equipping you with the skills you need to succeed in practice. It has the widest selection of vocational elective subjects available and offers three different LPC routes, allowing you to specialise in your chosen field: corporate, commercial and private and legal aid. The majority of teaching is in small, student-centred groups and the course features extensive use of multimedia learning resources. Students who complete this LPC earn credits towards the College's LL.M Masters degrees.

Bar Professional Training Course (full-time/part-time)

The College BPTC has been designed to resemble practice as closely as possible. Study follows a logical, realistic process from initial instruction to final appeal, and learning is based around the seven core skills and three knowledge areas stipulated by the Bar Standards Board. Most of your learning will be in small groups, and you'll have plenty of opportunities to put your learning into action through: practitioner evenings, mock trials, court visits, mooting, negotiating and advocacy competitions, and pro bono. Students who complete this BPTC will earn credits towards the College's LL.M Masters degrees.

Juris Doctor

The College of Law Juris Doctor qualification (JD) allows you to prepare to dual qualify in England and Wales and in the US by giving you access to the New York State Bar exam as well as the qualifications required to start either a training contract or pupillage here.

Masters Degrees (S-mode/A-mode)

The College's LL.M Masters degrees are truly professional qualifications and reflect cutting-edge approaches to legal practice. They offer a wide choice of flexible, specialist modules to suit your area of interest and enhance your expertise. These can be studied via S-mode (supervised online) modules, or by A-mode modules that combine online and face-to-face teaching and attendance at one of the college's UK centres. This will lead to an LL.M in either Professional Legal Practice or International Legal Practice.

Make a date

You can find out more by attending an open day or arranging a centre visit, or by coming to a taster session. For further details and to book a place, visit www.college-of-law.co.uk/events.

Contact
Freephone: 0800 289997
International:
+44 (0)1483 216000
Email: LLM@lawcol.co.uk
Website:
www.college-of-law.co.uk

GDL & LPC full-time
Apply to: Central Applications Board www.lawcabs.ac.uk

GDL & LPC part-time
Apply to: The College of Law
Contact:
admissions@lawcol.co.uk

BPTC full & part-time
Apply to Bar Standards Board (BSB)
www.barprofessionaltraining.org.uk

LL.M Masters Degrees
Apply to: The College of Law
Contact: LLM@lawcol.co.uk

Juris Doctor (JD)
Apply to: The College of Law
Contact:
admissions@lawcol.co.uk

The College of Law of England and Wales

Kaplan Law School

Kaplan Law School
Palace House, 3 Cathedral Street, London SE1 9DE
Tel: (020) 7367 6400
Email: admissions@kaplanlawschool.org.uk
Website: www.kaplanlawschool.org.uk

College profile

Kaplan Law School (KLS) offer Nottingham Law School's market-leading courses at their central London campus. Kaplan have achieved the highest ratings from the Solicitors Regulatory Authority (SRA), and have also secured a number of exclusive training deals with well-established law firms in London, reflecting the success of the partnership with Nottingham Law School (NLS) and the quality of training provided.

Kaplan's tutors are all qualified lawyers with a proven record in practice and legal education. They work in close collaboration with both firms and the NLS faculty to ensure the delivery of a consistently excellent student experience.

All students benefit from a proactive careers service led by a former Graduate Recruitment Manager of two major city law firms, as well as many pro bono schemes including a Legal Advice Clinic at the school.

The London campus overlooks the River Thames and has been custom-built with state of the art facilities designed to optimize the student and teaching experience. The South Bank location provides excellent transport links, proximity to the City's legal hub and a vibrant social and cultural community.

GDL: Graduate Diploma in Law (full-time)

This one-year intensive course is designed for any non-law graduate who intends to become a solicitor or barrister in the UK. Kaplan's GDL places the academic subjects into a work-related context so that students are more prepared for practice. All students who successfully complete the GDL will be guaranteed a place on Kaplan's LPC. Face to face tuition is a priority and the course is taught through interactive small group sessions and small lecture cohorts. See www.kaplanlawschool.org.uk/gdl for more information.

LPC: Legal Practice Course (full-time and part-time)

The NLS LPC has long been regarded as the industry leader and is the only LPC to receive the SRA's highest rating every year since its inception. Kaplan offer the same rigorous, professional standards of course design and delivery, reflected in the same highest rating received from the SRA. Kaplan's teaching model is based around smaller group sizes, which helps accelerate student learning and understanding and gives tutors more contact time with each student.

Kaplan offer you a choice of broad-based or specialist pathways through your LPC allowing you to tailor your LPC to a particular area of legal practice. Kaplan also aim to get you ready to practise through its Bridge to Practice programme. See www.kaplanlawschool.org.uk/lpc for more information.

BPTC: Bar Professional Training Course

Kaplan are delighted to have been validated by the Bar Standards Board (BSB) to deliver in London the NLS Bar Course as from September 2010. The NLS Bar Course is established as one of the best in the country with double the average pupillage rates and the highest student satisfaction rates.

The course was designed by tutors with experience of legal practice and will be delivered with the input of judges, barristers and other practitioners.

Kaplan's BPTC has high admission standards and includes a selection day to ensure a bright cohort of students and the best chance of securing a pupillage. See www.kaplanlawschool.org.uk/bptc for more information.

Summer School

Kaplan runs a highly successful two-day Summer School to introduce potential GDL, LPC and BPTC students to the skill sets necessary to become a transactional lawyer or barrister. See www.kaplanlawschool.org.uk/summerschool for more information.

Scholarships

Kaplan award a number of scholarships each year. See www.kaplanlawschool.org.uk/scholarship for more information.

Contact
Admissions:
admissions@kaplanlawschool.org.uk

GDL and LPC full time:
Apply to: Central Applications Board
Contact:
admissions@kaplanlawschool.org.uk

LPC part time:
Apply to Kaplan Law School
Contact:
admissions@kaplanlawschool.org.uk

BPTC
Apply to Bar Standards Board
www.barprofessionaltraining.org.uk

KAPLAN LAW SCHOOL

Nottingham Law School

Nottingham Law School, Belgrave Centre, Nottingham NG1 5LP
Tel: +44 (0)115 848 4460
Email: nls.enquiries@ntu.ac.uk
Website: www.ntu.ac.uk/nls

Legal Practice Course

Nottingham Law School's highly regarded Legal Practice Course has received the highest possible rating in every SRA assessment. The LPC is offered by full-time and part-time block study. This course has been designed to be challenging and stimulating for students and responsive to the needs of firms, varying from large commercial to smaller high street practices.

Nottingham Law School will help you make the best possible start to your legal career.

Nottingham Law School's LPC programme has been designed to allow you to select pathways that lead to a specific type of practice, or maintain a broad-based professional legal education if you are not sure yet what type of practice you intend to move to. In addition to the School's broad based LPC, corporate, commercial and public funding pathways are also offered. Nottingham's Legal Practice Course allows you to select your pathway when you start the course, rather than deciding on a particular route in advance.

Graduate Diploma in Law

The GDL is offered full-time or by distance-learning. Nottingham Law School's GDL is designed for any non-law graduate who intends to become a solicitor or barrister in the UK. The intensive course effectively covers the seven core subjects of an undergraduate law degree. It is the stepping stone to the LPC or BPTC, and a legal career thereafter. GDL students who embark on Nottingham Law School's LPC or BPTC will be eligible for a full LLB on successful completion of that professional course. Successful completion of the GDL (full-time) at first attempt guarantees students a place on the School's excellent-rated LPC and favourable consideration for the School's BPTC.

Bar Professional Training Course

Nottingham Law School has designed its BPTC to develop to a high standard a range of core practical skills, and to equip students to succeed in the fast-changing environment of practice at the Bar. Students are taught in small groups in high-quality teaching accommodation. The BPTC is taught entirely by qualified practitioners, and utilises the same integrated and interactive teaching methods as all of the School's other professional courses. Essentially, students learn by doing and Nottingham Law School provides an environment in which students are encouraged to realise, through practice and feedback, their full potential. The pupillage rate for Nottingham Law School is consistently above the national average.

LLM Professional Practice

Students who complete Nottingham Law School's LPC or BPTC can choose to 'top up' to an LLM which is valued by law firms as recognition of further expertise. You will need to complete both a week-long summer school programme in June after you have completed your LPC/BPTC, and a Professional Practice Dissertation (20,000 words) on a subject relevant to professional practice in the legal services sector. Students who have not completed their professional studies with Nottingham Law School are still eligible to take this qualification; please contact the university in advance as you may need to complete additional modules or provide evidence of learning.

Contact
Nottingham Law School
Belgrave Centre
Nottingham NG1 5LP
Tel: +44 (0)115 848 4460
Email: nls.enquiries@ntu.ac.uk
Website: www.ntu.ac.uk/nls

NOTTINGHAM
LAW SCHOOL
Nottingham Trent University

Northumbria Law School

City Campus East, Newcastle Upon Tyne, NE1 8ST
Tel: 0191 227 4453 Fax: 0191 227 4561
Email: et.admissions@northumbria.ac.uk
Website: www.northumbrialawschool.co.uk

Contact
Law Admissions
Tel: 0191 227 4453
Email:
et.admissions@northumbria.ac.uk

College profile

Northumbria Law School is justifiably renowned for excellence in learning and teaching and its ground-breaking portfolio of undergraduate, postgraduate and professional programmes. The School focuses on law in practice and is committed to ensuring that students develop the knowledge and skills needed to become successful legal professionals. This commitment is demonstrated through its academic staff, the majority of whom have considerable and often continuing experience of practice.

Graduate diploma in law (GDL)- full-time/ distance learning/ e-learning

The GDL provides the academic stage of legal education for non-law graduates who intend to practise law. It covers the seven foundations of legal knowledge. Students are also required to choose an eighth optional subject from a wide range available. Completion of the GDL allows entry to the Legal Practice Course (LPC) or Bar Professional Training Course (BPTC). Northumbria GDL students are entitled to a £1,000 discount off LPC or BPTC fees (must be studied over consecutive years).

Legal practice course (LPC)- full-time/ part-time

Northumbria's LPC was awarded the highest possible rating of 'commendable practice' in all areas of assessment by the Solicitors Regulation Authority (SRA). The programme provides vocational training across a range of subjects and practical skills, enabling students to learn how to apply their legal knowledge in a practical context. The course is taught in two blocks, stage 1 and stage 2. Students have the opportunity to tailor their LPC to their preferred career path as stage 1 is offered in two routes, general practice and commercial practice.

Bar professional training course* (BPTC) – full-time/part-time

Northumbria is one of only six institutions outside of London to offer the BPTC. In their last monitoring report, the Bar Standards Board wrote 'Northumbria University is clearly offering a high quality BPTC course in a first class facility'. The Law School is a short walk from Newcastle's legal centre – the Quayside – and many of the staff who teach on the programme are members of local chambers and practise regularly in local courts. Additionally, local practitioners regularly deliver lectures and run advocacy masterclasses for all students.

LLM – full-time/distance learning

The Law School offers a range of distinctive and innovative Masters programmes which focus on the practical operation of the law. LPC and BPTC students at Northumbria are able to study an LLM in Advanced Legal Practice at the same time. A newly validated MSc in Business with Legal Management is also available.

Facilities

The Law School is located on the award-winning City Campus East, in the heart of Newcastle. Based in a £70 million building, the School is justifiably proud of its facilities, with state-of-the-art lecture theatres, dedicated courtrooms, skills suites and an outstanding Law Practice Library.

northumbria UNIVERSITY Law School

* *Formerly the Bar Vocational Course*

Solicitors' Practice Areas

Banking and finance	90
Competition/antitrust	92
Construction and projects	94
Corporate	96
Crime	100
Employment	102
Environment	104
Family	106
Intellectual property	108
Litigation/dispute resolution	111
Personal injury and clinical negligence	114
Private client and charities	116
Property/real estate	118
Public interest	120
Restructuring/insolvency	122
Shipping and international trade	124
Sports, media and entertainment law	126
Tax	129
Technology, telecoms and outsourcing	130

Banking and finance

In a nutshell

Banking and finance lawyers may work in any one of the specialist areas described below, but all deal with the borrowing of money or the management of financial liabilities. Their task is to negotiate and document the contractual relationship between lenders and borrowers and ensure that their client's best legal and commercial interests are reflected in the terms of loan agreements. It is a hugely technical, ever-evolving and jargon-heavy area of law.

Straightforward bank lending: a bank lends money to a borrower on documented repayment terms. **Acquisition finance:** a loan made to a corporate borrower or private equity sponsor for the purpose of acquiring another company. This includes **leveraged finance**, where the borrower uses a very large amount of borrowed money to meet the cost of a significant acquisition without committing a lot of its own capital (as typically done in leveraged buyouts (LBOs): read our corporate law section). **Real estate finance:** a loan made to enable a borrower to acquire a property or finance the development of land and commonly secured by way of a mortgage on the acquired property/land. **Project finance:** the financing of long-term infrastructure (eg roads) and public services projects (eg hospitals), where the amounts borrowed to complete the project are paid back with the cash flow generated by the project. **Asset finance:** this enables the purchase and operation of large assets such as ships, aircraft and machinery. The lender normally takes security over the assets in question. **Islamic finance:** Muslim borrowers, lenders and investors must abide by Shari'a law, which prohibits the collection and payment of interest on a loan. Islamic finance specialists ensure that finance deals are structured in a Shari'a-compliant manner. **Debt capital markets:** this generic category covers many types of debt instruments, but generally speaking it deals with a borrower raising capital by selling tradable bonds to investors, who expect the full amount lent to be paid back to them with interest. **Securitisation:** essentially this is where a lender wants to sell its loans to create liquidity. It does so by selling them to a shell company, which then issues bonds to the markets. Bond investors get paid from the interest and principal on the loans owned by the shell company. **Structured finance:** a service offered by many large financial institutions for companies with unique financing needs that traditional loans cannot satisfy. Structured finance generally involves highly complex bespoke financial transactions. **Derivatives:** at its most basic, a derivative is a security used by banks and corporates to hedge risks to which they are exposed from factors outside of their control. They can also be used for speculative purposes by betting on the fluctuation of just about anything from currency exchange rates to the number of sunny days in a particular region. Futures, forwards, options and swaps are the most common types of derivatives. **Financial services regulation:** lawyers in this field ensure that their bank clients operate in compliance with the relevant financial legislation.

What lawyers do

- Meet with clients to establish their specific requirements and the commercial context of a deal.
- Carry out due diligence – an investigation exercise to verify the accuracy of information passed from the borrower to the lender or from the company raising finance to all parties investing in the deal. This can involve on-site meetings with the company's management, so lawyers can verify the company's credit profile. If financial instruments, such as bonds, are being offered to investors, the report will take the form of a prospectus, which must comply with the requirements of the EU prospectus and transparency directives.
- Negotiate with the opposite party to agree the terms of the deal and record them accurately in the facility documentation. Lenders' lawyers usually produce initial documents (often a standard form) and borrowers' lawyers try to negotiate more favourable terms for their clients. Lawyers on both sides must know when to compromise and when to hold out.
- Assist with the structuring of complicated or groundbreaking financing models and ensure innovative solutions comply with all relevant laws.
- Gather all parties to complete the transaction, ensuring all agreed terms are reflected in the loan and that all documents have been properly signed and witnessed. Just as in corporate deals, many decisions need to be made at properly convened board meetings and recorded in written resolutions.
- Finalise all post-completion registrations and procedures.

The realities of the job

- City firms act for investment banks on highly complex and often cross-border financings, whereas the work of regional firms generally involves acting for commercial banks on more mainstream domestic finance deals. If you want to be a hotshot in international finance then it's the City for you.
- Lawyers need to appreciate the needs and growth ambitions of their clients in order to deliver pertinent advice and warn of the legal risks involved in the transactions. Deals may involve the movement of money across borders and through different currencies and financial

products. International deals have an additional layer of difficulty: political changes in transitional economies can render a previously sound investment risky.

- Banking clients are ultra-demanding and the hours can be long. On the plus side your clients will be smart and dynamic. It is possible to build up long-term relationships with investment bank clients, even as a junior.
- Working on deals can be exciting. The team and the other side are all working to a common goal, often under significant time and other pressures. Deal closings bring adrenaline highs and a sense of satisfaction.
- You need to become absorbed in the finance world. Start reading the *FT* or the City pages in your daily newspaper for a taster.

Current issues

- By and large, the market is still feeling the effects of the credit crunch and the aftermath of the Lehman Brothers collapse. It has been a difficult year for both borrowers and lenders, with a relatively small number of new loans and deals. The banks' troubles have been well documented in the press, and a number of them have had to restructure their operations entirely.
- With fewer deals being done, many law firms have downsized their banking and finance teams. The big City firms were no exception, but they have fared better than initially expected due to their ability to adapt quickly in tougher market conditions. Those banking lawyers untouched by redundancies have had to be flexible, with clients needing advice on refinancings, recapitalisations and restructurings. Particularly noticeable is the trend for borrowers to buy back their own loans at a significant discount.
- Post-credit crunch, the cost of borrowing increased (as reflected in higher interest rates on borrowings and upfront fees). Banks are now more cautious, even towards borrowers with a strong credit profile and established relationships. Banks are, in theory, being encouraged to lend by the government and market analysts, but they face stringent credit committee conditions from within – eg enhanced security requirements and strict covenants.
- Commentators have observed a 'flight to quality' by clients, meaning magic circle firms are getting the lion's share of available work. Clients are also putting their faith (and money) into the hands of 'trusted advisers'.
- An area of particular interest to the magic circle firms is high-yield financing and the European bond market, traditionally the stomping grounds of US law firms. High-yield products provide an increasingly popular alternative financing strategy for clients struggling against the lack of traditional bank lending, and while investment banks were wary of the European bond market a decade or so ago, it now looks to be on the up.
- In order to curb the excesses of the banking community, governments are looking at strengthening regulatory controls. This is good news for regulatory lawyers, who can expect clients to ask for more advice on compliance issues and the implication of financial reforms.
- Secondments to banks are available, even for trainees, and subsequent moves in-house are common. In the past year many banks have laid off large numbers of their own legal personnel, which has increased their demand for law firm secondees at all levels of seniority. Some firms say this has put a strain on their own resources.

Read our True Pictures on...

Addleshaw Goddard	Jones Day
Allen & Overy LLP	K&L Gates
Ashurst	Kingsley Napley
Baker & McKenzie	Kirkland & Ellis
Beachcroft LLP	Latham & Watkins
Berwin Leighton Paisner	Lawrence Graham
Bingham McCutchen	Linklaters
Bird & Bird	Macfarlanes
Bond Pearce	Martineau
Brabners Chaffe Street	Mayer Brown
Browne Jacobson	Michelmores
Burges Salmon	Mills & Reeve
Charles Russell	Muckle
Clarke Willmott	Nabarro
Cleary Gottlieb	Norton Rose
Clifford Chance	Olswang
Clyde & Co	Orrick
CMS Cameron McKenna	Osborne Clarke
Cobbetts	Pannone
Dechert	Paul, Hastings
Dickinson Dees	Pinsent Masons
DLA Piper UK	Reed Smith
DMH Stallard	Shoosmiths
Dundas & Wilson	Sidley Austin
DWF	Simmons & Simmons
Eversheds	SJ Berwin
Farrer & Co	Skadden, Arps
Field Fisher Waterhouse	Slaughter and May
Foot Anstey Solicitors	SNR Denton
Freeth Cartwright	Speechly Bircham
Freshfields	Stephenson Harwood
Gordons	Stevens & Bolton
Hammonds	Taylor Wessing
Harbottle & Lewis	TLT
HBJ Gateley Wareing	Travers Smith
Herbert Smith	Trowers & Hamlins
Hill Dickinson	Veale Wasbrough Vizards
Hogan Lovells	Walker Morris
Holman Fenwick Willan	Ward Hadaway
Ince & Co	Watson, Farley & Williams
Irwin Mitchell	Weil, Gotshal & Manges

Competition/antitrust

In a nutshell

It is the job of the UK and EU regulatory authorities to ensure that markets function effectively on the basis of fair and open competition. The competition rules in the UK and EU are substantially similar, but the UK bodies concentrate on those rules that have their greatest effect domestically, while EU authorities deal with matters affecting multiple member states. The UK regulators are the Office of Fair Trade (OFT) and the Competition Commission; on matters also affecting other EU countries, it is the European Commission. Additionally, there are industry-specific regulatory bodies, such as Ofcom for the media and telecoms industry.

Competition authorities have extensive investigative powers – including the ability to carry out dawn raids – and can impose hefty fines. The OFT has become more proactive and litigation-minded in recent years, and you will certainly have heard about Intel's run-in with the European Commission. The computer chipmaker's record €1.06bn fine levied in May 2009 for anti-competitive practice is the largest ever and it shows that the Commission means business.

What lawyers do

- Negotiate clearance for acquisitions, mergers and joint ventures.
- Advise on the structure of commercial or co-operation agreements to ensure they can withstand a competition challenge.
- Deal with investigations into the way a client conducts business.
- Bring or defend claims in the Competition Appeal Tribunal (CAT).
- Advise on cross-border trade or anti-dumping measures (preventing companies exporting products at a lower price than it normally charges in its home market).
- Regulators investigate companies, bring prosecutions and advise on the application of new laws and regulations.

The realities of the job

- You won't get much independence; even junior lawyers work under the close supervision of experienced partners. In the early days the job involves a great deal of research into particular markets and how the authorities have approached different types of agreements in the past.
- You need to be interested in economics and politics.
- The work demands serious academic brainpower twinned with commercial acumen.
- As a popular area of practice it's hard to break into. Competition-specific studies – say a master's degree – will enhance your prospects.
- Advocacy is a relatively small part of the job, though you could end up appearing in the High Court or CAT.
- In international law firms you will travel abroad and may even work in an overseas office for a while, perhaps in Brussels, which is the hub for European competition work. Fluency in another language can be useful.

Current issues

- Competition law continues to increase its profile as greater regulatory activity is undertaken by the UK, EU and USA.
- The OFT continues to show its teeth, though it came under criticism after its four-year case against British Airways for price fixing with Virgin Atlantic collapsed in early 2010. It folded after the OFT failed to disclose key documents. The OFT is now under pressure to reform its approach to offering immunity in return for full co-operation in investigations, as it did with Virgin. Critics say the agency should perform its own investigations, rather than rely on the whistleblowers, who may become complacent or gain too much influence in the evidence gathering.
- The recession has caused a dip in merger control work, but there is plenty of cartel and competition litigation work to be had, particularly in damages actions.
- Competition lawyers are increasingly drawing on the experience of colleagues, such as financial regulation, tax and litigation specialists. They are also bringing in experts to address white-collar crime aspects.
- The remit of the CAT has been widened to allow claims for damages brought by third parties. Private enforcement can be a useful tool for competitor businesses and consumer groups, but thus far has had limited success.
- There are increased opportunities to work for the regulatory authorities; the OFT, for example, employs many more investigators than before. There is also a trend for lawyers to switch between private practice and working for the regulators.

Read our True Pictures on...

Addleshaw Goddard	Herbert Smith
Allen & Overy	Hogan Lovells
Arnold & Porter (UK)	Kingsley Napley
Ashurst	Latham & Watkins
Baker & McKenzie	Linklaters
Berwin Leighton Paisner	Macfarlanes
Bird & Bird	Mayer Brown
Bond Pearce	Nabarro
Burges Salmon	Norton Rose
Clifford Chance	Osborne Clarke
CMS Cameron McKenna	Pinsent Masons
Cobbetts	Reed Smith
Dickinson Dees	Simmons & Simmons
DLA Piper UK	SJ Berwin
Eversheds	Slaughter and May
Field Fisher Waterhouse	SNR Denton
Freshfields	TLT

Construction and projects

In a nutshell

Construction

Construction law can broadly be divided into non-contentious and contentious issues. The first involves lawyers helping clients at the procurement stage, pulling together all the contractual relationships prior to building work; the second sees them resolving disputes when things go wrong. In the past, the relatively high monetary stakes involved, and the industry trend for recovering building costs through the courts, made construction a litigation-happy practice. Since the 1990s most new contracts have contained mandatory procedures to be adopted in case of dispute. Adjudication of disputes has become the industry norm and these tend to follow a swift 28-day timetable. Others are resolved through mediation or arbitration; however, some disputes are so complex that the parties do still choose to slug it out in court.

Projects

Specialist construction lawyers work hand in hand with finance and corporate lawyers to enable projects to come to fruition. A few City firms and the largest US practices dominate the biggest international projects, but there's work countrywide. In the UK the Private Finance Initiative (PFI) – an aspect of Public Private Partnerships (PPP) – has been an important source of work. A key policy of the old government, it introduced private funding and management into areas that were previously public sector domains. Some law firms consistently represent the project companies, usually through a 'special purpose vehicle' (SPV) established to build, own and operate the end result of the project. Often the project company is a joint venture between various 'sponsor' companies. An SPV could also be partially owned by a government body or banks. Other firms consistently represent the organisations that commission projects. Then there are the firms that act purely on the finance side for banks, guarantors, export credit agencies, governments and international funding agencies.

What lawyers do

Construction: procurement

- Negotiate and draft contracts for programmes of building works. Any such programme involves a multitude of parties including landowners, main contractors, subcontractors, engineers and architects.
- Work in conjunction with property lawyers if the client has invested in land as well as undertaking a building project. Together, the lawyers seek and obtain all the necessary planning consents as well as local authority certifications.
- Where the developer does not own the land, liaise with the landowner's solicitors over matters such as stage payments, architects' certificates and other measures of performance.
- Make site visits during development.

Construction: disputes

- Assess the client's position and gather all related paperwork and evidence.
- Extract the important detail from huge volumes of technical documentation.
- Follow the resolution methods set out in the contracts between the parties.
- Where a settlement is impossible, issue, prepare for and attend proceedings with the client, usually instructing a barrister to advocate.

Projects

- Too varied to list. The field has specialists in the areas of funding, construction, real estate, planning, energy, telecoms and all aspects of the public sector, including health, education and housing.

The realities of the job

- Drafting requires attention to detail and careful thought.
- It's essential to keep up to date with industry standards and know contract law and tort inside out.
- People skills are fundamental. Contractors and subcontractors are generally earthy and direct; structural engineers live in a world of complicated technical reports; corporate types and in-house lawyers require smoother handling. You'll deal with them all.
- The construction world is often perceived as a male-dominated environment, but while some clients might see a visit to a lap-dancing club as par for the business entertainment course, there are many successful female construction lawyers, architects and engineers who avoid such activities.
- Most lawyers prefer either contentious or non-contentious work, and some firms like their construction lawyers to handle both, so pick your firm carefully.
- A background in construction or engineering is a major bonus because you'll already have industry contacts and will be able to combine legal know-how with practical advice.

- Projects require lawyers who enjoy the challenge of creating a complex scheme and figuring out all its possibilities and pitfalls. Projects can run for years, involving multidisciplinary legal work spanning finance, regulatory permissions, construction, employment law and much more.

Current issues

- There was a slight upturn in construction disputes during 2009/10, though not to the extent that some people had predicted. Ultimately, many claimants were unsure as to whether defendants would be able to pay the sums claimed, given the increase in contractors going bust all around the country. Mediation, arbitration and adjudication are definitely preferred.
- As the Brown government came to an end, it rubber-stamped quite a lot of public initiatives, such as Building Schools for the Future (BSF) and NHS LIFT projects. Shortly after the election of the coalition government, BSF came under the axe. The Olympics and Crossrail remain fairly significant for those contractors and lawyers lucky enough to have involvement.
- In domestic PFI, the market is likely to experience a huge shake-up. Contracts are likely to disappear and this will most likely lead to a contraction in all parts of the market, legal being no exception. Some firms have built their practices on the commoditised end of PFI, where they work through a large volume of standard contracts (such as BSF). It is these firms that are likely to suffer. Firms that focus on high-level one-off contracts like the Olympics and infrastructure projects should fare better.
- House building came to a standstill during the recession, but there is optimism in some quarters. The hope is that, having battened down the hatches in the downturn, developers will now have money to spare, perhaps for strategic land purchases of both green and brown-field sites in readiness for a revival in the building market.
- Social housing development became a hot area for firms to try and break into, but this sector is fearful for the period ahead as it presumes that previous levels of public spending will not be maintained.
- In Europe, energy security is a key concern for governments as recent political developments have emphasised the problematic nature of relying on a small number of sources for domestic energy requirements. An obvious example of the interest in energy security is the development of LNG storage and pipeline projects.
- Renewable energy continues to be a key area of investment and it satisfies both government commitments to energy security and carbon emission targets. These projects tend to have continued unabated despite the economic downturn due to their long-term nature.
- Nuclear technology is a key focus as, due to its relatively low carbon emissions, it too is able to satisfy reduction targets. The renewed interest can also be traced to a view that renewable energy sources may not be sufficient – in the short-term at least – to meet energy needs. This coincides with a reduction of interest and investment in traditional power generation, such as coal-powered stations. There is, however, investment in technology to make these old power stations more carbon efficient where possible.
- The Middle East continues to be a key area for investment. Other emerging markets that are rich in natural resources are also experiencing strong investment eg Africa.

Read our True Pictures on...

Addleshaw Goddard	Kennedys
Allen & Overy	Lawrence Graham
Ashurst	Lester Aldridge
Baker & McKenzie	Lewis Silkin
Barlow Lyde & Gilbert	Linklaters
Beachcroft	Macfarlanes
Berwin Leighton Paisner	Martineau
Bevan Brittan	Maxwell Winward
Bircham Dyson Bell	Mayer Brown
Bird & Bird	McGrigors
Bond Pearce	Michelmores
Brabners Chaffe Street	Mills & Reeve
Browne Jacobson	Muckle
Burges Salmon	Nabarro
Clarke Willmott	Norton Rose
Clifford Chance	Olswang
Clyde & Co	Osborne Clarke
CMS Cameron McKenna	Pannone
Cobbetts	Pinsent Masons
Cripps Harries Hall	Reed Smith
Dechert	Reynolds Porter Chamberlain
Dickinson Dees	Shoosmiths
DLA Piper UK	Simmons & Simmons
DMH Stallard	SJ Berwin
Dundas & Wilson	Slaughter and May
DWF	SNR Denton
Eversheds	Speechly Bircham
Field Fisher Waterhouse	Stephenson Harwood
Foot Anstey Solicitors	Stevens & Bolton
Freeth Cartwright	Taylor Wessing
Freshfields	TLT
Gordons	Travers Smith
Hammonds	Trowers & Hamlins
HBJ Gateley Wareing	Veale Wasbrough Vizards
Herbert Smith	Walker Morris
Hill Dickinson	Ward Hadaway
Hogan Lovells	Wedlake Bell
Jones Day	White & Case
K&L Gates	

Corporate law

In a nutshell

Corporate lawyers provide advice to companies on significant transactions affecting their activities, including internal operations, the buying and selling of businesses and business assets, and the arrangement of the finance to carry out these activities. Here are some of the terms you'll encounter.

Mergers and acquisitions (M&A): this is where one company acquires another by way of takeover (acquisition), or where two companies fuse to form a single larger entity (merger). The main reasons for a company to execute an M&A transaction are to grow its business (by acquiring or merging with a competitor) or add a new line of business to its existing activities. M&A can either be public (when it involves companies listed on a stock exchange) or private (when it concerns companies privately owned by individuals). **Equity capital markets:** where a private company raises capital by making its shares available to the public by listing itself on a stock exchange and executing an initial public offering (IPO), as a result of which it becomes a public company (or plc). The London Stock Exchange (LSE) and New York Stock Exchange (NYSE) are the most prestigious exchanges, but companies may list in many other exchanges worldwide. Once listed, the shares can be bought and sold by investors at a price determined by the market. **Private equity funds/houses:** manage multiple investment funds comprising investors who commit capital and mandate the private equity house to invest in numerous businesses on their behalf. **Private equity:** covers a range of transactions in which private equity funds are invested in or used to acquire privately held companies which have potential for growth. Private equity houses typically execute leveraged buyouts, using significant bank loans to complete the purchase of these businesses. A private equity fund's aim is to realise its investment by selling on portfolio companies at a profit or by way of an IPO of their shares on a stock exchange. **Venture capitalists:** groups of wealthy investors who provide capital to start-ups and small companies with perceived long-term growth potential. It typically entails high risk for investors but has the potential for above-average returns. **Corporate restructuring:** involves changes to the structure of a company and the disposal of certain assets, either because the company wants to concentrate on more profitable parts of its business, or because it is facing financial difficulties and needs to free up liquidity.

What lawyers do

- Negotiate and draft agreements – this will be done in conjunction with the client, the business that is being bought or sold, other advisers (eg accountants) and any financiers.
- Carry out due diligence – this is an investigation to verify the accuracy of information passed from the seller to the buyer, or from the company raising capital to the investor. It establishes the financial strength of the company, the outright ownership of all assets; whether there are outstanding debts or other claims against the company; any environmental or other liabilities that could reduce the value of the business in the future. If shares or bonds are being offered to the public, the report will take the form of a prospectus and must comply with statutory regulations.
- Arrange financing – this could come from banks or other types of investors; they will wish to have some kind of security for their investment, eg participation in the shareholding or a mortgage over property or other collateral.
- Gather all parties for the completion of the transaction, ensuring all assets have been properly covered by written documents that are properly signed and witnessed. Company law requires that decisions are made at properly convened board meetings and recorded in written resolutions.
- Finalise all post-completion registrations and procedures.

The realities of the job

- The type of clients your firm acts for will determine your experiences. Publicly listed companies, major private equity houses and the investment banks that underwrite deals can be extremely demanding and have a different attitude to risk than, say, rich entrepreneurs, owner-managed businesses (OMBs) and small to medium-sized enterprises (SMEs). To deal with such clients, a robust and confident manner is required and stamina is a must.
- Corporate transactions can be large and complicated, with many different aspects of the company affected in the process. Lawyers need to be conversant in a variety of legal disciplines and know when to refer matters to a specialist in, say, merger control (competition), employment, property or tax.
- Corporate deals involve mountains of paperwork, so you need to be well organised and have good drafting skills. Above all, corporate is a very practical area of

law, so commercial acumen and a good understanding of your clients' objectives is a must.

- Corporate work is cyclical and therefore the hours lawyers work can vary depending on the general state of the market and the particular needs of the clients, whose expectations have risen even further since the widespread use of instant modes of communication.
- The most junior member of a deal team normally gets stuck with the most boring or unrewarding tasks. The banes of the corporate trainee's life are data room management (putting together and caretaking all the factual information on which a deal relies) and bibling (the creation of files containing copies of all the agreed documents and deal information). More challenging tasks quickly become available to driven junior lawyers.
- You need to become absorbed in the corporate world. If you can't develop an interest in the business media then choose another area of practice pronto.

Read our True Pictures on...

Addleshaw Goddard	Jones Day
Allen & Overy	K&L Gates
Ashurst	Kirkland & Ellis
B P Collins	Latham & Watkins
Baker & McKenzie	Lawrence Graham
Barlow Lyde & Gilbert	Lewis Silkin
Bates Wells & Braithwaite	Linklaters
Beachcroft	Macfarlanes
Berwin Leighton Paisner	Manches
Bird & Bird	Martineau
Bond Pearce	Mayer Brown
Brabners Chaffe Street	Michelmores
Browne Jacobson	Mills & Reeve
Burges Salmon	Mishcon de Reya
Charles Russell	Muckle
Cleary Gottlieb	Nabarro
Clifford Chance	Norton Rose
Clyde & Co	Olswang
CMS Cameron McKenna	Orrick
Cobbetts	Osborne Clarke
Coffin Mew	Pannone
Covington & Burling	Paul, Hastings
Cripps Harries Hall	Penningtons Solicitors
Dechert	Pinsent Masons
Dewey & LeBoeuf	Reed Smith
Dickinson Dees	Reynolds Porter Chamberlain
DLA Piper UK	Shoosmiths
DMH Stallard	Sidley Austin
Dundas & Wilson	Simmons & Simmons
DWF	SJ Berwin
Eversheds	Skadden
Farrer & Co	Slaughter and May
Field Fisher Waterhouse	SNR Denton
Finers Stephens Innocent	Speechly Bircham
Foot Anstey Solicitors	Stephenson Harwood
Freeth Cartwright	Stevens & Bolton
Freshfields	Taylor Wessing
Gordons	TLT
Hammonds	Travers Smith
Harbottle & Lewis	Trethowans
HBJ Gateley Wareing	Trowers & Hamlins
Henmans	Veale Wasbrough Vizards
Herbert Smith	Walker Morris
Hill Dickinson	Ward Hadaway
Hogan Lovells	Weil, Gotshal & Manges
Howes Percival	
Irwin Mitchell	

Current issues

- Much of 2009 was marked by a dearth of M&A transactions, due to frozen credit markets. Distressed M&A deals, however, began to provide a stream of work as businesses facing financial difficulties sought alternative strategies to avoid insolvency. Such strategies include the disposal of non-core operations to free up cash or mergers with more financially stable entities.
- Companies have been finding it more difficult and expensive to borrow money from banks and, in such a volatile market, buyers and sellers have found it hard to reach agreement on the value of assets. The result has been a reduction in deal volume and value, with data providers pointing to a 30% decline in the overall M&A deal activity and a dramatic 95% drop in European IPO deals compared to the boom year of 2007.
- Leveraged buyouts, which are traditionally financed using a significant amount of borrowed money, have seen a particularly sharp decline in value and volume. Private equity players have focused on the restructuring of portfolio companies.
- Cash-rich investors have their pick of the best assets and often acquire businesses at a significant discount due to lower company valuations. There has been growing interest from emerging markets investors and sovereign wealth funds, particularly from the Middle East, in acquiring assets in the UK and elsewhere. Foreign bidders launched more than half the takeovers of UK-listed companies in the first quarter of 2010 – almost double the amount for the same period in 2008. Although the US is still the largest overseas bidder for UK companies, China and India are catching up fast.
- Private equity buyouts are on the rise, with the overall value of all UK buyouts in the first half of 2010 exceeding all transactions for 2009 by nearly 50%. Private equity has become a leading source of finance for buyouts. The average size of private equity-backed buyouts in 2010 is more than double what it was in 2009.
- Some UK regions did better than others in 2009/10. M&A activity in the North West of England held up

better than most regions, and companies there were the second biggest acquirers after London.

- Prior to the general election in 2010, investors were hesitant. After the announcement of the Emergency Budget in June 2010, they began to wonder about the ramifications of any increase in Capital Gains Tax (CGT). Some commentators felt that raising CGT could drive investment overseas and discourage international investors from placing equity investments in the UK.
- Big-ticket energy work – in both oil and gas and renewables – is on the up and up. Joint ventures between companies are increasingly popular on large projects, and government support for investments ensures greater regulatory stability.
- A sound grounding in corporate finance makes an excellent springboard for working in-house in major companies. Some lawyers move to banks to work as corporate finance execs or analysts. Company secretarial positions suit lawyers with a taste for internal management and compliance issues.

• **Be the best:** Excellent grades have never been more important. Do yourself a massive favour and resist the temptation to slack off. Recruiters tell us that a suprisingly high numbers of applicants cite mitigating circumstances for a poor degree grade. It doesn't wash. Critical illness; horrific accident; death of a parent = worth mentioning. Nasty cough; chipped nail = lame excuse.

top tip no. 9

Crime

In a nutshell

Criminal solicitors represent defendants in cases brought before the UK's criminal courts. Lesser offences are commonly dealt with exclusively by solicitors in the magistrates' courts; more serious charges go to the Crown Courts, which are essentially still the domain of barristers, not least because most defendants still prefer this. Everyday crime is the staple for most solicitors – theft, assault, drugs and driving offences. Fraud is the preserve of a more limited number of firms, and the cases require a different approach from, say, crimes of violence. Criminal practice is busy, often frantic, with a hectic schedule of visits to police stations, prisons and magistrates' courts meaning plenty of face-to-face client contact and advocacy.

What lawyers do

- Attend police stations to interview and advise people in police custody.
- Visit prisons to see clients on remand.
- Prepare the client's defence using medical and social workers' reports, liaising with witnesses, probation officers, the CPS and others.
- Attend conferences with counsel (ie barristers).
- Represent defendants at trial or brief barristers to do so.
- Represent clients at sentencing hearings, explaining any mitigating facts.
- Fraud solicitors need a head for business as they deal with a considerable volume of paperwork and financial analysis.

The realities of the job

- Hours are long and can disrupt your personal life. Lawyers who are accredited to work as Duty Solicitors will be on a rota and can be called to a police station at any time of the day or night.
- Confidence is essential. Without it you're doomed.
- In general crime you'll have a large caseload with a fast turnaround, meaning plenty of advocacy.
- The work is driven by the procedural rules and timetable of the court. Even so, recent figures show that almost a quarter of trials do not proceed on the appointed day.
- Your efforts can mean the difference between a person's liberty or incarceration. You have to be detail-conscious and constantly vigilant.
- You'll encounter horrible situations and difficult or distressed people. Murderers, rapists, drug dealers, conmen, paedophiles – if you have the ability to look beyond the labels and see these people as clients deserving of your best efforts then you've picked the right job.
- It can be disheartening to see clients repeat the same poor choices, returning to court again and again.
- Public funding of criminal defence means there's a good helping of bureaucracy. It also means you'll never be a millionaire.
- Trainees in fraud find the early years provide minimal advocacy and masses of trawling through warehouses full of documents. Caseloads are smaller but cases can run for years.

Current issues

- Huge changes in Legal Aid funding are ongoing and many firms that have previously excelled in crime are moving out of the area entirely or no longer accept publicly funded clients. Firms affected by the cuts (or those looking to pre-empt financial difficulties) are either abandoning Legal Aid altogether, merging, or shifting their focus from the more high street criminal cases to fraud and the more serious financial crimes.
- After failed attempts by Labour to rein in a ballooning Legal Aid budget, early-stage coalition government cuts will remove £325m from Legal Aid's £2.2bn budget. Currently, half of all criminal Legal Aid spending is spent on about 1% of cases and the UK has one of the most expensive Legal Aid schemes in the world. Read more about Legal Aid on our website.
- Past Ministry of Justice reforms aimed to address Legal Aid budgeting have been met with disapproval and led to extraordinary consequences. Recently, a defendant escaped confiscation proceedings because she was unable to find an advocate willing to accept the Legal Aid rates available for her representation.
- There has been talk of the government reducing the number of firms allowed to do criminal Legal Aid work, from around 400 firms nationally to around 40.
- A change in police station procedures means the police are cautioning more and charging less in an effort to meet government targets. This obviously has a knock-on effect on the number of available cases. The number of police officers will drop due to budgetary pressures.
- The nationwide rollout of the Legal Services Commission's Criminal Defence Service Direct is affecting the amount of work available for solicitors. The CDS now provides telephone advice to those detained at police stations for less serious matters – eg

drink driving, non-imprisonable offences, breach of bail and warrants.

- More fraud cases are popping up, and with authorities pushing for criminal charges for competition regulation violations, corporations are facing greater criminal liability. This kind of work tends to go to the firms that have traditionally handled white-collar crime. The Bribery Act 2010 aims to reform the criminal law to provide a comprehensive scheme of bribery offences in the UK or overseas. Companies will be held liable for corruption among staff and – for the first time – associated third parties. The Act comes into force in April 2011, but employers need to be in compliance with the new law well before then. White-collar crime lawyers will be busy advising companies on what the right anti-corruption policies and procedures are.
- Check out www.clsa.co.uk for other news and discussion on major developments in criminal practice.

Read our True Pictures on...

DLA Piper UK	Herbert Smith
Eversheds	Higgs & Sons
Finers Stephens Innocent	Hill Dickinson
Fisher Meredith	Irwin Mitchell
Foot Anstey Solicitors	Kingsley Napley
Forbes	Pannone

The criminal courts of England and Wales

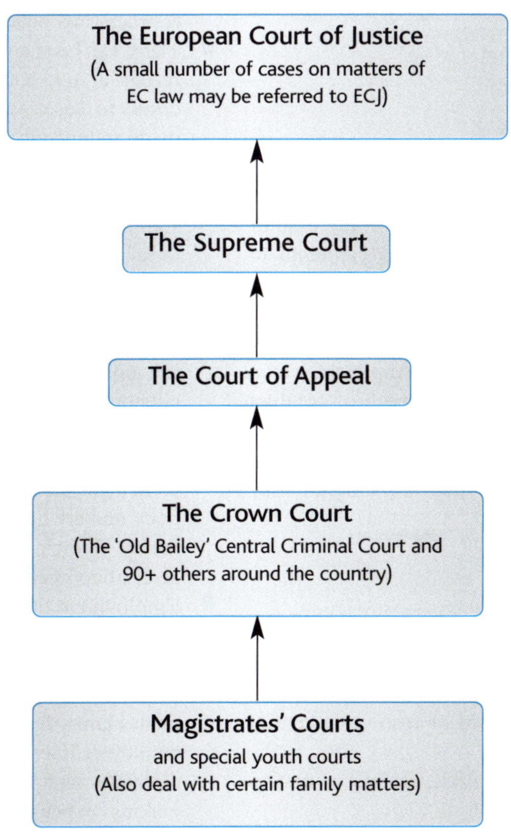

Employment

In a nutshell

Employment lawyers guide their clients through the ever-growing area of workplace-related legislation and are intimately involved in the relationship between employers and employees. The divide between employers' and employees' lawyers is often clear-cut, so bear this in mind when you pick your firm. Most will work either largely for employers or largely for employees; a few will straddle both sides of the fence. Usually the job includes both advisory work and litigation.

Disputes are almost always resolved at an Employment Tribunal, or before reaching one, and appeals are heard at the Employment Appeal Tribunal (EAT). The grievances leading to litigation fall into the following broad categories: redundancy; unlawful dismissal; breach of contract; harassment and discrimination. This last type of claim can be brought on the grounds of race, religious or philosophical belief, gender, sexual orientation, disability and age.

What lawyers do

Employees' solicitors

- Advise clients on whether they have suffered unlawful or unfair treatment and establish the amount to be claimed. This will either be capped or, in the case of discrimination, can include additional elements to cover loss of earnings, injury to feelings and aggravated damages.
- Gather evidence and witnesses to support the claim.
- Try to negotiate a payment from the employer or take the matter to tribunal. If there is a breach-of-contract element to the claim, it might be heard in a court rather than a tribunal.
- If the matter does reach tribunal, the solicitor may conduct the advocacy.

Employers' solicitors

- Defend or settle the sorts of claims described above.
- Negotiate employment contracts or exit packages for senior staff.
- Negotiate with unions to avoid or resolve industrial disputes.
- Formulate HR policies and provide training on how to avoid workplace problems.

Realities of the job

- You quickly develop an understanding of human foibles. By their very nature employment cases are filled with drama.
- Clients may assume your role is to provide emotional support as well as legal advice, so you need to take care to define your role appropriately.
- Solicitors who want to do their own advocacy thrive here, although barristers are commonly used for high-stakes or complicated hearings and trials.
- The work is driven by the procedural rules and timetable of the tribunals and courts.
- The law is extensive and changes frequently. You'll read more than your fair share of EU directives.

Current issues

- The appetite for redundancy exercises has not tailed off completely, and although not as strong as it was in 2008, many clients are still looking to make cost savings by restructuring, outsourcing or simply shedding staff.
- There has been a rise in TUPE work as staff are transferred or outsourced by companies looking to cut costs. In cases where staff have been dismissed or made redundant, or have had changes made to their contracts, there has been more scope for proceedings.
- Employers are more concerned than ever about their staff leaving to set up a competing business, leading to a rise in attempted enforcement of restrictive covenants and confidentiality agreements.
- Some law firms have retained the services of a team of HR specialists or a dedicated hotline to deal with low-cost, day-to-day employment queries. Many clients that have been looking to reduce their HR spend have noted the strong attraction of this service.
- Many organisations have consolidated their employment legal spend by putting out to tender just one contract, and are now looking for a sole legal provider to handle all their needs. This has naturally increased the level of competition between employment practices.
- Employment litigation has risen sharply as a result of a rise in redundancies. Workers have been much more willing to bring whistleblowing and discrimination claims to tribunal proceedings in a bid to force settlement claims from their former employers. Similarly, employers have been more likely to make use of disciplinary and breach of contract charges to avoid making expensive redundancy payoffs. Because of the depressed labour market, many employees have been reluctant to settle at an early stage and made

bolder gambles about extracting higher concessions from their previous employer.

- Those law firms with a successful track record in reducing costs, deterring claims against employers or winning at tribunals – and especially those that are willing to give an objective opinion on bringing or defeating a claim – are obviously the most sought after.
- The high average earnings and extravagant bonus schemes of many workers in the financial services sector has led to a spike in employment disputes as the recession bites. The Walker report on corporate governance in the banking industry and changes to the FSA code on remuneration have led to increased scrutiny of executive bonuses and incentive arrangements.
- Many companies are still leveraging the effects of the recession to make changes at board and senior management level. This has led to an increase in demand for advice on high-value contract termination work from both employees and respondents.
- Businesses are still failing and this has reaped benefits for law firms with a strong insolvency/administration specialism.

Read our True Pictures on...

Addleshaw Goddard
Allen & Overy
Ashurst
B P Collins
Baker & McKenzie
Barlow Lyde & Gilbert
Bates Wells & Braithwaite
Beachcroft
Berwin Leighton Paisner
Bevan Brittan
Bircham Dyson Bell
Bird & Bird
Bond Pearce
Brabners Chaffe Street
Browne Jacobson
Burges Salmon
Capsticks Solicitors
Charles Russell
Clarke Willmott
Clifford Chance
Clyde & Co
CMS Cameron McKenna
Cobbetts
Coffin Mew
Cripps Harries Hall
Dechert
Denton Wilde Sapte
Dickinson Dees
DLA Piper UK
DMH Stallard
Dundas & Wilson
DWF
Eversheds
Farrer & Co
Field Fisher Waterhouse
Finers Stephens Innocent
Foot Anstey Solicitors
Ford & Warren
Freeth Cartwright
Freshfields
Gordons
Hammonds
Harbottle & Lewis
HBJ Gateley Wareing
Henmans
Herbert Smith
Higgs & Sons
Hill Dickinson
Hogan Lovells
Howes Percival
Irwin Mitchell
Jones Day
Kennedys
Kingsley Napley
Latham & Watkins
Lawrence Graham
Lester Aldridge
Lewis Silkin
Linklaters
Macfarlanes
Manches
Martineau
Mayer Brown
McDermott Will & Emery UK
McGrigors
Michelmores
Mills & Reeve
Mishcon de Reya
Muckle
Nabarro
Norton Rose
Olswang
Osborne Clarke
Pannone
Penningtons Solicitors
Pinsent Masons
Reed Smith
Reynolds Porter Chamberlain
Shoosmiths
Simmons & Simmons
SJ Berwin
Slaughter and May
Speechly Bircham
Stephenson Harwood
Stevens & Bolton
Taylor Wessing
TLT
Travers Smith
Trethowans
Trowers & Hamlins
Veale Wasbrough Vizards
Walker Morris
Ward Hadaway
Watson, Farley & Williams
Wedlake Bell
White & Case
Withers

Environment

In a nutshell

Environment lawyers advise corporate clients on damage limitation and pre-emptive measures, and they defend them from prosecution. In other words, the majority of private practitioners work for, rather than stick it to, big business. Opportunities do exist at organisations like Greenpeace and Friends of the Earth, but these jobs are highly sought after. Another non-commercial option is to work for a local authority, a government department such as the Department for Environment, Food and Rural Affairs (Defra) or a regulatory body like the Environment Agency.

Environment law overlaps with other disciplines such as property, criminal law, corporate or EU law. Environmental issues can be deal breakers, especially in the modern era of corporate social responsibility. However, the small size of most law firms' environment teams means there are relatively few pure environmental specialists around.

What lawyers do

Lawyers in private practice

- Advise on the potential environmental consequences of corporate, property and projects transactions.
- Advise on compliance and regulatory issues to help clients operate within regulatory boundaries and avoid investigation or prosecution.
- Defend clients when they get into trouble over water or air pollution, waste disposal, emission levels or health and safety. Such cases can involve criminal or civil actions, judicial reviews and even statutory appeals. They may also be subject to damaging media coverage.

Lawyers with local authorities

- Handle a massive variety of work covering regulatory and planning issues plus waste management and air pollution prosecutions.
- Advise the authority on its own potential liability.

Lawyers working for Defra

- Are responsible for litigation, drafting of subordinate legislation, advisory work and contract drafting on any of Defra's varied mandates.
- Work in a team of over 80 lawyers, including trainees, on GLS-funded schemes. Defra aims to promote sustainable development without compromising the quality of life of future generations.

Lawyers working for the Environment Agency

- Prosecute environmental crimes – this involves gathering evidence, preparing cases and briefing barristers.
- Co-operate with government lawyers on the drafting and implementation of legislation.
- Work in Bristol and eight regional bases and are responsible for protecting and enhancing the environment. They also regulate corporate activities that have the capacity to pollute.

The realities of the job

- In this competitive and demanding field, all-round skills are best complemented by a genuine interest in a specific area. The way in which environmental law spans disciplines requires commercial nous and a good understanding of corporate structures.
- Excellent academics are essential to help wade through, extrapolate from and present research and complex legislation; so too are sound judgement, pragmatism and the ability to come up with inventive solutions.
- A basic grasp of science helps.
- If you want to change environmental laws or crusade for a better planet, then stick to the public or not for profit sectors. The sometimes uncomfortable realities of private practice won't be for you.
- Client contact is key and relationships can endure over many years. Environmental risks are difficult to quantify and clients will rely on your gut instincts and powers of lateral thinking.
- With visits to waste dumps or drying reservoirs, and a workload that can span health and safety matters, corporate transactions and regulatory advice all in one day, this is neither a desk-bound nor a quiet discipline.
- Research constantly advances and legislation is always changing in this field, so you'll spend a lot of time keeping up to date.
- A taste for European law is essential as more and more EU directives prescribe the boundaries of environmental law in the UK.

Current issues

- The biggest issue of 2010 has been the introduction of the Carbon Reduction Commitment Energy Efficiency Scheme (CRC), brought in to put a cap on the amount of carbon produced by organisations. There is a wave of other climate change-related legislation coming through, too, but CRC has been the most significant recently. This has resulted in an immense amount of regulatory compliance work, with many firms expecting an influx of litigation as enforcements come in to play later in the year.
- The Environmental Liability Directive was updated about a year ago, resulting in more companies taking up environmental insurance. Consequently, firms with an insurance focus have seen an increase in work on this front.
- The Environment Agency has been taking a more stringent approach to clamping down on regulatory offences. Where businesses might previously have dealt with them in-house, lawyers are now being instructed to negotiate with the EA. The costs involved can run into the millions.
- An increasingly well-informed public also means an increasingly litigious public. A surge in class actions, usually involving pollution, odour or other forms of nuisance, is being witnessed across the board. Some lawyers have speculated that the Environment Agency is slightly more 'trigger happy'.
- The increased focus on renewable energy in the UK has resulted in more work involving alternative forms of power, such as biomass, wind farm, nuclear and energy-from-waste projects. The energy-from-waste projects are especially topical as they have brought up issues regarding whether waste should be labelled as waste or a fuel.
- Climate change isn't just for academics any more. It's a whole legal area in itself. Top-flight international firms are encountering this type of work more often, and international issues are coming to the fore. Initiatives like the Equator Principles and Corporate Social Responsibility are now prominent.
- The carbon trading sector, at least in the UK, seems to be near dead in the water thanks to the recession. Manufacturers have been producing less, which has consequently meant they have needed to buy fewer carbon credits. This is an endemic problem at the moment, and carbon trading specialists are witnessing an all-time low in the volume of this type of work. This also means that no new blood/new lawyers have been entering the market, which could result in a dearth of specialists in the future. The failure of the Copenhagen Convention also added to the climate change sector's woes in that no real new, substantive legislation or changes were brought in to revitalise or rework the sector and its focus. Speak to a climate change lawyer and they're often quite despondent about the future.
- Keep on top of changes in environmental law courtesy of websites like www.endsreport.com. You should enhance your CV and prime yourself by joining organisations such as the Environmental Law Foundation (ELF) and the UK Environmental Law Association (www.ukela.org). Most environmental lawyers are members of UKELA and students are welcome to attend events across the country. The charity ELF (www.elflaw.org) provides a referral service for members of the public, organises lectures in London and produces regular newsletters for members.

Read our True Pictures on...

Addleshaw Goddard	Hogan Lovells
Allen & Overy	Irwin Mitchell
Ashurst	Jones Day
B P Collins	K&L Gates
Baker & McKenzie	Lawrence Graham
Barlow Lyde & Gilbert	Linklaters
Beachcroft	Macfarlanes
Berwin Leighton Paisner	Manches
Bircham Dyson Bell	Mayer Brown
Bond Pearce	Mills & Reeve
Browne Jacobson	Nabarro
Burges Salmon	Norton Rose
Clarke Willmott	Osborne Clarke
Clifford Chance	Pannone
CMS Cameron McKenna	Pinsent Masons
Dewey & LeBoeuf	Simmons & Simmons
Dickinson Dees	SJ Berwin
DLA Piper UK	Slaughter and May
DMH Stallard	SNR Denton
Dundas & Wilson	Stephenson Harwood
Eversheds	Stevens & Bolton
Freshfields	TLT
Hammonds	Travers Smith
Herbert Smith	

Family

In a nutshell

Lawyers are involved with almost every aspect of family life, from the legal mechanics and complications of marriage and civil partnerships to divorce, disputes between cohabitants, inheritance disputes between family members, prenuptial and cohabitation agreements and all matters relating to children. Whether working in a general high street practice with a large caseload of legally aided work, or for a specialist practice dealing with big-money divorces and complex child or international matters, family solicitors are in court a good deal and fully occupied back in the office.

There is effectively a division between child law and matrimonial law, with many practitioners devoting themselves exclusively to one or the other. Some plant a foot in each.

What lawyers do

Matrimonial lawyers

- Interview and advise clients on prenuptial agreements, cohabitation arrangements, divorce and the financial implications of divorce. This can involve issues like inheritance and wills, conveyancing, welfare benefits, company law, tax and trusts, pensions and even judicial review.
- Prepare the client's case for divorce and settlement hearings, including organising witnesses and providing summaries of assets/finances, which will require dealing with accountants, financial and pensions advisers.
- Attend conferences with barristers.
- Represent clients in hearings or brief barristers to do so.
- Negotiate settlements and associated financial terms.

Child law lawyers

- In private cases – interview and advise clients on the implications of divorce with regard to child contact and residence. In some instances this will result in court action. Deal with disputes between parents or other family members over the residence of, and contact with, children.
- In public cases – represent local authorities, parents, children's guardians or children themselves on matters such as children's care proceedings or abuse in care claims. Social workers, probation officers, psychologists and medical professionals will also be involved in cases.

The realities of the job

- When it comes to relationships and families, no two sets of circumstances will ever be the same. Advocacy is plentiful.
- You will encounter a real mix of clients, some at a joyful moment in their lives, others facing deeply traumatic times. A good family law practitioner combines the empathetic, sensitive qualities of a counsellor with the clarity of thought, and commercial acumen of a lawyer. You need to retain detachment to achieve the result your clients need.
- Tough negotiating skills and a strong nerve are vital as your work has immediate and practical consequences. The prospect of telling a client that they've lost a custody battle does much to sharpen the mind.
- A pragmatic and real-world outlook is useful, but you'll also need to spend time keeping abreast of legal developments.
- On publicly funded matters you'll face your share of bureaucracy and it certainly won't make you rich.

Current issues

- Pre-nuptial agreements were big in 2010 due to *Radmacher v Granatino*. Pre-nups are not automatically recognised by the English Courts, but in 2009 the Court of Appeal ruled that they should be taken into account in this case, which then went to the Supreme Court. That judgment is expected to clarify the status of pre-nups and whether or not they are enforceable under English law. Whatever the judgment, pre-nups have certainly gained credibility with the court and are likely to become more popular.
- London is arguably the divorce capital of Europe, and the most generous jurisdiction in the world for (usually) women in a divorce situation. International instructions regarding divorce are on the rise, as clients with a foot in two or more jurisdictions, not to mention a bundle of cash, seek to get the best outcome.
- The economic downturn has led to increased demand for advice on wealth protection and some family lawyers report an 'explosion' in the number of cohabiting couples seeking advice on relationship breakdown.
- Taxation is a major theme as, more than ever, clients seek to reach settlements that are structured to mitigate unnecessary tax or other liabilities. As in many other practice areas, it's worth getting close to a tax specialist.
- These are challenging times for the publicly funded lawyer. Many firms are feeling the squeeze and some

are choosing to limit, or even cease, legally aided work. This is the case with both matrimonial finance cases and childcare proceedings, although some firms have stuck with the latter on idealistic grounds.

- The Baby P case had a profound effect on public child law, and in 2008 the government's implementation of Care Proceedings Reforms (designed to speed up the resolution of cases involving children and avoid court) caused further consternation. For details see www.justice.gov.uk/guidance/careproceedings.htm.
- Social workers are under increased scrutiny and the family courts have been opened up to the press. Many lawyers say that this has made it much harder to do their jobs and has more to do with justice being seen to be done than anything else. The family courts have lately been heavily criticised for the length of time it takes to reach decisions in child law cases.

Read our True Pictures on...

B P Collins	Higgs & Sons
Bircham Dyson Bell	Hill Dickinson
Boodle Hatfield	Irwin Mitchell
Brabners Chaffe Street	Kingsley Napley
Burges Salmon	Lester Aldridge
Charles Russell	Manches
Clarke Willmott	Martineau
Coffin Mew	Michelmores
Cripps Harries Hall	Mills & Reeve
Dawsons	Mishcon de Reya
Dickinson Dees	Pannone
DWF	Speechly Bircham
Farrer & Co	TLT
Fisher Meredith	Trethowans
Foot Anstey Solicitors	Ward Hadaway
Harbottle & Lewis	Withers
Henmans	

Intellectual property

In a nutshell

Lawyers, patent attorneys and trade mark attorneys work to protect their clients' intellectual property assets. Technical solutions to technical problems are deemed to be inventions, usually protectable via **patents** that provide their proprietor with the exclusive right to stop others working in the claimed area for a period of usually up to 20 years. Preparing a patent specification is a highly specialised task requiring particular scientific/technical expertise and knowledge, combined with experience and knowledge of complex application procedures.

Trade marks used to sell goods or services are protectable by way of a registration procedure and provide a potentially perpetual monopoly right. The aesthetic shape and way a product is designed is also protectable via **registered design** protection for a limited period of time. **Unregistered rights** also exist for a time for various designs of products. Then there is **copyright**, which lasts during the lifetime of the creator and for a period after their death, and which arises automatically on the creation of music, artwork, works of literature or reference, databases and web pages, for example.

A single product such as a mobile phone will be protected by several different forms of IP in countries all around the world. For would-be competitors wanting to make or sell something similar, a first costly hurdle is simply finding out what these rights are and who owns them. Worst-case scenario, getting it wrong or overlooking an IP right might result in being on the wrong end of a court injunction or costly damages (fearsomely so in the USA) and innocence is no defence! The work of an IP lawyer is not only specialist in itself, but increasingly it requires close collaboration with other specialists in areas such as IT, media, competition, telecommunications, life sciences and employment.

What lawyers do

- Search domestic, European and international registers of patents, trade marks and registered designs to establish ownership of existing rights or the potential to register new rights.
- Take all steps to protect clients' interests by securing patents, trade marks and registered designs; appeal unfavourable decisions; attack decisions that benefit others but harm the lawyer's own client.
- Write letters to require that third parties desist from carrying out infringing activities or risk litigation for damages and an injunction.
- Issue court proceedings and prepare cases for trial, including taking witness statements, examining scientific or technical reports and commissioning experiments and tests. Junior lawyers may find themselves conducting consumer surveys and going on covert shopping expeditions.
- Instruct and consult with barristers. Solicitor-advocates can appear in the Patents County Court; the advantages of having a specialist IP barrister for higher court hearings are obvious.
- Draft commercial agreements between owners of IP rights and those who want to use the protected invention, design or artistic work. The most common documents will either transfer ownership or grant a licence for use.
- Work as part of a multidisciplinary team on corporate transactions, verifying ownership of IP rights and drafting documents enabling their transfer.

The realities of the job

- Lawyers must be able to handle everyone from company directors to mad inventors. Clients come from manufacturing, the hi-tech sector, engineering, pharmaceuticals, agrochemicals, universities and scientific institutions, media organisations and the arts.
- A degree in a relevant subject is common among patent lawyers. Brand and trade mark lawyers need a curiosity for all things creative and must keep up with consumer trends. Both need a good sense for commercial strategy.
- Attention to detail, precision and accuracy: you must be meticulous, particularly when drafting, as correct wording is imperative.
- In trade mark and design filings and prosecution, everything has a time limit. You will live by deadlines.
- In patent filing, procurement and strategy, you'll need to work seamlessly with a patent attorney. There are hardly any solicitors who are also patent attorneys (and vice versa).
- The volume of information and paperwork involved can be huge on patent matters, though on the plus side you could get the opportunity to visit research labs or factories to learn about production processes, etc.
- The stakes can be big. Commercial research and development in the pharmaceutical sector is motivated by profit not philanthropy. The investment involved will have been colossal, and even a day's loss of sales can be eye watering. Success or failure in litigation can dramatically affect a company's share price.

- Manufacturing, pharmaceutical and research companies usually employ patent specialists and there tend to be in-house legal teams at all the larger companies. In the media, major publishers and television companies employ in-house IP lawyers.

Current issues

- The liquidity crisis led to a growing awareness of intellectual property as a valuable asset. Businesses have become more aggressive in protecting their rights and litigation is on the rise. The English Courts' reputation for being patent-unfriendly has been challenged by recent judgments.
- International efforts are being made to harmonise aspects of patent procurement. The European, US and Japanese Patent Offices are testing out patent prosecution 'superhighways' to try and streamline the detailed processes of searching and examining patent applications. The European, US, Japanese, Korean and Chinese patent offices are looking at work sharing.
- The EU continues to move closer to getting a pan-European patent set up and there are raised hopes again, but politics over language has proved a monumental brake on progress for many years.
- Patent litigation costs continue to be a big issue (as highlighted by a £5.2m bill handed to BlackBerry by Allen & Overy in 2008 following a five-day trial) and the judges are most unhappy about it. Kitchin J gave assembled ranks of City solicitors a hard time in a seminar but the big litigators seem unrepentant, claiming that their clients have deep pockets and are entitled to spend vast amounts of money on having lawyers go through every document in fine detail and analysing them to death, if they so choose.
- In the trade mark arena many clients are seeking strategic advice on how to tackle the growing problem of counterfeit goods. L'Oréal's case concerning eBay's liability in relation to counterfeit goods sold on its auction site was referred to the ECJ by the French Courts. Its decision was heralded as a triumph for luxury brand owners utilising selective distribution channels. The trend for digitalisation is bringing online IP issues to prominence, and another eagerly awaited ECJ referral is that of *Interflora v Marks & Spencer*, in which the latter bought sponsored links from Google for the words Interflora, Inter-Flora and Intraflora. The law in the UK appears unclear on whether buying a keyword that matches another firm's trade mark is lawful. User-generated content is also an issue.
- Convergence between different forms of media and technology is giving rise to sensitive issues of data protection.
- European patent attorneys and trade mark attorneys now more than ever work as separate professions, but mostly still stick together in private practice partnerships. Some are LLPs and a very few are incorporated.
- Whilst historically some law firms have employed patent attorneys and/or trade mark attorneys, this model has not taken hold widely. Over in the patent attorney profession there are examples of a more joined-up approach to offering IP legal advice and litigation. Two good examples are HGF and Marks & Clerk. Both have patent and trade mark attorneys now working alongside solicitors' practices. If the new regime of Alternative Business Structures is a hit then the IP advice sector could see some interesting developments.

Read our True Pictures on...

Addleshaw Goddard	Hill Dickinson
Allen & Overy	Hogan Lovells
Arnold & Porter (UK)	Howes Percival
Ashurst	Jones Day
Baker & McKenzie	K&L Gates
Berwin Leighton Paisner	Latham & Watkins
Bird & Bird	Lewis Silkin
Bond Pearce	Linklaters
Brabners Chaffe Street	Macfarlanes
Bristows	Manches
Browne Jacobson	Martineau
Burges Salmon	Mayer Brown
Charles Russell	McDermott Will & Emery
Clarke Willmott	Mills & Reeve
Clifford Chance	Mishcon de Reya
CMS Cameron McKenna	Muckle
Cobbetts	Nabarro
Coffin Mew	Olswang
Cripps Harries Hall	Osborne Clarke
Dechert	Pannone
Dickinson Dees	Pinsent Masons
DLA Piper UK	Reed Smith
DMH Stallard	Reynolds Porter Chamberlain
DWF	Shoosmiths
Edwards Angell	Simmons & Simmons
Eversheds	SJ Berwin
Farrer & Co	Slaughter and May
Field Fisher Waterhouse	SNR Denton
Finers Stephens Innocent	Speechly Bircham
Foot Anstey Solicitors	Stephenson Harwood
Freshfields	Stevens & Bolton
Gordons	Taylor Wessing
Hammonds	TLT
Harbottle & Lewis	Walker Morris
HBJ Gateley Wareing	Ward Hadaway
Henmans	Wedlake Bell
Herbert Smith	Wiggin

- **Prestige' means nothing:** Don't apply to a firm just because some random survey says it's the 'best'. It may not be the best place for you. Choose a firm for the work, for the people, for the international opportunities or even just for the money. Don't choose it for the 'prestige' because when you're sitting in a room at four in the morning, knee deep in documents, surrounded by people you have nothing in common with, prestige means sod all.

top tip no. 10

Litigation/dispute resolution

In a nutshell

Litigation solicitors assist clients in resolving civil disputes. Disputes can concern anything from unpaid bills or unfulfilled contract terms to problems between landlords and tenants, infringement of IP rights, construction-related claims, the liabilities of insurers, shipping cases, defective products, media and entertainment industry wrangles… the list is endless. And that's just in the commercial sphere. The most common types of litigation involving private individuals are discussed at length in our personal injury overview.

If disputes are not settled by negotiation, they will be concluded by either court litigation or an alternative form of dispute resolution, hence the interchangeability of the terms 'litigation' and 'dispute resolution'. The most common of these other methods are arbitration and mediation; the former is often stipulated as the preferred method in commercial contracts, the latter is generally achieved through structured negotiations between the parties, overseen by an independent mediator. These methods can still be problematic: mediation is not necessarily adequate for complex matters and some argue that opponents can use it as a means of 'bleeding' money from each other or as covert interrogation.

Confusingly, there are two divisions of the High Court dealing with major cases – the Chancery Division and the Queen's Bench Division (QBD) – and each hears different types of case.

What litigators do

- Advise clients on whether they have a valid claim, or whether to settle or fight a claim made against them.
- Gather evidence and witnesses to support the client's position; develop case strategies.
- Issue court proceedings or embark on a process of alternative dispute resolution if correspondence with the defendant does not produce a satisfactory result.
- Represent clients at pre-trial hearings and case management conferences.
- Attend conferences with counsel (ie barristers) and brief them to conduct advocacy in hearings, trials and arbitrations.
- Attend trials, arbitrations and mediations with clients; provide assistance to barristers.

The realities of the job

- Work is driven by procedural rules and the timetable of the courts. Good litigators understand how best to manoeuvre within the system, while also developing winning case strategies.
- The phenomenal amount of paperwork generated means that young litigators spend much of their time sifting through documents, scheduling and copying them in order to provide the court and all other parties with an agreed bundle of evidence.
- Litigators need to express themselves succinctly and precisely.
- Unless the claim value is small, the solicitor's job is more about case preparation than court performance. Solicitor-advocates are gaining ground, and once properly qualified they can appear in the higher courts. Nonetheless, barristers still dominate court advocacy and recently the performance of some solicitor-advocates was criticised by the judiciary.
- Trainee workloads largely depend on the type of firm and the type of clients represented. Big City firms won't give trainees free rein on huge international banking disputes – they might not even go to court during their training contract – but they will be able to offer a small contribution to headline-making cases. Firms handling much smaller claims will often expect trainees to deal with all aspects of a case, from drafting correspondence and interim court applications to meetings with clients and settlement negotiations.
- There are a number of litigation-led law firms that handle cases of all sizes and these present the best opportunities for a litigation-heavy training contract.
- The Solicitors Regulation Authority (SRA) requires all trainee solicitors to gain some contentious experience. People tend to learn early on whether they are suited to this kind of work. Increasingly in big City firms, SRA requirements can be fulfilled by a litigation crash course.
- The competition for litigation jobs at NQ level is fierce. Concentrate on litigation-led firms if you are certain of your leanings.
- Despite a few firms like Herbert Smith and Hammonds starting up in-house advocacy units, the courts remain dominated by barristers, who are felt to have the edge when it comes to the skills and expertise needed to advocate. If you are determined to become both a solicitor and an advocate, certain areas of practice have more scope for advocacy – eg family, crime, employment and lower-value civil litigation.

Current issues

- Historically, London has been a popular forum for international litigation and arbitration. Some suggest this could be affected by an ECJ ruling that arbitration anti-suit injunctions are inconsistent with the Brussels regulation, but the sheer volume of cases (and from places as disparate as Russia and South America) does not appear to be slowing.
- Lord Falconer QC predicted a "*tsunami of* [post-credit crunch] *litigation,*" but the common consensus is that it either hasn't materialised or is taking longer to filter through. Since 2010, though, work has begun to pick up and litigators are generally pretty busy, with the expectation they will become even more so. Insurance litigation in particular has received a boost as more claims are filed and subsequently challenged.
- Several major cases concern Russian oligarchs and matters from the former CIS, as well as finance-related disputes in the BVI. The bank charges litigation was the biggest dispute to hit the English courts in recent years, with more or less everyone who's anyone involved.
- The Jackson Report has reviewed litigation funding; however, the common view is that it won't have a major impact for some time yet, if at all, not least because Parliament has more pressing concerns than this.
- Third-party litigation funding is emerging. Essentially an organisation that is not involved in a case, say a bank or private equity company, can choose to bank roll the cost of litigation for a share of the winnings.
- The challenges London now faces as an arbitration venue relate to costs and the increasing popularity of other locations, particularly Singapore. Some people worry that emerging economies such as China and India will look east for their preferred venue. Even if Singapore does become more popular, English law will still play a part, meaning UK arbitration lawyers would be likely to spend more time in Singapore.
- Bigger UK firms and US firms in London are handling more arbitration advocacy in-house and not instructing the Bar. There is debate as to how successful and effective this is, but it's certainly something these firms are pushing, especially for more run-of-the-mill cases.

Read our True Pictures on...

Addleshaw Goddard
Allen & Overy
Ashurst
B P Collins
Baker & McKenzie
Barlow Lyde & Gilbert
Bates Wells & Braithwaite
Beachcroft
Berwin Leighton Paisner
Bevan Brittan
Bingham McCutchen
Bird & Bird
Bond Pearce
Boodle Hatfield
Brabners Chaffe Street
Bristows
Browne Jacobson
Burges Salmon
Charles Russell
Clarke Willmott
Clifford Chance
Clyde & Co
CMS Cameron McKenna
Cobbetts
Coffin Mew
Covington & Burling
Cripps Harries Hall
Dawsons
Dechert
Dewey & LeBoeuf
Dickinson Dees
DLA Piper UK
DMH Stallard
DWF
Edwards Angell
Eversheds
Field Fisher Waterhouse
Finers Stephens Innocent
Foot Anstey Solicitors
Forbes
Ford & Warren
Freeth Cartwright
Freshfields
Gordons
Hammonds
HBJ Gateley Wareing
Henmans
Herbert Smith
Hill Dickinson
Hogan Lovells
Holman Fenwick Willan
Howes Percival
Ince & Co
Irwin Mitchell
Jones Day
K&L Gates
Kennedys
Kirkland & Ellis
Latham & Watkins
Lawrence Graham
Lester Aldridge
Lewis Silkin
Linklaters
Macfarlanes
Manches
Martineau
Mayer Brown
McGrigors
Michelmores
Mills & Reeve
Mishcon de Reya
Muckle
Nabarro
Norton Rose
Olswang
Osborne Clarke
Pannone
Penningtons Solicitors
Pinsent Masons
Reed Smith
Reynolds Porter Chamberlain
Shoosmiths
Simmons & Simmons
SJ Berwin
Skadden
Slaughter and May
SNR Denton
Speechly Bircham
Stephenson Harwood
Stevens & Bolton
Taylor Wessing
TLT
Travers Smith
Trethowans
Towers & Hamlins
Veale Wasbrough Vizards
Walker Morris
Ward Hadaway
Watson, Farley & Williams
White & Case
Winckworth Sherwood

The civil courts of England and Wales

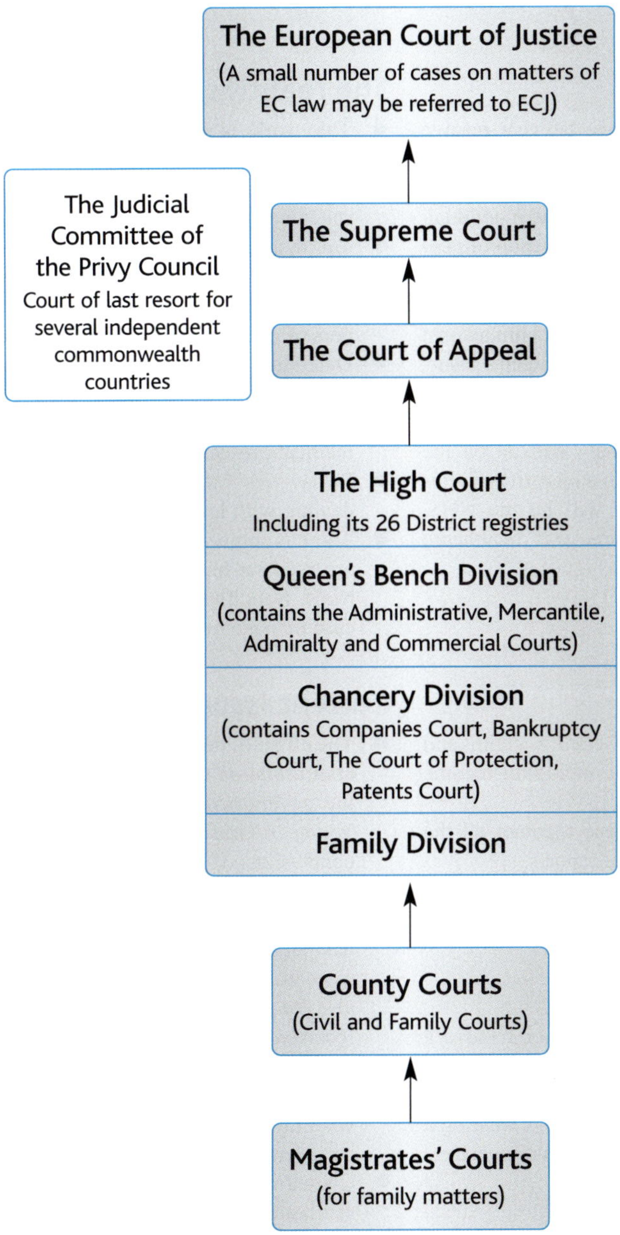

Other Specialist Courts

Employment Tribunals
Lands Tribunals
Leasehold Valuation Tribunals
VAT and Duties Tribunals
General and Special Commissioners (Tax)
Asylum & Immigration Tribunals

Europe

ECJ: Any UK court can refer a point of law for determination if it relates to EU law. The decision will be referred back to the court where the case originated.

European Court of Human Rights: Hears complaints regarding breaches of human rights.

Personal Injury and clinical negligence

In a nutshell

Personal injury and clinical negligence lawyers resolve claims brought by people who have been injured, either as a result of an accident or through flawed medical treatment. The claimant lawyer usually acts for one individual, but sometimes a claim may be brought by a group of people – this is a class action or multiparty claim. The defendant lawyer represents the party alleged to be responsible for the illness or injury. In most PI cases the claim against the defendant will be taken over by the defendant's insurance company, which will then be the solicitor's client. Local authorities are common defendants in relation to slips and trips, while employers usually end up on the hook for accidents in the workplace. In a majority of clinical negligence cases the defendant will be the NHS, although private medical practitioners and healthcare organisations are also sued.

What lawyers do

Claimant solicitors

- Determine the veracity of their client's claim and establish what they have suffered, including income lost and expenses incurred.
- Examine medical records and piece together all the facts. Commission further medical reports.
- Issue court proceedings if the defendant doesn't make an acceptable offer of compensation.

Defendant solicitors

- Try and avoid liability for their client or resolve a claim for as little as possible.
- Put all aspects of the case to the test. Perhaps the victim of a road traffic accident (RTA) wasn't wearing a seatbelt; perhaps the claimant has been malingering.

Both

- Manage the progress of the case over a period of months, even years, following an established set of procedural rules.
- Attempt to settle the claim before trial or, if a case goes to trial, brief a barrister and shepherd the client through the proceedings.

The realities of the job

- The work is driven by the procedural rules and timetable of the court.
- There is a mountain of paperwork, including witness statements and bundles of evidence.
- You'll spend a lot of time considering medical issues and records. Being squeamish is a no-no.
- Claimant lawyers have close contact with large numbers of clients and need good people skills.
- Defendant lawyers need to build long-term relationships with insurance companies. Clin neg defendant lawyers need to be able to communicate well with medical professionals and health sector managers.
- PI lawyers have large caseloads, especially when dealing with lower-value claims.
- There is some scope for advocacy, although barristers are used for high-stakes or complicated hearings and trials. Solicitors appear at preliminary hearings and case management conferences.

Current issues

- The effect of the much-anticipated Jackson Review of civil litigation costs is still unclear, although recently the government's new health and safety tsar, Lord Young of Graffham, lent his support to many of the conclusions of the report. He has been commissioned to review health and safety legislation and to deal with a perceived 'compensation culture'. Lord Young has particularly emphasised the need for compensation awards to better reflect the claimant's injury, and also for an end to the perceived disproportionate fees received by lawyers and referral agencies. It is not readily apparent whether this will lead to an adaptation of Conditional Fee Agreements (CFAs) – otherwise known as no-win, no-fee arrangements – or a complete overhaul of the current format.
- Claims management companies remain a controversial issue. Some practitioners see their involvement as a way to counteract the potential challenges from the entry of big high street names into the legal market when the Legal Services Act takes effect. However, many others regard them as a negative influence, and their power could be significantly curtailed if there is any implementation of Lord Justice Jackson's suggestions regarding banning the paying of referral fees to brokers and claims management companies.
- The impact of the imminent implementation of the Legal Services Act on the personal injury market remains to be seen. The opening up of the legal mar-

ket to alternative business structures has the potential to affect this practice area, as individual clients on the claimant side could be an ideal target group for the kind of service which might be offered by big high street names entering the legal market. Following the change of government it is possible that certain aspects of the Act may be altered, but currently it seems likely that at least the central ideas will remain.

- There has been a rise in the number of clinical negligence claims being brought. This may be attributed to the recession, with people in need of money more likely to pursue claims than previously. Alternatively it may be due to the greater availability of funding through CFAs, as well as greater public awareness of the feasibility of making a claim.
- Some concerns have been expressed about the quality of the defence available to clinicians. The NHS Litigation Authority continues to reduce the number of firms on its panel, and increasingly requires those that remain to adhere to very strict rules when responding to claims.
- The NHS Redress Act 2006 gives the power to introduce a scheme allowing lower-value claims to be handled by the NHS without going to court. Obviously this would cut away some of the lawyers' bread-and-butter work, and the proposal incites an important debate about health sector regulation in general.

Read our True Pictures on...

Barlow Lyde & Gilbert
Beachcroft
Bevan Brittan
Bond Pearce
Browne Jacobson
Capsticks Solicitors
Clarke Willmott
Coffin Mew
Cripps Harries Hall
DLA Piper UK
DWF
Eversheds
Field Fisher Waterhouse
Foot Anstey Solicitors
Forbes
Ford & Warren
Freeth Cartwright
Henmans
Hill Dickinson
Irwin Mitchell
Kennedys
Kingsley Napley
Michelmores
Mills & Reeve
Nabarro
Pannone
Penningtons Solicitors
Reynolds Porter Chamberlain
Shoosmiths
Trethowans
Veale Wasbrough Vizards

Private Client and charities

In a nutshell

You have money. You need to know how best to control it, preserve it and pass it on: enter the private client lawyer. Solicitors advise individuals, families and trusts on wealth management. Some offer additional matrimonial and small-scale commercial assistance; others focus exclusively on highly specialised tax and trusts issues, or wills and probate.

Charities lawyers advise on all aspects of not-for-profit organisations' activities. These specialists need exactly the same skills and knowledge as private client lawyers, but must also have the same kind of commercial knowledge as corporate lawyers.

What lawyers do

Private client lawyers

- Draft wills in consultation with clients and expedite their implementation after death. Probate involves the appointment of an executor and the settling of an estate. Organising a house clearance or even a funeral is not beyond the scope of a lawyer's duties.
- Advise clients on the most tax-efficient and appropriate structure for holding money and assets. Lawyers must ensure their clients understand the foreign law implications of trusts held in offshore jurisdictions.
- Advise overseas clients interested in investing in the UK, and banks whose overseas clients have UK interests.
- Assist clients with the very specific licensing, sales arrangement and tax planning issues related to ownership of heritage chattels (individual items or collections of cultural value or significance).
- Bring or defend litigation in relation to disputed legacies.

Charities lawyers

- Advise charities on registration, reorganisation, regulatory compliance and the implications of new legislation.
- Offer specialist trusts and investment advice.
- Advise on quasi-corporate and mainstream commercial matters; negotiate and draft contracts for sponsorship and the development of trading subsidiaries; manage property issues and handle IP concerns.
- Charities law still conjures up images of sleepy local fund-raising efforts or, alternatively, working on a trendy project for wealthy benefactors. The wide middle ground can incorporate working with a local authority, a local library and schools to establish an after-school homework programme, or rewriting the constitution of a 300-year-old church school to admit female pupils. Widespread international trust in British charity law means that you could also establish a study programme in Britain for a US university, or negotiate the formation of a zebra conservation charity in Tanzania.

The realities of the job

- An interest in other people's affairs is going to help. A capacity for empathy coupled with impartiality and absolute discretion are the hallmarks of a good private client lawyer. You'll need to be able to relate to and earn the trust of your many varied clients.
- Despite not being as chaotic as other fields, the technical demands of private client work can be exacting and an academic streak goes a long way.
- Despite not being as chaotic as other fields, the technical demands of private client work can be exacting and an academic streak goes a long way.
- The stereotype of the typical 'country gent' client is far from accurate: lottery wins, personal injury payouts, property portfolios, massive City salaries and successful businesses all feed the demand for legal advice.
- If you are wavering between private clients and commercial clients, charities law might offer a good balance.

Current issues

- The private client world is becoming increasingly internationalised. Wealthy people are selecting a wider geographical spread of assets, and London has become a hub for the management of these assets. Many clients come from Russia, the Middle East, the USA, India and France. The Finance Act 2008, which applies strict and complex tax rules to non-UK domiciliaries ('non-doms'), combined with the newly introduced 50% income tax rate, caused some high net worth individuals to consider leaving the UK. Those who've opted to stay have sought advice on restructuring their wealth. The UK is, nonetheless, still an attractive destination for foreign domiciled individuals to move to. There's been a steady flow of work from foreign nationals wishing to move to the UK.
- 2009 saw further pressure being applied to offshore financial centres in an attempt to obtain greater transparency as to the ownership and taxation of funds held there. This resulted in many enquiries about the

implications of the rapidly expanding network of international tax information exchange agreements and the consequences for those compliant individuals and families who legitimately wished to maintain their privacy. In addition, 2009 also saw greater efforts by the governments of western economies to facilitate the return of funds to their domestic economies by offering amnesties for the return of undeclared funds.

- More firms have dedicated teams handling legacy disputes. The RSPCA, for example, has been actively involved in these types of claims.
- After an interminably long wait, the Charities Act 2006 was finalised. The Act addresses fundamental questions about what constitutes a charity and what 'public benefit' means. It also provides for greater regulation in some areas, and greater freedom for charities in others.
- Economic uncertainty has brought many challenges for charities, particularly the large ones that rely heavily on public donations and/or government funding. Some charities have seen their budgets cut by up to 40% as a result of a reduction in corporate donations. As a result, many charities are restructuring or becoming more innovative with fund-raising, while others look towards collaborative working with other charities.
- There's been an upswing in charities mergers. The 2002 merger of Cancer Research and Macmillan proved it to be possible, and in 2008 there were just under 500 mergers registered with Charity Commission. One of the most publicised combinations was that of Age Concern and Help the Aged, to form Age UK.
- Other matters concerning charities are conflicts of interests, 'whistleblowing' and information management. A theme running through these areas is getting governance right – something that tends to come into focus in harder economic times. Economic difficulties aside, there are nearly 300,000 British millionaires donating 5% of their wealth, making the UK the second-largest charitable donor in the world.
- There is speculation that David Cameron's 'Big Society' will leave charities bidding for services previously provided by the public sector, and that these will become a source of extra funding. As a result, there will be competition between the private and public sectors for contracts.
- Loss of exempt charity status has affected numerous organisations – schools, religious institutions and museums, among others.
- Firms right across the country bemoan a dearth of young lawyers who can claim to be true private client specialists. It looks like a good time to put your hand up and be counted.

Read our True Pictures on...

Addleshaw Goddard	Higgs & Sons
Allen & Overy	Hill Dickinson
B P Collins	Howes Percival
Baker & McKenzie	Irwin Mitchell
Bates Wells & Braithwaite	Lawrence Graham
Berwin Leighton Paisner	Lester Aldridge
Bircham Dyson Bell	Macfarlanes
Boodle Hatfield	Manches
Brabners Chaffe Street	Martineau
Browne Jacobson	Michelmores
Burges Salmon	Mills & Reeve
Charles Russell	Mishcon de Reya
Clarke Willmott	Muckle
Clifford Chance	Osborne Clarke
Cobbetts	Pannone
Cripps Harries Hall	Penningtons Solicitors
Dawsons	Speechly Bircham
Dickinson Dees	Stevens & Bolton
Farrer & Co	Taylor Wessing
Foot Anstey Solicitors	TLT
Freeth Cartwright	Trethowans
Gordons	Trowers & Hamlins
Harbottle & Lewis	Veale Wasbrough Vizards
HBJ Gateley Wareing	Ward Hadaway
Henmans	Wedlake Bell
Herbert Smith	Winckworth Sherwood

Property/real estate

In a nutshell

Property lawyers, like their corporate law colleagues, are essentially transactional lawyers; the only real difference is that real estate deals require an extra layer of specialist legal and procedural knowledge and there aren't quite so many pesky regulatory authorities. The work centres on buildings and land of all types, and even the most oblique legal concepts have a bricks-and-mortar or human basis to them. It is common for lawyers to develop a specialism within this field, such as residential conveyancing, mortgage lending and property finance, social housing, or the leisure and hotels sector. Most firms have a property department, and the larger the department the more likely the lawyers are to specialise. Note: 'property' and 'real estate' are entirely interchangeable terms.

What lawyers do

- Negotiate sales, purchases and leases of land and buildings, and advise on the structure of deals. Record the terms of an agreement in legal documents.
- Gather and analyse factual information about properties from the owners, surveyors, local authorities and the Land Registry.
- Prepare reports for buyers and anyone lending money.
- Manage the transfer of money and the handover of properties to new owners or occupiers.
- Take the appropriate steps to register new owners and protect the interests of lenders or investors.
- Advise clients on their responsibilities in leasehold relationships, and how to take action if problems arise.
- Help developers get all the necessary permissions to build, alter or change the permitted use of properties.

The realities of the job

- Property lawyers have to multi-task. A single deal could involve many hundreds of properties and your caseload could contain scores of files, all at different stages in the process. You'll have to keep organised.
- Good drafting skills require attention to detail and careful thought. Plus you need to keep up to date with industry trends and standards.
- Some clients get antsy; you have to be able to explain legal problems in lay terms.
- Despite some site visits, this is mainly a desk job with a lot of time spent on the phone to other solicitors, estate agents, civil servants and consultants.
- Most instances of solicitor negligence occur in this area of practice. There is so much that can go wrong.
- Your days will be busy, but generally the hours are more sociable and predictable.

Current issues

- Arguably the most obviously cyclical legal area around, property practice will always and has always followed the market. In a down economy there's less demand for properties and new developments, values plummet and conventional bank lending becomes increasingly hard to find. Yes, the recession has hit the property sector hard, but this is nothing new. When the economy picks back up, so will this practice area.
- Generally, banks haven't been lending as much or as often, and it's been the cash-rich investors from foreign sovereign wealth funds (particularly Qatar) and big foreign companies (often German) who have been investing into the UK market. However, they've been actively and aggressively pursuing primary investment assets – the big office buildings, shopping centres and tower blocks, meaning that, at that level, there is a high demand and a low supply, keeping prices pretty high.
- There has been a shift towards refinancing of existing deals in the wake of the general downturn in new transactions, with landlords having to be much more flexible than in previous years. Landlords are keen to avoid the dreaded 'empty rates' scenario, where are forced to pay for buildings without occupiers.
- Apart from big projects like the Olympic Village and Crossrail, the public sector real estate market has slowed. This includes social housing. Firms with existing experience in these sectors largely have the market sewn up; however there are fears over a drier period ahead.
- The recession caused the real estate transactional market to implode, with some parties who had signed deals, especially buyers, examining/challenging purchase contracts and trying to pull out of deals. This triggered an increase in litigation and most firms have experienced an upturn in contentious work.
- Generally, property litigation is a booming area at the moment, even though matters are not necessarily going all the way to court due to cost implications. Many cash-strapped landlords and tenants are settling pre-court, or going to mediation.
- The slow economy means more insolvency, with the knock-on result that some former tenants are being pursued when their assignees default. There are also

more break clause disputes. The volume of general landlord and tenant and dilapidations work is also up, with landlords looking for somebody to blame; they are picking over every last detail.

- The trends in property finance have included a large number of loans being renegotiated, development finance thinner on the ground, increased fire sales, pre-syndication of new debt and anxiety that UK Real Estate Investment Trusts (REITs) may breach their financial covenants. Banks are beginning to lend again, and the market is now more receptive to new deals, although these are tightly controlled and generally at a much lower level than before. Deals under £100m are no longer considered small.
- German banks are a major presence, while Shari'a finance remains a small but significant area.

Read our True Pictures on...

Addleshaw Goddard	Howes Percival
Allen & Overy	Irwin Mitchell
Ashurst	Jones Day
B P Collins	K&L Gates
Baker & McKenzie	Kennedys
Barlow Lyde & Gilbert	Lawrence Graham
Bates Wells & Braithwaite	Lester Aldridge
Beachcroft	Lewis Silkin
Berwin Leighton Paisner	Linklaters
Bevan Brittan	Macfarlanes
Bond Pearce	Manches
Boodle Hatfield	Martineau
Brabners Chaffe Street	Maxwell Winward
Browne Jacobson	Mayer Brown
Burges Salmon	McGrigors
Charles Russell	Michelmores
Clarke Willmott	Mills & Reeve
Clifford Chance	Mishcon de Reya
Clyde & Co	Muckle
CMS Cameron McKenna	Nabarro
Cobbetts	Norton Rose
Coffin Mew	Olswang
Cripps Harries Hall	Orrick
Dechert	Osborne Clarke
Dickinson Dees	Pannone
DLA Piper UK	Paul, Hastings
DMH Stallard	Penningtons Solicitors
Dundas & Wilson	Pinsent Masons
DWF	Reed Smith
Eversheds	Shoosmiths
Farrer & Co	Sidley Austin
Field Fisher Waterhouse	Simmons & Simmons
Finers Stephens Innocent	SJ Berwin
Fisher Meredith	Slaughter and May
Foot Anstey Solicitors	SNR Denton
Forbes	Speechly Bircham
Freeth Cartwright	Stephenson Harwood
Freshfields	Stevens & Bolton
Gordons	Taylor Wessing
Hammonds	TLT
Harbottle & Lewis	Travers Smith
HBJ Gateley Wareing	Trethowans
Henmans	Trowers & Hamlins
Herbert Smith	Veale Wasbrough Vizards
Higgs & Sons	Walker Morris
Hill Dickinson	Ward Hadaway
Hogan Lovells	Wedlake Bell

Public interest

In a nutshell

Human rights lawyers protest injustice enshrined in law and fight for principle at the point of intersection between a state's powers and individuals' rights. Cases usually relate in some way to the UK's ratification of the European Convention on Human Rights through the Human Rights Act and crop up in criminal and civil contexts, often through the medium of judicial review, a key tool in questioning the decisions of public bodies. Civil contexts include claims regarding the right to education or community care under the Mental Health Act, cases of discrimination at work and even family issues. Criminal contexts could relate to complaints against the police, prisoners' issues, public order convictions following demonstrations, or perhaps extradition on terror charges.

Immigration lawyers deal with both business and personal immigration matters, the former having been embraced by the present government in its quest to manage economic migration. In this more lucrative area, lawyers assist highly skilled migrants to obtain residency or leave to remain in the UK, and help non-nationals to secure visas for travel abroad. They also work with companies that need to bring in employees from overseas. Personal immigration lawyers represent individuals who have fled persecution in their country of origin. They also take on cases for people whose right to stay in the UK is under threat or indeed entirely absent.

What lawyers do

Human rights lawyers

- Advise clients on how to appeal a decision made or action taken by a public body, such as the police, a local authority, a court, or a branch of government.
- Collect evidence, take witness statements, prepare cases and instruct barristers.
- Pursue cases through the procedural stages necessary to achieve the desired result. The final port of call for some cases is the European Court of Justice (ECJ), so lawyers need to be fully conversant with UK and European laws.

Business immigration lawyers

- Advise and assist businesses or their employees in relation to work permits and visas. They need to be up to speed on all current schemes, such as those for highly skilled migrants and investors.
- Prepare for, attend and advocate at tribunals or court hearings, where necessary instructing a barrister to do so.

Personal immigration lawyers

- Advise clients on their status and rights within the UK.
- Secure evidence of a client's identity, medical reports and witness statements and prepare cases for court hearings or appeals. Represent clients or instruct a barrister to do so.
- Undertake an immense amount of unremunerated form filling and Legal Aid paperwork.

The realities of the job

- A commitment to and belief in the values you're fighting for is essential in this relatively low-paid area. Work in the voluntary sector or taking on important cases pro bono can provide the greatest satisfaction.
- Sensitivity and empathy are absolutely essential because you'll often be dealing with highly emotional people, those with mental health issues or those who simply don't appreciate the full extent of their legal predicament.
- Strong analytical skills are required to pick out the legal issues you can change from the socio-economic ones beyond your control.
- In the battle against red tape, bureaucracy and institutional indifference, organisational skills and a vast store of patience are valuable assets.
- Opportunities for advocacy are abundant, which means that knowledge of court and tribunal procedures is a fundamental requirement. Often cases must pass through every possible stage of appeal before referral to judicial review or the ECJ.
- The competition for training contracts is huge. Voluntary work at a law centre or specialist voluntary organisation, or membership of Liberty or Justice, will help.
- Because much of the work is publicly funded, firms do not usually offer attractive trainee salaries or sponsorship through law school.
- If working within a commercial firm, the clients will be businesses and public sector organisations. As such there will be less of a campaigning element to the work and you will not necessarily feel you are 'on the side of the angels'.

Current issues

- Issues of asylum (including detention and deportation) and people seeking permission to stay in the UK on human rights grounds never cease to arouse strong opinions.
- The advent of the Freedom of Information Act, and increased transparency in the public sector in line with Article 6 of the Convention, mean law firms have seen a greater willingness from the public to challenge the decisions of authorities.
- Recent big human rights and civil liberties cases have mainly related to issues arising out of Guantanamo Bay, Iraq and control orders, and the use of information that might have detrimental consequences for national security. These cases have taken the form of judicial reviews and public inquiries. The much publicised Binyam Mohamed judicial review and Baha Mousa and Al-Sweady inquiries are examples of such investigations.
- There have also been a number of general social justice cases relating to equality rights and privacy rights, and a number of asylum seeker rights cases.
- The Points Based System (PBS) for immigration has now been fully implemented. Every employer now needs to obtain an immigration licence under the PBS before being able to issue a Certificate of Sponsorship for each employee it wishes to employ. Some argue that the scheme is now so technical that employers are constantly at risk of unlawful employment. Others believe that restricting highly skilled migrants from working in the UK is farcical.
- The government has amended its application of the PBS to allow the immigration status of members of religious communities to be dealt with outside the system. It has also agreed not to abolish the immigration category relating to Overseas Domestic Workers, which received significant publicity in the national press. The Home Office has lately been reworking the PBS.
- The past decade has seen enormous growth in human rights litigation, in UK court and in other European courts, as well as before the General Court (formerly the Court of First Instance), ECJ, European Court of Human Rights and international tribunals. This case-driven development of human rights law is based on fundamental rights standards which are common to the domestic legal systems throughout Europe.
- A recent example of a successful ECHR case is *S and Marper v UK*. The Grand Chamber of the court found the UK's policy of retaining DNA of innocent people to be a breach of Article 8 of the European Convention on Human Rights. This is the leading case on retention of biometric data and it received widespread media coverage.
- In July 2010, the Supreme Court recognised gay individuals' same right to have relationships as straight people. Previously, the Home Office could deport gay asylum seekers if it was 'reasonably tolerable' for them to conceal their sexuality to avoid persecution.

Read our True Pictures on...

Addleshaw Goddard	Hill Dickinson
Allen & Overy	Hogan Lovells
Ashurst	Irwin Mitchell
Baker & McKenzie	K&L Gates
Barlow Lyde & Gilbert	Kennedys
Bates Wells & Braithwaite	Kingsley Napley
Beachcroft	Lewis Silkin
Berwin Leighton Paisner	Manches
Bevan Brittan	Martineau
Bircham Dyson Bell	Mills & Reeve
Bird & Bird	Mishcon de Reya
Bond Pearce	Nabarro
Browne Jacobson	Norton Rose
Burges Salmon	Olswang
Capsticks Solicitors	Osborne Clarke
Charles Russell	Pannone
Clifford Chance	Penningtons Solicitors
Clyde & Co	Pinsent Masons
CMS Cameron McKenna	Reynolds Porter Chamberlain
Cobbetts	Shoosmiths
Cripps Harries Hall	Simmons & Simmons
Dickinson Dees	Slaughter and May
DLA Piper UK	SNR Denton
DMH Stallard	Speechly Bircham
DWF	Stephenson Harwood
Eversheds	Stevens & Bolton
Farrer & Co	TLT
Field Fisher Waterhouse	Trethowans
Fisher Meredith	Trowers & Hamlins
Foot Anstey Solicitors	Veale Wasbrough Vizards
Ford & Warren	Walker Morris
Freeth Cartwright	Ward Hadaway
Freshfields	Wiggin
Hammonds	Winckworth Sherwood
Herbert Smith	

- In immigration law there have been many modifications of late, with rules and regulations affecting the highly skilled migrant programme and people applying for leave to remain or settle in the UK. A new points-based immigration system (a source of considerable irritation for the majority of practitioners) means every employer now needs an immigration licence for each employee it wishes to employ. The risk of unlawful employment is high, if employers do not keep up with rule changes.
- Go to www.chambersstudent.co.uk for more current issues in the following public interest practice areas: Administrative Law, Civil Liberties, Education, Health & Safety, Health & Social Care, Licensing, Local Government, Parliamentary Law, Police Law, Professional Discipline, and Public Procurement.

Restructuring/insolvency

In a nutshell

Insolvency law governs the position of businesses and individuals who are in financial difficulties and unable to repay their debts as they become due. Such a situation may lead to insolvency proceedings, in which legal action is taken against the insolvent entity and assets may be liquidated to pay off outstanding debts. Before a company or individual gets involved in insolvency proceedings, they will likely be involved in a restructuring or an out-of-court arrangement with creditors to work out alternative repayment schedules. The work of lawyers in the field can therefore be non-contentious (restructuring) or contentious (insolvency litigation), and their role will vary depending on whether they act for debtors or their creditors. What follows are some of the terms you'll come across.

Debtor: an individual or company that owes money. **Creditor:** a person or institution that extends credit to another entity on condition that it is paid back at a later date. **Bankruptcy:** term used in the USA to describe insolvency procedures that apply to companies, but not in the UK, where the term applies to individuals only. **Restructuring:** a significant modification made to the debt, operations or structure of a company with its creditors' consent. After a restructuring, debt repayments become more manageable, making insolvency proceedings less likely. **Insolvency proceedings:** generic term that covers a variety of statutory proceedings aimed at rescuing or winding-up an insolvent company.

Insolvency proceedings include the following actions. **Company voluntary arrangement (CVA):** if it is clear that a business could survive if debt repayments were reduced, it can enter into a CVA agreement with its creditors. Under this legally binding agreement, a struggling company is allowed to repay some, or all, of its historic debts out of future profits, over an agreed period of time. **Administration:** when in administration, a company is protected from creditors enforcing their debts while an administrator takes over the management of its affairs. If the company is fundamentally sound, the administrator will implement a recovery plan aimed at streamlining the business and maximising profits. If it is apparent that the company has no future then it can be sold or liquidation can commence. **Receivership:** unlike administration, this is initiated by the company's creditors, not the company itself. A receiver is appointed by the court and must look to recover as much money as possible in order to settle the claims made by creditors. Under receivership, the interests of the creditors clearly take precedence over the survival of the company. **Liquidation:** procedure by which the assets of a company are placed under the control of a liquidator. In most cases, a company in liquidation ceases to trade, and the liquidator will sell the company's assets and distribute the proceeds to creditors. There are two forms: voluntary liquidation brought about by the company itself, or compulsory liquidation brought about by court order. **Distressed M&A:** the sale of all or a portion of an insolvent business in an efficient way to preserve going-concern value and avoid the potential for substantial loss of value through a piecemeal liquidation. **Pre-pack sale:** refers to a deal made with an interested buyer to sell the insolvent company's business and assets, negotiated before an administrator is appointed and completed immediately on appointment. Such schemes are becoming increasingly popular and more frequently used in the current economic climate.

What lawyers do

Debtors' lawyers

- Meet with clients to assess the gravity of the situation, highlight the available options and advise on the best course of action to follow.
- In a restructuring, advise the insolvent company on the reorganisation of its balance sheet (such as closing down unprofitable businesses or refinancing its debt) and assist in negotiations with creditors.
- Assist in insolvency filings, and once proceedings have commenced, work closely with the insolvency officeholders (ie those appointed as administrators, receivers or liquidators) and accountants, to achieve the goals set for the insolvent company.
- Provide advice to directors of insolvent companies, explaining their duties to creditors.
- Advise on the sale of assets or mergers and acquisitions of troubled companies.
- Assist clients in insolvency litigation and appeals.
- Provide preventative advice to debtor clients on liability management and ways to avoid insolvency proceedings.

Creditors' lawyers

- Meet with creditor clients to assess the validity of their security over the insolvent company, the strength of their position in the creditors' pool and the best course of action to ensure full recovery.
- Assist in negotiations with debtors and insolvency officeholders.

- Represent clients in insolvency litigation and appeals.
- Assist in the tracing and valuation of debtors' assets.
- Provide training to their clients on how to deal with insolvent companies.

The realities of the job

- Large City firms deal almost exclusively with large-scale corporate restructurings and insolvencies, and the representation of creditor groups in these matters. Smaller regional firms mostly assist on smaller corporate and personal insolvency cases.
- Corporate insolvency as a practice area is extremely varied, as proceedings affect every aspect of the insolvent company. Lawyers therefore need to be conversant in a variety of legal disciplines or know when to refer matters to specialists in employment, banking, property, litigation, corporate, etc.
- When financial difficulties arise in companies, the rapid deployment of a legal team is necessary to provide immediate assistance. This area of law is extremely fast paced, and lawyers are often asked to deliver solutions overnight.
- Insolvency and restructuring involves mountains of paperwork, so lawyers need to be organised and able to prioritise their workload, particularly when dealing with multiple assigments. With so much at stake, attention to detail is paramount when drafting asset sale agreements or documents to be filed at court.
- Restructuring and insolvency situations are understandably tense for both debtors and creditors, and lawyers sometimes need to deal with difficult people, so they must be able to hold their ground and show they are not easily intimidated.
- You will need to immerse yourself in both the financial and corporate worlds. Get started by reading the *FT* or City pages of your daily newspaper.

Read our True Pictures on...

Addleshaw Goddard	Irwin Mitchell
Allen & Overy	Jones Day
Ashurst	Kirkland & Ellis
Baker & McKenzie	Latham & Watkins
Barlow Lyde & Gilbert	Lawrence Graham
Beachcroft	Linklaters
Berwin Leighton Paisner	Martineau
Bingham McCutchen	Mayer Brown
Bond Pearce	Michelmores
Brabners Chaffe Street	Mills & Reeve
Browne Jacobson	Muckle
Burges Salmon	Nabarro
Charles Russell	Norton Rose
Clarke Willmott	Olswang
Clifford Chance	Osborne Clarke
Clyde & Co	Pannone
CMS Cameron McKenna	Pinsent Masons
Cobbetts	Shoosmiths
Coffin Mew	Sidley Austin
Dickinson Dees	Simmons & Simmons
DLA Piper UK	SJ Berwin
Dundas & Wilson	Skadden
DWF	Slaughter and May
Eversheds	SNR Denton
Field Fisher Waterhouse	Speechly Bircham
Freeth Cartwright	Stevens & Bolton
Freshfields	Taylor Wessing
Gordons	TLT
Hammonds	Travers Smith
HBJ Gateley Wareing	Veale Wasbrough Vizards
Herbert Smith	Walker Morris
Hill Dickinson	Ward Hadaway
Hogan Lovells	Weil, Gotshal & Manges
Howes Percival	

Current issues

- As the financial crisis unfolded, more businesses went bust. The predicted massive wave of formal insolvency instructions never came though and the jury is still out on whether it will come, or whether the volume of new instructions will remain slow and steady. By and large firms are gearing up for an increase.
- Not all insolvency lawyers can find enough work. Banks have been sitting on debt rather than litigating it, as assets aren't worth what they once were and litigation is expensive. In addition, the HMRC's Time to Pay Scheme has meant lenience towards small and medium enterprise owners who are in debt. This could be about to change.
- It is (or was) the accepted wisdom that it was better to have a business ticking over as a going concern, than to scrap everything (especially in the case of schools/charities/hotels). Low interest rates made that somewhat easier, but many lawyers expect the artificial bubble to burst.
- The sectors hardest hit by the recession – and therefore the busiest in relation to restructuring – are construction and property. Nonetheless, insolvency is cropping up everywhere, so lawyers need to be up to speed with a wider range of industry issues. As a result, firms are adapting a more cross-departmental, integrated approach.

Shipping and international trade

In a nutshell

Shipping lawyers deal with the carriage of goods or people by sea, plus any and every matter related to the financing, construction, use, insurance and decommissioning of the ships that carry them (or are arrested, sunk or salvaged while carrying them). Despite being the preserve of specialist firms, or relatively self-contained practice groups within larger firms, the discipline offers varied challenges. The major division is between wet work relating to accidents or misadventure at sea, and dry work involving the land-based, commercial and contractual side. In extension, disputes or litigation relating to contracts mean there is also a contentious side to dry work. While some lawyers in the area may be generalists, it is more common to specialise.

What lawyers do

Wet lawyers

- Act swiftly and decisively at a moment's notice to protect a client's interests and minimise any loss.
- Travel the world to assess the condition of ships, interview crew or witnesses and prepare cases.
- Take witness statements and advise clients on the merits of and strategy for cases.
- Handle court and arbitration appearances, conferences with barristers and client meetings.

Dry lawyers

- Negotiate and draft contracts for ship finance and shipbuilding, crew employment, sale and purchase agreements, affreightment contracts, and the registration and re-flagging of ships.
- May specialise in niche areas such as yachts or fishing, an area in which regulatory issues feature prominently.
- Handle similar tasks to wet lawyers in relation to contractual disputes but are less likely to jet off around the world at the drop of a hat.

The realities of the job

- Wet work offers the excitement of international assignments and clients, so lawyers need to react coolly to sudden emergencies and travel to far-flung places to offer practical and pragmatic analysis and advice.
- Despite the perils and pleasures of dealing with clients and instructions on the other side of the world, the hours are likely to be steady beyond those international-rescue moments.
- Non-contentious work touches on the intricacies of international trade, so it's as important to keep up with sector knowledge as legal developments.
- Dealing with a mixed clientele from all points on the social compass, you'll need to be just as comfortable extracting a comprehensible statement from a Norwegian merchant seaman as conducting negotiations with major financers.
- Contentious cases are driven by the procedural rules and timetable of the court or arbitration forum to which the matter has been referred. A solid grasp of procedure is as important as a strong foundation in tort and contract law.
- Some shipping lawyers do come from a naval background or are ex-mariners, but you won't be becalmed if the closest comparable experience you've had is steering Tommy Tugboat in the bath, as long as you can show a credible interest in the discipline.
- Though not an all-boys club, parts of the shipping world are still male dominated. Women lawyers and clients are more commonly found on the dry side.
- In the UK, shipping law is centred around London and a few other port cities. Major international centres include Piraeus in Greece, Hong Kong and Singapore. Some trainees even get to work in these locations.

Current issues

- Charter party contracts were put under pressure as the value fell out of the shipping industry. Some people suggested that the top end of the market plummeted between 90 and 100% in a matter of weeks. Commodities markets have stabilised to a degree, but shipowners are still finding it difficult to come by financing. Long-term recovery is likely to be slow.
- The collapse of freight rates led to an increase in contentious work. The amount of contentious work arising directly out of the economic crisis has tailed off to a degree, as contracts have been renegotiated and remaining businesses have stabilised their positions in the market.
- The level of ship financings remains low, although new deals are being made. Hotter areas are debt restructuring and recovery, and refund guarantees.
- Any increase in activity has been led by the Asian market, with China in particular singled out as a source of finance through both commercial banks and export credit agencies.

- Piracy remains a significant concern, but legal involvement tends to focus primarily on the status of a ship when seized – ie was it on hire during that period? – to establish who is responsible for the costs incurred. Actual prosecution of pirates remains rare, although in June 2010 a special court to try suspected pirates operating in the Gulf of Aden opened in the Shimo la Tewa prison in Mombasa, Kenya.

Read our True Pictures on...

Allen & Overy	Ince & Co
Barlow Lyde & Gilbert	Kennedys
Berwin Leighton Paisner	Linklaters
Clifford Chance	McGrigors
Clyde & Co	Norton Rose
DLA Piper UK	Orrick
Eversheds	Reed Smith
Field Fisher Waterhouse	Simmons & Simmons
HBJ Gateley Wareing	SNR Denton
Hill Dickinson	Stephenson Harwood
Hogan Lovells	Thomas Cooper
Holman Fenwick Willan	Watson, Farley & Williams

Sports, media and entertainment law

In a nutshell

Advertising and marketing lawyers offer advice to ensure a client's products or advertisements are compliant with industry standards, plus general advice on anything from contracts between clients, media and suppliers, to employment law, corporate transactions and litigation. Entertainment lawyers assist clients in the film, broadcasting, music, theatre and publishing industries with commercial legal advice or litigation.

Strictly speaking, sports lawyers work in an industry sector rather than a specific legal discipline, and firms draw on the expertise of individuals from several practice groups. Reputation management lawyers advise clients on how best to protect their own 'brand', be this through a defamation suit or an objection to invasion of privacy.

What lawyers do

Advertising and marketing lawyers

- Ensure advertising campaigns comply with legislation or regulatory codes controlled by the Advertising Standards Agency or Ofcom.
- Advise on comparative advertising, unauthorised references to living persons, potential trade mark or other intellectual property infringements.
- Defend clients against allegations that their work has infringed regulations or the rights of third parties. Bring complaints against competitors' advertising.

TV and film lawyers

- Offer production companies advice on every stage of the creation of programmes and films.
- Assist on the complicated banking and secured lending transactions that ensure financing for a film.
- Help engage performers; negotiate a multitude of ancillary contracts; negotiate distribution and worldwide rights; and manage defamation claims.

Music lawyers

- Advise major recording companies, independent labels and talent (including record producers and songwriters as well as artists).
- Advise on contracts, such as those between labels and bands, or between labels and third parties.
- Offer contentious and non-contentious copyright and trade mark advice relating to music, image rights and merchandising.
- Offer criminal advice when the things get old-school rock 'n' roll.
- Assist with immigration issues.

Theatre and publishing lawyers

- Advise theatre and opera companies, producers, agents and actors on contracts, funding and sponsorship/merchandising.
- Advise publishing companies and newspapers on contractual, licensing, copyright and libel matters.
- Assist with immigration issues.

Sports lawyers

- Assist with contract negotiations, be they between clubs and sportspeople, agents and players, sporting institutions and sponsors, or broadcasters and sports governing bodies.
- Handle varied employment law issues. Assist with immigration issues.
- Advise on corporate or commercial matters such as takeovers, public offerings, debt restructuring and bankruptcy, or the securing and structuring of credit.
- Enforce IP rights in the lucrative merchandise market and negotiate on matters affecting a sportsperson's image rights.
- Work on regulatory compliance issues within a sport or matters relating to the friction between sports regulations and EU/national law.
- Offer reputation management and criminal advice.

Reputation management

- Claimants' lawyers advise individuals – commonly celebrities, politicians or high-profile businessmen – on the nature of any potential libel action or breach of privacy claim, usually against broadcasters or publishers, before it either settles or goes to court.
- Defendants' lawyers advise broadcasters or other publishers on libel claims brought against them. With the burden of proof on the defendant, the lawyers must prove that what was published caused no loss to the claimant or was not libellous.

- Help clients stay out of hot water by giving pre-publication advice to authors, editors or production companies.

The realities of the job

- Advertising lawyers must have a good knowledge of advertising regulations, defamation and IP law. The work is real world and fast-paced.
- Clients are creative, lively and demanding. The issues thrown up can be fascinating and must be dealt with creatively.
- Many advertising disputes will be settled via regulatory bodies but some, particularly IP infringements, end in litigation.
- Entertainment lawyers need to be completely immersed in their chosen media and have a good grasp of copyright and contract law.
- Clients look to you for the rigour and discipline they may rarely exercise themselves. This is a sector where who you know makes a big difference, so expect to put in serious face time.
- Sports lawyers need to be proactive, passionate and have bags of commercial nous. They must be able to deal with people involved at all levels of all sports.
- Reputation management lawyers need a comprehensive understanding of libel and privacy laws and a willingness to think laterally.
- Individual claimants will be stressed and upset, so people skills, patience and resourcefulness are much needed.
- Solicitors prepare cases but barristers almost always get the glory.

Current issues

- In the world of broadcasting, both content providers and platform operators have been keen to introduce high definition services as a means of retaining viewer loyalty and enhancing revenues.
- At the heart of many developments is convergence, ie getting multiple services from a single provider. In particular, Apple's iPhone has started to reveal what consumers want to do with converged devices, and whether they are prepared to pay for the digital distribution of audio-visual content.
- Broadcasters are attempting to generate new revenue streams, in order to counteract the decline in advertising revenues. Online television has grown a great deal, but there has been no commensurate growth in revenues generated from this area. Firms are involved in fighting illegal online content.
- Advertising, news, drama, music, sport, interactive games and user-generated content are becoming increasingly undifferentiated as online access becomes routine. The attempt to regulate online content pursuant to the Audiovisual Media Services (AVMS) Directive is likely to create a spike in demand for legal services. Demand for competition advice is likely to show a long-term upward trend.
- The music industry continues to face challenges: illegal downloading and piracy are the biggest concerns. Sales of physical products are declining rapidly; however, 360° deals that incorporate physical sales with merchandising and live appearances (an area that still performs strongly) are going some way to redressing the balance.
- The UK tax credit for film financing has been firmly established and the weaker pound should boost foreign investment in the UK film and TV production sector. Still, a lot of previously finance-friendly banks have exited the market and the economic conditions will certainly constrain financing.
- The UK tax credit for film financing has been firmly established and the weaker pound should boost foreign investment in the UK film and TV production sector. Still, a lot of previously finance-friendly banks have exited the market and the economic conditions will certainly constrain financing.
- The economic downturn has intensified the public interest in sensitive areas such as gambling, alcohol and products targeting children. Following extensive consultations, there have also been changes made to the Committee of Advertising Practice (CAP) (non-broadcast) and BCAP (broadcast) codes in respect of health and nutritional claims.
- The recent implementation of the Consumer Protection Regulations and Business Protection

Read our True Pictures on...

Addleshaw Goddard	Herbert Smith
Baker & McKenzie	Hogan Lovells
Bates Wells & Braithwaite	Lewis Silkin
Berwin Leighton Paisner	Macfarlanes
Bird & Bird	Manches
Brabners Chaffe Street	Mayer Brown
Bristows	Mishcon de Reya
Charles Russell	Olswang
Clarke Willmott	Osborne Clarke
Clifford Chance	Pinsent Masons
CMS Cameron McKenna	Reed Smith
DLA Piper UK	Reynolds Porter Chamberlain
Eversheds	Sheridans
Farrer & Co	Slaughter and May
Field Fisher Waterhouse	SNR Denton
Finers Stephens Innocent	Speechly Bircham
Foot Anstey Solicitors	Taylor Wessing
Freshfields	Travers Smith
Hammonds	Wiggin
Harbottle & Lewis	

Regulations have re-codified the legislative framework to which all adverts (and commercial practices generally) must adhere. The new guidance also covers films and video games. The regulations have increased the demand for 'copy clearance' advice, as has the effects of the recession generally – for example, price wars tend to increase the amount of comparative advertising that is undertaken.

- Recent ECJ adjudications, such as those in the *Intel v CPM*, and *L'Oréal v Bellure* cases, have reignited the debate about the legal status of 'brand values' and shown how advertising and PR can have a direct consequence on the extent of registered trade mark protection that is available.
- Since issuing the draft regulations pursuant to the Audiovisual Media Services Directive, the government has made a u-turn and it now looks likely that product placement on UK-produced television programming will be permitted.
- This is supposed to be the 'golden decade' of sports event hosting in Britain. In addition to the 2012 Olympics, there is the 2010 Ryder Cup, the 2011 Champions League final, the 2014 Commonwealth Games (Glasgow), the 2015 Rugby (Union) World Cup, and the 2019 Cricket World Cup, as well as (hopefully) the FIFA World Cup in 2018.
- The 2012 Olympics are keeping lawyers busy, and the Premier League continues to attract significant media coverage. Sponsorship, advertising and corporate hospitality revenues have all taken a hit, but it's not been too bad at the élite level. Man United got a new £80m shirt sponsor, Liverpool's new shirt sponsorship deal is among its most lucrative ever, and Spurs has broken new ground by going for two different shirt sponsorship deals for different competitions.
- The Premier League's overseas broadcasting rights for 2010 to 2013 have doubled, from £625m to £1.4bn. Football clubs' finances and the transfer of clubs is big news. Portsmouth FC was the first-ever Premier League team to go into administration. The other biggest development in the world of football is the HMRC's decision to investigate image rights payments to footballers.
- There is a dispute between Ofcom and the Premier League over Ofcom's decision to make Sky reduce what it charges rival broadcasters to air its sports channels. It remains to be seen if Ofcom's wings will be clipped by the coalition government.
- One of the year's biggest sports disciplinary cases was rugby's Harlequins 'Bloodgate' scandal.

Tax

In a nutshell

Tax lawyers ensure that clients structure their business deals or day-to-day operations such that they take advantage of legal breaks and loopholes in tax legislation. Although predominantly an advisory practice area, on occasion matters can veer into litigation territory.

What lawyers do

Tax lawyers in private practice

- Handle tax planning for clients, making sure they understand the tax ramifications of the purchase, ownership and disposal of assets, including advice on structuring corporate portfolios in the most tax-efficient way.
- Offer transactional advice when working with corporate and other lawyers on matters such as an M&A deal, a joint venture or the acquisition of a large property portfolio.
- Deal with investigations or litigation resulting from prosecution by HM Revenue & Customs (HMRC). Litigation is always conducted against or brought by the government.

HMRC lawyers

- Investigate companies and bring prosecutions.
- Advise on how new laws apply to different situations.
- Defend cases brought against the government.

The realities of the job

- This is an intellectually rigorous, rather cloistered area of law and ideally suited to the more academic.
- Corporate tax lawyers are very well paid, treated with reverence by their colleagues and find intellectual stimulation in their work.
- Lawyers must not only have the ability to translate and implement complex tax legislation, but also be able to advise how to structure deals in a legitimate and tax-efficient way to avoid conflict with HMRC.
- If you don't already wear specs, expect to after a couple of years of poring over all that black letter law. The UK has more pages of tax legislation than almost any other country, and there are changes every year.
- In time, extra qualifications, such as the Chartered Tax Adviser exams, will be useful.
- It is not uncommon for lawyers to switch between government jobs and private practice. Some tax barristers were once solicitors.

Current issues

- There's been an increased focus on debt restructuring and equity raising. 2011 is likely to bring more major corporate restructurings.
- Funds work remains active. The restructuring of existing funds, launches of new funds and increases in capital flows all have tax consequences.
- A fall in transactional work has paved the way for other areas such as advisory and litigation to come to the fore. The significant savings achievable mean that tax lawyers' advice is valued more highly than ever.
- Significant changes to the UK tax regime and the introduction of specific anti-avoidance tax legislation will keep tax lawyers on their toes.
- Law firms have come into their own in relation to tax advice. Pre-Enron it seemed accountancy firms were taking over. However, companies now prefer to take advice from sources independent from their auditors.

Read our True Pictures on...

Addleshaw Goddard	Latham & Watkins
Allen & Overy	Linklaters
Ashurst	Macfarlanes
Baker & McKenzie	Mayer Brown
Berwin Leighton Paisner	McGrigors
Browne Jacobson	Mills & Reeve
Burges Salmon	Nabarro
Clifford Chance	Norton Rose
CMS Cameron McKenna	Olswang
Dechert	Osborne Clarke
Dewey & LeBoeuf	Penningtons Solicitors
DLA Piper UK	Pinsent Masons
Eversheds	Reynolds Porter Chamberlain
Field Fisher Waterhouse	Sidley Austin
Foot Anstey Solicitors	Simmons & Simmons
Freeth Cartwright	SJ Berwin
Freshfields	Skadden
Hammonds	Slaughter and May
HBJ Gateley Wareing	SNR Denton
Herbert Smith	Stephenson Harwood
Hogan Lovells	Stevens & Bolton
Irwin Mitchell	Travers Smith
Jones Day	Walker Morris
Kirkland & Ellis	

Technology, telecoms and outsourcing

In a nutshell

Technology lawyers distinguish themselves from general commercial advisers because of their specific industry know-how. They combine a keen understanding of the latest advances in various technologies with a thorough knowledge of the ever-changing law that regulates, protects and licenses them. As forms of media and new technologies converge, clients have come to rely on technology lawyers' innovation and imagination in offering rigorous legal solutions to maximise and protect income and ideas. The majority of the top 50 firms possess dedicated groups of lawyers. There are also specialists within many smaller commercial firms and a number of niche firms.

- In this frontier world, gut instinct matters. One in-house lawyer made what looked like a risky move from BT to little-known internet auction site eBay. Six years later he moved to head up Skype's legal team, a perfect example of the convergence of internet and telephone technology.
- High-end private sector outsourcing involves complex, high-value and increasingly multi-jurisdictional work. Mostly, it is the larger law firms that handle such deals. In the public sector, deals involve UK government departments, local authorities and the suppliers of services to those entities.

What lawyers do

- Advise on commercial transactions and draft the requisite documents. There is a heavy emphasis on risk management.
- Assist in the resolution of disputes, commonly by arbitration or other settlement procedures as this is a court-averse sector. Many disputes relate to faulty or unsatisfactory software or hardware.
- Help clients police their IT and web-based reputation and assets. Cyber-squatting, ownership of database information and the Data Protection Act are common topics.
- Give clients mainstream commercial, corporate and finance advice.
- Specialised outsourcing lawyers represent customers and suppliers in the negotiation and drafting of agreements for the provision of IT or other services by a third party.

The realities of the job

- You need to be familiar with the latest regulations and their potential impact on your client's business. Does a website need a disclaimer? What measures should your client take to protect data about individuals gathered from a website?
- You need a good grasp of the jargon of your chosen industry, firstly to write contracts but also so you can understand your clients' instructions. Read trade journals like *Media Lawyer* and *Wired*, or magazines such as *Computer Weekly* or *New Scientist*.
- The ability to think laterally and creatively is a must, especially when the application of a client's technology or content throws up entirely new issues.

Current issues

- Digital convergence throws up many legal problems as the business opportunities created by new technologies move beyond the capacity of existing legal or regulatory structures to contract or protect. Copyrighted content being transferred onto handheld devices; film or TV programme downloads from the internet… the list is practically endless.
- Many firms and their clients now believe that technology, media and telecoms are no longer three distinct markets, and structure their departments accordingly.
- The merger of Orange and T Mobile will create one of the largest mobile networks in the world, which will be called Everything Everywhere.
- The most interesting telecoms work is taking place overseas, particularly in Africa and Asia. Bharti's $9bn takeover of Zain (South African telecoms) is the ultimate example of this. India's Bharti Airtel is now the fifth-largest telecoms company in the world. There is plenty of room for manoeuvre in the emerging markets, unlike western Europe.
- There is still plenty to do in the regulatory arena. Telecoms companies in the UK continue to try to chip away the infrastructure that gives BT a massive competitive advantage over its rivals, particularly in terms of how much it pays for its cabling. In the wider world, similar battles are taking place, including in much of the Caribbean, which until very recently allowed monopoly markets to exist. These monopolies are slowly being eroded.
- 2010 is proving to be the first half-decent post-recession year for the IT industry. 2008 and 2009 were total disasters as overall IT spend plummeted, deal count and size both went down and lawyers found themselves with less work.

- Though a downturn in the economy traditionally hits technology spend, the outsourcing model suits recessionary times, particularly as a way to gain cost-effective access to specialist services. IT outsourcing began in the late 1980s, followed by business process outsourcings (BPOs) that involve handing responsibility to third-party service providers for functions like human resources, finance and accounting. Today, the lines between technology outsourcing (TO) and BPO are blurred. Smart outsourcing – the concept of outsourcing parts of a company, one part at a time, often using different suppliers – is in vogue at present, as is multisourcing (using many different suppliers on shorter term contracts).
- Legal process outsourcing is gaining momentum and many big firms have started sending work to India and South Africa. Even journalism is being outsourced. Trinity Mirror (publisher of the *Daily Mirror*), for example, recently outsourced some subediting.
- The BSkyB/EDS case was a rare example of an outsourcing dispute, which went all the way to court without settlement and was won by the company that paid for the outsourcing. It was one of the largest ever IT/outsourcing cases, and was also notable in the judge's unequivocal support for BSkyB (at one point EDS's expert witness was discredited when it was shown that a dog can gain a degree from his alma mater).

Read our True Pictures on...

Addleshaw Goddard
Allen & Overy
Ashurst
Baker & McKenzie
Barlow Lyde & Gilbert
Bates Wells & Braithwaite
Beachcroft
Berwin Leighton Paisner
Bevan Brittan
Bird & Bird
Bond Pearce
Brabners Chaffe Street
Bristows
Burges Salmon
Charles Russell
Clarke Willmott
Clifford Chance
Clyde & Co
CMS Cameron McKenna
Covington & Burling
DLA Piper UK
DMH Stallard
Dundas & Wilson
DWF
Eversheds
Field Fisher Waterhouse
Foot Anstey Solicitors
Freshfields
Hammonds
Harbottle & Lewis
Herbert Smith
Hogan Lovells
Jones Day
K&L Gates
Latham & Watkins
Linklaters
Manches
Martineau
Mayer Brown
Michelmores
Mills & Reeve
Nabarro
Norton Rose
Olswang
Osborne Clarke
Pannone
Pinsent Masons
Reynolds Porter Chamberlain
Shoosmiths
Simmons & Simmons
SJ Berwin
Slaughter and May
SNR Denton
Speechly Bircham
Stephenson Harwood
Stevens & Bolton
Taylor Wessing
TLT
Travers Smith
Veale Wasbrough Vizards
Walker Morris
Ward Hadaway
Wedlake Bell

- **Keep an open mind:** You might think you love litigation and hate corporate law, or vice versa, when you're studying, but trainees are often spectacularly converted when they start at a firm. Since you're going to have to sample a number of different departments whatever happens, it's best to approach every seat with a positive attitude. You might be surprised.

The True Picture

The True Picture reports on 125 firms in England and Wales, ranging from the international giants to small regional practices. Most handle commercial law, although many also offer private client experience.

The True Picture

Finding the right firm to train with is like finding a relationship: there has to be mutual attraction and you need to be well suited in terms of your interests and style.

Between them, the firms covered in the True Picture have up to 2,600 training contract vacancies to fill in 2011. With luck, one of them could be yours. Even if none of these 125 firms wants you, reading the reports will teach you a great deal about the nature of legal training and the experience of working within a law firm.

How we do our research

Every year we spend many months compiling the True Picture reports on law firms in England and Wales, ranging from the international giants to small regional practices. Our purpose is to get to the heart of what you need to know about a prospective employer – what it can offer you in terms of work and working environment. You'll want to know how many hours a day you'll be chained to your desk, the tasks that will keep you occupied and who you'll be working with. Importantly, you'll want to know about a firm's culture and whether colleagues will turn into party animals or party poopers come Friday night.

Most of our chosen firms handle commercial law, although many also offer private client experience. There are a few general practice firms offering publicly funded advice to their local communities. To take part in the True Picture a firm must provide a complete list of its trainees. After checking the list is complete, we randomly select a sample of individuals for telephone interviews. Our sources are guaranteed anonymity to give them the confidence to speak frankly. The True Picture is not shown to the law firms prior to publication; they see it for the first time when this book is published.

Trainees tell us why they chose their firm and why others might want to. We put on our serious faces and talk about seat allocation, the character and work of different departments, the level of supervision and what happens to people on qualification. And we flirt shamelessly to get the gossip on firm politics, office oddities and after-hours fun. We look for the things trainees agree upon, and if they don't agree we present both sides of the argument.

What kind of firm do you choose?

Your choice of firm will be based on location, size and the practice areas available... then it's a matter of chemistry. Some firms are stuffier, some are more industrious and some are very brand-aware, involving trainees heavily in marketing activities. Some work in modern open-plan offices; others occupy buildings long past their sell-by date. Some focus on international business; others are at the heart of their local business communities. Some concentrate on contentious work, others transactional. The combinations of these variables are endless.

What we found out this year

Coming after many months of redundancies and falling profits, our 2010 research was conducted at a time when law firms were starting to fight back and sound more positive about the future. Corporate activity had picked up somewhat, although most of our second-year trainee contacts remembered their first-year transactional seats as rather a quiet time. We've tended not to dwell on this fact, because it's due to the economy, not the firms in question, and because we know that by the time you, our readers, hopefully begin your training contracts in 2013 and beyond, market conditions might be very different. We've tried to make this a forward-looking guide and we've spent more time than ever speaking to training partners and managing partners about their strategies for the next few years. You'll notice their comments scattered throughout the True Picture features and published in more detail on our website.

Talk of recovery and fighting back should not disguise the fact that the UK economy is not out of the woods. The demise of Halliwells, a well-established national firm, in the summer of 2010 is proof of that. The aftershocks of the crisis of 2008 will be with us for a while yet. Budget cuts made by the coalition government will have profound effects on many law firms.

This year a number of firms announced their qualification job offers extremely late making it difficult for those who needed to look elsewhere for employment. We also noted reluctance on the part of many trainees to take overseas secondments: they wanted their face to be seen in their home office. Pre-recession, usually just over 80% of qualifiers stayed with the law firms that trained them, but in 2009 total retention at those firms we covered dropped to 74% – the worst for years. The class of 2010 fared marginally better, as 76% of those at our True Picture firms were retained, but that's still not a return to pre-credit crunch levels and no one can say what will happen to the market in the future.

If you intend to use retention rates as a determining factor in your choice of firm, do be wary of the statistics being bandied around. Law firms make their own rules on how to calculate retention rates – you may not be getting a full picture from them. We collect our own statistics and include them in each law firm feature. We have collated statistics since 2000 and publish them on our website.

A word on law firm mergers or closures. Mergers are a regular occurrence in the profession these days and we are presently seeing a spate of transatlantic ones. There have also been a few notable domestic mergers in the mid market. When firms merge, trainees' contracts are honoured, though of course it does mean that new recruits find themselves in a different firm to the one they signed up to. Closures are rarer, but as we've seen, they do happen and trainees can find themselves out on their ear. Those at Halliwells were in the main fortunate as several other firms came to the rescue when their employer went into administration.

It's not all bad news and there have been many success stories this year. One man's misfortune is another man's gold rush, and while real estate, corporate and finance-focused firms have continued to feel the pinch, insolvency lawyers and litigators remain busy and areas such as energy, life sciences and regulatory law are quite healthy.

What we hear every year

- Some seats like employment are more popular than others and there are no guarantees of getting a specific seat.
- Levels of responsibility vary between departments. In property you might have your own small files. In corporate you will generally work in a very junior capacity as part of a team.
- The experience in litigation depends entirely on the type of cases your firm handles; usually a trainee's responsibility is inversely proportionate to the value and complexity of a case.
- In times of plenty, corporate and finance seats mean long hours, commonly climaxing in all-nighters. The size and complexity of a deal will determine your role, but corporate and finance usually require the most teamwork.
- Most firms offer four six-month seats; some offer six four-month seats and others operate their own unique systems. Trainees switch departments and supervisors for each seat. Many share a room and work with a partner or senior assistant; others sit open-plan, either with the rest of the team or with other trainees. Occasionally trainees have their own room.
- All firms conduct appraisals: a minimum of one at the conclusion of each seat, and usually halfway through as well.
- Client secondments help you learn to understand clients' needs. They can be the highlight of a training contract.
- The Solicitors Regulation Authority requires all trainees to gain experience of both contentious and non-contentious work. Additionally, most firms have certain seats they require or prefer trainees to try. Some firms are very prescriptive, others flexible. Remember, a training contract is a time to explore legal practice to see what you're best at and most enjoy. You may surprise yourself.

And finally...

Use the True Picture to help you decide which firms to target. No matter how hard or easy securing a training contract is for you, you'll want to end up with the right one.

If when reading the True Picture you come across an unfamiliar term, turn to page 136 for our Jargonbuster.

Jargonbuster

- ABS – Alternative Business Structures: newly permitted arrangements for law firms, which allow non-lawyers to have a financial stake in the business.
- Agency work – making a court appearance for another firm that can't get to court.
- AIM – a 'junior' stock market run by the London Stock Exchange, which allows smaller companies to float stock within a more flexible system.
- Arbitration – a type of dispute resolution where the parties agree to abide by the decision of one or more arbitrators.
- Associate – a term used to denote solicitors who are not at partner level but are more senior than an assistant solicitor.
- Bench – the judge or judges in a courtroom.
- Best friends relationship – a situation where two firms have no organisational of financial ties, but use each other as the first port of call when referring work.
- Bibling – putting together sets of all the relevant documents for a transaction.
- Billing target/chargeable hours target – the number of hours lawyers are required to record working for a client; time is usually recorded in six-minute chunks; trainees do not usually have billing targets.
- Boutique – a firm which works primarily in one area of law.
- Brief – the instructing documents given to a barrister when they are instructed by a solicitor.
- Bundling – compiling bundles of documents for a court case.
- The City – the commercial and financial centre of London; also known as the Square Mile; not to be confused with the City of London Corporation, which is the public authority responsible for governing the City.
- CMC – case management conference.
- Coco – company-commercial department/work.
- Conditional fee arrangements – also called 'no win no fee'; an arrangement whereby a solicitor acting in a claim agrees only to be paid a fee if he wins the case.
- Contentious matters – legal disputes between parties.
- Conveyancing – the transfer of the ownership of property from one person to another.
- Counsel – a barrister.
- CSR – Corporate Social Responsibility; the practice of companies taking responsibility for the impact of their activities on society; in reality 'CSR committees' at firms will run projects where lawyers paint schools, plant trees and clean playgrounds.
- Data room duty – used to involve supervising visitors to rooms full of important documents, helping them find things and making sure they don't steal them. With electronic data rooms the job becomes more of a desktop exercise.
- Disclosure – making relevant documentation available to the other parties in a dispute.
- Dispute resolution – litigation, mediation, arbitration, etc.
- Document management – dealing with the more administrative side of deal documentation.
- Due diligence – the thorough investigation of a target company in a deal.
- Equity partner – a partner who receives a contractually agreed share of the firm's annual profits. A part owner of the firm. The other type of partner is a salaried partner.
- Fee earner – a lawyer whose time is paid for by a firm's clients.
- FTSE 100 (pronounced 'footsie') – an index of the 100 most valuable companies listed on the London Stock Exchange.
- Grunt work – administrative (and boring) yet essential tasks including photocopying, bundling, bibling, paginating, scheduling documents, data room duties and proof-reading or checking that documents are intact.
- High net worth individuals – rich people.
- Infant approval – court authorisation for a settlement involving a minor.
- In-house lawyer – a solicitor or barrister who is employed by a company or public body rather than a law firm or barristers' chambers.
- Injunction – a court order requiring a party to do, or to refrain from doing, certain acts.
- IPO – the Initial Public Offering of shares in a company to the public on a stock market; also known as a flotation.
- Junior Lawyers' Division – a sub-group within the Law Society set up in 2008 to represent student members of the Law Society, trainees and lawyers up to five years' PQE.
- Law Society – the official representative body of solicitors in England and Wales.
- Legal Aid – a government-funded system which pays for legal representation in criminal and some civil cases for individuals who would otherwise be unable to afford it.
- Legal Disciplinary Partnership (LDP) – a business structure whereby a law firm can take on non-lawyers as equity holders. Up to 25% of a partnership can be non-lawyers.
- Legal Services Act – the 2007 Act of Parliament aimed at liberalising and deregulating the legal market.
- Limited Liability Partnership (LLP) – a way of structuring a professional partnership such that no partner

is liable to any of the firm's creditors above and beyond a certain sum.

- Lockstep – the practice of increasing solicitors salaries based purely on seniority.
- M&A – mergers and acquisitions; the buying, selling and combining of companies; often the main focus of firm's corporate teams.
- Magic circle – the name given to five of the leading London-based law firms; it is generally held to consist of Allen & Overy, Clifford Chance, Freshfields Bruckhaus Deringer, Linklaters and Slaughter and May.
- Managing partner – the main boss of a law firm, who leads the partnership and/or management committee in running the business and devising its strategy.
- Master (in the High Court) – a judge in the High Court ranking lower than a High Court judge, chiefly responsible for case management. They are called 'Master' regardless of whether they are male or female.
- Mediation – a type of dispute resolution where a dispute is resolved with the help of a neutral third party.
- Moot – a mock trial used to train or test advocacy skills.
- Nearshoring – the outsourcing of work to another organisation, usually in a part of the UK where overheads and salary costs are lower.
- Niche practice area – a practice that is specialised and not in a mainstream area.
- Notary public – a person who is authorised to authenticate and certify estates, deeds, powers of attorney and other documents, especially for use abroad; the majorities of notaries are also solicitors.
- NQ – a newly qualified solicitor.
- (Offshore) outsourcing – hiring in an external organisation (overseas) to perform part of a company's activities.
- Paralegal – a non-qualified lawyer, often with some legal training, who assists qualified lawyers on legal matters.
- PLUS – a stock exchange in London founded in 2005, which lists small and mid-sized companies especially from the retail industry.
- Power of attorney – the legal authority to act on someone else's behalf.
- PQE – post-qualification experience.
- Pro bono – from the Latin 'pro bono publico', meaning 'for the public good'; legal work done without payment as a public service.
- Profits per equity partner (PEP) – the annual profits of a law firm divided by the total number of equity partners in the firm; this statistic is often used to indicate the financial health of a firm, but it can easily be manipulated by altering the number of equity partners.
- PSC – a compulsory course taken during the training contract.
- Reverse commute – living in a city, working on its outskirts (or even further away) and commuting that distance every day.
- Rights of audience – the right of a lawyer (either a solicitor or barrister) to appear and conduct proceedings in court.
- Salaried partner – a partner who receives a salary but has no contractual claim on the firm's profits; the other type of partner is an equity partner.
- Seat – a spell working in a department, usually four or six months.
- Secondment – the practice of 'lending' trainees and qualified solicitors to a firm's client to work in their in-house legal department for a certain period.
- Silo-ing – encouraging people to work in a specific field rather than being generalists; teams working very independently of others within a firm.
- Silver circle – a group of elite English law firms, generally considered as falling just outside the magic circle.
- SRA – Solicitors Regulation Authority.
- Swiss Verein – a business structure consisting of a number of independent offices, each of which is independently liable for its own obligations.
- Tesco Law – a nickname for the anticipated effect of the Legal Services Act.
- Tort – a breach of duty owed to someone else (a 'civil wrong') which leads to injury to a person or property.
- Training contract – a two-year period of working in legal practice in which someone who has completed their LPC is trained by an accredited organisation to become a qualified solicitor.
- Training partner – the partner who oversees the training scheme.
- Trainee partner – a trainee who acts like a partner.
- Vacation scheme – a placement with a law firm designed to familiarise a prospective trainee with a firm and vice versa; sometimes called 'vac schemes' or 'summer placements', they are usually held during the summer or at Easter and can last anywhere between one and four weeks.
- Verification – the aspect of a deal in which lawyers ensure stated information is accurate.

Firms by size in the UK

	Firm	London	S & Thames Valley	South West	Midlands	East	Yorkshire & NE	North West	Wales	Overseas	Trainees	Pages: True picture	Pages: A-Z solicitors
1	Government Legal Service	●						●			27	294	594
2	Eversheds	●			●	●	●	●	●	●	122	263	584
3	DLA Piper	●			●		●	●		●	170	249	580
4	Pinsent Masons	●		●	●		●	●		●	122	417	638
5	Clifford Chance	●								●	224	216	566
6	Linklaters	●								●	240	357	615
7	Herbert Smith	●								●	185	308	599
8	Allen & Overy	●								●	230	145	542
9	Freshfields Bruckhaus Deringer	●								●	197	289	592
10	Beachcroft	●	●	●	●		●	●	●	●	59	164	548
11	Addleshaw Goddard	●					●	●			83	141	541
12	Hogan Lovells	●								●	147	317	603
13	Hammonds	●			●		●	●		●	53	297	595
14	Berwin Leighton Paisner	●								●	79	167	550
15	Slaughter and May	●								●	170	446	651
16	Norton Rose	●								●	91	396	630
17	CMS Cameron McKenna	●		●						●	121	223	568
18	Hill Dickinson	●					●	●		●	40	313	602
19	Ashurst	●								●	108	151	544
20	Mills & Reeve	●			●	●	●	●			43	384	626
21=	Clyde & Co	●	●							●	50	219	567
21=	HBJ Gateley Wareing	●			●					●	29	302	597
23	Irwin Mitchell	●			●		●	●		●	76	330	606
24	DWF	●					●	●			38	257	582
25	SJ Berwin	●								●	73	441	649
26	Nabarro	●					●			●	58	392	629
27	Kennedys	●	●	●	●	●	●	●		●	32	339	609
28	McGrigors	●						●		●	21	379	623
29	SNR Denton	●	●							●	67	451	652
30	Shoosmiths	●	●		●			●			26	430	646
31	Bond Pearce	●	●	●							30	182	555
32	Simmons & Simmons	●								●	80	436	648
33	Cobbetts	●			●		●	●		●	31	227	569
34	Olswang	●	●							●	36	399	631
35	Field Fisher Waterhouse	●						●		●	19	270	586
36	Burges Salmon			●							43	201	561
37	Dundas & Wilson	●									20	255	581
38	Baker & McKenzie	●								●	79	155	545
39	Osborne Clarke	●	●	●						●	33	404	634
40	Charles Russell	●	●	●		●				●	23	207	563
41	Trowers & Hamlins	●		●				●		●	40	481	662
42	Barlow Lyde & Gilbert	●	●					●		●	30	159	546

Note: Firms are listed in order of size as measured by UK partner and solicitor figures provided to Chambers and Partners.

Firms by size in the UK

	Firm	London	S & Thames Valley	South West	Midlands	East	Yorkshire & NE	North West	Wales	Overseas	Trainees	Pages: True picture	Pages: A-Z solicitors
43	Mayer Brown	●								●	52	373	621
44	Dickinson Dees	●					●			●	26	245	579
45	Taylor Wessing	●				●				●	43	465	656
46	TLT Solicitors	●		●						●	26	471	659
47	Speechly Bircham	●								●	22	455	653
48	Bird & Bird	●								●	28	179	554
49	Reynolds Porter Chamberlain	●								●	30	425	642
50	Reed Smith	●								●	50	420	641
51	White & Case	●								●	62	507	671
52	Stephenson Harwood	●								●	29	459	654
53	Macfarlanes	●									60	360	616
54	Mishcon de Reya	●								●	26	387	627
55	Pannone	●						●			31	407	635
56	Travers Smith	●								●	48	475	660
57=	Browne Jacobson	●			●						16	197	560
57=	Clarke Willmott	●	●	●	●			●			19	210	564
59	Bevan Brittan	●		●	●						20	170	551
60	Farrer & Co	●									20	267	585
61	Lawrence Graham	●								●	23	349	612
62=	Walker Morris						●				20	488	665
62=	Withers	●								●	32	514	675
64	Brabners Chaffe Street							●			21	190	558
65	Freeth Cartwright	●			●			●			16	286	591
66	Holman Fenwick Willan	●								●	31	321	n/a
67	Michelmores	●		●							14	382	625
68	Jones Day	●								●	37	333	607
69	Ward Hadaway						●	●			18	491	666
70	Martineau	●			●						18	367	619
71	Latham & Watkins	●								●	28	346	611
72	Capsticks	●			●						11	204	562
73	Ince & Co	●								●	29	327	605
74	Penningtons Solicitors	●	●								18	412	637
75=	Foot Anstey			●							10	278	589
75=	K&L Gates	●								●	8	336	608
75=	Veale Wasbrough Vizards	●		●							16	484	663
78=	Lewis Silkin	●	●								12	354	614
78=	Manches	●	●								20	364	618
80	Bircham Dyson Bell	●									14	175	553
81	Watson, Farley & Williams	●								●	25	497	668
82	DMH Stallard	●	●								18	253	n/a
83	Dewey & LeBoeuf	●								●	20	242	578
84	Kingsley Napley	●									10	342	n/a

Notes: Firms are listed in order of size as measured by UK partner and solicitor figures provided to Chambers and Partners.

Firms by size in the UK

Firm	London	S & Thames Valley	South West	Midlands	East	Yorkshire & NE	North West	Wales	Overseas	Trainees	Pages: True picture	Pages: A-Z solicitors
85 Cripps Harries Hall	●	●								16	234	573
86 Forbes						●	●			16	281	590
87 Sidley Austin	●								●	17	433	647
88= Stevens & Bolton		●								8	462	655
88= Winckworth Sherwood	●	●			●					8	512	674
90= Bristows	●									16	193	559
90= Howes Percival		●		●	●					18	324	604
90= Wedlake Bell	●									6	500	669
93 Gordons						●				12	292	593
94 Weil, Gotshal & Manges	●								●	26	502	670
95 Dechert	●								●	17	239	577
96= Bates Wells & Braithwaite	●									8	162	547
96= Harbottle & Lewis	●									9	300	596
98 Skadden	●								●	13	444	650
99 Lester Aldridge	●	●								11	352	613
100= Coffin Mew		●								13	230	570
100= Finers Stephens Innocent	●									7	273	587
102 Covington & Burling	●								●	14	232	572
103 Higgs & Sons				●						8	311	601
104= Cleary Gottlieb Steen & Hamilton	●								●	19	213	565
104= Kirkland & Ellis	●								●	12	344	610
106= Boodle Hatfield	●	●								12	186	556
106= Fisher Meredith	●									14	276	n/a
108 Henmans		●								6	306/	598
109 Muckle						●				8	390	628
110 Ford & Warren						●				8	284	n/a
111 Trethowans		●	●							8	478	661
112 Paul Hastings	●								●	11	410	636
113 McDermott Will & Emery	●								●	5	376	622
114 Dawsons	●									9	236	576
115 Edwards Angell Palmer & Dodge	●								●	16	260	583
116 Orrick Herrington & Sutcliffe	●								●	10	402	633
117 Bingham McCutchen	●								●	4	173	552
118 Arnold & Porter	●								●	2	148	543
119= BP Collins		●								6	188	557
119= Sheridans	●									2	428	645
121 Maxwell Winward	●									5	370	620
122 Thomas Cooper	●								●	8	468	657
123 Wiggin	●		●							3	510	672
124 Warner Goodman		●								3	494	667
125 Vinson & Elkins	●								●	8	486	664

Note: Firms are listed in order of size as measured by UK partner and solicitor figures provided to Chambers and Partners.

Addleshaw Goddard LLP

The facts

Location: London, Manchester, Leeds

Number of UK partners/solicitors: 159/515

Total number of trainees: 83

Seats: 4x6 months

Alternative seats: Secondments

Extras: Pro bono – Springfield and University of Manchester Legal Advice Centres, Tiger11; language training

On chambersstudent.co.uk
- How to get into AG
- Team building in Romania
- More CSR initiatives
- AG's swish flagship office

This three-office commercial firm is one of the most successful 'national' firms and a contender in the City.

Addle-sure

Amid the chaos of campaign blunders, Clegg-mania and coalitions during the 2010 general election, one story in particular caught our eye: that of Jonathan Reynolds, who at 29 was one of the youngest MPs to be elected, easily securing the Labour seat of Stalybridge and Hyde, near Manchester. Unfortunately for Reynolds, his new political commitments meant giving up his traineeship at the Manchester office of Addleshaw Goddard. Far be it for us to speculate about the relative merits of these career trajectories, but what emerges from this story is evidence of AG's avowed commitment to investing in individuals, and those individuals' own sense of commitment. The trainees we spoke to could hardly have been a more mixed bunch, counting those with previous careers, those with a couple of gap years under their belt, those with families, and those from all sorts of universities and backgrounds among their cornucopian number. Their confidence is core to the spirit of the firm and a central component of 'the AG way'. It drives ambitions, in terms of both expansion and specialisation. The firm's profits may have dipped slightly in the 2009/10 financial year, but not significantly more or less than the competition, and with no deferrals to its graduate recruitment drive plus commercial litigation partner Monica Burch (herself originally a trainee at the firm) newly elected as chairman, Addleshaws appears to be fizzing with energy and dynamism.

Corporate work is where the firm really stakes its claim to dominance. It has always been a force to be reckoned with in the North, while London has gradually caught up in its operations to secure a place at the top of the mid-market rankings tree. Firm of choice in Leeds among the bigger building societies, Addleshaws has acted on behalf of the Dunfermline, Skipton and West Bromwich societies over the past year, advising the latter in a groundbreaking transaction dealing with the capital exchange of the society's subordinated debt of £182.5m. In fact, few major Yorkshire corporate transactions have slipped its reach in 2010, whether in M&A or private equity.

Meanwhile, in Manchester, the team receives its instructions from almost all the FTSE 350 located in the North West, while also attracting clients from further afield, such as Rolls-Royce and Capita Group. In London, the mid-market share continues to grow, with the office now flirting increasingly with the FTSE 100, counting HSBC, Sainsbury's and Diageo among its clients. One recently qualified solicitor told us that this was entirely consistent with the strategy when he first arrived, which was "*to win more FTSE 100 clients, develop talent within the business, put an emphasis on development and keep employees happy.*"

No one knows the northern real estate scene quite like Addleshaws, which has top-band *Chambers UK* rankings for both its Manchester and Leeds offices. Evidence of the high regard in which they are held can be seen in Blackpool Borough Council's selection of the firm to advise on its purchase of Blackpool Tower and a number of other local attractions, including Louis Tussaud's Waxworks and the Winter Gardens. The firm's London office is a dynamo in the construction world for its

Chambers UK rankings

Agriculture & Rural Affairs	Insurance
Banking & Finance	Intellectual Property
Banking Litigation	Life Sciences
Capital Markets	Local Government
Charities	Outsourcing
Competition/European Law	Partnership
Construction	Pensions
Consumer Finance	Planning
Corporate/M&A	Private Client
Defamation/Reputation Management	Private Equity
	Product Liability
Dispute Resolution	Projects
Education	Public Procurement
Employee Share Schemes	Real Estate
Employment	Real Estate Finance
Environment	Real Estate Litigation
Financial Services	Restructuring/Insolvency
Fraud	Retail
Health & Safety	Social Housing
Healthcare	Sports Law
Information Technology	Tax

education and healthcare sector work, and has also earned a considerable reputation in the more niche area of social housing finance, becoming *"a go-to law firm for a majority of funders."*

Bread(th) and butter

Talking of niche areas, one of the impressions emerging from our conversations with trainees was that they have a real opportunity to express their entrepreneurial side, especially if they attract the attention of smaller departments by taking less popular seats. In principle, the four-seat scheme can expose trainees to all four of the firm's main areas: contentious and commercial; corporate; finance and projects; and real estate. As such, new recruits have breadth of training but there is also scope for them to carve a niche early on. We spoke to a number of trainees who had been asked to repeat seats, sometimes in slightly more esoteric sub-practice areas. This gives anyone suffering from surface-scratching syndrome a chance to get rid of the itch. Graduate recruitment partner Geraint Harries was keen to emphasise this dual breadth-and-depth nature of the contract: *"Making your mark, yes, specialising too early, no. We still want the breadth of training. We will be supportive of trainees' interests, and there is a need to be flexible. There are times when you're working on a particular transaction, for example, when a trainee will be asked to stay on. We have the full range of niche seats, contentious seats and transactional seats, but we are also still primarily a transactional practice, with a focus on corporate, banking, and real estate."*

The independently minded Addleshaws trainees are quick to identify which seats suit them best and their experiences vary accordingly. A corporate seat for one trainee meant *"going back to what I understand more... working on private equity deals for private equity management houses."* Their work involved plenty of due diligence, document administration and ancillary assistance, but also a chance to look after *"all the client confidentiality agreements."* But if the *"fast-paced ride"* that is the corporate rollercoaster is one trainee's adrenaline, its *"unpredictability"* in both hours and workload can be another's vertigo. To give you some idea of just how busy it can get, March 2010 saw the corporate team up north advise on £680m worth of deals, including the £44.8m sale of The Guardian Media Group's regional business (incorporating the *Manchester Evening News*) to Trinity Mirror. Addleshaws' client base has allowed it to cope reasonably well with the recession, and if the transactional world does quieten at times, there are always partnership disputes to keep people busy, requiring empathy as well as professionalism. *"It was a baptism of fire – the clients would often burst into tears!"* recalled one source.

Even in such a transaction-minded firm, the contentious lawyers provide well-greased elbows. Contentious and commercial was actually last year's biggest billing division, bringing in £62.5m in revenue, and it was the only one to grow its income. Litigation at Addleshaws for the most part means commercial or construction cases, and as one trainee put it: *"You'll get the good, the bad and the ugly."* Because the work usually involves large disputes, you should expect a broad mix of tasks, from document bundling (*"it has to be done and is a good way for a trainee to cut their teeth on work that's going to be used by counsel!"*) to meeting with clients and going to court. Those who already had themselves marked down as litigators said that they often preferred the *"start-to-finish satisfaction"* that came with working on smaller cases, *"when you could tangibly see your contribution."* Said one: *"I love litigation; you just don't mind when it's the court giving you deadlines."* Fortunately, if there's a big case requiring long hours, *"you work late as a team, go out for team drinks and have team lunches. And after court, if things go our way, it's down the pub."*

It's horses for courses again when it comes to the other divisions – real estate, and finance and projects – but feedback was consistent on the degree of crossover between the two. Construction, for example, was described as *"quite a niche department, linked to projects,"* while a restructuring seat can find a trainee doing mostly property-related work. In projects, the work ranges from advising the Ministry of Defence, to the last government's pet project Building Schools for the Future and "*real bread-and-butter work in relation to the health sector.*" For the really diligent, hard work pays off: "*Once you put the effort in they will give you better opportunities.*" That said, it was also good to hear that face time is really farce time at Addleshaws. One source assured us that "*part of the firm's approach is that there's not a lot to be gained from just sitting around.*"

A-rootin' and a-TOOTin'

New trainees go on a pre-contract trip to Romania. It is an undisputed highlight of the entire two years, and to call it an icebreaker would be an understatement – it's more like a dam-buster. The new intake spends one week building houses and friendships in the city that spawned the Cheeky Girls, and the combination of holiday and humanitarianism has proved a success year after year. "*Getting to know everyone before you start makes you feel calmer and less nervous,*" said one source. Others described their impressions of Romania as "*totally unexpected,*" "*really vibrant*" and "*stunning.*" So what happens upon return, when the dust settles and the suits are donned? Our sources felt that the team building had been so effective that they had good friends in all three offices, despite the distance. These relationships are mostly limited to online interaction and annual events, but a particular highlight is the annual trainee conference. Whether it's "*talks from people within the firm on Addleshaws' initiatives,*" or "*more light-hearted things like quizzes and karaoke,*" the event is designed to remind of the ties that bind.

'Three Offices One Team' (TOOT) may be one of the firm's chief slogans, but it hasn't prevented some north-south differences from emerging, and it is inevitable that attitudes and atmosphere will vary slightly from office to office. London trainees do attract a small degree of jealousy over their new "*wow-factor*" office with its eco-friendly mod-cons. For example, "*lighting which is sensitive to movement*" was described by a northern trainee as "*very flashy*" and "*super hi-tech, so ours now seems a bit old by comparison.*" One Manchester trainee was fiercely loyal abut their workplace: "*I think we're quite lucky, the offices haven't dated at all – the only thing we envy is the canteen.*" The Leeds staff, meanwhile, occupy an entire building, which allows the firm to host events at its leisure, such as barbecues on the patio in the summer. Otherwise, organised social events tend to be department based, and come vac scheme time, Leeds trainees throw themselves into the programme's social aspect. The Shed bar is a particularly popular location year round.

Letting your hair down is an important part of the Manchester ethos: fortunately for them, staff have a favourite bar directly beneath the office. Barbirolli's ("*quite swanky*") is the designated location for monthly firm drinks. For a more relaxed scene, "*trainees have got into the habit of going to the 'little old man's pubs'*" in the vicinity, and being located in the centre of town makes the distance from pub to club not such a stretch. But if a night on the tiles has left you feeling a little sore, never fear: "*There's a physiotherapist that comes in once or twice a month!*" London, meanwhile, sounds the quietest of the three: "*We could do with more social stuff,*" moaned one interviewee, "*but it's a sign of the times.*" They have, however, adopted the office-wide drinks idea on the final Thursday of the month, and for want of other firm-organised events, trainees are still able to take the initiative. "*Even now there's a big group of us who go out,*" revealed a fourth-seat London recruit.

The AG Way

Post credit crunch, Addleshaws showed real determination to retain talent and not defer its new intake of trainees. Instead of looking at letting established staff go, it shuffled people between locations. "*The firm had to come up with innovative ways of retaining talent, such as client secondments,*" said one source, going on to say that there was a considerably more optimistic outlook for the next couple of years. "*The market will be better, and for a student, Addleshaws will offer everything it has in the past, with even more opportunities, such as the secondments programme and the likelihood that we'll have grown.*" Key to the firm's overall strategy is the idea of mobility. This means not just movement between the three offices (TOOT, remember?), but also a degree of flexibility and fluidity when it comes to inter-departmental work.

There are a few sweeping generalisations that can be made about this firm's trainees. They'll be energetic and enterprising without being the boisterous bully-boys of their chosen field. They will be bright and determined to succeed, generally having become used to impressive academic achievement. And they'll be personable ("*they're looking for 'people' people*") and proactive ("*the powers that be are always alive to new ideas*"). If this is what a 'From Me to You' mindset (and yes, that's another AG phrase) is all about, it was transmitted well From Them to Us.

And finally...

In 2010, a very healthy 40 of the firm's 46 qualifiers were able to take NQ jobs across the firm's four core practice lines.

Allen & Overy LLP

The facts

Location: London

Number of UK partners/solicitors: 184/564

Total number of trainees: 230

Seats: 3 or 6 months long

Alternative seats: Overseas seats, secondments

Extras: Pro bono – LawWorks, Bar Pro Bono Unit, Cambridge House legal advice centre, The Connection at St-Martin-in-the-Fields; language training

On chambersstudent.co.uk
- How to get into A&O
- The history of Allen & Overy
- A&Overseas

Landing a training contract at ultra-elite A&O will make Mum and Dad enormously proud, but how do you know if this international giant of finance sector wizardry is right for you?

Starting Overy

If you were one of those schoolchildren who dreamt about one day sitting behind your very own mahogany desk at a magic circle firm, the name Allen & Overy probably already sends shivers down your spine. With offices in 26 countries, and global revenue of more than £1bn in 2009/10, there's more than a little to get excited about. Even in the cooler economic climate, the firm has won roles on some of the biggest deals around, such as the £11.3bn shotgun acquisition of HBOS by Lloyds. It's one of the few firms in the world that has got away with a recruiting slogan like 'Start at the top' without being accused of getting ideas above its station.

The firm has grown from modest beginnings in six rooms behind the Bank of England to the pinnacle of legal prominence (to read more about its rise and rise to the top, see our website). Success in the UK wasn't enough and A&O first went global in the late 1970s, opening for business in Dubai and not looking back. Rather than seeking foreign mergers, the firm chose to expand under its own steam, developing a network of offices in Europe, Asia, the Middle East and the Americas. The decision to grow organically was a calculated one, and in February 2010, the firm moved into its fifth continent: Australasia.

A&O is unquestionably at the head of the class in all things finance. If you don't believe us, just ask our colleagues at *Chambers Global* who have ranked it in the highest tier year after year. The firm recently advised the arrangers of a $2.5bn bond for the government of Dubai, and was instructed by RBS in a $1.4bn securitisation of a portfolio of Airbus aircraft loans. A&O's international capital markets (ICM) division packs just as mighty a punch. Here, lawyers focus on large-scale bond and equity-linked offerings, as well as complex structured finance products. This jargon doesn't need to make sense to you yet, but if your idea of the practice of law is more *Ally McBeal* than *Wall Street*, best to look elsewhere.

In recent years A&O has invested heavily in an M&A practice to complement its finance expertise. Although A&O's corporate team's successes still lag slightly behind the likes of Freshfields' and Linklaters', the group runs some impressive deals, recently advising the world's largest ore producer, Vale SA, on the $4.9bn sale of its aluminium assets to Norsk Hydro. Together, finance, ICM and corporate account for three-quarters of the firm in London, but that proportion could be shifting. While environment, employment, restructuring, banking litigation and international arbitration are not the obvious practice areas that come to mind when one thinks of A&O, all are top-ranked in *Chambers UK*. Litigation is also on the rise: the group recently represented defence contractor BAE in its SFO investigation relating to the sale of fighter jets to Saudi Arabia.

A&O had to undergo a wide-scale restructuring in the face of the recession. There was a 9% reduction in global headcount, including approximately 47 partners. It was a

Chambers UK rankings

Administrative & Public Law	Insurance
Asset Finance	Intellectual Property
Banking & Finance	Investment Funds
Banking Litigation	Life Sciences
Capital Markets	Outsourcing
Commodities	Partnership
Competition/European Law	Pensions
Construction	Private Client
Corporate/M&A	Private Equity
Dispute Resolution	Projects
Employee Share Schemes	Public International Law
Employment	Public Procurement
Energy & Natural Resources	Real Estate
Environment	Real Estate Finance
Financial Services	Real Estate Litigation
Fraud	Restructuring/Insolvency
Information Technology	Tax
	Telecommunications
	Transport

painful and expensive overhaul, but one that the firm saw as ultimately necessary to preserve profitability. A&O comes out of the recession a leaner, meaner and more diversified machine.

Hard core

As you may have already guessed, banking, corporate and ICM are A&O's "*core practice areas*" and trainees must spend at least 12 months of their contract in at least two of those areas. Deal-loving trainees may opt out of a contentious seat altogether through a litigation course and 40 hours of practical experience at the Battersea Legal Advice Centre. Our sources advised that interested candidates recognise that "*there's room to do litigation at A&O, but this is a banking and corporate firm, and if you don't want to do banking and corporate maybe you should choose somewhere else.*"

A&O's training normally starts with a six-month seat in one of the core practice areas. About three months in, the firm hosts a seat-planning evening – kind of like a careers fair – in which trainees wander the tables picking up brochures and meeting departments' representatives. "*It's really good because they have partners and associates who explain what they do and answer your questions.*" Trainees then indicate their preferences to HR, including one "*priority seat,*" which they are guaranteed to do at some point during their contract.

In a general banking seat, one trainee had seen "*a variety of work including things like real estate finance, trade finance, emerging markets matters and general corporate lending.*" Another finance seat trainee spoke of plenty of chances to hone their drafting skills, while a third was pleased that their expectation of enjoying technical finance work was met. Of the "*fast-paced and deal-oriented*" atmosphere of the corporate department, trainees said: "*At the time it's stressful but it keeps you going.*" While "*there are no limitations on the amount of client contact you can have as a trainee,*" you do need to take the initiative as "*some partners are really good at inviting you straight away, and other times you have to suggest it.*" The work is deeply multi-jurisdictional – "*when you have to get up early to deal with comments from Asia, you realise how international it is.*" Needless to say, "*there is a lot interaction between the offices.*"

A seat in ICM involves working on the complicated types of product you may have read about in the news: derivates and structured finance. "*A lot of our clients were more hesitant about the stretching-the-boundary deals after Lehman collapsed,*" and of course these types of deals were getting a bashing in the press, but business was picking up at the time of our interviews. Said one source: "*Everyone who had Lehman as a counterparty required advice pretty quickly!*" The team also represents large investment banks on various equity-swap transactions. It's "*kind of bespoke*" work that requires real talent in order to "*form a decent structure in your mind and work out how everything fits together.*" Once trainees get the hang of it, they can pick up responsibility quite quickly. "*Last week I closed a deal because a senior associate and a partner were away,*" said a source. Despite peaks and troughs, it's a tough schedule in these departments and "*people should have no illusions; this is a very demanding place.*" One of the hardest things is "*getting used to your plans being cancelled. But that becomes part and parcel.*" We hear the firm is good about being flexible around fixed events like pre-booked tickets.

Finding your niche

Away from the mighty finance core, departments like competition, employment, regulatory and restructuring have become so popular among trainees that the perception is often that "*you have to put them in as a priority if you want to do them at all.*" Competition "*is a completely different shift from finance*" because of its "*analytical and considered approach.*" In this relatively small team, trainees receive a range of work on mergers, cartels and some litigation for banking sector and IT/telecommunications clients. The seat involves research galore as trainees "*have to run analysis to see if there would be problems globally should a merger occur.*" Their schedules are more predictable than in corporate or banking seats because deadlines are usually set in advance. That said, "*our work is closely tied with corporate, so if their deal is going up and down it can have a ripple effect.*" Restructuring is another "*problem-solving*" seat where trainees research technical legal questions and write memos during insolvency proceedings. This was a particularly demanding seat at the time of our interviews and sources were putting in long hours, "*but that's not always the firm's fault… as a trainee you want to absorb as much as you can.*"

Generally, trainees will sit with associates, and sometimes partners. Across all departments we got a sense of reverence for A&O's top brass. "*They're intimidating in that they know so much more than you do.*" But "*once you break down that initial fear of feeling you can't talk to them,*" we hear "*they're very approachable*" and "*definitely make you laugh once in a while.*" Naturally, they "*still expect quite a lot of you*" and "*will let you know gently*" if your work product isn't up to snuff.

The majority of trainees spend their final seat on an international or client secondment: see our website for a list of likely destinations. Who gets to go where is based on "*demand and your previous performance reviews.*" Our sources found the level of work abroad was higher, "*largely because there are fewer people in the office so you effectively have to step up a couple of notches.*" They also learned that other nations "*do business in a very different way.*" A trainee in the Middle East said: "*Everything is done face to face rather than by e-mail all the time. And clients do things at their own pace, so generally things tend to take longer.*" Across the globe, familiar IT and support systems and branded stationery soften the cultural differences. The firm provides luxury accommodation and "*an uplift in your salary*" to cover increased living costs. It also provides language classes, "*which is great despite the fact that my teacher despairs of me,*" joked a trainee. Client secondments are less in demand but equally rewarding: "*They needed someone to go and my supervisor suggested it to me. As it happened it was amazing!*" confirmed one source. Client secondments – often with banks – continue to be easily available to NQs: useful for those who want to work in-house one day.

Making the cut

A&O has a reputation for being "*the friendly magic circle firm.*" It's an idea that goes back years, and certainly the current trainees told us countless times that it's a place with "*a real emphasis on training,*" where "*the people are genuine and down to earth.*" We thought this quote was quite telling: "*There is an A&O type. Very sharp but not arrogant; very modestly on the ball. Really friendly and approachable, but also pretty cynical. We're all well aware of the fact that we're corporate lawyers! There are a lot of people who really do want to do this forever and are intent on partnership.*"

"*Some departments are more sociable than others,*" but there is definitely the opportunity for carousing if that's your thing. "*We have football teams, a badminton ladder, netball; there's an orchestra and a choir. They put on a production of The Magic Flute.*" Charitable events have included quizzes, a Three Peaks Challenge and "*a charity Wii Olympics,*" which saw lawyers from all departments duking it out on Mariokart. The firm's slick Foster-designed home in Spitalfields is so self-contained that trainees need not look beyond the office for socialising (though we would recommend it). A&O staff have access to all manner of services in the confines of their flashy building. There is a health practice, a canteen, a roof terrace (good for barbecues), a gym, and in the evenings the sixth-floor café morphs into a subsidised bar.

You'll know all too well that the recession did not give law firms an easy ride. While trainees were not directly affected by A&O's redundancies, "*the people you worked with were quite tense and there was some resentment of the trainees because we were insulated.*" For the record, most contacts felt the firm was "*pretty open*" about the process and "*put a lot of effort into handling it as sensitively as possible.*" While stressful, the qualification process is also quite transparent, and August finishers are normally informed exactly how many people each department will be taking on by early May. Once the numbers come out, the unofficial part of the process begins. "*You speak to the people you've worked with in the department where you want to qualify, and they'll give you an idea of whether you've got a good chance or whether you should reconsider.*" While "*you hear about people going really crazy and buying presents and taking people out for lunch,*" such tactics aren't likely to get you far. In 2010, 101 out of 128 qualifiers were kept on. While there is no detail this year as to which departments qualifiers went into, most years, the majority go into the banking, corporate and ICM departments.

And finally...

Sources feel that the training at A&O is *"the best in London."* A contract here will certainly expose you to the highest calibre of transactions; just be certain that you've got enough passion for finance to make the most of it.

Arnold & Porter (UK) LLP

The facts

Location: London

Number of UK partners/solicitors: 14/28

Total number of trainees: 2

Seats: 4x6 months

Alternative seats: Overseas seats, secondments

Extras: Pro bono – LawWorks

On chambersstudent.co.uk

- How to get into A&P
- More on A&P's pro bono opportunities
- We talk to managing partner Tim Frazer

You'll be highly visible as a trainee at this US-headquartered firm. That's a massive bonus, not a concern, say trainees.

Kings of the Hill

Arnold & Porter was founded in Washington, DC, in 1946 by government bigwigs Thurman Arnold, a former Assistant Attorney General, and Abe Fortas, who would later be appointed to the Supreme Court (and was known, incidentally, in his hometown of Memphis as 'Fiddlin' Abe Fortas' because of his talents with a violin). Former Chairman of the Federal Communications Commission Paul Porter joined them a year later.

All were veterans of the New Deal, the series of economic and political reforms that followed the Great Depression. Their firm attracted attention in high-profile pro bono cases, not least defending victims of McCarthyism at the height of the Communist witch-hunts. The founders' government connections and commitment to pro bono give the firm its flavour to this day.

A&P represents clients on both sides of the pond in numerous regulatory, litigation and transactional matters. Its 650-plus lawyers operate out of seven US offices plus London and Brussels. Long-term client Kraft used A&P on the competition aspects of its £11.5bn Cadburys acquisition (Clifford Chance advised on the M&A side). Lawyers from London, Brussels and several US offices collaborated on the deal. Meanwhile, in litigation, BP appointed Arnold & Porter along with Kirkland & Ellis to defend it against claims following the Gulf of Mexico oil well disaster.

London's approximately 40 lawyers work over three floors towards the top of Tower 42 in the City. Established in 1997 to bolster A&P's European capabilities, the office competes with larger rivals in its key practices: *Chambers UK* recognises its expertise with top or high rankings in life sciences, product liability, IP and media. Individual lawyers are also ranked in areas such as competition law, corporate/M&A and employment.

Smooth(er) criminal

A&P's life sciences practice is among the very best in London, and several of its practitioners have chemistry or medical backgrounds. It has advised the Association of British Pharmaceutical Industries on proposed new pricing regulation, and helped Allergan prevent fake Botox being brought into the EU. Clients such as GlaxoSmithKline, AstraZeneca and Pfizer benefit from the firm's wide-ranging expertise in matters including licensing, regulation, M&A, intellectual property and competition law. The strength of A&P's nationally ranked media and entertainment team is in part thanks to stellar IP and brand management capabilities. Having defended plagiarism claims concerning *The Da Vinci Code* a few years ago, the firm continues to advise its publisher Random House on various matters. Other clients include Virgin Media, Telegraph Media Group and Michael Jackson's Estate in connection with the *Thriller Live* West End show.

A&P currently recruits two trainees every two years. Despite being a relatively new scheme, competition for vacancies is fierce, with over 700 applications received last time round. The seat options are pharmaceuticals,

Chambers UK rankings

Competition/European Law	Life Sciences
Intellectual Property	Product Liability

IP, corporate, and another commercial seat like telecoms or competition, depending on the trainee's interests. A Brussels seat has been available, though recent expansion there may reduce the need for assistance from London. Each trainee gets to sit in a senior associate's office, enjoying some of the most majestic views in London.

Trainees here love the varied, cutting-edge work and high responsibility levels that come from being part of a close-knit team. Even on the vac scheme, one recalled: "*I was invited to go to client meetings with partners.*" The responsibility is there for vac schemers who want to grasp it: "*You're encouraged to go round, approach people and get your face out there. I thought if that was the experience even on the vacation scheme...*"

Pharma chameleons

The pharma seat, like others, offers a mix of contentious and non-contentious experiences. In one large case approaching trial, a trainee helped with "*continuing disclosure, case management and writing to the other side's solicitors. My supervisor was brilliant in getting me up to speed.*" Tasks on the regulatory and transactional side include "*research and drafting from scratch. I'd talk through my research with my supervisor, then draft an e-mail or letter.*" One interviewee enjoyed "*being involved from the start*" in writing a large report for a client. "*It was a fantastic feeling seeing my wording in print.*" Research topics range from Medicines and Healthcare Products Regulatory Agency guidelines to "*looking at the laws on embryo testing, or getting products to market.*" Working on a "*massive*" class action pharma case contrasted well with "*smaller IP cases*" for one source. On the litigation side, "*I did some bundling, but the associates allowed me to attend the hearing. I didn't need to be there but it was a good experience.*"

The sheer range of clients is one of the "*really great things*" in IP, sources said. They run from individual entrepreneurs to large global corporations in all sorts of sectors. The group doubled in size in 2008, grew further during 2009, and then further still in January 2010 with the arrival of top patent litigators from US firm Milbank. Recent highlights include the redesign of the Orange brand and advising US retailer Anthropologie on its European expansion. "*At first I did short-term tasks, then worked on longer cases,*" a trainee reported. "*I was handling all the admin for one of the medium-sized cases but was invited to client meetings.*" One rewarding task was helping to "*identify, source and interview experts.*" Work comes from various partners and senior associates, and one lucky trainee spent a few weeks in-house with a client in Switzerland. It gave them "*great exposure to what working in-house involves.*"

The corporate department "*isn't just M&A.*" For example, it recently advised UK cosmetics retailer Space NK on its expansion into the USA. "*I've done loads of stuff: private company acquisitions, asset acquisitions, due diligence for a take-private, employment work. Property too.*" Busy sectors for this team include technology, life sciences, retail, consumer products and real estate. Private equity has been more active recently.

Two's company

"*Because we're such a small office, things are very fluid and open,*" sources highlighted. "*All the groups work closely together,*" although generally "*it's a clean break between two seats.*" Culturally, the office "*isn't very American,*" and trainees have only occasional contact with partners in the USA. "*We're our own group,*" and London finds most of its own work. Everyone here is UK-qualified, and unlike some US firms in London there aren't any US partners permanently based here.

Being one of only two trainees means a quieter post-work experience. Our interviewees didn't mind too much. "*It's a shame we miss out on the social life, but I wouldn't change anything. It's allowed me to take on more responsibility from an early stage.*" There are Thursday 'Garden Room' drinks – named after a regular event held in the conservatory of the original DC office – allowing everyone to get together. "*They also do nice things like tea and cakes mid-afternoon for the whole firm if there's a forthcoming wedding or leaving do.*" Sports teams are non-existent, but on the plus side our sources felt more integrated into firm life.

General training includes "*lots of videocons from the US,*" and when external speakers visit the office, trainees are encouraged to attend. They normally pack up for the day around 6.30pm, though "*some days at 9pm or 10pm.*"

And finally...

The first trainees are due to complete their training in 2011. New qualifiers receive the added bonus of an invitation to attend the new associates' retreat in Washington, DC.

Ashurst

The facts

Location: London

Number of partners/solicitors: 132/312

Number of trainees: 108

Seats: 4x6 seats

Alternative seats: Overseas seats, secondments

Extras: Pro bono – Toynbee Hall Legal Advice Centre

On chambersstudent.co.uk
- How to get into Ashurst
- Ashurst's beginnings
- Overseas seats

"Ashurst is quite forward-thinking and an exciting place to work. It's really near the top in terms of quality, size, reach, experience and the deals it runs."

Bold decisions

Ashurst sits outside the magic circle and feels quite comfortable there, neither wanting to become part of this club nor seeing much significance in the categorisation. It knows its strengths, plays to them and builds on them. "*We're not big enough to claim we are the best at everything, but we are the best in the areas we specialise in: energy, corporate, international finance, real estate. In those areas we compete with the world's best firms,*" said recruitment partner David Carter. Corroborating this, a trainee added: "*Although we occasionally lose client pitches to the magic circle, we win more as our expertise grows. In corporate, finance and energy, we regularly win work that would have previously been done by the magic circle firms.*"

Over the past five years, Ashurst has improved its tally of FTSE 100 and FTSE 250 clients by 13 and, according to the annual FTSE survey by our colleagues on *The Chambers Magazine*, is now in seventh place in a list of the firms with the highest number of FTSE 100/250 clients. Said one source: "*Ashurst gets appointed to handle matters from clients who are conflicted out with other firms.*"

As tumbling profits, redundancies and an ambience of fear permeated the global economy, Ashurst took what was seen by some as a hubristic gamble. It scooped up a team of structured finance lawyers from a firm called McKee Nelson in New York. People questioned the move, saying that it would undermine morale (nobody wants to see new people being hired as their colleagues are being fired), harm the firm's relationship with its American allies (it won referral work from those firms on the basis that it didn't have a major US presence) and cost the firm money. Nevertheless, the decision proved to be astute: the new group generated £10m in revenue in its first year, despite the state of the financial markets. And the firm still gets US referrals. Take that, detractors. Back here in the UK, the energy, transport and infrastructure (ETI) department had continued to prosper during the weak economic conditions, and trainees also say: "*Now the finance and corporate departments are rebounding, they hit or exceeded budget – the recovery is in full flow.*"

Go east

In addition to the shock foray into US securities, Ashurst is following the emerging markets and expanding eastwards. "*We're a very powerful European firm with offices in key hubs, but comparatively light in Asia. The main push in the next five years will be eastwards, especially into Asia,*" managing partner Simon Bromwich told us. "*We opened in Hong Kong recently with 25 lawyers and it's the busiest office in the firm. We're desperate for more manpower in Tokyo, Singapore and Hong Kong.*" As per the UK market, the main practices are corporate and finance, but "*in terms of global strategy, energy is very strong and an important driver.*" As if to underline Bromwich's message, 2009/10 revenue figures show that some 36% of Ashurst's income came from its overseas offices (it now has 15 in Europe, five in Asia and two in the USA).

Chambers UK rankings

Banking & Finance	Insurance
Banking Litigation	Intellectual Property
Capital Markets	Investment Funds
Competition/European Law	Life Sciences
Construction	Local Government
Corporate/M&A	Pensions
Dispute Resolution	Planning
Employee Share Schemes	Private Equity
Employment	Product Liability
Energy & Natural Resources	Projects
Environment	Real Estate
Financial Services	Real Estate Finance
Fraud	Real Estate Litigation
Information Technology	Restructuring/Insolvency
	Tax
	Telecommunications
	Transport

Ashurst was the only foreign law firm to have a physical presence in India, but following the court-ordered closure of its Delhi liaison office (foreign firms are now prohibited from practising in India) it has needed to rethink its strategy regarding the subcontinent. It is now looking to tap into Indian business traffic via its bases in Hong Kong, Singapore, Abu Dhabi and Dubai. Ashurst partners have expressed their satisfaction with the relationships they fostered in India and the office had won some good *Chambers Global/Asia* rankings for its counsel in the areas of corporate, finance and projects.

Plastic bricks and motorways

All trainees complete four six-month seats, two of which are compulsory – international finance and corporate. "*Corporate and finance work are at the hub of what Ashurst does,*" so be sure you're after City-style work. "*If you want a more niche job, there are other firms more suitable,*" advised a source. For their other two seats, trainees can pick between a long list of commercial options and must select at least one contentious seat. They are encouraged to move around the firm, but if they show a real determination to do two seats in one department, it can be arranged, if the seats are in different subteams. All seats demand real effort, so leaving the office at 7pm is viewed as a good result. "*With hours it is the luck of the draw; it depends on the deal. There were times that were quite gritty, but afterwards you realise what you got out of it and what you achieved. Everyone has worked some late nights and some weekends – it's par for the course.*"

The compulsory international finance seat lives up to its name, according to trainees. Said one: "*I did a seat in structured finance, doing derivative trades, mainly for Goldman Sachs. I worked on deals that came from Hong Kong, London and New York. 70% of the work is international.*" Understandably, the mortgage-backed securities market (packaging up mortgages into a bond and selling it – one of the triggers of the credit crunch) isn't the busiest area right now, but trainees have been occupied on the restructuring of existing deals. "*It turned out that you get a lot of responsibility quickly, if you want it, and I got to go and meet the clients I'd been working for to complete the signing process.*"

Things are improving in the world of private equity – another hot area for the firm – and our sources had certainly noticed "*a definite pick up.*" Ashurst has lately handled deals like Apax's huge £975m purchase of pharmaceutical logistics company Marken and the sale of LGC Holdings (a provider of chemical and biological analytical services) to Bridgepoint for £275m. It's also been busy for Blackstone, owners of Merlin Entertainment Group, a theme park developer looking to build a $100m Legoland attraction in Florida.

Trainees spoke highly of corporate and, despite "*the crazy hours,*" argued: "*Even if you don't want to end up there, it's really good for understanding what Ashurst is all about.*" They described a "*self-confident*" department with "*a real deal-making atmosphere, whereas litigation and finance seem more academic and quieter.*" Trainees have "*self-contained tasks they can run with*" and, though there are proof-reading and document management tasks aplenty, the photocopier will never be their best friend. Said one source: "*I drafted a lot of documents and was in on a deal right up until post-completion, checking through everything. I did a lot of verifications near closing and reorganised the data rooms too, but I felt stretched enough and the work was typical NQ work.*"

Ashurst's ETI department is world class. Slovakian motorways, Swedish hospitals and a port in Jordan all pepper the list of recent work. In the UK, it advises Crossrail and is handling more waste projects than any other firm. Trainees say that the department is consistently busy and varied, adding that, as with finance or corporate, it is a good place to go to see mandates that affect the whole firm.

Sky's limit

Competition law is popular, and you can see why. The Ashurst team represented Intel in its appeal against a fine of over £1bn handed down by the European Commission – the largest fine ever to be levied for breach of EU competition rules. It also advised Virgin Media on the first-ever successful challenge to a Competition Commission merger control decision before the UK Competition Appeal Tribunal (CAT). BSkyB had wanted to buy a

17.9% stake in ITV but the CAT insisted that its holding be limited to less than 7.5%. These cases – both massive headline grabbers – demonstrate the strength of the firm's "*really, really busy*" and "*international*" team. Trainees spoke enthusiastically about price fixing, bid rigging and European Commission wrangles, describing their roles as varied and interesting, be it legal research, document bundling, letter writing or producing summaries for the Commission. There are eight competition partners in the London office and three trainee seats, meaning a good level of exposure for those sampling the department.

Litigation "*appeals to more academic, thoughtful types. People in the department aren't aggressive, but rather secure with what they know and can intimidate* [opponents] *with that.*" Finance-related litigation is a growth area and "*Ashurst gets a number of matters from banks when magic circle firms are conflicted out of representing them.*" A trainee on one such case described "*working for an investment bank in relation to a series of transactions that went wrong and have been unravelling in various locations around the world. I helped my supervisor co-ordinate the foreign lawyers and manage the case in the UK.*" A popular contentious option is employment law, but as with other niche seats "*you have to make your intentions clear.*" Many of the clients come via other departments, so expect work for private equity funds, real estate groups and telecoms companies, among others.

Those trainees who'd been abroad told us they'd loved their six-month overseas secondments. "*I don't see much difference in the work culture,*" insisted one; "*Ashurst manages to integrate all these foreign lawyers into one culture and, while I was in Paris, I found that the standard documents were the same too, so it was easy to fit in and it felt familiar.*" It's not a one-way street either: "*Spanish lawyers spend time in London, and the partners travel a lot*" so there is a "*good bond*" between them. There are also secondments to financial institutions and large corporates, with six or seven trainees visiting clients at any one time.

Stereotyping and the City

As you'd expect of a prominent old City firm (it was founded way back in 1822), Ashurst has its fair share of Oxbridge folk. The 27-person intake in March 2010 featured ten Oxbridge grads. The truth of the matter is that you don't have to have studied at a Russell Group university and (despite the stereotyping in the City) Ashurst's trainee group isn't terribly posh. According to recruiting partner David Carter: "*People who join tend to be those who turn down the magic circle because they don't like that style of firm, and those who turn us down tend to end up going to the magic circle.*" This view was supported by our sources. Characterwise, they are, of course, ambitious ("*we wouldn't be here if we weren't*"), but not to the point where they'd sacrifice all for their career or trample other people on their way up. At this stage it's worth mentioning that a lot of people are recruited through word of mouth, and some have relatives and friends already working at the firm. Trainees are aware of the posh stereotype, of course, and most hate it. "*People take the piss out of me a bit for it, but despite the misconceptions, it is very diverse here. There's a broad range of backgrounds,*" said one. "*There's a lot less drinking than I'd been led to believe,*" ventured another.

Trainees feel they get a good training in a friendly and minimally stressful environment that is conducive to hard work. The formal training is praised as much as the on-the-job tuition from attentive partners. Trainees say there is "*opportunity here to go as far as you want to. There's always support, but you can get as much independence as you want.*" A 360-degree appraisal system seems to work well and is "*not too formal.*"

Social events are usually team based and quite low key, but among the standout firm-wide jollies is a partners-v-the-rest cricket match that coincides with a summer party. Other sporting activities include netball, football, rugby and softball, and there is plenty for the non-sporty, such as a book club and regular networking events with canapés.

And finally...

Ashurst remains one of the City's thoroughbreds. It is praised highly by its trainees, who typically see themselves as continuing their careers with the firm. In 2010, 41 of the 53 qualifiers were able to do so.

Baker & McKenzie LLP

The facts

Location: London

Number of UK partners/solicitors: 81/203

Total number of trainees: 79

Seats: 4x6 months

Alternative seats: Overseas seats, secondments

Extras: Pro bono – United Nations High Commissioner for Refugees, Save the Children; language training

On chambersstudent.co.uk
- How to get into B&M
- B&M's culture in London
- The firm's history

Global giant Baker & McKenzie offers trainees more of a mid-sized firm experience in London. Mainstream and niche work can be explored in its non-hierarchical atmosphere.

Around the world in 67 offices

Jules Verne didn't come up with this one. It was Russell Baker and John McKenzie, who met in a taxi and went on to open their own firm in Chicago in 1949. "*It was the first firm to lay down global roots and to take that route,*" explained a trainee who clearly knew a thing or two about their employer's pioneering spirit. Today, with 67 offices, 'Baker Mac' is in more locations around the world than any other law firm. For more of the story, go to our website.

The firm operates in all the world's major financial centres and many other places besides. In terms of its organisation, it operates a Swiss Verein model, meaning each office is semi-autonomous. Said trainee principal Monica Kurnatowska: "*Each office will typically have a strong domestic practice, while also focusing on servicing international clients. Our aim is to be able to take on big global projects and big domestic clients. A big multinational would be sure to get the same quality of work, whether they are coming to the firm in London, Hong Kong or a smaller office.*" B&M believes that "*to call on a colleague anywhere should be the same as calling on a colleague down the corridor.*"

B&M's mid-sized, full-service London operation opened in 1961 and works in dozens of practice areas. The beauty of training here is that the firm combines the City's usual suspects of corporate and banking with specialist practice areas such as employee benefits and EU/competition and trade. *Chambers UK* ranks the firm highly for its niche expertise in areas such as administrative and public law; climate change; data protection; civil fraud; IT; telecoms; media and entertainment; outsourcing; and private client. Its more mainstream mid-market M&A, IP and employment work is also singled out for praise. In London, lawyers assist local clients such as the BBC Trust, advising on very UK-centric matters of public interest such as the BBC Executive's decision to allow the British National Party on *Question Time*. Other lawyers find their work is more international more of the time; for example Londoners recently advised Polish client Autostrada Wielkopolska in connection with a €1.6bn financing for the construction and operation of motorway sections in Poland, and for a major road between Berlin and Moscow. Other multinational clients of the office include HSBC, FedEx and Facebook. In 2009/10, London office revenues were up 4.6% to £120.3m – a reversal of the 3% drop in turnover in 2008/09.

Corporate compass

All trainees must do at least one seat (more if they like) in corporate, which is a cornerstone practice in this office. They may identify their preferences for the other three seats, one of which they'll be certain to get at either the second or third rotation. The corporate department is split into four different sub-groups. Corporate North (on the north side of the building) is the project finance and infrastructure group, where the work revolves around oil and gas, and recently environmental law. Corporate South

Chambers UK rankings

Administrative & Public Law	Immigration
Banking & Finance	Information Technology
Banking Litigation	Intellectual Property
Capital Markets	Investment Funds
Competition/European Law	Media & Entertainment
Construction	Outsourcing
Corporate/M&A	Pensions
Data Protection	Pensions Litigation
Dispute Resolution	Private Client
Employee Share Schemes	Private Equity
Employment	Product Liability
Energy & Natural Resources	Professional Discipline
Environment	Public International Law
Financial Services	Public Procurement
Franchising	Real Estate
Fraud	Restructuring/Insolvency
	Sports Law
	Tax
	Telecommunications

combines private equity and telecoms matters, whereas Corporate West concentrates on general M&A, reorganisations and insolvency/restructuring, as well as pharmaceutical clients. Corporate East works on a mix of US securitisations, financial services and private and public-listed companies work.

Corporate trainees carry a hefty load of document management chores, and the stop-and-start nature of some deals can lead to unpredictable hours. It's not so bad though, our sources said: "*The corporate department is very, very good. If you do get an all-nighter they'll say, 'Don't come in tomorrow.' Normally the partner will keep you in the loop as much as possible.*" Beyond grunt duties, trainee tasks range from drafting board minutes and shareholder resolutions to small agreements. Despite the administrative nature of the role and "*not much client interaction,*" one trainee assured us: "*I did feel very involved in the transactions.*"

Many trainees try the banking department, which a decade ago wasn't the hotbed of activity that it is today. Since then the office has built a team that is recognised by *Chambers UK* for its capital markets and securitisation work. B&M sits on the panel of a number of banks, including Calyon, Macquarie and JPMorgan Chase. The team's "*hugely international*" work often takes the form of "*mega-deals*" like the restructuring of BTA Bank, one of Kazakhstan's largest lenders, in which B&M represented the creditors' steering committee of 12 institutions including UBS, Deutsche and Fortis. The work is very varied for trainees, who find themselves having a go at drafting small bank agreements, proof-reading and managing other aspects of the documentation. The hours can occasionally be intense: "*I went through a solid two to three weeks of late nights and one horrible all-nighter until 5am.*"

Smells like team spirit

Employment law is a forte of B&M London – and worldwide – and the firm has been at the forefront of this relatively young area of commercial practice since the early days of the specialist employment lawyer in the 1980s. Working for an almost exclusively employer clientele that includes British Airways and Accenture, trainees attend pre-trial hearings and Employment Tribunals as well as more significant dates at the Employment Appeals Tribunal. The firm puts "*a great focus on ensuring fair allocations of those opportunities.*"

A "*highly respected IP group*" works for major brands like L'Oréal, which it recently represented at the European Court of Justice in a trade mark case about a look-and-smell-alike fragrance. According to one interviewee, the seat is "*totally global and involves you speaking to various lawyers around the world.*" The team frequently assists its London colleagues with general advice or anti-counterfeiting enforcement for brand-owning clients, which sees trainees "*reviewing responses from offending third parties and doing some administration.*"

Competition is another popular seat that involves a good deal of research and document review, as well as "*speaking to clients and corresponding with them on a regular basis.*" If you're lucky you might even help a client undergoing a dawn raid in a cartel investigation by the OFT. Trainees enjoy "*lots of responsibility*" in this team and are involved in "*chunky projects that you can really get your teeth into.*" The clients are "*often big household names*" like Apple, Nike and Pepsi.

And what of some of the other niche seats? The wealth management slot (an offshoot of the tax department) is all about "*helping high net worth individuals avoid paying too much tax*" and getting your head around complex trust structures. Pensions seats keep trainees busy researching, "*writing memos, doing technical drafting and meeting with clients and trustees.*" Over in the IT team, lawyers know all too well that technology "*moves faster than legislation*" and it's a job in itself to keep up with sector developments for clients like Apple/iTunes, Hewlett-Packard and Orange.

Trainees are "*guaranteed to get global exposure*" in almost every seat. One source told us: "*Every day I'm in touch with an overseas office or an overseas client.*" It's the nature of the beast here. The firm's global footprint and clientele ensure that "*you pick up key parts of international law and the way things are done in other juris-*

dictions." This all contributes to "*a sense that the work you're doing is a bit wider-reaching than just London.*" Some lucky trainees take an overseas seat, though interviewees warn against coming here with "*unrealistic expectations that you'll be guaranteed an overseas secondment,*" since competition is fierce. Trainees may apply to go to places such as Brussels, Abu Dhabi or Moscow, though the available locations often change from year to year. Wherever you want to go, seats are often tied to corporate work, and you'll have to make a good business case for going. There are also some excellent client secondment opportunities, recently at an investment bank, a mining company, a regulatory body, an internet search engine and a motor sports team.

Junior apprentices

Trainee work is distributed differently in each department but in all seats you should expect to be proactive. "*You have to get out there, show you're happy to help and flag up particular types of work you're interested in.*" Many times we heard that "*no matter what department, it's all very corporate-heavy.*" For that reason, "*it's useful to have an understanding of how big businesses work,*" and to "*have an interest in business in general.*" Trainee principal Monica Kurnatowska expanded on this when we spoke to her about what it takes to make it as a newbie at B&M. "*Trainees should get to grips with commercial drivers. People who do well here are interested from day one in what drives the client, and what drives our business. They are interested in understanding why clients want things a certain way.*"

Impress B&M folk enough to secure a training contract and the firm will give you plenty of attention, even while you're still at law school. "*The firm puts a focus on events for the future trainees,*" confirmed a source. Recruits bond while on the B&M LPC at the College of Law and this gives them a confidence boost when they start at the firm. Even new trainees say they feel comfortable approaching supervisors for guidance and feedback, although one trainee said: "*It would be nice to catch up with a neutral third party once a month.*" Many practice groups pair trainees up with an associate buddy, but there is no formal mentoring scheme across the office.

For trainees, the typical workday is 9am to 6.30pm, with the exception being corporate and banking. No cause for despair, though: "*People are quick to say thank you, particularly if you've done rubbish hours,*" a source revealed. These trainees are anything but a lazy bunch, and one was keen to stress how "*everyone got in on their own achievements and worked hard to get here.*" Head to our website for more on the classic B&M type.

A sense of community

"*It seems there's a committee for everything,*" remarked one trainee and certainly the firm promotes groups that champion LGBT, ethnicity and gender issues in the workplace. In sport, B&M takes part in the London Legal football league, and the firm hosts its own league called Euro Bakers. The most recent tournaments were held in Amsterdam and Munich. "*I think the London team is the best,*" claimed one source; "*it parties the first night it wins and then gets beaten by the German or Spanish office!*" Other popular sports include golf, hockey, sailing and netball. "*We're all pretty rubbish,*" laughed a trainee before talking excitedly about the social and networking opportunities that came hand in hand with matches. At Christmas, trainees put on an annual revue – a light-hearted "*pantomime type of thing.*" The firm sponsors monthly drinks for all (which coincides with wear-what-you-want day every Friday). At various other times, drinks trolleys roam the corridors.

The office decor is nothing trainees brag about. The firm is located "*right in the heart of things in the middle of the City, but the building isn't state of the art.*" One source described it as "*a massive issue,*" but others didn't seem too fussed either way. Trainees have big desks and find the workplace to be functional and "*comfortable enough to spend long hours.*" While "*the maroon carpet is looking faded,*" the "*bright*" and "*quirky artwork is a talking point.*" Trainees like the canteen and often drift in for a chat when they see a familiar face. In 2010, 33 out of 37 qualifying trainees remained with the firm, evidently feeling perfectly at home.

And finally...

Trainees love that B&M can offer them *"vast global opportunities as well as the chance to be a part of a smaller intake,"* in a firm with a distinctly non-hierarchical feel.

BARLOW LYDE & GILBERT
www.blg.co.uk
The Legal Week Awards 2005
WINNER Litigation Team of the Year
THE LAWYER AWARDS 2006
WINNER Litigation Team of the Year
LEGAL BUSINESS AWARDS
WINNER Dispute Resolution Team of the Year
Reactions LONDON MARKET AWARDS 2009
WINNER Best Law Firm in the London market
London Market LEADERS 2008
WINNER Best Law Firm in the London market
BEST RECRUIT
Medium City Fi
(2004)
For more information please contact Caroline Walsh, Head of Graduate Recruitment and Trainee Development
Barlow Lyde & Gilbert LLP
Beaufort House
15 St Botolph Street
London EC3A 7NJ
Telephone 020 7643 8065
Facsimile 020 7643 8500
grad.recruit@blg.co.uk

Barlow Lyde & Gilbert LLP

The facts

Location: London, Manchester, Oxford

Number of UK partners/solicitors: 76/187

Total number of trainees: 30

Seats: 4x6 months

Extras: Pro bono – LawWorks

On chambersstudent.co.uk
- How to get into BLG
- An interview with training principal John Flaherty
- The Equitable Life case

Should Barlow Lyde & Gilbert still be viewed as a litigation giant, or have its various efforts to boost transactional practice groups and revamp management turned it into a more rounded firm?

Time for change

BLG has built a reputation as one of the strongest insurance litigation firms in the country since it first set up shop in 1880. Its reputation for commercial litigation reached something of a climax in 2005/6 when its lawyers triumphed for Ernst & Young in the huge Equitable Life case, for which they received a whole clutch of awards. The 21st century has otherwise seen the firm try to shake up its old-fashioned image and structure, with which senior management was unhappy following a number of years of plateauing profitability. At the end of 2009, a more streamlined management structure was created: David Jabbari was appointed as chief operating officer, and he, along with senior partner Simon Konsta, now intends to drive the firm's ambitions further. Hopefully these changes will prove to be particularly timely, because as disputes practices elsewhere continue to charge ahead, BLG suffered a slide in litigation turnover in 2009/10, from £70m to £64.4m, in part a reflection of a number of partner departures.

One significant step has been the expansion of the firm's Asian investment, with new partner appointments to both Hong Kong and Singapore. At home, the recent collapse of northern law firm Halliwells has been very much to the benefit of BLG's new Manchester office. It took on over 200 people, including 17 partners. According to training principal John Flaherty, ensuring that *"the Manchester office will be completely embedded"* is a priority, and having rescued seven newly qualified solicitors and five trainees from the sinking Halliwells ship, BLG is giving strong signals that *"Manchester is likely to be relevant"* for those considering applying in the future.

The firm's giant insurance team, meanwhile, remains as strong as ever, and is described by our colleagues on *Chambers UK* as one that offers *"vast resources and excellent industry-specific expertise across the gamut of insurance and reinsurance, professional negligence, product liability, marine, aviation and personal injury matters."* The trainees we spoke to also seemed confident about the future, telling us: *"The changes that have been taking place are in the firm's best interests."* This should come as some reassurance to a firm that is widely seen as highly reliable but often reliably stagnant.

Taking off

As far as insurance litigation is concerned, the flight deck of this Starship Enterprise is its professional and financial disputes (PFD) team. For trainees it is an inevitable posting offering the best possible vantage point of the professional negligence and liability universe. It is certainly a good place to find your feet. New trainees should have some idea of what to expect as they will all have completed BLG's specially tailored insurance module during their LPC, and PFD as a first seat seems a logical extension of the necessary groundwork. *"I was keen to see what it was like, to find out if it really was for me,"* said one member of the crew. BLG is top-ranked in four out of five profes-

Chambers UK rankings

Aviation	Insurance
Banking Litigation	Outsourcing
Clinical Negligence	Personal Injury
Commodities	Police Law
Construction	Product Liability
Corporate/M&A	Professional Discipline
Dispute Resolution	Professional Negligence
Employment	Real Estate
Environment	Restructuring/Insolvency
Health & Safety	Shipping
	Travel

sional negligence categories (insurance, financial, high-end litigation and legal) by *Chambers UK*, and one of our sources helpfully explained just who this prestigious team is dealing with on a day-to-day basis. "*You're meeting the solicitors in trouble,*" he said. "*It's usually not their fault, they just haven't met clients' expectations. It's a real eye-opener, and humbling in a way, seeing how easy it might be to go wrong through no real fault of your own. It's a minefield they can get themselves into.*" Insurance brokers, accountants, financial institutions and construction companies also fill the client list.

And the work? "*In PFD you'll average somewhere around six on the responsibility scale, if ten is partnership and zero an outside observer. While you may do something extremely important, it goes through levels of scrutiny; you have exposure, but ultimate responsibility is not yours. The majority of work is research, preparing reports for insurers, forming a view on whether a case should be fought or settled, attending client meetings and taking notes.*" The fact that BLG has acted for a large number of the top 50 law firms in the country demonstrates the degree of confidence the team instils in other professionals.

On the directors' and officers' liability side of the practice there is both contentious and non-contentious work, and matters are often slightly more manageable in scale. "*I never did anything massive,*" said one interviewee. "*I'd be looking at insolvency arrangements, so if an entity in the UK went bust, I'd have to think about how that would impact on others. There was a lot of responsibility, looking at Civil Procedure Rules, deadlines and guidelines, and I was heavily involved in meetings when I was helping to prepare the disclosure bundle.*" Trainee contributions are obviously highly valued: "*What Barlows really tries to make you do is bring something extra to the table, to find that one bit of evidence that has been overlooked. When I was involved in acting for the insurers in a director's dispute with the administrator of a public company, as soon as the meeting was finished, I'd be thinking, 'I'm a director of a company – should I have traded when the company was obviously going to go into insolvency?' You have to add on that extra dimension of thinking about other elements.*" Supervisors are clearly keen to meet their trainees' expectations also: "*I sat with a partner who really took the time to sit down with me and asked whether I understood everything.*"

PFD is very closely aligned with another big-hitting practice group – the commercial litigation and arbitration (CLA) department. In 2009, the department ran a massive case relating to Ferrero chocolates. The firm was defending the hazelnut-consuming giant against fraud claims valued at €23m, from either side of the CLA/PFD divide. One CLA source described their role as "*very much trainee work – bundling and pagination – you're more of a back-seat trainee.*" They – and others – agreed that going to court was "*an excellent experience,*" and seeing barristers in action was not to be missed.

Risky business

Another widely respected department is called commercial risk and reinsurance (CRR). "*I know I sound like an advert for Barlows, but I enjoy this seat even more than the others,*" said one trainee. Another source was just as positive, telling us: "*I cannot speak highly enough of the department.*" Key to this enthusiasm is the spirit of the team itself, which is described as "*excellent.*" "*It's the best department in terms of personalities,*" and somewhere that "*senior fee earners take a genuine interest in your personal development.*" This is the place to go for cases worth billions, and budding insurance nerds should find plenty of food for thought among the large-scale coverage issues and notification claims that come through the department. Our sources spoke of "*research into quite obscure points of insurance law*" and "*drafting advice, reviewing policies and chatting to clients to see whether a particular policy applied to the situation.*" The recession caused reinsurance practices everywhere to take a battering, and BLG is no exception, but the view from the top is optimistic. "*It's been a tough market for the last few years, but we're seeing some green shoots there again,*" said John Flaherty.

If PFD doesn't entirely sate the appetite for upset, then the negligentsia need look no further than a seat in casualty and healthcare (CAH). This group deals mostly with clinical negligence and personal injury matters, and these can apparently leave some trainees feeling "*quite strongly about defending doctors and medical practitioners.*" The seat certainly offers good responsibility. Said one trainee: "*I got to experience running things on my own, going to court and doing my own advocacy.*" The aerospace team, meanwhile, "*deals with everything from air disasters to baggage losses or coffee spills causing personal injury,*" and unsurprisingly trainees were kept busy by the fallout from the Icelandic volcanic ash palaver. Again, this is an insurance-heavy seat in a top-rated department that goes down well with newcomers. One trainee described *"an amazing small claims experience where I was in charge of the whole disclosure."* We also asked our interviewees for tips on how to go about the key task of taking witness statements, and the simple advice was this: *"When you're there, ask every conceivable question, and don't be worried about taking up their time."*

In the smaller marine, energy and trade (MET) department, the divisions are well defined and the work is varied. *"There's marine, which is anything from charter parties, collisions with land or docks, personal injuries and piracy. Energy covers pipelines, oil and gas-related projects and oil spills. And trade covers commodities, a bit of trade finance and advising insurers on whether they need to pay out under a contract."* The work can be either contentious or non-contentious in nature, while the clients might be wealthy individuals, shipowners, shipbuilders or major insurers. While MET types tend to prefer *"the nitty-gritty law,"* they shouldn't lose sight of the fact that, here, as in other seats, *"you have to have quite good communication skills and learn to appear confident. People can be outspoken although they're not arrogant."*

Bones of contention

In reverse fashion to most other City firms, it is the non-contentious seats that are in the minority at BLG. While the compulsory transactional or advisory element of the training contract can be fulfilled by a client secondment, most trainees find themselves in either the corporate or commercial and technology departments. *"It had a great team,"* said one source of the latter. *"I got to draft some outsourcing contracts and agreements for streamlining. I was well supervised but did a lot on my own."* A less enthusiastic trainee confessed: *"I don't really enjoy corporate work. There was a lot of proof-reading of contracts, drafting terms and conditions, legal research and drafting articles."* One trainee simply announced: *"Don't come here for transactional work."* That said, no fewer than two trainees qualified into the transactional side of the firm in 2010, so we say don't dismiss the idea outright. The full 2010 qualification stats reveal that 15 of the 21 qualifiers stayed with BLG.

Prior to the arrival of ex-Halliwells lawyers, none of the London trainees spent time in Manchester, and the smaller Oxford office only hosted them on an ad hoc basis. Internationally, however, seats are available in both Hong Kong and Singapore, and we only heard *"amazing"* things about these locations. BLG has a Brazilian office, though anyone hoping to jet off for carnival shouldn't pack their costume just yet. *"We don't send trainees there on secondment yet, but that may well be an opportunity by 2013,"* said training principal John Flaherty. Client secondments include one of the world's largest banks, another renowned investment bank and a well-known risk management and insurance intermediary.

Gokking the office

The firm's outmoded office space is finally getting a makeover, with interior designers landing in summer 2010. BLG's digs are in a large building at Aldgate, which is shared with other businesses. As might be expected of a firm of litigators, the trainees at BLG are a gregarious bunch, though they haven't had as full a social life of late. *"The trainee social budget seems to have been blown out of the water,"* lamented one source. At least there is still a popular Friday night ritual: *"The drinks trolley is one saving grace; I always think it's great when you hear the clinking of the bottles."* Left to their own devices, trainees organise their own fun, which typically involves piling into the Slug & Lettuce on a Friday night. There are also firm-wide and departmental events, such as summer barbecues and Christmas parties. We understand that the CRR group is the one with the best Christmas party. BLG is big on sport, too, and we heard about keen participation in rugby, football and softball. A healthy post-work life is generally easier to achieve at litigation-heavy firms as the pace tends to be steadier and the workflow has fewer peaks and troughs.

And finally...

If disputes are your thing then you'll see plenty of great ones at BLG. The growth of the Manchester office should be a very positive step.

Bates Wells & Braithwaite London LLP

The facts

Location: London

Number of UK partners/solicitors: 26/50

Total number of trainees: 8

Seats: 2x6 + 3x4 months

Alternative seats: Secondments

Extras: Pro bono – Blackfriars Advice Centre

On chambersstudent.co.uk
- How to get into BWB
- The firm's pro bono efforts
- The Third Sector
- BWB's sport, media and entertainment work

"A City firm with a conscience," Bates Wells & Braithwaite manages to do good for society in a variety of sectors and offers a personal, hands-on training experience.

Benevolent BWB

The charitable sector is synonymous with the name Bates Wells & Braithwaite. In fact it helped write the law in this area – partner and Lib Dem Lord Phillips of Sudbury, in particular, has been instrumental in the creation of UK charities legislation. In 2009, BWB acted for 40 of the top 100 charities in the UK, including the British Red Cross, Oxfam, ActionAid International and the NSPCC. It also gained a significant new client in The Elders, an international organisation made up of the world's leading human rights figures, including Nelson Mandela, Jimmy Carter, Desmond Tutu and Kofi Annan.

In addition to its charities work, the firm is *"incredibly successful in taking niche areas* [like immigration, media and sport] *where we can become a dominant player. This has protected us in the downturn and given us a good market share. We sailed through the recession without any impact on growth or profitability,"* partnership executive officer Peter Bennett told us. *"We want our lawyers to be part of the sectors they're serving and major players in those worlds as people, not just as lawyers. The whole social policy tide is heading in our direction, and we're proud of our reputation for being at the cutting edge of that movement."*

The training contract consists of five seats (two in the first year, three in the second) which are mapped out in *"flight paths"* beforehand. Training co-ordinators create several flight paths and then it's up to the trainees to *"wrangle"* among themselves over who will take each. There is some flexibility: *"There was one path no one wanted to do, so we told the training partner and she changed it."* Trainees noted the advantages of *"knowing you've had input and what's coming up,"* but also acknowledged that *"your feelings can change – you may become more interested in a department* [not on your path] *but it's too late. You'd need a very plausible reason to switch."* Bennett insists that flight paths are *"a starting point, not an ending point,"* and that there's *"quite a lot of flexibility in the final seat."*

Human interest

"There's something inherently nice about working for charities," say trainees. *"The work and clients are so interesting, plus you're involved in doing some wider social good."* Another perk is that *"when you ring up and say, 'Sorry I haven't met that deadline', it's usually a human on the other end who understands, not just some corporate monster."* BWB claims to represent more than twice as many charities as its nearest rival: certainly 60% of its clientele is from the charitable and not-for-profit sector. It's not surprising, then, that the firm's largest department is *"really, really busy, and everything needs to be done immediately."* The clients trainees talk to can range from *"high-powered chief execs to just a little man wanting to set up his own charity."* For the latter, BWB often works pro bono – to find out more go to our website. It's not uncommon to repeat

Chambers UK rankings

Administrative & Public Law	Immigration
Charities	Media & Entertainment
Corporate/M&A	Partnership
Data Protection	Professional Discipline
Education	Real Estate
Employment	Real Estate Litigation
Healthcare	Sports Law

a seat in the department. The first time around *"you're given work from a larger number of fee earners,"* while in a second stint *"you're expected to know more, look after your own files and do more work in the smaller areas."* Those smaller areas include arts, media and sport: find out more about the work of these teams on our website.

The employment department offers plenty of contentious action. In a headline-making matter, BWB advised the mother of a disabled boy in a case against her former employer. It achieved a ground-breaking ruling on 'disability discrimination by association', giving greater protection in the workplace to individuals caring for disabled people. Omnipresence in the charity sector continues: lawyers advised Diabetes UK on a claimed breach of Northern Ireland's religious discrimination legislation, when an employee displayed a statue of Buddha. As a trainee you can expect to see real action: *"The firm really pushes for solicitors to do their own advocacy at tribunals, and trainees do get their chance."*

Drop it like it's Trott

BWB pulled mass headlines when P.I.M.P. (Prime IMmigration Partner, naturally) Phillip Trott won Snoop Dizzle's immigrizzle bizzle. Trott also helped rap's MVP 50 Cent put the game in a choke hold, passed the Courvoisier to Busta and even tipped off P. Diddy that it's all about the Benjamins. Okay… we admit he may have only advised on their legal entry to the UK and that's not as much of a G thang (baaaaaaby), but it ain't no fun if the homies can't have none. A few trainee sources had been involved in the Snoop case: taking witness statements, adding amendments, liaising with his management and briefing counsel. *"I was pretty involved, but you'd have to give the glory to Phillip… I guess,"* one joked. The seat also received rave reviews outside of its O.G. clientele because *"you get to deal with actual people and it really makes a difference to them."* Trainees get a kick out of *"to-ing and fro-ing with the Home Office and trying to achieve things from a bureaucratic organisation."*

Trainees can also do stints in the corporate, property, dispute resolution and public and regulatory law departments. BWB is a solid performer in lower mid-market corporate deals and takes on both company-commercial and partnership work. Dispute resolution is *"very fast paced"* and focuses on general commercial litigation, while the high-profile public and regulatory law team was instructed by the Liberal Democrats in the 2010 general election and helped *The Sunday Times* secure a Freedom of Information Act ruling making MPs' expenses public. And what a Pandora's box that turned out to be. Property clients include the YMCA and Save the Children. Trainees described this team as *"a friendly bunch"* and liked that the department offers *"varied work with quite a bit of responsibility."*

Besides their five seats, trainees must also develop a *"focus"* on a specific sector – either education, environment or healthcare. It doesn't exclude them from other work; in fact, it mainly involves *"research and going to meetings"* relating to the sector. Trainees can put as much effort in as they like, and sources say it *"gives continuity and helps build our awareness throughout the training contract."* Peter Bennett says this is *"a strategic development"* designed to *"make sure we have a grasp of what's going on in* [these areas] *and ensure we can meet clients' business needs."*

Life outside

With standard hours of 9am to 6pm, no working weekends and 8pm described as a late night, BWB is a haven of sanity within the City. *"We're expected to work hard, but not long hours,"* one explained. *"I was here until 7.30pm once and a couple of partners came in and told me to go home,"* another added. *"When it's busy, everyone thanks you for taking the extra time. When it's not busy, for goodness' sake go home!"* A committee organises pub quizzes and Christmas and summer parties, and there are people who go to the pub on Fridays, otherwise the social scene is relatively quiet.

BWB only takes on a handful of trainees per year, so expect stiff competition. While strong academics are important, the firm is more interested in well-rounded people with passionate and proven interests beyond the law. Read about how to impress on our website.

And finally...

BWB is ideal if you want a City firm that's not a corporate nightmare. It also manages to achieve excellent retention: all five qualifiers were offered jobs in 2010 and four accepted.

Beachcroft LLP

The facts

Location: Bristol, London, Leeds, Manchester, Birmingham, Winchester, Newcastle, Newport

Number of UK partners/solicitors: 144/584

Total number of trainees: 59

Seats: 4x6 months

Alternative seats: Secondments

Extras: Pro bono – Manuel Bravo, Prince's Trust, ProHelp, LawWorks

On chambersstudent.co.uk
- How to get into Beachcroft
- The firm's pro bono efforts
- The intricacies of insurance

This fast-expanding national firm is extending its healthcare and insurance practices while cross-selling its employment, real estate, corporate and public policy work to core clients. It all makes for a varied training experience.

Beachcroft 2.0

In the words of its trainees, Beachcroft is "*progressive and moving forward, always looking to build*" and "*very ambitious... constantly taking action.*" It employs over 1,500 staff and lawyers, and you should expect that number to rise. In 2008, senior partner Simon Hodson formulated a new strategy. Trainees gave us the lowdown: "*We are very much focusing on our core strengths – healthcare and insurance.*" A few years back we reported that this firm was expanding into more general corporate and commercial work; now though, it is back to concentrating on what it does best. Beachcroft earns top-tier *Chambers UK* rankings for healthcare and defendant personal injury and clinical negligence right across the country, and is also very strong for both education and public law. Its corporate capability is respectable but less renowned. "*We don't seek to be a full-service firm, but we seek to excel in the areas we work in,*" training partner Paul Parke says. "*It makes sense to cross-sell all our practices to the fantastic selection of clients we have.*" So, from the perspective of a future trainee, there is an almost endless supply of injury, professional and property risk litigation, and the firm offers training in corporate, property, employment, financial and public law, albeit that this is chiefly undertaken for insurance, public sector and health clients.

There have been many lateral hires of late. A 27-lawyer clin neg team arrived from Eversheds in 2008, which heralded Beachcroft's opening of a Newcastle office. The firm now has a panel place with the NHS Litigation Authority (NHSLA) in the North East. In 2009, a Dublin office was opened, as was a Wales-based specialist claims-handling outlet called 'B2'. It's designed to "*enlarge our capacity to do more volume and commoditised legal work,*" says Parke. Many firms have tried to make it in Ireland and few have succeeded, but Beachcroft is betting that the health and insurance markets will prove lucrative on the Emerald Isle.

More recently still, the Manchester office was expanded thanks to the arrival of a ten-partner healthcare team from Halliwells, while the London office brought insurance boutique Williams Holden Cooklin Gibbons on board. Trainees feel this is all part and parcel of the firm's innovative and competitive response to the Legal Services Act, which trainees are "*hearing about all the time.*" The firm is one of a number outsourcing much of its back-office work. Data support, reception, post, copying and filing will be done by Birmingham and Newport staff who transferred to outsourcing company Williams Lea.

The firm has something of a revolving door relationship with the worlds of public policy and healthcare. The hire of former chair of the Healthcare Commission (and MPs' expenses watchdog supremo) Sir Ian Kennedy as a consultant is one such example. Former senior partner – and former Employment Secretary – Lord Hunt of Wirral has compiled a report on the regulation of the legal professional for the Law Society. Head of strategic litigation

Chambers UK rankings

Administrative & Public Law	Insurance
Banking & Finance	Licensing
Clinical Negligence	Local Government
Construction	Personal Injury
Corporate/M&A	Product Liability
Debt Recovery	Professional Discipline
Dispute Resolution	Professional Negligence
Education	Projects
Employment	Public Procurement
Environment	Real Estate
Health & Safety	Real Estate Litigation
Healthcare	Restructuring/Insolvency
Information Technology	Retail

Andrew Parker advised Lord Justice Jackson on his litigation costs review and former managing partner Bob Heslett recently completed a term as president of the Law Society. Beachcroft is a well-connected place with its fingers in all sorts of appropriate pies.

Health issues

Trainee seats can be taken in Bristol, London, Manchester and Leeds. Birmingham, Newcastle and Winchester are smaller – the former specialises in injury risk and construction; the latter two in healthcare and insurance. There are no mandatory seats, but the fact that "*insurance and health work is our bread and butter*" means trainees "*will have to do an insurance seat at some point.*" The insurance seats are: injury risk, professional indemnity and commercial property risk. It's "*pretty much all defendant work, for employers* [like BP, British Airways and the MoD] *and professional indemnity insurers* [like Zurich and Allianz] *as well as NHS trusts.*"

Injury risk work covers injuries at work, stress, industrial deafness and disease-related issues. Professional indemnity involves defending professionals against negligence claims. Leeds lawyers acted for the managing partner of North Eastern law firm Raleys over the miners' health controversy, where a large number of firms and individual solicitors were accused of regulatory breaches over their handling of claims seeking compensation for sick miners. Read more about this topic on our website. In a property risk seat (which can be taken in London, Bristol and Manchester only), trainees experience "*a mix of defence and claimant work.*" Much of it involves defending insurers and property owners if, for instance, a warehouse is damaged by a contractor. Trainees report that in all three insurance seats, "*there is a lot of client interaction, either over the phone or in person.*"

The addition of the Halliwells team in Manchester means health advice and clin neg seats can now be taken in all locations except London. Clinical neg involves "*mostly NHS stuff... defending claims from people who get hurt in hospitals or are not treated properly.*" The health advice seat puts the trainee in what is effectively "*a one-stop shop for healthcare practitioners.*" Here, the work includes employment, mental capacity inquests, questions of patient consent, regulatory issues and public policy advice. To find out more about Beachcroft's core sectors, read the extra feature on our website.

Secondments are increasingly common, and there is a "*long-standing relationship*" with Unilever. The firm is looking to increase the number of secondments and has sent people on an ad hoc basis to a number of its insurer clients as well as household-name companies.

Hunt followers

One trainee said Beachcroft is "*not really a firm for people who want to do corporate-type work.*" Fair? Well, the reputation of the M&A team is comparable with that of, say, Reynolds Porter Chamberlain and Farrer in London's lower mid-market. A typical deal was the £31.5m sale by IT services company Xploite of its Anix data storage division. Elsewhere in the country the team gains *Chambers UK* rankings, but does tend to lag behind firms with larger, stronger corporate groups. In these other offices, corporate seats essentially involve acting for UK mid-market insurers on M&A deals, and small international clients. Together with commercial litigation, corporate is known for its longer hours – trainees might stay until 9pm. Insurance, health and employment seats are easier going: perhaps 8.30am to 6.30pm. "*They expect you to have a good work-life balance though, and to manage your time,*" one trainee said. "*When I was busy and staying behind, people asked what I was doing and told me to go home.*"

A real estate seat is fairly common, and the clients are mostly top-end commercial occupiers. "*The partner I sat with did a lot of work for the NHS, such as projects for Guy's and St Thomas' hospitals and planning for University College Hospital,*" said one source. Other clients include Balfour Beatty, Lloyd's of London and Waitrose.

London offers a financial services seat in the department headed up by Lord Hunt of Wirral. His lordship is something of a firm celebrity and future trainees will be given "*shadowing opportunities to follow him around in his London and Westminster activities.*" The financial institutions team was recently boosted by the addition of two partners from Norton Rose and Pinsent Masons. It specialises in corporate regulatory advice to the firm's top insurance clients.

Bristol offers a financial services litigation seat where work includes "*debt recovery claims, fraud work and breach of contact claims*" for clients including Citi, Imperial Tobacco and Orange. "*We advise clients strategically on what to do before a claim is brought,*" explained one source. The small size of the department means trainees run some files themselves and are "*on the phone to the client all the time.*"

A tour of the offices

The much-admired new office in Bristol has "*a village green type area in the middle, which is like an atrium where you can break away from your desk.*" Say trainees: "*It doesn't feel too lawyery here; the atmosphere is driven but relaxed.*" Bristolians get involved in the Hunt Cup – a debating competition at Bristol University which trainees judge – and they help people on work experience programmes that are run through the Society of Black Lawyers. Trainees also have a nice little perk in the form of corporate membership of Bristol Zoo.

The London office in Holborn is "*energetic and proactive*" and trainees frequently meet for lunch in its "*great canteen.*" A small City office on Eastcheap concentrates on insurance and litigation, and is "*very hard-working*" but also "*known for its nightlife... the junior lawyers all club together.*" Favourite haunts are Clause and the White Swan. London trainees stress the need to "*seek out opportunities for yourself and get your name known around the firm.*"

As in London, Beachcroft works from two locations in Leeds, and there is talk of moving into a new building to bring everyone together. The Leeds operations are "*very friendly. Everyone knows each other and says 'hi' in the corridors.*" The mood up here is fairly social and there are organised departmental drinks plus trips to the theatre and opera in the park. "*At the Christmas do there were lots of games. Everyone had balloons on their heads and mucked in with playing charades. No one was above joining in.*"

Manchester has a "*laid-back atmosphere,*" and the office's acquisition-based growth means that it "*feels a little more independent.*" At the same time as the ex-Halliwells crew joined in May 2010, the firm moved into new offices in the city. There are monthly drinks in Harry's Bar (the canteen) and annual events such as a Halloween party. Big on charity, the Manchester office is spearheading fund-raising and pro bono initiatives for The Prince's Trust. Go to our website for more information on this and tales of senior partners dressing up as hot dogs.

Immodest change in a modest world

Expect no hubris or boasting here. "*It doesn't feel like a massive firm; we've managed to keep a small-office culture,*" one trainee insisted. "*It's not a firm with big egos wandering around the place.*" Another added: "*We don't attract the hard-nosed, deal-making people that other firms do.*" A fair number of trainees come from non-Russell Group universities or previous careers. According to a survey in *The Lawyer*, Beachcroft is the second most female-friendly firm in the top 50. One-third of partners are women, as are two-thirds of trainees. "*I quite like the fact that there are a lot of women partners,*" said one source. "*They allow for flexible working. It's a firm that will always support its staff.*"

In 2010, 24 of the 31 qualifiers were retained and Beachcroft abandoned its annual recruitment round at short notice. It also deferred ten of the 29 September 2010 starters for a year. These measures seem to be in keeping with changes in the economy following the election of the coalition government and public sector spending cuts; however, the firm actually told us that it was the implications of changes brought about by the Legal Services Act and cost reviews by its insurer clients that was driving legal fees (and so the demand for trainees) down. Early in 2010 Beachcroft told us of its plans for the reform of its training contract, including the reduction of overall numbers from 60 to 30. The reduction just came sooner than anticipated. "*We're aiming at making our trainee intake more like a graduate intake in the civil service or insurance industry,*" Paul Parke explained. Visit our website to learn more about Beachcroft's thinking.

And finally...

Beachcroft may not define itself as full-service, but in truth it offers pretty much everything to trainees, including a pleasant working culture. Do bear in mind the health/insurance slant.

Berwin Leighton Paisner LLP

The facts

Location: London

Number of UK partners/solicitors: 180/366

Total number of trainees: 79

Seats: 4x6 months

Alternative seats: Overseas seats, secondments

Extras: Pro Bono – Sonali Gardens Legal Advice Centre

On chambersstudent.co.uk
- How to get into BLP
- BLP trainees on their bespoke LPC+ training
- BLP's recent big-name appointments

A noughties success story, Berwin Leighton Paisner has challenged the City's perception of it as merely a real estate specialist. With the firm having now marked its territory in other markets, trainees say they feel *"a part of something that's really going somewhere."*

Making its way up the food chain

BLP talks big. "*The aim is to be the best law firm in London – offering the best service and being the best place to work, which is important and clearly something* [management] *still bears in mind,*" said one source. All well and good, but the best how? "*The firm is trying to shape itself – not as a magic circle firm because we don't want to be that, we have a different culture – but we want to be a very full-service firm, right behind them and leading the rest.*"

"*Its ambition at the moment is quite impressive,*" one trainee told us. "*It's obvious that the firm is keen on pursuing opportunities as they arrive rather than just weathering the economic storm.*" According to managing partner Neville Eisenberg, that hits the nail on the head. The firm's appetite for rapid expansion has been clear for some time, but it became even more evident during the economic downturn. "*We saw the recession as an opportunity to accelerate our strategy,*" Eisenberg explained. BLP has indeed capitalised on the poor positioning of rival firms to lure away senior talent from magic circle, silver circle and US firms. See our website for more details. Prominent hires are giving BLP the strength to claw major work away from competitors; for example, striking a deal with Thames Water that will see the firm fulfil the majority of the utility company's legal requirements. Things have turned out well: the firm saw a 10% increase in per-partner profits and a 6% increase in turnover in the 2009/10 financial year.

Already the market leader in all things real estate, BLP is intent on growing the other four of its five 'pillars'– corporate, finance, dispute resolution and tax. Another aspect of BLP's strategy is to push into emerging markets. The firm opened offices in Moscow and Abu Dhabi mid-recession, adding to its existing list of branches in Paris, Brussels and Singapore. "*Abu Dhabi is already quite busy,*" Eisenberg told us, "*and we'll be planning some further organic growth there over the next few years.*" He also mentioned Singapore as a future target, but the firm's international strategy doesn't end there, as "*emerging markets are just one strand.*" BLP also partners with 'preferred firms' around the world. "*When you take the two* [growing international offices and preferred firms] *together there will be a lot more opportunity to get experience abroad, and those looking to join the firm should be aware of that,*" say trainees.

As it stands, one or two lucky trainees can already take seats in Brussels and Moscow. Domestically, trainees should expect to complete one of their four seats in the real estate department. As for the other three, "*there are always going to be people who don't get their choices,*" but "*you're guaranteed your first-choice seat at least once.*"

Chambers UK rankings

Asset Finance	Licensing
Banking & Finance	Local Government
Banking Litigation	Media & Entertainment
Capital Markets	Outsourcing
Charities	Parliamentary & Public Affairs
Competition/European Law	Pensions
Construction	Planning
Corporate/M&A	Private Client
Dispute Resolution	Private Equity
Employment	Projects
Energy & Natural Resources	Public Procurement
Environment	Real Estate
Financial Services	Real Estate Finance
Fraud	Real Estate Litigation
Information Technology	Restructuring/Insolvency
Insurance	Retail
Intellectual Property	Tax
Investment Funds	Telecommunications
	Transport

From Primark to landmark

For real estate matters of any kind, you'll be hard pressed to find a better place to train. From big-ticket deals, to real estate finance and litigation, to planning and construction law, BLP does it all. Long-standing client Tesco sends masses and masses of work BLP's way, and there are many lawyers for whom the retail giant is their core client. As well as more ordinary day-to-day property instructions, Tesco recently instructed the firm on the market's first commercial mortgage-backed securitisations (CMBS) since 2007. The retail sector is a key one for the firm, and among its clients are high-street names like Argos, Primark, Krispy Kreme, Mango, Burberry, Homebase, Monsoon, French Connection, Laura Ashley and Tie Rack. Another sector of key importance is hotels, leisure and gaming. Also worth knowing, BLP has developed particular expertise in managing distressed real estate, for example acting for Ernst & Young on the sale of the White Tower portfolio of nine London office buildings worth over £1bn which were used to back a CMBS deal.

Regeneration continues to be an important area of activity for BLP, and it was recently appointed by the London Borough of Tower Hamlets to advise on the regeneration of Blackwall Reach, one of the UK's most deprived areas. BLP is also assisting Barclays and RBS with financing the development of a £170m St Pancras luxury hotel scheme, bringing a Gothic Grade I-listed King's Cross building back into full use. Landmark buildings often crop up when there are BLP lawyers on the scene: the firm recently advised South Korea's National Pension Service and its asset manager/adviser JPMorgan on the acquisition of HSBC Tower in Canary Wharf for £772.5m.

Despite such big-ticket deals, the real estate department "*has a reputation for really decent hours*" and compared to some others "*is more of a lifestyle choice*" as "*people are quite relaxed.*" The department isn't short of "*phenomenal work*" for trainees: our sources had sampled "*everything from scheduling all the deeds for the Millennium Dome site, to looking after a small portfolio of Hilton hotels.*" Some sources found the "*market-leading*" real estate finance team to be "*inspiring,*" and its work to be "*very topical.*"

High-end priorities

"*Corporate is our number-one strategic priority of the moment,*" Neville Eisenberg told us. "*We're planning to continue to grow and expand at the higher-quality end considerably in the next couple of years. We really want to drive it.*" The corporate department is split into a number of groups. The four main subsections are M&A; private equity; funds/financial services; and investment banks/intermediaries. Recent highlights include advising investor Blackstone on a joint venture with British Land to acquire a 50% interest in the Broadgate office estate in the City. BLP was also on hand to advise on the deal's real estate and tax issues. The firm is additionally home to one of the finest AIM-focused groups in London. Trainees were pleased to "*get involved in some of the large deals, going to client meetings and drafting board minutes and other short template-based documents.*"

The firm's commercial group, formerly known as Business Technology Services (BTS), falls under the corporate umbrella, too, as the team handles commercial contracts relating to outsourcing, telecoms, media and technology matters. The group recently advised Barclays on its sponsorship of the London Cycle Hire Scheme. Take a seat in this department and "*you're guaranteed a secondment to* [one of the firm's clients, including major retailers and banks]." BLP has a "*good system*" in place whereby trainees spend three months away with one of these clients and three back with the commercial group. One trainee on secondment was kept busy "*drafting and negotiating contracts, and pretty much running everything on* [their] *own.*" They freely admitted: "*You feel overwhelmed at first but it's strange how quickly you adapt.*"

The evolution of BLP's finance department is "*a long-term project.*" The trainees we spoke to reckoned the department was "*busier than it's ever been*" and they spoke of "*a broad variety of work.*" For example, lawyers were advising the administrators of the Reader's Digest Association as it went into administration, and the Olympic Delivery Authority on the financing of the Olympic Village.

After shocks?

The dispute resolution group is "*extremely busy at the moment*" and recently met with success representing National Grid in a follow-on claim in the biggest cartel damages action to surface in the English courts. The energy company sued a number of European businesses including ABB, Alstom, Areva and Siemens for more than £200m, over a conspiracy to carve up the gas-insulated switchgear market (we didn't know what this is either, but Wikipedia is your friend here). The importance of the case lies in the fact that the Chancellor of the High Court agreed with National Grid in allowing the claim to continue despite the cartelists' appeal to the European Commission. The trainee experience in litigation sounds incredibly varied: some we spoke to "*loved it,*" while others found it "*very hierarchical.*" The firm is evidently "*attracting a lot of big cases,*" but that can mean trainees experience less interesting tasks and more document review. Some we spoke to had been spared drudgery and talked to us about "*drafting instructions to counsel, witness statements and statutory demands.*" Disparity in tasks aside, trainees agreed: "*It's nice to see stuff you're working on appear in the press, and see that what you're doing is relevant.*"

Neville Eisenberg cites the growth of BLP's tax department as "*quite a good case study of what one can do during a downturn. UK law firms had generally been a bit weak* [in the tax market], *so we saw opportunity, invested heavily and have grown dramatically.*" There are now over 50 lawyers in the department. Other seat options are plentiful within the five pillars. They range from EU/competition, to employment, to property planning, to real estate litigation, to IP and more.

Trainees were positive about the firm's growth, but acknowledged that "*inevitably some of that magic circle culture will come with it... we're supposed to be the antithesis of all that.*" BLP is known for being a place where "*everyone is very approachable and very happy,*" working with partners who are "*quite pleased and flattered if you come to them seeking advice.*" You can understand why the firm would want to take steps to maintain that kind of environment. "*Obviously, new partners bring in their own working practices from wherever they come from, but there certainly hasn't been a seismic shift in the approach. It's not as if it's suddenly all noses to the grindstone,*" one source insisted. "[Management has] *recruited partners who they thought were likely to fit in.*"

Lean on me

We reckon there's a classic BLP trainee. It used to be that the firm attracted and hired solid, sensible types and a fair few of them were already quite settled with established career plans and established personal relationships. We used to see BLP as a place for a steady and rewarding career. As it changes and becomes more and more popular among students, we sense it has recruited a livelier, more vibrant trainee group than ever before. Certainly all our sources were very enthusiastic about their role in the firm's future. Describing the ideal recruit, one source said it is "*someone who will try to make every piece of work their best piece.*"

Trainees appreciated the abundance of support available to them. Said one: "*We've got it all – mentors, buddies, and the most approachable HR I've ever encountered. I really can't sing their praises enough.*" Trainees also found the support of peers helpful, "*especially if you're having a bad day. It really makes a difference to be able to e-mail them and know they're there for you.*" It's clear that trainees are genuinely able to make "*very good friends,*" and most attributed this to the fact that they all study the LPC together. To find out more about the pros and cons of teaming up with future colleagues while on the course, go to our website. "*Trainees socialise quite a lot after work,*" heading to The Monument, The Fine Line or The Brit. The social scene itself is described as "*quite good, but could be better.*" It is far from lacking on the sports front – "*you name it, we have a team for it. And if we don't, the games committee is always open to being propositioned for a new venture.*"

Retention rates took a slight dip in 2009, but bounced back in 2010, when 30 out of 37 qualifiers stayed on. The transparency of the NQ job allocation system also "*improved dramatically*" this past year. "*We had regular meetings and a timetable was set down and followed. Everything was made very clear to us.*" Also worth mentioning is that "*the HR team here are very good about looking after people who are not kept on, providing internal and external career coaching.*"

And finally...

This is a great place to get a larger-mid-sized City-firm training in a slightly less hardcore environment. But don't forget: *"BLP is dynamic and thinks of itself as going places. It wants people who reflect that ambition."*

Bevan Brittan LLP

The facts

Location: Bristol, London, Birmingham

Number of UK partners/solicitors: 48/137

Total number of trainees: 20

Seats: 4x6 months

Alternative seats: None

Extras: Pro bono – ProHelp, South Westminster Legal Advice Centre

On chambersstudent.co.uk

- How to get into BB
- BB's CSR and pro bono schemes
- We chat to CEO Andrew Manning

Bevan Brittan's priorities are heath and communities, local government and major corporates. It specialises in public sector matters, and projects that fall within the public-private interface. Is this a genius time to join the firm or would you be taking a gamble on Dave Cameron's Big Society?

Public interest

This firm is close to both local government and the companies that have worked with them in public-private partnerships throughout the Labour years. "*There's a mix of local authorities who want to procure projects, and private sector and consortiums bidding to do projects,*" said a trainee as they attempted to explain the firm's pivotal position at the junction between the two parts of the UK economy. Will BB's vast experience assist it or hold it back as we enter an era of deep public spending cuts and ideological shift? We quizzed the firm's chief exec Andrew Manning on this and he assured us that the firm sees ample opportunities in the changing UK economy. For extended highlights of that discussion go to our website.

The coalition government's decisions on how to shrink the national deficit will affect all public sector bodies. They make up BB's core client base and, in the words of one trainee, "*are going to need a lot of legal help making changes,*" so "*the question for people more senior at the firm than me, is how we can help out public sector clients to cut those costs.*" Within the firm "*people are on the case,*" and we had to agree once we'd chatted to management. There's much to look at: among the firm's clients are around 40% of all NHS trusts and 50% of all Strategic Health Authorities; the NHS Litigation Authority; 140 local authorities (25% of the UK's total); and various central government departments, such as the Department for Culture, Media & Sport. Around 80% of BB's work relies on the public sector.

"*Obviously schools and hospitals will still have to be built,*" argued one trainee just a couple of months before the coalition government applied the brakes to the mammoth Building Schools for the Future (BSF) programme. But is this true? Will there even be BSF work in two years after existing projects are completed? As Andrew Manning pointed out: "*We've done a lot of that kind of work for the past couple of years, but new opportunities are coming out, such as the Academies programme and schemes in waste management and renewable energy.*" Go back three or four years and BB's projects lawyers were undertaking masses of work in relation to big health PFI schemes, then it was LIFT projects (also health-related), and only then came BSF. "*It's always been a changing market,*" said Manning; "*it's not as if we were doing BSF for 20 years.*" Another growth area emerges from the fact that local authorities are now likely to partner with each other to provide various services, and there will also be structural changes within the NHS on which BB will advise.

Project Change

Bevan Brittan's four-seat training scheme operates in each of its three offices in Bristol (the HQ, and where 11 trainees presently work), Birmingham (four trainees) and

Chambers UK rankings

Administrative & Public Law	Local Government
Clinical Negligence	Personal Injury
Construction	Professional Discipline
Dispute Resolution	Projects
Education	Public Procurement
Employment	Real Estate
Healthcare	Real Estate Litigation
Information Technology	Social Housing

London (five). The seats and experiences available to them are broadly the same in the different offices, and the current seat list looks like this: medical law/personal injury (MLPI); commercial dispute resolution; projects; property; construction and engineering; commercial (local government/corporate); commercial (healthcare); and employment. No seat is compulsory and trainees usually stay put in the office to which they are recruited, although they may from time to time make short visits to others and occasionally qualify into another office. The training scheme starts with an induction in Bristol, which is a good networking opportunity and allows new starters to meet the various support departments.

Projects is "*an enormous area*" in which trainees are introduced to massive agreements and complicated financing arrangements for major schemes, commonly in the health, education, street lighting and waste management arenas. They can often run for two to three years; for example BB worked for the North Bristol NHS Trust, advising it on the £430m redevelopment of Southmead Hospital, which will be Bristol's major acute hospital from 2013. Towards the start of projects, trainees have a lot to get their heads around and "*might even be asked to do research into potential areas where we can bid for work.*" Document management is a core part of the trainee's role, too, as "*we need to keep everyone up to date with information and queries as they come in.*" Then there's "*reviewing amendments or notations made to agreements by fee earners*" and "*a lot of shadowing and taking notes at meetings.*" With so many themes to understand, and so much information to pick up on and then review with their supervisors, trainees say: "*You've got to be extremely well organised.*"

Projects work can be "*quite daunting if it's a first seat, as you don't know a single thing about it,*" but time and effort bring rewards. "*I was in a meeting myself as the sole legal rep advising the client,*" recalled one more experienced trainee, adding: "*Trainees never hide behind qualified solicitors.*" The hours vary between "*averagely busy at normal times, to your life just being taken over for about three weeks.*" And then, "*completions are always exciting, with champagne!*" In the growing Academies market, the firm has already assisted Buckinghamshire County Council in relation to the Aylesbury Academy.

Icelandic woes

Much of BB's corporate work is a little different to most firms'. "*It's standard M&A, just with an extra layer of required knowledge, and it's often not knowledge you can ever learn at law school – local government, private healthcare and regulatory modules don't exist.*" Recent deals have included Plymouth City Council's £20m sale of its Citybus service to the Go-Ahead Group, and the reorganisation, debt restructuring and eventual sale of fitness business Esporta Group to Société Générale. These deals were handled by the Bristol team, but trainees say London is actually the hottest of the three offices for corporate deals. More generally, trainees reckon that "*if you're interested in massive international M&A, you're at the wrong firm.*" Bearing in mind that 80% public sector stat, they're probably right.

Commercial litigation covers financial services issues, general debt recovery, injunctions, insolvency, commercial contracts and more. The clientele is rather impressive: a shedload of local authorities plus major corporates such as Motorola; Halfords; Pernod Ricard; Zurich Financial Services; PwC and Sony Ericsson. Lawyers have lately advised ten universities, among them The Open University and Cambridge, on the recovery of funds invested with those collapsed Icelandic banks. This class action involves many UK local authorities, too, and has required lawyers to ensure that the Icelandic banks' assets are worked out according to best international practice. "*There are a lot of judicial reviews for the public sector,*" one source mentioned, while another spoke of going to court alone to secure an order – the experience was "*really cool.*"

Stranger than fiction

In commercial healthcare seats, "*various requests might seem a bit strange,*" revealed one trainee. "*There was one individual who lost a specially designed false leg on an aeroplane and the airline was asking for a replacement leg.*" Part of the workload involves regulatory matters, "*making sure procedures are followed, and advising clients who haven't followed them.*" Pluses include regularly "*picking up the phone to clients*" and the fact that the subject matter is "*quite a mental challenge.*"

In MLPI, trainees are exposed to injury litigation but also wider questions affecting healthcare clients. Their assignments might take them to inquests or require them to address incoming requests for procedural advice. For example: "*What do you do if someone is in a morgue and no one will claim them? Sometimes it's just about checking statute.*" Injury claims, including those arising from clinical errors, can relate to anything from botched surgery to failure to provide appropriate mental health services to patients. Trainees "*visit witnesses and doctors at hospitals,*" draft letters of instruction to medical experts, and prepare reports for core client the NHS Litigation Authority, which manages claims against the health service. Operations go wrong, and "*there are loads of cerebral palsy cases.*" Work comes from many sources as "*you're very much the department's trainee.*" One trainee spent "*three days in a mental asylum compiling a disclosure list for action.*" For some, "*reading a file about a patient's condition can be a bit morbid.*" Perhaps to compensate, the team is known for its "*great sense of humour.*"

Masters of stand up

Training workshops and presentations are well attended by trainees. "*Lawyers tend to get rusty on the basics and need updates on the new stuff,*" explained one source. "*They get you to do research and then deliver the findings to everyone else.*" Ideally, trainees are "*willing to stand up in front of people and speak, and to pick up the phone and ring someone without seeming embarrassed.*" Departments organise their own specialist training and there are also soft skills sessions on things like "*communicating with impact, and ways to spark up conversation.*"

The less "*artificial*" way of learning is through visible and approachable role models. "*Because it's open-plan here, you just walk up to people.*" Desks are typically grouped in fours, so "*if I had any questions, my supervisor was only ever over my shoulder. I bothered him as much as I needed to.*" All trainees are assigned a formal mentor and a buddy from the year above. Secretarial and back-office support also got a big thumbs-up from our sources.

Each office is quite new and similarly decorated; they are described as "*modern,*" "*shiny,*" "*spacious,*" and "*really nice and fresh.*" Said one Bristol trainee: "*It's a bit like a nice hotel!*" Maybe so, but trainees don't typically spend "*silly amounts of hours working.*" They normally show up from around 9am and leave at around 6pm, unless there's something big coming to a boil. "*The Bristol office is like a glass palace,*" said one Brum trainee; "*it's big and has a headquarters feel. We're called 'the family' here in Birmingham, because everyone knows everyone.*" Some trainees from outside Bristol shared a common criticism – that the West Country city is the centre of the firm's universe. "*It would be nice to get someone from outside Bristol in HR,*" said one. As with many multi-site firms, BB pushes a 'one firm' ethos with decisions and policies made on a cross-office basis rather than location by location.

The firm never runs short of sports and social events. Each office has regular pubs and each pub has its BB regulars. Each office also has a social committee that organises monthly drinks (which coincides with a charity dress-down day). Sports include netball, softball, football, hockey and basketball, and there's a firm-wide interdepartmental football match (watch out for the feisty MLPI team). The firm also comes together as a whole during the autumn for a charity day that is spent painting schools or homeless shelters and then finishes off with a party. Each office has its own Christmas party at which the trainees are the main entertainment – they put on a show that pokes fun at the partners. It has to be done delicately though: "*They'll be interviewing me for an NQ job!*" chuckled one source. Apparently, "*one of the best things about the firm is there's no strong sense of hierarchy.*" In the pub, for example, "*everyone mingles, from secretaries to partners.*"

Redundancies have blighted the legal profession over the past two years, and we heard about another round of staff being let go by BB in September 2009. "*Some went in employment and commercial litigation. Corporate in London was hit, but employment was the biggest shock,*" said a trainee. What we have here is a firm that needs to respond swiftly to the changing needs of its clientele. This can't be an easy task as many of those needs are still undefined. As for the 2010 qualification round, nine of the 17 people reaching the end of their training contracts were awarded jobs at the firm, three in Bristol, two in Birmingham and four in London.

And finally...

"If you're interested in politics you'd be interested in what we do," remarked a trainee. This is so true right now given the (r)evolution in the public sector.

Bingham McCutchen LLP

The facts

Location: London

Number of UK partners/solicitors: 15/28 (+ 4 US qualified)

Total number of trainees: 4

Seats: 4x6 months

Alternative seats: Hong Kong

Extras: Pro Bono – LawWorks

On chambersstudent.co.uk
- How to get into Bingham
- We talk to global managing partner Jay Zimmerman
- Bingham's history

"It could be easier somewhere else," say trainees, *"but certainly not better."* The downturn has brought a bounty of work to this restructuring-oriented international firm, along with *"a genuine sense of momentum."*

Perfect storm

If ever a firm was well positioned to handle an economic crisis, it's Bingham McCutchen. As the 2009/10 financial results of US firms in the City trickled in, it proved to be one of the few to have bucked the trend of decreasing revenues, thanks largely to its particular focus on the counter-cyclical areas of restructuring and finance litigation. Bingham's strategy is simple: to establish a presence in all the world's major financial centres – it most recently opened a German outpost. The 36-year-old London office has solidly stuck to its "*boutiquey finance work*" rather than going full service. This has proved to be a good choice as the ten-year growth picture shows that office revenue has stepped up slightly each year, with a jump of nearly 32% (to £40.8m) in 2009/10. To read more about Bingham's strategy and aims for the future, see our website for an interview with global managing partner Jay Zimmerman.

Despite the revenue growth, "*we will keep our trainee numbers low. 'Steady as you go' has treated us very well,*" training partner Natasha Harrison said. Bingham takes just two trainees per year. "*We hire* [in this way] *because we want to grow organically and give the office real roots.*" There are four departments available to trainees at the moment – the financial restructuring group (FRG), litigation, finance and corporate. Seat allocation is very straightforward: trainees visit every department for six months. The office has newly established tax and EU/competition practices, which may host trainees in the future. If business needs permit, there could also be a seat in Hong Kong.

It should be obvious that this is a training contract for people with a genuine interest in finance and bankruptcy matters. You don't have to be an NYSE-nerd or a FTSE-fanatic to be hired, but being able to talk with confidence about what you read in the *FT* is a must.

FRG yeah you know me!

Bingham London's FRG has just under 30 lawyers, making it one of the largest restructuring groups in the City. It's had one of its busiest years to date, acting on some of the largest European restructurings in the downturn, such as advising the senior secured noteholders on the €3.1bn restructuring of Wind Hellas, a Greek mobile phone operator, and acting for bondholders on the restructuring of all three nationalised Icelandic banks – Kaupthing, Landsbanki and Glitnir. Bingham also worked with lenders on bingo chain Gala Coral's debt restructuring, and with the ad hoc committee of bondholders on the restructuring of INM (publishers of *The Independent*). The FRG seat is "*very hands-on – from day one you have to be completely ready to work, and work hard. It's very high pressure as the transactions move very quickly. It's quick-fire but it's fun.*" Trainees are responsible for "*bits of drafting, a lot of research, and really making sure you're on top of the deals.*"

Chambers UK rankings

Banking Litigation	Restructuring/Insolvency
Financial Services	

The small but mighty financial litigation group has become increasingly active in the area of banking and structured products litigation, and had a hand in some of the most high-value and complex banking disputes recently, including litigation surrounding the collapse of Lehman Brothers. It's also been working on a long-running matter for Polish blue-chip company Elektrim, which has to date resulted in more than ten successful judgments before the English High Court. "*Smaller matters like pensions litigations come and go as well.*" The seat offers "*a lot of drafting and document review,*" and plenty of client contact. One trainee "*liaised with bondholders, providing them with fee estimates, reconciling their claims and basically just dealing with their day-to-day queries.*"

In the finance seat, "*you're almost expected on day one to know the same stuff as an associate.*" Tough? "*It was awful at times, but it really sets you up and* [can be] *the best seat in hindsight.*" As well as supporting FRG, the finance team also specialises in private placement note issuance for international investors. The firm has a separate financial regulatory group that typically advises hedge funds, banks, brokerages, insurance intermediaries and other financial services institutions in connection with FSA investigations and enforcement actions. Bingham recently advised a large overseas bank in a dispute with the FSA concerning the opening of a branch in the UK. Non-contentious highlights include working with the risk management team of a British retail bank, reviewing the ways in which it was complying with the FSA's requirement that firms treat customers fairly.

The corporate practice also works closely with the restructuring practice, providing clients with M&A advice following restructuring or recovery efforts. Collaboration with the Tokyo and Hong Kong offices on cross-border transactions is not uncommon. In 2009, Bingham advised on the takeover of a football club by Asian investors. Bingham predicts its M&A practice, specifically in London and Asia, will be an area of growth for the firm. Trainees agreed it's "*a fantastic department*" that's partner-heavy, so "*you work directly with them consistently,*" usually handling most things "*on your own with light supervision by a local partner or one in Hong Kong.*"

Bingham state of mind

Global managing partner Jay Zimmerman (fondly referred to as Jay-Z) headed up the London office for seven years before taking the top job in 1994. "*He has a soft spot for London – he knows who everybody is here and knows them by name,*" a source revealed. That's got to be good news for the future of Bingham's British operation, which is now under the leadership of James Roome. He recently celebrated his tenth year at the firm and received rave reviews from our interviewees. "*I can go into his office and just have a chat, sharing what I saw in the paper or whatever,*" said one. "*There's a huge culture of open-door,*" another agreed.

Sources also appreciated that "*no one will put you in a year-based box, so you'll always be pushed and given as much as you want and can handle,*" and that the small office headcount means "*everyone knows everyone else and you'll do a lot of one-on-one work with partners.*" The other side to the coin is that "*there are fewer places to hide. You can't just walk out at 5pm* [without a good excuse] *because everyone will see you leaving.*"

Bingham is "*quite an efficient place,*" said one source. "*Usually you come to work and get your head down, then you want to go home and spend time with your friends and family.*" However, "*there is quite a good social budget, trainees are always welcome and firm socials are always good fun.*" The trainees and younger associates sound like a "*collegial*" bunch. "*We all went to see Priscilla Queen of the Desert a few weeks ago and did dinner and drinks.*"

In 2009, salaries for Bingham NQs hit £100,000, putting the firm top of the market in the City. "*You can't lie and say you're not aware of it, but I wouldn't be here just for the money,*" one source insisted. "*HR will root it out quite quickly if that's why you're applying... I think it will be quite obvious.*" Plus, if you're not willing to put in the graft, "*you'll get bored of the hours very quickly.*" They are "*consistently long: it just comes with the terrain.*" Our sources agreed that the media buzz surrounding the salary was "*just a bit of hype, and journalists getting over-excited.*" As lowly hacks ourselves, we can understand why that would be, but truthfully the salary simply works out as about the same paid to the NQs' peers in America. One of the two 2010 qualifiers stayed on to take advantage of the super-generous salary.

And finally...

"You've got to be good, you've got to be serious and you've got to really, really be ready to get stuck in." Tick those boxes? Find out more about the application process on our website.

Bircham Dyson Bell

The facts

Location: London, Edinburgh

Number of UK partners/solicitors: 47/71

Total number of trainees: 14

Seats: 4x6 months

Alternative seats: Secondments

Extras: Pro bono – Migrants Resource Centre

On chambersstudent.co.uk
- How to get into BDB
- We talk to training partner Nick Evans
- An overview of the Planning Act

After a revamp of its marketing campaign a few years ago, Bircham Dyson Bell has succeeded in widening its reputation beyond its stalwart practices.

Public interest

BDB is best known for Parliamentary, public affairs and planning work (PPP), perhaps because there are so few firms that operate in this sphere. This year, however, we found "*the main driving force*" behind most trainees choosing the firm was "*variety – variety of practice and variety of clients.*" Many also see BDB as a place where they wouldn't "*feel like just a cog in a big wheel.*" While PPP and things like charities law "*stand out because they're different,*" the firm is set on reinforcing its reputation as a full-service outfit.

The structure of the four-seat training contract reflects this goal, as seats are available in real estate; corporate; commercial; employment; litigation; private client; charities; and, of course, PPP. None are compulsory and all are punctuated by regular feedback and appraisals. Trainees with a hankering for in-house experience can be seconded to Esso, and it's usually a popular choice despite its Sussex location.

The PPP team is considered a significant force in relation to the planning, authorisation, procurement, construction and delivery of major infrastructure and other projects. In this seat, "*you're almost always working on very large matters, but your role will be really small.*" Trainees advised that it's important to realise that while the firm's legacy may be in pure Parliamentary issues, it is now much more focused on major infrastructure projects. There are usually multiple trainees in the department, and they're much needed as "*there's always so much going on.*"

While most Parliamentary work involves securing consent for projects, the firm still tackles some more traditional issues. Trainees reported "*assisting in drafting a private bill for a peer who wanted to submit it to the House of Lords*" and "*advising on a how a bill could be amended and then preparing the appropriate papers to be submitted to the relevant committee.*" On the public affairs side, the firm provides advice on lobbying and Select Committee preparation, as well as media relations and crisis management. It's known for its public sector law expertise, representing numerous city and borough councils. BDB also undertakes a significant amount of public procurement work for a range of public sector bodies, bidders and contractors, often providing advice on large-scale regeneration schemes – guiding them through the detailed requirements of the UK regulations, EU directives and relevant case law.

On the planning side, BDB works with the big names like British Land, National Grid and Thames Water. The firm is currently advising National Grid on the Hinkley Point power station, Transport for London and London Underground on a major upgrade to Victoria Tube Station, and English Heritage on its opposition to proposals by P&O for three very tall buildings next to Waterloo Station. BDB is leading the way on developing advice surrounding the Planning Act 2008, a new regime that came into effect in March 2010. See our website for more information.

Chambers UK rankings

Administrative & Public Law	Parliamentary & Public Affairs
Agriculture & Rural Affairs	Planning
Charities	Police Law
Employment	Private Client
Environment	Public Procurement
Family/Matrimonial	Transport
Local Government	

Money makes the world go around

BDB's real estate practice handles standard commercial property matters, like advising Centrepoint Soho on its acquisition of a 60-year lease of social housing accommodation, along with standard portfolio management for the likes of ExxonMobil and Docklands Light Railway. It is known, too, for its specialist leasehold enfranchisement team. This team attracts a large number of residential tenant clients and investors on the main London estates, and frequently acts on the highest-value and most significant residential cases in Central London, recently completing the leasehold enfranchisement of Lincoln House, Basil Street, SW3 for £9.7m. The firm is making strides in the property finance arena, working with the likes of Santander, Clydesdale Bank and RBS. Recent highlights include advising RBS on a number of loans to charities including the Mothers Union and the Terrence Higgins Trust. Trainees said the real estate department has *"a great atmosphere." "You get a lot of your own files; one of mine was really big and I was working on it almost every day, contacting a very large client. It's a really good experience to have a file like that; it's really good for your confidence."*

Advice to charities runs through every department of the firm, but the charities department itself is *"a fairly small team."* Trainees found it *"an interesting area because of its mixture of all the different types of law, from corporate to trusts."* They also enjoyed being able to have their own files to manage. Some reported the rewarding feeling of seeing files through from start to finish – *"setting charities up and having them registered, and then advising on any constitutional changes or conflicts."* The files made available to trainees tend to be small, but the firm assists some of the nation's leading charities like WWF UK, the BBC Children in Need Appeal and Arts Council England. In the run up to the general election, BDB used its public affairs expertise to assist charities with lobbying.

Trainees receive *"a similar level of responsibility"* in private wealth seats. *"We have our own files* [which can include] *anything from preparing a will to basic tax planning or ongoing probate files. There's also a fair amount of Court of Protection work as well."* As in the charities seat, the more modest files will be designated for trainees, but some of the firm's bigger work includes advising a notable family from the Middle East and their offshore trustees on international wealth structuring, trusts and UK tax issues. Private wealth is the firm's second-largest department after PPP, and sources described the team as *"very intelligent and quite cerebral, as it can be quite academic at times since everything is looked at from a tax perspective."*

The family team gets involved in private wealth matters when there are divorce or guardian issues at hand, and the private wealth team will step into family matters when there are issues like cross-jurisdictional tax obligations. Yet the family team is more than capable of standing on its own two feet. It has been involved in an ongoing case combining matrimonial work with the after-effects of white-collar crime. The clients, both resident in Switzerland, are the second and third ex-wives of an individual who was found guilty several years ago of a tax fraud that was said to have cheated HMRC out of nearly £100m.

The employment group focuses on complex Employment Tribunal and High Court claims and employer restructurings. It has a diverse clientele that includes Royal Mail, National Express, Qatar Airlines, NHS trusts, charities, educators, retailers and law firms. The firm additionally has a specialty in industrial relations and acted for nine separate London bus companies in successful challenges to a London-wide bus strike by 14,000 drivers, organised by the union Unite in 2008. According to trainees, it's *"a brilliant seat. The mix of contentious and non-contentious makes for really interesting work. You'll be involved in high-profile matters as well as smaller ones, and there's so much client contact with the tribunals."*

The last three seat options are corporate, commercial and litigation. Corporate *"is not one of the firm's big areas. We advise organisations of a certain size* [in the lower mid-market]*, but because of that – and the size of the department – I found that as a trainee I was doing things that were handled by associates and senior assistants on the other side. It's a much sharper learning curve here than it would be in the magic circle,"* one source told us. The commercial seat *"generally speaking is contract negotiation and contract drafting,"* but trainees are also tasked with giving weekly presentations on commercial law updates. There's *"an awful lot of advocacy"* in the litigation seat. *"One of our clients is a large social landlord, and trainees are expected to go to court and litigate on their behalf. You do the entire process from beginning to end. In the past five months I think I've done seven hearings by myself."*

Budget cuts

Scotland Yard is one of the firm's neighbours and the Metropolitan Police Force is a client. Lawyers handle many issues, from allegations made against officers to the supply of IT systems. On the other side of BDB's office is St James's Park – not too shabby a back yard. You'll find groups of trainees and other staff lunching there in the summer. Trainees found working in Westminster a "*very pleasant*" alternative to the City. "*One of the nice things is that you see all the tourists. It's nice to think that you're working in an area that people want to come visit.*" The location proved to be even more exciting during the general election. "*The best bit about it was that you could hear the booming helicopters overhead. Everyone was rushing around to look out the windows; some people rushed out to see Cameron's speech. There was a real sense of excitement and buzz about the area.*"

However, as the coalition government announced its plans for public-sector budget cuts, the atmosphere changed. "*Everyone is kind of just watching the space,*" one trainee told us. This wait-and-see worry only adds to the pre-existing "*slight morale problem. I don't know whether it's recession cynicism or something deeper. The context in which law firms operate now is changing quite quickly. They are afraid of 'Tesco law' and the Ryanairs of legal service... budget law where clients can pay less and end up with the same thing. It's already shown that clients are getting more picky about paying their bills; expecting more and more from less and less, and it's starting to get a little bit depressing. There are no more sandwiches at our lunchtime meetings. Will they ever return?*" We put these issues to training partner Nick Evans; see his responses on our website.

Other than those two nagging issues, trainees were generally happy with the firm's atmosphere. "*It's certainly not a flashy firm. Everything's a bit more old-school here and it's not a particularly loud office.*" Indeed, whilst most firms are sporting modern minimalist leather sofas in the lobby, at BDB you'll find plush green velvet that could have been imported from your grandparents' house. Most trainees seemed more than happy to trade 'flash' for "*decent hours,*" "*a good work-life balance*" and "*a subtle, non-dictated*" social scene. The firms' annual rowing regatta is attended by most, and there are football and netball teams. "*We don't have that culture of everyone always heading to the pub after work, but there's a good group of people who like to go out.*"

Real progress

In 2010, four jobs were made available for the seven qualifiers. After a formal interview process for each, all four were filled. While some of the qualifiers were moving on to other firms, they did make it clear that "*the support throughout* [their] *training was fantastic. It's a really good place to train for that reason. There are so many people that are encouraging and always giving advice.*" Another reason none regretted choosing BDB was "*the amount of responsibility given to you when you prove you're ready to accept it: that can't be underrated. If you do a good job on one piece of work you will get more responsibility on the next. You can really chart your progress and by the end of a seat you'll be doing ten times more and taking ownership. People really want to invest in trainees, you're not just a resource.*"

This firm puts a lot of emphasis on previous work experience and there tends to be just as many mature candidates as those who have come straight through university and law school. If you want to get hired here, "*you need to show that while law is what you want to do professionally, you have other attributes and interests outside of it.*" Go online for more recruitment tips.

And finally...

"It won't suit everyone, but it certainly suited me. From day one I felt like I was making a difference."

- **Interview advice:** An HR manager says, "Show work experience and transferable skills, but make it relevant. Tell us why it will benefit the firm and why what you have learnt will make you a good lawyer."

Bird & Bird LLP

The facts

Location: London

Number of UK partners/solicitors: 75/172

Total number of trainees: 28

Seats: 4x6 months

Alternative seats: Overseas seats, secondments

Extras: Pro bono – various Law Centres, Toynbee Hall, Red Cross, Oxfam International; language training

On chambersstudent.co.uk
- How to get into Bird & Bird
- Pro bono opportunities at the firm
- Recent IP highlights

Monumental in IP and commercial advice, magnificent in sports, IT and aviation, and good at pretty much everything else, Bird & Bird continues to soar.

Bigger and better

While trainees at Bird & Bird insist that this is "*not a big corporate City law firm,*" its clients are as big as they come and range from the highbrow (Woody Allen) to the lowbrow (the Crazy Frog). They include Adobe, Airbus, Amazon, easyJet, Ericsson, Facebook, Flybe, Jack Daniels, lastminute.com, Nestlé, Nokia, PayPal, Mattel (for Polly Pocket), T-Mobile, Sega, various pharmaceutical companies and many, many more names you'll be familiar with. The firm has also built up some 17 offices across mainland Europe, plus others in Beijing, Hong Kong and Shanghai. No minnow this.

But we do see where our sources are coming from. Twobirds, as you might sometimes see it referred to, is not your classic corporate/finance-focused firm, although it does achieve respectable *Chambers UK* rankings in those areas. Instead, it is particularly well known for its intellectual property practice, which partly explains all those household-name clients.

While the firm is sometimes portrayed as heavily IP-focused (and don't worry: we'll go on at great length about that practice), it is "*actually more of a commercial firm.*" In addition to IP, Twobirds is ranked in the top tier in the UK for aviation, data protection, IT, life sciences, sports law, telecommunications and dispute resolution. New starters are asked to state their seat preferences before joining, and after that to let the recruiters know what they want in a more informal way. With the demand for certain seats very high, it's important to be clear and vocal about what you want. "*Stake your claim early, right at the start,*" advised our sources.

The IP crowd

For intellectual property, Bird & Bird is recognised by *Chambers* as one of the best in Europe, never mind the UK. To keep up the quality of the department, the firm looks for excellence in trainees. In turn, they have a reputation for being rather brainy. While a PhD in chemistry (or engineering, physics, maths, biology…) isn't essential in order to get involved in IP, it certainly won't hurt. In 2010, two of the three people taken on as newly qualified solicitors in the IP department had a background in science. The majority of the work in the department is so-called 'hard IP', which covers patents and industrial designs. However, former scientists also qualify into non-IP areas, and the so-called 'soft IP' seat (which deals with copyright, trade marks, design rights and database rights) is incredibly popular among trainees with no specialist scientific knowledge.

There has been an increase in the volume of trade mark litigation of late. The recession is an important factor in this, as companies appear to be more prepared to fight to keep competitors out of their market. Bird & Bird acted for Chinese company Sany Group against car manufacturer Daimler, successfully arguing that the logo Sany used on its diggers, cranes and concrete pumps was unlikely to cause confusion with the famous Mercedes three-pointed star. In another matter, the firm was instructed by Chippendales USA in an attempt to prevent unauthorised use of its name by a newly formed male dance troupe called 'Here Come the Boys'. This new troupe included a number of former Chippendales and raised the interesting legal question of how far former employees can go in

Chambers UK rankings

Asset Finance	Information Technology
Aviation	Intellectual Property
Banking & Finance	Life Sciences
Competition/European Law	Media & Entertainment
Construction	Outsourcing
Corporate/M&A	Private Equity
Data Protection	Product Liability
Dispute Resolution	Public Procurement
Employment	Sports Law
Fraud	Telecommunications
Immigration	Travel

referring to their previous employer in relation to a new venture. During this case, Bird & Bird's corridors were packed with handsome young men, their modesty covered by nothing but a skimpy thong, their tightly packed abs glistening with baby oil, their mighty torsos thrusting, solid and proud... sorry, we got distracted there for a minute. Nothing of the sort has ever been seen in the corridors of Bird & Bird. As far as we know.

Trainees are likely to be able to bag a seat in IP if they want it, but because of the specialised nature of the work they tend not to have huge responsibility or too much client contact. There aren't many paralegals so trainees end up doing bundling, filing and research. Other tasks include small bits of drafting, writing letters to people who have infringed copyright and advising companies on IP rights. There may also be some visits to court and sitting in on mediations.

The IP department is "*a whole separate world*" and "*almost like a separate firm.*" Especially at trainee level, you can go for two years without knowing anyone there, as they are in a separate office and have their own social events. There have been some attempts at increased interaction recently, but these have met with "*limited success.*" While the division is "*not at all acrimonious,*" the IP lawyers do seem to quite enjoy the separation as it allows them to maintain their own departmental persona and slightly more informal atmosphere. A common complaint is the fact that the firm is split into three very separate offices, one of which is "*much nicer than the others.*" Most of our sources felt that a single building "*would be so much better*" as it would build a more cohesive atmosphere and make it easier to know everyone else in the firm.

Commercial success

The IP and commercial departments are of similar size and prestige, and there is "*a bit of friendly rivalry*" between the two. The commercial team's work spans technology, telecoms, data protection, outsourcing and IT, and there's also a top-notch sports subgroup that counts among its clients Andy Murray, the International Olympic Committee, UEFA, FIFA, the Premier League, Wembley Stadium, Chelsea and Tottenham Hotspur FCs, Nike, the Rugby Football Union, the Rugby Football League, the Lawn Tennis Association, the International Cricket Council, the International Tennis Federation, the British Darts Organisation and many more. The sports law seat is highly sought after but "*notoriously hard work,*" and there are only one or two seats available at a time.

The IT subgroup advised BT on a new £2.6bn system for the NHS, which was designed to save it money and connect hundreds of thousands of doctors, nurses and other professionals to each other. In a separate matter, Twobirds advised Guy's & St Thomas' NHS Foundation Trust on its outsourcing of pathology services to a newly created LLP. Lord Carter of Coles is well known for his report on the provision of Legal Aid, but he also led a review of NHS pathology services in which he challenged the sector to deliver 'beneficial change' to pathology needs. This outsourcing is a direct response to that review.

As you can see, the commercial department attracts high-profile work and this is perhaps why it is always oversubscribed, for both seats and NQ jobs. The supervisors are "*brilliant,*" the team is large, sociable and lively but also "*laid-back,*" and there are always things going on. Trainee tasks typically include research, contract drafting, marketing and admin duties, and there is scope to get involved in deal negotiations.

The dispute resolution department, which doubled in size when Twobirds merged with specialist aviation law firm Lane & Partners in 2008, is also very popular. This busy and friendly team provides trainees with good responsibility and loads of client contact. The team has been acting for the claimants in a $100m High Court case – a family affair involving wealthy shipowner Loucas Haji-Ioannou (and, latterly, his heirs) and John Frangos, another shipowner and the former's ex-son-in-law. Disputes involving family members are normally humdingers, so we'd love to have been in court for a few days of that trial! Other cases relate to things such as video games, the motor industry and an individual who tried to sell his house by way of an online competition. You might think that sounds crazy, but apparently it's an increasingly popular thing to do. In that case the firm's client was PayPal, and one of the lawyers working on the case had previously been on secondment to that organisation.

Other teams offering seats include corporate, employment, real estate and banking. The banking group has a more traditional vibe, and as "*you can be the main point of contact with a client,*" trainees may take care of some matters entirely on their own. Tasks include daily e-mail contact with clients, registering land and sending out draft loan documents. In the busy corporate seat the hours can be long, but trainees are given good levels of responsibility.

Flying the nest

Overseas seats are available to some, and if you express clear interest you're quite likely to be able to take advantage of this part of the scheme. Possible destinations include Düsseldorf, Munich, Frankfurt, The Hague, Helsinki, Milan, Madrid, Stockholm, Brussels, Warsaw and Hong Kong, and these seats usually last either three or six months. Except for the English-speaking Helsinki, Stockholm and Brussels seats, trainees will need proficiency in the local language, but the firm does provide several months of language training in advance. There are also some exciting client secondments available. Trainees with some previous experience in the client's field are often favoured over those who arrive straight from uni and law school.

We received mixed comments about working hours. Some trainees were pleasantly surprised at how rarely they had to work late, but a couple of people were equally surprised to find that "*the hours are properly City.*" Overall, the consensus seemed to be that the average day runs from 8.30am to 6.30pm, with a few late nights where necessary, especially in corporate.

Because of its techy clients, some people "*expect the firm to be funky,*" but trainees say it's quite down-to-earth, "*not stuffy, but also not so zany.*" On the 'wacky office culture' front, Twobirds isn't exactly Google, but it does have table football games dotted around its offices. Watch out for the more eccentric partners, probably best described as "*big personalities,*" who make the firm an even more interesting place to work.

Golf, burlesque and karaoke

The Fetter Lane offices are not far from Lincoln's Inn Fields and the Royal Courts of Justice. The area is "*leafy, pleasant and buzzing,*" with lots of good places for lunch. There are two pubs in the short space between the three offices, the White Swan and the Castle, where you're guaranteed to bump into familiar faces on a Friday might. That said, there isn't "*a really macho hard-drinking culture.*" Karaoke at Lucky Voice is also a regular occurrence. A while ago, a burlesque bar called Volupté opened downstairs from one of the offices, but despite the club's positively chaste no-nipple policy, Bird & Bird's employees are discouraged from attending. Instead they can get involved in softball, football (male and female – there's an annual tournament between all the European offices), netball, cricket, golf and yoga. Some have also participated in a cycle ride to Paris and gone mountain biking in the Czech Republic. The firm's organised social life "*could be better,*" say some trainees, but firm-wide drinks parties occur every few months and there is a monthly film night with pizza. However, the majority of events are aimed at different departments, which is not ideal for integration.

Thanks to the variety of the firm's work and the fact that it "*doesn't keep all its eggs in one basket*" (over half of its lawyers operate outside the UK), Bird & Bird has fared quite well during the recession. Turnover rose by nearly 30% in the 2008/09 financial year to £186.3m, and in 2009/10 rose a further 10% to a record £201.8m. There were some redundancies and associate salaries were cut, but on the brighter side there were no trainee deferrals and 100% retention of qualifying trainees in 2009. In 2010, the firm managed to keep on 15 out of 19. Of those, three went to IP and four to the commercial department. One further qualifier was offered a six-month contract in Sweden.

And finally...

While the IP and commercial departments have most clout, the rest of the firm is expanding and improving. Clamour loudly about your preferences and you'll get a fine training.

Bond Pearce LLP

The facts

Location: Bristol, Plymouth, Southampton, London, Aberdeen

Number of UK partners/solicitors: 78/271

Total number of trainees: 30

Seats: 4x6 months

Alternative seats: Secondments

On chambersstudent.co.uk
- How to get into Bond Pearce
- Some of the firm's highlight cases and deals
- An idiot's guide to wind farms

Born in 1885 in the land of clotted cream and scrumpy, this West Country native is anything but a country bumpkin.

Shout out

Only last year trainees bemoaned the fact that Bond Pearce wasn't really on enough students' radars. "*It's a shame more graduates don't know about us,*" one lamented. As well as local clients like The Eden Project, the firm has a national client list to make you drool – Carlsberg, HSBC, Marks & Sparks, English Heritage and AIG to name but a few – plus an expanding London office. The firm has been pretty steady throughout the recession, with revenue only dipping slightly from £47.5m to £47m in 2009/10 and partner profits actually increasing by 10%. There's certainly plenty to shout about.

Bond Pearce's expertise frequently extends far beyond its hunting grounds in the South and South West. The firm is *Chambers UK*-ranked nationally for energy sector matters, retail, health and safety, local government and education. It earns best-in-the-region rankings in corporate/M&A; banking and finance; employment; IT; planning; licensing; product liability; real estate; and real estate litigation. The quality of its work and clients is important to trainees: our interviewees chose Bond Pearce because they had a connection with one of the office locations or a "*hatred*" of London – or both – but they wanted to do London-style work. "*I love the big client list and the big-money deals,*" one said.

Trainees are recruited to Bristol (the largest office) Plymouth and Southampton. "*As Bond Pearce has national clients,*" a trainee explained, "*there's collaboration between offices. The work isn't split by location.*" So, for example, Plymouth lawyers recover debts for Southampton-based B&Q, which is a major client, "*because we have the best team here.*" Similarly, if a trainee's supervisor isn't around, they may pick up the phone to "*the next best person to ask,*" even if that person is in another office.

In 2008, the firm almost pruned its Exeter office out of existence, as part of a new strategy to consolidate the Devon practice in one location. New buds of offices in London and Aberdeen appeared in its place, and two years on are starting to blossom. Bond Pearce's energy work has gone from strength to strength, while the London branch recently attracted big names including Barlow Lyde & Gilbert's former senior partner Richard Dedman, who is one of the UK's top professional liability and insurance lawyers. "*I get the feeling we're a firm on the move,*" a trainee commented. "*We aspire to reach the top 30.*" At the AGM earlier in 2010, mergers were mooted as a possible growth strategy, according to sources. "*In order to jump from a top 50 to a top 30 firm, we'd need to merge,*" one trainee suggested.

The range of seat options for trainees is impressive. Bristol has the most, and trainees list their five preferences before they join. In Plymouth and Southampton they list their top three. The seat allocation system is "*quite fair – if you don't get your first choice they'll try and make sure you get it the next time.*" Each department makes a business case for having a trainee and this ensures everyone stays busy. New starters spend the first four days in Bristol for an induction, and the non-Bristolians then disperse to their offices on the Friday. In each location, they're given a buddy to help settle them in.

Chambers UK rankings

Banking & Finance	Intellectual Property
Competition/European Law	Licensing
Construction	Local Government
Corporate/M&A	Pensions
Debt Recovery	Personal Injury
Dispute Resolution	Planning
Education	Product Liability
Employment	Professional Negligence
Energy & Natural Resources	Real Estate
Environment	Real Estate Litigation
Health & Safety	Restructuring/Insolvency
Information Technology	Retail

Green army

Bond Pearce is literally making waves in the buoyant renewable energy sector: it is advising on several tidal energy projects including an offshore wave-hub project in the South West. The 50-strong team is increasingly active further afield in both traditional and renewable energy, in the North and Irish Seas, and internationally. For example, it advised client Blue Oil on bids for assets put up for sale by Shell and ExxonMobil in Central America, and has advised UK oil explorer Afren in Nigeria. The corporate seat features "*quite a lot of oil and gas now,*" a trainee confirmed, while energy assignments are also keeping other departments like commercial property busy. Here, trainees have helped draw up option agreements for wind farms. A client like npower might do site surveys for a new wind farm, find a good one, then approach the landowner with a view to having first dibs if he ever chooses to sell up. "*Then we'd come in and sort out an option, say for 25 years.*" This type of work involves "*a lot of research, and I got to draft some option agreements myself, under a senior associate,*" a source reported. The sites are all around the country, including north of the border, though the complexities of Scottish law are apparently sometimes "*a pain.*"

Trainees in the planning seat have lately encountered plenty of infrastructure projects, particularly public sector-led regeneration schemes involving waste and housing. There's often cross-over with the work of other departments, like real estate and tax. The team recently advised East Devon District Council on a retail-led regeneration project, and Veolia Environmental Services sought assistance in respect of a waste-to-energy facility at a former Nottinghamshire colliery. There's a steady stream of renewable energy work. "*I liked the seat because it's interesting,*" a trainee told us, even though it's "*difficult, dense law*" dealing with "*thick pieces of legislation with pages and pages to plough through.*" Other key clients include ScottishPower Renewables, Ecotricity and Bristol City Council.

You've got mail

Nearly half of Bond Pearce's work is contentious, and trainees like the professional indemnity seat because it offers a useful overview of the litigation process, albeit in a niche area. The firm represents insurers including Aon and Royal & SunAlliance in negligence claims against surveyors, accountants and lawyers. Bond Pearce has one of the largest regional professional indemnity departments in the UK, and *Chambers UK* ranks it top of the tree. "*The quality of the training has been fantastic,*" one trainee reported, and "*you can run low-value claims yourself.*" In multimillion-pound cases, expect the "*usual trainee tasks*" like document bundling. The focus of an insurance seat varies between offices, but the defence of general liability claims and personal injury cases features heavily. "*They really pushed me and gave me a good range of tasks like disclosure, dealing with financial queries and looking at detailed assessments for costs,*" recalled one source. Trainees may even get to interview witnesses and prepare their statements. A typical scenario might involve a car crash; the team would represent the insurer and try to negotiate a settlement. "*Much bigger cases include spinal and brain injury claims.*"

Bond Pearce has over 40 years' experience in the retail sector and represents over 45 national and international retailers, including Sainsbury's, Marks & Spencer, GAME, Specsavers and The Post Office. Such clients seek assistance with property issues, competition and regulatory law, IP, employment and commercial matters. B&Q offers secondment opportunities to trainees – "*the commercial awareness gained is invaluable. I was constantly busy,*" said an interviewee who'd spent a seat with the company. The dispute resolution team – one of the largest outside London – helped The Post Office complete its 2,500-branch closure programme, advising on the complex legal risks involved. Other national clients include 3 Mobile, QVC and Skandia. Retail litigation offers trainees "*a complete mixed bag. It's research-based and very different to corporate, which was mainly document management and production.*" Research assignments can include anything from "*Sunday trading to the migration of silicone into food.*" The small banking team in Southampton is "*awesome,*" not only for the quality of the supervision but also the work. The commercial seat, meanwhile, involves drafting experience galore, often IP-related.

Video creates training stars

Training events include monthly departmental videoconferences, when Bristol, Southampton and Plymouth might each present for 20 minutes. "*Throughout the training contract I've been encouraged to go to as many sessions and events as possible,*" a source assured us. Each department has its own internal training; for example, the litigation department might congregate in Bristol for a day. The commercial department is starting a new programme whereby junior lawyers take it in turns to give a monthly lunchtime presentation on an area of commercial law, before opening up the floor for discussion. "*There's a lot of training in commercial teams especially, as the law changes all the time.*"

Mid and end-of-seat reviews currently use the same "*lengthy*" form. Several trainees told us they'd prefer a shorter, "*easier form for the mid-seat seat review, and to keep the current meaty document for the end-of-seat appraisal. It's slightly frustrating in some respects because it's burdensome to have to fill it out all the time.*" Apparently, HR is considering revising this process in light of the feedback.

Putting your head above the parapet

The Bristol office, two minutes from Temple Meads station in a new business district, is in an "*ultra-modern*" steel and glass building. The semi-open plan office layout is similar to the one in Southampton, with support staff in the centre of the office and fee earners around the outside, separated by "*lime-coloured dividers and white partition walls.*" Vending machines are on hand in a break-out area to satisfy chocolate and sandwich cravings. The big screen in one of the meeting rooms came in handy during the World Cup. Trainees say Bristol is "*more family-oriented,*" while Southampton is "*more social.*" In Southampton, too, a pod seating system helps create a friendly vibe and aids communication. Approaching partners isn't a big deal: "*You can just pop your head over the parapet.*" The London office was founded in 2003 as a 'touchpad' office, but since moving buildings in 2008 and making a number of lateral hires, it's clear that Bond Pearce has greater ambitions for the capital. There is now a seat option for trainees, although at present there are no plans to launch a full training scheme here. Also available is a secondment to the Aberdeen office, where the trainee works on oil and gas matters.

Plymouth is the "*most unique Bond Pearce office,*" said interviewees. Situated in Millbay "*near the flash West Hoe area,*" the building is a "*concrete monstrosity*" but "*brand-new inside.*" The firm occupies the top three floors of this six-storey building so there are "*fab views of the sea.*" Warships entering and leaving the nearby naval base complement the picture postcard scene and trainees tell us that Plymouth "*really comes to life in the summer when the tourists are here.*" A big screen in the Piazza in the city centre shows Wimbledon, plus opera and family films at other times. "*Plymouth's nice in summer, windy in winter.*" The pub of choice here is Sippers "*on the corner, 200 yards away. Not the best, but we go,*" a trainee confessed.

Are you ready to have fun?

Bond Pearce has a warm culture, and charitable and social activities fill up the calendar. The property team recently completed a sponsored cycle ride from Bristol to Southampton, camping outside Bath on the way down. Bristol lawyers, meanwhile, abseiled from their rooftop terrace, while another team completed the Three Peaks Challenge – Snowdon, Scafell Pike and Ben Nevis – in under 24 hours. "*We had perfect weather, luckily!*" one explained. On another occasion, partners (including the chairman and managing partner) "*jumped out of a plane for The Prince's Trust.*" In Southampton, the Bond Pearce triathletes competed in a local charity fundraiser, and Plymouth staff completed a half-marathon, doubtless egged along by chants of "*Green Arm-y!*"

The Bristol social committee organises subsidised events such as tickets for the cricket or a boat trip. There's also a monthly prize draw to win £50 of Marks & Sparks vouchers. Safe to say, the Bristol lawyers never run out of pants and socks. Their preferred watering hole is Toto's on the waterfront, next to the old office Bond Pearce left nearly five years ago. Delightful Southampton nightlife includes the re-launched Oceana nightclub in the pre-fab Leisureworld by the busy dual carriageway, and the more up-market Jo Daflo's, which is in a converted church. The sociable Bond Pearce trainees go out "*most Fridays,*" and are often more likely to be spotted in the trendy Bedford Place bars and eateries. They are active in the Junior Lawyers Division, and there's a good sports and social committee in the office.

Bond Pearce's friendly culture is assisted by decent work hours – 9am till 5.15pm, with 75 minutes for lunch. The downside is the pay, trainees said. A Bristol source, for example, told us: "*Compared to other firms we're not as well paid... but I'm happy. It's just a little surprising that other Bristol firms do the same work and their people get more.*"

And finally...

Such is the trainees' obvious affection for the firm, we weren't in the least surprised that so many wanted to stay on after their training contracts. In 2010 all 11 qualifiers did so.

- **Be flexible:** "Have a varied CV so that you can talk about a lot of different things in your interviews. It will relax you to talk about things that you're comfortable and happy with, and it will give the interviewers a better idea of who you are."

Boodle Hatfield

The facts

Location: London

Number of UK partners/solicitors: 32/31

Total number of trainees: 12

Seats: 4x6 months

Alternative seats: Oxford

Extras: Pro bono – Fulham Legal Advice Centre

On chambersstudent.co.uk
- How to get into Boodle Hatfield
- Digested Dukes of Westminster
- The Boodle pedigree

Soon to celebrate its third centenary, Boodle Hatfield achieves a sophisticated blend of the old and the new.

Life is Boodiful

Traditionally associated with Regency refinement, Boodle Hatfield's 21st century script reads less like an Austen adaptation and more like a *Dynasty*-style modern melodrama. Vast wealth, family feuding, sprawling estates and acrimonious divorce cases all form part of its storyline, with titled aristocrats and international entrepreneurs among the characters. The lawyers seem to have remained modest and unassuming in the face of such a clientele, and the environment in their Bond Street offices is one of a studious calm in contrast to the retail chaos going on outside. Realistically, only those shopping for firms strong on private client and property law should think of investing their time in a Boodle application, but the launch of an arts and culture practice group following the widely publicised success of an action taken against Christie's auction house on behalf of the former owners of a Titian painting demonstrates that the firm's interests are expanding. Lateral hiring continues apace, with three new partners being taken on at the beginning of 2010 and another corporate partner joining towards the end of 2010.

Lording it

The estate of the nation's richest man, the Duke of Westminster, bestrides many of London's more exclusive districts and much of the British rural landscape too. It's unsurprising then that the Grosvenor Estate manages to predominate Boodle's property practice. For one trainee, their property seat was "*85 to 90% Grosvenor.*" Due to its size, the work of this department can be a lot more varied than it might at first sound. As well as servicing Grosvenor's requirements, it acts for a couple of big pension funds and the Marriott Hotel chain, and is split into a number of different teams for residential, construction, development, environment and agriculture. All trainees spoke highly of their almost-inevitable seat in the department. Charged from the outset with managing their own "*cupboard full of files,*" it might come as quite a shock to be "*speaking to clients from the start,*" but in a fast-paced and busy environment, hitting the ground running soon launches into an exhilarating ride. Given the firm's experience with landed estates and penchant for noble clients, it should come as no surprise that it is also highly ranked by *Chambers UK* in the field of agriculture and rural affairs.

In the private client seat, the individuals who instruct Boodle unsurprisingly demand its best, which often means that trainees will find their phones ring a lot less than seniors'. As one source put it: "*Because the clients are very wealthy individuals and very important, they are also quite fussy about who their solicitors are.*" In an environment of hothouse academia, expect a good deal more research and microscopic discussions over the "*incredibly difficult technical details*" of black letter law. "*It's a very different culture with very clever people,*" was one interviewee's summation. The non-contentious side of the department deals with offshore tax and trust issues, while the contentious side is often occupied with complex litigation. Their hard work is obviously paying off as Boodle Hatfield has recently broken into *Chambers UK*'s top tier for contentious trust work.

Chambers UK rankings

Agriculture & Rural Affairs	Real Estate
Family/Matrimonial	Real Estate Litigation
Private Client	

The trials and tribulations of a family seat are a far cry from law school studies. "*It can't be taught,*" said one interviewee; "*you don't appreciate the fact that you'll be in court a lot, and you have a lot of client contact.*" That said, attending client conferences, working on high-profile divorce settlements and Children Act cases lacks nothing in drama and job satisfaction. "*I really, really enjoyed it,*" a source gushed. For those who, on leaving university, were torn between a life in the law and scriptwriting courtroom drama, the seat also gives the chance to be creative (though not with the truth, of course) in drafting long witness statements. Boodle Hatfield also has a small commercial litigation practice that nonetheless handles some substantial cases. Its eight-strong team is headed by a partner who is working on a dispute that is tied both to the travails of the Icelandic bank Kaupthing and to the recent sale of the Somerfield supermarket chain to the Co-op. The team also handles interesting art disputes.

With just two partners, three assistant solicitors and two trainees, the corporate department is intimate to say the least, but "*you learn so much*" when it's like that. The team focuses on privately held or controlled companies, high net worth individuals and entrepreneurs. It recently acted on the refurbishment of the Crowne Plaza Blackfriars hotel and advises whisky brand Cutty Sark on its international distribution network. "*If you feel confident with it, they're happy to let you do it,*" trainees said of the work here, and though the deals are smaller than those of the big boys in the City, a nice consequence is that you can see them through "*from beginning to end.*"

A break from the bustle of London comes in the form of Boodle's one secondment opportunity, a private client seat among Oxford's dreaming spires. The Oxford team is also ranked in the top tier by *Chambers UK* for private client work, which at trainee level involves a good deal of research. "*My drafting skills have come along a hell of a lot,*" claimed a source. The firm provides accommodation, and with the Oxford Tube coach shuttle doing the 100-minute ride every ten minutes, a night on the tiles – or cobbles – is really only a stone's throw away.

Don't tell them what they can't do

Trainees were adamant that "*we are not a City firm, and we are not pretending to be,*" and were also keen to assure us that Boodle was significantly more contemporary than its long history might lead an outsider to believe. "*It was definitely not as stuffy as I was expecting,*" one admitted. This assertion was backed up by others who described a "*supportive, open and friendly*" place. Pure academic qualifications may not be enough to get you in – trainees say that "*everyone's trekked to base camp, been in a blues band, has something different.*" You can read more about the application process on our website. In 2010, three of the seven qualifying trainees stayed with the firm.

Boodle Hatfield's social calendar is as easy-going as its solicitors, so while it is not jam-packed with formal balls and team-building events, on Fridays senior and junior employees alike mingle happily at the Duke of York (notice a theme?) around the corner. Quiz nights, book and film clubs – the latter with pizza thrown in – are likewise opportunities to loosen ties and tongues. Although Boodle Hatfield may have taken a while to warm up to CSR-related activities, it was particularly encouraging to hear that one trainee had not only been given permission to continue working with a domestic violence charity but had also made a presentation about it and started giving training to others interested in helping the organisation.

For the most part, trainees enjoy being located in the hubbub of the West End, often citing the commercial and theatrical surrounds as a conscious preference to City-slicking. The negatives – one interviewee compared the eerie noise echoing up from Oxford Street as being uncannily "*like the island in Lost every time the black smoke arrives*" – are vastly outweighed by the positives, such as easy access to Christmas shopping and Ben's Cookies. Just don't fall into the trap of becoming a personal shopper for all your friends: "*As you're there, can you pick me up so-and-so...*"

And finally...

You won't see Boodle Hatfield much at law fairs, but the firm consistently turns out happy trainees, so seek it out if you think that property and private client work in the West End sounds appealing.

B P Collins LLP

The facts

Location: Gerrards Cross

Number of UK partners/solicitors: 18/23

Total number of trainees: 6

Seats: 4x5 + 1x4 months

Alternative seats: Secondments

On chambersstudent.co.uk
- How to get into BPC
- A detailed examination of the seats on offer
- The lowdown on Gerrards Cross

Located in leafy Gerrards Cross, this commercial/private client hybrid attracts clients from both country and City. It is a full-service law firm with a strong interest in renewable energy.

Butchers, bakers, lawyers

A law firm that opened in 1966 over a butcher's shop in Gerrards Cross might at first sound like something out of the darkly surreal TV show *The League of Gentlemen*. But B P Collins is anything but ominous. Safely nestled between a Boots, a WHSmith and a Café Rouge, the firm's two offices are right in the centre of the small, affluent commuter town. Many of its partners and fee earners are former City lawyers who put their commuting days behind them for "*a higher quality of lifestyle.*" The charming village-y atmosphere belies the firm's strategic location between the M25 and the M40: a liminal position between London and the Northern Home Counties that allows it both a private and a commercial clientele.

Local private clients range from little old ladies with £500 under their mattresses to wealthy individuals with WAG-style estates. BPC's private client team specialises in family cases, wills and probate, tax planning, trusts and charities law. On the commercial side, national, local and London businesses take advantage of the firm's more affordable prices, and this frequently puts its lawyers opposite major City firms. BPC is well placed to serve the eastern Thames Valley's business community, for which it handles corporate/commercial matters, commercial property and commercial litigation. Clients include Pinewood Studios, Brentford Football Club, pesto brand Sacla and international air cargo company Transafrik.

4x5+1x4

BPC's unusual seat system is an arrangement that works rather well. Achieving a happy medium between four and six-seat training contracts, BPC lets its recruits take five. The final four-month seat is usually in the area in which they intend to qualify, and "*this gives you a few months to bolster your knowledge base – I'm all for it!*" declared one trainee. Seat selections are discussed in monthly meetings with "*fantastic*" training partner Matt Brandis, whose claim to legal fame was a notable Court of Appeal case involving a woman doctor who was sued for libel by her former father in law – a Worcester magistrate – after she complained to police that he had assaulted her and her son. The appeal court upheld a High Court decision in the doctor's favour. The case was important as it confirmed that oral and written complaints to the police are protected by absolute privilege and cannot be subject to a defamation action. Prior to the case, a complainant was only protected when the police had started their investigations.

In the words of one satisfied trainee, the firm "*gives us a sizeable amount of responsibility, and when I say sizeable I mean to say it's huge.*" This is backed up with a good amount of supervision, as "*no letters or e-mails go out without being checked by a fee earner.*" Trainees tackle a good range of tasks: drafting letters, e-mails and various legal documents, and explaining things to clients over the phone, all the while "*picking up advice from the partner sat opposite you.*" BPC is notable for the amount of advocacy opportunities it grants its trainees, especially in the

Chambers UK rankings

Charities	Family/Matrimonial
Corporate/M&A	Private Client
Dispute Resolution	Real Estate
Employment	Real Estate Litigation
Environment	

family and litigation seats. "*All of us have been in front of a master – it's almost a rite of passage and it's quite terrifying,*" chuckled a source. The seats on offer are litigation, private client, employment, coco, family and property. We heard plenty of good things about each, so go to our website for the full skinny. There are occasional opportunities for trainee secondments to IT companies Unisys in Uxbridge and SAS in Marlow, and the latter occasionally sends its own trainees on secondment to BPC.

myPod

In the open-plan litigation department there is "*a pod-based system*" – each pod has a partner, an associate, a secretary, and either a trainee or a paralegal. This works out well for trainees, who are within easy reach of a partner and of their supervisor, typically a senior associate. The general atmosphere at the firm is "*quite friendly*" and "*fairly relaxed, as far as law firms go.*" Partners are "*approachable – I'm constantly talking to them,*" a source confirmed. BPC has "*really good working hours,*" usually 8.30am to 6.30pm. This is the kind of environment in which "*there aren't more than one or two people kicking about after 7pm.*" According to one trainee, "*not many people take their full lunch break so they don't have to stay and work late.*" Every few weeks there may be late finishes (say, around 10.30pm, although we did hear '2am' mentioned once), especially in corporate and litigation. However, trainees are happy to put in extra time and effort when needed. The salary, incidentally, is "*not bad for the area*" and "*perfectly liveable.*" Trainees start on £23,000, and this rises to £24,000 in the second-year. Qualifiers' salaries vary depending on the practice area they go into.

Far from the madding crowd

Oh Gerrards Cross, how the trainees love thee. Well, kind of. "*It's pretty and quiet. I don't live there,*" said one. "*It has a Boots and an M&S,*" said another. Overall, "*it's quite... village-like.*" Many people drive in, and the Chiltern Line means that Marylebone Station is only 25 minutes away, making Gerrards Cross perfectly commutable from London. "*It's pleasant on a sunny day, and much better than getting out of the office and being surrounded by thousands of people on Oxford Street.*" Trainees, NQs and paralegals occasionally go for post-work drinks: the local favourite is The Ethorpe, and the group sometimes heads into London to continue the entertainment. However, verdicts on the social life ranged from "*very, very poor*" to "*not huge.*" There used to be a social committee, but it was put on hold "*due to lack of enthusiasm.*" It will be regrouping in the new year. It's not that there aren't any organised socials. The past year or so has seen bowling, a book club, a boat trip and a day at the Windsor Races, plus different departments also have days out to promote team bonding. In terms of sport, there is five-a-side football, rounders ("*it's not particularly a world-class team!*"), golf, cricket, netball and a running club. Charitable activities are well supported, so this year there was a fun run for the National Society for Epilepsy, and each department has "*a day where you do some CSR activity.*" There is "*a lot of talk about organising pro bono environmental activities*" and all the trainees are members of an environmental committee that suggests ways for the firm to reduce its carbon footprint. BPC also helps out some of its charity clients on a pro bono basis.

Escape from the country

BPC dealt with the recession "*very well,*" according to our sources. Some departments were hit harder than others: there were a few redundancies and reduced working hours, but they're back up to normal now. Chief Operating Officer Karl Wingfield has an accountancy background and is described as "*extremely capable.*" So yes, "*all seems to be going very well.*" This may be the case from a trainee's point of view, but the legal press reveals that the firm has lost some staff, including senior associates and partners, commonly to London firms. One trainee worried at how little incentive associates have to stay long term: the "*lack of promotion prospects causes some to look elsewhere.*" The recession has given pause to plans for expansion, but if there is to be growth in the future then it's going to be local.

Assessment days take place in September or October, but training contracts start at various times, depending on business needs. This means everyone qualifies at a different time. Between September 2009 and September 2010, five trainees qualified and three of them stayed on in the litigation, employment and private client departments.

And finally...

Our sources liked BPC for its range of practice areas, five-seat system and Bucks location. It is within easy reach of the capital and offers lower stress levels and shorter working hours than City firms.

Brabners Chaffe Street

The facts

Location: Liverpool, Manchester, Preston

Number of UK partners/solicitors: 71/97

Total number of trainees: 21

Seats: 4x6 months

Alternative seats: Occasional secondments

Extras: Pro bono – Liverpool University Law Clinic

On chambersstudent.co.uk
- How to get into Brabners
- Recent highlight cases and deals
- From sportsman to solicitor

Over the past ten years this North West firm has quadrupled in size.

Busy B

Liverpool's Brabners merged with Manchester's Chaffe Street in 2001, but that was only the first of a series of combinations that have taken place over the past decade. In 2006 the commercial team of James Chapman & Co joined the firm. In 2009 Liverpool-based Bremners Solicitors came on board, bulking up the social housing platform. And in 2010, sole practitioner David Bishop joined the firm's 22-strong private client practice.

A mixture of mid-market and high-end clients use the firm. "*Big businesses based locally,*" is how one trainee put it. Brabners has a significant presence in the region's social housing market and is well regarded on the corporate scene. *Chambers UK* gives the firm's charities practice a top rating for its representation of local and national charities on constitutional and governance issues, as well as wider employment, property and IP matters. For example, the Trust of the Royal Court Theatre in Liverpool sought advice on the grade II-listed building's regeneration.

Charity begins at Brabners

Brabners takes on 11 trainees each year, give or take one or two: usually five in Liverpool, five in Manchester and one in Preston. They spend the whole training contract in one office, but there is talk of introducing cross-office training in the future. Trainees say the firm is flexible if they aren't "*enamoured*" with one of their seats, or if they have a keen interest in a team that trainees don't usually visit, say, the matrimonial department. Everyone visits some combination from the following seats, with the chance to return to their favourite. On offer: property; private client; employment; corporate; commercial; sports; charity; social housing; and litigation. Some of these overlap; for instance "*the commercial department is closely connected with sport.*"

Property is an important area for Brabners, and it represents Associated British Foods, UK Land and DHL, which it assisted with the property aspects of the sale of part of its business to Home Delivery Network. Trainees encounter "*a lot of landlord and tenant work,*" focusing on lease negotiation, as well as the property aspects of corporate deals and general client enquiries. For example: "*A major retailer could be having particular issues with a shop.*" In other areas of the property department, work revolves around "*large estates and the issues that affect people who own a lot of agricultural land.*" Client contact is normally telephone and email-based.

Trainees' varied corporate experiences "*range from M&A, company reorganisations, share purchase agreements, warranties and disclosure, to due diligence, commercial agreements and company formation.*" All these tasks involve "*quite a lot of client contact.*" The corporate seat puts "*a large emphasis on charity,*" said a Liverpool trainee. Charity clients, that is: Autism Initiatives UK, Dudley Zoological Gardens and The Fisheries Society of the British Isles are all regulars. "*I was given files from their inception,*" said one source. The trainee experience includes taking minutes at meetings and being exposed to the "*stresses and strains that charities go through.*" That could mean property disputes, insolvency or "*directors not behaving themselves.*" Regular corporate clients include a major supermarket and a well-known drinks brand, plus MD Insurance Services and renewable energy project advisers Phoenix Greenworks Capital.

Chambers UK rankings

Banking & Finance	Information Technology
Charities	Intellectual Property
Construction	Private Client
Corporate/M&A	Real Estate
Defamation/Reputation Management	Real Estate Litigation
	Restructuring/Insolvency
Dispute Resolution	Social Housing
Employment	Sports Law
Family/Matrimonial	

Golden briefs

The standalone sports seat is hugely popular. It offers regulatory and transactional experiences and exposure to numerous top-level football clubs in England and abroad. Lawyers advised West Ham United after crowd trouble at Millwall; Manchester United on the £80m sale of Cristiano Ronaldo to Real Madrid; and LA Galaxy on David Beckham's loan to AC Milan. Trainees learn about "*loan agreements, transfer agreements and option agreements to buy young players in the future.*" Expect the hours to run on "*when transfer windows are open.*"

Commercial sports instructions focus on sponsorship, endorsement and image rights, as well as "*contracts surrounding merchandising and broadcasting agreements.*" Trainees see it all "*by attending meetings and through a great deal of client contact.*" Highlights for one included going to London for "*a high-level negotiation process*" regarding sponsorship deals for the London 2012 Olympics. Brabners is heavily involved with the Games on behalf of adidas, Thomas Cook and others. Whether you're into sports or not, "*one of the attractions is how varied the work can be.*" Sports law "*incorporates aspects of other areas, like employment and contractual issues.*"

Memory Street

Nineties kids: let your attention wander for a moment. But for children of the 80s: do you remember SodaStream? Get busy with the fizzy! Awesome. Brabners' litigators recently represented former directors of the company that manufactured the 'home carbonation system' and classic piece of nostalgia after it went into liquidation. A claim seeking £12m in damages was made against the individuals, involving allegations of breach of directors' duties. SodaStream has since been revived and is now manufactured in Israel and China.

The litigation team has seen increased activity in property disputes, insolvency, media and professional negligence. Acting for the claimant this time, Brabners sought damages from a defendant based in Costa Rica following the breach of an insurance contract. It also worked on a claim relating to money outstanding and alleged defects in a blackcurrant juice plant. Litigation gives trainees "*excellent experience*" – they conduct legal research and due diligence, draft witness statements and attend hearings and mediations. Trainees "*sometimes have sole responsibility for meeting with counsel before going into a hearing.*" The social housing seat offers another "*good opportunity to go to court,*" as does the varied employment seat with its unfair dismissals, redundancies and "*weird and wonderful cases coming out of Christmas parties.*"

The banking team has some good work; for example, advising Bank of Scotland on £100m of revolving credit facilities to a major developer. It's also been reappointed to the RBS panel and recently advised on the acquisition of helicopter flight training school Helicentre Liverpool, which is based at John Lennon Airport. A final word should be reserved for the excellent private client department, which is another ideal place to gain client contact. "*There are meetings quite often, and a lot of elderly clients. They like you coming round to the house, and you often have to tactically say that you need to leave now...*"

Sweet tooth and funny bone

The larger Liverpool and Manchester offices are modern, while Preston's is in the heart of Winckley Square, among other "*old, nice, traditional buildings.*" Trainees usually sit near to their "*really informative and approachable*" supervisors in the semi-open plan offices. Sources say the Brabners family is "*friendly and down to earth*" and, socially, "*there's always something being arranged, if you're that way inclined. When something is organised on a Friday night, you pretty much always get an office-wide e-mail.*" Once a month, each office holds a staff drinks event, and there are also 'Cake Fridays', for which people take turns to bring in home-baked treats.

"*All partners appreciate a good sense of humour,*" and the firm-wide Christmas party tradition is for trainees to "*organise something ridiculous and make a fool out of themselves.*" There's also "*a fair bit of socialising that goes on between the firm's two largest offices,*" and trainees from all three locations get together a few times a year.

And finally...

In 2010, Brabners was listed for the fifth consecutive year in *The Sunday Times'* list of '100 Best Companies To Work For'. The happy trainees we spoke to certainly didn't disagree with that analysis. Five out of 2010's ten qualifiers took jobs with the firm.

Bristows

The facts

Location: London

Number of UK partners/solicitors: 30/58

Total number of trainees: 16

Seats: Seats of 3 to 6 months

Alternative seats: Secondments

Extras: Pro bono – A4ID; language classes

On chambersstudent.co.uk
- How to get into Bristows
- We chat with managing partner Pat Treacy
- A history of Unilever House

Bristows is a top-flight, IP-led firm that is expanding beyond its traditional expertise without losing sight of its traditions.

iPeak

Founded in 1837, Bristows combines pedigree with the modernity one would expect of an IP specialist. The firm has excelled in patent litigation since before UK patent law even existed, advising on history-making inventions as wide-ranging as the first electrical telegraph to the arguably equally critical Y-front. Its current client roster includes marquee brands like Samsung, IBM, Canon, British Airways, Novartis and Sony Computer Entertainment, and with turnover up 9.8% even in the challenging 2009/10 fiscal year, business is looking good.

The firm's healthy financials stem from its specialised legal services: even in a recession, trade mark and patent owners still need to protect their valuable assets. On the contentious side, Bristows has been representing Siemens in a patent infringement suit over its magnetoresistive sensor technology (translation: it's what allows computers to read music and video files). In addition to defending the patent that helps run your iPod, Bristows has also recently advised University College London in a licensing deal with Pfizer for a new stem cell therapy that could potentially cure AMD, one of the most common causes of blindness.

For those who prefer chocolate and booze to medical breakthroughs, Bristows excels at so-called 'soft IP' work including copyright, trade mark, and design rights instructions for fashion, consumer products and media companies. Cadbury is a long-time client, and recently the firm advised Diageo in a trade mark infringement action against Sainsbury's for its summer cocktail drink Pitchers, which the beverage conglomerate found suspiciously similar to its beloved brand Pimm's.

While IP remains a key part of Bristows' identity, the firm's recent casework attests that it has expanded its practice in other areas, including commercial disputes, regulatory issues, data protection and IT. On the commercial/telecommunications end, the firm is acting for T-Mobile in a clash with another mobile phone service provider. Bristows also handles regulatory compliance for Rovi, a company you may not have heard of but whose products you definitely use – they create the electronic programme guides used by digital television providers like Sky. Last but not least, following three partner hires (two from rival Bird & Bird) in the past year alone, data protection has recently become a top-tier practice, according to *Chambers UK*. The team advises British Airways on a number of matters, from direct marketing to anti-terrorism and security initiatives, and has been designing a massive privacy compliance programme for food/finance/agriculture giant Cargill, the largest private company in the US.

Perhaps that was a long round-up but it's been a busy year for Bristows. Plus, as the firm's graduate recruitment team will tell you, while a science degree isn't a prequisite for admission into this always-popular club, bringing something extra to the party, like commercial awareness, is. So whether you're a science junkie looking for a ticket out of the lab, or a law or arts student with a keen analytical mind, as long as the chance to work with

Chambers UK rankings

Data Protection	Life Sciences
Dispute Resolution	Media & Entertainment
Information Technology	Partnership
Intellectual Property	

stellar clients on cutting-edge projects makes you salivate, read on.

Sweet deal

The firm's kaleidoscope logo is an apt metaphor for its seating system – what could be an arbitrary arrangement of puzzle pieces becomes a beautiful and symmetrical pattern, uniquely suited to each trainee. "*With such a broad range of practices, I think four seats wouldn't do Bristows justice,*" claimed one source. Luckily, the firm's seating system allows for both three and six-month seats. On arrival at the firm, trainees receive a plan that may contain five, six, or occasionally seven seats. The aim is to find the right combination based on client needs and trainee interests. There is flexibility and we heard of several trainees who made changes. "*They do try to accommodate you,*" insisted one.

Virtually all trainees will complete stints in four core areas: IP, commercial disputes, corporate and real estate. IP litigation is by far the most popular and trainees will typically spend six months there. They work on contentious trade mark, copyright, design and patent matters, many of which go to trial. While "*there's definitely document bundling to do,*" people "*would much rather have you do things where you are challenged*" and trainees really value the "*face-to-face time with clients and being in court seeing the outcome of your work; it's a great feeling to be asked to do something that you know matters.*" With clients like Novartis, L'Oréal and Cadbury you get "*exceptional quality work.*" How exceptional? We heard of trainees doing "*opposition research on a well-known chocolate brand,*" including comparing logos and the shape of the chocolate bars. Officially sanctioned trips to the sweet shop? We like it!

Commercial disputes is a growing department, and trainees can now opt to spend three months there and three more in IP litigation, rather than a full six months in IP. In commercial disputes, trainees typically "*prepare questions for counsel or to send to a client, liaise with barristers or their clerks, and occasionally handle small claims.*"

In addition to its core seats, the firm also offers time in regulatory, competition/EU and employment. The non-contentious commercial IP department is a popular one involving "*quite a bit of drafting and research. There's always going to be some administrative stuff, but never loads of it.*" Commercial IP work overlaps with the activities of the corporate department as "*the departments don't operate in isolation.*" Recent corporate deals have included financing agreements for technology-focused and property investment companies.

Corporate seats can occasionally involve late nights before a deal closing, but across departments trainees typically get out of the office before 7pm. "*Bristows expects you to do your job well, but if you're on top of your work, you go home.*" Trainees navigate through their seats with the support of senior associate mentors and their training diary review partner, with whom they meet regularly to discuss progress. End-of-seat appraisals are attended by the partner from their completed seat and the one they'll work for in their next. It's all designed to "*make sure you can develop on lessons learned and have the opportunity to do work you didn't already try.*"

Nearly every trainee spends three months on secondment with a client's in-house legal team, usually after a commercial IP seat because secondments "*are focused on using those skills.*" Bristows doesn't like to name-drop, but a number of top clients in the pharmaceutical and IT sectors regularly host trainees. "*At first it was daunting, like going to a new job,*" a source said. "*But I really enjoyed seeing things from the other side and the pressures a client company could be under.*"

Embrace your inner geek

So, how do you get the chance to get paid for buying chocolate? It's true that many trainees are lapsed scientists who "*didn't want to be shut away in a lab.*" But while they agreed that "*Bristows will always attract scientists,*" our sources insisted that now, perhaps more than ever, you don't need to be a physicist or engineer to land a training contract. As the firm increasingly pushes into other practice areas, a variety of academic experience is equally valued. "*You definitely don't need a science background. Somebody who did English is going to understand most cases just as well as I am,*" said one. "*There's only a limited number of cases where your specific knowledge will help.*" While 88% of the 2009 trainees had science degrees, just 25% of the 2010 intake did. The incoming 2011 trainees are more evenly proportioned – 40% have a science background.

Even if being able to recite the periodic table from memory isn't necessary, Bristows trainees are still "*horrendously clever.*" One source said of her peers: "*Their level of intelligence sometimes astounds me. If they weren't so normal and sociable they might be considered geeks.*" The sociability shows in weekly trips to local pubs like The Albion, monthly drinks, quizzes and poker nights where "*everyone is encouraged to get involved, partners too.*"

Sports teams for football, cricket and netball are also part of the scene, and there is a running club. "*People actually want to spend time together instead of rushing home.*" Every day at 1pm unoccupied trainees flock to break room "*the Hub,*" which has a flat screen, a PlayStation, table football and a library that isn't stocked with work-related reading material (unless you count John Grisham).

Located on the first two floors of the art deco Unilever House, Bristows' digs are state of the art with glass and style to spare. When the firm moved there in 2008, staff were consulted about the details, including what to name the conference rooms. The consensus was to name the external client meeting rooms after scientists and great thinkers (Michael Faraday and Adam Smith) and to name the internal rooms after pubs local to the former offices in Lincoln's Inn (eg The Seven Stars). There is some nostalgia for the firm's quaint old offices, which were spread across four buildings in Lincoln's Inn, but while it was "*a beautiful place,*" the new modern office is "*much more convenient and inclusive*" because "*it's easier to wander into each other's offices and discuss things.*" The new space fits Bristows' character, trainees said. "*We're a quite well-mannered, old-school firm that's racing into the 21st century with hi-tech clients and modern facilities. It's the best of both worlds.*"

Bristows has a strong track record of offering qualifying trainees full-time positions and all seven were retained in 2010. In recent years the IP litigation department has been a much sought-after destination. Last year alone, three trainees became IP litigators amid stiff competition. Five out of six second-year trainees were vying for spots in the group at the time of our calls. In the end, two of them got the positions. Despite the pressures, interviewees agreed that the spring of their second year was not a time for in-fighting or backstabbing. "*We were quite open about it because we're all good friends and everyone goes through it together. It's nice to have that support.*"

And finally...

Offering a stellar experience without forcing you to sacrifice your personal life, Bristows is a great match for techies and can make even non-scientists feel at home.

- **University v the real world:**
  Law at university is very academic, essay-based and analytical. In practice it's more procedural and there's a lot of form-filling. Plus, you have real clients, conflicting demands on your time and colleagues to contend with.

Browne Jacobson LLP

The facts

Location: Birmingham, Nottingham, London

Number of UK partners/solicitors: 69/130

Total number of trainees: 16

Seats: 4x6 months

Alternative seats: Occasional secondments

Extras: Pro bono – CAB, ProHelp, The Prince's Trust, Criminal Injuries Compensation scheme, Birmingham Employment Rights Advice Line

On chambersstudent.co.uk
- How to get into Browne Jacobson
- Pro bono at the firm
- We talk to training partner Brian Smith

This Midlands-based commercial firm is big on litigation and insurance. Offering a wide variety of practice areas, it has a good deal of public sector work and prioritises pro bono activities.

Law, less ordinary

Founded in 1832, Browne Jacobson is a medium-sized firm with its head office in Nottingham, a second office in Birmingham and a small base in London. As a result of organic growth, rather than mergers, the firm is now many times bigger than it was at the turn of the millennium. Broadly speaking, BJ specialises in four areas: health, insurance, corporate and the public sector. Its leading clients include Alliance Boots, Lloyds Bank, insurer Hiscox, the National Trust, the Welsh Assembly Government, the Treasury Solicitor's Department and a huge swathe of local authorities and NHS trusts.

BJ's future is likely to include an increased commercial aspect, as well as growth in the coco, health, insurance and public sector departments. Training partner (and former managing partner) Brian Smith says there are "*no plans to put any more dots on the map, but you can never rule anything out.*"

East and west

The training scheme is centred on Nottingham, where the firm is one of the biggest in the city. If you are thinking of doing a Birmingham-only training contract, be aware that there are only three different seats trainees can do in Brum (down from eight in 2009). They are health, employment, and a split stint in corporate and private client, so trainees hired to the Birmingham office have to repeat a seat if they aren't willing to commute to Nottingham for six months. Basically, "*there are more seats in Nottingham. If you're set on not moving from Birmingham, you'll be quite limited in what you can do.*" Trainees realise that they "*can't be precious about it in this climate,*" but this issue was definitely a sore point for some. The 20-person London office, opened 16 years ago, focuses on insurance, including personal injury and social care. It is "*much smaller and specialised: a bit distant.*" London usually accepts one Midlands trainee per seat rotation, although had none in situ at the time of our calls.

A clean bill of health

Of a trainee's four seats, the first is chosen by the firm, and for subsequent assignments trainees list three preferences. Second-years are given priority. There is usually a decent mix of those trainees who fancy litigation and those who are into deals, so everyone is usually happy with what they get. This next bit can be complicated to get your head around so take it slow. The firm is organised into the following areas: business and professional risk (BPR); business services; insurance and public risk (IPR); and property. This translates into a wealth of seat options: employment, professional indemnity, commercial litigation and construction and property risk sit within BPR; commercial, corporate and private client sit within business services; environment, social care and education, health, and personal injury within IPR; and property is split into development, retail and public authority seats.

Chambers UK rankings

Administrative & Public Law	Intellectual Property
Banking & Finance	Local Government
Clinical Negligence	Personal Injury
Construction	Planning
Corporate/M&A	Private Client
Dispute Resolution	Professional Negligence
Education	Real Estate
Employment	Real Estate Litigation
Environment	Restructuring/Insolvency
Healthcare	Social Housing
	Tax

Trainees spend at least six months in the core IPR department, which handles nearly a third of the firm's business. Some trainees will focus on personal injury, clinical negligence and stress-at-work cases, mainly on behalf of insurers. Big-name clients include Aviva, AXA and Hiscox. Trainees say the work here is *"really hands-on,"* quite technical and *"feels like real law,"* which means plenty of drafting, instructing counsel and going to hearings and mediations. Trainees may be the first port of call on lower-value claims, but always work with adequate supervision. They even have opportunities for advocacy in the county court.

Clinical negligence is a key area. *Chambers UK* ranks BJ among the best in the country, and the firm is one of just ten firms on the clinical legal panel of the NHS Litigation Authority. It also takes direct instructions from NHS trusts and primary care trusts across the Midlands and beyond. Dealing with birth and catastrophic injuries worth several million pounds, it's *"daunting"* and emotionally demanding for trainees, but also very rewarding. There isn't a huge amount of client contact, but trainees may occasionally take on their own files *"under a lot of supervision."* Their duties include corresponding with claimant solicitors, trips to the Royal Courts of Justice, reviewing medical records, attending conferences and writing articles. Since cases tend to outlast the lifespan of a six-month seat, trainees work with other fee earners and dip in and out of a number of them. In addition to handling clin neg matters, the firm was appointed to the panel of the Care Quality Commission, which has provided it with a stream of healthcare regulatory instructions.

Public relations

Chambers UK regards Browne Jacobson as one of the best in the East Midlands for M&A deals, alongside Eversheds and Freeth Cartwright. It acted on the £17m management buyout of Tropical Marine Centre and Cranswick Pet Products; assisted KeTech Group in a funding deal with government fund Capital for Enterprise; and – in case only household names impress you – a major high-street retailer is also a client. The corporate and commercial seats are *"quite popular"* among trainees despite the fact that it's been *"quite a quiet time."*

The public sector property team's remit covers local authorities, education and social care – three areas that are facing major change since the arrival of the coalition government. Other property areas include retail, transport and logistics, major corporates, fire, government agencies, housing associations and health trusts. The firm works for 200 of the 400 English and Welsh local authorities, and is a leader in the East Midlands for all kinds of social housing matters – site acquisitions and developments; portfolio financing; tenancies, right-to-buy and shared-ownership schemes; corporate governance; repossessions and evictions; and antisocial behaviour cases. The social housing sector has already been challenged by the contraction in bank lending and now faces scrutiny following the change in government.

In the area of environmental law, BJ is very highly regarded. The environment team offers broad experience to its trainees: it deals with pollution contamination cases, and assists the government and key agencies on Sites of Special Scientific Interest (SSSIs) and areas of natural beauty. One partner has successfully prosecuted several matters on behalf of Natural England. In one case, three people were convicted of setting fires on peat land within an SSSI; another related to an individual who had overgrazed an SSSI. The related administrative law team exposes trainees to regulatory issues, various points of dispute including nuisance claims, research and small trial matters that may involve advocacy in the early stages. Trainees might also get to travel around the country for meetings, and one source said they *"spent half the week with clients"* and were *"given access to people who are really important."*

The education team works mainly for providers, special educational needs co-ordinators (SENCOs) and governing bodies rather than students or parents. Trainees in this seat may find their workload also includes writing for national journals and blogs. The social care seat can be quite gritty as there are cases of child abuse to contend with. These are *"not pleasant but interesting,"* and trainees help out by interviewing witnesses, attending conferences and taking notes. The intellectual property team, meanwhile, offers both contentious and non-contentious experience, and has recently advised exciting clients such as Avon Cosmetics, Siemens and Goodyear. The firm has an excellent private client practice in the Midlands, so the firm often bags clients who are pretty wealthy or own *"large swathes of land."* The seat involves *"a lot of intricate stuff"* such as drafting wills and variations of wills, the management and administration of estates, tax schemes, tax planning, employee benefits, trusts and charity law. This last area sees trainees researching, setting up, amending and dissolving charities.

A property litigation team and a non-contentious commercial property team both offer a good mix of small and large cases. The lawyers represent clients such as Wilkinsons, LVMH, Prada and Zadig et Voltaire. The sports department represents local cricket clubs and football teams, and the varied employment team works for fire services, healthcare clients and retailers such as TK Maxx. There are also some secondments, which sadly we can't name.

Hogwarts does Nottingham

All trainees start with a thorough two-week induction, complete with bonding activities. During their training contracts, they also attend several courses that are "*bespoke to the firm,*" including lunchtime seminars, legal updates and practical skills sessions. The other standout feature is plenty of time in court, with opportunities for small-scale advocacy. In the past, trainees have told us that inter-office cohesion has not been amazing, and it doesn't look like too much has changed, but having said that, there are a few video-linked or live team meetings across offices.

The firm is known for being friendly and fun, and its culture is definitely a non-hierarchical one. Everyone goes to the pub together and there is an open-door policy. Not a 'people factory', the firm is big enough to attract big clients but small enough to put "*an emphasis on the people who work for them.*" It has an "*appropriate amount of laid-backness*" and partners are approachable. The offices themselves are pleasant places to work. The Nottingham one was variously described as "*ramshackle,*" "*a rabbit hole*" and "*Hogwarts*" as it is several buildings amalgamated into one, with the four departments split into different areas, and with many different entrances. It "*takes a while to get your head round it*" but once you do it's "*really nice,*" with a courtyard in the middle, comfy chairs and a good café downstairs (No. 44). It's also "*right in the centre*" and close to shops. The open-plan Birmingham office near Victoria Square is "*lovely*" and within reach of nice bars. The London office is centrally located on Gracechurch Street near The Bank of England.

In terms of working hours, BJ is "*not a nine-to-five firm.*" But don't worry: what this means is that it's actually more like "*nine to six.*" In a very busy seat you may expect to work until 6.30pm with some rare 10pm finishes. A few of the trainees we spoke to were happy to take work home with them or come in over the weekend if they hadn't finished everything during the week, or even just to catch up on admin tasks. However, "*if you stay late it's recognised.*" The firm has "*plenty of benefits and perks,*" such as a good holiday allowance and pension scheme, and there were no complaints about salary, although the increase between the first and second years of training was this year considered "*minimal.*"

The Nottingham office social life is "*fun and inclusive*" and revolves around two pubs: The Royal Children (known as The Kids) or a pricier establishment called The Castle. There is a sports and social committee, so trainees can get involved in football, rounders, badminton, squash, netball, the running team, golf days and the yearly Browne Jacobson cup, which features hockey, football and rugby. There are also things like quizzes, ballroom dancing competitions, a treasure hunt in Birmingham and "*a lot of bonding-type things.*" The end-of-year party is a firm-wide event, as is the summer ball, with Birmingham staff transported to and from Nottingham by bus. In each of the different offices there are four or five organised events during the year, and trainees are given a social budget. In Birmingham, there is "*usually someone up for a drink*" and trainees often go out for lunch on Fridays. One Friday a month there are office drinks from 5pm onwards.

A couple of years ago, the firm optimistically recruited 12 trainees, but the numbers are now back down to roughly eight per year. Morale "*has dropped a little bit,*" but seeing as partners "*all got together and didn't take equity out of the firm,*" the effect of the fragile economy has not entirely dampened the mood. Trainees say the firm was "*very open*" about what was happening, and is now seeing "*a pick-up in terms of business.*" The firm notched up a very decent NQ retention statistic in 2010, with ten of 12 qualifiers staying. These were all in Nottingham: three in business services, five in IPR, one in BPR and one in property. As one happy source said: "*There is a huge emphasis on retaining trainees. We were all fairly confident we weren't going to be shafted and we really weren't.*" It was a different story in the competitive Birmingham legal market where none of the 2010 qualifiers took jobs, comparing poorly to the three who stayed last year.

And finally...

This Midlands big hitter has loyal clients, good working hours and a strong insurance litigation practice, but don't forget that its focal point is Nottingham.

Burges Salmon LLP

The facts

Location: Bristol

Number of UK partners/solicitors: 65/230

Total number of trainees: 43

Seats: 6x4 months

Alternative seats: Secondments

Extras: Pro Bono – Bristol University Law Clinic; language classes

On chambersstudent.co.uk
- The way into Burges Salmon
- The new office
- BS's top 250 clients by sector

Burges Salmon has arguably achieved its goal of being the elite firm outside London. So what's next? With swanky new offices and unflinching drive, anything's possible for this Bristol success story.

Salmon run

Burges Salmon is a Bristol firm with a magic circle CV. You probably know the name (and maybe you've even heard about the famous pink stationery), but for all its ambitions the firm keeps a relatively low profile. Unless you've read previous editions of this guide, you probably won't know that the firm counts Coca-Cola, Chanel, Virgin, the MoD and Orange among its clients. Or that it is ranked among the best in the country for its environment and transport work – and is a top dog in the South West in just about every practice area you could care to mention. The firm's biggest sectors are financial services (21% of its top 250 clients come from this area), energy and natural resources (17%), real estate and construction (12%) and transport (11%), but it also gains major instructions from the worlds of agriculture, private client, IT, retail, aerospace and more.

While its modesty is endearing, some trainees said they wished Burges Salmon would cast gentility aside and shout its accomplishments from the rooftops. "*Sometimes I don't think the firm exploits what it has to offer and doesn't broadcast its massive achievements*," mused one source. According to training partner Roger Bull, that is exactly what the firm has planned for the future. "*We are developing a louder corporate voice so that we can continue to get across the message of the extremely impressive offering that we have.*" In the meantime, we're not too polite to tell you the good news. The firm's adverts are true. You *can* get London-quality work in a city where your daily commute doesn't make you feel like a contestant on some sadistic reality show.

BS only has the one office and is ferociously loyal to Bristol, so don't expect it to branch out into other cities. It is by no means parochial, however, and something like 70% of its work comes from beyond the South West. The firm also has a 'better friends' relationship with US outfit Thompson Hine.

Hot seats

Burges Salmon trainees get a well-rounded experience through the firm's six four-month seat plan. "*It's a bit of a nightmare to organise the two extra seats, but the benefit to the trainees far outweighs that*," said recruitment manager Katy Main. Our sources appreciated the effort because "*it really gives you the opportunity to explore different parts of the firm*" and "*make contacts.*"

Property is the only strictly compulsory seat. Trainees then choose between corporate, banking or commercial; either tax/trusts or employment, pensions and incentives (EPI); and finally (a long list is coming here) commercial disputes or construction or agriculture or property disputes or environment and planning. The fifth seat is a free choice, and trainees may either opt to try something completely new or repeat a favourite seat. They usually spend their final seat in the department in which they hope to qualify.

Chambers UK rankings

Agriculture & Rural Affairs	Intellectual Property
Banking & Finance	Investment Funds
Charities	Outsourcing
Competition/European Law	Partnership
Construction	Pensions
Corporate/M&A	Pensions Litigation
Debt Recovery	Planning
Dispute Resolution	Private Client
Employment	Private Equity
Energy & Natural Resources	Projects
Environment	Public Procurement
Family/Matrimonial	Real Estate
Health & Safety	Real Estate Litigation
Information Technology	Restructuring/Insolvency
	Tax
	Transport

In the large commercial department, interviewees reported a range of work so broad that *"you never get pigeon-holed into one area."* The seat entails a lot of contract negotiation, and one massive recent matter was advising the MoD on a multibillion-dollar search-and-rescue helicopter private finance initiative for the UK and the Falkland Islands. As you might expect, *"the size of the deal will affect the level of work you're doing"* and the biggest projects involve a lot of document review. Rest assured *"you do get to see what's going on higher up the chain,"* and *"with smaller clients you're involved in drafting."* Partners also *"make a real effort to take you to meetings."*

A commercial disputes seat is also varied, with trainees working on professional negligence, fraud and product liability cases, particularly for agricultural and food clients. This department also undertakes recoveries work for banks and building societies, including household names like Lloyds TSB and Nationwide, for which lawyers recently acted in a contract dispute with a supplier of software. The seat is hands-on, with plenty of research, drafting, liaising with clients and opposing lawyers, and even some advocacy in the form of summary judgment applications and small claims trials.

Also with a contentious element, the employment seat is an ever-popular destination. It was *"screamingly busy"* at the time of our interviews. Immigration work may come into play, for example corporate clients may need to understand how to work their way through the points-based system. Trainees say it's *"kind of a privilege"* to spend a seat in the firm's renowned environment department. Some of the recent *"cutting-edge"* work involved helping the Nuclear Decommissioning Authority dispose of some former nuclear sites. The seat encompasses both transactional matters and litigation, at times even including criminal environmental prosecutions.

Client secondments are prized as *"an invaluable experience because you have to stand on your own two feet and speak to directors. It's a confidence builder."* Plus, *"it also provides an understanding of our client's limitations. They don't have the support that we have here at the firm."* Recent destinations have included Lloyds, Airbus and the MoD.

Bristol: gorge-ous

As early as the vacation scheme, Burges Salmon loves to show off one of its most appealing assets – Bristol. Our sources had nothing but love for a laid-back and youthful city that, in addition to BS, is also the home of Banksy, Wallace and Gromit and the spectacular natural beauty of the Avon Gorge. Lucky vac schemers enjoy barbecues, wine-tasting evenings and events like the Bristol Balloon Fiesta or the chance to see famous stand-up acts warm up before heading to the Edinburgh Festival.

Trainees raved about their quality of life. They can afford flats in Georgian buildings in the upmarket areas of Clifton and Redland, and walk to work in the mornings. *"When I hear about my London friends with their daily nightmare commutes I thank my lucky stars my journey is so pleasant,"* one source rejoiced. We sound like tour guides, but it really is a lovely place to live and work, and for all trainees *"the lifestyle was a massive factor"* in their choice of BS.

Our sources reported *"really reasonable, steady hours"* with only the occasional late nights during deal completions. One interviewee told us: *"What I consider to be a long day, my friends at London consider to be a normal day."* While trainees are given BlackBerrys, *"there's no pressure from the firm to use them on the weekends or on holiday."* Flexible working arrangements are supported: Burges Salmon has the second highest percentage of part-time partners in the UK top 50, according to a 2009 survey by *The Lawyer*. Flexibility like that accounts for why so many trainees see a long-term future with BS. *"This isn't a firm where you're just a number and a source of cheap labour,"* an interviewee said. *"We've got a culture of respect and you're seen as an investment for the firm."*

Swimming with the Salmon

So how can you swim with the Salmon? Training solicitors is expensive and BS *"is cautious about people who want to use the firm to train and then go off to London."* While most trainees had some bond with the firm's home city, we learned that many also applied to the top London firms. You need to be the sort of person who craves the challenge and rigour of City work but cherishes your life outside it. "*Many of my contemporaries turned down training contracts at major City firms because they made the choice for the better quality of life here*," a source explained.

In addition to strong academics, the firm also looks for life experience and has brought in trainees with backgrounds in marketing, management consulting, engineering and the armed forces. If you want to impress the powers that be during an interview or a vac scheme, recruitment manager Katy Main advises: "*Ask loads of questions. Sometimes not asking questions can be perceived as a lack of interest*." But trainees warned against going overboard. "*It's fairly obvious when people aren't being themselves. There's no point trying to impress people for two weeks and getting a job based on something you're not.*" "*Soft skills*" and "*being able to socialise and be funny*" are important, but broadcasting your knowledge of every major deal you've read about in the *FT* could backfire and end up annoying people.

The firm has had consistently high NQ retention rates in recent years, and 21 out of 22 qualifiers stayed on in 2010. The qualification process was competitive, particularly in popular departments like commercial and commercial litigation, but trainees stressed that the firm works hard to find a place for people, even if it can't always be in their first-choice department. Nor does it prevaricate. "*We know quite early on where we stand. There would be quite a lot of time to find another job if the firm couldn't offer one*." September 2010 qualifiers knew whether they would be getting a job offer as early as April.

With 22 lawyers and 18 support staff made redundant in 2009, the firm has not escaped the recession unscathed, but trainees were not directly affected and applauded their employer for being "*very transparent about the process*." While BS did offer deferral options to incoming 2009 and 2010 trainees, it was on a voluntary basis. The firm has also historically been very generous with its trainee compensation and, in addition to paying for GDL and LPC fees, offers the highest maintenance grant outside of London at £7,000 per annum. NQ salaries fell in 2009, but our sources did not seem to mind. "*We'd rather have jobs at £40,000 than not have jobs at all. Plus, I think we're still probably the highest-paid young professionals in Bristol,*" said one.

In a New Quay

We've often mentioned in the past Burges Salmon's reputation as more traditional compared to its big rival in Bristol, Osborne Clarke. While a couple of trainees agreed that the firm "*can be a bit conservative and could take some more chances*," they say the distinction between the two firms holds less truth today. "*Because of our historical link to agricultural work, we will always have that air externally, but it's not entirely fair*," one thoughtful source mused. Training partner Roger Bull argued: "*It's an unfair description in the sense that we're cutting-edge with a number of our practices, including energy, and we've got clients we simply wouldn't get if we didn't understand 21st century business needs.*"

The firm moved into One Glass Wharf, a sleek, new, eco-friendly waterside office next to Bristol Temple Meads station, in the summer of 2010. The building is kitted out with a café, a rooftop terrace and environmentally sound features such as an air conditioning system that uses river water to cool the building. This last development was of particular importance to trainees, who had suffered through sweltering summers in the old building where "*we were boiling from lack of air conditioning*."

Thankfully the new location is still within spitting distance of favoured watering hole The Famous Royal Navy Volunteer (aka the Volley), where trainees congregate on Friday nights. After-work athletics are as popular as after-work drinks, and the firm has hockey, netball, basketball, softball, touch rugby, tennis and cricket teams. During our interviews trainees were in the midst of a heated inter-departmental football tournament. Most also opt in to the firm's social club, which offers subsidised film, theatre and concert tickets in Bristol in exchange for just a couple of pounds taken out of each month's pay cheque.

Though some firm-sponsored activities, like the summer party, have been put on hold during the recession, trainees are adept at making their own fun. *"Bristol is great for outdoorsy stuff"* and our sources were a rugged bunch of mountain bikers, surfers and *"really serious runners."* The intakes we spoke to had organised multiple weekends to country cottages for hiking, golf or beach time.

And finally...

Now that air conditioning has been brought to the entirety of the office, Burges Salmon trainees really have nothing to complain about. Students seeking top-quality work and a little humanity to boot will not be disappointed.

Capsticks Solicitors LLP

The facts

Location: London, Birmingham

Number of UK partners/solicitors: 34/106

Total number of trainees: 11

Seats: 6x4 months

Alternative seats: Secondments

Extras: Pro bono – Putney Law Centre

On chambersstudent.co.uk
- How to get into Capsticks
- Health sector overview
- We talk to training partner Majid Hassan

Created less than 30 years ago from an in-house legal team at the NHS, Capsticks is now a leading authority on healthcare law.

Healthy outlook?

Capsticks' client list speaks volumes: around 200 NHS trusts, PCTs, health authorities and other healthcare bodies from the private and voluntary sectors across the UK come here for their legal care. It's at the forefront of clinical law and recently advised on the Baby P inquiry, the Tamil hunger strike, an E. coli outbreak at a Surrey farm and the swine flu epidemic.

A relocation to Wimbledon from Putney and an upgrade to a "*nice modern*" office that provides "*a really open, teamworking environment*" has suited Capsticks well. It has also "*consolidated* [its] *position in Birmingham*" since launching there in summer 2008. The firm is now "*looking to expand further into the North. We already have clients there so we want to be able to provide for them locally and reach out to new ones,*" confirmed training partner Majid Hassan. While the coalition government's plans for the public sector could either make or break the firm's ability to finance this expansion, Hassan insists that management remains confident. "*We've always had to be on the ball when it comes to changes that are happening, or might happen, so that we can alert and advise our clients. We have to adapt as policies change; there will be things we do differently, but we're optimistic. We're growing as a practice and we see that continuing.*"

At Capsticks, trainees are a part of this plan. In 2010 it kept all four qualifiers for the fourth year in a row. "*We've been very lucky with the candidates we've been able to select. We've always attracted high-calibre applicants because of the kind of work we do, but surprisingly we don't recruit many with a healthcare background,*" Hassan added. "*I tried to identify a firm that correlated with my values,*" a source recalled; "*I wanted to do law, but I'm much more suited for work in the public sector, so Capsticks is a good compromise. You get the feeling that you're doing something positive, using law for public utility.*"

No pain, no gain

Trainees take six four-month seats chosen from clinical negligence; commercial; dispute resolution; employment; and real estate. With just five departments available, trainees repeat at least one seat, if not two. Capsticks' clinical practice is central to matters. "*It's a lot of negligence work, but you might also be involved in mental health issues, judicial reviews or trusts' decisions.*" Capsticks has been on the NHS Litigation Authority's clinical negligence legal panel since its inception in 1998. The significance of its instructions can range from monetary (amounting to tens of millions of pounds) to social (eg questions over the state funding of care). "*It's really interesting stuff... the reality is that in these cases it's not black and white, and 99% of the time when there's a breach of duty* [the healthcare provider] *will own up to it and move on. But some will go to trial, so Capsticks has to be very sensitive to not only our clients' needs but also the patient on the other side.*" Some recent cases involving severe neurological injuries, chronic pain syndrome and even death illustrate that "*you need that degree of sensitivity. Certain things that happen to people are horrific, but you have to be able to rationally remove yourself from the situation.*" Then again, there are also cases like that of a

Chambers UK rankings

Administrative & Public Law	Healthcare
Clinical Negligence	Professional Discipline
Employment	

hairdresser who sought around £1.4m after claiming an NHS trust failed to treat his fractured wrist. Capsticks' clin neg team was able to settle the case for a tenth of the original sum when it discovered he had continued to style at international fashion shows. Trainees experience "*a good range of work – drafting documents and correspondence, case analysis, witness prep.*" There's also bags of client contact. "*It's great, really deep-end stuff. To get that experience and attention is brilliant.*"

The dispute resolution seat brings "*an array of matters*" in three main categories: commercial litigation; property litigation; and regulatory law. Commercial litigators handle "*contracting matters for primary care trusts*" and "*public/private agreements,*" while property litigation can range from squatters' rights to leasehold disputes. The department is home to "*a big regulatory team*" that handles fitness-to-practise cases for various bodies such as the Nursing and Midwifery Council. "*You become involved in serious work quite quickly,*" one trainee said. "*You're given two or three cases where you're the case holder and you're expected to run them. The first two to three weeks are very scary, but the support network is really emphasised. Supervisors are selected very carefully and you'll get patted on the back for even the mundane tasks.*"

Sticky changes

Trainees have "*direct responsibility for cases*" in the commercial department too, usually small matters like "*hospital contracts with suppliers.*" The commercial team works with the real estate department on projects, many of them having been PPP schemes under the NHS LIFT initiative for the construction of new clinic facilities. The firm has also been busy overseeing the new wave of London polyclinics – essentially super-surgeries with up to 25 GPs, which provide some hospital services such as X-rays, minor surgery and outpatient treatment all under one roof. Of course the coalition government has major structural change lined up for the NHS and this will affect the firm's business. We spoke with Capsticks at length about the subject, so go to our website to find out more. Trainees agreed that the real estate team is "*definitely the nicest, they're so friendly,*" and they loved that "*it's a bit more chilled out, probably since it's all non-contentious so there aren't any crazy deadlines.*"

Capsticks' employment department has mastered the ability to be nimble and responsive in an ever-changing area of law. It's amazing these lawyers ever have time to catch their breath as the NHS is one of Europe's biggest employers. Again, there will be major change in this department once public sector spending cuts take effect, but this could mean more work for lawyers. In addition to handling complex claims against the NHS, the team also runs an HR advisory service and frequently gives talks at board level. Those complex claims have included defending Cumbria PCT against an age discrimination matter brought by a former chief exec who was removed from his post just prior to his 50th birthday, when he would have received a large pension enhancement of over £500,000. Before the change in government, the firm was also busy developing employment models for NHS community services in light of a policy to separate the commissioning and provision of NHS services. This involved looking at the protection of the pensions of those moving from the public to the private sector, as well as the usual TUPE considerations.

To cap it off

"*They bang on about work-life balance here, but it's true compared to our commercial neighbours in the City. On average I'm out of the office by 6.30 or 7pm, although long hours will happen from time to time,*" one source reported. Trainees also appreciated the "*brilliant*" support and training on offer. "*You get good exposure as a trainee, but in a safe environment,*" one said. "*There's a mentality where early responsibility is encouraged, rather than you just doing mediocre tasks,*" and at the same time "*people are looking after you. Everyone is willing to help, check your work, give you feedback; it never feels like your opinion doesn't matter.*"

"*It's a very approachable firm on all levels,*" one trainee enthused. "*I was amazed by the interaction between partners and trainees when I started,*" another added. "*I sit down and have drinks with partners after work... they're all very jovial and friendly*" and some will even send trainees in-joke e-mails. "*You would never, never, never get those scary shouting types at Capsticks: if you muck up they understand.*" In terms of nightlife, "*every Friday a lot of us, including an army of brilliant paralegals, head out for a drink. We're still feeling our way around Wimbledon to find the perfect spot. Putney Station* [the firm's old haunt] *has probably lost half its profits by now!*" one source joked.

And finally...

Capsticks may be a specialist firm in terms of its clientele but this doesn't mean a limited range of work to try out as a trainee.

- **Don't be anxious about starting your training:** A trainee tells us, "It's not as scary as you think it's going to be. People will be keen to help you and I wish I hadn't worried so much."

Charles Russell LLP

The facts

Location: London, Guildford, Cheltenham, Oxford, Cambridge

Number of UK partners/solicitors: 91/186

Total number of trainees: 23

Seats: 4x6 months

Alternative seats: Overseas seats, secondments

Extras: Pro bono – LawWorks, Bethnal Green Legal Advice Centre, Surrey Law Centre, RJC Advice Centre

On chambersstudent.co.uk
- How to get into Charles Russell
- The charms of Cheltenham
- A guide to Guildford

This town and country firm has a huge range of commercial and private client experiences to offer trainees. Its expanding network of offices now stretches beyond the South of England to Geneva and Bahrain.

Jack (Russell) of all trades

Charles Russell traces its origins back over 200 years. Historically a very English private client and family law firm, it has grown into quite the international business with eight offices, two of them overseas. Today its workload is around 70% commercial. On this larger side of the business the main areas are: corporate and commercial; employment (particularly prominent in the firm's Cambridge office); real estate; and litigation. The firm also has a strong reputation in such diverse sectors as telecommunications, media, sport, education and charities. This diversity is reflected in its client list, which includes the odd government and major international companies such as J.P. Morgan Cazenove, Virgin Media and Cable & Wireless. Also on the roster are scores of wealthy individuals and bastions of the English Establishment such as RAF Benevolent Fund, The City and Guilds of London Institute and The Church Commissioners for England. Private client and family practice are still at Charles Russell's core, and they still help define the firm's character. As one trainee was keen to point out, the firm is "*not an attack-dog litigator.*"

And yet in the past few years management has sniffed out opportunities both at home and overseas, leading to expansion in several areas. Charles Russell has more than doubled its number of offices in the past five years, adding Oxford, Cambridge and a small branch in the capital's St James's neighbourhood to its established office network in London, Guildford and Cheltenham. It's almost as if the firm has thrown a lasso around the City. Not content with UK expansion alone, it has also added an international dimension by opening in Geneva and Bahrain, key areas for private client and corporate/commercial work respectively. Top dog (and senior partner) Patrick Russell gave us the example of telecommunications work for various Middle Eastern clients being "*the springboard for the Bahrain office.*"

Potential globetrotters should know that further expansion is not on the cards for now and the firm is instead focusing on consolidating its current practices. This means developing its international arbitration offering in Geneva, for example, and focusing on inward investment in the tech sector in Oxford and Cambridge. We are "*looking at ways to combine the best of both* [private client and commercial]*... providing a full service to a wide range of clients with specific focus in particular sector areas,*" elaborated Russell.

A la carte

The London office recruits the greatest number of trainees, followed by Guildford and Cheltenham, with Cambridge and Bahrain taking only one each per year. Apparently competition for places is fiercest in the City, with around three-quarters of all applicants applying to the London office. The small size of teams in the regions does have its advantages, however, as trainees report having more responsibility.

Chambers UK rankings

Agriculture & Rural Affairs	Family/Matrimonial
Banking & Finance	Fraud
Capital Markets	Intellectual Property
Charities	Private Client
Corporate/M&A	Professional Discipline
Defamation/Reputation Management	Public Procurement
	Real Estate
Dispute Resolution	Real Estate Litigation
Education	Restructuring/Insolvency
Employment	Sports Law
Energy & Natural Resources	Telecommunications

It should be noted that not all offices cover all of the firm's practice areas, so let's examine what's on offer in each. London, as the largest training centre, offers seats in pretty much everything the firm does. Nothing is compulsory and it's possible to either restrict your training to commercial seats or combine commercial and private client seats. Go online for a full list of the seats. In Cheltenham the choice is limited to private client, corporate/commercial, real estate and litigation dispute resolution (LDR). Guildford has coco, employment & pensions, family, LDR, real estate and private client; Cambridge offers employment and coco. Geneva and Bahrain will take visiting trainees from the other offices and some people get the chance to go on client secondments. London trainees sometimes have a better chance of securing client secondments as the regional offices cannot always cope with losing anyone.

Fast cars, sport and fame

In London the corporate/commercial team focuses on a range of areas including charities, capital markets and IP. Certainly the client list is impressive and international, however, as one senior source conceded, this is no "*City-type banking and finance firm.*" Instead, Charles Russell's corporate team mines the mid-market, where it is ranked highly by *Chambers UK* and works on M&A and fund-raising, often for AIM-listed companies, especially in the natural resources sector. The firm recently advised J.P. Morgan Cazenove on a $92m fund-raising for AIM-listed client Coal of Africa, and Australian Allied Gold on share placements in the UK and Canada to raise approximately £88m. For trainees, the work "*can be quite varied; it depends what end of the floor you sit on, but you muck in with whatever's going.*" "*There's an interesting range of clients as the department covers everything from capital markets to charities. There are very large charities that are almost like companies and then smaller charities that are a little bit more eccentric.*" Corporate/commercial is proving a popular seat and several of the 2010 cohort of trainees wanted to qualify there. The hours can be longer than average, and it's the "*nature of the beast*" to do a few midnight stints.

Charles Russell has itself struck gold in the sports sector, with a dream team client list that includes West Ham Utd, Wembley Stadium, Fabio Capello, various county cricket clubs and Thierry Henry, who sought advice on the potential consequences of his controversial hand ball in the France v Ireland World Cup qualifying match. The practice has also recently worked on cyclist Bradley Wiggins' move to Team Sky, and with Nike on various sponsorship and merchandising deals. There is no specific sports law seat, but interested trainees may be able to work for clients in this sector during their corporate/commercial or dispute resolution (LDR) seat. A client secondment is also available to The FA.

It's not all diamonds and goals. If the name Charles Russell sounds familiar, you may have read about some of its sexier media work, namely in TV libel and privacy. The firm landed a place on ITV's legal panel and advised the Storm modelling agency (Kate Moss, Sophie Dahl, Lily Cole and other beauties) on a joint venture with the parent company of Simon Fuller's 19 Entertainment. Other clients include Brawn/Mercedes and the organisers of the V Festival. A defamation team works with Channel 4, The Catholic Church of England & Wales and an alleged girlfriend of Tiger Woods (though we can't say which). As with sports work, there is no dedicated media seat and work in this sector crops up in the corporate/commercial and LDR seats.

LDR is a popular seat. Trainees assist partners in writing correspondence and preparing arbitration documents and witness statements. There's "*lots of drafting,*" but grunt work on bundling and disclosure exercises are also "*par for the course... as a trainee you've got to expect it.*" The work is both domestic and international. Illustrating this fact is the firm's appointment by the Central Bank of Bahrain as external administrator in 2009 in the insolvency of Saudi-owned Awal Bank, which held assets worth more than $5bn. In quite a different case, lawyers are representing UK Athletics in a dispute with BBC Worldwide over the ownership of the international television rights to two new British athletics meetings – the London Grand Prix and the British Grand Prix.

Perhaps most responsibility is to be found in the real estate department where "*you manage quite a lot of your own files.*" As many cases are "*quite process-driven, it's a lot easier for a trainee to pick things up and get involved, and there's a lot of support.*" Clients here include Eton College, Bank of Ireland and The Random House Group.

Wealth of nations

Trainees typically form two camps: those attracted to the firm's reputation for private client and family matters, and those keen to try different areas as they're less certain about what's going to be right for them. Said one source: "*I knew I was interested in private client but didn't want to exclude the possibility of other things.*" Others noted that Charles Russell was "*unusual in that it's strong in private client and commercial.*"

Seats in family law revolve around client contact, although this varies between offices. The team handles divorce, financial settlements and other related issues such as private child cases (although it is not concerned with public child law). They say that London is the divorce capital of the world, and the international feel of the family team's clientele certainly reflects this. The seat will expose the trainee to the concept of 'forum shopping' and conflicts between different jurisdictions' laws. Many of the cases are worth tens of millions and some of the parties feel there is so much at stake that they'll push things as far as the Supreme Court. But it's not all about the money: "*The human element is really rewarding.*"

Private client on the other hand is all about the money. The practice acts for rich individuals from Japan to Georgia, and South Africa to Switzerland. The firm's Geneva office handles plenty of this type of work and, along with the outpost in Bahrain, has proved a good source of clients. The international wealth club has been in need of more advice than ever of late; it's not only in the UK that non-doms and their taxation have come under the spotlight. The department's work also spills over into Shari'a law and corporate advice. In the UK, trainee tasks include "*drawing up wills, powers of attorney, estate planning and a lot of research.*" Apparently one corner of the UK practice that deals mainly with historic English estates is so traditional that it's forgone modern technology and "*still does everything by letter.*"

International seats and client secondments to Cable & Wireless, Virgin Media and private equity firm Actis Capital, among others, are understandably popular. The Geneva and Bahrain offices are small and our sources reported high responsibility and client contact. Everything in Bahrain is apparently "*done on who you know, networking, business cards and socialising...*"

Mind your manners

Charles Russell is very conscious of its history and strives to balance the traditional and the modern. "*You don't feel like you are at a fuddy duddy firm,*" insisted one trainee. Senior partner Patrick Russell, a descendant of the original Charles Russell, sees the firm's strength in the traditional values of "*respect and manners... arrogance is not acceptable or accepted.*" All the trainees we spoke to cited work/life balance as a reason for choosing the firm and they stressed its role in the firm's ethos. "*There isn't a culture of presentee-ism here.*" The sleek London office, situated just off Fleet Street, has elements of environmentally intelligent design, although we're a little more envious of the staff in the Geneva office, which is apparently situated right by the lake. A 'one firm' policy is promoted across the offices, and our sources generally felt that the offices were well integrated. However, some noted a slight London/regional divide. "*The London office would like to think we're closer than we maybe are,*" suggested one.

Anyone interested in pro bono and charitable activities might like the "*Apprentice-style challenge*" that faced recent newbies before the start of their first seat. "*They sent us off into London to get as much free stuff as possible to raffle for a children's charity.*"

The social scene varies between offices. Party animals should head to London, and in Guildford there's also "*a vibrant group of trainees through to 7PQE that you can always find in one of three pubs within 500 metres of the office on Friday evenings.*" Each month the fairer sex in Guildford head to the White House, Keystone or a local piano bar for a girls' night out. "*The boys try and crash it!*" Smaller offices such as Cambridge have "*office lunches every so often,*" whereas Cheltenham has everything for the shopaholic as the office is located in "*a nice area of town with boutique-y shops and cafés.*" The firm has recently organised several larger events including boat parties, sailing days and tennis tournaments. In this sport-loving firm, teams have been formed for football, netball and cricket. Many of the players (and spectators) converge annually for the "*notorious*" and "*legendary*" sports dinner. Sadly, no trainee would elaborate. The firm's innate sense of fun seeps into its recruitment process too. For more on that, see our website.

And finally...

Keen to maintain its historic reputation for private client and family practice but looking also to strengthen its capabilities, both in the UK and abroad, Charles Russell knows how to spread its bets. In 2010, 16 of 20 trainees took up newly qualified positions at the firm.

Clarke Willmott LLP

The facts

Location: Birmingham, Bristol, Taunton, Southampton, London, Manchester

Number of UK partners/solicitors: 67/132

Total number of trainees: 19

Seats: 4x6 months

Alternative seats: None

On chambersstudent.co.uk
- How to get into CW
- More on paralegalling at the firm
- Equitable Life for dummies

Offering commercial and private client experiences, fast-growing Clarke Willmott is revealing its appetite for high-value work and national recognition.

Revving up

Officially, Clarke Willmott has its headquarters in Birmingham, and yet this is actually one of its smallest offices. Its biggest is in Bristol, and next in the size stakes comes Taunton, where the firm was founded way back in 1898. There's also an office in Southampton and tiny outposts in London and Manchester. Due to its high-street roots in Taunton, CW has traditionally had a South Western private client persona, but its arrival in several UK cities and subsequent commercial successes now mark it out as something more. Having at least doubled in size and turnover since 2000, the firm is ambitious and proud of it. It is a top-65 law firm, with 67 partners, almost 500 personnel and a turnover of £40.8m.

Along the way, mergers have supplemented organic growth. A 2002 tie-up with Southampton firm Ensor Byfield boosted CW's reputation for sports-related law. More recently, the 2010 merger with Bristol-based David Gist Solicitors "*has met with a lot of positivity*" and is set to strengthen the PI and clinical negligence divisions.

CW has won some major clients. In real estate litigation, its customers include Oddbins, Burger King and various high-street banks. It manages debt recovery cases for the London Borough of Harrow, the Ministry of Defence and the Department for Transport, and its sports clients include Bristol City and West Bromwich Albion Football Clubs, UK Sport, the Greyhound Board of Great Britain, the British Olympic Association and various tennis, rugby and cricket associations. Lawyers also gave IP rights advice to Silverstone F1GP and – wait for it – the Stig.

Following the client's lead

CW offers a range of legal services but claims not to be oriented towards any particular specialism: as it says on its website, 'we're just client led'. Certain client sectors have a degree of dominance: agriculture, real estate and construction, renewable energy, retail, sport, private client and international clients. The firm assists its overseas clients on corporate and commercial issues, business immigration, employment and property matters. Particular emphasis is placed on Australia, Brazil, Portugal, China, the Indian Subcontinent, Poland and North America. This approach makes use of some dual-qualified and/or bilingual lawyers and recognises the rise of the BRIC nations. Our trainees had largely domestic experiences; however, these international desks signify a forward-looking partnership.

Except for London and the newly opened Manchester office, all offices have trainees: usually about four in Southampton, four in Taunton, six in Bristol and five in Birmingham. New trainees are allocated their first seat, but are subsequently able to state their preferences. Securing a desired seat takes skill and a little luck, and one trainee's advice was this: "*Don't wait for handouts; if you want to work in a team go talk to them.*" Another's was to not "*waste time harassing HR.*" The different seats' popularity varies year on year, but litigation is always sought after. The litigation department focuses on commercial and financial disputes and CW litigators deal with the firm's "*crown jewel clients.*" Trainees tell us that it's easy to "*feel like part of the team*" and that their experiences are more "*research and drafting-based*" than lim-

Chambers UK rankings

Agriculture & Rural Affairs	Personal Injury
Banking & Finance	Planning
Construction	Private Client
Debt Recovery	Real Estate
Dispute Resolution	Real Estate Litigation
Employment	Restructuring/Insolvency
Environment	Retail
Family/Matrimonial	Social Housing
Information Technology	Sports Law
Intellectual Property	

ited to administrative tasks. Frequent court visits, including to the High Court, are a real plus, and there are also opportunities to interact with clients, both on the phone and in person. Most of the cases are large, but trainees may be able to run smaller ones on their own. The firm handles plenty of claims relating to the financial services sector, including fraud and pensions mis-selling. Claims against Equitable Life have been a key area of work and this issue led to CW partner Robert Morfee being interviewed on the BBC show *Working Lunch*. For more on Equitable Life, go to our website.

The corporate seat in Bristol is hugely popular as it incorporates some sports matters. The team is supportive and the supervisor always close at hand. A trainee will get stuck into due diligence and document management, and some smaller files are entrusted entirely to their care. But be warned: the workload can be "*feast or famine,*" so you might be really busy or twiddling your thumbs. This can play havoc with your social life, but that's the nature of corporate transactional practice. If you grow tomatoes (gardening is the new rock 'n' roll by the way) then you'll be familiar with Miracle Gro. CW represented a UK subsidiary of this New York-based business when it acquired another British horticulture business last year. This deal put CW lawyers opposite Eversheds. On others they have squared up to Allen & Overy, Freshfields, Jones Day, Trowers & Hamlins in the Middle East, Field Fisher Waterhouse and Osborne Clarke.

During a recession, insolvency lawyers move to centre stage. CW's insolvency team is divided into two sections to handle administrations and bankruptcies. A seat in this part of the firm exposes the trainee to both contentious and non-contentious matters, and there is plenty of crossover work with the corporate, property, litigation, and even family teams. A common first seat, new trainees learn a lot about other areas of the law quite quickly while also improving their drafting skills and being introduced to the courts. Partners are said to be very encouraging and keen that trainees speak directly to clients. "*It's nice to feel trusted,*" said one source.

Homes, hearts and minds

Property is another good first seat. The team has some big clients including national house builders, local authorities and housing associations, British Waterways and wine retailer Nicolas. Bristol City Football Club sought advice on its proposed £90m stadium relocation from Ashton Gate to Ashton Vale and its involvement in Bristol's successful application to be a host city as part of England's 2018 World Cup bid. It's not all sexy sports sector deals though: CW is a master of the humble residential conveyance and a large number of its staff are employed on this type of work across its offices. Property trainees sort through deeds, draft leases, register land or rights over land, prepare licences for alterations to buildings and liaise with clients. Even when trainees haven't chosen this seat, they typically find it "*really useful, as property rears its ugly head in everything.*" Deals are also more interesting by virtue of the fact that some have an immediate impact on the trainees' own surroundings. A construction seat involves plenty of research, reviewing contracts, drafting letters and preparing for court hearings plus a dollop of marketing activities. The department also runs a helpline giving free advice on construction topics. According to some sources, "*it doesn't lend itself so well as a trainee seat*" due to the large cases and trainees not being given much autonomy; others thought it was good "*to be thrown in at the deep end.*"

The private client department is a strong suit in Taunton, where it accounts for around a quarter of the office's work. Trainees assist seniors and are also given some of their own files. Tasks include drafting wills, writing letters, administrating probate, lifetime tax planning and research assignments on larger taxable estates and disputes. Given the location, the work often relates to agricultural assets and this requires experienced private client lawyers to also be well versed in business law. Other seats are available with the busy catastrophic injury team, which is excellent for hands-on experience and "*a good one for seeing a litigation matter from start to finish.*" The clinical negligence team has somewhat similar work, and here a source had really enjoyed their exposure to serious cases relating to brain injuries. In these more 'human interest' departments – as in others – our CW sources felt they were given a wide variety of work and a good mix of responsibility and support.

A Clarke's life

The distance between most of the CW offices is considerable, so there isn't a massively close rapport between them. Trainees generally stay put in the office they start in. That said, there is regular trainee interchange between

Bristol and Taunton, although trainees in Taunton "*shouldn't expect to get their first-choice seat in Bristol.*" It also depends on the seats you want: Southampton is very litigation-based; Bristol is particularly strong on commercial property and personal injury; and Taunton does a great deal of private client and agriculture work. There is no family department in Southampton and not much of one in Birmingham, so trainees need to go to Taunton or Bristol if it's of interest.

The hours are generally good and "*there's not a stay-late-for-the-sake-of-it culture.*" Most trainees leave around 6pm, and 7.30pm is considered late. The general atmosphere at the offices is professional: "*Relaxed but not too relaxed, and not stuffy.*" Seniors are "*very generous with their time,*" and larger teams, especially, are ready to give trainees the help they need. With only two guys out of 16 trainees in 2010, the gender balance has been somewhat wonky. This is anything but intentional and the demographics become more balanced among more senior lawyers. It's "*not a female-dominated firm,*" a source insisted. Indeed not: the partnership is just 22% female, not that this is low – it's towards the higher end of the average range for larger UK firms.

The offices are described as "*lovely,*" with the Bristol one taking the cake. Overlooking the river and Castle Park, with a huge atrium, it is "*the envy of most people who work in Bristol.*" The office also has its own café, called Berry Blue, where you can enjoy "*amazing breakfasts.*" The Birmingham office is in the city centre, and the Taunton office is in a green, leafy area with lots of parking and within easy reach of the motorway. The Southampton office is on a business park in Hedge End, near to the motorway and a large retail park.

Every month, on 'First Fridays of Fun' (FFF) staff can enjoy drinks after work on the partners' tab. Every now and then this also means casual dress. In each office a social committee organises quiz nights and outings to different bars. Each office also hosts a summer barbecue and a Christmas party (Bristol staff went to the Brasserie Blanc last year), but the distance between offices prevents firm-wide partying. When they start, trainees take training together at the Bristol office, but after this they "*don't really see each other.*" The social life in Taunton is made harder by the fact that many people drive there. Bristol trainees attend Junior Lawyers Division events, and the smaller Birmingham and Southampton offices' trainees also socialise with young lawyers from other firms in their respective cities. There is "*quite a lot you can do but not a lot organised for you,*" a source explained. Anyone with a passion for sport can indulge it with netball, softball, cricket or football, often playing against other professional services firms.

Dig out that vuvuzela?

CW hasn't been immune to the worldwide economic downturn, and there were some redundancies, among both fee earners and secretaries. The firm is currently outsourcing typing work to South Africa, but some trainees found this inefficient and mourned the loss of local secretarial support, which is now "*down to the bare bones.*" There were some staff on four-day weeks last year to avoid job cuts, but hours had returned to normal by the time we interviewed at the firm. During the darkest days of the credit crunch, the firm also suggested job-sharing and sabbaticals and trainees cited this as an example of management's ability to "*think creatively.*" There were no trainee deferrals, and three NQs who were not offered permanent jobs on qualification last year were kept on as legal assistants. All three were subsequently offered permanent positions at the firm. In the run up to 2010 qualification, the second-years we spoke to were "*not being naïve about being offered jobs*" and keeping their options open. In the end, seven of 11 trainees were kept on across all the offices in various departments.

And finally...

Big clients and big ambition – this mid-sized firm is aiming high. For regional private client and increasingly national and international business law this is a good bet.

Cleary Gottlieb Steen & Hamilton LLP

The facts

Location: London

Number of UK partners/solicitors: 9/38 (+US: 6/13)

Total number of trainees: 19

Seats: 4x6 months

Alternative seats: Overseas seats

Extras: Pro bono – LawWorks, FRU

On chambersstudent.co.uk
- **How to get into Cleary**
- **Cleary's brand of internationalism**
- **A new emphasis on litigation**

The London office of this nonconformist international firm is small, select, and a paradise for top performers hungry for hard work.

International by nature

Cleary Gottlieb took its first steps across the Atlantic only three years after it was founded in New York in 1946. Internationally minded from the beginning, when the US sent post-war Europe millions of dollars and hundreds of intellectuals to help rebuild the shattered continent, the firm made its mark by advising Jean Monnet (a chief architect of the European Community) on the implementation of the Marshall Plan aid package. The firm became exceedingly well versed on the European legal and financial structures and has always kept an eagle eye on emerging markets, swooping in to do business in Russia, the Middle East and Africa ahead of its competitors. To read more on Cleary's brand of internationalism go to our website.

The London office opened in 1971. Still relatively small, it is nonetheless respected for its strengths in capital markets, finance and M&A. Its litigation practice is a current focus of attention. Prominent partner Jonathan Blackman has been imported from the New York office, and former Simmons & Simmons finance litigation head Jonathan Kelly was brought on board to further cultivate Cleary's contentious presence in the City.

Renaissance lawyers

The firm's nonconformist style is central to its identity. It operates without departments and shapes its lawyers as generalists. "*Although we recognise the importance of specialised lawyers, we've always encouraged people to have a broader practice. It's more fun, and when you're having fun you do a good job. As a consequence it's easier for us to adapt to the market – we've never had a slew of lawyers with nothing to do when the market changes,*" London managing partner Mark Walker told us. This certainly proved to be true over the past two years as the financial meltdown brought a bounty of work to the firm, including its representation of Barclays Capital in its Lehman Brothers investment banking and capital markets acquisitions.

The generalist approach means that although trainees may be assigned to a particular seat, they're also likely to undertake work that is completely unrelated to it. Our sources viewed this "*flexibility to pick out the practice areas you like*" as "*the Cleary difference.*" Most said that if they expressed an interest in a certain area of practice, a project would be plonked on their desk within a week, if not the next day. Becoming an expert in many areas of law may seem daunting, but Cleary trainees seem up to the challenge. "*You learn to be very adaptable and to not shy away from anything. It's about being able to find an answer, even if you have an unfamiliar question.*" They don't lack support – first-year trainees are assigned second-year and associate mentors, and "*you'll always be approached by other people offering themselves as a resource.*" There is extensive formal training covering all subjects.

Full steam ahead

Despite the absence of formal departments, it's easy to identify finance, capital markets and M&A activities as

Chambers UK rankings

Banking & Finance	Corporate/M&A
Capital Markets	Private Equity

the firm's forte in London. Trainees reported *"a lot of derivatives work"* in the finance seat, where time is spent *"drafting agreements and schedules, and attending a lot of negotiations."* Cleary followed the shift in the market and was on call for some major restructurings, like that of Russian metals and mining company RUSAL. The firm was lead counsel in its restructuring of approximately $15bn of loans from both Russian and international banks, and also advised on its $2.2bn IPO in Hong Kong – the city's highest-profile foreign listing to date. Locally, Cleary took to the UK courts to represent Oaktree Capital, Cheyne Capital, Sandelman Partners and JPMorgan as super-senior revolving credit facility lenders in the TI Automotive restructuring. Most trainees hadn't done much capital markets work, even if they'd sat in the department, because of the sluggish market; however, it was on the up when we rang them.

The M&A practice stayed at full steam ahead despite the recession, partly because it was focused on Russia and emerging markets in the Middle East. On the home front, Cleary represented Goldman Sachs, Morgan Stanley and UBS Investment Bank as joint financial advisers to Cadbury in its takeover by Kraft. The firm also recently acted for private equity house TPG Capital on its acquisition of fashion outlet Republic, where you can find the likes of Diesel, G-Star and Miss Sixty as well as the Republic range. Besides the standard due diligence and research tasks, trainees are responsible for *"a fair bit of general transaction management – keeping on top of everything and pushing things towards closing."*

Traditionally, there has been a *"default view"* that trainees should undergo one finance and two corporate seats, along with the mandatory contentious one. Now, *"if you can present a compelling reason why you want to do two contentious seats, they'll try to accommodate you."* We expect that with the two new Jonathans in the office, contentious options will become more available and even more exciting.

Also on the rise is the number of overseas options. The firm's established arbitration seat in Paris is a definite (a first-seater recently starting his training contract there), as is a competition seat in Brussels. New York is now up and running again and the firm is also sending its first trainees to Hong Kong and Moscow. If you don't fancy a long stretch away, there are still plenty of travel opportunities. Besides the almost inevitable business trips, trainees are invited to *"acculturation"* seminars and bi-annual practice group meetings, usually in fancy European cities.

No easy answers

No matter what country or seat they are in, trainees are guaranteed intense responsibility. *"It can be scary at times how much you are trusted to do,"* but Cleary trainees get a thrill out of it and seem honoured, as *"it's a reflection of the fact the firm trusts you from day one."* Not a place for the meek or those who shy away from hard work, *"it's very rare to have an easy answer to give, and it's very often the case that you'll be the one asked to answer difficult questions."*

There are *"a lot of pressures and demands on your time."* Trainees admitted that *"you'll have to work weekends, late at night, cancel holidays."* To them, *"the question should be whether your work is more rewarding. It's unequivocally more worth it here than at magic circle firms, because there's more responsibility across the board. Getting exposure to some of the firm's most important clients during your training contract makes a big difference. You're not just BCC'd on client e-mails – they have your mobile number. You're given a BlackBerry because you're an indispensable part of the team. I'm quite amazed at my friends* [at other firms] *who don't have to do anything over weekends, but it makes me wonder how essential they are to the firm."* Despite the (often self-inflicted) hard-driving, *"when you close your first deal you realise it is all actually worth it."*

"There are no weak links" at Cleary. Out of about 2,000 applications per year, the firm generally limits its intake to between ten and 12. There are about 35 vac scheme places up for grabs annually, and for tips on how to get one and what to expect, see our website. You'll need an absolutely stellar CV, which should probably include a top degree from Oxbridge (although we were told this is becoming less important) and a substantial list of other achievements to boot. Speaking a second language or sporting a Master's degree isn't a prerequisite; however, you'll find them on most Cleary CVs as being *"academically curious"* is something the firm looks for. Cleary lawyers are *"all geeks"* – in an endearing way, of course. *"Traditionally they would have gone to the Bar. They are people who feel at home in library-like surroundings."*

A healthy haven

For a group of such high-achieving workaholics, we were impressed by Cleary's relaxed environment. There wasn't even a hint of competition and the social scene is in full swing. *"Everyone comes in with the same academic level so there's no need to prove yourself in that respect."* Trainees attributed the more *"chilled out"* atmosphere to a lack of billing targets and the lockstep compensation system. Additionally, "*there's not the same level of competition to get a job here, so it's healthier and kind of a haven compared to what other firms are doing.*" This haven is "*small and collegial*" with "*a strong sense of mutual support – everyone is approachable. Because it's such a small office you don't get cliques.*" The lack of departments also helps because "*everyone is mixed in, so you feel at home walking around.*" There is a distinct "*emphasis on people who are not purely black letter lawyers, but who are interesting, engaging and bright.*"

Most weeks, Cleary lawyers can be found at the Corney & Barrow "*on informally organised nights out. People tend to meet up on weekends too. The rumour that if you go to Cleary you're chained to your desk is definitely not true.*" There is a football team and a squash group, and some lawyers also bond through Cleary's many pro bono activities. "*You can take it or leave it,*" one source said of the social life, "*but most people take it.*"

And finally...

If you're not convinced by now, there's one final temptation. *"Financially, it's a lot more rewarding here."* The NQ salary is £92,000, currently the fourth highest in the market. In 2010, jobs were offered to all seven qualifiers and five stayed on.

Clifford Chance LLP

The facts

Location: London

Number of UK partners/solicitors: 191/610

Total number of trainees: 224

Seats: 4x6 months

Alternative seats: Overseas seats, secondments

Extras: Pro bono – various law centres, death row appeals; language classes

On chambersstudent.co.uk

- How to get into CC
- The firm's history
- Around the world in 50 seats
- A look at the more niche seats

Clifford Chance's far-reaching international network and unbridled ambition have seen it expand to become a firm of global pre-eminence.

Where the sun never sets

If you have ever considered a career in commercial law you will probably have heard of this firm. The 1987 merger between Clifford Turner and Coward Chance created the first 'mega-firm', and since then further mergers and organic growth have seen it amass 3,500 lawyers in 28 offices around the globe. It became the world's biggest law firm by the late 2000s. CC is usually among the first to land in new emerging markets and most recently it set up co-operation agreements with firms in India and Saudi Arabia.

The fatted years came to an abrupt end in 2008/09, with revenue tumbling 5% and equity partner profits down by a third. Since then billing systems have been overhauled, associate salaries rethought, partnership tracks redesigned, new practice heads appointed and grad recruitment responsibilities shifted from one partner to a committee of nine. Restructuring resulted in the firm culling 15% of its partnership and significant numbers of associates (80 in London, and the US was badly hit). Revenue dropped a further 5% in 2009/10, to just below £1.2bn, although CC regained its crown as the largest UK firm by revenue, overtaking Linklaters.

CC used to sit at the banking and finance end of the magic circle table, but now also has a strong presence in the areas of corporate, capital markets and high-end litigation. You name a top financial institution and you can almost guarantee CC is doing business with it. One of the biggest deals of the year saw lawyers acting for Santander, BNP Paribas, Citibank, HSBC and RBS on the refinancing of $15bn worth of debt for cement giant CEMEX. In another high-end matter, it acted for Lloyds over the potential protection of a whopping £260bn worth of its assets under the Government Asset Protection Scheme. Private equity is an area where CC is strong: it advised Warburg Pincus on its takeover of Poundland. In a still-fragile M&A market, CC was involved in one of the biggest M&A deals of 2010, advising Kraft on its much-publicised £11.9bn takeover of Cadbury. It also advised Barclays on the £8.2bn sale of an investment management subsidiary, and helped the Aluminum Corporation of China secure a $19.5bn partnership with Rio Tinto.

With all these megadeals to think about, it's easy to forget CC is a full-service firm with leading disputes, competition, tax, real estate, construction, employment, international arbitration, energy, environmental and public law departments. But trainees do focus on CC's core: over two-thirds of seats done by our randomly selected interviewees were in the capital markets, finance or corporate departments. Trainees will generally sit in at least two of these three departments. To visit a non-core seat it helps to "*push and push and push*" from the start of your contract. "*HR made it clear that if you compromise a bit and do an unpopular seat, you are more likely to get a niche one,*" a source claimed. Most of our sources strenuously denied any "*brown-nosing*" to get into niche seats or secure a job on qualification. Trainees did say however that "*the most important thing to do if you want to be a success here is to build relationships with colleagues. To some trainees, that comes naturally. With others, their people skills can let them down.*" This and other soft skills

Chambers UK rankings

Administrative & Public Law	Investment Funds
Asset Finance	Outsourcing
Banking & Finance	Parliamentary & Public Affairs
Banking Litigation	Pensions
Capital Markets	Planning
Commodities	Private Client
Competition/European Law	Private Equity
Construction	Product Liability
Corporate/M&A	Professional Negligence
Data Protection	Projects
Defamation/Reputation Management	Public International Law
Dispute Resolution	Real Estate
Employee Share Schemes	Real Estate Finance
Employment	Real Estate Litigation
Energy & Natural Resources	Restructuring/Insolvency
Environment	Retail
Financial Services	Social Housing
Fraud	Tax
Information Technology	Telecommunications
Insurance	Transport
Intellectual Property	

are addressed by the firm's extensive programme of ongoing training sessions.

It can't be said enough that this is an international business dealing 24/7 with the legal requirements of international clients. This comment from a trainee illustrates the point well: "*A client might instruct a partner in São Paulo and they might involve the London M&A and New York teams. A foreign client might also instruct London, and a deal based out of London might require foreign law advice. I worked on a recent matter where a lot of European jurisdictions were involved. There was no English player, but the documents used English law and the Central European offices were involved.*" For information on the dozens of overseas seats and client secondments, go to our website.

Groundhogs and tiny cogs

The banking team classically "*acts for banks and borrowers in the process of lending money and getting it from A to B to acquire companies and finance takeovers.*" For example, the team has been involved in the financing of part of the Athletes Village at the 2012 Olympics site. The team also advised Man Group, the world's largest hedge fund, on the UK part of a $1.6bn buyout. The recession has meant a change in the type of instructions the team has been getting and trainees might have found themselves "*acting for big international banks which lent billions of dollars to large Russian companies that, because the way things were priced in the boom times, are now struggling to pay it back.*" Refinancing and restructurings have dominated the department: lately lawyers recently advised on the £1bn restructuring of airport caterers Select Service Partners, and on the multibillion-dollar restructurings of Dubai World and RUSAL. "*It's exciting to be able to watch the mechanics of really high-profile restructurings like Dubai World, getting approvals and sign-offs from the UAE government and being a very tiny person in that.*"

Trainees have mixed experiences of the tiny-ness of their role in a finance seat. Some take a sunny view: "*I sat with a superstar asset finance partner and got immense responsibility. There's a very steep learning curve – transaction management is entirely left to you, and clients call you directly with difficult questions.*" Others see clouds: "*The work is all quite similar, whether you're managing a checklist, drafting a legal opinion or reviewing board minutes. Often the only difference is the number of jurisdictions a deal involves. An obvious trainee task is the bibling, which is not very varied.*" One trainee quipped that the repetition means "*sometimes it's a bit like Groundhog Day.*" The general attitude to the whole experience is: "*You have to accept the drudgery for the benefit, which is exposure to a high level of work.*"

Capital markets trainees usually specialise in equity, funds or, most commonly, structured debt ("*it's securitisation, but it's been called structured debt since the credit crunch to make it sound more appealing*"). Structured debt involves "*a lot of residential mortgage-backed securities* [RMBS], *loan receivables, credit card securities*" and collateralised debt obligations. Once you've managed to pronounce these financial tongue twisters you'll need to get your head round what they actually involve. Luckily, the departmental training "*explains all the concepts to you.*"

At it from the lit-co

Besides the Kraft deal, CC's corporate team acted for International Power on the sale of its £738m business in the Czech Republic, advised Anheuser-Busch InBev on the $2.2bn sale of its business in South-Eastern Europe, and helped Suntory (the Japanese whisky brand made infamous by the movie *Lost in Translation*) on its €2.6bn purchase of sexy French soft drinks brand Orangina-Schweppes. "*Corporate tends to have slightly bigger teams,*" which means "*work that comes down to trainees is on the drier side – document management, due diligence, ensuring amendments have gone into documents and making sure meeting rooms are booked.*" Trainees are not disappointed though and feel they have "*a good level of client contact.*" In harder-to-wangle corporate subgroups like media and technology, or competition and regulation, trainees are able to try "*a wider variety of work,*" including legal research and drafting.

Corporate, capital markets and banking seats are known to have the worst hours, particularly when the economy is not dragging along at a slow pace. "*You will sometimes have breakfast and dinner in the office. It can start to feel like you're in a bubble.*" Although no one forces face time upon trainees, the source who claimed that "*there are a few people who impose on themselves a culture of face time*" was probably onto something. Some say that in order to impress and get better work, it helps to put in the extra hours. This is just how some trainees like it though. "*Sometimes you do get a buzz from the long hours. You don't notice it's midnight as you're so involved in what you're doing.*"

CC's litigation department "*does everything from contract disputes to credit-crunch related issues.*" For example, its lawyers acted for Barclays in its appeal against the Competition Commission's decision to ban the sale of payment protection insurance alongside credit cards and loans. Other clients include Siemens, Société Générale and credit rating agency Standard & Poor's. The department "*is known to be hierarchical and is quite partner-driven.*" Partners and associates get the best pickings: "*As the trainee you sometimes end up going to meetings and court, but otherwise there's not much opportunity to have client contact.*" As a trainee, expect your share of "*photocopying and bundling and a lot of the grunt work.*" As far as supervisors go, some trainees reckon it's "*far more useful to sit with someone more senior to have more visibility and increase your chances on qualification.*" Space limitations restrict us from talking more about niche seats, which are known for their generally "*more relaxed*" nature, but visit our website for more info.

Reach out and touch the sky

CC is the only magic circle firm based at Canary Wharf. The office has its own dentist, dry cleaner, hairdressers, bar, gym, 24-hour canteen and subterranean entrance from the Tube. "*Even in the middle of the night you can always call down to the kitchen and ask them to bring you a hot snack.*" All this led us to ask whether trainees were chiefly attracted by the glamour, lifestyle and sheer prestige of working for the UK's biggest firm. Although "*people here like the idea of being known as Clifford Chance lawyers,*" the consensus is that it's "*less to do with lifestyle and more to do with the calibre of work.*" The message is: love the toils not the spoils. "*There might be people here who think they live a swanky life, but when they are proof-reading at 1am they will be brought back down to earth.*" One trainee explained CC's position in the trainee market: "*If you wanted the money you'd go to an American firm, and if you wanted the nice lifestyle you'd go to a smaller firm. CC doesn't give you the ultimate lifestyle or money, but it does give you brilliant training and the best calibre work you can get.*"

"*There are a lot of subcultures*" within CC, and "*different personality types will be attracted to different departments.*" Sources said they couldn't "*pinpoint any traits that the majority of trainees have*" and denied that CC-ers are the ultra-ambitious types we suspected them to be. A number of sources noted that trainees are "*quite diverse*" in ethnicity, background, international origin and personality. "*You need both the quiet types and the loud, brash types.*" They also say there's a strong meritocracy here, and that there's "*no particular prejudices – some of the people in other law firms seem a bit more elitist than those here.*" All in all, we'd suggest that the attitude of trainees here chimes with the first-mover, pioneering spirit CC is renowned for. Certainly, they are "*not people to be pushed around very easily.*"

Long hours do mean that CC doesn't have a massively active social scene, although the banking, finance and capital markets teams in particular do their best. "*Funds has an event every couple of months, like bowling or go-karting, while in capital markets everyone will end up in a bar.*" Trainees like to stick together: "*Quite often people have drinks in the fourth-floor Budgie bar, or more often use that as an initial meeting point. And if we're having a good time, we'll jump on the DLR to somewhere more central.*"

CC was an early adopter of legal process outsourcing: it set up its own knowledge centre just south of Delhi more than four years ago to carry out admin, research and documentation tasks more economically than possible in the UK. Said one trainee: "*It's really useful shifting some of the work elsewhere. I have got them to run in-depth research, and they will do it overnight. I haven't had any problems, although with anything you don't do yourself, it needs to be checked. I don't think it has had an impact on the number of NQs or trainees taken on; it's had more of an effect at paralegal level.*" Retention dropped from typically over 95% to below 80% in 2009. Reflecting the hesitant recovery of the economy, 102 of 136 qualifiers remained with the firm in 2010.

And finally...

Trainees really value what this firm gives them, whether they stay beyond qualification or not. If you don't mind long hours or working your way up from the bottom, we say, go for it.

Clyde & Co LLP

The facts

Location: London, Guildford

Number of UK partners/solicitors: 111/329

Total number of trainees: 50

Seats: 4x6 months

Alternative Seats: Overseas

Extras: Pro bono – Lambeth and Surrey Law Centres, Brent and RCJ CABs, Legal Literacy Programme

On chambersstudent.co.uk
- How to get into Clyde & Co
- An interview with managing partner Ben Knowles
- Clydes' foray into the Middle East

Has your aeroplane crashed into the ocean? Ship's cargo lost in stormy seas? Fire devastated your factory? Then you need Clyde & Co.

Sea of change

Clydes is the champion of heavy litigation. Flying high in the *Chambers UK* aviation rankings since its 2005 merger with UK specialists Beaumont & Son, the firm also maintains its traditional strength in shipping, advising on major piracy incidents, shipwrecks and high-seas collisions. With 23 offices worldwide, it is certainly well placed to do so in every corner of the globe. Naturally connected to these sectors are the fields of insurance, trade and energy, and Clydes excels in all of these on behalf of its multinational clients.

The firm's international reach now stretches from London to San Francisco via Dar es Salaam and Hong Kong. Revenue was up 4% to £192m in 2009/10, with 42% of that amount generated beyond the UK. The firm is keen to capitalise on the growing network of offices. Managing partner Ben Knowles elaborated: "*The strategy is to be the 'go-to' firm for complex cross-border international matters in our key sectors. The biggest push at the moment is in the energy sector.*" Trainees tell us the firm is "*completely open to any opportunity*" and will "*expand in any direction it thinks would be profitable.*" In the past few years Clydes has settled in New York (2006) and New Jersey (2010), servicing stateside insurance clients. It also forged an alliance with Indian firm ALMT Legal in 2009.

Clydes offers a mixture of transactional and contentious seats across its core sectors. It also offers recruits experience in real estate, employment and corporate/commercial. A stint in the firm's Guildford office is non negotiable, although not everyone will be allocated a seat there. While this has led to moans in the past, trainees often find that they quite like the calmer atmosphere of Surrey, and some know "*right from the off*" that they're GU through and through.

Calamity covered

"*Insurance and shipping are the darlings of the firm,*" and most trainees will spend at least one seat in one of "*many insurance teams.*" General insurance litigators "*act for underwriters on large losses* [when] *trains crash into each other or things catch fire.*" Trainees attend trials and arbitrations, take witness statements and conduct research. Reinsurance work can be really complex and so it's little wonder that those who go on to qualify here are described as "*a pretty studious bunch.*" Elsewhere, "*sexy*" political risk matters can cover wars, coups d'état and riots, although the run-of-the-mill work is international investment treaties, nationalisations and expropriations. Claims are often worth in excess of $100m and the clients are huge multinational insurers. "*You play a trainee role,*" said one of our sources, "*putting bundles together, dealing with all the expert reports – big admin tasks.*"

Declaring a love of insurance is probably the fastest way to kill the average dinner party conversation, so perhaps that's why there's "*an awful lot of client entertaining*" – like minds and all that. Trainees socialise with their counterparts in the insurance market ("*it's good fun and good business*"), although sadly they don't usually get to attend the big-ticket events. For now, the insurance team occupies space in the Corn Exchange, just around the corner from

Chambers UK rankings

Asset Finance	Information Technology
Aviation	Insurance
Commodities	Product Liability
Construction	Professional Negligence
Corporate/M&A	Projects
Dispute Resolution	Public International Law
Employment	Real Estate
Energy & Natural Resources	Restructuring/Insolvency
	Retail
Fraud	Shipping
Immigration	Transport

the rest of the firm on Eastcheap. Trainees observed that "*everything appears more efficient in the insurance department; that plays down into the way that they work – you have to be very organised.*" In 2011, Clydes will move everyone together in a single, larger office.

Seats in marine and international trade cover a range of practice areas from shipping to commodities. Shipping is split between tort-based 'wet' work (collisions, salvage, piracy, etc – also a focus of the Guildford office), and contract-based 'dry' work (cargo disputes, time charters, voyage charters, etc). One of the many wet cases we could mention is the May 2010 sinking of cargo ship 'Bright Century' following a crash with the 'Sea Success' in foggy conditions approximately 23 miles east of China's Shandong Peninsula. Clydes is advising on cargo claims.

A "*good variety*" of work awaits London shipping recruits: "*Lots of charter party disputes, cases involving fires on ships, late delivery of vessels, non-delivery of vessels...*" for everything from fancy yachts to hulking cargo ships. The firm employs master mariners for emergency response missions to investigate maritime collisions. Trainees don't take to the high seas themselves; instead they spend their time liaising with experts and drafting initial letters of claim, opinions and instructions to counsel. Shipping trainees are "*thrown in at the deep end,*" and we've heard that it's "*quite full-on between 9am and 6.30pm,*" but afterwards the shipping crew are "*good fun to have a drink with – and that happens quite a lot!*"

Commodities lawyers deal with the global trade of fungibles such as coal, cereals, gold, oil and gas, but also futures, derivatives and, lately, carbon trading. Confused? Don't worry, Clydes runs comprehensive induction programmes and offers continued training during these seats. That said, we've heard of a partner welcoming one trainee with "*here's the files,* [go] *run them,*" so you're expected to find your feet quickly. There's typically crate loads of "*non-payment of goods cases.*" Clydes advises traders including Glencore International, a large supplier of raw materials to industry. These experienced traders do most of the negotiation themselves, but if unsuccessful they get Clydes in to handle litigation, or more likely to arbitrate the dispute. Trainees in this seat liaise with clients and get stuck in with research and drafting correspondence.

Get your passport

Despite all the litigation talk, Clydes' corporate/commercial practice counts for almost 30% of its worldwide turnover. "*We have a growing transactional practice,*" one trainee explained; "*people are coming here more and more for that sort of thing.*" Corporate work spans the firm's core client sectors as well as the real estate and life sciences industries. Our trainee sources had worked with a Jersey-based investment house; on a big deal in the Congo; and on the setting up of Middle Eastern charities. Trainees take on proof-reading and straightforward drafting tasks, and liaise with clients. "*I was in charge of verification on a deal,*" one source told us; "*I had to go through an admission document line by line with the CEO of an investment bank.*" This high level of responsibility was a theme that ran through our interviews with trainees. "*They'll give you as much responsibility as they think you can take – it's a Clydes thing,*" one said. The hours are "*fairly civilised*" and the attitude is "*you work hard during the day and go home in good time.*" One trainee told us: "*I've never had to do an all-nighter,*" but towards the end of a deal "*I stopped making social plans during the week.*"

The aviation finance team acts for banks and airlines including Emirates, Air France, Credit Suisse and JPMorgan on the financing and leasing of aircraft, from small private jets to A380s. Trainees may find themselves "*dealing with counsel every day on multi-jurisdictional matters,*" or taking responsibility for smaller transactions under supervision. Sadly, however, there's no avoiding "*quite a lot of post-transaction bibling.*" One of the most popular seats is aviation litigation. If you weren't afraid of flying before this seat then you certainly will be after. Propellers hang on the walls in this department, which specialises in disasters. Take any major helicopter or plane crash and the odds are that Clydes lawyers have picked up some of the pieces. "*Generally speaking, we act for insurers on cargo losses, some personal injury and crashes,*" one hardened trainee explained. Trainees run their own small files and work directly with partners and associates on the major cases. Recently the firm advised on claims arising from the loss of Air France flight 447, which crashed into the Atlantic en route from Rio de Janeiro to Paris in June 2009. Despite its focus on disaster, aviation lit is apparently quite a sociable team that organises "*lots of lunches with major insurance clients.*"

Clydes also has an employment group and notable mid-market real estate practice. Employment trainees have the "*opportunity for advocacy,*" making applications in county courts. The department has "*a lot of retail clients*" and trainees can often be found "*drafting employee handbooks and contractual variations.*" In real estate there's the usual landlord and tenant matters, but also large developments and investments such as the £115m acquisition of property just a stone's throw from Buckingham Palace by a Hong Kong purchaser.

We haven't yet mentioned Clydes' prowess in the Middle East. It was one of the first to set up offices in the region and prizes local talent highly. The firm recently represented the government of Yemen in a multimillion-dollar international arbitration over the termination of oil production and distribution rights in the country. See our website for more information. Some trainees are able to jet off to an overseas seat. The potential locations are: Dubai, Abu Dhabi and Piraeus, and then (less frequently) Hong Kong, Shanghai and Singapore. No news as yet on the firm's Dar es Salaam office, acquired after Clydes' takeover of lawyers from specialist construction firm Shadbolt. Advice on handling overseas seats can be found on the firm's intranet or in *Clyde-o-scope* (a trainee/HR joint venture publication, and a pun we wish we'd thought of first). Our sources tell us you just have to "*turn up at the airport and the rest sorts itself out.*" One happy trainee enthused: "*I got a car and the apartment had tennis courts and a swimming pool.*" Very nice, although it's "*only at the weekends*" that trainees find the time to use these perks. Client secondments are also available for trainees who want to stay on home soil.

Welcome to the Hotel California

London lawyers generally go for Friday drinks at the aptly named Ship pub, where it's "*expected that the partners will buy the drinks.*" In Guildford, Clydes' lawyers commandeer the nearby Tup or head to the livelier King's Head in town. Our sources confessed that "*you probably don't go out so much in Guildford as London,*" since many people drive to work or have family commitments. Nevertheless, trainees have a special budget to organise drinks as and when, and departmental parties bring everyone together. On a far grander scale is the "*fabulous*" firm-wide Christmas party, last year hosted in a huge decorated marquee on London's Embankment. "*It's a swish sit-down dinner with lashings of wine, entertainment and dancing.*" The firm also cooks up a summer party and barbecue to which future joiners are invited. Football, cricket, rugby, netball and rounders are on the sporting roster for outdoorsy types, while for the indoorsy types there are things like pub quizzes in Guildford and karaoke in London.

Trainees are attracted to Clydes for its international reach and reputation for litigation. Most of our contacts had "*some kind of international aspect*" to their CV. The firm's website claims: 'Ask any of [our] lawyers what characterises the firm and they will answer entrepreneurialism', and when questioned, our sources certainly talked up the official line, with one observing that "*if you find a niche, you're allowed to develop it.*" Another noted that some partners cultivate "*personal little fiefdoms.*" Trainees think confidence is a must-have attribute, as is a willingness to handle responsibility, but it's "*quite a laid-back firm by most standards.*" One trainee confided that in his department, "*the team are almost like a bunch of old friends.*" Managing partner Ben Knowles put a slightly more sinister twist on it, joking: "*We're looking for future partners at the firm. It's a bit like Hotel California – you can never leave!*" In 2010, a very healthy 23 of the 25 qualifying trainees decided that this wouldn't be such a bad thing and accepted jobs.

And finally...

Sources within the firm observe that there's *"not one cohesive culture, but that's part of the charm!"* At Clyde & Co you'll find an eclectic and interesting bunch of lawyers doing excellent international work.

CMS Cameron McKenna LLP

The facts

Location: London, Bristol, Edinburgh, Aberdeen

Number of UK partners/solicitors: 129/346

Total number of trainees: 121

Seats: 4x6 months

Alternative Seats: Overseas seats, secondments

Extras: Pro bono – LawWorks, A4ID, TrustLaw Connect and others; language training

On chambersstudent.co.uk
- How to get into Camerons
- Environmental expertise
- Combining training with Olympic aspirations

Big in Central and Eastern Europe, and with a sky-scraping reputation for insurance, energy, projects and construction law, this City firm is keen to shake off its *"nice"* image.

Fe-fi-fo-fum

Nice. It's the word that haunts CMS Cameron McKenna, following it around like Mary's little lamb and generally ruining the firm's street-cred. This is the big bad City. No one wants to be known as 'nice'. So here are some monster figures. Revenue-wise, Camerons is the 13th largest firm in the UK, raking in £214m in 2009/10. In *Chambers UK*, it ranks in over 50 areas of practice, scoring particularly highly in the construction, projects/energy and insurance fields. This is a giant of a firm, and not one prone to letting others walk all over it. It's not afraid to make some big business decisions, recently looking into transferring the majority of its back-office staff to business services provider Integreon via a £600m outsourcing deal.

And yet... this is a firm that regularly features in the *Sunday Times*' '100 Best Companies to Work For' list, and a firm that worked hard to avoid making redundancies during the recession (although measures including four-day weeks, sabbaticals and partners volunteering to be de-equitised weren't enough to prevent some staff from losing their jobs).

Camerons was one of the first UK firms to establish offices in Eastern Europe. The Iron Curtain had barely fallen when it set up shop in Warsaw and Budapest, and it now boasts a smattering of offices from the Black Sea to the Baltic. For multi-jurisdictional issues, Camerons can also call on comrades in its wider CMS network – this group, established in 1999, is an organisation of nine independent European law firms banded together under one banner. The pan-European capability that it brings is Camerons' unique selling point, and its future strategy revolves around strengthening CMS ties. So don't expect this firm to be courting for an American merger, although senior sources admitted: "*We're never going to say we're not interested.*" The firm has, however, expressed a tentative interest in South America, setting up a "*temporary base*" in Brazil to advise various energy clients on projects work. This makes real sense. The firm is also looking at the Indian legal services market (currently off-limits to non-Indian firms) and is building relations with local lawyers Khaitan & Co so that "*when things open up, we will be there to take advantage of it.*"

Full of energy

Trainees can select from seats right across the firm's core sectors – energy; projects; construction; corporate; EU/competition; tax; insurance; banking; commercial litigation; real estate; financial services; immigration; and employment and pensions. They will also spend six months on either a client secondment or in another Camerons office during their second seat. However, there is limited scope to tailor the training contract, since a seat in either corporate or banking is compulsory, overseas seats are popular (some more than others), and trainees have no choice over their first seat. To compensate, they do get one priority choice that they are almost guaranteed to be granted at some stage during their two years.

Chambers UK rankings

Banking & Finance	Life Sciences
Banking Litigation	Media & Entertainment
Capital Markets	Outsourcing
Competition/European Law	Pensions
Construction	Pensions Litigation
Corporate/M&A	Planning
Data Protection	Private Equity
Dispute Resolution	Professional Negligence
Employee Share Schemes	Projects
Employment	Public Procurement
Energy & Natural Resources	Real Estate
Environment	Real Estate Finance
Financial Services	Real Estate Litigation
Immigration	Restructuring/Insolvency
Information Technology	Tax
Insurance	Telecommunications
Intellectual Property	Transport

Camerons' corporate department is "*quite broad... and we're encouraged to get involved in all kinds of stuff.*" The group recently advised the Department for Transport on the $4.9bn acquisition of London & Continental Railways (owner of the Eurostar operator) and its associated debt restructuring. The firm also represented Kulczyk Holding on the £735m sale of its minority interest in Polish brewer Kompania Piwowarska. Trainees typically handle due diligence and board minutes and amend clauses within shareholder agreements. When it comes to drafting, "*people are generally happy for a trainee to have a first stab at it.*" The department (universally described as "*fantastic*") has a strong social scene forged in part through many late nights (or early mornings). "*There is a sense of camaraderie as you all go to dinner at nine and then go back to work.*" Hard work is not without its rewards: one trainee told us that to compensate for slaving away until 3am, they were "*taken out a few days later on a boozy lunch.*" Typical of corporate departments across the City, there's "*a degree of laddish culture and bravado,*" but at Camerons there's "*not a lot of arrogance.*" Rather, "*it's all about the deals.*"

This firm is an energy powerhouse – this type of work is a key focus of Aberdeen and many of the European offices – and the practice covers both disputes and transactional matters. The Scottish office assisted five major oil and gas companies on the sale of their interests in North Sea oil fields and, sensing which way the breeze is blowing, lawyers are also advising on the development of offshore wind farms, the biggest being a £1.65bn project near Wales. RWE npower sought help with regard to nuclear new build proposals and BP wanted advice regarding the negotiation of a technical services agreement with the government of Iraq, essential for the company's investment in that country's Rumaila oil field.

The specialist energy disputes team, meanwhile, is "*extremely busy and works very long hours.*" It gets involved with huge international arbitrations, often concerning price review clauses in oil and gas supply contracts. Given the value and complexity of some of the disputes, trainees are given "*quite discrete tasks*" – bundling, looking after witnesses and organising exhibits. "*I will never pick up the phone and speak to clients or directly e-mail them,*" one confessed.

The general commercial litigation seat also incorporates technology and IP work. The department was involved with the Fiona litigation – a massive shipping case involving allegations of bribery and corruption, and one of the biggest disputes of 2009/10. Some trainees are able to manage low-value claims, say over minor trade mark infringements. "*I got quite a bit of advertising and marketing stuff,*" said one; "*advising corporate clients if they're featured on Watchdog and Panorama.*" As in the energy disputes seat, there's "*a good degree of bundling to be done.*"

A few trainees we spoke to were surprised to find themselves landing an immigration seat. "*Having signed up to a City law firm, I didn't expect it,*" admitted one, but it's a good area for developing soft skills as trainees "*manage their own files from start to finish*" and work closely with major banks and large companies. In this respect it can be an ideal first seat. Insurance, by contrast, gives trainees less responsibility because the team is "*so big and successful.*" It works in a separate office close to Lloyd's of London (this quirk is not unique to Camerons: we once heard a partner joke that insurance lawyers' heads explode if they go more than 100 metres from the Lloyd's building). This smaller office advises major insurers on policy coverage issues, which could be anything from the collapse of global businesses to cancelled concerts to international fraud. "*Most of the work is litigation,*" and trainees are mostly kept busy researching, bundling and document checking. Over in the construction seat, there's "*a lot of exposure to pretty technical drafting.*" The team mainly works on PFI/PPP projects such as "*the construction of waste facilities, schools and hospitals,*" and at present is working with major contractors on the 2012 London Olympics.

Sun, CEE and secondments

"*Camerons actively says, 'We want you out of here for six months,'*" and trainees spend their second seat either on a client secondment or at one of the firm's own offices outside London. A bunch of Central and Eastern European locations are up for grabs; closer to home, Bristol, Edinburgh and Aberdeen are also available. These more commutable locations have a certain appeal to those who have greater commitments in the UK. Aberdeen offers energy work, Edinburgh real estate and Bristol insurance. Energy and corporate work is high on the agenda in the continental European seats. Trainees rate their preferences and put forward a case for a visit to their chosen destination. Some cities, such as Moscow and Prague, are sometimes heavily oversubscribed and "*it's very difficult if everyone wants the same thing.*" Whereas some trainees thought that "*people who really push for something and stick to their guns are more likely to get what they want than those who are flexible,*" this is not how the graduate recruitment team views the situation. Their advice is to consider seats other than your top choice as this gives more room for manoeuvre. Overseas seats remain "*the highlight of the training contract*" for many. Prague is "*amazing*;" in Budapest, it's "*cheaper to go out for dinner than to the supermarket;*" and in Aberdeen "*bacon sandwiches*" are the order of the day. More in-depth information on non-London seats can be found on our website. Additionally, the firm offers a wide range of client secondments, both in and around London and one in Vienna. In terms of gaining a realistic understanding of clients' needs and the differences between being a lawyer in-house and in private practice, it's an unmissable experience.

A trainee committee meets monthly with the graduate recruitment team to raise any issues; one of which could be the points-based appraisal system which trainees are still rather unhappy about. "*Some people are inclined to give higher grades than others,*" they told us, also admitting that they were unable to suggest a better method. The firm recently introduced a 360° scheme whereby trainees also appraise supervisors. As one saw it: "*It's going to be quite obvious who's given feedback, so you can never give an honest opinion of somebody.*" Sources praised the training seminars organised by the firm. "*For corporate it's perfect; it's exactly what we need and there's so much that I hardly have time to prep for it!*"

CMS united

"*You don't get your City types here who are in law to screw people over,*" said one source. "*Everyone is nice. I don't want to say it, but it's true.*" There's that word again, so once again we'll report something more edgy. One trainee told us how they had booked holiday for their birthday, "*worked 9am to 1am every day*" to get all their work done beforehand, "*then until 3am... and I still had to spend my whole birthday at work.*" This tale illustrates the fact that you must be "*willing to work hard and accept that you will be making sacrifices every so often.*" Trainees say that, generally, Camerons "*does strike a good balance between getting you involved but not murdering you with work,*" but long hours were still cited as the low point for most. It's not that the hours are longer than at comparable firms, rather that these people tend to be a little more concerned with achieving some kind of work-life balance. Some 47 out of 61 qualifiers took up jobs in 2010, keen to continue working with others of the same mindset. For more on who the firm wants to recruit, see our website.

The firm doesn't drag its feet when it comes to CSR. "*The charity thing is taken very seriously... there's dress-down Fridays, people jumping off things or into things, marathons...*" One trainee "*stupidly agreed to do something involving singing*" at a 'Corporate's Got Talent' departmental fund-raiser. Alas, we're informed that "*corporate didn't have much talent*" after all. The members of firm band 'The Stragglers' must come from a different department: they won the 2009 Law Rocks competition, raising some decent money for their selected charity.

There's "*pretty much always someone at the pub on Friday,*" and usually it's the Hand and Shears, "*a little old man's pub.*" The trainee committee has an annual budget for social activities and the firm also puts on a summer party and regular departmental drinks. We've also heard stories of fancy dress socials and treasure hunting on departmental away days. Sport is a big thing: every year football teams from across the CMS network converge on a European city for the CMS World Cup, a "*three-day weekend where there's a bit of football and a lot of drinking... and the firm supplies the budget.*"

And finally...

This firm puts its own stamp on Big City Law, both in terms of its core practices and the slightly softer edges to its office culture. A particularly good pick for anyone keen on Eastern Europe or more tangible/physical sectors such as energy and construction.

Cobbetts LLP

The facts

Location: Manchester, Birmingham, Leeds, London

Number of UK partners/solicitors: 83/242

Total number of trainees: 31

Seats: 5x5 months

Alternative seats: Secondments

On chambersstudent.co.uk
- How to get into Cobbetts
- We talk to Cobbetts' managing partner, Michael Shaw
- The buzz in the mining sector

Cobbetts is an expansive regional firm headquartered in Manchester and with offices in Leeds, Birmingham and London. It handles regional and national work, with some international work too, especially relating to energy and projects.

ReaShawed

With the exception of the smallest branch in London, each of Cobbetts' offices *"do the same sort of stuff,"* which is to say they offer a full service with an emphasis on property and corporate. Historically, trainees have always enjoyed working here, and this year proved no exception. It all sounds grand, but tread carefully: Cobbetts has been through some tough years and had to lay low and take flak from the legal press. With property and corporate at the core of its business, the recession has had a real impact: last year trainees said that these engines of the firm were running slower.

In 2009, Cobbetts froze lawyers' pay and introduced a four-day week for some staff. It wasn't alone in doing so, of course, but we did also learn that trainees' salaries were cut by *"10% for nine months."* When revenue fell down by 18% for 2008/09, the tone was ominous. When profits were eventually announced for that financial year, they showed a drop of 53%. Average partner profits were just £96,000 last year. The 2009/10 financial results weren't released by the time we went to press, so check the online version of this feature to find out more.

Luckily, the banking litigation, projects and business restructuring teams broke Cobbetts' fall and, now that these markets are coming back to life, the firm will be glad it retained its private equity and capital markets specialists, who are said to be handling some sizeable IPOs and public-to-private deals for clients in the mining/minerals sector. One trainee happily reported: *"We did the first AIM listing to emerge in the last 18 months,"* and Nicola Frost, a partner in the 15-person private equity team, said that the firm now represents 14 private equity houses nationwide and is looking to expand its presence in London. The firm's long-standing managing partner Michael Shaw talked to us at some length about how the firm has negotiated the recession, and he stressed that Cobbetts' approach is *"not to allow any knee-jerk reactions or rewrite the strategy around a once-in-a-lifetime economic crisis."* Instead, the firm will look to boost its private equity practice; go for bigger, project-based work requiring a combination of skill sets and departments beyond the real estate group; and continue improving its standing in the mining/mineral extraction market, including in Africa. Expansion of the London office is *"a steady-as-she-goes exercise,"* said Shaw, who emphasised the importance of *"being realistic in your self-perception – some regional firms think they are more significant than they actually are, which we want to avoid by restricting our play around public markets where we're a recognised player, and in private equity where we have a strong base."*

Hope reigns supreme once more as trainees optimistically pointed to things like the opening of an office in Cairo, an emergent mining practice and a rebounding corporate market as signs of a new dawn. Shaw emphasised that

Chambers UK rankings

Banking & Finance	Intellectual Property
Banking Litigation	Licensing
Capital Markets	Pensions
Charities	Planning
Competition/European Law	Private Client
Corporate/M&A	Real Estate
Debt Recovery	Real Estate Litigation
Dispute Resolution	Restructuring/Insolvency
Employment	Social Housing

Cobbetts' debt gearing is still lower than many of its competitors', and that the firm has reduced its debt from £11.25m in April 2009 to £8.25m in April 2010.

High five

Let's talk about the training scheme. The Manchester HQ, because of its larger size, offers more seats, both mainstream and niche. It has the largest trainee intake, hoovering up half of the trainees. At the other end of the scale, the London office, which isn't full-service at present, offers corporate secondments to trainees from other offices as and when business needs require. Leeds presently has seven trainees and Birmingham 11. The seats available in Manchester are banking; commercial litigation; corporate; banking litigation; restructuring; private capital; TMTI (telecoms, media, trade and infrastructure); employment; real estate and property litigation. In Leeds there's banking; commercial litigation; banking litigation; corporate (with some TMTI); real estate; and employment (including pensions). In Birmingham there's commercial litigation; corporate; restructuring; TMTI; employment; real estate; and construction.

Cobbetts runs a five-seat scheme and trainees can repeat a seat. There are no compulsory seats, and trainees said they got the ones they wanted fairly easily. The system allows them to try a decent range of departments and, if they repeat a seat in the area they intend on qualifying into, puts them on a sturdy footing before the step up to NQ level. Apart from the occasional foray into London, trainees stay in their home office for the entire two years. They can apply for jobs outside their home office when they qualify.

Going for gold

In recent years, the firm has sought to build up its corporate side. The *Chambers UK*-ranked corporate practice mainly caters for AIM-listed companies, mid-sized corporates and regional businesses. Dr Oetker, the well-known manufacturer of pizzas and yoghurt, is a client, as is the less well-known Yorkshire-based healthcare sector IT provider EMIS Group, which the firm helped float on AIM in early 2010. The placement raised £50m for the company. Another exciting deal for the corporate team was a £5.7m placing for Central African Gold plc. Back in 2008, the firm represented the company's nominated adviser, Strand Partners, and its broker, Royal Bank of Canada Europe, on a share placing that raised £15.6m for the business. Another mining company, AIM-listed Peninsular Gold, sought advice lately too: it repurchased $20m of convertible loan notes with the team's assistance. As well as helping out by performing smaller tasks on large matters like these, trainees reported doing *"a lot of company secretarial work and dealing with companies' books."*

All of which segues rather nicely into some quick puns about mining. Cobbetts is prospecting for new work and tapping into a seam of mining clients in the Middle East. To help it pick into the market and cart off new business, it's entered into a joint venture with Cairo-based law firm El Said, Darwish & Partners, whose clients are reported to include Barclays, BNP Paribas, various airlines and some hotel developers. As well as mining-related work, Cobbetts has also won some infrastructure instructions in the region and will be looking to advise Egyptian investors buying real estate in the UK. Avoiding the expensive option of acquiring a firm abroad, Cobbetts set up a Swiss Verein (a legal structure in which members have very little exposure to each other's liabilities) called Cobbetts International. Suffice to say that it could give the firm an easy – and cost-effective – way of adding international partners. Further expansion into the Gulf region (Qatar, Oman) and to Moscow has been mooted.

Tales from the property market

Five years ago Cobbetts' Manchester real estate team was incandescent with talent and *Chambers UK* had it ranked in its top band. As the firm has moved away from being viewed largely as 'a property firm', it has slipped down the rankings to the third tier. As the recession bit hard, the department generated less revenue and was forced to make job cuts. Sanguine trainees say the group is stable and that key clients (eg Premier Inn Hotels and office space provider Bruntwood) have been retained, while the firm has won admirable mandates from the public sector. It represents Salford City Council and has also been working on one of Manchester's best-known projects, the building of Media City. This is ideal fodder for Cobbetts, which has a good track record in the field of regeneration and social housing. Media City is a £500m, 200-acre waterfront development funded by a mixture of public and private money. Trainees enjoy their seats there, doing work for clients like the Whitbread group of restaurants and hotels.

"The team is really friendly and, though you don't get dropped in at the deep end, you learn well, and quickly."

The banking litigation department has been a real boon during the recession. Here, trainees are involved in professional negligence cases, suing solicitors or valuers who had 'misled' mortgage lenders over property values or made some other kind of slip up. Upon taking control of properties after mortgage defaults, lenders like Bradford & Bingley and Yorkshire Building Society may find that the property is worth a lot less than the amount loaned to the homeowners. They then go looking for someone to take responsibility for the shortfall. *"It's bulk work, for which the firm doesn't charge hourly fees. Everyone just ploughs through it, bringing in a lot of money. It's not particularly exciting as it's the same kind of claim over and over again."* What the cases do teach trainees is the art of managing litigation and the essential steps in the court process. In Leeds *"the department does some fraud work, too, but the other stuff provides the vast majority of the work."*

"The TMTI seat offers experience in different types of disciplines. There's trade marks, patents, patent infringement and I felt like I was doing proper fee-earning work," said one source who'd loved the world of IP. It's one of the areas where the firm takes on international work, from the USA usually. Trainees help with a variety of matters for clients from various industry sectors, among them Orange, First Light Movies, Emap and London's *Evening Standard* newspaper. The firm's charities team works for clients such as *The Big Issue* and The Multiple Sclerosis Society. Its trainees get to handle a mixture of matters relating to property, corporate governance and litigation.

Playing it straight

At Cobbetts, you can get good, practical experience. Matters like a dispute over the improper building of a conservatory, though low-value, will involve the trainee in face-to-face client contact, writing witness statements, developing a strategy that best deals with the case, picking up case management skills and maybe even court appearances too. Working on only high-value, complex disputes may sound more glamorous, but what experience will a trainee get? Will they spend most of their time bundling up documents? Cobbetts offers a good mixture of high-profile matters and smaller, more hands-on assignments. The firm additionally encourages early networking through its 'Cobbetts Young Professionals' network, and trainees also told us about other networking events. They may be expected to organise *"seminars, training sessions and develop new business by doing tenders and pitches."* It's all good practice for later on in their careers.

A concern for values permeates the firm. Managing partner Michael Shaw told us he feels that some firms treated people rather badly during the recession. It was a matter of pride for him that Cobbetts *"did not lose sight of our values and ideas of how people should behave within the business."* He reckons Cobbetts *"retained its integrity by being straight and honest about redundancies."* The firm looks for *"people who value integrity and their relationships with all the people they work with, whether at a peer level or working in support functions."* Though trainees must be ambitious, Shaw said it should be *"an ambition for the firm rather than a very narrow personal ambition; one of 'if the firm does well, I will do well'."* This resonated with trainees: *"The culture is supportive. I have had jobs at other places that didn't have that supportive culture, and to have it here, you realise how valuable it is. People are glad to give their time to you and it makes a world of difference."*

According to the Competitiveness Index 2010 – and there's no arguing with those guys – Manchester has the highest levels of happiness in the country, despite the near constant rain. *"It just has a really good vibe about it. It's not like London, not as stuffy; a bit younger and a bit more fun,"* confirmed one trainee. Cobbetts doesn't organise many social events for its trainees, which didn't seem to bother them since they arrange plenty themselves. Some trainees clearly preferred to keep their working and social lives separate, while others said they were keen on going out with workmates.

Last year, Cobbetts gave permanent NQ jobs to 15 out of 25 qualifying trainees and the two trainees who were given temporary contracts now have permanent jobs with the firm. In 2010 the firm advertised 16 job vacancies to the 21 qualifiers, 13 of which were filled. Everyone in Leeds was successful. In Birmingham, where only two jobs were announced initially, a further two qualifiers were given 12-month fixed-term contracts following the success of a major tender for business. The weakest offering was in the large Manchester office, where there were only four NQ positions available for 11 qualifiers.

And finally...

This is a hugely likeable firm that's toughing out a lousy economy with good grace and by pulling one or two smart tricks from up its sleeve.

Coffin Mew LLP

The facts

Location: Southampton, Fareham, Portsmouth, Gosport

Number of UK partners/solicitors: 28/45

Total number of trainees: 13

Seats: 6x4 months

Alternative seats: Occasional secondments

Extras: Pro bono – Legal work for various charities including Honeypot

On chambersstudent.co.uk
- How to get into Coffin Mew
- Social housing at Coffin Mew
- CEO Vincent Denham on the future challenges facing lawyers

Coffin Mew retains its private client side but more than ever represents an excellent choice for commercial practice.

Living on the edge

At this Solent stalwart full service really means full service. Coffin Mew began in the 1800s with a private client focus and as recently as the early 1990s it had a network of tiny offices in equally tiny villages dotted throughout the region. It has since grown its corporate and commercial side extensively, becoming a major player in the region along the way. Today the firm has just four offices, the largest of which is in Southampton and the others being located in Portsmouth, Fareham and Gosport. According to its website, its most important client sectors range from aerospace and pharmaceuticals to garden centres and care homes: profitable areas not to be sniffed at and the latter reflecting the changing needs of Britain's ageing population. Why not take a look at the 'Sector Selector' page of Coffin Mew's website to better understand the nature of its target industries? On the private client side, Coffin Mew acts for many members of the armed forces; hardly surprising given its location. *Chambers UK* further underlines the firm's broad scope. It ranks highly in areas as diverse as clinical negligence and social housing.

In 2009, the firm appointed its first ever CEO, Vincent Denham, who has made a career of managing law firms and barristers' chambers, moving from Birmingham to London to Bristol and now Southampton. He was involved in the creation of Brum's first superset, St Philip's Chambers. As a man with a track record and big plans, he'll be pushing the firm to grow "*via merger and acquisition, and by bolting on individuals and groups of individuals.*" His vision for the future is unashamedly commercial, though that doesn't mean Coffin Mew will abandon its traditional high-street practices. "*The perception of private client being unprofitable exists because it's done by the wrong people at the wrong prices,*" Denham said.

The first tangible result of this new direction came in May 2010, when Coffin Mew was rebranded as, in Denham's words, an "*edgy*" firm. A new 'rhodamine red' and 'duck-egg blue' colour scheme replaced a rather more conservative blue and grey. Trainees talked about a "*buzz*" of "*nervous excitement*" around the office.

Padgett, placements and preferences

Six four-month seats make the training experience as broad as possible and there are a potential 11 destinations to choose from – commercial litigation; commercial services; commercial property; corporate; employment; family; insolvency; personal injury; private client and contentious and non-contentious seats in the renowned social housing department. People do blend commercial and private client seats.

Trainees have no say in their first seat choice. However, early on in their two years, they go for an informal lunch with training partner Malcolm Padgett and can express preferences for future seats. There's no guarantee that the next five seats will feature all three of their favourites; in fact, one trainee revealed: "*I know they do tend to mark you on how you do in your worst nightmare of a seat.*" The system was described as "*absolutely responsive. It's an ongoing conversation that allows trainees to develop into the fields we're most interested in.*" The firm tries to place trainees in their preferred qualification department for their last seat, so they can impress future teammates. There are

Chambers UK rankings

Clinical Negligence	Personal Injury
Corporate/M&A	Real Estate
Employment	Real Estate Litigation
Family/Matrimonial	Restructuring/Insolvency
Intellectual Property	Social Housing

no compulsory seats, although stints in corporate and property are more than likely. Since the whole purpose of the six-seat system is to give trainees as broad an experience as possible, consecutive seats are often *"like chalk and cheese."* Trainees move between Portsmouth, Fareham and Southampton (though not Gosport) for their seats and are unlikely to stay in one location. This makes a car essential, as *"without one you're restricted."* The Fareham office, for example, is just off the motorway. The Pompey and Southampton offices are both in the city centre.

Someone to watch over you

There are a few common themes linking the different seats. Because the firm has a small annual trainee intake (generally five) they aren't just cheap labour to be thrown at files. Said one: *"You're not just stuck at a photocopier."* In contentious areas, that might mean being given *"your own mini caseload"* or doing simple advocacy on matters like rent arrears. Departments like corporate or property involve plenty of drafting things like shareholders' agreements or board minutes. Small teams do mean that trainees must chip in with grunt work – *"it's sometimes a bit like pulling teeth"* – but the hours spent manhandling bundles of documents are generally kept to a minimum.

The corporate practice has grown significantly since the mid-1990s, making it a likely destination for trainees. A seat in this department encompasses corporate finance, commercial services, financial services and business regulation. Clients include national businesses like The Co-operative Bank, but regional clients are just as important – the University of Portsmouth being one good example. Our sources told us that their work was varied, but mainly consisted of *"drafting a lot of documents – shareholders' agreements, asset purchase agreements, that kind of thing,"* all under the watchful eye of senior fee earners.

The personal injury and clinical negligence team acts exclusively for claimants and is renowned for its work on serious brain injury cases. Recently, lawyers represented the estate of a patient negligently prescribed a fatal dose of morphine (intended for a patient in an adjoining bed) and a woman suffering severe facial disfigurement resulting from a procedure she underwent following negligent advice. Trainees said: *"It's juicy subject matter, although not for everyone – it can be a bit gory."* Typically, trainees find themselves managing costs case files, *"chasing down the cheques"* as well as doing odds and ends from the team's fee earners. For more on the experiences available in other seats, go to our website.

The appraisal system is, in a word, thorough. It's a three-stage process including a mid-seat appraisal that identifies *"areas where you may not be fully achieving, which gives you two months left in the seat to push in the right direction,"* an end-of-seat appraisal, and a further chat with training partner Malcolm Padgett.

Solent social scene

Coffin Mew is very much a suit-and-tie kinda place, but trainees don't think it has a buttoned-up atmosphere. Our sources reminisced about practical jokes in the social housing litigation seat, and it was accepted that *"you have to be able to have a laugh."* The firm involves itself in the community, doing work for children's charity Honeypot, and organising social events with other local businesses and clients – five-a-side football is one of the most popular. For a South Coast side, the team is doing well: it's not yet been docked points or put into administration.

After work, trainees in Southampton can be found either in The Alex, a self-styled 'Beer Emporium' (in actuality *"more of a spit and sawdust pub"*) or the more upmarket Chambers. They report a good, lively social scene among themselves and a few of the junior solicitors. In part, that's a function of the work-life balance that trainees manage to strike. *"It's not nine to five, but it's not that far off."* It's rare to see a trainee in the office after 7.30pm, and none of our interviewees had worked over a weekend. However, they did strike a note of caution. *"Because we're in the South you might think you can be in the pub at five past five. Not at all. Equally, it's tempting to think that because we're not in London, the quality of work and clients will be lower: that's nonsense."* Coffin Mew has always made it clear that this is not a soft-touch training contract and that it is looking for applicants who are talented enough to work in the City but have a good reason not to be there. The majority of trainees have links to the South, either through family or university, and no desire for a London 'big firm' career, which they imagine will be all cash, weekend work and lurching from crisis to crisis.

And finally...

Coffin Mew trainees value broad, meaningful experience and a balanced lifestyle. Both of 2010's second-years stayed with the firm on qualification.

Covington & Burling LLP

The facts

Location: London

Number of UK partners/solicitors: 18/54

Total number of trainees: 14

Seats: 4x6 months

Alternative seats: Secondments

Extras: Pro Bono – LawWorks

On chambersstudent.co.uk
- How to get into Covington
- The importance of good writing
- Covington's pro bono schemes
- A distinguished history

Come to Covington for life sciences, pharma and technology regulation as well as contentious and transactional work for substantive industry clients.

Partly political

Covington & Burling has been part of the political landscape in the United States for almost a century. Founded in 1919, one of its early partners was Dean Acheson, who went on to become US Secretary of State. In the US, the firm is known for its regulatory work, government advice, and life sciences and technology/IP practices. In its US political persuasions, the firm colours both red and blue. The 'Obama revolution' saw Covington partner Eric Holder become the States' first ever African-American Attorney General. At the same time, the "*revolving door*" the firm has with the government brought in former Homeland Security chief Michael Chertoff. Covington is expanding into all major global markets. "*We have a growing network of strategic relationships in the Middle East, India and Asia, as well as a number of active matters in Latin America. Our view is that we don't need offices in all of the regions where we are assisting clients on projects,*" firmwide managing partner Tim Hester told us from DC. He hit the nail on the head with what we think the firm's UK presence is all about: "*In London we do transactional and litigation work as well as international arbitration. Our presence in Brussels is strategic… and related to EU regulation.*"

Covington has been in London since 1988 and, despite its small size, services many major clients like Bacardi, British American Tobacco, Harley Davidson, Microsoft and Procter & Gamble. The London office retains a focus on the firm's US mainstays, but is becoming increasingly full-service. Legislative regulation is still a key strength, with the firm acting mostly for life sciences, pharmaceutical and technology clients in this regard.

Regulation nation

Litigation and corporate are both technically compulsory seats for trainees, although in practice contentious experience can be gained in a seat like employment instead. Client secondments are increasingly common, and more than half of trainees now spend a seat working for a big pharma company. On secondment, trainees "*do any work that comes in,*" including "*looking at contracts worth up to five million quid.*" They tell us they enjoy the insight it gives into "*how to advise general counsel.*" Overseas seats may be forthcoming in the future but are not a cert. "*We have sent people abroad in the past on an ad hoc basis when they have expressed an interest, but I don't think that will become formal in the upcoming few years,*" training principal Grant Castle told us.

IP/IT and life sciences seats nicely encompass the firm's key speciality: in both, almost all work is related to government regulation. For a number of our contacts these seats were a key draw when choosing Covington. The firm serves the great and the good of the pharmaceutical world: GE Healthcare, AstraZeneca, Pfizer, Genentech, Merck, Novartis, GlaxoSmithKline and Schering-Plough. A good example of the regulatory work that the team has undertaken is the advice it gave to pharma innovator Emergent BioSolutions on the development of a TB vaccine with Oxford University.

A seat in IP/IT sees trainees acting for technology-led clients like Microsoft, Boeing and O2, and there's "*a lot of EU-based stuff to do with how the UK has implemented EU law.*" The pace of technological change keeps the

Chambers UK rankings

Data Protection	Life Sciences
Dispute Resolution	Private Equity
Insurance	Product Liability

group innovative and "*academic.*" Trainees might find themselves looking at "*how you apply existing laws to new situations which they weren't designed for.*" For example, the team helped the NFL prevent the live online broadcast of the Super Bowl without its consent.

Cov-ering all your bases

The corporate team is quite small, which means trainees and associates have to be generalists. One trainee reported working on "*a few gentle reviewing tasks to begin with and then a cross-border acquisition in my third week.*" Corporate and dispute resolution clients often hail from the core pharma and technology client base. For example, the team represented Procter & Gamble during the acquisition of its pharmaceutical business by Warner Chilcott. Another part of the firm's clientele is the 'branded goods' sector, where you'll find the likes of Bacardi, Chiquita (the banana people) and Giorgio Armani. Deputy London managing partner Louise Nash told us that Covington is advising the latter on the development of "*a worldwide chain of Armani-branded hotels and resorts and Armani-branded residences in Egypt.*" We assume you don't have to find that a tasteful idea to enjoy the lawyering aspects.

The litigation group works on product liability, denials of insurance coverage and IP. It recently defended animal health company Merial over claims that it had leaked a strain of the foot-and-mouth virus from its Surrey plant in 2007. In this seat, trainees work on both "*arbitration and litigation, depending on what work comes in.*" A number of partner hires in the area indicate that Covington is becoming more interested in cross-border arbitration.

Following the lead of its DC mothership, government lobbying is increasingly important to the London office. The data protection group has given advice to the government on ID cards. Energy and 'cleantech'– for clients including ExxonMobil – is also a growing area of work, as are deals relating to India and the Middle East. London is set to play a key role in linking the rest of the firm to its Asian operations, and together with Dorsey & Whitney, Covington advised wind farm developer Indian Energy on its London Stock Exchange AIM flotation. Work is done in "*teams of three or four people*" and trainees are expected to "*take responsibility and take your own approach,*" with "*a fair amount of client contact.*" The reasonably high level of responsibility stems from the firm's American roots: "[US partners] *don't understand the concept of trainees: they will think you're an NQ or a first-year associate.*"

Renaissance (wo)men

A distinctive feature of Covington's culture is the "*academic*" nature of work and the "*importance of writing and doing a Rolls-Royce job.*" One trainee described "*a love of the craft of being a lawyer,*" reflecting the exact words of managing partner Tim Hester. The firm's offices are right next to the Royal Courts of Justice, and training partner Grant Castle says working at the firm can at times be more like being a barrister than a solicitor. He perhaps means that the academic nature of regulatory and arbitration work allows room for abstract legal pondering. "*People take pride in knowing the law and will read a lot,*" one trainee said. Castle says: "*A number of the partners are renowned artists or writers – one writes spy novels – and there is a real 'Renaissance man' culture.*"

Trainees describe the firm as "*a bit traditional and conservative with a small c.*" Despite this, "*they encourage you to be entrepreneurial – I introduced a couple of potential clients,*" one source said. The atmosphere is "*not overly formal. I talk to my supervisor about sports and getting hammered at the weekend,*" revealed one source. The dress code is "*business appropriate,*" which can even mean jumpers and chinos, and there's a Manhattan loft-style espresso bar on the office's first floor, where the IP/IT team likes to hang out.

Trainees report "*softball and cricket matches in the summer and quizzes every now and again.*" There is also a netball team known as the Covington Cupcakes, because one partner buys the team cupcakes after matches. There is a definite mix of US and UK events and culture here. "*We had a St George's Day thing last year and there was a Thanksgiving lunch.*" After-work drinks spring up by department: every month a drinks trolley is wheeled out for "*informal life sciences team drinks, which starts in Grant* [Castle]*'s office and proceeds to the pub,*" the most popular of which are The George and The Old Bank of England on Fleet Street. "*For the Christmas party we hired a converted church,*" one source told us, before hinting that the event may not entirely have met with puritan approval…

And finally...

Seemingly unfazed by the recession, Covington has expanded its trainee intake, and kept on all four qualifiers in 2010.

Cripps Harries Hall LLP

The facts

Location: Tunbridge Wells, London

Number of UK partners/solicitors: 39/62

Total number of trainees: 16

Seats: 6x4 months

Alternative seats: Occasional secondments

Extras: Pro bono – CAB

On chambersstudent.co.uk
- How to get into Cripps
- The full skinny on Tunbridge Wells
- Cripps' history

Cripps Harries Hall offers a solid grounding in private and commercial law away from the hectic late nights of the City.

Riding the Mexican wave

Founded in 1852, Cripps is one of the largest law firms in Kent. It is widely regarded as one of the most prestigious in the region, and its client base has traditionally been a mix of private clients and commercial entities. The wealthy folk in and around Tunbridge Wells provide a substantial private clientele (about a third of the firm's total), bringing in property, wills and wealth management instructions. The family department also attracts private clients from London looking for first-rate advice at a more affordable price.

In addition to a reassuringly solid private practice, Cripps is not short of decent commercial work. Important clients include PwC and Wagamama, and Cripps is currently advising Crossrail, High Speed 1 (aka the Channel Tunnel Rail Link), The Goring Hotel, which is adjacent to Buckingham Palace, and major construction company the Wates Group. For some years Cripps has been subcontracting work from major City law firm Lovells, managing to turn it around far more cheaply. This phenomenon, dubbed 'the Mexican wave', has brought in high-profile clients, raising Cripps' visibility and brand name in the process. With many trainees keen to specialise in it, property is certainly Cripps' strong point: it is "*the largest money-maker*" and Cripps is ranked in *Chambers UK*'s top band for construction, real estate and real estate litigation in the South. Another project that has helped fill the firm's coffers is the centre:mk shopping centre in Milton Keynes. The firm's total revenue for 2009/10 was £19.2m, the same as the previous year.

The joys of six

Cripps' training contract is divided into six seats of four months. Trainees generally view the six-seat system positively due to its variety and wider range of experience, but some expressed frustration at having to move on before they felt quite ready to leave a seat. The six seats are chosen at the start of the contract, although it's worth noting that the HR team does allow changes, especially for second-years. Expect at least two seats to be in a property-related area of practice, and the final seat to usually be a repeat seat in the department you want to specialise in on qualification, although this is not a guarantee. Property dispute resolution (PDR) is a popular choice, as are private client, employment and family. Most trainees will complete a seat in residential property, as it helps build confidence in the basics.

The real estate team is organised in three groups dealing with portfolio property, public sector matters and development. The portfolio team represents larger institutional property owners, such as Mexican wave fan Prudential. Trainees work on plenty of investment sales and purchases, plus day-to-day management of leasehold interests in portfolio properties. They deal with big-name clients and senior partners, which is quite exciting but "*you have to be on your guard.*" The development team has faced a tough market since the downturn but has an excellent track record with house builders, social housing clients and other developers.

Corporate departments are often assumed to be where the most important clients are found. In Cripps' case, property

Chambers UK rankings

Agriculture & Rural Affairs	Licensing
Charities	Local Government
Construction	Partnership
Corporate/M&A	Personal Injury
Debt Recovery	Planning
Dispute Resolution	Private Client
Employment	Real Estate
Family/Matrimonial	Real Estate Litigation
Intellectual Property	Social Housing

trumps corporate, and one trainee revealed that although there is a wide range of work on offer, they wish they'd known *"just how much of an emphasis is placed on property. I didn't quite realise how much."* The corporate team does have an interesting angle: dual-qualified partner Olivier Morel brings in work from French companies such as Brioche Dorée and its parent company Le Duff Group.

Cripplingly irrational

The private client team is still at the heart of the firm. A seat here focuses on wills, trusts and estates, and is a *"good one to go to first: you are thrown into things and instantly given free rein."* Private client trainees *"meet clients and deal with other professionals, banks and stockbrokers."* It takes skill to look after individuals who don't have much experience of professional advisers and who are *"not entirely rational with their money."* In one matter, a group of family trusts worth several million pounds had to be reorganised after family members fell out with each other.

The other seats available include family, employment, commercial dispute resolution, wealth preservation, private client disputes, inward investment, planning, construction and residential conveyancing. There are none in London and no regular client secondments, but recently two trainees went to HS1 to help with a major project. In all seats, although there is admin and form filling, trainees reckon they have a higher level of responsibility than they would in bigger firms. They feel consistently busy and challenged, but pleasantly so. There is day-to-day feedback, and trainees are appraised at the end of each seat by HR and the managing partner. Extensive training includes IT sessions and practice-based seminars. All first-years have a mentor and we're told that seniors are easily approached.

The location of the offices is a point of debate within the firm. Clients are always favourably impressed: Cripps' four Regency buildings are *"really beautiful,"* spacious and centrally located, just across the road from the pedestrian zone of Tunbridge Wells. Having to cross the road to reach another department is usually a welcome chance for a breath of fresh air (provided it isn't raining); however, there is talk of moving to a single building to achieve greater cohesion. Some of the quieter departments can feel isolated, with trainees sometimes spending weeks sitting *"in an empty room on your own."* The lack of air-conditioning was mentioned a few times, and since there isn't always parking for trainees they're on a rota for the few available slots.

75-minute lunches and top 100s

The well-being of employees is a priority, and as if to prove this, Cripps featured as just one of seven law firms in the *Sunday Times*' list of 100 Best Companies to Work For. If you are fantastically ambitious and want to do massive corporate deals, Cripps isn't the place for you: our sources were happy to swap the City's high salaries for a better work-life balance and the *"aesthetically pleasing"* surroundings of Tunbridge Wells. Their contracted hours are 9am till 5.15pm, with 75 minutes for lunch, and rarely do people stay beyond 6pm. The firm is said to be very accommodating where family is concerned.

The local nightlife is what it is, and the town is *"not teeming with recent graduates,"* so trainees grow to be quite close, becoming the main social group for many. Employees regularly socialise at Sankey's, which is both a wine bar and a seafood brasserie. There are quarterly drinks on the partners' tab, which tend to be well attended. There is football every Monday, cricket and tennis in the summer, netball, touch rugby and even a polo team. Charity is *"pushed quite strongly,"* so there are designated charity days and every year staff select a main charity (usually a regional one, but last time round they picked Help for Heroes). There is an annual summer ball, a choir, and rounds of *Come Dine With Me* have become popular among trainees.

Cripps used to have 100% retention rates for its qualifiers, but the poor economy has put paid to that. On the other hand, trainee recruitment hasn't been cut and the firm is aiming for gradual organic growth and hoping to expand its Mexican wave business to include other larger firms. Read Cripps' annual review on its website and note the useful practice area stats, as well as great pics of the Georgian architecture.

And finally...

In 2010 six of the eight qualifying trainees stayed with the firm, two of them on a one-year contract. The others knew that having the firm's name on their CV would take them a long way, both regionally and in London.

Dawsons LLP

The facts

Location: London

Number of UK partners/solicitors: 19/30

Total number of trainees: 9

Seats: 4x6 months

Alternative seats: Occasional secondments

Extras: Pro bono – South Westminster Legal Advice Centre

On chambersstudent.co.uk
- How to get into Dawsons
- Pro bono at the firm
- We talk to training partner Harender Branch

This mid-sized firm in the heart of London's legal district is a stylish and impressive place to train.

From coco to PC

On 16 March 1729, Edward Woodcock became the first solicitor in the country to register his trade. The firm he founded all those years ago later became known as Dawson & Co in 1918, and in 2002, Dawsons. It has seven different departments: corporate; employment; family; litigation; partnerships; private client; and property. Trainees say Dawsons is "*in a very good place at the moment.*" It has recently acquired a new CEO: Mark Dembovsky, former chief strategy officer at US giant Reed Smith. He keeps everyone in the loop with a weekly update via 'Mark's Blog,' in which he also explains any future plans. It is "*no secret*" that departments like property suffer in a recession, and some secretaries in that team were temporarily put on four-day working weeks, but the litigation and employment teams' "*booming*" business made up for that. Overall turnover has increased during the recession, which led to "*a lot of back-patting.*"

There are only four or five trainees in each annual intake, so they receive plenty of attention and support. It's a good place for people who "*don't want to be just a number,*" our sources said. New training partner Harender Branch received universal praise from trainees: "*Things have got better since she's been here*" as "*she remembers what being a trainee is like.*" Which is good news, seeing as trainees "*have a lot of contact with her... she does our seat allocations and gets to know us quite well.*" There are no compulsory seats: the firm endeavours to meet trainee wishes, and trainees can request to take a favourite seat twice. Overall, the process is managed "*incredibly well*" and "*in a very thoughtful way.*" Family and employment seats are popular, and corporate doesn't rate badly either.

Dawsons' week

As a trainee you "*must be prepared to roll your sleeves up.*" The levels of responsibility are high, and one source assured us: "*The client exposure in every seat has really been spectacular.*" Trainees are likely to go to court and may conduct advocacy, especially in the family department. There is, of course, some grunt work such as document bundling, but certainly "*not to the extent where you'd get fed up with it.*" Trainees sit in a room with two or three qualified lawyers, including a partner, meaning they can learn a lot by observation. A checklist of tasks is drawn up for each department so that new joiners know they will gain as wide an experience as possible. Dawsons has an international aspect to its business, with quite a lot of cross-jurisdictional work in the family, private client, corporate and litigation departments. Foreign language skills may come in handy but are not a necessity. The hours are "*very reasonable,*" usually 9am to 6pm, with rare post-8pm finishes. Applicants will be pleased to hear that "*everybody has a life*" and "*trainees don't have BlackBerrys.*" The salary's not bad either: first years get £31,000, rising to £33,000 in the second year, and £48,500 for an NQ position.

The ever-popular family department is headed by Suzanne Kingston, who is a trained mediator and often works on amicable splits. Because of this, trainees are exposed to mediation and collaborative law. Kingston states that about 50% of the pre and post-nuptial agreements she completed last year were done collaboratively. Since she is "*very well connected in the family law world, she gets a lot of good referrals in,*" typically quite wealthy individuals. The family seat is rewardingly "*hands-on*" and "*fast-paced and busy.*" Trainees draft documents and letters, do

Chambers UK rankings

Dispute Resolution	Partnership
Family/Matrimonial	Private Client

research, attend client meetings, prepare disclosure and go to court regularly. Our interviewees were *"really impressed with the amount of client contact."*

Out with the old

Employment is *"one of the firm's core departments,"* making up 20% of its business. After losing two partners, the team welcomed Paul Mander from Berwin Leighton Paisner as its new head and early indications suggest that the department's work has become more weighted towards employers than before. The seat offers a learning curve that is described as *"astronomical,"* presumably because trainees can take on their own files and give advice to clients over the phone. Expect cases covering discrimination, unfair dismissal and compromise agreements for departing City execs.

Litigation makes up another fifth of the firm's business and this department has several sub-teams for property, travel, commercial cases and international arbitration. The work may range from *"smaller breach of trust cases right up to huge claims,"* and trainees can take on some matters themselves. The seat is *"increasingly popular"* and the department is *"really growing and thriving."* It recently acted on a trade mark infringement case for cooldiamonds.com, and for two defendants in a claim for unpaid freight charges for the transportation of pineapples from the Ivory Coast to Europe.

Meanwhile, corporate trainees work on share purchase agreements and deal with company directors. Theirs is a different type of experience to those of their peers at the City giants: instead of feeling *"like a small cog in a big machine,"* trainees witness first hand how their efforts are impacting on their clients' lives. The department's work is more international than you might imagine for a firm of this size: there are bags of German clients and last year one of the main deals was for a large Russian mobile telecoms company.

A private client team advises on tax investigation, tax planning, international tax structuring and the establishment and administration of charities. Dawsons recently assisted a well-known educational charity, letting one of its buildings to a professional firm that required a new London HQ, and advised a naval charity in connection with a regeneration project in South East London. Trainees can expect research and drafting assignments as well as more procedural tasks relating to wills, probates and trusts. In the reasonably large property department, trainees encounter wealthy estates, several housing associations and trusts, education sector clients and corporate occupiers such as Emap. Residential developments and deals are central to much of the work.

Dawsons Dynamo

Dawsons' trainees commonly have previous careers and/or unusual non-law degrees, and their ages range from early 20s to mid-30s. One described the group as *"confident, bright and fun but hard-working."* This lot are certainly *"very close"* and often meet up for lunch. When an after-work pint or vino is needed they head for the Seven Stars, *"a tiny bar at the back of the Royal Courts of Justice"* (also beloved by barristers) and it doesn't hurt that the firm gives trainees a regular social budget. The social life is *"not overbearing, but there are things to do."* There are departmental events (eg 'Wine Fridays' in the family group), get-togethers for future trainees and firm-wide events such as the Christmas party and a summer family day. Staff play tennis with various private banks and law firms, while a team named 'Dawsons Dynamo' upholds firm honour on the football pitch.

Trainees described their firm as *"a modern and commercial City law firm,"* as evidenced by the fact it often acts opposite big City players. But it doesn't plan on expanding: if it grew, its lawyers would have to leave their beloved Lincoln's Inn location. Dawsons' office in 2 New Square is right in the heart of barrister-country and has quite a scholarly feel as a result. The location is *"really beautiful – we are surrounded by busy roads but here it's an oasis of green and calm."* The building, originally constructed in 1697, was destroyed in a fire that burned for three days in 1842 and was rebuilt in 1850. Because of the firm's age and location, some might expect it to be a stuffy place, but this is *"definitely not the case."* Admittedly, trainees don't *"slop around in jeans,"* but Dawsons is *"not particularly formal."* Sources say there's *"a cohesiveness to the firm"* and *"a collegiate atmosphere and sense of belonging."* Partners say hello to everybody and there's *"a 'thank you' culture."*

And finally...

In 2010, all four qualifiers stayed on, going into the litigation, corporate, private client and family departments.

- **This is a client-focused profession:** If you can't interact and put clients at ease then your career will be harmed. It's not just about the law, it's about being responsive to clients.

top tip no. 16

Dechert LLP

The facts

Location: London

Number of UK partners/solicitors: 29/54 (US: 7/4)

Total number of trainees: 17

Seats: 6x4 months

Alternative seats: Overseas seats, secondments

Extras: Pro bono – North Kensington Law Centre

On chambersstudent.co.uk
- How to get into Dechert
- We talk to director of training Bernard George
- Trainee life in Brussels

A *"decent firm with decent people"* that *"sets high standards for itself,"* Dechert has made some truly big strides since its beginnings in 1930s Philadelphia.

East coast, West coast, Emerald isle

This highly successful international firm has 11 US offices (reaching from Orange County to New York... check out what they've been up to at www.chambers-associate.com), two branches in Asia (Beijing and Hong Kong) and seven in Europe (Paris, Brussels, Luxembourg, Munich, Moscow, London and, as of 2010, Dublin). There may be 20 offices, but it's important to realise that *"London is a key cog in the Dechert mechanism."* The office became a part of the Dechert Empire in 2000, when it gave up the independence it had as a well-known City mid-sizer called Titmuss Sainer. *"Dechert* [in London] *is an odd one because it's really not a US firm; it's still more Titmuss than Dechert in some departments,"* one trainee told us. *"It really tried to keep hold of its English traditions, like cricket."* The game is massive at this firm, but we'll get to that later.

One thing that will definitely identify the firm's American roots is the nature of its work. Most of our sources *"wanted to go to a US firm because of the transatlantic aspect."* Another obvious attraction is its focus on financial services (FS) and corporate deals, and the most repeated advice trainees gave us was that it is absolutely vital for applicants to be interested in those two areas. Although the office is pretty much full-service, FS and corporate are at the forefront; so much so that qualifiers into these departments have an extra £5,000 per annum tacked onto their salary. Dechert trainees take six four-month seats during their two years, choosing from FS; corporate; finance and real estate (FRE); litigation; tax; employment; IP; and competition in Brussels. Repeating a seat is very likely, which makes the transition to qualified lawyer all the easier, especially in the more technical and complex areas of practice.

Metaphorical bodies of water

With over 120 lawyers dedicated to it across the Dechert network, FS is certainly the firm's largest and most profitable department. It's also a market leader on both sides of the Atlantic. According to trainees, calling it 'financial services' is *"a bit of a misnomer; it's basically investments, whether they're hedge funds, asset-backed, debt-based or securities."* The name does fit the firm's activity in the regulatory sphere. Dechert continues to provide compliance advice for asset managers and investment funds regulated by the Financial Services Authority here in the UK and by the Securities & Exchange Commission in the USA. These regulators are very much in the spotlight so be sure to keep up with developments via the business media. The other side of the work involves setting up funds, management companies and distribution operations in various jurisdictions around the world. It takes experience and real application before you can become confident when advising on the creation of new open-ended, closed-ended, domestic and offshore funds, CDOs and related structured products. That's exactly why NQ jobs here are awarded premium salaries.

Chambers UK rankings

Capital Markets	Investment Funds
Corporate/M&A	Planning
Dispute Resolution	Real Estate
Employment	Real Estate Litigation
Financial Services	Retail
Intellectual Property	Tax

Trainees definitely viewed FS as "*very different to any other department – it's a very specialised area.*" Indeed, last year we harped on about director of training Bernard George's advice on the differences between a Loch Ness lawyer and a Mississippi lawyer. To understand exactly what this means, check out our website, where you'll find his insightful musings on multiple subjects. "*It's very good, very challenging work,*" one source described the experience in FS. "*It's very transactional so there's not a lot of research, but there is a lot of drafting documents, prospectus agreements, written resolutions, letters to shareholders, board minutes... There's not as much client contact, but the matters are massive so it makes sense.*"

The firm's other leading department, corporate, is certainly warming up after a recession-induced lull. Trainees assured us that even in slow times "*there was still a lot of work, and I was given all the work I could be given.*" Dechert has built a good reputation in both the M&A and private equity arenas and recently won a role advising PanGenetics on its $190m sale of global rights for an experimental drug. The owners of clothing chain Jaeger also used the firm on their acquisition of 158-year-old Aquascutum from its Japanese owner. Proving their international reach, the London private equity lawyers recently advised investor Campos Verdes (backed by a $3bn London-based hedge and private equity fund) on its $613.2m merger with an Argentine agricultural giant across multiple Latin American jurisdictions. Corporate seat trainees' main responsibilities include "*drafting due diligence reports, lots of research, looking at core contracts and reviewing the financial health of UK companies that clients are looking to invest in.*"

Deck-urt, not De-shirt

"*It's a very good seat for a trainee,*" one source said of FRE, Dechert's finance and real estate group. Not only is it "*a very enjoyable, very friendly department,*" but "*you're given a lot of responsibility, and under supervision you'll be allowed to essentially run your own files through all stages of a real estate transaction.*" FRE's core strengths lie in sizeable acquisitions, developments, investments, tax structuring, occupier and financing transactions. It represents bags of retailers like Marks & Spencer, Bhs and Waitrose plus the likes of the Tussauds Group and News International. Dechert also has a small planning team taking on big work such as a 27,000 sq m Blackfriars office and retail development, just steps away from the firm's own office. Dechert's property litigators have also been involved in the development, and recently represented Blackfriars Investments in judicial review proceedings against Network Rail.

The commercial litigation practice mustn't be ignored. The team has been representing Israeli entrepreneur and industrialist Michael Cherney in his claims against the Russian oligarch Oleg Deripaska. It is one of the most substantial commercial cases pending in London. The firm has also been busy with a number of disputes arising from the Lehman and Kaupthing (Icelandic bank) collapses; it played a key role in the highly publicised Re Sigma Finance Corporation litigation (the first case to ever be decided by the UK's Supreme Court); and just to round things out, it is representing Argos in two sets of proceedings for malicious falsehood and trade mark infringement against Currys. Needless to say, "*it's the most varied department*" and trainee work "*really depends on the matters that come through the door. But there's no marking or dividing line between all the different areas in the department, like insurance, financial services, competition, etc.*"

If competition work is what you're after, you'll be keen to try the overseas seat in Brussels. "*It's competitive, but to my knowledge everyone who has wanted to go has gone,*" said one trainee. "*There are no rules about having to be a second-year or anything like that; it's really down to personal commitment, dedication and proving you have an interest in European Law.*" To find out more about this overseas opportunity, check out our Brussels feature online. At present, this is the only consistent overseas seat, but other opportunities come up when there are business needs.

Tax, employment and IP/business are the last three seat options. Tax seats "*are quite competitive,*" so the team must be keeping trainees happy. Most tax work comes from the FS and corporate departments, and Dechert has been seeing increasing private equity activity by hedge funds, which requires intensive international tax structuring advice in order to avoid local taxes on income and capital gains. The employment team takes on both contentious (tribunals) and non-contentious work (share schemes, contracts, policy advice and training). Trainees "*are involved more on the tribunal side; taking notes, drafting witness statements, etc. But there is some contracts work and there's a lot of research and loads of seminars and articles to prepare for.*" The IP department was described as "*very, very nice,*" with "*lovely people to work with.*" The team handles traditional IP matters along with data protection; trainees agreed that "*it's all very technical.*" Also worth noting this year was the presence in the department of a lot of junior associates, "*so less work got handed down to the trainee.*"

Stronger together

Besides the work on offer, trainees also praised the hours. "*It's no worse than anywhere else; it might even be marginally better. I've only worked one weekend and it was my own fault; I've certainly not had my life dominated.*" This is a decent summary of the general experience, but long hours should be expected in FS and corporate when the teams are operating at top speed. Our sources also appreciated the supervision they received, particularly the good partner contact. "*Both the firm and the trainees make lots of effort to be a team. We're a close group and no one is unreachable. This friendly approach is what has made my experience. We're competitive, but in a good way. We all try to work together to get a good result.*" We were pleased to hear just how much the trainees "*all get on like a house on fire.*" Said one: "*It's quite a small group so you don't get cliques. It's just the right size where we can all go out together, whether it's to the pub on Friday night or taking the weekend to visit the trainee in Brussels.*" We also heard plenty about the 'trainee code of honour'. "*I know I could call any trainee and say, 'Oh God how do I do this?' and they wouldn't blab on me.*" "*Certainly among trainees there's a fantastic spirit. The cohesion is very high and you do make lifelong friends.*"

Mushy feelings aside, there is one thing Dechert is pretty hardcore about – cricket. Apparently the team that typically competes against other firms and clients is so good that it's off to play in Brussels next year. At the time of our research, everyone was "*very much looking forward*" to the partners v staff match, not least because it tends to produce "*some legendary stories.*" Dechert also has football, netball and softball teams, as well as groups that play tennis together. If sports aren't your thing, there are quiz nights and we heard great things about a Thanksgiving party that involved bowling and karaoke – always an epic combo.

Lastly, a word to the wise from a pragmatist within the trainee group. "*Future applicants should probably know about retention. There are firms out there that will have spaces for all of their trainees no matter what – Dechert isn't one of them. It may improve and go up to 80%, but it will never be able to keep everyone. If job security is the main thing you're after, it's probably not the place.*" In 2010, six jobs were on offer for the ten qualifiers, and five accepted them.

And finally...

"I work very hard, but I'm happy. The smaller intake means we're looked after in a much more individual way; we're not being moulded into a type. There's been real flexibility about how they make the best of my qualities."

Dewey & LeBoeuf

The facts

Location: London
Number of UK partners/solicitors: 37/66
Total number of trainees: 20
Seats: 4x6 months
Alternative seats: Overseas seats
Extras: Pro Bono - Liberty Advice Line, East London Small Business Centre, The Medical Foundation, LawWorks; language classes

On chambersstudent.co.uk
- How to get into D&L
- D&L's bond-based innovation
- Dewey & De Vil
- We talk to managing partner Peter Sharp

A top-20 US firm, Dewey & LeBoeuf's London office offers trainees an array of almost exclusively international work. London is key to the firm's expansion in Russia, the Middle East and China.

Not mincing LeBoeuf

Dewey & LeBoeuf saw the light of day as recently as 2007. It came about through the merger of two big US players: Dewey Ballantine and LeBoeuf, Lamb, Greene & MacRae. Both were already established in London and each had offices across the globe and tons of international work. The global networks meshed well: "*In Europe LeBoeuf was in London, Paris and Brussels, while Dewey had Frankfurt, Milan, Warsaw... We were like two pirates, each with one half of the treasure map,*" London managing partner Peter Sharp told us.

In 2009, global revenue tumbled 11% to below the $1bn mark, as real estate, corporate and banking instructions dried up in the recession. The international work in which both Dewey and LeBoeuf were involved has kept the London branch ticking over nicely though. "*We've just posted our fifth consecutive month with revenue higher than that same month a year before,*" Peter Sharp told us back in spring 2010. When the London employment team jumped ship to Morgan Lewis in March of that year, the firm was quick to hire a new partner to replace them and keep the wheels turning.

Management don't mince their words about plans for global dominance. "*We have to have a strategy for the 15 or so largest economies in the world... We probably currently have a physical presence in two-thirds or more,*" global managing partner Steve Davis told us from New York. In 2008 D&L opened offices in Doha and Dubai, followed by Madrid in 2009 and Abu Dhabi in 2010. "*The London office is our global hub for our international practice,*" Sharp reiterated.

The "*international aspect of the work*" is a big attraction for trainees. And the 2010 group hasn't been disappointed. One spoke of working with lawyers across six far-flung jurisdictions on the same deal. "*I've come across nothing that's UK to UK,*" another told us; "*everything has at least one party that is international, and about 85% of the work is international to international.*" Overseas seats are available in the firm's Dubai, Moscow and Paris offices at every rotation, and we are told in hushed tones that a Beijing seat is on the cards too. "*People wouldn't struggle to get an overseas seat,*" one trainee said categorically, adding: "*Sometimes it errs on the side that nobody wants to go.*" Language skills can mean you're pushed towards certain overseas seats.

They MENA lot to us

LeBoeuf Lamb provided D&L with a substantial international energy and projects practice. Major clients include Gulf International Bank, Shell, Statoil, OPEC and the City of St Petersburg. Trainees find plenty to do on "*big deals*" for oil, gas and LNG companies and investors. And when trainees say big, they mean big. Recent deals included a $4.2bn asset sale to Gazprom by Italian energy giant Eni, and a $3.3bn acquisition for the China National Petroleum Corporation. And there's more where that came from.

Chambers UK rankings

Capital Markets	Environment
Dispute Resolution	Insurance
Energy & Natural Resources	Projects
	Tax

Listing all the countries where the firm has done deals will leave you short of breath: Uzbekistan, Russia, Azerbaijan, Bahrain, Jordan, the UAE, Angola, the Democratic Republic of Congo, Ghana, Kenya, Mozambique, Namibia, Sierra Leone, South Africa, Uganda and Zambia are just a few. Energy doesn't just mean oil and gas. The team advised Canada's Uranium Participation Corporation during its takeover of Guernsey's Uranium Limited. And work in the developing world isn't all about big money digging in: the firm's New York and Johannesburg offices advised athlete Castar Semenya on a pro bono basis during her gender testing.

Besides energy, projects work covers aviation and mining. One trainee described their "*biggest accomplishment*" as "*when the Russian office asked me to help them out on a $200m acquisition and gave it to me to deal with in London.*" Moscow is a big deal for the London office, as is the Middle East and North Africa (MENA). The energy team has lately advised Russia's Redbell on the acquisition of Timan Oil & Gas and Saudi Arabia's Kingdom Holding Company in a $370m takeover.

Insurance is another LeBoeuf legacy focus. There is a seat dedicated to insurance law, which according to Peter Sharp is a "*small nugget*" of what D&L does. "*We aim to represent* [energy and insurance companies] *in everything they need lawyers for.*" Clients include Aviva, Pacific Life Re and a number of top US insurers and reinsurers. As one trainee pointed out: "*A lot of insurance work has a New York component.*" On the contentious side of things the team advised Northern Rock's insurers on their liability after its nationalisation.

Lost in translation

All this talk of the LeBoeuf side of things could almost make you forget that Dewey brought with it an international M&A practice. Although there is "*a strong insurance presence*" in both the firm's litigation and M&A work, Peter Sharp says trainees shouldn't expect to "*spend* [their] *entire life representing insurance companies.*" D&L's high-end M&A practice is increasingly well regarded, and trainee experience reflects this. One reported working on "*a $1.2bn deal... not one of the biggest.*" Well, we're impressed! Trainees find they have ample client contact, which you "*don't always get the opportunity for in some of the other departments.*" Trainees liaise frequently with overseas lawyers, often finding "*the people from the other firm are partners and associates.*"

Make sure your passport is to hand because trainees head as far afield as China for closings. "*I've worked on some big cross-border M&A deals in African countries, where I got to use my language skills,*" one trainee recalled. This reflects the importance D&L places on those with second languages. "*We have a growing practice representing Japanese manufacturers... so if an applicant speaks Japanese that would be great,*" Peter Sharp confirmed. It's official: if you speak French, Spanish, Russian, Japanese, Arabic or Mandarin then the firm wants to hear from you.

Capital markets, banking and funds work is also a Dewey hangover. The group represents the likes of Barclays, BNP Paribas, Deutsche Bank, JPMorgan and RBS on structured funds, derivatives, IPOs and stock listings. Although trainees say they get "*a lot of responsibility in terms of holding the pen on deals,*" there are also "*boring jobs... from verification to incorporating comments into documents.*" Trainees can additionally take seats in litigation, competition and employment, and real estate may be on offer in the future too.

How about a seat in the competition department? It advises clients such as Panasonic, Hitachi and AIG on EU competition law compliance and the work includes "*random research on companies and checking merger thresholds in multiple jurisdictions.*" The general litigation seat is quite common and fairly popular among trainees. You're "*allowed to get really involved*" and this includes making "*calls with the barristers and some clients.*" Almost all the work is multi-jurisdictional, say, advising energy companies and other multinationals on fraud, risk management and arbitrations.

Dewey & LeTough

As a new first-year trainee, you'll be assigned a second-year as a 'LeBuddy' (they say this with a straight face) to "*show you the ropes,*" particularly "*the admin things.*" When we started hearing about the nitty gritty of the workplace we wondered to what extent it felt like an American firm and to what extent it felt British. "*I think its culture is definitely American, in the sense that it is less structured and a bit more individual-focused,*" one trainee concluded.

The recession has hit firms in all sorts of ways, but commonly the slowdown in work made it harder for relatively inexperienced trainees to gain that all-important experience. Across the profession we've heard about more senior lawyers (with billing targets to meet) clinging on to the available work with a grip tighter than Thing T. Thing with rigor mortis. "*I'm satisfied with the latter half of the contract,*" said one trainee; "*the recession in the first half killed the opportunities.*" A first-year told us: "*I wish I could learn more. You get exposure to international work... whether you can participate a lot is another question.*" Trainees certainly agree it's important to take initiative to win good assignments and be noticed by colleagues. "*If you're not focused you can fall through the cracks, but if you seek out opportunities you will get pulled along.*" Tough love.

Seek out good opportunities and you'll then need to put in the hours, especially in departments like corporate, litigation and banking. "*In my litigation seat there were a lot of late nights and a lot of weekends.*" Trainees are clear that there is "*no face-time culture – if there is work they'd love you to be here, but if you leave at 6pm and work comes up later, you can do it from home.*" One trainee in a particularly busy phase said: "*I've been working till about midnight.*" For others, working weekends and staying until the wee hours is more of a once-monthly affair.

A little pooped after a long day in the office? You're sure to find some junior colleagues at Bertorelli's, which is just across the road from the faux-gothic building that is Dewey's London base. The location served as Cruella De Vil's lair in the live-action *101 Dalmatians*. More online. People sometimes go out, "*even if they are working until 2am,*" although "*partners don't socialise much unless it's the yearly ball or wine tasting.*" One trainee reflected the feelings of most when they said: "*It's up to you to make your own social life – you're not forced to have fun.*"

Sharp-ening up the act

Trainees find that "*generally the partners treat you as equals... well not equals but with a lot of respect.*" Trainees were keen to mention an "*open-door policy*" and "*nice*" atmosphere, but we sensed a slight dampening of morale too. Although most agree that "*a* [post-merger] *divide can be overemphasised,*" one described the office as "*a bit Balkanised*" and added that "*it's hard to know as a whole where it's going.*" A number agree on this last point. Peter Sharp was installed as London managing partner earlier in 2010 after a two-year office managing partner hiatus. He is familiar with the role as he managed LeBoeuf London before the merger. "*It's the habit of some English firms to be very regimented and organised,*" he told us. "*We encourage the partners here to be open, entrepreneurial and innovative in looking for new work.*" A go-get-it attitude is key, right down to trainee level. "*If you show you are keen it probably does well for you,*" said a trainee. In 2010, 14 of the 15 qualifiers passed muster and accepted jobs.

And finally...

If you are interested in international work in London, D&L is looking for trainees with the right skill set, an appetite for hard work and a little understanding about the areas in which it works.

Dickinson Dees LLP

The facts

Location: Newcastle, Stockton-on-Tees, York, London

Number of UK partners/solicitors: 59/200

Total number of trainees: 26

Seats: 4x6 months

Alternative seats: Brussels, secondments

On chambersstudent.co.uk
- How to get into Dickinson Dees
- The firm's plans for the future
- The Newcastle legal scene

Dickinson Dees is undeniably *"the market leader in the North East."* If you're a blue-chip company doing business in the region it's Dickie Dees you'll be wanting – and that's exactly what the trainees love about the firm.

Grand-daddy

Dickinson Dees has been a Newcastle institution for over 200 years and today it sits firmly at the top of the North East legal market. Dozens of its practices are ranked highly in *Chambers UK*. It picks up top-tier placements for planning, property, private client, IP, family, environment, dispute resolution, corporate/M&A, construction, charities, banking and finance and agriculture. "*The fact it has been around for so long makes people feel proud, although others do sometimes think we consider ourselves superior,*" a trainee told us. Another quickly added that "*there is no air of arrogance*" wafting along the corridors. What attracted most of our sources to the firm was its prestigious client roster and the fact that "*on paper it's the biggest and the best in the city.*"

Offices in Stockton-on-Tees and York (the latter in the old Terry's chocolate factory) give North Eastern coverage beyond Tyneside, and the firm now has its sights set on the big time. "*We're a North East-based and focused firm but with a national outlook and national clients.*" Some trainees even detect "*aspirations to build a presence throughout the UK.*" A small service office in London provides a base for lawyers visiting City clients – there's almost always someone working there these days. When we spoke to trainees in late spring 2010, the partnership was in the midst of mulling over future strategy. Senior partner John Marshall's lips were sealed on what the outcome would be, but he promised he would reveal more about "*setting the strategic direction.*" Head to our website to find out more.

A wide array of practice groups amounts to a whopping 38 trainee seat options in Newcastle. They include both commercial and private client options. York offers a smaller number – property, corporate, charities and employment law; while Teesside has property, litigation, corporate and employment. Stints in the firm's three main property, litigation and coco divisions are mandatory for all, but there is still plenty of choice within each of these divisions. For each seat rotation, trainees rank three preferences and the system "*stops you being too restrictive in your choices.*"

More variety is provided by a secondment to Northern Rock as well as a six-week stint in Brussels. Here, too, the firm is the guiding hand that shapes trainees' destiny: "*They choose people to go on secondment for a reason – you have to have shown some confidence.*"

Full steam ahead

A general corporate seat will see you doing "*pretty standard*" work, including "*company sales and purchases, flotations and buyouts,*" as well as "*investments in different companies and listings.*" Clients include the Daily Mail & General Trust and gaming company NetPlay. Trainees have been "*involved in a number of big deals,*" including recently "*the restructuring of a football club and an engineering business.*" Although there are some "*boring tasks,*" the main body of trainee work entails "*drafting board minutes, proof-reading, talking with clients*" and "*heading up some of your own smaller files.*"

Chambers UK rankings

Agriculture & Rural Affairs	Environment
Banking & Finance	Family/Matrimonial
Charities	Intellectual Property
Competition/European Law	Local Government
Construction	Pensions
Corporate/M&A	Planning
Debt Recovery	Private Client
Dispute Resolution	Projects
Education	Real Estate
Employment	Real Estate Litigation
Energy & Natural Resources	Restructuring/Insolvency
	Social Housing
	Transport

Given the economy, the corporate recovery seat is "*extremely busy*" and trainees see plenty of court time, "*quite a lot of research and long hours.*" Besides corporate clients, the team advises professional regulators and industry bodies such as the Law Society, the Solicitors Regulation Authority and the Confederation of British Industry (CBI).

The mighty corporate rail team has helped Govia and Nexus with franchise bids for South Central and the Tyne and Wear Metro respectively. At the other end of the country, it advised three rail companies on the introduction of Oyster ticketing systems in London, and helped Southeastern Trains with the introduction of Britain's first domestic high-speed rail service. Although "*it's not the kind of seat you have in mind at law school,*" six months in this specialised department is "*quite good fun.*" Client relations tend to be long-standing and therefore close, and "*the supervisor is very, very good.*" Work varies from "*photocopying to sitting down with the client to talk about legal points*" and "*taking charge of data for certain transactions.*" This means you "*always feel part of the project you're on.*"

Back to school?

The commercial litigation team has lately advised universities, rail clients, local authorities and a Spanish telecom company on disputes and arbitrations. York lawyers work for a number of charity clients on contentious matters, including Barnardo's, NSPCC and Cancer Research UK. The experience in property litigation is "*a good mix between commercial leases and work for Registered Social Landlords on problems they have with their tenants – mainly anti-social behaviour.*" In contentious seats (as well as corporate recovery and planning seats) you'll frequently head off to court and there's always a chance of doing your own advocacy.

The employment team works on both contentious and non-contentious matters, almost exclusively for employers. Clients include Northern Rock, Siemens, Black & Decker, Nike and Formica (of plastic table fame). The team has advised the London Borough of Croydon, Northumberland County Council and other local authorities on the employment aspects of converting schools to Academy status, and one trainee spoke enthusiastically about "*a tribunal for a large NHS equal pay claim.*"

Real estate clients include major property owners and users like Procter & Gamble, Sainsbury's and GAP, as well as universities and house builders. "*The bulk of my work was on very large deals, like the sale of a part of a new development by a national house builder,*" a trainee told us. The Teesside property team represents several charities as well as a number of chemical and industrial companies. The projects team – also part of the property division – has been "*carving out a bit of niche for itself*" in PFI work and procurement. This has lately included "*building hospitals as well as Academies and schools for the Building Schools for the Future project.*" This work lives or dies at the behest of government policy.

Private client or 'wealth management' advice is the firm's fourth pillar. The private capital seat is "*the least popular*" and "*the black sheep of the family.*" We don't really see why, as trainees "*get to see a lot of clients.*" Said one: "*My supervisor was a partner and he took me to meetings just to learn and take notes.*" The team helps both major private landowners and business entrepreneurs deal sensibly with their mounting wads of cash. "*Some people have been clients for over 100 years and own vast swathes of Northumberland or County Durham. Others may have just started a business.*" One particularly candid trainee told us that private capital is "*basically a tax avoidance seat.*" In 2009, the team was involved in the administration of over 120 estates with a combined value of £350m. In summer 2010, however, the firm did wave goodbye to its family team, which left to become Silk Family Law. Dickinson Dees maintains a 'best friends' relationship with Silk.

Pitcher-ing in

The lawyers in Newcastle are split between two offices and trainees were keen to point out the differences. "*Trinity is a modern air-conditioned building in an excellent location for buying lunch: it's got a café and roof terrace.*" By contrast, "*a negative of the St Ann's Wharf building is that the canteen is on the ground floor with no windows,*" although "*it is in a prestigious location on the riverfront and the client rooms are very plush.*" Trainees spend time in both as St Ann's houses the coco and litigation departments ("*with a head-down, get on with the work feel*") while Trinity has property and private client (and "*a lot more people popping their head into each other's offices*"). York employs about 60 people, "*which means everyone says hello in the corridor, while people in Newcastle tend to keep themselves to themselves.*" Teesside is smaller still but packs a punch with "*heavy-weight DD branding behind it.*"

Dickie Dees' trainees invariably like the teams they work in. "*It's very friendly and you can chat with any-one from a partner down to a trainee.*" One source was happier still: "*The people you work with are very much your friends. I feel I can be myself and be silly at times and they don't mind.*" Supervisors and colleagues don't demand the world on your first day: "*It's a no-blame culture, so if you make a mistake they will just help you out.*"

One trainee gripe is that, partly because of redundancies during the recession, "*there are just too many partners up at the top of the firm*" and "*there are certain partners who are maybe a little bit insular.*" Questions about where the firm is headed in the future – regional top dog or national mid-sizer – also lead to debate. "*I would say the firm is quite forward-facing. It has quite a young management team, but expansion is contrary to the views of some of the more traditional people here,*" mused one source. Internal debates are perhaps the reason why "*sometimes management don't communicate enough with those lower down the chain.*" A recent employee satisfaction survey means that senior partner John Marshall is fully aware of this. "*Could we communicate better at times?*" he says. "*Yes we could.*" It's an area on which management will focus more attention in the future.

Trainees say the firm "*strikes a relatively good work-life balance*" and they usually manage to stick to an 8.30am to 6pm working day. "*8am to 7pm is probably at the longer end.*" In a corporate seat, "*if you have deadlines looming you stay late and then the next week you can leave at 5.30pm.*" All in all, "*it's sort of a half-way house*" between a smaller regional firm and a big City player. "*It's like a City firm, but it's up North,*" one trainee helpfully offered.

So what are Dickie Dees' people like? "*We all get along well so we must have something in common, but I'm not sure what it is,*" one trainee pondered, adding: "*Well, I suppose it's being sociable.*" The Teesside office recently hosted a Nintendo Wii tournament and York has "*events like business development drinks once every three or four months.*" In Newcastle, there are departmental Christmas and summer parties as well as curry nights, movie trips and race days, not to mention "*a lot of nights out – and Fridays are quite alcoholic. It's just accepted that in pub X down the street there will be trainees and if you want to go, you go.*" Trainees were just a little coy about the identity of 'pub X'. It's the Pitcher and Piano.

If you want to be a part of all this, take note: around two-thirds of the 2009 starters were recruited via the firm's vacation scheme. Go to our website to read more about the application process. Dickinson Dees has a history of doing its best for NQs, even if it can't find them jobs within the firm (three NQs were sent off on client secondments in 2009). In 2010, nine of 19 qualifiers took up jobs with the firm.

And finally...

If you're looking for training in the North East and you believe that big is beautiful, then prestigious Dickinson Dees should be on your list.

DLA Piper UK LLP

The facts

Location: Birmingham, Leeds, Liverpool, London, Manchester, Sheffield, Scotland

Number of UK partners/solicitors: 309/647

Total number of trainees: 170

Seats: 4x6 months

Alternative seats: Overseas seats, secondments

Extras: Pro bono – various programmes across the offices

On chambersstudent.co.uk
- How to get into DLA Piper
- DLA Piper overseas
- The firm's pro bono activities

'Gee, DLA, what do you want to do tonight?' 'The same thing we do every night...'

Try to take over the world!

DLA Piper is a big 'un. With offices on six continents, it has a presence in Baltimore, Bangkok, Beijing, Birmingham, Boston, Bratislava, Brisbane, Brussels and Bucharest – and that's just branches starting with the letter B! With over 3,500 lawyers, it's one of the largest firms on the planet, with global revenue surpassing $1bn and 69 offices in 30 countries (as well as a further 18 associate offices at last count). And what's it all for? "*DLA's aim is to be the biggest legal provider in the world,*" one trainee told us breezily.

DLA was born in 1996 out of the merger between two UK firms, Dibb Lupton Broomhead and Alsop Wilkinson. It was thinking big even back then, but it was the three-way merger in 2005 between DLA and the US's Piper Rudnick and Gray Cary Ware & Friendenrich that catapulted the firm into its current position. This was one of the largest transatlantic mergers in history. Since then, new offices or exclusive tie-ups have sprung up every few months – 2010 alone has seen expansion into Kenya, Brazil and Turkey. "*People are very proud of where DLA has come from and how we are doing,*" a trainee revealed.

The global strategy is to "*let the clients lead us, rather than leading the clients,*" says training partner Sian Croxon. "*But if there is an imperative, we will take it.*" It should come as no surprise that all this growth costs money. In 2009 the firm saw its debt grow by 80% to £53m. "*If you've got a business you have to invest,*" says Croxon, "*but we are tightly managed financially.*" The UK and Asian aspects of the business showed good financial health in 2009, with revenue falling just 1%, while the US part of the business shrunk by 13.9% (the firm still keeps separate accounts for the two sides of the Atlantic). The Middle East fared worst of all, with turnover dropping 40% from £20.5m to £12.4m. DLA was one of the first firms to jump into Dubai in order to capitalise on the expanding market there, but overstretch and the collapse of the Dubai property market saw the firm scale back its presence in the region. It is clear that at a management level DLA Piper is not a firm afraid of taking risks. On the global stage it has relished the challenge of attempting major leaps forward, even if there have been occasional setbacks along the way.

Despite the fact that it has hit the big time, the firm maintains offices not just in London, but in Birmingham, Leeds, Liverpool, Manchester and its hometown of Sheffield as well. So what you might be wondering is how much a new office in Kenya matters to a trainee who lives in, say, Garforth, and works next to Leeds railway station? "*I think we are still trying to take over the world, but it doesn't feel like you're part of a massive organisation all the time. Prestigious international work is balanced with work at a local level,*" said one source, reflecting the experience of most trainees in the regions. *Chambers UK* ranks the firm in 50 areas for its London and UK-wide practice alone. Add on the many regional rankings and you'll begin to understand the breadth and variety of DLA Piper's practice.

Chambers UK rankings

Administrative & Public Law	Intellectual Property
Asset Finance	Investment Funds
Aviation	Media & Entertainment
Banking & Finance	Outsourcing
Banking Litigation	Parliamentary & Public Affairs
Capital Markets	Pensions
Commodities	Planning
Competition/European Law	Private Equity
Construction	Projects
Corporate/M&A	Public International Law
Data Protection	Real Estate
Dispute Resolution	Real Estate Finance
Employment	Real Estate Litigation
Financial Services	Restructuring/Insolvency
Franchising	Retail
Fraud	Sports Law
Information Technology	Tax
Insurance	Telecommunications
	Transport

Globalocalisation

Across its practice groups, DLA Piper works on three tiers of matters: local/regional; national; and international. All offices provide a mix of the three, with London and Leeds leaning most towards the international end, Liverpool and Manchester most towards the regional, and Sheffield and Birmingham somewhere in the middle. Equally, certain departments (finance, corporate, employment) offer more scope for an international experience. DLA's recruitment motto ('Be local – go global') mostly holds true: "*In litigation we have worked across European jurisdictions,*" a Liverpool trainee said, adding: "*We've also had some German lawyers come over for a mediation.*" It can sometimes be more of a question of think global, go local: "*As long as we do well in Manchester, people are not too bothered about what we are doing internationally,*" a trainee from that city told us.

There are plenty of seats on offer, and while commercial litigation, real estate and corporate are the most common (especially in the regions), the firm doesn't force any seats upon trainees beyond the SRA's requirements to gain both contentious and non-contentious experience. "*Grad recruitment will do its best to fit you in where you want,*" seemed the most common view. Beyond the core departments, London offers the greatest variety of seats, including construction; sport and media; leveraged finance; projects; employment; pensions; and litigation and regulation. Regional offerings include IP and technology; planning; restructuring; property litigation; banking; and tax. International secondments to Tokyo, Moscow, Hong Kong and Singapore are available. There are also client secondments to a range of household names and financial institutions, with around ten trainees out on secondment at any one time.

Moscow to Merseyside

DLA Piper's litigation department has sub-teams specialising in property, finance, regulation, aviation, construction and insurance. The latter three are particular specialisations of the London office, while insurance lit – including personal injury and negligence – is hot in Birmingham. London trainees can do a 'litigation and regulation' seat, where they mostly concentrate on financial services issues. Clients include Barclays, RBS, BNP Paribas, Fortis and Deutsche Bank. You might find yourself doing "*investigations into issues within banks where you then put your findings forward to the FSA.*" There is a taste of international work, too, for clients like Gazprom and the governments of Cyprus and Zambia. Sheffield acts for "*some very large, some medium-sized and some smaller clients,*" including household names like Boots, ITV and Mothercare. "*I was fortunate to be involved in one big piece of litigation that was going on,*" reported a Manchester source; "*I was involved in all the pleadings and large meetings and got a real understanding of tactics and procedure.*" Experience is pretty hands-on: "*Most trainees get to do advocacy once or twice.*"

The London corporate team does "*primarily M&A, as well as capital markets work and a little bit of private equity.*" Clients include international organisations like anti-virus software people Sophos, the Oman Investment Fund and Kraft. Leeds and Birmingham serve both regional and national clients like Nottingham City Transport, Britannia Building Society, corner-shop chain Nisa, Amazon and freight airline Swissport. Liverpool and Manchester's work is more region-focused. There's a "*real buzz*" in the Leeds corporate team, which handles "*quite a lot of work with our St Petersburg and Moscow offices for international clients who have businesses in Russia.*" Trainees are fully involved: "*Sometimes I'm sat in on calls, half of which are being held in Russian.*" Restructuring is a "*busy seat,*" as DLA Piper capitalises on the woes of the downturn. The London team advised Icelandic bank Kaupthing and Deloitte on the restructuring of the retailer owners of Oasis and Warehouse, while a Manchester trainee reported "*spending the majority of my seat working on the Zavvi administration.*"

DLA's property teams are a mixed bag. Retail is big in Leeds: "*It's great; you can walk along the high street and say, 'Oh, I did work on that.*'" Sheffield handles a lot of residential property matters and trainees get "*hands-on practical experience, doing exchanges of contract and dealing with completions.*" Birmingham represents retail and institutional property owners like Birmingham City Council and EAT. The Manchester office recently advised

Vue on a new 3,000-seat cinema at London's Westfield Shopping Centre, while other clients range from Ernst & Young to the University of Bolton. The smaller nature of some work in the Northern offices means trainees sometimes "*get to run their own files under close supervision.*"

End of the world as we knew it

In London, finance takes over the key role played by property in the other offices, and London trainees invariably take a finance or corporate seat, sometimes both. Outside the capital, finance is a generalist seat and DLA Piper is a market leader in most regional locations. London trainees, however, can specialise in structured finance, leveraged finance and asset finance (dealing primarily with aviation). Work is "*on the banking side, so we're acting for lenders.*" One finance trainee told us that during the downturn they were left "*twiddling their thumbs watching banking lawyers run around thinking the world was coming to an end.*" Trainees are now more active, and though it's a complex seat, "*the finance elective on the LPC will give you enough knowledge to cope with it.*" More about seat experiences, and overseas opportunities, on our website.

"*You do tailor your training contract to the way you want it to be. In terms of responsibility and amount of work, it's up to you how much you want to take on.*" Across the firm it holds true that "*you're definitely encouraged to get out there and show your face around the department. The onus is on you to get the work you want to do.*" You're definitely not just doing the grunt tasks. Said one source: "*I've had a number of experiences where I was put onto conference calls that were way above my head, and I've been taken to completion meetings purely to gain experience.*" If there was one trainee regret it was that "*the induction was cut back from two weeks to three days.*"

Honourable mentions

In previous years trainees often waxed lyrical about co-CEO Sir Nigel Knowles (who was knighted in the 2009 New Year's Honours list). It was he who took over in 1996 and spearheaded Dibb Lupton Alsop's remarkable transformation into DLA Piper. This year, although we did hear a little about the Knowles cult of personality and the plans for world domination, trainees were equally keen to tell us about DLA's more intimate side, and what makes the firm such an appealing prospect. "*I live on the doorstep of the Peak District and work for a big international firm,*" a Sheffield trainee explained, "*so what attracted me to DLA was more the fact that I can take great pride in working for a firm as good as this, and the high quality of clients.*"

There's a "*close-knit*" culture focused on the idea that "*everyone gets on and goes out together,*" which leads to a lively social scene. Leeds has football and netball teams, and trainees enjoy a Friday night out. "*Last week I went out for a drink with a fellow trainee and a partner and two senior associates who I had never met before,*" said one. The smaller Liverpool office has "*office drinks once a month,*" while in Sheffield there's the Junior Lawyers Division ball to look forward to, and the firm pays for its sports teams to attend the York College of Law's sports day. The Birmingham office, meanwhile, boasts its own band called The Sued, which consists of "*a trainee, an NQ, a partner and a secretary.*" There are also "*sports league tournaments, quizzes and wine tastings – all good for networking.*"

Across its offices DLA attracts similar trainees. They are, by their own definition, "*team players who are prepared to work hard;*" "*goal-driven and motivated;*" "*positive and enthusiastic;*" and "*ambitious.*" Said one: "*You have to be, just because of the nature of the firm.*" You also need to be "*resilient*" and "*excited about where the firm is going...*" which obviously means you need to know where the firm is going. To find out, see our website.

Even those trainees we spoke to without NQ jobs remained positive about the top-notch training they had received at DLA Piper. In 2010, 72 of 97 qualifiers took up jobs with the firm. Retention was lower than elsewhere in Manchester – a city that's suffered badly during the recession. The small Liverpool office managed to keep on all its trainees and as in 2009 at least one trainee qualified into an overseas office. After grumbles in 2009, the 2010 NQ process was brought forward by a few weeks and trainees had no complaints about it this time around. Our interviewees took a realistic and measured approach to qualification and advised: "*The people who stay are those who demonstrate initiative, are generally up for it and act as if they are a fee earner in the team rather than just a trainee.*" Nuff said.

And finally...

The firm's unashamed willingness to shout about what it's good at should give you a few clues as to how to approach your application. Think big and think ambitious.

- **A training partner tells us:** "I love seeing on people's CVs that they have done paper rounds or run a small business. And team sport – I love that. Team sport makes you ideal for working in a law firm."

DMH Stallard LLP

The facts

Location: Brighton, Crawley, London

Number of UK partners/solicitors: 53/54

Total number of trainees: 18

Seats: 4x6 months

Alternative seats: Occasional secondments

On chambersstudent.co.uk
• How to get into DMH
• DMH in London: a closer look
• The firm's social scene

This full-service firm is happy in the 'Gatwick Diamond', yet doesn't look like halting its assault on London.

Diamond geezers

DMH Stallard started life in Brighton following the merger of three high street firms to create Donne, Mileham & Haddock. The firm rebranded itself as DMH (possibly to avoid fish gags) and expanded by opening a large Crawley office. Further mergers with London firms Stallards (in 2005) and Courts & Co (in 2008) gave it its current shape. It now acts for clients like Tesco, London Borough of Croydon and EDF Energy, presently the UK's largest energy generator. Crawley is the largest office, and it houses most of the firm's commercial departments. DMH prefers to call the office 'Gatwick'– presumably that name has connotations of international jet-setting and dynamism thanks to the airport, while Crawley has connotations of… well, nothing much. Actually this Sussex town has grown hugely and is a great business centre. DMH has found success acting for clients connected to the nearby airport.

While trainees say DMH's "*heart is still in Brighton,*" the majority of administrative departments, like HR, are now based in Crawley. They describe their employer as "*primarily a regional firm with a London base.*" Managing partner Tim Aspinall splits his time between Brighton and London, and the firm's interest in the capital is undeniable: go to our website to read about what DMH gets up to in the City.

Best foot forward

Trainees can expect a broad-based training with seats chosen from dispute resolution; corporate-commercial; property; property litigation; contentious IP; employment; planning; personal injury; and private client. You usually end up doing a property seat and in 2010 half of the trainees qualified into this department. Trainees must undertake seats in at least two offices, and new starters are fully aware that "*commuting is going to be part of the training contract.*" The office-switching policy is based on "*who fits with what team*" and provides the benefit of "*getting to know people in all the offices.*"

The Gatwick corporate-commercial team works on M&A, banking and commercial matters, and there is also "*a technology focus with lots of IT-related agreements.*" Clients come from the retail, media, leisure, professional services and finance industries and include the likes of KPMG and Deloitte. Lawyers also act for the owners of *Noostar*, an online talent show partly funded by Graham Norton. London corporate work is more financial in nature, with clients including insurer Swiss Re, main occupier of the iconic Gherkin building. "*I've been involved in a public company merger and done stuff on the buying and selling of shares,*" one satisfied trainee told us.

In litigation, trainees tackle "*whatever comes in the door: it's one mountain after another.*" Some cases are multi-million-pound matters, and so it's only natural that one London trainee reported "*having to do some dogsbody work.*" Their peers in Crawley were keener: "*I was given a good amount of responsibility and was able to talk to clients a lot.*" Said clients include famed guitar-makers Fender, Ramsay Health Care, Lloyds and the Arcadia

Chambers UK rankings

Banking & Finance	Environment
Construction	Information Technology
Corporate/M&A	Intellectual Property
Debt Recovery	Local Government
Dispute Resolution	Planning
Employment	Real Estate
	Real Estate Litigation

group, owner of Dorothy Perkins, Miss Selfridge and Topshop. In December 2008, the firm was appointed to the Treasury Solicitor's Department's Lit-Cat panel. Other clients include the University of Sussex and the Parliamentary and Health Service Ombudsman. Trainees enjoy the contentious IP seat, where they conduct research into "*trade mark, design right and copyright*" issues. There's enjoyable work on "*combating counterfeit products*" for retailers such as Arcadia companies, Office (the shoe people) and Havaiana flip-flops.

Noise annoys

A commercial property seat sees trainees supporting Brighton & Hove Albion FC. The construction of the club's £60m new Falmer Stadium has run into all manner of legal and environmental difficulties, so it's kept the lawyers on their toes. Other work includes "*regeneration and bread-and-butter landlord and tenant work such as drafting leases and licences to assign.*" There's "*quite a lot of client contact and the vast majority of work is assisting partners on larger files.*" Property clients include Aviva, London Borough of Croydon and the City of Westminster as well as top international banks. In property litigation you might run into some surprising work on ASBOs. "*If someone in social housing is breaking a clause in their tenancy by having loud parties, we'll act for the council on how to deal with the situation.*" Some trainees get their own caseload, which would typically include rent arrears and insolvency matters.

DMH's employment advice is mainly given to employers, and "*around 30 to 40% of clients are in the public sector.*" These include the London boroughs of Croydon, Bromley, Merton, Southwark, and Kensington and Chelsea, as well as Dover, Crawley, Brighton and Medway councils. Trainee tasks include "*reviewing staff handbooks and policies*" plus more contentious tribunal matters. Private sector clients include Sussex County Cricket Club and the National Geographic Channel.

Seats in personal injury and private client are taken in Brighton. In PI "*you get your own caseload of maybe 60 or 70 cases.*" The team acts for claimants who have been involved with car crashes and accidents at work or on holiday. One client was a passenger in a car where the driver was killed. The driver was drunk and did not have a full driving licence or any insurance. The client lost his left (dominant) arm and suffered a psychological reaction. A key factor in the case was whether the claimant knew the driver was drunk. The private client team advises wealthy individuals or their surviving family members on wills, inheritance and wealth management. Recently, this included unmasking a forged will with the help of genealogists and handwriting experts.

Fess up

Trainees see DMH as "*extremely well-managed,*" "*entrepreneurial*" and "*business-focused.*" While one source claimed there are "*perhaps too many systems,*" others admired the innovation. DHM Direct, the firm's case management system, means "*clients can look at their own matters remotely and see how they are progressing.*" One trainee reported on "*a streamlining initiative where different departments meet up to discuss how things can be organised more similarly.*" The AGM, which is both social and informational, was cancelled in 2010, but trainees still "*got their time with* [managing partner] *Tim* [Aspinall]" to discuss targets, fees and job prospects, and they felt the firm was "*open.*" Describing their employer, our sources used all the usual happy buzzwords: "*friendly,*" "*approachable*" and "*down to earth.*" Despite a move "*towards being a larger London-led regional organisation,*" there is still "*a lot of DMH in the firm,*" which means that "*if there is a problem and you 'fess up, they'll support you and help you.*" The firm's history of good retention speaks for itself. In 2010, six of nine second-year trainees were retained on qualification.

And finally...

If broad commercial/private client training in a respected South East and London firm is what you're after then this is a good pick.

Dundas & Wilson

The facts

Location: London, Edinburgh, Glasgow

Number of UK partners/solicitors: 82/207

Total number of trainees: 20 (in England)

Seats: 4x6 months

Alternative seats: Occasional secondments

On chambersstudent.co.uk
- How to get into D&W
- Recent highlight deals and cases
- Rabbie Burns: a guide for non-Scots

Since moving to London in 2002, tartan titan Dundas & Wilson is developing some real clout in the City.

Great chieftain

1759 was a big year for Scotland. Not only does it mark the birth year of national bard Robert Burns, but also that of Dundas & Wilson. Cream of the Scottish crop, the firm has a host of heavyweight clients on its books – RBS, KPMG, Standard Life, EDF and Samsung Europe – and is consistently ranked by *Chambers UK* in almost all areas of corporate and commercial practice north of the border. The firm has expanded beyond its tartan roots and now views London as a part of its patch. "*We're not quite as well known down here yet, but the quality of work is still very good and clients take us seriously because we've got such a good reputation in Scotland,*" explained a source. Now, "*it's a very different beast to when the firm first came down. At the beginning a lot of work was coming down from Scotland, but that's all changed.*"

The increasingly prominent corporate practice is evidence of the firm's rise in the London mid-market, and 2010 saw the office win a number of new clients, including E.ON and business software company SAP. Dundas also advised Evergreen Group, a Taiwanese conglomerate, on its share swap with Hutchison Whampoa and received some toothy instructions on the £136m MBO of Associated Dental Practices. The office now picks up *Chambers UK* rankings for restructuring, real estate and construction, among others.

Growth in the City has seen the London office surpass Glasgow to become the firm's second-largest office. In its commitment to becoming a "*seamless UK law firm,*" Dundas overhauled its management structure in 2010 and consolidated its practice groups according to location. In a move away from a joint-managing partner model, London-based Donald Shaw will continue at the helm of a newly unified board that includes partners in each location. "*Going forward, we see the main driver as being growth in London,*" commented training partner Martin Thomas. "*Now that our managing partner is based in London, I think that's significant as to where the firm is and where it's going.*"

All for one and one for all

"*Don't come here if you don't like corporate,*" warned a source. Corporate and property are the most common seats for trainees, though they can also select from litigation; corporate recovery; EU/competition; banking and finance; IP/IT; environment; and employment. As for securing their preferred seats, trainees "*usually get their choices eventually.*" Client secondments are sometimes available, although a seat in Scotland was taken out of the mix this past year. Trainees can still apply for any NQ job in any of the offices. In 2009, two of the seven London qualifiers were kept on and two people were brought down from Scotland. On this point, trainees insisted that English qualifiers have "*no need to worry about people in Scotland. At the end of the day if you're good enough, they'll find a way to keep you.*" In 2010, eight out of 11 London qualifiers stayed.

Trainees are assigned a mentor and an appraiser in every seat. Though this structure "*encourages you to take the official route,*" our sources gushed that "*other people are always*

Chambers UK rankings

Administrative & Public Law	Local Government
Banking & Finance	Media & Entertainment
Charities	Outsourcing
Construction	Parliamentary & Public Affairs
Corporate/M&A	Partnership
Dispute Resolution	Pensions
Education	Planning
Employee Share Schemes	Professional Negligence
Employment	Projects
Energy & Natural Resources	Public Procurement
Environment	Real Estate
Financial Services	Real Estate Litigation
Franchising	Restructuring/Insolvency
Healthcare	Sports Law
Immigration	Tax
Information Technology	Transport
Intellectual Property	
Investment Funds	

really approachable." Certainly the "*fantastic*" open-plan office bolsters this feeling – "*all the partners are approachable, and sitting among everyone harbours a better team atmosphere.*" Learning by osmosis, "*you can hear what senior members are doing*" and might even find yourself sitting near the managing partner. "*He sits at the end of the open-plan* [floor], *in front of the water machine, on a same-sized desk as everyone else.*" So no office gossip when you're filling up! Our sources also felt included in their teams. "*Even if you get asked to do a really minor task as part of a deal, they'll write the whole deal out on the whiteboard for you, so you really get an idea of the bigger picture.*"

Corporate trainees "*get real breadth of work – from the very beginnings of a company, to the end of a transaction.*" Our sources enjoyed drafting, "*sometimes ancillary documents, sometimes a few clauses of the main document.*" They also get stuck into research and helping out with completion meetings, which is "*really exciting when it runs like clockwork.*" The team itself is praised as being "*helpful and friendly – I couldn't really fault it.*"

With clients such as Scottish Widows, National Grid and Land Securities on the books, real estate trainees handle day-to-day portfolio management and liaise with the clients' agents. "*I've never felt like I've been hidden away,*" said one. "*You're running your own files, negotiating with the other side and getting instructions from the agent.*" While the construction department has had a couple of partner departures recently, trainees remain confident that "*it'll be exciting to build it up again.*" We heard about the great responsibility on offer in the department. "*Sometimes people were off doing other things and I was left with the deadline. It was like, 'So, I guess I'd better go to the meeting with the client now!'*"

I'm gonna be (414 miles)

When the recession dampened corporate activity in the Square Mile, finance and insolvency-related litigation became the silver lining. At Dundas, litigators worked on aspects of the Madoff scandal, advising the provisional liquidators to Madoff Securities International. The firm has been fighting to recover assets, including a $3m yacht owned by Mrs Madoff. The department also helped to obtain a judgment from the English Courts to allow the disclosure of data to the Madoff US trustee. Lucky trainees had some great exposure to this case, "*preparing interview bundles, attending long meetings and taking attendance notes to report to the client.*" Led by Martin Thomas, former head of property litigation at Herbert Smith, the department is split between commercial and property litigation, though trainees "*get work from both.*" Property litigation involves "*responsibility for your own files,*" while commercial litigation is "*less independent – you can't really do the particulars of a claim by yourself.*" Comm lit does at least provide "*lots of visits to the Royal Courts of Justice.*" One source told us that "*the meatiest work I've ever got was setting up a mediation,*" and we heard of another trainee who'd had the chance to do some small-scale advocacy. "*The first time's the hardest; the second is a million times easier.*"

The firm's "*long-term objective is to be 'one firm', allowing people to move and interact between offices.*" As far as work goes, "*you're often on the phone to someone in Scotland or vice versa*" and "*the teams frequently work together.*" Trainees attend induction days in Edinburgh with their Scottish counterparts and share video-conferenced training sessions with them. One innovative chap has taken the 'one firm' idea to extremes and actually run between the offices: banking lawyer Chris Friel made his way from London to Glasgow for the Haiti earthquake appeal, covering more than 25 marathons in 20 days.

Trainees "*spearhead the social organising;*" many play in one of the sports teams (football, volleyball and cricket) and the group regularly meets up for dinner or drinks. Daly's and Wellington's are popular pit stops on Friday night.

And finally...

For those who want solid commercial training in an office where people know each other, D&W is a good choice. Its roots may be in Scotland, but the firm's eyes are on London right now.

DWF LLP

The facts

Location: Liverpool, Manchester, Leeds, Preston, London

Number of UK partners/solicitors: 129/285

Total number of trainees: 38

Seats: 4x4 + 1x8 months

Alternative seats: Secondments

On chambersstudent.co.uk
- How to get into DWF
- Interesting recent DWF cases
- Some of the firm's tasty clients

This northern but increasingly national firm just keeps on growing.

Land of Leaither

Between the millennium and 2007, Liverpool and Manchester-based DWF doubled in size. Then a merger with fellow northerner Ricksons added another £21m of annual turnover plus additional offices in Preston and Leeds. Incredibly, the Leeds office has shot up from 24 to 170 staff in the three years since, while DWF's first ever London office opened in May 2008 and already has 70 staff. Not bad work during the worst recession in generations. This hair-raising expansion helped turnover jump 17% in 2009/10 to £71.5m.

Impressive earnings have enabled DWF to continue a strategy of lateral recruiting and invest in new offices in Liverpool and Leeds. Manchester will upgrade soon. DWF now ranks well inside the UK's top 50 law firms, but managing partner Andrew Leaitherland – who became top dog in 2006, aged just 36 – told us he's hungry for more growth. This success is "*a start rather than a finish,*" he said. "*Our strategy is to be in the top 30 in two years, and I think it's eminently achievable.*"

With an ever-expanding roster of regional and big-name clients like Santander, Allianz Cornhill, HBOS and ASDA, it's hard to disagree. Team hires since 2007 include a top-ranked private client and family team from Cobbetts, real estate teams from DLA Piper and Hammonds, and most recently insurance lawyers from Barlow Lyde & Gilbert in London. A torrent of individual lateral hires includes Hammonds' Manchester office head into the banking team. As a glance at DWF's recent press releases shows, other bolstered groups include litigation, pensions, competition, corporate, commercial and corporate recovery. What about the dangers of expanding too quickly? Leaitherland said DWF has the right infrastructure in place, and high-calibre support includes a new finance director hired in August 2009 from Baker & McKenzie. Also, DWF's balance of business and heavyweight insurance practice mean it is cash-generative, he added.

DWF was founded in Liverpool in 1977 by current senior partner Jim Davies and property lawyer Guy Wallis. The 'F' arrived a decade later when a merger with Manchester-based Foysters created Davies Wallis Foysters. *Chambers UK* ranks the firm in over 20 separate practice areas, and trainees have a raft of seat options to sample. An almost infinite variety of insurance work provides several, ranging from motor insurance and occupational health to professional negligence claims and coverage disputes. Trainees are likely to encounter other larger departments, too, including real estate, debt recovery, private client, commercial litigation and corporate. The firm as a whole has seven national practice groups: corporate; family law and private client; finance and restructuring; insurance; litigation; people (employment and pensions); and real estate.

DWF's unique seat system is a big draw for some applicants. "*One of the things that attracted me here was the four four-month seats followed by an eight-month seat in the department you then qualify into,*" one trainee reported. In the debate over the advantages of four-month seats, here's what one trainee had to say: "*Some complain that seats are too short, and just as you're getting into one you move on, but I don't think six-month seats are any different. The extra months in your final seat are certainly*

Chambers UK rankings

Banking & Finance	Information Technology
Banking Litigation	Insurance
Construction	Intellectual Property
Corporate/M&A	Partnership
Debt Recovery	Personal Injury
Dispute Resolution	Police Law
Employment	Real Estate
Family/Matrimonial	Real Estate Litigation
Health & Safety	Restructuring/Insolvency

helpful though." Seats are available in all of the offices, including London, which plans to recruit its own trainees in the future. DWF tries to accommodate everyone's preferences but ultimately allocates them according to business need, which might require working in another office. Don't worry, the firm will pay for your commute. Plus, "*they do try to make sure you don't have to commute more than once.*"

As in previous years, some trainees weren't overly happy with not learning what their next seat would be until the last minute, especially if they have to move offices. The firm is trying to improve the rotation process, and HR now gets together with first-years to have "*an open discussion about what seats they want to do next.*" Training principal David Blaquière told us that he's "*acutely aware*" of some trainees' unhappiness with the uncertainty surrounding their next seat, but that business needs change quickly and this system ensures they're sent where they'll be busiest. What follows is a whistle-stop tour of the main seats.

Faked accidents and hit squads

Insurance-related activities account for around 45% of DWF's manpower and revenue. The firm offers a full range of services to insurers, loss adjusters, corporate clients, local authorities and police forces. RSA is the main client of the department's motor fraud team. "*As soon as cases become litigated they come in quick,*" a trainee explained, "*and there are lots of deadlines.*" Cases range from drivers faking accidents to people who weren't even driving their car when it had a prang, but claim they were. Trainees in the (defendant) motor insurance seat are responsible for running lower-value files, drafting defences and reviewing medical records. They may also attend trials. "*I wouldn't want to qualify here, but it was good to run my own files from start to finish,*" one admitted.

The commercial insurance department acts for the likes of Admiral and Brit Insurance in areas such as professional negligence and recovery (where an insurer tries to recover what it can from whoever's fault it was for a particular mishap). Other work involves defending the Met Police against claims. This is "*very complex work with a lot of legal research,*" according to one trainee. The department became unpopular among trainees at the start of 2010 because of a major SRA intervention into a troubled law firm. "*It was a case of DWF going into another firm* [Wolstenholmes] *and taking away all the papers,*" one explained. "*We went in like a hit squad and then had to put 500 to 600 boxes of documents on a database.*" Not the most riveting work, we agree, but that wasn't the end of it. Once Wolstenholmes' clients found out what was happening there was a flood of anxious and/or angry phone calls, which trainees handled after emergency coaching.

Insurance seats like occupational health and catastrophic injury are "*usually pretty safe, as you're almost guaranteed a job,*" our sources believed. In the occupational health team, a typical scenario sees an insurer instructing DWF to represent an employer accused of being liable for an accident. "*We did a lot of work for scaffolding companies and nightclubs where people have fallen over.*" Volume is the name of the game in 'Resolution Law', which is the firm's separately branded claimant PI practice. Not for the squeamish, the department advises on every kind of personal injury A&E units have ever patched up, from car crash bashes to workplace wounds to childbirth injuries. DWF has conducted over 40,000 PI claims over the past decade, ranging from minor scrapes to the most severe situations including brain damage. There is additionally a volume-based defendant PI team.

Unpaid bills and dodgy wills

Tasks in the popular employment seat include the usual bundling and helping fee earners prepare for tribunals, but also taking witness statements and attending small hearings where advocacy is a possibility. One source enthused: "*I've enjoyed all my seats, but especially employment because of the advocacy. There's contentious and non-contentious work, so it covers the full range of legal skills you might ever need.*" This team has been busy advising clients on redundancy, restructuring, reduced hours, increased litigation, strikes and other issues. The team also provides employment training to clients such as the College of Law, BPP, BAE, Kellogg, M&S and the Methodist Church.

In the family seat, there are "*a lot of high-value divorces*" involving businesspeople, sports stars and other wealthy individuals, which means there's "*not a lot you can run on your own.*" One case in the related private client seat concerned an alleged forged will: one daughter of the deceased was left just £1 by her mother, while her sister received £300,000. Non-contentious private client work brings masses of client contact and trainees are "*constantly out of the office,*" visiting clients' homes or care homes to sort out wills or trusts.

The debt recovery department has boomed during the recession, and DWF has consolidated its position as a leading provider of such services. In the final months of 2009 and the first months of 2010, it was instructed on over 84,000 commercial and consumer debt cases, with a value of £133m. One trainee described their experience here as "*a bit of a strange one, just chasing payments on behalf of administrators for companies in administration. I didn't enjoy it,*" even if it was "*character-building... I'd call lists of debtors and ask if they were willing to reduce the debt, and negotiate repayment schedules.*" On the consumer side, ASDA recently appointed DWF to track down motorists who fail to pay for fuel at its pumps. Focusing on slightly higher-value claims, the finance litigation team represents banks and other lenders. "*For example, if you got a finance deal on a car and defaulted on payment, we'd draft the claim form.*" Our sources had enjoyed "*decent responsibility running files and attending hearings.*"

In the deal zone

Owing to the economy, this year fewer of our interviewees had spent time in the real estate group – actually one of DWF's biggest practices. The group has continued to tick along, however, including advising Manchester and Liverpool city councils on regeneration projects. DWF is legal adviser to John Moores University on various issues including real estate, and the Liverpool real estate team was recently appointed to Santander's legal panel. The team frequently collaborates with other specialist teams, like planning, construction, property litigation and property tax, all of which have grown. Turnover from property litigation shot up 50% in 2008/09 as the credit crisis caused havoc. It rose another 30% in 2009/10.

Corporate deal flow slowed but DWF kept its teams relatively busy, for example advising entrepreneur Ranjit Boparan on the acquisition of restaurant chain FishWorks out of administration. Key industries are food (Burton's Foods and Princes are clients), retail (Lidl and Iceland), real estate, limited liability partnerships, charities, education and insurance. Trainees described the experience as "*very pressured, and the hours had peaks and troughs.*" It's perfectly possible that at times corporate trainees will also be asked to assist another group, such as the "*academically challenging*" commercial/IP team.

VIP offices

The Liverpool office is in the trendy St Paul's Square development. "*The building is fantastic,*" a trainee gushed, telling us about a subsidised bistro on the seventh floor. Catering staff also "*come down at 3pm every day and hand out drinks and nibbles.*" The Manchester staff will leave dated premises at the end of 2010, and their move can't come soon enough as their old "*tall, thin building has a lot of floors*" so "*it can be tricky to meet others.*" The newish office in Leeds at Bridgewater Place is "*very nice, open-plan and on just two floors.*" The insurance-led Preston branch is "*very different;*" it's an old office on the "*beautiful*" and historic Winckley Square, where once upon an industrial revolution, Preston's nouveau riche built their homes. Today, "*it's where all the law firms are based.*" On King William Street in the City, the London office celebrated its second anniversary in summer 2010. Two trainees from northern offices were doing a seat here when we conducted interviews, and in future DWF aims to recruit trainees directly to the capital and provide a full-service offering in time. As a smaller office, London has "*fabulous camaraderie,*" although "*funnily enough there's not a massive social life.*"

A formal training programme includes monthly breakfast meetings. "*I feel we get a lot of training, and you can request it,*" said one source. "*I've noticed training improve,*" another observed. "*As there are more trainees now, they have inductions for some departments like commercial litigation and real estate.*"

Trainees are attracted by DWF's friendly, down-to-earth nature. "*I liked the culture and the values. This was the only large firm I met that appealed,*" one said. Last year Liverpool trainees organised their own long weekend away together in Bremen, home of Beck's beer. Alas, the brewery was closed and there "*wasn't much to do,*" but a good time was had by all nevertheless. Manchester's "*friendly, sociable*" activities have included trips to the Comedy Store, pub quizzes, and a skiing/snowboarding trip to The Chill Factore near Junction 10 on the M60. Departmental Christmas parties usually involve a "*nice meal*" and sometimes ice-skating. There are fewer trainees in Leeds and we hear "*they don't go out as much.*" Sports include footy, netball, cricket and running, and we can't sign off without mentioning the ever-popular 'Friday Fridge'. Every last Friday of the month, staff down tools at 4.30pm and dash to a booze-filled chiller.

And finally...

DWF's *"very entrepreneurial, innovative, energetic"* culture goes hand in hand with a good work-life balance. In 2010, qualification numbers were finalised as late as mid-September, but a very healthy 17 of the 19 qualifiers stayed on.

Edwards Angell Palmer & Dodge UK LLP

The facts

Location: London

Number of UK partners/solicitors: 22/24

Total number of trainees: 16

Seats: 4x6 months

Alternative seats: Secondments

Extras: Pro bono – RCJ CAB, Fair Trials International, LawWorks

On chambersstudent.co.uk

- How to get into EAPD
- Pro bono at the firm
- EAPD's varied litigation caseload
- The City's ancient Coffee houses

Insurance is at the heart of this litigation-focused transatlantic firm. A push in IP, private equity and competition law is, however, expanding the seat menu.

Make room

Since its creation in 2005, when Boston firm Edwards & Angell united with Rhode Island firm Palmer & Dodge, EAPD has grown across 11 US cities. On 1 January 2008 it acquired a UK base in the form of London insurance law stalwart Kendall Freeman. London was EAPD's first office abroad, but it quickly also established an offshore insurance and reinsurance practice in Bermuda, and a few months later opened in Hong Kong. During that one year, EAPD took a giant step closer to becoming a major international law firm. Today, it has some 600 lawyers worldwide, though with just 46 (+16 trainees) in London, the UK arm remains relatively small.

London has leveraged EAPD's reputation in the USA to further strengthen its core insurance litigation business. Similarly, to match the firm's profile on the other side of the pond, it is growing an IP team and private equity and venture capital practices. Competition law is another area of investment. Lateral hires are helping the push forward, and as one trainee commented: "*The old office will still be recognisable in a few years' time but there will be a new balance.*"

Growth in London led to a move from Fetter Lane to Old Broad Street, where the firm now occupies the ninth to 11th storeys of Dashwood House. The new office is more modern and significantly more spacious than EAPD's previous digs, although new hires are expected to fill vacant areas over time. The trainee intake remains consistent, however, with up to eight newbies joining each year.

Insurance and Co.

At the heart of any discussion about EAPD is its international insurance practice. Lawyers have been involved in the litigation and arbitration of insurance and reinsurance claims arising out of many, many things – asbestos, the credit crisis, aviation, natural disasters such as hurricanes Katrina, Rita and Ike (including damage caused to oil wells in the Gulf of Mexico), large-scale personal injury reinsurance and professional liability claims. New points of law are sometimes made when parties get into "*a fight,*" and trainees quickly learn that insurance policies must be visited and revisited to determine just who is eligible for what coverage. The work is complex and "*a bit alien when you first come to it,*" and tends to revolve around "*disputes between big and sophisticated companies.*" It's contract law "*but with more technical elements,*" and "*disputes are often more academic than other types of litigation.*"

Insurance cases can also be of such high value that they entail "*endless meetings to discuss two words*" and this makes it "*more partner and associate-led.*" Whether trainees are drafting witness statements, listening in on negotiations or proof-reading, "*you have to use your brain.*" Moving away from disputes, EAPD also advises insurance companies on transactional and regulatory matters. With such a clear focus for so many of the firm's lawyers, it should not surprise you that the training scheme reflects this sector bias.

Chambers UK rankings

Dispute Resolution	Intellectual Property
Insurance	Public International Law

Dodgy dealings

EAPD trainees feel the firm successfully accommodates their practice preferences but warn that applicants should expect at least two contentious seats, usually insurance litigation and commercial litigation. They can also rotate between competition, employment, insolvency, IP and private equity options, splitting their time across emerging areas where full-time seats aren't yet established. Secondments to clients such as the Enforcement Division of the FSA, Shell and Harrods are popular and leave trainees feeling like "*part of a legal team where there's no divide.*" Overseas postings are available in Hong Kong and the US. The nature of the work in these seats is dependent entirely on business needs.

Let's look at some of the seats, first visiting the contentious departments. Here, "*disputes can go on for years,*" which means no guarantee of court time for a trainee, as everything depends on the stage a case has reached in the litigation lifecycle. Luckily, the trainees we spoke to had been to court, sometimes on their own for small pre-trial tasks. They might go along to hearings with witnesses, and they sometimes meet with clients alone, "*which is scary but good.*" Commercial litigation, in particular, can offer "*fantastic client contact.*" EAPD is one of the few firms in the UK that offers exposure to public international law (PIL). Anyone interested in high-stakes anti-corruption and government-related issues will love it but must be flexible about the work they get. "*Cases don't come along regularly, but when they do they are huge,*" said a trainee. The PIL team recently advised the government of the Turks & Caicos Islands following an inquiry that unearthed serious corruption by several of its members and other parties. Partner James Maton also gives pro bono support to anti-corruption NGOs. For more on this very rare training opportunity, plus examples of commercial and insurance cases, go to our website.

The regulatory and transactional group now works on an even more international basis than before the EAPD tie-up. The transatlantic influence is unmistakable in London, where workloads and practice groups intertwine with the US offices. That said, the UK operation still has its own markets and is the closest tie to the firm's Hong Kong branch. The Bermuda law capability is also an important addition. Transactional seats combine "*a lot of classic trainee jobs like producing bundles and first drafts of documents*" with "*involvement with clients right away.*" On huge matters trainees find themselves closely supervised, but they can take on decent responsibility on "*side issues.*" One of EAPD's typical smaller mid-market deals might involve investment into or a merger between insurance-related companies. The relatively new private equity team does not yet take its own trainee but "*can utilise any associate or trainee within the broader corporate department,*" and the firm has said that making a seat possible here is a priority.

Food for thought

Some trainees report ten-hour days in busy seats. Staying until 8pm "*wouldn't be exceptional, but 1am would be.*" Our sources felt well supported: they sit with an associate or partner and are also allocated a partner-level mentor and a junior-level buddy – "*someone to take us out for lunch and another for coffee!*" Trainees easily develop relationships. "*You'll work with most lawyers in your department and, a year in, you'll know most of the people in the office.*" Furthermore, "*you're not ever given a task and just told to come back with the answer.*"

The in-house training and development programme includes department-specific presentations, workshops, advocacy training and guest speakers. "*Most supervisors are happy to help you develop your interests*" and encourage trainees along to marketing events. Firm socials are another networking must. "*They really want you to be yourself,*" insisted a source. Office managing partner Laurence Harris "*makes a big effort*" by including trainees in 'thinking dinners', during which they can ask questions about EAPD's strategy. A social committee organises big summer and winter bashes, comedy nights, paintball sessions and sports events, for example an annual football match that pitches staff against each other. "*I don't think the partners have ever won, but they did quite well last year,*" chuckled a trainee. Ahead of Friday afternoon drinks "*e-mails start going around at about 12 noon,*" though no one feels pressured into "*compulsory socialising.*" In 2010, five out of seven qualifying trainees stayed with the firm.

And finally...

"*You won't have studied it at law school,*" but insurance can be a very engaging field. The industry sector accounts for at least two-thirds of EAPD's business, so take the time to learn more about it.

Stefanie Sahla
Trainee Solicitor, London

Eversheds LLP

The facts

Location: Birmingham, Cambridge, Cardiff, Ipswich, Leeds, London, Manchester, Newcastle, Nottingham

Number of UK partners/solicitors: 293/1216

Total number of trainees: 122

Seats: 4x6 months

Alternative seats: Overseas seats, secondments

Extras: Pro bono – Mary Ward Centre and various other schemes; language training

On chambersstudent.co.uk
- How to get into Eversheds
- GAMS and The Clients' Revolution
- More info on seats

"There's a lot more ambition in the firm, I would say. If you wanted to plod, it's not the right place to be any more."

All things to all men

Eversheds' metamorphosis from regional to international firm continues apace. A leaner business model, more decisive leadership, new offices speckling the globe, a changing culture and an increasing presence in London are clarion calls for a new kind of applicant.

Changes in the legal market were expedited by the recession and, as revenues of many top UK firms level out, new growth strategies are being pursued. Rather than targeting a certain type or value of work, Eversheds wants to provide full-service advice on everything from 'nuts and bolts' matters through to more complicated issues. It wants to do this all over the world, but does not want to diminish its UK regional presence. Bold ambitions.

To achieve this, 'Networked Law' is Eversheds' secret weapon, and this basically means the ability to move work between offices, making use of regional specialties, capacity and regional price differences to tackle a greater range of work at a greater range of prices. Eversheds is already doing this for Tyco, Nestlé and software company Polaris, which it advises on all European, Middle Eastern and African matters. In July 2010, R&R Ice Cream selected Eversheds to assist on the takeover of French ice cream company Rolland – a cross-border deal for a company that has a presence in 18 countries worldwide and therefore needs an adviser with people on the ground in several places.

Eversheds' rampant expansion overseas – it has 47 offices globally – doesn't mean that its UK base has lost importance. Its lawyers get more *Chambers UK* rankings than any other firm; the London office is being scaled-up to become the firm's major international hub; and in addition to working on matters passed to them through the network, the regional offices are still winning local mandates. As one Leeds trainee pointed out: "*There are plenty of national companies based in the regions, and some international ones – it's not all centred on London.*"

All systems go

A key element of the firm's plan is to improve its international finance offering in London. To get the ball rolling, it has hired two new partners to target the big financial institutions. Another area in which the firm is performing strongly is pensions. Alongside Lovells and A&O, Eversheds has advised on pensions issues following the demerger of Wireless Worldwide from the Cable & Wireless Group. And, with Linklaters, it's worked on a pension recovery agreement between British Airways and two final-salary pension funds in order to clear the way for the airline's merger with Iberia. In both matters, billions were at stake.

A significant step in the firm's mission to become more "*client centred*" was the ground-breaking relationship with Tyco, for which the firm developed its Global Account Management System (GAMS) and new billing methods to meet the demands of a more price-sensitive client base. Understanding this 'partnership' style relationship is important so go online for more info. For now, let's examine the training contract.

Chambers UK rankings

Administrative & Public Law	Licensing
Aviation	Local Government
Banking & Finance	Media & Entertainment
Banking Litigation	Outsourcing
Capital Markets	Parliamentary & Public Affairs
Competition/European Law	Partnership
Construction	Pensions
Consumer Finance	Pensions Litigation
Corporate/M&A	Personal Injury
Data Protection	Planning
Debt Recovery	Private Equity
Defamation/Reputation Management	Product Liability
Dispute Resolution	Professional Discipline
Education	Professional Negligence
Employee Share Schemes	Projects
Employment	Public International Law
Energy & Natural Resources	Public Procurement
Environment	Real Estate
Financial Services	Real Estate Finance
Fraud	Real Estate Litigation
Health & Safety	Restructuring/Insolvency
Healthcare	Retail
Information Technology	Shipping
Insurance	Tax
Intellectual Property	Telecommunications
Investment Funds	Transport

Around the network: pt1

Trainees are hired by individual offices, but all seats across the network are available to all trainees, and it is possible for them to qualify into another office. All offices have seats available in the core sectors of corporate, commercial, HR and pensions, litigation and real estate, and some have niche practices – eg the shipping practice is in Newcastle and the bulk of the renewable energy team is in Cardiff. If taking London seats, regional trainees get bumped up to the London salary, and those who venture beyond the capital for a single seat retain their higher salary. As a result there's more competition for London seats and NQ roles than those in the regions. The most important message on seats though is that if a trainee consistently hankers after a certain department, they'll probably get it. We didn't hear any complaints over seat allocation, which is pretty remarkable for a firm of this size. Overseas seats and client secondments are open to trainees in all locations.

In the far north, although the office is not the biggest in Newcastle – Dickinson Dees and Ward Hadaway are larger – Eversheds is the biggest firm with a Newcastle office. The Newcastle market took a hit from the recession but, according to trainees, Networked Law "*helped out, although it's no panacea because only so much can be sent our way.*" Nonetheless, trainees report interesting public sector work for universities, councils, hospitals, regional development agencies and PFIs, much of which goes through the "*interesting and well-supervised*" construction team. Public sector clients are important to the firm as a whole: they have lately provided one fifth of its revenue. The Newcastle office is strong in core areas like dispute resolution, real estate, employment and corporate, and differentiates itself from the rest of the network by having a shipping team that handles wet and dry matters. One satisfied trainee was exposed to "*ship finance, charter party disputes, contract writing and some salvage-related stuff – it's different every day.*" The office is open plan and trainees "*know most people.*" Its Friday drinks crew is "*a solid crowd,*" and trainees usually go for a meal together at seat change time.

The office in "*always pretty*" Cambridge is grouped together with the one in "*not as pretty*" Ipswich. East of England trainees take seats in both, and because of the lower overheads in the region, "*see a lot of the more cost-sensitive work, in addition to work from the region and some London work too.*" They consider themselves to be integrated with the local market and "*have a lot of regional clients who you get to go out and meet.*" Differentiating them from other firms, they say "*people at Mills & Reeve across the road* [in Cambridge] *might disagree, but this is the most ambitious firm in the area.*" As in the other regional offices, there's a London tinge to things, with slightly longer hours creeping in and flexible working systems being touted as the future. "*We're not in London so I don't think it will ever be terrible,*" said one trainee. Cambridge has a specialist education practice, which is particularly noted for setting up international collaborations and overseas franchises for UK institutions. Ipswich has a highly regarded personal injury team.

The Nottingham office has around 120 people and handles plenty of cross-office work with Manchester, Leeds, Birmingham, Cambridge and London. Its smaller size promotes a sociable atmosphere and recent events have included spring and Christmas parties, team lunches, cycling in the Peak District and a trip to Alton Towers ("*conference and meetings in the morning, rides in the afternoon*"). With it being smaller, "*your reputation travels through the office, so if you can handle a lot of responsibility and client contact, the firm will give it to you.*" Nottingham is a key location for IT work, which is to be found within the broader commercial department.

Around the network: pt 2

Trainees in the cities of Cardiff, Birmingham, Leeds and Manchester all felt they received the quality work they'd expected, and were pleased by the calibre of Eversheds' clients. Trainees in Birmingham and Manchester commented that their local markets had been hit hard during the recession, but said that the size of Eversheds' clients had insulated them against the worst of it. Some explained that they spent most of their time working on large matters for national clients based in the regions, and that although there was some cross-office work and certainly some 'London scale' work, it mostly came from their own region. Some experienced internationally flavoured deals, and the work of the renewable energy team, mainly based in Cardiff, is a good example. This team handles various high-profile matters, including one of the world's largest offshore wind projects for npower renewables at Gwynt-y-Mor. Based off the North Wales coast, it will have 160 turbines. Another deal was the £1.3bn acquisition of a 50% interest in the Sheringham Shoal offshore wind project, which is just off the north Norfolk coast. Eversheds' Legal Systems Group (LSG), based in Cardiff, provides volume legal services to the UK's leading banks, building societies, insurance companies, self-insured organisations in both private and public sectors, insurance brokers, major plcs and private companies.

Capital concerns

In a network that aims eventually to bridge the whole world, London is being developed as the firm's keystone. Here, talented lawyers will draw in new, higher-value instructions from international clients. "*London offers so much that you can't get elsewhere. Not just work, but also the networks and the people you meet.*" Yes, the firm offers 'London-style work in the regions', but really the best place for 'London work' is… London. When the office building at 1 Wood Street opened, Eversheds commissioned a video in which some guy starts leaping and flipping energetically around the new HQ. Vaulting ambition being Eversheds' new modus operandi, the supporting cast of receptionists don't look too shocked.

So what have the London teams been up to? One deal will ring bells with many law students: Eversheds acted as lead adviser to Apollo on the £303m takeover of BPP Holdings, one of the largest UK public company takeovers in 2009. BPP is not only a law school, it's actually Europe's largest accountancy training company. Litigators, meanwhile, worked for Lion Apparel Systems, which is part of the world's largest supplier of personal protective equipment. Eversheds assisted the company in challenging the public procurement process followed by Firebuy, which is part of the Department for Communities and Local Government. Up for grabs was a 15-year contract to supply fire fighters' protective clothing, valued at £400m.

For much more on the different seat experiences around the network, go online.

New era Eversheds

Do your research on Eversheds and you may unearth some press reports that suggest a scene of Promethean toil and blunt dissatisfaction. Current trainees admitted that "*the push towards being an international firm, and the move away from being a smaller regional firm, do make for some tension because some people had always wanted to work for a small firm.*" For the new breed of Eversheds trainee, "*phasing in the magic circle way of doing things*" has been a positive thing. Said one: "*It's a change I'm happy to embrace.*" Another suggested that if people don't like the new direction, "*they should just move firm, not ask why we can't go back to how we were.*" As the focus on billing becomes more profound and the working hours lengthen, pay packets get fatter too. Trainees seemed happy.

Simply put, the culture is being toughened up. "*Decision by committee has definitely disappeared so we can make business decisions quicker. Performance has risen. One change that might have upset people is we used to do AGMs where there'd be pantomimes and things. Sports days… stuff like that… some would say that the fun has gone out of it…*" said a source, wandering down a cul-de-sac of nostalgia. "*That sort of thing isn't ruled out for the future, but you don't want to be doing that during a recession when you have to be more performance-driven.*" The other key thing to know about the culture is how commercially oriented it is. Said one super-savvy trainee: "*Clients comment on how much more commercially aware Eversheds is than its competitors. In the background there's still loads of legal research and looking at the law, but reporting to the client we try not to quote the law back at them, but put it in terms they understand; ones that are meaningful commercially.*"

This revolution within the firm has come at a cost. Post-credit crunch, Eversheds laid off more people than any other law firm in the UK. Arguably it would have restructured anyway and the recession was merely the catalyst. "*The firm was a bit flabby and inefficient. It needed to be more efficient.*" Cuts were made from the partnership all the way down through the business – no doubt a major factor in the firm's poor placing in recent satisfaction surveys. Now it is leaner, has outsourced many support functions overseas and boasts a higher profit margin. In 2009/10, partner profits rose despite a not-too-bad 3% drop in revenue to £355m. This figure places it in the UK's top-ten law firms as measured by revenue.

And what of the qualification prospects for those completing their training contracts in the new-look firm? In 2010, 71 out of 87 qualifiers took positions across the UK offices.

And finally...

Eversheds saw a new era approaching and responded quickly. This required steely pragmatism and a change in the working culture, but for current applicants with an ambitious streak, this is all good news.

- **Commercial awareness:** One recruiter told us just how much sympathy he has for 20-year-olds who are asked to be commercially aware. "It's about a state of mind, not just quoting the FT. You get it from thinking about the world from a business standpoint."

Farrer & Co LLP

The facts

Location: London

Number of UK partners/solicitors: 77/100

Total number of trainees: 20

Seats: 6x4 months

Alternative seats: Secondments

Extras: Language classes

On chambersstudent.co.uk
- How to get into Farrer
- The firm's CSR initiatives
- Farrer's fabulous history

With a spread of departments, A-list clients and charming eccentricities to spare, Farrer & Co is a London institution without being an antique.

Banks, bangers and bris

Farrer can officially mark its history from 1701, though according to the comprehensive timeline on its website, it was actually founded earlier. We're not going to quibble with the Queen's solicitors over a couple of years of history. It's probably enough that The Bank of England's charter was sealed in the Peacock Room on the ground floor of Farrer's Lincoln's Inn office in 1694. And we love the fact that Charles Dickens was a client. For those with affection for the past, there's no question that Farrer is steeped in lore. But it is also evolving, with refurbished facilities, innovative clients outside its traditional sectors and a vision for future growth.

Since 1769 when Mr Oliver Farrer became sole partner, the name has been synonymous with refined legal service to the aristocracy. Farrer solicitors quite literally wrote the book on farms and estates (see *Farms and Estates – A Conveyancing Handbook* by Henry Goulding and Christopher Jessel). With clients like the Duchy of Cornwall (a major source of income for the Prince of Wales and the birthplace of Duchy Originals sausages) and the Duchy of Lancaster it's easy to see why the firm is in the top tier of *Chambers UK* for agricultural and rural affairs.

The charities team is also exceptional: clients include the Royal British Legion, 12 out of the 15 London national museums, and universities including Oxford and Imperial College. The broad practice handles advisory and contentious work and has counselled various organisations on loss of exempt charity status because of changing rules in the past year. Recently, the team represented United Synagogue (the largest synagogal body in Europe) before the new Supreme Court, contesting a Court of Appeal ruling that a Jewish voluntary-aided school's use of a strict definition of Jewish heritage in its admissions criteria constituted racial discrimination.

From blue bloods to red tops

In addition to well-heeled individuals and venerable institutions, Farrer also represents journalists. While it counsels erudite publications like *The Economist* and the *Financial Times*, its big-money work comes from advising a slew of tabloid newspapers (*The Sun*, *The Daily Mail*, *News of the World*) on matters where there are clashes between individuals' rights to privacy and newspapers' rights to freedom of expression. Farrer's media team is particularly savvy at pre-publication review and defamation law and recently represented News Group Newspapers in a privacy claim brought by Ashley Cole over accounts of his alleged extramarital affairs. In less salacious news, the team also represented *The Economist* in a libel claim brought by a Russian billionaire who was unhappy with his company's portrayal in an article about the oil industry.

While proud of its heritage and history, Farrer is not opposed to changing with the times. Recently, it has made a push to develop areas outside of its traditional strengths. Chief Operating Officer Ben Bennett explained: *"Farrer has always had a reputation for private client work, and the personal service that comes with that is very much*

Chambers UK rankings

Agriculture & Rural Affairs	Financial Services
Charities	Intellectual Property
Corporate/M&A	Media & Entertainment
Defamation/Reputation Management	Partnership
	Private Client
Education	Professional Discipline
Employment	Real Estate
Family/Matrimonial	Sports Law

part of our ethos. But the firm is much more than that now and we are continuing to enhance our corporate and commercial areas to provide the specialist services that our business and institutional clients require." In November 2009, the firm brought property finance partner John Clark to its banking team, and in January 2010 took on three partners and a consultant from City firms to boost its corporate group. Sources also reported an influx of junior and mid-level hires. Time will tell if this growth alters the atmosphere, work-life balance and quirks that are uniquely Farrer's, but our contented trainee sources certainly hoped not.

Trainees "*think six seats are 100% necessary for a firm where there are so many practice areas,*" and fortunately six seats are exactly what is offered. Trainees had nothing but kind words for the seat allocation system and "*fantastic*" grad recruitment guru Donna Davies. They must complete seats in one department from each of four main practice blocks: property (estates and private property or commercial), litigation (media and disputes or family), commercial (corporate; banking and financial services; IP or employment), and private client (onshore; offshore; tax or charities). The fifth seat is a "*wild card,*" while the last is typically a repeat in the department in which they hope to qualify. If past years are any indication, trainees will stay beyond the final seat as Farrer has a stellar retention rate. "*There's still the philosophy that trainees are here to stay, not just to train,*" and all ten stayed put in 2010.

Lives of the rich and infamous

Of the "*really quirky and really interesting*" private client department, trainees say: "*We have the sort of clients who would be at the top of anyone's wish list.*" It's no longer just royalty and landed gentry; we're talking about entrepreneurs and charitable foundations, schools and universities, Russian oligarchs, media moguls and politicians. This seat can involve field trips, including running off to a deceased person's home to turn off the gas, making "*probate runs*" to the courts and the occasional deathbed will.

Trainees have less interaction with the superwealthy since partners tend to have established relationships as their trusted advisers. In the highly ranked family law team, however, they have "*a lot of client contact early on.*" With London such a favourable jurisdiction for wives separating from wealthy husbands, these lawyers see many international divorces involving complex assets. Prenuptial agreements, custody issues and even child abductions also come into play. While the firm has some "*less affluent*" clients, most work is "*big-money stuff. I'm scared by all the zeros,*" one source said. In the family seat, clients will often call trainees directly with questions, which is "*terrifying but great.*"

The recently combined media and disputes seat is extremely popular given the "*glamorous*" work on offer. With the firm's many newspaper clients, injunctive work is prevalent: "*It's very sensitive, confidential and time-pressured, but really exciting.*" Trainees will do a lot of Internet research and "*hands-on work taking evidence from a witness*" to evaluate whether a story is accurate and in the public interest. What sort of stories are we talking about? "*The newspapers will call up the partners and say, 'We want to print this about X, is that okay?' And the partners will say, 'Don't use that word. Better to use this word.'*"

In IP and commercial seats, trainees tackle work in unexpected areas. These departments serve the galleries and museums sector, and one recent IP matter involved the copyright of paintings. Sports law also falls under the commercial umbrella and the group represents four of the top six British sports governing bodies. For the Rugby Football Union, Farrer advised on its successful bid to host the 2015 Rugby World Cup in England for the first time in almost 20 years. Our sources worked on sponsorship matters, disciplinary actions and breach of contract disputes.

While trainees freely admit that "*if you have a burning desire to be a corporate lawyer, Farrer might not be your first choice,*" its corporate group has grown in recent years. While deals are smaller than you'd find at a big City firm, there are some bigger clients like Emap and the owners of delicious dim sum chain Ping Pong. Trainees particularly enjoyed working with entrepreneurs who came to the firm as private clients but then formed companies. Several reported trying lesser-known departments like corporate, financial services and banking and "*being surprised I enjoyed it quite so much.*" Several of our sources had worked on partnership agreements, especially issues arising from departures and redundancies during the recession. On a smaller-scale deal for a private company, "*you get good experience and aren't always having your hand held.*"

Tweed v Twitter?

Trainees were quick to clarify some of the misconceptions about Farrer. "*The firm is nowhere near as stuffy as it's reputed to be*" and "*it's not full of people who know the Queen and went to Eton.*" Of course, "*there are people who move in those circles.*" But while Farrer cherishes its history and retains its curiosities (including rumours of a secret vault haunted by a ghost), the firm is not stuck in the past or uptight. We encountered an array of different backgrounds and accents among the trainees.

While the main office has remained at 66 Lincoln's Inn since 1790, the firm has expanded into three other buildings (64, 65 and 67). Trainees told us they relish the "*stunning*" original offices, explaining that "*being in touch with the historical past of London did tick a few boxes. It's good to walk in and feel proud.*" They also loved "*working in this part of London, as opposed to the City which can feel sterile.*" The new buildings have recently been refurbished and are equipped with the sort of floor-to-ceiling glass conference rooms you'd expect to see in the City. They are even eco-friendly: new rooftop solar panels provide energy to heat water.

Although everyone agrees there is no Farrer "*type,*" the right sort of student will have a special engagement with the place and what it has to offer. "*It attracts people who want the whole package with their job,*" an interviewee said. While a few pointed out that the Farrer package does not include top-market compensation, all agree that "*our work-life balance is better. A couple of grand more pay is not worth sacrificing all of the great things we have here.*" Trainees really appreciated Farrer's more relaxed culture and its "*fairly reasonable and fairly predictable*" hours. Some departments (corporate, disputes, media) can involve later nights, but most trainees usually leave by 6.30pm.

The social life is robust and trainees genuinely seem to be friends. "*I'd be amazed if you didn't run into someone from Farrer at the White Horse on a Friday at 6pm,*" said one. There are plenty of other bonding opportunities. The annual staff v partners cricket match "*is quite funny,*" and an active football team plays in Kennington. Rugby is popular, with an annual "*grudge match*" against long-time client Coutts. For the musically inclined, the office has a choir.

A Christmas revue, written, performed and directed by the trainees, is a "*nerve-racking*" rite of passage and "*a bonding experience.*" Its "*typically pantomimey*" nature is quite fitting given that the father of English panto, John Rich, performed in Lincoln's Inn Fields back in 1717. Everyone at the firm is fair game for some playful mockery, although the senior partner does have to approve the script prior to the show. Boooo! Hiss! The summer party is another beloved event involving cocktails and sports. Last year's was held in Gray's Inn and involved a boules competition.

With so much fun and games going on, it's no wonder people say getting into Farrer "*is like winning the lottery.*" So how do you beat the odds? "*You have to have a bit of sparkle about you.*" And we don't mean the sparkle of diamonds. You won't find exclusively public school and Oxbridge grads at Farrer. Several sources had a previous career under their belt and the firm tells us a forty-something trainee is set to start in 2011.

And finally...

Trainees tell us: *"You have to have something about you that makes people want to talk to you and want to work with you."* After our interviews with Farrer folk, we think they're spot on.

Field Fisher Waterhouse LLP

The facts

Location: London, Manchester

Number of UK partners/solicitors: 120/179

Total number of trainees: 19

Seats: 4x6 months

Alternative seats: Brussels, secondments

Extras: Pro bono – Queen Mary Legal Advice Centre

On chambersstudent.co.uk
- How to get into FFW
- Londinium and the Square Mile
- The professional disciplinary arena

FFW's practice kaleidoscope allows for real breadth of training. Beyond corporate, IP/IT and regulatory matters there's a collection of niches to sample.

FFW®

In 2008 FFW set itself an ambitious revenue target of £200m by 2012 – more than double what it is currently. Though its profits are still on the slide, the firm remains confident. "*Obviously that goal was set before the banks fell off a cliff,*" said training partner Matthew Lohn. "*But it's still a good point to aim at. We might have to revise our time scale but we're heading towards it.*" The secret weapon? The 'Virtuous Triangle' of corporate, IP/IT and regulatory practice. "*That's where the firm sees its strengths and wants to market itself to those clients.*" FFW has even trademarked the slogan.

Geographical expansion and a growth in lawyer numbers are part of the plan too. The firm made up ten new partners in 2010 and more offices may also be on the cards. As well as London and a nine-lawyer Manchester outpost, FFW has branches in Brussels, Hamburg and Paris, and is "*looking at further European offices to reflect the demands of our clients,*" continued Lohn. "*All I can say is that we're considering two offices.*" Watch this space.

After taking the decision to defer its 2009 starters, cancelling recruitment for 2011 starts, a new team has refreshed the recruitment strategy and training contract. New from 2012 is a four-by-six-month seat rotation. Though the old six-by-four-month calendar was popular, our sources accepted that change would be good. "*Sometimes you get to the point where you're really enjoying a seat and have to move.*" Another innovation is the seat allocation system. Previously some trainees had felt aggrieved so HR introduced a spreadsheet showing everyone's previous seats and where they ranked in the trainees' choices. In a further bid "*to make it fairer,*" at each rotation trainees submit a CV and covering letter to apply for their first-choice department. Appraisals are now completed online – "*you get to appraise yourself, which is hard at first but if you do it after you complete your trainee diary you can really sell yourself.*"

The Virtuous Triangle

The corporate team is "*a very, very friendly bunch,*" and though there's always "*sheaths and sheaths*" of due diligence for trainees, "*there's interesting work too,*" such as drafting agreements and board minutes. Trainees were involved with the re-admission of Micro Focus International to the FTSE Official List, following the acquisition and reverse takeover of Borland Software Corporation for $113m. Under the corporate umbrella falls banking and finance, tax, financial services and funds. Finance trainees often "*work on bank lending to high-powered individuals, so you're involved with taking security over planes and yachts,*" and we heard of one who was invited to Biggin Hill Airport to celebrate a completion with "*champagne on a jet.*" The financial services and funds seat combines contentious and non-contentious activities, while those in the derivatives seat learn the ins and outs of industry standard agreements. The derivatives team is "*one of the friendliest*" and the only one to sit open-plan, so "*there's always someone to answer questions.*" On the downside, trainees think more bespoke training would be helpful, especially at the beginning because "*it's a complicated area that's hard to*

Chambers UK rankings

Administrative & Public Law	Outsourcing
Capital Markets	Partnership
Clinical Negligence	Pensions
Commodities	Personal Injury
Competition/European Law	Planning
Corporate/M&A	Private Equity
Data Protection	Professional Discipline
Dispute Resolution	Public Procurement
Employee Share Schemes	Real Estate
Employment	Real Estate Litigation
Financial Services	Restructuring/Insolvency
Franchising	Retail
Healthcare	Sports Law
Information Technology	Tax
Intellectual Property	Telecommunications
Investment Funds	Transport
Media & Entertainment	Travel

grasp." As yet there's no seat in FFW's Paris office, but keen linguists can faire entendre leurs voix in the corporate department, where a 'French desk' advises French clients on their UK plans.

"*Learning from amazing lawyers*" is the best thing about the IP department. It is split into three subgroups: trade marks; disputes; and commercial. The litigators are apparently "*more than happy to let you handle some things by yourself.*" Said one satisfied source: "*When I arrived I had to take notes at the Royal Courts of Justice and the Technology and Construction Court.*" FFW has one of the largest IP disputes teams in the UK and was involved in the high-profile 'smell-a-like' *L'Oréal v Bellure* case, in which the ECJ ruled that copycat products had infringed trade marks and contravened the Comparative Advertising Directive. When an Italian record producer released an unlicensed CD – *Elvis Presley Christmas Remixes* – FFW was there to advise Elvis Presley Enterprises on trade mark infringement and passing-off claims. The commercial IP team attracted almost 100 new clients in 2009, including Fortnum & Mason, Twentieth Century Fox and the Beckhams. "*You get really interesting and varied work, from franchising agreements to film financing, advertising law and sports law, as well as more general IP work,*" a trainee explained. Though events like the Cannes Film Festival are the preserve of seniors, trainees do have client contact – "*the firm's not afraid to put us in front of them.*"

The large technology team advises the likes of Google, Nectar and Mothercare plus numerous government departments. To give just two examples, as the Labour government was pushing the controversial ID card agenda, the firm was busy advising the Identity and Passport Service, and the Ministry of Justice sought assistance with arrangements for the supply of e-voting and e-counting services. The politics doesn't end there – technology partner Hamish Sandison stood for Labour in the last general election, hoping (but failing) to take Tory David Davies' seat.

Completing the Virtuous Triangle, the regulatory department "*advises regulatory bodies on their standards, develops policy guidelines and helps them run disciplinary cases.*" Clients include the General Dental Council, the Solicitors Regulation Authority, the General Social Care Council and the Rugby Football Union. FFW is also the principal external legal adviser of the General Medical Council, which it assisted with disciplinary proceedings involving Dr James Wakefield and the MMR vaccine. "*It's very hands on,*" a source explained; "*you talk to a variety of people, including clients and barristers.*" Go to our website for more on this area of practice.

If medical matters set your pulse racing, then consider the personal injury and clinical negligence department. "*It's what I came here for,*" admitted a source. "*You're dealing with people who've contracted industrial diseases in the course of their employment, so you have to locate and trawl through their insurance documents, which adds a personal investigator aspect to it.*" Trainees relish the "*human element*" to the work, as well as "*the high responsibility that comes from running your own cases.*" Charles Russell's team recently absconded to FFW.

Driving forward

"*Everyone should do a property seat,*" enthused one trainee. "*It's brilliant because you learn how to be a solicitor.*" The department works across a variety of client sectors, not least among them energy and infrastructure, the public sector and hotels and leisure. It recently advised National Grid on its natural gas pipeline system from Milford Haven to Gloucestershire – one of the largest UK civil engineering projects ever; it also acted for Donington Park racing circuit on the property and security elements of its proposed £135m bond issue, which was unable to proceed due to lack of investors. The 150-year lease then reverted to the freehold owners, the Wheatcroft family, which then granted a new one to Worcestershire-based company, the Adroit Group. Other clients include the Grand Hilton; Macquarie Bank; the trustees of the British Museum; and Luminar, the UK's largest operator of licensed late-night venues.

The stand-alone dispute resolution department offers "*the opportunity to get stuck in on some high-quality cases,*" as the team's work spans everything from arbitration and insurance/reinsurance disputes to telecommunications and travel cases. Lawyers recently represented insurer Assurant in its claim against another company, Willis, in a case that related to mid-1990s activities in the London personal accident reinsurance market. The lawyers achieved a $139m settlement for the client. "*You don't just have to do bundling and administrative jobs,*" assured a source. "*Of course there's some of that, but you get the proper work too, such as drafting witness statements and particulars of claim.*" We also heard of some who'd made court applications, as well as those who'd "*worked through the night, rushing to get an affidavit to freeze a fraudster's assets.*"

With a little understanding

A swathe of seat options – including EU and competition ("*great*") and employment ("*really interesting*") – means that the legal world really is your oyster at FFW. "*The seats on offer depend on business needs,*" recruiter Sonia Cochet explained, adding that trainees should "*just ask and we'll try to make it happen.*" Since its opening in 2007, FFW's Brussels office has been building pace, recently recruiting from A&O. A Brussels stint offers trainees a classic overseas experience, and there are also several client secondments that crop up. Lately these have included Viacom subsidiary Turner, Citibank and the Homes and Communities Agency. To say the rolling secondment gig with MTV is popular would be an understatement. Backing onto the canal at Camden Lock, MTV's open-office is "*always exciting and lively, everyone's just walking about.*" And by everyone, we include the likes of Dizzee Rascal and Sophie Ellis Bextor.

Our sources were enthusiastic about their experiences: "*The individual departments are great and you feel like part of the team.*" But examine FFW as a whole and it's a different story. Our guide once described FFW as a 'patchwork' law firm with excellent pockets of practice and slightly loose stitching. Trainee interviews still leave us with the impression the firm's different departments could be better connected. Certainly one thing our sources believed would promote cohesion is a better communal area. The office is currently split between two buildings, which "*translates to a split socially – it'd be great to have somewhere you can see everybody.*" Trainees do have "*the Bolthole*" in the basement, with pool table and wide screen TV, but "*it's very dark and nobody goes down there.*" Historians might be keen for a peek at the ancient Roman London wall that runs through the Bolthole – "*you can touch it if you like.*" A move to a single united building could be on the cards, however.

The qualification process was another area trainees said had room for improvement. "*A trainee committee meets with HR and the training partner, but with regards to qualification, the firm was too silent.*" Though our sources conceded "*it's a difficult time in the market,*" they did feel as though more information would have been helpful. Sonia Cochet explained that it can be hard for managers to predict their NQ needs well in advance, especially in this economy, so it wasn't a case of the firm deliberately withholding information from trainees. In 2010, 15 out of 21 qualifiers took jobs at the firm.

Despite grumbles about insufficient communication, there's still plenty of love for FFW. "*The firm proves that you can be human, approachable and friendly while still providing a high standard of work. It's the perfect blend.*" Supervisors are "*mostly friendly and easy to get along with,*" and "*people stay in touch when you leave a seat.*" There's no expectation to routinely stay late or, to use the old cliché, "*there's no need to hang your jacket on the back of a chair.*"

Organised socials have "*taken a nosedive recently,*" but Friday night pub-stops at Chamberlains continue to mark the end of the week. "*If a partner's there, they might end up putting their card behind the bar.*" Trainees can also get involved with football, hockey, netball, rounders and squash – there are in-house courts – as well as pro bono activities in conjunction with the Richard House care home and the Own It IP rights service.

And finally...

As well as streamlining its training contract and recruitment strategy, the firm is pushing its corporate, IP/IT and regulatory practices and looking to expand its European horizons.

Finers Stephens Innocent

The facts

Location: London

Number of UK partners/solicitors: 39/34

Total number of trainees: 7

Seats: 4x6 months

Alternative seats: None

Extras: Pro bono – LawWorks

On chambersstudent.co.uk
- How to get into FSI
- The history of the firm
- Image matters

It's aiming for *"a fresh and vibrant approach to law while still maintaining technical discipline."* Is West End firm Finers Stephens Innocent hitting the mark?

Pressing for freedom

FSI is a firm that's constantly evolving. Its history records several interesting mergers, but everything can be traced back to 1935, to a one-man shop in EC4. These days you'll find the firm just off Oxford Street in an office that features acres of glass, unique art and bright pink chairs. You'll also find it on the TV and radio, especially name partner Mark Stephens, who's provided legal commentary on current affairs more often than most lawyers have had hot dinners.

The high profile of Finers' IP/media department is the reason why. The firm's Rolodex includes international broadcasters and newspapers, publishers and distributors, dot.coms and telecoms, schools and universities, museums and galleries, artists, designers and photographers. Finers also represents celebrities like Lewis Hamilton and The Killers, although "*it would be wrong to say that* [the celeb world] *was the focus.*" Publishing is the team's stronghold. In a recent media intervention dubbed 'Alphabet Soup', a number of major publications – such as *The Guardian*, *The Times* and *The Economist*, along with news agency Associated Press – relied on FSI for their application to the Supreme Court to remove the anonymity orders granted to four terror suspects. This case – A, K, M & G v HM Treasury – was actually the first substantive matter to be heard by the new Supreme Court in October 2009. Other media and business clients look to FSI for guidance and representation in relation to reporting restrictions, defamation cases, reputation management, privacy and the avoidance of injunctions and super injunctions (as in the much-discussed Trafigura case).

In terms of IP, FSI has long represented media organisations in both contentious and non-contentious situations and is now building a presence in the fashion, art and cultural property sectors. Unsurprisingly, the IP/media seat is "*quite sought after*" by trainees and a slot there is not guaranteed. Trainees said it's the firm's "*most stressful*" department: "*There's such a high level of responsibility, but the team is quite good at figuring out who can take it. That's what sets the department apart.*"

We mustn't get carried away with all this media talk because the real estate practice is very much the backbone of the firm and completing a seat there is a given. The firm has good connections in the retail and leisure sectors, including long-standing relationships with Calvin Klein and Monsoon. More recent client wins include Sunglass Hut, Bare Escentuals and Original Penguin. Finers also has an involvement in the 2012 Olympics and Crossrail projects. The team advised over 100 businesses in the Olympic zone on their relocation as part of the largest compulsory purchase order in Europe to date. Our sources "*enjoyed the property seat more than expected,*" working on "*a lot of negotiations for leases and licences, and researching and drafting specialised clauses.*" They also "*have the opportunity to take individual responsibility for smaller files*" and never worry about back up: this

Chambers UK rankings

Corporate/M&A	Intellectual Property
Defamation/Reputation Management	Media & Entertainment
Dispute Resolution	Partnership
Employment	Real Estate
Fraud	Retail

is often the only department to have two or more trainees at the same time.

Rock legends and incredible teachers

Seats in the corporate and litigation departments are also on offer. The corporate practice specialises in AIM-related matters and recently directed NASDAQ-listed Global Traffic Network in its £15m acquisition of AIM-listed UBC Media Group's commercial division. "*There's a really nice balance between young associates and quite experienced partners,*" and trainees enjoy "*lots of client face time*" in addition to the standard "*due diligence, bibling, document management, drafting ancillary documents and big disclosure exercises.*" Meanwhile, the dispute resolution team acts on a good number of financial services disputes and is attempting to diversify its workload to include FSA regulatory work, Privy Council appellate litigation and more. The hours can become "*manic,*" especially if there's a big trial on. Nevertheless, "*the department is so gelled that if you're working late it's fine because you're working with one of the nicest teams at the firm.*" Across the firm, "*the hours are not that diabolical at all,*" with trainees reporting average days of 9.30am to between 5.30pm and 6.30pm.

The family department has a star-studded client list and recently represented the wife of an Oscar-winning film director in a cross-border divorce spanning Italy, the USA and the UK. This "*very small team*" is also developing a niche in children's cases after recently working on a high-profile abduction involving Russian parents. The seat "*is not particularly structured, but you do get exposed to all types of work and you go to a lot of magistrates' and family court hearings.*" The private client team works closely with the family team, as divorces often create the need for further estate planning. Divorced or not, clients with the 'wow' factor continue to seek out this branch of the firm – from rock legends to football stars to royalty. Trainees described the department as "*interesting, calm and open to discussion,*" and praised private client head Robert Craig for being "*a mentor for many: an incredible teacher.*"

Finers is fine

While trainees had stellar supervisors in some of their seats, they admitted to "*not having much support*" in others. It was agreed by and large that the firm is "*very friendly,*" but "*you do notice in some areas that it is a bit more hierarchical*" and "*you can feel like you're just at the bottom of a big pile at times.*" There are three graduate recruitment partners with whom trainees meet monthly, but generally they find that asserting themselves is the best way to get things done. "*Sitting back and letting things wash over you wouldn't be the best thing: you need to decide what you need and make that clear. No one is just going to come to you – you have to get out there and speak to the right people,*" one explained. "*You've got to be outgoing and have a certain amount of confidence and the ability to put yourself forward because you can be trampled if you're not standing up for yourself.*"

Assertiveness seems to be key when it comes to qualification. Jobs are announced as they become available, and announcements were left quite late in 2010 – "*a function of how tricky the market has been in the past couple of years,*" training partner Sara Wax explained. "*We do want to try and keep people as we've invested quite a lot of time in them. We're not one of those places that takes on swathes of people just to keep our numbers up. Our qualifiers have a lot more responsibility to really fill a hole rather than just be one of a block number the firm needs – it's a much more individual process.*" In 2010, three out of six qualifiers stayed at the firm.

The firm usually takes six trainees per year. "*They're not very rigid in who they recruit in terms of background,*" sources said. "*They don't discriminate against second careerers – they see that as an advantage. There are people from a lot of different backgrounds, from marketing to the army.*" To find out more about the recruitment process check our website.

A social life "*is there if you want it.*" The firm's social committee, FX, puts on wine tasting evenings, softball games, summer parties and the like. When it comes to impromptu nights out, "*different departments are very distinct – some say, 'It's Friday, let's go for a drink' and other departments don't.*"

And finally...

Trainees are invariably drawn to the firm's size, its West End location and its array of practice areas. One commented: *"At a firm like this you're involved in matters at a deeper level. There's no room to hide."*

- **Experience is vital:** You have to choose your area of law carefully because the job is very different depending on what you practise. Investigate things at an early stage so you know what you want to aim for.

Fisher Meredith LLP

The facts

Location: London

Number of UK partners/solicitors: 12/51

Total number of trainees: 14

Seats: 4x6 months

Alternative seats: Occasional secondments

On chambersstudent.co.uk
- How to get into FM
- Much more detail on the available seats
- We talk to managing partner Stephen Hewitt

If you're interested in human rights, you can't not apply to Fisher Meredith. Headquartered in Kennington in South London, it combines a Legal Aid practice with commercial and private work.

Big fish, little fish

FM is a 'mixed economy' firm – that is, it represents both publicly and privately funded clients. Currently, about 60% of its work is legally aided and 40% is privately funded, but the aim over the next few years is to reach more of a 50/50 split, or even reverse the balance in favour of private work. In a climate where Legal Aid funding is set to be cut to its bare bones, this shift is the only way the firm can remain profitable and continue Legal Aid services, to which it remains firmly committed.

FM was founded in Stockwell in 1975, and in 2010 opened a second office in Richmond. There is also talk of having a central London office one day. Litigation-focused, the firm is particularly strong on police and prison law, immigration, debt recovery, education and social housing. Its clients include individuals referred by organisations and charities such as domestic violence support group The Gaia Centre and The Refugee Council. Many of the cases are high-profile: in the past FM has acted for Sonia Sutcliffe, wife of the Yorkshire Ripper, and a suspect in the failed London bombings of July 2005. It additionally worked on the Deptford Fire and Damilola Taylor cases. Business clients include major companies, trades unions, charities and foreign embassies, among them John Lewis, the National Association of Head Teachers, Shelter and the Royal Embassy of Saudi Arabia.

Trainees can take seats in the following fields: civil litigation; police and prison law; children and family; housing; public service law (PSL, which includes education); and immigration. From next year "*there will be more seats in private areas.*" There is also a permanent trainee position at the private-only Richmond office. The firm's private departments include family, employment, property and private client. In the largely private civil litigation department, the work "*could be anything*" – negligence claims, actions against local authorities, disputes under the Water Act, landlord and tenant disputes or contract disputes. In order to maximise their experience during the four-seat contract, trainees are likely to complete two stints in the area they're most interested in. An HR source also told us that while there are no client secondments, FM "*has sometimes offered secondments to other law firms. One of our trainees wanted to experience a criminal seat, so was seconded to a Legal Aid crime firm.*"

FM's own crime department has been private-only since 2008. Its work covers commercial fraud, white-collar crime, affray, actual bodily harm, rape, drink driving and benefit fraud. The police and prison law seat involves civil actions against the police and the Home Office, and cases of people who are in the wrong category of prison or whose rights are being abused. The firm is currently representing 12 women who claim they were unnecessarily detained, assaulted and racially abused by officers at the Yarl's Wood detention centre, following a hunger strike.

Chambers UK rankings

Civil Liberties	Immigration
Debt Recovery	Police Law
Family/Matrimonial	Social Housing

Normally we'd go into much more detail about the available seats, but with so much else to talk about, we're going to skip that bit. Never fear: just go to our website for the full story on life in all the different departments.

Anger management

One thing to keep in mind is that at this firm *"you will meet vulnerable or difficult clients from day one."* We're talking about asylum seekers, suicidal clients and clients with mental health problems. For this reason, the firm looks for trainees who have had experience in a people-facing role, and especially contact with individuals in difficult situations. Clients *"can be challenging quite regularly, especially prisoners and young offenders, who often have a lot of baggage."* If they're distressed or angry, you have to understand that *"it's a stressful and upsetting time for them, especially when children are involved."* When you have *"two parents at each other's throats in a waiting room, it's up to you to keep the peace. You have to make sure your client doesn't do something to damage their case."*

So it's not just about legal magnificence. The job requires *"a lot of diplomacy and skills of persuasion,"* as you need to make sure clients understand that you're on their side and that *"you have their best interests at heart and are doing the best you can for them."* Sometimes they just won't take your advice, and they often have an unrealistic view of how things should pan out, so trainees have to be careful in managing expectations. At times you will need to be firm, and on occasion you *"have to accept there is very little you can do."* The whole thing can be *"very emotionally draining."* The open-plan set-up is good for picking up tips *"by overhearing how other people deal with difficult clients on the phone."*

The working day is officially 9.30am to 5pm, but trainees usually leave between 6.30pm and 7pm. A 10pm finish is not unheard of in the immigration and PSL teams; however, *"in most departments staying late is not expected, especially for trainees."* If it all gets a bit much, people are there to help. Trainees agreed that the *"level of supervision is really good. We get a lot of support."* Responsibility increases over time, but *"everything has to be checked, even very short letters in your fourth seat – the firm takes it seriously."*

For love, not money

"No one comes into Legal Aid for the money, that's for sure." First-year trainees start on £21,000 while the salary is £30,000 for NQs. There's talk of a salary review soon, and as one trainee said: *"If the firm becomes more private client-oriented, people will expect a raise."* But basically, *"if you're going to whinge about the salary, don't apply."* What do trainees get out of their job if not a huge wad of cash? The really rewarding bit, they told us, is when cases go well. High points included *"getting clients into accommodation," "tracking local authorities who were not doing what they should for young people"* and *"winning cases for clients in immigration."* As one source told us: *"One client was extremely vulnerable – she had been abused by different people in her home country – and her reaction was amazing. It was unbelievably rewarding. You become attached to your clients, some of whom have had the most awful backgrounds, and you're desperate for them to win. You see them a few weeks later and they're completely transformed. They send you cards. It's more rewarding than a big pay cheque."* If you scoffed at that, FM is not for you.

Trend-bucking and fund-cutting

The firm's style is *"fairly informal: it's not a place where everyone is suited and booted every day."* The open-plan offices at Blue Sky House in Kennington are *"pretty spacious and nice, but not super-flash."* The immediate area has few shops but *"lots of independent restaurants and cafés,"* and a nearby park is fantastic during the summer for tennis or a lunchtime run. Trainees become close friends and regularly wind down in local pubs such as The Dog House or The White Hart. The firm also organises beer and pizza nights in its boardroom, an annual summer outing (to the Isle of Wight last year) and a Christmas party. Trainees tend to be quite active in Legal Aid circles and volunteer with women's centres, charities and NGOs.

One unfortunate fact is that trainees are *"not guaranteed a place at the end here."* Retention rates are not usually particularly high, and second-years tend to be kept in the dark about jobs until relatively late in the day. In 2010, however, five of seven stayed on in PSL, family, immigration and housing.

And finally...

While Legal Aid firms nationwide face brutal cuts and possible closure, FM's blended practice should keep it stable, even in this difficult time.

Foot Anstey Solicitors

The facts

Location: Exeter, Plymouth, Taunton, Truro

Number of UK partners/solicitors: 40/95

Total number of trainees: 10

Seats: 4x6 months

Alternative seats: Occasional secondments

On chambersstudent.co.uk
- How to get into Foot Anstey
- We talk to partner and media guru Tony Jaffa
- Mumsnet v Gina Ford

Progressive, with commercial ambitions and some multimillion-pound cases, Foot Anstey is intent on earning a reputation as the premier law firm of the South West peninsula.

Playing footsie with ambition

Foot Anstey, the largest law firm in Devon, Cornwall and Somerset, is a full-service commercial operation with "*experts in various fields you wouldn't expect.*" It's not aiming to go national: its goal is to be the best firm west of Bristol, and with that in mind it has expanded significantly over the past five years or so. In 2005, the firm scooped up local player Alms & Young in Taunton; a team from major rival Clarke Willmott followed; and then came another merger in 2007 with ten-lawyer Plymouth firm Serpell Eaton Solicitors, which specialised in commercial property, private client and charity law. That year also saw the opening of an office in Truro. Although the firm is based in the South West, its clients come from all over the country and include Halfords, Lloyds TSB, Associated Newspapers and the National Farmers Union.

Foot Anstey trainees each take four six-month seats and can sample from a really good spread of practice groups. They indicate their first and second choices at each rotation, writing "*a little blurb*" about why they want them. For some of the most popular seats the process is more formal and may require a written submission and an interview. The extra effort is not wasted: it does make you think about your choices more carefully. The firm tries to give all trainees a broad experience, in terms of both practice areas and geographical location. To be clear, "*most people do a seat in a different office, and most want to do it. It's good to move around and meet a whole range of people in the firm.*" Truro to Taunton is a 125-mile trip (though we didn't speak to anyone who had done a seat in both), and even Exeter to Plymouth is a 45-mile drive along the edge of Dartmoor, so while some trainees choose to commute, many move house for the duration of their seat. We're told that "*most teams work on quite a collective basis, with frequent team meetings,*" and that many fee earners have desks in both Exeter and Plymouth. The seats on offer vary from year to year, but usually include insurance/personal injury; employment; clin neg; private client; childcare and family; financial and commercial; coco; construction and property; and commercial real estate.

Wake me up before you coco

Corporate commercial (coco) is a strong area for the firm, and it has some prestigious clients like the Wrigley Company, the Odeon cinema chain, Devon Wind Power and the Progressive Digital Media Group. From a trainee's point of view, it's a varied seat: there are M&A deals, share purchase agreements, business transfers, company sales and public procurement deals. Unsurprisingly, some of the work relates to local tourism and there are always instructions from local businessmen on which trainees can be let loose to practise their drafting. The trainee's role also involves company secretarial duties for between 40 and 50 companies. Client contact is mainly e-mail-based, making it slightly "*more faceless*" than other departments in that respect.

Chambers UK rankings

Agriculture & Rural Affairs	Employment
Banking & Finance	Family/Matrimonial
Banking Litigation	Information Technology
Charities	Intellectual Property
Clinical Negligence	Licensing
Corporate/M&A	Personal Injury
Crime	Planning
Debt Recovery	Private Client
Defamation/Reputation Management	Real Estate
	Real Estate Litigation
Dispute Resolution	Tax

Exeter is the place to be for commercial litigation. This popular team is "*doing very well and expanding rapidly,*" and luckily for trainees it can take a number of them at a time. The work covers bankruptcy and fraud, million-pound claims for professional negligence and lots of smaller disputes; for example, in 2009 alone, the group advised on over 150 debt recovery cases for a single client. It's a satisfying seat because smaller cases can be resolved quickly, giving trainees a chance both to run them and to see them all the way through to the end. Exeter Combined Court Centre is "*just round the corner*" on Southernhay, which is very much the city's legal district. Importantly, "*client contact is there if you want it.*" On the property litigation side, cases largely relate to residential rather than commercial properties, and involve landlord and tenant disputes, possession orders, boundary disputes and the division of large estates. As the seat requires some technical knowledge, there is more initial shadowing than in the commercial litigation seat. The Plymouth office also offers some exposure to sports litigation.

The downturn was probably felt most keenly in the firm's less-busy-than-usual commercial property department. It is, however, "*a good first seat,*" offering a gradual but stimulating learning curve. The department has worked on the Portland Harbour scheme for the 2012 Olympics, for the Royal Shakespeare Company and for the MoD.

Parent trouble

The media team is led by experienced lawyer Tony Jaffa, who is one of a handful of solicitors forming a panel put together by the last government to consider potential changes to the law on libel. As it happens the new coalition government also wants to review UK libel laws. Back in 2006, Jaffa advised writer Gina Ford, who tried to shut down the parenting website Mumsnet after site members allegedly posted defamatory comments about her. Needless to say, the website is still running and of course became a key battleground in the last general election, but Ford got an apology and a tidy sum. More recently, the media team has defended several newspaper groups against claims brought by the likes of Kate Winslet, Roman Abramovich and the chief executive of the Professional Footballers' Association, Gordon Taylor. The media/tech/IP seat can be quite a tricky one as some of the knowledge required is very technical, but within the seat there are also some more straightforward corporate and property matters trainees can sink their teeth into.

The hectic family seat focuses on divorce and children's cases and provides good opportunities for advocacy. Trainees spend a lot more time "*out and about with clients*" and can be in court as often as twice a week. "*Emotional*" domestic violence and children's cases can be rewarding but require quite a hardy disposition. The same can be said of the clinical negligence team, where trainees are given "*quite a lot of authority*" and their own files to run under supervision. Much of the work involves group litigation with up to 150 claimants, which unsurprisingly offers "*a great deal of client contact.*" The firm has won a place on the referral panel for a major legal expenses insurance company and this ensures a good flow of new instructions. One interesting set of cases involved men who were diagnosed with cancer and advised to undergo chemotherapy. Given the risk of infertility, each stored sperm samples that were then lost or damaged by their NHS trusts. Claims for lost sperm had never previously arisen in English law, but luckily Foot Anstey has a history of cases relating to cryogenics and andrology/IVF treatment. One of its lawyers ended up representing three groups of claimants in Southmead, Sheffield and Edinburgh, leading to the landmark Court of Appeal decision in *Yearworth and others v North Bristol NHS Trust.*

And loads more...

There are many more different seats on offer. The employment department is one of the largest in the South West and ranks in *Chambers UK*'s top tier for the region. Expect "*lots of tribunal work.*" The construction seat involves chasing up unpaid invoices for clients, drafting instructions to barristers, dealing with experts' reports, applications to the court for summary judgments, and sometimes trips to the High Court. The banking and finance team is doing well, as its list of client attests: Bank of Ireland, Clydesdale Bank, HSBC, NatWest and Peugeot Finance all use the firm. Seats in the education, charities and crime teams are also available (the latter in Plymouth and Taunton only). What's more, Foot Anstey offers secondments to clients, although unfortunately we can't name any this year.

Normal working hours are 9am to 5.15pm, with no work at weekends. It's on "*very rare*" occasions that trainees stay as late as 9.30pm. "*I can't remember the last time I left after six,*" claimed one source. Everyone is also given an hour a week off – called the 'lifestyle hour' – and a day off at the end of the year for Christmas shopping. There were some grumbles about poor benefits (no gym membership, private dental or medical care), but an improved package is "*in discussion.*" Trainees consider the salary "*competitive for the area.*"

We've noticed an increasingly distinct ambitious streak emerge in the firm in the past couple of years, and certainly a greater emphasis on recording hours and billing. It seems as if trainees too are taking on this characteristic. "*It can get competitive,*" said one trainee, "*but we all get along quite well.*" Another said: "*we're all irritatingly competitive – it's very friendly, but it's a difficult situation.*" Despite this, sources described the firm as "*relaxed and not intimidating.*" Managing partner John Westwell "*knows trainees by name and always says hello,*" and regularly lunches with juniors, briefing them on the firm's strategy and plans for the future.

Fit Anstey

You don't need to be South West born and bred, but many of the trainees went to a university west of Bristol. Basically, the firm is looking for "*people who want to work and stay here.*" The South West offers "*the best of both worlds: both city and beach.*" The brand new and "*absolutely stunning*" Plymouth office in Salt Quay House makes the most of its location. Its roof terrace overlooks the harbour and "*it's one of the best locations in Plymouth.*" The office in Exeter is a modern building in the city centre, within easy reach of green areas and the courts. The small but sociable Taunton office is conveniently located by the M5 in a business park, while the Truro office is split between two buildings (one a pretty Georgian townhouse) but there is talk of moving to a single site in the near future.

Trainees should be "*prepared to be involved – there are lots of things to do.*" Apart from the sailing, surfing and other water sports easily enjoyed locally, the firm has football, netball, volleyball, cricket and rugby teams, golfers and a squash ladder ("*Squashies Wednesday*"). Exeter trainees regularly go for a lunchtime swim, and there's an annual Taunton triathlon, a biathlon, an aquathlon and a fun run. And the local Junior Lawyers Division organises snowboarding holidays. We're exhausted just thinking about it all! Anyone less sporty can enjoy quarterly firm-wide drinks, some quiz evenings, barbecues and curry nights. Staff from the Plymouth office crowd into local pub The China House, and the Rendezvous wine bar attracts many Exeter trainees. The Christmas bash is usually held in Torquay so that "*everyone has to travel only a little.*"

No training contracts were cancelled or deferred last year, but there were only four trainees in the 2009 intake, down from 12 the previous year. Six new trainees joined in 2010 and the firm is now looking to hire six to eight per year. The choice of NQ jobs was narrowed for 2010's qualifiers, so trainees hoping for private client and property jobs had to look elsewhere – but this may change in the future. All in all, nine of the 13 qualifiers stayed on at the firm: three in Plymouth, three in Exeter, two in Taunton and one in Truro.

The firm's main aim for the future is "*to become the premier law firm in the South West*" and there is "*no suggestion of a Bristol office.*" While it is still committed to remaining a full-service firm, trainees predicted a decline in areas such as family in favour of a "*more commercial spin.*" The Legal Aid work at Foot Anstey depends on what the LSC decides, but the firm intends to continue it as long as it can. We're told that in the past "*80% of trainees wanted to try family law, so I think the firm has deliberately hired more commercially minded people recently.*" Private client work still has its place at the firm, although it seems likely that the teams will focus on more bespoke higher value work rather than high-volume, low-value services.

And finally...

If you're looking for commercial or high-value private client work in Devon, Cornwall and Somerset, ambitious Foot Anstey simply has to be on your list.

Forbes

The facts

Location: Manchester, Leeds, Blackburn, Accrington, Preston, Chorley

Number of UK partners/solicitors: 35/65

Total number of trainees: 16

Seats: 4x6 months

Alternative seats: Occasional secondments

Extras: Pro bono – Legal advice clinics in Blackburn, Preston, Chorley and Accrington

On chambersstudent.co.uk
- How to get into Forbes
- A life of crime: what to expect
- How Forbes is addressing the Legal Aid crisis

'Variety' and 'reputation' are the chief buzzwords among trainees at Forbes.

A foot in each camp

Straddling the high street and business district, Forbes has positioned itself as a multidisciplinary leader in the North West, with practices ranging from crime and family law to domestic conveyancing, commercial litigation, employment and insurance. This means it's possible for trainees to encounter small-time drug dealers, big-con fraudsters, the police, commercial movers and shakers and divorcing parents all in one training contract. On the commercial side, clients include AIG, Zurich, the Co-operative Group, and Blackburn Rovers and Burnley football clubs. A number of public sector bodies are on the client list, too, so it's ideal for someone who wants to try a bit of everything.

Legal Aid is being overhauled and public spending is being cut, yet Forbes is optimistic – how? Fortunately, the firm's reputation in these areas has meant that it was chosen for new consolidated panels charged with handling this kind of work. So, with various other firms failing to make the grade, Forbes is actually getting a better share of the work that is still available. Meanwhile, its commercial side – the larger part of the firm – is doing well. Good work done by the employment and insurance teams for several clients, both public and private, has won them mandates in other areas, like litigation or social housing. The firm is now planning to increase its geographical spread by opening in a location "*south of Manchester – not in London, but south.*"

Trainees take four six-month seats and the firm will take into account what sort of path they want to tread. Some choose to mix and match, oscillating between the private client and commercial seats, while others with a more steadfast idea of what they want to become can opt for seats in complementary areas.

The Blackburn offices have the most diverse selection of seats, with crime; family; personal injury; commercial litigation; business law; insurance litigation; employment; commercial property; and residential property all available. The Leeds and Manchester offices are insurance-focused, while Preston has Crown Court (crime); personal injury; wills and probate; commercial property; residential property; and housing litigation. Chorley offers seats in family and crime, and the smaller Accrington office tends not to take trainees. There are also occasional client secondments. "*The firm gives people the opportunity to move between offices, and usually trainees will do so at some point, but some people choose to stay in the same place all the time – it depends on which seats you want to do.*" A factor in deciding whether to move offices was often the allure/dislike of the city in question.

Out and about

In crime seats "*it's not a desk job at all,*" so trainees travel between witnesses, the accused and the police, taking statements, juggling documents and attending court. In other seats it's boardroom wrangles and high-stakes contractual nit-picking. For people who "*enjoy the excitement and constant challenge of crime work,*" Forbes is going to be pretty high on their list, as it is one of the region's biggest crime specialists. Time here is by no means compulsory, and it's easy for trainees to steer a different course. Go to our website for more detail on the three crime seats.

Chambers UK rankings

Crime	Personal Injury
Dispute Resolution	Social Housing

If you prefer not to be tied to a desk but don't fancy the grit of criminal work, the wills and probate seat is a good option. "*You travel around a lot*" and do "*different types of work, not just drafting wills. There's Lasting Powers of Attorney, Court of Protection, probate and other private client issues too.*" You may be privy to some eccentric wills or the revelation of familial rifts and mistresses, as people set up secret trusts to, for example, ensure that money can be gifted to someone without arousing suspicion. Trips to nursing homes, hospitals and care homes for the mentally ill to take last-minute requests from the dying can be emotionally taxing, but rewarding too. "*I had to do an emergency will in a hospital that was really dramatic. The client had an operation in half an hour, so it was really tense to hear all their most confidential and secret information, especially when you are thinking there's a good possibility that you'll be the last person they speak to.*" Residential conveyancing, meanwhile, is "*very much a technical area with a lot of letter drafting, deed reading and drawing up leases.*" It's a fairly straightforward process, so trainees are handed a lot of responsibility and quickly get used to dealing with clients.

Every little helps...

Insurance is a growing area for the firm and the lifeblood of the offices in Manchester and Leeds. Again, the variety of the work was praised: "*There's employers' liability, occupiers' liability, housing disrepair, motor claims, personal injury...*" Forbes believes that the quality and reputation of its personal injury department will save it from being totally ravaged by 'Tesco law', despite the prospect of new entrants into this marketplace. Starting by taking details from clients, trainees guide each case through its different stages, drafting witness statements, court documents and occasionally attending court. "*There was a good variety of tasks to be completed and a range of claims from damages caused by potholes to disaster claims.*" The department also handles interesting insurance fraud cases.

Employment is a popular destination and the team is "*expanding rapidly.*" The firm tells us the department's revenue has increased by 150% since 2007, as it wins yet more mandates to represent county councils across the North West. "*There's an equal balance between public and commercial clients,*" and trainees can expect plenty of tribunals but also contractual advice. Forbes' commercial litigation department has scaled up its debt collection capacity, and it also handles things like land disputes, breach of contract and construction disputes. Trainees enjoyed this seat and praised the level of responsibility available.

Roll out the red carpet

Forbes' appraisal system is described as "*excellent*" and we hear that it runs smoothly. Early on in their seat, trainees have an informal chat with their supervisor. At the end, the supervisor compiles a report based on feedback from the department and then goes through it with the trainee. At this point, the trainee meets with the training partner to discuss the previous seat and where they want to go next.

Trainees' social lives depend on their location, but all our sources were happy and told us about a decent Friday scene. As well as informal drinks and meals out, there are "*scheduled events like bowling and the Christmas party at Ewood Park, where there's the Forbes Oscars and a free bar.*" Forbes lawyers are down to earth with some quirks (in a good way!) and committed to their career. It sounds as if the firm is equally committed to them: in 2010, four of the five qualifiers took jobs with Forbes.

And finally...

'Tesco law' and the assault on the Legal Aid budget don't scare this firm. A good bet, we'd say.

- **Philately will get you everywhere:** Extra-curricular activities prove you are more than just a lean mean legal machine. There's no point in just listing your personal qualities in an application – you need to demonstrate them by way of example.

Ford & Warren

The facts

Location: Leeds

Number of UK partners/solicitors: 19/35

Total number of trainees: 8

Seats: 4x6 months

Alternative seats: None

On chambersstudent.co.uk
- How to get into F&W
- F&W's distinguished alumni
- The Yorkshire legal market

Like the modest Yorkshire pudding, Ford & Warren is no-nonsense. It's all about loyalty, hard work, high standards and, above all, *"giving a damned good service to the client."*

Heard it through the grapevine

What do YouTube, Facebook and Ford & Warren have in common? The popularity of all three has grown through word of mouth. "*We believe in organic growth and rely upon personal recommendation rather than paying for expensive marketing,*" commented one trainee. With a "*no-frills*" ideology, "*it's all about giving the client your best work at the best possible cost.*" But this isn't the Ryanair of law firms. Recently, F&W joined Primerus, a North American organisation that selects members who "*subscribe to achieving an excellent client service.*"

With Leeds roots stretching to 1816, this one-office firm, renamed Ford & Warren in 1878, has eschewed expansion via the merger route, instead growing organically and in response to client needs. F&W has gradually taken over all seven floors of Westgate Point – a redbrick, open-plan, "*imposing and impressive*" building that stands tall amid the buzzing city centre traffic. Certainly an "*efficient*" firm, it didn't make any redundancies during the harsh period following the credit crunch.

As well as strong real estate and litigation practices, F&W has a number of specialist departments such as transport and sport, and it also caters for private clients. "*You get really small clients and really big clients here. Getting a good range keeps it interesting and ensures great exposure.*" The firm counts major names like National Express and Punch Taverns among its clientele.

Pit stops

F&W trainees visit four seats, usually spending the last one in the department they wish to qualify into. Managing partner Keith Hearn sends an e-mail to trainees to ascertain their preferences, and "*after that it's down to business needs.*" Trainees sit together in 'trainee banks' on each floor. "*It's really helpful to have somebody to quickly turn to and ask for help.*"

Roaring ahead with a *Chambers UK* top-tier ranking, the transport department counts Eddie Stobart and Fastline UK among its clients. Partner Gary Hodgson has had an exciting year, acting in a gross negligence manslaughter prosecution, before several public inquiries, and successfully arguing a PSV (public service vehicle) fine from £11,000 all the way down to £1,750. Though there's no assigned seat in the department, trainees can cadge work from one of the partners and are likely to encounter transport clients elsewhere in the firm. For example, National Express instructs the employment team, where trainees enjoy having a go at "*all sorts of work*" from drafting claims and pleadings to attending client meetings and tribunals.

Trainees in the litigation department encounter cases of all shapes and sizes, and have court exposure from early on. "*Working on small claims is a great way to pick up the process really quickly, while with the larger ones you get to deal with experts and take witness statements.*" There is the dull matter of court bundling to be

Chambers UK rankings

Debt Recovery	Licensing
Dispute Resolution	Personal Injury
Employment	Transport

dealt with, but our sources realised that "*it comes with the territory – you need to do it to understand how it works.*" F&W's litigation department handles general commercial, insurance and personal injury cases, IP and fraud, finance litigation and sports matters. The firm advises numerous Premiership footballers, teams and agents. It was a game of two halves for Leeds United when Melvyn Levi, a former director of the club, launched a defamation claim against Chairman Ken Bates. F&W carried Mr Levi to victory, landing him £50,000 in damages and indemnity costs. Other work highlights include acting for the British Bobsleigh Association and representing Dwain Chambers in his battle to lift the lifetime ban that prevented him from competing in Grand Prix race events.

In keeping with its efficient nature and 'full service to the client' ideology, F&W conducts the majority of its own advocacy. "*There's a progression. They want to give you experience first by watching others – they don't throw you in at the deep end.*" But as one trainee told us: "*I'm certainly not mothered. I have a good amount of responsibility and if there's ever anything too complicated, I'll get it checked.*" Trainees are "*free to go and speak to anyone.*" And, as always, the client's interests come first. "*The training experience is also led by the client – they say how much they want you involved.*"

In commercial property, trainees find they get "*excellent hands-on experience.*" Drafting leases and licences, they're expected to "*have a go at producing a final document and then pass it on to get checked.*" Working with companies big and small – eg Punch Taverns and Thomas Cook – trainees experience acquisitions, disposals and leases. "*You see both sides of the coin,*" said one, "*and it gives you a really rounded picture.*" Over in the licensing department, trainees advise clients on how to comply with all relevant legislation.

A seat in F&W's private client department mostly involves "*drafting wills and some government work.*" Trainees found their colleagues very friendly and even worked alongside the managing partner. "*In total contrast to what I expected, there was really no intimidation at all,*" said one.

This is a firm that takes pride in appearances, from its strict dress code to its tidy-desk policy. "*Clients expect us to look smart,*" commented one trainee. "*They pay us so many pounds and expect us to appear in a way that reflects that.*" As for the tidy desks, trainees say "*it teaches you to how manage your files, as well as yourself.*"

On the side

F&W isn't big on marketing speak and empty jargon. On its website, it claims to offer 'just a high quality, value for money service'. "*The firm strives for excellence in everything we do; delivering a quality service on time at the cost estimated,*" we were told. "*This certainly isn't a firm where there's any dicking about.*" That's not to say folk don't know how to have a good time. Aside from the Christmas parties (firm-wide and departmental), the social scene is fairly informal. "*There's as much or as little as you want, and it's not shoved down your throat.*" Trainees enjoy popping out for coffee at lunchtime, or dinner and drinks after work, frequenting city-centre haunts such as Prohibition and Jupiter. The firm has a football team, and trainees also get involved with the Junior Lawyers Division.

And let's not forget the F&W resident band, Red Light Revival. "*Oh… I don't really know how to describe them. Funky electro?*" We checked them out on MySpace, where we discovered that they are actually… really quite good. Hum along to *Need Me Too* when applying and rage to *Bad Bitch Woman* should you get rejected. Comprised of fee earners, the band made it to the *Live and Unsigned* regional final this year.

"*This isn't the type of place where you do two years and then they throw you out,*" our sources insisted. True enough, in 2010 three out of the four qualifiers stayed on.

And finally...

The F&W ethos is plain and simple. Take pride in yourself, take pride in your work and give *"a damned good service"* to clients. You can't really argue with that.

Freeth Cartwright LLP

The facts

Location: Nottingham, Leicester, Derby, Birmingham, Manchester, London

Number of UK partners/solicitors: 81/86

Total number of trainees: 16

Seats: 4x6 months

Alternative seats: Secondments

On chambersstudent.co.uk
- How to get into Freeth
- Piloting the SRA's work-based learning scheme
- Workplace satisfaction

Nottingham-headquartered Freeth Cartwright has shifted its focus and grown its commercial practice in the past ten years. With a toe now tentatively dipped in the London market, it has signalled its ambitions beyond the Midlands.

When the drugs don't work

Freeth Cartwright's reputation was founded on headline class action civil litigation over things like breast implants and the MMR vaccine. A legacy of this is an exceptionally well-regarded product liability practice specialising in claims over allegedly faulty products, such as Cadbury's chocolate (in the salmonella contamination dispute) and Zyprexa, an antipsychotic drug alleged to cause diabetes. In one recent case, superstar products liability lawyer Paul Balen represented an 11-year-old boy who had claimed brain damage following use of an anti-meningitis vaccine manufactured by French pharmaceutical company Sanofi Pasteur. The manufacturer's UK distribution subsidiary has just wriggled off the hook in the Supreme Court, so the case has some odd angles to it. Another hangover, albeit a welcome one, is a strong claimant-based personal injury and clinical negligence practice. Recently the firm achieved three settlements worth in excess of £1m for injured clients, and it regularly represents bereaved families in high-profile inquests.

However, for over a decade the firm has been shifting its priorities away from the high street and into commerce, dropping, for example, a relatively unprofitable crime practice. Nowadays, Freeth is a corporate beast. As a trainee pointed out: "*It's very much a commercial business. It's not quite so 'look at the good we're doing,' although we are doing some good.*" The business focus has certainly brought success, and the firm achieves plenty of top-tier *Chambers UK* rankings in the East Midlands, as well as national recognition for construction and product liability work. There are several heavy hitters in the region, so it's impressive that Freeth can match Browne Jacobson and Eversheds (and beat the likes of Shoosmiths and Hewitsons) in the corporate, litigation and real estate league tables.

Corporate and property instructions now make up the bulk of Freeth's caseload, however, so the firm felt the impact of the global economic downturn. In 2009, profitability fell a heart-stopping 36%, and the firm made around 80 staff cuts, although it began recruiting again at the junior end quickly enough, and also recruited some senior-level laterals.

New shoots

Freeth has grown to six offices that extend from the East Midlands to Birmingham, Manchester and – as of 2010 – London. For the moment, this newest office is just a three-partner beachhead focused on corporate work. "*It's going to be very much a wait-and-see situation,*" said senior HR manager Carole Wigley. "*It really is a wholly different marketplace down there. But clients have said they would be very happy to see us in London.*" The Manchester office is now as big as those in Derby and Leicester, and trainees sense Birmingham is the current focus of attention. "*In a year it's got five new people in an office of 13 or 14. It's really busy.*"

Chambers UK rankings

Banking & Finance	Personal Injury
Clinical Negligence	Private Client
Construction	Product Liability
Corporate/M&A	Real Estate
Dispute Resolution	Real Estate Litigation
Employment	Restructuring/Insolvency
Energy & Natural Resources	Social Housing
Licensing	Tax

Nottingham remains the largest office by quite some margin and is still the firm's mothership. Consequently trainees spend the majority of their time in Robin Hood country – only four of the 13 at the firm in February 2010 were working outside the city, although from September 2010 it's expected that more trainees will work in other locations. However, "*if you're a Nottingham trainee, then it's expected that you'll be able to do a seat in Derby or Leicester.*" Indeed, a seat in another office is "*actively encouraged.*" The Leicester office is a "*posh new building*" right next to the train station and "*much nicer looking than Nottingham.*" We're also told it has a "*more relaxed*" atmosphere. Given that Birmingham is slightly further afield, this is a voluntary option, and Freeth helps trainees out by "*paying for parking costs and train travel.*" Given the distances involved, trainees do tend to relocate to Brum if they take up that option, and they sometimes stay on. Thankfully, there's no pressure to commute to the Manchester office, which has a couple of its own trainees. Birmingham, too, may get homegrown trainees by 2012; it seems unlikely that London will be taking any in the near future, although who knows what the longer term might bring?

The seat allocation process is more of a conversation than a paperwork exercise and second-year trainees are given priority. "*Having been through the system, I think that's the best way,*" one averred. It means that generally, a trainee's last seat will be in the practice area into which they hope to qualify. There are no compulsory seats, but given the importance of property, a stint getting to know the old bricks and mortar is highly likely. "*There might be five or six trainees within the broad real estate practice, each doing slightly different things.*"

Real estate of mind

The real estate group is by far the largest department and the firm used commercial property as a spearhead to penetrate the Birmingham market a couple of years back. Within the real estate bracket, there are a number of different subpractices. Broadly that means leasehold and freehold work, private developer and public work, and litigation as well. Despite a sluggish market, the firm has met with success servicing clients from healthcare, education and other parts of the public sector, and has been seeing work in the regeneration sphere as well as instructions from corporate occupiers. Recent highlights include acting for swimwear giant Speedo in the development of a new 35,000 sq ft global headquarters, and representing Lloyds Bank in the £40m refinancing of a privately owned house-building and investment group. Trainees speak enthusiastically about the seat. "*There's quite a lot of junior lawyer work, by which I mean work above the level of a trainee,*" said one. The nuts and bolts of the seat include "*plenty of drafting, be it a provision in a transfer document or other contract.*" Less glamorous, there's also a good deal of collating documents and the like, but "*you don't ever feel like a tea boy.*"

Commercial litigation is another big gun for Freeth, and it picks up quality work from both national and regional clients. Insolvencies have played a bigger part in this practice since the recession, and many have been the source of more general disputes. Also on the rise are disputes over the termination of contracts with suppliers when customers deem the terms too unfavourable. Corporate clients include Gala Coral Group, Coors, Carlsberg Tetley, Brit Insurance, Centaur Media (owners of *The Lawyer*) and British School of Motoring. Trainees work with a number of different fee earners because of the size of the practice (around 25 lawyers in total), which gives them a decent go at tasks such as "*drafting pre-action letters and witness statements, sitting in on hearings, and even sitting behind counsel at the Royal Courts of Justice in London.*" The flipside, according to one trainee, is that "*you don't necessarily feel like any one person is responsible for you directly.*" Quality-wise, trainee tasks are generally substantive, although "*donkey work*" is also "*par for the course*" in litigation seats. "*It's all well and good grumbling about menial tasks, but if you're learning litigation how can you expect to train without doing the basic preparation yourself?*" one reasonable source asked.

Trainees praised the corporate department for providing "*good exposure*" to deals. "*I was the partner's right-hand man,*" said one. "*It wasn't just getting documents from Companies House. There was one job where I effectively drafted the agreement from scratch.*" Another had a similar experience on a small corporate transaction. "*I was asked to take charge of it as best I could. Watching it complete was like giving away a child for adoption. I'd put my heart and soul into it for a month.*" The team acted on one of the Midlands' biggest private equity deals in 2009, the £23m buyout of Funeral Services Partnership by August Equity, and on Maven Capital Partners' £10m cash injection into a recycling and waste management company.

Trainees can still gain exposure to the private client side of the firm through clinical negligence, personal injury and private litigation seats. While we've played up the fact that the firm is much more commercially oriented these days, it shouldn't be forgotten that Freeth still gains a top *Chambers UK* ranking in the Midlands for clin neg. However, "*clin neg and private client are fairly steady in terms of growth. Their client bases aren't growing ridiculously, so they aren't crying out for trainees.*" It follows, then, that there are fewer qualification opportunities in these areas. With that proviso, there's no obstacle to working in them. Freeth does a fair amount of traditional personal injury work: think death, brain damage, amputation and other such cheerful subjects. It represents claimants on some cases and defendants (usually insurance companies) on others. Over in the clin neg team, it's a case of trying to right wrongs for patients who have received negligent surgery, treatment or diagnosis, leading some of them to suffer life-long disability or discomfort as a result.

In private litigation, the firm is frequently instructed in contentious probate matters, such as unscrupulous family members exerting undue influence over elderly relatives, and paternity testing to determine beneficiaries. Very Jeremy Kyle. A trainee talked about "*taking on an assistant's role half of the time, and spending the rest dealing with less high-value cases.*" Trainees attend hearings, although since Freeth "*instructs counsel in everything,*" they aren't generally involved in advocacy.

Appraisals start with the trainee assessing their own performance. Their supervisor then does the same thing, before they sit down together and compare the two. While "*it's worked well*" for some, others felt there are "*sometimes issues in finding the time to talk*" and that the system "*could be improved... It depends who you get.*" The salary "*on the whole is market rate*" and "*you are expected to work for it.*" Gasped one bleary-eyed trainee: "*On one deal I had four hours' sleep in three days.*" This isn't the norm, however, and the hours are "*generally not bad at all.*"

Tastes like chicken

The Nottingham office is spread over five open-plan floors. "*Property has the fourth, commercial and corporate have the third. Floor 3a at the back of the building is clin neg.*" They don't mix too much, so the culture varies by department. "*Private client tends to be quite bustling: they have to be sympathetic and listen to people day in, day out. It's quite a noisy floor, there's always someone on the phone. Business is more 'snap to it.' There's more pressure.*" Across the whole firm, numerous trainees agreed: "*You don't have to be a stuffy stereotype.*"

"*The trainees are a bit of a mixed bunch, so some tend to go out more than others.*" For the more outgoing, there's occasional bowling and go-karting, a popular mixed touch-rugby team, pub quizzes and drinking-based ribaldry at The Malt Cross or The Castle, which is "*the pub that every lawyer in Nottingham goes to.*" There are even occasional excursions to the UK's first branch of American gastronomic institution Hooters. "*It's fine if you go there with girls, like we do,*" we were told, "*and they do really good chicken wings.*" Trainees didn't comment on the quality of the breast or leg on offer.

Our sources were "*a bit cagey*" about their qualification prospects in 2010: a product of the economic conditions as much as anything else. When we last spoke to Freeth, five out of seven of its second-years had been offered NQ jobs.

And finally...

An ambitious firm with an enviable reputation in the East Midlands, Freeth's historical assets – PI, clinical negligence and the like – remain strong but now play second fiddle to commercial and property practices.

Freshfields Bruckhaus Deringer LLP

The facts

Location: London

Number of UK partners/solicitors: 161/551

Total number of trainees: 197

Seats: 3 or 6 months long

Alternative seats: Secondments, overseas seats

Extras: Pro bono – Tower Hamlets Law Centre, Liberty, Oxfam, US death row appeals; language training

On chambersstudent.co.uk
- How to get into Freshfields
- We talk to recruitment partner Simon Johnson
- 'A History of Freshfields': we read it so you don't have to

Freshfields Bruckhaus Deringer has combined British class with Teutonic efficiency to produce one of the world's finest corporate law firms.

Power play

With over 2,000 lawyers, 28 offices worldwide and revenue exceeding £1.14bn in 2009/10, Freshfields is one of the world's biggest law firms however you care to measure it. It's also one of the oldest, tracing its history back to at least 1743, when a chap by the name of Samuel Dodd became solicitor to The Bank of England.

It has long been the accepted wisdom that Freshfields is one of the more corporate-focused magic circle firms; however, "*there's a real feeling now,*" say trainees, "*that if you look at the make-up of our clients, the idea of corporate being more important than finance is quite archaic.*" Our parent publication *Chambers UK* broadly agrees with this assessment, although we'd say that the firm's reputation for banking work is still not quite the equal of its best-of-the-best corporate practice. Nor should Freshfields' litigation capability be ignored – particularly the arbitration group, which *Chambers Global*, in an uncharacteristic outburst of finality, cites as 'undoubtedly the number-one in the world'.

Freshfields has powered through the recession without excessive grief (although revenue did fall by 11.3% in 2009/10) and the firm avoided making the swathes of redundancies that affected its rivals. How did it manage this? According to trainee recruitment partner Simon Johnson: "*Over the last year or two there has been a flight to quality*" and this has probably insulated the top firms to some extent. However, a pretty comprehensive restructuring of the business in 2006 evidently came at just the right time. Departments were slimmed, older partners retired and others were de-equitised, leaving the firm toned and gym-fit when the recession struck. As for the future, Freshfields has worked out that "*a large portion of our billings come from a small number of our clients*" and so it wants to devote more resources to those key relationships. You can read much more about the firm's strategy on our website, but a key trend to note is its American ambitions. Freshfields has had some success in breaking into the US market but there is a long way to go and it has been concentrating on bringing litigators to its New York office of late.

Finding your flightpath

Trainees' seats are either three or six months long and our sources absolutely loved this. "*For me it has proved to be one of the best things about the training contract,*" said one. "*It's so flexible. You can start off somewhere and if it's not for you, you can get out without wasting half a year.*" It's generally the case that trainees will spend their first six months in corporate, finance or dispute resolution (DR). Then smart thinking is advised. There are tactical considerations when choosing seats – if you want to qualify into a certain department, three months might not be long enough to show how good you are. Therefore, it's best to devise a coherent seating plan early on and remember that qualification is the goal. Client secondments and overseas opportunities are also available – check our website for more on these.

This is a corporate firm so it would be weird if you came to Freshfields wanting to dodge this department entirely.

Chambers UK rankings

Administrative & Public Law	Investment Funds
Asset Finance	Outsourcing
Banking & Finance	Pensions
Banking Litigation	Private Equity
Capital Markets	Product Liability
Competition/European Law	Professional Negligence
Construction	Projects
Corporate/M&A	Public International Law
Dispute Resolution	Public Procurement
Employee Share Schemes	Real Estate
Employment	Real Estate Finance
Energy & Natural Resources	Restructuring/Insolvency
Environment	Retail
Financial Services	Sports Law
Fraud	Tax
Information Technology	Telecommunications
Insurance	Transport
Intellectual Property	

But why would you, when some of the biggest deals in the world are coming through the doors? Potential applicants should check the legal press for examples, but here are two corkers: in 2009 the team acted on BAA Airports' £1.5bn sale of its interest in Gatwick, and the $3bn purchase of Anheuser-Busch InBev's Central and Eastern European operations by CVC Capital Partners – the largest European buyout of the year. Big names like British Land, BAE Systems, BP and Tesco have also recently sought the firm's help. "*The deals I was doing were on the front page of the FT. If that gets you excited, you'll love it,*" said one source.

Let's cut to the chase: many of our contacts had worked "*crazy long hours for quite a long time*" in this department, kissing goodbye to evenings and weekends for the cause. Sounds horrible in black and white, but even litigation-minded trainees "*really did enjoy it.*" "*I can see the draw of corporate now,*" said one. Remaining brutally frank, much of the work is document management and the department has cut down on paralegals recently, "*so if there's a crap task it's trainees doing it.*" If you can prove yourself, there's better work to be had – "*drafting little bits of a prospectus,*" getting "*fully involved in every conference call*" and being "*sent to client meetings and allowed to talk.*" Making up for the long hours in corporate is the fact that "*the social aspect is very good.*"

That restructuring of 2006 saw Freshfields streamline its finance department, leading to claims that it was putting all its eggs in the corporate basket and no longer valued finance work. This analysis is off the mark: trainees are encouraged to spend time either in the banking and restructuring or structured asset finance (SAF) subgroups. They work for all the big names of banking – RBS, Deutsche, JPMorgan, Morgan Stanley, Barclays, HSBC and of course the Old Lady of Threadneedle Street herself. The firm tends to take on specialised, cutting-edge matters as opposed to commoditised transactions. For example, it advised Israeli shipping container company Zim on its "*fiendishly complicated*" debt restructuring. The SAF team has particular strength in the aviation sector, acting for clients such as Ryanair and Airbus. As in corporate, work "*can be very good and can be very menial.*" There's "*everything from your classic proof-reading to being in charge of conditions precedent at closing.*"

Smokin'

Trainees can opt for a two-week course if they don't want to do a full litigation seat, but the work coming into this department is as impressive as that in the transactional ones. Lately there have been matters related to the bank charges litigation, fallout from the Icelandic banking crisis, the death of Woolworths and the battle between Formula One and some of its competing teams. Some sources were heavily involved on a matter for JTI, the Japanese tobacco giant. "*It's probably not what I'd want to do for ever,*" admitted one source who added that the work was fascinating nonetheless.

Trainees tend to sit in one of a number of litigation subgroups (international arbitration; general commercial; and financial institutions disputes are just three) but may find themselves able to search for work from outside it. "*I was able to get on a relatively small dispute and saw associate tasks from early on – going to client meetings, helping to draft the defence, taking the statements from key technical witnesses,*" said one source, before adding: "*I'm on a dull document review at the moment.*" Then there's "*research, obviously: as a trainee people do ask you for your opinion because you are the one who's done all the reading.*"

Competition is one of the most in-demand seats, for myriad reasons. One contact reeled off a list. "*One of the best competition teams in the world; perceived as a law-heavy seat; the team is really nice; they take their role as trainee mentors seriously; good quality of work...*" Because it's so popular, only three-month stints are allowed in this team.

Balls of steel

The level of responsibility trainees receive depends not only on what's going on but also on their supervisor. Our sources said they'd "*been very lucky*" to consistently get "*really approachable*" and "*fantastic*" associates watching over them, but had also "*heard stories*" of people who weren't so good. A point of note: partners don't supervise and contact with them varies. In some departments (real estate, competition and banking were mentioned) partners are in the main very friendly and "*make a point to come and say hi when you arrive.*" In other areas, "*certain partners don't look below the senior associates. They are harder to approach and you wouldn't just knock on their door.*" If you've got the cojones, why not follow the advice of this confident soul? "*There's more a trainee can do. I said hello and smiled at partners in the corridor. Some blanked me at first, but I kept on doing it and now they all say hello and smile back.*"

In order to provide a clearer career path, the firm has introduced "*milestones*" that associates should be aiming to hit as they reach a certain level. "*There is a big booklet on what it all means. It does cover everything and should lead to more rounded associates.*" The formal training is "*brilliant, and that is one of the main advantages of coming somewhere like this.*" Beyond the trainee training there are many more general sessions. At a recent restructuring one, "*you couldn't get a seat – the lecture theatre was crammed.*"

Dignity, always dignity

Within collegial Freshfields, people "*don't take themselves too seriously*" and are confident that it is not a place for puffed-up, self-important types. "*Professionalism*" is the watchword and we sense that trainees are always mindful of maintaining the firm's reputation for utmost propriety. We did manage to get a peek behind the face Freshfields presents to the world, however, via an anecdote about the Christmas pantomime. This tradition had long been consigned to history but four trainees "*put their necks on the line*" and revived it last year, writing and producing the whole thing. It was largely based on a popular musical (though our sources wouldn't say which in case they got sued for infringement), had parts for five dames (all lawyers love drag) and some good-natured partners even got involved. Apparently one scene revolved around spoofing the many catchphrases on Linklaters' website. Sadly it wasn't videoed, presumably to stop copies falling into the unscrupulous hands of legal gossip websites. "*We've just got photos... and memories,*" said one source, wistfully.

There has long been a stereotype that Freshfields likes recruiting 'blues and blondes' but it's quite clear that the firm is no longer a bastion of "*sporty Aryan types.*" We note with interest that the proportion of trainees coming from a minority ethnic background jumped sharply in 2007 and the August 2010/February 2011 intake is set to be the most diverse ever. We also noticed, however, a trend that hasn't changed: most of our randomly selected interviewees do still hail from Oxbridge. Oxford in particular has proved a happy hunting ground – "*several partners have special relationships with the colleges.*" "*To be fair, the firm does make a lot of effort to recruit from a range of universities,*" and one trainee estimated that "*about half*" of trainees come from Oxbridge, with another quarter from redbricks and another quarter from overseas universities. The firm says this assessment is not far off the mark, but doesn't take into account the "*significant number*" who come from unis that don't fit into these categories.

Remuneration remains excellent, although trainees debated the benefits or otherwise of having a lockstep system that pays people at a set amount for their level of seniority. The firm hinted that, while it has no plans to abandon lockstep entirely, merit-based forms of compensation may play more of a role in the future. "*We could get paid a little more if they didn't plough so much money into the sports teams,*" said one source. That wasn't a complaint – "*it's a good way of getting people involved.*" Freshfields has a team for every possible sport and a gym in the basement to boot. The Harrow or The Witness Box near the firm's home off Fleet Street are always "*awash with Freshfields employees,*" and certain departments are also very socially active, particularly corporate. The competition team went to a medieval banquet at St Katherine Docks, and "*when structured finance had their spring party they invited all the trainees who had come though the department in the past.*"

Qualification prospects have traditionally been excellent but dropped to a merely good 80% in 2009 (still well above the national average for that year). The qualifiers of 2010 were clearly more nervous than usual about their prospects, but as it turned out, 78 out of 95 of them were retained.

And finally...

"No one joining us should be naïve about what it entails. You do have to work hard, but if you find the work interesting and you like the people it's not a deal breaker." That's the long and short of training at Freshfields.

Gordons LLP

The facts

Location: Leeds, Bradford

Number of UK partners/solicitors: 33/52

Total number of trainees: 12

Seats: 4x6 months

Alternative Seats: None

Extras: Pro bono – ProHelp, Be Involved

On chambersstudent.co.uk
- How to get into Gordons
- The Yorkshire legal market
- We talk to managing partner Paul Ayre

Successive mergers in the past decade have propelled this old Bradford-born firm from mid-tier regional outfit to among Yorkshire's best.

Let's grow

Founded in 1844, Gordons only established a Leeds presence in 2000 when it merged with Cranswick Watson. Further mergers followed in both Leeds and Bradford, which are 20 minutes apart by train. Staff are divided evenly between the two cities. Although it has big clients, such as supermarket giant Morrisons, the firm remains a proud Yorkshire operation with strong ties to its local community. It is keen to let the world know about its burgeoning profile and sees itself as a competitor to the Leeds 'Big Six'. Gordons became a top-100 law firm for the first time two years ago.

"*Students don't realise how many areas of law we cover, or how 'up there' we are,*" one trainee claimed. "*I confess I hadn't heard of Gordons until late into my LPC.*" In fact, *Chambers UK* ranks the firm in several categories in Yorkshire, both for business and personal law. "*If you're looking to work in Leeds you should definitely apply,*" a trainee advised. "*You'll get more exposure here than at the big national firms.*" The lateral hire of corporate partner Andrew Morris from DLA Piper in early 2010 highlights Gordons' increased pulling power.

Bradford-based Morrisons uses Gordons for everything from employment law to retail development. Along with City firms Herbert Smith and SJ Berwin, Gordons assisted the supermarket on the purchases of a massive distribution centre in Kent and then 38 Co-op and Somerfield stores for £223m. Other clients include Halfords, brewer Coors and Alliance & Leicester.

Tell it how it is

Gordons recruits six trainees a year and dictates their first two seats. Second-years indicate their preferred final two and usually get them. They like the range of options in both personal and commercial law: there's commercial property (the largest department); commercial litigation; corporate; family; personal injury; insolvency; construction; employment; and risk and compliance.

Trainees primarily pass their time in the Leeds office but typically spend at least six months in Bradford. "*My initial reaction to being sent to Bradford was, 'Oh no', but it's not that bad,*" said a source. The newly refurbished office is next to the station – ideal for trainees who commute in together. "*Bradford's a lot smaller than Leeds,*" but handy amenities include "*an M&S across the road from the office and lots of places to eat out.*" Trainees spoke enthusiastically about the supportive environment in each office. "*I enjoy working here. It's a good atmosphere,*" several confirmed. The Leeds office is "*really nice – everyone you pass in the corridor says hello,*" not least managing partner Paul Ayre, who "*always stops and makes an effort. He asks how you're getting on and which department you're going to next.*"

Making it personal

Ironically, Ayre's commercial property department evoked mixed responses from interviewees. Some found the work "*very procedural*" and the reams of post-completion documents less than riveting. One concluded: "*It's just not for*

Chambers UK rankings

Banking & Finance	Employment
Construction	Intellectual Property
	Private Client
Corporate/M&A	Real Estate
Dispute Resolution	Restructuring/Insolvency

me. I don't enjoy the law, though I had at law school. It's also less friendly than other departments because it's bigger and more serious." Another told us: "*I enjoyed this seat and the variety.*" Tasks include helping negotiate and draft leases, assisting in completing transactions and preparing auction packs. One trainee put the occasional "*frayed tempers*" and "*stressed environment*" down to the bottom having fallen out of the real estate market.

The personal law seat sees trainees looking at the legal affairs of individuals: probate files, wills, inheritance tax and trusts. "*The opportunity to manage your own files*" is perhaps its greatest selling point. Some more business-minded trainees can have negative preconceptions before starting this seat, but the work is more commercial than expected because "*these clients have their own businesses or big estates.*" Furthermore, the department is "*really friendly and people are very approachable.*" The business-minded are similarly "*less keen to do personal injury on the claimant side, because they see themselves more as commercial lawyers.*" There is defendant work on issues like road traffic accidents, and trainees again reported managing their own files. If Morrisons' lorry drivers have prangs – or worse – the Gordons team swings into action. A trainee might set up a diary system to keep track of claims. "*If anything got to the stage where I thought we had to issue proceedings against the other driver, I'd speak to the partner.*" Trips to court and client visits to "*hear them talk through what happened*" are par for the course.

A small family team handles divorce and other related matters, often for wealthy individuals. Trainees "*draft financial forms for divorces.*" These then need to be scrutinised to ensure all is as it seems. Recently, the press got hold of a story about a husband (Gordons' client) who was suing his ex-wife for substantial damages after he discovered that two of their three kids (who he'd been supporting financially) weren't actually his. "*Each case is different; you have to approach each with a blank canvas and not get sucked into emotional crises because you're trying to get the biggest monetary settlement for your client,*" a trainee wisely reflected.

The popular commercial litigation department offers "*varied and well-structured*" work but is more likely than most to demand the occasional late night. "*I was in until 11pm once, but on the plus side we got pizza,*" one trainee recalled. If that wasn't arduous enough, "*the next day I had to get up at 6am!*" Such long hours are rare and 8am or 9am until 5.30pm or 6pm is more standard. The team recently acted for Hallmark Cards in a contract dispute with a builder, and Leeds Building Society against defaulting developers in a multimillion-pound case.

Going postal

Trainees must take it in turns to open the post, following a fortnightly rotation. Those on post duty start at 8am. This chore is "*quite a good way to get to know all the names of the fee earners,*" one trainee acknowledged, "*and to see the types of work coming in.*" However, by the second year the novelty wears off. There's frequent contact between the Leeds and Bradford offices, including by video-link. Each month, different departments take it in turns to provide lunch and give 'What I Do' presentations. Trainees like the unstuffy, open-plan Leeds office but have a slight grumble about its "*not ideal location*" out by the canal: "*At lunch time it's a good ten to 15 minutes' walk into town.*" There's "*some sports rivalry*" on the football and cricket pitches with nearby law firm Cobbetts and accountants Grant Thornton. Favoured bars and eateries are Toast and Lazy Lounge, both conveniently located between BPP Law School and the Leeds office. Team socials have included cinema nights, horse racing trips and bowling.

Each year Gordons nominates a charity and pledges to raise it a certain amount of money. This year's was CandleLighters, which supports children with cancer. Around two dozen Gordonites braved hot coals in a fire walk to raise £3,000. That everyone accomplished this act of reckless altruism is apparently thanks to "*an inspirational speaker*" and some "*silly games*" beforehand. For the less adventurous, a dress-down Friday once a month with home-baked cakes also raises cash. Another popular fund-raiser is the annual 10 km 'Abbey Dash' from Leeds city centre to picturesque Kirkstall Abbey and back.

And finally...

Gordons is growing in size and reputation and offers something different to the Leeds 'Big Six'. All eight qualifiers took up NQ positions with the firm in 2010.

Government Legal Service (GLS)

The facts

Location: London

Number of UK lawyers: 1,978

Total number of trainees: 27

Seats: 4x6 months

Alternative seats: None

Extras: GLS Pro Bono Network; language training

On chambersstudent.co.uk
- **How to get into the GLS**
- **GLS trainees tell us more about their role**

"If I look out the window and tilt my head I can see Big Ben!" one of our interviewees said. It's an apt metaphor for GLS trainees' proximity to the machinery of government.

Crown jewels

GLS lawyers officially only have one client: it's big, sparkly and sits on the head of the most recognisable lady in the world. It's the Crown. Her Maj's government employs over half a million civil servants: just under 2,000 of those are lawyers and they come into the picture when the rest need legal advice – which is basically all the time.

Trainees work for specific government departments; many of them (11 out of 29 in 2010) find themselves under the wing of the Treasury Solicitor's department (TSol), which considers itself "*a law firm for the government: we charge other departments for our litigation.*" The other departments in the frame for trainees in 2010 were Her Majesty's Revenue and Customs (HMRC), the Department for Business, Innovation and Skills (BIS), the Department for Communities and Local Government (DCLG), the Department for Work and Pensions/ Department of Health (DWP/H), the Department for Food and Rural Affairs (Defra), the Ministry of Justice (MoJ) and the Department for Transport (DfT). In the past, further departments have also taken trainees, but public spending decisions have seen the list shorten.

Our TSol trainee sources had all spent their first two seats working on contentious matters ("*they try to give you one public law seat and one private law seat*"). In their second year they then spend either one or two seats on secondment to other departments in a non-contentious advisory role. The ministries that take seconded TSol-ers include Culture, Media and Sport, the Department for Education, the Attorney General's Office, the MoD and the Ministry of Justice. Elsewhere, trainees in departments like HMRC, BIS and DWP/H are able to complete their full training contract in-house, while in others, say Defra or DfT, they are seconded out to gain contentious experience. After the training contract, those who stay on spend one year as a 'legal officer' before becoming a Grade 7 lawyer.

There is no heavy competition for seats. Said one source: "*Everyone expresses preferences and the training principal will try to accommodate as many of those as possible.*" Almost all our interviewees' seats had been ones they had expressed some kind of preference for.

Getting into the GLS is increasingly tough: in 2010 it received over 2,500 applications for just 20 training contracts. By the way, it recruits both solicitors and barristers and you can leave yourself open to either route when first applying. See page 710 for our Chambers Report on the GLS pupillage experience. The application process is truly meritocratic and skills-based: "*Throughout the recruitment process* [during the online tests and face-to-face interviews] *no one sees any more than the applicant's name and whether they are a law or non-law student,*" explained James Murphy of the GLS Secretariat.

Yes minister

TSol is most "*akin to a corporate firm,*" and at times the work and environment can be "*quite intense.*" Lawyers fill out time slips and bill their hours, "*treating other departments as clients.*" The majority of its work is litigation and there are teams for things like immigration, employment, planning and tribunals, as well as more unusual problems like the mysterious-sounding bona vacantia, a "*strange backwater of English law*" that deals with "*the estates of people who have died intestate*" and "companies *which are wound up but don't deal with their assets.*" There's grittier work too. "*One team specialises in security-related immigration matters, but you wouldn't deal with the most sensitive things as a trainee.*" Newbies do get to work on "*judicial review cases against the UK Border Agency, and sometimes on the bigger cases, where you help with the disclosure.*" Lawyers also have to defend government decisions, such as whether or not to return refugees to Iraq. There are occasions when "*whole families get removed from the country or a criminal is deported.*" Immigration is TSol's largest and busiest team, closely followed by the employment group. In an employment seat, trainees manage "*about 15 active files, all at different stages*" and "*draft witness statements, instruct counsel and attend hearings across the country.*" TSol has also been heavily involved in mistreatment cases brought against the British Army by Iraqi civilians.

HMRC blends litigation with advisory work and has dozens of teams that all take trainees. They include tax insolvency ("*we have been involved in some significant football cases, which was interesting*"); ratings and valuations; European and international advisory; personal tax litigation; and corporate tax. Our interviewees had done "*advocacy in the bankruptcy courts*" and been involved with "*notifying departments on decisions of the European Court of Justice and whether cases in other EU member states influence the tax system here.*" Meanwhile, at the MoJ trainees "*advise prison governors on the Secretary of State's guidelines,*" as well as assisting with the drafting of bills and statutory instruments.

DWP/H share a legal team. Trainees are involved with everything from Jobcentre Plus employee disputes to the apology issued by the then Prime Minister Gordon Brown to orphans who were sent to Australia and Canada from the 1920s to the 1960s under a programme that aimed to improve their life chances but often led to distressing outcomes. At the Department for Education, lawyers advised on the judicial review of Sharon Shoesmith's dismissal from her post as Director of Children's Services at the London Borough of Haringey following the tragic Baby P case. They may also encounter List 99, an 80-year-old register of people who are barred from working with children by the Secretary of State. At BIS, lawyers looked at the controversy that arose after steel manufacturers Sheffield Forgemasters had an £80m government loan offer cancelled by the coalition government. They also ensure that "*British companies aren't exporting things to countries they shouldn't be.*"

We've touched upon the departments that take the most trainees but acknowledge that we've barely scratched the surface. There are plenty of other departments and dozens of other seats, so further research is highly recommended, and we've detailed more of the kind of work trainees do on our website.

A recurring theme among our interviewees was that you are "*given a lot of responsibility, sometimes from a frighteningly early stage.*" Genially badmouthing private practice was also popular: "*I know trainees in the private sector who spent their first year picking up dry cleaning, getting flowers for their supervisor's wife and photocopying – not here.*" In reality, private sector training isn't generally like that, but it is certainly true that GLS trainees are exposed to key work an awful lot of the time.

Invitation to join the government of Britain

Policy advice is the real meat of GLS lawyers' work. So how do trainees deal with contradictions between personal opinions and government policies? Here's the vanilla version: "*You have to make sure your work is balanced and fair; you have to remind yourself of your obligation to remain neutral, perhaps more so than private firm lawyers do with their clients.*" In this election year, we were curious about trainees' opinion on politics. "*I was impressed by the way people dealt with* [the change of government] *so easily,*" one commented. "*I have an interest in politics, but not from a perspective of wanting to be involved in it,*" said another; "*it's a detached interest.*" Beyond talk of "*professional duty*" and objectivity, one source offered an elegant constitutional explanation of the ethos of the civil servant. "*In a democracy it is the party who gets the most votes who is in power. Part of democracy is that civil servants work to the best of their ability, regardless of their own views, to carry out the government's policy. It's not me who has been elected to carry out a manifesto.*"

So what should the GLS expect from the new coalition government's budget axe? Our junior sources were not wholly optimistic about the future of trainees and qualified lawyers. "*Last year you wrote that one of the advantages of the GLS is job security,*" said one, "*but I don't think you can say that any more.*" What we can say is that the GLS has been partially ringfenced from the public sector job freeze and will continue to recruit, albeit in smaller numbers. All qualifying trainees were kept on as usual in 2010 and were also promised pay rises on qualification. "*There will be cuts and lawyers won't be immune from that, although probably we will be better protected than other groups,*" said one trainee; "*litigation is not an optional spend for government.*" Although wide-ranging government cuts may bring new legal issues of their own, trainees say this would be a minimal addition to the GLS's heavy caseload. "*We may have to do the same amount of work with less people,*" one mused.

For Queen and country

"*Public service*" was a phrase that cropped up again and again when we asked our interviewees why they chose the GLS. If you want to do "*varied and interesting*" work, but you're "*not fascinated by the City and its culture, then the GLS is an option worth considering.*" Trainees love it: "*Sometimes a piece of advice you give can touch on something very sensitive and you really feel in the thick of it.*"

Private practice attracted some of our trainees, but all were very happy to have chosen the GLS. "*I did work in the private sector and didn't really like the atmosphere of working for the good of someone else's share options,*" said one particularly keen public sector fan. Besides early responsibility, work/life balance is a big pull. "*If a bill is going through, you do have to work longer hours, but you're not expected to stay until stupid o'clock.*" The salary is one of the few negatives. "*If you are motivated purely by money, you won't find a place here,*" said one source. "*It's no secret that you don't get paid as well as you would in the City,*" another added, "*but we certainly don't get terrible wages.*" A qualification wage of between £32,000 and £40,000 is certainly not to be sniffed at. "*You work 38 or 40 hours a week, so hourly you're probably paid just as well as a City lawyer.*"

Unlike their commercial peers, GLS lawyers are usually expected to remain generalists throughout their careers. In fact, "*if you stay in one area for more than three years people sense there is something up with you.*" Trainee reports suggest that TSol is the only department moving towards a degree of specialisation: at the moment the rule is that "*once you join, you have to stay in a team for four years.*"

The party line

Our interviewees suggested that the legal teams are quite similar across the departments. Ministries do differ though: the MoD, for example, is "*slightly more old-fashioned*" and "*generally a lot more male and older*" than departments like Education or DWP/H. Trainees were positive about the "*support and supervision*" they received as well as the friendliness of colleagues. Though there are administrative tasks to do, "*the culture seems to be that everyone is responsible for their own bundles rather than dumping it all on the trainee.*" Overall, the culture of the GLS closely reflects that of the civil service in general. There's a need to "*know what the political sensitivities are and sometimes liaise with a higher authority* [like a ministerial team] *if work touches on something very sensitive.*" Ultimately, lawyers like rules and civil servants like rules, so the two gel rather well.

"*Trainees are spread out so in practice we don't see a lot of each other unless we arrange to.*" That said, there is a trainee network that organises monthly events like drinks evenings, picnics in St James's Park and ice skating. The Union of Government Lawyers, Youngish (UGLY) is also open to trainees and organises its own social events. We got the strong sense that (unlike some in the private sector) GLS lawyers aren't fully married to their work, and trainees agreed that most like to allow themselves a social and private life outside of the office. Of course, they are paid from the public purse, so no one expects a lavish lifestyle. "*Our job has precious little perks,*" said one source. "*Our Christmas parties are 'Bring Your Own' or we pay a fiver, and we bring in our own tea and coffee to work.*"

And finally...

If you want to combine your love of law with *"a public service ethos"* then do give the GLS closer attention. Expect to be put through your paces during the application procedure.

Hammonds LLP

The facts

Location: Birmingham, Leeds, London, Manchester

Number of UK partners/solicitors: 170/400

Total number of trainees: 53

Seats: 6x4 months

Alternative seats: Overseas seats secondments

On chambersstudent.co.uk
- How to get into Hammonds
- Deferrals with a difference
- We talk to Manchester office head Jane Haxby

After some trying times in the early noughties, multi-site, full-service firm Hammonds is looking to a bright future.

Squammonds?

In the days when Blur and Oasis were duking it out in the Battle of Britpop, Hammonds was rising to the top of some very different charts. From humble beginnings in Bradford, the firm popped up in Leeds, Manchester, Birmingham and London over the course of the 90s and rapidly ascended the table of the UK's highest-billing law firms. Then, proving that what goes up must come down, some difficult years took the wind from its sails. More about that on our website; all you really need to know right now is that the firm is back to business as usual.

Well, we say business as usual: the latest news (as of August 2010) put Hammonds in the 'advanced stages' of merger talks with Squire Sanders & Dempsey, a US firm with 32 offices in 15 countries. Hammonds has just ten in six countries, but it could help the American firm in its avowed aim to boost its presence in the UK and Western Europe. We won't jump the gun and say much more here, but we'll keep our website updated as this story develops.

When we talked to the new office chief in Manchester, Jane Haxby, before all this was announced, she said that Hammonds wanted to grow, both in profitability and quality of clients, but that it didn't want "*just to be the biggest.*" In bringing about growth, Hammonds understands that "*it's important to recognise the specialisms that you already have.*"

According to Haxby, "*it's a place where ambitious people really can fulfil their ambitions,*" and that confidence is shared by a loyal client base: Hammonds maintained its relationships with major clients through the years when it was in the doldrums (unlike rival Halliwells, for example, which crashed out of the market in spectacular fashion in mid 2010). Just as importantly, Hammonds added some excellent new clients, too, including retail giant Tesco and Royal Mail. By the way, in 2010 the firm invited some clients to join the vacation scheme panel of interviewers. "*Clients do have a vested interest in who the firm takes on as trainees,*" our sources argued. "*They need to be able to trust us as legal advisers.*"

Location, location, location

Applicants to Hammonds select a specific office to train in. Until recently, Hammonds' training scheme sent people around the office network, and so one consequence of the switch to location-specific training is that qualifying into another office is now "*obviously not as easy.*" What remains a major attraction is the six-seat set-up. "*It can be a whirlwind tour,*" said trainees, but it does ensure that "*you get a good array of experience, and you can also repeat a seat without missing out elsewhere.*"

There are three compulsory stop-offs over the course of the two years: property; litigation; and corporate strategy and finance, although due to a lack of corporate work this seat wasn't mandatory last year. Within these departments there are an assortment of seat choices. Under the property banner are the options of straightforward real estate or construction law. The usual buying and selling, leases and

Chambers UK rankings

Banking & Finance	Intellectual Property
Banking Litigation	Licensing
Capital Markets	Media & Entertainment
Construction	Pensions
Corporate/M&A	Pensions Litigation
Dispute Resolution	Planning
Employment	Real Estate
Environment	Real Estate Litigation
Health & Safety	Restructuring/Insolvency
Information Technology	Sports Law
	Tax

lease renewals await property trainees, along with regeneration and other development projects. The firm advised London Underground on the King's Cross Northern Ticket Hall improvement, which is part of a wider £900m plan to link King's Cross Tube station with St Pancras railway station in time for the 2012 Olympics. Client contact is welcomed in a "*generally upbeat department – the clients and people you deal with on a daily basis are mostly happy, unlike in a contentious seat!*" Over in the construction department, trainees are exposed to a variety of forms of dispute resolution; mostly they work on arbitrations and litigation in the Technology and Construction Court. The construction team does also have a non-contentious side, and here trainees work their way around development contracts and are left to "*run the smaller matters, with supervision when you need it.*" Hammonds provides trainees with both a partner supervisor and solicitor supervisor. "*They've all been really approachable – they become your friends by the end of the seat,*" raved one trainee. "*You can never ask too many questions.*"

Whale of a time

Though times have been hard for corporate finance teams across the UK, trainees spoke of a department where "*things are picking up*" and getting "*busier and busier.*" In 2009, the firm worked on 54 transactions with a total value in excess of £2bn. One kitschy deal involved advising the shareholders of retailer Cath Kidston on their £106m sale to private equity outfit TA Associates. When they assist on transactions, trainees discover that "*if you're willing and show that you want to do more than the traditional trainee tasks, they'll let you.*" Our sources were certainly encouraged to interact with clients, even though everything they produce needs to be checked. "*You can't just go Free Willy,*" warned one. Shouldering the responsibility of organising documents in completion meetings improves trainees' organisational skills, while working on due diligence requires them to "*liaise with other departments, which helps to get you a name within the firm.*"

Banking trainees spoke of the "*high involvement in completion meetings*" and the satisfaction of seeing deals through from start to finish. "*Even though I'd finished my seat, I was still able to go to the completion meetings,*" said one. A stint in the EU, competition, trade and regulatory team can also fulfil the corporate requirement, where the small team size offers "*a different dynamic.*" Work highlights include advising Aldi on its involvement in the Competition Commission's consultation on remedies, which led to the Commission's adoption of the Groceries Supply Code of Practice Order; and counselling T-Mobile UK and Orange on the planning aspects of their proposed merger. Trainees did admit, however, that because the supervisor for this seat is located in Manchester, "*you can feel a bit isolated if you're in another office.*"

Hammonds is no stranger to international business and it has both its own overseas branches and firms with which it is closely associated. There is exactly such an association with a five-office Italian firm, which looks to be rather good in the fields of IP, technology and employment law. Hammonds' own overseas branches are to be found in Beijing; Hong Kong; Moscow; St Petersburg; Madrid (highly rated for litigation); Brussels (excellent for international trade work); Paris and Berlin. At the time of our interviews, trainees had a chance to visit the Paris or Brussels offices for a seat. Hong Kong secondments were on hold, though this option may make a comeback. Would a Squire Sanders merger open up new overseas opportunities in the Americas? Watch this space.

Experience of a commercial department is "*preferred*" for those trainees wanting a client secondment. Music fans will be excited to hear that there's a regular spot at Live Nation, and we learned of people being seconded to Barclays and Northern Rock. "*Others come up now and again,*" we were informed. As to who gets to go, "*if there's a good relationship with a client, the firm wants to send people who will be good ambassadors.*" Visitors to Live Nation help its business team with general commercial contracts, sponsorship agreements and bringing claims against ticket touts. Plus they have the enviable perk of "*being sent a gig list every Monday and asked what tickets you want.*" Secondees enjoy high levels of responsibility and involvement, though "*you never feel like you're on your own – you can ring up Hammonds at any time.*" Cannily, the firm also offered the trainees it deferred during the recession the chance to work at one of its clients. Visit our website to read about one future starter's experience at the Birmingham Chamber of Commerce.

A league of their own

On to litigation at Hammonds. One source described the work they'd done in a mediation for a major client: "*At the end of the matter, they sent an e-mail to my partner to thank us for all the work we'd done. They copied in the managing partner, so it was great to get that recognition.*" Advocacy is also on the cards, and we heard of trainees who'd appeared before High Court masters, making interim applications and negotiating the admission of court documents. Our sources were all rather matter-of-fact about this exciting aspect to a contentious seat. "*They tell you to go and do it, and you do it!*" Property litigation and insolvency seats both fulfil the contentious requirement: in the latter, "*you get out in the market and do lots of networking.*" Demonstrating Hammonds' down-to-earth attitude, "*the firm organised a tongue-in-cheek kebab and darts night once.*"

Despite the fact that it is "*quite a complex and technical area,*" most trainees "*have a dabble*" in pensions, "*taking advantage of the firm's fantastic reputation.*" The seat involves plenty of "*hypothetical research,*" and many trainees enjoy starting with "*a clean slate*" in this unfamiliar area of law. Responsibility certainly ups for those who repeat the seat. Said one source: "*A file came in from a new client and I was given it from inception to the end. It almost turned me into a fee earner.*"

Trainees raved about London's "*amazing*" sports law department. "*It was such hard work... I basically gave up my life for four months, but I really didn't care.*" Working late here is "*more your prerogative than an expectation.*" And you can see why trainees want to give the seat their all. Hammonds acted as the main adviser to Chelsea FC, Fulham FC, and Aston Villa FC in 2009, and represented several other Premier League clubs as well. New clients include Roberto Mancini and Brit Insurance, whom the firm advised on its sponsorship agreement with the ECB – the largest ever sponsorship agreement in English cricket. Drafting notes of advice for football teams and employment terms and conditions for footballers, our sources "*learned loads about arbitration and doping regulations.*"

Dancing like dad

As soon as future starters sign up to the firm, they're invited along to socials. After-work drinks are a regular occurrence, especially in London where "*all the bars on the doorstep stop you from going straight home.*" Hammonds' summer and winter parties are ever-popular – "*it might not be the flashiest Christmas party, but everyone has a great time. There's a lot of university-style dancing where people are thrown into the circle to do a dance on their own.*" There are a good range of sports teams to get involved with – football, netball, cricket and rugby – and trainees can also support the efforts of the charity committee or take on pro bono activities. The induction for new starters at St Catherine's College, Oxford is "*basically a three-week jolly,*" although a recruitment source insisted it was hard work too. One memorable activity was an *Apprentice*-style pitch of a pasta machine to Alex Wotherspoon (the pretty-boy contestant in the 2008 series). "*We were working all through the night,*" confessed one trainee. "*But we were fed on good food and wine. Most importantly, we became great mates.*"

"*Why do I love it here?*" asked one trainee. "*It's the people. They really know what they're doing and are so passionate about their work, but they love life too.*" Don't expect any stuffiness or ego. "*That traditional image of a lawyer in his bowler hat? There's none of that here.*" We lost count of the number of times our sources described the firm as "*friendly*" and "*down-to-earth*" with "*approachable people who can get on with anybody.*" This ethos was evident to trainees right from the start. "*I wasn't traumatised in the slightest,*" one said of his training contract interview. "*We just had a discussion and talked for so long that recruitment had to come in and tell us to hurry it along as there were others waiting outside.*"

With trainees forming such a close-knit group, the run-up to qualification "*is made all the more difficult,*" but "*it doesn't feel like people are biting at each other's heels.*" Said one source: "*We just all have to do our best. It's not about trampling on each other.*" In 2010, 31 out of 39 qualifiers took up jobs with the firm.

And finally...

Hammonds appears to have moved on from its previous financial woes and our sources seemed delighted that the firm is full of *"real people"* who are committed to giving them a good training. Keep an eye on that Squire Sanders story.

Harbottle & Lewis LLP

The facts

Location: London

Number of UK partners/solicitors: 31/48

Total number of trainees: 9

Seats: 4x6 months

Alternative seats: Secondments

On chambersstudent.co.uk
- How to get into Harbottle
- The history of Hanover Square
- A law firm for the digital age

In 1955 in London's West End, Harbottle & Lewis's founders brought together an interest in the legal aspects of film production with a passion for theatre.

Stars and Skypes

In those early days, they concentrated on working for theatre and film producers, writers, actors and technicians. Television and music industry clients followed, and were eventually joined by new media businesses. Harbottle's work is now heavily influenced by the convergence of technologies and digitisation, and the firm is committed to advising companies on how to use new tech within the framework of sector-specific regulation and general competition and commercial law.

Those old-school theatre clients are still important: the firm has worked on successful titles such as *Billy Elliot*, *We Will Rock You* and *The 39 Steps*, and trainees get "*to see how a theatre production transfers from West End to Broadway*" and other behind-the-scenes aspects of this creative world. Famous clients are a part of daily life and you need to keep your cool. Harbottle represents people such as The Royal Household, Kate Middleton (she was awarded £5,000 in a privacy case), Gok Wan, Sophie Dahl, Postman Pat and Kate Moss. It also advised an ad agency on a campaign featuring Iggy Pop, and some very lucky souls have worked for our nation's true Lionheart, David Beckham. Well known corporates include News International, *The Evening Standard*, EMI Music Publishing, Universal Music Group and Comic Relief. But it is in the digital arena that Harbottle stands out from other specialist entertainment firms. One recently acted in a dispute against Skype in relation to its use of computer software licensed from client Joltid. For more on this kind of work, go to our website.

Media glory

New recruits to the four-seat training scheme learn of their assignments during their initial induction. Everyone must do a contentious seat, which can be either litigation, IP or employment. The media seat (called 4Is) combines interactive entertainment, IP, sport, TV, broadcasting, film, theatre and music work, and is naturally a favourite. Standalone IP and employment seats are also popular. Property and commercial are options too. The latter seat can be replaced by a secondment, lately to the London Organising Committee of the Olympic Games and Paralympic Games, or to long-standing client Virgin Atlantic in Crawley. At Virgin, trainees are "*shoved in at the deep end, but not in a bad way*" and work on contract drafting, reviewing all types of agreements used in the aviation industry and dealing with passenger claims. There is also a private client seat covering family and charity as well as the usual tax, wills and trusts.

A trainee's experience in litigation could be IP-oriented, in which case they will deal with big brands, investigate potential infringements and draft letters. High-profile and smaller companies are rewarding in different ways. "*You can see your work in action when you go home and turn on the TV. At the other end of the scale, you're working for clients that genuinely need your help.*" Other cases relate to everything from defamation to contract claims. Litigation trainees appear in court to take notes and are expected to undertake "*inevitable bundling*" duties in preparation for trials. "*It's vitally important that it gets done correctly,*" reported a source, explaining that all

Chambers UK rankings

Asset Finance	Information Technology
Charities	Intellectual Property
Corporate/M&A	Media & Entertainment
Defamation/Reputation Management	Private Client
Employment	Real Estate
Family/Matrimonial	Sports Law

eyes will be on the trainee if a flaw emerges. Speaking of court, the employment team has had a big year. As adviser to Gillian Switalski in one of the UK's most high-profile employment claims, it was all set to go to the Court of Appeal in late 2009, until the £19m discrimination and bullying claim against her former City employer was finally settled.

It's in the game!

The 4Is seat deals with IP, sport and all forms of entertainment media. Harbottle is building its contentious and regulatory sports practice: clients include a leading tennis player and the England Cricket Team, and lawyers recently negotiated licensing arrangements on behalf of EA SPORTS for brands such as FIFA, Tiger Woods and Need for Speed. The IP practice excels in areas such as personality rights and copyright infringement. It protects the Virgin brand and has worked on anti-piracy matters involving *Star Wars* and *Indiana Jones* properties. Media seat trainees explore actors' contracts, learn how theatre royalties work, draft agreements for writers and creative teams, and help on financing deals. Property seats involve "*large-scale residential transactions and commercial leases,*" plus support work for corporate deals, for example "*sales of night clubs and music venues.*"

Trainees agree that high-quality work is what gets them ahead and sets them up for qualification. They also speak about an environment in which "*everyone knows everyone else.*" The office isn't open-plan, and trainees typically sit with one or two lawyers of differing seniority, which is great for seeing how your career might look like in a few years. "*The most important thing is to make an effort and to get involved. It's not a place where you can hide away, and you don't want to be forgotten.*" The firm's "*homely feel*" (complete with fireplaces and bay windows) reinforces a sense of intimacy. "*You can walk into an associate's or partner's office and sit down and have a conversation with them, whether it's about work or the weekend's activities.*"

No BlackBerrys allowed

Every lunchtime, staff and partners can mingle over a free hot meal. This tradition requires everyone to put away phones and reading material and engage in good old-fashioned conversation. "*People tend to be fairly gregarious, open and easy-going,*" said a source. "*There's definitely a culture of not doing crazy hours,*" said one trainee. Work demands are less agonising than in big City firms but in no way equal to la dolce vita. "*Applicants should be made aware of that,*" one source stressed; "*people who give you work expect you to do it on time.*" Seniors are equipped with BlackBerrys, but dare ask for one as a junior and people will think you're "*bonkers!*" Passion for the client sector or the subject matter lends itself to diligent work. "*You do it for love, not money,*" said a trainee, referring to the fact that the Harbottle salary is lower than big City firms but "*certainly not peanuts.*"

The typical day runs from 9am to 6.30pm, but longer hours (say, to 8pm) crop up consistently in some seats. Working all night can be "*pretty miserable,*" but is the rare exception as supervisors step in to prevent trainees from becoming too stretched. The social scene involves bowling and karaoke, quiz nights, a Christmas party and sponsored charity events. Sports activities centre on touch rugby, football, cricket, netball and golf. Perks include backstage passes to the British Comedy Awards, soap awards and fashion shows.

And finally...

Harbottle focuses on a range of media sectors and seeks an equally colourful cross-section of personalities, according to training partner Sandi Simons. In 2010, five out of six qualifiers were offered positions; all accepted.

HBJ Gateley Wareing

The facts

Location: Birmingham, Leicester, Nottingham, London, Manchester, Scotland

Number of UK partners/solicitors: 140/300

Total number of trainees: 29 (English offices)

Seats: 4x6 months

Alternative seats: None

On chambersstudent.co.uk
- How to get into HBJ Gateley Wareing
- Charity at HBJ
- Past mergers and the new Halliwells add-on

HBJ Gateley Wareing is a dark horse. Without much fuss or fanfare, this national outfit is creeping up the list of the UK's top 100 firms.

In one fell swoop

A long and complicated history of mergers lies behind the now rather cumbersomely named HBJ Gateley Wareing, which now has bases in Scotland, Birmingham, Leicester, Nottingham, Manchester, London and Dubai. This report covers the firm's English training scheme. Property and corporate are HBJ's biggest departments, and it is ranked as one of the nation's best firms for legal advice to the transportation sector by *Chambers UK*. The firm also rates well in corporate/M&A; tax; banking; restructuring/insolvency; construction; real estate; dispute resolution; private client; pensions; and employment.

When northern law firm Halliwells collapsed spectacularly in summer 2010 (and if you don't know about this story yet, get online and read *The Chambers Magazine*'s article *Dangerous Ambition*), HBJ jumped in to take on the defunct firm's entire Manchester commercial practice. At one stroke, it gained more than 200 members of staff, including 40 partners and 13 trainees. The office is strong on corporate and real estate, and also has good banking and finance, real estate litigation, corporate recovery, commercial litigation, intellectual property, employment, pensions and construction groups. HBJ had apparently been thinking about building a Manchester office, so it wasn't exactly an overnight decision, but the Halliwells meltdown was a perfect opportunity. It has transformed the firm into an undeniably national outfit of significant weight in a new part of the country. We did speak to some Manchester trainees, but it was while they were still training at Halliwells. You can learn more about that office and its work and people online.

In past years, trainees could take seats in all the different English offices, with London and Birmingham the most popular options. During the recession, however, trainees were kept in the offices to which they were hired, which caused some discontent among our sources. Fortunately, in the future trainees should again be able to move around between the different branches, including the new Manchester office. At the time of our calls, Birmingham was still the largest office (230-240 staff) and had ten trainees. Nottingham had three, London two and Leicester one. The Manchester office is now the second biggest (210-220 staff) and it has 13 trainees, all of whom came over from Halliwells.

As for the relationships between the different locations, the Midlands people "*see quite a lot of each other*" at joint socials, while London trainees and lawyers have regular contact with colleagues in Birmingham. Some departments, such as insolvency, collaborate across the Midlands offices and meet quite regularly, either in person or via videoconference. While a handful of people from Edinburgh and Glasgow sometimes come down to Birmingham for meetings and work, the Scottish trainees remain largely a mystery to their English peers, but there's evidence to suggest there will be more of a connection with them in the future.

HBJ's seat rules require trainees to take one seat in corporate, one in property and a contentious option. Within these parameters there is room for variation and personal preference. For their fourth seat, trainees are asked to identify their first and second choices. Our sources generally

Chambers UK rankings

Agriculture & Rural Affairs	Pensions
Banking & Finance	Personal Injury
Construction	Private Client
Consumer Finance	Real Estate
Corporate/M&A	Restructuring/Insolvency
Debt Recovery	Shipping
Dispute Resolution	Social Housing
Employment	Tax
Family/Matrimonial	Transport
Intellectual Property	

understood the rationale behind this system and found the seating arrangements surprisingly flexible; nevertheless, they did express a wish for slightly more choice and better communication with HR about the process.

Hong Kong Brummie

The corporate department is the largest at the firm: its clients include insurer Allianz and recruitment company Pertemps, and its "*really big deals*" regularly appear in the press. Lawyers acted for Birmingham City plc (the AIM-listed parent of the football club) in its £81.5m takeover by Hong Kong businessman Carson Yeung, and for Maven Capital Partners on its £23m secondary buyout of Funeral Service Partnership. The old 'work hard, play hard' chestnut is at its truest in the corporate department: trainees find it incredibly busy, and the hours are decidedly longer than in the rest of the firm. Trainees get involved in "*a fairly broad spectrum of work"*– listings, private equity transactions, share and asset sales, drafting articles, research, etc. Our sources had made presentations, both within and outside the firm, travelled around to see different clients and attended completion meetings in other offices. In addition to the larger "*multimillion-pound deals*," there are also some "*hands-on smaller jobs*" that are ideal for trainees. It is also a good seat for developing organisational skills, as trainees sometimes have to juggle five or six things at a time. Alternatively, under the 'corporate' banner, trainees can do a seat in banking.

After corporate, property is the second biggest department, and the seat options here are property, property finance and the residential development unit. Despite the recession, some of our sources were given a lot of responsibility and found the seat to have been a busy one, often involving long hours. Trainees have daily contact with "*a wide variety of clients*" including Alfred McAlpine, British Telecom, Wolverhampton City Council and a number of big retailers. Our sources had run their own meetings, provided clients with advice and taken on drafting and research tasks. The residential development unit targets social housing organisations and has doubled its client base since 2008, though the climate for new development in the sector is now nowhere near as healthy as it was before the recession. Trainees in this seat found it "*surprising: I thought the market would be dead, but it was arguably my busiest six months*." The seat is varied, with "*lots of research*" and dealings with social landlords and house builders. Trainees were also given the opportunity to have direct client contact and run their own meetings.

The recovery/insolvency team combines disputes and transactional work, making it a popular seat for trainees. Riding the wave of the recession, the team is "*extremely busy.*" Trainees can look forward to a tremendous amount of advocacy as well as "*a lot of communication with clients*," plus negotiation and business development activities. One Birmingham trainee gushed that the team is "*lovely*," another that it is "*fantastic*." However, in London the seat can be less exciting and there was a suggestion that the trainee is underutilised.

Trainees may hone their litigation skills in employment, commercial dispute resolution or real estate/construction litigation seats. Since October 2006, HBJ has defended BT in over 280 employment cases, with a 100% success rate (the national average success rate is 76%). Cases have included the full range of employment tribunal jurisdictions, including unfair dismissal and discrimination on the grounds of race, sex and disability. Trainees found that the employment seat offered quite a lot of research; all sorts of drafting of agreements, tribunal documents and witness statements; client meetings and "*plenty more*."

Little Britain?

HBJ has a Dubai office that concentrates on construction and shipping but also handles some corporate transactions. Some UK fee earners "*go out there a lot*," but trainees hoping for a seat in Dubai shouldn't hold their breath. Despite this international aspect to the firm, trainee seats don't tend to involve much overseas work, although we are aware of some interesting links with China in the new Manchester office. Elsewhere, there are European elements to some asset finance matters, and in property there may be foreign buyers. The exception is the shipping department, which by nature is "*very international – at least 60%*," and trainees in this department often liaise with foreign lawyers. The seat can cover all sorts of unexpected issues, including employment and injury claims as well as collisions and contract disputes. The shipping team recently acted for Tom Perkins, venture capitalist and former husband of novelist Danielle Steele, in connection with the sale of the iconic 88-metre yacht, 'The Maltese Falcon', the only Dyna-rig sailing yacht in the world. The transaction, which involved four legal jurisdictions, is believed to be the most high-value megayacht sale in the world for at least the previous twelve months.

Overall, trainees were happy – and often pleasantly surprised – with the amount of responsibility and client contact they got (*"loads, absolutely loads"*), although this naturally varied between different offices, teams and supervisors. In general, working hours allow for *"a good work/life balance,"* and it's *"not frowned upon if you leave at 5.30pm,"* although late nights are sometimes required. The salary, on the other hand, was a sore point: it was variously described as *"disappointing to say the least"* and *"pretty bad."* In the Midlands offices, the starting salary is £20,000, rising to £32,000 for an NQ, while in London the figures are respectively £22,000 and £45,000. The arrival of better-paid Manchester trainees and NQs will undoubtedly mean the issue will be addressed one way or another.

Ghost walks and team games

Despite its mouthful of a name, HBJ Gateley Wareing is a firm with a reputation for being *"down to earth"* and where people *"go out of their way to organise social events and encourage team spirit."* Trainees aren't shy about asking stupid questions, employees are *"not expected to wear a tie every day,"* and there is a dress-down Friday once every month. Additionally, there is a buddy system in place and a staff council for discussing any problems that may arise.

One trainee related some words of wisdom: *"50% of the work is winning clients; 50% is keeping them,"* and for this reason, HBJ offers a number of networking courses. These come in handy as there can be client events once or twice a week in some departments. Public speaking and advocacy skills are also taught through presentation workshops, and there's also more specialised training sessions; for example, the shipping team in London has a series of lunchtime lectures and the real estate department is *"really good for training."* Other teams, such as corporate, are less focused on formal sessions, with trainees tending to pick up most of their knowledge as they go along.

In the past, HBJ was known as a step-up-to-the-plate sort of firm with rough-and-tumble lawyers who liked a drink or two. If this sounds like your sort of place, you might be a little late. One trainee said that *"as the firm has got bigger it has become less intense;"* while employees still *"like to let their hair down"* and are *"not afraid to get their hands dirty,"* HBJ has a calmer reputation these days. That said, there are plenty of sports teams, trainees regularly get involved with local Junior Lawyers Division initiatives, and those in Birmingham are members of the active Birmingham Trainee Solicitors' Society.

The Birmingham office building has an old façade and modern interior. It's in the legal heart of the city, close to the courts, so *"it makes you feel like a City lawyer"* as there are always *"lots of people around and the bars are busy in the evenings."* The other offices are all quite centrally located within their cities, and each has regular social events organised by trainees. Londoners arrange theatre trips, ghostly guided walks and bowling; in Leicester there are networking events; Nottingham trainees love ice-skating and barbecues; while the Birmingham crew is into karaoke, quizzes and pub games. There are also annual events that feature team games between the English offices.

Trainees understand that the firm is aiming to consolidate its presence in London, which should be helped by the addition of 11 people from Halliwells. The office on Holborn Viaduct currently only has two trainees but is *"growing quite significantly"* and *"desperately needs more."* The biggest change, of course, is the arrival of 200 Mancunians. With a not dissimilar approach to work and clients, we reckon the Halliwells rescue could turn out to be the game-changing move for HBJ. It has already pushed it into the top-50 UK firms, by revenue.

In 2010, seven out of ten HBJ qualifiers were kept on at the new-look firm, four of them in the Birmingham office. In general, trainees felt a strong *"sense of loyalty"* to their employer and found their training contract *"a very positive experience." "People are really supportive,"* said one; *"I made the right decision coming here."* Early noises from the firm's new Manchester branch suggests a sense of relief that the commercial (non-contentious) practice groups have remained largely intact and have been welcomed so positively by HBJ. Within a couple of months of the tie-up Manchester staff quit the expensive office they'd been occupying in the Spinningfields district and moved into Cobbetts' old digs at Ship Canal House on King Street.

And finally...

As it has grown, HBJ Gateley Wareing has become a serious player, but there's plenty to suggest it's still fun at heart. The Manchester deal should take the firm to the next level.

- **Researching firms:** Want to know how to do it properly? Go to www.chambersstudent.co.uk where we'll teach you the tricks of the trade.

Henmans LLP

The facts

Location: Oxford

Number of UK partners/solicitors: 22/38

Total number of trainees: 6

Seats: 4x6 months

Alternative seats: None

Extras: Pro bono – Oxford CAB

On chambersstudent.co.uk
• How to get into Henmans
• Henmans' main practice areas
• A closer look at clinical negligence and personal injury

A sharper focus on management and a growing corporate practice is giving this Thames Valley player an extra dimension.

Commercial relief

In 2007 Henmans moved from offices in central Oxford and Woodstock (think "*village location, brass plaque on the door*") to a business park off the Oxford ring road. "*There's plenty of space for more desks and people,*" said training principal Paul Thompson, explaining that "*room to expand*" was the incentive for the move. The firm's largest department is a private client team that accounts for almost a quarter of all income and is top-ranked in the Thames Valley by *Chambers UK*. Henmans is also one of the region's top clinical negligence, personal injury, agriculture and charities firms. It is additionally recognised for M&A, dispute resolution, employment and property, though it's fair to say that the commercial side of the business is less developed. Keen to change that, Henmans is making a push in its commercial offering. Accountant Matthew Keegan joined from Allen & Overy in 2008 as head of finance, and has led the drive.

The training contract offers seats in private client (incorporating charities), corporate, property, employment and dispute resolution, as well as a combined personal injury and clinical negligence seat. The absence of family seats has been a "*bone of contention*" for some trainees.

Cotswold life

The good folk of Oxfordshire provide rich pickings for the private client group. The county is home to wealthy professionals, successful academics, affluent grey-hairs, entrepreneurs and businessmen, plus the owners of landed and farming estates. The firm even has a few household-name actors and authors on its client list. Within the private client department, trainee tasks include technical tax planning advice and ample opportunities to "*have a go at the first draft of a will.*" Trainees like "*seeing the process through, which you can't necessarily do with, say, litigation.*" Dealing with death "*can be depressing,*" but the team's good humour lightens things. "*The client contact helps as well, rather than just researching points of law.*"

The personal injury lawyers represent both claimants and defendants, and "*big insurers and companies everyone's heard of*" including several well-known car manufacturers. The clin neg lawyers have seen the volume of instructions increase by 120% in the past year. Trainees in these seats are exposed to the staples of the sector – road traffic accidents, asbestos-related illness, botched surgery, dodgy doctoring and so on. They carry out research, "*go to court and take trial notes, and draft witness statements and instructions to counsel.*" Fans of the seat cite it as an "*amazing experience working with some real leaders in the field.*"

Henmans "*realises it's got to grow its corporate department,*" said one source. "*It's a regional firm that's got aspirations for national reach. It has that in some areas, but not corporate yet, and there is a focus on bringing more people in.*" The firm says the team's turnover grew by 20% in the past year, and interdepartmental referrals have helped bring in business. For example, company sales and restructurings came across from the land and agriculture practice. Expect lots of drafting and research

Chambers UK rankings

Agriculture & Rural Affairs	Family/Matrimonial
Charities	Intellectual Property
Clinical Negligence	Personal Injury
Corporate/M&A	Private Client
Dispute Resolution	Professional Negligence
Employment	Real Estate

in this "*document-heavy*" seat. One trainee got a "*buzz*" from a "*late-night deal,*" proving that while long hours don't come regularly, they can't be avoided completely.

The property department represents several prominent local businesses, estates and councils, plus some national clients including the Clydesdale and Co-operative Banks and builders' merchant Travis Perkins. Those familiar with London's arts scene will know the Roundhouse – Henmans acted on the Camden venue's sale. Contentious property features in the dispute resolution seat, which also offers a mixture of professional negligence, contentious probate and commercial litigation. Here, research topics range from human rights to bankruptcy, mortgage fraud to Land Registry rules. Trainees run some cases solo, including a debt recovery files. When it comes to professional indemnity matters – and the firm has a great track record – "*a lot tends to come from London insurance houses*" that manage the claims brought against their policyholders.

In Henmans' more business-driven world, marketing is important right from the get go. "*As trainees, we're encouraged to start cementing relationships with people who in five years' time will be sources of work.*" Typical activities include meet-and-greets and "*lunches with potential referrers.*"

The best things in life are free

Henmans is quite unusual in that it is presently two-thirds female with an almost 50-50 split at partner level. If you like the sound of this, put it high on your shortlist because you'll not see that kind of balance in many firms of its size. Managing partner Julia Iball trained with the firm, qualifying in 1987. Arguably it's the predominance of women that makes the work-life balance here so reasonable: flexible work schemes are available to everybody, not just parents.

It may be a one-office firm but trainees "*don't feel like we're this little provincial business*" and dispute that Henmans is an attractive option only for people from the region. Visually, the "*airy and modern*" office is, "*in terms of driving forward the corporate aspirations, dead on.*" There's "*lots of glass and a lovely big atrium in the middle.*" It's open-plan so "*there's always a bit of a buzz. You hear what's going on – how people interact and talk on the phone. You pick up loads.*" There aren't too many pubs and restaurants in the firm's neck of the woods but fortunately its subsidised cafeteria is "*very good indeed.*" If trainees had a complaint, it was about pay. "*The salary seems to be lagging behind the firm's aspirations,*" one grumbled. That said, the NQ salary of £34,000 is perfectly standard for a firm of Henmans' size and location.

A match made in Henmans

Henmans "*is sociable, so you'll meet people,*" but don't count on mingling at the pub with workmates every single Friday. The firm's business park location means everyone has to drive – not ideal for big nights out – but the firm does have the occasional barbecue and trips to the dogs. Trainees regularly co-ordinate local events for young lawyers in "*beautiful Oxford,*" and there are plenty of opportunities to click with others on the sports field. Tennis ace Tim's great-grandfather founded Henmans in 1890, so the firm-wide tennis tournament is only fitting. We also happen to know that the managing partner (presumably tongue in cheek) invested in table tennis set-up for corporate events. With "*netball matches against local accountants,*" a regular football scene and cricket during the summer months, there's no shortage of sporting chances. Joggers can bring their running shoes for a lunchtime group run, and the firm also had "*someone who used to do pilates on a weekly basis in one of the conference rooms,*" said a trainee, relieved it was "*optional rather than compulsory.*"

When not in tracksuits, the dress code is smart. "*Occasionally partners walk around in jeans, but that hasn't made its way down the pecking order just yet.*" There are dress-down days for charity, and one costume party inspired a partner to come dressed as Count Dracula, "*which was disconcerting at first.*"

And finally...

Henmans has a top private client practice and is developing well in the commercial sphere. In 2010, the firm was disappointed to not be able to keep its three qualifying trainees. Jobs simply weren't available in their preferred areas of practice.

Herbert Smith LLP

The facts

Location: London

Number of UK partners/solicitors: 170/600

Total number of trainees: 185

Seats: 4x6 months

Alternative seats: Overseas seats, secondments

Extras: Pro bono – Whitechapel Legal Advice Centre, Fair Trial International, FRU, RCJ CAB; language training

On chambersstudent.co.uk
- How to get into Herbert Smith
- We talk to managing partner David Willis
- Herbies' in-house advocacy unit

Undeniable quality and an enviable client list make upwardly mobile Herbert Smith an appealing choice for both disputes fans and transactionalists.

Twins

The twin pillars of this firm are disputes and corporate work; both are strong nationally and internationally. At last count, some 39% of UK revenue was generated by corporate lawyers, 41% by litigators, 10% by finance lawyers and another 10% by property lawyers. In 2009/10, Herbies' revenue was up a touch to £450m. "*Our objective is to be regarded as one of the world's elite law firms,*" managing partner David Willis told us, emphasising that to a client, law firms are more than percentages on balance sheets.

As any elite law firm will tell you, the most important thing is the quality of the work and the quality of the clients. Between 2004 and 2009, Herbert Smith gained more new FTSE 100/250 clients than any other firm (according to *The Chambers Magazine*), taking it to fifth place when it comes to FTSE 100 clients and third for combined FTSE 100/FTSE 250 clients. This shift to wider appeal has come during a period in which the firm has undergone global diversification and expansion. Some 18% of the firm's revenue was generated in offices outside the UK in 2005; now it is 33%.

The firm has grown its finance practice globally, adding partners who specialise in Islamic finance, structured finance, derivatives, general banking and restructuring. One recent success was getting onto the JPMorgan legal panel. In addition to 13 offices in Europe, Russia, the Middle East, South-East Asia, China and Japan, it is afforded further coverage by an alliance with German firm Gleiss Lutz and Benelux-based Stibbe.

Herbies doesn't have an office in Africa, but *Chambers Global* describes it as "*one of the clear leaders for oil and gas work in Africa... it consistently features on the continent's most high-profile petrochemicals transactions.*" India's closed legal market hasn't prevented Herbert Smith making a name for itself there either: it advised Tata Motors in its acquisition of Jaguar Land Rover from Ford for $2.3bn, helped Tata Steel with its £6.2bn takeover bid for the Anglo-Dutch steelmaker Corus, and worked with the Temasek Group on arrangements for an indirect investment in Indian mobile operator Bharti Airtel.

Financial jiggery-pokery

Trainees complete four seats of six months each. Litigation and corporate are both compulsory seats, but the other options are numerous. In what trainees describe as a "*really well-structured*" seat allocation process, they send a form to HR detailing up to eight preferred choices. The first thing HR does is allocate the overseas seats and the coveted spots in the firm's in-house advocacy unit. Other seats are then allocated after taking into account trainees' motivations.

Litigation runs deep. Herbies was long known as a disputes specialist and, though now more diversified, it still handles some of the most complex disputes in the world. This has always been a major draw for trainees, who quickly find that there are many specialised sub-teams to choose from. "*In my group there is sport, media, defamation; there's a*

Chambers UK rankings

Administrative & Public Law	Media & Entertainment
Banking & Finance	Outsourcing
Banking Litigation	Partnership
Capital Markets	Pensions
Competition/European Law	Pensions Litigation
Construction	Planning
Corporate/M&A	Private Client
Data Protection	Private Equity
Dispute Resolution	Product Liability
Employee Share Schemes	Professional Discipline
Employment	Professional Negligence
Energy & Natural Resources	Projects
Environment	Public International Law
Financial Services	Public Procurement
Fraud	Real Estate
Health & Safety	Real Estate Finance
Information Technology	Real Estate Litigation
Insurance	Restructuring/Insolvency
Intellectual Property	Retail
Investment Funds	Tax
Life Sciences	Telecommunications
Local Government	Transport

team that does construction, oil, gas and energy; then others do stuff like banking litigation and property litigation. Further groups handle financial services litigation, fraud investigations and public law; and there are plenty of others too." Irrespective of group, the consensus is that the work "*is really interesting and intellectually stimulating.*" Trainees felt they were "*on the cutting edge of the recession,*" handling "*lots of collateralised debt obligation litigation*" and other matters pertaining to super-technical financial jiggery-pokery. They loved it, not least because they worked closely with partners much of the time and were able to attend court hearings. Unusually, Herbert Smith has an advocacy unit comprising an in-house group of barristers and solicitors who handle the firm's courtroom advocacy and advise on case strategy. For more information go to our website.

Client events, drinks, strategy meetings and an hours culture in which "*people try to be considerate of your plans*" add to the appeal, making disputes teams very popular for qualification. Clients range from sovereign states to corporations, banks, energy providers and just about anything big enough to afford the firm's fees. To name just a few, the firm represents BAE Systems, Gazprom, Abbott Laboratories, Citi and Zurich. One landmark piece of work was the advice given to Mabey & Johnson, which instigated the first ever self-reporting case to the SFO following corruption in Jamaica, Ghana and Iraq.

Hitting your peak

In the deal-striking maelstrom of the corporate department, there is "*an emphasis on technical ability and still a good amount of intellectual challenge.*" People are "*motivated – they're not aggressive, but they are firm... a bit louder and more deal-driven too, wanting just the answer, not necessarily the reason for the answer. That's unlike litigation, where it's more academic and they'll want to know how you got to your solution.*" Some trainees love the corporate environment: "*It's really sociable and less hierarchical than in litigation; people have a good laugh at work. They hit their peak at around 6pm and continue to work later.*" What this means is that the department is "*best suited to someone who doesn't mind unpredictability.*" Trainees also say that "*there's a lot of opportunity to get stuck in and manage a transaction, and this can teach you how to work at pace and deal with practical issues. Corporate gives a lot of responsibility, though less client contact than in litigation.*"

It's no utopia though; some sources moaned that they'd had more "*rubbish work*" than expected. One person, for example, estimated that "*80% of my work was indexing and bibling,*" suggesting that this was "*a common complaint*" among their peers. Another spoke of a variety of duties – "*reviewing documents, putting together chronological plans of what would happen when, and tweaking standard documents to fit each matter, then filling them in.*" By the end of the seat, trainees start to "*negotiate over the phone and do fairly complicated tasks, which is essentially associate-level work.*" Clients include KPMG, Time Warner, Ernst & Young, The Blackstone Group, Deutsche Bank, BP and Rio Tinto. Lately lawyers have been working on BSkyB's £7.8bn takeover by News Corp and Arriva's €2.8bn takeover by German rail company Deutsche Bahn.

In the finance department, trainees have ample client contact. Said one: "*Finance directors or company secretaries could call me up at any time, which was cool.*" Although the nature of the deals often means trainees don't see a matter from start to finish, within the department there are always a variety of deals at various stages and "*they like it when you ask for responsibility.*" Refinancing and company reorganisations have flooded in lately. One trainee felt they'd been given fairly free rein. "*I had to do some intra-company reorganisation where certain parties had to accede as intercreditors to the main financing document. I handled things on my own, supervised by an associate.*" Clients include EDF, Standard Chartered Bank, Société Générale, BNP Paribas and Credit Suisse. Working with several major international banks, Herbies helped create a $2bn reserve-based facility for Tullow Oil, the largest borrowing base facility in the market. It also restructured a massive debt raised by EDF for the purchase of British Energy.

Long haul

The competition group is broad, going beyond just merger control work to include market investigations, cartel investigations, competition litigation, state aid, public procurement and utilities regulation. Clients include Coca-Cola, BSkyB and Virgin Atlantic, which the firm advised in relation to the OFT's criminal and civil investigations into long-haul passenger fuel surcharges. The real estate team worked on some huge matters in 2009, like the £1.51bn sale of Gatwick Airport and Qatari Diar Investment Company's acquisition of the US Embassy building in Grosvenor Square. The employment group, meanwhile, follows the international work trend, advising Ernst & Young as the administrators of Nortel Networks UK on the employment issues flowing from the administration of more than 30 subsidiaries in Europe, the Middle East and Africa. Other employment matters include strike prevention, executive governance issues of large companies, bonus disputes and High Court disputes.

Overseas seats are available in Abu Dhabi, Dubai, Singapore, Hong Kong, Shanghai, Bangkok, Tokyo, Brussels, Paris and Moscow. You don't necessarily need to visit a department with which you are already familiar in London, and there are only one or two locations where you need language skills. Trainees said their overseas placements were *"really enjoyable,"* citing heightened responsibility, good access to partners and a great social life. Their only gripes were that applying for NQ roles while overseas can be more difficult and that *"HR shouldn't let people go overseas if they're not sure they can find them an NQ job."* This is a complaint we have heard at other firms too. Client secondments are available to companies such as easyJet, Coca-Cola, BSkyB, UBS, Credit Suisse and rights organisation Liberty.

Lend a hand

The trainees we spoke to were expansive and fairly outspoken characters who obviously hadn't been pushed into the docile acceptance of menial work; they seem to be fans of the more technical aspect of law and relish nothing more than *"a rigorous, substantial discussion."* They like to provide not only answers to questions but also details as to how they arrived at them. There's a range of training sessions, of which *"the lunchtime lectures are most popular because you get fed."* Before entering departments, trainees attend inductions. The corporate one is *"an intensive three-day affair with practical and research tasks to get you up to speed."* As for mentoring, everyone is assigned a 'trainee review partner' from outside the pool of supervisors. *"They mediate between people, and it's a godsend for some people to have that independent person to help with work allocation or if they feel they are getting too much work."*

Despite making sacrifices for their careers, trainees do find time for a personal life. Gossip-wise, *"the two trainees caught doing monkey business in the office"* following enthusiastic use of a drinks trolley was *"the most interesting thing to have happened in the past six months."* There's also been a Wii party, a barbecue and a trip to watch the cricket at Lord's. A trainee camping trip to Devon was being organised as we conducted our interviews. Many people go for drinks after work on Fridays and there are *"loads of sports societies."* One trainee set up an evening legal clinic for Fair Trials International at which people spend three hours on a Thursday writing to lawyers, conducting legal research and providing support for domestic legal proceedings. The initiative was incredibly popular among trainees.

"There's an intangible thing called culture, and I think our culture is different," said managing partner David Willis. Trainees had picked up on the vibe too: *"Even on my vac scheme, I realised that it has a feel of being a genuine partnership instead of being like a plc."* This doesn't make it a stuffy place and there's no kowtowing: *"Partners are really nice and do stop and chat... and there's a good variety of younger people and old guard."* Emblematic of Herbies' team ethos (and the trainees' food fixation) is a canteen discussion group that *"puts forward concerns, like whether the mayonnaise in the sandwiches is low fat."* (It is. Phew!) There's also a trainee discussion group, which is *"a really good forum"* at which *"some quite leftfield questions get raised."* Trainees are additionally kept in the loop on bigger issues via communication sessions with the managing partner and senior partner.

And finally...

Continuing the trend of recent years, we sensed a really positive vibe at Herbert Smith. In 2010, the only downer was that just 76 out of 100 qualifiers stayed on.

Higgs & Sons

The facts

Locations: Brierley Hill, Kingswinford

Number of UK partners/solicitors: 30/38

Total number of trainees: 8

Seats: 4x4 months + 1x8 month

Alternative seats: None

Extras: Pro bono – Business Link, Birmingham Employment Advice Clinic

On chambersstudent.co.uk
- How to get into Higgs
- We talk to managing partner Paul Hunt
- Higgs' new home
- A synopsis of the social scene

Proud of its roots but not parochial, Higgs & Sons is the Black Country firm of choice and has the clients and offices to prove it.

Black Country boom

Since its creation in 1875, this firm has become a genuine force in the West Midlands' legal market. One source told us: "*We're not really competing with George Green any more,*" and it's certainly true that Higgs now sees its competition as the bigger Birmingham firms. Indeed, it has recruited partners from Birmingham big boys Martineau, Eversheds and Wragge & Co in recent years. While Higgs is rightly proud of its Black Country roots and the clientele it has built, it's a measure of the firm's progress that it attracts clients with a national presence, including Habib Bank AG Zurich and IT training company Computeach.

There's no better indication of the firm's recent ambition and growth than its brand new Brierley Hill office (go to our website to read more about it). A £1.5m investment, its 30,000 sq ft houses the vast majority of Higgs' personnel. The move is interesting for two reasons. First, it shows Higgs' size – having incorporated the old Brierley Hill and Stourbridge offices (some 150 people) under one roof, it is now the biggest legal office in the Black Country. Second, it shows the firm's strategy is not to expand geographically, despite a plan to grow both Higgs' brand and its staff numbers. According to managing partner Paul Hunt, the firm is "*committed to this region and has been for 135 years, but we're not parochial. My job is to get the message out; we've almost been a well-kept secret until now.*"

Fourmidable

Higgs has a well thought-out system when it comes to training contracts. After four four-month seats, there's a fifth super-long eight-month stint. That final seat is usually in the practice area into which a trainee hopes to qualify, the idea being that it smooths the transition process to qualified solicitor. Partner Catherine Junor says: "*The last eight months offer trainees a springboard.*"

A schedule is published at the beginning of the trainees' first year, listing their first four seats. That might seem a pretty prescriptive process, but our sources assured us that if you really want to change something, it can be arranged, though it should be sorted out sooner rather than later. "*It's obviously a bad idea to leave it until the last minute,*" stressed one source, "*but if you go and talk to HR, they will do their best to fix it for you.*" Another agreed: "*The schedule isn't set in stone, so people always get shuffled round a bit. I don't think anyone has ended up disappointed.*" The final seat is, naturally enough, a choice for trainees themselves to make in consultation with HR.

The private client department is a major part of Higgs' practice. It brings in roughly 25% of the firm's revenue, has the highest head count and earns the highest ranking in *Chambers UK*. All that makes it a likely destination for trainees, who described the department's wills, general probate and trust work as "*really varied.*" It involves plenty of drafting and client contact with "*really quite wealthy high net worth individuals, as well as the occasional old lady off the high street.*" A certain type of

Chambers UK rankings

Crime	Private Client
Employment	Real Estate
Family/Matrimonial	

person thrives here. One trainee reflected: "*You need to be able to communicate with clients on a personal level. It takes somebody who is quite down to earth.*" Another commented: "*You have to deal with emotive situations, and it's your job to take away all the little difficulties, the stresses and strains the client is under.*"

Those soft skills are just as important in clinical negligence or personal injury seats. It can be "*very, very personal. Clients are real people who have suffered, and in some cases they have really atrocious injuries.*" It isn't a seat for the squeamish, with one source reporting how "*some of the things I saw made me never want to go to see a doctor again. You have to have a strong stomach.*" Higgs frequently acts on claims worth hundreds of thousands of pounds, and sometimes millions. Trainees spend much of their time sifting through medical records, talking to hospital representatives and attending meetings and hearings with barristers. Our sources talked of "*negotiating possible settlements*" as well as effectively "*running a Criminal Injuries Compensation Authority claim through to fruition.*" The work is definitely demanding. "*You have to get a sense of both the medicine and the law, and that's not always easy.*"

Smooth criminal

Higgs has a team dealing exclusively with private defence work for motoring and criminal offences. Although small – just one partner and an associate – trainees get a chance to spend time in an area that is "*about as contentious as it gets!*" They are exposed to a range of cases, although generally motoring "*comprises about 80% of the work.*" Our contacts had sat in on Crown Court trials, conferences with barristers, and client conferences at the police station. Again, there's a strong human element to the work: "*You have to keep an open mind. There are two sides to every story, and generally these are people who have never been in trouble with the police before.*"

Another seat offers dispute resolution of all sorts, with "*referrals coming from all areas of the firm.*" Litigation is a growing department that began a few years ago with only three fee earners, and now has around ten. Our sources had been to court independently "*on six or seven occasions,*" particularly for matters like debt recovery where trainees are encouraged to run their own files. While perhaps initially a little daunting, trainees soon learn to harness their inner advocate when stood in front of a district judge. Our sources enthused about making applications to strike out claims, as well as for and against summary judgment. It's an excellent seat for anyone who wants to be on their feet.

All this talk of crime, clin neg and private client work might give the impression that Higgs lacks a commercial side. It doesn't. In fact, one of the most appealing aspects of the training contract is its broad scope. Trainees might be placed in a range of other seats – employment (very popular), commercial property, residential property, commercial, corporate and family. Across all the seats, our sources were happy with the work fed to them by supervisors and other fee earners.

Higgledy-Piggledy

The new office has added to Higgs' sense of professionalism but hasn't detracted from a family-firm feel. One trainee said: "*I can safely say that I could name every single person who works here,*" while another reflected: "*I'm quite comfortable saying hello to everybody in the corridor.*" There's plenty of information about the firm's social life on our website.

Potential applicants shouldn't feel intimidated at the prospect of walking into such a tight-knit firm as this. Higgs operates a buddy system for the two years before successful applicants start at the firm. That means "*you're allocated a buddy who's a trainee, and given their e-mail address so you can ask them questions.*" A good portion of employees have West Midlands roots, and current managing partner Paul Hunt is by no means alone in having joined the firm as a trainee and then worked his way up. The firm's long-termism is reflected in its retention rates: three out of four qualifiers stayed on in 2010, qualifying into insolvency, dispute resolution and private client.

And finally...

With a substantive and broad training contract, sociable staff and a bostin reputation in the West Midlands and increasingly beyond, Higgs is an excellent choice for friendly folk with a regional focus.

Hill Dickinson LLP

The facts

Location: London, Liverpool, Manchester, Chester, Sheffield

Number of UK partners/solicitors: 195/255

Total number of trainees: 40

Seats: 4x6 months

Alternative seats: Overseas seats, secondments

On chambersstudent.co.uk
- How to get into Hill Dickinson
- The firm's history
- Clinical negligence and healthcare practice

Celebrating its 200th birthday in 2010, Hill Dickinson is a North West institution with a strong reputation for negligence litigation and a great shipping practice in London.

Fab four

The firm was founded in Liverpool in 1810 by Edward Morrall, whose trade was maritime law; Messrs Hill and Dickinson didn't lend their names until much later. The 20th century saw mergers with law firms Wayman-Hales, Bullivant Jones and Middleton Potts significantly boost individual practice areas, and a split between the London (marine) practice and HD's large northern contingent in 1989. The 2006 reunification of the northern and southern parts of the business has made the firm what it is today: a regional behemoth with "*a breadth of experience in different areas*" to serve the every legal whim of the North West, and a watertight shipping practice in London and Liverpool. HD's history is steeped in shipping – it even acted on the legal aftermath of the loss of the 'Titanic' – but trainees up north tell us it's possible to "*forget that shipping is a massive part of the firm.*" In contrast to the office in the capital, the breadth of work up north is impressive; for example a sports law team advises Premiership players, promoters, management companies and professional bodies, while construction lawyers recently assisted contractors in an £80m PFI waste project. Of the northern offices, Liverpool is the largest, followed by Manchester, Chester and Sheffield. A small number of lawyers are also stationed in the shipping hubs of Singapore and Piraeus in Greece.

Trainees say the firm has a "*reputation of not going 'gung ho' into anything without thinking about it,*" and this is worth bearing in mind given a certain major development in summer 2010. HD rescued 129 staff in Liverpool and Sheffield from collapsing law firm Halliwells (previously a major rival), thereby strengthening its own commercial capabilities in the region. Training partner Alastair Gillespie explained to us that this acquisition is consistent with HD's past growth trajectory and has been made to "*complement what we've already got.*" It also achieves what trainees told us is HD's objective to become "*a £100m law firm.*"

Even in a reunited HD, there is the perpetual problem of long-distance relationships, or "*knock-on-door versus e-mail,*" as one trainee put it. "*We don't integrate with the trainees up north a lot* [except for] *a monthly video link,*" said London recruits, although it is possible for them to take seats in northern offices.

Life in HD

Trainees in Liverpool and Manchester can opt for seats in coco; employment; health; insurance and litigation; marine; professional risks; private client; and property and construction. Sheffield has options in property; commercial litigation; healthcare; and corporate. In London the options are coco; employment; insurance; and litigation and marine. Chester offers insurance and litigation plus property (which concentrates on agricultural matters for farming clients). Applicants apply on a largely office-by-office basis to Liverpool, Manchester, Sheffield or London, but those in the North West should be aware of

Chambers UK rankings

Banking & Finance	Insurance
Clinical Negligence	Intellectual Property
Commodities	Pensions
Construction	Personal Injury
Corporate/M&A	Private Client
Debt Recovery	Professional Discipline
Dispute Resolution	Professional Negligence
Employment	Real Estate
Family/Matrimonial	Real Estate Litigation
Fraud	Restructuring/Insolvency
Health & Safety	Shipping
Healthcare	Transport
	Travel

the strong possibility of moving offices during the training contract, sometimes with just a few weeks' notice. "*We don't know our seats early enough,*" some trainees moaned, many of them disliking the commute from Liverpool to Manchester, Chester or Sheffield. The best advice is to maintain an attitude of "*flexibility;*" most trainees sign only six-month residential leases or just take the long commute on the chin. An office move doesn't seem to have an impact on the quality of supervision on offer, which sounds great across the board. Said one trainee: "*My supervisor sends me out and about, and takes me to every client meeting. And I'm always on the phone answering questions.*" Furthermore, trainees have regular Q&A sessions with senior partners when, according to Alastair Gillespie, they can "*fire whatever they like at them and get straight answers.*"

Negligence, in the form of insurance litigation, drives Hill Dickinson's caseload in the North, where perhaps the most popular department among trainees is professional risks. This team acts for insurers such as Aviva on high-value claims against solicitors, accountants, surveyors and other professionals when they mess up. We've heard it's a fairly "*young*" department and trainees report "*lots of exposure to clients.*" Trainees can work on some claims from start to finish, taking witness statements, compiling disclosure documents, quantifying claims, assessing liability and drafting defences. When sometimes "*liability can't be defended,*" then it's a matter of "*fire control.*" For example, the department recently handled claims over the defective design and workmanship of a supermarket that required a full demolition and rebuild. As HD represents insurers, many cases settle before trial, but if something does go to court then trainees will attend, travelling as far as London to the High Court or the Supreme Court. One trainee recounted how they'd "*been to court for a hearing* [alone] *where the other side was represented by a partner.*"

Slips, trips and intravenous drips

A seat in employers' liability and disease litigation (ELD) is contagiously popular and it covers all those tort cases you memorised at law school. Remember Fairchild v Glenhaven or the case with the one-eyed garage mechanic? "*Slips and trips*" are serious work at HD and there's always "*a lot going on,*" from "*mesothelioma, accidents on ships and fatal car crashes,*" to workplace-related hand-arm vibration syndrome and noise-induced hearing loss claims. Consequently, trainees describe the department as a "*bit mad and louder*" than its professional risks counterpart. There's bags of drafting to be done, and trainees also review claimants' medical records and get stuck in on disclosure tasks.

HD has a standalone travel team that works on personal injury claims suffered by holidaymakers as well as commercial and employment issues. It counts among its clients the likes of Butlins and First Choice, plus various cruise liners, airlines such as Qantas and several adventure travel companies you may have solicited for your gap year. This team has worked on newsworthy accidents such as the 2009 inquest into the death of a Raleigh expedition volunteer in Namibia who fell from a zipwire on a high-ropes course. It also worked on the food-poisoning scare at Heston Blumenthal's Fat Duck restaurant.

Hill Dickinson has a strong healthcare practice fighting the cause for public bodies including Liverpool Primary Care Trust and University Hospital of South Manchester. The firm also maintains a coveted place on the NHS Litigation Authority panels for clinical negligence and employer's liability work. NHS litigation is huge and HD lawyers are "*absolutely run off* [their] *feet*" defending the health service on issues of clin neg ("*botched operations, misdiagnoses, etc.*") or employers' liability cases where NHS employees are injured at work. Typically HD sees "*lots of claims relating to stress, patient assaults and not providing a safe work environment.*" Trainees set up conferences with barristers and clients, draft defences and liaise with experts, while trying to keep on top of "*loads of deadlines.*" The healthcare team also focuses on the non-contentious needs of the NHS; for example, it was involved in the much-publicised Redfern Inquiry into post-mortem organ retention at Liverpool's Alder Hey Children's Hospital. The employment team works on NHS matters, too, and it also has commercial clients such as Iceland and Matalan.

Elementary, my dear Dickinson

Liverpool has a "*massive marine team,*" but it's in London where the main business is shipping, trade and energy. You will "*probably have to do at least one, if not two, shipping seats,*" trainees in the capital confessed. There's shipping litigation, marine personal injury and aspects of yacht finance and insurance to be found, all of which may bring interesting scenarios. Shipping litigation covers 'wet' (tort-based issues including salvage and collisions) and 'dry' work (contract-based matters such as damaged cargo). HD lawyers are well placed to handle wet work as *"a lot of the senior partners are master mariners"* and they've *"always got stories to tell."* When not listening to tales from the high seas, trainees will research points of law, *"draft letters of advice and run small charter party disputes."* Common in this sector are *"lots of arbitrations to get your teeth into,"* but thankfully not much grunt work, which is done by an army of paralegals. *"I've not spent much time at the photocopier at all!"* said one relieved source. Among the firm's top cases was the representation of 140 NVOCCs (Non Vessel Owning Common Carriers) on legal matters regarding the beaching of the 'MSC Napoli' in 2007. Marine-focused secondments are available to Singapore and Piraeus.

HD's crack criminal fraud team can be found pursuing cases relating to everything from mortgage fraud and fraudulent applications for European grants to large-scale global people trafficking, tax evasion and motor frauds. Trainees get the *"full experience of litigation... dealing with files right from first claim to* [court judgment]*."* Motor fraud lawyers assist insurers when they have suspicions that an accident claim is fraudulent. *"We have specialist intelligence analysts who can detect fraud rings,"* revealed a source. One such clan of conmen conspired to cause a collision between a car and a taxi full of passengers. After some detective work by HD (which trainees also got involved in), it transpired that the drivers shared an address and had previously made claims for staged accidents.

HD has an excellent reputation for private client work in the North, where it assists *"Mr and Mrs* [Affluent] *on the street"* on tax, wills and estate management. The firm seems to be popular with *"big lottery winners,"* many of whom are referred by lottery operator Camelot. Trainees in this department run probate files and relish the levels of client contact and responsibility they are afforded. Property is another great seat for managing your own files: in this field of practice the Chester office works closely with the University of Chester, Chester Zoo, and Chester Cathedral. In fact, roughly 60% of this small office's clientele are local to the city or North Wales.

Fortune favoured

All our interviewees in the North West had a connection to the region and cited HD's *"genuine local reputation"* as the main reason for choosing the firm. The Liverpool office, situated right on the docks, *"feels a lot more corporate"* than the other HD offices, but trainees still stressed a *"small-firm"* feel. *"The senior partner knows what football team I support,"* said one. The office in historic Chester is described as *"more laidback,"* while Manchester's has *"a homely atmosphere."* London trainees loved their more intimate-sized departments but reckoned that a renovation of the *"pretty shabby"* building is *"long overdue,"* especially when it's compared to the purpose-built home of their Liverpool colleagues. We have it on good authority that the firm is *"very keen to sort out its position on premises in Manchester and London."* Whether stationed by the Mersey or the Thames, trainees commented on an *"excellent work life balance,"* confirming that an average day is *"nine to six."*

Trainees insist that the firm is *"very business development-oriented now."* It organises *"networking and presentation skills days,"* pays for membership of the regional Junior Lawyers Division units, and sends trainees off to entertain clients. *"Trainees are ambassadors of the firm,"* explains Gillespie. *"You never know how valuable* [those connections can be]*."* The Merseyside Junior Lawyers Division puts on events nearly every month, from barbecues to balls and comedy nights, while client socials have taken the form of *"football afternoons and sailing weekends."* HD also *"matches up younger members of the firm with clients of the same age."* We hear that the *"trainee committee is quite good at funding things such as go-karting"* or days at the races. On Friday nights HD staff can be found in the Cross Keys in Liverpool or at the White Horse in London's Aldgate area. The year 2010 marked the firm's 200th anniversary, which it celebrated in style with a night of lavish entertainment. Liverpool's Echo Arena played host to a caricaturist, a fortune teller, one of the *Britain's Got Talent* dance troupes and the operatic abilities of HD's director of finance, Colin Wardale.

HD's charity committee is constantly promoting events. There have been *"dress-down days"* and some more daring endeavours including a ski-a-thon and the 2010 Caledonian challenge. *"We walked for 24 hours... it was hell on earth but a great laugh,"* said one participant. Subsidised gym membership possibly eased the pain. There's a five-a-side league for football fans, plus netball and poker teams that compete in the annual Corporate Games.

And finally...

Hill Dickinson doesn't recruit a lot of trainees for its size. *"Our aim is to keep all our trainees on qualification,"* adds Alastair Gillespie. In 2010, despite having taken over some of Halliwells' traineeships, 22 of the 26 qualifiers took up NQ positions.

Hogan Lovells International LLP

The facts

Location: London

Number of UK partners/solicitors: 161/434

Total number of trainees: 147

Seats: 4x6 months

Alternative seats: Overseas seats, secondments

Extras: Pro bono – eg Royal British Legion war pensions tribunals, Bow County Court Advice Network, anti-trafficking initiative with the Met Police; language training

On chambersstudent.co.uk

- How to get into Hogan Lovells
- The firm's CSR initiatives
- Hogan meets Lovells

On 1 May 2010 an era ended as an old and venerable City firm finally merged with an American suitor. What lies in store for the newborn Hogan Lovells International?

Hart-broken or Loved-up?

The news that Lovells was to merge with US giant Hogan & Hartson in a transatlantic romance set legal tongues wagging. After all, such a large venture had not been attempted for some time due to the economic climate and the fact that these mergers are considered notoriously difficult to achieve. Almost a year down the line, however, not only has the merger become legally binding in a ceremony complete with "*balloons and goody bags, mugs and mouse mats, and lime green ducks in the water fountain,*" but Hogan Lovells may even be setting a new trend, with Denton Wilde Sapte already following suit and others also looking across the pond for their own 'special relationship'.

How does this new household look? Not vastly different, said trainees. The ironing out of technical creases and minor domestic differences (do you say 'remuneration' or 'compensation'?) still had to be dealt with, and there were various potential client conflicts with, for example, both News International (Hogan) and ITV (Lovells) now vying for attention. But for trainees – at least the Lovells lot – business is very much as usual. "*At our level it has been seamless,*" reported one. There are some small differences in the day to day – "*There are lot more people walking around with American accents,*" and the H&H tradition of dress-down Fridays has been imported (with a caveat on 'provocative' clothing). Inevitably, it is the Hogan & Hartson UK trainees who have experienced a greater degree of change, being transplanted from a small London office into a much larger one, but for the most part the attitude was one of symbiotic energy. "*The culture hasn't changed much – both firms have strived individually to create a great place to work,*" were the words of one trainee.

In the pipeline

In the honeymoon period during which we made our calls, the confidence and optimism was evident at all levels. "*I think there is a real feeling of contentment among the troops, a feeling that the quality of the business is on a par with any of the magic circle firms,*" was the view of an associate familiar with both the old and new. All the essential ingredients for a Hog-Love coalition should be in place, with the two firms bringing a number of complementary practice areas into the mix, not least in dispute resolution, insurance and restructuring. By its own admission, top-end corporate work was never Lovells' strongest point. At the same time, management believes that the firm "*hasn't suffered over the last couple of years because we haven't been exposed in the same way. We feel that there will be corporate life after the crunch, and we do believe that we need to strengthen that area of the practice. It is a key policy objective.*" This objective has clearly been transmitted to trainees as well, with one telling us: "*I think they're planning to beef up corporate and finance, I think that's where we're trying to get to us a firm, to be competitive with the magic circle.*" Hogan & Hartson lawyers have certainly beefed up the department.

Chambers UK rankings

Administrative & Public Law	Life Sciences
Asset Finance	Media & Entertainment
Banking & Finance	Outsourcing
Banking Litigation	Parliamentary & Public Affairs
Capital Markets	Pensions
Commodities	Pensions Litigation
Competition/European Law	Planning
Construction	Product Liability
Consumer Finance	Professional Negligence
Corporate/M&A	Projects
Data Protection	Public International Law
Dispute Resolution	Public Procurement
Employee Share Schemes	Real Estate
Employment	Real Estate Finance
Energy & Natural Resources	Real Estate Litigation
Environment	Restructuring/Insolvency
Financial Services	Retail
Fraud	Tax
Information Technology	Telecommunications
Insurance	Transport
Intellectual Property	
Investment Funds	

May 19th 2010 saw the merged firm complete its first corporate deal, the £138m buyout of NBA team New Jersey Jets on behalf of Russian investment fund Onexim, a long-term client of Hogan & Hartson.

It's amazing how important Russian business is in the City of London, and the firm is getting in on a decent share of the available deals, particularly since the merger. One key matter involves advising one of the world's largest energy companies, Gazprom, on the structuring of its headline-hitting South Stream pipeline, estimated to have a capital cost of $31bn. The pipeline will transport gas to much of Western Europe, and Hogan Lovells' lawyers are doing everything to ensure that all the joint ventures are in place, and that its passage is smoothed by compliance with every aspect of local law in the six transit countries through which it passes. What's more, the recent Euro 100 survey by *The Chambers Magazine* shows that Hogan Lovells is trumping the magic circle for European clients in numerous areas, including commercial, regulatory and dispute resolution.

Tax(ing) work

Trainees at Hogan Lovells must currently take either a corporate seat or a finance seat but there's plenty to choose from. The corporate department is made up of several smaller, more focused teams. One deals with private equity matters, an area of the corporate market that has an interesting phase ahead of it. A source spoke of how friendly they had found the team members: "*There was a real family feeling and people were all very helpful in explaining stuff and keen to get you involved.*" Some trainees talked about how much crossover work they'd experienced during the quieter economy. In more normal times, big deals may be the order of the day, but the past couple of years have at least reinforced in trainees' minds just how interconnected the work of some departments can be.

Other subdivisions in corporate include corporate real estate and the ever-popular tax seat. One trainee fortunate enough to have landed the tax gig described it as "*interesting technically, but very difficult at times. Towards the end I had a lot more responsibility, supporting the banking team.*" The seat's popularity is down to a work ethic as much as quality of work itself. "*The culture in tax is completely different. In general the social life of that group was much more developed, and we'd all go down to the pub at five on Fridays.*" Retail banking, a niche seat within the specialist commercial team, is just one example: "*We were dealing with personal finance products, current accounts and credit card offerings. We were also heavily involved in claims management and lots of technical consumer credit legislation.*"

Beyond this tax haven lies the more ruthless world of finance, both more conventional banking and capital markets. Described by one trainee as "*one of the most gruelling seats,*" the banking stint can feel like "*a baptism of fire*" at times. This is where the quality of supervision, and seniors' attentiveness really helps. "*My supervisor was fantastic, she built me up slowly. To begin with I was helping with board minutes and bibling, towards the middle I began to have more of a free rein on smaller deals around the £30m value, and by the end I felt confident enough that when an associate went on holiday I put myself forward to fill their shoes.*" Here's one trainee's experience of the business restructuring and insolvency team: "*There were a lot of companies who had borrowed large amounts but are now struggling with large debts that are crippling them. We act for banks in restructuring the debt or reducing the debt by writing some of it off. In a seat like this, there's more classic trainee work, more getting documentation together, company searches, getting information off the company and generally doing all the due diligence around that. On top of that, we might do bits and pieces of drafting and legal research.*" Hard graft pays off though, with the team reporting that it's had its "*best year ever,*" advising on some extremely complex matters including the £3.5bn financial restructuring of Pearl Group, the UK manager of closed funds. Clients are a *Who's Who* of all the country's major banks, and the firm has further cemented its reputation by becoming one of only three to be appointed to HM Treasury's legal panel for financial stability.

Hogan Lovells' litigators have achieved a formidable status in a number of specialised areas: pensions, civil fraud, product liability and international arbitration, among others. A seat in the contentious department makes for content trainees. "*In terms of work it was absolutely fascinating,*" said one. "*I was working on a big multibillion-dollar fraud case – you couldn't ask for a better litigation experience!*" Our sources weren't disappointed with the highly regarded IP department either. They dealt with "*a mix of pre-action and contentious work, domain name issues, drafting and filing, gathering evidence and investigating claims.*" With a client list that includes Deutsche Telecom, adidas and play.com, there are plenty of recognisable brands.

Foreign investment

For many, one of the principal attractions of a training contract at legacy Lovells was its international presence and the prospect of overseas secondment opportunities. There are European seats as well as positions in more far-flung locations including Hong Kong, Singapore and Dubai, and all are highly coveted. For most, the foreign offices usually mean a greater degree of responsibility. "*If you show interest you're encouraged to just go with it. There's loads of networking and making your own waves with clients.*" Needless to say, few were ready to return. The merger throws open some exciting new secondments possibilities in the future, particularly in the Americas. London's managing partner Andrew Gamble told us: "*There will be opportunities to work in different offices, and indeed there may be opportunities to work in the US, though we can't say as yet exactly how, where and how many.*" At home, numerous client secondments are available with the likes of Barclays, Ford, John Lewis, Lloyds TSB, Save the Children and Standard Chartered Bank.

If there was one common gripe among trainees, it had to do with the qualification process. It was described as "*transparent but very stressful*" by one, "*a bit of a downer*" by another, and a system that leaves you "*potentially disadvantaged*" by a third. The issue is this: "*Hogan Lovells had an interview process for most departments and we didn't find out until up to two or three weeks after the other major firms.*" Trainees worried that those who were unfortunate enough not to be retained started on the back foot when it came to applying elsewhere. The simple fact of the matter is that the timing of the merger necessarily added an additional layer of complexity, so there is no reason why future trainees should encounter this problem. In 2010, 54 out of 79 qualifiers took up jobs with the firm, and can rest assured that lockstep progression (set pay rises for each year of experience) has started anew and that associate salaries will be increasing in the next financial year.

Loving Hogans' good-heartedness

Our sources were smarting a little from the fact that "*post-credit crunch, the budget of the trainee committee has been cut.*" While regular pub get-togethers are organised, all-out decadence is not the order of the day. Instead, the firm encourages solidarity and sociability in other ways. Hogan & Hartson was serious about corporate social responsibility, picking up awards for its commitment to pro bono work in London and around the world. Lovells also had a great track record on pro bono. For one trainee giving back involved "*doing some work for a social enterprise on a criminal injuries compensation case. I drafted submissions and a witness statement.*" In other charitable endeavours, daredevils (or deathwishers) can partake in one of the more extreme events we've encountered – an annual abseil down the side of the firm's Holborn Viaduct office. Name a reality show and these lawyers have emulated it: Legally Ballroom, Lovells' Got Talent, Lovells Apprentice… The latter even secured Sir Alan's right-hand woman and corporate matriarch Margaret Mountford as arbitress of their challenges. There are also a large number of sports teams, one of the most popular being softball because "*there's a social element to it – last Monday we were all sitting on Primrose Hill drinking beer.*"

"*Ambitious*" and "*nice*" might seem paradoxical as the most frequently recurring qualities of a Hogan Lovells lawyer, but they were affirmed by almost everyone we spoke to. "*I'm ambitious and I wanted a top-tier firm that everyone had heard of, but wasn't bothered about the magic circle thing. And I was looking for the kind of people I would want to go to the pub with.*" 'Nice' has previously been a label that Lovells lovelies had tried to shake off, but they're becoming increasingly comfortable with it again, with more senior sources saying that "*the firm has sometimes had the reputation for being too nice, and not cut-throat enough. But we don't see 'nice' as being a pejorative.*" Or in the words of a trainee: "*We are not the Dobermans of the legal world, but we're certainly not the fluffy pussycat types either.*"

And finally...

If legacy Lovells had the reputation of being nice, ambitious and international, Hogan Lovells may now just be a little nicer, a little more ambitious, and a little more international.

- **Calling all linguists:** As law firms become increasingly global, language skills are becoming more advantageous. Why let one slip when you can improve it while at university or law school?

Holman Fenwick Willan LLP

The facts

Location: London

Number of UK partners/solicitors: 66/100

Total number of trainees: 31

Seats: 4x6 months

Alternative Seats: Overseas seats, secondments

Extras: Pro bono – Morden Legal Advice Centre; language training

On chambersstudent.co.uk
- How to get into HFW
- More on the 'Limnos' litigation
- The firm's history

Holman Fenwick Willan is one of the world's best shipping firms, and with a large complement of other practices and overseas secondments to boot, there's plenty for a trainee to get stuck into.

Much more than shipping

Holman Fenwick Willan has a long and illustrious history in shipping, beginning in the early 19th century when the Holman family were Devonshire sailing-ship owners. In 1883, Frank Holman set sail for London where he became a solicitor. In 1899, E.A. Fenwick climbed aboard, and six years later W.C. Willan added his name to the crew: the threesome has been a big name in shipping law ever since. *Chambers UK* ranks it alongside Ince & Co as the world leader in the field. In fact, such is the firm's reputation that we've heard rumours that some companies instruct HFW simply so that "*the P&I clubs* [Protection and Indemnity shipping insurance societies] *will take them seriously.*" HFW has been riding the recessionary wave of litigation recently and turnover was up 0.9% to £99.6m in 2009/10. The firm draws on expertise across a global network of 11 offices – including three in Australia – and is building ties with local lawyers in Abu Dhabi and Saudi Arabia. HFW's strategy is simple, according to HR and training director James Collinge: "*It's about continual growth* [and] *setting up offices where our clients need us.*" The firm is at present considering adding further outposts in Europe and Australia, and is set to launch in Geneva in October 2010.

Over the years, HFW has cast its net wider into the trade and energy, finance, corporate and insurance sectors, all of it consistent with the firm's aim to be "*a leading firm in international commerce*" and not just in shipping. It now numbers Kuwait Oil Company, SeaDrill and DHL among its clients. At present contentious work makes up 70% of HFW's offering, but the plan is to "*think in a more rounded way about the sectors in which* [the firm] *is active*" – offering corporate services to energy clients, for example. In a deal that is typical of the firm's shipping/trade/corporate/finance mash-up, HFW recently advised APM Terminals on the sale of its 25% stake in Zeebrugge port to Chinese company Shanghai International Port Group for €27m.

Trainee seats are available in trade and energy; shipping and transport; ship finance; insurance/reinsurance; commercial litigation; corporate, projects and finance; and the smaller area of EU/competition law. None are compulsory, although since HFW's main line of work is litigation, trainees will spend time in either corporate, projects and finance or the "*pure transactional seat*" of ship finance to satisfy SRA requirements.

Wet, dry and soggy

"*People are grouped very loosely in teams,*" explained one source. Trainees commonly work for several partners at a time, and we've heard that some seats are "*a bit of a free for all.*" The trade and energy, and shipping and transport practice groups both handle shipping litigation. Trade and energy tends to focus on 'dry' matters – contract-based law like freight futures, charter party and sale contract disputes. "*It's real law, just like the problems you see at uni.*" Contract fans should check out HFW's

Chambers UK rankings

Asset Finance	Insurance
Commodities	Shipping
Dispute Resolution	Transport
Fraud	

work on the 'Limnos' litigation. To get started go to our website.

The shipping and transport seat, meanwhile, leans towards 'wet' matters – tort-based law covering collisions between ships and salvage issues. "*It's quite exciting,*" trainees tell us, as "*you have to act very quickly.*" The firm responded rapidly to the 2007 grounding of the 'MSC Napoli' off the coast of Devon, acting for the ship's owners and their P&I club. It also advised on a collision in the Aegean Sea between the 'Marti Princess' and the 'Renate Schulte' (do check out the photos of this). Seafaring is left to the 19 master mariners employed by HFW to investigate maritime collisions: trainees keep their feet on dry land drafting articles of claim and taking witness statements. One confessed: "*It would be good to go and see the boats,*" before admitting that they "*get a bit seasick.*" In addition to wet and dry, the firm also has a "*soggy section*" that handles a variety of issues including piracy.

Best enemies

One of our sources commented: "*In shipping, all people do is sue each other... but the weird thing is that, by and large, they will remain friends.*" The same camaraderie can be found among shipping lawyers. We've heard of some "*really big personalities*" at HFW, and some partners who can be "*a bit overpowering,*" but trainees assured us that "*you don't wait trembling outside the partner's door.*" There appears to be a difference between some of the senior partners and the new blood coming through. "*Some partners are the pure intellectual type – if you ask about a case or a point of law they'll recite it back to you. Then you get the more commercial guys.*" The latter fit well into HFW's ship finance department, which is "*as 21st century as Holmans gets,*" according to one interviewee. The firm acts for major banks, shipowners and charterers, drafting "*loans for fleets of ships and loans to fund purchases or refinancing.*"

Typically deals relate to "*oil tankers or bulk carriers,*" although there's the odd yacht finance matter for a super-rich client. "*You get responsibility early on*" when drafting documents, "*though obviously they'd be read a thousand times by someone else before they go out.*" The firm assisted tanker and container ship owner Aries Maritime Transport, advising on the restructuring of its $240m debt and negotiating the "*super-swapsy*" of almost 19 million shares in the company in exchange for three Capesize bulkers (a type of cargo ship). Closer to home HFW has acted for Swedish bank Handelsbanken, setting up €170m loan facilities for ferry operator Stena to part finance two new passenger ferries. Newbuilds aren't the only trade in this seat. "*I tended to do recycling deals,*" one trainee recalled, where "*the heap of rust in the port*" is bought for scrap, then "*sold on to a breakage yard in Bangladesh or India.*"

Time away

The commercial litigation team is relatively small and deals mainly with banking fraud and trusts disputes, also employment, construction, real estate and insolvency work. Trainees get up to the usual litigation tasks and there's always a lot of research to be done. "*It's all quite interesting points of law,*" trainees explained, and we've heard that there are a few old and wise partners who greet legal questions with: "*Now, you remember this point from 1880...*" HFW lawyers recently assisted a UAE investment bank recovering loans in excess of $600m from two companies.

Many trainees take a seat in corporate, projects and finance (CPF) to tick off the SRA's transactional requirement, but shipping is never far away as CPF takes on aspects of ship finance, shipbuilding contracts and project work on offshore oil and gas fields. Trainees have a go at the first drafts of loan agreements and guarantees, and attend "*big client meetings.*" A seat in insurance is similarly varied as "*a bunch of key clients throw anything its way.*" Trainees muck in with bundling, "*if it has to be done,*" draft correspondence to clients and barristers and prepare initial notes on new files for partners. HFW also maintains a seat in EU/competition law, although it has only a small team.

Client secondments are available and trainees say HFW "*is very good at sending people abroad.*" Paris, Piraeus, Hong Kong, Singapore and Dubai all host trainees from time to time. There's "*always a lot of interest in Dubai,*" but "*the ones that people really want to go to*" – Hong Kong and Singapore – aren't always available at each seat rotation. Languages generally aren't a prerequisite, although "*for Paris they tend to want French.*"

Mischief managed

While they stopped short of using the phrase 'old-school', trainees admitted there is a "*sense of tradition with maritime law.*" Though "*you can pick up on the fact that some partners don't like the pace of change,*" compared to a few years ago HFW "*is almost completely different in terms of corporate profile and the way it conducts itself.*" There's a new website, more women coming through into associate roles, and although the partnership is still largely white, male and public school, at trainee and NQ level the people are definitely more international and diverse. To facilitate integration there's a buffet lunch, every other month, to which everyone from back-office staff to partners are invited on a rolling basis.

Integration is one thing, but the "*sensible*" folk at HFW don't do "*stupid team-building.*" Nevertheless, its lawyers are not averse to novelty-ing it up for big events such as the Christmas party, where the firm set up a hog roast and "*closed off the bottom of the office to fill it with booze.*" "*I think there was a theme,*" one source recollected hazily. "*There were a lot of pirate hats.*" The last summer party – "*HFW Fest*" – was described as "*a cross between village fair and school fête, themed on Harry Potter,*" trainees told us. "*On paper it looked awful, but those who went enjoyed it.*" We've heard stories of welly wanging, jousting, free food and drink and a departmental tug-of-war. Regular sport involves golf and netball, and "*a lot of client events*" with the big P&I clubs, including cricket, tennis and rugby tournaments. Rugby, in particular is a "*big thing*" at HFW. It sponsors an international Rugby Sevens team called the HFW Wailers, about which there is information on the firm's website. Aptly enough, water-based events are popular among staff, from "*dragon boat racing to rowing.*" The trade and energy group hosts an open bar every Friday in different drinking holes across the City, while other departments descend to a bar below the office called Habit, or hang out in the firm's café and garden.

The firm receives applications from ex-mariners and those with connections to the shipping industry. Don't despair if you thought that port was only to be found on the starboard of your parents' drinks cabinet, HFW will consider people whose closest experience to life on the open seas is the 8am ferry to Calais. Nonetheless, all the trainees we spoke to had a thirst for international work and a desire to avoid "*standard City firms doing straight-up corporate law.*" For them, the "*slightly academic atmosphere*" at HFW offers the internationality they craved and they loved the fact that you can see the "*effect of your work on the ground.*" The firm is "*quite keen on languages,*" confided one interviewee: "*French, Spanish, Chinese, Greek...*" if you can converse with foreign shipowners then you're an asset to the firm.

And finally...

Trainees say the best thing at HFW is the work and the clients. *"It's just so international, and different time zones make everything more interesting!"* In 2010; 13 of the 15 qualifiers accepted jobs with the firm.

Howes Percival LLP

The facts

Location: Leicester, Northampton, Norwich, Milton Keynes

Number of UK partners/solicitors: 32/56

Total number of trainees: 18

Seats: 4x6 months

Alternative seats: None

On chambersstudent.co.uk
- How to get into HP
- We talk to HP's training principal Geraint Davies
- HP's CSR activities

Full-service Howes Percival is particularly known for its commercial work in the East Midlands and its private client and agricultural estates work in Norwich.

Where's Percival?

As has been the case with many firms, the past couple of years have brought challenges for this Leicester, Northampton, Norwich and Milton Keynes-based business, but it maintains its traditional strengths in areas like corporate, litigation and employment while branching out into new practices. It recently launched a family law group in Leicester with the hire of Harvey Ingram partner Jane Cowley, who will also spearhead growth of the firm's private client presence in the East Midlands offices. In 2008 the loss of the bulk of its Milton Keynes office when 30 lawyers defected to Denton Wilde Sapte was definitely a blow. HP's presence in that city is now reduced to a small residential and conveyancing practice with no training scheme. However, in March 2010 it announced the establishment of a small London office dedicated to insolvency and corporate recovery, expected to open in late 2010. Partner Nick Oliver's team is still tiny, but who knows, maybe some day trainees will be able to work in the capital.

HP is weathering the double-whammy of the recession plus reduced fee income from Milton Keynes fairly well. In the midst of it all, it picked up some high-profile bankruptcy litigation, including one of *The Lawyer*'s 'Top 10 cases for 2010', defending the administrators and the purchasers of a law firm that went into pre-packaged administration against claims that the firm was undervalued when it was sold.

HP wins a great deal of public sector instructions, including assisting HM Revenue & Customs on MTIC (Missing Trader Intra Community) cases – a kind of VAT fraud that costs the government billions every year. Is that what Nick Clegg was referring to in those TV debates, we wonder? The firm also attracts business from national and international companies looking to buy legal services below City prices. Considering the firm has big-name clients like Welcome Break, Nampak, Shanks and The British Racing Drivers Club, the formula appears to be working. With high-quality clients and exciting opportunities on offer, trainees told us the firm makes good on the promise of what HR Officer Katy Pattle describes as "*London-quality work with the lifestyle and time outside work that you wouldn't get in London.*"

Meeting in the Midlands

HP's two fairly independent limbs operate wholly separate recruitment schemes. Prospective applicants choose either the East Midlands arm (Leicester and Northampton) or the Norwich office. East Midlands trainees rotate through four six-month seats, with a choice between commercial property; commercial litigation; company commercial; employment; private client and family law (only available in Leicester). The sole requirement is a contentious seat in either litigation or employment.

Chambers UK rankings

Agriculture & Rural Affairs	Intellectual Property
Corporate/M&A	Private Client
Dispute Resolution	Real Estate
Employment	Restructuring/Insolvency

Most Midlands trainees spend time in both Leicester and Northampton before committing to one or other upon qualification. Our sources were grateful to experience what each had to offer, though occasionally people need to make inconvenient moves. Second-years have priority in seat allocation and *"it can be a real bugbear for first-years to get posted to Leicester when your family's in Northampton"* while *"the exciting seats get taken by second-years."* Ultimately *"it comes down to whether they can accommodate you and the business need."* But most agreed: *"They do their best to give you what you want."*

A seat in company commercial involves a range of corporate work including share and asset sales for big clients, many of whom are in the automotive or financial sectors. Trainees *"get an awful lot of responsibility"* that goes beyond due diligence to *"drafting contracts"* and *"all the ancillary documents."* One newbie told us: *"Quite often the partner will take you to a meeting with the clients to hear instructions and then you'll get to prepare the first draft."* In the popular employment seat, newbies tackle contentious and advisory work. They pay their dues with administrative tasks like preparing bundles for tribunals, but *"also take witness statements and draft responses to claims."* One lucky person got to craft a company's policy on immigration, while another was *"given a small claim to handle from beginning to end, including negotiating the settlement."* Employment brings some of the longest hours, *"but by City standards they're quite good,"* with ten to eleven-hour days normally the maximum.

Commercial litigation trainees work with a host of Midlands-based and some multinational clients including waste management companies, clothing manufacturers and the aforementioned Welcome Break. Sources reported substantive tasks like *"liaising with partners at other law firms"* and even conducting smaller hearings in judges' chambers and applications at the High Court. *"I've done work I would never have had the opportunity to do at my level at other firms,"* one happy source boasted. *"While my peers have been in the backroom, I've had direct contact with our biggest clients."*

All our interviewees stressed that *"the level of responsibility"* and the *"supportive environment"* set HP apart. *"One of the best things is that the partners are approachable"* and *"you get really good feedback."* We heard over and over that *"students should know they can get excellent-quality work outside London."* Trainees were also eager to tell us that the hours are not quite so strenuous as we have previously reported. *"For all the talk about the hours, it really isn't bad,"* one said. Others reported that, in the poorer economy, *"I've rarely stayed later than 6.30pm."* Not bad considering the *"salary is definitely higher in comparison to other local firms."*

A tale of two firms

Norwich and East Midlands trainees see little of each other. Said one: *"It feels completely separate; we're effectively two different firms."* As befits their East Anglian location, the agricultural estates and private client teams are each ranked well in *Chambers UK*. *"We get old-school landed gentry types who wear hunting clothes,"* a Norfolk source explained. But the office is also recognised for litigation, banking and finance, and employment. Seats are available to trainees in commercial litigation; agricultural and estates/tax planning; corporate; commercial property; and in the increasingly busy insolvency department. One source enjoyed *"working with clients in businesses I grew up with."*

Corporate restructuring and insolvency has become a major focus since the recession, and the Norwich team's expertise earns a top *Chambers UK* rating in East Anglia. The CIAR (Civil Interventions and Asset Recovery) department serves several government creditor clients, including the Insolvency Service, for which it conducts directors' disqualifications work, and HM Revenue & Customs, which the firm advised on an application to place Southend United FC into administration.

Northampton is *"the traditional base from which Howes Percival grew."* This *"cosier and quieter"* office is located in an older building complete with *"chandeliers, fancy meeting rooms and portraits on the wall."* While the Northampton office is *"at the nicer end of a charming market town,"* the Leicester office is in a business park. Leicester *"has more of a buzz about it"* and serves some of the firm's bigger commercial clients. It is *"very much seen as the slick, city office,"* which some newbies say makes it feel *"more driven and hierarchical."* Leicester also offers trainees more social opportunities in a wider selection of bars, restaurants and nightclubs. Plus the *"shops are open until 8pm,"* an important distinction from Northampton's five o'clock. While the Midlands trainees will refer to Norwich as being *"out in the sticks,"* it's own trainees praise it for being *"more laid-back"* and like that *"you can't walk through town without seeing someone you know."* Plus it's pretty nice that on a typical day the office empties by 6pm.

Communication between the offices has been a challenge, sources said, though interaction has improved of late. The fissure between the Midlands and Norwich offices was most acutely felt when Midlands trainees found out about Norwich's plans to open a London office through an article in *The Lawyer*. It was exciting news, but "*we knew nothing about it*" because "*there was no official announcement.*" One irritated source said: "*It was kind of unprofessional because a client mentioned it and I didn't even know about it.*" While not as overt as that communication failure, even Leicester and Northampton do not operate as closely as they could, trainees said. Management is "*trying to unify the firm*" through department-wide meetings and "*in the past year there's been a noticeable emphasis on the offices working together.*" While Leicester and Northampton tend to have separate clients, "*we will sometimes refer work to each other.*"

Trainees also called for more transparency from the top. "*There is sometimes the feeling that it's cloak and dagger and the partners don't let trainees or even fee earners know what's going on.*" For example, "*quite often they'll appoint a new solicitor or someone will resign and people will not find out about it except via office gossip.*" Naturally, one thing second-year trainees were really eager to learn was whether or not they would be taken on as NQs. In the end, four of 2010's seven qualifiers stayed.

Moving on

Many trainees had chosen HP specifically because they wanted to live near family and "*the location was one of the main attractions.*" Other than this, it was hard to pinpoint an HP type, save that they are "*straightforward*" and "*without any airs.*" For applicants, regional ties "*aren't a requirement but they do help.*" "*You must show that you genuinely want to work in a regional firm,*" one source advised. "*I know people from my LPC who applied to regional firms as a back-up to London firms. The people who are here really do want to be here.*" Others explained that "*work-life balance is one of the main reasons you choose the regions.*" And as one sage source noted: "*London firms sell themselves with a good salary and good clients without letting on that you have to work really long hours.*"

The social scene prompted mixed reviews. Leicester sounds more active than the other two, with Friday night drinks fairly regular even if the party is tempered by the fact that "*most people have to drive home.*" In Northampton and Norwich, "*people tend to go home straight after work*" so there is more of a lunch culture helped by the fact that the offices are in town centres rather than on business parks. In terms of sports, there's a squash ladder, football tournaments and table tennis. Some blame a lack of closeness among trainees on the multi-location training scheme. "*I think our bond's weakened,*" one source concluded. HP encourages bonding through firmwide events like the AGM and summer trainee party – usually a barbecue followed by "*a night out in town.*"

And how is morale generally? "*We went through a period when Milton Keynes went and then came the recession redundancies*" so "*morale was naturally a bit low.*" Our interviewees were hopeful for the future though. "*After Milton Keynes, there was work to be done to improve the firm's status,*" one mused, "*but I think that's been done.*" Trainees were happy with their choice. "*The firm does what it says on the tin,*" one commented. "*It's a regional firm with a very strong client base. It's what I expected and what I wanted.*" Another agreed: "*I get exposure to good clients without working the long hours I would in London. It's exactly what I thought it would be.*"

And finally...

If you want quality work without London stress and you've got the East Midlands or Norfolk in your blood, or in your mind, HP could be a perfect match.

Ince & Co

The facts

Location: London

Number of UK partners/solicitors: 54/84

Total number of trainees: 29

Seats: Notionally 4x6 months

Alternative seats: Ad hoc overseas seats

Extras: Language classes

On chambersstudent.co.uk
- How to get into Ince & Co
- A blagger's guide to shipping
- Piracy: an international problem

If shipping and insurance float your boat, climb aboard and get ready to captain your training contract.

Desert islands

British-built in 1870, Ince still stands tall on the Thames. The firm saw its turnover rise again to a healthy £86.3m in the 2009/10 financial year, rising from £79.4m in the perilous 2008/09 year. As a litigation-focused business, the economic downturn didn't hit it in the same way as other more transactionally oriented City players. Ince has seven core practice areas (or 'strands'). It is best known for shipping and insurance/reinsurance, and picks up top-tier *Chambers UK* rankings for each. The other five strands are aviation; commercial disputes; energy and offshore; international trade; and business and finance, this last one being the sole transactional area.

Ince lawyers haven't always been 'stranded'. In days gone by, they could float from practice area to practice area as they wished – aviation one day, insurance the next. But the tides have changed. Depending on the work they have been engaged in, lawyers are now allocated a "*home strand,*" and a second for flexibility one year after qualification. "*The strands are departments by any other name,*" explained one trainee. "*Before, you could switch between strands, but now you're unable to cross.*" But recruitment partner Jeremy Farr maintains that the system is not so rigid: it is still open to people to change strands, though it's perhaps not as easy as before. "*Essentially, it's all about career development so that those coming up to partnership have a real knowledge of their area and the clients.*"

Unlike their seniors, trainees are free to drift between strands, experiencing as much or as little of each as they wish. Though they are placed with a different partner every six months, "*you're free to get work from anyone.*" Some sources did note, however, that "*sitting with a partner in the field you're working in helps as you pick things up from them.*" When the six months are up, trainees take their caseload with them. "*It's a great learning experience,*" commented one. "*It helps you build client relationships because they know you'll be with them from beginning to end.*"

Go fish

Sitting in their office, pondering where to wet their feet, how do trainees actually get work? Simple: free enterprise. "*You can wander round the firm and look for work,*" said one. "*The partners are your clients – you've got to sell yourself to them. If you want to get work in a specific sector, go and tell the relevant partner.*" After that, "*one thing leads to another.*" This approach "*can be a little daunting at first,*" but trainees were complimentary about "*approachable*" and "*welcoming*" partners. "*They've all been in our shoes,*" said one, "*so they understand what it's like.*" Ince also operates a 'traffic lights' system – not speed dating, rather an online system where trainees evaluate their workload for themselves. Most trainees advertise themselves as being on amber, which translates as "*I've got some work but I'm not snowed under.*" "*If I've got a deadline I'll put myself on red,*" explained one, "*and if I'm on green I'll usually get an e-mail offering work.*" And it's "*fastest finger first*" when 'capacity e-mails' are sent out requesting trainees' assistance.

Chambers UK rankings

Asset Finance	Insurance
Aviation	Professional Negligence
Commodities	Shipping
Dispute Resolution	

In the face of "*challenging, interesting and varied work,*" trainees have to dig deep. "*On a lot of cases, it's just me and the partner,*" said one. "*It's quite a responsibility and privilege at the same time.*" Though some grunt work is "*inevitable on massive cases,*" trainees enjoy drafting case management directions and pleadings, taking witness statements, meeting clients and instructing experts and international lawyers. "*This isn't a 'cushy' firm – you don't come here to do two years of photocopying.*" On smaller cases, trainees do the "*day-to-day running of the case, and the partners check it at the end.*" Simply, "*you can just get on with things.*"

Trainees do need to be careful not to take on too much – they can't say yes to everything. "*You need to balance what you've promised to other people, otherwise you'll stay late.*" But, while they are thrown in at the deep end, "*there's always someone on hand with a life jacket.*" "*When I get stuck, I can go back to the partner who gave me the work and ask them for help,*" said one trainee. "*They know we're still learning.*"

Worse things happen at sea

"*It's going to be hard to avoid doing any shipping work,*" commented one trainee. But don't worry if you don't know your 'Hebei Spirit' from your Smirnoff Ice: shipping law is grounded in contract and tort and offers "*a good mix of heavy black letter law and its practical application.*" "*It's a real cerebral challenge,*" said one source. There's also "*a big focus*" on training to get trainees up to speed with the workings of the industry.

Ever fancied yourself as a lifesaver? The Ince website has an 'International Emergency Response' hotline. Manned 24 hours a day, 365 days a year, an Ince lawyer is on hand for all your emergencies. Well, shipping emergencies, anyway. The firm has recently been involved in a number of high-profile piracy cases, including the 'Faina' off the coast of Somalia and the 'Front Comor' in the Gulf of Aden. Ince lawyers also represented the Russian shipping company Sovcomflot in the hugely important Fiona Trust litigation, which was one of the biggest in the Commercial Court in recent times and involved claims amounting to more than $800m. In the 'Prestige' case, Ince lawyers considered the human rights implications of a captain's bail at the European Court of Human Rights.

When pirates (or, slightly less excitingly, rocks) are smashing holes in your ship, when oil's polluting the sea, when the ship's en route to Davy Jones' locker, it's Ince to the rescue! "*We all had our hopes up that we'd be going out to save sinking ships but that doesn't really happen,*" explained one trainee. The problem is you need experience for this kind of trip. Ince has lawyers who are ex-mariners who've spent more than 15 years at sea, so it's these guys who will be the ones on the scene. Trainees assist on the legal aspects back in London.

It doesn't take a genius to see the strong link between shipping and insurance, so it's little wonder Ince has its fingers deep in the insurance pie. The firm was recently called in to give expert legal opinion to the High Court of Justice of the Netherlands Antilles and Aruba in a marine insurance dispute and counselled the Canadian government's export credit agency. Trainees aren't likely to do any advocacy themselves – "*the disputes we're involved in are too high-value to leave to anyone but a barrister*" – but they do get involved in trials. "*I was handing witness bundles to witnesses, listening to witness evidence and generally getting to see quite a bit,*" a source confirmed.

Those wanting a break from the contentious can head over to the business and finance strand. Trainees are increasingly encouraged to take work from this area, although it is certainly the least popular. "*It's nothing to do with the people there,*" said one; "*it's just that I came to Ince because I wanted to do shipping.*" Many clients come from the shipping and energy sectors, others include traders and insurance companies plus a variety of privately owned businesses from media companies to chemical groups.

Yo, ho, ho...

Remember that emergency hotline? Ince hasn't reported any hoax calls (yet), but we did hear about a late-night phone call from another City firm. After trying to deliver some documents, the other firm went into panic mode when it discovered Ince's offices were in fact closed and rang the hotline. The caller was promptly told: "*This is not an emergency!*" A late night at Ince is somewhere between 8pm and 10pm. "*If I get in at 8am, it's empty,*" said one source; "*there's no face time here – if there's work that needs doing you pull your weight, but if not, you go home.*" Trainees occasionally need to cancel weekend or other plans: "*It's not something you have to do, but partners appreciate it if you can rearrange things.*"

Trainees are a "*tight-knit group*" and often lunch together in the breakout room, even though "*soup is the only hot option available.*" The firm organises monthly drinks at which "*everyone socialises – partners, lawyers and support staff too,*" and the carol service, Christmas party, family drinks evening, and black-tie May Ball are popular. On Marathon Sunday the firm invites friends and family to spectate from its Tower Bridge location. Trainees have an annual budget to organise two social events of their own and also enjoy impromptu get-togethers, whether it's dinner at Café Rouge or drinks at Prohibition. Generally, "*if there's something you want to do, you'll get the money to do it.*" There are a number of sports teams and even a sailing club. Being a member of the choir might come in handy at the firm's annual quiz night, where the losers belt out a karaoke rendition of 'We are the Champions'. Win or lose, it's important to remember that social events are a good way of increasing your profile within the office.

An Ince in every port

Sandwiched between St Katherine Docks and Tower Bridge, Ince's offices are "*very nice indeed.*" They're also just a stone's throw away from Execution Dock, where pirates of the high seas met their fate until the early 19th century. The floor-to-ceiling window in the reception area perfectly frames the yachts floating in the docks, six floors below.

"*Quite a British firm,*" Ince is "*professionally traditional,*" so no dress-down Fridays here. "*As a litigator, you're in court a lot so you have to be smart.*" Trainees "*have a bit about them,*" apparently, and are "*very driven and enthusiastic.*" Owing to the nature of the training structure, "*you need to be proactive,*" and this is "*definitely not a firm for shrinking violets.*" Confidence should not be confused with arrogance. "*No matter how clever you think you are, shipping law is challenging and always changing. If you come in thinking you know it all already, you're in for a rude awakening.*"

Trainees come from a range of backgrounds and universities. "*Some are highly academic and some have worked previously, but we're all enthusiastic and hard-working.*" Several come from other countries and speak other languages. In the 1990s, Ince expanded its global influence and now has offices in Dubai, Hamburg, Hong Kong, Le Havre, Paris, Piraeus, Shanghai and Singapore. Trainees have the opportunity to do an overseas seat if there's work available, and in the last few years a stint in Piraeus, Hamburg or Dubai has been the most likely. Even without a seat abroad, we heard of some who had travelled to such exotic locations as South Africa and Venezuela on business. Those with language skills can also help with document translation and meeting foreign clients when they come to London.

In a 2010 study of gender diversity at the UK's top 50 law firms, Ince floundered at the bottom. Only 11% of the partnership is female, and trainees admitted that the firm could "*no doubt do better.*" It's "*male-heavy at the top,*" said one, "*but at the bottom it's fairly equal.*" Others contended that "*it seems* [to have] *more* [to do with] *the women's choice than anything the firm is doing.*"

A place to drop anchor

"*I'd like to grow old here,*" said one content trainee. "*There's no reason why you wouldn't want to stay on: there's great work, great people and great offices.*" "*It would take a lot for me to want to leave,*" added another; "*the work-life balance is pretty good.*" With 70% of partners having trained at the firm, Ince could be a promising place to set up home. Yet we did hear of some disquiet among the ranks. Though Ince recorded a bumper year, it reduced its salary bands in 2009. "*It seems that purely because there were no other jobs to go to, they thought they could cut salaries,*" one disappointed source grumbled. Some argued, however, that "*in this market you can't be too complacent and you have to look ahead.*" Still, the firm posts consistently high NQ retention rates and kept on ten out of 12 qualifiers in 2010. Trainees find out whether they're on track during six-monthly appraisals, learning their fate in the final meeting at the end of May. There shouldn't be any nasty shocks, though. As one source put it: "*I'm not an optimistic person, but I'm busy, I'm working hard and I'm earning the firm money. I don't think there should be any surprises.*"

And finally...

At the end of the training contract, *"nothing changes except your salary."* This really is a firm that gets you ready for qualification.

Irwin Mitchell

The facts

Location: Birmingham, Bristol, Glasgow, Leeds, London, Manchester, Newcastle, Sheffield

Number of UK partners/solicitors: 119/298

Total number of trainees: 76

Seats: 3x4 +1x12 months

Alternative seats: None

Extras: Pro bono – LawWorks

On chambersstudent.co.uk
- How to get into IM
- More on trainees' seat options
- Business development at IM

With one of the top personal injury, clinical negligence and liability practices in the country, Irwin Mitchell aims for nationwide coverage and the continued expansion of its commercial practice.

IM moving on up

Irwin Mitchell is a firm with a strong history in personal injury (PI), clin neg and Court of Protection work. It is now also increasingly known for commercial law, and fields successful property, employment, commercial litigation and corporate practices. A national firm, IM has offices in Birmingham, Bristol, Glasgow, London, Leeds, Manchester, Newcastle, Sheffield and, perhaps surprisingly, Madrid and Málaga.

This is a very profitable organisation. Profits per equity partner stood at £514,000 in 2009/10, and revenue continues to rise. According to training partner Jane Horton, this is partly because the firm "*manages things very prudently,*" but also because "*PI, insurance and lender recovery work are pretty much safe from the recession – when times are tough people are more happy to pursue a PI claim.*" Trainees see "*plans for expansion everywhere.*" A new Bristol office and a "*satellite*" consulting office in Leicester were announced in 2010, while hires in Birmingham and London's commercial teams reveal a clear desire to grow that part of the business: it currently accounts for only around £40m of the firm's £157m turnover.

Where is IM going next? The answer seems to be everywhere: "*If you put pins in a map of the country where our offices are, it becomes obvious where the gaps are,*" Jane Horton says. The strategy seems to be to open offices focused on PI (as Bristol is currently) and then beef up the commercial side with lateral hires. The firm sees the implications of the Legal Services Act as presenting "*an opportunity rather than a threat*" – go to our website to see what it all means for IM, along with an insight into its 'no win, no fee' and pro bono work.

Training takes place in Birmingham, London, Leeds, Sheffield, Newcastle and, from autumn 2010, Bristol. Trainee numbers have been hiked over the past few years and in 2009 the firm brought in a new two-stream system of training. New starters now choose between a 'personal injury' or 'business and private client' stream. Trainees stay in one office for the duration of their training and conform to an unusual seat system. They take three seats of four months followed by a 12-month 'long seat'. The system has been through some teething problems, but trainees have no fundamental gripes with it. "*It's an advantage if you know what you want to do from the outset, but if you're not sure it's a negative thing,*" said one source, so do bear this in mind when you're applying. Again, see our website for an in-depth explanation of the seat system and a greater insight into what trainees think of it.

No PI in the sky

Despite the growth of commercial, PI is still a key focus. Depending on the office, trainees can take seats in clin neg, neuro-trauma and asbestos disease as well as Court of Protection; industrial disease; abuse; workplace injury;

Chambers UK rankings

Administrative & Public Law	Health & Safety
Banking & Finance	Personal Injury
Civil Liberties	Police Law
Clinical Negligence	Private Client
Corporate/M&A	Product Liability
Debt Recovery	Professional Discipline
Dispute Resolution	Real Estate
Employment	Real Estate Litigation
Environment	Restructuring/Insolvency
Family/Matrimonial	Tax
Fraud	Travel

armed forces litigation; group actions; travel; and general PI. A full breakdown of the seats you can try in each office can be found on our website. Clients are almost exclusively claimants and compensation ranges from "*a couple of hundred thousand to a couple of million pounds.*" In the past the PI team has represented victims of the 2006 London bombings in a pro bono compensation claim, as well as acting on litigation over the Lockerbie bombing and the King's Cross tube fire.

In a clin neg seat (also called 'medical law and patient rights') you might work for "*people who have had knee and hip operations which have gone wrong.*" Other cases have involved "*patients being infected with hepatitis B by blood products,*" "*injuries that women sustained in childbirth*" (a big focus in Manchester and Birmingham), treatment delays, failure to diagnose cancer and disabilities caused by malpractice. Working on cases for individuals, you get "*lots of hands-on experience and client contact,*" as well as "*responsibility for a lot of routine new client enquiries.*" In Sheffield "*the majority of work is on a large group action*" and "*at least two-thirds of work is against the NHS Litigation Authority.*" Other defendants include private clinics or big pharmaceutical companies. The team is acting for 200 clients, including children, who were misdiagnosed as suffering from epilepsy and unnecessarily prescribed powerful drugs.

The neuro-trauma team acts "*predominantly for people who have had a brain or spinal injury as the result of a road traffic accident.*" It won £3.2m for a young man with Asperger's and OCD who was hit by a car. The team also won an illegal immigrant from Turkey the right to stay in Britain to receive healthcare after a road traffic accident. Then there are workplace injury cases, including a £5m win for someone who was paralysed by falling boxes in a warehouse. Trainees are involved in "*everything from instructing counsel and medical experts to client meetings, taking and drafting witness statements, setting up meetings and seeing things through court.*" One Manchester trainee reported that most low-value work is being moved to Sheffield and that "*trainees tend to assist partners and associates, so their exposure is more to high-value stuff.*"

The asbestos team won over £10m in compensation in 2009 for groups and individuals who contracted mesothelioma from exposure to the mineral. Cases can go back to the 1940s and require medical and regulatory research by trainees. There's plenty of direct contact with clients who "*have six to twelve months left to live and who'll experience a really horrible death.*" As a lawyer you can be "*almost a release for their spouses.*"

Dealing with clients like this requires an attitude that balances professionalism with empathy. As one trainee put it: "*I think you have to be sensitive, genuinely have empathy and want to do whatever you can for clients, but sometimes you have to step back and not get too involved. You do have to be a certain type of person.*" Another agreed: "*You can't wither away under the stress of the emotion. You have to be strong for your clients. Some of the cases are very distressing.*"

Lawyers sans frontières

Work for the Court of Protection means "*being responsible for someone's finances or property*" if they are mentally or physically incapable of doing so. You'll be "*meeting clients straight away*" here too, and dealing with wills and trusts. The armed forces team, meanwhile, is suing the MoD on behalf of a civilian engineer who lost his shoulder in a roadside bomb blast in Basra. It also acted for paratrooper Ben Parkinson (perhaps the most injured member of the armed forces) in a case that led to the MoD to change its multiple injury compensation rules.

Ongoing product liability claims include one against Cadbury for salmonella poisoning, an illness that also pops up in the work of the travel team. It acts for groups of victims or their surviving relatives in "*bringing cases against package holiday companies over people who caught salmonella*" or were involved in road or plane crashes. This is the role of the Málaga and Madrid branches. "*A lot of work centres around expats and the local community,*" so trainees are unlikely to see much of the Spanish offices.

Hitting it for six

Although Newcastle and Bristol only do PI, Sheffield, Birmingham, Manchester, Leeds and London also offer commercial training contracts. One Manchester trainee spoke of "*big visions planned for the future,*" not least "*bringing all the different practice areas to Manchester.*" It's the same story in London where "*there's a conscious effort to improve the profile of the London business team.*" Commercial seats include property; commercial litigation; employment; insolvency; corporate and transactions; regulatory investigation; family law; and public law.

Property seats cover everything from "*individual residential purchases and sales through to commercial leases on buildings.*" The department acts for the likes of Thorntons, River Island and Sheffield Hallam University, as well as banks such as Santander. In one typical matter, lawyers advised HSBC over its funding of the new cricket pavilion at Headingley. Trainee work involves "*quite a lot of research into landlord and tenant matters.*" Commercial litigation, meanwhile, ranges from "*professional negligence to contractual claims and some property and regulatory cases.*" London and Manchester attract clients like InBev, the largest beer brewer in the world. Trainees gain "*good exposure working alongside the partners*" and tackle "*witness statements, entire bundles, settlement offers and letters of claim.*"

The employment team often acts for organisations like Age UK (formerly Age Concern and Help The Aged), Sheffcare, Sheffield Wednesday FC and a number of mid-market companies. One trainee spoke of "*running* [their] *supervisor's files*" and working on "*unfair dismissal claims, discrimination and whistle-blowing*" for employees. A corporate seat will involve buying and selling mid-market regional businesses, together with a few refinancing and funding matters for top international banks.

A family law seat (taken in the business stream as, hopefully, no one gets physically hurt) sees trainees dealing with assets after divorces and deaths, as well as parental access rights. The work is "*really interesting,*" although "*the clients are demanding and sometimes don't appreciate what you do.*" The public law team acts for charities and individuals against public bodies on "*health and social care, education, professional discipline, planning and environmental matters.*" "*Decisions could have wider consequences for social policy or the law*" – challenging the default retirement age is just one example.

Pinning things down

A good work/life balance is one of IM's top attractions, with hours not too long in any department. PI trainees work 9am to 5pm or sometimes an hour or two longer "*when a trial is due in a couple of weeks.*" Even in the business stream, late nights are a rarity, with one trainee telling us they'd "*stayed past 8pm only a handful of times.*"

Trainees say the firm is exactly "*like it said in the brochure.*" It's "*an approachable place. You'll wander into other teams and say, 'What do you know about this?'*" We agree with the trainee who asserted that IM takes on "*fun, normal people who you can have a laugh with.*" A common trait is a previous link to Birmingham, Manchester, Sheffield, Leeds or Newcastle – be it a (well or misspent) youth or an education at one of those cities' redbricks. Trainees don't just come from elite universities, and some confessed that they "*didn't do very well at A level.*" Recruitment is heavily merit-based, and a number of trainees have previously worked as paralegals, either at IM or elsewhere.

These common traits mean "*there is an overall culture, although each office is very individual.*" In most locations the firm has recently moved into new digs that are all "*similar in layout*" with "*IM branding throughout.*" Trainees in Manchester and Leeds feel their offices are "*much more intimate across all the different floors.*" People don't take themselves too seriously: "*All the PI partners in Leeds have caricatures of themselves on the outside of their pods,*" the result of professional handiwork at a Chinese New Year party. Although Sheffield is physically larger, and you "*could be sitting ten metres from someone and not know their name,*" trainees generally feel the office is "*really friendly,*" and there's "*lots of interaction between departments.*" London is described as "*relaxed*" yet "*entrepreneurial.*" Although lawyers refer cases to other offices, PI work is usually divided up by geographic area. Business instructions are easier to share across the network.

This firm is described as "*really sociable.*" In all offices there are a number of firm-sponsored social events, like end-of-year drinks, a client party at Manchester's Museum of Science and Industry and a "*Champagne Friday with partners buying goodness knows how much champagne.*" Trainees go out for pub drinks "*quite regularly,*" and other events have included trips to the dogs or the horses (that's in the North, of course), paintballing, brewery visits and charity quiz nights.

And finally...

The firm's decent retention record meant trainees were not too nervous about qualification in 2010. A total of 21 of 25 qualifiers were retained.

Jones Day

The facts

Location: London

Number of UK partners/solicitors: 50/106

Total number of trainees: 37

Seats: None

Alternative seats: None

Extras: Pro bono – Waterloo Legal Advice Service, LawWorks, FRU

On chambersstudent.co.uk
- How to get into Jones Day
- A potted history of the firm
- The Supreme Court and the STD

A bespoke training at Jones Day is just the ticket for independent go-getters. This London mid-sizer is part of a worldwide network of more than 2,400 commercial lawyers in 32 offices around the world.

Be a part of it

It all starts with a firm called Gouldens. The single-site London firm was known for its strong-minded spirit and lively culture. In 2003 its management lived up to a reputation for being somewhat ahead of the curve, and Gouldens merged with global player Jones Day. The US-born big hitter was a giant full-service machine, and becoming a part of the JD family certainly brought benefits to the Londoners. "*We get the big-ticket work while still retaining the intimacy of a medium-sized office,*" said one source.

Jones Day London claims that it's different to other American-run firms in the Square Mile. It assumes that many of its rivals have little independence from the USA and that they operate merely as satellites. While this is true of some, it certainly is not the case at Jones Day, where "*the London office is a UK business in its own right.*"

At the start of their contracts, new trainees fly out for an 'academy' week in Washington, DC to meet newbies from all corners of the planet. This Stateside induction certainly helps cement the 'one firm worldwide' mantra in their minds. "*There's a good feeling that it is one firm,*" commented a source. "*The academy was great to bring us all together, and we made contacts with people from around the world.*" This early-stage networking comes in handy for when trainees are working on international deals and cases. "*There's such an easy communication between offices – work is assigned to whomever is best suited to do it. It's not competitive. We were all researching similar points of law and rang each other up to ask questions and offer advice.*" As for the common assertion that JD has no 'satellite' or 'branch' offices, well, don't try to call its founding Cleveland, Ohio office the HQ. The firm is adamant that it doesn't have one.

So far, so good? Try this for size. In 2009 – for the tenth year in a row – Jones Day topped global M&A league tables, achieving deal completions in no less than 299 transactions. In London, the firm recently advised Orange on its acquisition of Unanimis Holdings, the UK's largest exclusive digital advertising network. It also worked for British Land on the formation of a joint venture partnership for the freehold ownership of Sheffield's Meadowhill Shopping Centre.

But it's not all big deals… Jones Day triumphed in the very first UK Supreme Court decision, which involved the interpretation of a clause within a security trust deed. Other cases handled by the London litigators relate to such varied topics as cricket and the liberalisation of the telecoms markets in various Caribbean jurisdictions; the financing and guarantee of an Uzbekistani cotton purchase contract; and the largest prosecution in the history of the Serious Fraud Office (a case that went as far as the House of Lords).

So it looks as if there's little to distinguish the firm from any other successful mid-sizer in the City … until, that is, you look at its training contract. Jones Day is one of the few firms that runs a non-rotational training scheme without any set seats in different departments. It instead

Chambers UK rankings

Banking Litigation	Outsourcing
Capital Markets	Pensions
Construction	Private Equity
Corporate/M&A	Real Estate
Dispute Resolution	Real Estate Finance
Employment	Real Estate Litigation
Environment	Restructuring/Insolvency
Fraud	Tax
Intellectual Property	

expects its recruits to "*go and hunt for work*" from wherever they like within the firm. Those who've found their feet within the scheme tell us: "*It's not that daunting once you get the hang of it.*" Still, feedback over the years suggests that this is not a great system for the faint-hearted. "*To a certain extent, it's the law of the jungle out there,*" admitted one source. "*A shrinking violet wouldn't survive.*" If you're up for the adventure, read on.

Welcome to the jungle

As trainees each have their own offices and "*no one to rely on to give you work,*" they must quickly get used to the idea of touting for business. "*The key trait you need for this is confidence,*" confirmed one contact. And yet, "*it's not about going into someone's office, being all loud and gregarious and trying to be their best friend right away.*" Indeed, graduate recruitment partner David Smith confirms that "*we want confident people, but not too confident. Confident enough to ask questions, but not people who think they can come in and run before they can walk.*" Jones Dayers certainly aren't "*those annoying Type A people you meet at parties.*" As for knocking on doors, "*it's expected*" and "*everyone's really friendly so doors are only closed if people are on an important phone call.*" According to one candid source, the main difference with a non-rotational training contract is that "*you have to get off your arse a bit more.*"

Jones Day trainees give the system a thumbs-up. "*I feel much more in control than if I was in a seat pattern,*" said one. There's "*not the same frustration of having to leave a case after six months. Here you're on it from beginning to end.*" Often newbies are unsure of where their interests lie, so most "*float around different departments for about six months.*" During that time, a programme of lunchtime seminars helps them become aware of the various departments and the differences between them. Trainees move within the building to a new office after a year, usually into an area populated by lawyers in the field in which they want to qualify. Despite aligning themselves more closely with a certain breed of lawyer, trainees can still take on work of any and all types. As long as trainees fulfil SRA requirements, they're free to roam as near or far as they choose. "*In eight months, I've done work in nine or ten different areas,*" said one source, who believed it had helped them "*understand all sides of a transaction.*" Picking and mixing is also great for those areas of law that trainees are less keen on. "*If there's something you don't like, you can do it in a short, sharp burst. It's quick and painful, but at least there's light at the end of the tunnel.*"

It's worth asking yourself if you have the right temperament for Jones Day's training scheme. One source emphasised that "*you make your own opportunities here.*" Another added: "*You can't be reactive; you can't just wait for things to come to you. You've got take the initiative and go out and learn how to be a solicitor.*" Letting people know that you want to work for them ensures that there are no disappointments in terms of missing out on a seat, but the downside is that you have to create a good buzz about you. If your reputation goes down after a poor contribution on Partner A's work then Partner B may not be so inclined to give you a try-out. "*You just have to hope something will come up and they'll come back to you.*"

The system allows people to orient themselves towards the work they prefer, even from an early stage. Don't expect to avoid mundane tasks entirely, although there's certainly a sense that you can tease out good responsibility. In litigation, "*there's a mix of cases of all sizes. There is always the less glamorous bundling and admin to be done,*" and although disclosure exercises can be dry, "*if you uncover that little nugget to drive the case forward, it's a really nice find.*" Trainees are also able to interview witnesses and draft their statements, and on smaller cases they take tasks like drafting correspondence and court documents. Over in corporate, there's "*nothing like the buzz of completion meetings.*" Some grunt work is unavoidable over on this side of the business too: trainees take care of due diligence, which "*has to be done if you want to get on the big deals... you will get more responsibility as you progress.*"

Working on matters from beginning to end, trainees "*often end up being the factual expert,*" which also means that "*you build up people's trust.*" And, the longer you spend with one department, the juicier the work. At Jones Day, responsibility is afforded to the able. "*It's about matching someone's capability to a job, rather than their level of qualification,*" said one contact. "*If you show you can cope, they'll give you as much responsibility as you want.*" This matches the firm's eat-what-you-kill approach – there's no lockstep remuneration – so "*people are rewarded on their ability rather than how long they've been with the firm, resulting in not a massive amount of hierarchy,*" explained David Smith. The firm didn't make any large-scale redundancies in the recession – "*we don't eat our young!*" he added. Our trainee sources described a supportive working environment, and one remembered wisdom imparted by a senior: "*A partner once said to me that you should always be working outside your comfort zone, otherwise you'll stagnate.*" On a corporate deal, one trainee was "*surprised by how much client contact I got. I was reporting to the client on everything that I was in charge of.*" It seems that "*once they work out you're not a lunatic,* [seniors] *are generally happy to let you get on with things.*"

No ladder without a snake

So, Jones Dayers pick and choose much of their work, see things through to completion and enjoy as much responsibility as they can handle. But, like the law of attraction, there's no positive without a negative. "*Super keen*" starters beware: "*One of the hardest things is learning how to manage your own workload.*" In a classic feast or famine scenario, "*you can find yourself frantically busy, but then you'll have nothing and you need to go looking again.*" And "*if everything tees off at the same time, you're in trouble!*" The juggling act does get easier over time, and trainees soon learn that "*there's nothing more annoying for people than when you don't get your work done when you say you will. Sometimes you have to suck it up and do the hours; other times you have to be realistic*" about what work you agree to take on.

When late nights come – as inevitably they will – "*there's a good team spirit and everybody mucks in.*" Though some sources did compare the training experience to "*a jungle,*" most were surprised by the lack of competition between trainees. "*Perhaps if there were seats, people would be more competitive,*" one mused, "*but if you're on the radar with people here you'll get the work you want eventually.*" All trainees now have monthly partner-mentor meetings, as well as regular guidance from trainee mentors and a graduate development manager who makes sure that they see a variety of work. Though one frank source conceded that "*sometimes you can feel that you're not being comprehensively supervised,*" when trainees do find work "*it's normally very good and you're thanked for what you do.*"

Men in tights

Our sources described the typical Jones Day recruit as "*friendly*" and confirmed that most seniors will "*want to have a chat with you about how you are and how your weekend was.*" As one source confirmed: "*You feel like a human being, not just a due diligence robot.*" There's a good mix of personalities too: "*Election time brought forward some healthy debates!*"

A social life "*is there if you want it.*" The local pub, The Harrow, is a popular watering hole on Fridays, and trainees often get together for a 'pay day' dinner. There are plenty of sports teams to join and someone recently started a book group. Another benefit of the non-rotational training is that "*you end up getting invited to loads of different departmental Christmas parties.*" And, what has to be the Christmas calendar highlight – the pantomime. A remnant from the Gouldens era, this is possibly the ultimate proof of Jones Day London's British character and proof that it has not become overly influenced by its colleagues across the pond. Each year, trainees add a few "*plot twists*" and Jones Day jokes to the chosen fairytale. Last year, Snow White's Prince Charming was played by a pensions partner. "*It was quite fitting really to have them charging in to save the day, as they're quite involved in pro bono.*" Illustrating the firm's American influence, perhaps, there are "*as many pro bono opportunities as you like.*" Trainees can apply to the pro bono partner for work and are also encouraged to get involved with advice evenings at the Waterloo Legal Advice Service and the Free Representation Unit.

Despite Jones Day's huge international network, there is no programme of overseas secondments. Still, lucky trainees might get to tag a long on business trips – we heard of some who'd managed a short spell in New York. There may also be the chance to go overseas or on client secondment once qualified. When it comes to qualification, like their predecessors, our sources confirmed that the transition from trainee to NQ is "*almost seamless.*" As one admitted, "*it was almost a non-event. I picked up the same case I'd been doing the day before. It was almost like, 'so what's happened?'*" In 2010, seven out of 11 qualifiers stayed with the firm.

And finally...

Non-rotational training effectively guarantees experience in anything the firm has to offer. For a confident and independent individual, it could be one heck of an adventure.

K&L Gates

The facts

Location: London

Number of UK partners/solicitors: 60/75

Total number of trainees: 8

Seats: 4x6 months

Alternative seats: Occasional secondments

Extras: Pro bono – LawWorks, Battersea Legal Advice Centre; language training

On chambersstudent.co.uk
• How to get into K&L Gates
• The firm's history and strategy
• Local landmark London Stone

With global revenue topping $1bn and 36 offices worldwide, K&L Gates is one of the big boys from the US, and yet its London office retains an English personality.

Merger king

K&L Gates, as it exists today, is the result of a flurry of national and international mergers. The 'K&L' comes from East Coast firm Kirkpatrick & Lockhart, while the 'Gates' in question is Bill's dad, former partner at California's Preston, Gates & Ellis. The two merged in 2007, just two years after K&L had taken over London mid-sizer Nicholson Graham & Jones. A desire to "*expand into more jurisdictions*" has recently seen K&L Gates open up shop in Paris, Dubai, Moscow, Tokyo and Warsaw in the space of 18 months. Go to our website to read more about the firm's international strategy.

Global revenue topped $1bn for the first time in 2009, up 8% on the previous year, but the London office fared less well, seeing its revenue drop by 28% to just under £30m. Redundancies in 2009 were followed by trainee deferrals in both 2009 and 2010. All this meant there was no recruitment round in 2009. In 2010, trainees told us: "*The echelons of power have been positive about the future,*" and demonstrating the firm's commitment to the City, K&L is set to move into brand-new premises next to St Paul's Cathedral in spring 2011, which is just as well as "*you can tell we've outgrown the old office.*"

The London office is a solid, full-service, mid-market player. However, there is still a clear focus on Nicholson Graham & Jones' old strengths of corporate and property ("*it is 99.9% likely that you will be doing those two seats*"). Seats are also available in projects; planning; construction litigation; commercial litigation; IP; banking and finance; insurance; pensions; environment and employment. Deferrals meant that recent trainees were asked to do more seats than normal in property and corporate, although "*they did take into account the fact that trainees wanted more variety*" and introduced a temporary four-month seat system to remedy the problem.

Blackpool rock

In a property seat, trainees are "*primarily in charge*" of 20 to 30 files ranging from "*negotiating smaller leases to rent reviews.*" They also help out on major transactions, so for example trainees might be responsible for "*the administrative stuff*" on big deals like a £150m property transaction for investment manager Henderson's UK retail fund. Other clients include Laing O'Rourke, Rushmoor Borough Council and AOL, while the property finance team acts for RBS, Anglo Irish Bank and Nationwide. As a bit of a sideline, property partner Piers Coleman advises the Liberal Democrats and various returning officers on electoral law. Over this past election year, the Lib Dems "*got in touch with him as and when they needed*" and trainees "*had to do some quick research and send back an answer.*"

One trainee estimated that 70% of the activity in the corporate department is international ("*in real estate it's almost 0%*"). You might, as one trainee did, "*act for a US company selling a Dutch subsidiary to an English company.*" Head of

Chambers UK rankings

Capital Markets	Licensing
Construction	Parliamentary & Public Affairs
Corporate/M&A	Planning
Dispute Resolution	Real Estate
Environment	Real Estate Finance
Information Technology	Travel
Insurance	
Intellectual Property	

legal recruiting Tina Two tells us that "*globally the firm is going through a period of exceptional and sustainable growth,*" and that trainees should expect to be involved in even more international work in future.

M&A lawyers helped out long-standing client Leisure Parcs on the £40m sale of the Blackpool Tower to Blackpool Borough Council. And listings are a big source of work: "*We've got five or six AIM floats on at the moment,*" said one source. The team also acts for Teledyne Technologies and Arena Leisure, the UK's largest horse racing operator, while international clients include KBR and Halliburton, both of which have had heavy involvement with the war in Iraq. In corporate, trainees do their share of due diligence, "*getting documents uploaded*" and preparing deal bibles, but there's plenty of "*general commercial drafting*" too. The firm's small size also means that "*it's not as if, when a deal is being done, the partners shove you out of the room.*"

The projects department advises local authorities on regeneration schemes and handles PFI projects and other property developments. It also advises London Underground on issues which crop up because of EU procurement regulations. This seat is "*similar to corporate*" for trainees, who have lately found themselves working on things like "*the building of a new hospital or school*" or on a social housing scheme. The planning department, meanwhile, helps "*local authorities, big property funds and individuals*" stick to planning rules and with "*Section 106 agreements and planning appeals.*"

Up the redcoats

The litigation department has a mixed client roster and trainees can get pretty involved. The team recently acted for Eurotunnel in a dispute with its insurers over damage claims for the September 2008 Channel Tunnel fire. It has said yes to the men from Del Monte, supported the West Indies Cricket Board and acted for three of the five directors of Farepak in litigation related to the collapse of their Christmas hamper business back in 2006. Other clients hail from the oil and technology industries.

Rumours of forthcoming overseas seats have been bouncing around for over half a decade. Our sources say international secondments are now not likely to be immediately forthcoming, although NQs have travelled as far afield as Singapore and Dubai for work. The trainees we spoke to also spent a week in Washington, DC at the start of their training, where they met new joiners from across the globe. This jaunt to the States was cancelled in 2009, but is likely to return. There is usually at least one trainee on secondment to a client: in the past trainees have spent time with major international and UK businesses.

Working hours remain surprisingly good for the City. In property, said one source, "*you can be out of the door by 6.30pm, and I've very rarely had to work weekends.*" In corporate, trainees must be prepared to "*work late for the same money,*" although "*there's more banter.*"

A rather English marriage

Anglo-American mergers are funny things. Sometimes they pay off in spades and sometimes the cultural differences between the firms produce unexpected consequences. However, five years on from the hook-up between Nicholson Graham & Jones and Kirkpatrick & Lockhart, this seems a happy union. "*Nothing really strikes me as having become Americanised,*" one source concluded. The consensus is that, despite the international work, the office "*has kept its individuality as an English part of the network.*" NGJ was always a rather nice, laid-back type of place, which is why it was no surprise to hear a trainee describe its successor as "*very friendly and quite confidence-instilling. I've always been able to learn from people: they forgive your mistakes and are always helpful.*" We don't think there's really a 'K&L type', but our sources all seemed to have been angling for "*mid-sized firms*" with perhaps "*some international presence.*" Well, they angled right.

And finally...

What we have here is a little corner of England in a vast global network. Expect stints in corporate and real estate at this pleasant and sometimes underrated office. Five of seven qualifiers stayed on in 2010.

- **Invest time in career planning:** "I used to spend a day or two on each application form. At my training contract interview at my firm, what impressed the recruiters was my general knowledge of current affairs."

Kennedys

The facts

Location: London, Manchester, Birmingham, Cambridge, Chelmsford, Maidstone, Belfast, Taunton, Sheffield

Number of UK partners/solicitors: 145/240

Total number of trainees: 32

Seats: 4x6 months

Alternative seats: Potentially overseas seats, occasional secondments

Extras: Language classes

On chambersstudent.co.uk
- How to get into Kennedys
- More on the firm's social life
- Pro bono opportunities at Kennedys

Seemingly recession-proof, this national – and now international – law firm with a focus on insurance litigation has been expanding rapidly.

What recession?

You may not yet have heard of Kennedys but this law firm is definitely one to watch. It has experienced a veritable flurry of activity in the past two or three years, and has been thrust headfirst into the legal public eye. Its training scheme is going to receive a lot more attention following a refocus on the programme.

Kennedys became a top-50 law firm just two years ago, after its revenue rose 30% to £67.3m in 2008/09. This past financial year saw another rise of 31% to £88.25m. There are two key factors that explain this recession-defying trend: first is Kennedys' countercyclical practice focus on contentious areas of law; second is the fact that it has grown the size of its fee earning staff, through both regular hires and the acquisition of additional offices. Kennedys has 145 partners and over 800 staff around the world now, over 400 of which are in London. In bold defiance of the down economy, last year it hired over 100 people and the number of trainees actually increased from 25 to 32. It also took on seven extra partners, a new business director and a development manager. In 2008 Kennedys merged with insurance litigation boutique Davies Lavery, which provided bases in Birmingham and Maidstone as well as additional staff and premises in Chelmsford. In July 2010, Kennedys opened an office in Sheffield with 11 partners and over 70 staff from the Sheffield insurance team of now defunct law firm Halliwells.

As if all that weren't enough, Kennedys converted its business model to an LLP, won various awards and is now on the SRA's legal panel. The firm has "*a lot of ambition, a lot of drive,*" and its recent successes have imbued it with extra confidence.

Who's that Guy?

An important bit of news is that Guy Stobart (of managing-partner-at-Burges-Salmon fame) joined Kennedys as its Chief Executive Officer. Saying he is "*a good character to lead the way forward*" may be a bit of an understatement. During his time at elite Bristol firm Burges Salmon, its turnover and staff numbers multiplied five-fold, so keep your eyes peeled to see what happens here. The mighty Stobart must have spotted some serious potential in Kennedys. He is also a "*very forthcoming and approachable chap*" and regularly attends trainee meetings and monthly staff drinks.

Kennedys dates back to 1899, and until a decade ago was based in just London and Brentwood in Essex. The firm's expansion has now given it nine offices around the UK: in London, Manchester, Birmingham, Cambridge, Chelmsford, Maidstone, Belfast, Taunton, and most recently Sheffield. This is only the beginning: it has also opened offices in Australia, Hong Kong, New Zealand, Singapore, Spain and the United Arab Emirates. As if that weren't enough, the firm also has associated offices in eight more countries, including Chile, France and Pakistan. In the last couple of years Kennedys has had some very important cases on its hands: litigation over a fire in the Channel Tunnel; massive claims over the Buncefield oil depot explosion in Hertfordshire; heavy industry problems in Mexico and Venezuela; the sinking

Chambers UK rankings

Clinical Negligence	Partnership
Construction	Personal Injury
Dispute Resolution	Product Liability
Employment	Professional Negligence
Health & Safety	Real Estate
Insurance	Shipping

of a dredger in Sierra Leone; a business interruption claim arising from the time of Madeleine McCann's disappearance; and the missing billions that Bernie Madoff, well, made off with.

Litigation time

This firm really *"does what it says on the box,"* say trainees. It has always described itself as direct, pragmatic and straightforward, and its motto is 'legal advice in black and white.' As such, the firm is clear about its heavy focus on litigation, and especially insurance litigation. Disputes have been the firm's strong point as far back as anyone can remember, and they account for around 80% of its work. Essentially, *"if you don't want to do litigation, then don't apply to Kennedys."* Kennedys' dispute resolution services take all forms – negotiation, litigation, arbitration and mediation. Our sources say that *"if it's litigation you want to do, you get a really good selection,"* as usually three out of four trainee seats are contentious in nature.

There are about 15 different seat options for trainees, nine of which are London-only, and only a handful of which are non-contentious. The key options are insurance/reinsurance, construction litigation, clinical negligence, defendant personal injury, corporate and commercial, workplace (employment and health and safety), product liability and professional negligence. Staff are organised into teams and identified by not entirely logical numbers: Team 1a, for example, works on professional indemnity issues, and Team 1b on insurance/reinsurance, as does Team 33. The level of responsibility varies a lot between seats, so you may have plenty in your first seat and do grunt work in your third seat, which *"doesn't feel like much of a progression."* Kennedys may offer secondments depending on client demand.

Construction litigation is one of the biggest teams at Kennedys. It is described as young and friendly with *"good banter."* Its work is usually in some way related to insurance and, given that many millions of pounds can be at stake, there is a fair amount of document bundling for trainees. The cases are huge, document-heavy affairs, often involving *"long trials and long hours."* The subject matter of major cases has lately included hurricane damage, defective windows in an office development in Paternoster Square, power stations, oil refineries, roads and poorly built houses. Trainees are involved in plenty of the more exciting aspects of the team's work, including meetings with experts and barristers, sitting in on witness interviews and then drafting statements. Some of our sources also went along to trials in the High Court. The hours here can be longer than in other seats, with trainees rarely leaving before 7.30pm, often doing late nights and occasionally working over the weekend.

Within the large insurance/reinsurance team there is a good variety of work, for example relating to healthcare and pharmaceuticals, the rail sector and maritime and international trade. As one of the insurance sector's legal big hitters, the cases Kennedys handles are *"really interesting."* The firm represents over 50 of the world's leading insurers, among them AIG, AXA, Zurich, Swiss Re, Munich Re and Lloyd's Syndicates. Trainees can't always be given huge amounts of responsibility in this seat, but they can expect to assist with disclosure, data handling and document bundling. They also conduct research on jurisdictional questions, international disputes, foreign arbitration and other countries' laws.

There is *"variety every day"* in the international arbitration and products liability seat, as the team works on shipping, aviation, professional indemnity, arbitration and fraud matters. Trainees are also very happy with the level of responsibility they get: our sources were *"involved in every stage"* of cases, with *"daily client contact and drafting letters and reports... basically the work of an NQ."* The clinical negligence defence team is another popular option and is ranked among the very best in the country by *Chambers UK*. *"Amazing supervisors"* teach trainees good habits early on by exposing them to the ins and outs of this field of practice. Kennedys is one of 11 firms on the legal panel of the NHS Litigation Authority, which co-ordinates the defence of negligence claims made against different parts of the health service. The causes and treatment of brain injuries are a common theme, particularly in relation to cerebral palsy and other birth injuries. Settlements or court awards can be worth millions of pounds as they are designed to ensure long-term care for those who have suffered injury. The question of who pays for long-term care is one of the most crucial at the moment, and the direction the courts take will be significant to the NHS and the insurers of private health providers.

Get out of town

If you have a strong preference for a seat, don't be shy about making it known to HR early on as *"they will bend over backwards"* to help. The popularity of different seats seems to vary between intakes, but the majority of recruits are quite set on becoming litigators. The employment/health and safety team is always popular: it is smaller, trainees are given good responsibility and they spend time out of the office at hearings and liaising with barristers. If a trainee does decide that disputes are not for them, there is a non-contentious seat to try. The commercial/corporate team is "*more of a support department,*" trainees tell us, but it provides useful advice to clients (mainly but not always in the insurance industry) on property, commercial contracts, insolvency, outsourcing, franchising, procurement and regulation matters, among others.

While trainees' work tends to be UK-based, in the shipping team especially you can expect to be involved in arbitrations for international clients. One lucky trainee spent six months in the firm's Hong Kong office, but whether or not overseas seats will be available in the future remains to be seen. Most trainees are hired to work in the London office, and then there are a handful scattered around Chelmsford, Cambridge, Manchester and Birmingham. While trainees tend to stay put in their original locations, regional recruits may spend six months in another office. Some of the regional offices specialise in certain fields: Chelmsford and Maidstone, for example, work mainly on personal injury claims; Cambridge focuses on clinical negligence; and Taunton on professional indemnity claims, but Sheffield, Manchester and Birmingham are multi-practice area offices.

In most seats, trainees were surprised to find that Kennedys really does live up to its promises of work-life balance. Especially in the regional offices, the hours are generally very manageable, usually around 9am until 6.30pm. One source mentioned that they were pleased to see that several people with children had come back to work part-time. But trainees do need to stay at the office when things hot up, and in certain seats that happens on a not infrequent basis.

Lunchtime wanders

Kennedys' shiny modern office in London is "*in the insurance industry centre of the world.*" It's next door to the Lloyd's Building and the Gherkin, and its terrace offers views of Tower 42, the London Eye, Tower Bridge, Monument and Canary Wharf. Employees are entitled to a free breakfast and have access throughout the day to free fruit and toast. The canteen (named 'The Witz') is a good option for lunch if you don't fancy picturesque 14th century Leadenhall Market just two minutes away. The latter has everything from shoeshine boys, butchers and florists to cheese shops, sushi, salad bars and pubs. It even featured in *The Imaginarium of Dr Parnassus* and served as the location for Diagon Alley in the *Harry Potter* films.

The London office is within easy reach of wine bar Corney & Barrow, but for trainees this is "*a bit swanky, so we go to this horrible and dingy place called Bar Britannia where they do £5 bottles of wine.*" Mmmm. Trainees typically have a GSOH and enjoy a few drinks, but depending on their team the informal social life is "*not always the most active.*" This might be because trainees are often busy with client events and, many of them being a little older, tend to have a social life outside work. That said, every month there are staff events with free food and drinks on the roof terrace, and there is an annual summer barbecue. Last year Kennedys organised a softball game in Primrose Hill, where the firm provided a picnic, beer and wine for an enjoyable evening in the park. Other sports include football, netball and cricket, sometimes with clients.

Growing steadily throughout the recession, Kennedys was "*not affected by it whatsoever,*" trainees insist. "*It's terrible to say, but litigators do quite well when things go bad for everyone else.*" It also helps that Kennedys is a "*cost-effective*" firm and has always "*pitched itself as quite good value within the market, and now clients are looking for better value in their lawyers.*" So proud were they of their achievements, that "*internal exuberance*" forced the team in the Sheffield office to shoot a video of an office sing-along (and dance-along) to Queen's *Don't Stop Me Now*, which made a temporary appearance on the internet. We rather liked it.

The firm prides itself on its NQ retention rates, which tend to be around 80–85%. Given that Kennedys is seemingly impervious to the recession, it was no surprise that seven of the ten qualifiers were kept on in 2010. As one trainee said: "*Everyone seems pretty happy and the firm is expanding, so whatever they're doing seems to be working.*"

And finally...

Ambitious and still growing, Kennedys is a great destination for wannabe litigators or anyone in tune with the insurance industry.

Kingsley Napley LLP

The facts

Location: London

Number of UK partners/solicitors: 44/58

Total number of trainees: 10

Seats: 4x6 months

Alternative seats: None

On chambersstudent.co.uk
- How to get into Kingsley Napley
- More on seat options
- We talk to managing partner Linda Woolley

Based in Clerkenwell's historic Knights Quarter, mid-sized Kingsley Napley is perhaps best known for representing famous people in sticky situations.

Crime pays

This firm's past and present client list reads like a *Who's Who* of the great, the good and the unusual. From former Liberal Party leader Jeremy Thorpe – charged with attempting to murder an alleged ex-boyfriend over 30 years ago – to General Pinochet, former Met Police chief Sir Ian Blair, ex-Bosnian president Ejup Ganic, Kate and Gerry McCann, and former England football captain John Terry, KN has represented all manner of rich and famous people. Litigation accounts for over 70% of its activities, and its criminal team is among London's finest, achieving *Chambers UK* top rankings. Historically, trainees were always attracted by KN's criminal practice, managing partner Linda Woolley told us. While seats in this department remain popular, trainees today gain broader contentious and non-contentious experience across the firm's private client (including clinical negligence and family) and business services (including corporate/commercial, employment and real estate) teams. Turnover rose £2m in 2009/10 to £21.5m, making it the firm's best ever year – thanks to increased billings in litigation groups, especially criminal/regulatory, clinical negligence and employment. The goal for 2010/11 is £24m.

After a hiatus lasting several years, KN's training programme re-emerged in 2007 and is here to stay. The seat options are: criminal; regulatory; clinical negligence; dispute resolution; corporate/commercial; family; private client; real estate; employment; and immigration. Trainees' four seats are mapped out in advance and they usually get at least two of their preferences. One source praised the system: "*I like knowing where I'm going to be. You can get to know the people you'll be working with in advance.*" Crime and family are the most popular seats, hence they are sometimes over-subscribed so compromises have to be made. Trainees sit with a senior associate or partner in each seat.

Traditionally, the criminal and regulatory department, private client areas, and business services groups have each contributed roughly a third of the firm's turnover. In 2009/10, crime contributed over 40%. Sidestepping the Legal Aid arena, KN's clients are usually wealthy and have recently included a surgeon accused of rape, a solicitor accused of GBH, a barrister accused of assault, and various footballers facing things such as motoring offence charges. A running joke is that KN's clients are more likely to have glassed someone with a champagne bottle than a pint glass. Trainees make police station visits to see clients, who have been charged with anything from criminal damage, punch-ups or domestic violence to white-collar crime. Pretty scary for first-timers, we'd imagine, but thankfully "*I never go on my own,*" an interviewee said.

Beware hypochondria

KN prosecutes and defends those accused of corporate crimes – City fraud, SFO, DTI and Inland Revenue investigations, asset tracing and money laundering. The team is internationally recognised for extradition matters. "*The partners are excellent and even the three or four-year qualified solicitors are good enough to be partners elsewhere.*" Work highlights include defending BA's former commercial director against price-fixing allegations and representing Premier League player Calum Davenport, whose legs were stabbed by his sister's boyfriend. In 2002, partner Michael Caplan became the first criminal solicitor to be made a QC.

Chambers UK rankings

Administrative & Public Law	Family/Matrimonial
Clinical Negligence	Financial Services
Competition/European Law	Fraud
Crime	Immigration
Employment	Professional Discipline

Top-ranked by *Chambers UK*, the large claimant-only clinical negligence practice was boosted by the arrival of two high-profile partners in 2009. It handles complex cases such as brain damage, spinal injury, fatal accidents, orthopaedic injury, GP negligence and wrongful birth (alleged failure to warn of the risks of a baby being born with a serious genetic disorder or illness). Trainees' medical knowledge increases dramatically during this seat, so much so for one source that "*it made me paranoid. I used go home thinking I had every ailment.*" Nevertheless, our source enjoyed the seat: "*It's fascinating – you have to get a handle on the condition a client or client's relative has and know the medical background.*" With their years of experience, partners "*probably know as much as the doctors.*" Trainees run their own files under supervision, draft witness statements and get out of the office from time to time – even if it is to attend a car crash site. Though sometimes upsetting, "*it's nice dealing with clients who in the main appreciate your help very much.*"

A different world

The clin neg team refers clients who've won significant damages to KN's small but growing private client department, which can advise on how to manage the money. Private client work might not hold obvious appeal to "*the younger generation who aren't interested in trusts and tax and wills,*" according to one trainee who found "*six months of drafting wills*" less than riveting. On the flip side there's "*loads of responsibility.*" Another source found the work "*more interesting than expected. These guys live in a different world.*" Clients tend to be "*upper-middle class liberal types, 99% of whom are really lovely.*" Celebrity clients have included Jade Goody.

In corporate/commercial, fee earners are "*not afraid*" to give trainees substantive work, whether it's drafting, helping with due diligence exercises or looking after clients. "*You get closer to the action than at other firms,*" one believed; "*I was treated like a qualified solicitor.*" As elsewhere, during the recession the department has had "*a rough ride, obviously,*" but there has been a decent flow of commercial and contractual queries coming in. In the sports sector, for example, this has meant sponsorship, wages and book deal negotiations for well-known players. KN is the legal adviser to the Players' Committee of the England football team. The sports law team itself comprises lawyers from the crime and regulatory, corporate/commercial, dispute resolution, employment and personal injury practices. To read about seat experiences in the family, immigration, employment and property teams go to our website.

One interviewee summed up what several said about the quality of supervision across departments: "*My supervisor and a couple of partners are very attentive to the type of work I'm getting, so if a solicitor takes the mick by giving out admin tasks, they say, 'Do it yourself' because they want trainees doing substantive tasks.*" Trainees undertake their share of grunt work but it's not excessive. In all seats, mid and end-of-seat reviews are based on feedback from everyone in the team, including secretaries and paralegals (assuming everyone completes and returns the assessment form). Some departments have a checklist of things they want trainees to experience: in family, for example, this will include drafting a divorce petition.

KNice guys

Our interviewees emphasised the firm's congenial culture, and some joked that KN actually stands for "*Kind and Nice.*" "*It's very different here compared to big City firms,*" one believed; "*people are very enthusiastic about their jobs and incredibly friendly.*" Senior partner Christopher Murray and managing partner Linda Woolley "*know who each trainee is,*" we're assured. Woolley qualified with the firm in 1992 and is "*very hands-on. She makes a point of meeting with all the trainees every six months and ensures that everyone's getting their appraisals and receives plenty of feedback.*" Mostly, trainees say that the environment is "*incredibly respectful and you'd struggle to think of anyone who is arrogant or conceited.*"

Trainees are spoilt for choice for pubs near the office. The tiny, quaint Jerusalem Tavern just round the corner is a favourite, but it's always packed so the not-as-cute Puncheon, Fence and 250-year-old One Tun are more regular haunts. Second careerers are welcome at KN, and in 2010 we noted an ex-physiotherapist and a former local newspaper journalist among the trainees. Another had worked in the music industry, while others had paralegalled around the City. "*If you can come with some life experience, that helps,*" a trainee believed. There's much more on how to get into KN on our website.

And finally...

In 2010, all five qualifying trainees stayed with the firm, two joining the criminal practice and one joining each of the coco, family and dispute resolution teams.

Kirkland & Ellis International LLP

The facts

Location: London

Number of UK partners/solicitors: 27/39 (US: 5/9)

Total number of trainees: 12

Seats: 4x6 months

Alternative seats: Overseas seats

Extras: Pro bono – LawWorks

On chambersstudent.co.uk
• How to get into Kirkland
• A brief history of the firm
• The world of private equity

International heavyweight Kirkland & Ellis has a brand new London training contract. We caught up with its first trainees.

Blown in from the Windy City

Chicago-based Kirkland & Ellis has six offices spread across the USA and four more outposts overseas, in Munich, London, Hong Kong and Shanghai. It employs more than 1,500 lawyers and is one of the USA's top-ten law firms, as measured by revenue. Kirkland opened its London office back in 1994 and welcomed its first batch of trainees in September 2009. Our interviewees were "*excited rather than hesitant*" to be the inaugural class and most were attracted by "*the American firm ethos: hard work and big deals.*" The office, based in the iconic Gherkin, has lately focused on ramping up its private equity capability and the June 2010 hire of two heavy-hitting partners from Ashurst got the legal media chatting about Kirkland's rising profile in the City. Growth was further reflected in K&E's decision to promote nine London lawyers to partner later in the year.

Private equity houses make up the majority of the office's clientele, and trainees told us: "*We're doing a bit of M&A for them, buying portfolio companies, renegotiating terms, and doing hush-hush deals like taking companies off the stock exchange.*" During the recession the firm stayed busy helping those private equity houses acquire failing companies to turn them around; for example, advising New York-based KPS Capital Partners on its acquisition of luxury goods manufacturer Waterford Wedgwood. The private equity sector looks like it has a lot of life in it right now, so this should be a fruitful area for the firm. Read more about it on our website.

You got the love

As the biggest department, corporate seat trainees couldn't help feeling "*thrown in at the deep end*" and expected to "*either sink or swim.*" Luckily, our sources had handled the waters well and thrived under the pressure, "*taking on as much responsibility as we could handle.*" Gushed one: "*The first month, I was pulled into a huge, incredibly exciting deal that was gaining speed and felt really intense.*" So what's their role on those deals? Well, Kirkland trainees "*aren't putting together bibles and filing,*" they're "*drafting and going to client meetings and conferences.*" Basically, "*the quality of work is ridiculous*" and our sources "*literally loved it to pieces.*"

Trainees also "*absolutely loved*" their stints in the private funds seat. This top-grade team migrated from SJ Berwin so "*they've worked together for quite a long time and that brings a good team feel.*" As the market steadies, the firm is starting to set up new funds again, recently helping first-time fund manager ESB Novus Modus on its inaugural fund formation, raising €200m of capital for investment in the renewable energy and energy efficiency sectors. Our sources raved about being "*properly involved from the beginning*" on similar deals, "*doing quite a bit of drafting.*" Added pressure comes from "*doing a lot more work for the client directly, so everything has to be perfect.*" Over in the banking seat, "*there are more transactions turning over a lot quicker, making for a lot more work to be done quickly.*" This team is a sponsor-side specialist but has a strong borrow-side finance practice as well. It is best known for advising private equity houses

Chambers UK rankings

Banking & Finance	Private Equity
Dispute Resolution	Restructuring/Insolvency
Investment Funds	Tax

on debt investments and remains active at the top of the leveraged buyout market.

The restructuring team took leading roles in the travails of Lehman Brothers, chemicals company Almatis, Japan Airlines and Reader's Digest. When asked if they enjoyed this seat, our interviewees said that they "*loved it.*" Noticing a theme? Trainees "*undertake a lot of research, dealing with actual problems and live business needs.*" They praised the team for being "*technically sound and knowledgeable,*" one adding: "*When you're there, you actually feel cleverer just by association.*"

The arbitration team mustn't be overlooked, working as it does with big-name clients on complex multi-jurisdictional disputes. Lawyers represented Samsung in a dispute with a German electronics company, which included bankruptcy proceedings in the USA, arbitration proceedings under the ICC, ad hoc arbitration in Paris and state court litigation in Germany. Trainees described the seat as "*very different*" and clearly enjoyed their "*varied work,*" like "*drafting, getting bundles together and sometimes some research.*" This department is also "*very close-knit, always helping each other out.*"

Small world

"*I was in the pub with my friend, who is at another firm, and a partner came in. He came up to me and we had a chat – not work-related at all, just a normal conversation, and my friend was floored that I could talk to a partner like that.*" Kirkland is a small office, so everyone knows each other. "*In the corridors there's plenty of smiling and saying hi. Everyone gets on very well and there is a closeness.*" There's "*no shouting down the corridors, unless it's 'Do you want some popcorn?' There are not a lot of angry people and that whole temper-losing mentality is really frowned upon. You don't come here if you're a volatile person; you've got to be quite chilled.*"

The office's small size ensures that trainees are "*integral members of the team. Every piece of work we do will be going to the client, which is quite daunting but does make you feel like you have a lot of responsibility. Other partners and associates* [besides your supervisor] *will come to you directly as there's only one trainee in each department except corporate. It's quite a good position to be in.*"

"*The attitude of the firm is that it's very open to how you want to manage your training contract. It's down to you really: whatever you put in you'll get out,*" our sources said. "*It's great being the first-ever intake because if we say something is good or bad, they will look into it.*" Trainees have had plenty of input into the lunchtime training programme, filling out feedback forms after each session. "*There were four a week for a while, which is quite a lot. We spoke up and said it was a bit too much, so now they're looking into it.*" They also had a say on the question of overseas seats. "*We all arrived and were quite keen to do one, so we raised it with a senior partner and told him which offices we were interested in. Now two of us are off to New York and Hong Kong.*" It's probably worth saying that as the training programme becomes more established, a little more rigidity will probably set in.

It seems the only downside of Kirkland's size is the social life. "*There have been a couple of nights out but it's lacking,*" one trainee reported. "*As a trainee class, we're close and meet up for lunch when we can, but as a firm we're so small it's hard to do lots of incredible stuff. Each department has its own social agenda, and every so often my team has really fun nights out,*" another added. Of course, the arrival of a new intake in September 2010 will double trainee numbers at a stroke (to 12) and our sources hoped that would liven things up.

It was clear that the trainees "*really love this firm,*" to the point where they are "*quite protective*" of who K&E takes in as new trainees. "*I was at a vac scheme event and a lot of the people there didn't really know about Kirkland and why it was special. It upset me in a way,*" said one. "*The US firms are not all the same.*" For its part, Kirkland seems just as invested in the trainees, saying it hopes to keep all of them when they qualify in 2011 (no one was set to finish in 2010). "*It's a massive relief to know that as long we keep working hard, we can just relax and get on with it. We all feel really blessed,*" said one trainee.

And finally...

Our loved-up trainee sources were clearly hard-grafting go-getters who don't mind putting in long hours for the sake of the team and absolutely thrive under pressure. If this isn't you, don't expect to fall quite so head-over-heels.

Latham & Watkins LLP

The facts

Location: London

Number of UK partners/solicitors: 32/74 (US: 12/27)

Total number of trainees: 28

Seats: 4x6 months

Alternative seats: Overseas seats

Extras: Pro bono – legal advice for Read International, Kingfisher Kids Club, Esuubi Trust; language classes

On chambersstudent.co.uk

- How to get into Latham
- More on the firm's pro bono initiatives
- We talk to training partner Dominic Newcomb

Latham's London branch is increasingly *"upwardly mobile"* and the excitement surrounding its expansion is undeniable.

Elementary, my dear Watkins

This "*top-tier international firm*" boasts a head count of 2,000 lawyers throughout 30 offices across the globe, so needless to say it has come a long way since its founding in 1934 Los Angeles. Fast-forward 74 years and Latham became the first firm to break the $2bn revenue barrier, proving its focus on capital markets, private equity and leveraged buyouts to be a good choice. Virtually every Chambers and Partners guide commends the quality of Latham's core practices, and the firm's transactional track record is hard to beat. It has represented the likes of Bank of America, Bear Stearns, Citi, Credit Suisse, Deutsche Bank, Goldman Sachs, Merrill Lynch, JPMorgan and Morgan Stanley, to name just a few. That said, *Chambers UK* also recognises Latham's public international law, technology and outsourcing, and energy projects practices as among the best in the nation, a taster perhaps of things to come. Latham's strategy is quite elementary – "*to deepen its presence in the major business, financial and regulatory centres of the world*" and not be "*just a US firm dabbling outside of the States.*" In the past two decades the firm has created a bounty of international outposts: ten in Europe, four in Asia and four in the Middle East. Despite the expansion, Latham sticks to its 'one firm' ethos. Though California is home to most of its lawyers, there is no 'headquarters' and each branch has notable autonomy.

Where does London fit into the global puzzle? Opened in 1990 as a finance boutique, it has since grown into a full commercial operation with around 150 lawyers. Rather than merely taking on the UK aspects of deals sourced in the USA, London is a hub for the firm's European and Middle Eastern work. Latham is presently making substantial efforts to further strengthen its UK arm, and at the time of research the buzz among trainees was undeniable – 'exciting' was certainly the catchphrase, and it's obvious why. After nabbing 13 partners from White & Case, the finance department is making waves – we were advised to "*watch this space.*" Growing the London corporate practice is next on the to-do list and trainees are sure to benefit as "*there are more options being created all the time and* [seatwise] *they're being really flexible about who goes where.*"

Ask, and you just might receive

The training scheme began in 2006 with just two trainees. By 2009 the intake was 15-strong, and Latham intends to see it "*get slightly bigger each year.*" As well as a mandatory contentious seat, trainees do stints in the finance and corporate departments. With only four seats in total, we wondered if this felt restrictive, but trainees couldn't say enough about how flexible they found the system. "*The whole training programme is run by a committee of mainly associates who are really great at taking your case and running with it. It's a much more visible process.*" The array of subgroups within each main department encourages varied experiences. Finance, for example, can encompass banking, restructuring, structured finance or project finance, while corporate includes general M&A and capital markets, and as well as IP/IT/outsourcing, there is also a standalone tax practice. Contentious options include securities litigation, general dispute

Chambers UK rankings

Banking & Finance	Information Technology
Banking Litigation	Intellectual Property
Capital Markets	Investment Funds
Competition/European Law	Outsourcing
Corporate/M&A	Private Equity
Dispute Resolution	Projects
Employment	Public International Law
Energy & Natural Resources	Restructuring/Insolvency
	Tax

resolution, competition, employment and public international law. This last option is a very interesting area that's rarely offered to UK trainees.

Trainees nominate their preferred subgroups but "*there's no cast-iron guarantee*" of securing these seats, especially if they're in smaller groups like tax, employment or IP/IT/outsourcing. Although trainees sit within particular teams, they're considered a resource for the entire department. For example, during a seat in structured finance, one source "*did a lot of restructuring, some project finance, some derivatives, some leveraged and only one structured deal.*" We were impressed by how much leeway trainees were given to pursue their interests beyond the office's designated practices. The firm helped one person gain Islamic finance qualifications, sponsored another's UK Environmental Law Association membership and even created an overseas seat at an office that had never hosted trainees because someone voiced interest. Trainees also have a say over the department into which they would like to qualify, and once in their NQ role they remain relatively 'unassigned', leaving them free to try their hand at a variety of projects. In 2010, the firm offered all nine qualifiers a spot and seven stayed.

Latham's international scope must be at the heart of any discussion. "*100% of the work I've done has been international; even on the smallest scale it's at least UK-France,*" one source revealed. If operating internationally from London isn't enough for you, Latham offers overseas seats in most of its other offices. "*There's enough space to go where you want,*" and it's not the rat race you may find at firms with larger training schemes. "*It was just so laissez-faire; I sent an e-mail saying I wanted to go to an office and they e-mailed me back within a few days saying, 'Great, we'll organise a spot there for you.' There was no 500-word essay or scary interview.*" Trainees who had spent their third or fourth seat abroad praised the logistics, telling us: "*It's quite a slick process.*" In addition to "*a really, really nice flat,*" there are personal allowances and plenty of support from HR. From September 2010, there were trainees litigating in Brussels and taking on corporate and finance work in Hong Kong, Singapore and Riyadh. Seats in Moscow and Dubai are also often on offer.

From Qatar to Old Trafford

"*People here may have a perception that they definitely want to be deal lawyers and they're perhaps not giving contentious work much of a chance,*" one trainee let on. That's a shame because Latham acts on some interesting disputes: its competition team recently had a fine against Fujifilm reduced by 40% in the Video Tapes cartel investigation by the European Commission. The public international law group worked with Barbados in maritime negotiations with France – its other clients include Ecuador, Croatia, Azerbaijan, Grenada, Ukraine and Malaysia – and if IP is what you're after, you can look forward to a clientele that includes Yahoo!, Facebook and Nike. Trainees say the contentious seats involve them in "*lots of initial advice to clients, correspondence, interviewing witnesses,*" "*first cracks at drafting*" and often becoming point person for barristers. A few had even handled small claims from start to finish. "*Some of the work has been mind-blowing,*" one said excitedly. "*I got to meet the GCs of our clients, MDs too. I've also been on conference calls with a head of state on a million-dollar dispute.*"

The finance teams have kept themselves busy with "*proper headline-grabbing cross-border work*" like the restructuring of the United Nations' International Maritime Organization or advising major export credit agencies like the Bank of China and Japan Bank for International Cooperation, along with commercial banks and underwriters in the $14bn financing of an LNG project in Papua New Guinea. Lawyers also advised the banking syndicate financing Manchester United's £500m bond. Trainees take on the usual due diligence, research, drafting and proof-reading tasks required on such deals, but they also get involved in business development, such as putting together pitches for new work.

"*It's really tough work and long hours in the transactional seats,*" a trainee warned. Yet it can be hugely rewarding "*when you get given a really meaty document that you didn't think you'd ever be able to touch and you have a go at the first draft.*" The M&A team advised the fabulously wealthy Qatar Investment Authority when NYSE Euronext agreed to buy a 25% stake in the Doha securities market for $250m. It was the largest investment ever made by NYSE in a foreign exchange and involved beating the British and German exchanges, which were also eyeing up the deal. On the capital markets side, Latham is considered a pioneer of the European high-yield market and is still the firm to beat despite a sluggish 2009.

Elf warning

Besides the international scope of the work, there are a few other things that mark Latham out as a US firm. For starters, a dazzling salary – on qualification you're looking at a not-too-shabby £96,970, currently the second highest in the market. "*It can't be ignored really,*" a trainee said of the impact the salary had on their choice of firm, "*but if that was the only good thing, it would really be quite miserable.*" A third US characteristic is the tendency for lean staffing of matters. Trainees "*always* [have a] *designated role,*" and our sources confirmed that they experienced "*80-90% great work, and about 10% 'standard trainee work.'*" As for the perennial rumour that American firms are more of a time suck, of course there will be long nights, weekends and cancelled plans, but "*it's much rarer than people would have you believe; people say things that make it sound scarier than it is.*" Fair enough, but there's no escaping the fact that qualified solicitors have a hefty annual billing target of 1,900 hours, and even trainees are supposed to hit a loose target of 1,200 hours. Luckily, legal pro bono work (which is prioritised heavily stateside) can count as billable time. To read more on Latham's pro bono efforts check out our website. Despite the preservation of certain US traits, trainees reject the idea of the London office as an American dominion and point out that the lack of a head office throughout the firm allows each branch to stand on its own two feet.

"*There are very few partners you would label as scary,*" our sources insisted. We'd suggest imagining them dressed in silly costumes – say, a Christmas elf – but you could simply get your hands on photos from the last Christmas party. Every year Latham raises money for charity by allowing staff to pay a pound to nominate the partner they think should don fancy dress. Those with the most nominations must not only suit up but prance around on stage. "*They're all really game for it – I think they actually secretly like it,*" a source sniggered.

Way out, way in

"*Latham is really transparent and non-hierarchical,*" possibly because it "*really buys into the laid-back California mentality – it's not just a gimmick.*" It's a place where "*public schoolboy arrogance does not go over well*" and you "*definitely need to be social.*" Play the game and get involved but don't be overly keen, trainees warned, as there's not a competitive atmosphere. Group training sessions are plentiful: they start with a full induction and continue with practice-specific sessions. Newly qualified lawyers attend a First Year Academy, usually in the USA. Appraisals take place quarterly, and trainees get a chance to tell the firm how they think it is doing through surveys circulated among staff.

As for nights out, Latham "*really likes to think it's lively,*" but a few frustrated trainees admitted that the scene was a bit too "*ad hoc.*" Every once in a while they can be found at Rocket (the upmarket bar and restaurant in the Square Mile, not the Euston pub with amazing student nights) and The Wall. Every couple of months management will run a tab and there are also occasional events like trips to the National Gallery or Italian cooking lessons.

Trainees described Latham as "*a unique culture of individuals*" and stressed the importance of "*being yourself.*" Also stressed was the simple but important fact that the vac scheme is definitely the preferred way in – all but two of the trainees taken on in 2009 had done one.

And finally...

Latham may have been slow to start a training contract in London, but this BigLaw pin-up is showing excellent form and has plans for continued organic growth in the capital.

Lawrence Graham LLP

The facts

Location: London

Number of UK partners/solicitors: 68/103

Total number of trainees: 31

Seats: 4x6 months

Alternative seats: Occasional overseas seats, secondments

On chambersstudent.co.uk
- How to get into LG
- The More London development
- What is AIM?

Mid-sizer LG's traditional property expertise is being balanced out by its growing corporate and litigation capabilities.

Cider summer

A few years ago, slightly stuffy old City firm Lawrence Graham underwent a bit of a renaissance. It rebranded itself as LG and moved from "*tired*" offices on The Strand to a fantastic new Foster-designed building in the More London development on the South Bank of the Thames, within spitting distance of Darth Vader's Helmet, aka Mayor Boris's City Hall. The spectacular view from LG's reception on the 8th floor takes in Tower Bridge, HMS Belfast and the skyscrapers across on the north side of the Thames. Back in 2005, before the revamp and office move, we described Lawrence Graham as a successful, much loved and "*thoroughly nice*" place that was traditionally strongest in property. We used to say that nothing much changed from year to year.

These days, it is clear LG has greater ambitions. A Dubai office opened in 2008 and a Moscow joint venture followed a year later. The firm wanted the world to know about its expanding corporate practice. "*The rebranding was happening when I applied,*" a current trainee recalled. "*There's still real pride in the new office,*" which "*shows the outside world the firm has high standards. It's a pleasure to welcome clients, who admire the view.*" The corporate upgrade hasn't compromised the firm's culture, sources claimed. "*It was known as a friendly firm, and they've kept that.*"

The credit crisis spoilt the welcome party, though, hitting the core corporate and real estate practices in particular. This difficult time saw two redundancy rounds, turnover fall 10% and partner profits down too. However, things picked up and LG posted a whopping 64% increase in partner profits and a 7.6% revenue hike for 2009/10. Dispute resolution, finance, corporate recovery and restructuring teams have all been busy, while the real estate practice has held together better than expected and the team has even started recruiting again. Marking this success, everyone at LG received "*a little bonus*" in June 2010. Recent highlights include advising C&C (the company behind Magners cider) on its £180m acquisition of Scottish tipple Tennent's and subsequent purchase of Blackthorn Cider. Whitbread recently used the firm for advice on the sale and leaseback of five Premier Inns, and LG was also instructed on the acquisition of 60 Walkabout, Jongleurs and Old Orleans branches out of administration by the former management.

Speak up

There are usually around 35 trainees in total – "*a nice size*" – although only 31 this year: a light hangover from the recession. Their four seats must include a transactional seat (corporate, banking, tax or corporate recovery), real estate, and a contentious area. LG allocates the first seat, then before each subsequent one, trainees list three preferences from the numerous options within LG's seven practice groups: commerce and technology; corporate; tax and private capital; dispute resolution; employment and pensions; finance; and real estate. This firm doesn't spoon-feed its trainees, so a little research when deciding what to list as preferences never goes amiss. "*It does help if you're quite vocal,*" one trainee believed. "*Most departments expect you to express an interest in joining them rather than just stick them down on a list and hope for the*

Chambers UK rankings

Capital Markets	Investment Funds
Charities	Pensions
Construction	Planning
Corporate/M&A	Private Client
Dispute Resolution	Public Procurement
Employment	Real Estate
Environment	Real Estate Finance
Fraud	Real Estate Litigation
Insurance	Restructuring/Insolvency

best. You have to take control, know what you want and show you want it." Not that this is a group of individuals who only look out for themselves; on the contrary. "*We don't push against each other,*" one source said, "*we all get along well and are supportive.*" This is a helpful approach in a firm that believes trainees should take ultimate responsibility for their career management.

Institutional clients in the real estate department include Legal & General and fund manager Hermes. The likes of Sainsbury's and Whitbread also come for advice on matters bricks and mortar matters. This integrated group advises on all types of property work, including sales and acquisitions, leases and lease disputes, debt refinancing and regeneration projects. The real estate finance team, for example, has lately advised on over £3bn of restructurings on behalf of banks, borrowers and funds. Sources reported a "*lovely*" working environment. "*My partner was always very happy to answer questions, and the associates were very welcoming and took me to as many client meetings as they could,*" said one trainee. They give you "*proper things to do,*" such as drafting leases and sale contracts, compiling sellers' packs, research and "*all the post-completion stuff including filing things at the Land Registry.*" On property disputes, trainees take on bundling duties, liaise with courts and may have the opportunity to attend hearings.

Trainees like the decent work-life balance in real estate. The department is "*bustling*" as people do their work but they then go home at a reasonable hour; unlike in some other transactional departments, there "*isn't a culture of sending marked-up agreements to clients at midnight.*" Though the group was affected by the recession and suffered redundancies, things have picked up noticeably. LG took on a lot of property management for institutional clients, "*so managed to avoid the worst of the slump,*" one source believed.

The corporate group is known for the quality of its mid-market M&A, joint venture and capital markets work and the jewel in the crown is its AIM practice, which is top-ranked nationally by *Chambers UK*. LG has attracted numerous assignments from the Indian subcontinent in recent years, for example advising Indian company KSK Power on its move up from AIM to the Main Market of the London Stock Exchange. Another highlight was advising the AIM-traded Clipper Windpower on a $270m equity and cash investment by United Technologies. As with real estate, AIM work had been "*quiet but has started to pick up.*" In this "*challenging*" seat, trainee tasks include "*general corporate governance, manning data rooms and drafting board minutes and letters.*" Said one: "*I worked closely with an associate who was putting together a circular and felt I was given quite a bit of responsibility.*" Smaller assignments offer "*more varied work*" and "*make a nice change.*" If a deal's hot, expect unsociable hours: "*You don't know when you're going to be able to leave,*" said one source. "*I often didn't get home until 10pm or 11pm.*"

Beyond Blighty

The popular dispute resolution team's global clients include mega-brewer InBev and GlaxoSmithKline, for which it secured a permanent injunction against animal rights extremists. It also won an *FT* award for its innovative anti-corruption and fraud work in asset-tracing for Brazil's government. Recent hires into the financial services team have helped increase LG's involvement in credit crunch-related disputes, particularly arbitration for clients reluctant to be drawn into costly court cases. Trainees can look forward to "*a lot of bundling*" and document review during the disclosure phase of cases, as well as drafting various court documents. One source was "*hand-held but given responsibility and my own files... I've been able to issue claims myself.*" The pace here is "*slightly slower than corporate because they are different beasts.*" That said, commercial litigation still feels "*dynamic*" thanks to the recent addition of some new partners.

It's not all inbound traffic at LG this year though: four of the eight London private client partners left to set up their own firm. Private client seats are still available to trainees and the locations of LG's overseas offices – Monaco, Moscow and the Middle East – indicate the importance of its private client practice, which earns excellent *Chambers UK* and *Chambers Global* rankings.

Advising Russian oligarchs, Gulf ruling families, Indian and Far Eastern billionaire industrialists and the heir of one of the 20th century's most famous artists isn't the be-all and end-all of these offices, however, and London-based commercial lawyers increasingly work on a range of international matters too. LG recently assisted Saudi-based Saad Group on a multibillion-pound debt restructuring and associated litigation, which occupied over 25 London lawyers as well as a Dubai-based team. The

Emirate has experienced an upswing in construction disputes in the past 18 months, some involving famous projects in the region. While LG does not have a formal programme of overseas secondments for trainees, the opportunity to spend time in Dubai does occasionally crop up if there is a business need. In Russia, the firm is working for Gazprom on the development of a huge offshore gas field, while the London-based commerce and technology team is also advising Russian clients. According to one trainee, LG is focusing more on overseas assignments "*because our clients are becoming more international.*"

"*Niche departments like IP and employment are always popular,*" and other seat possibilities include insurance/reinsurance, civil fraud, pensions and tax. The quality of supervision is good. "*All the partners are willing and happy to answer questions,*" said an experienced second-year. "*You're sitting with partners so you're being supervised all the time.*" There are regular departmental training workshops, though "*not too many or you wouldn't have time to do the job.*" Mid and end-of-seat appraisals also keep people on track.

Snap to it

On any given day, the development around LG's offices at 4 More London Riverside is usually teeming with tourists and buskers and politicians on their way to and from City Hall. Just outside, the Scoop, an 800-seat amphitheatre built into the pedestrianised thoroughfare, hosts free open-air theatre productions, music performances and movies throughout the summer. With plenty of bars, eateries and shops around Tooley Street and the Hays Galleria, LG lawyers can really enjoy the vibe. "*It feels like you get away from the suits,*" one trainee said, contrasting the area with that of the City proper, just across the river. "*The only hassle is when you're in a hurry and tourists ask you to take their photo.*"

Among the trainee intake you'll always find a few Oxbridge candidates who don't fancy the magic circle lifestyle, but LG also recruits from other universities with good law courses, among them Cardiff, Durham, Leicester, Nottingham and so on. "*They seem quite keen on people with a bit of life experience... I can't think of one person in my intake who hasn't lived abroad or done interesting things,*" claimed one source. Sixteen out of 23 qualifiers took up jobs with the firm in 2010.

Socially, "*there are always e-mails going out.*" There's a netball team, some staff run the Standard Chartered Great City Race in the Square Mile, and a group recently completed the 54-mile Caledonian Challenge in Scotland, walking the entire distance non-stop in under 24 hours. Trainees can celebrate Christmas three times with the trainee bash, departmental knees-up and client Yuletide party. Regular drinking haunts include The Bridge on Tooley Street, All Bar One and Hays Galleria, where you can sit outside by the river, pint in hand. Speaking of which, "*I was worried there'd be a drinking culture,*" said one source, "*but there's not. On Friday, if you just want one drink, that's fine. There's no pressure to be macho. People work hard and do a good job, but that doesn't get in the way of them being pleasant and reasonable human beings.*" LG may be a slicker, trendier beast than it was five years ago, but it's reassuring to find some things never change.

And finally...

Lawrence Graham provides a really good, rounded London training that isn't too hardcore. Keep your eye on its growing international profile.

Lester Aldridge LLP

The facts

Location: Bournemouth, Southampton, London

Number of UK partners/solicitors: 42/32

Total number of trainees: 11

Seats: 4x6 months

Alternative seats: Occasional secondments

On chambersstudent.co.uk
- How to get into Lester Aldridge
- We talk to managing partner Michael Giddins
- Advising GPs' practices

Bournemouth-born Lester Aldridge has a reputation for being a nice place to work. With a head office only minutes from the beach, it's easy to see why.

Choices choices

LA offers an appealing mix of commercial and private client work. Expect a decent roster of national clients including Lloyds TSB and mobile operator 3UK, as well as South Coast businesses and private individuals. Through its membership of MSI, a global alliance of lawyers and accountants, LA also has some international reach. The London office came into being in 2004 when LA merged with 200-year-old real estate-heavy firm Park Nelson. Another office in Milton Keynes was opened and then closed fairly soon after. Fortunately, this and other restructuring measures put LA in a good position to cope with the ravages of the recession. In 2010, the firm has been in hiring mode.

Trainee seats are available in Bournemouth and the smaller Southampton and London offices. "*There's quite a bit of movement between offices,*" a trainee explained. "*The training contract is with the firm as a whole,*" rather than an individual office, so it's likely trainees will work in more than one location over the course of their four seats. Most spend at least one seat in Bournemouth, which has the broadest selection. Trainees list three preferences before each seat change, and the firm also takes into account where people live. Preference is given to second-years at each seat rotation, and "*if you have a burning desire for a particular seat, you'll probably get it eventually.*" Options include property; corporate; marine; Fast Track debt recovery (litigation); dispute resolution; care; employment; family; and trusts, tax and wills (TTW). These are all available in Southampton/Bournemouth. The London seats are listed later. Most trainees take a property seat, and employment and corporate are usually rather popular.

Court time aplenty

The recession quietened real estate departments across the country, and one trainee confessed that during the worst of the credit crisis "*I didn't have a lot to do.*" Nevertheless, LA's team actually grew, and with over 25 people, it is actually one of Hampshire and Dorset's largest. Commercial property clients include retailers, care and retirement home operators and developers, ports and marinas, house builders and lenders. The firm recently advised Balfour Beatty on the public-private partnership (PPP) development of Salisbury Law Court, and Lloyds TSB on acquisition finance for a £10m portfolio of mobile homes. Trainees add that "*there are a lot of insolvency issues right now because of the recession. You do get responsibility and there's always partner support. They let you do the work but always check it.*"

Corporate seats involve "*a lot of drafting. It's been more commercial work such as agreements or share transfers than M&A recently,*" a trainee explained. M&A has been slow but not dead, and recently the team advised an engineering firm on its £15m sale to a French energy multinational. It also advised a plc on its disposal of a subsidiary, and a care homes operator on several acquisitions. Our sources again enjoyed "*a lot of client contact.*" The marine team handles all manner of cases for cruise operator Carnival – owner of P&O, Cunard and Princess Cruises – including personal injury and damage-to-cargo claims. On

Chambers UK rankings

Banking Litigation	Partnership
Charities	Planning
Debt Recovery	Private Client
Dispute Resolution	Real Estate
Employment	Real Estate Litigation
Family/Matrimonial	Shipping
Healthcare	

the transactional side, the team advised HSBC on loans for the purchase of yachts and commercial vessels.

Trainee tasks in the expanding dispute resolution department, headed by managing partner Michael Giddins, can range from "*the mundane,*" like photocopying and document bundling, to research, meeting clients ("*primarily taking notes*"), interviewing witnesses and attending court. Giddins also sits as a part-time judge, and according to one distinctly untrembly-kneed trainee, he "*likes people to fear him but he's not scary!*" Clients include individuals and businesses, and a major Premier League football team even instructs the firm. The cases are "*completely varied.*" Said one source: "*I ran smaller files including debt collection, plus simpler personal injury and marine claims.*" The busy banking litigation team advises on finance and security-related disputes for banks, building societies, mortgage lenders and other financial institutions. Its work is very timely, given the recession. Major clients include Abbey National and specialist lender Aldermore.

Traditionally, trainees haven't been that thrilled to work in the Fast Track debt recovery team, "*but the last few have enjoyed it.*" The team focuses on bulk recoveries for clients from a variety of sectors, including banking, utilities, media, energy and local authorities. For example, the team might assist a finance client in relation to someone who's stopped repayments on a car. Other work includes recovery of commercial debt, which some sources found "*a bit repetitive, but there is good contact with clients and the court. It's one of the younger teams and has a nice vibe.*"

Family is a "*fantastic*" seat with plenty of opportunities to go to court. Some of the more interesting cases cover fertility, surrogacy and advice to same-sex couples. The team frequently cross-refers work to other practices, especially the company-commercial, real estate and wills teams. The number of children's cases with an international element is increasing, and there are tricky contact and residence issues, as well as surrogacy matters and immigration complications. There's also bags of "*more traditional family work.*"

Appraisals are "*quite detailed.*" Trainees talk through with a partner "*whether your needs were met and what you've achieved over the past six months, then you are rated for core skills.*" Michael Giddins makes a point of meeting trainees for lunch every year, so they can raise any issues. Over a curry in Bournemouth, trainees asked for a mid-seat as well as an end-of-seat review, and this has now been implemented.

Happy meals

Near to the train station, the main seven-floor Bournemouth office "*isn't that pretty from the outside but is nice inside. There are colourful corporate colours and it's light and airy.*" The growing London team, currently based near St Paul's Cathedral, is likely to move before long. "*It's a million times more social here,*" a trainee enthused, as the office is only on one floor. There's a monthly 'happy breakfast' or 'happy lunch' when the office manager brings in food for everyone. London hosts one or two trainees at a time and they receive a salary increase of £500 for the duration of the seat and an additional £500 per month tax-free on top. The office has around 25 staff in total and offers seats in marine, property and private client.

Like London, Southampton is a single-floor branch and "*it's generally accepted that it is more social than Bournemouth because it's smaller. We go to the pub for lunch on Fridays.*" Its location in the smart Bedford Place neighbourhood makes The Cricketers (famous for its chilli chips) a venue of choice among trainees. "*The work-life balance is good,*" trainees agreed. As well as monthly happy-hour drinks in the office, one of Bournemouth's post room staff organises occasional outings to the Ringwood Brewery in the New Forest, where he works a second job. In 2010, everyone in the firm was invited on a September hiking weekend in Sussex, staying in a youth hostel, and we also heard about a trainee jolly to Bristol. "*There's quite a good footy team,*" and rumours from the sports committee suggest a netball team may emerge.

Gripes? "*It would be nice to be paid more.*" The £17,500 first-seat salary rises by £500 every six months, and is currently under review. But it's not all about the money: "*I chose LA over local firms that pay more because of the friendly culture and the London presence,*" a trainee concluded.

And finally...

Want a South Coast firm with a London dimension? Stepping into Lester Aldridge's world could be a perfect move. Four of the five qualifying trainees stayed on with the firm in 2010.

Lewis Silkin LLP

The facts

Location: London

Number of UK partners/solicitors: 56/76

Total number of trainees: 12

Seats: 6x4 months

Alternative seats: Secondments

On chambersstudent.co.uk
- How to get into Lewis Silkin
- Employment law highlights
- A brief history of legal advertising

At Lewis Silkin *"people feel free to be themselves, and the eclectic-ness of people within the firm strikes you."*

The scoop on 'scapes

Lewis Silkin has cool clients, dressed-down lawyers and modern attitudes, but it vigorously asserts that its defining trait is not its trendy presentation, its youthful Podcasting managing partner or vibrant culture but rather the work on offer. When pressed on cultural matters, our sources usually drew us back to the subject of work, maintaining that the firm's philosophy was that it ought to be as enjoyable as play.

The firm's founder, Mr Lewis Silkin, was a post-WWII government minister for planning, housing, new towns and the like. His legacy is a renowned social housing and regeneration practice that remains a large part of one of the firm's three sector-based departments: Landscape, Peoplescape and Mediascape. Dividing the firm up in this way *"creates more opportunities as a lot of things can fit into each 'scape. For example, there are eight subsections within media,"* training partner Cliff Fluet told us. Trainees complete six four-month seats, allowing them to experience each 'scape once and also take seats in corporate and dispute resolution before then repeating their favourite or perhaps going on a client secondment. *"Priority is given to second-years,"* but the small intake of five or six trainees per year means *"you will eventually get your first choice."*

The firm's largest department – employment – dominates the peoplescape division and the legal market. It's nearly impossible to match in terms of size, breadth and quality of service and receives a top-tier ranking in *Chambers UK*. Known to insiders as EID (employment and incentives department), it has grown dramatically in both headcount and revenue over the years. Being at the top of the market, EID sports an amazing Rolodex of clients including Apple, Credit Suisse, Freshfields, Ford, Marks & Spencer and the Viacom Group (MTV Networks Europe, Universal, Nickelodeon). The department splits its work about 85:15 employer:employee, with the employee representation usually reserved for City high flyers or cases of legal importance. One such case was that of whistleblower Pickett, a former employee of Citigroup; another was the Beck race discrimination claim against Canadian Imperial Bank of Commerce. Read more about these cases on our website.

Trainees found their stints in EID to be *"really, really enjoyable"* due to *"the department's excellent reputation and exposure to a wide range of matters with a good mix of respondent and claimant work."* They also appreciated that the team is *"very engaged in pro bono,"* providing even first-year trainees with the opportunity to effectively run their own files. *"I did advocacy at the tribunal for one,"* a source said proudly. In this department *"you're actually taking responsibility – drafting amendments from day one, negotiating with clients, taking calls from unions."*

A thriving immigration team handles work for its own clients (eg various prominent entertainment businesses and retailers including the BBC, Warner Bros., Bulgari and Berghaus) and for other major law firms without their own immigration capability. The team also has a profile in the sports sector, where its clients include Saracens,

Chambers UK rankings

Construction	Intellectual Property
Corporate/M&A	Media & Entertainment
Defamation/Reputation Management	Partnership
	Real Estate
Dispute Resolution	Real Estate Litigation
Education	Social Housing
Employment	Sports Law
Immigration	

Bath, Cardiff Blues and Bedford Blues rugby clubs and a handful of Premier League football clubs.

Promoted to the Premiership

The Sports Law Group (SLG) took an innovative step of appointing Brian Barwick as department chairman. Barwick was previously CEO of The FA and head of sport at the BBC and ITV – positions allowing him to significantly raise the profile of the SLG within the industry, particularly in relation to football. Barwick's appointment was swiftly followed by the hire of partner Andrew Osborne, formerly one of Hammonds' key sports lawyers. He brought with him a wealth of experience and contacts in relation to football transfer, immigration and player issues, as well as sporting disputes. The most exciting recent development for the SLG has been a critical breakthrough with the football Premiership. Prior to 2009, the firm acted for Fulham and Hull but has since added four more clubs from the league, advising on various issues including commercial contracts, intellectual property, transfers, employment, immigration and corporate matters. In the rugby world, LS represented Harlequins' winger Tom Williams during the 'bloodgate' scandal and was also instructed by the New Zealand All Blacks, South African Springboks and Australian Wallabies on their autumn tours.

In case you haven't picked up on the very obvious theme, LS is firmly rooted in the media landscape. Ex-chairman Roger Alexander is hailed as the nation's top advertising law guru. It sits oddly, and yet almost appropriately, alongside the fact that one of the firm's previous senior partners – former Labour MP John Fraser – established much of the UK consumer protection legislation while a government minister in the 1970s. Proving its frontrunner status in the industry, the firm was chosen to provide interim legal cover for the Institute of Practitioners in Advertising's (IPA) legal advice service following the departure of its in-house team. Other recent important work included the submission of a response to the Advertising Standards Authority (ASA) Code Review, which is reviewing the terms on which the ASA regulates advertisements. The firm also worked with long-standing ad agency client AMV on its new client agreement with insurer Aviva, including advising on a key talent agreement with Paul Whitehouse, who appears in the insurer's TV commercials.

Besides being *"a very diverse seat, with a music deal one day and a social landlord data protection matter the next, and a brand owner advertising campaign the next,"* MBT (media, brands and technology) *"is quite a cool department with well-known clients that relate to your everyday life."* The firm acts as Bacardi's key UK adviser, for example; LS has been helping it with the Bacardi.com content strategy, its 'B-Live' music strategy and its unique model of signing an artist to its label (rather than merely contracting for brand endorsement). The artist in question is Groove Armada. The firm advised Bacardi on all aspects of the deal with the band – negotiating terms with its music publishers and various media platforms and rights owners to circulate the material via its unique viral marketing 'Bacardi Share' free download mechanism. Mixing alcohol and music? Genius. Other MBT teams have been advising Ministry of Sound (now renamed MSHK) in relation to things such as its negotiations with iTunes and Amazon.com, music licensing issues, proposed musical productions and brand and IP licensing issues. Trainees are *"given quite a lot of responsibility"* in MBT seats and also get involved in some business development tasks. It's quite clear that part of their enjoyment comes from *"seeing the work we're doing is relevant to matters you can read about in the papers."*

Gimme shelter

On to landscape, which in another firm would probably be described simply as the property department. The property team works with a range of clients including Electronic Arts, Agilent Technologies, Nasdaq Omx, Rio Tinto, Royal Albert Hall and Gondola Group. The firm also has a long history of being *"very committed to social housing."* It stands out in the legal market for its activity in this sector and recently advised on regeneration and development schemes in Elephant & Castle, King's Cross and Notting Hill. The last of these saw the construction team getting involved as client Notting Hill Housing Group negotiated with a major house builder for the purchase of land and the construction of affordable homes at three locations. The firm frequently assists housing associations in securing loans from banks, and on other matters of a regulatory, corporate or restructuring nature. Real estate litigators step into the social housing arena, too, taking on anti-social behaviour cases and actions relating to unlawful sub-lettings. It's also worth mentioning the firm's experience in the education sector, and in particular the Academies programme. It had been involved in the establishment of some 50 Academies in England prior to the change of government and this should stand it in good stead in the new coalition government education era. Said one trainee of their landscape seat: *"It's great because it really gets you into file management from an early stage. There were a lot of files which my supervisor felt comfortable delegating to me, so I was managing them, organising the Land Registry aspects and doing due diligence."*

One of the two departments falling outside the 'scapes' structure is dispute resolution, which famously represented Mohamed Al Fayed in the inquest into the deaths of Princess Diana and his son Dodi. Trainees *"get given free rein on some matters and are expected to manage* [their] *own workloads."* Our sources talked about *"going to hearings"* and *"taking witness statements"* as typical tasks. The other non-'scape department is corporate, home to one of the top M&A teams operating in London's lower mid-market. Besides M&A, the department also handles capital markets, AIM and LSE matters. Trainees *"start off just working on documents,"* but progress fairly quickly. *"You can run your own deals once you know what's going on,"* said a past occupant of the corporate seat. The firm's small Oxford office concentrates on employment and does not offer trainee seats. The only option for time away from LS's Chancery Lane HQ is the occasional client secondment.

Speaking generally of their experiences, our sources insisted that *"trainees are expected to do real work"* and to *"work late when there are client needs."* That said, this is a firm where one's personal life is respected. It's also worth noting that LS was one of the early adopters of industry sector-led legal practice in its modern form, and it is thriving as a result in several industries. You *"really do get in-depth knowledge"* and *"feel really well prepared,"* said trainees.

They like to mov it mov it

There's a certain quality that sets LS apart from other firms in the City, and yet, rather disappointingly, it's difficult to define. *"I certainly can't put my finger on what it is exactly,"* one trainee told us. Here, you'll find ex-violinists and music producers alongside people who've worked as paralegals and those for whom LS represents a first career step. Training partner Cliff Fluet agrees: *"There's no Lewis Silkin type, but rather a Lewis Silkin person."* There are no hard-and-fast rules to who the firm might be interested in recruiting but *"it's definitely not cookie-cutter."* The firm has a working environment in which *"you can go and speak to anybody"* and *"there's a real desire to cascade knowledge and experience."* Something must be working as the firm has made the *Sunday Times'* 'Best Companies to Work For' list two years in a row. It is now the second-highest placed law firm in the list. As for the firm's finances, it saw marginal increases in revenue and profitability for the 2009/10 financial year.

If we gave an award for the most creative social scene, this firm would be hard to beat. Serious effort is put into department-sponsored parties for the whole firm. For example, MBT organised a *Strictly Come Dancing* soirée for their colleagues in other departments. This included mandatory ballroom classes for some! The *Eurovision* party planned by property lawyers had all staff rehearsing horribly cheesy continental pop songs for weeks, and the corporate team's school sports day featured all the classics, such as an egg-and-spoon race. It's not all song and dance: the firm had a very successful and *"very, very embarrassing"* Movember last year. Movember is a month when, across the City, guys grow moustaches for charity. Some of the LS boys really got into the idea and even produced a *Magnum PI*-inspired comic book. Breaks can be spent playing table football or having a go on the office Wii, and after hours you can join one of the firm's sports teams or venture out for drinks at the Slug and Lettuce, The Blue Anchor or Seven Stars.

We can assure you that LS trainees are a happy bunch. They couldn't think of anything they'd like to change about the firm, except of course to *"fill up the office's massive glass atrium with water and then put a shark in there. It'd be great – we could all be James Bond. We could have a trap door in one of the meeting rooms so that if the other side wasn't agreeing to our terms, we'd just press a button and they'd fall in with the shark."* We're not sure that would be SRA compliant.

And finally...

In 2010 three out of five qualifiers were retained, going into EID, MBT and corporate (there was another opening in litigation but no one applied for it). They continue their careers at a firm with a refreshingly contemporary ethos and genuine interest in staff satisfaction.

Linklaters

The facts

Location: London

Number of UK partners/solicitors: 200/600

Total number of trainees: 240

Seats: 4x6 months

Alternative seats: Overseas seats, secondments

Extras: Pro bono – Mary Ward Legal Advice Centre, RCJ CAB, Disability Law Service, A4ID and others; language training

On chambersstudent.co.uk
- How to get into Linklaters
- More on Linklaters' LPC
- The firm's diversity stats
- Linklaters' pro bono work

Training at Linklaters is no snoozy job to pay the bills. It takes real commitment and demands a tough, can-do attitude. If you've got the desire to succeed and the will to push your career hard, Linklaters should be worth all your effort.

Premium goals

Huge revenue, big profits and more than 2,000 lawyers in 26 cities worldwide: Linklaters' driving ambition has earned it a position among the world's elite law firms. This magic circle player has the second-highest turnover of any UK law firm (a decline of 9% for 2009/10 saw it cede top spot to Clifford Chance) and a breathtaking client list. Its stated goal is simply to be the number-one law firm in the world. Breaking that grand plan down a little, a key short-term aim is to build up Linklaters' standing in the USA.

The firm's clients are large, usually multinational and well known; smaller clients are gradually disappearing from the picture. More FTSE 100 companies instructed it than any other firm in 2009, according to the FTSE survey conducted by *The Chambers Magazine*. One such client is BP, which has sought the firm's counsel on a number of matters including litigation relating to the Buncefield oil storage depot explosion, in which there was more than £1bn at stake. Although often pegged as more corporate-led, Linklaters also won more FTSE 100 and FTSE 250 finance-related clients than any other firm, according to the same survey. Its avowed targeting of 'premium work' is clearly going well.

Early 2009 saw the axe swing at Linklaters and around 100 London lawyers – including partners – lost their jobs. It was one of the City's biggest culls and, inevitably, people questioned the firm's loyalty to its employees. It must be said that our sources thought morale has bounced back in 2010, and that the cuts were understandable. "*As a firm it is well-run... ruthlessly well-run. It is run as a business for the best interests of the business, not in the interests of the lawyers. Things are done as efficiently as possible for profits.*" Trainees say: "*It's the only way to run a business.*"

The art of compromise

Over the course of the four-seat scheme, most trainees will visit both a corporate seat and a finance seat. They will usually take three seats out of the following: asset finance; banking; capital markets; derivatives and structured products; projects; structured finance; litigation; and real estate. Some lucky trainees get exactly what they want every time, while others never seem to land the seat they are desperate for. There were suggestions that if you badger the partners in charge of a certain department sufficiently, you should be able to wangle the route you want. The firm denies this is the case, but there is certainly a perception among some trainees that the system works better for some people than others. It can't be easy for HR to please 240 demanding graduates, so the best advice is probably to press your case early and then consistently, but be prepared to give a little as well. Trainees are allowed a period of grace in which they can request to swap seats if they really don't like where they've ended up.

Chambers UK rankings

Asset Finance	Investment Funds
Banking & Finance	Life Sciences
Banking Litigation	Outsourcing
Capital Markets	Partnership
Commodities	Pensions
Competition/European Law	Pensions Litigation
Construction	Planning
Corporate/M&A	Private Equity
Data Protection	Professional Negligence
Dispute Resolution	Projects
Employee Share Schemes	Public Procurement
Employment	Real Estate
Energy & Natural Resources	Real Estate Finance
	Real Estate Litigation
Environment	Restructuring/Insolvency
Financial Services	Retail
Fraud	Tax
Information Technology	Telecommunications
Insurance	Transport
Intellectual Property	

The corporate department demands the most time from its trainees. "*Some people really thrive on being in corporate; it has a real team atmosphere and they love seeing their deals in the papers,*" but for others it's "*horrendous.*" One interviewee had left before 9pm only eight times in three months, and worked weekends too. You obviously need the right mindset. Client contact comes in the form of answering calls and e-mails, which trainees are free to do without much micro-management. Some people work directly for one partner; others take work from around their group, depending on what the firm has on its plate at the time. The pursuit of the biggest and best mandates means that trainees often have to be content with lower-level tasks than you would perhaps see at a smaller firm working on smaller deals. Nevertheless, there is definitely some truth in the idea that bigger means better quality (ie more difficult, profitable and complicated) work. Many of our sources were working on matters that crossed continents, involved several banks and drew on the resources of departments across the whole firm. "*You have to expect some grunt work, but you can't help but learn during these matters – you just soak it up.*" The firm's recent instructions include advising RBS on the £2bn sale of a majority stake in its Global Merchant Services arm to private equity houses Bain Capital and Advent International, and advising the seller in the £104.5m disposal of Channel 5 to Richard Desmond's publishing group Northern & Shell.

The financial teams deal with similar clients to the corporate ones and have a similarly hectic atmosphere. The training in these seats is "*excellent, due to both the actual tuition and the exposure. The deals are big and complex and you learn a lot.*" Among many prized deals, Linklaters' lawyers advised the lead arrangers in connection with KKR's £955m bid to acquire Pets at Home from Bridgepoint, and worked on the financing of seven Boeing B737 aircraft for Norwegian Air Shuttle. Linklaters' broad practice means there is a lot to choose from and trainees, although positioned within one specific and specialised team, can often work with as many people and sub-teams as they like. A banking seat trainee described their time as "*a baptism of fire*" as they worked on large restructurings. The quality of the experience is excellent though; "*there's a perception that there's not much law, that it's a lot of document churning and all that. But you get a lot of legal questions too,*" one source insisted. "*It was very rare that I just proof-read things.*" In discussions about the derivatives team, the word "*technical*" cropped up a fair amount. This area is rather dense and complex, meaning that even by the end of the seat many trainees aren't entirely up to speed, but they all enjoyed the experience. One told us about helping out with the drafting of a bond issue and working on a derivatives contract, which involved "*quite a lot of responsibility and attending client meetings, dealing with queries and helping to manage the transaction.*"

Don't forget your toothbrush

The energy and infrastructure seat is very busy, but trainees don't feel dragged down because it's "*quite a young group and there's lots of chat during the day.*" It's a seat that draws on many different disciplines. "*There are elements of property law when it comes to sustainable building; banking in working with the financial markets; issues linked to environmental concerns, including stuff to do with carbon trading; and even pensions came into it when we worked on a pension scheme with climate risk considerations.*" Trainees eagerly noted "*transactions that relate to emissions trading,*" which required them to conduct research and keep clients and colleagues abreast of legislative changes. Some matters can be finalised quickly, meaning that trainees observe them from start to finish. Others continue for years – some trainees had "*worked on a matter that has been going since 1994.*"

Telecoms, media and telecommunications (TMT) seats involve "*software licensing, telecoms regulations – like stuff relating to advertising and content – and supply agreements too.*" This is a small group so it may be hard to get a seat, but those who do can expect "*a lot of independence, more than elsewhere. You can do your own agreements and there are lots of different matters so you pick things up quickly.*" TMT is "*exceptionally busy. The guys here stay until 2am as standard and leaving at 10pm is our equivalent of going at 6pm.*" For a full list of all the seat options, go to our website.

Every trainee mentioned the hours they work. Here are some of their highlights: "*It's amazing how quickly you start to think that leaving at 9pm is early;*" "*people who moan about long hours and hard work are boring;*" "*when I finished at 7am, I'd go home, have a shower and a ten-minute nap and go back in. The shower is the key!*" At least work is fairly shared, thanks to an allocation system whereby trainees fill in spreadsheets detailing their workload and these are regularly monitored by HR. Trainees can take 25 days' holiday a year. Most people make sure they use them all and, mused one source: "*In the instances where people don't, I'd say it is because they live for work.*"

Hone and away

Overseas secondments are plentiful and the firm wants trainees to take full advantage of them to instil a spirit of internationalism right at the start of their careers. Two-thirds of trainees complete overseas secondments. Some posts require applicants to be conversant in the native language, but in others – such as Hong Kong – English is the lingua franca. Trainees working overseas used to be required to visit a department they already had experience of in the UK, but this is being phased out. For a list of likely overseas destinations, see page 536 or our website. Client secondments are available too, and these were described by one source as "*really beneficial, giving valuable in-house experience I wouldn't otherwise have had.*" Opportunities crop up with the likes of The Prince's Trust and the Mary Ward Centre as well as major corporates and banks. Trainees needn't worry about scotching their qualification chances by taking a seat away from the firm's London HQ. "*They don't encourage you to go unless you're in a strong position.*" Around a quarter of trainees will complete a client secondment.

The appraisal system was variously described as "*good,*" "*okay*" and "*not good.*" At the end of each seat, around ten different criteria are graded, letting people know the areas in which they need to up their game. Trainees nominate the lawyers they wish to receive feedback from and, if someone important is missed out, the supervisor will ask for their opinion too. One trainee complained that "*there can be a bit of a clash between what actually makes a good trainee and what is a load of HR mumbo-jumbo. For example, 'Are you driven by the firm's values?' Nobody knows what it actually means!*" They did acknowledge that the appraisal system was worthwhile overall.

The gas man cometh

So trainees work long hours on high-stakes matters without complaining or expressing desires for a gentler pace. Is oxygen pumped through the air con to keep them energised, productive and mildly high? The answer is that the firm has somehow created an atmosphere of easy humour and relatively quiet ambition, while its recruiters look for people whose natural curiosity will keep them awake and working, even in the wee small hours. We're talking about the type likely to say things like "*better busy than bored.*" Working in teams helps: "*If you had to stay late on your own it would be harder to bear, but when everyone is in it together, working well together, it's much easier. Most days we're here until pretty late, so the onus is on having fun while you're doing it, rather than getting it over and done with and out of the door a little earlier.*" Linklaters' trainees seem fairly happy, "*fiercely loyal*" and simply want to work. They generally all know each other before starting at the firm, having studied the Linklaters LPC at the College of Law's Moorgate branch. More on this on our website.

Asking trainees who should apply proved difficult and the annual intakes are diverse (see our website), so instead we asked who ought not apply. "*People shouldn't apply who have the wrong idea about what Linklaters is about – some people come in wanting to do something good, save the world, save the whales... it's not like that. You need to know what you're here for. You're not here for the dolphins.*" Telling our pragmatist we'd use that quote, they happily responded that doing so "*should get rid of a lot of annoying people.*"

Linklaters' office is modern and expansive, with a gym, beautician, dentist, physiotherapist and doctor on site. Meals in its popular canteen are served by "*a great French guy who is very funny and puts a smile on people's faces by joking about their long hours and asking why on earth they'd want to be lawyers.*" Linklaters doesn't skimp on the perks: to name just a few there are free phones, taxis paid for and a concierge service that means "*someone else will wait for the gas man or whatever so you can work.*"

Trainees don't venture out much during the week and tend not to socialise en masse, but there are organised parties including a well-attended summer ball. And the drinks trolley that does the rounds on Fridays "*makes working life a lot more fun!*"

And finally...

Linklaters remains the firm of choice for the ultra-ambitious. A total of 109 out of 136 qualifiers took up jobs with the firm in 2010.

Macfarlanes LLP

The facts

Location: London

Number of UK partners/assistants: 75/150

Total number of trainees: 60

Seats: 4x6 months

Alternative seats: Secondments

Extras: Pro bono – Cambridge House, LawWorks, Bar Pro Bono Unit; language training

On chambersstudent.co.uk
- How to get into Macfarlanes
- Macfarlanes' pro bono and charity work
- Recent highlight deals and cases

Macfarlanes is currently undergoing some nip-and-tuck cosmetic surgery. A PR revamp is underway and evident on its web pages. 'Discernibly different', reads the new slogan.

Mac-facelift

So what's new, from whom does it wish to differentiate itself, and how does it propose to do so? Smaller than the magic circle firms, Macfarlanes believes that its teams offer quality over quantity – a more tailored approach for a more discerning client. It is for this reason that the tight-knit partnership has felt no need to expand beyond its home just off Chancery Lane and close to the Royal Courts of Justice, although a fair amount of its work has an international angle. Macfarlanes remains "*staunchly independent*" and feels that is often the key to securing the trust of its foreign clients. Put succinctly by the firm's graduate recruitment partner John Hornby: "*We are not pursuing growth for growth's sake, we are pursuing quality for quality's sake.*" Macfarlanes loves that word 'quality' and it gets applied to the firm in many situations.

While offering a full service, Macfarlanes is most notable for its corporate department and a small but elite private client team. Evidence from the corporate team suggests that it still has the muscle to size up to the heavyweights: it represented DC Thomson on its acquisition of Friends Reunited from ITV at the end of 2009, and it made headline news at the beginning of 2010 by advising Four Seasons Healthcare – Britain's biggest care home group – on a deal for the restructuring of its £1.6bn debt package, one of the largest of its kind in Europe during the financial crisis. There is every reason to expect that more such commercial mortgage-backed securities (CMBS) restructurings will be heading its way. Long-term client Incisive Media was also in need of advice on the restructuring of its UK arm, while the team continued to increase its activity in the sports sector, giving advice to a number of Formula 1 racing teams (Red Bull Racing, Toro Rosso) and acting on several deals involving Premiership football clubs, most notably client E. Stanley Kroenke's investment in Arsenal FC. Another client is Paramount Restaurants, whose portfolio includes Chez Gérard, Bertorelli and Caffè Uno.

Low down or down-low?

Glamorous as it might sound, the second-year trainees had unsurprisingly found their first taste of the corporate scene less like the Monaco Grand Prix and often more like an interminable safety car lap. With markets crashing around them and people being laid off, the mood in the corporate department was described as having "*bad energy*" and being on occasion "*demoralising.*" Things now seem to be back on track, with the third and fourth quarters of 2009 showing an almost magic wand-like turnaround in M&A. Trainees reported that the quality of work was "*definitely picking up,*" that "*confidence was coming back into the market*" and "*a good deal more responsibility* [was] *being thrown our way.*" There's a phrase that's been bandied around the legal market during the recession – 'a flight to quality' – and Macfarlanes certainly fits the bill. The workload in this department will always be more "*peak-trough*" than elsewhere in the firm, but then there are always those who thrive on "*doing the really late hours one week and then easing off a little the next.*"

Chambers UK rankings

Agriculture & Rural Affairs	Intellectual Property
Banking & Finance	Investment Funds
Charities	Media & Entertainment
Competition/European Law	Pensions
Construction	Planning
Corporate/M&A	Private Client
Dispute Resolution	Private Equity
Employee Share Schemes	Real Estate
Employment	Real Estate Finance
Environment	Real Estate Litigation
Financial Services	Sports Law
Franchising	Tax

Whatever works

Two seats are compulsory in Macfarlanes' four-seat set-up. We've talked about the first, corporate; now let's discuss the second, real estate. This department makes up about a quarter of the firm and is divided into nine discrete areas. It is known to be *"a very friendly department – the friendliest even,"* and most interviewees spoke enthusiastically of their time there, especially having *"a lot of files of your own to look after."* Trainees like the client contact and the mixture of commercial and residential property deals. Asset management, the auction of properties, *"helping out with the sale of a large shopping centre,"* negotiating leases, writing to the Land Registry to remove a notice or request official copies of deeds, and drafting break notices on leases were all part of trainees' varied experiences. On the agenda in property finance is everything from *"people buying properties, doing them up and letting them,"* through to more complex and high-value deals for the likes of RBS and ING Bank, which lawyers advised on the £374m restructuring of its shopping centre portfolio. Those with *"a serious appetite for responsibility"* will find their hunger more than satisfied with their own files and a constantly ringing phone. Property seats generally go down well with people who like some independence right from the start of their training. All that time spent on property law as a student really does pay off.

Clearly the 'quirky' internal reputation of certain members of the private client department has done nothing to harm their significant standing in this legal field: the firm has national and international top-tier listings in *Chambers UK* and *Chambers Global* respectively. A big wave of 'non-dom' client queries provided much of the increased workload in this department over the past year. Despite changes in legislation, it's clear that the UK is still a hugely attractive destination for foreign domiciled individuals. One interviewee told us about some substantial work involving a new Charities Act that affects *"how charities should handle big-money claims."* Getting to grips with legislative change had proved a rewarding experience. As is often the case with a private client seat, the work at trainee level can be *"quite academic with not a lot of client contact,"* but there are few better places to specialise, particularly if you have an interest in the complexities of offshore funds and technicalities of tax.

While extremely stable at its core, Macfarlanes has also been slowly expanding in other areas, notably in its litigation department, now an eight-partner team that incorporates a wide variety of areas, such as IP, commercial and pensions litigation. The firm was in the spotlight when its lawyers defended Trafigura in Britain's largest-ever group litigation action (over 31,000 claimants) after the well-publicised Ivory Coast scandal. Much smaller issues also crop up, such as *"people with broken ponds or getting upset with stuff they've bought, or not paying their rent."* An employment seat, meanwhile, can throw up some *"really crazy, off-the-wall claimants,"* although this scenario usually arises when unrepresented individuals bring cases against Macfarlanes' employer clients.

Other seats are available in banking and finance; corporate tax; pensions; and competition. The firm's London-centricity means no overseas seats for trainees, while client secondments are rare but not unknown.

Facebook or face-in-a-book?

So why choose Macfarlanes over the magic circle? Speaking to the most recent set of trainees, the answer is fairly clear. In their minds it's all a matter of size, superiority and swagger. Applicants *"who don't want to be small cogs in a big machine"* are drawn to the firm's *"reputation for excellence"* and the website's promise of *"discernible difference."* Macfarlanes represents *"an alternative to the world's legal giants"* that suits the *"quietly confident"* over the *"cocky and arrogant."* Oxbridge and redbrick candidates predominate, but then *"quality"* – as if we haven't said it enough – is the most reiterated word in all the literature by and about Macfarlanes. John Hornby again: *"There are no Macfarlanes clones. People need to have a due measure of all talents, not just have a planet-sized brain, as we can't hide people in back rooms."* High expectations come with being a high-flyer, so a self-starting nature is important. It may not be a case of the gloves coming off, but the kid gloves are certainly nowhere to be seen – *"it's a small firm, and you can't hide if you make a mistake,"* said one trainee.

Still, its more petite nature means the training is good. Training sessions are conducted in the morning and at lunchtime and there are occasional evening seminars. Programmes tend to be *"front-loaded at the beginning of each seat."* They are mostly conducted by solicitors, although some are even led by the trainees themselves. In terms of appraisals, feedback opportunities are provided both midway through and at the end of each seat. Every six months, trainees and principals (partner supervisors) get together for a review of progress thus far. "*I've been really pleased with my supervisors,*" said one source. "*I've never been swamped with admin-type stuff.*" And – despite several trainees highlighting the "*corporate culture*" of the firm – Macfarlanes has never been a place where cigar-chomping partners roam free, feeding their egos by beasting their underlings. "*You are treated really well as a trainee. This is a nice, friendly, pleasant place.*"

Macfarlanes has long had the reputation of being traditionalist, conservative and slightly stuffy – an image trainees were keen to dispel. "*I thought it would be like the bankers' boardroom in Mary Poppins,*" said one, "*but it actually feels quite youthful.*" Departments have clearly cultivated their own personalities. Private client partners and associates are often said to be "*eccentric,*" "*quirky*" or "*bookish;*" the property lawyers more "*gregarious and outgoing;*" and the work-hard, play-hard corporate cats tend to "*take themselves quite seriously.*" This is never going to be a "*beers on trolleys on a Friday night*" crowd; instead the Macfarlanes clan, young and old, prefer to regroup at popular watering hole The Castle – famed for its good selection of real ales.

Perhaps it's not stuffy, but there is an area where Macfarlanes is undeniably behind the times. There's no dodging the issue: this firm is distinctly lacking in the diversity department. Of the 75 partners at the firm in July 2010, 64 were male and all were white. While the trainee group is more balanced gender-wise, it is far from diverse in its ethnic make-up. We discuss this in further detail on our website and get the firm's comment.

Life in the Macfastlane

Stately without being overly self-publicising, "*a bit like Judi Dench*" seemed to us a particularly apt description of the firm as a whole. A sense of decorum still seems to prevail in the social life of trainees, with the summer event seeing them take to the races at Ascot, and an annual classical concert also forming part of the firm-wide summer calendar. The antidote to the latter – a cabaret at Camden Town venue Koko – "*is definitely a high point*" and sounds as much *Moulin Rouge* as it does Minnelli. The line-up invariably includes the Macfarlanes choir and departmental dances. One trainee choreographed a performance of *Saturday Night Fever*. The event raises a significant amount for charity, as do the collectors "*going round with a bucket*" at events at Silverstone and the Emirates Stadium.

And finally...

Macfarlanes has an aura of class about it that comes from consistent excellence. It breeds loyal trainees and 22 out of its 27 qualifiers took up jobs with the firm in 2010.

- **Why be a lawyer?**

  "It wasn't just the money; it was always my intention to try and help people. I think I do, but not in the way I thought."

  "The job is intellectually challenging and I'm always learning something new."

  "There's a danger that some people get onto a treadmill, imagining long-term fulfilment. But just because it's an obvious and well-known career path doesn't mean it is for everyone."

top tip no. 24

Manches LLP

The facts

Location: London, Oxford, Reading

Number of UK partners/solicitors: 51/81

Total number of trainees: 20

Seats: 4x6 months

Alternative seats: Secondments

On chambersstudent.co.uk
- How to get into Manches
- We look at the firm's renowned partners
- Splitsville: divorce facts and figures

With crown jewel clients, an international reputation for family law, strong property work and a brilliant tech/media department in Oxford, Manches continues to concentrate on its strengths.

Family values

Manches is a family firm in more ways than one. Not only does it excel in family law, but there have also been three generations of Manches working at the firm. Sidney and Judith founded it in 1936 and were the first husband and wife to practise law in partnership together. Their daughter Jane Simpson is the current chair of the firm, and her brother Louis Manches heads the London office. A third-generation Manches is an associate in litigation. But it's not only Manches: the stellar partner list includes names such as Lady Helen Ward, Jane Craig and James Stewart, any one of whom you'd want on side if you were a seriously wealthy or famous person in the midst of a marriage breakdown.

In addition to family, the firm's most obvious interests are in property, retail and commercial technologies in London, and publishing, life sciences and IT in Oxford and Reading. Over the years, Manches has grown both organically and through the annexation of four smaller law firms, including a 2005 merger with seven-partner property boutique Marshall Ross & Prevezer.

Hot property

First-year trainees are often given seats in the two biggest departments: property and family, which latterly have accounted for 31% and 21% of the firm's work respectively. Property is divided into three teams: commercial property, property litigation, and construction, the last of which is only active in London. During the height of the recession, trainees were generally allocated to the busy prop lit team rather than the other two. The department has strong retail links, and the client list speaks for itself: All Saints, Moss Bros, Gap, Kookai, FCUK, Pizza Hut and WHSmith, which seeks the firm's advice on its arrangements with Railtrack to have stores in stations across the country, as well as its agreements with the Post Office and Costa Coffee. Headed by the "*very friendly*" Louis Manches, the property department is a good place for an early seat as it teaches trainees the basics. Hours can be long, but trainees are given their own small files to run, "*a lot of client contact*" and "*hardly any document bundling.*" Prop lit trainees' work includes writing loads of letters and e-mails, some disclosure exercises, negotiation meetings, mediations and attending hearings.

Being so strong on property, Manches was bound to take a hit during the recession. However, trainees feel that the firm has "*managed it well all along the way*" with moderate cuts in strategic sectors. It also helps that Manches is "*weighted towards litigation.*"

Family time

The family department is the leading light of the firm. It consistently features in *Chambers UK*'s top band and is "*slightly aloof*" from the other departments. A seat here can involve long hours and hard work, but "*the quality of work and people you're exposed to is something else.*"

Chambers UK rankings

Corporate/M&A	Intellectual Property
Dispute Resolution	Media & Entertainment
Education	Private Client
Employment	Real Estate
Environment	Real Estate Litigation
Family/Matrimonial	Retail
Information Technology	Social Housing

Recession means divorces. Job losses and monetary trouble means extra pressure on already-tense marriages, and many trophy wives (and husbands) walk out before the cash vanishes. Manches' family department has seen a rise in the number of divorce cases recently and its ethos is to minimise confrontation and attempt to go down the mediation route. The clients tend to be wealthy individuals, many of them from outside the UK. Working mainly on ancillary relief and child cases, trainees will take notes at client meetings, draft letters and sometimes go to court. They can expect client contact – sometimes daily – and should be prepared to see clients crying on a regular basis. London trainees are guaranteed six months in family, usually as their first seat, but it is unlikely that a trainee will do this (or any other) seat twice, as the firm is keen to make everyone work in a variety of departments.

Because family is so often given to first-seat trainees, the levels of responsibility are notoriously low. There is definitely "*lots of grunt work*:" trainees report masses of bundling and hours at the photocopier, as the cases are generally too complex for them to run solo. Compared to property, the trainee has a different type of responsibility in family: they will act as the intermediary between the client and the partner – although they "*wouldn't even dream of offering the client advice.*" Our sources said they were happy to learn largely by observing partners at work: one "*really enjoyed client meetings and mediations because you really get to see the partner you work for in action.*" The Oxford office also has a small but high-quality family department, which offers lots of client contact and time in court.

The busy litigation team is well regarded, and trainees say it is "*catching up in terms of business and prestige.*" Clients include British American Tobacco, Eurotunnel and Equitable Life, and it has also picked up some credit crunch-related inter-bank claims. Commercial litigation cases are generally quite big so trainees often become immersed in disclosure exercises. They are also given "*a fair amount of responsibility*" and at least one source enjoyed helping to "*chase down international fraudsters.*"

The other seats on offer are employment and tech/IP, plus there is a secondment to client London Underground which is generally given to a second-year trainee. This non-contentious construction seat is also open to Oxford trainees. Other shorter secondments are available in corporate, and there are some ad hoc secondments to clients such as All Saints and Universal. A fair amount of the UK-based cases involve work on overseas jurisdictions, usually related to fraud, international arbitration, seizure of assets, third homes, offshore accounts and international wealth protection. The family department has many Russian clients, and tech/IP is "*very international.*" Languages are helpful but not a requirement in this respect.

Lords of the ringroad

The Oxford office takes on two or three trainees each year and offers corporate, litigation, property, employment, tech/IP and family seats. Trainees will sometimes go to London for the day to meet a client, but "*there is little crossover – the two offices are almost two separate firms.*" So much so that there was once talk of the Oxford office joining Mills & Reeve, but negotiations apparently ceased after a number of meetings. In Oxford, Manches has strong links to local academic and educational publishing businesses. IP clients include the Oxford University Press, the Tolkien Estate, Blackwell, Macmillan, JD Salinger and Marvel Entertainment. Other clients include Endemol, Universal Pictures, the Telegraph Media Group, the National Trust, Chloe handbags and Damien Hirst. Manches has also done work for the University of Oxford, the University of Sussex and Royal Holloway. The Oxford office is building up its name in biotechnology and there is a brand new sustainability department. There is also outsourcing advice to videogame software development companies.

The first and second seats for Oxford trainees are tech/IP followed by corporate. The popular tech/IP seat focuses on trade marks, defamation, domain name disputes, publishing agreements and charities. Trainee tasks include addressing simple queries, taking notes at client meetings, "*an awful lot of very interesting research*" and very little grunt work. There is plenty of client interaction, and one trainee said that "*with simple trade mark stuff, the fee earner was happy for me to be the first point of contact.*" The corporate department is not client contact-heavy and its trainee work centres on drafting, due diligence, disclosure and company secretarial tasks: not always too popular with our sources, but the usually small size of transactions allowed them to see things from start to finish. Seats in Oxford were generally praised for the variety of the day-to-day work: trainees are "*encouraged to have a go at everything and are not just stuck at a photocopier.*" In both locations, the firm organises "*very, very useful*" know-how seminars, with internal and external speakers presenting on topics of interest. The newer Reading office focuses on technology and life sciences and does not yet offer trainee seats.

Balancing work and life

While most of the trainees we spoke to had experienced a handful of long nights and the occasional weekend of work, "*long hours are the exception rather than the norm.*" One said: "*I didn't want to sell my soul for a few years then retire exhausted,*" confirming that they had found a good work-life balance at Manches. It does of course depend on which partner you sit with, how they work, and how you work. At the Oxford office, late hours "*don't happen very often at all.*" Several people have small children and the firm is "*excellent*" for respecting family commitments.

Partners at all levels are "*absolutely brilliant,*" many of them are quite young and supervisors will "*really take a personal interest, which makes a world of difference.*" The only caveat is that the family team does have a reputation for being more hierarchical and full of sticklers. Should you be surprised by this? Probably not: the senior lawyers have a lot at stake, not least their phenomenal reputation as leaders in their field. If you have a problem as a trainee, our sources say you can always "*go back to your previous supervisor in another department, if you were quite close, to ask about qualification and skills.*" This is not an especially stuffy firm and while "*no one is going to turn up dressing like a slob,*" some departments are less formal than others.

Mountain and sea

In addition to the usual netball, football, softball and cricket, there's a yearly ski trip for London trainees and associates. At the famous Manches Cup sailing regatta, trainees, associates and partners spend two days racing against several other law firms. The days of the Cup bring extended partying and some serious fancy dress. This is all well documented online, so use your Google skills to find photos. Because of the recession, recent summer and Christmas parties were downgraded to smaller departmental affairs; however, trainees manage to find their own entertainment. The West End office location at Aldwych is variously described as "*great,*" "*ideal*" and "*brilliant,*" with Covent Garden and the Royal Courts of Justice just five minutes away in opposite directions. On Fridays, trainees go for drinks at the nearby Bierodrome or Pagliacci.

The Oxford office, on a business park three miles outside the city centre, is "*not one for parties.*" Oxford trainees tend to be slightly older and more settled, so there are "*regular but not constant*" events: a bit of bowling here, a beer and a curry there. The Oxford office, however, is "*really lovely*" and the resident chef recently won a Masterchef award. "*Never did I dream I would be fed as well as here,*" said one trainee, patting their belly.

Manches' qualification process is fairly informal and varies between departments, some of which interview trainees, some of which don't. The large family department always offers jobs, tech/IP is quite busy at the moment, and property is picking up as well. In 2010, five of the seven London qualifiers and all three Oxford trainees accepted jobs.

And finally...

In some ways still a traditional firm, Manches has top-quality work and a decent work-life balance. Definitely a good pick for family, retail, IP and publishing experience.

Martineau

The facts

Location: Birmingham, London

Number of UK partners/solicitors: 47/100

Total number of trainees: 18

Seats: 6x4 months

Alternative seats: None

On chambersstudent.co.uk
- How to get into Martineau
- The firm's plans for London and Birmingham
- Trends in the education sector

Martineau is a Birmingham institution with *"very approachable"* partners and key clients in banking, education and energy, among other sectors.

Old roots, green shoots

Martineau is a Birmingham firm with nearly two centuries' experience under its belt. One of the second city's leading independent law firms, it has a healthy spread of highly regarded practices and sector-focused teams. It's neck and neck with the likes of Eversheds and Pinsent Masons in the *Chambers UK* rankings for education (advising universities around the UK, including Lancaster, Cardiff, Warwick, Exeter, Teesside and Nottingham) and banking work (it has represented Lloyds since it conducted the legal work on the bank's incorporation), and with Mills & Reeve for private client matters.

Increasing instructions from energy and investment fund clients are proving lucrative. The firm represents companies like British Energy, National Grid and npower, and venture capital trusts Baronsmead on renewables projects, cleantech financings, and fund formations, fund-raising and mergers. Check out the firm's climate change 'portal' (www.cc-forum.co.uk) for the skinny on climate change legislation and policy. It is Martineau's senior partner Andrew Whitehead, elected in 2009, who heads this practice. Energy and funds, alongside banking, education and technology, make up the firm's 'chosen sectors'.

The firm is hoping to achieve growth in 2010, with core groups corporate, commercial and litigation expected to be the biggest breadwinners. Martineau's other two core practice areas are private capital (private client) and property. Trainees are obliged to take a spin in either property or corporate. Each core group is composed of sub-teams such as banking, corporate finance, M&A, commercial disputes, banking litigation, family, tax planning, commercial property, energy, education, employment and IP, among others.

Education, education, education

Martineau operates a six-seat rotation system. New arrivals have no say in where they go first but do get input into every subsequent seat. Second-years always have priority and it's not unusual to repeat a favoured seat. Work comes from many fee earners and partners, and supervisors play an active role in soliciting it. Trainees are also free to ask for work on their own.

Trainees in the corporate finance and M&A teams can expect to be *"proof-reading, taking minutes, drafting share certificates and resolutions, and filing things with Companies House."* When it's busy, trainees could be in the office until 10pm or 11pm, but that's about the latest it will get. Most normally head home around 6pm. Presumably, the recession allowed for many early nights: *"There was nothing coming in. It was so dull,"* one source recalled. Fortunately, the corporate department forecasts growth and has written the increase into its budget, according to long-standing managing partner Bill Barker. Banking also sits under the corporate umbrella, and two trainees were lucky enough to be sent on ad hoc secondments to one of the firm's banking clients.

Education is the bedrock of prosperous societies and a cornerstone of Martineau's business. One of the firm's 'chosen sectors', it has a team of lawyers who do nothing but advise universities and further education colleges (but not schools) on constitutional issues and *"the knotty*

Chambers UK rankings

Agriculture & Rural Affairs	Family/Matrimonial
Banking & Finance	Information Technology
Charities	Intellectual Property
Construction	Private Client
Corporate/M&A	Private Equity
Debt Recovery	Real Estate
Dispute Resolution	Real Estate Litigation
Education	Restructuring/Insolvency
Employment	

problems they get themselves into." Aside from this team, fee earners from all practice groups contribute to a cross-firm focus on the education sector. It all adds up to 100-odd lawyers servicing education clients. So trainees in IP and employment seats, for instance, could find themselves working exclusively for institutions of higher learning. Interviewees tell us the education team is "*really good at getting trainees involved,*" which can mean "*everything from witness statements through to making bundles.*" Sources also spoke of "*reviewing contracts and advising on consultancy agreements.*" The firm recently won new instructions from Nottingham and Nottingham Trent universities, but trainees worry that coalition government budget cuts will cause work to dry up and that national firms like Eversheds are already doing the job for less money. When we asked him about this, managing partner Bill Barker said: "*Although there is less transactional work, we have an awful lot of employment and restructuring matters in the education sector, and universities continue to have land and buildings that require legal work.*" Barker was also keen to stress that the firm does more than just service education clients. "*Our second biggest client in 2009 was a pension fund, and the fourth biggest was* [Midlands-based investment fund] *Harris Watson.*"

That said, the property group does indeed undertake a lot of work for educational clients, recently representing Lancaster University in its proposed wind farm development to generate electricity for both its campus and the National Grid. This seat is "*a real baptism of fire,*" as each of our sources recalled being assigned "*20-odd files of my own straight away.*" Fortunately the group is "*very team-oriented and passionate about the work it does.*" Trainees will probably assist either the commercial property or the corporate support team, the latter's function being to advise on the property aspects of corporate transactions. Trainees described "*negotiating terms, drafting contracts and licences, filling out stamp duty forms, doing all the post-completion stuff and researching.*" The kind of work you get "*depends on the partner you're working with – some will just have you researching, while others will get you drafting and going to client meetings.*" Those interested in the London property market can apply to take a commercial property seat down there – one of the two available each rotation in the capital.

The other London – and London only – seat is in banking litigation, and it's a "*brilliant*" option by all accounts. Following the recent passing of the much-loved group head and London managing partner Heather Leeson ("*an excellent tutor*"), the firm's head of dispute resolution has stepped in to fill the breach. Martineau has every intention of staying the course in the capital and, when we rang, was looking for a permanent replacement. With the office a stone's throw from St Paul's Cathedral, free accommodation in a company flat (shared with the property trainee) and "*a lot of files to run with,*" what's not to love? Clients include stalwart Lloyds and the trainee will find themselves fully occupied, often "*going to court and filing submissions.*" In Birmingham, the dispute resolution group has "*a great team dynamic.*" Trainees report being "*really busy,*" regardless of how busy the group as a whole is. One source recalled that their schedule involved "*forever going to court to file documents, drafting instructions for counsel and going to conferences with counsel.*" Martineau also has dedicated construction and property disputes teams.

Grave concerns

Over in the commercial department is the energy, projects and commerce (EPC) team. Trainees are "*encouraged to get involved in all aspects of the sector*" and are given "*files to run under supervision.*" Work typically involves "*dealing with commercial contracts for businesses or niche contracts for energy providers*" on matters like "*energy trading across jurisdictions*" and "*franchise agreements.*" Other commercial subgroups include employment, construction and IP – each of which do a great deal of work for education clients.

The fifth department is private capital, which is a "*relaxed and approachable*" group that houses family; tax planning and charities; and probate and trust teams. Trainees in a family seat will focus primarily on contentious matters and handle "*a lot of administrative tasks to get you used to the clients and cases.*" Here, divorce cases tend to be financial in nature, rather than dealing with child custody, and as such trainees help to research and produce financial statements. The tax and planning group handles "*everything to do with the dead and the dying*" and keeps trainees busy with "*quite a bit of research around things such as business tax relief and agricultural tax relief related to landed estates.*"

The view from the top

With such a variety of groups and seats, you'd be forgiven for thinking there were plenty of NQ spaces to go around. The sad truth, however, is that only five out of ten qualifiers were made offers in 2010 (they all accepted). You might put that down to the state of the economy and the Birmingham legal market, but some trainees put it down to Martineau. In short, they questioned the firm's practice of bringing in partners while not investing in the lower ranks. "*We have a top-heavy leverage structure, and there is a real lack of growth at the bottom,*" one explained. What's more, sources complain the new partners "*don't always bring work with them, and some have been here for 18 months and haven't brought in any yet,*" meaning "*people are hanging on to the good bits of work*" and even "*partners are doing fee-earning work that they should hand down.*" What this means ultimately is that there is less (and less good-quality) work for trainees and NQs. What does Bill Barker say to all of this? "*I'm not surprised to hear trainees say that. It will take time for partners' clients to come with them, but once that happens, we'll grow the associate and assistant ranks.*" Asked about the partners who've allegedly gone a year and a half without bringing in any new work, Barker replied: "*You've always got a combination of finders, minders and grinders, and as managing partner it's my job to recognise partners' different skills.*"

To Martineau's credit, trainees say the firm handled the qualification process well. "*They advertised quite a long time in advance – about four months ahead of time,*" one said, while another added: "*It's purely down to finances across the board.*" Barker is regretful that offers could not be made to all, telling us: "*I am very much a managing partner who wants to recruit all of our trainees every year. I am loath to let anyone leave.*"

Pods, pakoras and play time

Martineau is a friendly firm with a good work-life balance in almost all departments. "*The latest I've ever stayed was 7.50pm*" and "*I like to leave at 5.30pm*" were common refrains. The whole 'nice' vibe is heightened by the open-plan layout of the office, where people sit in four-person 'pods'. "*You get to see all the other trainees walking past and have a chat if you want.*" And if you want to chat with the managing partner or senior partner, you can do so at one of the regular meetings they both have with trainees and solicitors. "*They want to know how we're doing, what's on our minds and how we think things can be improved,*" a source explained. "*They do a really good job of reaching out to us.*"

On Fridays, "*there's usually an e-mail sent out by the social group.*" It's generally an invite to Asha's, a well-loved curry house with a bar serving half-price drinks from 5pm to 7pm. Expect to see trainees and solicitors from other firms there, too. Events like "*bowling or trips to comedy clubs are organised every few months*" and individual teams will often plan their own events. Christmas, for instance, was celebrated in each department with a meal or party. Sporty folk will be pleased to hear that the firm has football and netball teams that play in trainee and general leagues.

And finally...

Martineau is a welcoming firm with good clients, though it may take another year or two for its current strategy to bear fruit. There may be a salary increase coming for trainees. *"I'm looking to see if we can get more competitive on that front,"* said Bill Barker.

Maxwell Winward LLP

The facts

Location: London

Number of UK partners/solicitors: 22/18

Total number of trainees: 5

Seats: 4x6 months or 3x6 + 2x3 months

Alternative seats: None

On chambersstudent.co.uk
- How to get into Maxwell Winward
- The King's Cross regeneration project
- An idiot's guide to wind farms

Real estate-heavy Maxwell Batley and construction expert Winward Fearon tied the knot in 2007. They even took up residence in a building that's *"shaped like a wedding cake!"*

Firm foundation

Despite the battering taken by the property sector during the recession, real estate is still the firm's biggest department. Partners have joined the department from bigger firms LG and Pinsent Masons, while another joined the construction department from national firm Addleshaw Goddard. Maxwell Winward's strategy is to keep building its brand name and service offering, and to price its services more competitively than bigger players.

Chambers UK acknowledges the firm's impressive credentials in mid-market property and construction. Its talents span the development chain – developers, architects, investors, consultants, contractors and subcontractors all send business its way. The bulk of its non-contentious construction work is on the owner/employer side (for big institutional developers such as Hermes) and MW carries out contentious work for both contractors and purchasers. The economic downturn led to "*plenty of contentious work,*" said a trainee, explaining that this has helped the firm get through the transactional slump. "*Many contractors ran out of money and there's been a lot of unfinished work.*"

The change of government has added an extra element of uncertainty in the construction and property sectors, particularly in relation to the public sector. Public spending cuts will naturally have an impact going forwards, but there are other areas where there's good news: take renewable energy, biomass and new technologies, for example. All these things will probably receive extra investment. The firm has already acted for Bilfinger Berger, which bid in a joint venture with a Danish construction company to build the world's first 1 GW offshore wind farm in the Thames Estuary. The project could supply enough power for around three-quarters of a million homes.

Another high-profile project is the regeneration of the King's Cross railway lands in the London boroughs of Camden and Islington. It's one of the largest transformation projects in Europe, and the firm's involvement in such a grand scheme is a major feather in its cap. It has played a key role advising the main player – Argent King's Cross Limited Partnership – and you can read more about it all on our website.

Another London project is the refurbishment and further development of Tottenham Hale Retail Park, which the commercial property team has had a hand in. This group mainly advises blue-chip property companies plus domestic and overseas investment companies and pension funds on the management of their retail, industrial and office asset around the UK. Clients include The BT Pensions Scheme, Sun Life of Canada and The British Land Company.

Trainee terrain

So how does a humble trainee fit into major, long-running schemes? The answer is, of course, that at first they can

Chambers UK rankings

Construction	Real Estate

only make a small contribution. Trainee seats are available in four areas: construction, property, dispute resolution/commercial litigation and corporate/projects (CoPro). Trainees generally spend six months in each but are at liberty to revisit their preferred area instead of trying a fourth. There is also a chance to take two three-month seats. By the end of it all they know just how they fit in and they feel they're *"treated as an associate."*

In dispute resolution, *"the front line of the department is property litigation."* It makes up about half the unit's activities and includes plenty of landlord and tenant matters, including residential leasehold enfranchisement. Other cases rest on general commercial contracts, bankruptcy and even employment. Typical tasks include drafting instructions to counsel and a fair amount of research. Trainees regularly attend the Royal Courts of Justice and *"get to know the High Court quite well,"* albeit that their responsibilities don't tend to involve advocacy. Back in the office, *"people are constantly bouncing ideas off each other"* and the team is *"always busy on a number of matters."* The working day can stretch to 7.30pm.

Real estate is *"similar to dispute resolution"* in that trainees have good access to clients and work on some of their own files. Landlord and tenant issues are just as common, and when we spoke with trainees in spring 2010, development work from private investors was starting to pick up again. They also talked about acquisitions, sales and big pension funds, drafting deal documentation and negotiations.

Cranes on the brain

Law students often don't realise that they already know tons about construction law, which is essentially contract law and tort. When the parties to a building contract fall into dispute, adjudication is normally the way forward. *"The contractor could be behind schedule, or the architect's plans may not have been followed correctly,"* explained a trainee; *"various matters could lead to a dispute."* Whatever the case, adjudication requires a lot of early-stage work and is fast-paced (unlike litigation which can take years). *"You've got to prepare for it like you would for court,"* so that means *"the obligatory document bundling, collating and organising,"* along with research and proof-reading. Time is spent working up pleadings and witness statements, *"and the easiest way is to hop on the train and spend time chatting with clients."* They are *"keen to meet with lawyers because by the time they get to us they're usually in a pretty sticky situation."* This can lead to *"a mad rush to get things done, and a call for trainees."* Be aware that the disclosure part of the process involves *"digging through thousands of files."* While real estate work is largely domestic, the Middle East is an increasingly busy market for the construction team and we heard whispers about future possibilities for trainees to spend time there *"depending on client needs."* The volume of work in construction is up and down, bringing some *"weekends and late nights."* Otherwise it's a 9am-6.30pm seat.

In the CoPro seat, trainees learn that the *"wide-ranging commercial/corporate team"* covers M&A and general commercial advice, including company formations, advice on group structures and company law. One key area of activity is large hotel operators. There's a projects unit as well, which *"works on renewables and gas pipelines."* The seat offers good client contact but is *"definitely not your typical banking and corporate finance."*

Social landscape

Networking with clients adds an interesting dimension. Whether it's *"golf or dinner"* or *"simply getting to know clients,"* trainees take part. They're expected to attend the firm's big events *"to help out and chat with guests."* Back in the office, *"everyone takes an interest in trainees"* and *"there's always someone there to ask if you're feeling swamped."* Despite the support, *"people who aren't prepared to pick up the phone and talk to clients"* won't fit the bill. *"It's not a back office sort of job. You have to be client-facing."* In 2010, regrettably only one of the three qualifying trainees was able to take up a position with the firm.

When it's time to relax, the social committee recognises its cue. On one occasion everyone headed out for a night of pool; they've also sung karaoke, ice-skated and paintballed. That 'wedding cake' office building just off Ludgate Hill by St Paul's Cathedral is *"very nice... lovely."* On the inside, workspaces are separated by *"smart glass panels."* On the outside there are terraces. Favourite local pubs include the nearby White Swan and Hoop & Grapes: *"It all depends on who sends the first e-mail!"*

And finally...

Trainees see themselves as having *"a strong, firm character," "the confidence and the ability to smile and stay calm"* and a willingness *"to muck in when a work call goes round at 6pm on Friday."*

Mayer Brown International LLP

The facts

Location: London

Number of UK partners/solicitors: 100/160

Total number of trainees: 52

Seats: 4x6 months

Alternative seats: Overseas seats, secondments

Extras: Pro bono – LawWorks, Islington Law Centre, RCJ Advice Bureau and more; language training

On chambersstudent.co.uk
- How to get into Mayer Brown
- The firm's success in Asia
- A few of the firm's headline cases and deals

International giant Mayer Brown seeks students with an appetite for the hardcore City experience, particularly in its corporate and finance divisions.

The wars of the Roweses

Mayer Brown's story in London is a long one, but it's crucial to understanding what the firm is today. So... back in the day there was a City mid-sizer called Rowe & Maw. It was well respected but had something of a staid and conservative reputation, to the extent that some people nicknamed it Slow & Bore. Within this firm, however, was a clutch of young partners with big ambitions, and the most ambitious of the lot was a chap named Paul Maher.

In 2002, Rowe & Maw entered into a merger with Chicago's Mayer Brown, which already had a bunch of sophisticated finance lawyers in London. The tie-up came as a surprise to many but it boosted the Brits' prospects significantly, giving them access to new international clients. The London operation now acts for many global brands including the likes of Dow Chemical, EMI, Fujitsu, Independent News & Media, Morgan Stanley, Nando's, Sega, Thomson Reuters, Unilever and the 'Big Four' accounting firms. Paul Maher won himself a place on the firm's global management board, giving London plenty of clout within the worldwide network.

Another merger in 2008 with Asian firm Johnson Stokes & Master increased Mayer Brown's reach even further, and anyone considering applying to the firm should be aware that "*world domination*" is most definitely a goal. "*It wants to regard the magic circle as its peers,*" and with that in mind has been on a mission to strengthen its corporate and finance departments in particular, recently hiring partners from Allen & Overy and Clifford Chance. A seat in either corporate, finance or real estate is compulsory for trainees.

We said that the firm's history was vital in understanding where it is now: here's why. "*There are people who have come here for the Mayer Brown experience, and there are ex-Rowe & Maw people who have been here 30 years.*" It's fair to say that we detected evidence of some residual differences between the two groups. It also means that the training contract experience can vary wildly depending on which departments you end up working in. "*They all have a different ethos, even in terms of dress code and the atmosphere in the hallways.*" Bear that in mind when reading the rest of this feature.

Secondment chances

Let's start with the banking and finance department. We said it wanted to compete with the magic circle – does it? Answer: not yet, but the firm will be encouraged that it rose in the *Chambers UK* rankings this year. Football fans will be aware of Portsmouth FC's woes: the firm advised Al Fahim Asia Associates in its acquisition – and subsequent disposal of 90% – of the ailing club. It also acted for Nevsun Resources in its $235m project financing for the operation and construction of a gold, silver, zinc and copper mine in Eritrea. "*The most American part of the firm,*" this is a "*very, very driven department*" with "*pulverising*" hours much of the time. "*I found it awful; the other trainee there at the same time as me absolutely loved it,*" said one source, summing up the love-or-hate nature of the lifestyle.

Chambers UK rankings

Banking & Finance	Investment Funds
Banking Litigation	Media & Entertainment
Capital Markets	Outsourcing
Competition/European Law	Pensions
Construction	Pensions Litigation
Dispute Resolution	Professional Negligence
Employment	Real Estate
Energy & Natural Resources	Real Estate Finance
Environment	Real Estate Litigation
Information Technology	Restructuring/Insolvency
Insurance	Tax
Intellectual Property	Telecommunications

Corporate is "*slightly more relaxed*" than finance. "*It's the friendliest department I have sat in,*" testified one source. "*The junior partners are really quite approachable, and the associates are fairly young and easygoing.*" Nevertheless, it shares the same driven nature and the hours can be equally long. "*My average hours are 9.30am to 10pm,*" said one source with an especially busy workload. "*Then this week is going to be horrific: 1am or 2am finishes, plus I know I will lose this weekend.*" Corporate is a "*generalist*" department, so there are no subgroups for M&A, private equity, capital markets and so on. Trainees receive a broad, rather than a specialist training here. A "*pod system*" sees every trainee allocated to a defined group of associates and partners, "*but you can pick up work from anyone else as well.*" In both corporate and finance, trainees noted that the level of work on offer can be mixed. One source said: "*I had a supervisor who was very into teaching me and getting me drafting. Then there are people who see you as there to do the grunt work.*"

At least one secondment, either to a foreign office or a client, is also now compulsory. Client secondments are numerous, with placements at all sorts of interesting organisations including financial institutions, a pharma company, a news agency and more. Some are more glamorous than others so, for example, the firm occasionally has trouble persuading people to go off to work in Slough for six months. That said, our sources were uniformly positive about time spent on secondment, praising the higher level of responsibility on offer and the level of commercial awareness that can be gained. "*You learn about how businesses actually work. It's all very well reading the FT, but it doesn't give you that level of insight.*" Hong Kong and São Paulo were the only overseas seats available at the time of our calls, but New York and Brussels placements are likely to be reinstated and others may follow.

Putting the kart before the hours

Contentious seat options include commercial dispute resolution (CDR); construction litigation; property litigation; and insurance and reinsurance. CDR is the largest of these departments, and it came in for a good deal of criticism from trainees last year. If corporate and finance are American in tone, this department is "*very English,*" and previously we'd heard about how some "*austere*" partners left some trainees feeling uncomfortable at times. The good news is that things have improved. "*Changing the culture goes against the grain for them, but they were really hurt by the Chambers write-up and are doing a big PR assault on the trainees,*" including drinks nights and go-karting. Furthermore, work-wise the department is on a roll: "*The quality of instructions is improving all the time. It used to be work passed on by the corporate clients; now we're getting lots of Madoff stuff and instructions from the big accountancy firms. It's very much the plan to go for big-ticket litigation.*" However, it must be said that the kind of tasks on offer for trainees are still "*quite menial*" for the most part: "*Doc review, eight hours a day for four months,*" one typical source groaned. An attitude that trainees are for grunt work still seems to prevail in corners of the firm, and some sources highlighted a lack of paralegals as an issue. "*Litigation is naturally document-heavy, and partners and associates are never going to bundle. There's an attitude that a trainee is cheaper than a paralegal. You don't have to pay trainees overtime.*"

The smaller litigation teams gain better reviews. "*I really enjoyed it,*" one source said of construction litigation. "*On my third day I went to a big meeting with eight builders.*" Tasks can be as low-level as in CDR but there is a way to help yourself. "*Establish a working relationship with your supervisor, be prepared to do the menial tasks with a good attitude, ask questions and create a rapport*" and better work will follow. Hopefully, now that an olive branch has been sped round the go-kart track, this advice can also be taken on board by trainees entering the CDR group. The small insurance department is wildly popular among trainees. "*There is a big focus on your training. I was always doing the first draft of everything: I came on massively in that seat,*" raved one contact.

It's good to talk

The most recent chapter in the Mayer Brown story is, of course, entitled 'Recession'. Trainees admit the main departments were "*in the doldrums*" for a time, and the London office's turnover dropped 16% to £93.8m in 2009/10. Politics at the top of the firm also shook things up. Paul Maher, left out of the new global management board, departed to set up the London office of US firm Greenberg Traurig. He was an "*inspirational*" figure to some of our sources though not universally popular across the firm.

All this made for uncertain times at Mayer Brown, and in uncertain times clear communication is key. Unfortunately, it hasn't always been forthcoming. Sources were particularly miffed about the way a salary freeze for second-years was handled. "*We were asking for six months beforehand if it was going to affect us. They kept on saying it hadn't been decided yet and the announcement finally came a week and a half before we were due to get the pay raise.*" Procedures for seat allocation and qualification were also described as "*opaque*." One trainee summed it up thus: "*In the absence of being told something, speculation runs riot. The firm hasn't quite figured out that it's better to say something even if it's negative.*" More good news, though! "*We are much more positive now than we were 12 months ago,*" say trainees. "*We have a new training principal and there's a much higher level of interaction than before.*" Sources were pleased that a new, fairer appraisal system involving an element of self-assessment has been brought in. It also takes into account the quality of non-billable work trainees have undertaken – Mayer Brown is keen to get its people involved in pro bono, marketing and grad recruitment activities, all of which will undoubtedly help raise their status within the firm.

A recent move into "*extremely fancy*" premises in Bishopsgate has also helped improve the mood. "*There are at least two departments on every floor so we're becoming more homogenous. Everybody sees each other now.*" The offices have an "*open and airy*" feel and there are "*glass doors everywhere so you can see what people are up to.*" Trainees also liked the all-hours canteen, where they meet for lunch, and the views of East London. "*You can see the Millennium Dome from our window,*" said one.

On the road

Trainees have a "*competitive*" streak, but it's a healthy one and there's no backstabbing. Future intakes all study the LPC at Kaplan in London, "*so we are all really good friends before joining.*" Proving this point, some trainees were planning a group getaway to Seville at the time of our calls. The social life "*mainly centres around drinking.*" The local pub used to be the Light Bar "*but now it's full of trendy Shoreditch types and the music's really loud,*" so trainees have branched out. Departmental outings are fairly regular and trainees also participate in client events. A legal five-a-side football tournament was keenly contested by teams from the firm.

Our contacts noticed how "*the calibre of the trainee intake is increasing year on year.*" We've said in the past that MB isn't snobby about where its recruits studied, and as usual we spoke to trainees who had attended universities outside the Russell Group. However, sources say the firm is "*increasingly focused on getting people from Oxbridge and the top redbricks. It wants to build up Mayer Brown as a prestige brand at the top universities, although it won't discriminate against those who didn't go there.*"

We think Mayer Brown London is an ultra-ambitious place that will appeal to gutsy trainees. We spoke to many trainees who were unafraid to criticise the firm and yet were still thankful they'd made the choice to train here. "*Put it like this, I would never have joined Rowe & Maw but I'm happy to be at Mayer Brown,*" said one. "*We all joined a firm that wanted to go places,*" said another. This is a firm that's going places. The journey may be a bumpy one at times but the type of person who is attracted to Mayer Brown probably feels the journey is as important as the destination. If you're that type, jump on board. If you're not, get out of the road.

And finally...

Mayer Brown is smaller than the City giants but keen to compete with them. Some 15 of its 28 qualifiers were retained in 2010.

McDermott Will & Emery UK LLP

The facts

Location: London

Number of UK partners/solicitors: 22/28

Total number of trainees: 5

Seats: 4x6 months

Alternative seats: None

On chambersstudent.co.uk
- How to get into McDermott
- We talk to training partner Prajakt Samant
- McDermott stateside

Change has been the name of the game at Chicago-born McDermott Will & Emery, which has around 1,000 lawyers across 16 offices worldwide.

Do what you do best

The worldwide recession prompted self-examination and a full-scale strategic review at McDermott. In 2009, the year it celebrated its 75th birthday, its top brass changed, globally and in London, with two co-chairmen replacing the outgoing head honcho Harvey Freishtat, and ex-Lovells corporate legend Hugh Nineham becoming London head. Stateside, the firm laid off around 200 lawyers and staff, restructured or rebranded practice groups, and overhauled associate compensation and training. For more background, go online and read what new co-chairman Peter Sacripanti told our US sister publication *Chambers Associate* about the re-focusing of the business.

Founded in 1998, the London office is one of McDermott's six European branches and it employs around 60 lawyers and tax professionals. In January 2010, Nineham assumed the additional role of head of Europe and joined a new ten-person executive committee alongside US colleagues. A new private client group was set up in London, reflecting one of McDermott's core strengths in the USA. The hire of a partner from Denton Wilde Sapte added to the energy team, while a new head of European M&A joined from White & Case as part of the drive to boost the corporate practice. In 2011, McDermott will relocate to the City's tallest skyscraper, the brand new Heron Tower on Bishopsgate.

Meanwhile, partner departures in London caused the structured finance, competition and international arbitration groups to disappear. "*The London office is changing, re-focusing,*" a trainee explained. "*We can't be everything to everybody.*" Now the focus is on corporate, energy, employment, intellectual property and international private client and tax – "*what we do best.*" Firmwide, the four new core business groups are transactions; controversies; tax; and regulatory and government affairs. "*We've restructured the entire firm. We're a more focused office, more focused on clients, more aligned to the US.*"

Getting personal

Seat allocation is a fairly informal affair and, because of the small trainee group, "*you know you'll get your preferred seat.*" If there's a clash and another person wants to do the same seat, "*we work it out.*" Some groups like corporate, IP and employment can take on two trainees at a time. Whatever the seat, you'll usually share a room with a senior associate.

The new private client department is "*becoming one of the most popular seats.*" *Chambers USA* ranks McDermott in the top tier for wealth management in the States, and the hire of heavyweight lawyers in London suggests there's every chance it will become a force to be reckoned with here. Trainees get the chance to become "*a jack of all trades: I've drafted a will, done immigration and employment work, and there's the possibility of some contentious work too.*" Far from being out on a limb among the commercial teams, "*they're looking for this group to be a feeder for other departments;*" for example if a mega-rich client buys an aircraft, there may be an opportunity to provide advice on leasing.

The "*fast-paced*" corporate department handles predominantly mid-market M&A, often helping overseas businesses expand in the UK. By leveraging existing strengths

Chambers UK rankings

Employment	Life Sciences
Intellectual Property	Projects

in tax and IP, London lawyers help their US colleagues to build relationships with American businesses in Europe. McDermott has over 300 corporate lawyers worldwide advising clients ranging in size from start-ups to Fortune 500 and FTSE 100 companies, plus private equity firms. Energy and healthcare are key areas of focus and clients include Honeywell, Japanese oil company Nippon and accountants Baker Tilly. A small insolvency team operates within the corporate group. Here, trainee tasks include drafting letters and e-mails, preparing confidentiality agreements and making company searches. There is also "*decent*" direct client and partner contact. Trainees noticed "*quite a lot of overlap*" with the expanding energy group, where the work includes renewables matters. Recently lawyers advised a Goldman Sachs subsidiary on its acquisition of a major energy commodities trading business from US power giant Constellation Energy.

Brace yourself

A trainee who'd completed an energy seat told us: "*I immediately got involved on big projects, checking reports that came in, looking at due diligence questionnaires and writing memos and updates for clients.*" Meanwhile, the IP team recently represented ABSOLUT vodka in a dispute with the former Virgin Radio, and helped techy wizards Visto win $267.5m in damages from BlackBerry makers Research In Motion following a global patent dispute.

Tax is "*a research-heavy seat.*" Clients might, for example, ask whether they are liable for capital gains tax in a particular situation and it would be up to the trainee to check that the firm's advice is up to date. They quickly learn that "*HMRC tends to change the law regularly.*" Other tasks might include setting up an overseas company for a client to make it as tax efficient as possible.

Employment is a "*fantastic*" team: "*friendly, approachable, supportive*" and offering a "*good mix*" of contentious and non-contentious work. The department is "*very family-oriented. Everyone's at the same life stage and prefers to start early and leave early.*" McDermott advises corporate clients – and "*rarely individuals*" – on everything from team poaching to discrimination. Dresdner Kleinwort sought help during its sale to Commerzbank and on the subsequent integration of the two businesses. The team also defended F&C Asset Management in a record £19m discrimination claim brought by its former head of legal Gillian Switalski. You can expect plenty of drafting and research in this seat, although if a case reaches the High Court, brace yourself for high-pressure meetings with other lawyers and plenty of document bundling. Clients include Nike, UEFA, Formula One, BAE and Caterpillar.

Keeping up with the Californians

Working with US colleagues means "*you can't leave as early as normal, especially when it's West Coast colleagues.*" Particularly in the corporate seat, if a transaction is hot the hours can be "*horrific – it could be all night.*" On the flip side, "*if you have nothing to do you can leave at 6pm and go to the gym.*" Some trainees sounded super-busy when we called to arrange interviews, one having to reschedule twice because of work pressures. "*Because we're such a small trainee group,*" said one interviewee, "*we've even had to cancel holidays*" and the work intensity "*can make it difficult on that trainee who hasn't had a holiday for five or six months.*" In the view of some, recruiting temp paralegals would help. Then again, as one of only a few trainees, "*you get to do difficult work early*" and people are usually more than willing to help each other out. "*What goes around comes around!*"

"*Everyone gets to know you very quickly. When you start they send out your photo and a brief bio*" to the rest of the firm. Trainees have a buddy when they start, and an associate mentor from a different department in each seat. Our sources repeatedly praised the lack of hierarchy and said: "*You can interact with anyone. I've never felt nervous going into a partner's office.*"

The culture is friendly, if seriously hard-working. There's a newly appointed social committee and trainees have a budget for occasional meals or drinks. Favourite watering holes include posh Bond's and Pacific Oriental. Recent socials have included cocktail-making at Vinopolis and Middle Eastern dining with belly-dancing. Last year's Christmas party was informal and held in a boardroom; trainees also went to a gastropub for extra festive cheer, although "*it was a difficult time as we were all working until about 10pm.*" Free breakfasts each Friday are a nice perk, and there's subsidised membership of Bannatyne's gym.

And finally...

No longer drifting, McDermott London has a clear plan. Four out of five 2010 qualifiers stayed with the firm, joining the corporate, private client, IP and energy groups.

McGrigors LLP

The facts

Location: London, Manchester, Belfast, Scotland

Number of UK partners/solicitors: 100/281

Total number of trainees: 21 (in England)

Seats: 4x6 months

Alternative seats: Scotland, Falklands, secondments

On chambersstudent.co.uk
• How to get into McGrigors
• Secondment opportunities
• Alternative Business Structures in Scotland

This national firm with Scottish roots is currently undergoing a growth spurt.

Big Four meets Big Four

McGrigors is one of the Big Four Scottish law firms, and its recent history is intertwined with a member of a different Big Four. After the collapse of Texan energy giant Enron following years of poor practice by it and its auditor Arthur Andersen, there was a shift in attitudes towards the wisdom of multidisciplinary practices (MDPs), which effectively linked up all kinds of services such as legal and auditing. KPMG (one of the worldwide accountancy majors) had been fully into the idea of the MDP but then decided to sever its relationship with its legal arm, KLegal. KLegal in London was set adrift and McGrigors saw a perfect opportunity to set up a base in the capital. In 2002, the firm merged with KLegal and it seems to have worked out well. McGrigors is still able to count on KPMG for client referrals, some of them blue-chips, and the London lawyers know that they can rely on their Scots siblings' strong reputation and client connections. While the recession may have put a stop to regular London trainee secondments to KPMG, McGrigors continues to "*work quite closely with them*" and "*gets a lot of referrals in.*"

The firm extended its English operations in 2007 by opening an office in Manchester. In 2009 it scooped up West End firm Reid Minty, which specialised in commercial litigation and real estate. That year it also absorbed Belfast big-hitter L'Estrange & Brett, which now makes McGrigors one of the biggest law firms in Northern Ireland. With other offices in Edinburgh (its home), Glasgow and Aberdeen, this is presently the only firm to operate across all three UK jurisdictions in any significant manner. In addition, it has an office in the Falkland Islands and an associated office in Baku, Azerbaijan.

Trainees predict further "*organic growth,*" as well as consolidation in the Manchester and Belfast offices. All of our interviewees agreed that "*McGrigors will be a heavyweight in Manchester as well,*" pointing to the fact that it has grown from a one-man office to nearly 30 people already. David Moss, the former international head of construction and engineering at Hammonds, quit his firm and took his team with him to McGrigors' Manchester office. There is one permanent trainee seat here and one that crops up on a rolling basis.

McMagic

While top-ranked by *Chambers UK* in just about every practice area in Scotland, McGrigors' London office has a narrower range of hot practice areas. It is strong in the fields of projects and energy, real estate and construction; however, tax litigation (a KLegal legacy) is its standout practice. The firm's clients are impressive to say the least: Bank of Ireland, Bank of Scotland, Barclays, BP, Celtic FC, The Co-operative Bank, Deloitte, Deutsche Bank, HBOS, HSBC, Lloyds TSB, the MoD, RBS, Royal Mail, Taylor Wimpey, Thresher Group, Tote Bookmakers, the University of Aberdeen and West Coast Capital. Enough said. As the recession saw companies narrow their legal panels, McGrigors was among the select few kept on by heavyweights such as ASDA and BAA.

McGrigors' trainees may take seats in dispute resolution; commercial litigation; tax litigation; employment and pensions; construction; corporate; energy and infrastructure;

Chambers UK rankings

Administrative & Public Law	Intellectual Property
Banking & Finance	Licensing
Charities	Local Government
Construction	Parliamentary & Public Affairs
Corporate/M&A	Pensions
Dispute Resolution	Planning
Employee Share Schemes	Projects
Employment	Real Estate
Energy & Natural Resources	Real Estate Litigation
Environment	Retail
Health & Safety	Shipping
Information Technology	Tax

banking; and IP. Trainees submit their three preferences and provide a couple of sentences on why they want them. Energy, employment and litigation tend to be extremely popular, so it's "*very important*" you make your reasons for wanting to visit those departments extra-convincing. Trainees usually get at least two of their preferred choices. Many trainees also take a seat in another office, either elsewhere in the UK or in the Falkland Islands. Due to the recession, some client secondments were no longer available this year; nevertheless, a small number of them are still on offer.

The prestigious tax litigation team deals with many things including tax credit reclaims from HMRC, compound interest claims and fraud investigations. It also helps manage 100 of the UK's largest pension funds. McGrigors recently bolstered the team by hiring three non-lawyer tax investigation specialists from top-ten accountancy firm Tenon Group. Tax lit trainees work on big High Court claims, prepare cases for tribunals, attend hearings and get stuck into their share of document bundling. Some of the work is in the evolving field of group litigation, which we understand can involve as many as 120 claimants. The tax client base is "*enormously international*" and includes some large beer companies. Hopefully the lawyers don't find themselves thinking about work every time they've a pint in their hands… Working on HMRC cases is interesting and trainees learn to use a different set of skills from other types of litigation and "*have to be gentle and persuasive.*" Tax lit is a good seat to do later on: the hard work, long hours and complex cases are best suited to those with more experience. The department has a rather hierarchical structure; there isn't a great deal of direct client contact and trainees are "*heavily supervised.*" But the slog is worth it as the team is truly at "*the cutting edge of the law.*"

Right ideas, right place, right time

In timely fashion, McGrigors has launched a business crime and commercial fraud practice with a double-partner hire from the Khan Partnership. There has been a rise in white-collar crime cases and this type of work has been identified as a core growth area for McGrigors. The team advises corporate clients on corruption issues and pre-emptive measures to avoid civil and commercial fraud. For trainees, the level of responsibility is "*incredible*" (their work includes witness statements and advocacy in front of High Court masters) and they say they are "*extremely well supervised.*" Trainees see trials from start to finish, run small-scale cases and have plenty of client contact.

In the corporate team, trainees can look forward to long hours and quite a bit of drafting. M&A deals have been scarcer of late but the team still does a decent amount of AIM listings. The energy and infrastructure department, which has some overlap with corporate and banking, is also doing well and is likely to expand. It deals with oil and gas matters, power stations, wind farms, biofuels and renewable and nuclear energy projects. Deals are big and clients are "*pretty enormous*" – National Grid is just one. British company Rockhopper is presently prospecting for oil in the Falklands and is advised by McGrigors, which is the only UK law firm with a presence in the Islands. While it is not yet certain whether the resources are viable for commercial exploitation, it's worth keeping an eye on how this develops, as it may prove an extremely lucrative source of work for McGrigors.

The employment team's remit includes defending unfair dismissal claims and recently a number of redundancy claims. Trainees are "*able to build a real rapport with the clients,*" which range "*from large financial institutions down to individuals.*" Business immigration issues crop up, often with regard to US citizens. The recent government decisions have left everyone "*wondering what's going to happen*" to the flow of immigration work, but it's likely that clients will still need guidance, at least in the short term.

The commercial litigators recently celebrated a victory on behalf of steel firm Cleveland Bridge UK in a dispute regarding Wembley Stadium, securing it £3m in damages from its Clifford Chance-advised opposition. Litigation trainee tasks include helping with witness statements, making court bundles and completing court forms. There are also some smaller cases kicking about on which they can take even more responsibility.

The real estate seat involves work for O2, and the team recently advised Jimmy Choo on relocating its headquarters from Chelsea to Kensington. Trainees frequently manage their own small files and are *"left to get on with things,"* which makes this a popular seat. Tasks include negotiations, sales, drafting leases and licences, and dealing with the Land Registry. Construction is another department that offers a lot of responsibility. Clients include Morrisons and the architects of the Olympic Aquatics Centre. The team focuses on both procurement and dispute resolution, and work may involve property litigation, insolvency and debt disputes. Trainees regularly talk to clients and barristers, frequently working on things like witness statements and the negotiation of warranties. The Scottish offices also offer a seat in English real estate.

Out of kilter?

The working hours can sometimes be tough, with litigation and corporate the usual guilty parties. Especially in tax litigation, you should be prepared to *"work exceptionally hard and very long hours"* and know that *"people won't ask how busy you are before they give you work."* Leaving at 8pm is almost an everyday occurrence here, and even later nights, perhaps until 3am, are not at all uncommon. On the plus side, weekends in tax lit are always work-free, and after a certain time trainees get a free dinner, a taxi home and *"a pat on the back."* In non-London offices and in other departments such as employment, the hours are *"pretty reasonable."*

Through mergers and rebranding, McGrigors is becoming *"less and less a Scottish firm,"* but in spite of this in London it is still sometimes perceived as a Highland intruder. Admittedly, *"look at the name"* – it is *"a very Scottish-sounding firm."* This is a sore point for some, seeing as the firm now spans the length and breadth of the country, both in terms of office locations and clients. To complicate matters, the proposed introduction of alternative business structures (ABSs) has been causing a huge divide between Scotland's Big Four law firms and its high-street firms. The Big Four, which support ABSs, are threatening to leave Scotland – not in a literal sense, but to have their lawyers regulated by the English SRA. Do keep an eye on this developing story – there's more detail on our website.

Trainees claimed they were *"not a serious bunch"* and *"are all really close."* McGrigors is *"definitely a social firm."* The London office is *"at the heart of things,"* 30 seconds away from St Paul's Cathedral and right next to the Old Bailey. *"It gives you a feeling of pride; you know you're working in a proper law firm."* Our sources had a *"love-hate relationship"* with the All Bar One downstairs: *"We go there literally all the time."* There are several partner-funded drinks nights and events to celebrate St George's Day, St Patrick's Day and Halloween. An annual ceilidh is organised for Burns Night. For prospective trainees and vac scheme students, *"the social life is incredible; they treat you to all manner of wonders."* There are also rumours of a mysterious 'Ladies Day', which seems to be a fledgling client event of some description. The recession introduced *"an element of belt tightening,"* but then again we also heard that the Christmas party was an *"all-singing, all-dancing affair at an old gentlemen's club where we were treated to dinner and lots of champagne."* Football, netball, softball, baseball, rugby and cricket are on offer, and the hockey team plays against the KPMG offices in Amsterdam every year.

Trainees agreed that McGrigors has coped with the recession *"really well"* and that they were *"exceptional in their efforts to retain staff."* Cost-cutting measures *"were not taken lightly,"* but did ensure that there were *"hardly any"* redundancies and no trainee deferrals. Nationwide, 22 out of 36 trainees were given NQ positions this year, plus one more was awarded a six-month contract. In England, however, only six out of 18 qualifying trainees took up jobs with the firm (five in London, one in Manchester).

And finally...

Don't let the name fool you. McGrigors truly is a national firm.

Michelmores LLP

The facts

Location: Exeter, Sidmouth, London

Number of UK partners/solicitors: 45/113

Total number of trainees: 14

Seats: 4x6 months

Alternative seats: None

On chambersstudent.co.uk
- How to get into Michelmores
- We talk to training partner Tim Richards
- A few of the firm's headline cases and deals

Over the past five years Michelmores' headcount increased by 25% and its turnover shot up by 99%.

Monopoly moves

Since moving from its home next to the city's Cathedral to a state-of-the-art building on the outskirts of Exeter, and opening up in London's Piccadilly in 2005, Michelmores has experienced rapid growth. Even in the depths of the recession, turnover increased – up to £18.9m for 2008/09 – although at the time of going to press the figures for 2009/10 were unavailable. The grand plan has been to break into the list of the top 100 law firms and achieve a turnover of £50m within the next few years. As trainees acknowledge, there's no doubt that "*the firm has changed dramatically – it's much more commercially driven now.*" Michelmores appointed its first ever managing partner in 2009, introduced a two-year leadership programme for associates, and created the new position of client services director. "*There's a very positive attitude at the moment,*" our interviewees said. "*We're hitting our targets and bringing in new teams and new staff.*"

HM Prison Service, the Ministry of Justice, The Met Office and other national organisations instruct the firm, signifying that this is not merely a regional operation. Nor is the London office "*just a conduit for bumping work out to the South West – we genuinely undertake work up there and have teams that are flying. There are always people going up and down between the two offices to meet clients and bring work back.*" However, training partner Tim Richards maintains: "*We will always be a South West firm with a London office, as opposed to the other way round.*" Interviewees conceded that formalisation of the training contract and other systems was an inevitable consequence of growth, but said that "*beneath that commercial stamp the people are still the same.*"

Champignon pickings

The firm's tripartite division between commercial property, business, and private client matters leads to a good selection of seat options, and there's also the chance to spend six months in the London office, where the firm welcomed its first full-time trainee in 2008. "*Come in with an open mind – they don't like the word 'no' here,*" advised one interviewee, though another saw things quite differently, telling us: "*It helps if people come to the firm with an idea of the seats they want to do.*" Though the firm likes it if trainees spend time in each of the departments, "*nothing is set in stone.*" In any case, most of our sources had been able to take their first-choice seat.

With the largest commercial property department in the South West open to them, trainees have a feast of experiences. Clients include Blackpool Airport, Barratt Homes and Exeter University, which the firm recently advised on the £40m construction and operation of five new student halls and an international student centre. "*It was really exciting to go and see what progress had been made on the sites,*" said one trainee. Michelmores' ties to the university go deep – at one time the majority of trainees came from the campus, though they now hail from a wider range of institutions. The real estate group works alongside a number of other practices including planning, construction and property litigation, and there's also a team dedicated to public sector work, with a track record for representing over 50 local authorities plus central government departments and agencies.

Michelmores' excellent dispute resolution department recently advised one of the world's leading mushroom

Chambers UK rankings

Agriculture & Rural Affairs	Family/Matrimonial
Banking & Finance	Information Technology
Clinical Negligence	Planning
Construction	Private Client
Corporate/M&A	Real Estate
Dispute Resolution	Restructuring/Insolvency
Employment	

producers in a dispute with its energy broker and acted for a green services provider in a contract dispute concerning the provision of compostable waste recycling facilities. Smelling slightly rosier, the hire of Charles Metherell (who heads up an 'interventions' practice) from Bevan Brittan has proved a good move: Michelmores was then appointed to the SRA's panel of intervention agents. Intervention lawyers take control of law firms where there is a risk of dodgy dealings with client money. While there's no specified seat on the interventions team, trainees can get involved with the work and can also try out more specialist areas such as IP, professional and clinical negligence and insolvency.

Hound of the Michelmores

Headed by senior partner Will Michelmore, whose great-grandfather founded the firm in 1887, the top-tier private client department is the largest in the South West. It has the region's best-known landed families on its books – over 400 retain the firm – and also deals with more international and entrepreneurial clients. Increasingly, the team works alongside the corporate and commercial groups. Trainees "*do things beyond what you'd expect,*" but are confident that any mistakes will be picked up. "*If anything's wrong, it doesn't matter – you're still encouraged to go for it.*" Some partners are viewed as "*young and dynamic,*" while others are "*more traditional but with a great sense of humour.*" Very popular among trainees is Will Michelmore's trusty Labrador, Archie. "*I haven't been able to go walkies yet,*" one source said, "*but I always give him a good pat.*"

Court experience is par for the course in insolvency and clinical negligence seats. "*Once you've had enough experience watching others, you can do it yourself.*" We heard of one trainee who successfully defended a bankruptcy petition. "*It was great that the client could reopen the next day, and after having dealt with the client for a few months it was really satisfying on a personal level too.*" Trainees are let loose on clients early on. "*If* [seniors] *are going for drinks or meeting with clients, they're keen to take you,*" said one source. This is all a welcome change from a few years ago, when "*they expected you to give out canapés at client events, or show people where to park their cars.*" After trainees spoke up, such "*rubbish tasks*" have become a thing of the past. Other seats on offer include contentious probate; projects and procurement; corporate; family; employment; and commercial.

Those keen to swap Devon's rolling hills for London's dizzying tube station escalators can opt for a seat in the capital. "*It's brilliant,*" declared one source. "*Everyone is very supportive and encouraging. They push you as much as you want to be pushed... You don't always know what you'll be doing when you arrive in the morning.*" This can be to a trainee's advantage. "*I've been taken to lots of quite complicated meetings,*" and "*going up and down to the Royal Courts of Justice really helps you to get to know the City.*" Though Tim Richards confirmed that the recession has "*of course had an effect on the growth of the London practice,*" in the future "*it's high on the agenda to bring in international work.*"

Nobody's Inn

"*I know it sounds soppy but you do feel that the partners care about you as a person and about your development.*" After rolling our eyes, we asked why else Michelmores consistently breeds satisfied trainees. "*It's the little things that make the place more staff-focused,*" we learned, from the in-house gym, monthly hairdresser and nail technician, to the Michelmores bus link, dry-cleaning and car-washing service. "*Some of my closest friends are here,*" someone confessed. And of course, "*you look out to the estuary of the River Exe and the moorland commons – it's good to know that you'll be out there at the end of day.*" Our sources loved Exeter life and "*surfing and kayaking at the weekend,*" which starts promptly at half past five on a Friday.

Though the business park location doesn't foster after-work drinks, the social life "*is there to be organised*" and people "*are very inclusive, sending round random e-mails or posting plans on the intranet.*" Some lawyers enjoy running to the River Exe at lunchtime or cycling to the Nobody Inn for an evening meal. Firm-wide bashes take place quarterly and include a Christmas party ("*relatively tame considering the open bar*"), a quiz and treasure hunts. The firm also organises the Michelmores Cup, an annual corporate yacht race around Torbay.

And finally...

The last word goes to one trainee who pleaded: *"I hope you give it a good review because it's a pretty damned good place to work."* All in all, a happy bunch, and six out of nine qualifiers stayed with the firm in 2010.

Mills & Reeve LLP

The facts

Location: Birmingham, Cambridge, Norwich, London, Leeds, Manchester

Number of UK partners/solicitors: 92/350

Total number of trainees: 43

Seats: 6x4 months

Alternative seats: Occasional secondments

Extras: Pro Bono – Free Legal Advice Group

On chambersstudent.co.uk
- How to get into M&R
- Training contract applications: girls v boys
- M&R's charitable nature

As it continues its transitions from 'regional' to 'national' firm, top-50 player Mills & Reeve maintains a focus on healthcare and the public sector, while also expanding its commercial offering to the private sector.

Mills & Boom

Since first opening in Norwich in 1880, M&R has dominated the East Anglian market. A second office launched in Cambridge in 1987 and it has done well to attract a good amount of the region's hi-tech and life sciences business. M&R then broke out of its comfort zone and opened in Birmingham in 1998 and London in 2000. The latest advance of the M&R army led it to Leeds and Manchester in 2008, where it took on family law partners from Addleshaw Goddard. These newest offices currently have fewer than 20 staff members each, although "*whispers are going round that they are to recruit quite heavily in the coming months and years.*" Consider the fact that managing partner Guy Hinchley works out of the Birmingham office, and you have a clear shift towards a more nationally oriented strategy.

2008 saw the launch of a 'Strategic Plan to 2012', which focused on six core practice areas: higher education; health; private client; significant business; local authorities; and insurance. The firm's 'values and visions' statement – 'Infectious Ambition' – inspires trainees across the firm, although we suspect their attitudes are somewhat more down to earth than this cheesy slogan suggests. Having almost doubled its revenue in the past ten years, the firm maintains a clear and ardent desire to expand further. Attempts to open another office were thwarted in January 2010 when an idea to tie up with the 25-partner Oxford operation of London-based Manches went nowhere, but last June some very exciting news was announced. Along with South West-headquartered TLT Solicitors, M&R has been made an official referral partner by magic circle firm Freshfields. The City giant will pass on work that cannot be handled cheaply enough by its own lawyers.

M&R has seen solid financial results since the credit crunch and even posted a small increase in turnover for 2009/10. Besides this, M&R is ranked 72nd in the *Sunday Times*' '100 Best Companies to Work For' survey in 2010, the only top-50 law firm to make it onto the list. The firm's collegiality shines through in many situations, not least in the way Norwich lawyers responded to the downturn in business in 2008/09. "*Some teams proactively took the decision to work a four-day week, but it wasn't something which was imposed upon them,*" a senior source explained. Trainee retention stands at a good rate too, with 21 out of 23 qualifiers staying with the firm in 2010. All will be hoping that the firm's good fortune is not dented by public sector budget cuts.

Wherever I lay my Kaplan

There are three main reasons why you might consider this firm. First, it operates in a part of the country you want to work in – probably the West Midlands or East Anglia. Second, you have an interest in healthcare, education or the public sector. Third, you want a varied training at a firm with a reputation for quality.

Let's look first at the breadth of the training. M&R's six by four-month seat system is perfect in this respect as

Chambers UK rankings

Agriculture & Rural Affairs	Intellectual Property
Banking & Finance	Licensing
Charities	Local Government
Clinical Negligence	Pensions
Construction	Planning
Corporate/M&A	Private Client
Dispute Resolution	Private Equity
Education	Professional Discipline
Employment	Professional Negligence
Energy & Natural Resources	Projects
Environment	Public Procurement
Family/Matrimonial	Real Estate
Healthcare	Real Estate Litigation
Information Technology	Restructuring/Insolvency
	Tax

seats are offered in so many areas: agriculture, construction law, banking, insurance, real estate, employment, education, healthcare, dispute resolution, corporate/commercial, regulation, family, technology and tax. No seats are obligatory or ubiquitous across the firm, but property is something of a given in Norwich and Cambridge, as are healthcare and dispute resolution in Birmingham. "*Litigation and property are popular seats, as is family law,*" a trainee revealed.

Trainees' preferences are taken into account at each seat change. "*The first is chosen for you and after that we compile a wish list of seats.*" Second-years have priority. Trainees are based in the Cambridge, Birmingham and Norwich offices, but seats can also be taken in London, Leeds and Manchester from time to time. Postings to another office are sometimes "*offered to you,*" or can be requested if a certain practice area tickles your fancy. "*It's a smooth transition and they subsidise your accommodation,*" a source confirmed. On the subject of relocations, the firm has signed a deal to send its future trainees to Kaplan Law School in London for their LPC. Attending Kaplan is mandatory if you want to study in the capital.

Healthy shoots

Healthcare is a standout practice group, especially in the Midlands. "*Birmingham has a lot of public sector, healthcare and education work,*" and this includes dealing with negligence, regulation, governance and employment issues. "*We represent a lot of NHS trusts and do work related to mental health review tribunals,*" said a fan of the seat. The team also advised the Department of Health on its preparedness programme for the swine flu pandemic. In light of government plans to restructure aspects of the NHS, the firm is presumably readying itself for a new era in healthcare in which private companies could well play more of a role.

Having started with healthcare clients, the Brum office is becoming more of a full-service outfit, with insurance, construction, employment, family, corporate, real estate and private client work now on the menu. The employment seat is "*mainly contentious and you get a lot of work in tribunals, and negotiating and entering into settlements on behalf of clients.*" Insurance is the seat where trainees might come closest to being a bit of a dogsbody. The work is "*more formal and based on Civil Procedure Rules,*" which means chores such as "*indexing bundles, running up to court to get documents issued and served, and going through 600-page documents.*" In a regulatory seat one trainee reported doing work for the "*Care Quality Commission in their regulation of care homes.*" Another added: "*We prosecute dentists for the General Dental Council in misconduct cases.*"

In Cambridge and Birmingham, clients include a number of higher education institutions like Manchester Business College and Royal Holloway, which lawyers advise on real estate, employment and student matters. Combining its educational and healthcare expertise, M&R has done work for the Academic Health Science Centres of Imperial College London and Oxford and Cambridge universities. Taking advantage of its location at the heart of the burgeoning 'Silicon Fen', the Cambridge office has a notable intellectual property focus. "*We're ideally placed for developing science and technology companies in the region,*" said one source.

Of cabbages and King's

Commercial property is a big deal in both Cambridge and Norwich. In this seat "*you get a lot of responsibility and they allow you to develop as much as you want. I've worked for large commercial clients on multimillion-pound transactions.*" Norwich is the only office to offer property litigation: "*I got to do a bit of advocacy in the county court,*" one proud source recalled. The public sector, healthcare and education remit is evident here too, with lawyers acting for Norwich City Council, Addenbrooke's Hospital and various subsidiaries of Cambridge University. "*We've done work for Birmingham City Council and Norwich City Football Club... but no, I didn't get to meet Delia Smith,*" said one trainee. Representing public sector or higher education clients can be as newsworthy as acting for major private companies: for example, the property team recently helped Trinity College, Cambridge, buy a £24m stake in the O2 in Greenwich. M&R also sits on King's College's panel of legal advisers. Despite being the firm's place of birth,

Norwich is now only its third largest office, marking the rapid expansion of business elsewhere. Reflecting the characteristics of the region, the office has an important focus on private client, family and agriculture work. It's not all strapping Norfolk farm hands though: the team advises over a dozen of the wealthiest Oxbridge colleges on their agricultural holdings.

The Leeds and Manchester offices focus mainly on family law, although there is an insurance presence too. Actually there are family teams in all offices except London, making the firm one of the main family law players in the UK. A family seat means working on divorce and guardianship matters, quite often where the assets of the parties are substantial. "*It's good in terms of client contact as you get to work for individuals on their more private concerns.*" Bear in mind that the team is following the market in "*moving away from court-based disputes towards mediation and alternative approaches.*"

Although one trainee told us the firm is "*not for people who are really into banking or corporate work,*" there are growing banking and corporate teams in Cambridge and Norwich. "*Our main client is RBS,*" revealed a source; others include Santander and Lloyds TSB. Over half of the staff in London deal with insurance and reinsurance matters. The team commonly tackles small to medium-sized claims with a focus on property damage.

Grow your own

Although trainees report that their colleagues are "*down to earth*" and "*approachable*" across the firm, each office has its own personality. This derives in part from their different clients and work emphases, but also from more general regional differences. In Birmingham "*a lot of partners are very young,*" so the atmosphere is "*buzzing,*" "*fast-paced*" and "*entrepreneurial.*" The office is open-plan, with trainees sitting in 'pods' with other fee earners, which means "*you get to know the other teams on your floor really well.*" As for decor, "*some of the furnishings are a bit dated and the colours aren't quite right,*" one source whispered. Most people feel plugged in to the "*close-knit trainee community*" in the city. The firm pays for tickets to the annual ball organised by the Birmingham Futures young professionals group, and an M&R solicitor was recently the organisation's chair. The trainees' favoured Friday hangouts are on New Hall Street and Broad Street, plus there's the well-lawyered Old Joint Stock next door. A sports and social committee organises comedy nights and theatre trips plus lots of on-field competition.

Life in Norwich is described as more "*middle-aged*" – admittedly usually by those who don't live there – but trainees do know how to enjoy themselves. There are choir events and beer festivals, and "*trainees get together informally.*" Drinks in the office on the last Friday of the month, regular events like pool and bowling – everyone joins in. "*I've been on bike rides with partners and we once even went Zorbing down a dry ski slope.*" The Norwich office is "*modern with good facilities,*" even if its culture is described as "*traditional and respectable,*" which could well be a result of the influence of "*some private clients who have big landed estates.*"

The Cambridge branch has two floors, "*one is open-plan and the other has offices.*" For trainees, open-plan wins hands down. "*When I was in real estate, the* [office] *managing partner was in the same pod as me,*" a source recalled. The increasingly businesslike and innovative approach of Oxbridge colleges is reflected in the ethos here: "*I think we're entrepreneurial; with no clients have I seen a traditional approach,*" one trainee concluded. Although our sources suggested a little competition was in evidence around the office, getting on here is "*not a question of who shouts the loudest or who you play tennis with.*" Sport is popular, however: there are football and netball teams as well as "*a firm-wide cricket match of partners against players*" and a north-south inter-office football match. The small Manchester outlet is in leased accommodation in a semi-commercial building, which means "*you meet some interesting people in the lift!*" There are social events here too: "*A team leader might stand up at 5.30pm on a Friday and say, 'Let's go for drinks.'*"

Summer and Christmas parties alternate between firm-wide and single-office events. The branches meet up for "*business away-days*" organised by practice group, and we noted a penchant for charitable giving. In 2008 the firm topped a poll of the most charitable law firms, with almost 25% of employees donating via the payroll. The firm's annual charity event for 2010 was a Three Peaks Challenge.

And finally...

Interested in healthcare, education or the public sector? Is East Anglia or the West Midlands your stomping ground? Just want a high-quality training contract that exposes you to a variety of clients and practices? Mills & Reeve ticks many boxes.

Mishcon de Reya

The facts

Location: London

Number of UK partners/solicitors: 59/153

Total number of trainees: 26

Seats: 4x6 months

Alternative seats: Occasional secondments

Extras: Pro Bono – Pink Law Legal Advice Centre

On chambersstudent.co.uk
- How to get into Mishcon
- Deciphering Mishconspeak
- We talk to training partner Daniel Levy

Mishcon de Reya: it's business, but it's personal too.

Perception v Reality

Mishcon is notorious for handling famous divorces, from Princess Diana to Heather Mills. *The Times* once said that simply seeing the name of the firm could strike fear into any man's heart. Yet Mishcon is no one-trick pony – the firm's commercial departments (corporate, employment, property and litigation) account for around 90% of its revenue. Family law is most definitely an important but small part of the business. Even within that department it's not all about the divorce work. Although the team recently advised on Galina Berezovsky's rumoured £100m separation from exiled Russian oligarch Boris, it also launched a campaign to address issues in relation to private law Children Act proceedings and is lobbying for the Act to establish 'conflict clinics' as an alternative to legal proceedings.

One of a pack of smaller mid-market firms in London, Mishcon has seemingly decided to make a few waves in the profession. The most major item of news to report is that it opened a New York office in January 2010 – not many firms of similar a size have tried that. The new outpost is headed by fraud specialist Jim McGuire, who joined along with a group from US firm Sheppard Mullin. The small team has already taken on big work, including a copyright infringement class action against Google.

It can't be said enough: "*The firm is really buying into its commerciality at the moment and really looking into developing that side of the business.*" For this, read: 'The firm is fed up of being famous for its private clients and is shamelessly flaunting its commercial wares around town'. Nothing wrong with that. Many a firm has stagnated because it didn't have the gumption to market itself properly. We've certainly noticed Mishcon's name cropping up in the legal press more often of late and it literally made news when it became the first law firm to partner with the *FT* for a four-part editorial series called 'Deals and Dealmakers'.

Fraudsters and fakers

The firm excels in lower mid-market M&A and has some big-name clients like online poker room PKR and a well-known Mayfair hotel. It acted for Osem UK, a Nestlé-owned Kosher food importer and distributor, as it acquired the business of Yarden GB, and for Indian film production company UMP on its $45m takeover by UTV Software Communications. "*You get quite involved,*" one trainee said of the corporate seat. "*If it's a big deal you're assisting with document management and drafting ancillary documents and board minutes.*"

Mishcon's employment group specialises in high-level matters against well-known financial institutions, lately in relation to bonuses. One such case sees Mishcon going up against Linklaters, representing 21 Dresden bankers in a group action. The bankers are chasing bonuses promised before the sale of Dresdner Bank to Commerzbank during the recession. According to trainees, there's "*a relatively equal balance of litigious and non-litigious*" work within the department, and trainee tasks are also "*quite varied,*" ranging from "*big disclosure exercises*" to "*drafting contracts.*" The department is one of the firm's best when it comes to formal training. "*Every week there are case discussions to make sure we're on top of new developments.*"

Chambers UK rankings

Corporate/M&A	Immigration
Defamation/Reputation Management	Intellectual Property
Dispute Resolution	Licensing
Employment	Private Client
Family/Matrimonial	Real Estate
Fraud	Real Estate Litigation

There were numerous comments on the "*fantastic atmosphere*" and "*really good team dynamic*" of the property department. Like employment, it offers "*well-structured training.*" Trainees see "*a lot of big deals,*" like the one in which the team helped online luxury fashion retailer Net-a-Porter secure an office space in the Westfield mall. Small deals are just as frequent and, even better, trainees are entrusted to "*run and progress some matters basically on* [their] *own.*" "*It's great because you can really see the total lifetime of the case,*" one raved.

Mishcon's litigators undertake work for both individuals and companies. Trainees "*really get into the nitty-gritty because* [they] *spend so much time with the documents*" and "*get to know the background.*" The ever-popular fraud team has had its best year yet and saw its revenue grow by 25% and account for over half of the firm's total litigation-based earnings. The practice boasts some of the most exciting work around, allowing solicitors to don their detective hats as they co-ordinate international, big-money fraud investigations. The firm is currently acting for one of the world's largest hotel developers, Resort Properties Group, in a multimillion-dollar fraud perpetrated by ex-employees and consultants of large construction projects in the Caribbean. Mishcon lawyers went to Jamaica, the British Virgin Islands, the Cayman Islands, China, Taiwan, Canada, the USA and Brunei in order to prepare and execute a series of simultaneous search orders, asset freezing orders and third-party disclosure orders to preserve evidence. The firm is now investigating and tracing bribes paid to the conspirators throughout the US, Canada and Asia.

Trainees who had sampled the contentious trusts and probates group said "*cases were never boring*" and that they enjoyed "*investigating family histories and fallouts*" when dealing with contested wills. The media/reputation management team likewise offers "*incredible work*" that would be hard to find dull. Apparently there are some "*big characters*" in the department – fitting considering its big clients, which include some of the most well-known MPs. Shopaholics take note: during a stint in the IP department you're likely to be "*surrounded by designer shoes and handbags,*" comparing real to fake for trade mark and design rights cases. You may even be lucky enough to score a secondment to one of the firm's luxury group clients.

Party animals

Mishcon trainees don't necessarily need the designer perks. At the time of research, there were 22 trainees, only four of them guys. Furthermore, we couldn't help but notice that the ladies were looking pretty stylish in their corporate head shots. "*We do have a lot of attractive trainees – it certainly has been noted and remarked upon,*" one of the four males blushed. As for the gender imbalance: "*Apparently it just ended up that way. What can I say? Lucky me.*" You can often find trainees kicking back at the Square Pig or Bountiful Cow next to Mishcon's Red Lion Square offices, where "*there's always someone any given night – mainly Thursdays and Fridays as long as there isn't football on.*"

Trainees agreed that this is a "*very, very social place*" with plenty on besides trips to the pub, such as ski trips and summer parties. The Christmas party always proves entertaining as the first-year trainees put on a performance. The last intake came up with their own rendition of the *Chicago* number *Cell Block Tango*, murdering off their supervisors with staplers and photocopiers. "*It's fun but really quite scary. The partners and everyone else find it hilarious because they know it's awful for you, but it is a good way to bond with your intake – we're all in it together.*"

Good as Gold

Mishcon is happy to be different. Last year we joked that it might as well have stuffed alligators hanging from the ceilings; this year we can officially report that while no progress has been made on the taxidermy front, there is a rooster in reception in the form of a sizeable Warhol-esque painting. Only a little offbeat, but certainly a nice break from the standard geometric prints. "*We've got lots of personality here,*" trainees said proudly. "*It's part of what makes us quite successful. Not only are our clients quite entrepreneurial, our solicitors are too. You're allowed to develop your own style and you're encouraged to pursue your outside interests, however wacky they are.*" The firm "*doesn't want you to lose your identity.*"

While our sources agreed there was a 'Mishcon type', no one could put their finger on what it is exactly. "*I guess it's just a state of mind,*" one attempted. "*Everyone's got that same sort of spark that makes us slightly different.*" Somehow the firm has managed to bring all these sparks of different personalities together and provided an arena in which they can flourish. In fact, Mishcon has been so successful in doing so that it earned a place in *The Sunday*

Times' '100 Best Companies to Work For' list in 2010. It's clear managing partner Kevin Gold, who "*you could definitely call a character,*" has something to do with this. Our sources showed a lot of love for the man. "*He's one of those people who is just very good natured,*" and many put the fact that "*the firm is still run in that familiar way*" with "*community values showing through*" down to him.

"*There's a lot of interaction between the fee earners and everyone else about what they're thinking. There's a lot of sharing, which is really useful, especially for a young lawyer.*" Most trainees agreed that one of Mishcon's best qualities is its "*openness – you can go into any office, as long as it's not fiendishly busy of course, introduce yourself and ask for guidance.*" Supervisors are not just responsible for assigning work, "*they look after your growth, development and general wellbeing.*" The firm also has a group of 'legal director lawyers' responsible for knowledge building and trainee support. Formal systems aside, "*everyone makes time and they're quite happy to answer even stupid questions. There's no, 'Oh shush that's a partner, you can't talk to them'. If you were in a room whispering they'd ask you to speak up.*" Being able to form an opinion and speak out is one of Mishcon's key values; it's the type of place where "*if you have a good idea, they'll say go for it. My supervisor likes the fact that I come up to him with suggestions, or even tell him he's wrong.*" HR manager Ann-Marie Comer says the ability to voice opinions is something the firm looks for during vacation schemes and assessment centres – find more recruitment tips on our website.

In conclusion, Mishcon is "*really trying to go forward. It's great – all very gung ho!*" The firm has produced loads of new initiatives and products in its rebranding phase: if you need help keeping them straight, check out our Mishcon dictionary, or 'Mishconary' if you will, online. All this marching on together is instilling major pride through all levels of staff. "*It's a really, really good place to be. You feel like you can see your future here, make a career for yourself,*" one trainee summed up.

And finally...

In 2010, the firm offered 13 jobs to its 15 qualifiers, but with a few trainees going for some of the same positions, only 12 stayed.

Muckle LLP

The facts

Location: Newcastle

Number of UK partners/solicitors: 24/32

Total number of trainees: 8

Seats: 4x6 months

Alternative seats: None

On chambersstudent.co.uk
- How to get into Muckle
- We talk to managing partner Steve McNicol
- The Newcastle legal scene

Newcastle firm Muckle combines *"ambition and drive"* with an egalitarian culture in which *"people feel valued."*

Many a McNicol

While a less-familiar name in the student market than Newcastle's biggest players, Muckle is nevertheless highly regarded by *Chambers UK* and pops up in its rankings for banking, charities, corporate, debt recovery, dispute resolution, employment, IP and property matters.

Its 24 partners make Muckle the fourth-largest commercial firm in Newcastle; however, managing partner Steve McNicol tells us: "*We're proud to say we are a truly North East-based firm. Many of our competitors have decided to open in new locations, but we feel very strongly that we can service client needs right across the country whilst maintaining the very strong culture that a one-office firm has.*" Muckle does indeed have a few national businesses on its books, among them Greggs the bakers. Trainees agree with the boss: "*We've not opened a satellite office. That would dilute what we have as a single-site firm. It would develop a sense of other-ness.*"

Sitting pretty in Toon town, the firm has weathered the recession. Like other firms, it was forced to make some redundancies and trainee deferrals at the height of the recession. 2008/09 saw a 33% drop in profits per equity partner and a small drop in revenue. But innovation in 'service excellence' ("*our brand-marker in the region*") goes hand in hand with a steady and sure outlook for the future: trainees and management feel "*everything seems back on track.*" The firm received a boost in 2010 with the arrival of Robert Langley, construction big-shot and former senior partner at rival firm Watson Burton.

... makes a Muckle

The firm is a full-service operation, offering trainee seats in corporate; dispute resolution; property; banking; commercial; employment; contentious construction; and private client. "*Corporate finance and property are the two anchor teams within the business,*" but no seats are compulsory. The corporate team deals with "*acquisitions, mergers and sales for local small and medium enterprises and plcs.*" It helped Vertu Motors raise £30m through an AIM listing, and assisted on the restructuring of menswear retailer The Officers Club. "*When there are lots of deals on, trainees will be responsible for the more mundane tasks, but that's not the main thing you will be doing,*" sources said. Expect to take on other essential tasks like "*drafting board minutes and resolutions.*" Supervisors "*make an effort to get you involved in the juicier parts of the deal.*"

Property trainees assist developers and institutional investors and have lately worked on various hotel projects around the country. The team represented developer Metnor in the sale of land to Northumbria University; Barratt Homes, Millhouse Developments, Durham Country Cricket Club and Arriva also send work. Trainees are responsible for post-completion tasks and enjoy "*going to client meetings and drafting leases and licences.*"

A well-respected banking department services the likes of Bank of Scotland, Lloyds Banking Group and RBS. The team has been "*shifting towards insolvency in the past year,*" and at the time of our calls people were "*busy with*

Chambers UK rankings

Banking & Finance	Employment
Charities	Intellectual Property
Construction	Real Estate
Corporate/M&A	Real Estate Litigation
Debt Recovery	Restructuring/Insolvency
Dispute Resolution	

refinancing, restructuring and administrations." The Muckle debt recovery team is top-ranked in the North East by *Chambers UK* and winning plenty of new clients. It helps creditor clients with the recovery of rent arrears, unpaid college fees and other types of unpaid bills. Clients include Newcastle College, Bastion Security and the Department for Education. The team does not take trainees itself, but those doing a litigation seat are likely to handle some debt recovery tasks on the side.

Find your own

In a litigation seat, trainees can expect to be "*managing cases through the court process*" and "*doing advocacy in district judges' chambers.*" North Eastern small businesses make up the lion's share of the client base, but lawyers are also instructed by London South Bank University and CAV Aerospace. They "*work on anything from contentious debt recovery to insolvency, shareholder disputes, contractual disputes and partnership disputes,*" as well as warranty and construction claims, professional negligence and IP infringements. The employment team acts mainly for employers (eg Sunderland AFC; Tyne & Wear Fire and Rescue Service) and some individual claimants. Trainees have "*fantastic exposure to clients*" and enjoy "*advising on best practice, disciplinary action and grievances, and equality and diversity training.*"

Commercial seats bring commercial contracts plus IT, IP and data protection issues. IP clients include NHS Surrey, Newcastle Science City and renewable energy champion NaREC. Renewable energy is an area where Muckle is "*looking at new markets which are untapped.*" Trainees told us innovation is the key to new business: this is not a firm intent on "*stealing work off our rivals' plates.*"

Muck-ling about

So much for the work on offer. What about Muckle office life? Managing partner McNicol asserts that "*to purely focus on customers will not necessarily mean that you will become an excellent service provider. It's all about getting recruitment right, retaining excellent people and having a strong culture.*" Trainees agree. "*People feel valued here. You're not viewed as being less important if you are lower paid,*" one said. "*Even if you're in admin, you should still be able to have a laugh and a joke with an equity partner.*" Management gives quarterly briefings on Muckle's plans, finances and strategy. "*They make a real effort to involve the whole firm in fundamental decisions and the direction the firm goes in.*" None of this makes Muckle a soft-touch employer. People are expected to adopt a strong and clear commercial work ethos: "*As lawyers we wrap ourselves around clients.*" But, as McNicol explains: "*Most business people are not interested in the legal technicalities – their primary objective is to deliver what the business needs on time and within budget. Our role is to find a way for them to do that without boring them with the detail.*"

The firm recently moved into "*fantastic*" new offices near St James' Park ("*before, we were in a minging rabbit warren*"). The break-out room is fondly nicknamed 'time out' and boasts its own pool table. Office egalitarianism is reflected in the fact that trainees refer to the print room (which keeps photocopying work out of trainees' hands) as 'the Hub' – "*everyone is treated as an important part of the firm.*" There are many social events. On Fridays, trainees can be found in Fluid, a sports bar opposite the office although there's a movement to get more people going to the smarter Soho bar. Departments go out for meals and drinks, and "*the commercial team rented out a cinema to watch Top Gun.*" Sports are a big thing too, particularly netball, football and squash. Summer rounders pits Muckle against other Newcastle firms, and "*for Sport Relief there was a boys-v-girls netball match.*" The summer party is open to employees' kids and there's "*a bouncy castle and then a dinner and disco in the evening.*"

All six qualifiers were kept on in 2009. Muckle deferred three of its four 2008 starters to 2009, meaning only one second-year qualified in 2010, although sadly they were not retained.

And finally...

Muckle is looking for trainees who can show it real commitment. Tip: the firm places *"a lot of emphasis on its vac scheme,"* so check out our website for more info.

Nabarro LLP

The facts

Location: London, Sheffield

Number of UK partners/solicitors: 125/277

Total number of trainees: 58

Seats: 6x4 months

Alternative seats: Brussels, secondments

Extras: Pro bono – LawWorks, St Luke's Community Centre; language classes

On chambersstudent.co.uk

- How to get into Nabarro
- We talk to graduate recruitment partner Justin Cornelius
- Pro bono initiatives
- Networking 101

Flying the flag of brand clarity in the north and south of England, Nabarro's castles have weathered the recessionary storm to prove they were certainly not built on sand. But what is the reality beyond real estate renown?

Keeping it real?

1958: brothers Felix and Alan Nabarro merge their law practice with Leslie Nathanson to form Nabarro Nathanson, a firm built from strong foundations in property law and litigation. Some 50 years on from its conception, Nabarro's real estate prestige is still towering. Major clients include Land Securities, JPMorgan and Great Portland Estates, which its lawyers recently advised on the sale of a 50% interest in The 100 Bishopsgate Partnership to Brookfield Properties, worth a whopping £42.975m. Another highlight saw the lawyers help to secure a lease on behalf of Hermes Real Estate, one of the biggest property lettings in the City of London since the economic downturn. With insecurity abounding in property markets, following the credit crunch, the real estate litigation team has risen to the challenges of an increasing number of disputes over development agreements, and vendor and purchaser feuds in light of falling property prices. Important, too, was the firm's ability to offer its services at competitive prices through canny use of its smaller Sheffield base.

Understandably, Nabarro is always keen to stress that it has expanded beyond the bricks and mortar of its real estate reputation to establish itself as a key player in other practice areas, particularly corporate and finance. As with almost all firms, Nabarro's M&A and related activity slowed after the world economy fell off a cliff, in part due to the encroachment of magic circle and other big City firms on the mid-market territory in which Nabarro had been making a name. Senior sources suggest that this is likely to be a short-lived trespass, and the firm is confident about not only regaining ground, but also looking to size up to the magic circle on international deals. Graduate recruitment partner Justin Cornelius was positive when we spoke to him in summer 2010: "*There has already been a real upturn in the last three months, and over the next couple of years corporate finance and related areas will be a core tenet of our growth.*" While it was never fully frozen over, the ice in Nabarro's corporate Narnia was obviously melting: of the three associates promoted to partnership in April 2010, one was in corporate and another in finance.

In other areas, intellectual property is just one example of a discipline in which Nabarro is really beginning to assert itself, leading particularly in trade mark work for familiar labels such as Levi Strauss & Co, Ryanair, HMV and Diesel. No surprises that such popular brands make for a popular seat as well, which along with employment is one of the most sought after.

Swinging six-ies

So let's look at the seats in Nabarro's six-seat training contract. The rotation system allows the new starter to sample five different areas of law, with their last seat being a return to the department into which they want to qualify. Trainees, in particular first-years, must be prepared to find themselves both spoilt for choice ("*I don't*

Chambers UK rankings

Banking & Finance	Investment Funds
Capital Markets	Local Government
Clinical Negligence	Pensions
Competition/European Law	Pensions Litigation
Construction	Personal Injury
Corporate/M&A	Planning
Dispute Resolution	Private Equity
Education	Professional Discipline
Employment	Projects
Energy & Natural Resources	Public Procurement
	Real Estate
Environment	Real Estate Finance
Health & Safety	Real Estate Litigation
Healthcare	Restructuring/Insolvency
Information Technology	Retail
Intellectual Property	Tax

really know why so few firms offer six seats") and frustrated with the faster cycle ("*people hate the seat change*"). An extensive range of choices makes for a happy trainee group, particularly since seat allocation is nothing like the frenzied game of musical chairs played at some firms. It satisfies both those with a strong conviction about which area they want to qualify in and those who are keen to pick and choose before committing. "*The six-seat system has been a definite advantage,*" one trainee assured us. "*It has enabled me to really tailor my training contract, and even though I always knew I wanted to qualify in property, I have been able to do planning and insolvency, which will come in useful later on.*"

Property seats are compulsory. In this department, trainees manage their own files and plenty of them told us just how much they liked the responsibility and the opportunity to get your hands dirty and impress supervisors and colleagues. The work of the department runs right across the spectrum from landlord and tenant issues to development and complex sales and purchases that are structured more like corporate deals than traditional property transfers. Working hours are manageable. Said one source: "*They were usually 8.30am to 6.30pm, sometimes later on particularly difficult transactions. I stayed until 4am twice.*"

Because the firm's reputation relies heavily on its real estate lawyers, it's no surprise that property litigation has been considered a hot seat in the past. Today, however, this veritable Hell's Kitchen does seem to have cooled a little and "*people actually volunteer for it nowadays!*" Hours and deadlines can still be both demanding and unpredictable, with a lot of research, writing letters of advice, drafting instructions to counsel and attending conferences at barristers chambers all thrown into the mix. Nabarro's litigators have been active on all sorts of disputes of late, including spats over a shopping centre in Hemel Hempstead, a deal for Middlesex Uni, a fancy Mayfair development and the Crossrail project.

Every trainee will complete either a corporate seat or a banking seat. Latterly the corporate department – which performs very well in the mid-market – has been quieter than usual but no dodo. The options available to trainees are: the public companies team, the private companies/private equity team and the indirect investment team. And what better way to reassert the firm's name in the capital markets arena than by advising on three emerging market-oriented company admissions to the London markets in quick succession in early 2010? An alternative to a corporate seat is banking, which involves liaising with property associates handling real estate financing deals and the welcome bonus of working closely with clients.

Elsewhere, an insolvency seat encourages trainees to step up to the plate in a department with fewer associates. We heard about trainees rising to interesting challenges from creditor clients keen to protect their interests in corporate restructurings and insolvencies. Commercial litigation can throw up the odd high point too. "*The best experience was going down to court and appearing in front of a master. Coming out unscathed gave me a real buzz,*" said one satisfied trainee.

For those with an interest in all things EU, a first-year seat is available in Nabarro's sole overseas office in Brussels. Rather than build a network of foreign offices, Nabarro has instead hooked up with a firm called August & Debouzy in France, another called GSK Stockmann + Kollegen in Germany and a third, Nunziante Magrone, in Italy. It shares its Brussels office with the first two. As part of a team of three, the trainee who gets the Brussels posting will quickly find their role to be more research-based, with monitoring EU developments and writing alerts and articles for firm newsletters comprising much of the day-to-day. The firm rents a "*fully kitted-out*" one-bed apartment just 20 minutes' walk from the office, and there is a mailing list putting all Brussels trainees in touch with each other so no one need feel set adrift.

Closer to home, secondment opportunities are available with Oxford University, Mercedes-Benz, Essex County Council and hedge fund RAB Capital, assisting a team of six analysts and three full-time lawyers. Secondments are always a great way to see how clients work and understand their priorities. Back in the office, trainees say there is a highly supportive infrastructure. The firm's collective embrace provides newbies with both buddies and mentors, putting new arrivals in contact with second-year trainees and partners respectively. By contrast, it is very unlikely for Nabarro trainees to be supervised directly by partners, and more common for them to be sat alongside four to six-year PQEs. This is not generally seen as a negative, but simply a question of striking a balance between challenging work and a not-so-challenging working relationship.

Sheffield united

"*It's nice to visit, but I wouldn't want to live there,*" was the chorus that came from Sheffield trainees when asked if they fancied a move to London. Nabarro's Sheffield office maintains its historical links with the coal mining industry. Its origins are rooted in work for the UK's former nationalised mining industry, British Coal, and as such the branch's health team continues to defend mining-related illness or injury cases. Whether in health claims or clinical negligence seats, new trainees are given plenty of responsibility, with trips to court and drafting witness statements par for the course. The office's wider profile, however, allows it to offer further seat options in real estate litigation, construction and environment law. In construction, for example, both contentious and non-contentious experiences are available, and large cases can land on your desk from the off.

The two locations understandably have different characters. Sitting quietly next to the canal in the emerging business district of Victoria Quays, the pace in Sheffield is less frantic in comparison to Holborn, which is close to London's legal heart. Sheffield's trainee intake is usually five per year. When we noted that all five trainees in one cohort were female, a source told us: "*It would be nice to have some boys!*" At least the smaller group is tightly knit.

Clear skies ahead?

A standard-bearer for rooting out fussy rhetoric in legalese, Nabarro's 'Clarity matters' mantra can give the impression of successful sloganisation masquerading as stripped-down sincerity. But all those we spoke to declared the firm's clarity campaign to be more than just cosmetic, with all staff receiving training in expurgating florid magniloquence in favour of plain speaking. Compare the graduate website with the Nabarro-commissioned Bird and Fortune sketches on YouTube (Search 'Ungobbledegooked') for some idea of this transformation.

A lack of clarity is not an issue when it comes to firm identity. Trainees all described Nabarro as friendly, and senior sources put this down to the right combination of individualism and collective ambition. Nabarro isn't known as a firm that has targeted the Oxbridge confluence to fill its trainee positions; instead it has always placed its faith in personality over a top academic pedigree. "*My feeling was that they look beyond your grades and see if there was something else you have to offer,*" commented one interviewee. This is not to say Nabarro compromises on quality: its vacation scheme, consistently rated as one of the country's best undergraduate internships, is described by trainees as rigorous and rewarding in equal measure. Said one: "*If you can get through the vac scheme, you can get through anything.*" As such, this three-weeker is sure to unmask any Nabarro no-nos: the best advice from current trainees on how to approach the scheme's fast-paced mix of group activities, presentations and social events was simply "*act naturally.*" For much more on the scheme, go to our website.

The social scene is lively if unobtrusive. The end of the week often finds the Londoners lifting spirits at either the nearby Dolphin tavern or the Enterprise, and while the Sheffield clan have lamented the lack of an immediate local, there is certainly no shortage of social occasions: buddy nights, charity balls and 'Contact Nabarro' events fill the communal calendar. The latter is an initiative that encourages trainee lawyers to develop their networking skills via things like wine-tasting evenings, legal updates and various other presentations. Firm band Music Matters is well received at both ends of the country, and performed respectably as one of six groups to compete in the 'Law Rocks' finals.

And finally...

Despite continued recessionary unrest, Nabarro did well in 2010 when 29 out of 34 qualifiers were able to take up NQ positions. It's largely business as almost usual for this very likeable firm that's increasingly popular with students.

- **In English please?** Capital whats? Wet and dry shipping? Restructuring? Our Practice Area pages explain the mysteries of all the main fields of law, describe what lawyers actually do within them and tell you which firms covered in the True Picture section are the best regarded for such work.

Norton Rose LLP

The facts

Location: London

Number of UK partners/solicitors: 138/346

Total number of trainees: 91

Seats: 6x4 months

Alternative seats: Overseas seats, secondments

Extras: Pro bono – Tooting and Tower Hamlets Law Centres, FRU, CAB; language training

On chambersstudent.co.uk
- How to get into Norton Rose
- Career progression at the firm
- More on More London

Think getting into the magic circle is more competitive than other City firms? Norton Rose receives at least as many applications as Slaughters or Clifford Chance, thanks to its reputation as a jolly nice firm doing top-drawer international work.

Norton R'Oz

While many City firms were throwing themselves at potential American partners in 2010, Norton Rose took the less conventional step of looking down under for merger opportunities. Stepping up to the crease was Deacons Australia, the nation's number eight bat (in terms of revenue and partner numbers) and an excellent signing for Norton Rose, which was looking to raise its game in the Asia-Pacific league. The move allowed the firm to extend its talent pool, get feet on the ground in Australia's five major cities and boost its presence in Bangkok, Singapore, Tokyo and Jakarta. This may well prove to be a savvy tie-up, not least because of both firms' acknowledged expertise in complex banking, finance and corporate issues. A shared love of beer, barbecues and cricket has proved an added bonus.

Norton Rose's asset finance team is a consistent top performer, being the only City practice to have earned *Chambers UK* top-tier rankings in all aspects of transport finance. These are the people to turn to for advice on all things aviation, whether financing aircraft or transferring assets from one airline to another, and confidence in their expertise is evidenced by a client list that includes Italy's Alitalia, KLM of The Netherlands, and easyJet. The same goes for the rail department, whose faithful client base includes the Department for Transport, the Office for Rail Regulation and HSBC Rail (UK). From a trainee's perspective it helps that there are "*some people who are extremely interested, even in the technical side; the* [non-fee-earning] *know-how lawyers can explain everything to us.*"

Asset finance is just one strand – albeit a major one – in the massive banking division. Also covered are syndicated loans, structured finance, acquisition finance, project finance, securitisation, derivatives, telecoms finance, real estate finance, restructuring and insolvency and international securities work. The firm regularly acts for all the major banks as well as several major borrowers. In the expanding world of Islamic finance, Norton Rose has a great name, in part thanks to its long-term involvement in the Middle East, which goes back three decades. It is still gaining ground here, and was recently appointed as primary legal adviser to the Saudi Capital Markets Authority. Here in the UK, the FSA has begun to flex its muscles more, and Norton Rose has a team to assist clients in this new, more demanding regulatory era.

Norton Rose is equally adept in the AIM arena, recently advising Latin American independent oil and gas explorer Geopark Holdings on two multimillion-dollar placings to institutional investors in the USA, Chile and the UK. And while Norton Rose may not be a paid-up member of the magic circle, it is happy to take them on at their own corporate finance game, lining up opposite Slaughter and May in two of 2010's more sizeable M&A deals: the collapsed Prudential takeover of AIG and the £2.75bn

Chambers UK rankings

Administrative & Public Law	Information Technology
Asset Finance	Insurance
Aviation	Investment Funds
Banking & Finance	Outsourcing
Banking Litigation	Pensions
Capital Markets	Private Equity
Commodities	Professional Negligence
Competition/European Law	Projects
Construction	Public Procurement
Corporate/M&A	Real Estate
Dispute Resolution	Real Estate Finance
Employee Share Schemes	Restructuring/Insolvency
Employment	Shipping
Energy & Natural Resources	Tax
Environment	Telecommunications
Financial Services	Transport
Fraud	Travel

takeover of AXA's UK life assurance business to buyout fund Resolution. Recent partner recruitment has thrown a spotlight on the investment funds practice, which is now advising on more structured products and gaining new hedge funds and private equity clients.

In the past, Norton Rose has emphasised its corporate credentials and underplayed its dispute resolution practice, not wanting to attract too many potential litigators when it didn't have space for them. One trainee wanted us to make it clear that *"a lot of people want disputes, but when it comes to qualification people need to have realistic expectations."* Two recent partner hires brings the total number of litigators in the group to nearly 70, however, and clients include HSBC, Citi, Nestlé and ExxonMobil, so this department is no mere adornment. Do bear in mind, though, that a training contract here is likely to be heavily grounded in finance and corporate.

Flying high, digging deep

Norton Rose runs a six-seat training programme, with compulsory stops in corporate finance and banking. The advantages and disadvantages of six seats are plain enough: *"I definitely do feel that sometimes into your fourth month you're starting to feel useful to someone and then you have to move on,"* said one interviewee. But another reminded us that *"the six-seat system is a good one, particularly if you're not quite sure which area you want to do."*

By land, sea or air, transport is a big part of Norton Rose's banking department. Inevitably, then, aviation, shipping and rail finance are often considered *"core first-seater seats,"* perhaps because the likelihood that you might find yourself there again later on makes them a good place to find your feet. Second-year sources who had started in late 2008 and early 2009 understandably found the place very quiet. By contrast, reports from first-years in 2010 were much more positive. They told us about the jet-set lifestyle of working in aviation, where trainees are often given full responsibility for taking documents to locations such as Toulouse or Hamburg and getting them signed off in person. *"The clients will often take you for dinner afterwards,"* said one, *"and then fly back in the plane they just bought."* Sewers may not be as glamorous as a peek at the jet set, but Norton Rose has found plenty of work in relation to the funding of water and waste water projects. More than this, it's also heavily involved in electricity; oil and gas; nuclear; renewables; and international infrastructure more generally.

One interviewee in the corporate department reported having been involved *"predominantly in mining deals, but the work was of the type you see in newspapers, and it's quite cool to see these deals actually happening."* Norton Rose's corporate team is described as *"approachable,"* though it apparently *"doesn't suffer fools gladly."* The advantages to this are that you'll get as much responsibility as you choose to take on, but on the other hand *"if you're not very confident or you underperform it could be difficult."* One source told us how much they had enjoyed sitting with a partner in this department: *"I definitely got along with him and really like the people in the team."* This was echoed by another source who had seen more work from the insurance sector. *"It was a really good seat,"* they said; *"I was thrown straight in and given a transaction of my own."* They had experienced some long hours but *"only a few occasions when I was working late on my own. One day an associate was supposed to go home but then returned to help me out with some research. Even though everyone was working hard they still had a smile on their face."*

While it *"takes a long time to be able to develop the knowledge base"* in the tax department, trainees of a more academic bent (*"everyone in the team wears cardigans, and they're all experts"*) will enjoy *"lots of research tasks and drafting of technical analysis."* And when you're playing a role for clients such as HSBC on matters such as a rights issue worth £12.5bn – *"the biggest there had been at the time"* – it sounds like a good seat all round. And the hours are better too.

Fortunately, the training scheme has the flexibility to allow those who are already set on finance work to try a number of seats in this area, while others can dip their toes in a variety of practices before making a commitment. These include competition/EC; property; planning and environment; incentives and pensions; and media and technology. And then, of course, there are all the client secondments (eg Nestlé; Chartis, AXA and Constellation Europe) and overseas seats.

World view

Melbourne, Sydney, Perth, Canberra, Brisbane, Jakarta, Bangkok and Tokyo... the list of overseas offices goes on. While not all these destinations are available as international seats, one thing is for sure: Norton Rose's promise of a truly international training need not fall short if that's what you're hungry for. Six seats to fill and such a wide variety of options mean that it might even be possible to secure two postings overseas. According to HR sources, about 80% of trainees will take international seats at some point, with some of the more popular ones being Singapore, Hong Kong and Dubai. There's the odd cultural difference – late in and late to leave in Italy, a strong culture of face time in Germany – but secondees were mostly happy with both the quality of the work abroad and the standard of living. "*I had a really nice place with a guest room as well, in a great location near the canals,*" said a Milan secondee. We didn't know Milan even had canals but apparently they're three times longer than Venice's and have been undergoing a bit of a revival lately. Trainees are offered 30 hours of basic language training for some destinations. Go to page 536 for the full list of overseas seat options.

Norty but nice

The celebrations for the merger with Deacons included a 'summer sizzler' at the Honourable Artillery Company, "*where everyone had to go in boardies and flip-flops.*" The event was an impressive affair with "*a huge marquee, hundreds of barbecues, dodgems, fairground rides and a disco.*" Not always so lavish in their tastes, trainees are more commonly found in local favourite The Bridge on Tooley Street on a Friday night, mingling with associates and the odd partner. And now that the "*social budget is definitely back on track,*" extended nights out are more common again.

Norton Rose is big on sport. "*There seems to be a sporting team for everything,*" said one trainee. "*There are cricket tours, where they go off and play in different countries, and there was a football tour to Dublin.*" A highlight of the sporting calendar is the annual City Scrum touch rugby tournament, organised by Norton Rose along with Harlequins, which the firm sponsors. Quins have long-standing ties to the world of finance, and members of the club take on the role of coach to each of the corporate sponsors' teams (Norton Rose, HSBC, Ernst & Young, Credit Suisse, etc). Thus far, JPMorgan remain undefeated on the field.

For those not so exercise-inclined, there are plenty of extra-curricular alternatives on offer. Highly commended by all was the firm choir, which gathers pace with every performance and is run by "*a very enthusiastic trainee.*" From the former managing partner to secretaries, all are encouraged to join in a lively repertoire that includes "*everything from Mozart to Glee songs. We even had a request for Joyful, Joyful from Sister Act!*" There are mentoring schemes with Southwark schools to get involved with, as well as football coaching for eight to 11-year-olds. The more serious side of pro bono work finds staff offering advice to the public at both the Tooting and Tower Hamlets Law Centres.

Norton Rose consistently notches up high rankings as a great place to work. We haven't forgotten that while many firms were getting rid of people in droves during the worst phase of the recession, Norton Rose bent over backwards to avoid making redundancies. This fact wasn't lost on the trainees. "*I don't think I could go through this interview without mentioning Flex,*" said one. "*It is a flexible working scheme, meaning that during the recession people could work four-day weeks or take a 12-week sabbatical. It has been a real demonstration of the culture of Norton Rose.*" The scheme saved jobs but must have taken a toll on the firm's financials. It reported a 2% drop in turnover and 6% fall in equity partner profits in 2009/10. All things considered (merger costs no exception) this is a very respectable result. Salaries have risen recently and NQ retention rates were okay – 45 out of 58 qualifiers stayed on in 2010.

If there was one blot on the work-life balance sheet, it was a familiar cause of complaint. "*Something that falls short is the fact that trainees* [in some departments] *are given BlackBerrys,*" moaned one source. "*It can be good, but a lot of people get used to constantly keeping you on the hook. You're often asked to come back in.*" Every rose has its thorns, eh? It's obviously not enough to put people off, as trainees had a lot of difficulty imagining themselves elsewhere. The 'nice' adjective was maybe one that didn't sit too well with some, but then again, "*if by nice you mean that pretty much everyone you work with is supportive and you feel appreciated, then it's true.*"

And finally...

In bad times, firms show their true colours. Norton Rose proved itself to be solid gold.

Olswang

The facts

Location: London, Reading

Number of UK partners/solicitors: 92/218

Total number of trainees: 36

Seats: 4x6 months

Alternative seats: Brussels, secondments

Extras: Pro bono – LawWorks

On chambersstudent.co.uk

- How to get into Olswang
- A few of the firm's headline cases and deals
- Olswang's corporate social responsibility push

Olswang's reputation for film, broadcasting and digital advice is second to none. Its clients include eBay, *The Guardian* and the BBC – but don't ever call it a media firm.

Full phat

Remember the millennium? Britain's biggest problem was a slightly wobbly bridge and saying you'd Googled someone still raised a juvenile snigger. Truly it was a brave new world. As a firm focused on media and stuffed with sexy, techy clients, Olswang slotted into this dynamic, go-ahead era of Cool Britannia perfectly. You'd spot its trainees at law fairs wearing combat trousers when everyone else was in suits. It had MTV playing in reception. It grew like the blazes and was Chambers and Partners' Firm of the Year in 2000.

You're probably waiting for us to tell you how, a decade on, everything's gone to hell in a handcart and Olswang is a shadow of its former self. Far from it: the firm is stable and successful. Turnover increased to £91m in 2009/10, and this at a time when some equally well-known firms were still suffering a recession-induced slump. But that's not to say Olswang is the same firm it was ten years ago. It's turned from a trendy, swaggering teenager to a responsible 29-year-old: still young enough to be with it, but aware that it needs a steady income to pay the bills. With this in mind, it has broadened its practice, initially through major investment in property lawyers and then more recently by pushing further into corporate services. The firm competes well in London's corporate mid-market, ranking in *Chambers UK* alongside the likes of LG, Pinsent Masons and SNR Denton for M&A work. In property matters, the firm rates alongside the likes of Eversheds and Norton Rose. With other top rankings in litigation, capital markets and telecoms advice, there's no doubt that this is a very capable full-service firm.

Some law students, however, are a bit behind the times in their perception of Olswang. So let's be clear: a corporate seat is compulsory and there is no guarantee of time in the very popular media, communications and telecoms (MCT) or commercial litigation teams. "*Applicants should ask themselves the question: would I be happy if I never got to do a media seat?*" advised one trainee, although we're told that HR tries to ensure everyone gets their first-choice seat at some point.

Skype high

The corporate department closed 45 deals in the first quarter of 2010 – a new record for it. The biggest transaction of late was the takeover of Pearl Group (the largest closed life and pension fund consolidator in the UK) by Liberty Acquisition. That deal was valued at $6.7bn: huge for Olswang, which typically handles matters in the multimillion-pound bracket. PartyGaming's £71.9m acquisition of online bingo company Cashcade and the sale of Aussie media business Southern Star to Endemol for AU$75m are two good examples.

The corporate group is essentially one of generalists, although there are a few who concentrate on private equity. Trainees will find themselves doing the usual chores such as drafting board minutes and Companies House

Chambers UK rankings

Administrative & Public Law	Life Sciences
Banking & Finance	Media & Entertainment
Capital Markets	Outsourcing
Construction	Planning
Corporate/M&A	Private Equity
Data Protection	Real Estate
Defamation/Reputation Management	Real Estate Finance
	Real Estate Litigation
Dispute Resolution	Restructuring/Insolvency
Employee Share Schemes	Retail
Employment	Sports Law
Information Technology	Tax
Intellectual Property	Telecommunications
Licensing	

forms, although bigger deals will see them doing "*very basic disclosure tasks.*" Many of our sources had worked in the department during its recession-y quiet patch, but later visitors said it had "*definitely recovered: we are extremely busy.*"

Real estate is a key department, and it allows trainees independence and autonomy. Said one source: "*You are in charge of your own files and do all the legwork. You do the drafting, you write replies to enquiries and check it all off with your supervisor. You're the first port of call, so there's a lot of client contact.*" Royal Mail and Legal & General both instruct the group.

The "*thriving*" commercial litigation group is popular. We learned that "*eight or nine*" second-years applied for a qualification job in the department in 2010, several putting it as "*their first and only choice.*" Considering the cases it handles, that's hardly surprising. Department head Steven Baker led a team defending Skype from a US lawsuit brought by a company called Joltid that was claiming Skype had infringed its copyright in the peer-to-peer technology underlying Skype's Internet telephony service. The case was set for trial in June 2010 and eventually settled out of court. The firm is also representing ITV in a confrontation with Scottish Television over advertising revenues (STV's opt-out of programmes like *The Bill* and *Midsomer Murders* is set to be a key aspect of the dispute), and acting for BBC Worldwide against the administrators of Woolworths. The Beeb had been in a joint venture with Woolies regarding DVD publishing before the retailer became insolvent. One litigation partner has become known for his expertise in internet libel – "*Facebook defamation, anonymous e-mails, that sort of stuff.*"

Trainees on the Skype case found themselves in an essentially "*administrative*" role, "*helping manage the disclosure process rather than getting your teeth into the intricacies of the law.*" At least it involved "*going to the client, interviewing witnesses and meeting some very eminent QCs.*" Others sources, however, got files of their own and could "*issue the proceedings, write up the claim and deal with everything.*" With commercial lit so popular, other contentious options tend to be overshadowed. Employment is one of these, and yet we spoke to several trainees who enjoyed it enormously. An "*intimate*" team, since the recession it has had more litigation than transactional work, reflecting a surge in constructive dismissal claims (Olswang tends to act for the defendant). "*Lots of small matters plus ongoing work that isn't all-consuming*" make the perfect environment for good trainee responsibility, and although there's plenty of document bundling to do trainees will also draft compromise agreements and witness statements and attend tribunal hearings.

This is the best place you will ever work. FACT.

And so to the commercial group. The BBC, ITV, Channel 4, Sky, M & C Saatchi, Microsoft and Trinny and Susannah are but a few of the names who use the department, so no wonder it's perpetually in demand. But is it all it's cracked up to be?

"*Fantastic!*" was the verdict of one trainee. "*I've really been given the opportunity to get talking to clients and to draft documents. If you're in the film finance team, you'll definitely get on the phone to agents and try and negotiate certain points. It's really interesting, and it is actually quite glamorous at times. The associate I sit with has become quite blasé about it; he forgets how exciting it is!*" The team has been advising the UK Film Council (now to be axed by the coalition government) on its investment in British movies, and it provided the production lawyers for Sony Pictures Entertainment on the film *Cemetery Junction*, negotiating contracts for stars Ralph Fiennes and Emily Watson and writer/producers Ricky Gervais and Stephen Merchant.

Again, a word of warning. Olswang's media operation is so successful that it has just about reached its maximum size. Media work will remain important, but the commercial department is increasingly concentrating on bringing in lucrative outsourcing and telecoms deals. Good news for the firm, but it does mean there's no guarantee trainees will see the sexiest work, even in an MCT seat. Actually, outsourcing work is pretty interesting in itself: the firm advised the Post Office as it embarked on an arrangement with the DVLA to allow people to enrol their biometric details at a Post Office branch and so renew their driving licences. Sources say that getting "*a mix*" of all kinds of work is likely, but it's the luck of the draw whether you get lots of one thing and little of others.

Unmentioned so far is Olswang's small Reading office, which handles commercial, employment, real estate and banking matters. It recruits a small number of its own trainees every year, and the general expectation is that they will spend their whole training contract in that town. Trainees in each location can go on secondment to a client, and it could even be a well-known broadcasting company. Here, they are "*basically part of the in-house team,*" gaining "*experience that would be harder to get in a law firm.*" A competition law seat in Brussels is also often available. On the subject of international work, Olswang additionally has a Berlin office and recently signed up to a 'non-exclusive alliance' with US firm Cooley.

The ex files

Our interviewees recognised "*the tongue-in-cheek image of the semi-trendy media trainee.*" To us, they came across as chirpy, unpretentious and socially graceful rather than ultra-cool types who'd wear sunglasses indoors given half a chance. "*Some of the MCT solicitors are genuinely glam and go to all the right parties, but if you look at the trainees I'm not sure we're the coolest,*" said one. "*I wouldn't say we are particularly un-cool,*" he continued, adding that "*mutual respect*" and "*working together*" were more important defining characteristics. Others agreed. "*The firm does well; even as a trainee you really feel proud to be part of Olswang.*"

While the firm takes plenty of applicants straight from academia, there is usually a clutch who've had previous careers. This year, we heard about "*a former TV script editor, someone who worked in advertising for a bit and someone with a year's experience at a film production company,*" but also an ex-teacher, an ex-accountant and "*people who have paralegalled here, there and everywhere.*"

With no trainee social budget to play with, beyond an end-of-month drinks event, our contacts "*wouldn't say there's lots and lots of organised fun*" and so they generally make their own entertainment. They seem an adventurous crew and, in addition to the standard movie nights and house parties, some had been rage-buggying during a weekend in the West Country. We also heard about a polo day ("*Oh no, that will make us sound like we're all really posh and we're not!*") and some people went to Rebel Bingo in Shoreditch (Google it). Sporty types can get into five-a-side football and softball.

The elephant in the room

Qualification is a rigorous process. Trainees need to apply for a position, make a good impression at an interview and sometimes take exams as well. This ensures everything is fair and above board, especially important given how popular some departments are. It's stressful though, and our sources acknowledged that "*there will be good people who will leave*" because they can't get into the departments they want. In the end, just 13 out of 24 qualifiers stayed. A total of 19 vacancies were actually advertised: as already mentioned, commercial litigation was heavily oversubscribed.

MTV may have vanished from the reception area but when we poked our head around the door in summer 2010, in its place was a large pachyderm. Olswang had adopted a colourfully decorated statue on behalf of the Elephant Family charity. The firm has made "*a big push*" in its pro bono and corporate social responsibility activities in the past couple of years: visit our website to find out more. It also takes diversity issues seriously and anyone can set up an affinity group, although we're told that so far there are only three: an LGBT society, a Christian society and a real ale society. To our beer-loving, gay, devout readers: never let it be said there isn't a firm for you.

And finally...

A bright and breezy mid-market firm, Olswang is right for people who want mainstream commercial experience with a media slant.

Orrick Herrington & Sutcliffe (Europe) LLP

The facts

Location: London

Number of UK partners/solicitors: 13/32

Total number of trainees: 10

Seats: 4x6 months

Alternative seats: Potentially overseas seats

Extras: Pro bono – A4ID, LawWorks, Citizens Advice Bureau

On chambersstudent.co.uk
- How to get into Orrick
- Ralph Baxter: the man behind modern Orrick
- A history of many mergers

Global Orrick = massive. Orrick in London = petite. It's a winning combination if you want huge multinational deals but don't fancy being one of a hundred trainees.

Global conqueror

Orrick is sitting pretty these days in new offices on Cheapside. After a 12-year stint in Tower 42, this San Francisco-founded firm is stepping it up. "*We are an ambitious firm in growth mode,*" says London managing partner Anne O'Neill. In fact, Orrick has been growing for the last 20 years, evolving from a 200-lawyer California outfit to a global one with 1,100 lawyers in 22 offices. Its traditional strength is in finance, so when the London office opened in 1998, it was logical that focus was put on the structured finance market. The credit crisis virtually stopped such transactions but created a windfall of restructuring and refinancing that has kept lawyers busy.

What is London's place in the wider network? "*We're not just a satellite office. Three-quarters of the London business originates in London,*" says Anne O'Neill. Trainees think that "*sometimes we have our leash yanked from across the Atlantic,*" but that management has "*taken a keener interest in all our overseas offices since 2009.*" They point to scuppered merger talks with SJ Berwin as evidence of Orrick's commitment to growing in London. Don't read too much into the failure of merger talks, though. "*We talk to other people all the time,*" assured O'Neill. Orrick has intended to increase the size of the London office for a while, but the recession put a stop to that. The new building has two empty floors just itching to be populated. "*We are looking to double in size ASAP,*" said O'Neill, adding: "*We want to compete with the magic and silver circles.*"

With major international growth already, and more likely, the challenge for Orrick worldwide is to remain unified despite its size. How's it going so far? "*There's a lot of talk about being one big family, but I think we operate as different firms,*" opined one trainee. Another said: "*As far as work is concerned, there's a lot of collaboration and information exchange, but beyond that I don't know.*" Perhaps it's quite hard to see beyond London's four walls.

Pick a team, any team

Considering Orrick London only has around 50 lawyers, there's a decent spread of practice areas to keep trainees on their toes. Of their four seats, at least one needs to be contentious, chosen from commercial litigation, competition, employment or restructuring, while transactional options include corporate, finance and real estate. The firm is also considering reinstating a Hong Kong seat and "*looking at the possibility*" of a Paris seat, according to training principal Simon Cockshutt. Trainees don't find out "*until the very last moment*" what their first seat will be, but are encouraged to make clear in their mid-seat appraisals where they'd like to go for the others. The firm does its best to give them their first choice. The work allocation system has also become slightly less structured. A "*first-come, first-served*" approach now means trainees can receive work from anyone, though much of it will still come from their assigned supervisor.

Chambers UK rankings

Asset Finance	Social Housing
Private Equity	

Central to making London a "*key strategic office*" is a plan to grow the corporate group. Doing so should prove interesting, since a good chunk of the team departed in early 2010, leaving only three full-time partners. The firm says it is actively looking for replacements who will bring M&A and private equity expertise. The current partners focus on M&A and venture capital, with trainees taking charge of many of the easier assignments – "*the usual Companies House filings, drafting minutes and resolutions, etc.*" Despite the team's small size, the deals can be massive. A good example is the recent $23.8bn merger completed for Norwegian telecoms client Telenor – one of the biggest mergers in Europe in 2009. One trainee reported "*completely manic*" hours in corporate during one part of their seat, although "*things eased up eventually.*"

Those who land in the global finance group – a cornerstone practice with "*great camaraderie*" but "*unpredictable hours*" – will sample either structured, project or asset finance. One trainee worked on shipping finance, which involves "*learning arcane terminology and resolving insurance issues.*" Another example of the team's work is its recent representation of Standard Bank in the refinancing of Total Kenya's purchase of Chevron service stations in Kenya. As you can tell, much of Orrick's work is international in nature. Of course, there's also "*run-of-the-mill finance,*" and there's no avoiding some of the "*classic trainee stuff – proof-reading, checking things and filling out Form 395s for Companies House.*"

Apron strings not included

With only two partners (including training principal Simon Cockshutt) and two to three trainees in the litigation team, expect "*loads of responsibility.*" That may mean "*handling your own cases*" with partner supervision, "*going to court*" or "*meeting with clients and third parties.*" A bit less exciting is the research and memo drafting, although it depends what subjects you're looking at. The small but perfectly formed team has been representing media conglomerate Vivendi in a dispute with Deutsche Telekom and Elektrim over the control of a Polish mobile phone company worth more than $5bn.

The "*fantastic*" real estate seat is in a well-established team that's been together for 20 years. The group recently advised old and loyal client Capital Shopping Centres on the St David's Dewi Sant development in Cardiff, one of the largest shopping centres of its kind in Europe. Trainees normally join this team in their first year. "*It's a great way to start,*" said one; "*they look out for their team members and get you involved as much as possible.*" Getting involved means "*liaising with clients and other solicitors on a daily basis.*" The small (one partner, one associate) restructuring department, meanwhile, offers "*a huge variety of high-level work with a ton of responsibility. You're treated more like an associate.*" The team has recently been involved in large cross-border insolvencies involving hedge funds that imploded after the Madoff scandal broke.

Trainees are appraised twice a seat but "*that may be the only feedback you get,*" said one who'd experienced "*people sitting on my paperwork for weeks without letting me know if I did it well or not.*" Others agreed that, with some exceptions, supervisors could be a bit more on the ball with day-to-day feedback. Trainees also bemoaned that they no longer share offices with associates and now room with each other. This was disappointing for some of our sources but we're told the office layout makes it difficult to arrange anything different.

A-ten-hut!

Trainees roundly agree that people at the firm are "*friendly*" and that Orrick operates a "*non-hierarchical structure. It's not every firm where trainees go out for a beer with a partner just because.*" Another notable feature of Orrick lawyers is that many "*did other things before becoming a lawyer.*" Cockshutt confirms: "*We actively look for people with interesting CVs. Those candidates possess a level of maturity we find attractive.*" Commercial experience in the City is especially valued, and past and present trainees have worked for organisations ranging from multinational conglomorates to the military.

Military organisational skills could come in handy. At the annual Christmas party, it's up to trainees to provide the entertainment. In 2009, they debuted the 'O Factor', a singing contest in which all in attendance let loose their inner Eltons and Arethas. "*It was a big success – even the partners sang!*"

And finally...

Orrick is going to appeal to students interested in international practice. The London office is likely to evolve over the coming years and, in 2010, eight out of ten qualifiers stayed on to find out how.

Osborne Clarke

The facts

Location: Bristol, London, Reading

Number of UK partners/solicitors: 84/198

Total number of trainees: 33

Seats: 4x6 months

Alternative seats: Secondments

On chambersstudent.co.uk
- How to get into OC
- OC's overseas interests
- Trainees describe OC's culture

With three UK offices and a reputation for innovation, Osborne Clarke is a regional top cat with its eye on a bigger piece of the City's corporate pie.

Fortune favours the brave

Osborne Clarke is a venerable and established name in the South West, with a history that dates back to 1748. In the 1830s, founder Jeremiah Osborne's grandson helped the Great Western Railway survey its route along the River Avon and, 180-odd years later, the firm continues to win big clients. The corporate team recently advised Carphone Warehouse on its demerger from TalkTalk and its subsequent £450m refinancing. The firm's 'puma' logo (nicely revamped to coincide with the fresh and funky redesign of the website) encapsulates its reputation in Bristol: it's a fierce contender vying with long-time rival Burges Salmon for the top spot. *Chambers UK* ranks it as one of the best in the region for construction, corporate finance, dispute resolution, employment, insolvency, IT, IP, pensions, real estate and tax.

Beyond Bristol, the firm's smaller Reading office was opened in 1998 at the height of the dotcom boom: its reputation rests on work for technology companies in the Thames Valley. One of the first regional firms to move into the City in the 1980s, OC has worked hard to become a corporate force and now competes with mid-tier London firms.

According to managing partner Simon Beswick, OC is thinking even bigger and increasingly branching out from its technology expertise. After the dotcom bubble burst, the firm was forced to re-evaluate its strategy. "*From that point on, we appreciated that if you become overly reliant on one sector your fortunes follow that sector,*" Beswick said. "*We took a very conscious decision that we needed to have a broader approach to the market.*" The recent past has seen OC apply its tech strengths to other types of transactions, like banking and finance. "*We recently pitched against two magic circle firms to advise a private equity firm on setting up a new bank. We won it because we understood that it was a technology play as much as a financial services regulatory matter,*" Beswick explained.

The firm revamped its practice model again in 2010, cutting back its target sectors to four. "*First: digital business, because a lot of business is conducted electronically now. We bring that digital electronic experience,*" says Beswick. "*The second is financial services; the third is real estate and infrastructure; and the fourth is energy and natural resources. We're trying to be famous in those four market sectors, and famous for higher-value services.*" The firm has also been savvy in making the most of its overseas network. A base in Silicon Valley serves a valuable marketing function and has won lucrative referrals from American firms, while offices in Germany account for 18% of annual revenue. With exciting deals and international work, trainees get to experience Beswick's assertion first-hand: "*The forefathers of Osborne Clarke would have never in their wildest dreams imagined the high level of work we do today.*"

Root down

Until the September 2009 intake, trainees were hired to work for the firm as a whole, rather than in one particular office. It was expected that trainees would move between the three locations based on their own preferences and,

Chambers UK rankings

Agriculture & Rural Affairs	Investment Funds
Banking & Finance	Media & Entertainment
Banking Litigation	Outsourcing
Capital Markets	Pensions
Charities	Pensions Litigation
Competition/European Law	Planning
Construction	Private Client
Corporate/M&A	Private Equity
Data Protection	Real Estate
Dispute Resolution	Real Estate Litigation
Employee Share Schemes	Restructuring/Insolvency
Employment	Retail
Environment	Sports Law
Health & Safety	Tax
Healthcare	Telecommunications
Information Technology	Transport
Intellectual Property	

sometimes, business needs. The planning became a logistical nightmare and now training contracts are location-specific. Those who had experienced both the old and new systems were happy with the change. "*In the past there was always a danger that you could be uprooted... it works far better now.*" If a trainee has a burning desire to try another office, it can be arranged. "*We assess that on a case-by-case basis,*" said grad recruiter Zoe Reid.

OC newbies speak with the grad team to come up with a tentative plan for their four six-month seats. "*We ask trainees to look at the contract as a whole and not pick seat by seat,*" said Reid. All three locations offer corporate, banking, commercial litigation and property. In addition, in Reading there are general commercial and employment seats; in London you can do general commercial, employment, media and technology and insolvency; while Bristol has the biggest menu with further options in construction, pensions, private client, tax and incentives.

Though there are many options, potential trainees should be aware that with the SRA's contentious/non-contentious requirements, and the firm's requirement for a corporate and either a property or a tax seat, "*things are more rigid*" than they first appear. Commercial and employment seats are always particularly popular; property is less so, but several said they ultimately enjoyed the department more than expected. "*The team is great and because you work on smaller matters you can almost run your own files, so it's good for developing skills and dealing with clients.*"

Climbing the corporate ladder

Corporate is the one seat that every trainee will complete. It's one of the firm's largest departments, but "*because there are fewer trainees than at other firms, work doesn't get diluted down the chain.*" The team handles plenty of M&A and private equity deals, but our sources had also seen quite a bit of public company finance deals. Clients include several financial institutions and retail and energy companies, and it's worth noting that OC is among the best in the UK for private equity deals. Said one source: "*On the private equity side it's the usual mix of VC guys and private equity houses of varying sizes.*" The London office recently advised French Connection on its £5m sale of the Nicole Farhi label to OpenGate Capital. "*You get some typical trainee tasks like verification but you also get involved in drafting.*" The team is "*very inclusive*" and "*makes sure trainees come to every meeting to understand the background of deals.*" Unsurprisingly, corporate seats tend to have the most unpredictable hours, and even in relatively laid-back Bristol can require "*2am finishes.*" Our sources didn't seem to mind: "*You get used to it when the adrenaline kicks in.*" Despite, or perhaps because of the long hours, "*corporate is a very social department.*" When things are slower, "*there's no culture of people staying for no reason and they're quite happy for you to go.*"

Commercial litigation seats are "*very interesting and kind of high-pressure.*" The team acts for financial institutions, technology companies and even some rich Russians. "*Everyone has their own specialities and you're very much encouraged to request work in the sectors you're most interested in.*" One speciality is IP litigation, where trainees assist social networking sites and big-name video game publishers on "*some pretty cutting-edge stuff.*" The different offices collaborate and it's quite common for a London trainee to make a court run to the RCJ on behalf of the Bristol office.

Property is a big area for the firm, and seats might focus on retail clients, regeneration projects (for the likes of big developers such as St Modwen, Persimmon and Barratt), sports venues (stadiums in Poole, Swindon and Reading and the management and refurbishment of the Milton Keynes Bowl), property funds, student accommodation and residential developments. As is often found by trainees everywhere, the hands-on nature of property seats can bring a great sense of achievement, even for relatively new trainees.

London's media seats can be difficult to land. The group is split into a marketing/advertising team and a video and computer games team. The marketing bunch take instructions from clients like Vodafone and M&S, and sometimes a day at the office can involve watching adverts to ensure they comply with the CAP Code. Then there's work for US companies running promotional campaigns for film premieres in the UK. Trainees often deal with terms and conditions for online contests and "*have the first go at redrafting privacy policies.*" The video games team advises major publishers like Nintendo, which "*we are helping with some services through their Wii.*" Sadly, this doesn't mean trainees play MarioKart at work, but we hear "*the client contact is fantastic.*"

Employment is popular too, and trainees report a good mix of contentious and advisory work for financial institutions and media clients. They help prepare for tribunals and with the defence of sexual discrimination and equal pay claims. The seat involves due diligence, but also the drafting of service agreements and contracts plus a great deal of research. "*I was able to negotiate a compromise agreement with the opposition myself,*" said one trainee. Various client secondments are also on offer: the most established is with RAB Capital.

Puma power

Trainees feel the firm's "*quirky*" puma logo embodies its spirit because "*it's fresh, fun and contemporary.*" "*We've even got puma T-shirts for our sport teams.*" OC has open-plan offices in all UK locations, which trainees say is "*really useful for learning because there's more face-to-face contact.*" It also exemplifies the firm's "*non-hierarchical*" ethos: "*If a stranger were to walk into the office, they wouldn't be able to tell who is a partner and who is a trainee.*"

Our sources reckoned Bristol to be "*the most social*" and "*relaxed*" of the three branches. The culture is "*professional but laid-back,*" with an average day ending between 6 and 7pm. Presumably the sting of an occasional later night is alleviated by being able to walk home to a flat in "*a nice Georgian square.*" The city itself has "*quite a buzz about it*" and a bustling arts and music scene. While some claimed "*there aren't a ton of firm-organised activities,*" monthly drinks have recently been reinstated in the office atrium. Trainees regularly kick off the weekend at local watering hole Cornubia and have organised paintball and surfing and camping trips. Rugby, cricket and netball are also popular. Associates and trainees come out and play but "*there's not as much involvement from partners.*"

Evening activities in London "*tend to be more off the cuff*" and departmental rather than office-wide. Look for trainees at local haunt The Spectator on Friday nights. Sources who had enjoyed Bristol's canteen lamented the lack of communal eating space, even though lively Paternoster Square is just around the corner. The office is also conveniently situated by a lovely patch of green known as Postman's Park, home to what is perhaps London's most unusual memorial (more info on our website). It may lack a canteen but the London office, like Bristol, does have a Friday afternoon cake trolley. "*One of the trainees will send an e-mail around the office when it's coming. There's definitely a buzz on Friday afternoons.*" Sounds sugar-induced.

Reading trainees rave about a "*spacious, airy and quite calm*" environment where "*it's easy to get to know everyone.*" The after-work social scene is "*mostly ad hoc,*" but people take advantage of the "*fantastic location virtually on top of the train station and within two minutes of a huge range of places to eat and shop.*"

The three offices will occasionally gather for work, training or play. An annual fancy-dress party is always much anticipated. Before the recession, the firm hired a country estate for a 1980s-themed extravaganza complete with rollerskating, breakdancing and "*alcoholic slush puppies.*" Recent parties have been more modest, but trainees did embrace the wild west theme last year. The firm also hosts an annual "*alliance day,*" so that junior staff can meet their counterparts at affiliated firms across Europe.

The fact that trainee retention was poor in 2009 (and to be honest the firm has an up-and-down record) was making 2010 qualifiers anxious at the time of our calls. Unnecessarily so, it seems: in 2010, 16 out of 18 qualifiers were retained.

And finally...

Whether it's the big name in the South West, the corporate scene in London or the techie vibe of the Thames Valley, OC has a range of attractions.

Pannone LLP

The facts

Location: Manchester, Hale, Alderley Edge, London

Number of UK partners/solicitors: 107/103

Total number of trainees: 31

Seats: 4x6 months

Alternative seats: Occasional secondments

Extras: Pro bono – Manchester University and Manchester Metropolitan University Legal Advice Centres

On chambersstudent.co.uk
- How to get into Pannone
- We talk to training partner Andrea Cohen
- PI and clin neg highlights

If you want to enjoy your days at work and access a variety of different areas of practice during your training then Manchester's Pannone is a smart choice.

Best of the best

With its impressive list of clients spread evenly between private client and commercial practice, *Chambers UK* rankings in a whopping 21 practice areas and a consistent position as the top-ranked law firm in the *Sunday Times*' '100 Best Companies to Work For' list, Pannone sounds too good to be true. However, fiercely loyal trainees insisted that "*all the good things* [they'd] *heard about the firm turned out to be right*" and that while it's a successful law firm, Pannone is "*actually quite a fun place to work.*" Apparently, "*there's a different work ethos here; it's not as old fashioned.*" As one trainee put it: "*You feel like you're part of the team rather than just a resource, even when working with senior partners.*" "*Everyone is treated as you'd expect to be treated,*" training partner Andrea Cohen revealed as the firm's big secret. "*Nothing we do is rocket science. I actually wonder sometimes why other firms don't do what we do.*"

Naturally, there was a lot of hype and speculation when Manchester through-and-through Pannone made its first – albeit baby-steps into London in 2010. "*We don't know* [how it will develop] *at the moment. We opened it because there were requirements and now we're going to see how it goes,*" explained Cohen. Some of the trainees we spoke to mentioned that "*it came as a bit of a surprise*" and "*it was more of a rumour at first – everyone was running around like, 'What? We have a London office? Does it actually exist?'*" However, this is a firm that makes substantial effort to keep its staff in the know. Weekly bulletins are sent out and the firm recently established an 'information consultation' group, which sees representatives from each department meeting every two months.

Pannone's roots lie within its personal injury and clinical negligence practices, both of which are consistently ranked top in the North West by *Chambers UK*. Rodger Pannone, descendent of the original founder, is now a consultant at the firm. During his time in practice Rodger worked on the Opren and thalidomide cases, the Manchester air crash and the Piper Alpha and Lockerbie disasters, which gives some insight into the calibre of work this firm is involved with. But it is not just clinical negligence and PI that draw trainees to the firm; it is the rare breadth of practice areas that they find particularly appealing. "*Like many, I really wasn't sure what kind of law I wanted to practise. It's hard to know when you're just out of uni; that's why Pannone really appealed to me. I knew I'd be able to do a variety of seats,*" said one source.

The seats on offer are personal injury; clinical negligence; family; private client; commercial property; commercial litigation; corporate; employment; construction; insolvency; and regulatory (previously known as business crime). Trainees generally stick to either a commercial or a private client 'stream', but "*some do cross over to get a bit of everything.*" With no compulsory seats it's a perfect system for those who want to pick and mix; however, several trainees mentioned that "*you can't really avoid personal injury.*"

Getting personal

As it is the firm's largest department, half a dozen trainees sit in the personal injury department at any one time. Each is assigned to a team with specialisms ranging from catastrophic head injuries, industrial diseases and death in

Chambers UK rankings

Banking & Finance	Information Technology
Clinical Negligence	Intellectual Property
Construction	Local Government
Corporate/M&A	Partnership
Debt Recovery	Personal Injury
Dispute Resolution	Private Client
Employment	Real Estate
Environment	Real Estate Litigation
Family/Matrimonial	Restructuring/Insolvency
Fraud	Travel

custody, to sports injuries, child abuse issues and holiday accidents. The seat experience can vary depending on what team you're on. For example, if you're working on "*fast-track RTAs* [road traffic accidents]," you're "*given a file to pick up and run with – they're smaller claims, so easy to get into. You'll be the first port of call for many of the clients and will even attend hearings by yourself.*" On the other hand, in relation to serious injuries and industrial diseases, the cases are "*high-value, long-running matters*" where trainees "*play the assistant role but still have a lot of client contact.*" The PI department works closely with the clinical negligence practice, which also offers trainees "*a really, really good experience.*" Trainee time in clin neg will typically be spent "*drafting instructions to counsel and letters to medical experts.*"

The private client department takes on standard wills and trusts instructions and trainees have an opportunity to "*run smaller probate files.*" The team is continuing to grow its Court of Protection practice, and with the help of a significant number of referrals from the clinical negligence department it saw a 50% increase in turnover last year. Pannone's offices in the affluent areas of Alderley Edge (where loads of footballers live) and Hale also offer wills, probate and family advice to private clients. Trainees are sent to these offices when there's a requirement, but they are not official full-seat secondments.

Trainees are exposed to "*quite a good variety of work*" in the family department. Expect to be "*drafting petitions, affidavits and applications for court.*" You'll also "*attend court quiet often, accompanying other fee earners.*" The department represents wealthy individuals and a few quite famous people, and clients' assets sometimes amount to tens of millions of pounds. The department is also developing a system that makes it possible for clients to supply documents for divorce proceedings online.

Pannone's employment group is called upon by the likes of The Bank of England and Toyota Financial Services. It was also recently instructed by Reebok and adidas in relation to a fuller integration of their respective businesses to a single site in Stockport. "*There's a really strong team dynamic and the partners will sort out any questions you have if you go to them,*" one trainee enthused. They also stressed the "*very, very good quality of work, with lots of drafting and client contact.*" Some trainees even had their own "*small advocacy opportunities.*"

Business time

The flourishing commercial litigation department incorporates general commercial, property, IP, debt and professional negligence teams. Pannone's litigators are favourites with some big names including Kellogg and The Co-operative Bank. The firm recently went up against Herbert Smith, representing the former chief executive of JJB Sports, Christopher Ronnie, in a contractual dispute with JJB following his widely reported resignation. "*There's quite a lot of pressure and everything is really last-minute,*" one trainee said; "*it's one of those seats where some people definitely don't like it and some definitely do – I loved it.*" Others described being "*thrown in at the deep end*" of "*large-scale, high-volume matters.*" As with most contentious seats, the majority of trainees' time is spent researching and preparing documents and bundles, but there is also client contact and plenty of time in court. Working on High Court cases or major mediations may even involve trips to London.

When it comes to corporate work, "*it's more small company transactions and private acquisitions.*" However, there are plenty of big companies, like Chevron, that call on Pannone's corporate lawyers. Trainees have "*lots of involvement in those transactions, normally handling due diligence, drafting disclosure letters and other not-so-sophisticated documents.*" They are also invited to meetings with clients. A seat in this department additionally exposes trainees to IP and environmental issues. The firm recently handled the £1.8m public offering for Windpower (Wales), which not only raised money for its ongoing capital requirements, but also brought in community ownership from the surrounding area. This had the effect of creating a 'buy in' to the projects and enabled the company to gain political support in local councils and the Welsh Assembly Government. On the IP side, trainees conduct plenty of research.

The firm's regulatory department has been busy "*handling very interesting high-value fraud work*" in every possible area from money laundering to international corruption. The firm is also heavily involved in internal investigations for corporate clients. A seat in this department involves "*regular trips to court*" and extensive research. Seats in Pannone's insolvency and corporate recovery department are also on offer and are likely to involve working for big-name lenders such as Nationwide and Anglo Irish Bank.

That brings us to commercial property and construction. The recession put the real estate market in a slump, but Pannone has thus far benefited from its established public sector team and experience on development and regeneration work. The firm assists Lancashire County Council to manage the bulk of its property portfolio and has worked on key regeneration projects for Manchester City Council and new clients such as St Helens Council. Of course the safety net provided by the public sector now looks like it will be weakened because of major spending cuts, so bring on the private sector recovery. The construction department works closely with the property and corporate teams and has been busy advising the Greater Manchester Transport Executive on procurement contracts for the Manchester Metrolink Light Rail System. Construction trainees appreciated the fact that the seat had both contentious and non-contentious experiences to offer, albeit that recently it's been "*more contentious because everyone's falling out with each other due to the recession.*"

Let them eat cake

A recent shuffle in management saw managing partner Steven Grant take his predecessor Joy Kingsley's place as senior partner when she left the firm for JMW Solicitors after an amazingly successful career at Pannone. Former head of the clinical negligence department Emma Holt has now stepped into the managing partner position. "*What she's doing is building on what we've got already, and looking into the challenges of the Legal Services Act – looking forward to how we'll tackle it as the changes come about,*" Andrea Cohen told us. Not only does Pannone have a female managing partner, but the partnership itself is over 40% female, which is high for a firm of this size.

It could be this rare gender balance at senior level, family mentality and "*genuine open-door policy*" that make Pannone one of the happiest of all law firms. Or perhaps it is "*being treated like an equal part of the team,*" perks like additional holiday time for good performance or the ubiquitous cake eating. We're putting our money on the cake. "*The rumours are true, you do get a lot of it,*" one source revealed. "*You get cake if you meet targets, if it's someone's birthday, if you've just gone too long without it... any reason you can think of really.*" Praise for baked goods aside, decent work-life balance is another reason why Pannone is a happy workplace. "*It's flexible, as long as they know you're getting your work done; there's no sort of competition for who stays longest,*" one trainee explained. "*There's quite a big 5.01pm club, especially on a Friday,*" another added.

Pannone has a "*cracking*" social scene. "*Everyone* [from the partners to the support staff] *always goes along to the set pieces like the Christmas party and summer barbecue, along with monthly drinks nights.*" Besides that, it's not uncommon to have departmental shindigs and the firm also has a social committee that co-ordinates "*all sorts of events: trips to Madrid and the Christmas markets all over Europe, paintballing, comedy nights, cocktail mixology sessions – they try to accommodate all types of people.*" At trainee-only level, hitting the pub on a Friday, and sometimes Thursday, is a given, and Pannone trainees are heavily involved in the Manchester Trainee Solicitors Group, which puts on "*loads of events.*" Clearly, the firm recruits those who are "*outgoing and willing to get involved.*" Strong Manchester ties are also key, as the firm "*has a bit of a complex that people will use* [their Pannone training] *to go off to London. They want to protect their investment.*" Find more Pannone recruitment tips on our website.

No firm is perfect, and besides its lack of toasters ("*we'll always remember 'toastgate: the day they took all the toasters away' after they kept setting off fire alarms*") the only fault we could dig up on Pannone related to its "*very difficult*" qualification process in 2010. This was mainly down to the fact that it all happened rather late in the day. For 2010 qualifying trainees it was "*a mixed bag*" of outcomes, with most "*being held with a maybe*" during our time of research in early August. "*In the future it might be better to have an answer by a certain date, as this has forced myself and others to apply elsewhere,*" one trainee told us. Cohen explained: "*I appreciate the position they're in, but it is due to the difficult market. It's not because we don't want to keep people on; we are taking extra time to find positions because they are all so good.*" In the end, the firm kept only seven of its 14 trainees.

And finally...

The poor NQ retention result aside, top marks go to the Pannone training scheme again this year. Ingrained within the firm's DNA is an atmosphere that is strong, positive and definitely worthy of emulation.

Paul, Hastings, Janofsky & Walker LLP

The facts

Location: London

Number of UK partners/solicitors: 13/31 (US: 4)

Total number of trainees: 11

Seats: 4x6 months

Alternative seats: Secondments

Extras: Pro bono – LawWorks, Addaction

On chambersstudent.co.uk
- How to get into Paul Hastings
- The strategy for London
- Paul Hastings stateside

Paul Hastings wants London to become its second largest office on the back of finance and banking work. This US BigLaw firm looks for *"robust," "ambitious"* and *"driven"* trainees.

Looking Feder afield

Founded in Los Angeles in 1951, Paul Hastings has expanded to become a global heavyweight, now employing approximately 1,000 lawyers worldwide. It has nine offices in the USA and nine elsewhere. Global chief of real estate Philip Feder recently became head of the UK office, showing the firm's commitment to the City. *"We want to spearhead growth with a deep focus on London,"* Feder told us. Read more on how this office is key to Paul Hastings' future plans on our website.

Despite being on the scene since 1997, Paul Hastings still needs to make a big push before it can claim to be a serious force in the City. It gains considerably fewer rankings in *Chambers UK* than other US firms of a comparable size in London; however, our parent publication does recognise its skills and achievements in real estate finance and capital markets work. Finance is most certainly Paul Hastings' main focus in the Big Smoke. Training partner Christian Parker says that potential trainees must have *"a serious interest in finance, as you may find yourself immersed in that for 16 hours a day."*

Although firm-wide revenue fell almost 10% in 2009, the London office saw turnover rise 40% to £25m. This was in part due to the hire of a seven-partner team from fellow US firm Cadwalader, Wickersham & Taft. They brought a number of trainees with them and it seems they have settled in well. *"There were lots of social events aimed at integration,"* said one ex-Cads trainee. *"We definitely feel part of the Paul Hastings culture: they did as much as they could."* The new hires have given the firm greater strength in several areas and a positive consequence for trainees has been the creation of new seats in restructuring and capital markets, as well as bigger regulation and banking/finance teams. Paul Hastings' existing seats included project finance; real estate; litigation; employment; corporate/M&A; and tax.

A finance romance

No seat is compulsory and trainees are pretty happy with the way they are allocated to the different departments every six months. There are four seats in capital markets, which means that everyone will spend time in this department in one way or another. Capital markets is divided into sub-teams for investment management, commercial mortgage-backed securities (CMBS) and structured funds. But even if your seat is in a particular sub-team, *"you get to do a mixture of things."* In CMBS, for example, trainees might look at *"distressed deals needing restructuring, liquidations and servicing underlying loans."* Structured funds work could include *"working for an investment bank, changing the terms and conditions of notes so that bond-holders didn't make redemptions."* One source felt the work was *"very hands-on,"* adding: *"Clients would call me directly for some of the questions."* Trainees do find themselves *"dropped in at the deep end." "I was asked to do a first draft of a document in my second week,"* one recalled, *"although I knew who to ask for help when I was struggling."*

Chambers UK rankings

Capital Markets	Real Estate Finance

The project finance team handles a great deal of infrastructure work in Southeastern Europe, recently representing the Republika Srpska (a constituent part of Bosnia & Herzegovina) in the construction of over 400 km of motorway. The firm also acts for companies with air and seaport projects in Croatia. This is "*the seat to do if you are interested in working overseas, or if you want to travel: people have spent time in Croatia and Bosnia*" and have met "*high-powered representatives of those countries.*" Although there are no overseas seats, sources also spoke of trips to Brussels and Luxembourg during deals.

Lately, the corporate team has mainly represented investment managers on joint ventures, acquisitions, debt financing and bankruptcy. The workload demands long hours. Said one source: "*I'm pretty much always here past 7pm and usually here until about 8pm; we've done some pretty long all-nighters, perhaps about three or four of those in the last year.*" Clients include Amgen, Visa International and Société Générale.

The magnificent seven

The Cadwalader Seven included a litigation partner and a financial services expert, bringing Paul Hastings new contentious powers. Litigation centres on banking and finance, and the team represented some of Lehman's creditors after its collapse. Regulatory work is "*quite topical*" and has lately included matters relating to "*the Payments Services Directive, which has just been implemented.*" There's "*lots of client contact, but you're expected to work hard and to have the ethic and the drive to get yourself that exposure.*"

In employment, lawyers only act for employers – typically investment banks and other financial institutions, insurers and life sciences companies. "*I worked on a potential litigation and wrote memos to clients,*" one trainee recalled. There are also pro bono matters to attend to, for example "*helping a respondent defend a claim of unfair dismissal.*" Trainees are given greater autonomy on pro bono cases and see it as "*a good way of learning.*"

The Cadwalader team brought with it a secondment to Credit Suisse. Another one in the HR/legal department at Bank of America Merrill Lynch is available through Paul Hastings' employment department, and we understand that position has been a very interesting one, not least because of the bank's merger. Newly qualified lawyers might also have the chance to go on secondment to the likes of Wells Fargo or Société Générale.

Bigger, longer and Uncle Sam

The atmosphere at Paul Hastings is "*entrepreneurial and go-get-it*" so trainees have to be pretty tough. "*You need to be robust here, as well as flexible and easy to get along with.*" There is "*lots of ambition: everyone is quite driven.*" Although one source admitted that "*among the trainees there are competitive people,*" another claimed that you "*don't need to be aggressive*" to get ahead. What you must do is "*show that you're keen,*" and helping out with business development is a good way of demonstrating your eagerness. In terms of the work, it's accepted that while "*you'll be challenged and there is nowhere to hide,*" colleagues are "*supportive*" and the firm is very good in terms of "*approachability and a friendly culture.*" Trainees say that "*there are quite a few eccentric partners and there will be the occasional e-mail which gets a giggle, but that's as extreme as it gets.*" All this chimes with what office chief Phil Feder tells us about the work culture: "*We're in this together: no one is exempt from working hard.*"

The dreaded (to us at least) phrase "*work hard, play hard*" came up, with one source explaining that "*you're expected to put in the hours, but I haven't had to miss out on anything in my private life.*" Others said their social life did sometimes take a back seat. One trainee summarised: "*You need to be available – we're given BlackBerrys on day one for a reason.*" The fact that there is "*more a focus on work*" means firm social events are not constant. "*We do have drinks every few months or so, but it's not a particularly frequent occurrence.*" Phil Feder did invite all London lawyers to a Thanksgiving party at his house, however. One of our sources revealed that there are "*quite a few American lawyers and it does feel like an American firm.*" Trainees have a social budget of their own, which in the past has been spent on cookery classes and a casino night. There is a football team and tennis and squash competitions, and lawyers are "*keen to go out for a drink on special occasions.*"

Four out of the seven qualifiers stayed on with the firm in 2010 and took advantage of the generous pay packet on offer. Trainees start on £40,000 and earn £80,000 on qualification.

And finally...

Paul Hastings offers a refreshing and challenging training that would suit someone interested in top finance clients and willing to show their worth through hard graft.

Penningtons Solicitors LLP

The facts

Location: Basingstoke, Godalming, London

Number of UK partners/solicitors: 51/85

Total number of trainees: 18

Seats: 4x6 months

Alternative seats: None

On chambersstudent.co.uk
- How to get into Penningtons
- The firm's CSR initiatives
- A few of the firm's headline cases and deals

Remodelled for the 21st century, but retaining a hint of 'Establishment' tradition, 200-year-old Penningtons is cementing its one-firm approach in the Home Counties and London.

All change for South West services

Penningtons' reputation as one of the South's more traditional firms has been challenged of late. A strategic review in 2007 has led it to a 'one-firm policy' by which its work is shared between its three offices in Basingstoke, Godalming and London. Chief executive David Raine has set the goal of doubling revenue and profits by 2012 and tells us he is "*confident we will achieve that.*" Penningtons came in at number 89 on *The Lawyer*'s 2009 list of the top 100 firms, with revenue of £22.5m and profits per partner at a low £85,000. Raine explained this is a result of "*the costs of restructuring in what was a pretty disastrous year for the industry as a whole,*" which included reducing costs, trainee deferrals, redundancies and moving people between departments. "*The last year has been much better,*" he was pleased to tell us.

One trainee described Penningtons as having "*traditional qualities because it's quite an old firm but it's not backwards.*" A fair enough statement, but perhaps not the whole story. There's a "*drive to be more entrepreneurial*" and "*a mix of international and good old Home Counties clients.*" Although it is becoming more innovative – introducing new trainee seats and practice groups – trainees say the firm "*will never forget its history and existing clients.*"

All this talk of tradition stems from the fact that Penningtons has retained practices and work that many other commercial firms dropped in the 1990s, and it still acts for wealthy private individuals and ancient institutions. Said one source: "*Our private clients do include people who've had money for generations, but we also serve entrepreneurs.*" Having said this, the bulk of Penningtons' work is commercial, covering property, dispute resolution, employment, professional regulation and business immigration. Attempts to attract instructions from big corporate and international clients are ongoing, and the corporate finance team has had some success on this front, acting for tongue-twisting Danish pensions fund Kommunernes Pensionforsikring as well as clients in Greece and Norway.

Of the 16 trainees beavering away at Penningtons when we rang in April 2010, four were based in Basingstoke, five in Godalming and seven in London. The seats trainees take are usually determined by friendly "*negotiation*" among themselves. "*If we can make up our minds and there are no clashes, HR will go with our decision; otherwise they will discuss it with us.*" Trainees complete four six-month seats, with repeats not only permitted but frequent. "*I'm doing a particular seat again because I wanted to have a good stab at it,*" confirmed one source.

An interesting side effect of the recession-triggered slowdown in work has been that it is now possible for trainees to switch between offices, something that was unlikely in the past. "*They do let you go to other offices if there is a spare seat,*" although it is still dependent on business

Chambers UK rankings

Clinical Negligence	Professional Discipline
Corporate/M&A	Real Estate
Employment	Real Estate Litigation
Immigration	Social Housing
Personal Injury	Tax
Private Client	Travel

needs. Moving is an "*effortless*" process. "*It's all part of the one-firm policy, I suppose,*" a trainee mused. Godalming and Basingstoke are each a 45-minute commute from Waterloo, so easy enough to get to from the capital. The ride out should be smooth and uncrowded, courtesy of Penningtons' client South West Trains.

Negligence pays

The firm is divided into three pan-office divisions: business services, commercial property and private individuals. There is a decentralised element to the work, however, and the different branches of these divisions still work on different types of cases and deals. In Basingstoke a good chunk of the private individuals practice involves clinical negligence. Take, for example, the case of a schoolgirl who won a six-figure sum after doctors failed to treat her properly when she dislocated her knee during netball practice. Non-contentious work in Basingstoke includes drafting wills and giving tax advice, and this is the only office offering contentious private client experience on disputed wills. "*I worked on quite a few cases where we went to court,*" one trainee was happy to report.

The Godalming private individuals team chiefly handles personal injury cases relating to accidents and injuries abroad. With a niche in travel law, the team acts both for big insurance companies like AXA and Allianz, and for holidaying Brits who have come a cropper. "*In the PI and travel departments, there's good hands-on action as soon as you start.*"

In a London private individuals seat, trainees are more likely to work on massive trust funds, capital gains tax and non-dom issues for offshore pension providers and wealthy families. On occasion, international financial work spills over into the Godalming and Basingstoke offices too. The London team has been busy advising clients with substantial overseas-held assets that could become liable for UK tax.

From Basingstoke to Belize

Although property seats are technically not compulsory, "*everyone will do a property seat*" in London and they are almost ubiquitous elsewhere. The Basingstoke and Godalming property groups handle both residential and commercial matters, with part of the Basingstoke team also working on social housing. "*There's a lot of development and landlord and tenant work. We work for quite big organisations: for example, looking at the leasing of one company's shop units across the country.*" Within the property department, London's small but growing construction group deals with numerous matters relating to PFIs, as well as commercial developments. The team will often do work for lenders and institutional property clients like Abbey, Allied Irish Banks and Aviva, mainly on mid-market deals. The team also assists charities and non-profit organisations like The Trustees of Borough Market and The Fire Fighters Charity.

The business service division is the firm's largest and it covers commercial dispute resolution, employment, professional regulation and business immigration. A dispute resolution seat is pretty much a cert in London and common elsewhere. You get to "*run parts of large ongoing projects and debt recovery files,*" although there is plenty of supervision. "*You don't work on things in a throw-the-file-at-you type of way.*" Long-standing banking litigation clients include two from the Indian subcontinent: Syndicate Bank and Bank of India.

In an employment seat in Basingstoke, trainees might find themselves representing senior corporate managers or major UK or international companies like GMTV, Twentieth Century Fox and Irish banana people Fyffes – which apparently dominates banana production in Belize. Other clients include Godalming's Charterhouse School and Italian train signal manufacturers Ansaldo STS. In London's professional regulation department, trainees might find themselves acting for the Royal College of Veterinary Surgeons, not to mention the legal profession's very own Solicitors Regulatory Authority. "*You get to prosecute rogue solicitors and rogue vets, which is quite satisfying.*" Penningtons lawyers were also involved when the SRA struck off Andrew Nulty, a solicitor at another firm who made £13m out of compensation claims for sick miners. You can read the incredible story of Nulty's rise and fall on our website.

London's immigration team saw a boost in its operations in November 2009, when it took on two people from KPMG. This means immigration is now a trainee seat in its own right, and a "*popular one*" at that. Clients include Richard Rogers' firm of architects and Tetleys (of tea, not beer, fame) as well as a host of other commercial, leisure and art world clients. Lawyers also handle immigration and asylum cases for private individuals, winning refugee status for *Big Brother 6* contestant Makosi Musambasi in 2005. Since then, Penningtons has built a niche in representing Zimbabweans, as well as Latin American and West African asylum seekers.

Scenic Surrey and lively London

The cobblestoned streets of picturesque Godalming play host to commuters and local celeb residents like Alan Hansen and Ashley Cole. The town is also the location for Penningtons' annual firm-wide sports day, which is "*a big day in everyone's calendar.*" The sports and social committee organises cinema trips, curry nights and pub quizzes, which "*everyone comes along to.*" Italian restaurant chain Prezzo is a popular lunchtime haunt, and lunches tend to be solid rather than liquid.

"*We've got a bowling event tomorrow,*" one Basingstoke trainee told us, adding that social events were reasonably frequent. This office is sited on a business park – think *The Office* without the creepy people – and "*most people commute in.*" As such, impromptu lunches are infrequent and there is "*no culture of the whole office going to the pub.*" Finally, the London office is "*sociable*" and "*inclusive,*" with "*big events organised once every two or three months.*" These include theatre trips and curry nights. "*Everyone goes out together*" for Friday night drinks and popular haunts include The Livery, The Red Herring, The Lord Raglan and Williamson's Tavern.

In both London and Godalming, Penningtons people have moved into "*spanking new*" offices in the past couple of years. The open-plan layout in London means "*it's scary when you are on the phone and you've just started a new seat, but it does make you learn quicker.*" It also means that partners are "*easy to approach.*" Said one trainee: "*I can hear when my supervisor is having a good or a bad day.*" Although the offices have different social scenes and work purview, Penningtons' culture and character remains essentially the same across all three. It's "*open,*" "*respectful of your personal life,*" "*not massively lively but never that quiet*" and "*dangerously middle class.*"

Quality of, and enthusiasm for, work is what gets people ahead here. "*There's no 'jackets on the back of seats' culture and no one expects you to behave a certain way to impress people.*" Sources also say that "*the partners themselves are against a focus on chargeable hours*" over the quality of trainees' learning experiences. Standard working hours in London are a reasonable 9am to 6pm. "*Sometimes I might have to stay until 7.30pm or 8pm at the latest,*" one source said, but all-nighters are largely out of the question. Elsewhere, the trainees tend to get in earlier and sometimes leave earlier too.

Although some of our sources thought Penningtons needs to "*blow its own trumpet a bit more,*" one described it as "*confident not arrogant,*" adding that "*it's not a show-offy firm, but we're pretty damned good at what we do.*" Trainees get involved with marketing events: indeed, one won the annual 'Firmwide Networker' award, which usually goes to a qualified fee earner. In 2010, six out of ten qualifiers stayed on.

And finally...

With mainstream work plus some interesting specialities, Penningtons is an attractive option for anyone wanting to encounter private individuals and corporate clients.

- **Street Fighter? Space Invader? Tomb Raider?**
  Harbottle & Lewis and Osborne Clarke are the top dogs for computer games law. You might also consider Bird & Bird, Bristows, DLA Piper, Hogan Lovells, Davenport Lyons, Lawrence Graham, Sheridans, Speechly Bircham and Weightmans. www.chambersandpartners.com can tell you which firms specialise in all kinds of niche areas of law.

Pinsent Masons

The facts

Location: London, Birmingham, Manchester, Leeds, Bristol, Scotland

Number of UK partners/solicitors: 253/626

Total number of trainees: 122

Seats: 4x6 months

Alternative seats: Overseas seats, secondments

Extras: Pro bono – eg Business in the Community, Leeds Ahead

On chambersstudent.co.uk
• How to get into PM
• Pinsent Masons across the UK
• We talk to HR director Jonathan Bond

Pinsent Masons is an extensive full-service commercial firm with multiple UK offices, international interests and defined client sectors, one of the more notable being construction and engineering.

Sectorise and internationalise

In spite of the Arctic chill in the economy and two relatively disappointing years in the core property and corporate departments, our sources at PM were full of respect for those who have trained them. Their mood music was upbeat, and why not? PM has cosied up with international firm Salans in what looks set to become an almost exclusive relationship. Whispers of a merger have amounted to little, but in Shanghai the firm is taking the step of moving in with its international alliance partner. Then there is the firm's latest joint venture in Singapore alongside local firm MPillay. This could see its Asia-Pacific investment expand further and its international presence strengthen. PM has also taken a long look at its business model and made a move to what it calls a 'sectoral' approach. This allows it to identify with clients' commercial interests and, as HR Director Jonathan Bond says: "*Our clients want to know that we understand their sector, not if we're either banking or corporate lawyers.*" Then there is also the hope that the last couple of years' poorer NQ retention rates and dwindling partnership promotions have reached their lowest ebb.

PM has established credentials and strong foundations. The firm has a whole clutch of impressive *Chambers UK* rankings to its name right across the commercial landscape. This all equates to a four-seat training scheme that is full of promise for trainees. Our report covers the English scheme, where trainees are recruited to London, Manchester, Leeds and Birmingham and typically stay in their 'home' office for all four seats, although some will go to Dubai or a client for six months. The range of seats in each office is detailed on our website. A separate Scottish training scheme operates, too, as does one in Hong Kong.

One fir all and all fir one

While no seats are compulsory "*it's more than likely that you'll do one in either corporate or property,*" says graduate recruitment manager Edward Walker. The corporate deal arena slowed considerably during the recession, though the firm's AIM machine remained finely tuned: look no further than that team's role advising Regal Petroleum – a top 50 FTSE AIM-quoted oil and gas company – on its secondary placing to raise $104.7m. But even corporate kings sometimes have to settle for smaller fare, such as the £2.3m buyout of the production company HandMade by Almorah Services, a measly amount considering it owns the rights to such cult classics as *Life of Brian*, *Withnail & I* and *Lock, Stock and Two Smoking Barrels*. Trainees were satisfied with their corporate experience; it was "*never crazy out of control busy, but good busy.*" The work can get a little repetitive at times ("*I could do completion documents in my sleep*"), but it's not all hard graft. "*After one completion we dressed as Christmas trees and went out for quite a few drinks!*" We suppose that happened in December, but kind of hope not.

Property is hot at PM, and so is the seat. "*It was all hands to the pump,*" reminisced one source who had spent some

Chambers UK rankings

Banking & Finance	Local Government
Capital Markets	Media & Entertainment
Competition/European Law	Outsourcing
Construction	Pensions
Corporate/M&A	Pensions Litigation
Data Protection	Planning
Dispute Resolution	Private Equity
Education	Professional Negligence
Employee Share Schemes	Projects
Employment	Public Procurement
Energy & Natural Resources	Real Estate
Environment	Real Estate Litigation
Health & Safety	Restructuring/Insolvency
Healthcare	Retail
Information Technology	Tax
Insurance	Telecommunications
Intellectual Property	Transport
Life Sciences	

time working on a large portfolio sale for an investment client. Evidently the lawyers make a real effort with trainees. "*I had a great supervisor; it was a really nice department... really friendly and sociable, and they gave me a lot of guidance.*" If property gives you the chance to run a lot of your own files because some transactions are fairly small, tasks in the projects team are very different because the projects are "*much bigger and longer term.*" The department's work covers everything from roads to energy to health sector projects, and with offices in Dubai, Singapore, Shanghai and Beijing, the work has "*a very international feel.*" As part of the sectoral drive, there is a newly merged projects and construction department that has both contentious and non-contentious work teams.

PM's construction lawyers represent some of the country's biggest industry players, including Carillion, Bovis Lend Lease and Balfour Beatty. Its long-term collaboration with the first of these most recently saw the firm land a role advising an MoD consortium led by the construction company on the redevelopment of Aldershot barracks and Salisbury Plain garrisons. The construction lawyers have developed a formidable reputation abroad, particularly in the UAE where they often lead in significant transactions involving pipelines and international airports. Trainees told us that while there was rarely any need for "*full-blown litigation,*" when preparing for trial they would be "*looking after trial bundles, liaising with counsel, drafting witness statements, sending letters to court, dropping off documents and doing research on points of law.*" Said one: "*What's good is that you are taken under the wing of partners in the disputes team and are encouraged to actively participate. Often what happens is that, even if letters don't go out in my name, I'll at least get to do a first draft.*" On the non-contentious side, trainees encountered matters such as a Highways Agency project for the M25 motorway, worth in excess of £6bn, and a £2.4bn Building Schools for the Future project in Birmingham – the most expensive of its kind to come to market (never mind the fact that BSF is now defunct).

Back to school

Tax and employment seats are always popular. Tax seats are "*really hands-on,*" with different queries coming from a variety of other departments. "*They're not the typical tax-type people – I really enjoyed it and everyone was so friendly*" recalled one source. Another trainee was equally enthusiastic about employment: "*The best thing was the quality of the work. It was real black letter law, and there is always a claimant at the end. I was doing the sexy stuff like discrimination.*" Another said it was "*a nice change of pace. The law is changing from week to week, from case to case, so it's great from an academic point of view.*" Ultimately, it is the client contact that makes this seat so appealing: "*It's more of a personal seat. You're asking the witness to give their thoughts and feelings, so you feel a little bit closer to the clients.*" PM also has a renowned pensions practice that represents the likes of Cadbury Pension Schemes, Premier Foods Pension Scheme, AXA UK and Friends Provident. The department received a further boost in London when it hired Taylor Wessing's practice head in May 2010.

The old 'outsourcing, technology and commercial' department has now combined with the dispute resolution department to form a new division called 'strategic business services'. Trainees taking a seat in the area of outsourcing and technology find that the work has two aspects: one is more transactional in nature and involves close working with data protection and information law teams; the other is "*analysis of big-name contracts and agency agreements.*" Having household names such as Bird's Eye, Odeon Cinemas and Manchester United as clients is what makes for "*a really enjoyable seat, because you get to see behind the scenes.*" The attraction is similar when it comes to client secondments: there's one to Müller – complete with plenty of free yoghurt – and others include John Lewis, AXA, AIG and Man U. Naturally, secondments may change from time to time. Currently the only overseas seat is in Dubai, although the firm is considering Hong Kong and other locations within Salans' international network.

The general view is that PM's training contract remains thorough and well run. "*If you look at it from the point of view of having a great portfolio and training then it's a fantastic experience.*" Particular appreciation was reserved for the quality of supervision: "*I had very good supervisors; they could have been teachers in another life,*" said one source. Feedback suggests that people at all levels are keen to give trainees as much exposure as possible: "*They're always asking, 'Have you drafted a response? Have you been to a tribunal? Have you been to a mediation? If not, come along!'*"

Hold the line

"*Six years on, the different cultures have been fully assimilated into one firm,*" HR Director Jonathan Bond told us. It was as long ago as 2004 that Masons merged with Pinsents, and yet London staff will only start working together under one roof in early 2011, when three separate offices will be replaced by shiny new digs at 30 Crown Place. We discuss the English office specs in more detail online.

Sportsmen and women will receive a warm embrace at PM, where teams are as much about the collegiate atmosphere as competition. "*I play touch rugby, cricket, softball, netball,*" said one trainee. "*It's really good for getting to know people from different levels and other practices, and meeting the people from the other side of the conference table.*" An introduction to this breaking down of barriers can be experienced as early as the vac scheme, where one trainee relished the opportunity of "*playing for the firm's football team and telling partners to hold the line or pull back!*" On the pitch or off, PM are a sociable lot and they see playing hard as a natural counterbalance to working hard. The Manchester and Birmingham offices appear to be leaders in this respect, with the former having implemented a Friday evening drinks trolley in the office's deli – an opportunity for partners and trainees to graze on the same turf (though one of the trainees assured us "*it's not Club 18-30*"). In the spirit of one-upmanship, "*the weekend starts on Thursday*" in Birmingham, with a night at nearby Asha's bar offering two-for-one cocktails leading into a dress-down jeans day on Friday. The Yorkshire trainees may lack numbers "*but we can usually get a crowd of ten or more for any birthdays.*" Down south the Londoners will no doubt be on the hunt for new favourite watering holes when they move offices.

Bound together

Is there much inter-regional exchange between Masonic lodges? Well the entire new intake does get together at the beginning of the contract, going away for a week in Bedford. Sadly, 2010 saw the cancellation of the hugely popular National Trainee Day, but sources in the know were able to confirm that it will be resurrected as there is "*nothing quite so useful as getting everyone together.*" Another tie that binds is a strong corporate social responsibility drive, with numerous charity initiatives, mentoring programmes and reading schemes to participate in. We heard about a long-running business advice clinic in Birmingham; organisations called Heart of the City and Arts & Business; and the charities Starfish and SOS Children's Villages International. PM is also rightly proud of its diversity achievements and as well as being the first firm to be made part of the Stonewall Workplace Equality Index, it now also has LGBT, black and minority ethnic, women, family, disability and faith diversity groups.

In weighing up this feature, we find ourselves caught between the firm's rock-steady reputation and obvious investment in the training process, and the hard fact that for the second year running PM's NQ retention figures have been very low. A total of just 37 out of 61 qualifiers took up NQ jobs in 2010. Trainees admitted that it was "*difficult to be positive when the retention rates are what they are*" but pointed the finger of blame at the recession (indeed, the firm's retention was always respectable before 2009). One stoically said: "*What I would say to anyone thinking of applying is that PM's training contracts are held in high esteem and will stand you in good stead whatever happens. In the long run, if you've got a rubbish training contract under your belt, your chances of getting a job anywhere else are that much worse. People shouldn't be put off by retention rates: it's the nature of the beast at the moment. Look for quality.*"

And finally...

Pinsent Masons has a very respected name in the marketplace and a timely 'sectorised' approach to business.

Reed Smith LLP

The facts

Location: London

Number of UK partners/solicitors: 103/140

Total number of trainees: 50

Seats: 4x6 months

Alternative seats: Overseas seats, secondments

Extras: Pro bono – Liberty, Queen Mary Legal Advice Centre, U-Turn; language classes

On chambersstudent.co.uk
- How to get into Reed Smith
- More on CareeRS
- U-Turn: a Reed Smith pro bono project

During its meteoric rise from regional US firm to international juggernaut, Reed Smith has experienced some growing pains. A new office and a sharper focus in London could take it out of its awkward stage.

Reed it and weep

In just ten years, Reed Smith has transformed a small London outpost into the largest office in a global network of 1,600 lawyers in 23 offices, 15 of them in the USA, four in Europe, two in Asia and two in the Middle East. After a breakthrough merger with mid-market City firm Richards Butler (RB) in 2007, Reed Smith seemed to lose its sense of direction. It gained 250 lawyers and RB's specialist shipping and media law teams, but rather than exploiting those areas and consolidating its assets, it went on a hiring spree, attracting a slew of partners from big players like Freshfields and Herbert Smith in such a wide range of fields that it seemed like it was growing for growth's sake.

The timing of the firm's aggressive expansion couldn't have been less fortuitous. The recession took its toll and UK revenue dropped 11% to $141.1m in 2009 from $159m the year before. Management made some tough decisions involving two modest rounds of UK redundancies. Trainees felt the squeeze too, with compulsory six-month deferrals for all intakes between September 2009 and March 2011. In the midst of these difficult choices, Reed Smith made some innovative and market-leading changes to its business model. Lockstep compensation for associates has given way to a merit-based pay structure. Non-equity partners in the US were also asked to contribute 15% of their base salary back to the firm or lose partnership status. This brought them in line with their UK partners. It is hoped that these changes will place the firm in a stronger position after the downturn.

Along with a move to stunning new offices in London's Broadgate Tower, Reed Smith has now also come forward with a more explicit strategy. Roger Parker, managing partner for Europe and the Middle East, outlined the plan for us: "*We want to have an ever-stronger presence in transactional areas like corporate and finance in the UK market and to develop sectors in which we have a strong name, such as energy, media, real estate and transport.*" Even trainees seemed tuned in to a renewed sense of focus and commented on the firm's emphasis on winning big work from a smaller number of premium clients and its targeted financial industries group (FIG). While the goal of financial sector dominance hasn't yet been realised, the firm remains a leader in RB's traditional strong suits of shipping and media. Reed Smith has big dreams and the trick will be to ensure that trainees aren't lost in the shuffle of its ambitions.

Nice work if you can get it

Reed Smith covers virtually every area of practice from shipping to employment. Plus, there are no prescribed seats, so other than fulfilling SRA requirements, trainees have flexibility. The only catch is that some of the more popular or niche departments can be nearly impossible to get into. Since priority is based on seniority, the media and the energy, trade and commodities (ETC) seats, for

Chambers UK rankings

Asset Finance	Insurance
Banking Litigation	Intellectual Property
Commodities	Life Sciences
Competition/European Law	Media & Entertainment
Construction	Pensions
Corporate/M&A	Product Liability
Defamation/Reputation Management	Professional Negligence
	Real Estate
Dispute Resolution	Real Estate Finance
Employment	Real Estate Litigation
Fraud	Shipping

example, are sometimes just pipe dreams until you're in your third or often fourth seat, and even then there's no guarantee.

The situation was aggravated at the time of our interviews because of the economy, and we did hear that "*seat allocation has been the one major disappointment in our training contract.*" By the time readers join the firm things should have normalised. These are the available options: corporate (subgroups in media, competition and life sciences); ETC; shipping; real estate; employment; FIG (subgroups in general finance, leveraged finance, funds, restructuring, transport finance, real estate finance); commercial disputes; and tax. The most common seats are corporate, commercial disputes, shipping and real estate.

Wonderbras and social networking

A general corporate seat involves a month of 'CoSec' in which trainees play company secretary for clients, drafting board minutes and dealing with annual accounts. "*It's not particularly thrilling,*" but you do work with some of the firm's more exciting clients. After CoSec come other commercial tasks, such as drafting conditions for online promotions or working on public listings. With clients like Wonderbra alongside banks and pharmaceutical and media companies, there is a "*broad range*" of experiences to be had. But be warned, sometimes "*you'll have the most mundane task in the world,*" like extensive due diligence, "*which can get repetitive.*" Expect some unplanned nights "*when you have a client who says, 'I want this tomorrow.*'" Otherwise, "*if you're not on a deal your hours are good.*"

The corporate media subgroup always offered a highly coveted seat with exciting Hollywood production and digital media work. Sadly, "*there have been significant departures from the film and TV division, which have changed the department,*" although the firm has made hires into its advertising team. Managing Partner Roger Parker explained: "*The impact of the merger is that the media department is a smaller part of the whole. But we're committed to the media sector and within a three-year period we will be stronger and more diverse in our range of capabilities. We will be recruiting.*" That commitment has become increasingly focused on advising new media clients like social networking websites and online music services. The seat now involves "*quite a bit of research*" plus "*they let you sit in on meetings with high-profile clients.*" Not bad when these include the likes of Microsoft, AOL, MTV, Lastfm and the BBC.

In the "*huge*" commercial disputes department, trainees experience all sorts. There are subgroups for professional negligence, IP, media litigation and banking litigation, but most trainees try a bit of everything. Litigation is "*quite buzzy and more vibrant*" than some of the other departments, but the work can be "*more administrative, and if you get involved with a trial it's inevitable you'll do bundling.*" At least during the occasional late nights "*you bond with people and you're never there alone.*" Plus there are opportunities for drafting witness statements.

Come sail away

Shipping was a core part of RB's business and this department retains its culture more than any other. "*It wasn't so much a merger for them because all of the people are still ex-Richards Butler.*" Trainees are assigned to either 'wet' or 'dry' teams, with 'wet' particularly suited to people with maritime expertise because "*you actually need to know the parts of ships.*" The 'wet' (or Admiralty) team recently represented Steamship Mutual in an $11m damages claim over a collision involving one of the world's largest luxury yachts.

'Dry' shipping involves contract disputes, cargo damage claims, unsafe port claims, delays and wrongful termination of charter parties. With "*new and bizarre problems cropping up every day,*" it's never boring. The department is "*quite academic and very proud of it,*" and while there are some mundane tasks like bundling, trainees also have "*great responsibility,*" including drafting claim submissions and witness statements, "*going to all of the client meetings*" and "*liaising with experts and instructing counsel.*" Clients come from around the world and lawyers recently advised on a $1.4bn contract dispute. Expect to work consistently hard and "*rarely finish before 8pm.*" Shipping sometimes overlaps with the ETC department's work. Here, trainees will see contentious and non-contentious matters, including cargo disputes and advice on changing pricing mechanisms for commodities like minerals and precious metals. In addition to representing "*massive banks,*" the firm sometimes has smaller clients such as international art brokers who buy in one country and sell in another.

Client secondments are popular, though these have been "*harder to come by*" during the recession. New for 2010, Reed Smith introduced a secondment to human rights organisation Liberty. A bigger issue is the cancellation of some international seats, the availability of which had been the prime reason why several of our sources had chosen the firm. At the time of research, Hong Kong was off the table. Abu Dhabi, Dubai and Piraeus remained but few people applied to them, which is especially surprising given that the Abu Dhabi office has three Jacuzzis and a pool on the roof. One source speculated: "*People were nervous about being away from the office because fewer qualification jobs have been available.*"

Reed between the lines

Trainees say you mustn't expect the stereotypical 'American firm' experience of long, gruelling hours. "*I had avoided US firms because of the reputation, but it's nothing like that here,*" said one. "*We don't have BlackBerrys so there's not that expectation of being on call 24/7.*" The overwhelming view was that "*everyone recognises the value of work-life balance.*" Trainees "*don't notice a massive American influence*" or feel they are working in "*an American firm with a London outpost.*" Because London is the firm's largest office, its role is *"quite pivotal as the midpoint between America and the rest of Europe."* One marginal transatlantic nuisance is that IT support is stateside and "*if you want something done you have to phone America first.*"

Where the US does exert control is on job prospects for NQs. "*A lot of the senior management team are in the States and the job list has to be approved there first,*" we learned. In 2010, this meant a longer wait for anxious fourth-seaters. "*We were sent the timetable in an e-mail and it said 'subject to change' about five times.*" Roger Parker spoke to us about this. "*We rely on our practice group leaders to make decisions and in some cases – not many – they will be based in other countries. It's an example of how international businesses work.*" Recruiters also confirmed that the qualification process is run by practice groups, rather than specific offices, and therefore decisions are necessarily global.

Another issue related to communication from management. Several sources agreed "*it would be good to have more knowledge filtering down.*" To be fair to the firm, "*communication is something they're really trying to work on*" and trainees had "*noticed improvements in the past year,*" especially through Roger Parker's presentations and global managing partner Greg Jordan's frequent visits. "*He'll do a trainee meeting and you're allowed to ask tough questions, if you've got the guts.*" Trainees say it's essential to be clued-up on the big picture because "*you need to know which groups they're intending to grow so that you can decide where you want to qualify.*" An official job list is released, but "*you get unofficial hints so people tend to know where there will be jobs.*" Trainees apply for roles with a CV and covering letter. The firm also conducts two rounds of interviews. "*It's stressful even when the economy's good,*" sources said. In 2010, 18 of the 25 qualifiers took jobs with the firm.

Tower of song

Broadgate Tower's 538 feet of glass and steel presides over Liverpool Street. "*It's an absolutely stunning building*" and "*the views never cease to amaze you.*" The skyscraper's canteen, Thirty-One, boasts sweeping views of the City and landmarks like St Paul's Cathedral and Tower Bridge. We heard praise for the food, especially the "*theatre bar*" where they cook pasta and stir fry in front of you. Trainees eat there together most days, for the views and also convenience because "*the building's so big it takes ages to get outside.*" Some people miss the low prices of the canteen in the old building: "*Trainees resent that they used to pay 50p for soup and now have to pay £1.30.*" Nobody misses eating in the old basement though.

The 31st floor is also used for activities and rehearsal space. A choir was preparing for a June recital at the time of our interviews. For rock and roller solicitors, the firm even has a few different bands including the aptly named The Reed Smiths. In addition to headlining functions like the Christmas party, they've also competed at the charity battle of the bands 'Law Rocks'. Those not musically inclined can opt for sports like netball, football, cricket and firm-organised golf lessons. "*I have a sneaking suspicion there's a table tennis league,*" added a source. Departmental colleagues enjoy catching up over drinks in the office on a Thursday and trainees' Friday nights are spent in Piccolino at Exchange Square, the Light Bar or one of the area's few "*genuine pubs.*"

And finally...

Reed Smith has grown quickly and with that comes the potential for more change. But if you're looking for a wide array of big-ticket international work without being chained to a BlackBerry this Anglo-American hybrid could be a good fit.

- **A managing partner advises:** "Perseverence is going to be the order of the day – it's all about supply and demand, although perhaps it's the other way round today. I've seen a huge number of good candidates who are finding it difficult to get hold of a position, and it's not personal, it's just there are fewer positions. Energy, personality and enthusiasm all help."

Reynolds Porter Chamberlain LLP

The facts

Location: London

Number of UK partners/solicitors: 65/180

Total number of trainees: 30

Seats: 4x6 months

Alternative seats: Secondments

Extras: Pro bono - Mencap

On chambersstudent.co.uk
- How to get into RPC
- St Katharine Docks
- Some of the firm's highlight cases and deals

City firm Reynolds Porter Chamberlain has become rather popular with prospective trainee solicitors and it's not hard to see why.

Clearly buzzing

RPC's 260-plus lawyers operate out of two divisions: insurance (the largest) and commercial (which does everything else). Litigation accounts for around 70% of business and is a big draw for many applicants. "*If you want to be a litigator, an insurance law firm is a great place to be,*" partner and training principal Alex Anderson explained. Insurance "*throws up a broad array of work,*" a trainee concurred; "*I wasn't looking for a firm that did huge corporate deals.*"

In 2006, the firm made a big statement about its future ambitions by moving from a grotty 1960s block on High Holborn to a trendy, Richard Rogers-designed palace overlooking St Katharine Docks, next to the Tower of London. The entire building is made almost entirely of glass, giving it an extremely open feel and uninterrupted views of the City, the Tower, docks and rising 'Shard' skyscraper over on the south bank of the Thames. Around the same time, management changed and a string of new partners started joining. The big plan was to make RPC slicker and more successful. Trainees still feel there is "*a buzz*" about the firm and say "*it's going places.*" A senior source agreed: "*We're bolder and more confident about what we have to offer.*"

The credit crunch led to a rise in big-ticket litigation, and RPC has continued to expand its service offering through lateral hires into various practices. These include Eversheds' former insurance/reinsurance head – one of ten partner hires in 2009 – and most recently two employment law partners from Wragge & Co, an IP partner from Arnold & Porter and Clyde & Co's former head of dispute resolution and co-head of international arbitration. The firm has also revamped certain HR procedures and, for example, launched a sophisticated programme to aid career feedback and development. Also new is a deal with BPP for all future trainees to study their LPC with this provider.

All change

In the 2005 *Student Guide* we pointed out that in the old offices the partners used to take lunch together in their own dining room, and a trainee at that time told us that RPC was "*perceived as being quite traditional.*" Things have certainly changed in a relatively short period of time. "*It's becoming a much more driven and ambitious firm.*" RPC is increasingly handling international assignments, thanks to certain senior lateral hires and its long-time membership of TerraLex, an international law firm network. There have been numerous partner hires on the commercial side. "*You can push change through quicker with laterals,*" a senior source reflected, whether by upping the work rate or just bringing in fresh ideas and ways of doing things. "*I joined the firm at just the right time!*" a second-year proudly told us. Check out the amusing comic-book style recruiting brochure on RPC's website to see for yourself the "*buzz*" it's trying to create.

The 15 trainees recruited each year don't need prior insurance knowledge and are pleasantly surprised at how varied this type of legal practice can be. Pretty much everything under the sun can be insured, after all. RPC has

Chambers UK rankings

Clinical Negligence	Intellectual Property
Construction	Media & Entertainment
Corporate/M&A	Partnership
Defamation/Reputation Management	Personal Injury
Dispute Resolution	Product Liability
Education	Professional Discipline
Employment	Professional Negligence
Information Technology	Real Estate Litigation
Insurance	Tax

advised some of the biggest names in insurance and reinsurance, including Zurich and Swiss Re. This division of the firm works on a wide range of disputes. Key areas of focus are: financial institutions and directors' and officers' liabilities; energy; property; political risk and accident and health; product liability and recall; and reinsurance. Recent highlights include a £250m claim over the construction of Wembley Stadium; cases arising from Bernie Madoff's mammoth Ponzi scheme; and issues deriving from 9/11 and Hurricane Katrina.

On the non-contentious side, RPC advises several major players in both the Lloyd's and company (ie non-Lloyd's) insurance markets on transactions and day-to-day commercial and regulatory matters. The insurance world hasn't done too badly during the recession and some of RPC's clients have looked to expand their operations by opening new Lloyd's syndicates and other ventures. This, and the fact that there's a greater emphasis on keeping the FSA happy, has meant non-contentious insurance lawyers have been busy. A two-week induction, which includes a tour of the Lloyd's Building, means *"you do pick knowledge up quickly, plus the partners are good at explaining things."*

When professionals slip up

Chambers UK ranks RPC in no less than 25 different areas of legal practice, and while trainees are likely to spend at least two of their six-month seats in an insurance-related group, the possibilities of work in more specialist areas are many. There are smaller teams for things like IP, media, construction, defamation and employment, for example. Before each seat change, trainees list their three preferences and discuss them with the training principal.

The sizable professional risks department was particularly popular with the current trainee group (last year IP was popular, and media before that). The team advises professionals including accountants, lawyers, insurance brokers, surveyors and construction advisers on their professional liability to clients. The firm tells us, for example, that mortgage fraud claims against solicitors and surveyors are on the rise and expected to increase dramatically over the next year. *"I really love this department as the work's so interesting,"* one source said. Trainees assist on *"huge, document-heavy cases"* and there's also opportunity to run smaller ones pretty much solo. Another source liked how colleagues *"made a big effort to make us feel involved."* By the end of the seat, trainees said they had *"good responsibility, including writing reports for insurers and giving* [their] *views."* Our sources were also pleased to be able to attend mediations.

Unlike the big-ticket litigation in other departments, the general liability and medical department mainly acts for medical malpractice insurers, defending health practitioners, clinics and other organisations against negligence claims. Cases have involved abortion clinics as well as a hospice that mistakenly administered an overdose of insulin to a patient. Trainee tasks include drafting witness statements, research and writing reports. The seat *"can be more scary because straightaway you're doing what a solicitor would do."* One of the most challenging things about it is staffing the department's 24/7 helpline for doctors with queries. Trainees take calls, *"initially on a speakerphone with a supervisor."*

The construction team advises on both transactional and contentious matters. *"I did mainly litigation,"* said one source; *"for example, concrete that hadn't formed properly or problems with rust."* Another recalled: *"When I started there was a lot of research. People gave me bits and pieces, and later on I got into the cases."* Tasks also include looking at building contracts and ensuring they reflect the clients' best interests. *"I had to draft warrantees for subcontractors and speak to clients to update them,"* a source said. The department's roster of big-name clients includes Carillion and Bovis Homes, plus Akzo Nobel, Shanks Waste Management and AstraZeneca, whom RPC advised on a head office move to the Paddington Central development.

Scream if you wanna go faster

Recalling their time in the expanding real estate group, one trainee said: *"I had my own files – around 15 to 20 of them – and client contact, so responsibility levels were good."* The team recently helped HMV acquire 14 retail leases from the administrator of Zavvi. It's a *"really sociable department,"* and as well as bowling, staff were recently whisked up and down the Thames in a speedboat before being treated to dinner. Presumably they were glad it wasn't the other way around.

In commercial disputes, *"you could be acting for an individual or a multinational."* Responsibility levels are good, although as one trainee admitted: "*I'd be lying if I said I didn't do a fair amount of document management... though this is still a partner or senior associate trusting you to do a good job.*" You might even get to attend court on your own. "*Once you get over the initial fear, it's really good fun.*" Similarly, our interviewees liked the IP, technology and outsourcing seat because the work is so interesting. There's "*a real range of clients*" and the "*people are great.*" Evidence of IP rights is everywhere: "*Even the shape of a Coke bottle in the supermarket is trade marked,*" one trainee reminded us. New client Universal Music benefits from RPC's advice on commercial IP matters, particularly in relation to downloads and licensing arrangements. Sports Direct, meanwhile, has entrusted famous brands like Slazenger and Lonsdale to RPC's experts.

RPC has one of the most highly regarded media defence practices in the UK, as shown by a national *Chambers UK* top-tier ranking. It represented the publishers of several newspapers including the *Daily Mail*, the *Daily Mirror*, the *Daily Express* and *The Sun* in the Robert Murat libel case, which followed on from Madeleine McCann's disappearance. It also successfully defended Google in a ground-breaking High Court libel action regarding the appearance of defamatory search engine results. Client secondments are possible, with Sports Direct and Carillion both regular options. Two new 2010 secondments with household-name clients are bound to whip up interest. We'd love to tell you who they are with but sadly we're not allowed to.

Stage and screen

Utterly open-plan offices create a sociable culture where "*you don't have a scary door to knock on.*" Initial fears about distracting noise levels were allayed by the installation of 'white noise' machines. Having visited the firm, we can testify to the weird peace and quiet in what should be a noisy office. Each trainee normally sits in a 'pod' (or bank of desks) for up to four people, and "*wherever you're sat, you're close to your supervisor.*" High-backed, black leather-and-chrome designer chairs with built-in coat hangers complete the über-slick look.

Just 15 new trainees arrive each year. "*It's a nice number;*" not so many you're lost in the crowd and "*not so few that it's cliquey and tiresome.*" Trainees spoke warmly of the firm's friendliness and decent work-life balance, as well as regular trips to Prohibition – the bar at the foot of the building. Football and netball are reasonably popular after-work pastimes, and the firm enters the Lloyds Rugby Sevens tournament. RPC also boasts a decent choir.

"*Even during the recession we've had cool parties,*" an interviewee cooed. For the Christmas party at "*a rather nice hotel,*" trainees recorded a spoof TV newsreel, RPC News. One dressed as a pig for a piece-to-camera about swine flu; rugby players dressed in netball kit for a story about the Royal Mail strikes; while Michael Jackson and *Star Wars* characters with light sabers were spotted fighting on the high-level walkways within the office. The news team also daringly ran a story about the new HR initiatives, inspired by the TV show *The Apprentice*.

The firm really seems to get people of all levels involved in RPC life and feeling like they are all part of the same team. Secretaries, for example, aren't closeted away in their own areas; instead they sit with the fee earners in the pods. Even management sits in the pods. New starters' nerves are taken into consideration: RPC welcomes incoming trainees with introductory training sessions and a lunch on day one. "*It took the edge off the first day,*" said an appreciative source.

RPC is making strides in the areas of diversity and community activities. These include supporting gay network Interlaw and backing anyone who wants to set up an affinity organisation for a particular minority. For chariddy, a partner climbed Kilimanjaro; a group of staff members hiked up Snowdonia's peaks; and others did a sponsored 'Tube run' covering 26 stops on the London Underground, starting at A and working their way through the alphabet. Mencap is this year's nominated charity. Some people also volunteer as ushers at Wilton's – the oldest surviving music hall in the world – but they don't like to make a song and dance about it.

And finally...

We've been loving RPC more and more with each passing year. It seems its trainees do too: in 2010, ten of the 12 qualifiers stayed for the long haul.

Sheridans

The facts

Location: London

Number of UK partners/solicitors: 27/14

Total number of trainees: 2

Seats: 4x6 months

Alternative seats: None

On chambersstudent.co.uk
- How to get into Sheridans
- The amazing life of Bernard Sheridan
- The Digital Economy Act

In an entertainment capital as rich and lively as London, this media firm has plenty to keep it busy.

What's the line up?

In 1953, art-lover Bernard Sheridan founded a small law firm specialising in entertainment and public law issues, with an emphasis on pro bono civil liberties cases. As Sheridans expanded, he continued to work seven days a week for a list of celebrated clients including The Hollies and later Pink Floyd and Kate Bush. Over time, the firm grew into one of the leading West End media practices, thanks to the patronage of Sir Andrew Lloyd Webber, The Rolling Stones, Sir Paul McCartney, Natasha Bedingfield, Kylie Minogue, Leona Lewis, Phil Collins, David Gray and many more. The firm has also advised artists including Damien Hirst, and today it focuses not just on music but also computer games, broadcasting, sport and theatre. While litigation is still a core activity, company/commercial, property and planning advice are also important.

Sheridans' lawyers assist clients across the creative industries – in sports, TV, film, technology, telecoms (especially mobile), marketing, online content delivery, music, gaming, fashion and branding. They seek advice on commerce and IP, employment, licensing, funding and business and property transactions. Partner Keith Ashby confirmed that the firm's approach is *"to meet clients' requirements under one roof."* Trainees clearly know the drill: *"Creative clients use the firm for their various legal needs, which may be unrelated to entertainment."*

You presumably want to learn more about the firm's meeja credentials. You won't be disappointed. Sheridans recently won Pink Floyd's digital royalties dispute with EMI over how royalties were calculated and whether EMI was entitled to sell the band's tracks separately online. The definition of the word 'record' was at the heart of the conflict. This type of work dates back to early days when founder Bernard Sheridan strove to improve royalty terms for his clients.

Let's get digital

Of course, these days it's all about new technology, and the good news is that Sheridans attracts the cream of the gaming industry crop, including the makers of *Batman: Arkham Asylum* and *Need for Speed SHIFT*, and has dealt with crossover matters concerning the use of music in games like *SingStar*. Lately the entertainment software team has expanded, and the firm also buffed up its cross-media capability by bringing in leading sports lawyers from Bird & Bird. Rights acquisitions surrounding the Indian Cricket League raised questions for the firm's broadcast clients. Domestic football's governing bodies have also used Sheridans, and the firm is advising sports rights agency Sportfive on a range of matters involving its marketing and sales of European media rights to the 2014 and 2016 winter and summer Olympic Games.

In the film and TV industry, the firm advises broadcasters (including BBC, Channel 4 and National Geographic), film and TV production companies, distribution and sales agents, film finance investors and talent. Their advice covers: licensing; franchising; e-commerce; domain name, trade mark and copyright issues; and contract-focused employment issues. The firm

Chambers UK rankings

Media & Entertainment

advised RDF Media, for example, on a £10m co-production with the BBC.

There have been new hires on the corporate/commercial side. Property and planning work centres on investments, leasehold buildings and secured lending, and the coco crew negotiate and settle commercial contracts, mergers, acquisitions and disposals, while also getting their feet wet with corporate reorganisations and insolvencies, fraud issues and company formations.

Get yourself a pen with a light

Trainees complete four of the following seats: dispute resolution (simultaneously taking in commercial litigation and employment); film, TV, and sport; music, theatre and media; company/commercial; and property (although this seat hasn't been occupied over the past couple of years). All trainees spend at least six months in an area of entertainment law. In the film, TV and sport group, trainees encounter "*low-budget films, which need a lot of work from start to finish... from the first client meetings all the way through to the grand gala opening night.*" On top of that "*in film and TV you've got investment that comes in from all over the place. It requires a lot of research into the different rules and tax regimes that apply if investors come from different countries.*" The very best assignments have to be "*watching films with a notepad and listing problematic issues and potential future disputes.*" But it's not all about watching movies: "*We're encouraged to meet with clients and to get to know them.*"s

The exploitation of sports rights needs to be looked at too. Sports broadcast rights involve "*different platforms – TV, broadband, online – as well as different territories such as Australasia and the Middle East and Africa.*" In the music, theatre and media department, there's "*loads, absolutely loads*" to do. For trainees this involves "*drafting agreements for artist clients, or producer and mixer agreements.*" Other clients include independent labels and events companies. One trainee told us just how rewarding it is to "*watch TV and see someone singing because I've pushed for them to be there.*"

Gaining contentious experience simultaneously across litigation and employment is a demanding feat but it "*improves you as a lawyer, especially in terms of time management.*" The contentious seat exposes trainees to "*every aspect*" of cases and requires them to interact with clients and barristers. Trainees have "*made appearances in front of district judges, taken notes on applications and worked on advocacy skills.*" They sometimes run cases solo, usually small debt claims at first. Other tasks include writing letters, checking case law and preparing notes of advice for clients, with whom they frequently meet. Their hours can run on longer than the typical 9am to 6pm, but when it's all over, trainees are always welcome to mingle with colleagues over after-work drinks. Generally, the social scene is "*very laid back*" and less dressy than the firm's swanky Christmas and summer bashes.

Sundeck and superstars

For some fresh air join the firm's football team for weekly meets in Hyde Park, or simply visit the office's terrace, which overlooks the city from above Tottenham Court Road. "*You can see Wembley on a good day.*" Inside there's an entertainment space that doubles up as a boardroom, and recently the firm exhibited the work of a new artist there. The office has "*a modern feel to it*" and is partly open-plan, allowing trainees to "*take work from all members of a team, which broadens the experience.*" There's "*assistance on tap really,*" as well as partner-led training sessions and webinars. "*You do actually know everyone within a short period of time. If you have anything you want to discuss, you feel free to walk up to someone's desk and have a conversation about it,*" said a source. It sounds like trainees look up to senior mentors as "*superstars in what they do.*"

We heard that "*there's no actual Sheridans fit,*" yet the firm is interested in candidates who will get on well with the rest of the firm. It's clear too that you need the right mindset. The creative industries are fast-paced and constantly shaped and reshaped by legislation and the growth of the digital economy. To help clients' businesses adapt, you have to "*really enjoy the things that get them up in the morning.*" That means keeping a close eye on regulatory developments and key trends as they emerge. Needless to say, "*everyone here knows what's going on in the entertainment industry as a whole.*" You'll also need the confidence to deal with strong-willed clients, and don't expect them all to be celebrities. For more information about who the firm is interested in visit our website.

And finally...

Sheridans may offer fun opportunities for films in Cannes, music awards in Texas and all that jazz, but remember, what matters most is a genuine interest in the evolution of its core client industries. In 2010, the one qualifying trainee stayed on as an NQ.

Shoosmiths

The facts

Location: Birmingham, Basingstoke, Milton Keynes, Northampton, Nottingham, Reading, Fareham, London, Manchester

Number of UK partners/solicitors: 110/249

Total number of trainees: 26

Seats: 4x6 months

Alternative seats: Secondments

On chambersstudent.co.uk
- How to get into Shoosmiths
- Closing the debate on 2009's infamous trainee deferrals
- We talk future strategy with chairman Andrew Tubbs

National firm Shoosmiths has offices dotted all over the country. A full commercial service offering is twinned with large-scale debt recovery, personal injury and conveyancing.

Walk a mile in their Shoos...

Shoosmiths was founded in Northampton and now has branches stretching from Manchester in the North to Fareham, near Southampton, in the South. Its newest offices in London and Manchester were opened in 2008 and 2009 respectively. Growth has been a key theme for the firm over the past decade; indeed Shoosmiths doubled in size between 2002 and 2008. Having once been best known for its volume services in the fields of debt recovery, personal injury, wills and conveyancing, Shoosmiths has now established itself as a full-on commercial operation covering all the usual corporate, litigation, property, employment, IP/IT and lender services work you might expect in a firm of this size and spread.

Affected by the recession, the firm's finances have been sluggish of late: 2009/10 results showed that revenue fell 9% to £90m, having dropped in 08/09 too. Profits per equity partner rollercoastered down 54% in 08/09 only to rise 69.5% to £256,000 in 09/10. The firm had to make more than 100 redundancies and required pay cuts and shorter hours. One trainee confirmed that they "[got] *the impression* [the firm] *had been plateauing,*" but they were also convinced that "*it's going to start growing again.*"

In early 2010, the firm hived off and rebranded its volume legal services teams, which are now known as 'Access Legal from Shoosmiths'. This spin-off operation handles all the firm's wills, personal injury and residential conveyancing business. Although Northampton offers two seats in the volume business (personal injury and private client), trainees generally stick to the commercial side of the fence. Innovation and strategy are important to firm chairman Andrew Tubbs. "*Shall I talk you through the strategy a bit, then?*" he said keenly during our interview. Why not wander over to our website to find out what he had to say about volume work, opening in Manchester and 'umbrella billing'.

So what is Shoosmiths particularly good at? Look in *Chambers UK* and you'll find it ranked for masses of different things from planning, IP and product liability to corporate deals, commercial litigation and social housing. Exactly where you work in the Shoosmiths network will determine what kind of work you are exposed to and how highly rated those teams are. Shoosmiths' clientele is as diverse as its talents, so you'll likely run into the likes of Volkswagen, SAMSUNG, AstraZeneca, HMV and WHSmith as you make your journey through your training.

Remain calm and return to your seats

Shoosmiths received a lot of press attention in 2009 when it deferred future starters without pay. The trainees we spoke to felt that the matter was "*blown out of proportion*" and "*something which had to happen at the time.*" Andrew Tubbs recognised that "*there are lessons to be*

Chambers UK rankings

Banking & Finance	Intellectual Property
Banking Litigation	Licensing
Clinical Negligence	Pensions
Consumer Finance	Personal Injury
Corporate/M&A	Planning
Debt Recovery	Product Liability
Dispute Resolution	Real Estate
Employment	Real Estate Litigation
Health & Safety	Restructuring/Insolvency
Information Technology	Retail
	Social Housing

learnt from last year," and several of our trainee sources agreed. Go to our website for more details. Suffice to say, deferred trainees came on board in 2010 and the firm is recruiting again.

At the moment, training can be completed in Northampton, Milton Keynes, Birmingham, Nottingham, Reading and Fareham (known as the Solent office). Northampton and Milton Keynes are treated as a single unit for training purposes, given their proximity to each other. London, Basingstoke and Manchester don't currently host any trainees, but the firm has recruited for the 2011 start in Manchester. Andrew Tubbs explained that "*Manchester is to be made a full-service office with all five practice areas within three years.*" Indeed, since our conversation with Tubbs, a three-lawyer team has arrived from collapsed firm Halliwells, launching a corporate practice.

Brand-new recruits spend a week together in a hotel in Northampton with jaunts to the various offices, and typically they "*bond quite a lot.*" In time, they take further training courses together, but there isn't too much else that gets them in direct contact again. Save for the Northampton-MK twinning, trainees tend not to take seats in other offices and also usually qualify into the office they trained in.

No seats are ubiquitous and it's a case of making the most of the options available in each office to ensure that you gain both contentious and non-contentious experiences. Client secondments (to Volkswagen as well as a number of other household names) are usually available at each seat rotation and the general consensus is that secondments are "*fantastic*" because "*you understand what clients actually need advice on and what's just extra.*"

Youth and experience

Lender services is a big thing in Northampton. The team helps top banks reclaim debts, and as you might imagine it's brisk business when recession bites. Trainees' work is "*mostly contentious and litigation-focused and includes payment protection claims, return-of-goods orders and money orders* [from the courts]." One of the best aspects is "*going to court and sitting behind the barrister to see how a case progresses.*" Mortgage-based litigation from lenders is supplemented with plenty of instructions from corporates and retailers. Other Northampton seat options are private client; insurance litigation and regulatory; lender services and personal injury. The regulatory team are a foody bunch. The lawyers advise manufacturers on product launches, labelling and recalls.

The seats offered in MK are IP; commercial property; commercial litigation; property litigation; corporate/banking; commercial; pensions; and employment. Unlike Northampton (which earns *Chambers UK* rankings in exclusively contentious areas of practice, mostly those that affect individuals), MK's rankings are much more commercially focused and cover quite specialist areas such as pensions, the retail sector and IP/IT. The journey by road from Northampton to MK is only 20 miles, so it's not a major problem for trainees to split their training between the two. As in past years we did hear a moan or two about the Northampton office's business park location, which can dampen the social scene a little.

The Birmingham branch's city centre location on Colmore Row means the office is "*a lot more sociable.*" Brum has a broad spread of teams in all the major commercial areas, and they earn respectable *Chambers UK* rankings in most. This office has a large and "*quite renowned*" property team that advises clients including AstraZeneca, Poundland and Jessops. Social housing is also on the cards and Birmingham City Council is a client. Besides property, other seats include construction; planning; corporate; commercial; commercial litigation; property litigation; lender services; PI/clin neg; employment; and insolvency/restructuring. The people in this busy and industrious office are described as "*fairly young.*" "*You can always find someone at Asha's on a Friday. And our social club puts on events every month, like trips to the Taste of Birmingham exhibition.*" Table football in the games room is also a nice perk.

Working for the Shoo people

Nottingham's city centre branch is conducive to a snappy social life. One trainee recalled "*some crazy wild times*" and we heard how "*lots of people go to The Nav*[igation Inn] *or the Canal House area.*" The office has an energetic feel about it, reflecting its practice orientation. Six seat options are available here – corporate; commercial;

competition; employment; property litigation; and commercial property. The property team's client roster includes IKEA, Nottingham City Council, Nottingham City Transport, British Waterways and Thomas Cook. An IP/IT focus in the commercial department sees it acting for Nottingham University, The Open University and BP on technology matters. In this seat trainee tasks amount to "*quite a lot of document drafting and reviewing agency agreements and contracts.*"

In the Thames Valley, the Basingstoke office doesn't take trainees and concentrates on high-volume, low-value personal injury cases. The Reading office, by contrast, offers a veritable commercial feast of employment; property; commercial litigation; tax; property litigation; corporate; banking; commercial; and IP seats. It collects a host of commercial practice rankings from *Chambers UK*. Appropriately, given its name, the firm acts for shoe retailers Jimmy Choo and LK Bennett. IP work includes "*research about trade marks and retail issues*" for clients like TK Maxx, Ducati, Mattel and Danone, as well as "*researching and updating clients on the Freedom of Information Act.*" The property team is "*very lively:* [you] *get a lot of responsibility, run* [your] *own files and have loads of client contact,*" mainly on landlord and tenant issues. Litigation experiences involve "*fast-track debt claims, enforcing personal guarantees, defendant-side personal injury claims* [and] *general commercial contract disputes.*" Being based in a commuter town means "*the social life isn't particularly wonderful as a lot of people rush to get their trains.*" As in all Shoosmiths offices, there is "*a Christmas party and other bits and pieces.*"

The seats in the successful Solent office are corporate; property/planning; commercial litigation; commercial; marine; and employment. Property is less landlord and tenant-focused than in other locations, instead offering trainees plenty of "*planning applications and Section 106* [so-called planning gain] *agreements with councils.*" Clients include Southampton City Council, English Heritage and retailer Spar. Litigation is a "*small team,* " but one happy trainee recalled three visits to the Royal Courts of Justice during their seat. The corporate team is bigger, with trainees somewhat at the "*bottom of the pile*" working on more administrative tasks like "*sending forms to Companies House.*" The out-of-town location is on a business park "*right on the motorway between Southampton and Portsmouth.*" Although "*it's in the middle of nowhere,*" trainees describe "*a fun atmosphere*" and head out together when they can. "*We have a night out every one or two months, and there's always about ten or 15 people who might go out for a drink fairly frequently.*"

Getting your Shoo in the door

Shoosmiths is "*a good firm for equality between the genders*" and some 32% of its partners are women. The appointment of Claire Rowe as managing partner in 2009 makes it one of the minority of large law firms with a female at the helm. So who fits in at Shoosmiths? It actually seems to suit people with local connections as well as those not so concerned about location. Although "*some people have quite strong connections*" to their chosen town, there are "*quite a number of fee earners who commute in from other places.*" One Northampton trainee summed up their motivation, which we think is common to maybe half of the trainees in that office: "*For me it had nothing to do with the area. I wanted a training contract with a good firm, so I was prepared to move.*"

"*There is a typical Shoosmiths trainee across the firm,*" sources concluded. This person is "*very open-minded, friendly and not dour or competitive – there are no climbing-the-ladder sort of personalities.*" One said: "*I don't think any of us are pretentious or stuffy; we're fun-loving and happy people... quite approachable and down to earth,*" although another believed "*the typical trainee is changing*" and that "*there have been some quite confident and self-assured people coming in.*" Even so, don't expect to be confronted with an army of hard chargers on your first day at the firm.

"*Shoosmiths has a good work-life balance*" was the verdict of our interviewees. "*I always feel valued if I stay later,*" stressed one. Good work-life balance doesn't mean soft though. "*Things have stepped up since I've been here,*" a trainee revealed; "*you can't leave at 5.30pm every day.*" Although normal hours are about 8.30am to 6pm in the core commercial departments, trainees may sometimes need to stay a good few hours longer. "*I have had quite a few late nights. A couple of weeks ago I worked until 10pm every night,*" a trainee admitted. In 2010, 15 of the 18 qualifying trainees accepted jobs at the firm.

And finally...

Keep an eye open for news on London and bear in mind that the firm is now recruiting for its fledgling Manchester office. If you are picking one of its other established locations, make sure you understand the practice spread on offer.

Sidley Austin LLP

The facts

Location: London

Number of UK partners/solicitors: 32/60 (US: 6/7)

Total number of trainees: 17

Seats: 4x6 months, some split seats available

Alternative seats: Overseas seats

Extras: Pro bono – LawWorks

On chambersstudent.co.uk
- How to get into Sidley Austin
- Capital markets for dummies
- Sidley stateside

At the London office of this US-headquartered firm, the focus is still on finance but not to the exclusion of all else.

Crunch time

The modern-day Sidley Austin was formed in May 2001 with the merger of long-time servant of corporate America, Chicago's Sidley & Austin, and internationally oriented Wall Street supremo Brown & Wood. The firms had 235 years of experience between them, so you'd guess the tie-up was carefully considered. A name change followed in January 2006, when the title Sidley Austin LLP was adopted. Since merging, the conjoined firm has strategically expanded into key financial and trade centres around the world, opening in Geneva (2002), Brussels (2003), Frankfurt (2006) and Sydney (2007), to add to pre-existing international offices in London, Beijing, Tokyo, Hong Kong, Shanghai and Singapore. Today the full-service firm has 1,800 employees in 17 offices, ten of which are outside its homeland. Sidley Austin's worldwide revenue and profits doubled between 2003 and 2007, and then in 2008 it recorded its highest-ever revenue – $1.5bn. After the credit crunch rode into town to spoil the party, the firm's worldwide revenue dropped by 9% in 2009.

Among its foreign locations, London was the first (opened in 1974) and it is arguably the most successful. Since its founding, the office has pushed itself to the forefront of the specialised financial work of the City, over time developing a focus on capital markets that is reflected in impressive *Chambers UK* rankings. In particular we're talking about debt and equity capital markets deals, structured finance, securitisation and derivatives, plus financial services regulation. Other noteworthy practices relate to tax, real estate finance and investment funds, particularly hedge funds.

Since late 2007, the firm has had to think quickly and smartly about the nature of its operations here in our world-beating financial hub. In the absence of strong demand for securitisation transactions, it uses its expertise "*as an industry leader in securitisations to deal with the restructuring elements of those deals.*" For example, it advised the equity investors and mezzanine lenders in the High Street/Fleet Street II CMBS restructuring. This was the first CMBS securitisation in Germany to be fundamentally restructured and was an extremely complex matter. If you want to read about what CMBS structures are, go to our website.

Over the past two years the firm has begun to diversify its London practice, reconfiguring departments such as insurance, funds and litigation. For example, the firm pushed into the insurance and reinsurance sector with a double partner hire in London in 2010. "*They are now standing alone and working on complicated trustee disputes or other contentious matters, which don't involve the financial industry at all,*" remarked a clued-up second-year.

Present tense

You need to know more about what Sidley London is up to now. Remember, what we have is a highly technically proficient group of lawyers who know the workings of the City inside-out and have a good track record in international

Chambers UK rankings

Capital Markets	Real Estate Finance
Financial Services	Restructuring/Insolvency
Insurance	Tax
Investment Funds	

high finance. The core International Finance Group (IFG) is still alive and kicking, but less emphasis is placed on trainees spending time here. Previously everyone would sit in this part of the firm for between six and 12 months, either working on structured finance, derivatives, regulatory or real estate matters. Once *"the key and the engine room,"* IFG seats are no longer compulsory and, for the first time, second-year trainees coming up for qualification in 2010 hadn't all experienced a finance seat. The full range of seat options in 2010 was as follows: M&A; hedge funds; competition; employment; insolvency; insurance and financial services; IP; dispute resolution (much of it financial); IFG; and tax. While seats open up according to business needs, trainees are generally happy with what is a fairly bespoke scheme, and as in many firms, second-years are given priority when it comes to selecting seats.

Inside that once mammoth (and still substantial) IFG department, trainees have been working on securities issues for big banks, often restructuring deals, redoing security packages and extending loans. There's also work involving the hard-hit residential mortgage backed securities market, and derivatives. Even with the drop in securitisation activities, trainees told us they had seen *"top-quality work"* and noted that it has very recently *"become more interesting to work in the financial sector."* Their assignments ranged from drafting security documents and agreements, to investigating and commenting on arrears for clients that manage residential mortgage portfolios, to monitoring Lehman Brothers' insolvency issues on a daily basis.

Capital markets seats tend to require *"a lot of document turning,"* whereas elements of marketing show up more in the investment funds practice, in which research-intensive regulatory assignments also feature in the mix. International elements crop up regularly, whether it's because clients are based abroad, or the nature of the deals require trainees to analyse European directives. Trainees can only dream of an overseas seat in the USA or the Far East as right now that's far from a top priority for Sidley Austin. Some do have the option of a seat in Brussels, if they're interested in competition law, and shorter overseas trips may crop up within a London seat.

The insolvency/corporate reorganisation seat may be split with tax, which itself is offered only for three months. Given the firm's finance expertise, we're told it's *"not traditional insolvency work."* Clients include Bank of America, GE Capital and Merrill Lynch. Sidley also has a nice sideline in insurance-related insolvency. Dispute resolution trainees get the chance to go to court, but don't be under any illusion as to how much control you'll have over cases as a newbie. The department gets some massive instructions, such as acting for the FIA in the Renault 'Crashgate' incident at the 2008 Singapore Grand Prix. There was an allegation that Renault team chiefs asked Nelson Piquet Junior to crash deliberately to benefit his team mate Fernando Alonso. Sidley lawyers investigated, analysing the technical data and interviewing all the main players at the later Belgian Grand Prix.

The f-word

All new trainees get the same induction, which includes sessions on how to write a basic e-mail, how to manage the paper on your desk, how to use support groups, document printing, library facilities, etc. Specialist training, for instance on drafting and research techniques, is also provided, and the IFG has had to put in real effort into explaining its direction vis-à-vis the ever evolving finance sector. Other training sessions include an eight-day litigation course provided by the College of Law for those who wish to sidestep a full litigation seat.

Trainees have their share of administrative tasks and paperwork, especially when in a new and unfamiliar practice group. But within no time they're also putting their brains to good use, grasping complex transactions by the scruff of the neck. *"If you're given something mundane like proof-reading or another laborious task, they'll be almost apologetic,"* commented one source. Trainees feel they're encouraged to ask questions and are *"impressed that people really do take time to explain things to you. They expect you to know it next time though..."* Client contact starts early and is the only occasion for which trainees are expected to wear suits.

Trainees seem comfortable asking the senior associates or partners they sit with for guidance, and our interviewees suggested that informal feedback was consistently available. More formal mid and end-of-seat reviews help them gauge where and how they'd like to further develop themselves professionally. Without doubt, our sources had fallen under the same spell – the belief that *"an American firm could give me the magic circle training and deals"* without the possibility of getting lost among a massive intake. This notion is far from hocus-pocus, but it is also true that by comparison, and despite the recent diversification, there are fewer seat choices and a narrower range of clients and activities dealt with by the firm. The comment from one trainee – *"you feel privileged to train at a firm like this if you want to focus on finance"* – perhaps says it all.

Earning your stripes

Trainees dismiss the notion that all American firms are slave drivers. The amount of work they undertake is to a degree self-controlled, especially in the run up to qualification, when trainees keep "*a nose-clean, head-down attitude.*" Generally they work a ten-hour day, with weekends, late evenings and the occasional all-nighter required whenever their team gets busy. Long hours are normally spent working alongside seniors, and sometimes clients, which in itself can be exhilarating. "*It's how you earn your stripes,*" explained one source. While you shouldn't expect a party atmosphere, people in some groups have a habit of "*laughing or joking, even in the wee hours of the morning.*"

Decent facilities also help reduce the strain. Sidley Austin's home in Basinghall Street near The Bank of England is modern and appealing. Said one appreciative source: "*It has warm wood tones, lots of glass, natural sunlight, fantastic views and great sunsets... although obviously I don't get to see them because I'm busy working.*" Good marks also go to the canteen, which was described as "*not gourmet, but not at all bad.*" One interesting observation from our sources related to the extent to which Chicago's influence can be felt day to day, even down to things such as claiming back money on taxi receipts. "*Chicago does seem to have a lot of control,*" said one source; "*at the same time, what this means is that the London office has access to huge, huge clients.*"

Social interaction isn't limited to lunchtime meets in the canteen, nor is it organised along hierarchical lines. "*Sidley's quite good in that respect, in that you can talk to partners and senior people socially.*" For many, Friday evenings are for the pub, more often than not the nearby olde worlde Old Doctor Butler's Head. If that doesn't appeal, "*Davy's has opened a wine bar practically in the basement of the building.*" Sidley Austin folk like the odd barbecue in warm weather and the sports and social committee is always on the lookout for active bodies for summer softball against rival law firms. Other favourite events are a big Christmas party, usually held at a swanky venue like Claridges, and a Halloween party, last time held in the office. A lot of effort was put into this second event and families were welcomed. Trainees say they can maintain something of a personal social life, only occasionally needing to cancel plans at the last minute.

Whether they've come to the firm straight out of university and law school or "*travelled around the world a couple of times,*" Sidley Austin looks for people who can bring something to the party. We came across quite a few non-Brits and quite a few coming from previous careers. Just as last year, we had discussions with trainees about the importance of client-wooing skills: it seems that the new broader path the firm is treading has inspired recruits to help win new business. For more on the recruitment process, see our website.

And finally...

In 2010, eight of the firm's ten qualifying trainees took jobs with the firm, going into a range of practice areas that reflect the firm's broadening interests in London.

Simmons & Simmons

The facts

Location: London

Number of UK partners/solicitors: 112/223

Total number of trainees: 80

Seats: 6x4 months

Alternative seats: Overseas seats, client secondments

Extras: Pro bono – Battersea Legal Advice Centre, LawWorks, London Legal Support Trust, A4ID; language training

On chambersstudent.co.uk
- How to get into Simmons
- The Simmons MBA
- Examining the firm's enviable art collection

Founded by twin brothers Percy and Edward in 1896, Simmons & Simmons is well known for its leading finance practice and has a host of other successful practice groups.

Mergers and emerging markets

Of all the trends under observation here in the hub of legal analysis that is Chambers and Partners, among the most closely scrutinised are the increasing appetite of UK firms to merge with US counterparts to establish a foothold in that powerful economy, and the influx of lawyers to new Asian offices, particularly in Hong Kong and China. Simmons is cautiously thinking about the States and is some way down the road with its Asian journey. In the summer of 2010 it coyly flirted with Mayer Brown, but failed to go all the way with the American-headquartered firm. Meanwhile, a Beijing office launched with the appointment of a partner from a Chinese firm. It follows earlier launches in Shanghai, Toyko and Hong Kong. In fact, about half of Simmons' revenue is generated outside the UK, even if it is simultaneously cooling some of its European operations (a Padua office closed and 20 lawyers defected from the Rome outpost in 2010).

The Mayer Brown merger talks might have come to nothing, but they indicate the firm's thought processes at the moment. Keep an eye on the legal press, as we wouldn't bet against Simmons casting lustful glances at other US firms. As a continent that avoided recession for the most part, Africa is now emerging as a hotbed of major transactions. Simmons recently advised on a major privatisation of an African telecommunications company for the Zambian Development Agency, described as the most significant in the history of the country.

Hedging its bets

When it comes to Simmons' training contract, seats can be taken in four categories: financial markets; corporate; contentious; and a miscellaneous fourth area covering anything left over. In general, one seat must be taken from each of the first three categories and a final choice is made from any of the four categories. The financial markets department has been a pioneer in advising the largest hedge fund managers in the UK and Europe, as well as institutional asset managers looking to set up hedge funds. As fund products become more diversified, the group has been at the forefront of the changing market and the growing convergence of hedge and regulated funds. Despite the tough conditions, the group has acted on successful launches. Retail, equity and property funds are all apparently on the up, bringing with them more client activity. May 2010 saw another coup for the finance team when, along with Allen & Overy, it snatched a key role in refinancing the travel company Thomas Cook – a deal worth nearly £2bn – from the jaws of three competing magic circle firms.

When finance is your firm's fodder, a seat in this department is always going to be a) mandatory and b) a crazy-busy ride. Simmons doesn't quite size up to the magic circle in the very biggest of deals, but one trainee was proud to say that "*it's nice to be seen as a firm that's very good at niche areas.*" So, if capital markets, funds, private equity or tax really are your bag, then Simmons has plenty to offer. "*It's a strong financial practice. They're a clever bunch of people. They've really taught me the relationship*

Chambers UK rankings

Asset Finance	Health & Safety
Banking & Finance	Information Technology
Banking Litigation	Intellectual Property
Capital Markets	Investment Funds
Commodities	Life Sciences
Competition/European Law	Outsourcing
Construction	Pensions
Corporate/M&A	Product Liability
Data Protection	Professional Negligence
Dispute Resolution	Projects
Employee Share Schemes	Real Estate
Employment	Real Estate Finance
Energy & Natural Resources	Restructuring/Insolvency
	Retail
Environment	Tax
Financial Services	Telecommunications
Fraud	Transport

between finance and law," said one source. The work, especially for the relatively uninitiated, will be about 50% grunt-type tasks and 50% "*meaningful,*" the latter ranging from "*amending and drafting documents*" to "*doing the first mark-ups, case management and getting documents signed off by trustees.*" Thinking caps are also required for "*more bespoke discussions about fund structures, how they work, and more difficult legal issues around funds.*"

Like most in the City, the Simmons corporate group has run slower than usual. It has nevertheless seen some interesting deals, such as HMV's purchase of live music event company Mean Fiddler Group. Lawyers also represented Lebedev Holdings as it bought a 75.1% stake in the *Evening Standard* – a deal which has revived the fortunes of the London paper. Alexander Lebedev is one of the so-called Russian oligarchs and his company also owns *The Independent*. It's "*substantial transactions*" such as this that trainees can expect to be involved with most of the time, but one was lucky enough to have a partner "*who let me play with one deal and run with it on my own.*" Corporate and finance seats are the usual suspects for long hours: while the past couple of years have generally been quieter in the City, and trainees assure us there is no face-time requirement, when deals demand it they must stay as long as it takes to get the job done.

It's not all corporate and finance though: Simmons has a leading employment practice, UK-wide and internationally. "*At first it was all very daunting,*" said a trainee who'd experienced a seat in the department, but fortunately: "*My supervisor still had a fresh memory of what it was like to be a trainee. She just told me, 'Don't be scared, everyone here is meant to be helping you!'*" The workload is varied, offering both smaller cases and more substantial ones, and there are always plenty of client training initiatives to assist with. Simmons is at the leading edge when it comes to delivering information on changes in the law and other pertinent issues to clients. The firm almost always represents employers, among them Deutsche Bank, UBS, Visa, GE and Virgin Media. Competition law is another strong suit, and a seat here will cover all sorts "*from cartel investigations to really relevant mergers that you see in the papers. When you actually see something in the FT it's like, 'That's great!'*"

There's plenty going on in the infrastructure and energy teams – areas that have proved particularly resilient in the face of the recession. One trainee who'd been deeply involved in green projects, including those concerned with generating energy from waste gases, was extremely pleased with both the supervision and the work. "*This isn't the Ally McBeal life I thought I was going to be living! I'm the rubbish trainee!*" they joked. Simmons' life sciences practice continues to be successful, with the firm's IP group one of the country's most highly regarded. Big-name pharmaceutical and biotech companies such as GlaxoSmithKline flock to the Simmons team, as do clients like Virgin Media, Abercrombie & Fitch and Coca-Cola. Science graduates converting to law can really marry their interests here.

Contentious seats provide a refreshing change from transactional ones. One source described their commercial litigation experience as "*wonderful – I got to work with a complete range of people on arbitration and professional negligence cases.*" "*I'm involved in one, liaising with counsel and going to meetings... I haven't attended a hearing. My supervisor had professional negligence cases, so generally they settle. A lot of the other trainees have been to court though.*" Another trainee had also loved their time in the department: "*It's important for a transactional lawyer to know how to avoid the pitfalls. We work directly with partners and it's good to sit with them.*" Something Simmons excels at is banking litigation. Of late there has been an increase in the number of complaints and claims relating to the mis-selling of financial products to investors. Other work results from the fallout from the Lehman collapse, the Icelandic banking crisis and the massive Madoff fraud.

TLC, and lots of it

The firm markets its internationalism to the max, and yet the overseas secondment system seems to have lost some of its appeal. "*One big element of surprise was that a lot of us were sent on secondments that we weren't prepared for at all,*" said one interviewee. "*It wasn't really what I was planning,*" was the hesitant response of another, while a third was more forthright still. How things have changed. Five years ago, we would have heard complaints across the City about not enough overseas opportunities. Much of the recent concern over secondments can be explained by trainees wanting to make their presence felt in London ahead of the all-important qualification decisions. "*The perception in the London office was that if you didn't stay you weren't going to get a job because of lack of face time, and the overseas secondment/client secondment was seen as a waste of a seat.*" These comments should be balanced against the fact that trainees went on to speak highly of their experiences abroad or with a client. Approximately 40% of trainees go on a client secondment at some point. Among the options offered on a regular basis are UBS, Barclays and GlaxoSmithKline.

One trainee who went to Dubai told us: "*The work there was really interesting, especially as it's an emerging market, and there were big deals going on when we first arrived.*" Tokyo, too, serves up an excellent blend of quality work. "*Even though my seat was nominally corporate, the office was really a one-stop shop for all sorts of employment, investment and other work.*" The Tokyo secondment also allows for quality time out – "*lots of drinks and karaoke... it's best to choose a Japanese favourite!*" Abu Dhabi, Hong Kong and Paris are the other options.

One thing all our interviewees particularly wanted to commend was just how accommodating partners and supervisors had been. In contrast to the 'stiff upper lip, stand to attention' ethos they envisioned, trainees here feel very much at ease with asking questions and talking things through. "*Some of the partners have this amazing way of explaining complex things in a simple way,*" was a typical comment. "*My supervisor was really good at always getting me involved,*" one source said. It seems this attentiveness is a firm-wide attribute, as one Dubai secondee remarked: "*Supervision there was excellent – they were very enthusiastic, always taking the time to explain things to you.* [My supervisor] *would even make me role-play out all the points for client meetings.*" Because the firm is full of niche areas and specialisations, this contributes to the sense of community. "*The unique thing about Simmons is that we work in small teams,*" one trainee told us. "*We're very tight-knit, so people are always buying each other chocolate or going out for dinner.*" These Simmons seduction techniques obviously work wonders. "*These are people I'd go the extra mile for,*" admitted one source.

We noted some confusion and apprehension surrounding the issue of qualification in 2010, not least because the number of trainees retained in 2009 dropped to a lowly 60%. In all honesty, even during the boom years retention at Simmons was consistently below the average for the firms we cover in the True Picture (head to our website to see how significantly), so we can't blame trainees for being a little nervy. In 2010, 36 out of 50 qualifiers took up jobs with the firm.

Emin-ently entertaining

Combining commercial acumen with social ease is obviously a winning formula here, and if you can add your own splash of innovation to the mix, it's more than likely you'll fit in. "*Simmons has always been about people,*" said one source. "*I've been allowed to play to my strengths, and I've always been asked for my input.*" Perhaps trainees should think about drawing their inspiration from the impressive collection of modern art that adorns the walls: it includes original Tracey Emins and Damien Hirsts.

Simmons' trainee social committee doesn't test its members' stamina to the limits, but whether it's going for "*a general knees-up at somewhere trendy in Shoreditch*" or just spilling into the "*inevitable*" Corney & Barrow or Rack and Tenter on a Friday evening, "*you are always able to find kindred spirits.*" You might even run into the odd partner "*to have a real heart-to-heart talk with.*" Indicative of a fairly easy-going nature at Simmons, interviewees described "*a nice culture and a nice work ethic.*" Not too nice though, warned one source. "*I don't think we are the cuddly law firm that we once were,*" they said, recognising that "*financial performance*" is far from unimportant.

And finally...

Simmons & Simmons is a top finance-focused firm with really decent people and international opportunities aplenty. Keep a lookout for more merger gossip.

- **Fewer training contracts:** From a high point in 2007/8 when 6,303 training contracts were registered by The Law Society, the number of new traineeships declined to 5,809 in 2008/9. The biggest drops were in The Midlands (20.82%) and Wales (15.93%). The smallest drops were in the South West (0.9%) and London (2.32%).

SJ Berwin LLP

The facts

Location: London

Number of UK partners/solicitors: 95/314

Total number of trainees: 73

Seats: 4x6 months

Alternative seats: Overseas seats, secondments

Extras: Pro bono – Toynbee Hall Law Centre; language classes

On chambersstudent.co.uk
- How to get into SJB
- We talk to outgoing managing partner Ralph Cohen
- The world of private equity

"It's all go around here. I should probably tell you that before we get started..."

Scaryfairytale?

Once upon a time, there was a charismatic City lawyer named Stanley Berwin. After founding Berwin & Co (now Berwin Leighton Paisner), he left to work in-house at Rothschild. Four years later, he returned to the firm expecting to seize back his throne as senior partner. He was disappointed. Berwin & Co had different ideas and it was so long Stanley. And so in 1982 he founded SJ Berwin instead. An ambitious, bullish, fast-paced child of the 80s, in two shakes of a pair of red braces, SJB was punching its way through the City Establishment, forcing its way into the UK's top 25 firms.

Underlying this guns-blazing work ethic was one simple consideration: the clients' interests. And it's still true today. As trainees commented: *"It's so important to go beyond client expectations... You need to keep surprising people, like telling them it'll be ready on Friday and giving it to them on Wednesday."* *"When SJB started, they wanted to make things easier for the client,"* confirmed another. *"We don't use legal jargon, and you've got to think creatively to get the right solution for them. It's not always the* [purely] *legal solution that fits, but if it works for the client, that's the way to go!"* Stanley would be proud.

Ever the innovative young 'un, SJB was one of the first City law firms to embrace private equity and fund formation work. Though it now faces strong competition from Clifford Chance and US firm Kirkland & Ellis, SJB is still ranked by *Chambers UK* as one of the leaders in this specialised field. Still, this full-service law firm isn't all about the transactional, and trainees believe that it will be more balanced in the future as the litigation practice *"gets busier and busier."* Real estate also remains a core area, along with banking and M&A. Indeed, SJB trainees usually spend two out of their four seats in the firm's corporate department, although the downturn required everyone to be a *"bit more flexible"* about seat allocation. *"We're becoming a more well-rounded firm,"* said one trainee, *"but corporate is definitely still king."*

Our sources were excited to be *"part of a law firm that you can help grow, rather than one that's already established."* *"I like the fact that it's forthright and ambitious,"* said one trainee. *"It sticks two fingers up to the Establishment."* Rebellion is all very well and good for a teenager, but is it time for SJB to grow up? The recession has forced firms to examine all parts of their businesses and their strategies for the future. The latest news puts SJB in merger talks with major US firm Proskauer Rose. Still to infiltrate the US market, SJB has previously had good relationships with several US firms. Though it has always denied merger rumours in the past, it is now evidently very open about the idea.

The SJB super-league

The corporate department is split into four teams: A, B, C and D. The A team is a *"mixture of M&A and flotations."* Though sluggish market conditions have prevailed, the firm acted for Australian packaging giant Amcor in its £1.2bn offer to purchase certain assets of the Alcan Packaging group. Step up to team B for all your private

Chambers UK rankings

Banking & Finance	Intellectual Property
Banking Litigation	Investment Funds
Capital Markets	Life Sciences
Competition/European Law	Outsourcing
Construction	Planning
Corporate/M&A	Private Equity
Dispute Resolution	Real Estate
Employment	Real Estate Finance
Environment	Real Estate Litigation
Financial Services	Restructuring/Insolvency
Fraud	Retail
Information Technology	Tax

equity buyout needs. One trainee found the work *"quite complex and way beyond what I thought I could do,"* revealing that they were responsible for *"project management"* and got some real hands-on tasks with *"a lot of scope for some blue-sky drafting."* The firm represented 3i in the sale of 30 portfolio companies to a consortium of investors in ten different jurisdictions, as well as Climate Change Capital Private Equity on financing its MBO of Climate Energy. Team C is all about private equity fund formation. *"It's clear that SJB sets the benchmark for other firms to catch up on,"* claimed one trainee, entirely with justification. This popular seat has trainees involved in limited partnership transfers, drafting and filing documents and coming up with legal opinions. Team D is *"more of a mixture of the others,"* handling smaller deals, buyouts and funds.

"There's a lot of interaction between departments, so it's not as if corporate is in a bubble." It will often be in touch with, for example, the tax team, which offers an extremely popular seat. Trainees say that the work is *"intellectually exciting,"* often requiring them to consider tax problems that have not been solved before. It's a good seat to do because, *"irrespective of where you qualify, tax experience will help those alarm bells to go off, alerting you that there might be a particular issue with a transaction."*

In SJB's renowned real estate department, trainees can be *"responsible for dozens of matters."* The department is split into three subgroups – one devoted to property finance, the other two split between different types of client. SJB's first-ever client, British Land, is still a major source of instructions, recently seeking advice on the pre-letting of its shiny new Ropemaker building (the biggest letting in the Square Mile in 2009). Other clients include AXA, The Crown Estate, Marks & Spencer and Hilton. *"The firm puts a big emphasis on getting to know what its clients are like,"* explained one source. No more so than in real estate, where trainees are *"trained from the outset about how certain clients want things done in a particular way."*

We heard of trainees who were the single point of contact for some clients; some who continued with deals even after moving seats; and some who were in charge of completions while their supervisors were away. *"You definitely get as much responsibility as you can handle, and sometimes more."* Make sure you've got a good pair of lungs: *"If you have too much responsibility, they tell you to shout!"*

Somebody's watching me

While SJB lawyers have previously been raised on a diet of private equity, their appetite is broadening. Though trainees warned, *"don't come here if you don't want to work in a firm that's corporate-focused,"* the litigation department is accessing meatier work and the majority of trainees rather like this. The department achieves *Chambers UK* top rankings, and while there's still the option to do a short litigation course instead of a full seat, trainees spoke of *"a busy department with interesting cases, where they really like you to get involved."* Their tasks include attending meetings, writing letters and drafting instructions to counsel on smaller cases. *"I've done two mediations,"* one source told us. *"They really want to train you and see you progress and stay at the firm."* Even for trainees who prefer transactional work, a contentious seat can be helpful. *"You need to have the paranoia that comes with it. It makes you more prudent: you square things off before they become issues."* Those in finance litigation found the market for this type of dispute has really picked up in the past year, while over in the EU and competition team, trainees waxed lyrical about cases in foreign jurisdictions and *"getting to take charge and giving your opinion all the time."*

Never one to shuffle its feet at the back, SJB was one of the first mid-tier City firms to expand into Europe. For a long time it was labelled 'a European law firm', but that tag is now a misnomer since it has further expanded its horizons and opened offices in Dubai, Hong Kong and Shanghai. Many of the international offices have secondment opportunities for trainees, and while there are no language requirements, we heard that it does help if you've already done a corresponding seat in London.

SJ Badass?

"From everything you read about the firm, it's the one you love to hate." To put it simply, SJB's got a bit of a rep. *"We grew from nowhere,"* said one trainee; *"you've got to be quite ballsy to do that."* The SJB stereotype is that of an aggressive corporate machine that works its people hard. What do trainees say? *"Obviously, in business clients*

want lawyers who will get them the best result. If that means aggression, that's the way it is," one stated. Said another: "*We're aggressive in that if the other side questions us, we're forthright. We know our stuff – we've won awards.*" As for the firm's internal relations, trainees say: "*In the heat of the moment, people have to be clear cut, and there's no nonsense when you're receiving information.*" They added that "*bitching among ourselves isn't in the spirit of the firm.*" SJB is no place for wallflowers because "*if you want to do something, if you want to get the real gems, you've got to be forceful. If you expect things to be handed to you on a plate, you'll get what they give you.*"

"*Everyone seems really motivated and enthusiastic – it's catching!*" What this actually means is that "*this isn't the place to come unless you're ambitious and capable of making that known. Otherwise you'll have a lot of work dumped on you.*" Everyone's confident, and yet "*I don't think that many people are arrogant,*" commented one source. It all means that if you want a certain seat, you'll need to argue your case. You've also got to want to get involved. "*This is a place where you can make your own destiny.*"

And what of the firm's reputation as a hard-driving employer? "*Obviously during the downturn it wasn't as busy,*" commented one trainee, "*but when it kicked off, it really kicked off.*" That's no understatement. Getting out of the office by 10pm was the trainees' measure of reasonable, though "*when you're working on a big deal, 10pm can seem like a delight.*" We heard of people who'd done all-nighters – three-day stints in some cases – without even the hope of making it to the sleeping pods. "*You are expected to work hard and pick things up quickly when you're really tired. This is an environment that's urgent and where the client is everything. It is challenging and can be terrifying.*" As one trainee aptly summarised: "*It's not nine to five, but that's the career choice you make at a City firm.*"

Before the recession this kind of pace was scaring people off qualifying into the corporate teams, but perhaps redundancies across the City have cast things in a different light. Now, as one corporate trainee revealed, "*people still crack a smile at 5am.*" Despite the long hours, trainees were confident that they were never in late for the sake of it. "*If you're able to leave at 5.30pm or before, and you're not involved in anything significant enough to stay late for, then you're probably not doing anything worthwhile.*" One source even confessed: "*The days I've stayed late and worked hard have been the best days of my training contract.*"

The SJB offices aren't a half bad place to spend all those hours. There are breakout rooms on every floor and table football and ping-pong when you need to let off steam. Trainees might even attempt some juggling, given that they completed circus training when they first started. Really! And let's not forget the rooftop terrace overlooking the Thames. It's the largest private roof terrace in London and when the weather's hot "*there are endless parties.*" Another hotspot is The Banker pub, where trainees can be found on Friday nights. When the weather's poor, they congregate for their free lunch in Stanley's, the SJB canteen with its "*big Wagamama-style tables.*" Here you might find yourself sitting with the most senior of partners. Some think the perk should be extended to a free breakfast too: "*If you've been there all night, it's just rude not to get one.*" Other perks include a dry-cleaning and shoe-shining pick-up service and an in-house doctor. As befits its international persona, the firm celebrates a variety of important dates – from St George's Day to Eid – when appropriate delicacies can be discovered in the canteen.

While trainees were confident that the firm is on the up, when it came to their qualification prospects they were slightly edgy. "*There aren't as many jobs to go round at the moment. You don't need to turn into a horrible lawyer stereotype to work here, but it does help if you've got a competitive edge.*" A total of 29 out of 37 qualifiers stayed on at the firm in 2010.

And finally...

The sky's the limit at this ambitious player. To fit in you need to be a driven and confident go-getter with real stamina. Don't underestimate the pace at which things move here.

Skadden, Arps, Slate, Meagher & Flom (UK) LLP

The facts

Location: London

Number of UK partners/solicitors: 19/59 (US: 11/13)

Total number of trainees: 13

Seats: 4x6 months

Alternative seats: Overseas seats

Extras: Pro bono – LawWorks, FRU

On chambersstudent.co.uk
- **How to get into Skadden**
- **The lowdown on legendary Skadden figures Joseph Flom and Peter Atkins**
- **Skadden stateside**

With 2,000 attorneys in 24 offices, Skadden truly is a Big Apple behemoth. Yet the firm's meteoric rise is a bit of an underdog story.

Showing the bastards

The book *Skadden: Power, Money, and the Rise of a Legal Empire* profiles the rough-and-tumble lawyers who founded what is now the world's second highest-grossing firm. Joe Flom, Skadden's last living name partner, joined as its first associate in 1948 and guided the firm through the wheeler-dealer 1980s and into its spot at the top of the M&A tables. The son of poor garment workers in Brooklyn, one of Flom's catchphrases was: "*We've got to show the bastards that you don't have to be born into it.*"

Skadden can trade punches with the magic circle in transactional work – banking, private equity, venture capital, M&A or capital markets. The *Chambers UK*-ranked M&A team recently advised reinsurance provider Validus Holdings in its $1.6bn acquisition of IPC Holdings. Other major instructions include representing pharma company UCB on a £1.5bn financing and advising reservation company Travelport on its planned public listing, which would have been the largest IPO in London since 2007 had it not fallen through.

Though Skadden is famous for corporate work, trainees said that international arbitration is becoming just as important too. In March 2009, the firm bolstered the practice by taking on partner David Kavanagh, who brought a team of three associates – not to mention the multibillion-euro Vivendi/T-Mobile arbitrations – with him from O'Melveny & Myers. The group was recently instructed by the Slovak Republic in the defence of a $1.1bn investment treaty dispute. While arbitration is on the rise, training partner Danny Tricot told us that Skadden will remain true to its roots. "*That area has been very productive given the downturn, but our strategy is to remain very corporate and M&A-driven.*"

The London office serves as Skadden's gateway to Europe, with particularly strong ties to Eastern Europe and Russia. Bruce Buck, the partner in charge of Europe (and also chairman of Chelsea FC), helps bring in high-profile Russian clients like his club's owner Roman Abramovich. The firm is representing him in a £3.12bn lawsuit brought by his former business partner, oligarch Boris Berezovsky.

Seat yourself

The London office was founded in 1988, and its trainee scheme is now six years old. The programme's flexibility is a highlight. "*At other firms you have to fill out applications and compete with people for a seat. Our system is informal.*" In the first year, corporate and litigation seats are compulsory but trainees are able to select the order in which they do them. Second-years are free to choose their final two seats from options including banking, tax, restructuring or even a repeat of corporate or litigation if that takes their fancy. Overseas seats in Hong Kong and possibly Moscow are also available.

Corporate seats involve research, document review and drafting, plus "*you get to deal directly with partners and clients*" because Skadden "*is not very hierarchical.*" The work is "*top-notch*" and almost entirely international, but given the high-stakes deals and "*manic deadlines*" the hours are "*very variable*" and sometimes "*quite long*" in the lead-up to a closing. At that stage "*you might work*

Chambers UK rankings

Banking & Finance	Energy & Natural Resources
Capital Markets	Private Equity
Corporate/M&A	Restructuring/Insolvency
Dispute Resolution	Tax

through the night." The type of corporate work taken on in the seat will vary depending on the firm's current dealflow but can run the gamut from capital markets to M&A to private equity.

In the litigation and international arbitration seats, trainees perform "*in-depth legal research*" and may participate in mediations, witness interviews and drafting statements in large cross-border disputes. Litigation partners at Skadden often perform their own advocacy and "*they're very keen to help you develop your skills and offer seminars for you to improve your public speaking.*" Pro bono contributions to organisations like the Free Representation Unit are also encouraged. The hours are more consistent in arbitration, with work typically ending at 8pm. Trainees in both corporate and arbitration have regular interaction with other Skadden offices across the globe.

Trainees must fill out applications for overseas appointments as Skadden sends just one trainee to Hong Kong every six months. This seat offers a mix of work from corporate and banking to international arbitration. "*It can be tailored to your interests,*" but "*there's a lot of capital markets work.*" We also heard tales of trainees who made shorter trips to the likes of Egypt, Greece and Los Angeles. "*There has to be a business need, but it does happen,*" graduate recruitment specialist Kate Harman confirmed.

Trainees get the bulk of their assignments from the senior associates they sit with, but one advantage to working in an international firm like this is access to a diverse group of senior attorneys with a wide range of specialties. Though trainees are supervised by UK-qualified solicitors, they sometimes work for foreign-qualified lawyers like former Washington, DC partner Gary DiBianco, who is developing a corporate investigations practice in London.

Born in the USA

While our sources had heard plenty of rumours that American firms drive trainees harder than their UK counterparts, they made it quite clear that Skadden doesn't treat trainees like conscripted soldiers. "*Don't be put off by our reputation,*" one said. "*The clients are very demanding*" and "*you have to demonstrate your dedication,*" but "*it's not cutthroat.*"

While the schedule can be gruelling, trainees insisted: "*The hours aren't any worse than at a magic circle firm.*" Plus, they argued, the intellectual (and financial) rewards are greater. Several said they chose Skadden because "*you get the same level of responsibility as a first-year qualified lawyer at another firm.*" Our sources speculated that this benefit stems from the firm's American roots. "*In the US they don't have the concept of a trainee, so you get more responsibility than at a UK firm. They treat you like a lawyer from day one.*" Skadden is also "*meritocratic: they allow the good people to progress, which is very much an American thing.*" Another US influence is the compensation; NQs here earn a tidy £94,000 in their first year. "*It's not all about the money, but you can't help but think – why would I go to another firm when I could do the same work here and earn 30 grand more?*"

Can see the Eye, but no NY

The current trainee group is "*quite close,*" and in addition to exploring Canary Wharf's watering holes on Friday nights, some see each other at the weekend for dinners and cinema outings. Other social opportunities include inter-firm football and netball leagues. One year Skadden hosted a *Strictly Come Dancing*-themed event, with competing solicitors wearing actual costumes from the BBC show. Sharing offices with senior associates also has social and educational benefits, not to mention the aesthetic appeal of "*splendid views*" of the London Eye and the Gherkin. Post-qualification, junior solicitors get their own digs but lose the scenery.

Until 2010, trainees were able to attend Skadden's *"brilliant"* global retreat in New York. Now the trip has been reserved for NQs, which our sources felt was *"slightly unfortunate." "We thought solicitors would get more out of it after they had qualified,"* training partner Danny Tricot said.

Because each intake is so small (just seven trainees started in 2009) the firm is usually able to offer jobs to all qualifiers and did just that in 2010 – keeping all five. What's more, "*it's fairly easy to qualify into the department you want.*"

And finally...

Plush parties aside, trainees agree that Skadden's greatest perks are high levels of responsibility and professional freedom. It may explain why one trainee insisted: *"Everyone turned down multiple magic circle offers to come here."*

Slaughter and May

The facts

Location: London

Number of UK partners/solicitors: 116/418

Total number of trainees: 170

Seats: 4x6 months

Alternative seats: Overseas seats; secondments

Extras: Pro bono – University House Legal Advice Centre, Islington and Battersea Law Centres, LawWorks, Citizenship Foundation; language classes

On chambersstudent.co.uk
- How to get into Slaughter and May
- We talk to executive partner Graham White
- The Oxbridge debate

Slaughters may be one of five members of the magic circle, but as far as it is concerned all the best tricks come from within its own four walls.

Slaughters sorcery

Clichéd as it might sound, Slaughter and May is a veritable Hogwarts of a law firm. Shrouded in the mystique of corporate conjuring, highly privileged access and closely contained practices, many are the myths that surround it. The truth is, the firm's consistency seems to breed a feeling of conspiracy among competitors, when actually Slaughters just employs reliably excellent lawyers to do a reliably excellent job in a competitive corporate environment. No magic wands, no consultation with talking hats. The firm's pared-down application process is designed to identify those individuals who have the intellect and concision to put across only what is necessary. The selected trainees can then expect to be intellectually challenged as much as commercially inducted. "*Often when you do corporate deals, a lot of what is involved is pro forma: you just jump through a series of hoops,*" said one of them. "*I wanted to do something that was slightly more innovative because when you have more complex subject matter, you come across issues that require you to really think about the law. The big sales like Cadbury and Prudential have aspects to them that make you do that.*"

Ah yes, Prudential. Not the story of the year for any of the key players concerned, but nevertheless one of the most widely covered. Slaughters was advising the men from the Pru on the attempted buyout of AIG Asia, but the deal collapsed after AIG refused to accept the reduced offer that Prudential's investors and shareholders had put on the table. The £12bn hostile takeover of Cadbury by Kraft Foods was altogether more successful (for the unsentimental in a Dairy Milk v Dairylea world, anyway), becoming one of the biggest bids in the City for years. Slaughters remains the FTSE 100's legal darling, advising the likes of GlaxoSmithKline, Centrica and British Airways on some often ground-breaking issues. Perhaps most importantly, it has been the firm of choice for HM Treasury, from which it generated £32.9m in fees between 2007 and 2010. That goes some way to explaining its incredibly high level of profitability. The partnership at Slaughters is famously close-knit and, like elsewhere in the City elite, difficult to break into, but it is also this that keeps it strong.

Refusing to gamble on international expansion also appears to have been a prudent move. It opened an office in China in 2009, but otherwise Slaughters is satisfied with a network of world-class 'best friend' firms across the globe and for work to be referred between them. So, succinctly put, Slaughter and May aims for "*the best-quality work, the best-quality clients and a best-friends strategy.*"

Generalism is a specialism at Slaughters – though it calls it a 'multi-specialist approach'. "*We concentrate on giving people as wide a range of work as possible. To avoid putting people in 'silos', we won't be encouraging people to specialise,*" says executive partner Graham White. For those of you not conversant with management-speak, putting people in 'silos' describes the practice of sectorising them so much that they cannot properly interact with each other, which naturally can be detrimental to business. "*It's a reflection of our client base: they're not the sort of people who have repetitive transactions, so they want*

Chambers UK rankings

Administrative & Public Law	Intellectual Property
Asset Finance	Investment Funds
Banking & Finance	Life Sciences
Banking Litigation	Outsourcing
Capital Markets	Partnership
Competition/European Law	Pensions
Construction	Pensions Litigation
Corporate/M&A	Private Equity
Dispute Resolution	Professional Negligence
Employee Share Schemes	Projects
Employment	Real Estate
Energy & Natural Resources	Restructuring/Insolvency
Environment	Retail
Financial Services	Sports Law
Fraud	Tax
Information Technology	Telecommunications
Insurance	

continuity in their legal team but also an ability to do whichever sort of work." This is an ethos that may initially be hard to grasp by trainees used to very structured study in well-defined disciplines; however, most respond well. "*I like the fact that the firm doesn't have rigid demarcations between practice areas; the parameters are very wide,*" said one disciple.

If you're wondering how order is maintained in such a loosely defined environment, the answer lies in a fairly well-established hierarchy. Most sources confirmed that "*at Slaughter and May as a whole, there is a definite division between trainee, associate and partner work,*" meaning that some found themselves "*feeling a bit useless*" when sat with a partner who "*just wasn't able to delegate work to me.*" But others extol the advantages: it teaches you to be proactive in seeking out your own work, and provides structure.

Making a killing

Trainees choose their seats prior to beginning their contract. Their flight paths will include at least two stints in corporate/commercial, though "*you'd be lucky to get away without doing two corporate and one finance*" (known internally as CoCoFin). Slaughter and May's grouping system operates not by conventional team titles, but instead there are seven corporate and finance teams, each named after the initials of the partner that heads it. Given the dips in corporate activity during the recession, it was no surprise to hear that mid and post-crunch trainees had witnessed CoCo flops and CoCo pops in their respective eras. "*We had quite an atypical experience,*" admitted one fourth-seater of his first seat. "*It was quite quiet; there was a lot of boring admin work, proofreading and zero client contact. Then it started to pick up just as I left.*" For first-years the difference in contextual conditions was notable: "*I've had a very enjoyable three and a half months. I've been very lucky – we're not running at absolute full tilt, so we get given more responsibility because the supervisors can give you more time. I'm drafting a new contract for a client, which is fantastic, and have loads of direct contact with clients.*" All too often the level of responsibility on offer will come down to the deals that any one supervisor is working on at the time. One of the trainees assisting with GlaxoSmithKline's "*huge joint venture*" with Pfizer to create a new HIV medication company saw a mixture of "*drafting board minutes and bibling. But then I did also get to do associate-level work, and it was great to see the transaction covered in the FT.*"

While 2009 was naturally a difficult year, trainees in Slaughter and May's finance groups appear to have been consistently busy. "*I did the most work in this seat, hitting the ground running and going straight into a transaction,*" explained one. Whether advising Global Infrastructure Partners on a £1.125bn acquisition of Gatwick Airport, or Premier Oil's $600m buy-up of Oilexco, there are clearly still big-money deals for new starters to dive into. Attending meetings, liaising with clients and helping to draw up transaction documents are the order of the day, and as one satisfied trainee told us: "*I was surprised about how much work I was allowed to do at the time.*"

Best friends in high places

Commercial real estate offers "*a lot of client contact and a lot more responsibility,*" with some trainees "*getting involved in big redevelopments and proper drafting.*" Others work on "*negotiating lease terms from getting instructions right through to completion.*" The development of the Olympic Village for the 2012 Games and Arsenal's redevelopment of Highbury with a new mixed-use development to the south of the Emirates Stadium are just some recent examples of matters handled. The department itself, in contrast to the "*boys' club*" atmosphere of the corporate groups, was described as being "*quite chirpy*" in tone.

Dispute resolution is popular, and much sought after when it comes to qualification. "*I really enjoyed it,*" enthused one source. "*I started off on a big document review exercise, going through various documents and e-mails, deciding which ones are relevant for a disclosure exercise.*" There is also a good deal of research involved, "*including jurisdictional and enforcement issues.*" Slaughters has a hand in some really big cases: acting for HM Treasury on issues arising from the Northern Rock debacle; representing British Airways during the European Commission's investigation into alleged cartel activity; and the Nationwide Building Society in a test case examining the validity of unarranged overdraft charges.

There shouldn't be an automatic assumption that a lack of foreign offices means a lack of secondment opportunities. While one trainee did inform us that "*everyone feels that the whole secondment procedure is really cloak and dagger,*" positions are available in glamorous and exciting locations (Hong Kong, New York, Sydney, etc.) as long as you're prepared to contend for them. The experience does not disappoint either, with trainees reporting that they actually preferred the 'best friends' approach to having their own outposts because it meant a fuller integration into the legal culture of another country. There is often an increased level of responsibility in those countries where the concept of a trainee is alien. Other London seat options include employment, competition, tax, pensions, IT and IP. There also some secondments to clients.

Total training

"*There are two aspects to the training: on the job with a supervisor and formal training sessions.*" The nature of the former means that "*everyone's experience is subjective according to their supervisor,*" but there was absolute unanimity in praise of the utility of the latter. "*One thing that has been really good is the training,*" said a source; "*things like accountancy master classes and talks from partners.*" Most new recruits worry that they're far from combat-ready – "*we're taught to be good trainees and becoming an NQ seems like a big leap,*" said one. Another mused more philosophically on life in the lower ranks: "*It's just the nature of the food chain.*"

There are plenty of preconceptions about Slaughter and May, but most new arrivals are pleasantly surprised by the lack of stereotypes walking around. "*People aren't as cocky or arrogant as others think; they're just really clever people who don't boast about it.*" Certainly our sources were eager to set the record straight. "*I had read that it was quite a blueblood firm and was surprised at how friendly it is,*" said one. There may not be a typical trainee at Slaughter and May, but you can be sure that "*independent,*" "*ambitious,*" "*academic*" and "*thick-skinned*" will be adjectives characteristic to all those who prosper there. "*I'm not very good at being micro-managed,*" said one interviewee. "*I like being told what I need to do and then getting on with it. Your supervisor's not going to want to know if you have a lot of questions.*"

Self-motivation and discipline are rewarded by an absence of billable-hour targets, something touted as one of the great benefits to working at Slaughters. But just because "*you don't have to be here if you don't have work to do,*" that doesn't mean that you'll always get out of doing long hours. Trainees spoke casually of all-nighters, and some were even able to look on the bright side of doing a late-night deal shortly after the Christmas party: "*We spent all night raiding hampers! It was actually quite fun!*"

Slaughterhouse thrives

Life at Slaughter and May is not marketed as laughter and play, and these trainees aren't the most hard-drinking, hard-partying group in the City. Perhaps due to the "*bit of a 'them and us' mentality among partners,*" those in the lower echelons tend to organise their own fairly sedate social activities ("*there is always someone who is happy to go for a drink*") or leave the office behind altogether. "*You don't get given BlackBerrys, and I never log on when I'm not in the office,*" said one interviewee, reflecting the 'work hard, play elsewhere' mentality. "*I like the fact we don't have a drycleaner, a hairdresser and dormitories – an office is an office.*" The canteen, it should be said, more than makes up for the lack of any of the above. It's not that extra-curricular activities don't exist: "*Once you're here there is a trainee solicitors' committee, lots of sports teams and dinners, and each department does a summer and autumn party.*" There is no underestimating the individualism inherent in the firm's culture, such that one person's interest in "*free art passes, free concert tickets, free theatre tickets*" is another's environment committee, literacy scheme with St Luke's primary school or participation in the in-house magazine.

NQ retention rates at Slaughters are consistently among the best in the City, and even a recession didn't dent them too much. In 2010, 75 out of 85 qualifiers took up jobs with the firm.

And finally...

"The thing that attracted me the most about Slaughter and May was its reputation for being outstanding at everything that it does. I was inspired by the fact that it values excellence." Excellence is a hard-earned achievement, so if you find excelling exhausting, think again.

- **In your prime?** "There's a great deal of value in trainees for whom law is a second career. They can often bring maturity and real-world commercial experience to the role." Training partner, City firm.

Can you
take the
HEAT?

SNR Denton

The facts

Location: London, Milton Keynes

Number of UK partners/solicitors: 120/249

Total number of trainees: 67

Seats: 4x6 months

Alternative seats: Overseas seats, secondments

Extras: Pro bono – PopLaw, CAB, legal advice to Camfed and UNICEF UK; language training

On chambersstudent.co.uk

- How to get into SNR Denton
- The firm's African ambition
- How a 'combination' differs from a 'merger'

The Denton Wilde Sapte we all knew and loved had a reputation as being ideal for *"someone who wants to work on big City deals but also wants to have a life."* Will that continue following its US tie-up?

All around the world

DWS grabbed headlines in May 2010 when it announced that as of 30 September 2010, it would enter into 'a combination' with US firm Sonnenschein, Nath & Rosenthal, forming a 1,400-lawyer giant in 18 countries called SNR Denton. Having recovered from some setbacks in the early noughties, DWS was already a firm on the up. Even before the merger announcement, it stood out when it posted a 20% increase in partner profits, accompanying stable revenue in the 2009/10 financial year. Its impressive global imprint already incorporated overseas offices in Paris, Singapore, Istanbul, Almaty (Kazakhstan), Moscow, Tashkent (Uzbekistan), Abu Dhabi, Cairo, Doha, Dubai, Muscat and, as of 2010, Bahrain. It had additionally gathered associate offices in St Petersburg, Lebanon, Ashgabat (Turkmenistan), Amman, Kuwait and Riyadh. That's more offices in the Middle East than any other firm. We mustn't leave out established links with nine African law firms. The firm has an established history in the now emerging market. With the SNR tie-up, DWS adds nine US offices plus outposts in Brussels and Zurich.

Right place, right time

Before the SNR deal, trainees' four six-month seats usually fell within DWS' four core areas: financial institutions; real estate and retail; energy, infrastructure and project finance (EIPF); and technology, media and telecoms (TMT). After the 'combination', the firm intends to focus on eight key sectors. To find out what they are, visit our website. We'll also detail any modification to the trainee seat system there. In London, banking has taken centre stage for some time. DWS' CEO Howard Morris spoke of the firm's ideal positioning: *"Back in '07, we looked at our practice areas and we figured that banking would be a big challenge because we didn't do the high-end stuff like securitisation and debt capital markets. However, through the downturn it's turned to our favour as clients are looking for more general advice and we are known for our large institutional knowledge and leading restructuring/insolvency practice."*

"Some students come in not wanting to do a banking seat and that's strange because not only is our banking department a very strong one but it's our specialty," one trainee added. The firm is frequently called upon by all the major UK players like RBS, Barclays, HSBC and Lloyds but does not fall short on international work. Dentons recently advised a syndicate of four Chinese banks on a $1bn loan to Standard Bank of South Africa, probably the largest deal of its kind for a South African financial institution in the Chinese market. A trainee's mandatory stint in the department could entail general banking, asset finance or trade finance. Asset finance is *"good for a first-seater"* as there's *"experience with day-to-day basic decisions, preparing all the documents and client contact."* The work consists of *"a lot of repeat deals and aircraft financing."* Trade finance involves *"loans for commodities,"* dealing with *"everything from tobacco to*

Chambers UK rankings

Asset Finance	Outsourcing
Banking & Finance	Pensions
Banking Litigation	Planning
Capital Markets	Projects
Commodities	Public Procurement
Competition/European Law	Real Estate
Construction	Real Estate Finance
Corporate/M&A	Real Estate Litigation
Data Protection	Restructuring/Insolvency
Dispute Resolution	Retail
Employment	Social Housing
Energy & Natural Resources	Sports Law
Environment	Tax
Information Technology	Telecommunications
Intellectual Property	Transport
Local Government	

cashew nuts and gold." It is a department notorious for its unpredictable, long hours, including a rare all-nighter or two. Our sources "*didn't find it too bad*" and appreciated "*you're never there alone; there's always another trainee or associate and there's no waiting around for the sake of it or waiting around for your supervisor to leave first.*"

Real estate is "*slightly more relaxed*" as it is "*less international, so there are fewer long hours.*" That's not to say the domestic work disappoints: the firm's real estate team advised in relation to the new Supreme Court and its ownership, including drafting and negotiating all construction documentation and negotiating with the Secretary of State for Communities and Local Government, from whom the site was acquired. Lawyers also helped Ambassador Theatre Group with its acquisition of Live Nation's UK portfolio of 16 theatres for £90m and mainstay client Sainsbury's on acquisition and redevelopment plans for some football stadiums. It's standard for trainees to have their own files and be "*told to get on with it,*" which our sources loved. "*I had files that were mine. It was my directions that were moving them forward and clients e-mail you directly and ask you to sort out their problems. It really boosted my confidence,*" one gushed. The firm also works in the social housing arena advising many of the major lenders that provide funding to the sector.

Going nuclear

Project finance is "*quite an up-and-down seat. You either have a lot going on, like when the closing of a big deal is coming up, or a little.*" Trainees are heavily involved on the legal research side and also find themselves "*dealing with the conditions precedent.*" The energy seat offers the opportunity to do "*loads of marketing and pitches and proposals.*" Here in the UK, EIPF teams advised EDF Energy Networks on the Olympic Park undergrounding project and handled the £2.8bn financing of the Birmingham Highways Maintenance PFI project. International deals are there too: lately lawyers have worked with Botswana Power Corporation as the host nation power utility in relation to the $3bn Mmamabula Power Project – the first IPP project in Botswana. It is likely to be viewed as a model project in the region. The nuclear practice is one to watch as the firm recently hired two experts from Hammonds.

There are also seats in some of the niche EIPF areas like rail, where lawyers advise on "*contracts for train procurement*" or "*bids for government contracts.*" "*It's all a bit geeky, but I really liked it,*" admitted one trainee. The firm advises Northern Rail (the UK's largest train operator) on day-to-day commercial issues, property transactions, disputes, regulatory and franchise advice and more. Other projects include National Express' InterCity Express Programme, which will supply the next generation of high-speed trains to the UK.

Technologic

The TMT department has scaled right back over the past few years. CEO Howard Morris cited losing most of the team to DLA Piper in 2004, along with the death of old media, as reasons. While none of our interviewees had done a seat in the department (only four are available), Morris assured us it is on the up as its increasing digital focus helped it achieve the highest rate of growth of any department last year – 25%. Those seeking red-carpet glamour should know that "*the media work within TMT is tiny now; it's really very techy,*" he added. Recent work has included advising a software developer on a supply contract to a government department, advising an international bank on an IT services agreement and helping a large retailer to outsource its IT support. On the telecoms side, the firm led legal work on the largest pre-pack administration to date, for Hellas Telecommunications.

Dentons had a hand in other high-profile restructurings, like those of Woolworths, Crystal Palace FC and Portsmouth FC, and sports broadcaster Setanta sought help when it tried to restructure its finances. A number of hedge and investment funds turned to the firm in connection with the UK administrations of Lehman. The trainee experience involves "*quite technical work*" along with "*some bundling and pagination, but paralegals and information assistants help with a lot of it.*" Doing a seat in restructuring/insolvency will fulfil contentious requirements, though a stint in dispute resolution is more common. Most cases come from the firm's existing finance and energy clients. Trainees assist with bigger cases and there may also be smaller ones "*where* [they'll] *have conduct from start to end.*" Expect "*a lot of drafting and attending pre-trial hearings.*"

The corporate department certainly deserves a shout out. Recent highlights include advising Sainsbury's on a joint venture leading to a new facilities management service model for its 850 stores. The London office teamed up with Dubai and Kuwait to assist Vodafone with its $952m IPO in Qatar – the first by an international company on the Qatar exchange, and the second largest IPO to date in the Gulf state.

Home and away

Client secondments abound, with the likes of Total, Shell, Thames Water, Goldman Sachs, RBS and Citi all taking trainees. When it comes to getting out of the office, the real story is the overseas seats. Abu Dhabi, Dubai, Muscat, Moscow, Istanbul and Paris have all been up for grabs in the past, but there are "*no hard and fast rules*" in terms of availability.

A City firm it may be, but "*everyone is very, very nice.*" Trainees are "*always banging on about how nice everyone is, but when you're working on something, you're all trying to get to the same end. Some firms can act unnecessarily aggressively, but Dentons isn't one to throw its weight around.*" This firm has a seemingly ideal "*relaxed, casual, lively and almost jokey*" office environment, where "*you do feel included. You get on with everyone right from the support staff to the senior partners. I know some senior partners you can go in and joke around with and have a good relationship. I haven't met any that are scary.*" CEO Howard Morris is always keen for a laugh, "*always says hello,*" and "*knows everyone by name.*" "*There's a lot of affection for him,*" even in tough times. In the wake of redundancies in 2008, he went around to see every member of staff and addressed their concerns individually. Decision makers are clearly held in high regard as trainees showed plenty of genuine gratitude for how "*human*" the firm was. "*It's not going to be a problem if you have to take some time off for personal reasons, and you can say no to work if you have a good reason,*" reported one trainee.

In the smaller Milton Keynes office, trainees were enjoying their time so much their only complaints were about parking permits. We were told the office offers a better work-life balance, which seems valid, as although it takes in "*mostly City work,*" this tends to be real estate, construction and litigation. Plus, there is no mandatory banking seat. A swoop on Howes Percival's MK office in 2008 has "*gone as well as it could have*" and the firm has picked up "*significant clients, some of which have nothing to do with London.*" New MK trainees head to London for their induction and are "*always invited to social events down there.*"

Feel like dancin' dancin'

Back in the City, a trainee social committee organises big events at Christmas and each September/March for leavers and joiners. When we rang, everyone was buzzing about a summer ball. In between times, there is occasionally a trainee budget behind the bar at the Corney & Barrow just next door to the office. Firm-wide events have been scaled back, but we did hear good things about a bowling night, where there was some celebratory singing of Scissor Sisters' *I Don't Feel Like Dancing*.

A glow of positivity permeates this firm; however, there was a thick cloud of worry over our second-year interviewees as they witnessed only one of seven March 2010 qualifiers being kept on. "*It was a function of taking a very hard look at business needs, and it would be unjust of us to take people on where there's not work for them,*" senior sources explained. Trainees didn't let it get them down too much: "*Even though I'm not sure if I'll get a job, it's okay because either way I've had the best time ever.*" The firm notified 25 vacancies for its 32 autumn qualifiers and 18 accepted offers.

And finally...

As the legal world waits to see how SNR Denton will live up to its potential, it is safe to say that supportive, well-rounded training at this firm is guaranteed.

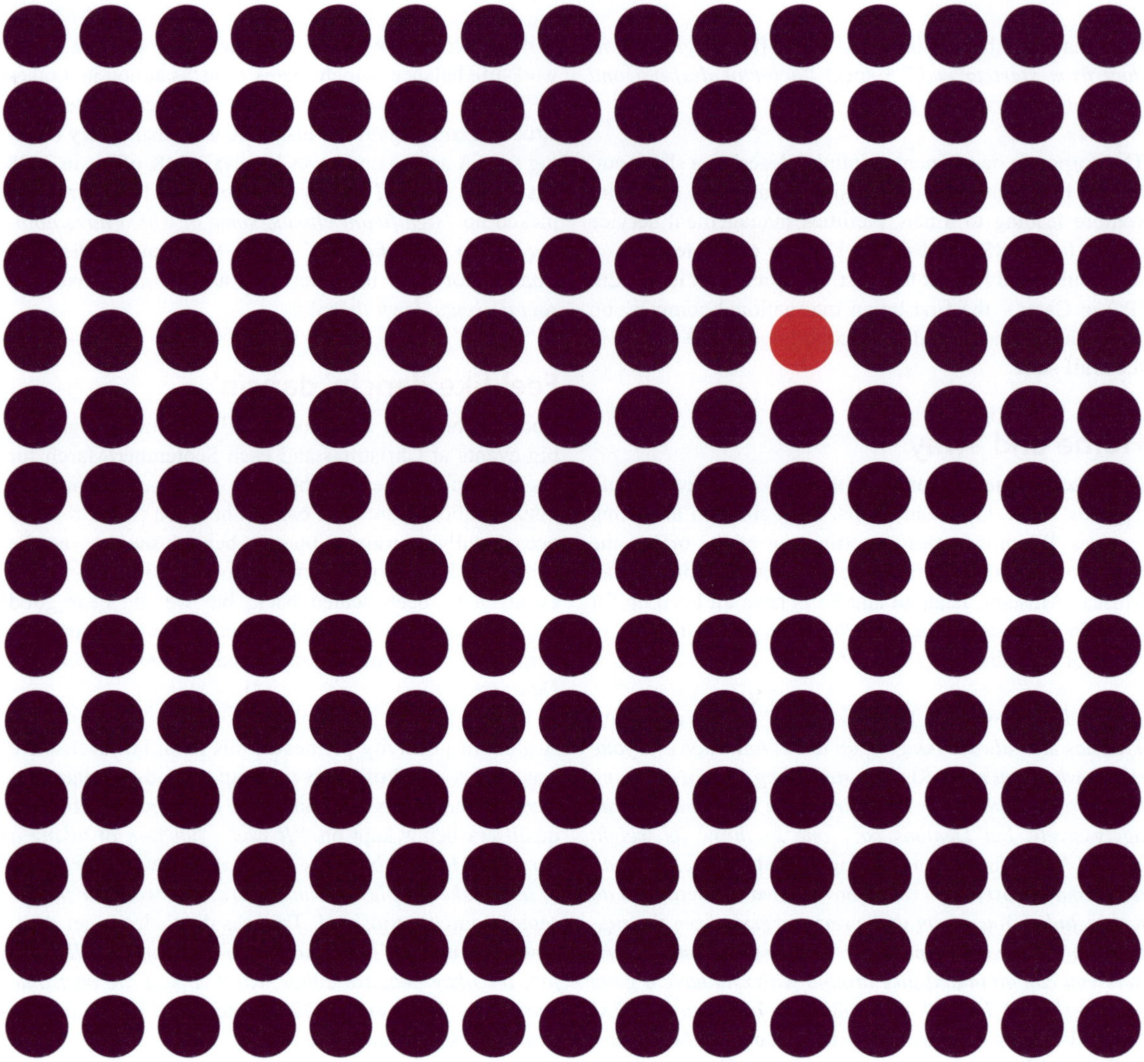

Speechly Bircham LLP

The facts

Location: London

Number of UK partners/solicitors: 87/165

Total number of trainees: 22

Seats: 6x4 months

Alternative seats: Potential secondment

Extras: Pro bono – Blackfriars Settlement

On chambersstudent.co.uk
- How to get into Speechly Bircham
- The Campbell Hooper factor
- A few of the firm's headline cases and deals

Speechly Bircham has been making its presence felt in the City playground over the past year. Following the integration of Campbell Hooper into its gang, it has since pursued a vigorous campaign of troop-gathering.

Ripped

This began with added muscle in the competition team in the form of a Nabarro partner. Then came an encounter with Farrer & Co, with Speechlys striking first by nabbing an experienced financial services partner, followed by Farrer taking one of Speechlys' trusts and tax planning partners. Speechlys next pumped up its pensions practice by hiring a Wedlake Bell partner, while adding some extra beef to its projects and infrastructure team by way of two ex-Shadbolt partners. All this brawn is obviously matched in brain, as the financials for 2009/10 were positive: a 29% increase in both annual turnover and partner profits.

Weighty is a good word to describe Speechlys' renowned private client practice, which with 21 partners to its name is probably the largest in the City. The division's reputation is bolstered by its clientele of ultra high net worth individuals such as Gulf billionaires and those worth in excess of £100m. Some of these people are busy buying up trophy assets across the UK, including hotels, country properties, marinas and one of the largest private jet hangars in the country. They are investing big over here, often as part of a global strategy to redistribute their wealth.

Big-name clients abound elsewhere too. As the strapline for her latest TV show declares, 'It takes one to know one', and who better to identify a model solicitor than one of Speechlys' most glamorous clients, supermodel Elle Macpherson. The businesswoman and now television personality has the IP and media departments busy working on matters relating to the Elle Macpherson Intimates lingerie range and television show *Britain's Next Top Model*. The IP, technology and commercial (IPTC) team, though only four years old, obviously knows an entrepreneur when it sees one, as it also counts among its clients *Dragons' Den* maverick Michael Pritchard, who successfully pitched his multi-directional household Anyway Spray to the poker-faced posse. One of the biggest stories for the department was the defence of software minnow World Programming against the monolithic SAS over a breach of software copyright terms. The case has been described as the most significant of its kind in over a decade.

Preferential treatment

One readily observable trend among Speechlys trainees this year was their early identification and ongoing investment in specific practice areas. Whether it was private client, IP or employment, a number narrated a complete lifecycle of embryonic interests at undergraduate level that were then pursued through LPCs and vac schemes, taken up again as seat choices, and often culminated in qualification in the very area they had aspired to work in. Speechlys seems to cater generously for each individual's pursuits and preferences, and all our sources were pleased with the fact that "*you definitely get at least two of your four choices*."

Chambers UK rankings

Agriculture & Rural Affairs	Intellectual Property
Charities	Investment Funds
Construction	Media & Entertainment
Corporate/M&A	Pensions
Data Protection	Private Client
Employment	Real Estate
Family/Matrimonial	Real Estate Litigation
Financial Services	Restructuring/Insolvency
Immigration	

Real estate is not a compulsory seat, but all our interviewees had sat in either the non-contentious or contentious teams within the department. The former covers regeneration, development, investors and occupiers, with plenty to keep a trainee interested. "*Real estate is different from other departments in that there is a very quick turnover. There will usually be about 15 matters on the go at any one time.*" Trainee tasks include "*preparing title packs for properties going to auction, registration applications, helping with the completion of developments*" and post-deal formalities. The construction department offers "*really good exposure*" on disputes. One trainee described their duties as a good deal of drafting court documents, plenty of research and attendance at court hearings. "*I've never been overworked and never been underworked,*" mused a source, adding: "*It's exciting to be part of it all – the people are inspiring and supportive.*" The real estate and construction teams certainly gained added clout with the arrival of the Campbell Hooper crowd, and they now have over 70 lawyers. Highlights of the past property year were ongoing work with Derwent London on the Portobello Dock Development, and acting for RBS on a major office move.

Private client is core to Speechlys' reputation, and as a trainee seat choice it does not disappoint. "*I really loved the seat,*" a euphoric trainee told us. "*I really enjoyed the work, I really liked drafting, I liked the way I got a variety of work, and I liked having lots of amazing clients.*" Said clients are mostly rather rich, such as the notorious non-doms, "*but we also have some from middle England.*" One interviewee was particularly impressed with the "*very sophisticated ways of managing wealth and estates,*" and another got a real kick from the fact that "*it's different to other aspects of law as it's not transactional as such. There is an intellectual challenge and I really enjoyed that.*" But trainees should also expect to entertain a certain degree of eccentricity from such a moneyed clientele: "*In the City everything is done by phone or e-mails, but private client is a bit more old school. Clients actually come into the office and some don't even have e-mails!*" Campbell Hooper also brought with it a specialist mental capacity group that represents mentally incapacitated individuals from the elderly to young victims of brain injury.

Speechlys is active on corporate finance transactions in the mid and lower mid-market arena, with its great strengths lying in AIM and capital markets deals. Trainees appreciated the greater commercial awareness this seat gave them: "*Sometimes when you go to a corporate firm you go into a more specialist team, but I got to do bits of everything – not just general M&A, but banking and restructuring as well.*" One second-year described a wide variety of work including "*buy-backs of shares and drafting shareholder resolutions, loan agreements and an investment proposal.*" Most of the corporate team's more interesting transactions remain confidential, but we can tell you that it has a strong clientele that includes Cable & Wireless and Citibank.

Niche-ly, niche-ly

Immigration is an unusual practice area for a City law firm, but it is for this reason that it can prove popular. Perhaps reading this you find yourself in the same position as the trainee who admitted: "*I didn't know much about immigration beforehand.*" Never fear, because essential to getting to grips with the seat is learning on the job and keeping pace with developments in immigration law (Article 39 of the EC Treaty anyone?). The team concentrates largely on business immigration but sees "*all sorts of clients from various different sectors, including banking, media and entertainment.*" These might be "*high net worth individuals wanting to undertake work in the UK, spouses of British citizens, or EEA nationals wanting to exercise their rights.*" To give just one example, Speechlys advised theatre company Cameron Mackintosh on immigration permissions for American guest stars Nick Jonas and Norm Lewis to come and perform in *Les Mis*.

Nearly half of the trainees we chatted with had sat in employment. "*It's an up-and-coming area of law, really interesting, and there's always a lot in the news about it.*" And what makes it so interesting? "*We have a range of clients from individuals to large companies and also individuals within those companies.*" With issues such as sex discrimination, whistle-blowing and equal pay filling their plates, and "*fantastic work*" that involves drafting witness statements, working on electronic disclosures and attending mediations, trainees sounded hungry for more. That said, when we asked one trainee just how oversubscribed the seat was, the response was qualified: "*Employment is a popular seat. Private client is also very popular. There's nothing that's not popular.*"

The fused IPTC group sounds every bit as lively as its list of clients might suggest. Aside from Ms Macpherson and

Mr Pritchard, the team counts Black & Decker, Munich Re and Gina Shoes among its clients. "*You choose IPTC because you want a challenge*," said one trainee who had taken up the gauntlet. "*I was heavily involved in document management, which sounds dull but was really quite interesting as you get to know the nuts and bolts of what's going on. On another case I got to go to a lot of client meetings to try and ascertain what the issues were and get the clients' perspectives*." The seat allows its occupants to see a good mix of contentious and non-contentious work and was described as "*a brilliant department for giving trainees responsibility; you're treated like a full member of the team.*" In addition, Speechlys' data protection experts run an interesting campaign called 'The i in online', designed to teach children and teenagers about sharing personal information and how to manage data, with a particular focus on social networking sites. We also heard positive feedback about experiences in seats such as family and contentious trusts, commercial dispute resolution and property litigation.

Making Speechlys special

Last year's *True Picture* predicted that the merger between Speechly Bircham and Campbell Hooper could be a meeting of minds. We pride ourselves on being good psychics, and just as we foresoothed, the two firms are singing from the same hymn sheet. The tie-up has left no discernible residue of resentment/nostalgia among employees, and a chorus of trainees confirmed that "*the integration was so smooth... you didn't have any idea who came from Campbell Hooper and who from Speechly Bircham*."

Not a single trainee failed to mention the benefits of their open-plan environment. Said one: "*I think open-plan is great because you don't have to go and wait to knock on someone else's door*." "*You can eat your partner's Maltesers, as well as fellow trainees' Maltesers*," seemed the more rational advantage. A word of warning though: if you're currently reading this in a small room that cries out for the full Kim and Aggie, you may want to reconsider your approach. "*We have a clean-desk policy*," explained one of our interviewees. "*It's about trying to keep your desk in order, filing electronically as much as possible so you don't generate more paper than you need to. And there are floor managers making sure we're sitting properly. It's just so we don't encroach on other people's space*." The offices and their location received unanimous approbation also: "*They certainly are shiny. They're very well situated, directly opposite the Technology and Construction Court and only ten minutes from the Family Court*."

Open-plan and clean desks apply to all and, like a corporate Febreze, they give the firm the impression of a refreshing lack of hierarchy both in its work and in its social ethics. Trainees don't have an independent social committee because "*most sports and social events are firm-wide*." These range from "*so many informal drinks*," either in the local Corney & Barrow or the White Swan just behind the office, to the hugely popular Halloween parties, Christmas extravaganzas and summer get-togethers. Biannual "*amazing pub quiz nights*," day trips to Paris, and even to the zoo, have also been on the agenda. The more cerebral may enjoy the comfort of a sandwich and a good book, to be shared with fellow literature lovers at book club meetings.

Our interviewees were enthusiastic about Speechlys' exclusively trainee-run CSR initiative – the 'Life Matters' presentations that they conduct in partnership with the Blackfriars Settlement charity. These talks are delivered to members of the elderly community to advise them on "*various legal topics such as nuisance neighbours, scams and benefits*." They are followed by a 30-minute discussion session. The programme has proved such a success that trainees have even encouraged vac schemers to go along, and one qualifying trainee was so sorry to be leaving it behind that he told us resolutely: "*I'm going to set up a new project*."

On the subject of the firm, trainee vocabulary soon has a familiar ring: "*friendly*," "*exciting*," "*friendly*," "*expanding*," "*friendly*," "*lovely*," "*friendly*." So perhaps our beefcake analogy was a little inappropriate for such a well-spoken and amenable legion. When the only complaint was that "*there's maybe a bit too much air-con*," it is clear that these are spirits that are hard to dampen. One trainee described herself as someone who "*tends to look at life in a glass-half-full sort of way rather than glass-half-empty*." Such cause for contemplation need never arise however, because from where we're standing, all their cups seem to be running over. And with more vacancies than qualifiers this year, the phenomenon needs little explanation.

And finally...

It's clean desks from now on for the 14 of the 15 qualifiers who stayed with the firm in 2010.

Stephenson Harwood

The facts

Location: London

Number of UK partners/solicitors: 96/142

Total number of trainees: 29

Seats: 4x6 months

Alternative seats: Overseas seats, secondments

Extras: Pro bono – Citizenship Foundation, CAB; language classes

On chambersstudent.co.uk

- How to get into SH
- We talk to training partner Neil Noble
- Fiona Trust litigation 101

Highly ranked in the mid-market, this international firm has lately attracted oodles of talent from the magic circle to bolster its finance team.

Something in the water

For a long time misconceived as mainly a shipping law firm, Stephenson Harwood has emerged happily from the bad place where it spent the early years of the new millennium. Since taking its lead from much-admired (former) managing partner Sunil Gadhia, who unravelled and fixed some key structural and morale problems during his tenure, it has returned to good health and prosperity. No longer adrift in the legal backwaters, SH has emerged from the fog and looks nothing like a boutique shipping operation. "*It's always been a mystery to us why we've been regarded that way,*" training partner Neil Noble told us, so let's get one thing straight: SH is more "*a mid-sized international corporate and commercial law firm than a niche shipping practice.*" Focusing on clients in energy, financial services, projects, real estate and transportation, it is highly ranked by *Chambers UK* for mid-market corporate and disputes, and is increasingly well regarded for asset finance deals. In terms of niches, the firm does maintain a strong shipping group and also has an intriguing reputation for defending high-value international civil fraud claims. More on each of these later.

The firm was founded in 1875 after William Harwood's return from China. A century later SH retraced his steps east along the trade route. It opened an office in Hong Kong in 1979 and added other outposts in China and Singapore in the 1990s. These forays east were undoubtedly guided by demand for legal services from the shipping industry, although today the firm has expanded deep into other areas. Most recently it bolstered its asset finance practice with lateral hires from City heavyweights such as Ashurst and Freshfields. In fact 50% of the partnership weren't at the firm five years ago – an astonishing statistic considering the recession. But SH is all about defying economic trends; growing when other firms were shrinking, and pulling stable revenue and profit figures out of a hat when competitors were reeling from double-digit drops. New partners have been bringing in clients and high-quality work, so the firm's healthy progress looks set to continue. It's all a far cry from just a few years earlier when many pundits assumed SH was a washed-up firm after several years of poor management.

The plan is to continue to "*grow head count*" with the aim of building the partnership up from 100 to 150 in the next five years. Further international growth is also on the cards in Singapore to meet "*huge demand there.*" Closer to home, the firm is looking to Germany to strengthen its existing European office network, which currently comprises London, Paris and Piraeus in Greece.

Something to SHout about

SH is starting to find its voice, although one trainee admitted: "*It doesn't shout about itself enough... we do really good-quality work but people outside don't know that.*" The firm has advised the administrators of the $4bn estate of Hong Kong multimillionairess Nina Wang, who seems to have left two wills upon her death. One purportedly leaves her vast fortune to her feng shui consultant, Tony Chan; the other to a charitable foundation she set up. A crisis of conscience, perhaps, or maybe Mr Chan designed the deceased's fountain of wealth to flow in his

Chambers UK rankings

Asset Finance	Intellectual Property
Aviation	Investment Funds
Banking Litigation	Outsourcing
Capital Markets	Pensions
Commodities	Planning
Construction	Private Equity
Corporate/M&A	Professional Negligence
Dispute Resolution	Real Estate
Education	Real Estate Finance
Employment	Real Estate Litigation
Environment	Shipping
Financial Services	Tax
Fraud	Transport
Information Technology	

direction? The SH corporate team needs no help from the three-legged toad of prosperity as its client pool already comprises major banks and corporates, including historically loyal client HSBC (whose relationship with the firm dates back to Will Harwood's stay in China). Also sending business are Lloyds, Shell, Total and Virgin.

Conflicting wills and corporate banking are tame compared to the more mysterious work of the firm's civil fraud squad, whose consistently high-value cases could each have formed the sub-plot of a 007 novel. Recent dramas include the Fiona Trust case (one of the largest in the Commercial Court recently), in which SH defended the former director general of Sovcomflot – now the largest shipping company in Russia – against allegations of conspiracy to defraud the company through unlawful shipping and banking transactions totalling over $600m. The department has also been working on a case involving a company that occupied the iconic Ark building next to the Hammersmith Flyover and allegations of asset stripping.

So where do trainees fit in to all this excitement? Six-month seats take them to four different teams chosen from corporate; real estate; employment and pensions; commercial litigation; shipping litigation; and finance. A contentious seat is compulsory, as is one in either corporate or finance.

Finance is a popular seat, we hear, in part because there are a lot of different types of work on offer, usually international in scope. Much of the work relates to asset financing, and there are aviation and shipping subgroups that advise many Asian companies on their financing arrangements. The department as a whole is picking up more clients as it diversifies into general finance and banking; indeed, activities now relate to land, sea and air rather than just maritime matters. Lawyers recently advised a consortium bidding to develop the new Dublin Metro North system; organised a $4.5bn luxury shipping credit facility with major international banks; and worked with HSBC on a £220m debt restructuring for a sinking cruise line. There is scope for client contact in this seat, although the work is largely *"collecting and sending out documents and keeping the mechanics of the transaction going."* Trainees need organisational talents as they spend their time collating conditions precedent and drafting or reviewing deeds of assignment and various security documents to support loans. *"I ran some small trade finance deals on my own,"* a source explained with pride.

Mid-market Olympians

Commercial litigation trainees enjoy a mix of bigger cases and smaller ones on which they have more freedom and control. The department is *"very, very busy"* and there are *"always loads of 'capacity e-mails' going around,"* so if they take the initiative trainees can get involved in different things. *"Massive cases do demand menial work like bundling,"* and one of our sources confessed to working consecutive late nights and a few weekends in a row for one big trial, but trainees generally find the work interesting *"because it's all headline stuff."* Front-page cases have lately included a Central Asian banking dispute and judicial review proceedings for the UK subsidiary of an Iranian bank against sanctions issued by the EU Council that prevented the company from trading in Europe. Among the smaller matters trainees typically run solo are debt collections and lower-value breach of contract disputes.

By contrast, the claims are rarely low-value in the shipping litigation seat, where trainees are *"thrown in at the deep end."* Said one: *"In my second week I was on the phone to a* [Middle Eastern] *company to find out why they had not paid a bill of lading."* This department works on everything from *"capsized boats and collisions"* to *"disputes with Korean shipyards"* and high-seas piracy. The hours tend to be quite long as *"with the economic downturn everyone was breaking agreements."*

The real estate practice has been working on a project of Olympic proportions, advising EDF Energy on the construction of power distribution systems for the Olympic Park. Trainees assist on bigger projects such as this and also run their own files for things like short tenancies and shopping centre leases. Over in corporate, trainees encounter investment trusts, AIM flotations, filling out shareholder proxy forms, drafting correspondence and attending client meetings. One trainee revealed that they'd *"acted as company secretary for about 150 companies."* The firm recently advised Motor Oil Hellas on a €245m acquisition of Shell's downstream business in Greece, and it also assisted on the £100m sale of several UK power stations.

Passepartout

If you're the sort who'd like to spend a seat away from the firm then what about a secondment to one of its clients? These seats offer "*a completely different perspective... and are the best way to develop and become fully independent.*" Or how about spending six months overseas? Postings to Hong Kong and Singapore are always attractive to the well-travelled trainees at SH, yet competition for places isn't too fierce as family ties and relationships keep some at home. "*If you have a family it's harder to leave for six months,*" so generally everyone who wants to go abroad does get to go.

The Asian offices handle a mix of asset finance and corporate work, mainly for Asian businesses. "*We listed lots of Asian companies on AIM,*" recalled one source. Trainees reported "*a lot of interconnection between the offices... associates come out when we're busy... and people also come out for conferences...*" In fact, a quarter of SH's fee earners are based abroad, so trainees in HK certainly don't feel isolated. Those we spoke to found the experience "*absolutely fantastic*" and cited the seat as a highlight of their time at the firm. Overseas seats usually mean greater responsibility, but the non-professional perks are another huge attraction. "*Living out there was incredible,*" recalled one jetsetter. The firm makes your move as smooth as possible: flights are provided and "*they put you up in a nice flat with a swimming pool.*" Luxury even extends to the workplace – "*our office is in the Bank of China Tower, the coolest building in Hong Kong.*" Trainees socialise with other London law firm expats, and some also relive their gap years, one weekend at a time. "*I think I went on about nine trips when I was out there... Taipei, Japan, Malaysia...*" Lucky so and so's.

On the move

When back on home turf, SH lawyers commandeer a local pub – Shores – every Friday. For some reason the shipping team has its own favourite – The Cockpit – which is apparently "*a bit of an old man's pub.*" However it might soon be a case of last orders at each as the firm is set to weigh anchor and move from picturesque St Paul's Churchyard to swanky new premises at One Finsbury Circus in 2011. The move is necessary as the firm's rapid expansion has left it "*bursting at the seams.*" Sad to be moving, trainees told us: "*It's going to be a shame because our front door literally looks onto St Paul's.*"

This firm has always liked a party. Firmwide socials include a Christmas bash and summer barbecues, although most activities are organised informally within departments. For sporting trainees there's the usual round-up of netball, football and bowling, and also cricket and golf events are organised with clients. Trainees have their own committee, which acts as "*the link between us, HR and the partners.*" It's something the relatively new HR team is looking to strengthen and it has already been used to organise a successful networking event for trainees and clients. Participation in pro bono and community activities is at each trainee's discretion. While associates can get involved in giving actual legal advice, there's "*very little*" organised for trainees. That said, if you're enthusiastic then you're encouraged to find things yourself. Last year, for example, the trainee committee organised fund-raising activities following the Haiti earthquake.

Stephenson Harwood "*draws people who have more than one dimension,*" remarked a source. Since the annual intake is fairly small, the firm wants "*people who take on responsibility from the first day; trainees who can hit the ground running.*" Our sources also stressed that "*you have to be quite outgoing, but not arrogant.*" To find out more on how to get into the firm, go to our website. Recent success has prompted SH to increase its trainee intake from 14 to 16 in order to meet business needs, and there's been a recent increase in application numbers to match the firm's resurgent reputation in the City.

So what really distinguishes Stephenson Harwood from the many other mid-sized firms with international interests? According to training partner Neil Noble, it's "*a balanced and well-hedged practice.*" According to trainees, it's "*because we do what we know we're best at, we stick to it and we work very hard to maintain our standards.*" Simples.

And finally...

Stephenson Harwood is increasing its trainee intake to meet demand, and according to our sources it is most definitely *"going places and has a story to tell!"* In 2010, nine out of 15 qualifiers accepted jobs at the firm.

Stevens & Bolton LLP

The facts

Location: Guildford

Number of UK partners/solicitors: 36/54

Total number of trainees: 8

Seats: 6x4 months

Alternative Seats: None

Extras: Pro bono – department-specific initiatives

On chambersstudent.co.uk
- How to get into S&B
- We talk with managing partner Richard Baxter
- The lowdown on Guildford

Dozens of ex-City lawyers have escaped the hustle of the Square Mile for the more sustainable pace of this single-office Surrey firm.

The City in minor key

Guildford-based Stevens & Bolton promises 'City work outside the City' for trainees attracted to the calmer pace of life on the banks of the River Wey. More than half of the firm's partnership are City-escapees who've bolted from the Big Smoke. For them, corporate-led S&B is a perfect match, especially since the firm's recent move into a flash new office. "*It's very swanky with floor-to-ceiling glass windows overlooking the river,*" and the goal is that S&B "*will attract more City business with this more City look.*"

It's only in recent decades that S&B has become a commercial contender with a clientele that includes the likes of Amazon.co.uk, Bank of Scotland and Kuoni Travel. "*We've also got some good, loyal, local clients,*" some of which date back to S&B's previous incarnation as a small firm focusing on private client and real estate services for the good folk of Surrey. Even now, private client matters still permeate several departments, clients are treated to croquet and golf socials and the firm's telephone hold music is Mozart's classic symphony no.40 in G minor.

Trainees describe S&B as a "*sensible*" firm. "*It likes to champion work-life balance,*" one pointed out, while another mulled over the extent to which lateral hires from the City had actually shed their Square-Mile mentality. "*Their attitude does influence the rest of the firm,*" they said of the high standards and professional expectations of seniors, "*but everyone is more relaxed here because of the environment we're in.*" That said, even beyond the M25 you'll face some late nights because there's "*no feeling that any less is expected of you.*"

Full-throttle training

Since 2009, S&B has offered a six-seat training contract that allows recruits to either experience all six core practice areas or repeat a favourite seat. Trainees admitted: "*It's difficult changing every four months because you lose the two months where you're comfortable,*" but they recognise that the added variety is ideal for those unsure of where to qualify.

At the risk of sounding like a socialist Chancellor of the Exchequer, we'll tell you that tax is popular. It's an academic seat with "*reasonably varied and technical*" tasks. There's "*more research and drafting than in other departments*" but, equally, partners "*are not afraid to put trainees in touch with clients directly.*" The department handles both corporate and private client issues – everything from deal structuring to trust funds, wills and probate. Surrey has oodles of rich City commuters and older landed wealth. Said one tax fan: "*You're always dealing with people who have assets abroad, and if possible they'll let a trainee deal with probate files from start to finish.*"

The employment team handles "*a lot of contentious work*" plus a range of non-contentious advice such as "*helping clients formulate policies*" and, increasingly, immigration queries for international companies such as Amazon or Paramount Pictures. "*It was really busy because of the economic downturn,*" one trainee recalled. "*I was taking witness statements from clients from the word go and drafting briefs to counsel.*"

Chambers UK rankings

Banking & Finance	Information Technology
Construction	Intellectual Property
Corporate/M&A	Partnership
Debt Recovery	Pensions
Dispute Resolution	Private Client
Employment	Real Estate
Environment	Restructuring/Insolvency
Immigration	Tax

Nuts and bolt-ons

Litigation wins the prize for most responsibility. Trainees run several debt collection files and are encouraged to go to court. "*I did my own advocacy at the county court and went on my own for a trial,*" enthused one trainee. "*It's a very good feeling when a decision goes your way!*" Trainees assist on larger cases, say, commercial disputes arising out of distribution agreements, partnership and shareholder dust-ups and IT disputes. Within the department, trainees are "*encouraged to seek a range of work... supervisors are not proprietary over trainees.*" Some also gain exposure to IP cases. A recent trade mark and copyright infringement dispute pitted P1, the world's leading supercar club, against new rival GP1. "*We were acting for the claimant and it was quite a cut-and-dried case. It was the trainee's job to gather evidence, manage documents and help prepare the mediation.*" Trainees get their hands on "*a fair bit of drafting,*" including particulars of claim and witness statements. "*I did have bundling to do,*" a source admitted, "*but not too much, and I got really good work as well.*" Another recounted how "*a partner helped trainees paginate until 2.15am one weekend.*"

Corporate powerhouse

The hours are less punishing in the family team, which takes cases involving divorce and children issues and gives trainees plenty of client contact and drafting experience. There's more drafting in property – "*there are always quite a lot of licences to assign*" and "*masses of landlord and tenant matters.*" Other common duties include compiling information packs and checking legal title for properties due to be sold.

"*The corporate department is our powerhouse,*" said one trainee when telling us about the mixed corporate/commercial seat. "*Most of the work I've been involved in has been M&A and banking... marking up shareholder agreements,*" due diligence, etc. Among the team's biggest recent transactions is a £45m refinancing by Santander of 140 Kia Motors dealerships. Trainees who stray into the realm of day-to-day commercial advice can end up looking at anything from "*Freedom of Information Act requests to agency agreements.*" One trainee recalled that they "*had a crack at first drafts of commercial agreements and trade mark licences.*" The partners are "*really good,*" trainees tell us; "*all top of their game and nice laid-back people.*" Despite enjoying the taste of success, "*they don't want to be here all night... they've moved out of the City for good reasons.*"

Buttercups and bouncy castles

Most of our sources had avoided the capital entirely when applying for training contracts. S&B is "*a regional firm in all the best senses,*" one trainee commented. "*Its size, set against the quality of work, does set it apart,*" we heard, plus "*you know everyone in the firm and that's really nice.*" Mostly our sources wanted students to know that "*it's certainly not an easy ride.*"

So what's it really like in Guildford? "*There's a nice mix of restaurants, pubs and shops*" and "*the nightlife serves most needs pretty well, but I'd stop short at recommending Guildford for its night clubs. It's pleasant but definitely not edgy.*" A firm-wide soirée is organised for the last Thursday of every month, and socials "*tend to be quiet drinks rather than crazy nights out.*" We've heard that S&B turned the dial up to 11 to celebrate its office move – there was "*karaoke and arcade games on the top floor and the trainees sang Build Me Up Buttercup.*" London is only 30 minutes away by train and around half of the trainee group reverse-commute every day. Firm-wide activities are commonly family-oriented, such as barbecues and an *It's a Knockout* fun day "*with big inflatables and partners getting buckets of water chucked over them.*" Other sports tend to be more traditional – "*staff v partners cricket matches,*" plus tennis, badminton and basketball at a local sports hall.

And finally...

S&B trainees give this City/Home Counties mash-up a big thumbs-up. In 2010, two of the four qualifiers accepted jobs with the firm. Other jobs were available but not in areas the qualifiers wanted.

- **Want to work for Chambers and Partners?** Our research team is over 100 strong and works on a range of legal guides. If you have good interviewing and writing skills, why not take a look at our website and find out more about us and what we do? Some of our researchers are with us while looking for a training contract or pupillage. We're especially interested in people who speak foreign languages.

Taylor Wessing LLP

The facts

Location: London, Cambridge

Number of UK partners/solicitors: 99/159

Total number of trainees: 43

Seats: 4x6 months

Alternative Seats: Secondments

Extras: Pro bono – Blackfriars Settlement, Oxfam's 1,000 City Lawyers; language training

On chambersstudent.co.uk
- How to get into Taylor Wessing
- Pro bono at the firm
- Venture capital 101

This mid-sized firm has a great reputation in IP and life sciences plus established transactional practices, and is pushing a more corporate image.

Brand on the run

The product of an Anglo-German merger in 2002, Taylor Wessing now has ten European offices and small footholds in the Middle East and China. The English and German partnerships operate as separate profit centres, although the German offices have lately structured themselves to more closely mirror the UK offices, including the introduction of cross-office industry groups. There are no overseas secondments for trainees, so the extent to which their training will feel international will depend on the departments in which they work and the nature of the work in each. This perhaps explains why some trainees felt the offices have "*operated as relatively distinct entities,*" while others saw that on multi-jurisdictional issues there's "*fairly frequent interaction.*"

Like the big brands it represents, TW knows that image counts for a lot. Managing partner Tim Eyles has set about defining and refocusing the firm's strategy around four brand values and five core industry sectors – technology, brands and communication; energy and utilities; financial services; life sciences and healthcare; and real estate, infrastructure and mobility. The plan is also to better align the international offices and make sure that clients are "*using all of our services in our different offices.*" The four brand values are detailed on TW's website, if you're interested. There is also a major focus on "*ten core clients*" – among them RBS, Deutsche Post, Google, easyJet, Nike and private equity firm Electra. It's been a tough time in the market and TW did not escape the recession unscathed: global turnover fell by 5.3% in 2009/10 to £178m, while UK turnover dipped 7.3% to £84.5m.

The training programme involves four seats and only one compulsory stop – in corporate, which reflects the fact that "*the core of the firm is its transactional hubs.*" Corporate seats can be taken in tax and incentives; finance; commercial and hotels; corporate, commercial/projects; private equity; financial institutions and markets (FIM); and technology and inward investment. Wherever they sit, trainees who prove their worth are given responsibility to match. "*In a way* [corporate tax was] *like being back at uni,*" one trainee remembered; "*I had to solve technical problems, dig down into statute books and get the right answer.*" In the finance seat, trainees work primarily for banks and other financial institutions on acquisition finance, securitisation and development finance. One trainee in this seat was "*running small deals* [up to £5m] *on my own,*" including drafting loan agreements and ancillary documents; they also found themselves negotiating contract terms for bank clients. It's "*deal after deal after deal*" here, and the long hours reflect this; nevertheless, finance seats are generally oversubscribed. The separate FIM seat involves giving regulatory and compliance advice on takeovers and restructurings, etc. to a range of financial institutions including investment banks. All very timely stuff, and yet there is an "*urban legend*" going around that "*trainees want to avoid FIM.*" Certainly the work can be detailed and technical. "*We act for a lot of AIM companies; I got to draft all documents for restructuring of a group of companies…*[My supervisor] *will say, 'off you go, draft everything.'*"

Chambers UK rankings

Agriculture & Rural Affairs	Life Sciences
Banking & Finance	Media & Entertainment
Banking Litigation	Outsourcing
Capital Markets	Pensions
Construction	Pensions Litigation
Corporate/M&A	Planning
Defamation/Reputation Management	Private Client
	Private Equity
Dispute Resolution	Product Liability
Employment	Real Estate
Financial Services	Real Estate Finance
Fraud	Real Estate Litigation
Information Technology	Restructuring/Insolvency
Intellectual Property	Telecommunications

Is TW the Schumacher of the corporate mid-market? It advised Ross Brawn on his purchase of the entire issued share capital of Brawn GP from Honda. It then advised on the sale of 75.1% of Brawn GP's shares. Off the track and onto the field, the firm helped Devondale Investments on the sale of Portsmouth City FC to a company run by Dubai-born real estate magnate Sulaiman Al Fahim. In a game of Premiership pass the parcel, TW lawyers then advised on the subsequent sale of 90% of the club's shares to a company controlled by Saudi businessman Ali Al Faraj. The corporate department is an exciting one to be in: trainees draft share purchase agreements and assist with other aspects of transactions, and one we spoke to was "*responsible for the disclosure letter on a small £4-5m transaction.*" Apparently a trainee was packed off to Rotterdam for a deal completion on their second day in the department.

These days the dust never settles over in the corporate restructuring and insolvency team, which offers a contentious seat. This team works with major banks and "*big accountancy firms*" such as PwC and Grant Thornton. The department has been superbusy during the downturn and has a reputation as one of the most "*work hard, play hard*" areas of the firm. Apparently one of the team's client social events involved a ten-car Scalextric track in one of the firm's top-floor boardrooms. Lawyers were "*grouped into teams with clients* [and were apparently] *supposed to let the client win.*"

Private client teams are rare in City firms; however, TW has a thriving practice group that offers a seat to trainees. Don't expect the old green-welly brigade though; "*we have a lot of corporate clients... the partners and fee earners reflect that some are young and dynamic and a few are much more old-school.*" The firm recently worked on a $4bn trust restructuring for a North American family and advised on the creation of a $100m Shari'a offshore trust to facilitate venture capital investments in Europe. It's "*high-stakes stuff,*" according to one source, and you "*have to be willing to turn your hand to anything... I got really good exposure to property and mortgages, finance, tax planning, trusts, estate administration... it's old-school lawyering.*" Trainees liaise with intermediaries such as accountants, bankers and HMRC, and there will be plenty of research, will drafting and contact with clients. "*Tax work is really high-level so you can't get a huge amount of responsibility, but you learn a lot.*" Further seats are available in construction; employment and pensions; real estate; real estate litigation; commercial disputes; IT/telecoms; trade marks, copyright and media; and patents.

Techy Wessing

TW's excellent reputation in the IP realm is worth knowing about because this is an acknowledged area for growth within the profession in an otherwise largely moribund economy. The firm has been ranked highly by *Chambers UK* for both 'hard' and 'soft' IP matters for a long time, and it represents clients such as Nokia, North Face, The Motley Fool, Pepsi, Christian Dior and LVMH. It also represents venture capitalists and there's a dedicated group working on inward investments into the UK by US clients, mainly "*big pharmas, Silicon Valley players and internet companies.*" For more information on this dynamic sector, see our website.

IP seats are popular. The 'hard' IP patents group advises on highly technical matters such as the development of nano-particle medications. The patents seat has "*big-scale cases that go on for a long time... you tend to work in a big team and it's not really possible to get a lot* [of client contact]." TW represents pharmaceuticals companies such as Abbott Laboratories and Tamiflu manufacturer Gilead, and lawyers recently advised Oxford Biomedica on the £34m development in collaboration with sanofi-aventis of new gene-based medicines for ocular diseases. On the contentious side, TW represented Apotex against Les Laboratoires Servier on a patent dispute relating to hypertension medication. The client was awarded £17.5m in damages. Trainee tasks are "*organisational and research-based.*"

Meanwhile, 'soft' IP embraces trade marks, copyright and passing off, among other things. Imagine an average day: you eat a bowl of Kellogg's for breakfast while reading the *Daily Mail*. At work you Google and print documents on a Hewlett-Packard printer; in the evening you buy a Burberry coat (okay, perhaps not so average) with your Visa, before heading to a Wetherspoons to kick back with a Heineken. These are all brands that the TW lawyers guard from infringement, and from the outset trainees are expected to get stuck in. A regular task for one was acting on "*e-mails from clients monitoring the market* [for trade mark infringements]" and drafting "*cease and desist letters*" on their behalf. In this seat, trainees find themselves in court and frequently liaise with clients and barristers.

The standalone IT/telecoms team is a pretty good place to wind up as it has some major clients such as Google and PartyGaming, the latter being a place trainees can do a client secondment. Defamation and reputation management is also serious business at TW, and trainees can see some of this work in the soft IP seat. The firm defends media companies including Associated Newspapers against libel claims made against them. Lawyers recently advised publisher Pan Macmillan on controversial references made about author and activist Erin Pizzey in Andrew Marr's *A History of Modern Britain*.

Trusted Taylors

Last year's report pondered on whether the abolition of dress-down Fridays by new managing partner Tim Eyles would be "*a death knell for a more relaxed TW.*" This year trainees noted "*a strict dress code*" and the need to respect "*a clear hierarchy.*" One trainee summed up this ethos as follows: "*You're at work... you have your individuality at the weekend.*"

TW is an ambitious firm with an atmosphere to match. Trainees have hinted that "*strong characters*" populate certain departments and some supervisors "*have a reputation for working* [trainees] *pretty hard.*" The grad recruitment team monitors trainee supervision, and one trainee observed that "*the worst offenders have either left or have quietly had their trainee taken away from them.*" In essence, this is not a place with a "*softly, softly*" approach and, according to our interviewees, "*you do sometimes need to be a bit thick-skinned.*" Being pushed is integral to the training experience here. "*It's the best way to learn,*" according to a senior source, and as trainees put it: "*You're expected to hit the ground running.*"

While trainees were generally very positive about their seats, we picked up on some gripes over other aspects of the experience. Several people told us they felt "*left out of things* [eg presentations] *and some e-mails that go to associates don't go round to us.*" A communications working group has now been formed. Some trainees also had difficulty communicating problems. Trainees have meetings with the grad recruitment team (HR staff and training partners) "*every couple of months*" to feed back on their experiences. "*Trainees are often nervous,*" one of our sources remarked; "*you're worried about putting someone's nose out of joint.*" Another advised "*not rocking the boat.*" All this said, "*the graduate recruitment team does listen to what we say,*" but trainees wondered if the "*nature of the hierarchy*" gave the grad recruitment team "*enough authority to get things done*" and suggested that this "*could be improved by having someone independent of the partnership to speak on our behalf.*" Finally, some second-year trainees were frustrated with the nature of the NQ recruitment process. More on this on our website. Nevertheless, 2010 was a good year for qualifiers: 19 out of 24 stayed on, ten of them going into corporate practice groups.

No messing with Wessing

Trainees are expected "*to contribute to the firm in more than just* [their] *work.*" The corporate and finance departments seem to conduct themselves in much the same way as an investment bank, and trainees are expected to step up and make their mark on business development. They help organise and attend client socials, including "*dinners, cocktail evenings and Wii sports tournaments.*"

When they're not entertaining clients, lawyers "*across the firm go out in smaller groups*" to the local Corney and Barrow. There's a social budget for trainees and "*the firm organises drinks events for future joiners.*" There's also "*quite a big karaoke crowd*" which heads off to K Box in the West End after the pub. "*We should have some kind of pass there!*" declared one trainee. The karaoke obsession goes some way to explaining the performances put on for the 2010 charity fund-raising extravaganza – 'TW Hot Talent', which was "*mostly singing with the occasional dance routine.*" Other events include a European football tour, "*cricket matches all the time,*" netball games and "*triathlons organised with clients.*" Trainees are "*heavily involved*" in pro bono matters, too.

And finally...

"*People who get their heads down go places in Taylor Wessing,*" said one trainee of the secret to success at this firm. Do this, prove your worth and you'll reap the rewards.

Thomas Cooper

The facts

Location: London

Number of UK partners/solicitors: 20/19

Total number of trainees: 8

Seats: 4x6 months

Alternative seats: Overseas seats

On chambersstudent.co.uk
- How to get into Thomas Cooper
- P&I clubs
- The under 10-metre fishing fleet debate

Though small in size, Thomas Cooper is a big name in the world of shipping.

Blow high, blow low

The Napoleonic Wars. A time of heroes, great deeds and really big hats. It was in the aftermath of this epic conflict that Mr Thomas Cooper, an Admiralty lawyer by trade, set up shop in London. His livelihood was in a now arcane area of law called prize, which was central to the Royal Navy's income. Following the end of the war, Crown and crew split the value of ships and cargo captured from enemy fleets – a lucrative affair. In 1870, Cooper's practice was sold to a private client, banking and commercial firm by the name of Stibbard Gibson, creating Thomas Cooper & Stibbard. The shipping side of the practice gradually reasserted itself over the years, and in 2007 the firm took back its original name.

Today a banking practice is all that remains of the Stibbard legacy, and Thomas Cooper's stock in trade is maritime, trade and finance law. Over the past few years the firm has grown significantly. It has offices in London, Athens, Madrid, Paris, Singapore and Vancouver, and recently won a place on the panel of Gard, the world's largest P&I club. Recently lawyers have advised the sub-charterers of the 'Delvina' vessel following its hijacking by pirates off the coast of Somalia, but *"piracy problems are generally resolved by someone paying money to someone else"* and this doesn't provide a significant volume of work, explained managing partner Timothy Goode. Of more importance is the area of commodities law, for which the firm is *Chambers UK*-ranked. Commodities are products such as sugar or oil that have no qualitative differentiation, and this area is all about sale of goods disputes. Lately, many charterers have been trying to get out of the long-term contracts they agreed to before the recession.

Seats on deck

The London office is split into three departments: shipping, commercial litigation and banking and finance. Seats can be taken in shipping; commercial litigation; personal injury; banking; and marine and commercial litigation (MCL). The nature of the shipping seat depends on the trainee's supervising partner and their area of speciality. 'Dry' shipping usually relates to contract disputes; for instance, if someone breaches a contract to supply goods or defaults on a hire agreement. By contrast, 'wet' shipping is all to do with problems encountered at sea, be it salt-water damage to a vessel or the loss of goods in a collision. The master of a ship that is leaning to one side might decide to push its cargo overboard to re-float the vessel and disputes over lost cargo could emerge. Wet or dry, shipping disputes are *"really interesting"* and trainees prepare for and attend arbitrations, draft notes for counsel, contact witnesses, gather evidence, research case law and meet clients in the UK and abroad.

Let's look at the MCL seat. Insurance companies often instruct the firm on behalf of a shipowner when someone has been injured on board. Take, for example, the case of a passenger who contracted a disease on board and died from it after allegedly negligent medical treatment back on land. Thomas Cooper argued responsibility for the death lay with the health professionals rather than the ship company. All manner of problems and unusual situations occur (worse things happen at sea, remember?) and it's worth making the point that the shipping practice area is *"robust, even when a financial downturn happens. Shipping lawyers will always be necessary."*

Chambers UK rankings

Commodities	Shipping

Don't imagine that shipping clients are all jolly Jack Tars with no experience of fancy-schmancy lawyerfolk. Our sources stressed that "*shipowners are very savvy. They work very hard and expect high levels of service.*" And remember, shipping problems don't just arise in normal working hours – "*you never know when a collision might occur.*" Trainees feel they get ample responsibility, despite unavoidable administrative work. Client contact is high – usually insurers rather than shipowners – and trainees sometimes visit ships at British ports.

Cod wars and MoD wars

The commercial litigation department picks up topical cases. Naturally its activities reflect the orientation of the wider firm, and it also has nautical clients of its own, such as the New Under Ten Fisherman's Association. Not some junior band of ichthyophiles, rather members of the under 10-metre English inshore fishing fleet, which applied for a judicial review of the government's decision to allocate cod quota in the eastern English Channel. Then there's the estate of Captain James Phillipson, the first British soldier killed on active duty in Helmand province, Afghanistan. The coroner concluded that Captain Phillipson's death was caused not by the Taliban but by "*the systematic failures of the Ministry of Defence to provide mission-essential equipment.*" Commercial litigation seats involve some bundling, photocopying and pagination duties, along with "*a lot of disclosure and putting together lists of documents.*"

An Athens secondment gives trainees excellent responsibility and their own files – "*people don't have time to constantly supervise you.*" Other secondments are available to the firm's offices in Madrid and Paris (where speaking French is a prerequisite).

Cruising along

If trainees had a criticism, it's that "*the firm isn't as organised as it could be*" and the distribution of work is "*more fluid, less structured.*" This is sometimes the case in firms with smaller training schemes, and smaller firms full stop. Spoon-feeding simply won't happen here. The firm is partner-heavy and so trainees work directly with these experts in their field, but there is the issue that "*the partner has been doing it for 20 years and might not think of the obvious questions you might have, so you have to be proactive about asking.*" We do get the impression that this is rather an old-school firm with a clutch of very experienced partners, but we're heartened to hear that they are "*approachable, laid-back and friendly*" and even those who are "*not the youngest*" are "*still fun to go out and have a drink with.*" Shipping is still largely a male-dominated industry, and that's also reflected in the higher echelons of Thomas Cooper. Looking at the fee earner biographies on the firm's website, however, we do note that it has hired a spate of female lawyers and retained plenty of female trainees in recent years. In 2010, all three qualifying trainees remained with the firm.

Some trainees admit they "*literally knew nothing*" about the technical aspects of shipping before joining. Get a head start by reading up on some maritime law "*and looking up every word that seems novel.*" Familiarise yourself with the basic terms, like bills of lading, charter parties and, of course, the concept of P&I clubs – the firm's main clients. You can start with the short feature on our website. Fortunately, the firm is "*very keen*" on thorough training and has an in-house lecture programme given by partners and other experts, including former mariners. "*There was a really good lecture on bunker claims involving bunker contamination, which was very useful,*" said one source. Lectures are also organised by the London Shipping Law Centre in affiliation with UCL.

The "*modern*" office is "*nice and airy,*" but comfortable as opposed to fantastically luxurious. "*Shipping clients are very practical. They don't want you to spend money on flashy offices.*" Trainees' average hours are from 9am to 6.30pm and "*never past 10pm.*" "*People are very sociable*" and regularly go out for drinks after work. Lawyers and clients mingle regularly, both "*because we're in roughly the same neighbourhood*" and because "*people do enjoy drinking – part of that is the nature of the shipping industry and P&I clubs.*" Annual social events include a boat party – how appropriate!

And finally...

Thomas Cooper is perfect for those who've a penchant for contract law and international disputes and are also looking for a small enough environment that "*when you get a firm-wide e-mail, you're not wondering who it's from.*"

TLT LLP

The facts

Location: Bristol, London

Number of UK partners/solicitors: 61/190

Total number of trainees: 26

Seats: 4x6 months

Alternative seats: Secondments

On chambersstudent.co.uk
- How to get into TLT
- We talk to managing partner David Pester
- Some of the firm's headline cases and deals

This *"go-getting"* Bristol firm has now become a go-getter in London too.

Top Trumps

"*One of the defining characteristics of the firm is that it's quite ambitious,*" declared one trainee, clearly aware of the firm's impressive progress in the UK legal market. TLT is a "*young firm*" that was formed in 2000 from the merger of West Country practices Trumps and Lawrence Tucketts. There must be something in the water that flows past its Bristol office because momentum has been building over the past decade. Two further mergers in London gifted TLT a foothold in the City and it has been attracting more and more high-profile clients, including several FTSE 100 companies and major banks. On the books are Barclays, Deutsche Bank, JPMorgan Chase and TUI Travel among others. All up, the firm now has around 650 partners and staff and scores a ranking in *The Sunday Times*' '100 Best Companies to Work For' list.

The firm works in five major sectors: the built environment; financial services; leisure; retail; and technology and media. TLT has particular strength in the domestic leisure industry, representing theme parks, attractions and large hotel and pub chains. It is also heavily invested in the financial services sector, providing well-priced services, both volume and more bespoke. There's "*a lot of focus on meeting and exceeding client expectations,*" onc marketing-focused source told us. The licensing team – top-ranked by *Chambers UK* – seems to typify this approach: it produced a commercial guide for publicans last summer on 'How to make the most out of the World Cup'. Also in relation to leisure, lawyers secured compensation for the London Dungeon, which was in dispute with a rival attraction over unlawful business practices, and in relation to the built environment TLT advised on a multimillion-pound redevelopment at Covent Garden. In the financial services sector, lawyers assisted Church House Trust Bank on its takeover by Virgin Money. TLT has aspirations to be a top-50 UK firm, and to help it achieve this it is now conjuring a variety of commercial instructions from magic circle firm Freshfields, with which it has a referral relationship. This sort of arrangement isn't entirely new to TLT, which already has other important referral relationships.

Responsibili-TLT

There's now so much for trainees to experience at this firm. The majority are hired to the Bristol office but you should expect London to take an increasingly bigger role in the training scheme as it now has trainees of its own. TLT regards the range of seats available as one of the best aspects of the training scheme, since apart from fulfilling the SRA's contentious/non-contentious requirement, no one seat is compulsory. TLT's core seats are to be found in its banking and financial services litigation, property and corporate divisions. Others crop up in teams like employment, insolvency, general commercial litigation, construction, pensions, planning and social housing. In addition the firm also has one seat in its Bristol family team.

Much of TLT's success so far is attributable to its financial services lawyers. Some focus on the 'now' area of regulation, assisting major banking clients with FSA compliance and things like anti-money laundering practices. London-based, this is "*quite an academic seat... for the first couple of days you just need to read and understand how the regulatory system works.*" Having got your

Chambers UK rankings

Banking & Finance	Information Technology
Banking Litigation	Intellectual Property
Competition/European Law	Licensing
Construction	Partnership
Corporate/M&A	Pensions
Debt Recovery	Planning
Dispute Resolution	Private Client
Employment	Real Estate
Energy & Natural Resources	Real Estate Litigation
Environment	Restructuring/Insolvency
Family/Matrimonial	Social Housing
Franchising	

head around the mind-bending subject matter, you'll then be asked to conduct loads of research and draft technical notes on changes in the law.

TLT's financial services litigation team has grown significantly over the past decade and been really busy since the credit crisis. In some respects you could say the recession has worked in the firm's favour. "*There's a lot of work and it's all pretty varied,*" one trainee told us. "*You get work off everyone in the team*" so "*in addition to your own caseload you also assist with larger cases where the value of claims is significantly more.*" Recent disputes have covered multimillion-pound mortgage frauds and claims for negligent overvaluations of properties. If the UK housing market suffers a further price drop, especially if interest rates rise, this could be the perfect storm that leads to a flood of negligence claims like this. "*I've been involved with high-value multiparty professional negligence claims,*" confirmed one trainee, clearly pleased with the work they'd experienced. Another element of the department's caseload is repossessions on behalf of mortgage lenders. "*I went to court on my own to conduct possession hearings and win the order for the client.*" Typically, trainees in this seat (offered in both Bristol and London) will work on pre-action correspondence, take witness statements, draft documents and deal with court applications – all of which add up to a good understanding of the litigation process.

On cue

TLT's success can also be attributed to its strategy of taking on those aspects of work for big multinationals that leading City firms don't want. This includes debt recovery and smaller-scale insolvency. TLT has one of the largest corporate recovery and insolvency teams in the UK and it's been acting for lenders and administrators including Barclays, KPMG and PwC. The firm undertakes "*security reviews for distressed businesses*" and recently advised on the restructuring of Rileys snooker club. Said one trainee: "*I got involved in a couple of purchases of companies in administration, company secretarial stuff, research, work for the official receiver... assigning causes of action where a bankrupt has a claim.*" Another spent "*plenty of time liaising with the courts to try and get things done quicker.*" At present, this seat is only on offer in Bristol. Getting things done quickly seems to be the way in this department: it rescued two financial litigation partners from collapsed Manchester firm Halliwells days after that firm announced it was intending to call in the administrators.

Both Bristol and London trainees can visit the broad-ranging commercial department, where they tend to see a variety of matters. "*I got to draft a few contracts for the Metropolitan Police, did some confidentially agreements, some competition, work on franchising, some data protection work for Orange.*" TLT is a five-star name in relation to the leisure industry and its client list includes Merlin Entertainments (Alton Towers, LEGOLAND, Madame Tussauds) and Punch Taverns. The team has also advised on music noise levels at the Larmer Tree Festival site.

Real estate is a diverse practice group; it works on everything from social housing and residential property to renewable energy projects, commercial transactions and developments. In Bristol and London, trainees will draft leases, deal with clients and the Land Registry over the phone, handle sales of smaller business properties and negotiate formal rights of way over land. Our sources relished the levels of responsibility they were given in this department. "*I got to run my own files through from instruction to completion,*" said one, while another told us: "*In my first week I was asked to complete a lease on my own.*" On bigger projects such as Somerfield's £1.7bn sale to the Co-operative Group, trainees were plunged into a sea of title investigation, drafting reports and "*quite a lot of corporate support work... dealing with quirky property points the corporate team wanted looking into.*" That Somerfield gig then turned into a full-blown place on the Co-op's main legal panel, which consists of just three firms.

The corporate department has experience of the Indian market. TLT has even featured in an Indian business game show designed to showcase British M&A advisory talent. On a more serious note, the firm advises major Indian banks including ICICI and Bank of India. The firm recently advised a syndicate of Indian lenders on a $110m loan to oil and gas exploration company Indus Gas and advised WHSmith on investment in the subcontinent. Don't assume this means the firm is internationally focused: it has a single overseas office in the Greek port of Piraeus – a legacy from one of its London merger partners. All training takes place in the UK.

Attending court seems to be fairly common for TLT trainees, especially in the small Bristol family department. "*I got a couple of chances to do advocacy on my own,*" one trainee enthused; "*the judge called me down and grilled me. It was good fun.*" In employment, too, where the firm works for clients such as the Energy Saving Trust, Imperial Tobacco, UPS and several tech companies, there is bags of responsibility for trainees; "*you're encouraged to make settlement offers to ACAS yourself.*"

Some seats are renowned for having excellent supervisors. "*Some are really hands-on; others are more laissez-faire,*" and although these differing management styles don't always suit everyone, most trainees felt that seniors "*pitched the level of supervision just right.*" Involvement in marketing and business development is encouraged among trainees and they are invited to client networking events. In addition, there is "*a networking drinks thing we do every month where trainees, NQs and others go to a bar. It's good to catch up with people from different departments.*"

The Wild South West

"*I can't think of anyone who is a lone ranger,*" one of our interviewees commented. Indeed, the firm's local bar in Bristol – Toto's – is "*very well attended*" by everyone from partners through to secretaries. This "*swanky, chilled-out place right next to the river*" has "*cult status*" among Bristol trainees. When we rang their London peers they were still scoping out new drinking holes having recently moved to bigger offices on Gresham Street. They now reside on the seventh floor of a building overlooking the Guildhall conservation area. As for the pub search: "*We're all taking it very seriously,*" a source revealed.

Another thing TLT takes seriously is dressing up, be it for the formal Christmas bash and "*big ol' summer party*" or for slightly less dignified occasions. "*At Christmas we did a charity run around Battersea Park in felt Santa suits*" and "*for Halloween there was a cowboys and Indians fancy dress party. I skulked home at 3am, leaving most of the partners on the dance floor in this trashy club we'd ended up in.*" Nice. Trainees also organise informal socials revolving around bowling, tapas and cocktails, and on sunny days in Bristol "*most people go and sit out on the grass in Castle Park*" to relax over lunch. One of the London partners is renowned for hosting summer parties at his home for the entire finance team, even setting up a bouncy castle in his garden.

For sporting types there's subsidised gym membership and football, netball, cricket and hockey teams. In Bristol, softball games are played "*up on the downs*" and the corporate team has an annual camping weekend in Wales for surfing and "*fun and games down by The Gower.*" Pro bono at TLT focuses on two main projects: one with school children and another with the homeless. Trainees can get involved in the Ablaze reading scheme in primary schools, and there's "*talk of starting up a mentoring scheme as well for GCSE students.*" The Business Action on Homelessness project in Bristol is about "*providing life coaching for people who've been through traumatic experiences and want to get back into employment.*"

Most trainees at TLT wanted to avoid the City and so applied exclusively to regional firms, or even just Bristol firms. Now that TLT is pushing its office in the capital this will probably change; nevertheless about half the current intake still have a Bristol or South West connection. Our sources admit that being in the City near major clients is important; however, the firm has no intention of "*losing its Bristol identity.*" This identity seems to be less about a certain way of doing things and more about not forgetting your roots. The firm has stayed close to long-standing clients and "*still acts for Bristol-based firms such as Aardman Animations,*" Bristol Cathedral and Arnolfini Arts Centre.

TLT trainees describe themselves as "*laid-back, confident people who are driven to push things forward.*" Said one: "*Everybody is ambitious for the firm; we're very proud of how far it's come so quickly.*" In the several years we've been interviewing TLT trainees, the most common reason for choosing the firm over others in Bristol was its one-time underdog status and "*the feeling that other firms in Bristol were resting on their laurels.*" It's clear that the firm's trainees chose well, not least the 2010 qualifiers – TLT offered all of the 11 people finishing their training contracts places at the firm. Nine stayed: four in London and five in Bristol.

And finally...

TLT is ten years young, and the next decade looks to be as exciting for the firm as its first.

Travers Smith LLP

The facts

Location: London

Number of UK partners/solicitors: 61/245

Total number of trainees: 48

Seats: 4x6 months

Alternative seats: Paris, secondments

Extras: Pro bono – Paddington Law Centre, City Law School Legal Advice Centre, Bar Pro Bono Unit, Caribbean death row appeals and more; language training

On chambersstudent.co.uk
- How to get into Travers
- Travers Smith: corporate kings
- Standing up to the vulture funds

Matching the magic circle for brainpower, if not manpower, City institution Travers Smith attracts graduates looking for quality work in a more intimate environment.

Pedigree

Over the course of its long history Travers has, for the most part, stuck to what it knows best and done it very well indeed. Never one of London's larger firms, it resisted the urge to balloon during the boom years that preceded the recent recession, and instead concentrated on its core strength – a corporate department that can compete with the best in the profession. Although deals have been scarcer of late, Travers has still picked up important instructions. One came from Clinton Cards, which lawyers advised on the administration of its subsidiary company, Birthdays, and the subsequent purchase of 196 of its better-performing stores from the administrator. It also acted for London Mining in its $45m investment in a Chinese iron ore joint venture. Travers' private equity team is known to be impressive. Lawyers were busy for Bridgepoint on its £955m sale of Pets at Home (where pets come first) in early 2010.

It's this mix of substantial instructions, coupled with a smaller office and more personal atmosphere than is possible in the magic circle, which continues to woo students to Travers. Several of our interviewees spoke favourably of an application process that, in the words of one, "*helped get the best out of me in a way that other firms didn't.*" For example, "*they just want an online CV and covering letter: they don't want to sift through a load of rubbish about a time you led a team. So you have to be incredibly concise about what you want to get over. It's just a page to say why you are applying and why you would be a good lawyer.*" At interview and on the vac scheme, trainees agreed, "*there's no formality to make you feel on edge. Initially I thought that not everybody could be this nice. They really are!*" Travers Smith employees are typically very loyal to the firm and this in turn contributes to consistently high NQ retention – 17 out of 21 stayed on in 2010 – and a high number of 'lifers'. Around 75% of Travers partners trained with the firm.

Three's company

Let's look at the basics of the training scheme. A visit to the corporate department is compulsory, be it to the corporate finance or private equity and funds teams. Trainees must also take a seat in either real estate or banking, and either litigation or employment. The final seat is, in Traversspeak, the "*wildcard*" – chosen from corporate recovery; commercial (including IP/IT); competition; financial services and markets; pensions; and tax. It's an equitable system in which most trainees get what they want, albeit that the commercial seats are often oversubscribed. Regular secondments to private equity houses Bridgepoint and 3i are also available.

"*For trainees, corporate is quite a big deal.*" It's the largest department and has the most high-profile work, meaning that "*everyone sees it as the toughest seat*" with the most demanding schedule. "*I've already done four or five days when I have worked into the small hours,*" said

Chambers UK rankings

Banking & Finance	Investment Funds
Banking Litigation	Media & Entertainment
Capital Markets	Outsourcing
Competition/European Law	Pensions
Corporate/M&A	Planning
Dispute Resolution	Private Equity
Employee Share Schemes	Real Estate
Employment	Real Estate Finance
Environment	Restructuring/Insolvency
Financial Services	Retail
Fraud	Tax
Information Technology	

a relatively new arrival to the group, although for the most part weekends are apparently respected. "*I had quite a lot of one-to-one work with partners,*" another recalled, telling us how they were "*writing up advice notes on some quite technical things and then sitting down with the partner and going through them.*" Trainees split their time between ongoing projects and "*one-off queries where a client rings you up with a question.*" For more on the type of work Travers' core corporate department handles and how it manages to give the big firms a run for their money, visit our website.

"*Known for giving trainees their own projects and making them first port of call for clients,*" the real estate team is always popular. It recently advised German fund HIH Global Invest on its £40m acquisition of Friary Court – the headquarters of London-based shipping firm Holman Fenwick Willan. The structure of the training scheme means trainees can't visit both the real estate and banking departments, but one of the banking seats focuses on property finance. A good example of the typical deal here is German real estate financier WestImmo's £190m refinancing of Value Retail, the owner of the Bicester Village retail park.

And so to commercial litigation. "*What's nice about it,*" said one source, "*is that there's a very good range. You get the really big matters as well as much smaller disputes where trainees can get involved in the nitty gritty.*" Among those big matters, Travers is defending the Royal Bank of Scotland Group against a £10m claim brought by Austria's Raiffeisen Zentralbank Österreich, arising out of one of RBS's Enron-related transactions. Yes, Enron is still making waves nearly ten years after its spectacular bankruptcy. The firm is also acting for the Argentine Republic as it seeks to beat off the vulture funds circling it following the collapse of the country's economy in 2001. Litigation inevitably involves grunt work: "*I was one of the unfortunate souls who spent a lot of time doing disclosure for 12 hours a day,*" said a trainee. "*Aside from that, it was very interesting. The first time you go to court and see the 'television' type of law, it's fascinating, and the department tries to ensure that all its trainees do get to see that.*"

Contentious experience can also be gained in the employment seat, but here "*there's also a corporate element and you assist clients with their training. We have a guy who does a radio show for one of our clients a couple of times a year.*" Trainees are heavily involved with the prep work for these training events, and one praised the fact that "*people value my opinion. It's often wrong, but it's always asked for.*" The team's clients include large employers such as AIG, Virgin Active, Pinewood Studios and the RAC.

All trainees share an office with two other people – usually a partner and an assistant. This is an excellent set-up for a trainee and our interviews praised it, both for the increased level of chumminess it fosters and for the learning opportunities it provides. "*You get to see how someone with 20 years' experience deals with clients on the phone. It's massively useful as you have a precedent in front of you every single day. There's no stewing for hours when you don't know the answer to something.*" Though not a deliberate policy, it seems that many trainees sit with a head of department at some point.

Spending time with the BF

"*I think the word that has to go in your feature is 'friendly,'*" said one trainee in an attempt to sum up the Travers Smith culture. We pointed out that 'friendly' was a terrible cliché and asked him to come up with something else instead (find out his response at the end of the feature). Cliché or not, 'friendly' does seem to be the operative word for this firm. An active social life revolves around the Bishop's Finger public house ("*the BF*"), and on Fridays there's "*always a contingent who manage to last the distance and end up in Karaoke Box at 2am*" – even if it means travelling right back across town to get there. Departmental outings are common (the banking lawyers are among the biggest partiers, apparently), as are trainee events. "*Last Friday we had a night that totally wrote off my weekend... again,*" one mumbled. It's also a tradition that "*partners will take their room out for dinner.*" Sporty types are well catered for: there are "*lots of teams, albeit playing at a low standard!*"

The book and its cover

So far, so positive. Now we come to the twist in the Travers Smith fairytale. We always used to point out that the trainee group was male-dominated. This is no longer the case, but looking at the profiles of the 46 trainees at the time of our interviews in March 2010, you can't help but notice some undeniable traits. Oxford, Cambridge, Durham and Bristol graduates make up 65% of the 08/09 intake (about the same as in previous years). We were also informed that, among the second-years at least, state school students were vastly outnumbered by those from private schools. At that time 98% of trainees were white.

As so often in life, there's more going on than meets the eye. "*There are a lot of people who seem like they might be very English who actually aren't,*" said one trainee. Most "*passionately*" disagreed that partners deliberately recruit in their own image, and the firm quite reasonably argues that it just looks for the best no matter who they are. We say: nobody should be put off applying, but Travers can do much more to diversify its workforce. See our website for more analysis and the firm's views.

Gilding the Lilley

Travers is "*careful and doesn't just follow trends. It hasn't tried to do things that it's not set up to do. That's a sustainable approach to surviving and thriving.*" The conservative policy has served the firm well. "*Yes, we're quite cautious, but when it comes to the crunch, we did the biggest private equity deals of 2009 at a time when there was nothing going on in the market.*" Trainees deny any accusation that Travers is set in its ways. "*I just think it doesn't buy into the more trendy way in which other firms market themselves. It cuts out the management consultancy bullshit. You know where you stand.*" The bottom line is, of course, the bottom line, and in 2009/10 Travers' revenue and profits both increased significantly, in contrast to many of its competitors. With its small, old-style partnership breeding stability, Travers is "*a firm sure of its identity.*"

In January 2010, Chris Carroll stood down as managing partner after nine years, and head of employment Andrew Lilley took the reins. By all accounts, Carroll (now senior partner) is a bit of a "*character*" who brought a relaxed management style to the table. Lilley, trainees say, is relatively young and a "*go-getter*" who may be more hands-on. "*I think there will be subtle changes,*" one contact mused. "*There are a lot of people looking forward to it.*" At the time of our interviews, Lilley was still getting the lie of the land, and trainees could only speculate about the changes he may introduce. These included building stronger links with overseas firms and further growth and diversification. "*All the talk in the corridors is about competing with the magic circle,*" one contact said. Of course, one major difference between Travers and the magic circle firms is that until now Travers has made minimal overseas investment. Its single Paris office takes one French-speaking London-based trainee every six months for mainly corporate work.

Whatever the future may have in store, trainees all agree that the firm won't ever change its essential 'Travers-ness'. They say it will remain an "*affable*" and "*collegiate*" place where there's "*never a 'too busy to train you' attitude*" and "*no one's scared to take the piss out of a partner.*" Apart from lobbying for a move into a single building (the firm is currently in two, which "*encourages the opinion that corporate is in a world of its own*") and nicer sandwiches for lunchtime meetings ("*There was carrot in one. Whoever heard of a carrot sandwich?*"), trainees couldn't find anything broken to fix. For the record, the firm says that moving buildings is not on the agenda, although there are "*plans afoot*" for greater integration between the offices. More positive news on the sandwich front: Travers admits they are currently awful but says its "*fantastic*" catering team will soon be hand-making sarnies on-site.

Remember the trainee who came up with the 'friendly' cliché? We asked him to sum up the firm in a more interesting and pithy way. "*A sound bite? I should get Tony Blair in here. Hmm, I was going to say that it's 'true blue' but that's descending into High School Musical territory. Let's just say... it's a classic firm that's always worthy of consideration.*" Yep. Got it in one.

And finally...

Travers will always be Travers. For those lucky enough to fit its mould, that will always mean great training, great clients and a great working environment.

Trethowans LLP

The facts

Location: Southampton, Salisbury

Number of UK partners/solicitors: 26/27

Total number of trainees: 8

Seats: 4x6 months

Alternative seats: None

On chambersstudent.co.uk
- How to get into Trethowans
- We talk to managing partner Simon Rhodes
- More on Trethowans' other departments

This long-established Hampshire and Wiltshire firm has patiently built a solid reputation in both the private client and commercial spheres.

Final destination

George Nodder founded Trethowans in Salisbury in 1866 for the wealthy folk of Wiltshire, and there it stayed for 130 years until a small merger in 1996 added an office in Southampton. This was done with commercial clients in mind and in order to add to the firm's prospering personal injury and clinical negligence practices.

Today, the Salisbury and Southampton offices are relatively equal in size and profitability. Commercial property, commercial litigation, personal injury and clin neg span both offices, and trainees also have access to seats in company commercial; residential property; private client; employment; family law and farms and estates. The commercial departments are mostly in Southampton, while the ones geared towards private individuals are over in Salisbury and still account for nearly half of the firm's business. In the years immediately preceding the recession, turnover increased rapidly and this pushed Trethowans into the list of the UK's 200 largest law firms.

A new management team has been in place since 2009, led by managing partner Simon Rhodes. Under a '2012 Destination' strategy, the firm is looking to grow all of its services. This has resulted in active recruitment in all departments.

In a split second

A trainee's first seat starts in November. The firm allocates seats based on both business needs and trainees' "*wish lists,*" which they update periodically in conversation with HR. Our sources' preferences were largely accommodated: in fact, "*they'll try to fit you in before the training contract actually starts,*" often in a secretarial position in order to help familiarise you with the firm. Over the course of their contract, trainees are likely to spend time in both offices and experience a mix of commercial and private law. Salisbury and Southampton are only about 20 miles apart, so the commute is fine, although since it's easier by road than rail, carpooling is a good idea.

We'll start our tour of seats in the personal injury and clinical negligence department as this is the area where Trethowans has its best showing in *Chambers UK* – it's top-ranked in the South of England. The PI team acts mainly for claimants: drivers, cyclists and pedestrians injured in road traffic accidents are the standard fare, but injuries sustained at work or from things like fireworks or asbestos also crop up. The clin neg team acts for claimants too, on cerebral palsy and other birth injuries and severe injuries sustained by adults. It excels in head and spinal injury cases and works in conjunction with Headway: the Brain Injury Association, the Spinal Injuries Association and the SRA's clin neg and PI panels. Trainees go along to care units to visit clients, which provides a big reality check. "*Some clients have had accidents and in a split second their lives have changed forever,*" said someone who felt a personal reward in assisting clients through rehabilitation and helping secure "*the best possible outcome.*" Our sources gained "*exposure to high-value claims*" as well as smaller cases. "*I tend to run those myself,*" said one contact of the smaller matters. "*I'm not just doing the easy bits, I'm*

Chambers UK rankings

Agriculture & Rural Affairs	Employment
Clinical Negligence	Family/Matrimonial
	Licensing
Corporate/M&A	Personal Injury
Dispute Resolution	Real Estate

responsible for what happens with the file and making sure things are progressing."

Boozing and betting

The commercial litigation department is now headed by Richard Cook, a 2009 hire from Southampton rival Shoosmiths. He oversees an increasing amount of professional negligence work, including recently a claim by the trustees of a pension fund against law firm Charles Russell, for a sum in the region of £4m. Litigators also represented a hotel in a dispute with an IT company over the fitness for purpose and quality of software that it had supplied. Both these cases went to trial in London and trainees were "*photocopying for two weeks in a row*" beforehand, but also "*went to court almost every day, sat behind counsel and took notes, before going back to chambers at lunchtime for meetings with barristers and clients.*" Household-name litigation clients include the Ministry of Defence, Bacardi and Ladbrokes.

Bacardi and Ladbrokes are also clients of the commercial property department, which has a big following from the agricultural sector thanks to an associate who handles sales and purchases of country houses, farms and equestrian properties. He also keeps bees as a hobby – not important, of course, but we just thought it was a nice thing to mention. A residential conveyancing seat is usually offered to those with private client interests due to the frequency of crossover cases. To read more about work in Trethowans' other departments, go to our website.

There's no official mentoring scheme at Trethowans, but trainees have a dedicated supervisor in each seat. Reviews are scheduled every other month and HR "*comes round once a month to check that we're okay.*"

"*This is a business that provides legal advice, not an academic or a professional body,*" says managing partner Simon Rhodes. "*We can teach our trainees the law, we're good at that, but that's a given. All future trainees need to be able to get on with people and show us how they can see a business opportunity.*" Trethowans puts an emphasis on teaching trainees about business development, client services and financial management. "*We're trying to choose entrepreneurial people,*" said Rhodes, adding that a business pedigree is an application booster. "*Everyone has got to get involved in marketing,*" said a trainee. "*Show you understand that.*" Lately female applicants have outnumbered males to such an extent that none of the current trainee group is male. The imbalance "*isn't a problem per se,*" says HR partner Nicola Richards, "*but it would be nice to have a more even spread.*" Get applying, lads.

Friday spirits

The trainee salary is at market level for this part of the world, even though this doesn't match what's available in many parts of the country. Nevertheless, trainees swear that "*this is a great place to apply for a training contract,*" not least because of the provincial beauty of medieval Salisbury. The office there is anything but medieval: it's brand-new and has an open-plan arrangement complete with grand spiral staircase. The Southampton office – "*a lovely old building*" – is also largely open-plan. "*Everyone keeps their voice down,*" but that's not to say people keep to themselves. "*It's quite lively and we have a laugh.*" Said one source: "*Everyone's so friendly, nice and down-to-earth. I can go to lunch with the finance director or go have a cup of tea with the managing partner. You don't feel like you're on your guard at all.*"

Official hours are 9am to 5pm, and "*it's entirely up to you if you want to put in more,*" said a trainee. "*I know all firms like to say they don't have a long-hours culture, but I can genuinely say there isn't one here.*" Big trials can bring longer hours, and life in employment is dictated by tribunal deadlines, so "*documents need to be turned out quickly,*" but generally "*it's a ghost town at 5.10pm on Fridays.*" The firm hosts Friday afternoon drinks once a month, alternating between the offices. Trainees are also given a quarterly social budget. Lawyers take part in "*light-hearted*" sports events, including football, cricket, netball, touch rugby and recently a charity swim-a-thon. Barbecues, pub nights and a Trethowans' Got Talent competition are some other highlights from the past year.

And finally...

The 2010 retention figures weren't finalised at the time of going to press: go to our website to find out how many qualifiers stayed with the firm.

Trowers & Hamlins LLP

The facts

Location: London, Manchester, Exeter

Number of UK partners/solicitors: 102/165

Total number of trainees: 40

Seats: 4x6 months

Alternative seats: Overseas seats

On chambersstudent.co.uk
- How to get into Trowers
- The social housing sector
- The Middle Eastern economies

Representing a cocktail of public and private sector clients in the UK and the Middle East, this firm offers a unique blend of some very different types of work.

Legal soup for the soul

Walking with kings yet keeping the common touch, Trowers is a "*two-faceted firm*" that acts for both public sector clients and corporate giants. It is renowned for its property-related activities, and in particular a strong social housing practice has proved to be its bedrock. We say strong; we mean mighty. Trowers has three UK offices – in London, Manchester and Exeter – and each is ranked top in its region for social housing by *Chambers UK*. Along with Eversheds, it's also top of the pile for advice to local government clients. The other side of the firm's character is shown in its London mid-market corporate practice (comparable with the likes of Beachcroft, Farrer and Reynolds Porter Chamberlain), a strong reputation for construction and an extensive Middle Eastern network. Out there, it has offices in Oman, Dubai, Abu Dhabi, Bahrain, Cairo and Saudi Arabia and is a leading firm in the region.

"*The private side allows it to be a profitable City firm, while the public element gives the firm stability – the one balances the other,*" said our interviewees. They were adamant that "*Trowers isn't a charity; it makes money but it sticks with public sector work because it's a leader in the field and there's a feeling that we're doing something good.*" In the rocky 2007/08 financial year, the combined turnover of the real estate practices at the top 20 UK firms fell by 18%, but at Trowers it grew, fuelled by the firm's position in what was then the safer haven of social housing. In 2009, the firm advised Plymouth Community Homes on the largest ever housing stock transfer in the South West of England, while in 2010 Worcestershire County Council and Worcester University turned to Trowers for advice on their pioneering venture to open the UK's first joint public and university library. Now add to this the firm's back catalogue – its partners have advised successive governments on crucial policy issues and written the sector's precedent agreements and leases – and it's easy to see why Trowers' client roster reads like the *Who's Who* of Registered Social Landlords (RSLs). One such client is the Peabody Trust, which has a huge portfolio of London properties, valued at around £1bn. In early 2010, Trowers was appointed to the national panel of the housing and regeneration body, the Homes and Communities Agency, and it recently advised Triathlon Homes on the acquisition and development of residential units at the London 2012 Athletes Village, which will provide over 1,300 affordable homes after the Olympic Games finish.

Marks... set... go!

Many trainees complete at least one property-related seat. "*Most go into housing projects for their first seat*" and can really get stuck in. "*There are big development projects on which we take a supporting role,*" explained one source, "*but from these projects come ancillary matters that can be delegated entirely to trainees.*" Such matters include residential conveyancing for housing associations, drafting Section 106 agreements (which, for

Chambers UK rankings

Administrative & Public Law	Healthcare
Agriculture & Rural Affairs	Local Government
Banking & Finance	Projects
Charities	Public Procurement
Construction	Real Estate
Corporate/M&A	Real Estate Litigation
Education	Social Housing
Employment	

example, bind developers to providing affordable housing within their schemes), remortgaging properties when housing associations refinance themselves, organising the 'easements' necessary to put in utilities, and "*working with central and local government in terms of policy and strategy.*"

Although trainees have "*a lot of plates to spin*" – one of this year's cohort apparently had 80 files – most found it a great way to develop their "*billing, transactional and case management*" skills. Unleashed immediately, new starters "*call clients and lawyers on a daily basis, and by lawyers I mean partners too.*" While it might be a little intimidating at first, "*there's no point learning to drive on a private road: you need to experience the real thing.*" With an instructor, naturally. "*If you make a mistake and admit to it, it's okay – you're never going to be responsible for a deal collapsing,*" say trainees, and "*supervisors are generally really helpful and accommodating.*"

Over in the public sector, communities and governance team, trainees do "*corporate-style work for public institutions*" such as housing associations, schools and hospitals. "*It's much more academic than I expected,*" said a source, though "*there is a lot of resolution drafting and registering things with the FSA.*" Our sources were also excited about working with charities. "*It's interesting – you set them up and find out how they fit into the legislative framework.*"

The social housing sector largely prospered under the Labour government but could now face a more challenging phase following the coalition government's decision to implement major spending cuts. Furthermore, RSLs' ability to raise private finance is still compromised by the delicate state of the bank lending market. As such, it is impossible to say with any degree of certainty exactly how the social housing sector will change over the next few years. What we do know is that it is likely to broaden in scope with the addition of participants from beyond the not-for-profit sector. Lawyers will need to assist clients in a variety of new ways, not least in relation to possible changes in security of tenure, joint ventures between RSLs and alternative ways of raising funds. Much will also depend on the fortunes of the residential property market. It is also worth pointing out that the joint procurement of legal services by pairs or groups of clients could force legal fees down.

More than one pillar

While there's no doubt that the firm's name is synonymous with social housing and the public sector, these areas are by no means the be-all and end-all. "*The thing about our corporate work is that it's extremely varied,*" said a source. The clients come "*from all over the place,*" and trainees "*just do whatever is thrown our way,*" often turning to a trusted copy of Dicey, Morris & Collins on *The Conflict of Laws*. There's a fair amount of interaction between the London, Manchester and Exeter offices. Trainees also told us about of "*lots of Middle East-related work, including Shari'a finance and setting up offshore companies, property funds and property investments.*" As elsewhere in the firm, they enjoy a good dollop of responsibility. "*I got the chance to complete a deal on my own,*" boasted one source. "*People are very apologetic if you have to work late,*" and as one trainee put it: "*I work longer hours than my non-law friends but less than my other law friends.*" Across the firm, a trainee's usual finishing time would be 7pm, occasionally later during deal closings. In corporate, for example, trainees can sometimes expect to be in "*until 4am and back in at 8am,*" but they confessed to "*loving the adrenalin of late-night completions.*"

The "*academic and esoteric*" tax department is also a hit. "*The kind of tax structuring we advise on is usually done by the Big Four* [accountancy firms], *but our clients are quite happy for the lawyers to deal with it, and we often have to review what the Big Four say anyway.*" Though some clients "*do still need the comfort of having it signed off by one of the Big Four,*" trainees "*research and analyse law and cases every day – you're a real lawyer's lawyer.*" The team works with many other departments in the firm.

Trowers' litigation group can accommodate half of all the trainees at the firm; the rest take a short litigation course run by Kaplan Law School. Those who visit the department can testify that "*it's a completely different experience to anywhere else in the firm.*" It's split into three teams – commercial, property and construction – and our sources enjoyed working on a variety of cases, some with human rights elements and others relating to breaches of confidentiality. The recession added more insolvency and bankruptcy work. "*Lots of bad debts have arisen in the City, so I've been doing a lot of debt chasing,*" said one trainee. "*It's been interesting, if a bit soulless.*"

Sheikh it up

For those looking for a break from the seemingly perpetual drizzle of the UK, Trowers brims with Middle Eastern promise. Unlike some firms, where there's a real tussle for overseas opportunities, here "*they have to make sure they've got enough trainees to send out, so sometimes they have to convince people to go.*" Trainees are seconded either to another UK office or to Dubai, Abu Dhabi, Oman or Bahrain. Hannah King, the firm's graduate development manager, says that "*50% of our trainees are seconded,*" and trainees assured us that "*if you want to go, you definitely can.*"

Time abroad means "*great commercial experience,*" and a chance to develop tactical skills. In the Gulf, the corporate department works with local and international companies and often needs to add caveats to its advice. "*The Sheikh could turn around tomorrow and change his mind about the law,*" a source explained. In Dubai, trainees focus on general corporate matters and either private finance or construction. After the city's property bubble burst in early 2009, construction work was "*really slow... clients were hoping for things to get really cheap so that they could start building again.*" Still, trainees were positive: "*We've been through bad patches before, but we'll always be someone out here.*" Trowers' sturdy footing in the Middle East is a product of its long investment in the region: it began sending lawyers out to assist the Bahrain government in the 1960s. "*Other firms come out here and set up shop, but locally they don't have good connections.*" Trowers also has links with Saudi Arabian law firm Feras Al Shawaf, and with Sultans Law in Syria. Go to our website to find out more about the Middle Eastern legal landscape.

Several trainees ranked their secondments as the "*highlight*" of their training contracts. "*They really encourage you to take on more responsibility and if you do your work well they'll give you higher-level stuff. They're keen for you to go out and meet clients, and you also have a lot of partner contact so you get a greater exposure than in the UK.*" It's also a "*great opportunity to travel*" and "*it's brilliant going to the beach at the weekend – you feel like you're on holiday.*" Some people mentioned watching Formula One in Abu Dhabi and Bahrain and "*dune-bashing in the desert.*" Guinness fans will be pleased to know "*there are a good few Irish and Indonesian pubs.*" While "*aware of a more conservative culture in the background,*" the trainees we spoke to didn't find it a problem. "*There are so many different nationalities out there that often you don't notice it.*"

Trimmer time

Though the firm was one of the UK's legal pioneers in the Gulf states, "*it never tried to expand too quickly or take on what's not possible.*" Undoubtedly influenced by its public sector clients, a source commented that the firm "*has a responsibility to them. We need to be quite steady and reliable to respect the fact that they've got responsibilities that are bigger than them.*" Trowers is "*very much a shirt-and-tie place.*" A tidy haircut is also required: "*Occasionally I'm told that I might think about getting one,*" said a source. But it's not all straightlaced. Trainees like the "*open-door environment,*" where "*you don't feel like an idiot if you have to ask a partner a question.*" Though some commented that the firm isn't "*massively sociable,*" others argued that "*there are usually a few beers to be had on a Friday night if you source them out,*" and trainees usually have lunch together before training sessions on a Monday. Firm-wide 'billing drive' drinks, held in the offices every two months, are popular. Trainees also enjoy mid-seat meals and there are three social events per year to which future joiners are invited. "*We've had a games night, softball and ten-pin bowling.*"

"*The firm is keen to keep on as many qualifiers as possible*" and in 2010 12 out of 17 were retained. "*You don't get the feeling that you're cannon fodder here.*"

And finally...

The mix of work at Trowers is unique and will be particularly appealing to anyone with a social conscience and/or an interest in the Middle East.

Veale Wasbrough Vizards

The facts

Location: Bristol, London

Number of UK partners/solicitors: 49/86

Total number of trainees: 16

Seats: 4x6 months

Alternative seats: Secondments

Extras: Pro bono – BRAVE, Avon & Bristol Law Centre

On chambersstudent.co.uk
- How to get into VWV
- The legal world of Dickens
- Issues in the education sector

Based in Bristol and London, this firm excels in education and charities law.

A tale of two cities

In November 2009, Bristol-based Veale Wasbrough merged with Vizards Tweedie, a 200-year-old London firm that holds the honour of being Charles Dickens' first employer when he was a legal clerk. In truth, the marriage between the two firms is more worthy of an Austen heroine's matchmaking than a Dickens novel. In addition to the "*personal chemistry*" and "*evident synergy*" between the two businesses, VT was aiming to expand, and its "*slightly older style*" has benefited from the connection with the more youthful VW. For its part, VW was looking for a London base to strengthen client relationships and gain new ones and, bingo, VT's "*lovely and modern*" offices are minutes away from the Royal Courts of Justice. Veale Wasbrough Vizards now has over 300 employees and a combined turnover of £22m. The union has also "*strengthened both firms' charities and private client teams.*" Some of the solicitors are now splitting their week between London and Bristol, and clients are passed between the offices. At the time of our calls in spring 2010, Bristol had 14 trainees and London just the two, but it's probably reasonable to assume that the capital's training programme will expand.

The reaction to the merger has been "*very, very good:*" you hear "*nothing but positive comments,*" said trainees. The firm specialises in education and charities law, but also covers a mixed bag of private and public sector work. In the public sector, the firm is involved in such diverse areas as health, motorways, infrastructure, waste disposal and street lighting, and it also counts the Ministry of Defence as a client. In the private sector, customers include PwC and Airbus UK, banks HSBC, Clydesdale and Allied Irish, and oil companies Esso and Total. Next door to the Bristol office are two sister divisions of the firm: Convey Direct, working on residential conveyancing, and Augustine Injury Law, which deals with 'no win, no fee' personal injury claims. The latter recovered over £6m in damages for clients last year. Neither Augustine nor Convey Direct currently offer seats to trainees.

Another positive result of the merger for Bristol trainees is that they now have a chance to spend a seat in the capital. Trainees are likely to take a seat in their first-choice area, and our sources had no real complaints about seat allocation. Even if they were dispatched to a team that wasn't one of their preferences, they "*understood later why the decision was made*" and invariably ended up enjoying the seat.

Education, education, education

Education is, without doubt, VWV's forte, and although there are no compulsory seats it's likely that trainees will spend time in this department. The firm represents over 900 educational and charitable institutions, including 700 independent schools. The recession has led to increased instructions for the firm on independent school mergers (between Brighton's Roedean School and St Mary's Hall, for example) and tuition fee disputes with parents. It's not just schools VWV acts for – the firm advised the University of Bristol on arrangements to establish its Students' Union as a new charitable company – and the current aim is to branch out even further, advising more maintained schools, universities, nurseries and Academies.

Chambers UK rankings

Banking & Finance	Information Technology
Charities	Partnership
Construction	Personal Injury
Corporate/M&A	Private Client
Debt Recovery	Real Estate
Dispute Resolution	Real Estate Litigation
Education	Restructuring/Insolvency
Employment	

The education department is divided into three teams: employment, charity/corporate and pastoral. The first of these deals with reorganisations, the hiring and dismissal of teachers, harassment and discrimination cases, and drafting staff contracts. The charity/corporate seat handles governance, reviewing school constitutions and real estate matters such as registering land. The pastoral team manages the relationships within schools, and between schools and parents. This covers things like policies, complaints, bullying, child protection and special needs. One source described it as "*the more pure side of education.*" This seat is "*hugely diverse and varied*" and involves visits to schools about twice a week. Trainees can also expect to write articles for education sector publications or VWV's school newsletter, which is "*great for learning about a subject.*" Seeing as there are only a handful of pastoral teams in the UK, this division is possibly the most niche of the three.

Fleeing from creditors

The real estate department is large but, as with the education department, split into teams including commercial, plot sales, construction, planning environmental and property litigation. As you might imagine, all those education clients hold many acres of real estate, and VWV assists with managing and exploiting them. It's also big on the student accommodation scene, recently acting for Quintain and The Wellcome Trust on developments in Bristol, Sheffield and Leeds. But there's more to the property department than this: a team devoted to healthcare developments has received instructions from several GP practices together wanting to develop new 'super surgery' premises. (Trainees say it's "*interesting acting for fellow professionals.*") The firm also represents 12 government departments including the MoD and the DVLA. Trainees become very involved in smaller matters: one twice managed to stop a landlord from increasing a client's rent and told us: "*It's a very good feeling to be able to help people.*"

The commercial litigation department has a varied caseload. Its lawyers have acted for Airbus UK in relation to the death of a visitor to one of its sites, for South Somerset District Council in a dispute over income from a car park, and for a computer games company in a spat over the ownership of the film and television rights to some well-known comic characters. The seat involves a great deal of time in court, sitting in on trials, and trainees may also be called on to assist with mediations. Other seats are available in corporate, private client, employment and 'commercial and projects', which covers the public sector and IT.

On the waterfront

The workforce at VWV Bristol is notably young, with many solicitors in their late twenties and early thirties, and "*there is always the sound of laughter in the air.*" Trainees are not usually expected to do incredibly long hours, and the office tends to be empty by 6.30pm. When there are major deadlines, however, they do stay longer, generally out of enthusiasm and "*respect for colleagues*" rather than because they feel pressured to do so.

While some Bristol law firms are relocating to the less picturesque Temple Meads area, VWV is only minutes away from the quayside. One source gushed that "*from the top floor you can see the countryside, the harbour and parks,*" and during interviews we could hear the cries of seagulls outside. Many trainees live in the leafy Clifton and Cotham areas, a leisurely 20 to 30-minute walk from the office. Bristol itself is a pleasant corner of these Isles and is home to a vibrant cultural scene. Every Friday, trainees head across the road to the recently refurbished Colston Hall. An active social committee organises wine and cheese evenings, charity quizzes, barbecues, sports teams and cake sales. A summer ball is attended by staff from both offices: in past years it has been held at Bristol Zoo, the Pump Rooms in Bath and most recently Ascot. With just two trainees in London, the social scene is office-wide. Favourite post-work jollies include quizzes and trips to the pub.

And finally...

VWV has a good record for internal career progression, and several of its partners used to be trainees at the firm. In 2010, a total of ten out of 12 qualifiers were retained.

Vinson & Elkins RLLP

The facts

Location: London

Number of UK partners/solicitors: 9/15

Total number of trainees: 8

Seats: 4x6 months

Alternative seats: Overseas seats

Extras: Pro bono – LawWorks

On chambersstudent.co.uk
- How to get into V&E
- An overview of the energy sector
- V&E stateside

Vinson & Elkins is famous for its energy sector work and looks for highly energetic trainees.

No one-trick pony

Vinson & Elkins' Texan heritage explains its reputation today as a global leader in energy law. Founded in Houston in 1917, it remained a single-office operation until 1971, when it became one of the first American law firms to open in London. Still a relatively small (though growing) operation, its London office frequently collaborates with V&E's 13 others on mega-deals all over the world. For example, one partner recently helped colleagues in Beijing, Shanghai, Hong Kong and Dubai advise Chinese state-run oil giant Sinopec on its $7.2bn acquisition of Canada's Addax Petroleum. This deal was the largest Chinese acquisition overseas in 2009 and it gave Sinopec assets in Iraq, Nigeria and Gabon, illustrating just how international V&E's work can be.

Although it's a leading energy firm, trainees were keen to tell us that V&E London is "*not a one-trick pony.*" It is active in several other industry sectors, including aviation, telecoms, pharmaceuticals and construction. Its finance team has advised on major non-energy transactions, including portfolios of distressed real estate loans and mortgage-backed securities. Clients include Bank of Scotland, Standard Bank and Commercial Bank of Qatar. The dispute resolution and arbitration team has similarly become increasingly involved in shipping and shareholder/finance disputes, and several construction cases have come its way involving allegations of bribery and fraud.

It must be said, however, that these other areas aren't yet recognised by *Chambers UK* rankings. The world of oil and gas and other forms of energy still dominate life here, so it's no coincidence that V&E was reportedly the first law firm BP called for help during the Deepwater Horizon disaster in the Gulf of Mexico. Likewise, private equity houses KKR and TPG got in touch when they needed legal advice on the $45bn buyout of energy giant TXU. "*In a recession everyone still needs food and fuel,*" one trainee reminded us.

As for the future, global managing partner Joe Dilg told our sister publication, *Chambers Associate*, that V&E has been working with management consultancy McKinsey to identify "*strengths at the firm that hold true in different economies,*" and that energy remains a core strength, fitting this bill. "*Renewables technology, energy M&A and the environmental practice, including litigation and the issues rising from the global warming debate, will all be a part of our future,*" he said.

Multitasking

The V&E training contract is pretty flexible and offers tremendous responsibility, trainees reported. "*Within energy there's a lot of scope for different types of work.*" Furthermore, although each trainee sits with a partner or senior associate for six months before moving to the next department, work can fly in from all directions so they can find themselves staffed on deals from several fields at any one time. "*I sat with an energy partner but ended up doing big financial assignments and arbitration,*" said one source. "*The training here gives you the opportunity to become a more rounded lawyer,*" another reported. "*Even in your contentious seat, you'll still work on other*

Chambers UK rankings

Energy & Natural Resources	Projects

things like M&A or finance. There's no typical day. Each depends on your flow of work and is at best erratic and unpredictable. My attitude towards this is that we're getting great experience." On the downside, "*you can end up with 20 different deadlines from different departments.*" This in turn means long hours, though schedules have "*complete peaks and troughs. You can have one month leaving at 6pm, then another at midnight or 4am.*" Trainees didn't seem to mind though, and assured us that "*if you're not busy, you go home.*"

"*You can steer your training contract according to your interests,*" so if finance is your thing, you can specialise more in that – provided, of course, that you impress the relevant lawyers. "*If you made a good impression on a particular person they'll probably use you more.*" For example, private equity tasks at trainee level include a lot of first drafts – "*all ancillary documents, board minutes, share certificates, all the filings.*"

The opportunity to spend six months abroad is a big draw, and second-years reported that they were still fed work by their host overseas office, even after returning to London. Our sources typically found the overseas seat "*very useful in terms of professional growth, with many opportunities to meet clients. I needed the corporate credit card a lot!*" Even in London, trainees feel they are treated like junior associates and have good exposure to clients. "*We're encouraged to invite our own contacts to marketing events along with their managers.*" Trainees are also treated like associates during the 'First Wednesday' meeting each month, when they give a ten or 15-minute presentation on recent developments in a particular area of law to the whole office – and any other offices that may be conferenced in. "*First-year trainees give presentations too, and we had to do one on our second day!*" recalled one source.

Lovin' the elevator

Deputy training principal Mark Beeley was recently identified as a 'future leader' in his field of international dispute resolution by *The Lawyer*. Trainees praised his supervising style, and that of supervisors generally. "*Mark is an exceptional trainer,*" one of his protégés explained. "*He has a very good attitude. Some lawyers might draft something and give it to trainees to check for typos. He'd give it to you to draft first, then check and correct it. You can trace your progress by the diminution of his markings.*" Scribbled-upon documents include internal and client memos, pleadings for arbitrations or litigations, other court documents and letters to the solicitors on the other side of a dispute. Contentious seat trainees also have opportunities to interview witnesses and go to court.

Trainees must be proactive with partners if they're interested in particular types of work. The office's size and culture makes partner-junior communication clear, "*and you can go and speak to Alex* [Msimang, London's managing partner] *quite freely. There's a very loose sense of hierarchy. You find yourself chatting to and socialising with people of all levels. As a trainee, your input is valued.*" Even global managing partner Joe Dilg took the trainees to the pub on a recent visit. Beeley and the office managing partner are in charge of appraisals. Trainees complete a self-evaluation and then discuss things with the two of them.

V&E's office is located on the 32nd and 33rd floors of Moorgate's CityPoint building. You'll be stunned by how quickly the lift gets you up there. "*It's the fastest in Europe,*" a source confirmed, "*or at least it was until people complained about feeling ill, then they slowed it down.*" The views from the office are phenomenal and the facilities include a basement gym. People often go for Thursday or Friday drinks if they're not too busy. Regular haunts are the Corney & Barrow and Rack and Tenter at the foot of CityPoint. Some staff enjoy an annual ski trip, and the firm celebrates its roots with a Texas Independence Day party with plenty of tequila and cowboy boots on show. With the World Cup nearing, our interviews veered off towards football at times, and in a moment of excitement the *Student Guide* challenged V&E's five-a-side team to a match. We won't bother you with trivialities such as the score, but will report that the game was played in good spirit and that Mark Beeley is a handy goalkeeper.

And finally...

V&E's small size in London allows it an informal kind of workplace, but this is still a top-quality firm with major clients. All three qualifiers stayed on in 2010.

Walker Morris

The facts

Location: Leeds

Number of UK partners/solicitors: 49/120

Total number of trainees: 20

Seats: 6x4 months

Alternative seats: Secondments

On chambersstudent.co.uk
• How to get into Walker Morris
• The Leeds legal market
• Football insolvencies

Walker Morris is a commercial success story with a distinctive Leeds character and an ambition that extends way beyond West Yorkshire.

Hen lihai (very impressive)

In the competitive Leeds legal market, the Big Six firms continue to reign supreme. Five of those six – DLA Piper, Addleshaw Goddard, Eversheds, Hammonds and Pinsent Masons – are firms with a national, if not international, footprint. The sixth, Walker Morris, is quite different. As the firm's own website puts it, 'The competition's all over the place.' It's a claim that's not without foundation: DLA has offices as far-flung as Qatar and Tanzania, and Eversheds has a presence in places like Bratislava and Kuala Lumpur. Walker Morris, in marked contrast, has a one-site, Leeds-only strategy (although technically there are two offices, some ten metres apart).

The firm's small footprint belies a full commercial service – check out its extensive rankings in *Chambers UK* – and an outlook that is anything but parochial. According to the firm's own calculations, around 70% of its work comes from outside Yorkshire. Recent highlights include advising a banking syndicate comprising Lloyds TSB, Bank of Scotland and National Australia Bank on a proposed £21m capital restructuring of the Heywood Williams Group, a Huddersfield-based international building supplies firm. Meanwhile, Walker Morris' property practice advised Leeds United on the £4m purchase of a new training ground and has acted for nearby local authorities like Kirklees Metropolitan Borough Council, as well as those as far afield as the London Borough of Bexley. The firm was also involved in the Court of Appeal case over Mayfair-based celebrity eatery Cipriani, which was forced to change its name in spring 2010 following a challenge from the Hotel Cipriani in Venice.

The firm's ambitions extend beyond Blighty, with China the next frontier. Walker Morris secured a major victory on behalf of Chinese electronics manufacturer (and sometime sponsor of F1 golden boy Lewis Hamilton) aigo in a trade mark infringement case. It was the first time a Chinese manufacturer has won such a case in the UK. This involvement with the People's Republic wasn't a one-off: the firm has employed a number of Chinese lawyers, has a China trade practice group and a Mandarin version of its website.

The firm's one-site structure is a source of enthusiasm among trainees. "*We know everybody by name as we're not spread out over hundreds of miles, and that helps us work together across departments.*" A firm source was quick to point out that during the downturn, the one-site blueprint has left no room for unhealthy inter-office competition. Nor was there – or is there – concern that a remote office dictates the firm's strategy and direction. For more on the advantages of single-site working and who the firm wants to recruit, see training partner Jo Ratcliff's words of wisdom on our website.

DIY seating

Walker Morris offers a programme of six four-month seats. Of the Big Six, only Hammonds' scheme has a comparable structure. During each phase, trainees sit with a supervisor who is invariably a partner. The aim is to ensure that the first year gives trainees broad experience, and that means dictating their first three seats. Typically newbies are exposed to property, general corporate and

Chambers UK rankings

Banking & Finance	Intellectual Property
Banking Litigation	Pensions
Construction	Planning
Corporate/M&A	Real Estate
Debt Recovery	Real Estate Litigation
Dispute Resolution	Restructuring/Insolvency
Employment	Retail
Environment	Tax
Information Technology	

litigation. If that seems a tad prescriptive, you should know that our sources were generally enthusiastic about the arrangement. Said one: "*It means you experience life in diverse practice areas. For example, I ended up in planning, a specialist department. I really enjoyed it, but I would never have thought of picking it.*"

Having got the compulsory placements out of the way, second-years have autonomy when choosing their remaining seats. Here's the full range of options: commercial property; planning and environmental; IP/trade marks; commercial contracts; commercial projects; corporate; banking; insolvency; commercial dispute resolution; regulatory (which is health and safety, consumer credit, data protection, etc); construction and engineering; real estate and banking litigation; employment; and pensions. There are usually client secondment options too. People can be fairly certain of being placed in their preferred departments, but "*if there are any conflicts, trainees sort it out among themselves. We all sit around a table and chat about it until we come up with a solution.*" It's a testament to the maturity of trainees and the efficacy of the process that rarely is a partner required to step in and toss the proverbial coin. At the time of going to press, the firm was experimenting with a preference system for first-year trainees, but it's not clear whether it will stick with the idea.

A trainee committee is a useful forum for putting across ideas and suggestions to management. Trainees appreciate the ease with which people can communicate at the firm, which they say has a straight-talking ethos and no love of bureaucracy. This ethos influences trainee appraisals. Mid-seat reviews are "*not formal*" and more a case of "*are we on track?*" Further, more formal reviews occur at the end of each seat, although "*sometimes they are delayed.*" On an ongoing basis, "*we're advised that it's best to ask, 'Is there anything I could be doing? Am I doing anything wrong?'*" As one source put it: "*You get told when you've done something badly and when you've done something well!*"

Kings of the high street

Commercial property is a core practice area. The firm achieves top rankings regionally in anything property-related and its client list reads like a census of most British regional town centres: LK Bennett, Starbucks, Netto and Specsavers have all used the firm. For trainees, the seat involves a fair bit of "*drafting option agreements, other types of contract and client correspondence,*" with "*the odd mundane task*" thrown in. Everything is overseen, but trainees reported "*a lot of autonomy.*" In this large team people "*tend to thrive on the buzz of doing deals.*"

Walker Morris also takes on a good chunk of property litigation, including topical matters such as mortgage fraud. A trainee enthused about "*assisting a partner with an emergency ex parte freezing injunction: I drafted all the documents, liaised and instructed counsel and went to the hearing.*" Advocacy isn't an alien concept to trainees. "*On a weekly basis I conducted hearings in front of a district judge. It's a good experience, but the first time I did it, it was literally the scariest thing I have ever done in my life. You learn quickly though.*"

Another contentious seat is available in banking litigation, where to a greater or lesser extent property issues regularly crop up. Think mortgage defaults and possession proceedings. "*There's a lot of court work and I love the fact you're given your own files and told to get on with it,*" said one source. Trainees need to get their game on, as according to one source, "*you need to be really, really organised. I've got 50 files at the moment.*" Some cases include chasing down people who bought flash wheels on the never-never. Other contentious options include IP, employment and general commercial litigation.

Corporate is a big team that's generally busy, although there was some thumb twiddling during the recession. First-year trainees usually take seats here and we encountered genuine enthusiasm. "*You're a jack of all trades. You liaise with loads of different people and it gives you a really good overview of the firm,*" claimed a second-year. Business has picked up, partly due to the team focusing more on insolvency and restructuring. Walker Morris has excellent form in interesting insolvency work: historically, it has enjoyed celebrated status in the niche area of football administrations. Local boys Leeds United, as well as Luton Town FC, AFC Bournemouth and Rotherham United have all been clients. In most seats, trainees' levels of responsibility are excellent. One source confirmed: "*Unless there's a lot to do, I don't find myself stood by a photocopier. It's less of a handholding scenario than I thought it might be... for example, I have looked after clients at hearings and taken them out for lunch and things.*"

Another redbrick in the wall

Many trainees come from local(ish) redbrick universities. Leeds Uni is a key supplier and you'll always see Walker Morris at its autumn law fair. Alumni of Durham, Newcastle, Sheffield, Manchester Met and the like also find their way to the firm. "*The most important thing is that a candidate is attracted to us, not to Leeds,*" said a recruitment source. Several of our contacts had no prior connection to the city, but had upped sticks purely on the basis of favourable impressions of Walker Morris.

Unquestionably, part of the attraction is the firm's collegial atmosphere, both during and after work. Several trainees described the firm as "*straightforward*" and "*no-nonsense.*" One told us he'd joined because the vacation scheme was "*accessible and not intimidating. It felt real.*" Recruitment sources denied that this was anything to do with a Yorkshire attitude – "*being down to earth doesn't make you Northern*" – but a second-year trainee revealed that "*the whole Northern identity thing is pretty crucial to the firm.*" It's a hard-working identity and, as such, "*probably doesn't suit people who always want to come in at 9am and leave at half five.*" The good news is that most people reckon "*weekends are still sacrosanct.*"

Extracurricular activities include sports (netball and football are popular), quizzes, bowling and barbecues. There's also a trainee day featuring a hog roast. This year our sources reported that the social whirlwind had slowed to a stiff breeze. "*I don't think it's quite what it used to be,*" said one; "*we don't have the budget we used to. People talk wistfully about the good old days when we were out on the lash every night.*" It's a revealing comment reflecting an underlying theme to many events. "*The social life is mainly drinking-based,*" one trainee sheepishly admitted, and others agreed. Local haunts include Barworks ("*it's quite cheap, so good for the end of the month*") and Sous le Nez, an altogether classier joint by all accounts. The humble institution that is the public house is a great leveller. Trainees go out with partners after a busy deal or case, and "*partners will buy trainees their drinks – it's an unwritten rule.*" Additionally, the pub is an opportunity to see what vac schemers are like outside the office. Trainees have input during the vac scheme and recruitment process, and they tell us: "*The people who did well on the vacation scheme are those who got involved and socialised after work. It meant we could see who had some decent chat.*"

Which takes us to an important point. "*You have to be confident and outgoing in order to thrive. There aren't many, if any, shy people here, and if you're not a social person then you would struggle.*" One source reflected: "*I suppose the firm is full of outgoing, bubbly, confident people.*" Trainees are expected to market themselves to colleagues, ask questions and get along well with others. Said another source: "*You need to be able to have a laugh, and to laugh at yourself. In Outlook, I have a file for e-mails marked 'Banter' for all the non-work office stuff that flies around.*" One thing that might appear in such a file is moans about the heating in the building – it's just too hot for some people and there's no air-con.

If by this point you've concluded that Walker Morris is a firm for people who work and play well with others, then you're right. Said one source: "*You overhear partners and fee earners at all levels and you learn that this is a very user-friendly firm. From a very early stage you know that no one is trying to trip you up and that people are very open.*" This approach is taken with clients too: "*The firm really engages with people's businesses.*" And as you might expect, trainees have to engage in the firm's business. As one of them advised: "*You have to market yourself to some extent, no matter how good you are at the work, as it also comes down to things like personality.*" In 2010, 15 of the 17 qualifiers were made of the right stuff and accepted jobs at the firm.

And finally...

This commercial player is a stable, hard-working kind of firm that is looking for bright, ambitious grafters. It particularly excels in property-related work, insolvency and various types of dispute resolution.

Ward Hadaway

The facts

Location: Newcastle, Leeds, Manchester

Number of UK partners/solicitors: 60/94

Total number of trainees: 18

Seats: 4x6 months

Alternative seats: None

On chambersstudent.co.uk
- How to get into WH
- WH's charitable nature
- The skinny on Newcastle's legal scene

Newcastle-headquartered Ward Hadaway has established a reputation as a strong player in the North East and has ambitions for further Northern expansion.

North by northeast

Ward Hadaway, as it exists today, is the result of the 1988 merger in Newcastle of the seemingly tautological Hadaway & Hadaway and the grandly named Septimus G. Ward & Rose. It is now firmly established as a top full-service outfit in the North East, and *Chambers UK* awards it a swathe of rankings in the region and a top-of-the-tree position for dispute resolution, employment and property. In recent years, the firm has opened a "*rapidly growing*" Leeds office and poached a ton of partners from Eversheds. A new hire from Trowers & Hamlins, meanwhile, won instructions to advise on a £350m schools project just two months after arriving. All this means WH is now right up there in the Newcastle élite and giving "*bigger and older*" Dickinson Dees a run for its money.

A drop in revenue and partner profits during the recession led to a number of redundancies, trainee deferrals and the implementation of a four-day week in some departments. The recession blues also put the planned opening of a full Manchester office on hold for a while. Current trainees "*get the impression that people think things are looking up,*" and in the spring of 2010 the firm planted a tiny seed in the North West. The Manchester venture is starting out with an IT focus, but training partner Paula Myers tells us that "*it's early days… in the fullness of time we're looking to go full-service.*" Trainees describe WH's ambition as being "*to consolidate as a leading firm in the North, not just the North East.*" Management has made it clear that WH will remain a regional firm that aims to bring in more and more work from Yorkshire and Humberside.

There is a growing ambition to "*win more big national clients*" to add to the list that already instruct the firm. These include ASDA, Speedo, Orange and bakers Greggs. WH is also keen to hold on to its core Northern following, some of the biggest names among them being Durham County Council, Northumbrian Water, the University of Northumbria and Yorkshire Building Society. NHS work is big business: WH is one of the few firms on the NHS Litigation Authority's legal panel. It is the only North East firm to act for the NHSLA in clinical negligence cases, and it also advises NHS trusts on employment and property matters.

A four-seat system takes trainees through WH's full-service offering. The seat options can include: corporate finance; company/commercial; commercial litigation; public sector property; property finance; insolvency; employment; healthcare (clin neg); personal injury; licensing and regulatory; property litigation; pensions; and IP. At present there is an employment seat available in the smaller Leeds office at every rotation, with the expectation being that trainees will be recruited directly into the office in the not too distant future.

No seats are compulsory and trainees are allowed to sample what they wish, although second-years' requests take priority. Looking at the typical seat patterns, it's clear that you might either blend healthcare/PI seats with commercial ones or perhaps even stick to commercial seats. One source said that in the end they were "*completely satisfied*" with the system; another added that HR "*does try to*

Chambers UK rankings

Agriculture & Rural Affairs	Healthcare
Banking & Finance	Information Technology
Charities	Intellectual Property
Clinical Negligence	Personal Injury
Construction	Planning
Corporate/M&A	Private Client
Debt Recovery	Professional Discipline
Dispute Resolution	Real Estate
Employment	Real Estate Litigation
Family/Matrimonial	Restructuring/Insolvency

accommodate everyone." The only gripe related to timing: "*You used to turn up on the morning of the rotation with your boxes, without knowing what seat you were going into.*" Things are "*getting better*" and trainees can now usually expect to find out the identity of their next department a month in advance. They certainly "*always have at least a week.*"

Hard/away at work

A property seat is likely to involve construction and regeneration projects, working for big house builders like Northumberland Estates, Future Builders England and Barratt Homes. For example, the team advised on a regeneration scheme to deliver a new school and 300 homes at the former Bates Colliery Site at Blyth, negotiating a joint venture between Banks Property and UK Coal along with Northumberland County Council and the Homes and Communities Agency. A subgroup within property services the public sector, including NHS bodies and local authorities. Other clients include banks and no-frills supermarket chain Aldi. Property trainees' responsibility levels vary, but managing "*30-odd files*" is not uncommon. Our sources "*reviewed, drafted and marked up leases*" and e-mailed plenty of solicitors acting on the other side of deals. The property litigation team also assists "*some of the large North East house builders*" as well as individual landlords and tenants in housing disputes.

A corporate finance seat is fairly common and puts trainees on deals that are sometimes "*worth hundreds of millions of pounds.*" Lawyers advise Barclays, Lloyds, Bank of Scotland, RBS, The Co-operative Bank and Santander on acquisition finance transactions, investment property financings and debt restructurings. Trainee involvement isn't as intense here as elsewhere. "*There's not very much opportunity to be at the coalface,*" said one. Another added that "*a trainee's task is very much one of organisation, like getting all the completion documents in a file and making sure that they've been tabbed correctly with a sticky tab.*" The consensus is that the seat is "*equally-valuable*" as the others, even if trainees are "*less involved in each transaction.*" Likewise, the company/commercial seat usually sees trainees staffed on "*a small part of quite a big transaction or project*" and the work is "*very similar to corporate finance.*" However, these trainees will "*actually deal with the directors and members of companies.*" We hear that corporate finance is "*the most entrepreneurial of the departments and most likely to go out lunching and golfing.*"

In contention

The *Chambers UK* top-ranked commercial litigation department handles professional negligence, insurance, public sector and private wealth claims, and trainees see work ranging from "*disputed wills and conflicts between shareholders and partnerships, to defamation and defence work for newspapers.*" Clients include Persimmon Homes and Newcastle Airport. WH represented the former against Redcar & Cleveland Borough Council in a tussle concerning the designation of a certain patch of land as a village green. Trainees get involved with case management conferences and are always "*rushing off down to court.*" It's certainly a popular seat and around half of our interviewees had managed to gain advocacy experience; they also agreed that in contentious seats they really got to follow the litigation process and were always under excellent supervision.

In healthcare, trainees mainly work on high-value clin neg cases for defendants and "*pretty much do the same things as a newly qualified.*" They spend their time "*drafting court documents, liaising with clients and attending round-table meetings with counsel.*" They often run their own matters and one source had been to two inquests "*and not just for a tag-along experience.*" Indeed, the seat is defined by hands-on work, which means you're "*in at the deep end, as opposed to having your hand held throughout.*" Expect to "*learn from your mistakes instead of being told what to do.*" In PI, defendant clients include the likes of North Yorkshire County Council and Newcastle University. The work revolves around "*lots of road traffic accidents, slips and trips, occupiers' liability and employers' liability,*" and the firm says that over the past few years the annual turnover of this group has quadrupled.

Training partner Paula Myers highlights employment as another key area for expansion, especially in Leeds. The department acts for employers like Barratt Homes, Orange and Yorkshire Building Society. There are also equal pay claims against NHS trusts and local councils. Trainees undertake "*a variety of work including drafting defences and schedules of loss, analysing positions in cases, doing small research tasks and dealing with client queries.*" Insolvency is a small team where trainees have "*a lot of hands-on experience*" and run their own files. Matters are both contentious and non-contentious and can cover anything from "*placing a company into administration*" to individual bankruptcies. And finally, a quick word on the IP seat, which one trainee praised for its focus on client contact. "*IP has to be congratulated on its networking and marketing events; they really encourage you to learn about the industry.*"

Tyne of your life

Trainees tell us that WH is "*an exciting firm*" with an "*influx of youth wanting to win work and open new offices.*" Said one trainee: "*People are encouraged to go to networking and business development events, and the firm encourages us to go to Junior Lawyers Division events. With certain partners, their job is simply to go out and win business.*" Trainees also describe WH as an "*enjoyable*" place to work. "*There are very few dragonish partners; everyone gets on with their job and laughs and jokes when it is appropriate.*" The culture is "*user-friendly, and no one here is a traditional or stereotypical sort of lawyer. People are easy to deal with.*" The main Sandgate building is close to the riverfront and houses property, IP, litigation and employment. Trainees sit with supervisors in offices, which means it's "*maybe more chatty and energetic*" than the modern Keel Row building opposite. Keel Row houses the commercial and private client departments and is open plan, which "*makes it quieter.*" In both buildings, "*people are quite approachable – you can go and talk to anyone.*" Trainees normally work from about 8.30am to 6pm, but in all departments when things get busy you can "*easily work till 7pm or 8pm.*"

All our trainee contacts were – like the firm itself – totally committed to a life in Newcastle. They either came from the North East or attended a local university. Besides the geographical connection, most also saw other similarities among themselves. "*We're all from a broadly similar background: none of us went to Edge Hill and none of us went to Cambridge either,*" said one. Indeed, all our sources went to reputable universities, though not always a redbrick one. Furthermore, "*we are all quite approachable and none of us are particularly quiet.*" With the Northumbrian countryside half an hour's drive away, several are into sports and outdoor activities.

Trainees "*tend to get on as a group*" – birds of a feather and all that, we guess. Although "*socially, the formal functions have been knocked on the head,*" we got the impression that WH trainees don't let that stop them. Budget cuts have not dampened morale, and trainees expect to see a new social budget "*soon.*" The "*staple diet*" is drinks at the Pitcher & Piano on Friday evenings. "*We don't really have to arrange that: you just pop over and there will be someone there.*" It's not just Friday nights either: "*Trainees see each other socially on the weekends*" and "*sometimes go to gigs or out for meals, or to the beach for barbecues.*"

And finally...

Ward Hadaway provides top training in the North East. Before the recession, it was known for its excellent retention rates, though in 2009 only two-thirds of trainees stayed on and in 2010 just five out of ten took up NQ jobs.

Warner Goodman LLP

The facts

Location: Fareham, Southampton, Portsmouth

Number of UK partners/solicitors: 13/22

Total number of trainees: 3

Seats: Flexible, minimum of 3

Alternative seats: None

On chambersstudent.co.uk
- How to get into Warner Goodman
- An interview with managing partner Ian Curtis

Warner Goodman has served the folk of Fareham since 1852 and retains a strong reputation for private client work. From larger offices in Southampton and Portsmouth, it also advises businesses in the Solent corridor.

Red, white and blue

Recent years have seen a big push to grow the commercial side of the business. In response to the changing legal marketplace, the firm converted to LLP status, ditched its crime department and separately rebranded its commercial practice as WG Commercial. Commercial activity currently accounts for roughly 25 to 30% of turnover, and managing partner Ian Curtis told us: "*Our objective is to make this 50% by the end of 2012.*"

Most of the commercial teams – commercial litigation, company/commercial, employment and commercial property – are based in Southampton, although there is a small spur in Portsmouth which also has trainee seats. Warner Goodman hasn't neglected its high street origins, and departments like personal injury and family continue to grow, too: the Southampton office houses one of the leading personal injury teams in the area. Family lawyers are present in all three offices, as this "*is one area we believe isn't easily centralised,*" Curtis says – not least because of local rivalries. A Southampton client would hardly be likely to hop on the train to Pompey just to see a solicitor, after all – especially if they're a Saints fan.

Warner Goodman's high street practice remains committed to Legal Aid work and recently re-secured its contract from the Legal Services Commission. That's not to say the sector won't see major change and an inevitable reduction in the availability of public funding for legal services. Elsewhere, the residential conveyancing team shrank through redundancies and natural wastage during the recession and now accounts for only around ten to 15% of turnover. However, the firm is still a regional leader for this type of work.

Family misfortunes

The firm expects trainees to complete a minimum of three seats but offers genuine flexibility over what they do and for how long they do it. In the past some trainees have completed as many as five seats; however, lately most have chosen to settle into a more conventional four-seat system. "*Generally people do four, and it's quite common to go back to a department you want to qualify into.*" Movement between offices is likely and the full seat list includes: commercial property; commercial litigation; company/commercial; employment; family; private client; conveyancing; personal injury; and financial services (usually the least popular). A three-month marketing seat is also available.

The family seat provides an excellent overview of the field. Cases cover children, divorce and domestic violence, often involving drugs and alcohol. "*I was surprised by the level of responsibility I got,*" said one source, referring to "*lots of client meetings to understand people's problems,*" and "*a first advocacy opportunity just four months in.*" This was "*daunting but rewarding.*" If trainees don't feel quite ready to "*get a buzz,*" a supervisor will step in and do the hearing instead. Our sources appreciated this support. All four of the current trainees had happily completed a family seat because "*it's very busy and hands-on with lots of new clients and a quick turnaround. It's good to see a case through from start to finish, though some do take ages.*" The split between Legal Aid and private work is roughly 50/50, but this could change with government cutbacks.

In personal injury, said one interviewee, "*I got to work with a range of people and see many different styles of working – like how to keep files organised and ways of dealing with clients.*" Cases range from road traffic accidents to "*much more complex cases like industrial disease and injuries at work.*" The department only handles claimant cases, mostly from Hampshire and Dorset. Trainees like the sheer variety of the seat – "*no two injuries are the same,*" after all. They're likely to spend quite a bit of time doing research to try and quantify claims.

Chain reaction

The employment team holds quarterly client seminars at the Rose Bowl, home of Hampshire County Cricket Club. Trainee participation is strongly encouraged: "*I did a couple in front of 100 people,*" recalled one. Three or four members of the team present on a topic, then lead interactive activities and discussions with the clients. "*It's also good for networking.*" The team represents both respondents and applicants, working for regular corporate clients and individuals. Our interviewees liked the mix of contentious and non-contentious work, and found the seat interesting because "*employment law is always changing.*" Trainees also help with tribunal preparation, take notes during hearings and work on a weekly client newsletter.

Managing your own files is a big bonus in the commercial litigation seat. "*It's nice that clients phone and ask for me specifically,*" one source enthused; "*I never felt out of my depth because there's always people around to help.*" Diverse assignments include insolvency, breach of contract and defective goods and services – perhaps a company with a gripe against a supplier, or a claim against a building contractor for shoddy work. "*I've been busy drafting particulars of a claim, which is always fun! You have to have a deep understanding of a matter, get your head down and make sure you get everything correct,*" explained one trainee. Face-to-face and phone client contact, disclosure, drafting witness statements, applications and visits to court are all par for the course in this seat.

A typical trainee task in commercial property is researching title for a plot of land that a client is interested in buying. You also need to check with the local authority to see "*if it was polluted in the past or has sewers or water mains running through it.*" There's a "*steady flow of clients*" and a lot of lease and lease extension work. One source "*really enjoyed residential conveyancing*" because "*there's a lot of talking on the phone to get things moving, trying to match up a chain. It's so busy, a really lovely department to work in,*" and it especially benefits from the firm's "*really good, up-to-date IT system*" because "*you can run so many searches at once.*"

Court in the act

Southampton is the largest office, followed by Portsmouth then Fareham. "*There's not a huge difference between the offices – all are very welcoming with no barriers between different seniorities.*" Regular group lunches are attended by directors (partners), associates, trainees and support staff. The trainee group also meets up fairly regularly. The Fareham office is on the high street, ideal for lunch-hour retail therapy. The Portsmouth office is near the university, close to the city centre and the county court. Southampton goes one better and is literally opposite the county court, with the magistrates' court close by. So close in fact that you can see the judges at work from part of the office. The Pompey office is next door to The Wig & Pen pub, and the Old Portsmouth area is home to a number of "*nice pubs.*" Fareham's building is quite a grand ex banking hall "*with lots of corridors and separate rooms,*" whereas Southampton is "*more open-plan.*"

WG's social club organises subsidised events like ten-pin bowling and a day out at Goodwood races. "*I didn't win much at all!*" one sourced moaned. The deal is simple: employees each throw a pound a month into the kitty, and the directors match the amount raised. There's a summer barbecue and annual party to which everyone's invited. Sports teams occasionally compete at footy, touch rugby and cricket.

Trainees' genuine affection for Warner Goodman is clear when they say things like: "*I can honestly say I've loved every day I've been here*" and "*I speak to friends at other firms and thank God I'm here.*" One source summed things up slightly less gushingly: "*I feel I've such a good basis for my future career. My skill base and confidence have grown tremendously. I just feel I'm very well equipped.*" In 2010, two of the firm's three qualifiers stayed on, while the third left purely for relocation reasons.

And finally...

Changes in the availability of Legal Aid funding are a major unknown for mixed-practice firms such as Warner Goodman, but it is already part way down the road to a more privately paying and commercial future.

Watson, Farley & Williams

The facts

Location: London

Number of UK partners/solicitors: 46/70

Total number of trainees: 25

Seats: 6x4 months

Alternative seats: Overseas seats

Extras: Pro bono – Toynbee Hall Legal Advice Centre

On chambersstudent.co.uk

- How to get into WFW
- We talk to managing partner Michael Greville
- The renewable energy sector

With a 100% guarantee of time abroad, budding lawyers in search of an international training experience need look no further than mid-sizer Watson, Farley & Williams.

Against the tide

Three Norton Rose partners jumped ship to set up Watson, Farley & Williams in 1982. Much has changed over the past three decades, not least the scale and orientation of the firm's business. There are now a dozen offices stretching from Western Europe to Asia and New York; the firm most recently opened up in Madrid in 2009, and before that it was Munich and Milan in 2008. Though London remains the biggest office in terms of headcount, WFW's international network has undoubtedly buoyed it in this undulating economy. The firm's overall turnover has actually increased during the recession, jumping by 9% during the 2009/10 financial year. "*In these sorts of times, the work goes to people at the top of the market in the sectors where they have the strongest competitive positions,*" said managing partner Michael Greville. "*For us that's shipping, energy and natural resources, and they've all generated legal work.*" Supporting Greville's position is the news that WFW hired four new partners in May 2010, including the former head of the energy and infrastructure finance team at Freshfields.

'International' is a term tossed about by every law firm with an outpost beyond the UK, but at WFW, the training experience really is just that. With a guaranteed seat abroad – Paris, Piraeus, Singapore or Bangkok – trainees forgo the usual four by six-month seat formula for six four-month stints. "*It gives you more choice and flexibility for qualification,*" a trainee explained. The international seats certainly helped in 2009 when three of the 13 qualifiers began NQ life in one of the firm's international offices. In 2010, ten of the 12 qualifiers took up qualification jobs with the firm. One involved a 12-month placement in Greece prior to a return to the London office. Other NQ positions led qualifiers to short-term visits to other offices. Time abroad "*isn't a jolly – it's hard work,*" so don't come here looking to make up for a missed backpacking opportunity. As for the six-seat system, "*it keeps you active,*" insisted one trainee. "*If you like a seat, it stops you getting too complacent. And if you don't, it's not long before you get to leave.*" Some even get the chance to redo a favourite seat.

Chain mail

Time in the finance department is compulsory. Though this world has been quieter since the credit crunch, our sources were kept busy with insolvency/restructuring and loan refinancing. They spoke of drafting loan documentation, monitoring conditions precedent, transactions for the funding, purchase and delivery of ships, and loan restructuring for liquid natural gas (LNG) companies. Clients include Credit Suisse, RBS, JPMorgan Chase Bank and ING Bank. WFW recently advised Citibank in its role as co-ordinator, agent and trustee in Korea Export Insurance Corporation's $850m financing of an ice-class drill ship – KEIC's largest-ever ship financing to date. Renewable energy is a key sector for the firm and the department advised in relation to a tender for six offshore wind farm projects.

Chambers UK rankings

Asset Finance	Employment
Commodities	Energy & Natural Resources
Dispute Resolution	

Shipping was a big part of the firm's early focus, and it still is today. Said one source: "*It really is the centre of the firm, so it's good to get in there to understand what people are talking about.*" "*It was quite a shock to the system at first,*" recalled one recruit. "*I didn't have a clue what a tanker was.*" As part of their two-week induction, trainees "*go through a lot of basics like the port and starboard stuff*" and have further departmental talks throughout their seats.

In several seats it's easy to see that "*the international offices are very much integrated,*" and "*it gets really obvious when you look at the e-mail chain of a big shipping case.*" On cross-jurisdictional cases "*you work with people in the international offices almost daily,*" but excitement can wane when you're locked into work in other time zones. Once a ship is delivered, trainees will often need to register a mortgage over it, and if that's happening in another country it can require "*sweet talking the registry office to open up at 2am.*" Recalling exactly this experience, one trainee said: "*It is good fun and a laugh, but it does mean having to ruin someone else's night.*" The firm acted for lenders Nordea and Lloyds TSB, after major shipping company Britannia Bulk collapsed in late 2008 and the lenders needed to enforce the security they had taken over 13 ships.

Paris and Piraeus, in Greece, are prime destinations for those hungry for more ship finance experience, but spending time in the London department is a pre-requisite for heading out there. "*It's similar to the work you do in London, except you're dealing with French banks so it has a continental twist,*" said one visitor to Paris. In the capital of romance, trainees stay in an apartment in the trendy Marais district and can watch the Bastille Day parade along the Champs-Élysées from the office's balcony. "*Because of the size of the teams overseas, there's no mid-layer of lawyers to dilute the work, so you get involved fairly quickly.*"

Working closely with a partner is commonplace at this firm, and by doing so trainees said they found it easier to "*understand more about what was going on.*" It's great for boosting confidence. Responsibility and client contact "*varies from seat to seat,*" we heard. "*In some litigation cases, it's natural that the partner might be more in contact with the client, while in shipping there's lots of document management to do, so you're talking to the client and the other side every day.*" Wherever trainees found themselves, it seems to be true that "*you're certainly not kept away from the client.*"

Nerdy, moi?

"*People often just think of shipping and energy finance when they think of WFW,*" said one source, "*but the corporate department has independent work of its own.*" Corporate is a compulsory seat, and here the pace and workload can be "*very up and down*" depending on deal flow – "*there's always a big rush when a project comes in.*" AIM-related matters are standard fare. And we heard about one trainee who was "*really heavily involved on an IPO and in the office for 30 or 40 hours straight.*" Such episodes are the exception to the rule, however. As well as first stabs at drafting transaction documents and getting involved with due diligence and conditions precedent, some of our sources were excited to be working in the department when the new Companies Act came into force. "*I know it sounds nerdy, but we needed to know how it was changing and affecting the law in practice.*" One recent deal involved advising Genesis Petroleum Corporation on its merger with Bayerngas Norge. A magic circle firm acted for Bayerngas, but it was WFW that was mandated to advise the new company on subsequent matters.

The third compulsory stop for WFW trainees is litigation. Like corporate, the department evolved out of the firm's shipping practice and now has "*its own clients – you can be doing anything,*" trainees tell us, from insolvency to international arbitration. It's possible to do a contentious seat in Singapore where, again, "*there's not a massive gap between the trainees and the partners you're working with. You're often asked about the merits of a case and you're encouraged to have an opinion.*"

Six appeal

"*There's a friendly, flat structure across the firm,*" trainees confirmed, telling us how often they are likely to bump into managing partner Michael Greville or founding partner Martin Watson. "*The culture is corporate but not cut-throat*" and "*the open-door and dress-down policies mean that it's not very stuffy.*" If things go wrong it's all about finding the solution: "*I've never been shouted at,*" insisted a source. Some supervisors were described as "*brilliant*" and "*good at explaining things that are quite specialised.*" These supervisory relationships tend to work well, which is important because "*you spend a hell of a lot of time together!*" Trainees sit with either a partner or associate, and there are pros and cons with each. "*With a partner you often get less interaction with them on a daily basis because they're so busy, but you get taught by somebody with that level of experience. Associates are there all the time, and it's also easier for them to remember what it was like being a trainee.*"

Six seats instead of four "*gets you across all the main areas, but also into a couple of the small ones too.*" Property, international tax and employment are all on offer, though at the time of our research there was no seat in employment as the supervisor was on maternity leave. Competition is now off the menu too following that team's exit in 2009, although the firm is developing its practice and hopes to offer the seat again soon. Tax seats offer a good variety of work and trainees experience not only the "*tax elements of shipping or energy contracts, but inheritance tax issues for individuals too.*" The property team has been "*surprisingly busy, especially in the renewables sector,*" where lawyers deal with the real estate aspects of LNG pipelines and onshore and offshore wind farms.

Climb every mountain

The musical chair-style seat rotation also gets trainees networking, and "*because it's a smaller firm everyone knows each other.*" The firm hosts two balls a year – one at Christmas and another in April when new partner announcements are made. For the second year running, no new partners were made up in the London office in 2010. Still, our sources maintained that "*you've just got to ride out the bad times – if anyone really thought they were hard done by, they would have left by now.*" Everyone cheered the firm's "*collegiality,*" and at firm events "*you can find yourself sitting next to a partner or someone from the print room.*" There's always a drinks event when vac schemers are in, and the corporate department "*has a habit of wheeling out a cart of wine and champagne when there's something to celebrate.*"

"*It's a social firm, but it's not die-hard partying,*" insisted one source. Still, trainees "*all get along well,*" eating lunch together every day and meeting for drinks on a Friday. "*On lazy days we'll go to All Bar One or Piccolino's nearby, where people can come down as they finish their work. But if we're feeling a bit more adventurous we'll go out to Spitalfields.*" There are football and netball teams – the footballers recently went on tour to Hamburg – and everyone can join in on the firm's annual golf and karting days for clients.

Those keen for pro bono can volunteer at the Toynbee Hall Legal Advice Centre, and WFW also has a policy of supporting individuals' own initiatives. One trainee climbed Mount Kilimanjaro to raise awareness for Help for Heroes, and their colleagues provided generous sponsorship. It's in keeping with the idea that management wants to look after staff. Even in the depths of the recession, the firm made no trainee deferrals and only a small number of redundancies. "*Their attitude seems to be that short-term solutions don't work.*" Perhaps this long-termist approach prevailed each time the firm has been courted for a merger. As yet no advances from other firms have led WFW to the church door.

The trainees we spoke to were well travelled; some had taken gap years and several were from international backgrounds. "*We're looking for trainees who can get along with most sorts of people,*" said grad recruiter Louise Turgoose. "*We do have loud people as well as those who are more introverted, but everyone gets along.*" Go to our website to read more about who the firm is looking for, its new recruitment process and what to expect on the vacation scheme.

And finally...

A close-knit culture, good responsibility and international experience by the bucket-load await recruits at this focused mid-sizer.

Wedlake Bell LLP

The facts

Location: London

Number of UK partners/solicitors: 43/45

Total number of trainees: 6

Seats: 4x6 months

Alternative seats: Secondments

On chambersstudent.co.uk

- How to get into Wedlake Bell
- We talk to managing partner Philip Matthews
- Bedford Row: a lawyer's natural habitat?

This mid-sizer is one of London's oldest firms but its appetite for fun is alive and well. Who's at the party? Lacoste, Diageo, Hyatt, Rolls-Royce and Dreamworks, among others.

Trench coats and text messaging

This 230-year-old firm excels in a number of traditional areas and a few contemporary ones. It is highlighted in *Chambers UK* for private client, real estate, construction, IT and IP, and trainees describe it as "*pretty full-service.*" Recently the firm has been busy on a number of commercial matters, advising retailer Aquascutum on trading arrangements with business partners in Asia and counselling clients like Tesco and Teletext on advertising disputes involving Google Adwords. Crimestoppers also came to the firm for guidance on the use of photos of notorious murderers in one of its information campaigns.

Since August 2009 the firm has added ten to the partnership (five came from outside the firm). Managing partner Philip Matthews walked us through the firm's current strategy: "*It's to grow by a series of targeted lateral hires, to deepen resources in core areas, and to add skill sets in complementary services. I don't think it's likely that we would invest in a new practice area we haven't done before. It's a fairly cautious process of expansion.*"

The firm's India group is a medium to long-term initiative made up of several lawyers who are interested in expanding their client connections in the subcontinent. In terms of doing business in the UK for Indian clients, the investment has already started paying dividends, said Matthews. Wedlake Bell's international presence and experience are also growing through an organisation called Trans European Law Firms Alliance (TELFA), of which the firm is a founding member. This referral network has a relationship with a similar American organisation called USLAW.

Although not compulsory, one near certainty in a Wedlake Bell training contract is a seat in a property-related area. This can be in commercial/residential property, property litigation or construction. There's also a distinct real estate finance team within the department and lately it's been working on plenty of debt restructuring. The firm recently assisted the UK arm of Fortis Bank on the restructuring of a £37m facility advanced to a property development company for funding a mixed-use development scheme in Wembley. Property sector clients range from retailers to airlines to sporting institutions. Trainees recalled working on a variety of big and small deals, the latter giving them "*numerous files that you can run yourself*" and a chance to "*manage your own caseload.*" Where small pieces of land are involved, they often take complete ownership of the matter. The commercial property team works closely with the rest of the firm, particularly the construction, tax and corporate teams. Expensive property acquisitions, estate re-mortgaging and other "*high-end stuff*" are often run in close contact with the firm's private client specialists, who have often built long-standing relationships with wealthy clients.

In the property litigation seat trainees' responsibilities include drafting claim forms, issuing proceedings,

Chambers UK rankings

Construction	Intellectual Property
Employment	Private Client
Information Technology	Real Estate

preparing trial bundles for summary and default applications, building witness statements and instructing counsel. Anyone who sits with the construction team soon learns that most disputes follow an established system of adjudication rather than being litigated in court. "*It's very fast-moving because it has to be decided in 28 days,*" said one source of the adjudication procedure. In this mixed contentious/non-contentious team, trainees draft collateral warranties, performance bonds and witness statements, and work in co-operation with the National Specialist Contractor's Council telephone helpline.

Corporate lawyers assisted Jaeger on new franchise arrangements in Russia and the United Arab Emirates, and advised on how to terminate franchises in Thailand, Taiwan and Japan. "*Here, you work as a team and don't have the responsibility of running a matter,*" revealed one source. Another referred to "*feeling like more of a cog in a big wheel*" as they provided assistance on deals – taking board minutes, concentrating on corporate governance and conducting due diligence. Trainees gain experience of partnership agreements, share purchases, M&A and other types of transaction, and feel they have access to companies that are "*large enough to have interesting work, but small enough to mean we're in touch with the best contacts on the client's side.*" The firm has close ties with drinks giant Diageo, which hosts trainees on secondment during their commercial/IP training. This opportunity to "*sit in a global procurement department*" exposes the trainee to Diageo's commercial contracts, franchising agreements, international licensing and highly brag-worthy (and heavily discounted) staff bar.

The rich and the bankrupt

Wedlake Bell's private clients include landed gentry and political figures, and some have been ranked in the *Sunday Times*' Rich List. Contentious trusts and probate work (ie wills disputes) are on the rise, as are the number of pre and post-nuptial agreements. Having said that, private client work at trainee level usually revolves around non-contentious matters. We heard that this seat is "*great for client contact*" as trainees attend many meetings. The rest of their time is largely spent drafting wills and trust documents, and generally helping wealthy individuals who hold UK assets with their tax and estate planning, be this on or offshore.

A corporate tax seat is "*predominantly research-based*" and "*quite complex.*" It's almost the polar opposite of the business recoveries seat, which combines contentious and non-contentious work. Debt recovery for liquidators is common, and this involves "*chasing debtors and then negotiating.*" Trainees have helped to represent liquidators in bankruptcy cases and assisted their supervisors to prepare for trial by updating bundles of documents and liaising with witnesses. One or two have also attended post-trial enforcement hearings. Actually conducting their own advocacy in front of a master was a high point for one source.

Time to go to the pub

Many departments conduct in-house seminars, and in some cases trainees participate in the presentations. They receive formal feedback on their work, "*sometimes as often as every month.*" Trainees told us: "*The firm pushes you, but I was supervised at every stage*" and "*you really run your own files; you're treated like a fee earner.*" While there is no official mentoring scheme, "*supervisors are always asking whether we're working too hard.*" Standard days are nine or ten hours, and on top of that, be ready to be "*quite sociable and get involved*" with fellow trainees, partners and clients. All fee earners' offices have glass doors that are "*always open*" and "*top to bottom, everyone's pretty nice.*" A hierarchy is not especially evident at this "*friendly*" firm, although one trainee revealed how "*everyone's approachable, but some departments are more old-fashioned than others*" (ahem, private client). Once a month the firm hosts drop-in drinks in its "*very modern, very nice office*" or at one of the local pubs. A "*Wedlake Bell type*" is happy to take part in the firm's lively social scene – there's a social committee, and charity and sporting events are popular. Lately staff have participated in the Race For Life, triathlon events and netball and cricket fixtures.

And finally...

In 2010, four out of six qualifying trainees stayed with this classic West End firm. Personality and client skills are as highly prized as legal prowess, so approach any interview with suitable confidence.

Weil, Gotshal & Manges LLP

The facts

Location: London

Number of UK partners/solicitors: 23/61 (US: 8)

Total number of trainees: 26

Seats: 4x6 months

Alternative seats: Overseas seats

Extras: Pro bono – LawWorks, Bar Pro Bono Unit, Battersea Law Centre, RCJ CAB

On chambersstudent.co.uk
- How to get into Weil
- The ins and outs of seat allocation
- Weil stateside

Are you interested in stepping out of your comfort zone to take part in key global transactions? The right applicants should love this hard-charging firm and the challenges it offers.

Name-dropping

Weil Gotshal & Manges (it rhymes with the River Ganges) was founded in New York in 1931 and now employs around 1,300 lawyers across 20 offices on three continents. Long known for its bankruptcy and restructuring practice (it advised on Enron back in the day), the firm grew steadily during the recent boom years but has really come into its own during the recession, advising both Lehman and General Motors after they collapsed.

Weil opened its London office in 1996, primarily to service a private equity client now known as HM Capital. As Weil's second largest outpost, London serves as its European hub. The firm gained its City presence by luring pockets of prominent partners from competitors, but now hopes to "*grow in a sustained and organic way.*" Senior partner Mark Soundy told us that part of the strategy is facing the "*key challenge to make up partners internally. Over 50% of our current partners were, but that's not high enough.*" In terms of work, Soundy says the private equity practice is "*relatively mature, but we would like to take it to another level.*" International public M&A is another one to watch, as the office is doing more work for the investment banks in an international context. Bankruptcy is important to any Weil office, but London recently lost the head of its department and so growth plans there are on hold in the short term. Soundy hopes to see litigation expand over the next few years, with other specialist areas following.

Manges munchies

Although private equity is its mainstay, the London office proved its versatility by rolling up its sleeves during the recession and taking on a massive role in both the Lehman and GM restructurings. The London team co-ordinated all non-US issues relating to Lehman's Chapter 11 process, ranging from filing applications to derivative portfolios to employment to proprietary IT. The group played a similar role in the GM restructuring, advising on the impact on its European businesses. Grabbing another headline, the firm helped AIG in the sale of its American Life Insurance Company, one of many in a series of sell-offs designed to help the insurer repay its substantial outstanding balance to the US government. The London office has also developed a strong corporate media niche.

Given the economy, Weil London has been able to combine its strength in private equity and restructuring to advise on significant private equity portfolio company restructurings. Lawyers represented Lion Capital and The Blackstone Group in one of the biggest private equity exits of 2009: the sale of Orangina Schweppes to its Japanese rival Suntory. It advised Lion Capital once again when US snacks group Diamond Foods acquired Kettle Chips. In 2010, the firm advised on Central Europe's largest ever IPO – the listing of Polish insurance company PZU, worth £1.7bn. It also oversaw Advent International's £500m acquisition of DFS and £190m acquisition of Xanify.

Chambers UK rankings

Banking & Finance	Private Equity
Capital Markets	Restructuring/Insolvency
Corporate/M&A	Tax

Trainees spend their (mandatory) corporate seat "*primarily keeping people up to date with what's going on, drafting agreements, keeping in touch with overseas counsel and keeping documents organised.*" They appreciate "*the broad range of work*" with "*good exposure to foreign counsel*" and "*good discrete tasks we can take the initiative on.*"

From Lehman to Littlewoods

A seat in the general finance department – the firm's merged securitisation and banking team – is also mandatory. Securitisation lawyers have been busy on the derivatives front, while their colleagues have been assisting sponsors in the private equity arena in raising capital for acquisitions. It recently represented Barclays in the restructuring of Bridgepoint's portfolio company, 1st Credit. Trainees described their finance stints as "*very document-heavy*" and noted how busy the team was. "*Some* [juniors] *can bill up to 250 or 260 hours a month, and a few did 300 for two months in a row.*"

It's clear that "*if you come to Weil in London, transactional work should be what you're about.*" Some trainees saw contentious seats as a haven within the office, however, and raved about the department's "*positive and dynamic environment*" where "*you never feel like your head is on the block.*" "*It's all high-profile stuff: Lehman, Iceland, AIG.*" The department also gets stuck into more local cases, representing Littlewoods in a High Court VAT case, for example. Trainees had good things to say about the competition team too. The firm sends those who prefer a transaction-heavy training contract on a litigation course at College of Law. Its smaller size allows more "*responsibility and visibility,*" and even the opportunity to take occasional trips to Brussels. Proving it's an area on the up, competition took on its first qualifier in 2010, and litigation took on two. Weil also brought on Juliet Blanch, who previously headed up McDermott Will & Emery's international disputes group. Besides that, the proximity of Weil's new office to the Commercial Courts should also aid further growth.

We discussed seat allocation and the qualification process with trainees. The basic gist of things is that while some stick to the formal process of applying for seats through HR, others pitch themselves directly to partners. Consequently, some sources felt: "*It's all about who you can charm and what strings you can pull.*" When we asked the firm about this, it indicated that it had at one point considered upfront allocation at the start of the training contract, but thought it would be even more problematic. Trainees do have plenty of opportunities to voice their concerns at various meetings with HR, but trying to accommodate both the trainees' requests and the firm's business needs is complicated. There were also complaints that the firm had shelved overseas secondments during the economic downturn. While naturally this was a great disappointment to some, it has to be said that this is not an issue that affected Weil alone, and some overseas seats (Paris, and probably New York soon) have made their return. For now, the firm makes the point that London trainees are first and foremost recruited to work in and assist the operations of the London office. Both the firm and trainees had more to say on these issues, so visit our website for the full skinny.

The 'for the London office' mentality does reinforce the idea that this branch stands on its own two feet and is certainly not an American enclave. Over 90% of its solicitors are UK-qualified. It can't be ignored that this is a US firm, and in many ways this is worth highlighting, not least because of its efforts in the areas of pro bono and diversity. Weil is "*quite big on pro bono*" and "*trainees get involved a lot and are in many ways the backbone of it.*" The firm plays to its strengths and helps private equity ventures that invest in social enterprises and sustainable property, but there are also contributions to the work of Battersea Legal Advice Centre and the Citizens Advice Bureau at the Royal Courts of Justice. Weil also helps run the LawWorks Community Business Clinic, which provides free commercial advice to social enterprises in deprived areas of London. It additionally sends one trainee to the Bar Pro Bono Unit every Friday.

Weil recently advised UNICEF UK on a pro bono basis on the drafting of the agreement between them, Endemol and ITV for the broadcast of the 2010 Soccer Aid celebrity/pro football game between England and the Rest of the World. On the charities side, the firm holds pub quizzes to raise money for Richard's House Children's Hospice and visits local schools as part of a CSR programme. "*Everyone gets involved*" and each solicitor is expected to rack up at least 50 pro bono hours per year. "*Clearly there's a hierarchy of work and fee payers do take precedence, but pro bono clients are treated with just as much importance.*" Weil was the first firm to have a full-time pro bono co-ordinator, and there is a day-to-day co-ordinator along with a pro bono and charities committee in the London office.

Weil you were sleeping

This is not a place for people who require handholding or spoon-feeding; trainees need to be robust with loads of drive and initiative. "*Rather than them sitting you down and explaining everything in detail, they ask you to give it a go first.*" Long nights do happen. Trainees admitted to "*staggering out at 3am,*" but insisted that their schedules were no worse than their magic circle peers. "*Your character can really be tested when you're leaving in the early hours for two weeks straight. Everyone can deal with a late night once or twice in a row, but when it's two consecutive weeks under pressure it can be quite tough. But when the deal closes, there's that huge sense of elation, like you've just finished your exams.*"

Lean staffing is common. "*There are deals where there won't even be a partner – it will be a senior associate, a mid-level, maybe a junior and a trainee. They squeeze a lot out of everyone – you get to know mid-level people who are worked to death, or literally until they go home sick.*" For those best suited to the firm, great responsibility feels like a blessing as they get to work "*beyond* [their] *level*" on "*quite big-ticket stuff. You do have to work hard, but it's great to be involved and alongside the big names.*" Others found their workload "*not challenging in complexity, just daunting in volume.*" That said, all our sources appreciated "*not being chained to the photocopier.*"

More goosebumps than R.L. Stine

In case you haven't picked up on it by now, Weil is not for the weak. Its recruitment campaign does enough to tell you that, with its ominous slogan of 'Do something that scares you' alongside keywords like 'challenging' and 'intense'. This all comes back to the idea of not being afraid to take on work beyond your presumed level. "*People aren't afraid to give you what you can take. The responsibility can be scary at times. Whenever you are faced with something you've never done before there's that sense of unease and discomfort, but you become more used to it. It is scary, but you just have to be someone who is willing to embrace that mindset. You can't stay under the radar here – everybody knows everybody, so you will be in the spotlight.*" If you "*have a genuine interest in getting deals done;*" if your reward comes simply through "*knowing that you're being tested and doing work beyond your level;*" if you can fill the unforgiving minute with 60 seconds' worth of distance run, yours is the earth, and everything that's in it. You'll probably fit in at Weil just fine, too.

There are more tangible perks than the warm glow of professional fulfilment, including "*working in a large corporate environment with a prestigious brand name*" and a sizeable salary that hits £90,000 upon qualification. In 2010, seven out of ten qualifying trainees stayed at the firm, all gaining positions in their preferred departments.

All shook up

"*If someone were to want a really social place I'd say go elsewhere,*" one trainee advised. It's not that people are unfriendly, it's more that they are busy! Weil's social scene is modest – "*there aren't really that many nights out*" – but trainees do get a drinks budget twice a year. There's also the Christmas party and annual charity pub quiz, which we heard very good things about as apparently a few partners donned Elvis costumes for the karaoke round of the quiz. The whole office and their families were recently invited to a summer party at managing partner Mike Francies' house. Top marks to him: not only was there a barbecue but also sushi, crepes and other "*amazing food choices.*" And let's not forget the band, face painters, superimposing photo booths, bouncy castle and a giant inflatable human football table. When they're not impersonating The King, putting their face on Superman's body or getting strapped in for life-size foosball, the "*vast majority of partners have their doors open and are happy for you to pop in if you have a question.*"

Speaking of those doors, on a little reconnaissance mission to Weil's old Moorgate home, we noticed many were adorned with entertaining posters, often football-related. Apparently Francies is always up for a chat about the beautiful game, and he and other seniors are reportedly "*very good at being appreciative of the work you do and saying thank you.*" We hope to see the posters in Weil's shiny new office in the Rolls Building on Fetter Lane, which it will share with HM Courts Service.

And finally...

Weil trainees have to be ready to jump in at the deep end of the corporate pool and swim power laps. Rewards: a mega-salary, top deals and working with the best in the biz.

- **Choose the right firm:** One of the biggest impediments to people moving successfully from a junior to a mid-level role is developing a genuine interest in the area in which they work. This requires great stamina. In order to do it for more than a couple of years, you must be interested in what you are doing, otherwise it's impossible.

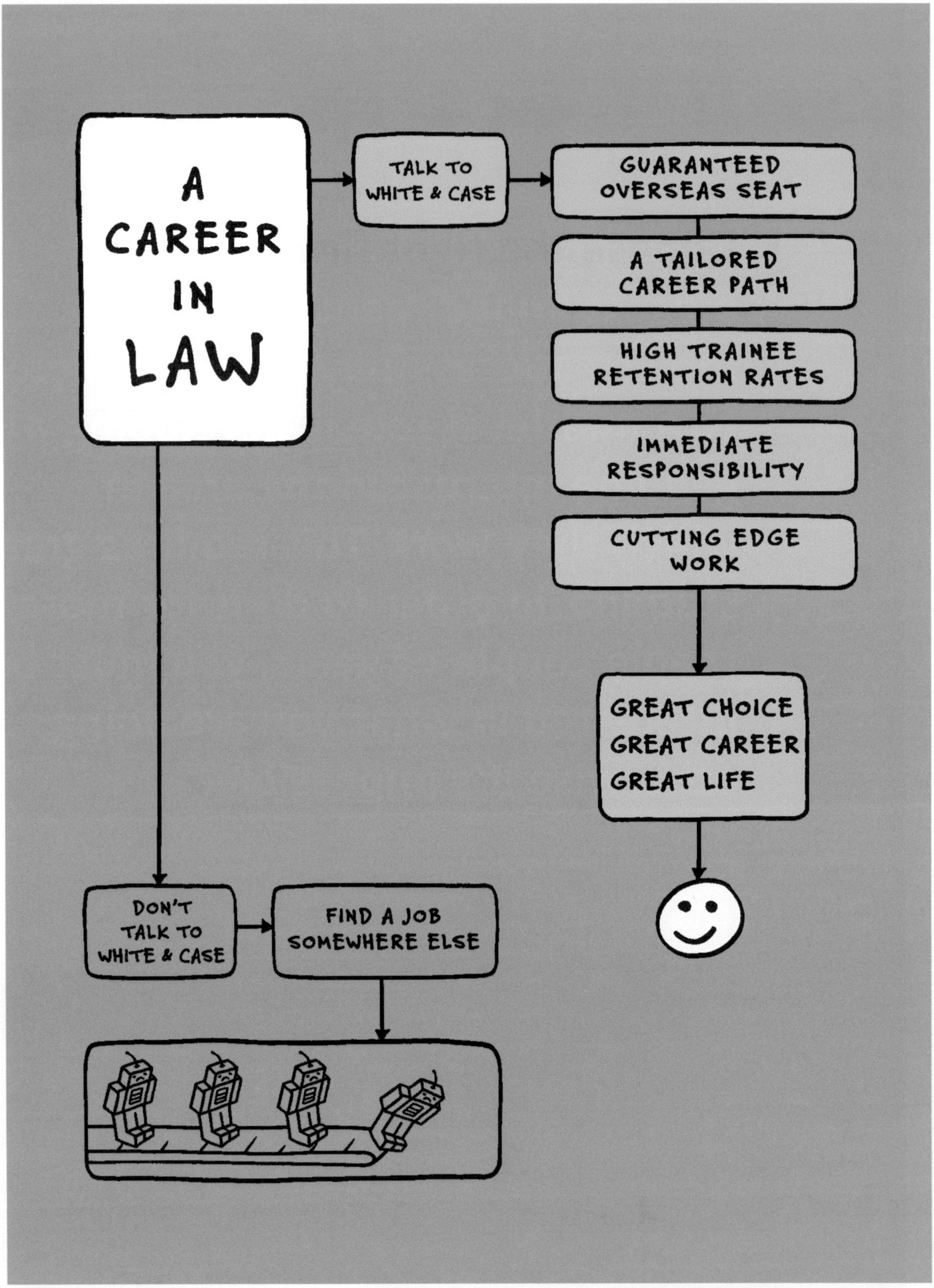
A CAREER IN LAW
TALK TO WHITE & CASE
GUARANTEED OVERSEAS SEAT
A TAILORED CAREER PATH
HIGH TRAINEE RETENTION RATES
IMMEDIATE RESPONSIBILITY
CUTTING EDGE WORK
GREAT CHOICE
GREAT CAREER
GREAT LIFE
DON'T TALK TO WHITE & CASE
FIND A JOB SOMEWHERE ELSE

White & Case LLP

The facts

Location: London

Number of UK partners/solicitors: 55/187

Total number of trainees: 62

Seats: 4x6 months

Alternative seats: Overseas seats

Extras: Pro bono – A4ID, LawWorks and more; language classes

On chambersstudent.co.uk
- How to get into White & Case
- Recent developments in the London office
- The history of W&C

A global firm of titanic sprawl and ambition, White & Case London has been navigating choppier waters than most. Have the storm clouds cleared?

No pain, no gain?

White & Case has had it rough lately. The international giant underwent two rounds of redundancies in November 2008 and March 2009, with around 100 fee earners and staff let go in London alone. Meanwhile, a spate of partner exits that continued into the first quarter of 2010 hit the firm's London banking practice and its Middle Eastern operations. The latter departures came in the wake of poor financial results: global gross revenue dropped 11% to $1.3bn in 2009/10.

The firm has been on the ground on London since 1971, and London managing partner Oliver Brettle tells us that it "*remains totally committed to this market.*" Indeed, the London finance group is a lynchpin in W&C's hugely successful global business. A large proportion of the office's rankings in *Chambers UK* are for finance-related matters, including banking, Islamic finance, capital markets, trade and asset finance, and project finance. W&C frequently plays opposite the big dogs of the magic circle on finance deals, particularly those relating to energy projects. It recently joined Clifford Chance and Linklaters in working on a £3.5bn deal to fund and build a pipeline that will transport gas from Russia to Europe. This is just one of many enormous, multi-jurisdictional transactions on which W&C lawyers work.

With a newly beefed-up Moscow office playing its part, you can expect to see an even greater concentration of Russian-related business, particularly in relation to international arbitration. W&C has outposts in far-flung places like Almaty, Johannesburg and São Paolo, and these are each indicative of its focus on emerging markets and growing economies, particularly those with an abundance of natural resources. Equally revealing is the firm's 20-year presence in Eastern Europe, where it now has six offices and plenty of lawyers scooping *Chambers Europe* rankings. All told, W&C has 36 offices in 25 countries, only five of which are in its original home nation – the USA. The firm's history is quite an interesting one and explains much of its persona: read more on our website.

White & Basics

Trainees complete four six-month seats. Most trainees sit in a room with their supervisor and take assignments from them, but work can also be sourced from others in the department. "*It just depends on how entrepreneurial you are.*" The allocation system is straightforward: trainees indicate their first, second and third preferences, and the firm "*does its best to make sure you get what you want,*" a trainee explained. Preferred supervisors may also be indicated if they specialise in an area of practice that particularly piques a trainee's interest. Trainees generally get the seats they want, but occasionally have to settle for a second or third-choice seat. Any disappointment is almost certainly washed away by the guarantee of a seat abroad, which is something that leads many trainees to choose the firm in the first place.

Because of its importance to the firm, a finance seat is a compulsory part of the training contract and some trainees take more than one. Around half of the finance division is made up of lawyers in the energy, infrastruc-

Chambers UK rankings

Asset Finance	Employment
Banking & Finance	Energy & Natural Resources
Banking Litigation	Financial Services
Capital Markets	Information Technology
Commodities	Investment Funds
Construction	Projects
Corporate/M&A	Restructuring/Insolvency
Data Protection	Telecommunications
Dispute Resolution	Transport

ture, projects and asset finance (EIPAF) practice. The other half focuses on more traditional bank finance and capital markets deals. Of late, much of the banking work has taken on a restructuring flavour. Recent matters included advising German bank West LB on the $1.7bn restructuring of Kuwait-based Global Investment House, which manages clients' wealth by investing in the Middle East, Africa and Asia.

Whether sitting in EIPAF or the banking and capital markets teams, trainees do much the same set of tasks. They collate and manage the conditions precedent on which transactions rely; they prepare 'bibles' containing copies of all deal documents (the job is "*tedious*"); they proofread, research, draft memos and make Form 395 registrations at Companies House; and they correspond with lawyers in other countries. Those in EIPAF encounter "*lots of oil and gas infrastructure projects in Russia*" or aircraft financing for clients like mid-market lender CIT Group. The projects team is "*very hard-working and expects trainees to function independently and to take on a large volume of work without asking too many questions. It's not as friendly as bank finance or corporate.*" Those concentrating on asset finance matters enjoy "*working on transactions from start to finish,*" even though "*grunt work seems more prevalent here than in other groups.*"

Banking and capital markets trainees can expect responsibility "*commensurate with or even exceeding*" their job title. Said one source: "*You can get involved as much as you like.*" Trainees here spend their time liaising with overseas lawyers and those on the other side of the deal; they draft board minutes, legal opinions and transaction documents; and once they have the requisite experience they can "*run simple transactions and negotiate amendments and changes to documents.*" The hours can be intense but we're pleased to report that, in contrast to feedback in recent years, the atmosphere is now said to be supportive. "*Given the backdrop of the redundancies and departures, it would have been easy for us to be neglected, but we haven't been,*" said one interviewee. What's more, the department makes "*a significant effort to bring everyone up to speed. Every two weeks we have a session on a different aspect of the practice,*" added another. Credit for these all-around good vibes is given to banking head Magdalene Bayim-Adomako and partner Mark Glengarry. "*They're two of the most decent and genuine people I know,*" said one admiring source. After a phase of heavy staff and partner losses, the team recently welcomed two new partners and, according to London managing partner Oliver Brettle, is looking to recruit more "*heavy-hitting, market-leading bank finance partners.*"

Ideal for adventurers

Corporate, though not considered a flagship practice, is a popular seat offering "*a real smorgasbord*" of work, although restructuring has been the dominant activity of late. Expect "*quite a lot of dogsbody work*" and "*quite a lot of client contact.*" When not at client meetings with a partner, trainees knuckle down to plenty of drafting tasks. Dogsbody work aside, they rather like this relatively small team. It may not remain small for long, though: "*In London, specifically, we've made clear that we need to further strengthen our corporate and M&A practice to build on our emerging markets work,*" admits Brettle.

The "*perennially popular*" litigation seat attracts people, despite the inevitability of "*the dreaded bundling.*" Attending court is always a treat, be it "*shadowing and note taking*" or making small applications. And the bundling chores, dreaded as they may be, have an upside: "*Because you know the documents inside-out, you become a key point of reference for the team.*" The other thing to note is that junior associates "*muck in to get things done when we're hellishly busy.*" The small size of the team ensures "*exposure to partners every day.*" The group has about 20 lawyers and, according to Brettle, "*is expanding quite markedly.*" It handles complex, multi-jurisdictional disputes, generally relating to banking, energy, infrastructure, funds and sovereign entities. Lawyers recently advised Turkish conglomerate Cukurova Holdings in the Eastern Caribbean Supreme Court in the British Virgin Islands on a case concerning a $1.3bn loan facility from the Russian Alfa group. A "*very big part*" of the disputes section is international arbitration, and there is also a dedicated construction disputes team. Both are ranked in *Chambers UK*.

"*All seats are pretty okay, but the overseas seat is amazing.*" Every trainee does one, and on rare occasions two. W&C has outposts in the usual legal hubs of Hong Kong, Paris, Moscow, Abu Dhabi and New York (which is very popular with trainees), but it also offers seats in some less likely locations – Kazakhstan's largest city, Almaty, for example, or Johannesburg (where W&C is the only firm to send a trainee). For a complete list of the locations that can be visited, see page 536. Client secondments are available post-qualification. The firm's attitude is to "*push you to get international experience.*" If staying put in the UK for the entire two years is a priority for you, then this is really not the right firm. W&C is all about international clients, deals and experiences, and there are "*examples of people qualifying into the offices where they did their overseas seat.*"

The internationalists

Successive trainee intakes have grown exponentially in size over the past decade. Inevitably, this means the level of a trainee's individual day-to-day involvement with a training partner is not at the same high level as it once was. The programme is, however, still small enough for trainees to be "*on a first-name basis with Shahnaz and Lara in HR. They're great,*" a source reported; "*they make a significant effort to reach out to us.*" Training opportunities are abundant and appraisals are carried out twice per seat. The hours vary according to workflow, but trainees tell us an average day begins around 9am and ends at 7.30pm. At the scary end, when "*things get crazy,*" the hours are jaw-droppingly long. "*In the past 11 weeks, I've done 790 hours,*" related one interviewee. You do the maths.

W&C has an eat-what-you-kill approach to its business – that is to say partners' earnings are dependent on the business they bring in, rather than on their seniority. "*The American stereotype is that you work horrendously long hours in a dog-eat-dog environment,*" said one source. While we have heard reports from trainees and juniors past that this is indeed how they felt, more recent interviewees did not see things the same way. "*I don't care for that assessment, or for those who speculate on it. I joined White & Case because of the people,*" said one. Trainees come to the London office from all over the world, and certainly from beyond Oxbridge. For more on the recruitment process and the firm's preferred candidates, see our website.

As for W&C's American roots, trainees describe the London-New York relationship as "*strangely absent. The London office tries very hard to maintain its Englishness and not be run out of New York, and it does a good job of it.*" One interviewee went so far as to add: "*I'm not sure New York likes that very much.*" Others thought the London office was a bit "*neglected*" by US management, and that it should be "*more of a player on the world stage.*" When asked for comment, Oliver Brettle insisted, "*London is very much a player on the world stage,*" and pointed to the importance of English law in international transactions.

In Bruges

In a "*concerted effort to do the whole 'team spirit' thing,*" the troops rallied for the firm's annual football and volleyball 'World Cup' in Turkey in 2010. London trainees also take part in a two-night retreat with their EU counterparts in the Belgian city of Bruges. They are quite likely to then encounter each other when working on deals. "*I've been very impressed with the level of interconnectivity between offices,*" said one source. "*I've even been on the phone with one of the Swedish trainees I met in Bruges!*" Friday drinks are usually held at local haunts The Phoenix, The Rocket ("*its only redeeming feature is that it's across the street*") or the more upscale Pacific Oriental. Litigation trainees went on a department-organised ski trip to Engelberg in Switzerland, while some others took the Eurostar to Paris to play football against client BNP Paribas.

W&C London has "*quite a committed programme*" of pro bono activities. As trainees rightly point out, "*it's such a big part of the culture in New York,*" and it's being pushed in London too. Trainees can get involved with the Citizens Advice Bureau ("*you can turn up with an associate and give advice to people with small claims, evictions and so on*") or provide legal assistance to charitable organisations. NQs are encouraged to apply for placements with Advocates for International Development and "*anyone can suggest an initiative.*" There are also plenty of community projects, such as mentoring A level students.

Historically, W&C has had a high retention rate and it maintained this record in 2010 when 25 out of 27 qualifiers took jobs with the firm, with six going into EIPAF and four into bank finance. One typical trainee moan is that "*they do leave it quite late to tell you if you've been kept on and where you're going.*"

And finally...

White & Case will suit outgoing, internationally minded individuals who have an interest in the world of global finance and don't need handholding.

Wiggin LLP

The facts

Location: Cheltenham, London

Number of UK partners/solicitors: 16/22

Total number of trainees: 3

Seats: 4x6 months

Alternative seats: Secondments

On chambersstudent.co.uk
- How to get into Wiggin
- The lowdown on Cheltenham
- The Digital Economy Act

Wiggin's base in a converted cinema on Cheltenham's historic Promenade is fitting, given its full immersion in the world of media and entertainment.

Channel surfing

As the country claws its way out of recession (or tries to), over in wealthy Cheltenham an "*injection of positivity*" has seen Wiggin become massively invested in re-invigorating its training contract. It's put in place added mentors and a higher salary (first-years £32,000; second-years £36,000). The firm has also changed which seats are available, nixing time in unpopular property in favour of a media-only four-seat rotation. To find out why, read our interview with training partner Simon Baggs online. Wiggin's strategic outlook is also being renewed. "*We want to be the best at what we do – indispensable to the point where media clients can't afford not to use us.*" All this makes for "*quite exciting times*" at the firm, which trainees say has "*a tangible momentum behind it.*"

In the world of film production, Wiggin advises major US studios (Twentieth Century Fox, Columbia Pictures, Miramax...) on their UK and European productions and also acts for some leading players in the independent film finance sector. Recent production undertakings include *The Imaginarium of Doctor Parnassus*, which involved dealing with the repercussions of Heath Ledger's death during production; *Gulliver's Travels*, starring frat packer Jack Black; and *The Voyage of the Dawn Treader*, third instalment of the Narnia series. Wiggin is active in TV production too, recently handling a big-budget series for HBO called *Game of Thrones*. Marvel Studios used the finance team in relation to investments in *Iron Man II* and *Thor*, and it also helped with the financings of *Never Let Me Go* and *Eagle of the Ninth*, which features heartthrob Channing Tatum. In short, scoring a seat in the team "*is great, and the client list is out of this world.*"

The broadcast team has been busy for NHK (Japan's BBC equivalent) on commercial and regulatory matters as it rolls out international services in the EU. The group has also tackled licensing matters for ITV in anticipation of the digital switchover. Although there's "*lots of TV-oriented work, there's also quite a bit of gambling, gaming and internet-slash-software-y work*" undertaken by the department. "*It's an extremely technical area,*" but luckily "*everyone in the department is great because they detail what's going on for you, even if you're only playing a minor role, say, drafting or researching.*"

While it's not likely you'd seek out Wiggin for corporate deal experience, a seat in this department is almost a given. Trainees say it's a great place to start as "*you'll learn the things you need to know as a solicitor,*" including "*a good amount of drafting experience.*"

World in motion

Wiggin's music department has advised Napster, Warner Bros. and Virgin Media on licensing and music services, and the BPI on rights protection. On the talent side, the likes of New Order and The Feeling have come knocking. And when training partner Simon Baggs isn't busy having trainees over for dinner, he's lead adviser on the British record industry's approach to online piracy – a hot topic given the introduction of the Digital Economy Act (more about that online too). As the BPI is such a mainstay

Chambers UK rankings

Defamation/Reputation Management	Licensing
	Media & Entertainment
Intellectual Property	Sports Law

client, Wiggin has a regular six-month secondment to its Westminster Bridge HQ and, unsurprisingly, it gets rave reviews. Whether "*dashing around Earls Court getting last-minute clearance for song samples at The BRITs*" or "*sitting in on meetings about all the big matters of the day,*" trainees loved being "*plopped right into the heart of the music industry.*" The firm owns a two-bedroom flat near the BPI, where secondees and other lawyers travelling in and out of Wiggin's small London office can stay.

Wiggin is also active in the publishing sector, with clients including Bauer Consumer Media (*Heat*, *Grazia*, *FHM*, *Q*, *Kerrang*); IPC (*NME*, *Marie Claire*, *Loaded*); HarperCollins; Random House; Oxford University Press and Times Newspapers. The firm was recently asked to defend *Grazia* against a privacy claim made by Victoria Beckham – the case concerned the degree of privacy to which über-celebs are entitled. Trainees can experience cases like these during their litigation stint – described as "*off-the-scale brilliant.*" The defamation group is "*only a three-person team so you really have to step up to the plate and do your part, but they really give you help when you need it. They make working hard fun, as cheesy as that sounds. It's a really tough seat, but opening The Guardian and seeing what you're working on right there is pretty awesome.*"

Sports law is a relatively recent focus for the firm, but the department is growing. In 2009 it assisted Perform Group with the ground-breaking Internet-only distribution of England's World Cup qualifier against Ukraine. The team also serves as the exclusive media advisers to Man U's legal panel and worked with UEFA in relation to the international licensing and distribution of the documentary *Kill the Referee*.

Hi-fidelity

Everyone's in agreement on the quality of the training experience so the next important question is: how does Cheltenham life compare with London? The training experience will largely be based in the 112,000-inhabitant Cotswold town. Luckily, we know a fair bit about the place so you can read our review online. Trainees tell us: "*The hours are comparable with London: we work ten or 12-hour days* [or longer if dealing with clients in Los Angeles], *but it helps a lot when your commute is a ten-minute walk across two parks.*" Another "*huge selling point*" is the laid-back dress code. "*We just wear jeans or whatever else we want, within reason. When people are really busy and working hard it helps you feel more relaxed.*" The Wiggin office itself is far from the stuffy City standard: there are bright colours and signed film posters everywhere. Office traditions include a Friday drinks trolley paired with the 'Friday night playlist' – staff all take a turn creating a playlist of five tunes everyone knows and five they don't but probably should.

The Wiggsters "*tend to be outgoing people with quite a bit of personality. You fit in better if you can switch in and out of professional mode – like going to make a cup of tea and having a few jokes and then knuckling down to work,*" one explained. "*Lots of us go out after work and unwind without actually talking about work. It's fairly easy to organise a night out and there are always e-mails going around for gigs and festivals.*" Five-a-side team The Wiggin Warriors is apparently "*having a bit of a golden period right now*" and has topped the (Cheltenham) Premier League a fair few times. While the boys have football to keep them fit, many of the girls attend spin classes.

"*There's certainly a good vibe, but at the same time it's still a law firm, and a very good, ambitious law firm.*" Remember: "*You can't think it's an easy ride just because we're in Cheltenham. There are incredibly high standards to meet all the time. As a trainee you've got to keep them.*" Meeting the firm's high standards is crucial when it comes to bagging a qualification job, but so is your attitude to building a life in the Cotswolds. Over the years, Wiggin's NQ retention rates have moved up and down depending on these two factors, and in 2010 one of two qualifiers stayed on.

And finally...

"We're niche. We're cutting-edge. We're the best at what we do and we have a lot of fun getting there." Wiggin presents a really unique opportunity, so it's understandable that recruiters will scrutinise applicants closely and want to be 100% sure a candidate is right for them.

Winckworth Sherwood

The facts

Location: London, Oxford, Chelmsford

Number of UK partners/solicitors: 37/53

Total number of trainees: 8

Seats: 4x6 months

Alternative seats: None

On chambersstudent.co.uk
- How to get into Winckworth
- Winckworth's history
- Working for public sector clients

You may have been told never to talk about religion or politics in polite company, but at Winckworth Sherwood you might just find yourself doing both. What other London firm can offer you a seat in ecclesiastical law?

That would be an ecumenical matter

This firm offers a range of work at the crossroads of the public and private sectors. As well as acting as a parliamentary agent, the firm deals with social housing, employment, property, planning and licensing matters, and also has a niche ecclesiastical law department. "*To put it grandly, our work revolves around church and state,*" managing partner Roger Fitton told us. Clients of the former group include the Church of England, the Westminster Roman Catholic Diocese and the Christian-Muslim Forum; the latter represents the Department for Transport, the City of London Corporation and the Northern Ireland Assembly.

The firm continues to expand and innovate. In 2008, Winckworth welcomed prominent social housing partners from Bircham Dyson Bell and Prince Evans and more recently it grew its employment team with four lawyers from Lincoln's Inn firm Dawsons. Although the firm did make a few redundancies during the recession, its ambition to expand was reflected by the move to new, larger offices in 2009.

All around the clock tower

Although there are minor outposts in Oxford and Chelmsford, the training scheme is based in London. All departments take trainees, so the unusual list of available seats adds up to: parliamentary agency; planning; housing and regeneration; private client; ecclesiastical law; education; employment; property and licensing; institutional property; and dispute resolution. Trainees don't choose their first seat, but after that they can discuss their interests with the training partner, both in meetings and informally. Special interests and prior exerience are taken into account, and we found that trainees were generally happy with the seat allocation system.

Parliamentary agency practice is one of Winckworth's "*unique selling points.*" Agents are licensed by Parliament to draft, promote and oppose Private Bills, that is to say, pieces of legislation promoted by third parties to obtain benefits or powers. Winckworth's parliamentary agency group deals chiefly with the planning of major domestic infrastructure projects. For example, it is advising BAA on a new Reading-Heathrow-Waterloo rail link and helping the government with "*permissions for the Crossrail project.*" In the past, the team worked on the enabling legislation for the Channel Tunnel and its rail link. Other clients include the Association of British Ports, the National Audit Office and the National Trust. Trainees undertake "*difficult drafting and research tasks, together with litigation and adversarial tasks.*"

Winckworth began representing charitable institutions over 100 years ago and has acted for the Church of England since the 1930s. The firm also assists a decent number of mid-sized charities. Part of the firm's charity work revolves around the Church and other religious organisations. A seat in the ecclesiastical department could include "*dealing*

Chambers UK rankings

Charities	Planning
Education	Real Estate Litigation
Local Government	Social Housing
Parliamentary & Public Affairs	

with defamation suits, technological matters like the placing of a mobile phone mast on a church, data protection work and Canon Law." Client contact is common here and involves meetings with "*priests in dog collars and church commercial figureheads.*" The work is highly varied and covers everything from the "*peculiar employment arrangements in the church*" to "*someone who fell through the floor of a clock tower and is suing for breach of health and safety.*" An offshoot of church work, the education team has made a name for itself representing diocesan education boards, local authorities and foundations. Already ranked in *Chambers UK*, the team is expanding and looking to represent more universities and colleges.

One of the most popular seats is private client. The focus here is on family and matrimonial law, and trainee work includes "*making applications in front of judges, arranging Powers of Attorney, writing wills and attending court for matrimonial hearings.*" If you're in luck, you might even get to try a spot of advocacy.

Traineesaurus rex

All this talk of church and state hides the fact that much of Winckworth's practice is property-related, and there are a large number of seats available in this area. An institutional property seat is "*essentially commercial property but for big institutional clients.*" To give a couple of examples, there are retail store acquisitions for T-Mobile and representing the Roman Catholic Archdiocese of Northampton on the redevelopment of its investments in Slough Town Centre. Trainees feel "*very much a member of the team*" and are kept busy with numerous tasks such as "*ordering property searches and attending auctions.*" There's a little light property litigation on the side.

Sainsbury's is an important client of the property and licensing department. "*We look after a huge database of their alcohol licences,*" a trainee explained. The licensing team also deals with one-off venues, such as the Parklife event space on London's Oxford Street, which recently hosted the Dinosaurs Unleashed exhibition. As well as dealing with plenty of paperwork, trainees are exposed to contentious matters in the magistrates' courts. This tendency to touch on the contentious is a recurring theme in most seats.

In the housing and regeneration seat, "*we act for mainly large house builders in developments, acquiring the land and drafting lease agreements.*" Clients include several London boroughs and Barratt Homes, which the firm assists with various projects in Docklands and other parts of Greater London. Regeneration assignments include planning and construction matters relating to developments like the new Dalston Junction complex in East London.

Solid and respectful

Winckworth's new offices near London Bridge sit in the shadows of Southwark Cathedral, a major client, and are close to Kaplan Law School. Trainees love that "*whenever you look outside there is some fantastic scenery.*" They sit with partners or senior solicitors in glass-fronted offices and tell us: "*You do feel the eyes going through the back of your head, but it focuses the mind and stops you wandering off on idle Google searches!*"

The firm is not at all "*aggressive*" or "*alpha male,*" but rather a "*friendly*" and "*normal*" kind of place. The varied clientele means that some people sense slight culture differences between departments so, for example, "*ecclesiastical and parliamentary are more traditional.*" Additionally, these teams, along with private client, are described as "*solid and respectful. There's more pearls and cashmere. The commercial, housing, property and licensing departments are more modern and progressive.*" "*A smaller number of trainees than perhaps the firm's size would merit*" means "*there's no politicking and positioning*" to get ahead. "*As long as you do a good job and are reasonably sociable you'll be fine.*" The firm has a strong record for keeping on qualifying trainees and retained all four in 2010.

The social scene "*has improved since moving to London Bridge.*" Last year's Christmas party at nearby Vinopolis was "*black tie and pretty swanky.*" There are cricket and football teams and the social committee is always pushing for more events. "*Last week we went to see Legally Blonde, and there was a pub quiz a few months ago.*" A drinks party takes place once a month and several trainees agreed that the lower frequency of social events "*keeps them special.*"

And finally...

If you are interested in parliamentary, ecclesiastical or social housing work – or if you think you might be – why not give this interesting firm some closer attention?

Withers LLP

The facts

Location: London

Number of UK partners/solicitors: 60/109

Total number of trainees: 32

Seats: 4x6 months

Alternative seats: Milan, client secondments

Extras: Pro Bono – CAB at the Principal Registry

On chambersstudent.co.uk
- How to get into Withers
- Unconventional literary heroines
- Landmark divorce cases

"*If you're interested in private client and family law, there aren't any other firms with this calibre of clients and international work,*" say trainees, and yet such high praise for one strand of the firm's practice shouldn't mask the broader training opportunities here.

Classical funk mash up

Withers has been a name in the UK legal profession since 1896. There's an interesting timeline graphic on the firm's website highlighting some of its more influential characters over the years. Why not take a look? Its most recent decade is of particular interest, and during this time the firm has gone through "*a huge period of expansion*" that looks to be far from over. "*Because we don't have all our eggs in one basket, we weren't stopped in our steps during the recession,*" training partner Daniel Isaac explained. The firm did what most of its peers couldn't during the downturn – it made the "*gutsy*" decision to open another office, in the British Virgin Islands of all places. "*We're not at the end,*" Isaac continued; "*there is definitely going to be further growth.*" So, before we go any further, let's do a quick roll call: Withers has more than 670 people across eight (soon to be nine) offices in six countries. The locations are each centres of wealth: London; Geneva; Milan; New York; New Haven and Greenwich in Connecticut; Hong Kong and now the BVI. All have an abundance of moneyed individuals in need of good advice as to how best to protect, invest and pass on their wealth. At the time of our research, Withers confirmed that it was to open another new office but wouldn't give any details. Just prior to going to press, news came of an interesting association with a financial services advisory firm in Shanghai.

Expansion is also on the cards for some of the firm's practice groups, particularly in the contentious sphere. The firm maintains an "*absolute commitment to litigation*" and tells us "*it's really growing.*" Withers may be best known as a top-notch private client firm that represents a quarter of the *Sunday Times'* Rich List and a significant proportion of the world's wealthiest families, but don't assume that's all it does. As one trainee put it: "*All that private client work lies alongside very straightforward commercial departments, albeit with the funky client edge.*"

They speak Prada!

Or, more accurately, Withers speaks Benetton, Jade Jagger, Luella, Matthew Williamson, MaxMara, Moschino, Valentino, Vivienne Westwood and Vera Wang, among many, many other names that any well-versed shopoholic would dream about. Recent highlights include advising Bono and his wife Ali Hewson on an investment by LVMH (behind Louis Vuitton, Fendi, Dior, Pucci, Givenchy, Marc Jacobs) into their ethical fashion brand Edun, and advising Natalie Massenet, founder of Net-a-Porter, on the company's £350m sale to Swiss luxury goods group Richemont. "*If you're set on doing big M&A with FTSE 100 companies then this wouldn't be the place for you,*" training partner Daniel Isaac warned. "*What we can do here is give you very good corporate experience, but we can also show you what it's like working with individuals, entrepreneurs and charities. You may well end up where you thought you would, but you could be some-*

Chambers UK rankings

Administrative & Public Law	Employment
Agriculture & Rural Affairs	Family/Matrimonial
Charities	Fraud
Defamation/Reputation Management	Intellectual Property
	Private Client
	Professional Negligence

where radically different." Who needs the FTSE when you have fashion?

Most of those who end up at Withers are drawn in by the emphasis on the individual. "*I found that when you've met the clients and you can really see their anxiety the work feels much more real,*" one trainee told us. "*You really need to know the ins and outs of their lives to understand how to structure their wealth,*" another added. The firm really makes an effort to tailor its practices and services to the clients, and it's often the case that clients use several different departments within the firm. Divorces, for example, can often involve contentious trusts issues. Wealth structuring might lead to the setting up or acquisition of a business or a purchase of rural property. Trainees work their way around the firm's various departments by way of four six-month seats, and the small intake means they have a decent amount of choice and freedom as to what they sample. While you might not get your first-choice seat every time, "*if you're keen on any seats you will be likely to do them.*"

FITT but you know it

Withers' core client base of wealthy UK residents, landed estates and businesses falls within the remit of the family and business (FAB) section of its private client department. In FAB you'll find "*families who have been with the firm for what seems like centuries.*" Trainees here can expect to spend most of their time drafting wills and various trust documents, "*trying to avoid Inheritance Tax and making sure assets are passed down in the right way.*" FAB also frequently works with the property team when there are real property assets. The FITT (funds, investments, trusts and tax) group will work closely with the corporate department handling issues related to tax structures. FITT trainees are kept busy with "*various investment proposals for structuring personal investment funds, preparing supporting documentation and looking at tax implications.*"

The international private client team is particularly active in Latin America, Hong Kong and the Far East, as well as Russia and the former Soviet states. Trainees "*loved the cross border nature of the work,*" which involves advising "*seriously high net worth clients who have really interesting businesses and lives.*" Be prepared for some major brain work as there are "*a lot of offshore tax issues.*" Brief descriptions of the type of work that goes on in the team suggest that there is a vast amount of knowledge to be gained from the outset.

The contentious trusts and successions group handles high-value, high-complexity international trust disputes. Trainees learn about contested probate claims, which basically involves "*people challenging the validity of a will, citing undue influence, forgery, even madness, so you really need to know the background. And it's important to be able to understand the law and be capable of explaining it.*" Despite the heavy subject material, our sources really enjoyed the seat, praising the "*really nice feeling within the team.*" The contentious trusts department frequently works with the firm's much-lauded family department. It usually helps protect trusts from divorce settlements, but did the opposite recently and helped secure part of a trust for a client.

Lifestyles of the rich and famous

Some of the issues you'll come across in the family department "*really make your jaw drop.*" Over the past couple of years, the firm has been embroiled in the Marco Pierre White divorce, representing the celeb chef's wife Mati. Other clients have included Melissa Miller of landmark case *Miller v Miller*, and John Charman of landmark case *Charman v Charman*. The department is described as "*a well-oiled machine*" that "*runs like clockwork.*" "*As a trainee you're not as involved in handling the client, but you do get a lot of exposure in court, acting as an assistant to the assistant solicitor and the partner.*" Trainees gushed about "*doing a fair bit of work*" with partner Diana Parker, "*who is a bit of a legend.*" Indeed she is. Besides handling some major divorces, back in 1999 Parker was the youngest and first female to become chairman of a top 100 UK firm.

If you're after yet more jaw-dropping work, look no further than Withers' defamation and reputation management group. This small and relatively young department advises Britney Spears' co-conservators, who recently achieved a significant apology published by a woman's weekly glossy mag over an unauthorised, purportedly exclusive interview. They've also been after a national Sunday tabloid over privacy and copyright infringement following the unauthorised publication of various photos. Withers' lawyers provide media advice to Sirs David and Frederick Barclay, and were successful in a complaint to *The Times* over an article that falsely accused the brothers of tax avoidance, resulting in a prominent correction. Back in 2009, ballroom star Anton Du Beke turned to the firm when various publications covered his relationship with *Strictly* partner Laila Rouass and, at the other end of the sporting spectrum, Withers provides ongoing media advice to Renault Formula 1. Our sources were pumped with adrenaline by the "*really quick work, as stories can break over the weekend*" and loved that there was "*always something new to handle.*"

La dolce vita

"*Extraordinarily wealthy, creative people will have diverse business needs,*" so there are plenty of other areas trainees can experience. Take commercial litigation: "*The breadth of work is absolutely huge.*" The department hosts various special interest groups, ranging from fraud to FSA regulation to professional negligence claims against solicitors and QCs to cross-border transfers of art. "*Literally no day is the same,*" one source said excitedly.

In employment, trainees are "*often just reporting straight to the partner.*" The team handles "*quite big matters*" for both employees and employers, but is particularly recognised for its work for senior executives and holds the record for acting for the claimant in what may be the highest-value and most complex whistle-blowing claim brought before an employment tribunal (*Hannoun v GLG Partners*). The three property seats (rural, commercial and residential) provide trainees with some real independence as they are expected to run their own files. Trainees in the charities department are "*very heavily involved in business development – co-ordinating a lot of seminars, putting together news bulletins and just pushing it to the forefront.*" IP offers work for premium clients such as London's Cipriani restaurant group.

A client secondment at the Tate Galleries or a seat in Milan (for fluent Italian-speakers only) offers a refreshing change of pace. The latter, particularly, is buzzing at the moment as the firm recently started practising Italian (as well as English) law to become a proper force in the Milan market. The seat offers "*a nice contrast to working in a big office with all the infrastructure.*" Plus you could entertain fantasies of living la dolce vita by whizzing to work on a Vespa!

Pride and prejudice

"*Withers is posh,*" one source acknowledged, "*but it's important not to confuse posh with stuck-up.*" "*I think you would have labelled the firm a certain way some time ago, but I don't think it's as true anymore,*" another insisted. We also heard that "*value was found in stepping out of the pool, as the client base is changing. People come from all walks of life and make money.*" We were pleased to hear that there's "*no arrogance*" among trainees, rather that they all seemed to be "*really impressed*" by each other. "*Putting aside modesty, everyone in my intake seems intelligent and confident in a quiet rather than macho way,*" a source observed. The trainees form "*quite a tight group*" and "*have a really good little support system: there are always e-mails going around.*" Most venture down to Jamie's in Fleet Place for after work drinks on a Friday.

Withers looks for "*a bit of personality*" and "*a spark of originality*" through its infamous application form question: 'Which literary character would you be?' Recruiters found it "*not ideal*" that some 90% of females are choosing Jo March, Elizabeth Bennet or Hermione Granger so we've done your homework for you and put together a list of alternatives; that as well as other top tips and an outline of the application process and vac scheme can be found on our website.

Withers' 2009 NQ retention rates may appear jarring, with only 11 out of 19 staying on after their training, but it's worth noting that since then the firm has brought back seven of the eight originally let go. In 2010, 15 out of 18 qualifiers were kept on.

And finally...

This *"premier"* firm offers trainees much more than *"green-wellied law."*

Refine Your Search

Application and selection methods of the top firms	519
Table of salaries and benefits	525
Picking a firm for its overseas opportunities	535

Refine your search

We know just how disorienting, disheartening and crazily time consuming it can be to get lost in acres and acres of recruitment material from law firms telling you how they're the best thing since sliced bread. We're sure they are, but how can you tell which are most suited to your undoubted talents?

Snap yourself out of that haze and glance at our crystal clear comparison tables. They show you the facts you really want to know, in an instant. Which firms are flashing the cash? Which have moths in their wallets? Which will post you to sunnier climes for a working holiday... ahem, overseas placement? What other carrots are firms prepared to dangle in front of you to secure your signature? Who will pay you to go to law school? And finally, how do you apply?

This section is divided into three easy-to-use reference tables that should help you shorten your long list of target firms. They show at a glance the application and selection procedures of each firm, the number of rival applicants you're likely to compete against for that coveted training contract place, the salaries and benefits on offer, and the locations of overseas seats among those firms that offer them. If you missed it there's a Vacation Schemes table on page 36.

Application and selection methods

The table on the following page lets you know how each law firm requires you to apply – whether by a letter crafted in your best joined-up handwriting, via a CV in the post or an application form online. It shows you what minimum degree is required and how many interviews and/or assessments you face. Finally, and equally crucially, it gives the number of training contracts available alongside how many applications each firm receives.

Salaries and law school sponsorships

Our table of salaries and law school sponsorships on page 525 reveals the current salaries on offer for first and second-year trainees at each firm plus the salary for newly qualified solicitors. It also gives details of sponsorship and awards available to help you pay for law school, along with information about other benefits once you join the firm, like gym membership and health insurance.

Overseas seats

The final table on page 536 lists the firms that ship trainees out to various international locations, so if you've a hankering for Hong Kong, a longing for Luxembourg or possibly even a fetish for the Falkland Islands, we'll show you where to apply before you can say, 'Money, tickets, passport!'

Applications and Selection

Firm name	Method of Application	Selection Process	Degree Class	Number of Contracts	Number of Applications
Addleshaw Goddard	See website	Interview + assessment centre	2:1	45-50	1,500
Allen & Overy	Online	Interview	2:1	105	2,500
Arnold & Porter	Online	Interview	2:1	2	700
Ashurst	Online	2 interviews	2:1	55	2,500
Baker & McKenzie	Online	Group exercise + interview	2:1	38	2,000
Barlow Lyde & Gilbert	Online	Assessment Centre	Not known	15	1,500
Bates Wells & Braithwaite	Online	Interviews	2:1	4	750+
Beachcroft	Online	Online test + assessment centre	2:1 preferred	16	Not known
Beale & Company	Application form	Interview + assessment	2:1	Not known	Not known
Berwin Leighton Paisner	Online	Phone interview, assessment day + interview	2:1	35-40	1,500
Bevan Brittan	Online	Not known	Not known	Not known	Not known
Bingham McCutchen	Online	Interviews	High 2:1	2	Not known
Bircham Dyson Bell	See website	2 interviews + assessment + online test	2:1 preferred	7	650
Bird & Bird	Online	Assessment day	2:1	16	1,400
Bond Pearce	Online	Assessment day	2:1	15-20	Not known
Boodle Hatfield	Online	Interviews + assessment	2:1	6	Not known
B P Collins	Handwritten letter & CV	Interview + assessment day	2:1	Not known	Not known
Brabners Chaffe Street	Online	Interview + assessment day	2:1	10	Not known
Bristows	Online	2 interviews	2:1 preferred	Up to 10	3,500
Browne Jacobson	Online or CV & covering letter	Telephone interview + assessment centre + interview	Not known	8	900
Burges Salmon	Online	Not known	2:1	20-25	1,500
Capsticks	Application form, CV & letter	Interview	2:1	5	200
Charles Russell	Online	Assessment day	2:1	20	1,500
Cleary Gottlieb Steen & Hamilton	CV & covering letter	Usually via vac scheme	High 2:1	10-12	Not known
Clifford Chance	Online	Assessment day + interview	2:1	120	Not known
Clyde & Co	Online	Interview + assessments	2:1	24	1,400+
CMS Cameron McKenna	Online	Online test, interview + assessment centre	2:1	60	1,500
Cobbetts	Online	Assessment days	2:1	12	1,000
Coffin Mew	See website	Interview	2:1 (usually)	4	400+
Collyer Bristow	Online	Online test + interview	2:1	Not known	Not known
Covington & Burling	Online	2 interviews	2:1	6	Not known
Cripps Harries Hall	Online	Interview	2:1	8	Up to 750
Davenport Lyons	Online	Interviews	2:1	8	800
Davies Arnold Cooper	Application form	Not known	2:1 (usually)	7	Not known

Applications and Selection

Firm name	Method of Application	Selection Process	Degree Class	Number of Contracts	Number of Applications
Dawsons	Online	2 Interviews	2:1	5	350-400
Dechert	Online	Interviews + assessments + written tests	2:1	10	1,000
Dewey & LeBoeuf	Online	2 interviews	2:1	15	850
Dickinson Dees	Online	Interview + assessments	2:1	Up to 17	800
DLA Piper	Online	2 interviews + assessments	2:1	85	2,600
Dundas & Wilson	Online	Assessment day + interview	2:1 preferred	35 (12 in London)	300
DWF	Online	Interview + assessment centre	2:1	21	1,200
Edwards Angell Palmer & Dodge	Online	Interview + assessments	2:1	Up to 8	700
Eversheds	Online	Assessment day + interview	2:1	50	3,000
Farrer & Co	Online	Interviews	2:1	10	900
Field Fisher Waterhouse	Online	Assessment centre	2:1	Up to 15	800
Finers Stephens Innocent	CV & covering letter	2 interviews	2:1	6	800
Fladgate	Application form	Assessment + interview	2:1	4	Not Known
Foot Anstey	Online	Assessment day	2:1 preferred	6	Not known
Forbes	Online	Interview	2:1	4	350+
Freeth Cartwright	Online	Interview + selection day	Not known	Not known	Not known
Freshfields Bruckhaus Deringer	Online	2 interviews + written test	2:1	90	2,000
Gordons	Online	Interviews + exercise	2:1	6	300
Government Legal Service	Online	Online test + interview + assessment day	2:1	22-30	2,000+
Hammonds	Online	Assessment + interview	2:1	25	1,300
Harbottle & Lewis	Application form	Interview	2:1	5	800
HBJ Gateley Wareing	Online	Not known	2:1	Not known	Not known
Henmans	Application form online	Assessment day + interview	Not known	3	300
Herbert Smith	Online	Online testing + assessment day	2:1	85	2,000
Hewitsons	Application form	Interview	2:1	10	850
Higgs & Sons	Online	Interview	2:1 will consider 2:2	4	250+
Hill Dickinson	Online	Telephone interviews + assessment day	Not known	Not known	Not known
Hogan Lovells	Online	Assessment day	2:1	90	1,500
Howes Percival	Online	Assessment centre	2:1	8	300
Ince & Co	Online	2 interviews + assessments	2:1	12	1,000
Irwin Mitchell	Online	Assessment centre + interview	None	40-45	2,000
Jones Day	CV & letter online	2 interviews	2:1	10-15	1,800
Kennedys	Online	Assessment day	2:1	15-18	400

Applications and Selection

Firm name	Method of Application	Selection Process	Degree Class	Number of Contracts	Number of Applications
Kirkland & Ellis	CV & letter	Interview	2:1	Not known	Not known
K&L Gates	Online	Assessment day	2:1	Not known	1,000
Latham & Watkins	Online	3 interviews	2:1	15	Not known
Lawrence Graham	Online	Interview + tests	2:1	20	800
Lester Aldridge	Application form	Interview + assessment	2:1	6	200
Lewis Silkin	Online	Assessment day + interview	2:1	6	600
Linklaters	Online	2 interviews + assessments	2:1	110	4,000
Macfarlanes	Online	Assessment day	2:1	Up to 30	800
Maclay Murray & Spens	Application form (online)	2 interviews + assessments	2:1	30 London & Scotland	150 (London)
Manches	Online	2 interviews	2:1	10	850
Martineau	Online	Half-day assessment centre	2:1	10-12	600
Maxwell Winward	CV & covering letter	2 interviews	2:1	2	600
Mayer Brown	Online	Interview + assessments	2:1	30	1,000+
McDermott, Will & Emery	Online	Interview + assessment day	Not known	Not known	Not known
McGrigors	Online	Half-day assessment centre	2:1	10-12 (London)	Not known
Memery Crystal	Online	Interview + assessment centre	2:1	4	180
Michelmores	Online	Assessment day	Usually 2:1	6	200
Mills & Reeve	Online	Assessment day	2:1	20	750
Mishcon de Reya	Online	Not known	2:1	8-12	1,500+
Muckle	Online	Interview + assessment day	2:1	4	120-130
Nabarro	Online	Assessment day + interview	2:1	35	2,000
Norton Rose	Online	Interview + assessments	2:1	55	2,500+
Olswang	Online	Interview + assessments	2:1	24	2,000
O'Melveny & Myers	Online	Interview	2:1	Up to 4	250-300
Orrick	Online	2 interviews	2:1	10	Not known
Osborne Clarke	Online	Assessment day + interview	2:1	20	1,200
Pannone	Online	2 interviews	2:1	12	1,200
Paul Hastings	Online	Interview	2:1	4-5	Not known
Penningtons Solicitors	Online	Not known	2:1	5-10	1,000
Pinsent Masons	Online	Assessment day + interview	2:1	60	2,000+
PricewaterhouseCoopers Legal	Online	Not known	2:1	8	Not known
Pritchard Englefield	Application form	Interview	Generally 2:1	3	300-400
Reed Smith	Online	Interview + assessment day	2:1	30	1,500
Reynolds Porter Chamberlain	Online	Assessment day + interview	2:1	15	800

Applications and Selection

Firm name	Method of Application	Selection Process	Degree Class	Number of Contracts	Number of Applications
Salans	Letter & CV	Interview + assessments	2:1	3-4	400-500
Shearman & Sterling	Online	Interview + assessment centre	2:1	15	Not known
Sheridans	CV & letter	2 interviews	2:1	1	Not known
Shoosmiths	Online	Full-day assessment centre	2:1	22	1,000
Sidley Austin	Application form	Interview(s)	2:1	10	300
Simmons & Simmons	Online	Interview or assessment day	2:1	c. 40	2,000
SJ Berwin	Online	2 interviews + assessments	2:1	40	2,000
Skadden	Online	Interview + exercise	2:1	10-12	700
Slaughter and May	Online	Interview	2:1	c. 90	2,000
SNR Denton	Application form	2 interviews + assessments	2:1	25-30	1,500
Speechly Bircham	Application form	Interview + assessment	2:1	12	800
Stephenson Harwood	Online	Telephone interview + assessment day	2:1	16	1,000
Stevens & Bolton	Online	2 interviews + assessments	2:1	4	250
Taylor Wessing	Online	Assessment centre + interview	2:1	c. 20	1,000
Thomas Cooper	Online	Interviews + assessments	2:1	Not known	Not known
Thomas Eggar	Online	Assessment centre + interview	2:1	8	Not known
TLT	Online	Assessment centre + telephone screening	2:1	Up to 15	700
Travers Smith	Online	2 interviews	2:1	25	2,000
Trethowans	Letter & application form	Interview + assessment day	2:1	3-4	100+
Trowers & Hamlins	Online	Interviews + assessments	2:1	22	1,600
Veale Wasbrough Vizards	Application form (online)	Interview	2:1 preferred	8-10	Not known
Vinson & Elkins	Online	Interview	2:1	3-4	405
Walker Morris	Online	Interviews + assessments	2:1	18	800
Ward Hadaway	Application form	Assessment centre + interview	2:1	10	600+

Applications and Selection

Firm name	Method of Application	Selection Process	Degree Class	Number of Contracts	Number of Applications
Warner Goodman	Online	Interview	2:1	2	Not known
Watson, Farley & Williams	Online	Assessment centre + interview	2:1	12-14	700
Wedlake Bell	Application form	2 interviews + open day	2:1	6	Not known
Weil, Gotshal & Manges	Online	Not known	2:1	10	Not known
White & Case	Online	Interview	2:1	30	1,600
Wiggin	Online	Interview + 2-day selection	2:1	3	250
Wilsons Solicitors	Online or CV	Interview + assessment day	2:1	4	Not known
Winckworth Sherwood	Online	2 interviews	2:1	5	200
Withers	Application form	2 interviews + assessments	2:1	16	700

- **Network, network, network:** While nepotism may be unfashionable, networking is very much in vogue. It's not pretty, it's not always fun, it is, however, necessary. Thankfully, it's easier than you might think, and not quite as soulless and mercenary. Go to www.chambersstudent.co.uk for advice on how to get started.

top tip no. 32

Salaries and Benefits

Firm name	1st Year Salary	2nd year salary	Sponsorship/ awards	Other Benefits	Qualification Salary
Addleshaw Goddard	£36,000 (London) £24,500 (Manch/Leeds)	£37,000 (London) £25,500 (Manch/Leeds)	GDL & LPC: fees + £7,000 (London) or £4,500 (elsewhere)	Corporate gym m'ship, STL, subsd restaurant, pension, pte healthcare	£58,000 (London) £36,500 (Manch/Leeds)
Allen & Overy	£38,000	£43,200	LPC: fees + £7,000 GDL: fees + £6,000 (London), £5,000 (elsewhere)	Pte healthcare, PMI, STL, subsd restaurant, in-house medical facilities, music rooms, gym, prayer rooms	£61,000
Arnold & Porter	Not known	Not known	GDL & LPC: fees + £7,250 maintainance	Bonuses, lunch vouchers, private health insurance, life assurance, STL.	Not Known
Ashurst	£37,000	£41,000	GDL & LPC: fees + £7,500, £500 for first-class degree or LPC distinction, language bursaries	PHI, pension, life assurance, STL, gym m'ship	£60,000
Baker & McKenzie	£37,500 + £3,000 'joining bonus'	£40,000	Not known	PHI, life ins, PMI, pension, subsd gym m'ship, STL, subsd restaurant	£61,000
Barlow Lyde & Gilbert	£34,000	£36,000	GDL & LPC: fees + maintenance	Not known	£56,000
Bates, Wells & Braithwaite	£30,000	£32,500	LPC fees paid, interest paid on student loan.	STL, subsd gym, subsd restaurant, one months unpaid leave on qualification, pension	£45,000
Beachcroft	£34,000 (London) £26,000 (Regions)	£37,000 (London) £29,000 (Regions)	GDL & LPC: fees + £5,000	Flexible scheme	Not known
Beale & Co	£28,000 (London) £23,800 (Regions)	£30,000 (London) £25,500 (Regions)	Not known	STL, discretionary bonus	Not known
Berwin Leighton Paisner	£37,000	£41,000	GDL & LPC: fees + £7,200	Not known	£59,000
Bevan Brittan	Not known	Not known	GDL & LPC: fees + bursary	Not known	Not known
Bingham McCutchen	£40,000	£45,000	GDL & LPC: fees + £8,000	PHI, travel ins, disability ins, STL, life ass, subsd gym, discretionary bonus + critical illness scheme	£100,000
Bircham Dyson Bell	£30,000	£31,000	Not known	Pte healthcare, life ass, STL, pension, subsd gym, bonus scheme	£49,000
Bird & Bird	£35,000	£37,000	Not known	Not known	£55,000
Bond Pearce	£24,000	£25,000	GDL & LPC: fees + £6,000	Not known	Not known
Boodle Hatfield	£32,000	£34,500	GDL & LPC: fees + maintenance	Pte healthcare, life ass, STL, pension, PHI, PMI, CTW, conveyancing grant, enhanced maternity pay, EAP	£50,000
BP Collins	£23,000	£24,000	Not known	Not known	Not known

PHI = Permanent Health Insurance; STL = Season Ticket Loan; PMI = Private Medical Insurance; EAP = Employee Assistance Programme; CTW= Cycle to work scheme

Salaries and Benefits

Firm name	1st Year Salary	2nd year salary	Sponsorship/ awards	Other Benefits	Qualification Salary
Brabners Chaffe Street	No less than £22,000	No less than £22,000	Assistance with LPC funding	Not known	Not known
Bristows	£33,000	£36,000	GDL & LPC: fees + £7,000	Pension, life ass, PMI, PHI, childcare vouchers, eye care, CTW STL, health assessment, EAP	£53,500
Browne Jacobson	£24,500	£25,500	GDL & LPC: fees + £5,000	Life ass, PMI, pension, income protection insurance, corporate discounts	Not known
Burges Salmon	£30,000	£31,000	GDL & LPC: fees + £7,000	Bonus, pension, pte healthcare, mobile phone, gym m'ship, Xmas gift, life ass, sports and social club	£40,000
Capsticks	£29,000	£30,000	GDL & LPC: financial support	Bonus, pension, PHI, PMI, death-in-service-cover, STL, childcare vouchers, CTW, gym membership	£46,000
Charles Russell	£31,500	£32,500	GDL & LPC: fees + £6,000 (London) £4,500 (Guildford) £3,500 (Cheltenham)	BUPA, PHI, life ass, pension, STL, subsidised canteen	£55,000
Clarke Willmott	£24,000	£25,500	GDL & LPC: funding	Life ass, pension, gym m'ship, bonus, STL, eyecare & childcare vouchers, CTW	£33,500- £36,000 (dependent on location)
Cleary Gottlieb Steen & Hamilton	£40,000	£45,000	GDL & LPC: fees + £8,000	PHI (personal & family), disability ins, life ins, EAP, subsd restaurant	£92,000
Clifford Chance	£38,000	£43,000	GDL & LPC: fees + maintenance	Subsd rest, fitness centre, pension, up to 6 weeks' leave on qual	£61,500
Clyde & Co	£35,000	£38,000	GDL & LPC: fees + £7,000 (Lon/Guild) £6,000 (elsewhere)	Interest-free loan on joining, pension, life ass, PMI, subsd gym m'ship, STL	£58,000
CMS Cameron McKenna	£37,500	£41,500	GDL & LPC: fees + up to £7,500	Bonus, gym m'ship, life ass, pension, pte healthcare, STL, care line, subs'd rest, buy-holiday scheme	£59,000

PHI = Permanent Health Insurance; STL = Season Ticket Loan; PMI = Private Medical Insurance; EAP = Employee Assistance Programme; CTW= Cycle to work scheme

Salaries and Benefits

Firm name	1st Year Salary	2nd year salary	Sponsorship/ awards	Other Benefits	Qualification Salary
Cobbetts	£23,000	£25,000	GDL & LPC: fees + £5,000 during LPC year	BUPA, gym m'ship, pension, STL, death-in-service cover, counselling, buy-holiday scheme	£30,000
Coffin Mew	Not known	Not known	LPC: discussed with candidates	Not known	Not known
Collyer Bristow	£28,000	£31,000	LPC: fees + £4,000	Pension, PMI, life ass, STL, childcare vouchers, CTW	Not known
Covington & Burling	£40,000	£44,000	GDL & LPC: fees + £8,000	Pension, life ass, pte healthcare, STL, income protection	Not known
Cripps Harries Hall	£21,500	£23,500	LPC fees: 50% interest-free loan, 50% bursary	Not known	£37,000
Davenport Lyons	£33,000-£33,666	£34,332-£35,000	No	Pension, STL, client intro bonus, subsd gym m'ship, discretionary bonus, life ass, pte healthcare, EAP	Not known
Davies Arnold Cooper	£35,000	Not known	GDL & LPC: fees + maintenance	PMI, STL	Not known
Dawsons	£31,000	£33,000	GDL & LPC: fees + maintenance	PMI, life ass, pension, STL	£48,500
Dechert	£38,000	£43,000	LPC: fees + £10,000	Not known	£65,000-£73,000
Dewey & LeBoeuf	£40,000	£45,000	GDL & LPC: fees + £8,500	PMI, PHI, life ass, EAP, private GP, STL, childcare vouchers, subsd gym, worldwide travel insurance, CTW, subsd dental care	£75,000
Dickinson Dees	£19,500	£20,500	GDL & LPC: fees + maintenance	Not known	Not known
DLA Piper	£36,000 (London) £25,000 (regions)	£38,000 (London) £27,000 (regions)	GDL & LPC: fees + up to £7,000	Not known	£60,000 (London) £38,000 (regions)
Dundas & Wilson	£30,000 (London)	£33,500 (London)	GDL & LPC: fees + maintenance	Life ass, PHI, pension, STL, holiday-purchase scheme	Not known
DWF	£25,000 (NW) £35,000 (London)	Not known	LPC: fees	Flexible scheme	Not known

PHI = Permanent Health Insurance; STL = Season Ticket Loan; PMI = Private Medical Insurance; EAP = Employee Assistance Programme; CTW= Cycle to work scheme

Salaries and Benefits

Firm name	1st Year Salary	2nd year salary	Sponsorship/ awards	Other Benefits	Qualification Salary
Edwards Angell Palmer & Dodge	£37,000	£41,000	GDL & LPC: fees + £6,500 (£7,000 in London)	BUPA, STL, subs'd gym, bonus, CTW, pension, EAP, life ass	£58,000
Eversheds	£35,000 (London)	£37,000 (London)	GDL & LPC: fees + maintenance	Not known	£57,000 (London)
Farrer & Co	£32,500	£35,000	GDL & LPC: fees + £6,000	Flexible scheme	£53,000
Field Fisher Waterhouse	£35,000	Not known	GDL: fees + £5,500 LPC: fees + £6,000	Flexible scheme	£54,000
Finers Stephens Innocent	£30,000	£32,000	GDL & LPC: fees	Pension, PMI, life ins, long-term disability ins, STL, EAP	£47,000
Fladgate	£30,000	Not known	Not known	Pension, PHI, life ass, STL, gym loan, PMI	£50,000
Foot Anstey	£19,500	£21,000	LPC: up to £9,600	Pension, life assurance, childcare vouchers, green travel scheme	£32,000-£33,000
Forbes	At least Law Soc min	£19,500	Not known	Not known	Not known
Freeth Cartwright	£22,000	Not known	Not known	Not known	Not known
Freshfields Bruckhaus Deringer	£39,000	£44,000	GDL & LPC: fees + maintenance	flexible & competitive	£60,000
Gordons	£20,000	£22,000	£5,000 towards LPC fees	Pension, life ass, death-in-service benefit, STL, childcare vouchers	£34,500
Government Legal Service	£23,280 - £25,600	£24,850-£27,335	BPTC & LPC: fees + £5,000-£7,000 GDL: possibly	Pension, subsd canteen	£32,000-£40,000
Hammonds	£32,000 (London) £22,000 (other)	£35,000 (London) £25,000 (other)	GDL: fees + £4,500 (£6,000 London) LPC: fees + £5,000 (£7,000 London)	Flexible: Pension, life ass, subsd gym m'ship, STL	£56,000 (London) £36,000 (other)
Harbottle & Lewis	£28,000	£29,000	LPC: fees + interest-free loan	Lunch, STL	£45,000
HBJ Gateley Wareing	£20,000-£22,000 (Midlands)	£22,000-£24,000 (Midlands)	LPC: fees + £5,000	Buddy system, library, private health, life ass, STL	£32,000 (Midlands)
Henmans	£22,000	£24,000	Not known	BUPA, pension, EAP, subs'd cafe, free parking, life ass	£34,000

PHI = Permanent Health Insurance; STL = Season Ticket Loan; PMI = Private Medical Insurance; EAP = Employee Assistance Programme; CTW= Cycle to work scheme

Salaries and Benefits

Firm name	1st Year Salary	2nd year salary	Sponsorship/ awards	Other Benefits	Qualification Salary
Herbert Smith	£38,000	£43,000	GDL: £5,000 outside London £6,000 in London LPC: £6,000	Bonus, PHI, STL, life ass, subsd gym m'ship, pension, pte healthcare	£61,000
Hewitsons	£23,500	under review	None	Not known	£35,000
Higgs & Sons	£21,500	£24,000	None	PMI, life ass, pension, BTSS membership	£32,000
Hill Dickinson	£24,000 (North) £32,000 (London)	£26,000 (North) £34,000 (London)	LPC sponsorship	Not known	Not known
Hogan Lovells	£37,000	£42,000	GDL & LPC: fees + maintenance grant	PMI, life ass, PHI, STL, in-house gym, staff rest, dentist, GP & physio, local retail discounts	£60,000
Howes Percival	£24,500 (East mids) £22,000 (Norwich)	£26,500 (East mids) £23,000 (Norwich)	GDL & LPC: funding	Pension, PHI	£38,500 (East mids) £33,500 (Norwich)
Ince & Co	£36,000	£39,000	GDL & LPC: fees + £6,000 (London and Guildford), £5,500 (elsewhere)	STL, corporate health cover, PHI, pension, subsd gym m'ship	£58,000
Irwin Mitchell	£22,450 (outside London)	£24,650 (outside London)	GDL & LPC: fees + £4,500	Healthcare, pension, subsd gym m'ship	Not known
Jones Day	£39,000 increasing to £41,000 after 6 months	£45,000 increasing to £50,000 after 18 months	GDL & LPC: fees + £8,000	Pte healthcare, sports club m'ship, group life cover, STL, pension, salary sacrifice scheme	£70,000
K&L Gates	£35,000	£38,000	GDL: fees + £5,000 LPC: fees + £7,000	STL, subsd gym m'ship, PHI, life ass, bonus, pension, medicare m'ship	£60,000
Kennedys	£32,000	£36,000	Not known	PHI, pension, PMI, life ins, STL, gym m'ship, CTW, EAP, GP, contribution to conveyancing fees, childcare assistance	£58,000
Kirkland & Ellis	£40,000	£43,000	GDL & LPC: fees + £7,500	PMI, travel ins, life ins, EAP, gym m'ship	Not known
Latham & Watkins	£41,000	£44,000	GDL & LPC: fees + £8,000	Healthcare & dental scheme, pension, life ass	£96,970
Lawrence Graham (LG)	Not known	Not known	GDL & LPC: fees + £6,500 (London) £6,000 (elsewhere)	STL, life ass	£55,000
Lewis Silkin	£32,000	£34,000	GDL & LPC: fees + £5,000	Life ass, critical illness cover, health ins, STL, pension, subsd gym m'ship, bonus	£50,000

PHI = Permanent Health Insurance; STL = Season Ticket Loan; PMI = Private Medical Insurance; EAP = Employee Assistance Programme; CTW= Cycle to work scheme

Salaries and Benefits

Firm name	1st Year Salary	2nd year salary	Sponsorship/ awards	Other Benefits	Qualification Salary
Linklaters	£37,400	Not known	GDL & LPC: fees + maintenance	Bonus, life ass, PMI, in-house healthcare & gym, travel ins, STL, income protection and others	£61,500 + discretionary bonus
Macfarlanes	£38,000	£43,000	GDL & LPC: fees + £7,000	Pension, life ass, pte health, STL, subsd gym m'ship, bonus, child care vouchers	£60,000
Maclay Murray & Spens	£32,000 (London)	Not known	Not known	Pension, death-in-service benefit, conveyancing, medical & dental, income protection	Not known
Manches	£30,000 (London)	£33,000 (London)	GDL & LPC: fees + £5,000	STL, PHI, pension, BUPA, life ins	£50,000 (London)
Martineau	c.£21,000	c.£22,500	Not known	Not known	£36,000
Maxwell Winward	£29,000	£31,500	GDL & LPC: contribution	STL, PHI	£48,000
Mayer Brown	£37,500	£42,300	GDL & LPC: fees + £7,000	STL, sports club m'ship, pte health	Not known
McDermott, Will & Emery	£39,000	£43,000	GDL & LPC: fees + maintenance	PMI, dental ins, life ass, EAP, PHI, STL, subsd gym m'ship	Not known
McGrigors	£32,000 (London)	£37,000 (London)	GDL & LPC: fees + £6,000	PMI, STL, life ass, pension	£56,000 (London)
Memery Crystal	£26,500	£29,500	GDL & LPC: fees	Life ass, health, STL, gym sub, pension, CTW, bonus	Not known
Michelmores	£20,000	£21,000	LPC: fees up to £8,000	Subsd rest, subsd gym, free parking, pension, PMI	£33,000
Mills & Reeve	£23,000	£24,000	GDL & LPC: fees + maintenance	Flexible: Life ass, pension, bonus, subsd gym & restaurant, STL, PMI	Not known
Mishcon de Reya	£32,000	Not known	GDL & LPC: fees + maintenance	PMI, travel ins, subsd gym m'ship, STL, life ass, pension, doctor, EAP, income protection, CTW	Not known
Muckle	£20,000	Not known	LPC: fees subject to eligibility	Pension, PHI, life ass, corporate discounts, salary sacrifice	£30,000

PHI = Permanent Health Insurance; STL = Season Ticket Loan; PMI = Private Medical Insurance; EAP = Employee Assistance Programme; CTW= Cycle to work scheme

Salaries and Benefits

Firm name	1st Year Salary	2nd year salary	Sponsorship/ awards	Other Benefits	Qualification Salary
Nabarro	£37,000 (London) £25,000 (Sheffield)	£40,000 (London) £28,000 (Sheffield)	GDL: fees + £6,000 (London) or £5,000 LPC: fees + £7,000 (London) or £6,000 [50% of fees, if paid retrospectively]	PMI, pension, STL, subsd restaurant, subsd gym m'ship	£58,000 (London) £38,000 (Sheffield)
Norton Rose	£37,000	£41,500	Not known	Life ass, PMI, STL, subsd gym m'ship EAP, subsd rest, pension, CTW	Not known
Olswang	£35,000	£39,000	GDL & LPC: fees + £7,000 (London) or £6,500 (elsewhere)	Pension, life cover, dental, STL, subsd gym m'ship and staff rest, PHI, medical cover	£59,000
O'Melveny & Myers	£39,000	£42,500	GDL & LPC: fees + £7,000	Pension, travel ins, subsd gym m'ship, PHI, life ass, STL, long term disability insurance	£72,500
Orrick, Herrington & Sutcliffe	£38,000	£42,500	GDL & LPC: fees + £7,000	Pension, health insurance, subsd gym m'ship, STL, PMI, dental care, childcare vouchers	Not known
Osborne Clarke	Not known	Not known	GDL & LPC: fees + £6,500	Pension, PMI, STL, PHI, life ass	Not known
Pannone	£23,000	£23,000	Half grant for LPC fees at COL, Manchester	Not known	£34,000
Paul Hastings	£40,000	£45,000	Funding available	Pte healthcare, life ass, pension, STL, subsd gym m'ship	£80,000
Penningtons Solicitors	£30,000 (London)	£32,000 (London)	LPC: fees + £5,000	Pension, life ass, PMI, STL, crit illness ins	£47,000 (London)
Pinsent Masons	£36,000 (London)	£39,000 (London)	GDL & LPC: fees + maintenance	Not known	£58,000 (London)
PricewaterhouseCoopers Legal	£30,000	£35,000	GDL & LPC: scholarship for fees + maintenance	Not known	Not known

PHI = Permanent Health Insurance; STL = Season Ticket Loan; PMI = Private Medical Insurance; EAP = Employee Assistance Programme; CTW= Cycle to work scheme

Salaries and Benefits

Firm name	1st Year Salary	2nd year salary	Sponsorship/ awards	Other Benefits	Qualification Salary
Pritchard Englefield	Not known	Not known	LPC: fees	Subsd training, lunch vouchers, PMI, STL	Not known
Reed Smith	£37,000 (London)	Not known	GDL: fees + £6,000 LPC: fees + £7,000	STL, life ins, pension, bonus, conveyancing, subsd rest, PHI	£57,000 + bonus (London)
Reynolds Porter Chamberlain	£37,000	£40,000	GDL & LPC: fees + £6,500	Flexible package	£58,000
Salans	£33,000	£35,000	LPC: fees	Pte healthcare, pension, life ass, STL, critical illness cover	£58,000
Shearman & Sterling	£39,000	£40,500	GDL & LPC: fees + £7,000	Not known	£73,000
Shoosmiths	Not known	Not known	GDL & LPC: fees + maintenance	Life ass, pension, staff discounts, Christmas bonus, flexible holidays scheme	Not known
Sidley Austin	£39,000	£43,000	GDL & LPC: fees + £7,000	PHI, life ass, subsd gym m'ship, STL, income protection, pension, subsd rest	Not known
Simmons & Simmons	£36,000	£40,000	GDL & LPC: fees + up to £7,500	Not known	£59,000
SJ Berwin	£37,500	£41,500	Not known	Pte health, subsd gym m'ship, life ass, pension, STL, free lunch	£59,000
Skadden	£40,000	£43,000	GDL & LPC: fees + £8,000	Life ins, PMI, PHI, travel ins, subsd gym m'ship & rest, technology budget, EAP	Not known
Slaughter and May	£38,000	£43,000	GDL & LPC: fees + maintenance	STL, pension, subsd health club m'ship, accident cover, PMI, interest free loan	£61,000
SNR Denton	£37,000	£40,000	GDL & LPC: fees + £6,000 (£7,000 London)	Flexible package	£59,000
Speechly Bircham	£32,000-£33,000	£34,000-£35,000	GDL & LPC: fees + maintenance	Not known	£54,000
Stephenson Harwood	£35,000	£40,000	GDL & LPC: fees + maintenance	pte health, STL, gym sub, PHI, pension, life ass, private GP, dental	£58,000
Stevens & Bolton	£24,500	Not known	GDL & LPC: fees + £4,000	life ass, pension, STL, PHI, private healthcare	Not known
Taylor Wessing	£35,000	£38,000	Not known	Not known	£59,000
Thomas Cooper	£32,000	£33,600	LPC: fees	life ass, pension, STL, gym loan, PMI, PHI	Not known

PHI = Permanent Health Insurance; STL = Season Ticket Loan; PMI = Private Medical Insurance; EAP = Employee Assistance Programme; CTW= Cycle to work scheme

Salaries and Benefits

Firm name	1st Year Salary	2nd year salary	Sponsorship/ awards	Other Benefits	Qualification Salary
Thomas Eggar	Not known	Not known	LPC: 50% grant, 50% loan	Not known	Not known
TLT Solicitors	Not known	Not known	GDL & LPC: fees + maintenance	Flexible package	Not known
Travers Smith	£38,000	£42,000	GDL & LPC: fees + £7,000 (London) or £6,500 (elsewhere)	PHI, PMI, life ass, STL, subsd bistro, health club m'ship	£60,000
Trethowans	Not known	Not known	LPC: fees	Pension, death-in-service cover, PHI, bonus, car parking childcare vouchers	Not known
Trowers & Hamlins	£35,000	£38,000	GDL & LPC: fees + £6,000	Not known	£55,000
Veale Wasbrough Vizards	£23,000	£25,000	GDL & LPC: fees + interest-free loan	Not known	£35,000
Vinson & Elkins	£40,000	£42,000	LPC: fees + up to £7,500	Pension, STL, life ass, priv med & dental	£80,000
Walker Morris	£24,000	£26,000	GDL & LPC: fees + £5,000	Not known	£37,000
Ward Hadaway	£20,000	£20,500	GDL & LPC: fees + maintenance	Death-in-service cover, pension, travel scheme	£35,000
Watson, Farley & Williams	£35,000	£40,000	GDL & LPC: fees + £6,500 (London) or £5,500 (elsewhere)	Life ass, STL, pension, subsd gym m'ship, EAP, income protection, pte healthcare	£59,000
Wedlake Bell	Not known	Not known	LPC: fees + £4,000	Pension, STL, subsd gym m'ship, life ass, health insurance	Not known
Weil, Gotshal & Manges	£41,000	Not known	Not known	Not known	Not known
White & Case	£41,000 rising by £1,000 every six months	Not known	GDL & LPC: fees + maintenance. Prize for LPC commendation or distinction	PMI, life ass, pension, dental, illness & travel ins, gym m'ship, retail vouchers, STL, green bikes	£70,000
Wiggin	£32,000	£36,000	GDL & LPC: fees + £3,500	Life ass, pte health cover, pension, PHI, subsd gym m'ship	£50,000
Wilsons Solicitors	Not known	Not known	LPC: interest-free loan up to £4,500	Pension, life ass, PMI	Not known
Winckworth Sherwood	Not known	Not known	GDL & LPC: financial assistance under certain conditions	PHI, STL, life ins, subsd gym mship	Not known
Withers	£33,000	£35,000	GDL & LPC: fees + £5,000	Not known	£53,000

PHI = Permanent Health Insurance; STL = Season Ticket Loan; PMI = Private Medical Insurance; EAP = Employee Assistance Programme; CTW= Cycle to work scheme

- **Practical experience can be the most eloquent and essential aspect of your CV:** As a leading human rights lawyer told us, "People always ask me, how do I show an interest in human rights law? But that's the wrong way round. People who are genuinely interested will already be involved."

Picking a firm for its overseas opportunities

The idea of the international law firm is far from new; UK firms have ventured overseas since the 19th century. What has changed is the number of firms with offices overseas and the increasing desire to plant flags all over the globe.

The big firms are canny operators. They understand that to thrive in a competitive international legal market it is necessary to have a network of offices (or relationships with overseas firms) in parts of the world where the economies are growing and/or busiest. China and India are of real interest at present, as are parts of the Middle East and the oil and gas-rich parts of Central Asia. The downturn in the world economy accelerated this process, with firms becoming ever more determined to invest in developing countries where growth has been affected less. Essentially, wherever commercial interests go, so law firms follow. Similarly, when a country begins to look stale, firms start to lose interest and scale back their offices.

There are so many firms with overseas networks that keeping track of the office openings and closings is almost a full-time occupation. Wherever possible, we have mentioned the main changes from the past year in our True Picture reports. What we can't predict is exactly who is going to merge with whom. Anglo-American mergers have been particularly in vogue in 2010, with Lovells and Denton Wilde Sapte securing transatlantic tie-ups and Simmons & Simmons and SJ Berwin among those openly courting US firms.

The following table summarises exactly where overseas seat opportunities lie this year. Because of the recession, they have decreased in number since 2008, although many firms are telling us that, as and when the economy recovers, they hope to reinstate some of those seats that have been taken off the table. As for international work back in the UK, the nature of a firm's clientele and worldwide office footprint determine what trainees see day to day. At White & Case there is a considerable amount of project finance work conducted in conjunction with Eastern European and Central Asian offices. CMS Cameron McKenna's superb energy practice brings in work, and at the likes of Dewey & LeBoeuf and SNR Denton, African LNG deals have flowed from the firm's energy clientele. Trowers & Hamlins' predominance in the Middle East brings work back to London, as do Lawrence Graham's Indian relationships.

If international work interests you then consider whether you would want to remain at home during your training or have the guarantee of an overseas seat. If it is the latter then pick a firm where you can be certain of securing an overseas posting. The competition at some firms is tough, while at others everyone who wants to go does. The True Picture reports should help you here. One other thing to bear in mind is your ability to speak another language. If you're fluent in Russian you may be collared for Moscow instead of the New York opening you've got your eye on. It also follows that where language skills would be useful – say in Italy – those who possess them prove to be more attractive at a training contract interview. Some firms actively recruit with language needs in mind. International private client firm Withers, for example, likes to have a couple of fluent Italian speakers in each intake to fill its coveted corporate seat in Milan.

Although time abroad gives you experience of working in another jurisdiction, you'll not normally practise foreign law. An overseas seat is without doubt a very rewarding and challenging experience. It will usually be taken in an office that is smaller than your home office, and you will normally have greater responsibility. The trick to securing the most popular overseas seats is to wage an effective campaign of self-promotion and perhaps also gain prerequisite experience in the UK office before you go.

On arrival in a new country you don't need to worry about feeling isolated as the local lawyers and staff invariably give a warm welcome to newcomers. In some cities with a large influx of UK trainees there is a ready-made social scene and it's likely that the first thing to pop into your inbox will be an invite to meet other new arrivals. In Singapore trainees make the most of the region by jetting off for group weekends on Malaysian or Indonesian islands. In Brussels they hook into the social scene attached to the vast EU machine. Another big plus is the free accommodation provided by the law firms. Usually, trainees are housed in their own apartments in smart areas close to a city's centre. It may be some time before they can afford such plush digs and domestic help back home. For more on life as a trainee in an overseas seat, check out our website where we report from the most frequented training locations around the world.

Overseas seats: Who goes where?

Location	Firm
Abu Dhabi	Allen & Overy, Baker & McKenzie, Clifford Chance, Clyde & Co, Dewey & LeBoeuf, Herbert Smith, Norton Rose, Reed Smith, Simmons & Simmons, Trowers & Hamlins, Vinson & Elkins, White & Case
Almaty	White & Case
Amsterdam	Allen & Overy, Clifford Chance, Linklaters, Norton Rose, Slaughter and May
Athens	Norton Rose, Thomas Cooper
Auckland	Slaughter and May
Bahrain	Charles Russell, Norton Rose, Trowers & Hamlins
Bangkok	Allen & Overy, Herbert Smith, Watson Farley & Williams
Beijing	Allen & Overy, Freshfields Bruckhaus Deringer, Linklaters, Norton Rose, Slaughter and May
Berlin	Freshfields Bruckhaus Deringer, SJ Berwin
Brussels	Allen & Overy, Ashurst, Baker & McKenzie, Berwin Leighton Paisner, Bird & Bird, Cleary Gottlieb Steen & Hamilton, Clifford Chance, Dechert, Dickinson Dees, Field Fisher Waterhouse, Freshfields Bruckhaus Deringer, Hammonds, Herbert Smith, Hogan Lovells, Latham & Watkins, Linklaters, Mayer Brown, Nabarro, Norton Rose, Olswang, Sidley Austin, SJ Berwin, Slaughter and May, White & Case
Bucharest	Allen & Overy, CMS Cameron McKenna
Budapest	Allen & Overy, CMS Cameron McKenna
Dubai	Allen & Overy, Ashurst, Clifford Chance, Clyde & Co, Dewey & LeBoeuf, Freshfields Bruckhaus Deringer, Herbert Smith, Hogan Lovells, Holman Fenwick Willan, Ince & Co, Latham & Watkins, Linklaters, Norton Rose, Pinsent Masons, Reed Smith, Simmons & Simmons, Slaughter and May, SNR Denton, Trowers & Hamlins, Vinson & Elkins
Düsseldorf	Bird & Bird, Freshfields Bruckhaus Deringer, Slaughter and May
Falkland Islands	McGrigors
Frankfurt	Allen & Overy, Ashurst, Bird & Bird, Clifford Chance, Freshfields Bruckhaus Deringer, Hogan Lovells, Linklaters, Norton Rose, SJ Berwin, White & Case
Geneva	Charles Russell
The Hague	Bird & Bird
Hamburg	Ince & Co
Helsinki	Bird & Bird
Hong Kong	Allen & Overy, Baker & McKenzie, Barlow Lyde & Gilbert, Bingham McCutchen, Cleary Gottlieb Steen & Hamilton, Clifford Chance, Clyde & Co, Dewey & LeBoeuf, DLA Piper, Edwards Angell Palmer & Dodge, Freshfields Bruckhaus Deringer, Herbert Smith, Hogan Lovells, Holman Fenwick Willan, Kirkland & Ellis, Latham & Watkins, Linklaters, Mayer Brown, Norton Rose, Orrick, Reed Smith, Simmons & Simmons, Skadden, Slaughter and May, Stephenson Harwood, White & Case
Johannesburg	White & Case
Kiev	CMS Cameron McKenna
Luxembourg	Clifford Chance
Madrid	Allen & Overy, Ashurst, Baker & McKenzie, Bird & Bird, Clifford Chance, Freshfields Bruckhaus Deringer, Linklaters, SJ Berwin, Slaughter and May
Milan	Allen & Overy, Bird & Bird, Clifford Chance, Freshfields Bruckhaus Deringer, Linklaters, Norton Rose, SJ Berwin, Slaughter and May, Withers
Moscow	Allen & Overy, Baker & McKenzie, Berwin Leighton Paisner, Cleary Gottlieb Steen & Hamilton, Clifford Chance, CMS Cameron McKenna, Dewey & LeBoeuf, DLA Piper, Herbert Smith, Latham & Watkins, Linklaters, White & Case

Note: The availability of overseas secondments is liable to change year by year, so if you have your heart set on a particular destination do check with firms before committing to them.

Overseas seats: Who goes where?

Location	Firm
Mumbai	Slaughter and May
Munich	Clifford Chance, Norton Rose, SJ Berwin, Slaughter and May
Muscat	SNR Denton, Towers & Hamlins
New York	Allen & Overy, Cleary Gottlieb Steen & Hamilton, Clifford Chance, Freshfields Bruckhaus Deringer, Kirkland & Ellis, Linklaters, Mayer Brown, Slaughter and May, Weil Gotshal & Manges, White & Case
Oslo	Slaughter and May
Paris	Allen & Overy, Ashurst, Baker & McKenzie, Cleary Gottlieb Steen & Hamilton, Clifford Chance, Dewey & LeBoeuf, Eversheds, Freshfields Bruckhaus Deringer, Hammonds, Herbert Smith, Hogan Lovells, Holman Fenwick Willan, Linklaters, Norton Rose, Simmons & Simmons, SJ Berwin, Slaughter and May, SNR Denton, Travers Smith, Watson Farley & Williams, Weil Gotshal & Manges, White & Case
Piraeus	Clyde & Co, Hill Dickinson, Holman Fenwick Willan, Ince & Co, Reed Smith, Watson Farley & Williams
Prague	Clifford Chance, CMS Cameron McKenna, White & Case
Riyadh	Freshfields Bruckhaus Deringer, Latham & Watkins
Rome	Allen & Overy
São Paulo	Clifford Chance, Mayer Brown
Shanghai	Allen & Overy, Clyde & Co, Eversheds, Freshfields Bruckhaus Deringer, Herbert Smith, Linklaters, Norton Rose
Singapore	Allen & Overy, Ashurst, Barlow Lyde & Gilbert, Clifford Chance, Clyde & Co, DLA Piper, Herbert Smith, Hill Dickinson, Hogan Lovells, Holman Fenwick William, Latham & Watkins, Linklaters, Norton Rose, Stephenson Harwood, Watson Farley & Williams, White & Case
Stockholm	Bird & Bird, Slaughter and May
Sydney	Slaughter and May
Tokyo	Allen & Overy, Ashurst, Baker & McKenzie, Clifford Chance, DLA Piper, Freshfields Bruckhaus Deringer, Herbert Smith, Linklaters, Norton Rose, Simmons & Simmons, Slaughter and May, White & Case
Toronto	Baker & McKenzie
Vienna	CMS Cameron McKenna (client secondment), Freshfields Bruckhaus Deringer
Warsaw	Bird & Bird
Washington, DC	Freshfields Bruckhaus Deringer

- **Things always take longer than you think:** However long you reckon it will take to complete an application form, double your estimate (and then add some more time). You can always go to the pub if you finish early.

A-Z of Solicitors

- **Think ahead:** You can read a legal or business article the day before you go for an interview and think you've got a feel for the topic, but it's probably just the latest update in an ongoing story. If you have been reading the same publication for two or threee months beforehand, you will be much more sound on the way stories have developed.

Addleshaw Goddard

Milton Gate, 60 Chiswell St, London, EC1Y 4AG
Sovereign House, PO Box 8, Sovereign Street, Leeds LS1 1HQ
100 Barbirolli Square, Manchester, M2 3AB
Website: www.addleshawgoddard.com/graduates
Tel: (020) 7606 8855 / (0161) 934 6000
Fax: (020) 7606 4390 / (0161) 934 6060

Firm profile

As a major force on the legal landscape, Addleshaw Goddard offers extensive and exciting opportunities to all its trainees across the entire spectrum of commercial law, from employment and banking to real estate, corporate finance, intellectual property, employment, PFI and litigation. As a trainee with this firm, you'll be a key member of the team from day one. Whether based in the London, Leeds or Manchester office (or out on secondment), you'll work closely with blue-chip clients within a supportive yet challenging environment, and be part of a structured training programme designed to ensure your success – now and in the future.

Main areas of work

The firm has four main business divisions: Finance and Projects, Contentious and Commercial, Corporate and Real Estate. Within these divisions as well as the main practice areas it also has specialist areas such as sport, intellectual property, employment and private client services such as trusts and tax.

Trainee profile

Graduates who are capable of achieving a 2:1 and can demonstrate commercial awareness, motivation and enthusiasm. Applications from law and non-law graduates are welcomed, as are applications from students who may be considering a change of direction. We also have a diversity access programme for applicants on GDL or LPC with less conventional academic backgrounds. Further details can be found on our website.

Training environment

During each six-month seat, there will be regular two-way performance reviews with the supervising partner or solicitor. Trainees have the opportunity to spend a seat in one of the firm's other offices and there are a number of secondments to clients available. Seated with a qualified solicitor or partner and working as part of a team enables trainees to develop the professional skills necessary to deal with the demanding and challenging work the firm carries out for its clients. Practical training is complemented by high-quality training courses provided by both the in-house team and external training providers.

Sponsorship & benefits

GDL and LPC fees are paid, plus a maintenance grant of £7,000 (London) or £4,500 (elsewhere in the UK). Benefits include corporate gym membership, season ticket loan, subsidised restaurant, pension and private healthcare.

Vacation placements

Places for 2011 – 90; Duration – 1, 2 or 3 weeks (over Easter and the summer); location – all offices; Apply by 31 January 2011.

Partners 166
Associates 500+
Trainees 91

Contact
The Graduate Recruitment Team
grad@addleshawgoddard.com

Selection procedure
Interview, assessment centre

Closing date for 2012
31 July 2011

Application
Training contracts p.a. 45-50
Applications p.a. 1,500
% interviewed 10%
Required degree grade 2:1

Training
Salary
1st year
London £36,000
Leeds/Manchester £24,500
2nd year
London £37,000
Leeds/Manchester £25,500
Holiday entitlement
25 days
% of trainees with a non-law degree p.a. 45%

Post-qualification
Salary
London £58,000
Leeds/Manchester £36,500
% of trainees accepting job on qualification (2010) 86%

Other offices
London, Leeds, Manchester

Allen & Overy LLP

One Bishops Square, London E1 6AD
Tel: (020) 3088 0000 Fax: (020) 3088 0088
Email: graduate.recruitment@allenovery.com
Website: www.allenovery.com/careeruk

Firm profile
Allen & Overy LLP is an international legal practice with approximately 5,000 people working across 36 major centres worldwide. The firm's client list includes many of the world's top businesses, financial institutions and governments.

Main areas of work
Banking, corporate, international capital markets, litigation and dispute resolution, tax, employment and benefits and real estate. Allen & Overy partners frequently lead the field in their particular areas of law and the firm can claim both an enviable reputation amongst clients and unrivalled success in major deals.

Training Contracts
We recruit around 105 trainee solicitors each year across two intakes (March and September). Applications are welcome from law and non-law graduates. Our current starting salary for trainee solicitors is £38,000, rising to £43,200 in the second year of training.

From 1st June 2011 - 31st July 2011, penultimate year law undergraduates and law graduates can apply for our training contracts for interview in September 2011. We will only be accepting applications for our September 2013 / March 2014 intakes.

Final year non-law undergraduates and non-law graduates can apply from the 1st November 2010 - 16th January 2011 for our September 2013 / March 2014 intakes.

Trainee profile
You will need to demonstrate a genuine enthusiasm for a legal career and Allen & Overy. The firm looks for a strong, consistent academic performance and you should have achieved or be predicted at least a 2:1 degree (or equivalent). At Allen & Overy you will be working in a team where you will use your initiative and manage your own time and workload, so evidence of teamwork, leadership and problem solving skills are also looked for.

Training environment
Allen & Overy offers a training contract characterised by flexibility and choice. The seat structure ensures that you get to see as many parts of the firm as possible and that your learning is hands-on, guided by an experienced associate or partner. Your choice of a priority seat is guaranteed when you begin your training contract. Given the strength of the firm's international finance practice, trainees are required to spend a minimum of 12 months in at least two of the three core departments of banking, corporate and international capital markets. The firm now offers its trainees the option of completing a litigation course. This means that trainees will no longer need to spend time in the firm's dispute resolution or employment departments to gain their contentious experience if they are sure their interests lie elsewhere. There are also opportunities for trainees to undertake an international or client secondment during their final year of training.

Vacation placements
Allen & Overy offers 65 vacation placements across the year. The winter placement is for non-law finalists and graduates who should apply from 1st October to 31st October 2010. Summer placements are for penultimate year law undergraduates and law graduates who should apply from 1st November 2010 to 16th January 2011.

Benefits
Private healthcare, private medical insurance, in-house medical facilities, interest-free season ticket loan, free in-house gym, subsidised staff restaurants, multi-faith prayer rooms and music rooms.

Sponsorship & awards
GDL and LPC course fees are paid in full along with contributions towards your maintenance costs. For the Allen & Overy LPC in London, a £7,000 maintenance grant is provided. For the GDL, £6,000 is provided in London and £5,000 elsewhere. Financial incentives are also offered to future trainees achieving a first class undergraduate degree or a distinction in the LPC.

Partners 470*
Associates 1969*
London Trainees 230
*Denotes world-wide number

Contact
Graduate Recruitment

Method of application
Online application form

Selection procedure
Interview

Closing date for 2013
Non Law candidates:
16th Jan 2011
Law candidates: 31st July 2011

Application
Training contracts p.a. 105
Applications p.a. 2,500
% interviewed p.a. 8-10%
Required degree grade 2:1
(or equivalent)

Training
Salary
£38,000 – Year 1
£43,200 – Year 2
£61,000 – NQ
Holiday entitlement 25 days
% of trainees with a
non-law degree p.a. 45%
% of trainees with a
law degree p.a. 55%
No. of seats available
in international offices
37 seats twice a year;
14 client secondments

Post-qualification
Salary £61,000 (2010)
% of trainees offered job
on qualification 81%
% of partners who joined as
trainees over 50%

International offices
Abu Dhabi, Amsterdam, Antwerp, Athens, Bangkok, Beijing, Bratislava, Brussels, Budapest, Bucharest*, Doha, Dubai, Dusseldorf, Frankfurt, Hamburg, Hong Kong, Jakarta*, London, Luxembourg, Madrid, Mannheim, Milan, Moscow, Munich, New York, Paris, Perth, Prague, Riyadh*, Rome, Sao Paulo, Shanghai, Singapore, Sydney, Tokyo, Warsaw
(*associated office)

Arnold & Porter (UK) LLP

Tower 42, 25 Old Broad Street, London, EC2N 1HQ
Tel: (020) 7786 6100 Fax: (020) 7786 6299
Email: graduates@aporter.com
Website: www.arnoldporter.com

Firm profile

Arnold & Porter is a US-based firm with a deserved reputation for its quality of service and expertise in handling the most complex legal and business problems requiring innovative and practical solutions. The firm's global reach, experience, and deep knowledge allows it to work across geographic, cultural, technological, and ideological borders, serving clients whose business needs require US, EU, or cross-border regulatory, litigation, and transactional services.

Main areas of work

The London office is home to the firm's European regulatory, life sciences, IP, competition, corporate, employment and telecoms practices. The UK Legal 500 recently ranked its London office as recommended in administrative and public policy, EU competition, IP, M&A, pharmaceuticals and biotechnology, product liability, publishing, rail, telecommunications, and venture capital.

Trainee profile

The firm looks for talented law and non-law graduates from all backgrounds who share the firm's commitment to excellence, and want to be part of the continued growth of its London office. Candidates need to demonstrate a consistently high academic background; the firm looks for well-rounded individuals who can demonstrate their participation in a range of extra curricular activities and achievements.

Training environment

Four six-month seats: pharmaceuticals, IP, corporate and securities and competition. The firm encourages individuals to work across specialisms, and emphasises teamwork, so trainees may find that whilst they are working in one group, they undertake work in a variety of different areas throughout the firm. Trainees will be expected to work on several matters at once, and assume responsibility at an early stage. Trainees may also have an opportunity to work in the firm's Brussels office and where the occasion permits, to work on projects in one of the firm's US offices.

An important aspect of the firm's culture is its commitment to pro bono. Trainees and all lawyers at the firm are encouraged to take part and devote 15% of their time to it, which helps young lawyers develop client managements skills from an early stage.

Vacation schemes

The firm takes up to eight summer vacation students each year. Whether you are a law or non-law student, the firm will introduce you to life in a busy City law firm, spending two weeks working on a variety of projects and workshops with partners and associates throughout the London office. Apply via the firm's website by 25 February 2011.

Benefits

Healthy incentive bonus, lunch vouchers, Christmas bonus, child care vouchers, private health insurance, life assurance, season ticket loan.

Sponsorship & awards

GDL/LPC: fees paid; £7,250 pa maintenance.

Partners 14
Assistant Solicitors 21
Total Trainees 2

Contact
Graduate Recruitment

Method of application
Apply via website

Selection procedure
Interview with partners and associates

Closing date for 2012
29 July 2011

Application
Training contracts p.a. 2
Applications p.a 700
% interviewed 2%
Required degree grade 2:1

Training salary
1st year US firm market rate
2nd year US firm market rate
Holiday entitlement 25 days

Post-qualification
% of trainees offered job on qualification 100%

Overseas, regional offices
London, Washington DC, New York, Los Angeles, Denver, Northern Virginia, San Francisco, Brussels

ARNOLD & PORTER (UK) LLP

Ashurst LLP

Broadwalk House, 5 Appold St, London EC2A 2HA
Tel: (020) 7638 1111 Fax: (020) 7638 1112
Email: gradrec@ashurst.com
Website: www.ashurst.com

Firm profile

Ashurst LLP is an elite law firm advising corporates and financial institutions, with core businesses in mergers and acquisitions, corporate and structured finance. The firm's strong and growing presence around the world is built on extensive experience in working with clients on the complex international legal and regulatory issues relating to cross-border transactions.

Main areas of work

Competition and EU; corporate; employment, incentives and pensions; energy, transport and infrastructure; international finance; litigation; real estate; tax; and technology and commercial.

Trainee profile

To become an Ashurst trainee you will need to show common sense and good judgement. The firm needs to know that you can handle responsibility because you will be involved in some of the highest quality international work on offer anywhere. The transactions and cases you will be involved in will be intellectually demanding, so Ashurst looks for high academic achievers who are able to think laterally. But it's not just academic results that matter. Ashurst wants people who have a range of interests outside of their studies. And they want outgoing people with a sense of humour who know how to laugh at themselves.

Training environment

Your training contract will consist of four seats. For each, you will sit with a partner or senior solicitor who will be the main source of your work and your principal supervisor during that seat. Seats are generally for six months. Anything less than that will not give you sufficient depth of experience for the responsibility Ashurst expects you to take on. The firm asks trainees to spend one seat in the Corporate Department and one seat in the International Finance Department. Trainees spend their two remaining seats in the firm's other practice areas, on secondment to a client or on secondment to an overseas office.

Benefits

Private health insurance, pension, life assurance, interest-free season ticket loan, subsidised gym membership and 25 days holiday per year during training. Other benefits can be found on the 'benefits and salaries' section of the firm's website.

Vacation placements

Places for 2011: A two-week Easter placement scheme primarily aimed at final-year non-law undergraduates and all graduates. Two three-week summer placement schemes primarily aimed at penultimate-year law undergraduates. Remuneration £275 p.w. Closing date 31 January 2011.

Sponsorship & awards

GDL and LPC funding plus maintenance allowances of £7,500 per annum. LPC distinction and first class degree awards of £500. Language tuition bursaries.

Partners 200+
Assistant Solicitors 500+
Total Trainees 100+

Contact
Stephen Trowbridge
Graduate Recruitment and Development Manager

Method of application
Online

Selection procedure
Interview with Graduate Recruitment and Development Manager followed by interview with two Partners

Closing date for 2013
31 July 2011

Application
Training contracts p.a. 55
Applications p.a. 2,500
% interviewed p.a. 10%
Required degree grade 2:1

Training
Salary (2010)
First year
£37,000
Second year
£41,000
Holiday entitlement 25 days
% of trainees with a non-law degree 50%
Number of seats abroad available p.a. 10

Post-qualification
Salary (2010) £60,000
% of trainees offered job on qualification (2010) 74%

Overseas offices
Abu Dhabi, Brussels, Dubai, Frankfurt, Hong Kong, Madrid, Milan, Munich, New York, Paris, Singapore, Stockholm, Tokyo, Washington DC

Baker & McKenzie LLP

100 New Bridge Street, London EC4V 6JA
Tel: (020) 7919 1000 Fax: (020) 7919 1999
Email: multiplyingyourpotential@bakermckenzie.com
Website: www.mutliplyingyourpotential.co.uk

Firm profile

Baker & McKenzie LLP is a leading global law firm based in 67 locations across 39 countries. With a presence in virtually every important financial and commercial centre in the world, the firm's strategy is to provide the best combination of local legal and commercial knowledge, international expertise and resources.

Main areas of work

Corporate; dispute resolution; banking; EU, competition and trade; employment; intellectual property; information technology and commercial; pensions; tax; projects; real estate; structured capital markets. In addition the firm has cross-departmental practice groups, such as media and communications, insurance and reinsurance, business recovery and environmental law.

Trainee profile

The firm is looking for trainee solicitors who are stimulated by intellectual challenge and want to be 'the best' at what they do. Effective communication together with the ability to be creative and practical problem solvers, team players and a sense of humour are qualities which will help them stand out from the crowd.

Training environment

Four six-month seats which include a corporate and a contentious seat, usually within the firm's highly regarded dispute resolution department. There is also the possibility of a secondment abroad or to a client. During each seat you will have a meeting to discuss individual seat preferences. In addition, you will receive formal and informal reviews to discuss your progress. Your training contract commences with a highly interactive and practical induction programme which focuses on key skills including practical problem solving, interviewing, presenting and the application of information technology. The firm's training programme includes important components on management and other business skills, as well as seminars and workshops on key legal topics for each practice area. There is a Trainee Solicitor Liaison Committee which acts as a forum for any new ideas or raises issues which may occur during your training contract. Trainees are actively encouraged to participate in a variety of pro bono issues and, outside office hours, there is a varied sporting and social life.

Benefits

Permanent health insurance, life insurance, private medical insurance, group personal pension, subsidised gym membership, season ticket loan, subsidised staff restaurant.

Vacation placements

London Summer Placement - Places for 2011: 35; Duration: 3 weeks; Remuneration (2010): £270 p.w.; Closing date: 31 January 2011.

International Summer Placement - Places for 2011: 3-5; Duration: 8-12 weeks divided between London and an overseas office; Remuneration (2010): £270 p.w.; Closing date: 31 January 2011.

Partners 83
Assistant Solicitors 213
Total Trainees 81

Contact
Justine Beedle

Method of application
Online application form

Selection procedure
Candidates to participate in an interactive group exercise, followed by a discussion with an associate and an interview with two partners based around a typical client problem

Closing date for 2013
Non-law 31 March 2011
Law 31 July 2011

Application
Training contracts p.a. 38
Applications p.a. 2,000
% interviewed p.a. 5%
Required degree grade 2:1

Training
Salary
1st year (2010) £37,500 + £3,000 'joining bonus'
2nd year (2009) £40,000
Holiday entitlement 25 days
% of trainees with a non-law degree p.a.
Approx 50%
No. of seats available abroad p.a. Variable
post-qualification
Salary (2010) £61,000
% of trainees offered job on qualification (2010) 94%

BAKER & McKENZIE

Barlow Lyde & Gilbert LLP

Beaufort House, 15 St Botolph Street, London EC3A 7NJ
Tel: (020) 7247 2277 Fax: (020) 7071 9000
Email: grad.recruit@blg.co.uk Website: www.blg.co.uk

Firm profile

Barlow Lyde & Gilbert LLP ("BLG") is a pre-eminent international law firm with an unrivalled reputation within major industry sectors including financial services, professional practices, aerospace, shipping, commodities, energy, construction, and healthcare, particularly where clients in those sectors also require insurance and reinsurance market expertise. The firm's Insurance and Reinsurance Practice is one of the largest in the world, providing services of unparalleled breadth across the sector. BLG was named "Best Law Firm" to the global insurance industry at Reactions London Market Awards 2009. BLG is also renowned for its Commercial Litigation and Arbitration Practice, providing an extensive range of high-value, multi-jurisdictional dispute resolutions to clients from many different industries across the world. The firm scooped "Litigation Team of the Year" at the Legal Week Awards in 2005, and again at both The Lawyer Awards and the Legal Business Awards in 2006. BLG's non-contentious expertise spans corporate, commercial, employment, pensions, insolvency, property, outsourcing, technology, and insurance risk transactions. The firm has over 80 partners and more than 200 lawyers in its offices in London, Singapore, Oxford, Manchester and São Paulo, together with its affiliated undertakings in Hong Kong and Shanghai. BLG was named "one to watch" in the Best Companies Guide 2009.

Trainee profile

The firm recruits 15 trainees a year. It looks for intelligent and motivated graduates with good academic qualifications and excellent communication skills. Trainees must be able to work independently or in a team, and are expected to display common sense and initiative. An appreciation of the client's commercial interests is essential.

Training environment

During your training contract you will have six-month seats in four different practice areas. The firm always try to accommodate a trainee's preference for a particular type of work. There are opportunities to spend time in its other offices, on secondment with clients or on exchange programmes with overseas law firms. A capable trainee will deal regularly with clients from an early stage in his or her training, subject to supervision. All trainees are expected to undertake and assist in practice development and client care. Successful candidates will enjoy a wide variety of social and sporting events at BLG, ensuring that trainees have the chance to meet and stay in contact with employees from across the firm.

Work placement scheme

An increasing number of the firm's trainees come through its summer vacation schemes. Whether you are a law or non-law student, the firm will introduce you to life in a City law firm. You can even choose which department you want to spend time in. The closing date for applications is 31 January 2011. The firm also runs open days and drop-in sessions throughout the year. Full details on these are available from the website - www.blg.co.uk.

Whether you wish to apply for an interview day or a vacation scheme, please apply via the firm's website at www.blg.co.uk. The closing date for interview days is 31 August 2011.

Sponsorship & awards

A maintenance grant is provided and law school fees are paid in full.

Partners 84
Vacancies 15
Trainees 41
Total staff 625

Contact
Caroline Walsh
Head of Graduate Recruitment & Trainee Development

Method of application
Online application form only

Selection procedure
Assessment Centre

Closing date for 2013
31 August 2011

Application
Training contracts p.a. 15
Applications p.a. 1,500
% interviewed p.a. 10%

Training
Salary
1st year £34,000
2nd year £36,000
Holiday entitlement
5 weeks
post-qualification
Salary £56,000
Trainees offered job on qualification (2010) 71%

Offices
London, Oxford, Manchester, Hong Kong, Shanghai, Singapore, São Paulo

BARLOW LYDE & GILBERT

Bates Wells & Braithwaite London LLP

2-6 Cannon Street, London EC4M 6YH
Tel: (020) 7551 7777 Fax: (020) 7551 7800
Email: training@bwbllp.com
Website: www.bwbllp.com

Firm profile

Bates Wells and Braithwaite is a commercial law firm servicing a wide range of commercial statutory, charity and social enterprises. The firm is expanding, progressive and is doing high quality work for clients and providing high quality training for those who work with the firm.

Whilst the firm is ranked first in three areas of law by the Legal 500 and ranked by them or Chambers in 15 other areas of law, the firm also believes in its staff enjoying a good work/life balance and living a life outside as well as inside the office.

Main areas of work

The firm is well known for its work for a wide range and variety of clients given its size. This includes working with the charities and social enterprise sector, commercial organisations, regulatory and individuals. The firm also has particular expertise in the arts and media, sports and immigration arenas together with strong departments dealing with employment, property and dispute resolution.

Trainee profile

The firm is looking for trainees with not only a sound academic background and the ability to communicate clearly and effectively, but most importantly it is looking for trainees who positively want to join a firm such as Bates Wells & Braithwaite.

Training environment

In the first year there are two six month seats, whilst in the second year there are three four month seats which, between them, cover a wide range of the work with which the firm is involved. From time to time the firm arranges secondments to clients on an ad hoc basis.

The firm runs a programme of internal seminars specifically addressed to trainees and operates a mentoring system, all designed to ensure that the trainees enjoy their time with the firm and to maximise the opportunities that are available for them during their training contract and beyond.

Benefits

Interest-free loan for season ticket travel, subsidised use of gym and squash court, subsidised restaurant, one month's unpaid leave on qualification and the firm's pension scheme with match funding provided.

Vacation placements

Places for 2011: 18 people for a duration of one week each. Closing date: 17th February 2011.

Sponsorship & awards

LPC course fees paid and interest paid on student loans during the training contract.

Partners 27
Assistant Solicitors 56
Trainees 8

Graduate recruitmentcontact
Peter Bennett (020) 7551 7777

Method of application
Online via website

Selection procedure
Interviews

Closing date for 2013
14 July 2011 - see website

Application
Training contracts per annum 4
Applications p.a. 750+
% interviewed p.a. 5%
Required degree 2:1

Training
Salary
1st year, £30,000
2nd year, £32,500
Holiday entitlement
5 weeks
Post-qualification
Salary £45,000
% of trainees offered job
on qualification (last 3 years)
100%

Beachcroft LLP

100 Fetter Lane, London EC4A 1BN
Tel: (020) 7242 1011 Fax: (020) 7831 6630
Email: trainee@beachcroft.co.uk
Website: www.beachcroft.com

Firm profile

Beachcroft LLP is one of the largest commercial firms in the UK, with a turnover of over £131m. The firm has over 1,500 people working from eight offices and it serves the broadest range of clients. This means the firm offers exceptional career opportunities for ambitious people who want to become leaders in their field.

Beachcroft is one of the largest law firms to obtain the 'Investors in People' award across all of its offices. The firm values its people and works with them to help them achieve excellence in legal knowledge and commercial understanding alike. The firm's working culture of mutual respect has led it to be seen as both a friendly firm – and one that literally means business.

Main areas of work

From routine insurance claims management to 'trusted adviser' work for major national and international organisations, the firm delivers integrated legal services to clients in six main industry groups; financial institutions, health and public sector, real estate, technology and telecommunications, industrial goods and services, and consumer goods and services.

Trainee profile

You're bright, articulate, inquisitive and adaptable. But what makes you right for Beachcroft is an unpretentious but real interest in the work, a respect for others, and ambitions to be a leader in your field. People from varied backgrounds convert to law with Beachcroft; the firm finds their experience an asset.

Training environment

The firm's aim is to develop its future leaders – not just to provide legal training. That's why its programme is tailored to ensuring that its trainees acquire the skills and knowledge that will enable them to lead its business in the future. The firm offers a programme that identifies individual skills and talents and directs these to parts of its business where they will develop and thrive. It goes without saying that the firm's scheme delivers the required SRA elements for qualification as a solicitor, but its programme also includes business and personal skills training modules, coaching groups and varied internal placements as swell as secondments with top clients. The firm offers support through individual mentors and challenge trainees with high quality work. It's all about attracting, nurturing and retaining the best talent.

Benefits

A flexible benefits package where you can personalise your rewards – 'buying' or 'selling' options such as pension entitlement and private healthcare. Additional benefits include well woman and man checks, free eye test, employee assistance programme, travel loans, discounted insurance, a bikes-to-work scheme and many other fringe benefits.

Vacation placements

Summer: June (apply by 1 March).

Partners 140
Assistant Solicitors 743
Total Trainees 49

Contact
Carrie Daniels
Recruitment Officer
Email:
trainee@beachcroft.co.uk

Method of application
Apply online at
www.beachcroft.com

Selection procedure
Online psychometric testing and assessment centre

Closing date
1 August each year

Application
Training contracts per annum 16
Required degree 2:1 preferred

Training
Salary
1st year, regions
£26,000 p.a.
2nd year, regions
£29,000 p.a.
1st year, London
£34,000 p.a.
2nd year, London
£37,000 p.a.
Holiday entitlement - 25 days
% of trainees with a non-law degree p.a. - 45%
Beachcroft provides payment for GDL, LPC and £5,000 bursary.

Offices
Birmingham, Leeds*, Bristol*, Manchester*, Winchester, Newcastle, Dublin (*training offices), Auckland

Beale and Company Solicitors LLP

Garrick House, 27-32 King Street, Covent Garden, London, WC2E 8JB
Tel: (020) 7240 3474 Fax: (020) 7240 9111
Email: h.kapadia@beale-law.com
Website: www.beale-law.com

Partners 13
Assistant Solicitors 25
Trainees 8

Contact
Mrs Heidi Kapadia

Method of application
Application form

Selection procedure
Interview and assessment

Closing date for 2010/2011
Not applicable

Training
Salary
1st year, £28,000 (London)
1st year, £23,800 (Regions)
2nd year, £30,000 (London)
2nd year, £25,500 (Regions)

Firm profile

Beale and Company is a specialist niche practice based in London, Bristol and Dublin. With the firm ranked as a leading practice for Technology and Construction Professional Negligence and Construction in London; and for Professional Negligence generally in the Regions, it provides the perfect opportunity for trainees to explore their legal capabilities in a range of challenging areas. It combines the cut and thrust of a practice focused on providing the best service to clients who are nationally and internationally recognised leaders in their fields with the community and balance that the ethos of a smaller firm embodies. With an active participation in a European Network of law firms, and a regular international dimension to the matters handled, trainees are able to experience a diversity of legal issues.

Main areas of work

The firm specialises in: construction, professional negligence; dispute resolution; insurance; IT; corporate and commercial; employment; health and safety; and property (domestic and commercial) together with some private client work.

Trainee profile

The firm is looking for candidates with a strong academic background (having obtained or being predicted a 2:1 honours degree in any subject), and a real interest in pursuing a career in the law. Trainees need to be commercial, motivated and analytical. A candidate should have the ability to work as a team player and have the initiative to be involved in the strategy and management of a matter from an early stage so as to achieve the most from the training experience.

Training environment

The two year training contract will include six month seats in the key areas of the practice, two of which will be within the Dispute Resolution Department. There may be opportunities to spend time in a different office within the firm, or to go on secondment to clients. Trainees also enjoy a number of social and sporting activities throughout the year, both internally and within the local business community.

Benefits

The firm's benefits include: holiday entitlement; interest free loan for a season ticket for travel; discretionary annual bonus and a competitive salary.

Berwin Leighton Paisner

Adelaide House, London Bridge, London EC4R 9HA
Tel: (020) 3400 1000 Fax: (020) 3400 1111
Email: traineerecruit@blplaw.com Website: www.blplaw.com

Firm profile

BLP is an exciting, ambitious, and dynamic full service City law firm. The firm has particular strengths in real estate, corporate, finance, tax and a strong litigation and dispute resolution capability. The firm has around 730 lawyers including 190 Partners. There is an open and friendly culture, combined with a strong commitment to career development. Its people are prized for their legal talent and renowned for being personally committed to helping clients succeed. It's a distinct BLP quality.

Main areas of work

BLP delivers first-rate, pragmatic legal advice that helps a wide portfolio of clients to achieve their goals. Clients are serviced by lawyers specialising in over 60 areas of legal expertise and a wide variety of key sectors. These include: commercial contracts; corporate finance; defence and aerospace; dispute resolution; energy and natural resources; EU and competition; finance; healthcare and education; hotels, leisure and gaming; human resources; insurance; intellectual property; outsourcing; public sector; real estate; retail; regulatory and compliance; restructuring and insolvency; tax; technology, media and telecoms; and transport and infrastructure.

LPC+

Trainees study at the College of Law for both the GDL and LPC. The firm runs the UK's first tailor-made LPC Course, called the LPC+ where tutors are joined by BLP lawyers and trainers who help to deliver some of the sessions, using BLP precedents and documents, discussing how theory is applied to real cases and transactions.

Trainee profile

The firm is looking for bright, business-minded individuals with a positive approach and a drive to succeed. Successful applicants are people-orientated, hungry to learn, and have the flexibility to work in different teams across the firm to find practical solutions for its clients.

Training environment

When recruiting trainees, the focus is on quality rather than quantity. As a result, trainees are rewarded with a high degree of responsibility and involvement underpinned by an exceptional standard of training and support. BLP has always worked hard to provide the right environment for people to grow. Each trainee is allocated a Partner mentor who provides invaluable support and guidance across the four seats. Trainee development is important to the firm and appraisals take place every three months. The trainee induction covers the practical aspects of working in a law firm, from billing to client care. There is technical training for each department, with weekly skills sessions and seminars for trainees as well as professional skills courses.

Vacation placements

Places for 2011: Assessment centres held during December, January and February at the firm's London office, applications accepted online before 31 January 2011 (at www.blplaw.com). The firm runs a one week Easter vacation scheme and two week Summer vacation schemes, aimed at those in their penultimate year and above (law and non-law).

Sponsorship

CPE/GDL and LPC+ fees paid and £7,200 maintenance p.a.

Partners 190
Assistant Solicitors 380
Total Trainees 80

Contact
Claire England

Method of application
Online application form

Selection procedure
Telephone Interview, Assessment day & partner interview

Closing date for 2013/2014
31 July 2011

Application
Training contracts p.a. 35-40
Applications p.a. 1,500
% interviewed p.a. 10%
Required degree grade 2:1

Training
Salary
1st year (2010)
£37,000
2nd year (2010)
£41,000
Holiday entitlement 25 days
% of trainees with a non-law degree p.a. 50%
No. of seats available abroad p.a. 2

Post-qualification
Salary (2010) £59,000
% of trainees offered job on qualification (Sept 2010) 90%

Offices
London, Brussels, Paris, Abu Dhabi, Moscow, Singapore, preferred firms network in over 65 countries

BERWIN LEIGHTON PAISNER

Bevan Brittan

Kings Orchard, 1 Queen Street, Bristol, BS2 0HQ
Tel: (0870) 194 3050 Fax: (0870) 194 8954
Email: hr.training@bevanbrittan.com
Website: www.bevanbrittan.com

Partners 48
Total Trainees 20

Contact
HR and Training
(0870) 194 3050

Method of application
Online application

Closing date for 2013
31 July 2011

Post-qualification
% of trainees offered job on qualification (2010) 53%

Other offices
Birmingham, London

Firm profile

Bevan Brittan is a major commercial law firm who provide a comprehensive range of services to clients throughout the country from its offices in London, Birmingham and Bristol. The firm is the largest specialist provider of commercial legal services to the Public Sector in the UK.

Main areas of work

The firm is structured around three primary areas of the UK economy: health, communities and local government and private sector interface with public sector organisations. The firm's clients include a third of all NHS Trusts, a quarter of all Local Authorities, 30 Housing Associations, and over 100 private sector firms who serve these sectors. The firm's services include advice covering outsourcing, major infrastructure projects and PFI, employment matters, regulation and governance, property, construction, litigation and dispute resolution, and general commercial issues.

Trainee profile

Bevan Brittan recognises that the firm's success depends upon a team of lawyers dedicated to service excellence. Its success is maintained by attracting and retaining enthusiastic, bright people with sound common sense, plenty of energy and the ability to work and communicate well with others.

Training environment

During each six-month seat, the core of your training will be practical work experience in conjunction with an extensive educational programme. Together the training is aimed at developing attitudes, skills and legal and commercial knowledge essential for your career success. You are encouraged to take on as much work and responsibility as you are able to handle, which will be reviewed on a regular basis with your supervising Partner. The firm is friendly and supportive with an open-door policy along with a range of social, sporting and cultural activities.

Vacation placements

Places available across the three offices for 2011: TBC. Closing date: 31st March 2011.

Sponsorship & awards

Bursary and funding for GDL and LPC.

Bingham McCutchen (London) LLP

41 Lothbury, London, EC2R 7HF
Tel: (020) 7661 5300 Fax: (020) 7661 5400
Email: graduaterecruitment@bingham.com Website: www.bingham.com

Firm profile

Bingham's London team of 40 leading finance, litigation and corporate lawyers is dedicated to providing a seamless and responsive service to international financial institution clients. The firm's London office capabilities have been carefully shaped to meet the complex needs of a demanding client segment. Through practical experience and in-depth study of the legal and business issues facing these clients, the firm's London lawyers provide counsel in an intelligent, savvy, forceful and focused way. Members of Bingham's London office represent many of the world's largest insurance companies, pension funds, investment banks, hedge funds, distressed debt investors, international agencies, governments and multinational corporate groups. Bingham has recently represented the creditors on the restructurings of numerous UK plcs, Lehman Brothers, Taylor Wimpey, M.J. Maillis, Phoenix Pharmahandel and Thomson; bondholders of the three Icelandic Banks (Glitnir, Kaupthing and Landsbanki); bondholders of, among others, Elektrim, Head, Independent News & Media, Kremikovtzi, LyondellBasell, Truvo and Wind Hellas; lenders to LBOs including European Directories S.A., Gala Coral, Ineos, Mauser, Monier, TI Automotive and Zapf; noteholders of real estate securitisation vehicles, including Level One, Plantation Place and White Tower; and bondholders in nearly all of the restructurings of high yield bonds in Norway including Petromena and Skeie Drilling. The Financial Restructuring Practice in London, which is closely integrated with our restructuring and insolvency practice in the United States, Frankfurt, Tokyo and Hong Kong, and has been awarded a top-tier ranking for restructuring and insolvency in England by *Practical Law Company* for four consecutive years. London lawyers also have extensive experience in the areas of finance, litigation, corporate, tax, financial services regulatory and competition.

Bingham's market-leading practices are focused on global financial services firms and Fortune 100 companies. The firm has 1,100 lawyers in 13 locations in the US, Europe and Asia.

Main areas of work

Bingham's London office capabilities include financial restructuring, finance, litigation, corporate, tax, financial regulatory and EU/UK competition.

Trainee profile

The firm is looking for top quality candidates who can demonstrate an exceptional academic record combined with evidence of extra-curricular achievement. Prospective trainees will show initiative, be solution driven and seek to be part of a challenging yet friendly environment.

Training environment

The firm currently recruits two trainee solicitors a year. The training contract consists of four six-month seats, rotating between the following practice areas: financial restructuring, finance, corporate and litigation. Trainees also have the opportunity to spend one of their second year seats in the firm's Hong Kong office. The intimate nature of the London office means that you will benefit from a bespoke training programme with a high level of partner involvement. With the firm's small team approach, you will assume responsibilities from day one.

Benefits

The firm offers an extensive compensation programme for trainees. As well as a highly competitive salary, the firm offers private health insurance, travel insurance, long term disability insurance, season ticket loan, life assurance, a critical illness scheme and subsidised gym membership. A discretionary bonus is also payable.

Sponsorship & awards

LPC fees and maintenance grant of £8,000 per annum. PgDL fees and maintenance grant of £8,000 per annum.

Assistant solicitors 25
Total Trainees 4

Contact
Nicola Matthews, Human Resources Officer.
(020) 7661 5300

Method of application
Online application via firm website at www.bingham.com or via CV Mail

Selection procedure
Currently face to face interviews

Closing date for 2013
31 July 2011

Application
Training contracts p.a. up to 2
Required degree grade: High 2:1 from a leading university and excellent A-levels

Training
Salary
1st year £40,000
2nd year £45,000
Holiday entitlement
25 days

Post-qualification
Salary (2010) £100,000

Overseas offices
Boston, Frankfurt, Hartford, Hong Kong, Los Angeles, New York, Orange County, San Francisco, Santa Monica, Silicon Valley, Tokyo, Washington

Bircham Dyson Bell LLP

50 Broadway, London SW1H 0BL
Tel: (020) 7227 7000 Fax: (020) 7222 3480

Firm profile

Bircham Dyson Bell is a leading London law firm. The firm's approach and track record has enabled it to attract and retain some of the most talented people in the profession. This is achieved through the breadth and variety of work that the firm does. As part of the firm's commitment to providing a high level of service, it has been accredited with the Law Society's Lexcel quality mark and are one of the first law firms to be awarded ISO 14001, the internationally recognised standard for Environmental Management Systems. The firm is a leading member of Lexwork International, a network of 34 mid-sized independent law firms with over 1,700 lawyers in major cities across North America and Europe.

Main areas of work

Bircham Dyson Bell is recognised as having leading departments in the charity, private wealth, parliamentary, planning and public law fields. The firm also has strong corporate, commercial, employment, litigation and real estate teams.

Trainee profile

Applications are welcome from both law and non-law students who can demonstrate a consistently high academic record. The firm is looking for forward thinkers with a practical outlook and lots of initiative to join in the firm's friendly, hard-working environment. If you're focused, positive and a confident leader, get in touch. Many of the firm's current trainees have diverse interests outside law.

Training environment

The firm's training is designed to produce its future partners. To achieve this they aim to provide a balance of both formal and practical training and will give early responsibility to those who show promise. The two-year training contract consists of four six-month seats during which you will work alongside partners and other senior lawyers, some of whom are leaders in their field. As the firm practises in a wide variety of legal disciplines, trainees benefit from a diverse experience. Trainees undergo specific technical training in each seat in addition to the mandatory Professional Skills Course (PSC). Great emphasis is also placed on soft skills training and development so when you qualify you have the breadth of skills required to be an excellent solicitor.

Benefits

Bonus scheme, group health care, life assurance, pension scheme, season ticket loan and corporate rate gym membership

Partners 48
Fee Earners 115
Total Trainees 14

Contact
Graduate Recruitment Team
(020) 7227 7000

Method of application
Please visit the firm's website, www.bdb-law.co.uk

Selection procedure
Two interviews with members of the Graduate Recruitment Team, comprising a number of partners, associates and HR. In addition you will be required to complete an online test and assessment centre exercise

Closing date for 2013
31 July 2011

Application
Training contracts p.a. 7
Applications p.a. 650
% interviewed p.a. 8%
Required degree grade:
2:1 or above degree preferred

Training
Salary
1st year £30,000
2nd year £31,000
Holiday entitlement
25 days

Post-qualification
Salary £49,000
% of trainees offered job on qualification (2010) 57%

Bird & Bird

15 Fetter Lane, London EC4A 1JP
Tel: (020) 7415 6003 Fax: (020) 7415 6111
Website: www.twobirds.com

Firm profile

Bird & Bird is an international law firm that operates on the basis of an in-depth understanding of key industry sectors, including: aviation and aerospace, financial services, communications, electronics, energy, IT, life sciences, media and sport. The firm is proud to be working with some of the world's most innovative and technologically advanced companies, each of which depend on cutting-edge legal advice to meet their business objectives.

The firm is ambitious and it manages to combine a resilient business approach with a hugely supportive attitude to its employees. With offices in Beijing, Bratislava, Brussels, Budapest, Düsseldorf, Frankfurt, The Hague, Helsinki, Hong Kong, London, Lyon, Madrid, Milan, Munich, Paris, Prague, Rome, Shanghai, Singapore, Stockholm, Warsaw and close ties with firms in other key centres in Europe, Asia and the United States, the firm is well placed to offer its clients local expertise within a global context.

The firm is proud of its friendly, stimulating environment where individuals are able to develop first class legal, business and interpersonal skills. It has an open and collegiate culture reflected in its strong retention rate and assistant involvement. The firm is structured with a very strong international perspective to its culture - integrated teams working for cross-border clients as well as a range of international sport and social activities enables this.

At Bird & Bird, there is a genuine commitment to acting as a responsible employer and also as a proactive member of its local and wider international communities. The firm has a full programme of corporate social responsibility initiatives and policies in place, which fall under three broad areas, people, community and environment.

Main areas of work

Aviation and aerospace, banking and finance, commercial, construction and engineering, corporate finance, dispute resolution, employment, energy and infrastructure, clean technology, EU and competition, restructuring and insolvency, intellectual property, IT, communications, life sciences, media, private equity and venture capital, real estate, sport and tax.

Trainee profile

The firm recognises that its lawyers are its most important asset and that is why the firm recruits strong graduates capable of developing expert legal skills and commercial acumen. A certain level of intelligence and common sense is a prerequisite (the firm looks for excellent A levels and a strong 2.1), but more importantly it looks for well-rounded individuals who will fit in.

The firm's trainee solicitors are outgoing, articulate team-players, willing to work hard when called upon and genuinely interested in progressing their careers. The firm aims to recruit people who will stay with the firm and therefore seek candidates who have a long-term interest in Bird & Bird and the sectors and areas of legal practice it focuses on.

Training environment

The firm's trainees take on responsibility from day one and enjoy varied and challenging work for industry-shaping clients. If you become a trainee with the firm, you will be given the chance to excel.

The firm runs a business skills development programme to provide you with the basic building blocks for your future development within the business of law.

Trainees will spend six months in three of the following practice areas: corporate, commercial, employment, banking, tax, intellectual property, dispute resolution and real estate.

Trainees are encouraged to join the number of sports teams at the firm and to attend various social events.

Partners 220*
Assistant Solicitors 595*
Total Trainees 28 in London
*denotes worldwide figures

Contact
Lynne Walters, Graduate & Trainee Manager
london.graduates@twobirds.com

Method of application
Online application form via the firm website.

Selection procedure
Insight and selection days in February 2011 for Summer placements and August 2011 for Training Contracts.

Closing date for 2013
31 May 2011 for law and non-law students.

Application
Training contracts p.a. 16
Applications p.a. 1,400
% interviewed p.a. 10%
Required degree grade 2:1

Training
Salary
1st year (2010) £35,000
2nd year (2010) £37,000
Holiday entitlement
25 days
% of trainees with a non-law degree p.a. Varies

Post-qualification
Salary (2010) £55,000
% of trainees offered job on qualification (2010) 84%

Overseas offices
Beijing, Bratislava, Brussels, Budapest, Düsseldorf, Frankfurt, The Hague, Helsinki, Hong Kong, London, Lyon, Madrid, Milan, Munich, Paris, Prague, Rome, Shanghai, Singapore, Stockholm, Warsaw

Bond Pearce LLP

3 Temple Quay, Temple Back East, Bristol, BS1 6DZ
Tel: 0845 415 0000 Fax: 0845 415 6900
Email: sam.lee@bondpearce.com
Website: www.bondpearce.com

Firm profile

You'll be surprised what this hidden gem has to offer you! Bond Pearce is a firm that is truly going places. With ambitious growth plans this is an exciting time to be thinking about joining the firm. As the business expands the firm continues to attract high calibre lawyers as a result of the quality and diversity of the work it undertakes both regionally and nationally.

As a trainee you will benefit from excellent supervision from lawyers who are ranked by Chambers as leaders in their fields and who have a breadth and depth of experience that is second to none.

The firm's recent growth and continued success is based on forging strong client relationships, providing effective business solutions and recruiting high calibre people across the firm.

Outstanding client service is something the firm is passionate about, as it helps to build and reinforce relationships, improve the timeliness of advice and encourage teamwork. The result: commercial legal advice that is proactive rather than simply reactive.

Main areas of work

The firm's particular strengths lie in its sector expertise and much of the work lies at the cutting edge of developments in key sectors such as energy, retail, financial services, real estate and the public sector. The firm boasts an impressive portfolio of clients which includes, for example: Lloyds TSB, BBC, QBE Group, RWE Npower Plc, Carnival Plc, Associated British Ports, English Heritage, The Crown Estate, MoD, Barclays Bank, Royal Mail, Kingfisher, B&Q, Virgin Group, Chemring Group, Carlsberg, Marks & Spencer.

Trainee profile

Bond Pearce LLP is looking for individuals who are capable of combining great legal knowledge with a sound commercial focus; people who are driven, creative and have a genuine enthusiasm for both the law and business and individuals with a natural ability in dealing with people.

Training environment

You couldn't ask for a better start to your legal career. The firm's first class training and development programme is recognised among the best in the industry and ensures that you qualify with the best possible legal, business and personal skills. The firm has worked hard to create a culture that encourages, inspires and challenges. Its Graduate Team, consisting of partners, associates and HR provide all the support and encouragement that you need to see you through your two years with the firm. Structured over four seats the firm offers a good range of practice areas for you to train and qualify into.

Trainees are an integral part of the firm's business and right from the start of your training contract you will enjoy early responsibility and exposure to high profile clients at the most senior level.

When & how to apply

Applications for a training contract should be made by 31 July 2011. You can apply using the firm's application form on the graduate pages of our website. The closing date for the summer vacation scheme is 9 April 2011.

Vacation placements

Two weeks in June/July.

Sponsorship & awards

Full GDL and LPC £6,000 maintenance grant for both.

Vacancies 15
Trainees 30
Partners 79
Total staff 650

Contact
Samantha Lee, Graduate Recruitment Manager

Method of application
Electronic application form

Selection procedure
Assessment days

Closing date
31 July 2010

Application
Training contracts p.a. 15-20
Minimum qualification 2:1 degree

Training
Salary
1st year £24,000
2nd year £25,000
Holiday entitlement
25 days

Offices
Bristol, Plymouth, Southampton, London, Aberdeen

Bond Pearce

Boodle Hatfield

89 New Bond Street, London, W1S 1DA
Tel: (020) 7629 7411 Fax: (020) 7629 2621
Email: traineesolicitors@boodlehatfield.com
Website: www.boodlehatfield.com

Firm profile

Boodle Hatfield is a highly successful medium-sized firm which has been providing bespoke legal services for more than 275 years. They still act for some of their very first clients and are proud to do so. The firm has grown into a substantial practice, serving the full spectrum of commercial and private clients, both domestically and internationally.

Main areas of work

The ethos of facilitating private capital activity and private businesses underpins the work of the whole firm. The interplay of skills between five major areas – private client and tax, property, family, corporate and litigation – makes Boodle Hatfield particularly well placed to serve these individuals and businesses.

Trainee profile

The qualities the firm looks for in its trainees are commitment, flexibility and the ability to work as part of a team. Applicants with a gained/ predicted 2:1 degree in any discipline and a minimum of ABB at A-level should apply.

Training environment

Trainees spend six months in up to four of the firm's main areas: property, corporate, family, private client and tax, and litigation. Boodle Hatfield is well known for the high quality of its training. All trainees are involved in client work from the start and are encouraged to handle their own files personally as soon as they are able to do so, (with the appropriate supervision). The firm's trainees therefore have a greater degree of client contact than in many firms with the result that they should be able to take on more responsibility at an early stage. Trainees are given formal appraisals every three months which are designed as a two-way process and give trainees the chance to discuss their progress and to indicate where more can be done to help in their ongoing training and development.

Benefits

Private healthcare, life assurance, season ticket loan, pension scheme, enhanced maternity pay, conveyancing grant, permanent health insurance, employee assistance line, childcare vouchers, cycle to work scheme, give as you earn scheme.

Vacation placements

Two week placement between June and September, for which 10 students are accepted each year. Applicants should apply via the application form on the website at www.boodlehatfield.com. The form will be available from 1st December 2010.

Sponsorship & awards

LPC and GDL fees paid in full plus maintenance grant.

Partners 32
Assistant Solicitors 33
Total Trainees 12

Contact
Bethan Guest
(020) 7079 8103

Method of application
Online application

Selection procedure
Interviews with the Training Principal, a Partner and the HR Director plus an ability test in verbal reasoning

Closing date for 2013
See website

Application
Training contracts p.a. 6
Required degree grade 2:1

Training
Salary
1st year £32,000
2nd year £34,500
Holiday entitlement
25 days

Post-qualification
Salary £50,000

Regional offices
Oxford

Bristows

100 Victoria Embankment, London EC4Y 0DH
Tel: (020) 7400 8000 Fax: (020) 7400 8050
Email: info@bristows.com
Website: www.bristows.com

Partners 30
Assistant Solicitors 61
Total Trainees 15

Contact
Trainee Recruitment & Training Officer

Method of application
Online

Selection procedure
2 individual interviews

Closing date for 2013
23 January 2011 for February interviews,
24 July 2011 for August interviews

Application
Training contracts p.a. Up to 10
Applications p.a. 3,500
% interviewed p.a. 6%
Required degree grade 2:1 (preferred)

Training
Salary
1st year (2010) £33,000
2nd year (2010) £36,000
Holiday entitlement 23 days
% of trainees with a non-law degree p.a. 94%

Post-qualification
Salary (2010) £53,500
% of trainees offered job on qualification (2010) 100%

Firm profile
Bristows is a medium-sized firm that handles the kind of work that might normally be associated with only the very largest firms. Established more than 170 years ago, the firm has built up a client list that includes leading businesses from a variety of sectors, whether global corporations, growing start-ups, charities or financial institutions. Working with so many ambitious organisations, the firm is often advising on issues that shape entire industries and on which a company's future might depend. For example, advising on whether the business is entitled to launch a new product or assisting a client to buy a rival business.

Main areas of work
Bristows might be known as one of the foremost intellectual property firms in the UK, but this only tells part of the story. The firm's lawyers are also recognised as leading authorities in a wide variety of other legal disciplines and as a firm offer a true breadth of expertise. These are our core practice areas: intellectual property-including patent, trademarks and brand protection; information technology; privacy and data protection; regulatory; EU and competition; advertising, marketing and promotion; corporate; commercial disputes; employment; real estate; product liability; tax; publishing and media.

Trainee profile
The size of the firm makes this an ideal environment for trainees. As part of a small intake, the trainees work alongside the partners dealing directly with clients right from the start. There's plenty of responsibility but this is matched by an extremely supportive and friendly culture so you're never far from encouragement and advice when you need it. The firm recognises that its reputation as a leading city law firm is entirely down to the individuals who work here, so it places great stock in attracting talented people and doing all it can to make sure they enjoy life at Bristows.

Training environment
Each year the firm has between 8-10 graduates join its team. The firm is extremely selective because its looking for the people who will be its future partners. As part of such a small and high calibre intake you'll have every chance to shine and the firm will give you real responsibility earlier than you might expect. During the two years' training, you'll spend time in each of the firm's main departments, developing your skills and knowledge. You'll also work closely with its partners, something which is guaranteed to speed up the learning process. Part of this training may also involve a secondment to one of a number of leading clients. With the international spread of its clients, the probability of overseas travel is high, especially following qualification.

Benefits
Life assurance, pension scheme; private medical insurance, permanent health insurance, eye care, health assessment, employee assistance programme, cycle to work scheme, childcare voucher scheme, season ticket loan.

Placement schemes
The firm runs placement schemes which give you the chance to work at Bristows over Spring, Summer or Winter. It's a great chance to assess whether law as a career, and Bristows as a firm, are for you. The kind of things you'll find yourself doing will include research, drafting documents, attending meetings and you might also go along to court hearings.

Sponsorship & awards
GDL and LPC fees paid in full, plus a maintenance grant of £7,000 for each.

Browne Jacobson

Nottingham, Birmingham, London
Tel: (0115) 976 6000 Fax: (0115) 947 5246
Email: traineeapplications@brownejacobson.com
Website: www.brownejacobson.com/trainees.aspx

Firm profile

Browne Jacobson is one of the largest full service commercial law firms in the Midlands with regional and national reach through its offices in Nottingham, Birmingham and London.

With around 500 people, Browne Jacobson is large enough to attract some of the best talent in the country, but small enough to foster a supportive and flexible working environment. The firm's people are the key to its success and it has a track record of attracting and retaining outstanding people. This was recognised by the Lawyer HR Awards in 2008 and 2010 when the firm picked up the Graduate Recruitment Campaign of the Year Award.

Browne Jacobson focuses on long-term relationships that are friendly, flexible and straightforward, both with its people and its clients. The firm's modern, progressive working environment and its friendly and open culture mean that its people enjoy working here so they stay. This allows good working relationships to develop and provides consistency for clients. It's a simple tactic yet one that works; a large proportion of the firm's client base has been with the firm for a number of years.

Main areas of work

The firm has a long established and nationwide reputation in all areas of its commercial, public sector, health and insurance practices and is recognised as regional heavyweight for corporate, property, public enquiry, litigation and professional risk work.

Trainee profile

Browne Jacobson is looking for talented law and non-law graduates who can bring with them enthusiasm, commitment, client focus and a flexible and friendly attitude.

Training environment

Trainees start with a comprehensive induction programme, a fast track professional skills course and then go onto a trainee development programme. They spend four periods of six months in some of the principle areas of the firm, gaining an overview of the practice. Trainees get great training, a friendly and supportive working environment, and real career opportunities. They are also given quality work and exposure to clients from early on, but are supported in achieving results and recognised for their contribution.

Sponsorship & awards

LPC/PGDL tuition fees paid, plus maintenance grant for LPC/PGDL of £5,000.

Open days

Browne Jacobson runs an open day in the spring - application deadline for the 2011 open day is 17 March 2011. Apply online or by CV and covering letter.

Benefits

Life assurance, income protection insurance, pension, private medical insurance and corporate discounts.

Partners 70
Associates 51
Assistant Solicitors 74
Total Trainees 16
Total Staff 500

Contact
Zena Comrie, HR Executive

Method of application
Apply online at www.brownejacobson.com/trainees.aspx or by CV and covering letter

Selection procedure
Telephone interview, assessment centre and partner interview

Closing date
31 July 2011 for 2013 training contracts

Application
Training contracts p.a. 8
Applications p.a. 900
% interviewed p.a. 5%

Training
Salary
1st year (2010) £24,500
2nd year (2010) £25,500
Holiday entitlement 25 days
% of trainees with a non-law degree p.a. 40%

Post-qualification
Salary Market Rate
Holiday entitlement 25 days
% of trainees offered a job on qualification (2010) 83%

brownejacobson
law, less ordinary

Burges Salmon

1 Glass Wharf, Bristol, BS2 0ZX
Tel: (0117) 902 7771 Fax: (0117) 902 4400
Email: natalie.byard@burges-salmon.com
Website: www.burges-salmon.com

Firm profile

Burges Salmon is proof that law doesn't have to mean London.

Based in Bristol, the firm's turnover has more than tripled in recent years as it continues to win prestigious clients out of the hands of City rivals. Clients such as Orange, the Ministry of Defence and Virgin rely on its legal expertise and in doing so have helped cement the firm's reputation for creative, lateral thinking. Burges Salmon's primary asset is its people. Trainees benefit from supervision by lawyers who are leaders in their field with a formidable depth of experience. All this against the backdrop of Bristol: a city with a quality of life you would be hard pressed to find anywhere else in the UK.

Main areas of work

Burges Salmon provides national and international clients such as The Crown Estate, Discovery Channel and Chanel with a full commercial service through five main departments: corporate and financial institutions; commercial; property; private client and wealth structuring; and disputes, environment and planning.

Trainee profile

Burges Salmon lawyers are hard working, motivated individuals with a strong academic background and enthusiasm for a career in law. Candidates must be commercially aware and possess excellent communication skills.

Training environment

Trainees play a vital role in shaping the future of the firm and Burges Salmon invests a great deal of time and resource into training and development. Training is personalised to suit each individual, and the six seat structure allows the opportunity to experience a wider range of practice areas before making a decision on qualification. This dedication to trainees is demonstrated by a high retention rate, which is well above the industry average.

Vacation placements

Burges Salmon runs two open days in February and offers 40 two-week vacation placements during the summer. Individuals visit two departments of their choice supervised by a Partner or senior solicitor, and attend court visits and client meetings. Current trainees run skills training sessions, sports and social events. Remuneration: £250 per week.

Sponsorship and awards

The firm pays GDL and LPC fees at the institution of your choice. Maintenance grants of £7,000 are paid to LPC students, and £14,000 to students studying for both the GDL and LPC (£7,000 p.a.).

Benefits

Annually reviewed competitive salary, 24 days paid annual leave, bonus scheme, pension scheme, private health care membership, life assurance, mobile phone, Christmas gift, corporate gym membership, sports and social club.

Partners 65
Assistant Solicitors 340 Total
Trainees 43

Contact
Natalie Byard, Recruitment Officer

Method of application
Employer's application form available on website

Selection procedure
Penultimate year law students, final year law and non-law students, recent graduates and those considering a change of career are considered for open days, vacation placements and/or training contracts.

Closing date for 2013
31 July 2011

Application
Training contracts p.a. 20-25
Applications p.a. 1,500
% interviewed p.a. 10%
Required degree grade 2:1

Training
Salary
1st year (2009) £30,000
2nd year (2009) £31,000
Holiday entitlement 24 days
% of trainees with a non-law degree p.a. 50%

Post-qualification
Salary (2009) £40,000
% of trainees offered job on qualification (2010) 91%
% of assistants who joined as trainees (2010) 50%
% of partners who joined as trainees (2010) 30%

BURGES SALMON

Capsticks

1 St George's Road, Wimbledon, SW19 4DR
Tel: (020) 8780 2211 Fax: (020) 8780 4811
Email: career@capsticks.com
Website: www.capsticks.com

Firm profile

Capsticks is the leading provider of legal services to the healthcare sector and has almost 150 lawyers focusing on healthcare across its offices in London and Birmingham. The firm has ambitious plans for further growth, both in its core market and by promoting its broader capability and expanding private sector client base. In 2010, Capsticks was awarded Niche firm of the year by "The Lawyer".

Main areas of work

The firm acts for a wide range of healthcare clients, including NHS Trusts and Health Authorities, the NHSLA, regulatory bodies, charities and independent healthcare providers. The firm's main practice areas are clinical law, corporate/commercial, dispute resolution, employment and real estate.

Trainee profile

The firm is committed to recruiting the best people to maintain its market leading position. The firm recruits five trainee solicitors each year and welcomes applications from candidates who are either on course for or have achieved at least a 2.1 (or equivalent) in their undergraduate degree. The firm expects candidates to be committed to a career in healthcare law and to be able to demonstrate they are highly driven, but well rounded, team players, with good problem solving and communication skills.

Training environment

The firm's broad range of practice areas and healthcare clients enables it to give its trainees an opportunity to experience a wide variety of legal work. Trainees are therefore able to acquire an in-depth knowledge of both healthcare law and the healthcare industry, in addition to developing the skills that any good lawyer needs.

The training contract is designed to give trainees maximum exposure to the work of the firm and trainees undertake seats in all of the firm's practice areas, including clinical law, corporate/commercial, dispute resolution, employment and real estate.

Benefits

Bonus scheme, 25 days holiday, pension contribution, permanent health insurance, private medical insurance, death in service benefit, cycle to work scheme, corporate gym 'membership' scheme, childcare voucher scheme and season ticket loan.

Vacation placements

The firm's vacation scheme runs from the end of June through to the middle of August and placements last for two weeks each. In order to be eligible for the 2011 vacation scheme you should be looking to secure a training contract with the firm in September 2013. The firm welcomes applications for a place on its 2011 vacation scheme between 15 November 2010 and 25 February 2011. Further details are available from the website.

The firm encourages all prospective trainee solicitors to participate in the vacation scheme as this is their primary means for selecting future trainee solicitors.

Sponsorship & awards

The firm offers its future trainees financial support for both the Graduate Diploma in Law and the Legal Practice Course.

Partners 34
Assistant Solicitors 106
Total Trainees 10
Other Fee-earners 43

Contact
HR department,
career@capsticks.com

Method of application
Application form, CV and covering letter

Selection procedure
Interview with Partner and Director of HR

Closing date for 2013
12 August 2011

Application
Training contracts p.a. 5
Applications p.a. 200
% interviewed p.a. 7%
Required degree grade
2:1 or above

Training
Salary
1st year £29,000 p.a.
2nd year £30,000 p.a.
Holiday entitlement
25 days p.a.
% of trainees with a non-law degree p.a. 40%

Post-qualification
Salary (2009)
£46,000 p.a.
% of trainees offered job on qualification (2009) 80%

Charles Russell LLP

5 Fleet Place, London, EC4M 7RD
Tel: (020) 7203 5000 Fax: (020) 7203 5307
Website: www.charlesrussell.co.uk

Firm profile

Charles Russell is a Top 50 full service law firm, with clients ranging from international FTSE and AIM businesses, to private companies, governments, not-for-profit organisations and private individuals. It has eight offices: two in London, Guildford, Cambridge, Cheltenham, Oxford, Geneva and Bahrain.

The practice is known for its client care, high quality, expertise and friendly approach. The strategy is simple – to develop relationships with clients, understand their needs and deliver a quality service. Experienced in carrying out cross-border corporate and commercial work, the practice also provides clients with access to 135 recommended law firms across the world as part of two major legal networks: ALFA International and the Association of European Lawyers.

The practice's lawyers and staff are highly motivated and talented people. Many lawyers are ranked as leaders in their field. The practice's commitment to training and development and a strong team spirit are key ingredients to being known as a friendly practice to work. There is a CSR committee that helps promote and organise pro bono, volunteering and fundraising initiatives. Staff can take two days off to participate in volunteering opportunities either organised by the practice or personally.

Main areas of work

Around 75% of the practice's work is commercial. Principal areas of work include corporate/commercial, media, technology and communications, sport and media, retail design and leisure, employment and pensions, charities, private client, family, intellectual property, litigation and dispute resolution, healthcare and real estate.

Trainee profile

Trainees should be rounded achievers, with an excellent academic background and outside interests.

Training environment

For a practice of its size, a small number of trainees are recruited each year. This allows trainees to undergo the best possible training. Trainees spend six months in four of the following areas: corporate/commercial, employment/pensions, family, litigation and dispute resolution, private client and real estate or on client or overseas office secondment. Wherever possible the practice will try to accommodate individual preferences. You will be seated with a partner/senior solicitor. Regular appraisals are held to discuss progress and direction. Trainees are encouraged to attend extensive in-house training. The Professional Skills Course is taught both internally and externally. Trainees are encouraged to take on as much responsibility as possible.

Benefits

BUPA; PHI and life assurance; pension; season ticket loan; 25 days' holiday plus an additional day's holiday or pay for house moves and a subsidised canteen in the London office.

Sponsorship & awards

The firm undertakes to pay GDL and/or LPC course fees together with a grant of £6,000 per annum (London), £4,500 per annum (Guildford), £3,500 per annum (Cheltenham) while you are at law school.

Partners 91
Other fee-earners 216
Total trainees 37
Total staff 594

Contact
trainee.recruitment@charlesrussell.co.uk

Method of application
Online application via www.charlesrussell.co.uk

Selection procedure
Assessment days to include an interview & other exercises designed to assess identified performance criteria

Closing date for 2013
31st July 2011

Application
Training contracts for 2013: 20
Applications p.a. Approx 1,500
% interviewed p.a. 7%
Preferred degree grade 2:1

Training
Salary (London)
1st year (2010) £31,500
2nd year (2010) £32,500
Holiday entitlement (2010) 25 days + additional day for house moves

Post-qualification
Salary (2010) £55,000

Regional offices
Also offers training contracts in its Cheltenham (2 places) and Guildford (4 places) offices.

CHARLES RUSSELL

Clarke Willmott LLP

138 Edmund Street, Birmingham, B3 2ES
Tel: (0845) 209 1729 Fax: (0845) 209 2516
Email: heather.cooper@clarkewillmott.com
Website: www.clarkewillmott.com/trainees

Firm profile

Clarke Willmott LLP is a UK law firm with a national reputation in key commercial and private client services. With 67 Partners and approximately 465 people in total, the firm operates from five locations: Bristol, Birmingham, Taunton, Southampton and London (serviced office).

The firm's lawyers are, first and foremost, business advisers whose objectives are to help clients achieve their goals and to enhance the value of their opportunities. The firm takes a straightforward, proactive approach, and has helped enterprises of all sizes and at all stages of the business lifecycle navigate a range of complex legal issues with positive results. Above all the firm understands that its clients are not looking for more legal advice, they are looking for more business. The firm sees it as its role to help them achieve it.

Main areas of work

Services include corporate, commercial, real estate and construction, business recovery, dispute resolution and insolvency, employment, health and safety, intellectual property, personal injury, insurance, property and private capital as well as a range of services to private clients. The firm has specialist industry experience in real estate (development, investment, social housing, construction and urban regeneration), retail, sport, agriculture, renewable energy and private client.

Trainee profile

The firm's trainees are commercially aware and can demonstrate a clear commitment to a career in law. Clarke Willmott's trainees have a confident, energetic approach and have the ability to work and communicate well with others.

Training environment

Trainees complete four six-month seats, providing a wide range of practical experience and skills in contentious and non-contentious work. Individual preference is sought and will be balanced with the firm's needs. Trainees work closely with partners and solicitors in a supportive team structure, and have regular reviews to ensure they are reaching their potential. Training in both legal and non-legal areas is provided to meet the needs of the individual trainee and the Professional Skills Course is undertaken in-house.

Sponsorship & benefits

Life assurance, group personal pension, gym membership, performance related bonus, funding for the GDL and LPC, occupational sick pay, season ticket loans, eyecare vouchers, childcare vouchers, and cycle to work scheme.

Partners 67
Solicitors 132
Trainees 19

Contact
Heather Cooper, Graduate Recruitment Manager

Training
Salary
1st year (2010) £24,000
2nd year (2010) £25,500
Holiday entitlement
25 days

Post-qualification
Salary (2010) £33,500-£36,000 (dependant on location)
% of trainees offered job on qualification (2009) 79%

Regional offices
Birmingham, Bristol, Southampton, Taunton, London

*clarke willmott

Cleary Gottlieb Steen & Hamilton LLP

City Place House, 55 Basinghall Street, London, EC2V 5EH
Tel: (020) 7614 2200 Fax: (020) 7600 1698
Email: longraduaterecruit@cgsh.com
Website: www.cgsh.com/careers/london

Firm profile

Cleary Gottlieb is one of the leading international law firms, with 12 closely integrated offices located in major financial and political centres around the world. For more than 60 years, the firm has been pre-eminent in shaping the internationalisation of the legal profession. Its worldwide practice has a proven track record for innovation and providing advice of the highest quality to meet the domestic and international needs of its clients.

Main areas of work

Core practice groups in London are mergers and acquisitions, private equity, financing, and debt and equity capital markets (IPOs), plus additional self-standing practices in international litigation and arbitration, competition, tax, financial regulation, intellectual property and information technology.

Trainee profile

Cleary looks for candidates who are enthusiastic about the practice of law in a challenging and dynamic international setting. Whilst academic excellence is a pre-requisite, the firm places particular emphasis on recruiting candidates that they and their clients will enjoy working with. A sense of humour is as important as the ability to think critically and creatively about cutting-edge legal issues.

Training environment

By limiting its graduate intake to just 10-12 trainees a year, Cleary is able to offer bespoke training that is individually tailored to the interests, experience and aptitudes of the individuals that join them. The firm does not believe that the transition from trainee solicitor to associate occurs overnight on qualification, but rather that the transition should be a smooth and gradual one. It therefore encourages its trainee solicitors to accept increased responsibility as soon as they are ready to do so. With appropriate levels of supervision, trainees operate as lawyers of the firm from the day that they join.

Benefits

Health club membership, private healthcare cover (personal and family), life insurance of twice annual salary, long-term disability insurance, employee assistance programme and subsidised staff restaurant.

Vacation schemes

The firm's London office offers 35 vacation places each year (five in winter, ten in spring and ten in each of two summer schemes). The firm actively encourages all candidates that are seriously considering applying for a trainee solicitor position to undertake a vacation placement with the firm. Applications for winter vacation placements should be received by November 15. The deadline for spring and summer vacation scheme applications is January 28.

Sponsorship & awards

Cleary funds the LPC for all future trainee solicitors. For non-law graduates, the firm also funds the GDL. A maintenance grant of £8,000 is paid for each year of professional study.

Trainees 19
Partners 193
(15 in London)
Total Staff 2500
(190 in London)

Contact
Graduate Recruitment

Method of application
Cover letter and CV

Selection procedure
Future trainees are primarily selected from among those having completed a vacation scheme with the firm

Closing date for 2013
July 31 2011

Application
Training contracts p.a. 10-12
Required degree grade
High 2:1

Training
Salary
1st year £40,000
2nd year £45,000

Post-qualification
Salary £92,000

Overseas offices
New York, Washington DC, Paris, Brussels, Moscow, Frankfurt, Cologne, Rome, Milan, Hong Kong and Beijing

Clifford Chance

10 Upper Bank Street, Canary Wharf, London, E14 5JJ
Tel: (020) 7006 3003
Email: Recruitment.London@CliffordChance.com
Website: www.cliffordchance.com/gradsuk

Firm profile

At Clifford Chance the firm's goal is to be at the forefront of the elite group of international law firms that is emerging. Clifford Chance advises its clients internationally and domestically; under common law and civil law systems; in local and cross-border transactions and disputes; on day-to-day operations and on 'game-changing' transformational deals and issues.

Trainee profile

The firm is looking for people who have the potential to become outstanding lawyers. That means you'll need to be able to think on your feet, to offer new ideas and to play your part in a team that is likely to span practice areas, offices and time zones. You'll also need energy and commitment – this is a demanding business and teamwork is also hard work. Beyond this, the firm is looking for people who are genuinely ambitious, not just to be successful but to fulfil all their potential and to help clients achieve their goals. Clifford Chance is organised into six global practices – corporate, capital markets, banking and finance, real estate, litigation and dispute resolution, and tax, pensions and employment. As a Clifford Chance trainee you will work in at least three of these practices, learning from professionals at the leading edge of our profession.

Training environment

Each seat will give you exposure to new clients and colleagues, and you can expect to work on a variety of deals and projects, both large and small, as you build your portfolio of skills. Clifford Chance is a firm of exceptional lawyers drawn from a wide range of backgrounds – there is no one 'type' here. The firm ask a lot of its trainees – focus and dedication are taken as read, but they will also need to be flexible and willing to adapt to new challenges and a lot of responsibility.

Benefits

As well as a competitive salary, you'll enjoy: a subsidised restaurant; free use of fitness centre, swimming pool, squash courts and wellness centre; the option of up to six weeks' leave on qualification and a pension.

Vacation placements

The best way to learn more about what the firm does and what it is like to work here, is to come and try it for yourself. The firm's summer vacation scheme is a structured four-week programme featuring workshops, seminars and the opportunity to work alongside a trainee lawyer or associate to gain first-hand experience of the work they do. The firm's winter and spring workshops provide a shorter, condensed version of the summer vacation scheme.

Sponsorship & awards

Fees for GDL and LPC covered. The level of contribution you are eligible to receive for both fees and maintenance will vary if you have already started the course before making your training contract application. Maintenance is also provided. Please refer to website for details.

London office
Partners 191
Lawyers 610
Trainees 228

Contact
Recruitment London (020) 7006 3003

Method of application
Applications for the firm's training contract, vacation schemes, spring and winter workshops shoud be made via www.cliffordchance.com/gradsuk

Selection procedure
Verbal reasoning test, group exercise, commercial question, competency-based interview

Application
Deadlines: Non-law - 31 January 2011, Law - 31 July 2011
Training contract vacancies: 120
320 (26) UCAS points at A-level or equivalent and minimum requirement: 320(26) UCAS, 2:1 degree

Training
Salary:
1st year £38,000
2nd year £43,000
Holiday entitlement: 25 days
% of trainees with a non-law degree p.a. 50%
No. of seats available abroad p.a. 53 in each six month seat

Post-qualification
Salary: £61,500
% of trainees offered job on qualification (2009): 82%

Overseas offices
Abu Dhabi, Amsterdam, Bangkok, Barcelona, Beijing, Brussels, Bucharest, Dubai, Düsseldorf, Frankfurt, Hong Kong, Kyiv, London, Luxembourg, Madrid, Milan, Moscow, Munich, New York, Paris, Prague, Riyadh (co-operative office), Rome, São Paulo, Shanghai, Singapore, Tokyo, Warsaw, Washington DC

Clyde & Co

51 Eastcheap, London EC3M 1JP
Tel: (020) 7623 1244 Fax: (020) 7623 5427
Email: theanswers@clydeco.com Website: www.clydeco.com/graduate

Firm profile

With roots in international trade, Clyde & Co LLP's main objective is to help clients do business in over 120 countries around the globe. The firm values entrepreneurialism, commercial problem solving, excellence and the freedom to be an individual. Clients value the firm's hands on, innovative approach. The firm's lawyers know their industries, their clients, and most importantly understand the commercial realities of business. Availability and responsiveness are key in the firm's core industries and these characteristics have become part of the mindset of a Clyde & Co lawyer.

The firm has expanded rapidly in recent years and is a dominant player in the insurance, reinsurance, international litigation, shipping, aviation, transport, international trade and energy, and commodities sectors. Clyde & Co has one of the largest Litigation practices in the UK.

Main areas of work

Aviation and Aerospace, Corporate/Commercial, Dispute Resolution, EC/Competition, Energy, Trade and Commodities, Insurance and Re-insurance, Real Estate, Shipping, Transport and Logistics.

Trainee profile

The firm is looking for graduates with excellent academic records, outgoing personalities and keen interests. Trainees need to have the social skills that will enable them to communicate effectively and build relationships with clients and colleagues. The ability to analyse problems, apply common sense and provide solutions to situations are all qualities the firm seeks. Ultimately Clyde & Co recruits to retain and is seeking candidates who will remain with the firm beyond qualification.

Training environment

You will gain early responsibility and be supported through close personal supervision and day-to-day coaching complemented by a wide range of training courses. You will undertake four six-month seats in London and Guildford, which will cover both transactional and contentious work. You may also choose to be seconded to one of the firm's overseas offices or have the opportunity for a client secondment.

Benefits

An optional £1,000 interest free loan on joining, pension, life assurance, private medical insurance, subsidised gym membership, interest-free season ticket loan and coffee shop.

Legal work experience

The firm runs two-week summer vacation schemes for 20 students. The 2011 schemes will take place in June and July. Applications are made online and the closing date is 31 January 2011. For more details please visit the website at www.clydeco.com/graduate.

Sponsorship & awards

GDL and LPC fees paid plus a maintenance grant of £7,000 in London/Guildford and £6,000 elsewhere.

Partners 177
Assistant Solicitors 738
Trainees 52

Contact
Emma Young
Graduate Manager

Method of application
Online via website
www.clydeco.com/graduate

Selection procedure
Assessment session with Graduate Recruitment followed by interview with 2 partners
Closing date for 2013
31 July 2011

Application
Training contracts p.a. 24
Applications p.a. 1,400 +
% interviewed p.a. 10%
Required degree grade 2:1

Training
Salary
1st year (2009) £35,000
2nd year (2009) £38,000
(Reviewed annually)
Holiday entitlement 25 days
% of trainees with a non-law degree p.a. 50%

Post-qualification
Salary (2010) £58,000

Overseas offices
Abu Dhabi, Caracas, Dar es Salaam, Doha, Dubai, Hong Kong, San Francisco, Moscow, Nantes, New Jersey, New York, Paris, Piraeus, Rio de Janeiro, Shanghai, Singapore, and associate offices in Bangalore, Belgrade, Mumbai, Riyadh and St Petersburg

CMS Cameron McKenna LLP

Mitre House, 160 Aldersgate Street, London EC1A 4DD
Tel: (0845) 300 0491 Fax: (020) 7367 2000
Email: gradrec@cms-cmck.com Website: www.cmstalklaw.com

Firm profile

CMS is the leading European organisation of law and tax firms with more offices across Europe than any other firm. CMS brings together nine unique firms including CMS Cameron McKenna, which operates in the UK and across Central and Eastern Europe. The firm advises on a wide range of transactions and issues, and has developed many long-term relationships throughout the business world, meaning that the firm's clients benefit from working with teams that really understand their issues and concerns.

Main areas of work

The firm's clients benefit from an extensive range of tailored services, delivered through offices in the UK, Central Europe, North America and Asia. The firm's services include banking and international finance, corporate, real estate, commercial, energy, projects and construction, insurance and re-insurance.

Trainee profile

The firm looks for high achieving team players with good communication, analytical and organisational skills. You will need to show initative and be able to accept personal responsibility, not only for your own work, but also for your career development. You will need to be resilient and focused on achieving results.

Training environment

The firm is highly supportive and puts no limits on a trainee's progress. It offers four six-months seats over a period of two years. You will be awarded a priority seat when you start your training contract and will undertake a compulsory seat in these areas: corporate or banking, and a contentious seat. To develop you and your legal skills even further, you can expect to be seconded to a client or spend time in one of their international and regional offices. In each seat you will be allocated high quality work on substantial transactions for a range of government and blue-chip clients. The three compulsory modules of the Professional Skills Course will be completed on a fast track basis during the trainee induction. This enables trainees to be effective and participate on a practical level as soon as possible. The Professional Skills Course is complimented by a comprehensive in-house training programme that continues up to qualification and beyond.

Vacation placements

Places for 2011: 60 over spring and summer. Duration: 2 weeks. Remuneration: £250pw. Closing date for applications: 31 January 2011.

Benefits

Annual bonus, gym membership/subsidy, life assurance, pensions scheme with firm contributions, private healthcare, season ticket loan, confidential care line, subsidised restaurant and 25 days holiday with options to buy a further five days.

Sponsorship & awards

GDL and LPC sponsorship is provided. London trainees will be required to undertake their LPC at BPP Law School London where the firm will pay their fees and provide a maintenance grant of up to £7,500. Further details will be supplied on offer of a Training Contract.

Partners 138
Assistant Solicitors 603
Total Trainees 120

Contact
Graduate Recruitment Team
(0845) 300 0491

Method of application
Online application form
www.cmstalklaw.com

Selection procedure
Online application form and psychometric test, Interview and presentation, analysis exercise, group exercise, partner interview

Closing date
31 July 2011

Application
Training contracts p.a. 60
Applications p.a. 1,500
% interviewed p.a. 35%
Required degree grade 2:1

Training
Salary
1st year (2010) £37,500
2nd year (2010) £41,500
Holiday entitlement
25 days + option of flexible holidays
% of trainees with a non-law degree p.a. 50%
No. of seats available abroad p.a. Currently 12

Post-qualification
Salary (2010) £59,000
% of trainees offered job on qualification (2009) 83%

Cobbetts LLP

58 Mosley Street, Manchester M2 3H2
Tel: (0845) 165 5100
Email: gr8training@cobbetts.com
Website: www.cobbettsgraduate.com

Firm profile

Cobbetts is a leading full service law firm with offices in the UK's most exciting commercial centres, Birmingham, Leeds, London and Manchester. The firm continues to place high-quality and long-term relationship building with clients at the forefront of its strategy for success. This leads to a requirement for talented individuals with first-class legal expertise and the people skills to really deliver value to both the firm and its clients. The firm's varied client base gives its trainees the opportunity to get involved in the legal work of PLCs, mid-sized corporates, financial institutions, public sector and not for profit clients. Working in a firm with a reputation for quality work and innovation, and surrounded by business focused, forward thinking individuals, trainees have the perfect opportunity to make their mark in a growing and successful legal business. The firm employs around 600 people (inc. 31 trainee solicitors) across the offices. Training contracts are offered in Birmingham, Leeds and Manchester.

Main areas of work

Cobbetts operates through a number of flexible service teams based on work type and managed across seven areas of practice: banking (including business restructuring), commercial, corporate, dispute resolution, employment, private capital and real estate. Cobbetts' legal expertise spans many industry sectors, especially banking and finance, leisure, retail, IT, media, local government, low carbon and regeneration.

Trainee profile

The firm looks for high academic achievers who show potential to offer something above and beyond the undertaking of legal work. Individuals must demonstrate the confidence and commitment to thrive in a strong client centred commercial environment and have a desire for responsibility early in their training. The firm welcomes applications from students of any discipline who are in the penultimate year or final year of study and from those who have already graduated.

Training environment

Trainee solicitors are supervised by partners and solicitors who have the expertise to turn trainees into confident and capable newly qualified solicitors. Trainees are supervised through five five-month seats to gain a broad depth of experience in the firm's core and specialist areas of law including corporate, real estate and dispute resolution. Depending on business needs, opportunities may also arise for a trainee to spend time on secondment at client or partner organisations.

Trainees are also developed through activities with students who have been offered a contract with the firm and through the firm's structured CSR initiatives. Trainees are supported with development before their training contract through the buddy scheme and LPC+ in conjunction with the College of Law, and during their training contract via practice area induction workshops and the PSC. In addition, once trainees qualify, they will undergo the Cobbetts NQ programme and gain benefit from "Springboard", the firm's structured legal training programme in their first two years of qualification.

Benefits

Opportunity to join the BUPA healthcare scheme after three months, gym membership, social club, pension scheme, season ticket travel loan, death in service and counselling service. In addition to annual holiday entitlement, employees are also entitled to a free day's holiday for moving house and wedding day and have an option to buy or sell additional holidays.

Sponsorship & awards

GDL and LPC fees paid. Maintenance grant of £5,000 during LPC year.

Partners 83
Other fee earners 242
Total Trainees 31

Contact
Paul Kendall
(0845) 165 5053
gr8training@cobbetts.com

Method of application
Online application form

Selection procedure
Assessment days

Closing dates
Training contracts 2013: 31 July 2011
Easter and Summer vacation schemes 2011: 13 February 2011

Application
Training contracts p.a. 12
Applications p.a. 1,000
% interviewed p.a. 7%
Required degree grade 2:1

Training
Salary for each year of training
1st year £23,000
2nd year £25,000
(both reviewed annually)
Holiday entitlement
Starting at 23 days

Post-qualification
Salary NQ £30,000
(reviewed annually)
% of trainees offered job on qualification 68%

Other offices
Birmingham, Leeds, London

Coffin Mew LLP

Fareham Point, Wickham Road, Fareham PO16 7AU
Tel: (01329) 825617 Fax: (01329) 825619
Email: annemorgan@coffinmew.co.uk
Website: www.coffinmew.co.uk

Firm profile

Coffin Mew LLP offers an exceptional training opportunity. The firm is rapidly expanding to become one of the larger southern regional firms with major offices located in the cities of Portsmouth and Southampton and just off the M27 Motorway at Fareham. The firm is in the enviable position of operating a balanced practice offering top quality commercial and private client services in approximately equal volume and is particularly noted for a number of niche practices with national reputations.

Main areas of work

The firm is structured through five business groups with eleven core training departments. These are corporate and corporate finance, commercial services, employment, commercial litigation, property litigation, personal injury, property; family, social housing, insolvency and trust/probate.

Trainee profile

The firm encourages applications from candidates with very good academic ability who seek a broad based training contract in a highly progressive and demanding but friendly and pleasant environment.

Training environment

The training contract is usually divided into six seats of four months each which will normally include a Property Department, a Litigation Department, a Private Client Department and a Commercial Department. The remainder of the training contract will be allocated after discussion with the trainee concerned. The firm aims, when possible to ensure that the trainee spends the final period of his or her training contract in the department in which he or she hopes to work after qualification.

Sponsorship & awards

LPC funding available by discussion with candidates.

Vacation placements

Open Week in July each year; applications for the 2011 Open Week are accepted between 1 November 2010 and 31 March 2011. For further details see the firm's website.

Partners 27
Associates 21
Assistant solicitors 23
Total trainees 13

Contact
Mrs Anne Morgan
Graduate Recruitment

Method of application
Please see firm's website

Selection procedure
Interview

Closing date for July 2013
31 July 2011 (not before January 1 2011)

Application
Training contracts p.a. 4
Applications p.a. 400+
% interviewed p.a. 5%
Required degree grade
2:1 (save in exceptional circumstances)

Training
Salary
1st year
Competitive market rate
2nd year
Competitive market rate
Holiday entitlement currently 24 days
% of trainees with a non-law degree p.a. 23%

Post-qualification
Salary Competitive market rate
% of trainees offered job on qualification (2010) 100%
% of assistants who joined as trainees 32.6%
% of partners who joined as trainees 25%

CoffinMew

Collyer Bristow LLP

4 Bedford Row, London, WC1R 4DF
Tel: (020) 7242 7363 Fax: (020) 7405 0555
Email: recruitment@collyerbristow.com
Website: www.collyerbristow.com

Partners 32
Trainees 7
Total Staff 130

Contact
recruitment@collyerbristow.com

Method of application
Online application form

Selection procedure
Online testing & interview

Training
Salary
1st year (2010) £28,000
2nd year (2010) £31,000
(Both reviewed annually)

Firm profile

London and Geneva based, the firm celebrates the breadth and diversity of its client base which includes multinationals, public and private companies, businesses and partnerships, public sector organisations and a substantial private client practice. Many of the firm's lawyers have trained and qualified with the firm and share their diverse experiences, outlooks and expertise with the firm's clients. The firm is famous for its ground-breaking in-house art gallery and is passionate in its support for the contemporary arts.

Main areas of work

The firm advises a diverse range of businesses and individuals on challenges of all shapes, sizes and complexity and offers top quality legal advice in private client, family, property, company commercial and dispute resolution.

Trainee profile

The firm is looking for individuals who are able to demonstrate a strong academic performance having gained a 2.1 or at least on track to achieve this. Successful candidates will be motivated individuals who possess strong commercial awareness, common sense and an ability to understand the client's business needs.

Training environment

You will spend six months in four of the firm's five key practice areas working with a range of people from senior Partners to more recently qualified solicitors. The firm has a mentoring, training and appraisal programme which nurtures the development of your technical expertise and client advisory skills. You will be encouraged at an early stage to take responsibility for your own files and to participate in managing the client's work.

Benefits

25 days holiday, pension, private medical insurance, life assurance, season ticket loan, Ride2work and childcare voucher schemes.

Sponsorship & awards

Full LPC funding and maintenance grant of £4,000.

Covington & Burling LLP

265 Strand, London WC2R 1BH
Tel: (020) 7067 2000 Fax: (020) 7067 2222
Email: graduate@cov.com
Website: www.cov.com

Firm profile

Covington & Burling LLP is a leading international law firm founded in Washington DC that has more than 750 lawyers in offices in Beijing, Brussels, London New York, San Francisco, San Diego, Silicon Valley and Washington. Covington London is dynamic and growing. The firm opened its London office in 1988, and now offers services to clients over a wide range of practice areas from its modern offices next to the Royal Courts of Justice.

Main areas of work

The principal practice groups in Covington's London office are corporate, dispute resolution, life sciences, and technology and media. The demarcation between these areas is not rigid and solicitors frequently work across several practice groups. In particular, lawyers in the corporate and dispute resolution groups often draw on Covington's vast regulatory experience in areas such as food and drug, communications, and new technologies. At a firm level, practice and industry groups work closely together across all offices. Household names for which the London office acts include Microsoft, the Business Software Alliance, Giorgio Armani, Bacardi, Procter & Gamble, Merck, GlaxoSmithKline, Piper Jaffray, Indian Energy and the British Horse Racing Authority.

Trainee profile

The firm is looking for outstanding students who are committed to providing quality legal advice in an imaginative way, so that it can maintain its ability to respond to the evolving needs and expectations of clients. The firm looks for team players, but above all else, it looks for intellectual distinction, imagination and integrity. The firm is looking for consistently high academic performers that have or expect to achieve a minimum of 2:1 degree in any discipline. In return the firm believes it can offer more challenging and dynamic opportunities for Covington lawyers.

Training environment

The firm splits the two year period into four six-month seats rotating between practice areas. All trainees will spend six months in the corporate and dispute resolution practice areas. Currently, the other seats are in the life sciences, employment, tax and information technology/intellectual property practice areas. A secondment to the in-house Legal Department of a client may also be possible. The size of the programme means that the firm is able to adopt a flexible approach, accommodating your wishes wherever possible.

You will sit and work closely with a senior associate or partner who will supervise your work during each training seat. In addition to their supervisors, trainees have the opportunity to work with other lawyers in the practice group relevant to their training seat. Much of the firm's work is cross-border in nature, and often trainees work with associates and partners in the Brussels and US offices. Their limited number helps ensure that the firm's trainees receive high quality, meaningful work in a supportive and open environment.

Benefits

Pension, income protection, private health cover, life assurance and season ticket loan.

Vacation placements

24 places during summer vacation. Closing date for applications 28 January 2011.

Sponsorship & awards

GDL and LPC fees paid. Maintenance grant of £8,000 per annum.

Partners: 230
Associate Lawyers & Other Fee-earners: 582
Total Trainees London:

2009	11
2010	14
2011	13

Contact
Graduate Recruitment Manager
(020) 7067 2098
graduate@cov.com

Method of application
Online Application Form
See website www.cov.com

Selection procedure
1st & 2nd interview

Closing date for 2013
31 July 2011

Application
Training contracts p.a. 6
Required degree grade 2:1

Training
Salary:
1st year £40,000
2nd year £44,000
Holiday entitlement 25 days

Overseas offices
Beijing, Brussels, New York, San Francisco, San Diego, Silicon Valley, Washington

COVINGTON
COVINGTON & BURLING LLP

Cripps Harries Hall LLP

Wallside House, 12 Mount Ephraim Road, Tunbridge Wells TN1 1EG
Tel: (01892) 506006 Fax: (01892) 506360
Email: graduates@crippslaw.com
Website: www.crippslaw.com

Firm profile

A leading regional law firm and one of the largest in the South East, the firm is recognised as being amongst the most progressive and innovative regional practices.

The firm's organisation into client-focused, industry sector groups promotes a strong ethos of client service and ensures the firm's solicitors are not only excellent legal practitioners but also experts in specialist business sectors. The firm is regarded by many businesses, institutions and wealthy individuals as the natural first choice among regional law firms. Although long-established, the firm's profile is young, professional, forward-thinking, friendly and informal.

The firm achieved the Lexcel quality mark in January 1999, the first 'Top 100' firm to do so. In 2008 the firm was awarded one star status in the Sunday Times Best Companies to work for accreditation.

Main areas of work

Commercial 18%, dispute resolution 18%, private client 26%, property 38%.

Trainee profile

Individuals who are confident and capable, with lively but well organised minds and a genuine interest in delivering client solutions through effective and pragmatic use of the law; keen to make a meaningful contribution both during their contract and long term career with the firm.

Training environment

The firm offers a comprehensive induction course, a well structured training programme, frequent one to one reviews, regular in-house courses and seminars, good levels of support and real responsibility.

The training programme is broader than most other firms and typically includes six seats in both commercial and private client areas. Trainees usually share a room with a partner or an associate and gain varied and challenging first hand experience.

Sponsorship awards

Discretionary LPC funding: Fees – 50% interest free loan, 50% bursary.

Partners 39
Assistant Solicitors 61
Total Trainees 16

Contact
Jim Fennell
Head of HR & Development

Method of application
Application form available on website

Selection procedure
One interview with Managing Partner and Head of Human Resources

Closing date for 2013
31 July 2011

Application
Training contracts p.a. 8
Applications p.a. Up to 750
% interviewed p.a. 6%
Required degree grade 2:1

Training
Salary
1st year (2009) £21,500
2nd year (2009) £23,500
Holiday entitlement 25 days
% of trainees with a non-law degree p.a. 37%

Post-qualification
Salary (2009) £37,000
% of trainees offered job on qualification (2009) 60%
% of assistants/associates (as at 1/5/09) who joined as trainees 52%
% of partners (as at 1/5/09) who joined as trainees 22%

CRIPPS HARRIES HALL LLP

Davenport Lyons

30 Old Burlington Street, London W1S 3NL
Tel: (020) 7468 2600 Fax: (020) 7437 8216
Website: www.davenportlyons.com

Firm profile

A leading business law firm offering a partner-led service. The firm provides commercial advice to its clients across a broad range of market sectors. The firm offers a unique combination of very strong corporate, tax, litigation and property capabilities coupled with specialist media and intellectual property expertise. Based in the luxurious surroundings of Mayfair, coupled with the firm's desire to retain its warm and friendly environment, Davenport Lyons is the ideal place to start your career as a successful solicitor.

Main areas of work

The firm provides comprehensive advice from its 17 legal services covering: corporate; intellectual property/rights; dispute resolution; property; commercial; tax; film and TV; employment and immigration; competition; defamation and privacy; information technology; insolvency and corporate reconstruction; licensing; aviation and travel; music; private client and wealth management; and family and children.

Trainee profile

Davenport Lyons is looking for candidates with excellent academic qualifications (2:1 and above, good A level results) and interesting backgrounds, who are practical and can demonstrate good business acumen. Candidates should have a breadth of interests and foreign language skills are an advantage. In short, the firm is looking for well-rounded individuals.

Training environment

The training programme consists of four six-month seats. During each seat trainees receive mid and end of the seat reviews, and each seat has a dedicated trainee supervisor. Davenport Lyons has an on-going in-house training and lecture programme. The firm prides itself on offering interesting, hands-on training with trainees being encouraged to develop their own client relationships and to handle their own files under appropriate supervision, therefore being treated as junior fee earners. The firm aims to make its training contract informative, educational, practical, supportive and, let us not forget, as enjoyable as possible.

Benefits

Season ticket loan; client introduction bonus; contribution to gym membership; discretionary bonus; 23 days holiday; life assurance; Employee Support Programme; pension and private health scheme.

Vacation placements

A limited number of places are available on the Summer Vacation Scheme, which runs during July and August. Remuneration is £250 per week.

Sponsorship & awards

The firm does not offer financial assistance.

Partners 49
Fee Earners 50
Total Staff 207
Trainees 16

Contact
Alan Geaney
Human Resources Director
Michael Hatchwell
Training Partner

Method of application
Apply online at
www.davenportlyons.com

Selection procedure
Interviews
Closing date for 2013
31 July 2011

Application
Training contracts p.a. 8
Applications p.a. c.800
% interviewed p.a. 6%
Required degree grade 2:1, AAB at A Level (320+ UCAS Points)

Training
Salary
1st Year trainee
£33,000 - £33,666
2nd Year trainee
£34,332 - £35,000
Holiday entitlement 23 days
% of trainees with a non-law degree p.a. 70%

Post-qualification
% of trainees offered job on qualification (2010) 75%

Office
London

Davenport Lyons

Davies Arnold Cooper LLP

6–8 Bouverie Street, London EC4Y 8DD
Tel: (020) 7936 2222 Fax: (020) 7936 2020
Email: gradrecruit@dac.co.uk
Website: www.dac.co.uk

Partners 81
Total Fee-earners 212
Total Trainees 13
Total Staff 376

Firm profile

Davies Arnold Cooper LLP is an international law firm specialising in insurance, real estate, construction, employment, corporate and product liability. The firm has offices in London, Manchester, Madrid and Mexico City.

Main areas of work

Dispute resolution: 65%; real estate: 35%.

Trainee profile

The world of law is vast and technical. You need to demonstrate that you will be up to the job intellectually. The firm looks for intellect (a UCAS tariff of 300, excluding General Studies, a 2:1 or first class degree is usual). The firm also looks for common sense and maturity. It relishes forthright views and social confidence but it doesn't care for arrogance.

Although it may sometimes seem to you that life consists of studying and sitting exams, the firm does look for a bit more. It is impressed by people who push themselves. What you have done with your life so far counts for much more than where you went to school or university. The firm is as interested in talking to those who are embarking on law as a second career as it is in seeing undergraduates.

Training programme & environment

The firm encourages you to take on responsibility as soon as you join and will give you as much as you can handle, although you will always be supervised and never left alone to struggle. You will experience both contentious and non-contentious work and because the firm only takes on up to ten trainees every year, the chances are you will be able to select your preferred seats. There are seven training contract positions available for September 2013. Applications should be made using the firm's application form which is available from the website.

Benefits

Current first year salary is £35,000 with 25 days holiday, private medical insurance and season ticket loan.

Sponsorship & awards

GDL and LPC fees paid plus maintenance grants.

Dawsons LLP

2 New Square, Lincoln's Inn, WC2A 3RZ
Tel: (020) 7421 4800 Fax: (020) 7421 4848
Email: recruit@dawsonsllp.com
Website: www.dawsonsllp.com

Firm profile

Positioned to offer a partner-led dynamic service for its clients, this successful practice differentiates itself with an international and high profile client base.

Dawsons' lawyers are as skilled at offering a broad range of legal advice to high net worth individuals and entrepreneurs as they are to private and quoted companies, professional partnerships, real estate developers, housing associations, charities and schools.

More than 50% of the firm's work has a strong international flavour.

Main areas of work

Dawsons LLP provides the full spectrum of corporate and commercial legal advice, including corporate finance and M&A; litigation; arbitration; real estate; professional partnerships; travel; employment; private client; and all aspects of family law advice.

Trainee profile

Candidates need to show excellent intellectual capabilities, a keen interest in the firm's areas of expertise and a practical and commercial approach to problem solving. The firm is looking for well-rounded individuals with a positive outlook, who are keen and able to take on early responsibility. Trainees are the future of the firm and an important part of building on its success.

Training Environment

The training consists of four six-month seats in the following departments: corporate, employment, family, litigation, private client and property. The firm will consider your areas of interest when making seat allocations. You will share an office with a Partner to assist development and provide easy access for support and guidance. You will have quarterly reviews. You will have client contact from an early stage. Trainees are involved in all social and marketing events and encouraged to partake in pro bono activities.

Benefits

Private health insurance, life assurance, pension, season ticket loan.

Vacation Placements

The firm offers a number of one week placements during Easter and Summer vacations.

Sponsorship

GDL and LPC funding plus maintenance allowance.

Partners 19
Assistant Solicitors 32
Total Trainees 9
Total staff 110

Contact
Harender Branch, Graduate Recruitment Partner

Method of application
Online

Selection procedure
Interview based on the facts of a typical client problem with two partners, followed by a second interview with two other partners from the interview panel

Closing date for 2013
31 July 2011 (closing date for vacation schemes 1 March 2011)

Application
Training contracts p.a. 5
Applications p.a. 350-400
% interviewed p.a. 10%
Required degree grade 2:1

Training
Salary (2010)
1st year £31,000
2nd year £33,000
Holiday entitlement 25 days
% of trainees with a non-law degree p.a. 50%

Post-qualification
Salary (2010) £48,500
% of trainees offered job on qualification (2010) 100%

Office
London

DAWSONS
SOLICITORS

Dechert LLP

160 Queen Victoria Street, London EC4V 4QQ
Tel: (020) 7184 7000 Fax: (020) 7184 7001
Email: application@dechert.com Website: www.dechert.com

Firm profile

Dechert LLP is a dynamic international law firm, with 2,000 people across the USA, Europe and Asia. London is the third largest office, after Philadelphia and New York.

Main areas of work

The London office has particular strengths in investment funds, corporate and securities including private equity, and finance and real estate; and smaller teams in employment, IP, litigation and tax.

Trainee profile

Dechert looks for enthusiasm, intelligence, an ability to find practical solutions, and for powers of expression and persuasion. Graduates from any discipline are welcome to apply.

Training environment

The highly personalised six seat rotation system allows trainees to structure their training contract to their interests and aspirations, and allows opportunity for secondments to Brussels, Munich, Paris or the USA as well as to clients. Your seat plan and professional development are guided by both the firm's Director of Training and by your dedicated trainee partner, who meet with you regularly. Your trainee partner is allocated to you when you start your training contract and acts as a sounding board and a source of support until you qualify.

Vacation placements

Work placement programmes at Easter, and in the summer. The firm's work placement programmes are aimed at penultimate year law students. The closing date for applications is 31 January 2011.

Sponsorship & awards

The firm pays LPC fees plus £10,000 sponsorship.

Partners 36*
Assistant Solicitors 48*
Total Trainees 19*
*denotes London figure

Contact
Graduate Recruitment Officer

Method of application
Online

Selection procedure
An assessment morning or afternoon which includes interviews with partners, associates and recruiters, and written tests

Closing date for 2013
31 July 2011

Application
Training contracts p.a. 10
Applications p.a. Approx 1,000
% interviewed p.a. Approx 10%
Required degree grade 2:1 (or capability of attaining a 2:1)

Training
Salary
1st year £38,000
2nd year £43,000
Holiday entitlement 25 days
% of trainees with a non-law degree p.a. Varies
No. of seats available abroad p.a. three in Brussels and other possibilities

Post-qualification
Salary c.£65,000 to £73,000 (depending on practice area)
% of trainees offered job on qualification 70%

Overseas offices
Austin, Beijing, Boston, Brussels, Charlotte, Dubai, Hartford, Hong Kong, Luxembourg, Moscow, Munich, New York, Orange County, Paris, Philadelphia, Princeton, San Francisco, Silicon Valley, Washington

Dewey & LeBoeuf

No 1 Minister Court, Mincing Lane, London, EC3R 7YL
Tel: (020) 7459 5000 Fax: (020) 7459 5099
Email: londongraduate@dl.com Website: www.dl.com

Firm profile

Dewey & LeBoeuf is a full-service global law firm advising a wide range of clients throughout the United States, Europe, Russia/the CIS, the Middle East, Asia and Africa. With more than 1,200 lawyers in virtually all major financial and commercial centres, the firm represents multinational corporations, financial institutions, government agencies and stateowned entities in their most complex legal matters. The London office of Dewey & LeBoeuf is the firm's largest international office with 34 partners and over 90 legal staff. The majority of the firm's London based partners and associates are English qualified solicitors, and the London office is the natural centre of some of the firm's most interesting and diverse work.

Main areas of work

Banking, mergers and acquisitions, corporate finance, project finance, litigation and dispute resolution, arbitration, intellectual property and information technology, EU/competition, tax, real estate, environmental and employment. The firm also possesses leading industry experience in sectors including insurance, energy and utilities and banking.

Trainee profile

Dewey & LeBoeuf is looking for dynamic, internationally-minded, versatile individuals who demonstrate commercial awareness and a genuine enthusiasm for the law. The firm wants people who are dedicated to delivering excellent advice and client service. Language skills are desirable but not essential.

Training environment

The firm encourages learning through one-on-one interaction with its partners and experienced associates. Trainees are encouraged to see and experience as much of the practice as possible and you can expect to be exposed to high quality work with early responsibility. Trainees undertake four six-month seats within different practice areas. Secondments to the firm's international offices in Abu Dhabi, Dubai, Moscow and Paris, as well as six-month client secondments, are available. The firm's training programme is comprehensive, and in addition to the professional skills course, covers an induction programme and attendance at internal and external courses. Trainees will also participate in regular training sessions run through its own internal 'Dewey & LeBoeuf University' (DLU), which offers regular seminars on law and practice. Progress and training needs are formally reviewed every three months.

Benefits

The firm offers 25 days' holiday per annum, private medical insurance, permanent health insurance, life assurance, employee assistance programme, private GP services, Ride2Work scheme, worldwide travel insurance, season ticket loan, childcare vouchers, and preferential rates for dental care and for gym membership.

Vacation placements

The firm offers one-week spring vacation and two-week summer vacation schemes for penultimate year law undergraduates and graduates of all disciplines. Places for 2011: 12; Remuneration: £400 per week; closing date 31 January 2011. Apply online at www.dl.com

Sponsorship & awards

Full payment of GDL/LPC fees and maintenance grant of £8,500 provided per annum.

Partners 34
Other lawyers 66
Total Trainees 26

Contact
Katharyn White,
Legal HR Manager

Method of application
Apply online www.dl.com

Selection procedure
Two interviews with the firm's partners, associates and graduate recruitment team

Closing date for 2013
31 July 2011

Application
Training contracts p.a. 15
Applications p.a. 850
% interviewed p.a. 9%
Required grades AAB at A-level and 2:1 degree or equivalent

Training
Salary
1st year (2010) £40,000
2nd year (2010) £45,000

Post-qualification
Salary (2010) £75,000
% of trainees offered job on qualification (2010) 93%

Offices
Abu Dhabi, Albany, Almaty, Beijing, Boston, Brussels, Chicago, Doha, Dubai, Frankfurt, Hong Kong, Houston, Johannesburg, London, Los Angeles, Madrid, Milan, Moscow, New York, Paris, Riyadh, Rome, San Francisco, Silicon Valley, Warsaw, Washington DC

Dickinson Dees LLP

St. Ann's Wharf, 112 Quayside, Newcastle upon Tyne NE1 3DX
Tel: (0844) 984 1500 Fax: (0844) 984 1501
Email: graduate.recruitment@dickinson-dees.com
Website: www.trainingcontract.com

Firm profile

Dickinson Dees enjoys an excellent reputation as one of the country's leading commercial law firms. Based in Newcastle upon Tyne with additional offices in Tees Valley, York and London the firm prides itself on the breadth of expertise across its 38 practice areas which enables it to offer services of the highest standards to clients. Whilst many of the firm's clients are based in the North, Dickinson Dees works on a national basis for national and internationally based businesses and organisations.

Main areas of work

The firm has 670 employees and is organised into four key departments (Company commercial, commercial property, litigation and wealth management) with 38 cross departmental teams advising on specific areas.

Trainee profile

The firm is looking for intellectually able, motivated and enthusiastic graduates from any discipline who have good communication skills. Successful applicants will understand the need to provide practical, commercial advice to clients. They will share the firm's commitment to self development and teamwork and its desire to provide clients with services which match their highest expectations.

Training environment

There are relatively few trainees for the size of the practice which ensures a supportive and friendly environment. You will be fully integrated into the firm and involved in all aspects of the firms business. The training contract consists of four seats across the different departments. Trainees sit with their supervisors and appraisals are carried out every three months. The firm has its own Training Department as well as a supportive Graduate Recruitment Team. There are induction courses for each seat move with opportunities for trainees to get involved in the firm's training programme. The firm offers a tailored in-house Professional Skills Course which is run in conjunction with the College of Law.

Work placements

Places for 2011: 40; Duration: 1 week; Remuneration: £200 p.w. The firm's work placement weeks are part of the recruitment process and all applicants should apply online at www.trainingcontract.com. Apply by 31 January 2011 for Easter and Summer placements.

Sponsorship & awards

GDL/LPC fees paid and maintenance grant offered.

Partners 68
Total Staff 670
Total Trainees 30

Contact
Joanne Smallwood, Graduate Recruitment Adviser

Method of application
Apply online at www.trainingcontract.com

Selection procedure
Aptitude and ability tests, negotiation exercise, personality questionnaire, presentation, interview
Closing date for 2013
31 July 2011

Application
Training contracts are based in Newcastle, Tees Valley and York (up to 17 across the three offices)
Applications p.a. 800
% interviewed p.a. 10%
Required degree grade 2:1 in any subject

Training
Salary
1st year £19,500
2nd year £20,500
Holiday entitlement 25 days
% of trainees with a non-law degree p.a. 50%
No. of seats available abroad p.a. 3
(3-month secondments)

Post-qualification
% of trainees offered job on qualification (2009) 84%(15/17)
% of partners (as at 01/07/2010) who joined as trainees 35%

Other offices
Tees Valley, York, London
Brussels (associated office)

DICKINSON DEES

DLA Piper UK LLP

3 Noble Street, London, EC2V 7EE
Tel: (0870) 0111 111
Email: recruitment.graduate@dlapiper.com
Website: www.dlapipergraduates.co.uk

Firm profile

DLA Piper is one of the world's largest full service commercial law firms. They now have more than 3,500 lawyers employees working from over 65 offices across Europe, Asia, the Middle East and the US. Their current vision is to be the leading global business law firm. Clients include some of the world's leading businesses, governments, banks and financial institutions. This impressive client base coupled with an emphasis on providing high quality service and teamwork, offers a challenging fast-paced working environment.

DLA Piper offers its trainees the opportunity to apply for international secondments to a range of its offices, as well as a number of client secondments.

In 2008 DLA Piper won the prestigious National Graduate Recruitment Awards' 'Diversity Recruitment Award' proving their commitment to recruiting people from a wide variety of backgrounds and ages. This progressive approach to recruitment creates a mix of talents that contributes to their success.

DLA Piper is committed to making sure you feel part of the firm once you accept a training contract with them. Future trainees have access to the website 'Inside DLA Piper' where they can, amongst other things, contact one another via chat forums, and keep up to date with what is going on in the firm wherever they are in the world.

Main areas of work

Corporate; employment, pensions and benefits; finance and projects; intellectual property and technology; litigation and regulatory; real estate; and restructuring.

Trainee profile

The firm is looking for individuals from either a law or non-law background who have a minimum ABB at A Level (or equivalent) and expect, or have achieved a 2.1 degree classification - however, a strong academic background alone is no longer sufficient. DLA Piper looks for highly motivated and energetic team players with sound commercial awareness, outstanding communication and organisational skills. As well as this, in line with the firm's main focus of work, a keen interest in the corporate world is essential - as is an appetite for life!

Training environment

Following a comprehensive residential induction, trainees complete four six month seats during the course of their training contract. If you want responsibility, the firm will give you as much as you can handle and your progress will be monitored through regular reviews and feedback. The compulsory Professional Skills Course is run in-house and is tailored to meet the needs of the firm's trainees. This combined with on-the-job experience, provides trainees with an excellent grounding on which to build their professional careers.

Summer placements

DLA Piper runs two week summer placement schemes across all of its UK offices. The scheme aims to give a thorough insight into life at the firm. There will be approximately 170 places available for 2011. The closing date is 31 January 2011.

Sponsorship & awards

Payment of LPC and GDL fees plus maintenance grant in both years of up to £7,000.

Partners 1230
Fee-earners 2080
Total Trainees 173

Contact
Sally Carthy, Head of Graduate Recruitment

Method of application
Online application form

Selection procedure
First interview, second interview, assessment afternoon

Closing date for 2011 (2013 Training Contracts)
31 July 2011

Application
Training contracts p.a. 85
Applications p.a. 2,600
% interviewed p.a. 15%
Required degree grade 2:1

Training
Salary 2009 (2010 TBC)
1st year (London) £36,000
2nd year (London) £38,000
1st year (Regions) £25,000
2nd year (Regions) £27,000
1st year (Scotland) £22,000
2nd year (Scotland) £24,000
% of trainees with a non-law degree p.a. 40%

Post-qualification
Salary 2010
£60,000 (London)
£38,000 (English Regional offices)
£34,000 (Scotland)

UK offices
Birmingham, Edinburgh, Glasgow, Leeds, Liverpool, London, Manchester, Sheffield

Overseas offices
Austria, Belgium, Bosnia-Herzegovina, Bulgaria, China, Croatia, Czech Republic, France, Georgia, Germany, Hong Kong, Hungary, Italy, Japan, Netherlands, Norway, Poland, Russia, Singapore, Slovak Republic, Spain, Thailand, Turkey, Ukraine, UAE, USA.

Dundas & Wilson LLP

Northwest Wing, Bush House, Aldwych, London, WC2B 4EZ
Tel: (020) 7240 2401 Fax: (020) 7240 2448
Email: lorraine.bale@dundas-wilson.com
Website: www.dundas-wilson.com

Firm profile

Dundas & Wilson is a leading UK commercial law firm with offices in London, Edinburgh and Glasgow. The firm services a wide range of prestigious clients, including major companies and public sector organisations, throughout the UK and abroad.

Main areas of work

Lawyers are grouped into key areas of expertise including debt, restructuring and resources construction and engineering, corporate, corporate recovery, dispute resolution, environment, employment, EU and competition, IP / IT, outsourcing, pensions, planning and funds, projects, property, property finance, public law, transport and tax.

Trainee profile

Dundas & Wilson are looking for applicants with enthusiasm, commitment, adaptability, strong written and oral communication skills, excellent interpersonal skills, commercial awareness and an aptitude for problem solving and analysis.

Training environment

The two year traineeship is split into four six-month seats. The firm aims to accommodate trainees' preferences when allocating seats as the firm wants to encourage trainees to take an active part in managing their career development.

During the traineeship trainees receive on-the-job training, two day seat training at the beginning of each seat, training in core skills such as drafting and effective legal writing and regular seminars. Trainees receive a formal performance review every three months and are allocated a mentor for each seat.

The firm's open plan environment means that trainees sit amongst assistants, associates, senior associates and Partners – this provides daily opportunities to observe how lawyers communicate both with clients and each other. This type of learning is invaluable and great preparation for life as a fully fledged lawyer.

Benefits

Life assurance, permanent health insurance, group personal pension, season ticket loan, holiday purchase scheme.

Vacation scheme

Dundas & Wilson offers three-week summer placements. To apply, please visit the website and complete the online application form. The closing date is 30 January 2011.

Sponsorship & awards

GDL/CPE and LPC fees paid plus maintenance grant.

Partners 82
Lawyers 364
Trainees 56

Contact
Lorraine Bale

Method of application
Online application

Selection procedure
Assessment day comprising interview, group exercise, occupational personality questionnaire and aptitude tests

Closing date for 2013
31 July 2011

Application
Training contracts p.a. 35 (12 in London)
Applications p.a. 300
% interviewed p.a. 15%
Required degree grade 2:1 preferred

Training
Salary
1st year (Scotland) £19,000 (England) £30,000
2nd year (Scotland) £22,000 (England) £33,500
Holiday entitlement 25 days

Offices
London, Edinburgh, Glasgow

DUNDAS & WILSON

DWF LLP

Bridgewater Place, Water Lane, Leeds, LS11 5DY
5 St Paul's Square, Old Hall Street, Liverpool, L3 9AE
Capital House, 85 King William Street, London, EC4N 7BL
Centurion House, 129 Deansgate, Manchester, M3 3AA
6 Winckley Square, Preston, PR1 3JJ
Tel: (0161) 603 5000 Fax: (0161) 603 5050

Firm profile

DWF LLP is a leading, full service law firm. The firm provides a full range of legal services to businesses and private clients across the UK.

The firm employs over 1,200 people, including 128 Partners and over 600 fee earners.

The firm is able to serve clients on a national basis from offices in Leeds, Liverpool, London, Manchester and Preston and internationally through its relationships with law firms around the world. The business continues to expand through a combination of organic growth, lateral hires and other consolidation activity.

The firm prides itself on providing outstanding client service that combines excellent commercial advice with an approachable style.

Main areas of work

DWF provides a full range of legal services: corporate, family law and private client, finance and restructuring, insurance, litigation, people and real estate. A full list of these services can be found on the firm's website at www.dwf.co.uk.

DWF also provides legal services across a range of different industries and sectors, and has developed particular expertise in a number of specific areas. To enable clients to benefit from this expertise, the firm has developed a series of sector-focused teams: charity, education, energy and infrastructure, food, healthcare, public sector, recruitment, retail and leisure.

Trainee profile

DWF's future depends on recruiting and retaining the right people. DWF only recruit people of the highest quality and are always on the look out for ambitious and driven professionals who are able to add value to their developing team. DWF wants its trainee solicitors to play a part in building on its success. The firm is looking for trainees who enjoy working as part of a busy team, respond positively to a challenge and have what it takes to deliver results for clients. The firm is looking for its partners of the future and in recent years virtually all of its qualifying trainees have been offered jobs. DWF is an equal opportunities employer and is committed to diversity in all aspects.

Training environment

DWF provides a well structured training programme for all trainee solicitors which combines the day to day practical experience of working with a Partner, associate or senior solicitor, backed by a comprehensive in-house lecture and workshop programme and the PSC course. As a trainee you will very quickly become a vital member of the team, being delegated the appropriate level of responsibility from an early stage in your training.

Full supervision is provided and there will be opportunities for up to six seats in different practice groups. This enables you to look at specialist areas of work within different departments.

Partners 128
Other fee-earners 600
Total Trainees 34

Contact
Claire Martin
Graduate Recruitment Officer

Method of application
Online application

Selection procedure
2 stage interview/selection process

Closing date for 2012/2013
Undergraduates 31 July 2011
Graduates 30 June 2011

Application
Training contracts p.a. 21
Applications p.a. c. 1200
% interviewed p.a. 15%
Required degree grade 2:1

Training
Salary
1st year (2010)
£25,000-NW
£35,000-London
Holiday entitlement
25 days p.a. minimum + option to buy & sell holidays

Post-qualification
% of trainees offered job on qualification (2009) 100%

Benefits
Flexible benefits scheme including insurance, life assurance, pension and other benefits

Vacation placements
Summer vacation placement schemes across all offices

Sponsorship & awards
LPC funding for tuition fees

Edwards Angell Palmer & Dodge UK LLP

Dashwood 69 Old Broad Street, London, EC2M 1QS
Tel: 020 7583 4055
Fax: 020 7353 7377
Email: traineerecruitment@eapdlaw.com
Website: www.eapdlaw.com

Firm profile

EAPD is an international commercial law firm combining the expertise of over 500 lawyers in 30 practice groups, across the US, UK and Hong Kong. The firm offers a full array of legal services to clients worldwide.

Main areas of work

The firm's work in London is expanding but currently covers thirteen practice areas: asset recovery; commercial litigation; competition; corporate; employment; energy and offshore engineering; insurance and reinsurance; IP; international arbitration; international law; private equity and venture capital; product liability and restructuring and insolvency.

Trainee profile

Academic excellence is important but the firm also seeks engaging and motivated individuals with the initiative and drive to make their mark. The firm values good commercial sense, adaptability and those capable of thinking on their feet. The firm's trainees work hard and have early responsibility and influence over the matters they work on. Therefore, you'll need to understand teamwork, show evidence of taking on responsibilities and communicating well with others. You'll also need great analytical skills and a rigorous approach. The firm looks for people with interesting achievements and those who've made the most of their non-academic opportunities. A range of work/life experiences demonstrating these skills and qualities is key.

Training environment

The firm believes you learn best by doing, getting involved in real work from the start and because of its size in London, the firm can offer excellent training with high-quality work in a more personal environment. Trainees get the chance to meet clients, be responsible for their own work and join in marketing and client development activities. Trainees spend six months in four of the firm's major practice areas. Frequent workshops on the firm's tailored training programme help develop the technical skills and knowledge needed in those areas. Secondment opportunities to major clients, or one of the firm's international offices, gives you the chance to build on and maximise the knowledge and skills gained. Regular structured feedback, reviews and constructive advice enable you to fulfil your true potential. A multi-level support network including buddies, partner mentors and the trainee recruitment team, ensures you have the correct level of guidance and support. Any suggestions or concerns can be voiced via the firm's trainee committee.

Benefits

Bupa, STL, subsidised gym membership, bonus scheme, pension scheme, life assurance, subsidised café, ride to work scheme, confidential employee assistance scheme.

Vacation placements

The firm offers a structured two-week placement for 8-10 students in June/July of each year. The firm also hosts open days at Easter, Summer and Christmas – check website for dates and details.

Sponsorship & awards

CPE/GDL and LPC funding, plus a maintenance grant of £7,000 (London) / £6,500 (outside London).

Partners 22
Assistant Solicitors 28
Total Trainees 15

Contact
Sarah Warnes 020 7556 4414

Method of application
Online applications only
www.trainee.eapdlaw.com

Selection procedure
Assessment morning plus one interview with two partners/senior associates

Closing date for 2013
31 July 2011

Application
Training contracts p.a. up to 8
Applications p.a. 700 approx
% interviewed p.a. 10%
Required degree grade 2:1

Training
Salary
1st year £37,000
2nd year £41,000
Holiday entitlement 25 days

Post-qualification
Salary £58,000
Summer placements up to 10 p.a.
Open days 4-5 accomodating up to 125 students in total
Closing date for summer placements 25 February 2011
Closing date for open days check website

Offices
UK-London, US-New York, Boston, Hartford, Providence, Stamford, Washington, West Palm Beach, Newport Beach, Wilmington, Madison, Ft Lauderdale, Asia-Hong Kong

Eversheds

1 Wood Street, London, EC2V 7WS
Tel: (0845) 497 9797 Fax: (0845) 497 4919
Email: gradrec@eversheds.com
Website: www.eversheds.com/graduaterecruitment

Firm profile

International law firm Eversheds is one of the largest full service firms in the world with over 4,100 people and 47 offices in major cities across Europe, the Middle East, Africa and Asia. As an innovative firm working for some of the world's most prestigious organisations, Eversheds offers a compelling mixture of straightforward advice, clear direction, predictable costs and outstanding service.

Eversheds' strategic plan will see the firm build on its achievements and continue expanding and the firm is looking for highly ambitious and focused trainees to to be a part of this growth/ expansion.

Main areas of work

Core work: company commercial, litigation and dispute management, real estate, human resources (employment and pensions) and legal systems group.

Trainee profile

People at Eversheds are valued for their drive and business acumen, as well as their legal expertise, and the firm develops the same qualities in its trainees. Taking a hands-on approach to learning and development, Eversheds will help you build the career you want.

Training environment

Eversheds offers a full training programme with the opportunity to focus your technical skills in each of the various practice groups as you rotate through four six-month seats. You will also take part in a full programme of personal and commercial development skills training, including finance and business, communication, presenting, business writing, client care, professional standards and advocacy.

Vacation placements

Two week summer placements are available across Eversheds' UK offices. Applications can be made at www.eversheds.com/graduaterecruitment. The application deadline for the 2011 Schemes is 31 January 2011. Please visit the website for the dates of the 2011 Schemes.

Sponsorship & awards

GDL and LPC fees and maintenance grants in accordance with the terms of the firm's offer.

Offices

Abu Dhabi, Amsterdam, Barcelona, Berne, Birmingham, Bratislava, Brussels, Budapest, Cambridge, Cardiff, Copenhagen, Doha, Dublin, Edinburgh, Geneva, Hong Kong, Ipswich, Jeddah, Johannesburg, Kuala Lumpur, Leeds, London, Madrid, Manchester, Milan, Munich, Newcastle, Nottingham, Ostrava, Paris, Port Louis, Prague, Riga, Riyadh, Rome, Rotterdam, Shanghai, Singapore, Stockholm, Tallinn, Tirana, Valladolid, Vienna, Vilnius, Warsaw, Wroclaw and Zurich. In addition the firm has close relationships with preferred law firms across Europe, Middle East and America. Further details are available on the firm's website.

Partners 540+
Lawyers 2,000+
Total Trainees 100+

Contact
gradrec@eversheds.com

Method of application
Apply online at www.eversheds.com/graduatesrecruitment

Selection procedure
Selection days include an interview, group and individual exercises
Closing date: Please visit the firm's website for details

Application
Training contracts p.a. 50
Applications p.a. 3,000
% interviewed p.a. 20%
Required degree grade 2:1 or 300 UCAS points

Training
Salary
1st year London (2009) £35,000
2nd year London (2009) £37,000
Holiday entitlement 25 days
% of trainees with a non-law degree p.a. 45%
No. of seats available abroad p.a. 5+

Post-qualification
Salary London (2009) £57,000
% of trainees offered job on qualification (2010) 83%

Farrer & Co LLP

66 Lincoln's Inn Fields, London WC2A 3LH
Tel: (020) 3375 7000 Fax: (020) 3375 7001
Email: training@farrer.co.uk
Website: www.farrer.co.uk

Firm profile

Farrer & Co is a mid-sized London law firm. The firm provides specialist advice to a large number of prominent private, institutional and commercial clients. Farrer & Co has built a successful law firm based on the goodwill of close client relationships, outstanding expertise in niche sectors and a careful attention to personal service and quality.

Main areas of work

The firm's breadth of expertise is reflected by the fact that it has an outstanding reputation in fields as diverse as matrimonial law, offshore tax planning, employment, heritage work, charity law, defamation and sports law.

Trainee profile

Trainees are expected to be highly motivated individuals with keen intellects and interesting and engaging personalities. Those applicants who appear to break the mould – as shown by their initiative for organisation, leadership, exploration, or enterprise – are far more likely to get an interview than the erudite, but otherwise unimpressive, student.

Training environment

The training programme involves each trainee in the widest range of cases, clients and issues possible in a single law firm, taking full advantage of the wide range of practice areas at Farrer & Co by offering six seats, rather than the more usual four. This provides a broad foundation of knowledge and experience and the opportunity to make an informed choice about the area of law in which to specialise. A high degree of involvement is encouraged under the direct supervision of solicitors and partners. Trainees attend an induction programme and regular internal lectures. The training partner reviews trainees' progress at the end of each seat and extensive feedback is given. The firm has a very friendly atmosphere and regular sporting and social events.

Benefits

Flexible benefits scheme, sporting teams/clubs, season ticket loan, 25 days' holiday, group income protection, group life assurance, company doctor, subsidised gym membership, subsidised yoga/pilates, pension scheme, private medical insurance after one year, wellwoman/wellman checks.

Vacation placements

Places for 2011: 30; Duration: 2 weeks at Easter, two schemes for 2 weeks in summer; Remuneration: £275 p.w.; Closing Date: 31 January 2011.

Sponsorship & awards

CPE Funding: Fees paid plus £6,000 maintenance. LPC Funding: Fees paid plus £6,000 maintenance.

Partners 75
Assistant Solicitors 138
Total Trainees 20

Contact
Trainee Recruitment Manager

Method of application
Online via the firm's website

Selection procedure
Interviews with Trainee Recruitment Partner and partners

Closing date for 2013
31 July 2011

Application
Training contracts p.a.10
Applications p.a. 900
% interviewed p.a. 5%
Required degree grade 2:1

Training
Salary
1st year (sept 2010) £32,500
2nd year (sept 2010) £35,000
Holiday entitlement 25 days
% of trainees with non-law degrees p.a. 40-60%

Post-qualification
Salary (2010) £53,000
trainees offered job on qualification (2009) 100%
% of partners (as at July 08) who joined as trainees: over 60%

Field Fisher Waterhouse LLP

35 Vine Street, London EC3N 2AA
Tel: (020) 7861 4000 Fax: (020) 7488 0084
Email: graduaterecruitment@ffw.com Website: www.ffw.com/careers

Firm profile

Field Fisher Waterhouse is a European law firm providing commercial solutions across a range of industry sectors. It has a particular focus on companies that are highly regulated and those with intellectual property and technology driven business models.

The firm's international client base choose to work with it because it provides exceptional lawyers with industry expertise and strong commercial knowledge of their businesses, enabling the firm to work with them to maximise their market opportunities. The firm is acknowledged as leading experts in sectors such as technology and communications, hotels and leisure and media as well as for its public sector work.

Clients that include listed and unlisted companies, multinationals, financial institutions, professional partnerships, trade associations and Government departments, value the firm's flexible approach to teamwork and that it will shape its structures and way of working to meet their specific needs.

Main areas of work

The firm's main areas of practice are corporate, IP, technology and regulatory law. It also has leading expertise in areas such as banking and finance, financial services, real estate, dispute resolution, personal injury and medical negligence.

Trainee profile

The people we're looking for need to be bright, ambitious and very commercial, but it's your ability to communicate, your experiences and attitude that really makes the difference and that is what the firm believes makes a great lawyer. The firm does not want another generation of legal clones, it is looking for well-rounded individuals because who you are as a person and what else you have achieved is just as important to us.

Training environment

The firm offers a four-seat training contract and our range of practice areas enable us to offer outstanding opportunities for training. Trainees are treated as a valued part of the team and are encouraged to assume early responsibility. Secondment opportunities include MTV, Fidelity and the Brussels office. Practical training is complemented by a comprehensive programme of in-house seminars, workshops and external courses, accompanied by regular feedback and a formal assessment at the end of each seat. The firm invests highly in the development and training of all its trainees and provides good-quality work within a friendly, relaxed and supportive working environment. You will also have additional support from your fellow trainees, the Graduate Recruitment Team and a supervisor who is a senior solicitor.

Sponsorship & benefits

Sponsorship and a GDL (£5,500) and LPC (£6,000) maintenance grant are paid. Other benefits include: 25 days' holiday, life assurance, season ticket loan, medical insurance, GP service, and pension in addition to having two squash courts in the firm's offices. The firm operates a flexible benefits scheme where you have the ability to flex your benefits according to your lifestyle (for example having more holiday or less insurance cover). The firm also offers its newly-qualified solicitors four weeks' unpaid leave to mark the end of their training contracts.

Vacation placements & open days

Increasingly, trainees have come to the firm through the vacation schemes, which provide a useful way of getting an insider's view of Field Fisher Waterhouse. The firm runs schemes at Easter and during June where you have the opportunity to spend two weeks working on real client matters and taking part in a variety of social activities.

Vacancies (2013) up to 15
Trainees (2010) 19
Partners 142
Staff 713

Contact
Amelia Goodwin, HR Officer

Method of application
Online via the firm website, www.ffw.com/careers

Selection procedure
Online form, psychometric tests, assessment centre

Closing date for 2011
Easter and Summer vacation scheme: 13 February 2011
2013 Training contracts: 31 July 2011

Application
Training contracts p.a. up to 15
Applications p.a. 800
Required degree grade 2:1, good A-levels

Training
Salary
starting salary (2010) £35,000
Holiday entitlement
25 days

Post-qualification
Salary (2010) £54,000
% of trainees offered job on qualification (2009) 71%

Offices
London, Manchester, Brussels, Hamburg and Paris

Finers Stephens Innocent

179 Great Portland St, London W1W 5LS
Tel: (020) 7323 4000 Fax: (020) 7580 7069
Email: gradrecruitment@fsilaw.com
Website: www.fsilaw.com

Firm profile

Finers Stephens Innocent is an expanding practice in Central London, providing a range of high quality legal services to corporate, commercial and private clients. The firm's philosophy includes close partner involvement and a cost-effective approach in all client matters. They have a working style which is unstuffy and informal, but still aspires to the highest quality of output, while offering a sensible work-life balance. The firm is a member of the Meritas international network of law firms.

Main areas of work

Commercial property, company commercial, employment, private client, family, media, defamation. See the website for further details.

Trainee profile

The firm requires academic excellence in all applicants. It also looks for maturity, personality, a broad range of interests, initiative, strong communication skills, and the ability to write clear English, and to think like a lawyer. The firm has for several years given equal consideration to applicants whether applying straight from university or having followed another career previously. Trainees get early responsibility, client contact and close involvement in transactions and litigation matters.

Training environment

Between offering you a training contract and the time you start, the firm aims to keep regularly in touch with you, including offering you some work experience with them. When you start they provide a careful induction programme, after which you complete four six-month seats in different departments, sharing a room with either a Partner or Senior Assistant. The firm has three Training Partners who keep a close eye on the welfare and progress of trainees. There are regular group meetings with trainees, and an appraisal process which enables you to know how you are progressing, as well as giving you a chance to provide feedback on your training. The firm runs a variety of in-house training courses for trainees.

Benefits

25 days holiday; pension; private medical insurance; life insurance; long-term disability insurance; season ticket loan, EAP scheme.

Sponsorship & awards

LPC and CPE course fees.

Partners 37
Assistant Solicitors 36
Total Trainees 12

Contact
Graduate Recruitment

Method of application
CV & covering letter

Selection procedure
2 interviews with the Training Partners

Closing date for 2013
30 June 2011

Application
Training contracts p.a. 6
Applications p.a. 800
% interviewed p.a. 3%
Required degree grade 2:1

Training
Salary
1st year £30,000
2nd year £32,000
Holiday entitlement 25 days
% of trainees with a non-law degree p.a. 0-50%

Post-qualification
Salary £47,000
% of trainees offered job on qualification (2010) 50%

Fladgate LLP

16 Great Queen Street, London, WC2B 5DG
Tel: (020) 3036 7000 Fax: (020) 3036 7600
Email: trainees@fladgate.com Website: www.fladgate.com

Firm profile

Fladgate LLP is an innovative, progressive and thriving law firm which prides itself on its friendly and professional working environment.

Main areas of work

The firm provides a wide range of legal services to a portfolio of prestigious clients in the UK and overseas, including multinationals, major institutions and listed companies, clearing banks, lenders and entrepreneurs. Fladgate LLP's lawyers have experience in most major areas of practice and the firm combines an accessible and responsive style of service with first-class technical skills and in-depth expertise.

The firm has a strong international dimension based on multi-lingual and multi-qualified lawyers working in London and complemented by access to an extensive network of overseas lawyers. The firm operates specialist teams which serve continental Europe, India, Israel, South Africa, the US and the Middle East.

The firm's three main departments comprise property (which includes separate planning, construction and property litigation teams), corporate (which includes tax, private capital, intellectual property, commercial and employment groups) and litigation. These are supported by a number of specialist cross-departmental teams that provide co-ordinated advice on a range of issues.

Trainee profile

Fladgate LLP seeks trainees with enthusiasm, leadership potential and excellent interpersonal skills. You must be able to work both independently and in a team, and will be expected to show common sense and initiative. Awareness of the commercial interests of clients is essential. You will have a minimum of a 2:1 degree, although not necessarily in law, together with three excellent A levels or equivalent.

Training environment

Typically, you will complete four six-month seats. Each seat will bring you into contact with new clients and colleagues, and you can expect to gain real hands-on experience of a variety of deals and projects, both large and small. In each seat you will work alongside senior lawyers who will supervise your development and ensure that you are involved in challenging and interesting work. In addition to on-the-job training, each department has a comprehensive training schedule of seminars and workshops covering a range of legal and skills training.

The firm has a modern culture and an open-door policy where trainees are given early responsibility and encouraged to achieve their full potential.

Benefits

Pension, permanent health insurance, life assurance, season ticket loan, sports club loan, private medical.

Partners 47
Assistant Solicitors 21
Total Trainees 8

Contact
Mrs Annaleen Stephens, Senior Human Resources Manager

Method of application
Please apply using the firm's application form. Further information and an application form are available at the firm's website www.fladgate.com

Selection procedure
Assessment day including interview

Application
For more details please visit www.fladgate.com
Training contracts p.a. 4
Required degree grade 2:1

Training
Starting salary £30,000
Holiday entitlement
22-25 days

Post-qualification
Salary £50,000

Foot Anstey

Salt Quay House, 4 North East Quay, Sutton Harbour, Plymouth, PL4 0BN
Tel: (01752) 675000 Fax: (01752) 675500
Email: training@footanstey.com Website: www.footanstey.com

Firm profile

Foot Anstey is the largest legal firm in Devon, Somerset and Cornwall with substantial offices in Exeter, Plymouth, Taunton and Truro. The firm offers specialist legal advice to businesses, public sector organisations and individuals both regionally and nationally and prides itself in the excellence of advice and service to clients. Foot Anstey has grown rapidly in recent years, doubling in size since 2005, to a turnover of over £20m. The firm was the first in the UK to achieve the Law Society's national award for excellence in practice standards and is both IIP and Lexcel accredited. The firm also holds a Legal Services Commission Specialist Quality Mark.

The firm recognises that a client focused strategy relies on the attraction and retention of the best lawyers. The firm has successfully attracted top lawyers from London and major regional centres seeking the combination of the quality of life offered by the south west region together with a high quality of work from an impressive regional and national client portfolio.

Main areas of work

As a full service law firm, Foot Anstey delivers the spectrum of services associated with a major regional law firm. Main areas of work include: agriculture and rural business, banking, charities, clinical negligence, construction, commercial property, company commercial, criminal advocates, dispute resolution, education, employment, family finance and childcare, financial services, insolvency, IT/IP, media and private client. The firm has an extensive range of clients from commercial, public and private sectors, acting for numerous local, regional and national companies and high net worth individuals.

Trainee profile

The firm welcomes applications from all law and non-law graduates who have a good academic background, exceptional communication skills and the ability to work as part of a dynamic team. Trainees are welcomed into a friendly and supportive environment where they will find the quality and variety of work both challenging and rewarding.

Training environment

The firm's wide range of legal services enable it to offer trainees experience in a wide range of disciplines. Trainees undertake four seats of six months. Seats are allocated following an application and internal interview process. Individual monthly meetings are held with supervisors and appraisals are conducted at the end of each seat. Regular communication between the trainees and supervisors ensures an open and friendly environment. The Professional Skills Course is taught externally.

Benefits

Contributory pension scheme, 25 days' holiday, childcare vouchers, green travel schemes and life assurance.

Vacation placements

The deadline for the 2011 summer placement scheme is 30 April 2011. Please apply using the online application form.

Sponsorship & awards

Up to £9,600 grant available towards LPC and living expenses.

Vacancies 6
Trainees 16
Partners 40
Total Staff 352

Contact
Kelly Cooke
(01752) 675069

Method of application
Applications for a training contract should be made by 3 July 2011 using the online application form available at www.footanstey.com

Selection procedure
Assessment day
application
Training contracts p.a. 6
Usually 2:1 degree

Closing date for 2012/2013
3 July 2011

Training
Salary
1st year (2010) £19,500
2nd year (2010) £21,000
Holiday entitlement 25 days

Post-qualification
Salary (2010) £32,000-£33,000
% of trainees offered job on qualification (2010) 100%
% of assistant solicitors who joined as trainees
(as at 30/04/10) 30%
% of partners who joined as trainees (as at 30/04/10) 13%

Offices
Exeter, Plymouth, Taunton & Truro

Foot Anstey

Forbes

73 Northgate, Blackburn BB2 1AA
Tel: (01254) 580000 Fax: (01254) 222216
Email: graduate.recruitment@forbessolicitors.co.uk

Firm profile

Forbes is one of the largest practices in the north with 35 partners and over 350 members of staff based in nine offices across the north of England. The firm has a broad based practice dealing with both commercial and private client work and can therefore provide a varied and exciting training contract. The firm is however especially noted for excellence in its business law; civil litigation; insurance; crime; family and employment departments. It has a number of Higher Court Advocates and the firm holds many Legal Service Commission Franchises. Underlying the practice is a strong commitment to quality, training and career development – a commitment underlined by the fact that Forbes was one of the first firms to be recognised as an Investor in People and its ISO 9001 accreditation. For applicants looking for a 'city' practice without the associated hassles of working in a city then Forbes could be it. The firm can offer the best of both worlds – a large firm with extensive resources and support combined with a commitment to quality, people and the personal touch.

Main areas of work

Business law, civil litigation, housing, insurance, crime, family and employment services.

Trainee profile

Forbes looks for high-calibre recruits with strong North West connections and good academic records, who are also keen team players. Candidates should have a total commitment to client service and identify with the firm's philosophy of providing practical straightforward legal advice.

Training environment

A tailored training programme involves six months in four of the following: crime, civil litigation, insurance in Leeds or Blackburn, housing, matrimonial, and non-contentious/business law.

Partners 35
Assistant Solicitors 65
Total Trainees 8

Contact
Graduate Recruitment Manager

Method of application
Online application

Selection procedure
Interview with partners

Closing date for 2013
31 July 2011
If no invite to interview is received by 31/08/11 applicants to assume they have been unsucesful.

Application
Training contracts p.a. 4
Applications p.a. 350 plus
% interviewed p.a. Varies
Required degree grade 2:1

Training
Salary
1st year At least Law Society minimum
2nd year £19,500
Holiday entitlement
20 days p.a.

Post-qualification
Salary
Highly competitive
% of trainees offered job on qualification (2010) 80%

Freeth Cartwright LLP

Cumberland Court, 80 Mount Street, Nottingham NG1 6HH
Tel: (0845) 634 2600 Fax: (0115) 859 9600
Email: carole.wigley@freethcartwright.co.uk
Website: www.freethcartwright.co.uk

Members 81
Assistant Solicitors 122
Total Trainees 13

Contact
Carole Wigley, Senior HR Manager

Method of application
Online application form

Selection procedure
Interview & selection day
Closing date for 2013
15 July 2011

Training
Starting salary (2010) £22,000

Offices
Birmingham, Derby, Leicester, London, Manchester and Nottingham

Firm profile

Tracing its origins back to 1805, Freeth Cartwright LLP became Nottingham's largest firm in 1994 with successful offices now established in Birmingham, Derby, Leicester, London and Manchester. Whilst Freeth Cartwright LLP is a heavyweight commercial firm, serving a wide variety of corporate and institutional clients, there is also a commitment to a range of legal services, which includes a substantial private client element. This enables it to give a breadth of experience in training which is not always available in firms of a similar size.

Freeth Cartwright is extremely pleased to have been awarded The Sunday Times 100 Best Companies to Work for status in 2008, 2009 and 2010 and was also winner of LawCareers.Net Training & Recruitment 2008 award for the 'Best Trainer' category for National/ Large Regional Firms and shortlisted in 2010.

Main areas of work

Real estate and construction, commercial services, private client and personal litigation.

Trainee profile

Freeth Cartwright LLP looks for people to bring their own perspective and individuality to the firm. The firm needs people who can cope with the intellectual demands of life as a lawyer and who possess the wider personal skills which are needed in its diverse practice.

Training environment

Freeth Cartwright LLP is committed to providing comprehensive training for all its staff. The firm's training programme is based on in-house training covering technical matters and personal skills, supplemented with external courses where appropriate. The firm endeavours to give the best possible experience during the training period, as it believes that informal training on-the-job is the most effective means of encouraging the skills required in a qualified solicitor. One of the firm's senior partners takes responsibility for all its trainees and their personal development, overseeing their progress through the firm and discussing performance based on feedback. Normally, the training contract will consist of four six month seats in different departments, most of which are available in the firm's Nottingham offices, although it is possible for trainees to spend at least one seat in another location.

Freeth
Cartwright
LLP

Freshfields Bruckhaus Deringer

Freshfields Bruckhaus Deringer LLP
65 Fleet Street, London EC4Y 1HS
Tel: (020) 7785 5554 Fax: (020) 7832 7001
Email: uktrainees@freshfields.com
Website: www.freshfields.com/uktrainees

Firm profile

Freshfields Bruckhaus Deringer is one of a handful of leading international law firms.

The firm's clients are mainly big commercial businesses whose names are well-known. The type of work the firm does divides into helping clients achieve what they want through doing deals, advising them on real and potential problems, and helping them sort out their disputes.

Main areas of work

Clients look to the firm to be able to answer any legal or regulatory questions that confront them. Organisationally, the firm's lawyers work in one of eight departments: corporate; finance; dispute resolution; real estate; intellectual property/IT; tax; employment, pensions and benefits; and antitrust, competition and trade. But the firm's practice is extremely broad, and dynamic: it is constantly changing to meet clients' needs.

Trainee profile

Trainees need to be intellectually talented and have excellent English skills. They need to enjoy working on difficult problems, working alongside others, and never doing less than the best they can.

Training environment

Trainees can move departments every three months: many other firms are not so flexible. All departments provide formal training. But trainees learn most by working for clients alongside the firm's more experienced lawyers, both in London and in other offices in the US, Europe and Asia. Some are also seconded to clients.

Benefits

The firm offers a flexible and competitive benefits package.

Vacation placements

The firm normally takes students on vacation schemes who are in the summer before their final undergraduate year. Some summer vacation students can spend time abroad as part of their placement. The application window for the summer 2011 schemes is from 1 October 2010 to 15 January 2011 but the sooner you apply, the better.

Sponsorship & awards

The firm pays the GDL and LPC fees for all its prospective trainees, and a maintenance grant for both courses.

Partners 468
Assistant Solicitors 1,682
Total Trainees 192
(London based)

Contact
uktrainees@freshfields.com

Method of application
Online application form

Selection procedure
2 interviews and written test

Closing date for 2013
31 July 2011

Application
Training contracts p.a. 90
Applications p.a. c.2,000
% interviewed p.a. c.12%
Required degree grade 2:1

Training
Salary
1st year £39,000
2nd year £44,000
Holiday entitlement 25 days
% of trainees with a non-law degree p.a. c.40%
No. of seats available abroad p.a. c.72

Post-qualification
Salary £60,000
% of trainees offered job on qualification c.86%

Overseas offices
Abu Dhabi, Amsterdam, Bahrain, Barcelona, Beijing, Berlin, Brussels, Cologne, Dubai, Düsseldorf, Frankfurt, Hamburg, Hanoi, Ho Chi Minh City, Hong Kong, Madrid, Milan, Moscow, Munich, New York, Paris, Riyadh, Rome, Shanghai, Tokyo, Vienna, Washington DC

Gordons LLP

Riverside West, Whitehall Road, Leeds, LS1 4AW
Tel: (0113) 227 0100 Fax: (0113) 227 0113
Forward House, 8 Duke Street, Bradford, BD1 3QX
Tel: (01274) 202202 Fax: (01274) 202100
Email: karen.mills@gordonsllp.com
Website: www.gordonsllp.com

Firm profile

Gordons is one of the largest law firms based entirely in Yorkshire, with offices in Leeds and Bradford. The firm provides commercial and personal legal services to a wide range of businesses and individuals across the region and beyond, from the individual entrepreneur and small family business to the large PLC, and the firm's private client service is equally as comprehensive. The firm's approach is that of a straight-talking, hard-working, ambitious law firm that puts its clients' success before its own.

Main areas of work

Commercial property; planning and environmental; construction; corporate; banking; insolvency; commercial litigation; intellectual property; employment; personal injury; personal law; family law and residential property.

Trainee profile

The firm is looking for trainees who are eager to learn, have good interpersonal skills, can relate well to clients and who welcome responsibility at an early stage. Initiative, commercial awareness, IT skills and a friendly and professional manner are all essential qualities along with ambition to succeed. The firm sees its trainees as its partners of tomorrow!

Training environment

The firm's trainees spend a minimum of six months in at least three of the following departments: company/ commercial; commercial property, litigation, private client. During the second year of the training contract trainees may state their preference for a particular department and the firm will try to accommodate the request where possible. The firm's trainees work closely with a partner or senior solicitor in each seat and get 'hands on' training with plenty of client contact. They are actively encouraged to get involved with marketing, networking, training, and other events hosted by the firm and/ or clients, and the firm itself has regular social activities on offer, both formal and informal. The environment is supportive and friendly with an open door policy across the firm, and the trainees have regular meetings with their supervisors to ensure their progress. The firm aims to offer its trainees positions within the firm on qualification wherever possible.

Benefits

Group personal pension; life assurance of three x salary death in service benefit; interest-free season ticket loan; childcare vouchers scheme; 24 days holiday per year plus statutory holidays, weekly yoga sessions.

Sponsorship & awards

The firm contributes £5,000 towards LPC course fees.

Partners 33
Assistant Solicitors 52
Total Trainees 12

Contact
Karen Mills, HR Manager
Philip Paget, Training Partner

Method of application
Online application via website www.gordonsllp.com

Selection procedure
One stage interview process, including practical exercise and opportunity to meet current trainees

Closing date for 2013
1st August 2011

Application
Training contracts p.a. 6
Applications p.a. 300
% interviewed p.a. 10%
Required degree grade 2:1

Training
Salary
1st year £20,000
2nd year £22,000
Holiday entitlement 24 days and statutory
% of trainees with a non-law degree p.a. 50%

Post-qualification
Salary £34,500 p.a.
% of trainees offered job on qualification 100%

Government Legal Service

11th Floor, Castlemead, Lower Castle Street, Bristol, BS1 3AG
Tel: 0845 3000 793
Email: glstrainees@tmpw.co.uk
Website: www.gls.gov.uk

Firm profile

The Government Legal Service (GLS) is the collective term for the 2000 lawyers working in the legal teams of over 30 of the largest government departments and agencies. GLS lawyers have one client, the government of the day, which requires advice and support across the entire spectrum of its activities.

Main areas of work

There are many parallels between the GLS' work and that found in private practice. The government employs staff, purchases goods and services, buys and sells land and enters into contracts. GLS lawyers advise and represent the government on a huge range of issues which are often high profile and politically sensitive.

In addition to interpreting existing laws, GLS lawyers also have the opportunity to make new legislation. GLS lawyers are part of the teams that breathe life into the policies pledged by governments. They advise ministers and policy officials on what can (and can't) be done under existing legislation. If new legislation is required, GLS lawyers will help to draft and take it through Parliament in the form of a Bill. They will work closely with policy officials and Ministers and even support Ministers in Parliamentary debates. This type of work is unique to the GLS.

Trainee profile

To join the GLS as a trainee solicitor or pupil barrister, you'll need at least a 2:1 degree (which need not be in law). You must also provide evidence of strong analytical ability, excellent communication and interpersonal skills and motivation for working in public service.

Training environment

The GLS provides a unique and varied training environment for trainees and pupils. Generally, trainee solicitors work in four different areas of practice over a two-year period in the government Department to which they are assigned. Pupil barristers divide their year's pupillage between their Department and chambers. The GLS prides itself on involving trainees and pupils in the full range of casework conducted by their Department. This frequently includes high profile matters and will be under the supervision of senior colleagues.

Benefits

These include professional development opportunities, excellent pension scheme, civilised working hours, generous holiday entitlement and subsidised restaurant facilities.

Vacation placements

Summer 2011 vacation placement scheme; approx 60 places. Duration: 2-3 weeks. Anticipated closing date: late January/ early February 2011. Remuneration: £200-£250 pw.

Sponsorship & awards

LPC and BVC fees as well as other compulsory Professional Skills Course fees. Funding may be available for the GDL. The GLS also provides a grant of around £5,000-7,000 for the vocational year.

Total Trainees around 50 currently working for the Government Legal Service

Contact
glstrainees@tmpw.co.uk or visit www.gls.gov.uk

Method of application
Online application form, situational judgement test and verbal reasoning test

Selection procedure
Half day assessment centre involving a written exercise, a competancy based interview and a technical interview

Closing date for 2013
29 July 2011

Application
Training contracts p.a. 22-30
Applications p.a. 2000+
% interviewed p.a. 5%
Required degree grade (need not be in law) 2:1

Training
Salary
1st year salary: £23,280-£25,600
2nd year salary £24,850-£27,335
Holiday entitlement 25 days on entry

Post-qualification
Salary
£32,000-£40,000
% of trainees accepting job on qualification (2009) over 95%

Hammonds LLP

Rutland House, 148 Edmund Street, Birmingham B3 2JR
7 Devonshire Square, Cutlers Gardens, London EC2M 4YH
2 Park Lane, Leeds LS3 1ES
Trinity Court, 16 John Dalton Street, Manchester M6O 8HS
Tel: (0800) 163 498
Email: traineerecruitment@hammonds.com Website: www.hammonds.com/trainees

Firm profile

Hammonds is one of Europe's largest corporate law firms and a member of the Global 100. In the UK alone, the firm advises over 200 London Stock Exchange quoted companies and 30 FTSE 100 companies. The firm has offices in London, Birmingham, Leeds, Manchester, Brussels, Paris, Berlin, Munich, Rome*, Milan*, Madrid, Turin*, Beijing and Hong Kong. The firm has over 1,000 staff, including 170 Partners, 400 solicitors and 50 trainees. The firm is regarded as innovative, opportunistic and highly successful in the markets in which it operates.

Main areas of work

Corporate; commercial dispute resolution; construction, engineering and projects; employment; EU and competition; finance law (including banking); intellectual property and commercial; media/IT; pensions; property; sports law; tax.

Trainee profile

Hammonds seeks applications from all disciplines for vacation work and training contracts. Consideration given to four elements in trainee selection: strong academic performance (2:1 degree classification), evidence of work experience in the legal sector, excellent communication skills and significant achievement in non-academic pursuits.

Training environment

25 trainee solicitors recruited each year. Trainees undertake six four-month seats during their training contract. Trainees have input in choice of seats and are encouraged to undertake a broad selection of seats to benefit their knowledge on qualification. Trainees benefit from two-tier supervision and challenging work. The firm provides a comprehensive induction programme including on-going departmental training, seminars and workshops throughout the training contract. Trainees undertake formal appraisal meetings with their supervisors during each seat. Hammonds' trainees benefit from exposure to clients, cross-border work and opportunity for seats on secondment.Trainees are involved in all aspects of professional life.

Benefits

Pension, life assurance, subsidised gym membership, interest free season ticket loan and a flexible benefits package.

Vacation placements

Places for 2011: 25 Summer Scheme; Duration: 2 weeks; Remuneration: £230 p.w. (London), £180 p.w. (Leeds, Manchester, Birmingham); Closing Date: 31 January 2011.

Sponsorship & awards

PgDL and LPC fees paid and maintenance grant provided. Maintenance grant presently:

GDL: London, £6,000; Regional, £4,500.

LPC: London, £7,000; Regional, £5,000.

*An association with the italian law firm R&P Legal - Rossotto, Colombatto & Partners.

Partners 170
Assistant Solicitors 400
Total Trainees 50

Contact
Graduate Recruitment Team

Method of application
Online application form

Selection procedure
Assessment and interview

Closing date for 2013
31 July 2011

Application
Training contracts p.a. 25
Applications p.a. 1,300
% interviewed p.a. 10%
Required degree grade 2:1

Training
Salary
1st year (2009)
£22,000 regional
£32,000 London
2nd year (2008)
£25,000 regional
£35,000 London
Holiday entitlement 25 days
% of trainees with a non-law degree p.a. 40%
No. of seats available abroad p.a. 4

Post-qualification
Salary (2010)
London £56,000
Other £36,000
% of trainees accepting job on qualification (2010) 71%

Overseas offices
Brussels,Beijing, Paris, Berlin, Munich, Rome, Milan, Turin, Hong Kong, Madrid

Harbottle & Lewis LLP

Hanover House, 14 Hanover Square, London W1S 1HP
Tel: (020) 7667 5000 Fax: (020) 7667 5100
Email: kathy.beilby@harbottle.com
Website: www.harbottle.com

Firm profile

Harbottle & Lewis LLP is a commercial law firm providing advice primarily to those in the media, entertainment and communications industries.

The firm has been at the centre of many of the media industry's largest and most high profile transactions and cases and its lawyers are recognised for some of the most pioneering work in the exploitation of digital media and content.

Main areas of work

The firm focuses on the provision of innovative and effective advice on corporate, employment, finance and asset leasing, intellectual property, litigation, property and tax law as well as more general commercial and regulatory advice.

It provides specialist advice to clients in all areas of the communications and creative industries including advertising, broadcasting, digital media, fashion, film, interactive entertainment, music, publishing, sponsorship, sport, television and theatre. The firm also advises on the legal issues faced by organisations and individuals in the media spotlight such as defamation, data protection, and privacy. It also has expertise in other areas such as aviation, charities, family, personal injury and private client.

Trainee profile

Trainees will have demonstrated the high academic abilities, commercial awareness, and initiative necessary to become part of a team advising clients in dynamic and demanding industries.

Training environment

The two year training contract is divided into four six-month seats where trainees will be given experience in a variety of legal skills. Seats include, corporate, employment, family/tax/private client, litigation property, a secondment to a long-standing client as well as seats in the firm's core industries, such as film, interactive entertainment, music, publishing, sport, television, and theatre. The firm has a policy of accepting a small number of trainees to ensure they are given relevant and challenging work and are exposed to and have responsibility for a full range of legal tasks. The firm has its own seminar programme in both legal topics and industry know-how. An open door policy and a pragmatic entrepreneurial approach to legal practice provides a stimulating working environment.

Benefits

Lunch provided; season ticket loans.

Sponsorship & awards

LPC fees paid and interest-free loans towards maintenance.

Partners 31
Assistant Solicitors 42
Total Trainees 10

Contact
Kathy Beilby

Method of application
Application form to download from website

Selection procedure
Interview

Closing date for 2013
31 July 2011

Application
Training contracts p.a. 5
Applications p.a. 800
% interviewed p.a. 10%
Required degree grade 2:1

Training
Salary
1st year £28,000 (2010)
2nd year £29,000 (2010)
Holiday entitlement
in the first year 23 days
in the second year 26 days
% of trainees with
a non-law degree p.a. 40%

Post-qualification
Salary (2010) £45k

HBJ Gateley Wareing LLP

One Eleven, Edmund Street, Birmingham B3 2HJ
Tel: (0121) 234 0000 Fax: (0121) 234 0079
Email: graduaterecruitment.england@hbj-gw.com
Website: www.hbjgateleywareing.com

Firm profile

A 100 partner, UK commercial based practice with an excellent reputation for general commercial work and particular expertise in corporate, plc, commercial, employment, property, construction, insolvency, commercial dispute resolution, banking, tax and shipping.

The firm also offers individual clients a complete private client service including FSA-approved financial advice. The firm is expanding (569 employees) and offers a highly practical, commercial and fast-paced environment. HBJ Gateley Wareing has built an outstanding reputation across the UK for its practical approach, sound advice and professional commitment to its clients. The firm is a full range, multi-disciplinary legal business with expertise in many areas.

HBJ Gateley Wareing has an enviable reputation as a friendly and sociable place to work. The firm is committed to equality and diversity across the firm.

Trainee profile

To apply for a placement in England: applications are invited from second year law students and final year non-law students and graduates. Applicants should have (or be heading for) a minimum 2.1 degree, and should have at least three Bs (or equivalent) at A-level. Individuals should be hardworking team players capable of using initiative and demonstrating commercial awareness.

Training environment

Four six-month seats with ongoing supervision and appraisals every three months. PSC taken internally. In-house courses on skills such as time management, negotiation, IT, drafting, business skills, marketing, presenting and writing in plain English.

Benefits

Current trainee offered as a 'buddy' – a point of contact within the firm, library available, private health, life assurance (death in service) and season ticket loan.

Vacation placements

Two-week placement over the summer. Deadline for next year's vacation placement scheme is 11 February 2011 and the closing date for 2013 training contracts is 31 July 2011. Apply online at www.hbjgateleywareing.com. Paper/email applications not accepted.

Sponsorship & awards

LPC maintenance grant of £5,000.

Partners 100 (firmwide)
Vacancies 12 (England)
Total Trainees 16 (England)
Total Staff 569 (firmwide)

Contact
HR Department

Closing date for 2013
Training contracts:
31 July 2011
Vacation placements:
11 February 2011

Training
Salary
1st year £20,000-22,000 (Midlands)
2nd year £22,000-24,000 (Midlands)

Post-qualification
Salary £32,000 (Midlands)

Offices
Birmingham, Dubai, Edinburgh, Glasgow, Leicester, London and Nottingham.

HBJ Gateley Wareing

Henmans LLP

5000 Oxford Business Park South, Oxford OX4 2BH
Tel: (01865) 780000 Fax: (01865) 778682
Email: welcome@henmansllp.co.uk
Website: www.henmansllp.co.uk

Firm profile

Henmans LLP is one of the leading law firms in Oxford, with several practice areas ranked as the leading experts in the Thames Valley by commentators. The firm has a national reputation in its specialist areas, handling commercial and personal matters for a wide range of clients both nationally and internationally. The firm also acts for a large number of third sector organisations and insurers.

More than half of its senior lawyers are acknowledged as experts within their fields, so clients are confident of receiving the most authoritative advice available. The firm believes that the best advisers are those who thoroughly understand your concerns, so it works hard to ensure that it has a detailed appreciation of your business or personal questions, and can offer the best possible advice.

Main areas of work

The firm's core service of litigation is nationally recognised for its high quality. The firm also has an excellent reputation for its personal injury, clinical negligence, property, private client and charity work. The breakdown of work is as follows: Personal injury and clinical negligence 19%, dispute resolution 18%, Private client (including family)/charities/trusts 33%, corporate employment 12% and Property 18%.

Trainee profile

Commercial awareness, sound academic accomplishment, intellectual capability, IT literacy, able to work as part of a team, good communication skills.

Training environment

Trainees are an important part of the firm's future. The firm is committed to providing a high standard of training throughout the contract. Trainees are introduced to the firm with a detailed induction and overview of its client base. A trainee manual is provided to familiarise the trainee with each department's procedures. Experience is likely to be within the PI, property, professional negligence/commercial litigation, corporate, employment and private client departments. The firm provides an ongoing programme of in-house education and regular appraisals within its supportive friendly environment. The firm values commitment and enthusiasm both professionally and socially as an integral part of its culture and trainees are encouraged to join in social activities and become involved with the life of the firm.

Benefits

Holiday entitlement 23 days + 2 firm days at Christmas. BUPA, pension, life assurance, EAP, scheme, free car parking, subsidised cafe, pilates.

Partners 23
Other Solicitors & Fee-earners 53
Total Trainees 6

Contact
Viv J Matthews (Mrs)
MA CH FCIPD
Head of HR

Method of application
Application form on website

Selection procedure
The interview process comprises an assessment day with Head of HR and partners, including an interview, presentation, verbal reasoning test, drafting and team exercise

Closing date for 2013
31 July 2011

Application
Training contracts p.a. 3
Applications p.a. 300

Training
Salary
1st year (2009/10) £22,000
2nd year (2009/10) £24,000
% of trainees with a non-law degree p.a. 40%

Post-qualification
Salary (2009) £34,000
% of assistants who joined as trainees 28%
% of partners who joined as trainees 15%

HENMANS LLP

Herbert Smith LLP

Exchange House, Primrose Street, London EC2A 2HA
Tel: (020) 7374 8000 Fax: (020) 7374 0888
Email: graduate.recruitment@herbertsmith.com
Website: www.herbertsmithgraduates.com

Firm profile

Pre-eminent in dispute resolution and with an outstanding reputation for high value transactional advice, Herbert Smith LLP is a leading international law firm. Its main clients are prominent global and national businesses that it serves from offices in Asia, Europe and the Middle East.

Main areas of work

Alongside Herbert Smith's outstanding reputation in dispute resolution and corporate work, the firm has leading practices in finance, real estate, competition and employment, pensions and incentives. It is also acknowledged as a leader in several industry sectors, including the energy and natural resources and financial institutions sectors.

Trainee profile

As well as a strong academic record, applicants require a strong level of commercial awareness and the common sense to be able to make their own way in a large firm. Combine these qualities with a creative and questioning mind, and Herbert Smith will offer you great challenges and rewards.

Training environment

The strength and breadth of the firm's practice areas, including corporate, dispute resolution and finance, guarantee excellent training and development opportunities for trainees. The training process balances contentious and non-contentious work; early responsibility and support. An emphasis is also placed on professional and personal development. Trainees rotate around four six-month seats, including a seat in a specialist area such as IP or competition. Trainees are also encouraged to go on secondment to a client or to one of the firm's international offices. Herbert Smith's global reach makes this a possibility for many.

Sponsorship & benefits

Herbert Smith offers £5,000 for the GDL outside of London; £6,000 GDL inside London and £6,000 for the LPC. Benefits include 25 days' holiday (rising to 27 after qualification), bonus scheme, gym membership subsidy, life assurance, pension scheme with company contributions, private healthcare, season ticket loan, permanent health insurance.

Vacation placements

Herbert Smith offers a two-week winter vacation scheme, a two-week spring vacation scheme and three summer vacation schemes. The vacation scheme will give you an excellent insight into working life at a leading international City firm. Placements are open to both law and non-law students, and during the scheme you will be exposed to the highest quality contentious and non-contentious work. You will be treated as one of the team and given real work for real clients.

Partners 270
Fee-earners 783
Total Trainees 238
*denotes worldwide figures

Contact
graduate.recruitment@herbertsmith.com
020 7374 8000

Method of application
Online at www.herbertsmithgraduates.com

Selection procedure
Online testing and face to face assessments

Closing date for March 2013/Sept 2013
31 July 2011

Application
Training contracts p.a. 85
Applications p.a. circa 2,000
% interviewed p.a. 20%
Required degree grade 2:1

Training
Salary
1st year £38,000
2nd year £43,000
Holiday entitlement
25 days, rising to 27 on qualification
ratio of law to non-law graduates is broadly equal

Post-qualification
Salary (2010) £61,000
% of trainees offered job on qualification (2010) 82%

Overseas offices
Abu Dhabi, Bangkok, Beijing, Brussels, Dubai, Hong Kong, London, Madrid, Moscow, Paris, Shanghai, Singapore, Tokyo
associated offices
Amsterdam, Berlin, Budapest, Dammam, Frankfurt, Jakarta, Jeddah, Munich, New York, Prague, Riyadh, Stuttgart, Warsaw

Herbert Smith

Hewitsons LLP

42 Newmarket Road, Cambridge CB5 8EP
Tel: (01604) 233233 Fax: (01223) 316511
Email: mail@hewitsons.com (for all offices)
Website: www.hewitsons.com (for all offices)

Firm profile

Established in 1865, the firm handles mostly company and commercial work, but has a growing body of public sector clients. The firm has three offices: Cambridge, Northampton and Milton Keynes.

Main areas of work

Three sections: corporate, property and private client.

Trainee profile

The firm is interested in applications from candidates who have achieved a high degree of success in academic studies and who are bright, personable and able to take the initiative.

Training environment

The firm offers four six-month seats.

Benefits

The PSC is provided during the first year of the training contract. This is coupled with an extensive programme of Trainee Solicitor Seminars provided by specialist in-house lawyers.

Vacation placements

Places for 2011: A few placements are available, application is by way of letter and CV to Caroline Lewis; Duration: 1 week.

Sponsorship & awards

Funding for the CPE and/or LPC is not provided.

Partners 38
Assistant Solicitors 37
Total Trainees 8

Contact
Caroline Lewis
7 Spencer Parade Northampton
NN1 5AB

Method of application
Firm's application form

Selection procedure
Interview

Closing date for 2013
End of August 2011

Application
Training contracts p.a. 10
Applications p.a. 850
% interviewed p.a. 10%
Required degree grade
2:1 min

Training
Salary
1st year £23,500
2nd year under review
Holiday entitlement 22 days
% of trainees with a
non-law degree p.a. 50%

Post-qualification
Salary £35,000
% of trainees offered job
on qualification (2010) 75%

Higgs & Sons

3 Waterfront Business Park, Brierley Hill, DY5 1LX
Tel: (0845) 111 5050 Fax: (01384) 327290
Email: graduaterecruitment@higgsandsons.co.uk
Website: www.higgsandsons.co.uk

Firm profile

Higgs & Sons is now one of the largest and most respected law firms in the West Midlands, operating out of two offices in Brierley Hill and Kingswinford and employing over 170 staff. During 2010 the firm moved its headquarters to a new purpose - designed facility at the prestigious Waterfront Business Park. The firm is well recognised in the Legal 500 and Chambers Guide to the Legal Profession.

Higgs & Sons is different from the typical law firm. The firm successfully combines traditional values with an innovative approach to legal problems which has helped to attract an impressive client base whilst also staying true to the local community. Clients and staff alike are attracted to Higgs' ability to offer an all round service in a number of areas. The firm is proud to provide a supportive and friendly working environment within which both colleagues and clients can thrive. The opportunity for career progression is also clear as more than half of the firm's partners trained with the firm.

Main areas of work

For the business client: corporate and commercial, insolvency, employment law, commercial litigation and commercial property.

For the private client: wills, probate, trusts and tax, employment law, personal injury, clinical negligence, conveyancing, dispute resolution, matrimonial/ family, motoring and private criminal.

Trainee profile

Applications are welcome from law and non law students who can demonstrate consistently high academic records, a broad range of interpersonal skills and extra curricular activities and interests. The firm would like to hear about what you have done to develop your wider skills and awareness. It is looking for people who want to get involved and participate fully in the business.

Candidates will preferably have a 2:1 class degree but graduates with a 2:2 class will be considered.

Training environment

A training contract at Higgs is different from those offered by other firms. There is the unique opportunity to undertake six four month seats in a variety of departments, including a double seat in the department in to which you wish to qualify as you approach the end of your training contract. Throughout the training contract you will receive a mix of contentious and non-contentious work and an open door policy means that there is always someone on hand to answer questions and supervise your work. Regular appraisals take place at the end of each seat and a designated Partner oversees you throughout the duration of your training contract, acting as a mentor. Participation in BTSS events and an active Higgs social environment ensures the work life balance.

Benefits

Private medical insurance, contributory pension, life assurance, 25 days holiday and BTSS Membership.

Sponsorship

Professional Skills Course.

Partners 29
Fee Earners 48
Total Trainees 8

Contact
Helena Tonks

Method of application
Online application form

Selection procedure
Interview with trainee committee

Closing date for 2013
18th August 2011

Application
Training contracts p.a. 4
Applications p.a. 250 plus
% interviewed p.a. varies
Required degree grade preferably 2:1, will consider 2:2

Training
Salary reviewed annually
1st year £21,500
2nd year £24,000
Holiday entitlement 25 days p.a.

Post-qualification
Salary £32,000
% of trainees offered job on qualification 80%

Hill Dickinson

No. 1 Street, Paul's Square, Liverpool, L3 9SJ
Tel: (0151) 600 8000
Email: emma.mcavinchey@hilldickinson.com; rebecca.o'regan@hilldickinson.com
Website: www.hilldickinson.com

Firm profile

Hill Dickinson offers the comprehensive range of commercial legal services fromm offices in Liverpool, Manchester, London, Chester, Piraeus and Singapore and Sheffield. It is a top 40 sized practice with over 190 partners and more than 1300 people.

Main areas of work

Hill Dickinson is a major force in insurance and is well respected in the corporate and commercial arena, its marine expertise is internationally renowned and it has award-winning property and construction and employment teams. The firm is widely regarded as a leader in the fields of commercial litigation, healthcare law, clinical negligence, professional risks, intellectual property and wealth management.

The firm is also committed to driving forward its sector offerings in areas such as retail, transport and logistics, the public sector, travel and leisure, energy and media and entertainment.

With a focus on enhancing its international presence, in March 2009, the firm opened a new office in Singapore and in July 2009, it merged with London-based commodities practice Middleton Potts, adding further weight to its global reputation for shipping and transport work.

Clients include multi-national companies, major corporations and UK plcs. insurance companies, UK and foreign banks and financial institutions as well as public and professional bodies and private individuals.

Trainee profile

Commercial awareness and academic ability are the key factors, together with a desire to succeed. Trainees are viewed as the partners of the future and the firm is looking for personable individuals with whom it wants to work.

Training environment

Trainees spend periods of six months in four different practice groups. Trainees are encouraged to accept responsibility and are expected to act with initiative. The firm has an active social committee and a larger than usual selection of competitive sporting teams.

Vacation placements

Four one week schemes. 40 places available for 2011. Apply online by 31 January 2011.

Partners 197
Assistant Solicitors 177
Associates 66
Total Trainees 40

Contact
emma.mcavinchey@
hilldickinson.com

Method of application
Online application form

Selection procedure
Telephone interviews,
pyschometric testing,
assessment day

Closing date for 2013
31st July 2011

Training
Salary
1st year (2010) £24,000
2nd year (2010) £26,000
1st year (London) £32,000
2nd year (London) £34,000
Sponsorship: LPC
Holiday entitlement
25 days & birthday day off

Post-qualification
% of trainees offered job
on qualification 86%

Offices
Liverpool, Manchester, London,
Chester, Sheffield, Singapore,

Hogan Lovells

Hogan Lovells, Atlantic House, Holborn Viaduct, London, EC1A 2FG
Tel (020) 7296 2000 Fax (020) 7296 2001
Email : recruit@hoganlovells.com
Website: www.hoganlovells.com/graduates

Firm profile

Hogan Lovells is one of the leading international legal practices, with over 40 offices in Asia, Europe, Latin America, the Middle East, and the United States.

Main areas of work

The firm's international strength across a wide range of practice areas gives it an exceptional reputation not only for corporate, finance, litigation, government regulatory and intellectual property, but also for other specialist areas including employment, EU/competition, insurance and tax.

Trainee profile

The practice is looking for people whose combination of academic excellence and specialist knowledge will develop Hogan Lovells' business and take it forward. As well as demonstrating strong academic and intellectual ability, candidates should have strong communication and interpersonal skills and a professional, commercial attitude. You should be happy working in a team, yet capable of, and used to, independent action. Above all candidates should have a single-minded ambition to succeed in a top legal practice.

Training environment

The training and development of the firm's trainee solicitors reflects the nature and ambitions of the firm as a whole; trainees are guaranteed to have a genuinely broad experience of its wide ranging practice areas and be immersed in Hogan Lovells' team-based structure.

Trainees at Hogan Lovells spend six months in four different areas of the practice to gain as much experience as possible. All trainees must spend six months in a corporate or finance seat, and six months gaining contentious experience in the firm's dispute resolution practice. In the second year of training, there is the option of spending a seat on secondment either to one of the international offices, or to the in-house legal team of a major client.

Benefits

PPP medical insurance, life assurance, season ticket loan, in-house gym, access to dentist, doctor and physiotherapist, subsidised staff restaurant, discounts at local retailers

Sponsorship

GDL and LPC course fees are paid, and maintenance grants are provided for both the GDL and LPC.

Partners 800+
Assistant Solicitors 2,500+
Total Trainees 148

Contact
recruit@hoganlovells.com
020 7296 2000

Method of application
Online application form

Selection procedure
Assessment day

Closing date for 2013/2014
31 July 2011

Application
Training contracts p.a. 90
Applications p.a. 1,500
% interviewed p.a. 25%
Required degree grade 2:1

Training
Salary
1st year (2010) £37,000
2nd year (2010) £42,000
Holiday entitlement 25 days
% of trainees with a non-law degree p.a. 50%
No. of seats available abroad p.a. 25

Post-qualification
Salary £60,000

International offices
Abu Dhabi, Alicante, Amsterdam, Baltimore, Beijing, Berlin, Boulder, Brussels, Budapest, Caracas, Colorado, Denver, Dubai, Dusseldorf, Frankfurt, Hamburg, Hanoi, Ho Chi Minh City, Hong Kong, Houston, Jeddah, London, Los Angeles, Madrid, Miami, Milan, Moscow, New York, Munich, Northern Virginia, Paris, Philadelphia, Prague, Riyadh, Rome, San Francisco, Shanghai, Silicon Valley, Singapore, Tokyo, Ulaanbaatar, Warsaw, Washington DC, Zagreb.

Howes Percival LLP

Oxford House, Cliftonville, Northampton NN1 5PN
Tel: (01604) 230400 Fax: (01604) 620956
Email: katy.pattle@howespercival.com
Website: www.howespercival.com

Firm profile

Howes Percival LLP is a leading commercial law firm with offices in Leicester, Milton Keynes, Northampton and Norwich. Previously the firm has won the Leicestershire Law Society Firm of the year award and the UK Regional Firm of the Year at the Legal Business Awards. The firm's working environment is progressive and highly professional and its corporate structure means that fee-earners are rewarded on merit and can progress to associate or partner status quickly. The type and high value of the work that the firm does places it in a position whereby it is recognised as being a regional firm by location only. The firm has the expertise, resources and Partner reputation that match a city firm.

Main areas of work

The practice is departmentalised and the breakdown of its work is as follows: corporate 30%; commercial property 25%; commercial litigation 20%; insolvency 10%; employment 10%; private client 5%.

Trainee profile

The firm is looking for eight well-educated, focused, enthusiastic, commercially aware graduates with a minimum 2:1 degree in any discipline. Howes Percival LLP welcomes confident communicators with strong interpersonal skills who share the firm's desire to be the best.

Training environment

Trainees complete four six-month seats, each one in a different department. Trainees joining the Norwich office will remain at Norwich for the duration of their training contract. Within the East Midlands region, there is the opportunity to gain experience in two of the three East Midlands offices. Trainees report direct to a partner, and after three months and again towards the end of each seat they will be formally assessed by the partner training them. Trainees will be given every assistance by the fee-earners in their department to develop quickly and will be given responsibility as soon as they are ready.

Benefits

Contributory pension scheme. Private health insurance. LPC/GDL/ maintenance grant. Details available upon request.

Vacation placements

Vacation placements are available in June, July and August. Please apply via the online application form found on the trainee page of the firm's website. The closing date is 30 April 2011.

Partners 32
Solicitors 57
Total Trainees 17

Contact
Miss Katy Pattle
HR Officer

Method of application
Online application form

Selection procedure
Assessment centres

Closing date for 2013
31 July 2011

Application
Training contracts p.a. 8
Applications p.a. 300
% interviewed p.a. 10%
Required degree grade 2:1

Training
Salary
1st year £24,500 (East Mids - Sept 10)
1st year £22,000 (Norwich - Sept 10)
2nd year £26,500 (East Mids- Sept 10)
2nd year (Norwich - Sept 10 £23,000)
Holiday entitlement
25 days p.a.

Post-qualification
Salary
£38,500 (East Midlands)
£33,500 (Norwich)

Ince & Co

International House, 1 St Katharine's Way, London E1W 1AY
Email: recruitment@incelaw.com

Firm profile

From its origins in maritime law, the firm's practice today encompasses all aspects of the work areas listed below. Ince & Co is frequently at the forefront of developments in contract and tort law.

Main areas of work

Aviation, business and finance, commercial disputes, energy and offshore, insurance and reinsurance, international trade and shipping.

Trainee profile

Hardworking, competitive individuals with initiative who relish challenge and responsibility within a team environment. Academic achievements, positions of responsibility, sport and travel are all taken into account.

Training environment

Trainees sit with four different partners for six months at a time throughout their training. Under close supervision, they are encouraged from an early stage to meet and visit clients, interview witnesses, liaise with counsel, deal with technical experts and handle opposing lawyers. They will quickly build up a portfolio of cases from a number of partners involved in a cross-section of the firm's practice and will see their cases through from start to finish. They will also attend in-house and external lectures, conferences and seminars on practical and legal topics.

Benefits

STL, corporate health cover, PHI, contributory pension scheme. Well Man/Well Woman health checks, subsidised gym membership.

Vacation placements

Places for 2011: 15; Duration: 2 weeks; Remuneration: £250 p.w.; Closing Date: 31 January 2011.

Sponsorship & awards

LPC/CPE fees, £6,000 grant for study in London & Guildford, £5,500 grant for study elsewhere.

Partners 88*
Senior Associates 40*
Solicitors 157*
Total Trainees 30*
* denotes worldwide figures

Contact
Helen Salisbury

Method of application
online at www.graduates.incelaw.com

Selection procedure
Interview with HR professional, interview with 2 partners from Recruitment Committee & 3 tests

Closing date for 2013
31 July 2011

Application
Training contracts p.a. 12
Applications p.a. 1,000
% interviewed p.a. 10%
Required degree grade 2:1

Training
Salary
1st year £36,000
2nd year £39,000
Holiday entitlement 25 days
% of trainees with a non-law degree p.a. 55%

Post-qualification
Salary £58,000
% of trainees offered job on qualification (2010) 83%. All accepted!
% of partners (as at 2010) who joined as trainees Approx 70%

Overseas offices
Dubai, Hamburg, Hong Kong, Le Havre, Paris, Piraeus, Shanghai, Singapore

Irwin Mitchell

Riverside East, 2 Millsands, Sheffield S3 8DT
Tel: (0870) 1500 100 Fax: (0870) 197 3549
Email: graduaterecruitment@irwinmitchell.com
Website: www.irwinmitchell.com

Firm profile

Founded in 1912, the firm has grown from strength to strength and today employ more than 2300 people through its office network of major cities within the UK and its two offices in Spain. Irwin Mitchell Solicitors has grown both organically and through a number of strategic mergers with firms and organisations in tune with the firm's values and culture. The firm is the largest full service law firm within the UK with its services divided into two main categories; legal services for individuals and those for businesses, institutions and organisations. As well as being recognised as the leading national personal injury firm in the UK, the firm has also developed a reputation for the delivery of strong commercial services that add real value to businesses, institutions and organisations. Over the last five years the firm as enjoyed substantial growth as its business strategies have reaped rewards.

Main areas of work

Corporate services and private client; insurance; personal injury.

Trainee profile

The firm is looking for ambitious and well-motivated individuals who have a real commitment to the law and who can demonstrate a positive approach to work-life balance. Irwin Mitchell recruits law and non-law graduates and views social ability as important as academic achievement. Irwin Mitchell believes trainees are an investment for the future and endeavours to retain trainees upon qualification. In addition to the firm's training contract vacancies it also runs a work placement scheme giving potential training contract candidates a chance to experience what it is like to be a solicitor within the firm.

Training environment

The firm's training contracts are streamed so that as a trainee you would either undertake a training contract based within the firm's Personal Injury Practice Area, (where you can gain experience in personal injury, clinical negligence and personal injury defence) or you would undertake a training contract based within the firm's business and private client practice area (where dependant on office location you could gain experience in departments such as insolvency, commercial litigation, court of protection, corporate, public law and family). Trainees spend the first year of their training contract undertaking three seats of four months in duration. During the second year trainees undertake a twelve month seat, in the area which they and the firm wish them to qualify into. The firm offers a structured induction programme to trainees joining the practice.

Benefits

Healthcare scheme, contributory pension scheme, subsidised gym membership, away day and Christmas party.

Sponsorship & awards

Payment of PGDL and LPC fees plus a £4,500 maintenance grant.

Partners 136
Assistant Solicitors 210
Total Trainees 76

Contact
Charlotte Beesley
Graduate Manager
graduaterecruitment@irwinmitchell.com

Method of application
Please visit the firm's website www.irwinmitchell.com and complete the online application

Selection procedure
Assessment centre & interview

Closing date for 2013
31 July 2011

Application
Training contracts p.a. 40-45
Applications p.a. 2,000
% interviewed p.a. 15%
Required degree grade: The firm does not require a specific degree grade

Training
Salary
1st year £22,450
2nd year £24,650
(outside London)
reviewed annually in September
Holiday entitlement
24.5 days

Post-qualification
% of trainees offered job on qualification 91%

Overseas offices/ Regional offices
Birmingham, Bristol, Leeds, London, Manchester, Newcastle, Sheffield, Glasgow, Madrid & Malaga

Jones Day

21 Tudor Street, London, EC4Y 0DJ
Tel: (020) 7039 5959 Fax: (020) 7039 5999
Email: recruit.london@jonesday.com
Website: www.jonesdaylondon.com

Firm profile

Jones Day operates as one firm worldwide with 2,500 lawyers in 32 offices. Jones Day in London is a key part of this international partnership and has around 200 lawyers, including around 50 partners and 30-40 trainees. This means that the firm can offer its lawyers a perfect combination - the intimacy and atmosphere of a medium sized City firm with access to both UK and multinational clients.

Main areas of work

Principal areas of practice at Jones Day include: corporate finance and M&A transactions; investment funds, private equity and corporate tax planning, banking, capital markets and structured finance, business restructuring, litigation, intellectual property, tax and real estate. The London office also has teams of lawyers who are experienced in such areas as competition/antitrust, environmental and employment and pensions law.

Trainee profile

The firm looks for candidates with either a law or non-law degree who have strong intellectual and analytical ability, good communication skills and who can demonstrate resourcefulness, drive, dedication and the ability to engage with clients and colleagues.

Training environment

The firm operates a unique, non-rotational system of training and trainees receive work simultaneously from all departments in the firm. The training is designed to provide flexibility and responsibility from the start. Trainees are encouraged to assume their own workload, which allows early responsibility, a faster development of potential and the opportunity to compare and contrast the different disciplines alongside one another. Work will vary from small cases which the trainee may handle alone (under the supervision of a senior lawyer) to larger matters where they will assist a partner or an associate solicitor. The firm runs a structured training programme with a regular schedule of seminars to support the thorough practical training and regular feedback that trainees receive from the associates and partners they work with.

Placement schemes

Places for 2010/11: Winter (non-law): closing date 31 October. Spring 2011 (non-law): closing date 31 January. Summer (law): closing date 31 January. Placements last for two weeks with an allowance of £400 per week. Students get to see how the firm's non-rotational training system works in practice by taking on real work from a variety of practice areas. They also get to meet a range of lawyers at various social events.

Trainee Benefits

Private healthcare, season ticket loan, subsidised sports club membership, group life cover, salary sacrifice schemes and access to stakeholder pension.

Sponsorship & awards

GDL/PgDL and LPC fees paid and £8,000 maintenance p.a.

Partners approx 50
Assistant Solicitors 90
Total Trainees 30-40

Contact
Diana Spoudeas
Graduate Recruitment Manager

Method of application
CV and letter online at www.jonesdaylondon.com

Selection procedure
2 interviews with partners
Closing date for 2013
31 July 2011

Application
Training contracts p.a. 10-15
Applications p.a. 1,800
% interviewed p.a. 12%
Required degree grade 2:1

Training
Salary
1st year (2010) £39,000 increasing to £41,000 after six months
2nd year (2010) £45,000 rising to £50,000 after 18 months
Holiday entitlement
5 weeks

Post-qualification
Salary (2010) £70,000
% of trainees offered job on qualification (2010) 58%

Overseas offices
Continental Europe, Asia, North America, Latin America, Middle East, Asia Pacific

K&L Gates LLP

110 Cannon Street, London, EC4N 6AR
Tel: (020) 7648 9000 Fax: (020) 7648 9001
Email: traineerecruitment@klgates.com
Website: www.klgates.com/europe_recruitment/graduate/

Firm profile

K&L Gates comprises approximately 2,000 lawyers who practice in 36 office locations on three continents, and represents capital markets participants, entrepreneurs, growth and middle market companies, leading FORTUNE 100 and FTSE 100 global corporations and public sector entities. Whilst the firm's international practice requires lawyers with diverse backgrounds and skills, the firm comes together in its shared values of investment and growth, both for the firm and the individual. The firm is committed to professional development and provides a cutting edge training programme.

Main areas of work

K&L Gates is active in the areas of investment management and related funds work, mergers and acquisitions, private equity, real estate, intellectual property, digital media and sport, travel and leisure, construction, insurance coverage, securities enforcement, environmental matters, regulatory work, PFI projects, litigation, international arbitration and other forms of dispute resolution.

Trainee profile

The firm welcomes applications from both law and non-law students. Law students should generally be in their penultimate year of study and non-law students should be in their final year of study. The firm also welcomes applications from relevant postgraduates or others who have satisfied the 'academic stage of training' as required by the Law Society. You should be highly motivated, intellectually curious, with an interest in commercial law and be looking for comprehensive training.

Training environment

The firm ensures each trainee is given exceptional opportunities to learn, experience and develop so that they can achieve their maximum potential. Trainees spend six month seats in four of the following areas: corporate, dispute resolution and litigation, intellectual property, construction, tax, real estate, employment, pensions and environment. Each trainee sits with a supervisor and is allocated an individual mentor to ensure all round supervision and training. The firm has a thorough induction scheme, and has won awards for its career development programme. High importance is placed on the acquisition of business and professional skills, with considerable emphasis on client contact and early responsibility. The training programme consists of weekly legal education seminars, workshops and a full programme of skills electives. Pro Bono and Corporate Social Responsibility activities are also encouraged.

Benefits

25 days holiday per annum, subsidised gym membership, season ticket loan, private health insurance, bonus scheme, life assurance, medicentre membership and pension.

Legal work placements

The firm's formal legal work placement scheme is open to penultimate year law students, final year non-law students, other relevant post graduates or others who have satisfied the 'academic stage of training' as required by the Law Society.

Sponsorship

GDL funding: fees paid plus £5,000 maintenance grant. LPC funding: fees paid plus £7,000 maintenance grant.

Partners 60
Trainees 8
Total Staff 275

Contact
Hayley Atherton

Method of application
Online at www.klgates.com/europe_recruitment/graduate/ or request a paper application

Selection procedure
Full assessment day

Closing date for 2013
31 July 2011

Application
Training contracts p.a. tbd
Applications p.a. 1,000
% interviewed p.a. 10%
Required degree grade 2:1

Training
Salary
1st year £35,000
2nd year £38,000
% of trainees with a non-law degree p.a. Varies

Post-qualification
Salary £60,000
% of trainees offered job on qualification (2009) 80%

Overseas offices
Anchorage, Austin, Beijing, Berlin, Boston, Charlotte, Chicago, Dallas, Dubai, Fort Worth, Frankfurt, Harrisburg, Hong Kong, Los Angeles, Miami, Moscow, Newark, New York, Orange County, Palo Alto, Paris, Pittsburgh, Portland, Raleigh, Research Triangle Park, San Diego, San Francisco, Seattle, Shanghai, Singapore, Spokane/Coeur D'Alene, Taipei, Tokyo, Warsaw, Washington

K&L | GATES

Kennedys

25 Fenchurch Avenue, London, EC3M 5AD
Tel: (020) 7667 9667 Fax: (020) 7667 9777
Email: bubb@kennedys-law.com
Website: www.kennedys-law.com

Firm profile

Kennedys is a specialist national and international legal firm with unrivalled expertise in litigation and dispute resolution. The firm has over 850 people globally, across nine UK and seven international locations. Kennedys is a top 50 law firm and The firm's growth and success has been recognised by the 2010 Legal Business Awards, where it was awarded 'Law Firm of the Year' as well as 'Insurance Team of the Year' in the Legal Business Awards. Kennedys is regarded as a leader, not just because it has some of the most respected legal minds in their field - but because they know the importance of being practical, commercial and approachable. Kennedys prides itself on offering its clients clear legal advice.

Main areas of work

Kennedys lawyers provide a range of specialist legal services for many industries including: insurance/reinsurance, healthcare, construction, rail, local government, maritime and international trade – with a particular focus on dispute resolution and litigation.

Trainee profile

The firm is looking for graduates who are articulate, self aware and resourceful. Kennedys' trainees experience early responsibility and client contact, therefore it essential to have a mature and confident approach. Trainees with the firm must have commercial awareness and a strong appreciation of the interests of the client. As Kennedys has a vibrant and supportive working environment it is also looking for sociable, energetic team players, with a wide range of interests outside of their studies.

Training environment

The purpose of the training contract is to give the trainees a mix of experience and skills that will set them up in their legal career as a solicitor with Kennedys. The firm's ability to consistently offer the majority of its trainees positions on qualification is attributable to producing newly qualified lawyers who are competent, confident and commercially driven. A balance of, responsibility, supervision and formal training achieves this. Kennedys ensures that their trainee solicitors are given sound training in the core disciplines. All partners and supervisors are readily accessible and always ready to offer support when needed.

Placement schemes

Kennedys runs summer vacation schemes during June and July. Applications should be made online for the 2011 schemes by 31 January 2011.

Benefits

Permanent health insurance, pension, private medial insurance, life insurance, 25 days holiday increasing to 27 days after five years, interest-free season ticket loan, gym membership, cycle to work scheme, child care assistance scheme, employee assistance scheme, corporate GP, contribution towards conveyancing fees and eye care vouchers.

Partners 145
Solicitors 240
Total Trainees 32

Contact
Rowena Bubb Graduate Recruitment Officer
r.bubb@kennedys-law.com

Method of application
Online Application Form

Selection procedure
Assessment Day

Closing date for 2011
30 November 2010
2012/2013 - 31 July 2011

Application
Training contracts approx 15-18
Applications 400 (London)
% interviewed 10%
Required degree grade 2:1 and 300 UCAS points or equivalent at A-level

Training
Salary
1st Year £32,000
2nd Year £36,000

Post-qualification
Salary £58,000
% of trainees offered job on qualification 85-90%

Offices
London, Chelmsford, Birmingham, Manchester, Taunton, Cambridge, Maidstone, Sheffield, Belfast, Hong Kong, Singapore, Madrid, Dubai, Sydney, Auckland

Kennedys
Legal advice in black and white

Kirkland & Ellis International LLP

30 St Mary Axe, London, EC3A 8AF
Tel: (020) 7469 2000 Fax: (020) 7469 2001
Website: www.kirkland.com/ukgraduate

Firm profile

Kirkland & Ellis International LLP is a 1,500-attorney law firm representing global clients in offices around the world.

For 100 years, major national and international clients have called upon Kirkland & Ellis to provide superior legal advice and client services. The firm's London office has been the hub of European operations since 1994. Here, approximately 80 lawyers offer detailed expertise to a wide range of UK and international clients.

Main areas of work

The firm handles complex corporate, restructuring, tax, intellectual property, litigation and counselling matters. Kirkland & Ellis operates as a strategic network, committing the full resources of an international firm to any matter in any territory as appropriate.

Trainee profile

Your academic record will be excellent, probably culminating in an expected or achieved 2.1. You will have the initiative, the drive and the work ethic to thrive in the firm's meritocratic culture and arrive with an understanding of the work undertaken in the firm's London office.

Training environment

As one of a select number of trainees, you will be given early responsibility to work on complex multi jurisdictional matters.

The principal focus of your training will be on corporate law with a specialism in private equity. You will complete four, six month seats and obtain training in areas such as banking, funds, arbitration, IP, restructuring and tax. In addition there will be opportunities to undertake an overseas secondment to enable you to experience the international resources and capabilities of Kirkland & Ellis.

Your on the job training will be actively supported by an extensive education programme, carefully tailored to meet your needs.

Benefits

Private medical insurance, travel insurance, life insurance, employee assistance plan, corporate gym membership.

Vacation placements

Places for 2011: up to 14. Duration: 2 weeks. Remuneration: £350 per week. Closing date for applications: 31/01/11.

Sponsorship & awards

GDL and LPC course fees and a maintenance grant of £7,500 p.a.

Partners 500
Assistant solicitors 1327

Contact
Kate Osborne

Method of application
CV and covering letter to include a full % breakdown of degree results per subject

Selection procedure
Interview

Closing date for 2013
31 July 2011

Training
Salary
1st year (2010) £40,000
2nd year (2010) £43,000
Holiday entitlement
25 days

Post-qualification
(currently no data)

Overseas/ regional offices
Chicago, Hong Kong, Los Angeles, Munich, New York, Palo Alto, San Francisco, Shanghai, Washington D.C.

KIRKLAND & ELLIS
INTERNATIONAL LLP

Latham & Watkins

99 Bishopsgate, London, EC2M 3XF
Tel: (020) 7710 1000 Fax: (020) 7374 4460
Email: london.trainees@lw.com
Website: www.lw.com

Firm profile

Latham & Watkins has more than 2,000 lawyers in 30 offices across Europe, America and Asia and the London office advises on some of the most significant and groundbreaking cross-border transactions in Europe. The firm believes that its non-hierarchical management style and 'one firm' culture makes Latham & Watkins unique.

Main areas of work

Corporate, finance, litigation, employment and tax.

Trainee profile

Candidates with a strong academic background, excellent communication skills and a consistent record of personal and/or professional achievement will be rewarded with first class training. The firm is dedicated to diversity and equal opportunity and values originality and creative thinking.

Training environment

Latham & Watkins can provide a very different training experience to that offered by the rest of the elite law firms. Each trainee receives bespoke supervision and outstanding support while being encouraged to recognise that they have their own part to play in the growth and success of the firm. Each trainee also has meaningful responsibility from the outset and significant legal experience on qualification. Trainees may also be given the opportunity to spend one of their four six-month seats in one of the firm's overseas offices.

Benefits

Healthcare and dental scheme, pension scheme and life assurance.

Sponsorship & awards

All GDL and LPC costs are paid and trainees receive a maintenance grant of £8,000 per year whilst studying.

Vacation placements

The firm has a two-week Easter vacation scheme and a two-week summer scheme. Students are paid £300 per week. The deadline for Easter scheme applications is 31st December and the deadline for summer scheme applications is 31st January.

Partners 54
Associates 107
Trainees 28

Contact
Alex Mitchell

Method of application
Online application form at www.lw.com

Selection procedure
3 x 30 minute interviews with a partner and an associate

Closing date for 2013
31 July 2011

Application
Training contracts p.a. 15
Required degree grade: 2:1

Training
Salary
1st year (2010) £41,000
2nd year (2010) £44,000

Post-qualification
Salary: £96,970

Overseas/regional offices
Abu Dhabi, Barcelona, Beijing, Brussels, Chicago, Doha, Dubai, Frankfurt, Hamburg, Hong Kong, Houston, Riyadh, Rome, London, Los Angeles, Madrid, Milan, Moscow, Munich, New Jersey, New York, Orange County, Paris, San Diego, San Francisco, Shanghai, Silicon Valley, Singapore, Tokyo, Washington DC.

Lawrence Graham LLP

4 More London Riverside, London, SE1 2AU
Tel: (020) 7379 0000 Fax: (020) 7173 8694
Email: graduate@lg-legal.com
Website: http://graduates.lg-legal.com

Firm profile

LG is a distinctive legal practice with a leading reputation in its chosen services and sectors. The firm's approach is relationship-driven and internationally minded, with great people dedicated to giving clients just what they need. A vibrant, agile firm which is, above all, just different.

The firm services its clients from international offices in London, Dubai, Monaco and Russia, and also through its close relationships with other advisers in its key jurisdictions. Together, LG advise seamlessly on the most complex cases, cross-border deals and disputes.

Main areas of work

LG offers a full range of legal services with particular focus on commerce and technology, corporate, dispute resolution, employment and pensions, finance, real estate and tax and private capital. It has a specific understanding of the issues facing businesses and individuals operating in its key sectors: Energy and natural resources, financial institutions, healthcare, hospitality and leisure, private capital, publishing and media, real estate, support services and technology.

Over 30% of the firm's transactions are now handled for companies outside the UK. The emerging markets of India, South East Asia and the Middle East remain of critical importance to the firm and its clients, while exciting new business opportunities in the more mature markets of Europe and North America keep it firmly centred on those regions.

LG is proud to have a culture that is open and refreshingly straightforward. It employs highly talented individuals, while valuing a strong team ethic - and that is fundamental to the way it works as a business.

Trainee profile

The firm is looking for individuals from a variety of backgrounds with refined communication skills who can demonstrate a commitment to a career in the commercial application of law. A strong academic track record with a minimum of 320 UCAS tariff points and a 2.1 degree is a basic requirement. Also required is a good record of achievement in other areas – indicative of the ability to succeed in a demanding career – and evidence of team working skills and the ability to handle responsibility.

Training environment

Under Partner supervision trainees will be given early responsibility. Training is structured to facilitate the ability to manage one's own files and interact with clients. In addition to the Professional Skills Course, there are departmental training and induction sessions as well as a two year rolling training programme, designed to develop well-rounded lawyers. Training consists of four six-month seats: real estate, transactional and contentious seats are compulsory.

Benefits

Season ticket loan, life assurance.

Vacation placements

Places for 2011: Duration: 3 x 2 weeks between June and July; Remuneration: £300 p.w; Closing Date: 31 January 2011.

Sponsorship & awards

GDL Funding: Course fees and maintenance grant. £6k outside London, £6.5k in London. LPC Funding: Course fees and maintenance grant. £6k outside London, £6.5k in London.

Partners 69
Assistant Solicitors 101
Total Trainees 31

Contact
Vicki Baldwin Graduate Recruitment Manager

Method of application
Firm's online application form.

Selection procedure
Verbal reasoning test, Partner interview and assessed case study

Closing date for 2013
31 July 2011

Application
Training contracts approx 20
Applications p.a. 800
Required degree grade 2:1

Training
Salary
Competitive
% of trainees with a non-law degree p.a. 40%

Post-qualification
Salary (2010) £55,000
% of trainees offered job on qualification (2010) 70%

Lester Aldridge LLP

Russell House, Oxford Road, Bournemouth BH8 8EX
Tel: (01202) 786161 Fax: (01202) 786110
Email: humanresources@LA-law.com
Website: www.lesteraldridge.com

Firm profile

Lester Aldridge LLP is an energetic business providing both commercial and private client services on a local, regional, national and international scale. The firm's reputation rests on the expertise of its people who are first-class in every respect, and on the firm's astute approach to its clients. Client satisfaction is always the firm's aim.

History is important in any business – it shows a commitment to its industry and its clients and the firm is proud of its own history. Lester Aldridge's positioning on the south coast offers a positive working environment and a great work life balance; while providing opportunities to work with first class lawyers, impressive clients, and opportunity for City experience via LA's London office.

Excellent legal advice is standard. Each client can expect a commitment of excellent service from its staff, a Partner led approach, leading legal expertise, comprehensive and cohesive advice, innovative and technological support and value for money.

Main areas of work

LA's work is divided up into 5 groups – dispute resolution, corporate and commercial, banking and finance, real estate and private client. Within these groups the firm has a number of sectors which offer a cross section of these work types – these include marine, charities, fertility and same sex couples, development, care and medical practices. As a trainee, you will get involved in the broad range giving you choice and experience for your future career in law.

Trainee profile

Candidates should have a consistently strong academic record, be commercially aware and possess a broad range of interpersonal skills. Applicants should be highly motivated and have a desire to succeed working with teams to advise clients in dynamic and demanding industries.

Training environment

When you start at LA you'll be given responsibilities and real jobs to get your teeth into. Direct client involvement is encouraged and you will become an integral part of each team you join.

During the course of your two year contract you will complete four seats of six months duration. This gives you exposure to different areas of the firm and hopefully will help you decide what you would like to specialise in.

Giving constructive feedback is always encouraged at LA, so you can expect to hear the good things about your work from your team (and a few things you need to improve). LA also has an appraisal system where you work with your team leader to set objectives and create an action plan that will measure your progress. In addition each trainee is assigned a mentor to provide guidance and encouragement and regular review meetings are arranged with the Managing Partner where you'll be encouraged to voice your views and opinions.

Work placements

The firm offers 2 week work placements in July and August of each year. The application deadline is usually 31 March but please check the firm's website for further details on how to apply.

Sponsorship

LPC currently under review.

Vacancies 6
Trainees 11
Total Staff 261

Contact
Juliet Artal

Method of application
Apply to human resources application form

Selection procedure
Interview by a panel of partners as part of assessment and development day

Closing date for 2013
To be confirmed

Application
Training contracts p.a. 6
Applications p.a. 200
% interviewed p.a. 5%
Minimum required degree grade 2:1

Training
Salary
Starting salary: Competitive market rate for a south coast firm plus additional London allowance where appropriate
Holiday entitlement 22 days

Offices
Bournemouth (2), Southampton & London

Lewis Silkin LLP

5 Chancery Lane, Clifford's Inn, London EC4A 1BL
Tel: (020) 7074 8000 Fax: (020) 7864 1200
Email: train@lewissilkin.com
Website: www.lewissilkin.com

Partners 56
Assistant Solicitors 76
Total Trainees 12

Contact
Human Resources

Method of application
Online application form

Selection procedure
Assessment day, including an interview with 2 partners, a group exercise, analytical and aptitude test

Closing date for 2013
Please refer to website

Application
Training contracts p.a. 6
Applications p.a. 600
Required degree grade 2:1

Training
Salary
1st year £32,000
2nd year £34,000
Holiday entitlement 25 days

Post-qualification
Salary (2010) £50,000

Firm profile

Lewis Silkin is a commercial firm with 56 partners. What distinguishes them is a matter of personality. For lawyers, they are notably informal, unstuffy...well, human really. They are 'people people'; as committed and professional as any good law firm, but perhaps more adept at the inter-personal skills that make relationships work and go on working. They place a high priority on the excellent technical ability and commercial thinking of their lawyers and also on their relationships with clients. Clients find them refreshingly easy to deal with. The firm has a friendly, lively style with a commitment to continuous improvement.

Main areas of work

The firm has a wide range of corporate clients and provides services through five departments: corporate, employment and incentives, litigation, property, housing and construction, and media, brands and technology. The major work areas are commercial litigation and dispute resolution; corporate services, which includes company commercial and corporate finance; defamation; employment; marketing services, embracing advertising and marketing law; property, construction, technology and communications, including IT, media and telecommunications. They are UK leaders in employment law and have a strong reputation within social housing and the media and advertising sectors.

Trainee profile

They are looking for trainees with keen minds and personalities, who will fit into a professional but informal team.

Training environment

The firm provides a comprehensive induction and training programme, with practical hands-on experience from day one. You will sit with either a partner or senior associate giving you access to day-to-day supervision and guidance. The training contract consists of six four-month seats, working in the firm's five departments and/ or client secondments.

Benefits

These include individual and firm bonus schemes, life assurance, critical illness cover, health insurance, season ticket loan, group pension plan and subsidised gym membership.

Work placements

The two-week work placement scheme which takes place during either June or July, gives participants the opportunity to gain first hand experience of life at Lewis Silkin. Applications should be made via the firm's website between November 2010 and the end of January 2011.

Open days

Open days will be held during spring 2011 to give participants an overview of the firm, its main areas of work and a chance to meet trainees and partners.

Applications should be made between November 2010 and the end of January 2011.

Sponsorship & awards

Funding for GDL and LPC fees is provided plus a £5,000 maintenance grant for each.

Linklaters LLP

One Silk Street, London EC2Y 8HQ
Tel: (020) 7456 2000 Fax: (020) 7456 2222
Email: graduate.recruitment@linklaters.com
Website: www.linklaters.com/ukgradsCSG

Firm profile

Join Linklaters and you become part of one of the world's most prestigious law firms – a global network of exceptionally talented, highly motivated lawyers working as a team and learning from one another to fulfil its ambition of becoming the premium global law firm.

Main areas of work

While many law firms are strong in particular areas, Linklaters is the only firm to have market-leading global teams across the full range of corporate, finance and commercial practice areas. This, partnered with its culture of innovation, teamwork and entrepreneurship, means that it has built strong relationships with the world's leading companies, financial institutions and governments and is asked to advise them on their most important and challenging transactions and assignments.

Trainee profile

A truly global firm, Linklaters has 19 practices across 26 cities worldwide, giving you the opportunity to connect with a diverse range of international colleagues and clients on a daily basis. As part of your training contract you will have the opportunity to be seconded to one of the firm's international offices or to the offices of one of its clients, giving you first hand experience of this global dimension.

Linklaters has high expectations of its trainees and recruits talented and motivated graduates who expect a lot from themselves. In return, the firm offers its trainees global opportunities, entrepreneurial freedom, world-class training and incredible rewards.

Training environment

Linklaters recruits a diverse mix of the most talented graduates from a wide range of universities and backgrounds. Non-law graduates spend a conversion year at law school taking the Graduate Diploma in Law (GDL) and all graduates complete the Legal Practice Course (LPC) before starting their training contracts. The firm meets the cost of the GDL and the LPC and provides a maintenance grant for both. The training contract is structured around four six-month seats, designed to build your knowledge, experience and contacts in a broad range of practice areas and to equip you for your long-term career.

Sponsorship & benefits

GDL and LPC fees are paid in full, plus a maintenance grant. Benefits include eligibility for a personal performance-related bonus, pension, private medical insurance, life assurance, income protection, in-house healthcare services, family friendly benefits, in-house gym, subsidised staff restaurant, interest-free season ticket loan, holiday travel insurance, time bank scheme, cycle2work and give as you earn.

Vacation placements

Linklaters offers a two-week winter Vacation Scheme for final year non-law students, and two summer Vacation Schemes (four weeks) for penultimate year law students.

Partners 480
Associates 2,200
Trainees 250+*
*(London)

Contact
Graduate Recruitment

Method of application
Online application form

Selection procedure
Critical reasoning test, 2 interviews including a commercial case study

Application
Training contracts p.a. 110
Applications p.a. 4,000
Required degree grade 2:1

Training
Salary
1st year (2010) £37,400
Holiday entitlement 25 days
% of trainees with a non-law degree p.a. 40%

Post-qualification
Salary £61,500 + discretionary performance-related bonus

Offices
Amsterdam, Antwerp, Bangkok, Beijing, Berlin, Brussels, Dubai, Düsseldorf, Frankfurt, Hong Kong, Lisbon, London, Luxembourg, Madrid, Milan, Moscow, Munich, New York, Paris, Rome, São Paulo, Shanghai, Singapore, Stockholm, Tokyo, Warsaw

Macfarlanes LLP

20 Cursitor Street, London, EC4A 1LT
Tel: (020) 7831 9222 Fax: (020) 7831 9607
Email: gradrec@macfarlanes.com
Website: www.macfarlanes.com

Firm profile

Macfarlanes is a leading City law firm. The firm is recognised for the quality of its work, not just in dealing with a full range of corporate and commercial matters, but in advising clients on their private affairs. Clients trust Macfarlanes' judgement and the firm is in a unique position to advise on their most complex matters, whilst at the same time remaining smaller than its competitors.

As advisers to many of the world's leading businesses and business leaders, the firm manages international matters in an effective and seamless manner. It gives clients a single point of contact and co-ordinates advice across all relevant jurisdictions.

Main areas of work

The firm's main areas of practice are in banking and finance; commercial; competition; corporate and M&A; employment, pensions and benefits; financial services regulatory; investment funds; IP and IT; litigation and dispute resolution; private equity; private client; real estate; restructuring and insolvency; and tax.

Trainee profile

Macfarlanes believes the strongest firm is achieved by choosing a mix of people – reflecting different styles so as to meet the needs that it – and its varied range of clients – will have in the future. The firm looks for a rare combination of intellectual curiosity, character and drive. It is looking for ambitious trainees who will thrive on responsibility and challenge and who are ready to begin their careers on day one.

Training environment

Woven into every aspect of life at the firm is an enduring commitment to the development of trainees. Training begins with tailored electives on the LPC and a week long induction course at the start of your training contract.

During the two-year training contract you'll be working on real cases, doing real work for real clients from day one. As a trainee you will complete four six-month seats in different areas of practice; typically it is one seat in corporate and M&A and one seat in real estate, one in either private client or litigation and then a seat in one of the firm's specialised practice areas within corporate. The precise allocation of seats is flexible so that it can offer you as broad a legal training as possible. Support and guidance are, of course, vital and you will find your supervisor a valuable source of information and inspiration.

Benefits

Life assurance, pension scheme with company contributions, private healthcare, discretionary performance related bonus scheme, season ticket loan, subsidised restaurant, gym membership subsidy, eyecare vouchers and childcare vouchers.

Vacation placements

Places for 2011: 55; Duration 2 weeks; Remuneration: £250 p.w.; Closing Date: 31 January 2011.

Sponsorship & awards

CPE/GDL and LPC fees paid in full and a £7,000 maintenance allowance.

Partners 75
Assistant Solicitors 150
Total Trainees 54

Contact
Vicki Dimmick

Method of application
Online via website

Selection procedure
Assessment day

Closing date for 2013
31 July 2011

Application
Training contracts p.a. up to 30
Applications p.a. 800
% interviewed p.a. 20%
Required degree grade 2:1

Training
Salary
1st year £38,000
2nd year £43,000
Holiday entitlement 25 days, rising to 26 on qualification
% of trainees with a non-law degree p.a. 65%

Post-qualification
Salary (2009) £60,000
% of trainees offered job on qualification (2010) 88%
% of partners (as at 1/9/10) who joined as trainees 52%

Maclay Murray & Spens LLP

151 St Vincent Street, Glasgow G2 5NJ
Tel: (0141) 248 5011
Website: www.mms.co.uk

Firm profile

Maclay Murray & Spens LLP is a full service, independent, commercial law firm offering legal solutions and advice to clients throughout the UK and beyond. With offices in Aberdeen, Glasgow, Edingburgh and London the firm's objective is to provide a consistently excellent quality of service across the firm's entire service range and from every UK office.

Main areas of work

Banking and finance, capital projects, commercial dispute resolution, construction and engineering, corporate, employment pensions and benefits, EU, competition and regulatory , IP and technology, oil and gas, planning and environmental, private client, property, public sector and tax.

Trainee profile

Applicants should have a strong academic background (minimum 2:1 degree) as well as demonstrate a number of key skills including an inquiring mind and a keenness to learn, commitment, professionalism, determination to see a job through, first class communication skills, the ability to get on with colleagues and clients at all levels, an ability to operate under pressure in a team environment, as well as a sense of humour. The firm welcomes bright non-law graduates.

Training environment

MMS will provide you with a very broad range of practice experience, including legal writing, drafting, research work, and an element of client contact. This is one of the firm's strengths as a business and a long standing attraction for candidates.

By working as a team member on more complex transactions, you are given the opportunity to gain experience over a broad range of work. You will also be encouraged to meet and work alongside clients from different backgrounds and diverse areas of industry and commerce.

Benefits

At MMS trainees are paid competitive salaries as well as provided with an attractive benefits package. All of the firm's employees receive a combination of fixed and variable holidays totalling 34 days each year. The firm also offers a contributory pension scheme, death in service benefit worth four times your annual salary, support with conveyancing fees, enhanced maternity and paternity pay, income protection insurance and discounted access to medical and dental plans.

Partners 62
Assistant Solicitors 170
Total Trainees 50

Contact
trainee.recruitment@mms.co.uk

Method of application
Application forms only, accessed at www.mms.co.uk/traineeship

Selection procedure
Following an initial interview a number of candidates will be invited to attend a second interview with 2 Partners, where they will also complete a roleplay and research exercise. Offers will be made to the successful candidates very soon after the second interview

Closing date for 2013
London traineeship Sept 2011
Scottish traineeship Oct 2011

Application
Training contracts p.a. 30
Applications p.a.
Scotland 300
London 150
Required degree grade 2:1

Training
Salary (2010)
(Scotland) 1st year £17,000
(London) 1st year £32,000
Holiday entitlement All of our employees receive a combination of fixed and variable holidays totalling 34 days per year.

Overseas/regional offices
Aberdeen, Edinburgh, Glasgow, London

Manches

Aldwych House, 81 Aldwych, London WC2B 4RP
Tel: (020) 7404 4433 Fax: (020) 7430 1133
Email: sheona.boldero@manches.com
Website: www.manches.com

Firm profile

Manches is a mid-sized commercial firm based in London and the Thames Valley with strengths across a range of services and industry sectors. Their current strategy will see a greater concentration and focus on the firm's core industry sectors, while continuing to be market leaders in family law. The firm offers 10 trainee places each September.

Main areas of work

Industry Sectors: real estate, international wealth protection, retail business, commercial technology.

Legal Groups: commercial property, commercial litigation, corporate finance, construction, family, trusts & estates, employment, intellectual property, information technology, biotechnology (Oxford and Reading offices only), and environment & planning.

Trainee profile

Manches aims to recruit a broad cross-section of candidates with different ranges of experiences and backgrounds. However, all candidates should demonstrate consistently good academic records, together with cheerful enthusiasm, high levels of commitment, an appreciation of commercial issues, the ability to think for themselves and have warm and approachable social skills. A sense of humour is an asset!

Training environment

The firm gives high-quality individual training. Trainees generally sit in four different seats for six months at a time. The firm's comprehensive induction week, followed by its practically based "learning by doing" training programme enables trainees to take responsibility from an early stage, ensuring that they become confident and competent solicitors at the point of qualification. Trainees have the opportunity to actively participate in departmental meetings, presentations, client seminars and briefings and they receive regular appraisals on their progress.

Benefits

Season ticket loan, BUPA after six months, permanent health insurance, life insurance, pension after six months.

Vacation placements

Places for 2011: 20 approx.; Duration: 1 week; Closing Date: 15th February 2011; Remuneration: £200 (under review).

Sponsorship & awards

GDL and LPC fees are paid in full together with an annual maintenance allowance (currently £5,000 p.a.).

Partners 59
Assistant Solicitors 65
Total Trainees 20

Contact
Sheona Boldero
sheona.boldero@manches.com

Method of application
Online application form

Selection procedure
1st interview with HR, 2nd Interview with partners.

Closing date for 2013
31 July 2011

Application
Training contracts p.a. 10
Applications p.a. 850
% interviewed p.a. 5%
Required degree grade 2:1 min

Training
Salary
1st year (2010)
London £30,000
2nd year (2010)
London £33,000
Holiday entitlement 24 days

Post-qualification
Salary
London £50,000
% of trainees offered job on qualification (2010) 80%

Martineau

No 1 Colmore Square, Birmingham B4 6AA
35 New Bridge Street, London, EC4V 6BW
Tel: (0870) 763 2000 Fax: (0870) 763 2001
Email: jennifer.seymour@martineau-uk.com
Website: www.martineau-uk.com

Firm profile

Martineau is a dynamic and passionate law firm that combines a commercial and vibrant atmosphere with a personal and caring attitude.

Brand values are based on the three 'i's - integrity, innovation and inspiration. They reflect the working cutlure where they are inspired to deliver innovative solutions to clients, ensuring to exceed their needs, wants and expectations.

Providing national and international advice to its clients, the firm is recognised as market leader in many of its areas of practice and is well known for providing high level expertise.

Martineau looks for enthusiastic and committed graduates with good degrees, not necessarily in law, to contribute to its successful practice.

State of the art premises in the heart of Birmingham city centre, coupled with its expanding London office, provide trainees with an ideal base to gain experience in a variety of core and niche practice areas.

As a founder member of Multilaw, an international network of law firms, opportunities also stretch far beyond the UK.

Martineau is also a member of State Law Resources which is a network of independent law firms with a focus on energy and climate across 43 State and Canada.

The firm's commitment to client care and quality is endorsed by the ISO 9001 standard.

Main areas of work

Commercial 26%; corporate 23%; disputes resolution 23%; property 18%; private client 10%. Focus areas include energy and utilities, education, banking, investment funds and technology.

Trainee profile

Trainees are vital to Martineau's future and no effort is spared to give the best possible experience and support to them, whilst treating them as individuals. There is a very high retention rate at the end of training contracts, when trainees are generally offered roles in their preferred departments and specialisms.

Training environment

Martineau's aim is to work in partnership with trainees, providing them with mentoring, supervision, support and an exposure to the key areas of the firm's practice. Trainees are actively encouraged to be an integral part of the team delivering legal solutions to its clients whilst benefiting from quality work, flexible seat rotation in a small and friendly team environment. Trainees gain experience in three main areas, corporate, dispute resolution, commercial property and they are then given the opportunity to experience commercial work in areas of their chosen specialism. There are opportunities for Birmingham-based trainees to be exposed to the London scene.

Trainees benefit from a bespoke career development and training programme which is tailored to their personal needs; it covers not only legal technical matters, but also a business and commercial approach which has never been more central to successful professional careers.

In giving training and offering experience that matches the best city firms Martineau offers a rare opportunity for trainees to lay great foundations for their legal career in a fast moving, ever changing but caring environment.

Partners 48
Assistant Solicitors 100
Total Trainees 20

Contact
Jennifer Seymour

Method of application
Online application form
www.martineau-uk.com

Selection procedure
Assessment centre - half day

Closing date for 2013
31 July 2011

Application
Training contracts p.a. 10-12
Applications p.a. 600
% interviewed p.a. 10%
Required degree grade 2:1

Training
Salary
1st year (2009) c. £21,000
2nd year (2009) c. £22,500
Holiday entitlement 25 days
% of trainees with a non-law degree (2009) 45%

Post-qualification
Salary (2010) £36,000
% of trainees offered job on qualification (2009) 70%
% of assistants (as at 01/07/10) who joined as trainees 33%
% of partners (as at 01/07/10) who joined as trainees 27%

martineau

Maxwell Winward LLP

100 Ludgate Hill, London EC4M 7RE
Tel: (020) 7651 0000 Fax: (020) 7651 4800
Email: recruitment@maxwellwinward.com
Website: www.maxwellwinward.com

Firm profile

Maxwell Winward is the successfully established and bedded down firm created by the merger of leading property firm Maxwell Batley and built environment specialists Winward Fearon back in 2007. Three years down the line, the merger has been demonstrably successful, as evidenced by the strengthened breadth and depth of the practice in its key areas and by the full service the firm is able to offer to its clients. The firm has proved itself to be a compelling alternative to larger firms in all aspects of advice provided in the firm's key areas. The firm has a modern focus and a friendly unstuffy ethos where trainees are treated as important members of the team and as future solicitors of the business. Trainees are encouraged to interact with everyone in the firm and become a part of the team from day one. This interaction provides trainees with the best possible opportunity to develop the abilities and skills needed on qualification to become the successful lawyers of the future.

Main areas of work

The firm specialises in Real Estate, Construction (both contentious and non-contentious), Corporate, Company/Commercial, Employment, Projects and Dispute Resolution. As well as acting for several high-profile blue-chip clients, the firm also acts for a number of smaller commercial clients and some high net worth individuals.

Trainee profile

Successful candidates will have at least a 2:1 in any discipline. It is important that candidates are willing to learn and have enthusiasm, common sense, sound judgement and commercial awareness as well as a genuine interest in the firm's specialist areas.

Training environment

The varied nature of the firm's work means that trainees are given a range of experience from all of the different practice areas. The training contract is split into four six-month seats in each of the different practice areas. Whilst trainees are closely supervised, the firm is keen to ensure that they are given valuable practical experience, as much client contact as possible and the responsibility to gradually gain the confidence to tackle matters with little supervision.

The firm arranges internal seminars for trainees in order to give them formal training to complement the day to day experience that comes with assisting on 'real-life' matters.

Benefits

20 days holiday, Season ticket loan, Private health insurance.

Sponsorship & awards

Contribution towards fees and maintenance for GDL and LPC.

Partners 22
Assistant Solicitors 18
Total Trainees 5

Contact
The HR Manager

Method of application
CV and covering letter

Selection procedure
Two interviews
closing date for 2013
01 July 2011

Application
Training contracts p.a. 2
Applications p.a. 600
% interviewed p.a. 7%
Required degree grade 2:1

Training
Salary
1st year (2010) £29,000
2nd year (2010) £31,500
Holiday entitlement 20 days

Post-qualification
Salary (2010) £48,000
% of trainees offered job
on qualification (2010) 33%

Mayer Brown[1]

201 Bishopsgate, London EC2M 3AF
Email: graduaterecruitment@mayerbrown.com
Website: www.mayerbrown.com/london

Firm profile

Mayer Brown is a leading international law firm with offices in key business centres across the Americas, Europe and Asia. The firm has more than 1,600 lawyers, including approximately 875 in the Americas, 425 in Europe and 300 in Asia. The firm's Asia presence was enhanced by its 2008 combination with Johnson Stokes & Master, the largest and oldest Asia law firm. (In Asia, the firm is known as Mayer Brown JSM.) In December 2009, Mayer Brown formed an association with Tauil & Chequer, a leading law firm in Brazil. This impressive on-the-ground presence in the world's leading markets for legal services enables Mayer Brown to offer clients access to local market expertise on a global basis.

Main areas of work

The firm's lawyers practise in a wide range of areas including corporate, finance, litigation and dispute resolution, real estate, insurance and reinsurance, pensions and employment, competition and trade, tax, intellectual property, and information technology. The firm advises many of the world's largest companies including a significant proportion of the Fortune 100, FTSE 100 and DAX and Hang Seng Index organizations from the worlds of banking, insurance, communications, industrials, energy, construction, professional services, media, pharmaceuticals, chemicals and mining.

Trainee profile

The firm is looking for candidates who not only have a consistently strong academic record, but also who have a wide range of interests and achievements outside their academic career. Additionally, the firm would like to see innovative candidates who can demonstrate a drive for results, good verbal and written communication skills, and an ability to analyse, with good judgement and excellent interpersonal skills.

Training environment

One of the advantages of joining Mayer Brown are the choices available to you. The firm's trainees can tailor their training contract from a range of different seats, including the firm's main practice areas in London and international secondments (Brussels, Hong Kong, New York and São Paulo). If you don't want to stray too far, a wealth of in-house experience is also available via the firm's client secondments within the UK. For a large international firm, its London office remains a tightly knit team with an open and inclusive culture. You will nevertheless be given significant opportunities to assist on matters which may be multi-disciplinary, cross-border, complex and high-profile in nature.

Benefits

Benefits include 25 days holiday per annum, an interest free season ticket loan, subsidised sports club membership and membership of private health scheme.

Work experience programmes

The firm runs three work experience programmes each year; two three-week schemes in the Summer and one two-week programme at Easter. You will gain experience in two key practice areas and be involved in seminars and social events, including a trip to Brussels.

Sponsorship & awards

The firm will cover the cost of the GDL and LPC fees and provide a maintenance grant of £7,000.

1 Mayer Brown is a global legal services organisation comprising legal practices that are separate entities (the "Mayer Brown Practices"). The Mayer Brown Practices are: Mayer Brown LLP, a limited liability partnership established in the United States; Mayer Brown International LLP, a limited liability partnership (regulated by the Solicitors Regulation Authority and registered in England and Wales number OC 303359); Mayer Brown JSM, a Hong Kong partnership, and its associated entities in Asia; and Tauil & Chequer Advogados, a Brazilian law partnership with which Mayer Brown is associated. "Mayer Brown" and the Mayer Brown logo are the trademarks of the individual Mayer Brown Practices in their respective jurisdictions.

Partners 100
Assistant Solicitors 160
Total Trainees 52

Contact
Jacqui Megson Graduate Recruitment Manager

Method of application
Online application form

Selection procedure
One stage assessment process including an interview, a written exercise, a group exercise and an online verbal reasoning test
Closing date for Sept 2013/March 2014
31 July 2011

Application
Training contracts p.a. approx 30
Applications p.a. 1,000+
% interviewed p.a. 10%
Required degree grade 2:1

Training
1st year £37,500
2nd year £42,300
Holiday entitlement 25 days
% of trainees with a non-law degree p.a. 50%

Post-qualification
% of trainees offered job on qualification 60% (2010)

Overseas offices
Bangkok, Beijing, Berlin, Brussels, Charlotte, Chicago, Cologne, Frankfurt, Guangzhou, Hanoi, Ho Chi Minh City, Hong Kong, Houston, London, Los Angeles, New York, Palo Alto, Paris, São Paulo, Shanghai and Washington DC.

McDermott Will & Emery UK LLP

7 Bishopsgate, London EC2N 3AR
Tel: (020) 7577 6900 Fax: (020) 7577 6950
Website: www.mwe.com
Email: graduate.recruitment@mwe.com

Firm profile

McDermott Will & Emery UK LLP is a leading international law firm with offices in Boston, Brussels, Chicago, Düsseldorf, Houston, London, Los Angeles, Miami, Milan, Munich, New York, Orange County, Rome, San Diego, Silicon Valley and Washington DC. The firm's client base includes some of the world's leading financial institutions, largest corporations, mid-cap businesses, and individuals. The firm represents more than 60% of the companies in the Fortune 100 in addition to clients in the FTSE 100 and FTSE 250. Rated as one of the leading firms in The American Lawyer's Top 100, by a number of indicators, including gross revenues and profits per Partner.

London Office: The London office was founded in 1998. It is already recognised as being in the top 10 of the 100 US law firms operating in London by the legal media. The firm has around 60 lawyers at present in London, almost all of whom are English-qualified. The firm provides business oriented legal advice to multinational and national corporates, financial institutions, investment banks and private clients. Many of the firm's partners were head of practice at their former firms and are recognised as leaders in their respective fields by the most respected professional directories and market commentators.

Main areas of work

Energy and commodities advisory; corporate advisory, financial institutions advisory; employee benefits, compensation, labour and employment; US and international tax; private client; international dispute avoidance and resolution; anti-trust/competition and IP litigation. London is the hub for the firm's European expansions and the firm coordinates legal advice from here for all multinational clients across Europe and elsewhere.

Trainee profile

The firm is looking for the brightest, best and most entrepreneurial trainees. You will need to convince the firm that you have made a deliberate choice to apply to McDermott Will & Emery.

Training environment

The primary focus is to provide a practical foundation for your career with the firm. You will experience four seats over the two-year period and a deliberately small number of trainees means that the firm is able to provide a degree of flexibility in tailoring seats to the individual. Trainees get regular support and feedback.

Benefits

Private medical and dental insurance, life assurance, permanent health insurance, season ticket loan, subsidised gym membership, employee assistance programme, 25 days holiday.

Sponsorship & awards

GDL and LPC funding and maintenance grant.

Partners 562 (worldwide)
Associate Lawyers & Other Fee-earners 697(worldwide)
Total Trainees 10 (London)

Contact
Emma Doran

Method of application
Apply online at www.mwe.com

Selection procedure
Assessment day, written test and one interview with Partners

Closing date for September 2013/ March 2014
31 July 2011

Training
Salary
1st year £39,000 (2009)
2nd year £43,000 (2009)

McGrigors LLP

5 Old Bailey, London, EC4M 7BA
Tel: (020) 7054 2500
Email: graduate.recruitment@mcgrigors.com
Website: www.mcgrigorsornot.com
Twitter: @mcgrigorsllp

Firm profile

McGrigors is a top-50 full-service law firm with around 800 people working from offices in London, Edinburgh, Manchester, Aberdeen, Belfast and Glasgow. This makes the firm the only to operate across all three UK jurisdictions. Its client list comprises 38% of the FTSE100 and 40 AIM-listed companies. The firm's big enough to offer exciting opportunities with heavyweight clients, but also small and friendly enough to know the name of every graduate who joins.

The firm's work covers virtually every area of commercial law, with opportunities to take on seats in several offices, as well as secondments to interesting clients. In June 2010, The Lawyer magazine awarded McGrigors the title of Regional/National Law Firm of the Year.

The firm takes its role in the community seriously and has won awards for its corporate social responsibility programme. Every month, staff are given half a day to spend volunteering within their local communities. The firm also supports a wide range of social projects, from mentoring school children to providing free advice to those who can't afford a solicitor's service.

Main areas of work

Energy: McGrigors has one of the biggest dedicated teams of energy lawyers in the UK, with experience of the entire energy spectrum and strong relationships with energy companies, regulatory bodies and the wider financial community.

Infrastructure: McGrigors' Infrastructure Team has established itself as a market-leader, having completed over 200 PPP/ PFI projects to date. McGrigors advises on urban regeneration, education, health, housing, prisons, waste, transport and roads with experience of all sides of the equation.

Professional & Financial Services: McGrigors advises all types of professional and financial services companies, including accountancy practices, insurers, banks and lenders, private equity houses, and pension companies and their trustees.

Banking & Finance: the McGrigors team's advice extends to all types of lending and security transactions, from the straightforward to the highly complex.

Corporate: the McGrigors Corporate Team offers a full range of corporate and commercial legal services with an understanding of the various pressures and sensitivities which affect corporate transactions.

Employment & Pensions: McGrigors' Employment and Pensions Team has more than 40 lawyers nationally advising some of the UK's largest businesses, and provides support as part of the firm's transactional work.

Litigation & Dispute Resolution: McGrigors has one of the largest, most diversified and fastest-growing litigation practices in the UK.

Tax Disputes & Investigations: a market-leading player offering a cutting-edge service to companies and individuals in dispute with the tax authorities, McGrigors focuses exclusively on actual or potentially contentious tax matters.

Real Estate: the team is a leader when it comes to transactions involving property development projects, brownfield and waterfront developments, structured finance, landlord and tenant work, portfolio management and advising the social housing sector.

Trainee profile

We are looking for candidates who have drive, ability and confidence. Potential Trainees need to prove that they are interested in business, not simply black letter law. Our trainees are highly visible throughout the Firm and are expected to get actively involved from both a business and social aspect..

Benefits

The firm offers private medical cover, life assurance, pension, 35 days annual leave (including bank holidays) and season ticket loans.

Sponsorship

CPE and LPC fees are paid plus an annual maintenance grant of £6,000 in England. The firm also provides shortfall funding up to £1,000 for those Scottish trainees who receive no or partial funding.

Partners 100*
Assistant Solicitors 281*
Total Trainees 63*
*denotes firm wide

Contact
Margaret-Ann Roy or Sandra Ward (Scotland & Belfast)
Nadine Hurwood (England)

Method of application
Online application

Selection procedure
Half day assessment including interview, and relevant aptitude tests
Closing date
30 Jan 2011 for Summer scheme (England)
30 July 2011 for 2013 (England) training contracts
Dates for application for Scotland & Belfast available on firm's website

Application
No. of training contracts p.a.
10-12 in London
15-20 in Scotland
% interviewed - 15%
Preferred degree grade realistic estimate of 2:1 or higher

Training
Salary
London 1st year £32,000
2nd year £37,000
Scotland 1st year £18,000
2nd year £21,000
Rates for other offices available on firm's website
Holiday 35 days including bank holidays

Post-qualification
Salary
London (2010/2011) £56,000
Scotland (2010/2011) £31,500
% offered job in 2010 64%

Overseas/regional offices
London, Edinburgh, Glasgow, Aberdeen, Manchester, Belfast & a satellite office in the Falklands

Memery Crystal LLP

44 Southampton Buildings, London, WC2A 1AP
Tel: (020) 7242 5905 Fax: (020) 7242 2058
Email: hcowen@memerycrystal.com Web: www.memerycrystal.com

Firm profile

Memery Crystal LLP is a medium sized city law firm that has grown from strength to strength and is now one of the UK's leading law firms in its specialist areas. The firm's ethos is that people come first, whether they are clients, members of the firm or fellow advisers. This philosophy has enabled the firm to bring out the best in the lawyers who work here and those to whom the firm provides a service have recognised Memery Crystal through numerous awards.

Main areas of work

The firm's main practice areas are company/commercial, dispute resolution and real estate. Within these areas, specialist groups deal with corporate finance, employment, property litigation, tax, insolvency, construction, insurance, corporate crime, regulatory law, digital technology and e-commerce.

Trainee profile

The firm is looking for candidates who have achieved a high standard of education, show a willingness to take on responsibility, are commercially aware, respond to challenges, have the drive and ambition to succeed, and are seeking fulfilment and recognition in their chosen profession.

Training environment

During your training you will have a balance of formal and practical training. Your development will be closely monitored with appraisals carried out every 3 months. You will sit either with a Partner, associate or senior assistant who will monitor your progress on a regular basis. During the course of your training contract, there will be a regular rotation of seats within the firm.

Benefits

The firm provides a bonus scheme, life assurance, health cover, travel insurance, season ticket loan, group pension plan subsidised gym membership and cycle to work scheme.

Sponsorship & awards

Funding for LPC and GDL fees is provided.

Partners 22
Assistant Solicitors 32
Total Trainees 8

Contact
Helen Cowen

Method of application
Online application form

Selection procedure
First interview followed by assessment centre
Closing date for 2013
31 July 2011 for training

Application
Training contracts p.a. 4
Applications p.a. 180
Required degree grade 2:1

Training
Salary
1st year (2010) £26,500
2nd year (2010) £29,500
Holiday entitlement
25 days p.a.
% of trainees with a non-law degree 40%

Post-qualification
Competitive Salary

Michelmores LLP

Woodwater House, Pynes Hill, Exeter, EX2 5WR
Tel: (01392) 688 688 Fax: (01392) 360 563 Email: claire.kearns@michelmores.com
Clarges House, 6-12 Clarges Street, London, W1J 8DH
Tel: (020) 7242 5905 Fax: (020) 7242 2058 Website: www.michelmores.com

Firm profile

Michelmores LLP, one of the fastest growing law firms in the South West, is a dynamic, full-service practice with a total complement of over 300 staff. Providing a first class service to a wide range of local, national and international clients (including several central government departments) the firm has an established track record of attracting quality recruits at every level, enabling its trainees to learn from solicitors who are leaders in their fields. Michelmores has created a great place to work and attracts and retains some of the very best lawyers. The partnership has retained a collegiate style, which has helped to foster a happy law firm renowned for the enthusiasm of its lawyers, from the Managing Partner down to the first year trainees. The firm has won a number of awards and accolades, culminating in being named UK Regional Law Firm of the Year at the British Legal Awards in December 2009.

Main areas of work

The firm has a good reputation for its work in company commercial law, dispute resolution and commercial property while the firm's Private Client Group (including the firm's Family Team) continues to thrive. The firm also has specialist teams in areas such as projects/PFI, technology, media and communications, construction and medical negligence.

Trainee profile

The firm welcomes applications from both law and non-law graduates. The firm is looking for trainees with a strong academic background who are team players and who genuinely want to share in the firm's success and help it to continue to grow and improve.

Training environment

As a Michelmores trainee you will usually spend 6 months in each of the firm's main departments (business, property and private client). You will work closely with your supervisor in each department and will be pleasantly surprised at the level of client exposure, responsibility and client involvement. The firm's trainees are given both the opportunity to handle work themselves (while under supervision) and to work as part of a team. The quality of the firm's training is high. You will be expected to attend relevant in-house training sessions on areas such as marketing, IT skills and time management, and will also be encouraged to attend external conferences, seminars and marketing events. The firm offers the opportunity of spending part of your training contract in the London office.

Sponsorship & benefits

Optional private medical insurance, pension scheme, payment of LPC fees (up to 8k), subsidised staff restaurant, subsidised gym with personal trainer, free parking.

Vacation placements

The firm runs an annual vacation placement scheme in July in the firm's Exeter office for one week. The online application form is available on the website. Completed forms should arrive by 28 February 2011.

Partners 45
Total Staff (inc. Partners) 315
Assistant solicitors 70

Contact
Claire Kearns
(Claire.Kearns@michelmores.com)

Method of application
Online application form

Selection procedure
Assessment days

Closing date for 2013
1 July 2011

Application
Training contracts p.a.6
Applications p.a. 200
% interviewed - 15%
Required degree grade 2:1
(occasional exceptions)

Training
Salary
1st year (2010) £20,000
2nd year (2011)£21,000
Holiday entitlement
28 days p.a.
% of trainees with a non-law degree 10%
Number of seats available abroad 0 (although occasional foreign secondments available)

Post-qualification
Salary (2010) £33,000
% offered job 70%

Mills & Reeve

112 Hills Road, Cambridge CB2 1PH
Tel: (01223) 222336 Fax: (01223) 355848
Email: graduate.recruitment@mills-reeve.com Web: www.mills-reeve.com/graduates

Firm profile

Mills & Reeve acts for commercial organisations; ranging from PLCs to multinationals to start-ups, as well as more than 70 universities and colleges, more than 100 healthcare trusts and NHS bodies, and over 65 local government institutions. The firm also has a national centre of excellence in private client services.

Mills & Reeve has offices in Birmingham, Cambridge, Leeds, London, Manchester and Norwich.

For the seventh year running Mills & Reeve has been listed in the Sunday Times Top 100 Best Companies to Work For, which recognises that the firm puts people at the centre of its business.

Main areas of work

A full-service law firm. Core sectors are: corporate and commercial, banking and finance, technology, insurance, real estate, healthcare, education and private client.

Trainee profile

The firm welcomes applications from both law and non-law disciplines. Candidates should already have or expect a 2.1 degree or equivalent. Trainee solicitors should display initiative and enthusiasm for their career, a professional approach to work and be ready to accept early responsibility.

Training environment

Trainees complete six four-month seats and are recruited to the Birmingham, Cambridge and Norwich offices. Trainees can temporarily move to another office, to complete a seat not practised in their base office. The firm will support the move with an accommodation allowance.

Trainees work alongside a partner or senior solicitor. Regular feedback is given to aid development. Performance is assessed by a formal review at the end of each seat.

The firm encourages early responsibility. Training is supported by a full induction, in-house training programme developed by the firm's team of professional support lawyers and the professional skills course (PSC).

Job opportunities on qualification are good and a high proportion of trainees remain with the firm.

Benefits

Life assurance, a contributory pension scheme, 25 days holiday, bonus scheme, sports and social club, subsidised staff restaurants and catering facilities, season ticket loan, discounted rate for private medical insurance, corporate gym membership. The firm runs a flexible benefits scheme.

Vacation placements

Applications for two week placements during the summer must be received by 31 January 2011.

Sponsorship & awards

The firm pays the full costs of the CPE/GDL and LPC fees and a maintenance grant during the GDL and LPC.

Partners 92
Assistant Solicitors 350
Total Trainees 43

Contact
Fiona Medlock

Method of application
Online

Selection procedure
Normally one day assessment centre

Closing date for 2013
31 July 2011 for training contracts
31st January 2011 for work placements

Application
Training contracts p.a 20
Applications p.a. Approx 750
% interviewed p.a. 10%
Required degree grade 2:1

Training
Salary
1st year £23,000
2nd year £24,000
Holiday entitlement
25 days p.a.
% of trainees with a non-law degree 40%

Post-qualification
% of trainees offered job on qualification 91% (2010)

Mishcon de Reya

Summit House, 12 Red Lion Square, London WC1R 4QD
Tel: (020) 7440 7000 Fax: (020) 7430 0691
Email: recruitment@mishcon.com
Website: www.mishcon.com

Firm profile

Mishcon de Reya, founded in 1937 is a London based law firm, offering services to companies and individuals. The firm offers every legal service and its expertise covers five areas: analysing risk, protection of assets, managing wealth, resolving disputes and building business.

Main areas of work

Organised internally into six main departments: corporate, employment, dispute resolution, real estate, private client and family, the firm also has a growing number of specialist groups which include: art; betting and gaming; banking and finance; defamation; fraud; immigration; insolvency; IP; private client and public advocacy.

Trainee profile

The firm's trainees are typically high-achieving and intelligent with good interpersonal skills. Strength of character and ability to think laterally are also important.

Training environment

Trainees have the opportunity to gain experience, skills and knowledge from across the firm in four different seats (each six months). These include both contentious and non contentious work. Because of the relatively few training contracts offered, trainees can be exposed to high quality work with early responsibility. Trainees are supported with a training and development programme, in addition to the professional Skills Course. Trainee performance is monitored closely and trainees can expect to receive regular feedback in addition to mid-seat and end-of-seat appraisals.

Benefits

Private medical insurance, travel insurance, EAP, subsidised gym membership, season ticket loan, group income protection, life assurance and stakeholder pension scheme, in-house doctor, yoga classes, childcare vouchers, cycle scheme, bonus scheme and charity donations through payroll.

Vacation placements

Places for 2011: 15+; Duration: 2 weeks; Salary: £250 p.w.; Closing Date: 31st January 2011.

Sponsorship & awards

GDL and LPC funding with annual allowance.

Partners 59
Assistant Solicitors 80
Total Trainees 26

Contact
Ann-Marie Comer, HR Manager
Sisa Sibanda, HR Advisor

Method of application
Online application form

Closing date for 2013
31 July 2011

Application
Training contracts p.a. 8-12
Applications p.a. 1,500+
% interviewed p.a. 5%
Required degree grade 2:1

Training
Salary
1st year £32,000
Holiday entitlement
25 days p.a.
Occasional secondments available

Mishcon de Reya

Muckle LLP

Time Central, 32 Gallowgate, Newcastle upon Tyne, NE1 4BF
Tel: (0191) 211 7777 Fax: (0191) 211 7788
Email: nsingh@muckle-llp.com Website: www.muckle-llp.com

Firm profile

Muckle LLP is a leading commercial law firm in the North East of England. The firm has an excellent client base of successful private and public companies, property developers, financial institutions, public sector and educational organisations, which recognise that its innovative commercial skills are a major benefit in enhancing its service delivery to them.

Main areas of work

The firm is divided into five main groups – commercial, property, employment, dispute resolution and private client. The specialist teams within these groups are: banking, business restructuring and insolvency, commercial services, corporate finance, intellectual property and technology, property investment and development, planning, construction, employment, education and private client.

Trainee profile

The firm recruits four trainees a year. The firm is looking to recruit talented individuals who can demonstrate their enthusiasm and desire to become business advisers and a commitment to building their career in the North East. Trainees must have good academic qualifications and communication skills and must be able to work in a team and also independently.

Training environment

The firm runs an excellent training programme that focuses on the trainees' legal, IT, management and business development skills. During your training contract you will experience training within four of the firm's six main service group areas: corporate, commercial, property, employment, dispute resolution and private client. Training is a combination of on-the-job experience, partner mentoring as well as in-house and external courses. Trainees are encouraged to join the social, charitable or graduate recruitment committees.

Benefits

25 days holiday a year and flexible holiday option; pension after six months service; permanent health insurance; life assurance; corporate discounts; wellbeing initiative; salary sacrifice schemes (eg public transport discount).

Sponsorship & awards

LPC fees are paid subject to eligibility.

Partners 24
Fee earners 60
Total Trainees 8

Contact
Neena Singh, Graduate Recruitment Co-ordinator 0191 211 7987

Method of application
Apply online via our website www.muckle-llp.com

Selection procedure
Interviews and an assessment day

Closing date for 2011 summer vacation scheme
Friday 25th February 2011

Closing date for 2013 training contracts
Sunday 31st July 2011

Application
Training contracts p.a. 4
Applications p.a. 120-130
% interviewed p.a. 25%
Required degree grade 2:1

Training
Salary
Starting salary £20,000 with regular reviews throughout training contract
Holiday entitlement
25 days holiday a year and flexible holiday option

Post-qualification
Salary
Starting salary £30,000 with regular reviews
100% trainees offered job on qualification

Office
Only Newcastle upon Tyne

Nabarro LLP

Lacon House, 84 Theobald's Road, London WC1X 8RW
Tel: (020) 7524 6000 Fax: (020) 7524 6524
Email: graduateinfo@nabarro.com
Website: www.nabarro.com

Firm profile

Nabarro is a major UK law firm renowned for its positive, practical approach. The firm operates across a number of industry sectors and legal disciplines and aims to deliver the highest quality legal advice as clearly and concisely as possible.

Main areas of work

Corporate and commercial law; real estate; IP/IT; projects; PPP; PFI; pensions; employment; dispute resolution; construction and engineering; planning; environmental law; banking, finance and restructuring; insolvency and tax.

Trainee profile

The firm is committed to making the most of diverse skills, expertise, experience, attitudes and backgrounds. Accordingly, there is no typical Nabarro trainee. You will need a strong academic record and, in keeping with clients' needs, the firm also wants you to demonstrate a flexibility of thinking and a flair for creative problem solving that will allow you to provide its clients with the best advice and assistance. The firm is also looking for students who demonstrate a proactive approach, strong interpersonal and team working skills as well as commercial acumen.

Training environment

Trainees undertake six four-month seats to ensure maximum exposure to the firm's core practice areas, as well as the opportunity to spend time in more specialist seats or possibly on secondment to a client or Brussels. Your development and future seats are discussed with you mid way through each seat.

Benefits

Private medical insurance, 26 days holidays, pension, season ticket loan, subsidised restaurant, subsidised gym membership. Trainee salaries are reviewed annually.

Vacation placements

Places for 2011: 65

Duration: 3 weeks between mid June and mid August. Closing date: 31 January 2011.

Nabarro's vacation scheme is an award winning three week scheme offering a comprehensive and structured programme of events. You will be based in one department with an allocated supervisor and buddy who will ensure you gain a good mix of work and an excellent insight into life at Nabarro. The firm recruits the majority of its trainees through its summer scheme.

Sponsorship & awards

Full fees paid for the GDL and LPC plus a maintenance grant: LPC London: £7000, regions £6,000. GDL London: £6,000, regions £5,000. The firm pays 50% of fees retrospectively if you have completed your GDL/ LPC.

Partners 130+
Assistant Solicitors 420+
Total Trainees 70

Contact
Jane Drew

Method of application
Online only

Selection procedure
Assessment Day (including interview)

Closing date for 2013
31 July 2011

Application
Training contracts p.a. 35
Applications p.a. 2,000
Required degree grade 2:1

Training
Salary
1st year (2010)
London £37,000
Sheffield £25,000
2nd year (2010)
London £40,000
Sheffield £28,000
Holiday entitlement 26 days

Post-qualification
Salary (2010)
London £58,000
Sheffield £38,000
(reviewed annually)

Overseas offices
Brussels. In Europe the firm has an alliance with GSK Stockmann & Kollegen in Germany, August & Debouzy in France and Nunziante Magrone in Italy.

Norton Rose

3 More London Riverside, London, SE1 2AQ
Tel: (020) 7444 2113 Fax: (020) 7283 6500
Email: grad.recruitment@nortonrose.com
Website: www.nortonrose.com/careers

Firm profile

Norton Rose Group is a leading international legal practice. The firm offers a full business law service from offices across Europe, the Middle East and Asia Pacific.

Knowing how its clients' businesses work and understanding what drives their industries is fundamental to the firm. The lawyers share industry knowledge and sector expertise across borders, enabling the firm to support its clients anywhere in the world. The firm is strong in financial institutions; energy; infrastructure and commodities; transport; and technology.

The firm has over 1800 lawyers operating from 30 offices in Abu Dhabi, Amsterdam, Athens, Bahrain, Bangkok, Beijing, Brisbane, Brussels, Canberra, Dubai, Frankfurt, Hong Kong, London, Melbourne, Milan, Moscow, Munich, Paris, Perth, Piraeus, Prague, Rome, Shanghai, Singapore, Sydney, Tokyo and Warsaw and from associate offices in Ho Chi Minh City, Jakarta and Riyadh.

Norton Rose Group comprises Norton Rose LLP, Norton Rose Australia and their respective affiliates.

Main areas of work

Corporate finance; banking; dispute resolution; property; planning and environmental; taxation; competition and regulatory; employment, pensions and incentives; intellectual property and technology.

Trainee profile

Norton Rose LLP operates an innovative six-seat system. The first four seats (16 months) include one seat in each of the practice's core departments - corporate finance, banking and dispute resolution - plus an optional seat in one of the firm's other, non-core departments - employment, pensions and incentives, tax, competition and EC, intellectual property and technology, or property, planning and environmental. The remaining eight months can be spent in the department in which you wish to qualify, or you can visit a different practice area for four months to help you decide, and spend the last four months in your qualification seat. Alternatively, from your third seat onwards, you can elect to spend four months in one of the practice's international offices or apply for a client secondment. The practice's flexible seat system makes the transition from trainee to qualified solicitor as smooth as possible. The system has won the practice's trainees' approval, and from their point of view, develops associates with the adaptability and expertise the firm needs for its future.

Benefits

Life assurance, private health insurance (optional), season ticket loan, cycle to work scheme, subsidised gym membership, employee assistance programme, subsidised staff restaurant, eligibility to join the firm's group personal pension scheme.

Placement programmes

Places for 2010: 20 Winter Scheme - duration two weeks; Places for 2011: 40 Summer Scheme - duration four weeks; remuneration: £250 p.w.

Closing Date: 31 October 2010 for Winter Scheme; 31 January 2011 for Summer Scheme. Approximately 5 open days per year are held each year; please see www.nortonrose.com/careers for more information..

Partners 431*
Assistant Solicitors 1157*
Total Trainees 96
*denotes worldwide figures

Contact
Lisa Millar

Method of application
Online only

Selection procedure
Verbal/inductive reasoning test, interview plus written and group exercise

Closing date for 2013
31 July 2011

Application
Training contracts p.a. 55
Applications p.a. 2,500+
% interviewed p.a. 9%
Required degree grade 2:1

Training
Salary
1st year £37,000
2nd year £41,500
Holiday entitlement 25days % of trainees with a non-law degree p.a. 40% No. of seats available abroad p.a. 22 (per seat move)

Overseas offices
Abu Dhabi, Amsterdam, Athens, Bahrain, Bangkok, Beijing, Brisbane, Brussels, Canberra, Dubai, Frankfurt, Ho Chi Minh City*, Hong Kong, Jakarta,* London, Melbourne, Milan, Moscow, Munich, Paris, Perth, Piraeus, Prague, Riyadh,* Rome, Shanghai, Singapore, Sydney, Tokyo, Warsaw
*Associated office

Olswang

90 High Holborn, London WC1V 6XX
Tel: (020) 7067 3000 Fax: (020) 7067 3999
Email: traineesolicitor@olswang.com
Website: www.olswang.com/traineesolicitor

Firm profile

Olswang LLP is a leading business law firm with a strong reputation for quality and innovation; its lawyers are renowned for understanding the clients' businesses and providing first class legal advice. The firm works for many of the leading names in the media, technology and real estate sectors, but today its clients come from an ever-wider range of sectors. Founded in 1981, the firm has grown to a staff of more than 600, including over 90 partners and five European offices.
The firm's sector focus supports the wealth of knowledge and interest among fee earners and attracts a distinct breadth of clients from across industries. The firm represents recognised brands and key industry players, as well as smaller, pioneering companies. These include Bloomberg, eBay, Guardian Media Group plc, ITV, Legal & General, Lloyds, Microsoft, MTV Networks Europe, Nationwide, Orange, Sony BMG, UBS and Warner Music International.

Main areas of work

The firm's principal practice areas include: corporate; data protection; employment; EU and competition; finance; intellectual property; litigation and arbitration; media transactions; outsourcing; real estate; restructuring; tax; and technology transactions.

Trainee profile

Being a trainee at Olswang is both demanding and rewarding. The firm is interested in hearing from individuals who have achieved, or are on course for, a 2:1 degree or above and possess exceptional drive and relevant commercial experience. In addition, it is absolutely critical that trainees fit well into the Olswang environment, which is challenging, busy, individualistic, meritocratic and fun.

Training environment

Olswang wants to help trainees match their expectations and needs with those of the firm. Training consists of four six-month seats in Corporate, Real Estate, Litigation, Finance, Commercial or IP groups. You will be assigned a mentor, usually a Partner, to assist and advise you throughout your training contract. In-house lectures supplement general training and six-monthly appraisals assess development. Regular social events with the other trainees not only encourage strong relationship building but add to the fun of work.

Benefits

Immediately: life cover, medical cover, dental scheme, subsidised gym membership, subsidised staff restaurant, season ticket loan. After six months: pension contributions. After 12 months: PHI.

Vacation placements

Places for 2011: June & July; Duration: 2 weeks; Remuneration: £275 p.w.; 17 students per scheme; Closing Date: 31 January 2011.

Sponsorship & awards

LPC and GDL fees paid in full. Maintenance grant of £7,000 (inside London), £6,500 (outside).

Partners 95
Fee-earners 225
Total Trainees 48

Contact
Sarmini Ghosh
Senior trainee solicitor recruitment officer

Method of application
Online

Selection procedure
Commercial case study, interview, psychometric test and written exercises

Closing date for 2013
31 July 2011

Application
Training contracts p.a. 24
Applications p.a. 2,000
% interviewed p.a. 4%
Required degree grade 2:1

Training
Salary
1st year (2010) £35,000
2nd year (2010) £39,000
Holiday entitlement 25 days
% of trainees with a non-law degree p.a. 50%

Post-qualification
Salary (2010) £59,000

Overseas offices
Brussels, Berlin, Madrid

O'Melveny & Myers LLP

Warwick Court, 5 Paternoster Square, London, EC4M 7DX
Tel: (020) 7088 0000 Fax: (020) 7088 0001
Email: graduate-recruitment@omm.com Website: www.omm.com

Firm profile

O'Melveny & Myers is a top 20 global law firm with over 1,000 lawyers practising in 14 offices in the key US, Asian and European economic and political centres. The London office was effectively re-launched in 2004 and provides transactional and litigation legal services to a diverse group of prominent private equity houses, financial institutions and corporate clients. The team in London comprises in the main English qualified lawyers, as well as some dual qualified (US and UK) lawyers, who advise on cross-border English law matters and work closely with the firm's international network to provide a seamless global service. The London office is known for its entrepreneurial leadership and commitment to excellence, both of which underpin its approach to recruitment. Each year a number of its Partners and Counsel are recognised in the Chambers UK guide as leaders in their practice areas.

Main areas of work

Globally, O'Melveny's capabilities span virtually every area of legal practice. The London office has both a Transactions Department, which focuses on private equity, corporate finance, M&A and investment funds matters, as well as an international Litigation Department, offering international arbitration and London High Court litigation services, with antitrust and competition services support provided through the Brussels office. London also has the key transactional support functions which are essential to a leading corporate practice; namely tax, regulatory and intellectual property/IT expertise.

Trainee profile

The London office recruits up to four high calibre graduates for training contracts each year. Successful candidates must have proven academic ability, high levels of determination with a desire to excel, good team working skills and sound commercial awareness.

Training environment

Individual preferences can be taken into account when tailoring the London training programme, subject to the trainee completing the core competencies. Trainees complete seats with Partners or senior lawyers usually in each of the corporate, finance, funds and litigation practices. O'Melveny trainees are also regularly seconded overseas to the Hong Kong, Singapore, Tokyo and Brussels offices. They are encouraged to be proactive and take responsibility at an early stage. OMM trainees are expected to work hard, but do so in a supportive and inclusive environment, with regular formal and informal feedback. Great importance is placed on training for lawyers at all levels, and so trainees participate in both legal and non-legal skills training programmes.

Vacation schemes

Vacation placements are available for two weeks between June and September. All applications for 2011 vacation placements must be submitted online via www.apply4law.com/omm by 31 January 2011.

Benefits

Flexible benefits include: 25 days holiday, pension, life assurance, long term disability insurance, private health insurance, travel insurance, interest-free season ticket loan, corporate rate gym membership.

Sponsorship & awards

O'Melveny & Myers sponsors GDL/LPC fees incurred post-recruitment and awards a maintenance grant (currently £7,000 per annum) during the GDL/LPC course.

Partners 9
Counsel & Associates 16
Trainees 8

Contact
Fiona McEwan
Human Resources Assistant

Method of application
Online application
www.apply4law.com/omm

Selection procedure
Interview

Application
Training contracts p.a. up to 4
Applications p.a. 250-300
% interviewed p.a. 5-10%
Required degree grade 2:1, any discipline

Closing date for 2013
31 July 2011

Training
Salary
1st year £39,000 (correct for 2010)
2nd year £42,500 (correct for 2010)

Post-qualification
£72,500 (correct for 2010)

Overseas offices/ regional offices
Beijing, Brussels, Century City, Hong Kong, Los Angeles, Newport Beach, New York, San Francisco, Shanghai, Silicon Valley, Singapore, Tokyo and Washington D.C.

Orrick, Herrington & Sutcliffe

107 Cheapside, London, EC2V 6DN
Tel: (020) 7862 4600 Fax: (020) 7862 4800
Email: recruitlondon@orrick.com
Website: www.orrick.com/london/gradrecruitment

Firm profile

Orrick is a leading international law firm with more than 1,000 lawyers in 21 offices located throughout Asia, Europe and North America. Orrick has earned a global reputation advising both established and emerging companies, banks and international financial institutions. Much of Orrick's client work involves cross-border transactions which have increased substantially in recent years with the development of the firm's network of global offices.

Main areas of work

Acquisition finance, arbitration and litigation, banking, capital markets, trade and asset finance, competition and European Union law, corporate and corporate finance, employment, energy and project finance, global bankruptcy and debt restructuring, international dispute resolution, private investment funds, real estate, structured finance and securitisation, tax.

Trainee profile

If you set your standards high, have a strong work ethic and are a bright, talented graduate of any discipline, you will be guaranteed broad-based experience. Applicants should have at least three A level passes at grades A and B and a 2.1 degree.

Training environment

Orrick is a firm for academically outstanding graduates. The firm values team players and reward collaboration over competition. It aims to give individuals the opportunity to flourish in a lively and supportive work environment and encourages interaction among lawyers across international offices at every level of experience within the firm. It supports learning through a steadfast focus on training and a mentoring programme that will provide you with the right foundation for building your legal career and for working with clients. Trainees work closely with fee earners and gain practical experience in research, drafting, procedural and client-related skills. There are regular training sessions and they draw on a range of speakers including in-house experts, clients and specialist professionals in their fields to provide an extensive and varied programme. The two-year training programme comprises four six-month seats with the opportunity to sit a seat in their Hong Kong office. Trainees undertake the Professional Skills Course during their induction programme.

Benefits

Pension, health insurance, subsidised gym membership, season ticket loan, private medical insurance, dental care and childcare voucher scheme.

Sponsorship & awards

GDL and LPC: fees paid plus £7,000 maintenance.

Open days

Orrick hold several open days each year. Applicants get to spend the day in Orrick's London office and these are a great way to see the office of a US law firm in action. See website for dates and details on how to apply.

Partners 16 (London)
Associates 32 (incl of Counsel) (London)
Total Trainees 10

Contact
Simon Cockshutt

Method of application
Online at www.orrick.com/london/gradrecruitment

Selection procedure
2 interviews: 1st round with senior associates, 2nd round with partners

Closing date for 2013
31 July 2011

Application
Training contracts p.a. 10
Required degree grade 2:1

Training
Salary
1st year (2010): £38,000
2nd year (2010): £42,500
Holiday entitlement 25 days
% of trainees retained on qualification (2010) 80%

Overseas offices
Beijing, Berlin, Dusseldorf, Frankfurt, Hong Kong, Los Angeles, Milan, Moscow, New York, Orange County, Pacific Northwest, Paris, Rome, Sacramento, San Francisco, Shanghai, Silicon Valley, Taipei, Tokyo and Washington DC.

Osborne Clarke

2 Temple Back East, Temple Quay, Bristol BS1 6EG
Tel: (0117) 917 3484
Email: trainee.recruitment@osborneclarke.com
Website:www.osborneclarke.com

Firm profile

Osborne Clarke turns its legal expertise into its clients' commercial gain. By using their lawyers' experience, expertise and imagination its clients are given tailored, practical advice that makes a difference to their business. Although professional, Osborne Clarke doesn't believe that means it has to be stuffy or over-complicate solutions.

The firm's sector focus means that it knows a range of important industry sectors inside out. Osborne Clarke has particular expertise in digital business, energy and natural resources, financial services and real estate and infrastructure. As you'd expect the firm is also expert in the full range of legal services, from business regulation to tax.

With offices in key European locations, including the UK and Germany, as well as in the US, the close working relationships Osborne Clarke has with other firms around the world gives its clients access to global expertise.

Main areas of work

Main areas of expertise include; banking and finance, business regulation, commercial, corporate, employment and benefits, litigation, pensions, projects, real estate, restructuring and insolvency and tax.

Trainee profile

Osborne Clarke is looking for candidates who can: communicate effectively; think commercially and practically; solve problems creatively; build effective relationships; and demonstrate initiative. Foreign language skills are also an advantage. Strong academic achievement is essential and candidates should have achieved, or expect to achieve, at least a 2.1 degree in any discipline with grades A – B at A Level or equivalent. Applications from candidates seeking a career change are welcomed.

Training environment

During the 2 year training contract trainees complete 4 six-month seats, with all trainees expected to undertake a seat in litigation, corporate, and either real estate or tax. Trainees at Osborne Clarke are coached by experienced lawyers in each department and have access to a real workload to enable them to qualify with experience and confidence in dealing with clients - essential at the start of their career.

In each seat trainees are assigned a training supervisor, who is responsible for their day-to-day supervision. In addition to regular informal feedback sessions trainees benefit from formal progress reviews held every 3 months which helps to track their development.

Benefits

25 days' holiday (plus a Christmas shopping day), pension, permanent health insurance, private medical insurance, life assurance and season ticket loan.

Vacation schemes

Each of Osborne Clarke's vacation scheme placements runs for two weeks over the summer and offers a great opportunity for candidates to really get to know the firm. The placement follows a structured programme which allows candidates to spend time in two different departments and get involved in real client work. Beyond work there are plenty of social events organised by our trainees.

Sponsorship & Awards

The firm will pay candidates tuition fees provided that they are no more than half way through either the GDL or LPC when they are recruited, along with a maintenance grant of £6,500 per course.

Partners 112
Lawyers 260
Trainees 34

Contact
Zoe Reid, Trainee Recruitment Officer

Method of application
Online application form

Selection procedure
Assessment centre comprises of group exercises, psychometric test, partner interview, written exercise

Closing date for 2013
31 July 2011

Application
Training contracts p.a. 20
Applications p.a. 1,200
% interviewed p.a. 10%
Required degree grade: 2:1, any discipline

Training
1st year Competitive
2nd year Competitive
Holiday entitlement 25 days
% of trainees with a non-law degree p.a. 35%

Post-qualification
Competitive

Offices
Bristol, Cologne, London, Munich, Silicon Valley, Thames Valley

Pannone LLP

123 Deansgate, Manchester M3 2BU
Tel: (0161) 909 3000 Fax: (0161) 909 4444
Email: graduaterecruitment@pannone.co.uk
Website: www.pannone.com

Firm profile

A high-profile Manchester firm offering a full range of legal services to a diverse client base which is split almost equally between private and commercial clients. The firm was the first to be awarded the quality standard ISO 9001 and is a founder member of Pannone Law Group – Europe's first integrated international law group. Pannone was voted the highest placed law firm in the Sunday Times 100 Best Companies To Work For in 2010 for the seventh year running.

Main areas of work

Commercial litigation 16%; personal injury 25%; corporate 13%; commercial property 8%; family 8%; clinical negligence 6%; private client 5%; employment 5%; construction 3%; regulatory 6%; residential property 5%.

Trainee profile

Selection criteria include a high level of academic achievement, teamwork, organisation and communication skills, a wide range of interests and a connection with the North West.

Training environment

An induction course helps trainees adjust to working life, and covers the firm's quality procedures and good practice. Regular trainee seminars cover the work of other departments within the firm, legal developments and practice. Additional departmental training sessions focus in more detail on legal and procedural matters in that department. Four seats of six months are spent in various departments and trainees' progress is monitored regularly. Trainees have easy access to support and guidance on any matters of concern. Work is tackled with gusto here, but so are the many social gatherings that take place.

Vacation placements

Places for 2011: 88; Duration: 1 week; Remuneration: None; Closing Date 30 April 2011. Recruitment for training contracts is primarily through vacation placements.

Sponsorship & awards

Half grant for LPC + fees at The College of Law, Manchester.

Partners 107
Assistant Solicitors 103
Total Trainees 36

Contact
Amy Bell

Method of application
Online only

Selection procedure
Individual interview, second interview comprises a tour of the firm & informal lunch

Closing date for 2013
31st July 2011

Application
Training contracts p.a. 12
Applications p.a. 1,200
% interviewed p.a. 10%
Required degree grade 2:1

Training
Salary
1st year (2009) £23,000
2nd year (2009) £23,000
Holiday entitlement 23 days
% of trainees with a non-law degree p.a. 33%

Post-qualification
Salary (2009) £34,000
% of trainees offered job on qualification (2009) 67%
% of solicitors who joined as trainees 54.9%
% of partners who joined as trainees 40.5%

Paul, Hastings, Janofsky & Walker (Europe) LLP

10 Bishops Square, 8th Floor, London, E1 6EG
Tel: (020) 3023 5100 Fax: (020) 3023 5109
Email: kellytaverner@paulhastings.com
Website: www.paulhastings.com

Firm profile

With 1,000+ lawyers serving clients from 18 worldwide offices, Paul Hastings provides a full range of services to clients around the globe.The firm has established long standing partnerships with many of the world's top financial institutions, Fortune 500 companies and other leading corporations. Paul Hastings represents and advises clients across a full range of practices, industries and regions.

Main areas of work

Paul Hastings' principle practice areas in London are capital markets, corporate, employment, finance, litigation, real estate, restructuring and tax.

Trainee profile

The firm seeks individuals with a wide variety of skills who combine intellectual ability with enthusiasm, creativity and a demonstrable ability to thrive in a challenging environment. The firm expects candidates to have a high level of achievement both at A level (or equivalent) and degree level. This would typically mean an upper second or first class degree and a majority of A grades at A level. The firm recruits both law and non-law graduates.

Training environment

Paul Hastings will provide you with a first class training and development programme, combining on-the-job training and professional courses. The firm will monitor your progress on a formal and informal basis to ensure you receive ongoing training and have the opportunity to give feedback on the programme itself and on those areas that are most important to you.

Trainees spend six months in four of the following practice areas: Capital markets, corporate, employment, finance, litigation, project finance, real estate, restructuring and tax.

Benefits

Private healthcare, life assurance, pension scheme, season ticket loan, gym subsidy.

Sponsorship & awards

Paul Hastings offers sponsorship and maintenance grants.

Vacation placements

Places for 2011: 6; Duration: 2 weeks; Remuneration: £350 per week; Closing date: 28th February 2011.

Partners 15
Assistant Solicitors 33
Total Trainees 11

Contact
Graduate Recruitment

Method of application
online application form available on website

Selection procedure
Interview

Closing date for 2013
31 July 2011

Application
Training contracts p.a. 4-5
Required degree grade 2:1

Training
Salary
1st year (2010) £40,000
2nd year (2010) £45,000
Holiday entitlement
25 days

Post-qualification
Salary (2010) £80,000

Overseas/regional offices
Atlanta, Beijing, Brussels, Chicago, Frankfurt, Hong Kong, London, Los Angeles, Milan, New York, Orange County, Palo Alto, Paris, San Diego, San Francisco, Shanghai, Tokyo, Washington DC

PaulHastings

Penningtons Solicitors LLP

Abacus House, 33 Gutter Lane, London, EC2V 8 AR
Tel: (020) 7457 3000 Fax: (020) 7457 3240
Website: www.penningtons.co.uk

Partners 51
Assistant Solicitors 108
Total Trainees 18
* denotes worldwide figures

Contact
Andrea Law

Method of application
Online via firm's website

Closing date for 2013
31 July 2011

Application
Training contracts p.a. 5-10
Applications p.a. 1,000
% interviewed p.a. 5%
Required degree grade 2:1

Training
Salary
1st year (2010)
£30,000 (London)
2nd year (2010)
£32,000 (London)
Holiday entitlement 23 days

Post-qualification
Salary (2010) £47,000 (London)

Firm profile

Penningtons Solicitors LLP is a thriving, modern law firm with a 200-year history and a deep commitment to top quality, partner-led services. Today, the firm is based in London and the South East with offices in London, Hampshire and Surrey.

Main areas of work

In the business sphere, Penningtons advises on matters relating to all aspects of commercial property, intellectual property, management buy-outs and buy-ins, mergers, acquisitions and joint ventures, as well as dispute resolution. Advice is also given on information technology, business recovery, commercial contracts, agricultural and environmental law, and company secretarial services are offered. The firm helps individuals with advice on property, tax and estate planning, general financial management, the administration of wills and trusts, charities, personal injury, clinical negligence and immigration. Clients often ask Penningtons to advise on both their private and commercial affairs.

Trainee profile

Penningtons seeks high calibre candidates with enthusiasm and resilience. A high standard of academic achievement is expected: three or more good A level passes and preferably a 2:1 or better at degree level, whether you are reading law or another discipline.

Training environment

You will be given a thorough grounding in the law, spending time in three or four of the firm's divisions; commercial property, business services and private individuals. The firm ensures a varied training is given, avoiding too specialised an approach before qualification. Nonetheless, the experience gained in each department gives you a solid foundation, equipping you to embark on your chosen specialisation at the end of your training contract with the firm. Penningtons knows its trainee solicitors are happiest and most successful when busy with good quality work. The firm believes in introducing trainees to challenging cases. The value of giving its trainees responsibility, and allowing direct contact with clients is recognised. However, experienced solicitors are always ready to give support when needed.

Benefits

Life assurance, critical illness cover, pension, private medical insurance, 23 days holiday, interest free season ticket loan, sports and social events.

Vacation placements

The firm offers both summer vacation placements and information days. Applications are accepted from 1 December 2010 to 31 March 2011.

Sponsorship & awards

Full fees and maintenance for the LPC plus a maintenance grant of £5,000.

Pinsent Masons LLP

CityPoint, One Ropemaker Street, London, EC2Y 9AH
Email: graduate@pinsentmasons.com
Website: www.pinsentmasons.com/graduate

Firm profile

Pinsent Masons is a top 15 UK law firm with a growing international presence, that is committed to sector focussed growth through it's core sector approach. Not constrained by the legacy of many larger commercial practices, this approach aligns the firm to specific business sectors to achieve market-leading positions. The firm is focused on providing a value added service developing a successful and innovative approach to building strong corporate relationships.
With a substantial range of FTSE 100, FTSE 250, Fortune 500 and AIM quoted organisations and public sector clients the firm has an impressive portfolio of clients operating in the global economy. Consequently the firm is constantly looking to extend its own international reach and capabilities. This means you'll be part of a team tackling business issues in some of the world's most dynamic markets. There may also be an opportunity to work overseas through the firm's European Alliance network with 'Salans' or in one of its offices in the Middle East and Asia.

Main areas of work

The firm offers depth, scope and opportunity for it's trainees in a culture of early responsibility and high quality work. As a member of a creative, resourceful and supportive team, you can expect a constant flow of stimulating assignments – developing your legal expertise, market knowledge and commercial vision to deliver commercial legal solutions. Main areas of work include: banking and insurance, corporate, dispute resolution, employment, intellectual property, projects and construction, property, tax and pensions.

Trainee profile

The firm welcomes applications from all backgrounds. Whether your degree is law or non law, there will be no barriers to what you can achieve in the firm's uniquely progressive, meritocratic and open culture. In addition to a strong academic background, the firm is looking for people who can combine a sharp mind with commercial acumen and strong people skills to work in partnership with their clients' businesses.

Training environment

Trainees sit in four seats of six months across the practice areas with supervision from partners and associates. There are also opportunities for trainees to be seconded to clients. There is a supportive team culture which derives from the firm's values of; ambition and excellence; being open and approachable; respect and co-operation.
In addition to the training required by the Law Societies, the firm offers a broad-ranging and custom-made training programme designed to deliver outstanding technical and management skills that link in with the needs of the business. This is the first stage in the firm's focussed to development programme that supports individuals on their route to partnership.
The firm has an open plan office environment and this no barriers focused approach encourages an informal team atmosphere with a positive focus on work-life balance.

Summer vacation placements

Places for 2011: 100; duration: 2 weeks; Closing Date: 31 January 2011.

Sponsorship & awards

In England, full sponsorship is offered for the GDL and LPC fees, as well as a maintenance grant. In Scotland, financial assistance is offered for Diploma fees, together with a maintenance grant.

Partners 280+
Lawyers 1,000
Total Trainees 135

Contact
Edward Walker

Method of application
Online application form
www.pinsentmasons.com/graduate

Selection procedure
Assessment day including interview

Closing date for 2013
31 July 2011 (English offices) and 21 October 2011 (Scottish offices)

Application
Training contracts p.a. 60
Applications p.a. 2,000+
Required degree grade 2:1

Training
Salary
1st year £36,000 (London)
2nd year £39,000 (London)
Holiday entitlement 25 days

Post-qualification
Salary (2010) £58,000 (London)

UK offices
London, Birmingham, Bristol, Leeds, Manchester, Edinburgh and Glasgow

PricewaterhouseCoopers Legal LLP

1 Embankment Place, London, WC2N 6DX
Tel: 0808 100 1500
Website: pwc.com/uk/careers

Vacancies 8
Trainees 18
Partners 26
Total staff 172
Work placement Yes

Method of application
Visit www.pwclegal.co.uk where you will be directed to our careers site to complete an online application

Closing date for 2013
Trainees: July 31 (2011)
Summer vacation scheme January 31 (2011)

Application
Required academic grade 2:1 honours degree in any degree discipline plus at least a 320 UCAS tariff or equivalent

Training
Salary London
1st year (2010) £30,000
2nd year (2010) £35,000

Firm profile

PricewaterhouseCoopers Legal LLP (PwC Legal) is an independent member of the PricewaterhouseCoopers (PwC) international network of firms. Its services include corporate restructuring, mergers and acquisitions, intellectual property, information technology, immigration, pensions, employment, financial services, banking, commercial contracts, real estate, litigation, private client and environment. The firm offers domestic and international clients both project-based, specialist legal advice and ongoing general counsel support. And not only does its ambitious growth plans make it an exciting place to launch a legal career; so does its working model, which is unique in the UK legal services market. PwC Legal can call upon the wider PwC network's specialists when it needs to offer complete, rounded solutions that incorporate multi-disciplinary advice. It often works with PwC tax advisers, human capital consultants, corporate finance experts, actuaries, management consultants and, of course, accountants. And it has access to legal expertise in over 70 countries and immigration expertise in over 112 countries. Thanks to such resources, the firm can deliver a superior client experience that goes beyond just legal services.

Trainee profile

PwC Legal recruits penultimate-year law students and final year non-law students with at least a 2:1 honours degree or equivalent, a 320+ UCAS tariff or equivalent and a keen interest in business law.

Training environment

Trainee solicitors develop into top lawyers in any of the mainstream practice groups: corporate, financial services, banking, litigation, real estate, intellectual property, employment, pensions or immigration. At the same time, exposure to the diverse skill sets of PwC hones strong business advisory skills. Trainees also develop lateral thinking skills, gain practical hands-on experience and help deliver creative solutions. Training includes: A thorough induction covering core practice groups, client care and time management skills, and IT, research and admin. Support to gain a professional qualification – trainees take the core modules of the Professional Skills Course (PSC) during their second seat. A range of electives during the fourth seat to complete the PSC. Extensive internal training to develop business, management and interpersonal skills. Exceptional prospects – throughout the training contract and beyond.

Vacation schemes

The firm's paid, three-week summer vacation scheme offers exposure to practice groups and invaluable work experience. Yet another plus point? The scheme is also a good route towards securing a training contract.

Sponsorship & awards

Trainees can apply for a scholarship award to help with the costs of the Graduate Diploma in Law Course and the Legal Practice Course. If successful, they receive the total cost of the tuition and examination fees plus a significant contribution towards living expenses. Details are on the firm's website.

PRICEWATERHOUSECOOPERS LEGAL

Pritchard Englefield

14 New St, London EC2M 4HE
Tel: (020) 7972 9720 Fax: (020) 7972 9722
Email: po@pe-legal.com
Website: www.pe-legal.com

Firm profile

A niche City firm practising a mix of general commercial and non-commercial law with many German and French clients. Despite its strong commercial departments, the firm still undertakes family and private client work and is renowned for its ever-present international flavour.

Main areas of work

All main areas of commercial practice including litigation, commercial/corporate/ banking (UK, German and French), IP/IT, property and employment, also estate and trusts (UK and off-shore), pensions, charities, personal injury and family.

Trainee profile

High academic achievers with fluent German and/or French.

Training environment

An induction course acquaints trainees with the computer network, online library and finance & administrative procedures and there is a formal in-house training programme during the first week. Four six-month seats make up most of your training. You can usually choose some departments, and you could spend two six-month periods in the same seat. Over two years, you learn advocacy, negotiating, drafting and interviewing, attend court, use your language skills every day and meet clients from day one. Occasional talks and seminars explain the work of the firm, and you can air concerns over bi-monthly lunches with the partners comprising the Trainee Panel. PSC is taken externally over two years. The Social Committee of the firm organises regular parties, French film evenings and quiz nights.

Benefits

Some subsidised training, monthly luncheon vouchers, and eligibility for membership of the firm's private medical insurance scheme as well as an interest free loan for an annual season ticket.

Sponsorship & awards

Full funding for LPC fees.

Partners 21
Assistant Solicitors 13
Other Fee Earners 7
Total Trainees 3

Contact
Graduate Recruitment

Method of application
Standard application form available from Graduate Recruitment or online

Selection procedure
1 interview only in September

Closing date for 2013
31 July 2011

Application
Training contracts p.a. 3
Applications p.a. 300–400
% interviewed p.a. 10%
Required degree grade
Generally 2:1

Training
Salary
Market rate
Subject to 6 month review
Holiday entitlement 25 days
% of trainees with a non-law degree p.a. Approx 50%

Post-qualification
Salary (2009)
Market rate
% of trainees offered job on qualification (2009) 100%
% of assistants (as at 01/09/09) who joined as trainees 60%
% of Partners (as at 01/09/09) who joined as trainees 20%

Reed Smith

The Broadgate Tower, 20 Primrose Street, London, EC2A 2RS
Tel: +44 (020) 3116 3000 Fax: +44 (020) 3116 3999
Email: graduate.recruitment@reedsmith.com
Website: www.reedsmith.com

Firm profile

Key to Reed Smith's success is its ability to build lasting relationships: with clients and with each other. United through a culture defined by commitment to professional development, team-work, diversity, pro bono and community support, the firm has grown to become one of the 15 largest law firms in the world. Its 22 offices span three continents and London is currently the largest with over 500 people. While the offices benefit from an international framework, each one retains key elements of the local business culture. Last year the team in London consolidated from two premises to one office space in The Broadgate Tower, which boasts fantastic views of the city.

Main areas of work

The firm is particularly well known for its work advising leading companies in the areas of financial services, life sciences, shipping, energy, trade and commodities, advertising, technology and media. It provides a wide range of commercial legal services for all these clients, including a full spectrum of corporate, commercial and financial services, dispute resolution, real estate and employment advice. Much of the work is multi-jurisdictional.

Trainee profile

The firm is looking for individuals with the drive and potential to become world-class business lawyers. They want 'players' rather than 'onlookers' with strong intellect, initiative, the ability to thrive in a challenging profession and the personal qualities to build strong relationships with colleagues and clients.

Training environment

On offer is a four-seat programme with opportunities for secondments to clients and the firm's overseas offices. Trainees also benefit from being able to take a wide range of courses in its award-winning corporate university, developed in partnership with the highly rated Wharton School of the University of Pennsylvania. There are vacancies for training contracts commencing in August 2013 and February 2014.

Benefits

Pension, life insurance, private health insurance, interest-free season ticket loan, bonus, subsidised staff restaurant and staff conveyancing allowance.

Vacation placements

The firm offers up to 20 places each year to applicants who will, on arrival, have completed at least two years of undergraduate study.

Sponsorship & awards

GDL Funding: Fees paid plus £6,000 maintenance. LPC Funding: Fees paid plus £7,000 maintenance

---

Partners 104*
Fee-earners 230*
Total Trainees 45
* denotes UK figures

Contact
Lucy Crittenden

Method of application
Online application form

Selection procedure
Selection exercise, interview, verbal reasoning assessment

Closing date for 2013/2014
31 July 2011

Application
Training contracts p.a. approximately 30
Applications p.a. 1500
% interviewed p.a. 7%
Required degree grade 2:1

Training
Salary
1st year (2010) £37,000
Holiday entitlement 25 days
% of trainees with a non-law degree p.a. 35%
No. of seats available abroad p.a. 6

Post-qualification
Salary (2010)
£57,000 plus bonus
% of assistants who joined as trainees 43%
% of partners who joined as trainees 45%

Overseas offices
New York, London, Hong Kong, Chicago, Washington DC, Beijing, Paris, Los Angeles, San Francisco, Philadelphia, Pittsburg, Oakland, Munich, Abu Dhabi, Princeton, N. Virginia, Wilmington, Dubai, Century City, Piraeus, Richmond, Silicon Valley

Reynolds Porter Chamberlain LLP

Tower Bridge House, St Katharine's Way, London, E1W 1AA
Tel: (020) 3060 6000 Fax: (020) 3070 7000
Email: training@rpc.co.uk
Website: www.rpc.co.uk/training

Firm profile

Reynolds Porter Chamberlain LLP (RPC) is a forward thinking, London-based law firm with a wide-ranging practice, some of the leading lawyers in their fields and great clients in both the UK and overseas. The firm offers a depth of knowledge and creativity that few firms can rival and is regularly praised in the leading directories for the quality of its training programmes.

Based in modern offices in the City, RPC works in an open, collaborative environment designed to bring out the best in its people and to ensure that the service offered to its clients is second to none. The firm strives to create a working environment in which knowledge is shared and access to Partners is a reality.

The firm has two divisions: its commercial division offers a full business law service across a wide range of sectors including publishing and media, retail and construction. The firm's insurance division stands alone in fulfilling the specialist needs of the insurance industry and handles some of the largest and most high-profile claims in the market, many of which span several jurisdictions.

Trainee profile

RPC appoints 15 trainees each year from a law or non-law background. Although proven academic ability is important (the firm requires a 2.1 degree or above) it also values energy, enthusiasm, business sense, commitment and the ability to communicate and relate well to others. Recruitment usually takes place in the September two years before commencement of the training contract. Shortlisted candidates will be invited to one of the firm's assessment days, during which they will have the opportunity to meet current trainees and Partners.

Training environment

As a trainee you will receive first-rate training in a supportive working environment. You will work closely with a Partner and will be given real responsibility as soon as you are ready to handle it. At least six months will be spent in four areas of the firm's practice and RPC encourages its trainees to express preferences for the areas in which they would like to train. In addition to the Professional Skills Course, the firm provides a complementary programme of in-house training. When you qualify, the firm hopes you will stay with RPC and it endeavours to place you in the area of law that suits you best.

Benefits

The firm feels it is important to offer its employees a creative and competitive benefits package with choice and flexibility. Its full range of benefits can be viewed via the website.

Vacation placements

RPC also runs summer vacation schemes each year to enable prospective trainees to spend time at the firm, getting a feel for its work and atmosphere. Twelve students at a time spend two weeks at RPC and are integrated as closely as possible with the real working life of the firm. You should get a good idea of whether a career at RPC is right for you.

Sponsorship & awards

Bursaries are available for the GDL, if applicable, and the LPC. Bursaries comprise course and examination fees and a maintenance grant of up to £6,500. The firm requests that all its trainees complete their LPC at BPP University College.

Partners 65
Associates 150
Total trainees 30

Contact
Trainee Recruitment Team

Method of application
Online application system

Selection procedure
First interview face-to-face (Group exercises, presentations, aptitude tests, case studies)

Closing date for 2013
31 July 2011

Application
Training contracts p.a. 15
Applications p.a. 800
% interviewed p.a. 7.5%
Required degree grade 2:1

Training
Salary
1st year £37,000
2nd year £40,000
Holiday entitlement 20 days
% of trainees with a non-law degree p.a. Approx 40%

Post-qualification
Salary (2010) £58,000
% of trainees offered job on qualification (2010) 83%
% of Associates (as at 01/05/10) who joined as trainees 28%
% of Partners (as at 01/05/09) who joined as trainees 33%

Salans

Millennium Bridge House, 2 Lambeth Hill, London EC4V 4AJ
Tel: (020) 7429 6000 Fax: (020) 7429 6001
Email: londonrecruitment@salans.com

Firm profile

Salans has an open and friendly culture with an informal, but hardworking environment. It is a multinational law firm with full-service offices in the City of London, Paris and New York, together with further offices in Almaty, Baku, Barcelona, Berlin, Beijing, Bratislava, Brussels, Bucharest, Budapest, Frankfurt, Hong Kong, Istanbul, Kyiv, Madrid, Moscow, Prague, Shanghai, St Petersburg and Warsaw. Building on the success of the firm's emerging markets practices and with a long established presence in Shanghai, the firm currently has over over 700 fee-earners, including 189 Partners worldwide, with 32 partners residing in the London office. Its lawyers strongly believe in assisting individuals and groups unable to access legal services, through a positive commitment to pro bono work. In 2007 and 2008 Salans were finalists at the Lawyer Awards for 'International Law Firm of the Year'.

Main areas of work

London Office: Banking and finance; corporate and commercial litigation; employment; real estate; reorganisation, restructuring and insolvency and corporate recovery; information technology and communications; betting and gaming; shipping and arbitration.

Trainee profile

You will have high academic qualifications, including good A-Level (or equivalent) results, and the ability to approach complex problems in a practical and commercial way. The firm is looking for highly motivated, creative and enthusiastic team players. It looks to recruit trainees who make a difference, want early responsibility and contribute to the ever-changing legal world. Relevant work experience demonstrating a desire to pursue a career in law will be viewed positively, and language and computer skills are also valued.

Benefits

Private healthcare, pension, life assurance, critical illness cover, interest free season ticket loan.

Sponsorship & awards

LPC tuition fees paid.

Partners 189 (Worldwide)
Assistant Solicitors (Worldwide) 400+
Total Trainees (London) 10

Contact
Keely Smith
HR Manager

Method of application
Covering letter & CV

Selection procedure
Interview written test and presentation

Closing date for 2013
8 July 2011

Application
Training contracts p.a. 3-4
Applications p.a. 400-500
% interviewed p.a. 5%
Required degree grade 2:1

Training
Salary
1st year £33,000
2nd year £35,000
Holiday entitlement 25 days
% of trainees with a non-law degree p.a. Variable
No. of seats available abroad p.a. One (occasional)

Post-qualification
Salary (2009) £58,000
% of trainees offered job on qualification (2009) 65%

Overseas offices
Almaty, Baku, Barcelona, Berlin, Beijing, Bratislava, Brussels, Bucharest, Budapest, Frankfurt, Hong Kong, Istanbul, Kyiv, Madrid, Moscow, New York, Paris, Prague, Shanghai, St Petersburg and Warsaw (22 in total)

Shearman & Sterling LLP

Broadgate West, 9 Appold Street, London EC2A 2AP
Tel: (020) 7655 5000 Fax: (020) 7655 5500

Firm profile

Shearman and Sterling LLP is one of the world's leading premier global law firms and was established over a century ago. The London office opened in 1972, and quickly became one of the leading practices, covering all aspects of English, European and US corporate and finance law. Globally there are approximately 900 attorneys, including around 200 partners.

Main areas of work

Our main areas of work include European Corporate (including Mergers & Acquisitions, Intellectual Property & US Capital Markets), Project Development & Finance, European Finance (including Capital Markets, Structured, Acquisition & Leveraged Finance), International Litigation & Arbitration, Antitrust, Tax, Financial Institutions Advisory & Asset Management, Property and Executive Compensation & Employee Benefits.

Trainee profile

The role of a trainee solicitor at Shearman and Sterling is as demanding as it is rewarding, with the chance to work on major deals with individuals at all levels, from partners to associates. The diverse range of practices and clients allows for a large variety of work for trainees, who are given real responsibility from day one. Trainees become an integrated part of the team working on deals, and will contribute work that adds significant value to the end result.

The 2 year training contract consists of 4 seats, each lasting 6 months. As part of a global firm, trainees have the opportunity to work in an overseas office for one of their seats. This includes: New York, Abu Dhabi, Hong Kong and Singapore. As well as potentially working in one of the other offices, trainees will frequently be part of cross-jurisdictional deals, interacting, and developing relationships with colleagues in other offices. As a result, trainees build up a strong network globally, which becomes invaluable throughout their career.

Sponsorship & awards

Sponsorship for the CPE/PgDL and LPC courses, together with a maintenance grant of £7,000.

Partners 26
Assistant Solicitors 127
Total Trainees 22

Contact
Charlotte Hannan
Tel: (020) 7655 5000

Method of application
Online at www.shearman.com

Selection procedure
Online testing, interviews, assessment centre

Closing date for 2013
30 June 2011

Application
Training contracts p.a. 15
Required degree grade 2:1, AAB A-levels (or equivalent) UCAS points minimum

Training
Salary
1st year (2009) £39,000
2nd year (2010) £40,500
Holiday entitlement
24 days p.a.
% of trainees with non-law degree p.a. 40%
No of seats available abroad 3-5

Post-qualification
Salary (2009) £73,000
% of trainees offered job on qualification (2010) 92%

Overseas offices
Abu Dhabi, Bejing, Brussels, Düsseldorf, Frankfurt, Hong Kong, Menlo Park, Milan, Munich, New York, Paris, Rome, San Francisco, Sao Paulo, Shanghai, Singapore, Tokyo, Toronto, Washington DC

Sheridans

Whittington House, Alfred Place, London, WC1E 7EA
Tel: (020) 7079 0100 Fax: (020) 7079 0200
Email: info@sheridans.co.uk
Website: www.sheridans.co.uk

Firm profile

Sheridans is a full-service law firm with an established reputation for its work in the creative industries. Representing many internationally recognised names in music, film, TV and theatre, it also has a thriving commercial practice offering corporate, private client, dispute resolution, property and employment services.

Main areas of work

ENTERTAINMENT & MEDIA: The music department advises recording artists and recording and management companies on contract negotiation, popular and classical music publishing, merchandising and sponsorship. The film and TV department advises broadcasters, TV and feature film production companies, distribution and sales agents, financiers and talent. Other specialist areas include the theatre, sport, book and magazine publishing, trademarks and domain names, computer games, online and digital media.

DISPUTE RESOLUTION: The firm provides advice and representation in relation to disputes arising in the media and entertainment industries. The disputes typically range from privacy and defamation claims against the national press to rights disputes.

CORPORATE/ COMMERCIAL: The firm advises on commercial contracts, mergers, acquisitions and disposals, management buy-outs and buy-ins, corporate finance, joint ventures, corporate reorganisations, company formations and insolvency.

PROPERTY: Services include the sale and purchase of commercial property, involving investment, leasehold and planning matters, secured lending, building and development schemes and property financing, as well as domestic conveyancing for high net worth individuals.

EMPLOYMENT: The employment practice handles contentious and non-contentious matters, representing both employers and employees, including senior executives.

Trainee profile

Excellent academic background (2.1 and above, good A levels), commercial awareness, great interpersonal skills and an ability to think strategically. Trainees should have an enthusiasm for and a demonstrable commitment to the firm's areas of practice.

Training

The training contract is divided into four six month seats, although trainees are expected to be flexible and assist any department as required. Trainees are given a challenging range of work and exposure to a significant level of responsibility.

Partners 27
Consultants 2
Assistant solicitors 14
Total trainees 2

Contact
Claire Lewis (Training Principal)

Method of application
CV and covering letter, by email to training@sheridans.co.uk (see website)

Selection procedure
2 stage interview process

Closing date for 2013
31 July 2011

Application
Training contracts p.a. 1
Required degree grade 2:1

Training
Salary
1st year competitive with similar firms
2nd year competitive with similar firms
Holiday entitlement
20 days

Post-qualification
Salary Competitive with similar firms
% of trainees offered job on qualification (in last two years) 50%

Shoosmiths

The Lakes, Northampton NN4 7SH
Tel: (0870) 086 3075 Fax: (0870) 086 3001
Email: join.us@shoosmiths.co.uk
Website: www.shoosmiths.co.uk

Firm profile

Shoosmiths is one of the UK's fastest-growing national law firms with offices across the midlands, the north west and the south of England. The firm is a progressive, forward-thinking law firm with a real spirit of enterprise. The firm really values its people by giving them the freedom, recognition and support to succeed.

Main areas of work

The firm is a full service law firm with numerous practice areas including commercial property, corporate, commercial and dispute resolution.

Trainee profile

You'll be open-minded, flexible, and will be looking to work in a non-hierarchical, open plan environment. You'll also value a life outside of the office. Workwise, you'll care about the quality of service you give to clients (both internal and external) and you'll want to make a real and direct contribution to the firm's success.

Training environment

Trainees are given real work from day one. Experience is built around a practical workload, complemented by technical and business skills training. Over the two years, trainees complete four six-month placements around the firm.

The firm only places one or two trainees in each department which means that you'll be listened to and valued, and will get a good level of access to your supervising Partner and colleagues.

Benefits

Flexible holidays, pension (after three months' service), life assurance, various staff discounts, Christmas bonus.

Vacation placements

The firm offers two-week placements during June and July. Please apply online via the website. The closing date for summer placements will be 5pm, 28 February 2011.

Sponsorship & awards

GDL & LPC funding; the firm pays fees plus a maintenance grant.

Partners 110
Vacancies c. 30
Total Staff 1,200
Total Trainees 30

Contact
Graduate Recruitment

Method of application
Online application form

Selection procedure
Full day assessment centre

Closing date for 2013
See website

Application
Training contracts p.a. 22
Applications p.a. 1,000
% interviewed p.a. 10%
Required degree grade 2:1

Training
Salary
£tbc
Holiday entitlement
23 days + option to flex

Post-qualification
Salary £tbc

Offices
Birmingham, Northampton, Nottingham, Manchester, Milton Keynes, Solent, Thames Valley, Basingstoke*, London*
*(not available for TC's or placements)

Sidley Austin LLP

Woolgate Exchange, 25 Basinghall Street, London EC2V 5HA
Tel: (020) 7360 3600
Email: ukrecruitment@sidley.com
Website: www.sidley.com

Firm profile

Sidley Austin LLP is one of the world's largest full-service law firms. With approximately 1,700 lawyers practising on four continents (North America, Europe, Australasia and Asia), the firm provides a broad range of integrated services to meet the needs of its clients across a multitude of industries.

Main areas of work

Corporate, competition, corporate reorganisation and bankruptcy, debt restructuring, debt finance and structured finance, equity capital markets, employment, financial services regulatory, hedge funds, insurance, IP/IT, litigation, real estate and real estate finance, tax.

Trainee profile

Sidley Austin LLP looks for focused, intelligent and enthusiastic individuals with personality and humour who have a real interest in practising law in the commercial world. Trainees should have a consistently strong academic record and a 2:1 degree (not necessarily in law).

Training environment

The firm is not a typical City firm and it is not a 'legal factory' so there is no risk of being just a number. Everyone is encouraged to be proactive and to create their own niche when they are ready to do so. Trainees spend time in the firm's main groups. In each group trainees will sit with a partner or senior associate to ensure individual training based on 'hands on' experience. You will be encouraged to take responsibility where appropriate. Regular meetings with your supervisor ensure both the quality and quantity of your experience. In addition, there is a structured timetable of training on a cross-section of subjects.

Benefits

Private health insurance, life assurance, contribution to gym membership, interest-free season ticket loan, income protection scheme, pension and subsidised restaurant.

Sponsorship & awards

Tuition fees for the GDL/CPE and the LPC. Maintenance grant of £7,000 p.a.

Sidley Austin LLP, a Delaware limited liability partnership which operates at the firm's offices other than Chicago, London, Hong Kong, Singapore and Sydney, is affiliated with other partnerships, including Sidley Austin LLP, an Illinois limited liability partnership (Chicago); Sidley Austin LLP, a separate Delaware limited liability partnership (London); Sidley Austin LLP, a separate Delaware limited liability partnership (Singapore); Sidley Austin, a New York general partnership (Hong Kong); Sidley Austin, a Delaware general partnership of registered foreign lawyers restricted to practicing foreign law (Sydney); and Sidley Austin Nishikawa Foreign Law Joint Enterprise (Tokyo). The affiliated partnerships are referred to herein collectively as Sidley Austin, Sidley, or the firm.

Partners 38
Assistant Solicitors 80
Total Trainees 17

Contact
Lucy Slater,
Graduate Recruitment Officer

Method of application
Application form

Selection procedure
Interview(s)

Closing date for 2013
31 July 2011

Application
Training contracts p.a. 10
Applications p.a. 300
% interviewed p.a. 15
Required degree grade 2:1

Training
Salary
1st year (2010) £39,000
2nd year (2010) £43,000
Holiday entitlement 25 days
% of trainees with a
non-law degree p.a. 50%

Overseas offices
Beijing, Brussels, Chicago, Dallas, Frankfurt, Geneva, Hong Kong, London, Los Angeles, New York, Palo Alto, San Francisco, Shanghai, Singapore, Sydney, Tokyo, Washington DC

Simmons & Simmons

CityPoint, One Ropemaker Street, London EC2Y 9SS
Tel: (020) 7628 2020 Fax: (020) 7628 2070
Email: recruitment@simmons-simmons.com
Website: www.simmons-simmons.com/graduates

Firm profile

Dynamic and innovative, Simmons & Simmons has a reputation for offering a superior legal service, wherever and whenever it is required. The firm's high quality advice and the positive working atmosphere in its international network of 18 offices has won admiration and praise from both the legal community and business clients.

Main areas of work

Simmons & Simmons offers its clients a full range of legal services across numerous industry sectors. The firm has a particular focus on the world's fastest growing sectors, namely: energy and infrastructure; financial institutions; life sciences; and TMT. Simmons & Simmons provides a wide choice of service areas in which its lawyers can specialise. These include corporate and commercial; information, communications and technology; dispute resolution; employment and benefits; EU, competition and regulatory; financial markets; IP; projects; real estate; taxation and pensions.

Trainee profile

Simmons & Simmons is interested to find out about your academic successes but will also explore your ability to form excellent interpersonal relations and work within a team environment, as well as your levels of motivation, drive and ambition.

Show evidence of a rich 'life experience' as well as examples of your intellectual capabilities and you will be provided with everything you need to become a successful member of the firm.

Training environment

The training programme at Simmons & Simmons is constantly evolving to build the skills you will need to be successful in the fast moving world of international business. The firm provides experience in a range of areas of law and a balanced approach to gaining the knowledge, expertise and abilities you will need to qualify in the practice area of your choice.

Vacation placements

The firm's internship schemes are one of the primary means of selecting candidates for a career at Simmons & Simmons. Your placement will enable you to gain first-hand experience of a busy and dynamic international law firm, as well as gain exposure to everything from the firm's service areas to the kinds of deals and transactions the firm works on.

The firm's three week summer internships are open to penultimate year law students, final year non law students, international and mature students, graduates and those changing career. Applications open 01 November 2010.

The spring internship scheme is a great opportunity for first year law students and penultimate year non-law students to get an in-depth view of the firm at an early stage of your studies. Applications open 01 November 2010.

Simmons & Simmons also runs winter insight workshops aimed specifically at final year non-law students, and non-law graduates. Applications open 01 October 2010.

Finally, a series of open days, available to all undergraduates, graduates, mature and international students are run throughout the year.

Sponsorship & awards

The firm will cover your full tuition fees at law school and offer a maintenance allowance of up to £7,500.

Partners 212
Assistant Solicitors 596
Total Trainees 106

Contact
Anna King Graduate Recruitment Manager

Method of application
Online application form, at www.simmons-simmons.com/graduates

Selection procedure
Interview or Assessment day

Closing date for 2013
31 July 2011

Application
Training contracts p.a. circa 40
Applications p.a. 2,000
Required degree grade 2:1

Training
Salary
£36,000, 1st and 2nd seat
£40,000, 3rd and 4th seat
Holiday entitlement 25 days
% of trainees with a non-law degree p.a. 50%
No. of seats available abroad p.a. varies

Post-qualification
Salary (2010) £59,000

Overseas offices
Abu Dhabi, Amsterdam, Brussels, Doha, Dubai, Düsseldorf, Frankfurt, Funchal*, Hong Kong, Lisbon*, London, Madrid, Milan, Paris, Rome, Rotterdam, Shanghai, Tokyo
*Sociedade Rebelo de Sousa in association with Simmons & Simmons

Simmons & Simmons

SJ Berwin

10 Queen Street Place, London, EC4R 1BE
Tel: (020) 7111 2268 Fax: (020) 7111 2000
Email: graduate.recruitment@sjberwin.com
Website: www.sjberwin.com

Partners 161
Assistant Solicitors 400
Total Trainees 73

Contact
Graduate Recruitment Team

Method of application
Online application form

Selection procedure
2 interviews/ case study/ critical reasoning test
Closing date for 2013
31 July 2011
Easter & summer vacation schemes 31 January 2011

Application
Training contracts p.a. 40
Applications p.a. 2,000
10% interviewed p.a.
Required degree grade 2:1

Training
Salary
£37,500, 1st year
£41,500, 2nd year
Holiday entitlement 25 days
% of trainees with a non-law degree p.a. 50%

Post-qualification
Salary (2010) £59,000
% of trainees offered job on qualification (2010) 78%

Overseas offices
Berlin, Brussels, Dubai, Frankfurt, Hong Kong, Madrid, Milan, Munich, Paris, Shanghai, Turin

Firm profile

SJ Berwin is an international corporate law firm. Clients range from major multinational business corporations and financial institutions to high net-worth individuals. As a result, the firm has established a strong reputation in corporate finance. The firm has 160 partners and over 400 fee-earners.

Main areas of work

SJ Berwin was created and continues to thrive as a leading-edge legal services business, focusing on the European and international marketplace. The firm's clients are sophisticated buyers of legal services, principally entrepreneurial companies and financial institutions, whom the firm advises on a comprehensive range of services including: corporate/M&A, commercial, communications and technology, energy and natural resources, employment and pensions, EU and competition, finance, financial markets, intellectual property, investment funds, litigation and dispute resolution, pharmaceuticals and life sciences, private equity, real estate, reconstruction and insolvency, retail and tax.

Trainee profile

The firm wants ambitious, commercially minded individuals who seek a high level of involvement from day one. Candidates must have a strong academic record, be on track for, or have achieved, a 2:1 or equivalent in their undergraduate degree, and have demonstrated strong team and leadership potential.

Training environment

The two-year training contract is divided into four six-month seats. Trainees will spend two seats (which may include a seat abroad) within the following areas: finance, mergers and aquisitions, equity capital markets, private equity, venture capital and investment funds. Trainees are given early responsibility and are supported throughout the training contract.

How to apply

The firm welcomes applications from all disciplines and all universities. Applications must be made using the firm's online form available at www.sjberwin.com. The same form can be used to indicate your interest in an open day, a vacation scheme and/or a training contract.

Benefits

25 days holiday, private healthcare, gym membership/subsidy, life assurance, pension scheme, season ticket loan, free lunch.

Skadden Arps, Slate, Meagher & Flom (UK) LLP

40 Bank Street, Canary Wharf, London E14 5DS
Tel: (020) 7519 7000 Fax: (020) 7519 7070
Email: graduate.hiring@skadden.com Website: www.skadden.com/uktraineesolicitors

Firm profile

Skadden is one of the leading law firms in the world with approximately 2,000 lawyers in 24 offices across the globe. Clients include corporate, industrial, financial institutions and government entities. The London office is the gateway to the firm's European practice and has some 250 lawyers dedicated to top-end, cross-border corporate transactions and international arbitration and litigation. The firm has handled matters in nearly every country in the greater European region, and in Africa and the Middle East. The firm is consistently ranked as a leader in all disciplines and amongst a whole host of accolades, the firm has been voted 'Global Corporate Law Firm of the Year' (*Chambers and Partners*), 'Best US Law Firm in London' (*Legal Business*) 'Best Trainer' and 'Best Recruiter' in the US law firm in London category (*Law Careers.Net Training and Recruitment Awards*).

Main areas of work

Lawyers across the European network focus primarily on corporate transactions, including domestic and cross-border mergers and acquisitions, private equity, capital markets, leveraged finance and banking, tax, corporate restructuring and energy and projects. The firm also advise in international arbitration, litigation and regulatory matters.

Trainee profile

The firm seeks to recruit a small number of high-calibre graduates from any discipline to join their highly successful London office as trainee solicitors. The firm is looking for candidates who combine intellectual ability with enthusiasm, creativity and a demonstrable ability to rise to a challenge and to work with others towards a common goal.

Training environment

The firm can offer you the chance to develop your career in a uniquely rewarding and professional environment. You will join a close-knit but diverse team in which you will be given ample opportunity to work on complex matters, almost all with an international aspect, whilst benefiting from highly personalised training and supervision in an informal and friendly environment. The first year of your training contract will be divided into two six month seats where you will gain experience in corporate transactions and international litigation and arbitration. In the second year of your training contract, you will have the opportunity to discuss your preferences for your remaining two seats. The firm also offers the opportunity for second year trainees to be seconded to our Hong Kong office for a six month seat.

Benefits

Life insurance, private health insurance, private medical insurance, travel insurance, joining fee paid at Canary Wharf gym, subsidised restaurant, employee assistance programme and technology allowance.

Work placements

Skadden offers the opportunity for penultimate year law and non-law students to experience the culture and working environment of the firm through two week work placements. Placements are paid and take place during Easter and over the course of the summer. The deadline for applications is 12 January 2011 for placements in 2011.

Sponsorship & awards

The firm pays for GDL and LPC course fees and provides a £8,000 grant for each year of these courses.

Partners 29*
Assistant Solicitors 80
Trainees 12*
*London office

Contact
Kate Harman
Graduate Recruitment Specialist

Method of application
Online application

Selection procedure
A selection event comprising of an interview and a short exercise

Closing date for 2013
31 July 2011

Application
Training contracts p.a. 10-12
Applications p.a. 700
% interviewed p.a. 8%
Required degree grade 2:1

Training
Salary
1st year £40,000
2nd year £43,000
Holiday entitlement 25 days
% of trainees with a non-law degree p.a. 50%

Overseas offices
Beijing, Boston, Brussels, Chicago, Frankfurt, Hong Kong, Houston, Los Angeles, Moscow, Munich, New York, Palo Alto, Paris, San Francisco, São Paulo, Shanghai, Singapore, Sydney, Tokyo, Toronto, Vienna, Washington DC, Wilmington.

Skadden

Slaughter and May

One Bunhill Row, London EC1Y 8YY
Tel: (020) 7600 1200 Fax: (020) 7090 5000
Email: trainee.recruit@slaughterandmay.com (enquiries only)
Website: www.slaughterandmay.com

Firm profile

One of the most prestigious law firms in the world, Slaughter and May enjoys a reputation for quality and expertise. The corporate, commercial and financing practice is particularly strong and lawyers are known for their business acumen and technical excellence. As well as its London, Paris, Brussels, Beijing and Hong Kong offices, the firm nurtures long-standing relationships with the leading independent law firms in other jurisdictions in order to provide the best advice and service across the world.

Main areas of work

Corporate, commercial and financing; tax; competition; financial regulation; dispute resolution; technology, media and telecommunications; intellectual property; commercial real estate; environment; pensions and employment.

Trainee profile

The work is demanding and the firm looks for intellectual agility and the ability to work with people from different countries and walks of life. Common sense, the ability to communicate clearly and the willingness to accept responsibility are all essential. The firm expects to provide training in everything except the fundamental principles of law, so does not expect applicants to know much of commercial life.

Training environment

Each trainee completes four or five seats of three or six months duration. Two or three seats will be spent in one of the firm's corporate, commercial and financing law groups. The remaining time can be divided between some of the specialist groups and can also include an overseas secondment to one or the firm's offices or to one of its best friend firms. In each seat a partner is responsible for monitoring your progress and reviewing your work. There is an extensive training programme which includes the PSC. There are also discussion groups covering general and specialised legal topics.

Benefits

Private medical insurance, season ticket loan, pension scheme, interest free loan, subsidised membership of health club, 24 hour accident cover.

Work experience:

One or two-week work experience schemes are available at Easter, Christmas and during the summer period for those considering a career in law. Please visit the website for full details.

Sponsorship & awards

GDL and LPC fees and maintenance grants are paid.

Partners 127
Associates Over 400
Total Trainees 192

Contact
The Trainee Recruitment Team

Method of application
Online (via website)

Selection procedure
Interview

Application
Training contracts p.a. Approx 90
Applications p.a. 2,000 approx
% interviewed p.a. 25% approx
Required degree grade Good 2:1 ability

Training
Salary (May 2010)
1st year £38,000
2nd year £43,000
Holiday entitlement 25 days p.a.
% of trainees with a non-law degree Approx 50%
No. of seats available abroad p.a. Approx 30-40

Post-qualification
Salary (May 2010) £61,000
% of trainees offered job on qualification (Sept 2010) 93%

Overseas offices
Paris, Brussels, Beijing and Hong Kong, plus "Best Friend" firms in all the major jurisdictions.

SNR Denton

One Fleet Place, London EC4M 7WS
Tel: (020) 7242 1212 Fax: (020) 7320 6555
Email: graduaterecruitment@snrdenton.com
Website: www.snrdenton/graduates.com

Firm profile

SNR Denton is a top 25 legal services provider worldwide, with a network spanning four continents, in 18 countries and 33 locations.

SNR Denton was formed on 30 September 2010 with the combination of Denton Wilde Sapte LLP and Sonnenschein Nath & Rosenthal LLP.

The firm works hard to maintain a friendly and open environment where ideas are shared and people work together to achieve goals.

Main areas of work

SNR Denton offers an international legal practice focused on quality in the following industry sectors: energy transport and infrastructure, financial institutions and funds, government, health and life sciences, insurance, manufacturing, real estate, retail and hotels, technology, media and telecommunications.

Trainee profile

The firm looks for candidates who are team players with a strong academic and extra curricular record of achievement. Given the diversity of the firm's business, it looks for people from a wide-range of skills, aptitudes and personalities. You will need drive and ambition, with the potential to contribute to the growing success of SNR Denton.

Training environment

The firm is looking for people to join its London, Milton Keynes and Middle East Offices. As a trainee you will undertake four six-month seats. This will include a contentious seat and a banking seat (training in London). You may also have the opportunity to work in one of the firm's international offices or with one of the firm's clients.

You will be given as much responsibility as you can handle, and will be working with the law, with your team and with clients in real business situations.

Benefits

Flexible benefit scheme including private health insurance and sports club membership allowance. Season ticket loan.

Vacation placements

One week summer scheme open to second, penultimate, final year law students and those who have already completed a law degree. Open days in December open to final year non-law students and those who have already completed a non-law degree. Open day in Spring for first year law students.

Sponsorship & awards

GDL and LPC tuition fees covered plus £6,000 maintenance grant in your actual year of study, £7,000 if studying in London. The firm will pay LPC fees retrospectively.

Partners 500
Fee-earners 1500
Total Trainees 60

Contact
Hemlata Shamji

Method of application
Application form

Selection procedure
First interview; selection test; second interview and case study

Closing date for 2013
Non-law 31 March 2011
Law 31 July 2011

Application
Training contracts p.a. 25-30
Applications p.a. 1,500
% interviewed p.a. 15%
Required degree grade 2:1

Training
Salary
1st year £37,000
2nd year £40,000
Holiday entitlement 24 days
% of trainees with a non-law degree p.a. 30%
No. of seats available abroad p.a. Currently 5

Post-qualification
Salary (2010) £59,000
% of trainees offered job on qualification (2010) 60%

SNR Denton Offices
Abu Dhabi, Almaty, Bahrain, Brussels, Cairo, Chicago, Dallas, Doha, Dubai, Kansas City, Los Angeles, London, Milton Keynes, Moscow, Muscat, Short Hills, New York, Paris, Phoenix, San Francisco, Silicon Valley, Singapore, St Louis, Tashkent Washington DC, Zurich

SNR Denton Associate Offices
Jordan, Kuwait, Saudi Arabia

SNR Denton Facilities
Boston, Miami, Walnut Creek

SNR Denton Associate Firms
Algeria, Beirut, Burundi, Ghana, Kenya, Mauritius, Rwanda, Russia, South Africa, Tanzania, Tripoli, Turkey, Turkmenistan, Uganda, Zambia

Speechly Bircham LLP

6 New Street Square, London, EC4A 3LX
Tel: (020) 7427 6400 Fax: (020) 7353 4368
Website: www.speechlys.com

Firm profile

Speechly Bircham works energetically to deliver commercial and practical solutions and to advise clients in an efficient and cost-effective way. With over 240 lawyers, the firm is organised around providing integrated transactional, advisory and disputes services to its three main client markets. Much of Speechly Bircham's work has an international dimension and close working relationships have been built with leading independent firms in all major financial, commercial and wealth management centres across the world.

Main areas of work

Business Services: UK and multinational organisations benefit from the breadth of experience of the specialist teams in the firm's Business Services Division. With more than 120 lawyers, teams provide businesses with a comprehensive legal service in corporate finance; banking; financial services; insolvency; tax; IP; technology; competition; data protection; employment; pensions; business immigration and all types of commercial disputes.

Private Client Services: The firm's leading private client practice is ranked as one of the top ten in the world (Chambers Global 2009), and is the second largest Private Client Group in London (Private Client Practitioner 2008). The firm is known for providing a complete service to UK and international individuals and families, wealth management organisations, trustees, family offices and charities. Providing integrated advice on wealth protection, tax succession planning, philanthropy, family and real estate issues is a key feature.

Real Estate; Construction and Engineering Services: Over 70 lawyers work in multidisciplinary teams to provide advice to lenders, investors, developers, occupiers, contractors and engineers. Clients include major quoted and international companies, blue chip financial institutions, funds, housebuilders, private investors and consultants. The firm operates across all major real estate sectors including commercial and industrial property, strategic land and regeneration, urban estates; healthcare, retail and leisure. The team of construction and engineering lawyers is one of the most significant in the UK and internationally.

Trainee profile

The firm welcomes applications from all degree disciplines from candidates who are capable of achieving or who have achieved 2:1.

Training environment

Trainees complete four six-month seats across the firm's three divisions and will therefore experience a varied and broad training contract and develop a wide range of skills. Trainees are supported by a partner or solicitor, given early responsibility and supervised client contact, complemented by comprehensive in-house legal training. Regular performance reviews are held to promote development and ensure trainees achieve their potential.

Summer scheme placements

The firm offers the opportunity to attend a three week summer placement scheme giving students an opportunity to experience its practice areas and an insight into what life at Speechly Bircham is really like. Students experience working within a different practice group each week and undertake fee-earning work which can include research, drafting letters, attending client meetings and going to court. However it is not all work and no play and the summer schemes are punctuated by a variety of sports and social events. Applications for 2011 summer placements to be submitted by 4 February 2011.

Sponsorship

GDL and LPC fees paid together with a maintenance grant.

Partners 87
Assistant Solicitors 138
Total Trainees 22

Contact
Helen Wiggs
Human Resources Manager

Method of application
Application form (available online)

Selection procedure
Interview and psychometric testing

Closing date for 2013
31 July 2011

Application
Training contracts p.a. 12
Applications p.a. 800
% interviewed p.a. 15%
Required degree grade 2:1

Training
Salary
1st year
£32,000-33,000
2nd year
£34,000-£35,000
Holiday entitlement 25 days

Post-qualification
Salary (2010) £54,000
Holiday entitlement 25 days

Stephenson Harwood

One St Paul's Churchyard, London EC4M 8SH
Tel: (020) 7809 2812 Fax: (020) 7003 8346
Email: graduate.recruitment@shlegal.com
Website: www.shlegal.com/graduate

Firm profile

Stephenson Harwood is an international law firm with over 100 partners and over 600 staff worldwide. With a fifth of the firm's people operating out of Asia, the China connection is stronger than ever. And from that first bank client, the firm has today built a formidable strength in the banking and wider financial services sector, accounting for twelve of the firm's top twenty clients. Stephenson Harwood is more than simply a City-based practice. Through its international network of offices and affiliates, it provides clients with quality resources and expert local knowledge in Africa, Asia, Europe, the Middle East and Latin America.

The UK offices are relocating in spring 2011 to Finsbury Circus.

Main areas of work

Corporate (including corporate finance, funds, corporate tax, business technology); employment, pensions, finance; dry and wet shipping litigation; commercial litigation; and real estate.

Trainee profile

The firm looks for high calibre graduates with excellent academic records, business awareness and excellent communication skills.

Training environment

As the graduate intake is relatively small, the firm gives trainees individual attention, coaching and monitoring. Your structured and challenging programme involves four six month seats in areas of the firm covering contentious and non-contentious areas, across any department within the firm's practice groups. These seats include 'on the job' training and you will share an office with a Partner or senior associate. In-house lectures complement your training and there is continuous review of your career development. You will have the opportunity to spend six months abroad and have free language tuition where appropriate. You will be given your own caseload and as much responsibility as you can shoulder. The firm plays a range of team sports, offers subsidised membership of a City health club (or a health club of your choice) and has privileged seats for concerts at the Royal Albert Hall and access to private views at the Tate Gallery.

Benefits

Subsidised membership of health clubs, private health insurance and screening, pension, life assurance, private GP services, critical illness cover, retail vouchers, dental insurance, season ticket loan and 25 days paid holiday per year.

Vacation placements

Places for 2010/2011: 40; Duration: 1 week Christmas; 2 weeks Easter and summer; Remuneration: £260 p.w.

Closing Date: 7 November 2010 for Christmas; 31 January 2011 for Easter and summer.

Sponsorship & awards

Fees paid for GDL and LPC and maintenance awards (if still studying).

Partners 111* (96 UK)
Associates 204* (142 UK)
Total Trainees 37* (27 UK)
* denotes world-wide figures

Contact
Rebecca Ryalls, Graduate Recruitment Assistant (graduate.recruitment@shlegal.com)

Method of application
Online application form via www.apply4law.com/sh

Selection procedure
Training contract - application screening, psychometric testing, telephone interview and assessment centre
Placement schemes - as above with face to face interview and the assessment centre during the scheme
Closing date for TC commencing March/Sept 2013 31st July 2011

Application
Applications p.a. circa 1,000
Training contracts p.a. 16
Required degree grade 2:1

Training
Salary
1st year £35,000
2nd year £40,000
Holiday entitlement 25 days
% of trainees with a non-law degree p.a. 50%
No. of seats available abroad p.a. 8 (4 per 6 month rotation

Post-qualification
Salary £58,000
% of trainees offered job on qualification for September (2010) 71%

Overseas offices
Paris, Piraeus, Hong Kong, Singapore, Shanghai, Guangzhou

Associated offices
Greece, Kuwait, Croatia, France, Romania

Stevens & Bolton LLP

Wey House, Farnham Road, Guildford GUI 4X5
Tel: (01483) 302264 Fax: (01483) 302254
Email: julie.bounden@stevens-bolton.com
Website: www.stevens-bolton.com

Firm profile

Stevens & Bolton LLP is a leading regional law firm in the south-east with a national practice. Its vision is to be the South's top independent law firm – and a great place to work. It was named National/Regional Law Firm of the Year at the 2009 Legal Business Awards and the firm was also named Corporate Law Firm of the Year at the Insider Dealmakers South East awards for the fourth year running.

Clients include household name PLCs and other major international groups, mid tier businesses (whether quoted or owner managed) and high net worth private clients.

The firm is a full service law firm and particular features of its approach to client service include the responsiveness of lawyers and strength in depth in all key areas; an emphasis on sound, practical advice aimed at achieving clients' commercial objectives; open, collaborative and friendly relationships with clients and a constructive approach with other advisers; a continuing investment in know how, training and technology to enhance the value of the firm's services. Increasingly its work involves an international element and the firm has established relationships with overseas firms in key jurisdictions.

There are number of active groups in the firm so that everyone is able to contribute ideas in areas such as marketing, profile raising, 'greening the office' and corporate and social responsibility.

Main areas of work

Corporate and commercial, real estate, dispute resolution, employment pensions and immigration, tax and trusts, private client and family.

Trainee profile

The firm would like to hear from you if you have (or expect) a 2:1 or first class degree. Just as important is the kind of person you are. Tell us about your motivations, achievements, interests and hobbies – what gets you out of bed in the morning? Initiative is a quality that the firm looks for too, so think about situations you have been in where your involvement has made a real difference.

Training environment

The firm provides excellent training to all its trainees, with real client contact and responsibility early on. To ensure that trainees get as broad a range of experience as possible you will do six four month seats with the aim of giving you the opportunity (where possible) to spend your final seat in the department you hope to qualify into. All trainees receive regular feedback and appraisals and sit either with a partner or a senior associate.

Benefits

Pension, private healthcare, life assurance, permanent health insurance and an interest free loan for rail travel or car parking.

Sponsorship & awards

The firm will pay the fees at the level set by the College of Law, Guildford for the CPE/GDL and LPC, (if no grant is available) and £4,000 maintenance grant for each course of study. Future trainees who have not taken the GDL/LPC are required to attend the College of Law, Guildford.

Vacation placements

The firm will run two programmes each summer of one week's duration. Please see the website for further information. Applications are accepted between 1 December 2010 and 31 January 2011.

Partners 36
Associates 54
Total Trainees 8

Contact
Julie Bounden
(01483) 302264

Method of application
Online application form available from website

Selection procedure
Two interviews & other processes

Closing date for 2013
Please see website

Application
Training contracts p.a. 4
Applications p.a. 250
% interviewed 10%
Required degree grade 2:1

Training
Salary
1st year (2010) £24,500
Holiday entitlement 25 days

Overseas/regional offices
Guildford only

Taylor Wessing LLP

5 New Street Square, London EC4 3TW
Tel: (020) 7300 7000 Fax: (020) 7300 7100
Email: graduate@taylorwessing.com
Website: www.taylorwessing.com/graduate

Firm profile

Taylor Wessing is a leading international law firm with a forward-thinking approach to serving clients. By thinking creatively, being proactive and staying close to its clients, the firm identifies better ways to help them achieve their ambitions and deliver innovative solutions that help their businesses grow.

The firm's clients include large and medium size, private and public companies, financial institutions, professional service firms, public sector bodies and wealthy individuals. Its focus is on the sectors that the firm believes are the industries of tomorrow: technology, communications and brands; life sciences and healthcare; energy and environment; real estate and infrastructure; financial institutions and services.

Taylor Wessing is an expert in providing a seamless, high-quality service to global clients across many jurisdictions. Combining a pan-European network with a strong presence in the Middle East, India, China and North America, it is the leading firm for inward investment from North America and experts in IP protection and enforcement rights across the globe. That's why Taylor Wessing works for 60% of the world's Top 50 brands.

Main areas of work

Taylor Wessing offers industry-focused advice by grouping together lawyers from different legal areas with in-depth sector experience and support their work with specialist practice areas:
Banking and finance; capital markets; copyright and media law; corporate; commercial agreements; construction and engineering; employment and pensions; EU competition, IT and telecoms; litigation and dispute resolution; logistics and transport; patents; pharmaceutical law; planning and environment; private client; projects; real estate; restructuring and corporate recovery; tax; trade marks and designs.

Trainee profile

Taylor Wessing looks for people with a minimum of ABB grades at A-level and a 2:1 degree in any discipline. You'll need to be a team player with the communication skills to build vibrant relationships with its clients. You'll have the energy, ambition and creativity to take responsibility and have a real impact on its business. You'll also be committed to a career in law, with a genuine drive to learn and explore new boundaries.

Training environment

Taylor Wessing's training programme combines the in-house Professional Skills Course with six-month seats in four different practice groups, including one contentious seat and one in its corporate or finance areas.

Working closely with partners and associates on high quality work from the outset, you'll get regular support and feedback every step of the way and ongoing discussions to match your interests to the growth and needs of the firm. There are also secondment opportunities to its clients.

Vacation placements

Taylor Wessing's vacation schemes are designed for you to experience life as a trainee solicitor in a uniquely innovative City law firm. You'll spend two weeks in two different practice groups gaining first-hand experience under the supervision of associates and partners.

Partners 280
Fee-earners 400
Trainees Circa 40 (UK)

Contact
Graduate Recruitment Department

Method of application
Online application form

Selection procedure
Assessment centre and partner interview

Closing date for 2013
31 July 2011

Application
Training contracts p.a. Circa 20
Applications p.a. Circa 1000
% interviewed p.a. 20%
Required degree grade 2:1

Training
Salary
1st year £35,000
2nd year £38,000
Holiday entitlement 25 days
% of trainees with a non-law degree p.a. 50%

Post-qualification
Salary £59,000
% of trainees offered jobs on qualification (2010) 79%

Overseas offices
Berlin, Brussels, Cambridge, Dubai, Düsseldorf, Frankfurt, Hamburg, London, Munich, Paris and representative offices in Beijing and Shanghai. Associate office in Warsaw

TaylorWessing

Thomas Cooper

Ibex House, 42-47 Minories, London EC3N 1HA
Tel: (020) 7481 8851 Fax: (020) 7480 6097
Email: recruitment@thomascooperlaw.com
Website: www.thomascooperlaw.com

Firm profile

Thomas Cooper is an international law firm which was founded in 1825.

Thomas Cooper has experience of dealing with the law in key jurisdictions around the world, with offices in London, Athens, Madrid, Paris, Singapore and Vancouver. The firm takes a pragmatic approach, providing clear advice that helps clients navigate through the complexity of international commerce.

The firm is recommended by and recognised by the major legal directories for its expertise.

The firm's clients operate globally and range from shipowners to charterers and traders, from banks and other financial institutions to underwriters and P&I clubs, from blue chip companies to small businesses and private individuals.

The firm gives insightful and pragmatic advice to clients and allows them to manage their exposure to risk more effectively.

Main Areas of Work

The firm's core practice areas are maritime, trade, finance, company and commercial, international arbitration, insurance, oil and gas.

Trainee Profile

As a trainee with the firm you will be exposed to clients and fee earning work from your first seat. Thomas Cooper works for a wide variety of clients and as such, you can expect to find yourself dealing with finance, personal injury, wet or dry shipping claims.

Thomas Cooper values its trainees because they are vital for the future of the business. If you are bright, confident and a self starter who has a keen interest in maritime then the firm would encourage you to apply to its trainee programme.

Training Environment

Thomas Cooper has a four-seat trainee programme over two years: two seats in shipping, one in defence and personal injury; and one in finance and international trade. There is also opportunity to do a seat in one of the firm's international offices, this is dependent upon language skills and team workload.

Benefits

Private medical insurance; permanent health insurance; life assurance; 25 days holiday; pension scheme; loan for dental insurance; season ticket loan; loan for gym membership. LPC course fees are paid by the firm.

Partners 29
Assistant solicitors 21
Total trainees 8

Contact
Karan Tapley - Human Resources Manager
Tel: (020) 7481 8851

Method of application
Online application form

Selection procedure
Interviews and assessments

Closing date for 2013
31 July 2011

Application
Required degree grade 2:1

Training
Salary
Starting salary for trainees is:
Year 1 £32,000
Year 2 £33,600 (based on 2010 salaries)
25 days holiday

Overseas/ regional offices
Athens, Madrid, Paris, Singapore & Vancouver

THOMAS COOPER

Thomas Eggar

The Corn Exchange, Baffins Lane, Chichester PO19 1GE
Tel: (01243) 813253
Email: recruitment@thomaseggar.com
Website: www.thomaseggar.com

Firm profile

Thomas Eggar is rated as one of the top 100 law firms in the UK. Based across the South, it is one of the country's leading regional law firms with a staff approaching 500. The firm offers both private client and commercial services to a diverse range of clients, locally, nationally and internationally. It also offers financial services through Thesis, the firm's investment management arm, which is the largest solicitor-based investment management unit in the UK.

Main areas of work

Apart from its strength in the private client sector, the firm handles property, employment, commercial and dispute resolution matters; among its major clients are banks, building societies and other financial institutions, railway and track operators and construction companies, football clubs and sports personalities.

Trainee profile

The firm seeks very able trainees who exhibit good business acumen, with a 2:1 degree in any discipline. Applications can be made up to 31 July 2011 for training contracts to commence in 2012 and 2013. Applications should be online. You should give details of your attachment to the South in your online application. The online application is www.apply4law.com/thomaseggar.

Training environment

Trainees would normally have four seats covering commercial property, commercial, dispute resolution and private client. In order to give good exposure to various specialisations, some of the seats are likely to be in different offices. Trainees should be prepared to undertake seats in any of the firm's six offices.

Vacation placements

There is a limited summer placement scheme in July and August each year: this runs for five days and can be within any one of our locations. Applications should be made online. Please give details of your accommodation plans in your application. Travel expenses are paid.

Sponsorship & awards

LPC 50% grant, 50% loan.

Vacancies 8
Partners 73
Trainees 16
Total Staff 475+

Contact
Donna Patterson

Method of application
On-line
www.apply4law.com/thomaseggar

Selection procedure
CV, assessment centre and interview

Closing date for 2012/2013
31 July 2011

Training
The firm aims to pay the going rate for a firm based in the South. A London weighting is paid to those who undertake seats in the London office.
Required degree grade
2:1 (any discipline)

Other offices
Chichester, Gatwick, London, Worthing, Newbury, Southampton

TLT LLP

One Redcliff St, Bristol BS1 6TP
Tel: (0117) 917 7586 Fax: (0117) 917 7649
Email: bee.yazdani@TLTsolicitors.com Website: www.TLTcareers.com/trainee

Firm profile

Here, the firm is open. Open to connected working, open plan and open minded. It has reshaped the traditional law firm model into a fresh, bright, inclusive and creative place to work. As a Top 100 firm - with 650 people across Bristol, London and Piraeus, Greece - it is confident that its way works. The firm has won awards and gathered accolades, but what matters more is that it has made an impact. The Financial Times called it one of Europe's most innovative law firms, and in 2009/2010, its turnover reached £41 million. The firm continues to win business from FTSE-listed, national and international companies including Punch Taverns, the Metropolitan Police Authority, Orange and Ecotricity. So the firm is going places – and quickly. If you want to make your mark in law, work progressively and with a conscience, then this is where your career really begins.

Main areas of work

The firm's full service legal offering spans the financial, leisure, retail, built environment, technology and media industries, and its core legal specialisms are real estate, banking and finance, commercial, corporate, employment, dispute resolution and litigation. But it believes there's more to legal work than being a lawyer – you need to embrace management, technology and business skills too.

Trainee profile

The firm's trainees are rather special. Genuinely ambitious, talented and technically impressive, you don't just tick all the boxes – you open them up, reshape them, and connect them all together. You'll stand out, stand up for what's right, and stand shoulder to shoulder with your colleagues – you must embrace team working and share a passion for exceptional client service. And while academic achievement is important, your personal qualities also count for a lot here.

Training environment

Whether you join us for your training contract or a one week vacation scheme placement, you'll work on live cases for real clients, get input from a Partner, and develop a broad range of skills across the full legal and business spectrum. Our training contracts are designed to have more in them so you get more out of them. So here you'll gain invaluable technical knowledge and professional skills, all backed up by a one-to-one mentor, expert guidance and unlimited support throughout.

Benefits

The firm is one of just ten Top 100 law firms to offer a full and flexible benefits plan, which means you can design your benefits package to meet your lifestyle needs, picking and choosing from a selection of rewards and benefits. As part of the firm's commitment to giving something back, you'll also be encouraged to get involved in community support work, pro bono legal advice, fundraising activities and environmental initiatives.

Vacation placements

Spend a week with TLT and you'll pick up unparalleled experience and a real taste of life at a leading law firm - especially when you consider the amount of Partner contact you'll enjoy. And we've built assessments into the week, which means you won't have to make a separate training contract application or attend an assessment day.

Sponsorship & awards

CPE and LPC fees plus maintenance grant.

Partners 62
Solicitors 200
Total Trainees 25

Contact
Bee Yazdani, Graduate Recruitment Officer
Tel: 0117 917 7586

Method of application
Online application form at www.TLTcareers.com/trainee

Selection procedure
Application form, telephone screening, verbal reasoning testing, assessment centre
Closing date: 31 July each year

Application
Training contracts: up to 15 p.a.
Applications: circa 700 p.a.
% interviewed: 12% p.a.
Required degree grade:
2:1 or above in any discipline at degree level and a minimum of 300/24 UCAS points at A level

Training
Salary: See website for details
Holiday entitlement: 25 days

Post-qualification
Salary:
See website for details
% trainees offered job on qualification: 80-100%

Offices
Bristol, London, Piraeus (Greece)

Travers Smith LLP

10 Snow Hill, London EC1A 2AL
Tel: (020) 7295 3000 Fax: (020) 7295 3500
Email: graduate.recruitment@traverssmith.com
Website: www.traverssmith.com

Firm profile

A leading City firm with a major Corporate and Commercial Practice. Although less than a quarter of the size of the dozen largest firms, they handle the highest quality work, much of which has an international dimension.

Main areas of work

Corporate law (including takeovers and mergers, private equity and funds), commercial law (which includes commercial contracts, IT and intellectual property), litigation, corporate recovery/insolvency, financial services and markets, tax, employment, EU/competition, pensions, banking and real estate. The firm also offers a range of pro bono opportunities within individual departments and on a firm wide basis and carries out commercial work for a number of UK charities.

Trainee profile

The firm looks for people who combine academic excellence with common sense; who are articulate, who think on their feet, who are determined and self motivated and who take their work but not themselves seriously. Applications are welcome from law and non-law graduates.

Training environment

Travers Smith has earned a phenomenal reputation in relation to its size. The work they undertake is exciting, intellectually demanding and top quality involving blue-chip clients and big numbers. This means that their trainees gain great experience right from the outset.

The firm has a comprehensive training programme which ensures that trainees experience a broad range of work. All trainee solicitors sit in rooms with partners and assistants, receive an individual and extensive training from experienced lawyers and enjoy client contact and the responsibility that goes with it from the beginning of their training contract.

Benefits

Private health insurance, permanent health insurance, life assurance, corporate health club membership, subsidised bistro, season ticket loan.

Vacation placements

Summer 2011: 3 schemes with 15 places on each; Duration: two weeks; Remuneration: £250; Closing Date: 31 January 2011. The firm also offers a two week Christmas scheme for 15 students.

Sponsorship & awards

GDL and LPC paid in full plus maintenance of £7,000 per annum to those in London and £6,500 per annum to those outside of London.

Partners 61
Assistant Solicitors 245
Total Trainees 48

Contact
Germaine VanGeyzel

Method of application
Online

Selection procedure
Interviews (2 stage process)

Closing date for 2013
31 July 2011

Application
Training contracts p.a. 25
Applications p.a. 2,000
% interviewed p.a. 15%
Required degree grade 2:1

Training
Salary
1st year (2009) £38,000
2nd year (2009) £42,000
Holiday entitlement 25 days

Post-qualification
Salary (2010) £60,000
% of trainees offered job
on qualification (2010) 81%

Trethowans LLP

London Road Office Park, London Road, Salisbury Wiltshire, SP1 3HP
Tel: 01722 412512 Fax: 01722 333011
Email: recruitment@trethowans.com Web: www.trethowans.com

Firm profile

Trethowans is a major law firm in the South, advising business and individual clients and has around 130 people, including 24 partners and over 40 lawyers across offices in Salisbury and Southampton. The firm represents international and national household brand names, owner-managed businesses, entrepreneurs and major regional employers across the UK. Service excellence is a priority - clients value the firm's ability to deliver top-quality, expert advice, on time, in a very personable manner and at a competitive price. The firm has expertise across six main industry sectors: property and pensions, healthcare, banking and finance, personal wealth, retail and leisure, media, manufacturing and distribution and agriculture and estates.

Main areas of work

The firm's business lawyers, who specialise in different areas of the law, work together to regularly advise international and national household brand names, owner-managed, entrepreneurial and major regional employers across the UK, Hampshire and Wiltshire. Five of the firm's six teams that advise business clients are rated in the two independent guides to the legal profession, Chambers Guide to the Legal Profession and Legal 500. Legal advice to businesses include: corporate, commercial, commercial property, commercial litigation, employment and licensing.

For individuals the firm's teams of expert lawyers deliver advice in a down-to-earth and approachable manner. The 'Trethowans' personality is particularly important so that individual clients can meet the 'real person' behind the lawyer. Four of the firm's five teams that advise individual clients are also rated in Chambers Guide to the Legal Profession and Legal 500. Legal advice to individuals include: personal injury, private client (Wills, trusts and tax), landed estates, family and residential property.

Trainee profile

Trainees should possess sound academic abilities and be able to demonstrate commercial acumen. Flexibility, ambition and enthusiasm are valued. Candidates should be good communicators and adopt a problem solving approach to client work.

Training environment

Trainee solicitors normally undertake four separate specialist seats, each lasting six months. The firm offers a flexible approach in deciding trainees' seats to suit individual needs, while providing a broad training programme in accordance with the Solicitors Regulation Authority guidelines. Trainees have their own desks and work closely with the supervising lawyer/Partner to whom they are responsible. They are considered an integral part of each team and become closely involved in the team's work to obtain first-hand legal experience. Each trainee is appraised every six months by their supervisor and the Training Partner. This enables the trainee scheme to be continually evaluated and also ensures that the highest possible standards are maintained. Prospects for trainees are excellent, most trainees are offered a post as an assistant solicitor at the end of their training contract.

Benefits

Incremental holiday entitlement up to 28 days, contributory pension scheme, death in service benefit, PHI scheme, performance-related bonus scheme, car parking, new staff recruitment bonus, childcare voucher scheme.

Sponsorship and awards

LPC course fees paid for if training contract secured prior to commencement of LPC.

Partners 24
Assistant Solicitors 20
Total Trainees 7

Contact
Kate Ellis
023 8082 0503

Method of application
Applications by application form (available online) and covering letter

Selection procedure
Two stage process; interview and assessment day

Closing date for 2013
29 July 2011

Application
Training contracts p.a. 3-4
Applications p.a. 100+
% interviewed p.a. 20-25%
Required degree grade
2:1

Training
Salary: in excess of Law Society minimum
Holiday entitlement 23 days

Post-qualification
Market rate
% of trainees offered position on qualification 100% (Nov 2009)

Regional offices
Salisbury, Southampton

TRETHOWANS
SOLICITORS

Trowers & Hamlins LLP

Sceptre Court, 40 Tower Hill, London EC3N 4DX
Tel: (020) 7423 8000 Fax: (020) 7423 8001
Email: hking@trowers.com Website: www.trowers.com

Firm profile

Trowers & Hamlins is a top 50, full service city law firm offering regional and international opportunities. The firm has UK offices in London, Manchester and Exeter and a long standing presence in the Middle East with offices in Abu Dhabi, Bahrain, Cairo, Dubai and Oman. Although known for its work in the Public Sector and Social Housing, there is far more to the firm than that and it is frequently listed as a key player in the corporate, banking and finance and commercial property sectors.

Main areas of work

Banking and finance, commercial property, corporate, dispute resolution and litigation, employment, housing projects, international, projects and construction, public sector communities and governance, public sector commercial and tax, trusts and pensions.

Trainee profile

The firm recruits twenty-two trainees each year split equally between September and March intakes. Each year the firm recruits one trainee to join the Exeter office and approximately three to join the Manchester office. The firm is naturally looking for an excellent academic record but in addition to this recognises that supplementary skills are required and actively seeks out candidates with exceptional commercial awareness, outstanding communication skills and a genuine passion for the law.

Training environment

The training contract is split into four six month seats. Offering secondment opportunities in the Middle East alongside seats in a wide range of departments, it is not surprising that trainees gain a varied and interesting experience. Trainees are paired with either a senior solicitor or Partner as their supervisor to ensure that a suitable level of support is provided. Assessment takes place constantly, with trainees completing both a mid seat and end of seat appraisal - providing the opportunity to gain regular feedback and continuously progress.

Responsibility is given from a very early stage with trainees in some departments running files on their own on joining the department. Trainees are encouraged to take as autonomous a role as is possible safe in the knowledge that there is a structured support system in place to provide assistance should they require it.

Training forms an integral part of the training contract with trainee solicitors receiving departmental training every week as part of the Monday Lunchtime Training Programme. In addition to this, further business skills training is provided covering vital skills such as presentation technique and negotiation practice.

Vacation placements

The firm runs three fortnight long vacation placements which are open to candidates wishing to commence training contracts in September 2013 and March 2014. Online applications should be submitted by 1 March via the firm's website.

Sponsorship & awards

GDL and LPC sponsorship is provided. In addition, those studying for either course will receive a maintenance grant of £6,000. All London based trainees will be required to undertake the LPC at Kaplan Law School.

Partners 106
Assistant Solicitors 179
Total Trainees 39

Contact
Hannah King, Graduate Development Manager

Method of application
Online application form

Selection procedure
Assessment centre, interviews, psychometric tests & practical test

Closing date for 2013
1 August 2011

Application
Training contracts p.a. 22
Applications p.a. 1,600
% interviewed p.a. 4%
Required degree grade 2:1 or higher

Training
Salary (subject to review)
1st year £35,000
2nd year £38,000
Holiday entitlement 25 days
% of trainees with a non-law degree p.a. 50%
No. of seats available abroad p.a. 12

Post-qualification
Salary (2010) £55,000
% of trainees offered job on qualification (2010) 70.5%

Offices
London, Exeter, Manchester, Abu Dhabi, Dubai, Oman, Bahrain and Cairo

Veale Wasbrough Vizards

Orchard Court, Orchard Lane, Bristol, BS1 5WS
Tel: (0117) 925 2020 Fax: (0117) 925 2025
Barnards Inn, 86 Fetter Lane, London, EC4A 1AD
Tel: (020) 7405 1234
Email: jobs@vwv.co.uk Website: www.vwv.co.uk

Firm profile

Veale Wasbrough Vizards acts nationally for clients in the education and charities, healthcare, public and family owned business sectors. VWV believes the quality of the service provided to clients is fundamental to the success and growth of the business.

The firm's combination of specialist expertise, genuine teamwork and client commitment sets us apart. Consequently the Partners have always made collaborative teamwork a high priority. The 300 staff at Veale Wasbrough Vizards are based at the firm's offices in the heart of two cities: Bristol and London.

Main areas of work

The firm provides full commercial law services and specialises in four key client sectors: education and charities, healthcare, public and family owned business sectors. VWV also offer a dedicated service to private clients, including estates and tax planning; as well as residential conveyancing through Convey Direct and personal injury claims through Augustines Injury Law.

Trainee profile

The firm recruits 8-10 trainees annually. It is looking for graduates who will become dynamic lawyers, who will make the most of the training opportunities and positively contribute to the future of the firm. Applicants should have proven academic ability, be good team players, with strong communication skills and commercial awareness.

Training environment

The firm offers its trainees early responsibility. It provides four seats of six months in a variety of departments, including, commercial and projects, commercial litigation, corporate, education, employment, private client and real estate (including construction and property litigation). Trainees therefore benefit from experience in a wide range of practice areas. Many of the firm's present Partners and senior lawyers trained with the firm and are now widely respected experts in their chosen field of specialism.

Sponsorship and awards

Successful candidates may be eligible for sponsorship for the Diploma in Law and/or Legal Practice Course, consisting of a grant for LPC fees and an interest-free loan.

Work experience/ schemes

The firm's summer vacation scheme offers a week's unpaid work experience, providing an insight into the day to day workings of a large firm of commercial lawyers, as students spend time in different legal teams.

Partners 49
Assistant Solicitors 86
Total Trainees 16

Contact
Angela Parfitt, Recruitment Manager

Method of application
Application form on website

Selection procedure
Interview

Closing date for September 2013
30 June 2011

Application
Training contracts p.a. 8-10
% interviewed (2009) 10%
Required degree grade
Preferably 2:1

Training
1st year £23,000
2nd year £25,000
Holiday entitlement 25 days plus bank holidays

Post-qualification
Salary £35,000
% of trainees offered job on qualification (2010) 87%

Vinson & Elkins

CityPoint, 33rd Floor, One Ropemaker Street, London, EC2Y 9UE
Tel: (020) 7065 6000 Fax: (020) 7065 6001

Firm profile

Vinson & Elkins is one of the largest international law firms and has been repeatedly ranked as the world's leading energy law firm. Founded in Houston in 1917 (and with an office in London for over 30 years), Vinson & Elkins currently has over 750 lawyers with offices in Abu Dhabi, Austin, Beijing, Dallas, Dubai, Hong Kong, Houston, London, Moscow, New York, Palo Alto, Shanghai, Tokyo and Washington, D.C.

Main areas of work

Cross-border M&A, private equity, corporate finance and securities advice (including London Main Market and AIM listings and international equity and debt capital markets), banking and finance, international energy transactions, project development and finance transactions, litigation and arbitration and tax.

Trainee profile

The firm is looking for ambitious individuals with strong academic results and sound commercial awareness. The ability to think laterally and creatively is essential, as is a need for common-sense and a willingness to take the initiative.

Training environment

The firm currently offers three to four training contracts commencing each September. These are not run on a rigid seat system, but instead a trainee will gain wide experience in many different areas, working with a wide variety of associates and partners from across the firm. V&E is proud of the fact it has twice won LawCareers Net awards for the quality of its training with a further three nominations.

Whilst the trainees are based in London, the firm is currently regularly seconding its trainees to other offices (particularly its offices in Abu Dhabi and Dubai).

Benefits

Private medical and dental, pension, season ticket loan, life assurance.

Vacation placements

Vinson & Elkins views vacation placements as a key part of its recruitment process. For summer 2011 apply by 28 February 2011, by way of online application form.

Sponsorship & awards

The firm pays all LPC course fees and a discretionary stipend (of up to £7,500) to assist with the LPC year.

Partners 10
Assistant Solicitors 17
Total Trainees 8

Contact
Mark Beeley (020) 7065 6046

Method of application
Online Application form

Selection procedure
Interview

Closing date for 2013
31 August 2011

Application
Training contracts p.a. 3-4
Applications p.a. 405
% interviewed p.a. 10%
Required degree grade 2:1

Training
Salary
1st year £40,000
2nd year £42,000
Holiday entitlement 25 days
% of trainees with a non-law degree p.a. 40%
No. of seats available abroad p.a. 4

Post-qualification
Salary £80,000
% of trainees offered job on qualification 95%

Overseas, Regional offices
Abu Dhabi, Austin, Beijing, Dallas, Dubai, Hong Kong, Houston, London, Moscow, New York, Palo Alto, Shanghai, Tokyo and Washington D.C.

Walker Morris

Kings Court, 12 King Street, Leeds LS1 2HL
Tel: (0113) 283 2500 Fax: (0113) 245 9412
Email: hellograduates@walkermorris.co.uk
Website: www.walkermorris.co.uk

Firm profile

Based in Leeds, Walker Morris is one of the largest commercial law firms in the North, with over 530 people, providing a full range of legal services to commercial and private clients both nationally and internationally.

Main areas of work

CDR, commercial, commercial property, construction, corporate, employment, finance, intellectual property, insolvency, liquor licensing and gaming, PFI/ public sector, planning and environmental, regulatory, sports, tax.

Trainee profile

Bright, articulate, highly motivated individuals who will thrive on early responsibility in a demanding yet friendly environment.

Training environment

Trainees commence with an induction programme, before spending four months in each main department (commercial property, corporate and commercial litigation). Trainees can choose in which departments they wish to spend their second year. Formal training will include lectures, interactive workshops, seminars and e-learning. The PSC covers the compulsory elements and the electives consist of a variety of specially tailored skills programmes. Individual IT training is provided. Opportunities can also arise for secondments to some of the firm's major clients. Emphasis is placed on teamwork, inside and outside the office. The firm's social and sporting activities are an important part of its culture and are organised by a committee drawn from all levels of the firm. A trainee solicitors' committee represents the trainees in the firm but also organises events and liaises with the Leeds Trainee Solicitors Group.

Vacation placements

Places for 2011: 48 over 3 weeks; Duration: 1 week; Remuneration: £250 p.w.; Closing Date: 31 January 2011.

Sponsorship & awards

LPC & PGDL fees plus maintenance of £5,000.

Partners 50
Assistant Solicitors 120
Total Trainees 28

Contact
Jo Ratcliffe

Method of application
Online application form

Selection procedure
Assessment centre & face-to-face interviews

Closing date for 2013
31 July 2011

Application
Training contracts p.a. 18
Applications p.a.
Approx. 800
% interviewed p.a.
Face to face 5%
Required degree grade 2:1

Training
Salary
1st year £24,000
2nd year £26,000
Holiday entitlement 24 days
% of trainees with a non-law degree p.a.
30% on average

Post-qualification
Salary £37,000
% of trainees offered job on qualification 82%
% of assistants who joined as trainees 55%
% of partners who joined as trainees 50%

Ward Hadaway

Sandgate House, 102 Quayside, Newcastle upon Tyne NE1 3DX
Tel: (0191) 204 4000 Fax: (0191) 204 4098
Email: recruitment@wardhadaway.com
Website: www.wardhadaway.com

Firm profile

Ward Hadaway is one of the most progressive law firms in the North East and is firmly established as one of the region's legal heavyweights. The firm attracts some of the most ambitious businesses in the region has a substantial client base of regional, national and international clients from the private and public sectors.

As a business founded and located in the North East, the firm has grown rapidly, investing heavily in developing its existing people, and recruiting further outstanding individuals from inside and outside of the region. The firm is listed in the top 100 UK law firms.

Main areas of work

The firm is divided into five main departments; litigation, property, corporate, commercial and private client, with a number of cross departmental teams. The firm is commercially based, satisfying the needs of the business community in both business and private life. Clients vary from international plcs to local, private clients. The firm is on a number of panels including; the Arts Council, NHS (four panels), English Heritage, Department of Education and the General Teaching Council.

Trainee profile

The usual academic and professional qualifications are sought. Sound commercial and business awareness are essential as is the need to demonstrate strong communication skills, enthusiasm and flexibility. Candidates will be able to demonstrate excellent interpersonal and analytical skills.

Training environment

The training contract is structured around four seats, each of six months duration. At regular intervals, and each time you are due to change seat, you will have the opportunity to discuss the experience you would like to gain during your training contract. The firm will give high priority to your preferences. You will work closely with a Partner or associate who will supervise and encourage you as you become involved in more complex work. Your practical experience will also be complemented by an extensive programme of seminars and lectures. All trainees are allocated a 'buddy', usually a second year trainee or newly qualified solicitor, who can provide as much practical advice and guidance as possible during your training. The firm has an active social committee and offers a full range of sporting and social events.

Benefits

25 days holiday (27 after five years service), death in service insurance, contributory pension, flexible holiday scheme, travel scheme.

Vacation placements

Vacation placements run spring/summer between June and July and are of 1 week's duration. Applications should be received by 28 February 2011.

Sponsorship & awards

CPE/GDL and LPC fees paid and maintenance grants in accordance with the terms of the firm's offer.

Partners 60
Total Trainees 18

Contact
Graduate recruitment team

Method of application
Firm's application form

Selection procedure
Assessment Centre and interview

Closing date for 2013
31 July 2011

Application
Training contracts p.a. 10
Applications p.a. 600+
% interviewed p.a. 10%
Required degree grade 2:1

Training
Salary
1st year (2009) £20,000
2nd year (2009) £20,500
Holiday entitlement 25 days
% of trainees with a non-law degree p.a. Varies

Post-qualification
Salary (2009) £35,000

Warner Goodman LLP

Portland Chambers, 66 West Street, Fareham, Hampshire, PO16 0JR
Tel: (01329) 288 121 Fax: (01329) 822 714
8/9 College Place, London Road, Southampton, SO15 2FF
Coleman House, 2-4 Landport Terrace, Portsmouth, PO1 2RG
Email: enquiries@warnergoodman.co.uk Website: www.warnergoodman.co.uk

Firm profile

Warner Goodman LLP is highly regarded in Hampshire as one of the county's most forward thinking and dynamic firms. The firm values its people highly and invests a lot of time in developing and nurturing their many talents. Work-life balance is respected and a flexible approach for those with caring responsibilities helps the firm retain many high performing fee earners. The firm takes particular pride in delivering professional client friendly services across its six legal disciplines. Advances in e-conveyancing, case management systems and paperless transactions are all exemplified at Warner Goodman.

Main areas of work

The firm is split into six business groups: WG Commercial (which handles all aspects of employment, company commercial, commercial litigation, commercial property, landlord and tenant and licensing), private client, injury, family, residential conveyancing and financial services.

Trainee profile

The firm seeks to recruit talented bright graduates with a good academic record together with a flair for communication and a common sense approach to business. The firm values an approachable, down to earth attitude. This way the firm can continue its track record in first-rate client service and can continue to put its clients first.

Training Environment

Training will comprise of four seats of six months' duration. Trainees may be asked to work at any of the firm's offices during the training contract giving trainees the opportunity of meeting as many people as possible throughout the firm and amongst the firm's clients, helping trainees to begin to establish their own reputation and following.

Sponsorship & awards

See website.

Partners 13
Total Trainees 3

Contact
Dan Thompson

Method of application
online application form

Selection procedure
Interview

Closing date for 2013
31 July 2011

Application
Average of 2 training contracts per year. Required degree grade 2:1

Training
Training is provided across the firms three offices, and covers each of the practice groups. Input from trainees is sought as to their preferred choice of seat

Post-qualification
Salary at market rate.
% of trainees offered job on qualification (2010) 66%

Regional offices
Fareham, Southampton, Portsmouth

Watson, Farley & Williams LLP

15 Appold Street, London EC2A 2HB
Tel: (020) 7814 8000 Fax: (020) 7814 8017
Email: graduates@wfw.com
Website: www.wfw.com/trainee

Firm profile

Watson, Farley & Williams was founded in 1982 in the City of London. It has since grown rapidly to 98 partners and a total staff of over 550. The firm now has offices in London, New York, Paris, Hamburg, Munich, Rome, Milan, Madrid, Athens, Piraeus, Singapore, Bangkok.

Watson, Farley & Williams is an international corporate and commercial law firm recognised for its excellence in banking, structured and asset financing, particularly in the transport and energy sectors. Through its international network the firm's lawyers are able to advise in many languages including English, French, German, Greek, Russian, Italian, Thai, as well as advising in US Federal law. The international offices work together, a structure of particular benefit to international clients.

Main areas of work

The firm is divided into five international practice groups: international corporate, international shipping finance, international project and structured finance, international litigation and international tax. These groups are not divided by location but work together internationally. The International Corporate Group is divided into several sub-groups: corporate, employment, EU/competition and commercial property.

Trainee profile

The firm looks to recruit graduates who, in addition to a sound academic background, exhibit enthusiasm, ambition, self-awareness, initiative and an understanding of the commerical world.

Training environment

Each trainee undertakes six four-month seats, one of which will be based in Paris, Piraeus, Singapore or Bangkok. From day one the firm aims to give trainees real experience by sitting them with a partner or a senior assistant.

Each trainee is also likely to have a seat in one of the firm's more specialised areas such as tax, property, employment or EU competition. Trainees undertake professional skills training during their training contract and the firm also holds regular in-house seminars at which it invites guest speakers and partners to speak.

Benefits

25 days holiday, Income Protection, Life Assurance, Employee Assistance Programme, Pension, Interest Free Season Ticket Loan, £250 towards Sports Club membership, Private Healthcare.

Vacation placements

Places for 2011: 30; Duration: 2 weeks; Remuneration: £250 p.w.; Closing Date: 31st January 2011.

Sponsorship & awards

GDL and LPC fees paid and £6,500 maintenance p.a. (£5,500 outside London).

Partners 98
Total fee-earners over 300
Total Trainees 26

Contact
Graduate Recruitment Manager

Method of application
Online application

Selection procedure
Assessment centre & Interview

Closing date for 2013
31 July 2011

Application
Training contracts p.a. 12-14
Applications p.a. 700
% interviewed p.a. 20-30%
Required degree grade
Minimum 2:1 & 300 UCAS points or above

Training
Salary
1st year (2010) £35,000
2nd year (2010) £40,000
Holiday entitlement 25 days
% of trainees with a non-law degree p.a. 50%
No. of seats available abroad p.a. 14

Post-qualification
Salary (2010)
£59,000
% of trainees offered job on qualification (2010) 90%
% of assistants (as at 01/09/10) who joined as trainees 52%
% of partners (as at 1/9/10) who joined as trainees 5%

Overseas offices
New York, Paris, Hamburg, Munich, Rome, Milan, Madrid, Athens, Piraeus, Singapore, Bangkok

Wedlake Bell

52 Bedford Row, London, WC1R 4LR
Tel: (020) 7395 3000 Fax: (020) 7395 3100
Email: recruitment@wedlakebell.com
Website: www.wedlakebell.com

Partners 43
Assistant Solicitors 49
Total Trainees 12

Contact
Natalie King

Method of application
Application form

Selection procedure
Two interviews & open day

Closing date for 2013
End of July 2011

Application
Training contracts p.a. 6
Required degree grade 2:1

Training
Holiday entitlement
1st year 23 days
2nd year 24 days
% of trainees with a non-law degree p.a. 50%

Firm profile

Wedlake Bell LLP is a medium-sized law firm providing legal advice to businesses and high net worth individuals from around the world. The firm's services are based on a high degree of partner involvement, extensive business and commercial experience and strong technical expertise. The firm has approximately 100 lawyers in central London and affiliations with law firms throughout Europe and in the United States.

Main areas of work

For the firm's business clients: banking & asset finance; corporate; corporate tax; business recoveries; commercial; intellectual property; information technology; media; commercial property; construction; residential property.

For private individuals: tax, trusts and wealth protection; offshore services; residential property.

Trainee profile

In addition to academic excellence, Wedlake Bell LLP looks for commercial aptitude, flexibility, enthusiasm, a personable nature, confidence, mental agility and computer literacy in its candidates. Languages are not crucial.

Training environment

Trainees have four seats of six months across the following areas: corporate, corporate tax, business recoveries, banking, construction, media and IP/IT, employment, pensions, litigation, property and private client. As a trainee, the firm encourages you to have direct contact and involvement with clients from an early stage. Trainees will work within highly specialised teams and have a high degree of responsibility. Trainees will be closely supervised by a partner or senior solicitor and become involved in high quality and varied work. The firm is committed to the training and career development of its lawyers and many of its trainees continue their careers with the firm, often through to partnership. Wedlake Bell has an informal, creative and co-operative culture with a balanced approach to life.

Sponsorship & benefits

LPC fees paid and £4,000 maintenance grant where local authority grant not available. During the training contract: pension, travel loans, corporate gym membership, health insurance and life assurance.

Vacation placements

Places for 2011: 8; Duration: 3 weeks in July; Remuneration: £250 p.w.; Closing Date: End of February, 2011.

Weil, Gotshal & Manges

One South Place, London EC2M 2WG
Tel: (020) 7903 1074 Fax: (020) 7903 0990
Email: graduate.recruitment@weil.com
Website: www.weil.com

Firm profile

International law firm Weil, Gotshal & Manges has over 1,200 lawyers, including 300 partners, in 20 cities throughout the US, Europe and Asia.

The London office was established in 1996 and has grown to become the second largest of the firm's worldwide offices, with over 110 lawyers, 85% of which are UK-qualified. The London office is the hub of the firm's European practice.

Main areas of work

The firm's Restructuring Practice is recognised as one of the leading practices in its field. The firm has been involved in virtually every major chapter 11 reorganisation case in the US, including Lehmans, Washington Mutual and Pilgrim's Pride, and in major international out-of-court debt restructurings. The London team continues to build on that market-leading reputation across Europe, coordinating international corporate aspects of Lehmans, advising Icelandic bank Kapustin and various SIC restructurings.

Balanced with its restructuring expertise, it is also one of the leading private equity law firms in London and Europe.

Lawyers in the office advise on all aspects of domestic and cross-border transactional and general corporate issues, including public and private mergers, acquisitions and disposals, demergers and re-organisations, equity capital markets, joint ventures and strategic alliances and corporate governance. Transactional support is provided by specialists in the fields of tax, real estate, commercial contracts, competition, employment/employee benefits, environment, IP/IT and pensions. The firm offers specialist sector focus across a range of industries including consumer brands, defence, energy, healthcare, technology, media and telecommunications.

Few firms can match the quality and depth of Weil Gotshal's experience in litigation, arbitration and other forms of dispute resolution. The firm helps clients solve their toughest problems in any forum throughout the world and has an impressive track record for winning extremely large and difficult cases.

The firm has an international Finance Practice including bank and institutional lending, acquisition finance (including senior and mezzanine debt), asset finance, derivatives, refinancings and recapitalisations, debt capital markets (including high yield), structured finance, lease financings and securitisation which continues to be among the very best practices in London.

The firm's Antitrust/Competition Practice is one of the largest, most diversified and highly respected in the legal and business community. The firm provides integrated global counseling, litigation, regulatory and transactional services to a wide range of industries.

Few firms place greater emphasis on pro bono work - the firm's award-winning programme is incredibly varied and upholds the highest standards of public service by the legal community.

Weil Gotshal also invests considerable time and effort in recruiting and retaining exceptional talent, from diverse backgrounds and cultures at all levels.

Vacation placements

Places for 2011 Summer: 15 places. Closing date for applications by online application form: 31 January 2011.

Partners 24
Assistant Solicitors 64
Total Trainees 24

Contact
Jillian Singh

Method of application
online application form

Closing date for 2013
31 July 2011

Application
Training contracts p.a. 10
Required degree grade 2:1

Training
Salary
1st year (2010) £41,000
Holiday entitlement 23 days

Overseas offices
Beijing, Boston, Budapest, Dallas, Dubai, Frankfurt, Hong Kong, Houston, Miami, Munich, New York, Paris, Prague, Providence, Silicon Valley, Singapore, Shanghai, Warsaw, Washington DC, Wilmington

Weil

White & Case LLP

5 Old Broad Street, London EC2N 1DW
Tel: (020) 7532 1000 Fax: (020) 7532 1001
Email: trainee@whitecase.com
Website: www.whitecasetrainee.com

Firm profile

White & Case LLP is a global law firm with more than 2,100 lawyers worldwide. The firm has a network of 36 offices, providing the full range of legal services of the highest quality in virtually every major commercial centre and emerging market. They work with international businesses, financial institutions and governments worldwide on corporate and financial transactions and dispute resolution proceedings. Their clients range from some of the world's longest established and most respected names to many start-up visionaries. The firm's lawyers work on a variety of sophisticated, high-value transactions, many of which feature in the legal press worldwide as the firm's clients achieve firsts in privatisation, cross-border business deals, or major development projects.

Main areas of work

Banking and capital markets; construction and engineering; corporate (including M&A and private equity); dispute resolution (including arbitration & mediation); employment & benefits; energy, infrastructure, project & asset finance; IP, PPP/PFI; real estate; tax; and telecommunications.

Trainee profile

Trainees should be ambitious, creative and work well in teams. They should have an understanding of international commercial issues and have a desire to be involved in high profile, cross-border legal matters.

Training environment

Trainees undertake four seats, each of six months in duration. The firm guarantees that one of these seats can be spent overseas. Regardless of where they work, trainees get a high level of partner and senior associate contact from day one, ensuring they receive high quality, stimulating and rewarding work. Trainees are encouraged to take early responsibility and there is a strong emphasis on practical hands-on training, together with plenty of support and feedback. The firm recruits and develops trainee solicitors with the aim of retaining them on qualification.

Benefits

The firm operates a flexible benefits scheme, through which you can select the benefits you wish to receive. Currently, the benefits include private medical insurance, dental insurance, life assurance, pension, critical illness insurance, travel insurance, retail vouchers, gym membership, season ticket loan and green bikes.

Vacation placements

Places for 2011: 12-15 two-week Easter placements and 40-50 two-week Summer placements available. Remuneration: £350 per week; Closing Date: 31 January 2011.

Sponsorship & awards

GDL and LPC fees and maintenance paid p.a. Awards for commendation and distinction for LPC.

Partners 55
Assistant Solicitors 187
Total Trainees 65

Contact
Shahnaz Begum

Method of application
Online application via firm website

Selection procedure
Interview
Closing date for August 2013/ February 2014
31 July 2011

Application
Training contracts p.a.30
Applications p.a. 1,600
Required degree grade 2:1

Training
Salary
£41,000, rising by £1,000 every 6 months
Holiday entitlement 25 days
All trainees are guaranteed to spend a seat overseas

Post-qualification
Salary £70,000

Overseas offices
Abu Dhabi, Almaty, Ankara, Beijing, Berlin, Bratislava, Brussels, Bucharest, Budapest, Düsseldorf, Frankfurt, Geneva, Hamburg, Helsinki, Hong Kong, Istanbul, Johannesburg, London, Los Angeles, Mexico City, Miami, Moscow, Munich, New York, Palo Alto, Paris, Prague, Riyadh, São Paulo, Singapore, Shanghai, Stockholm, Tokyo, Warsaw, Washington DC

Wiggin LLP

10th Floor, Met Building, 22 Percy Street, London, W1T 2BU
Tel: (020) 7612 9612 Fax (020) 7612 9611
The Promenade, Cheltenham GL50 1WG
Tel: (01242) 224114 Fax: (01242) 224223
Email: law@wiggin.co.uk Website: www.wiggin.co.uk

Firm profile

Wiggin are experts in the constantly evolving field of media law. They focus exclusively on media with particular emphasis on film, music, sport, gaming, technology, broadcast and publishing. They are recognised for the uncompromising excellence of their work and an unrelenting determination to deliver the best possible results for their media clients. They have an international reputation for their innovative approach, fresh thinking and cutting edge experience in media law; a sector that is changing with mesmerizing speed. The firm offers a highly personalised relationship, working in partnership with its clients to address the complex legal challenges that the fast evolving media industry presents. They have the knowledge and experience, as well as the commitment and confidence, to deliver straightforward and genuine advice motivated only by the need to achieve the best possible outcome for clients. Based primarily out of their Cheltenham office, and also in London, and with blue-chip clients based all over the World (primarily London and the west coast of America) the firm goes to where clients need them to be.

Main areas of work

Commercial 60%, Corporate 18%, Litigation 22%.

Trainee profile

If you want to experience high profile media issues in a forward thinking environment then contact Wiggin. They're looking for you if you can demonstrate a passion for media and the law, strong academic ability and a commitment to success. One word of warning though, their seats are not for the faint hearted! They need trainees that relish hard work and a challenge. They'll be at the law fairs so come and see what they are all about.

Training environment

Training is split into four seats and these will be allocated from company/commercial, commercial media (2 seats), media litigation, employment, film and property. Although based at the Cheltenham office, you will be meeting clients in London and could end up on a six-month secondment there with the British Phonographic Industry (the record industry's trade association).

They don't want you to do the photocopying. Their trainees are encouraged to take an active role in transactions, assume responsibility and deal directly with clients. In-house seminars are held regularly and training reviews are held every three months. You'll get an experience just like your friends in the City but within the exciting and niche area of media law and within a firm small enough to recognise the importance of a personal approach.

Benefits

Life assurance, private health cover, pension scheme, permanent health insurance, gym membership at corporate rates.

Sponsorship & awards

PgDL and LPC fees and £3,500 maintenance p.a.

Partners 16
Assistant Solicitors 22
Total Trainees 5

Contact
Office Manager

Method of application
Online application only – www.wiggin.co.uk

Selection procedure
Interview followed by two-day selection

Closing date for 2013
31 July 2011

Application
Training contracts p.a. 3
Applications p.a. 250
% interviewed p.a. 20%
Required degree grade 2:1

Training
Salary
1st year £32,000
2nd year £36,000
Holiday entitlement 20 days + one day per annum up to max 25 days
% of trainees with a non-law degree p.a. 50%

Post-qualification
Salary £50,000
% of trainees offered job on qualification (2009) 60%
% of assistants (as at 2009) who joined as trainees 20%
% of partners (as at 2009) who joined as trainees 19%

Wilsons Solicitors LLP

Steynings House, Summerlock Approach, Salisbury, Wiltshire, SP2 7RJ
Tel: (01722) 412 412 Fax: (01722) 427 610
Email: jo.ratcliffe@wilsonslaw.com
Website: www.wilsonslaw.com

Firm profile

Wilsons is ranked as one of the top private client and charity law firms in the country. The firm's 270-year heritage, combined with lawyers who are recognised leaders in their fields, enables the firm to provide a unique combination of skills and experience to wealthy individuals, entrepreneurs, companies, landed estates, trust companies and charities.
Working from the Salisbury and London offices, the firm currently employs 183 people, 61 of whom are lawyers and 32 are partners. The firm prides itself on the quality of its bespoke service delivery. Lawyers are dedicated to ensuring a detailed understanding of clients' interests and a seamless working relationship across the different specialities of the practice.

Main areas of work

Private Client: One of the largest private client teams outside of London, its leading practice delivers services which include tax, estate and succession planning, UK and Offshore tax and trusts, Wills, probate and trust administration, litigation and family.
Charities & Education: One of the top five charity practices in the country offering clients corporate and governance advice and both contentious and non-contentious legacy work for the charity.
Company Commercial: The team specialise in employment, commercial property, insolvency, mergers and acquisitions and corporate finance.
Agriculture & Rural Affairs: Many of the firm's clients are substantial land owners and the highly regarded team offer services including property transactions, litigation, tax planning and advice on diversification. The team also specialise in landowner development, working solely for landowners.

Trainee profile

The firm aims to employ the highest quality people. Its reputation relies upon this. The firm places considerable emphasis on teamwork and for this reason it looks for applicants who are clear team players. If quality of life is important to you, the firm would like to meet you.

Training environment

Despite the firm's national and international client base the centre of its operations are situated in Salisbury. During its 270 year history the firm has attracted several senior City lawyers and an enviable client base. This ensures an exceptional quality of work within beautiful surroundings. An open approach to management means information is available across the firm and a flat structure means plenty of potential for positions of responsibility.
A two year training contract enables trainees to samples four disciplines with six monthly seats in different practice areas.

Benefits

Pension (2% in first year, 3% in second year), life assurance (2 times salary), choice of optional benefits and private medical insurance.

Work experience placements

One week available in July at our head office in Salisbury.

Sponsorship & awards

On joining the firm as a trainee the firm can offer you an interest free loan of up to £4,500 for the Legal Practice Course. The firm is committed to your training contract and would hope to retain you once you qualify. If you stay with Wilsons for two years after qualifying the loan will be written off.

Partners 32
Trainees 8
Total Staff 183

Contact
Mrs J Ratcliffe
jo.ratcliffe@wilsonslaw.com

Method of application
Application via website or CV

Selection procedure
interview and assessment day

Closing dates for
training scheme:
31 July 2011 for training contract to commence in September 2012 and 2013

Application
Training contracts p.a. 4
Required degree grade 2:1
Salary
market rate
Holiday entitlement 22 days

Offices
Salisbury, London

Winckworth Sherwood

Minerva House, 5 Montague Close, London, SE1 9BB
Tel: (020) 7593 5000 Fax: (020) 7593 5099
Email: trainees@wslaw.co.uk
Website: www.wslaw.co.uk

Firm profile

Winckworth Sherwood is a dynamic law firm with a commitment to provide clients with more than just legal advice. The firm's diversity is its strength and its lawyers include leading specialists in their fields many with deep personal investment in the firm's clients sectors. This gives trainees a broad exposure to the law as well as a deeper understanding of the sectors which the firm supports. The firm is at the forefront of the private and public sector interface and its modern and collaborative approach enables it to adapt to its clients' individual businesses, providing them with pragmatic solutions to their whole range of requirements. The firm has offices in London, Oxford and Chelmsford although training only takes place at its London office.

Main areas of work

The firm's main specialist areas include real estate, social housing, house building, planning, parliamentary, transport, commercial, ecclesiastical, private client, licensing, dispute resolution and employment. Clients are diverse and include Genesis Housing Group, Barratt, Bellway, Sainsbury's, a number of public audit bodies, the Rail and Safety Standards Board (RSSB), the Church of England, the Port of London Authority and the Department for Transport.

Trainee profile

The firm requires a strong academic record both at school and university, but it also looks for attributes which demonstrate the potential for making a positive contribution to the firm. It is important to be able to empathise with clients whilst at the same time keeping a clear business head; the firm looks for evidence of these qualities at the outset. The firm is also interested in indications of high achievement in non-academic pursuits. It is a highly individual firm and wants independent, intelligent and personable trainees – not a type. It wants people who, after training, can provide a client with new ideas, bring a fresh approach and help them achieve desired results in a changing legal environment.

Training environment

The firm recruits five trainee solicitors a year; it keeps the number deliberately low to maximise the staff/trainee ratio, so that its trainees are fully involved in all aspects of each department in their two year training period. As a trainee you will rotate through four departments in six month placements or 'seats'. The purpose of each seat is to give you a solid grounding in that area of the law. The firm encourages substantial client contact from the start and you will be involved in all phases of a matter. As a trainee you will usually sit with a partner or senior solicitor and may be given the opportunity to manage your own files, subject to suitable supervision. The firm has a well developed in-house continuing education programme which draws upon the expertise of partners, qualified staff and guest professionals, in which trainees are encouraged to participate.

Benefits

Private health insurance, season ticket loan, life insurance, corporate gym membership. Holiday entitlement is 24 days plus public holidays.

Sponsorship & awards

Under certain conditions the firm also provides financial assistance to trainees attending the Legal Practice Course (LPC) or Graduate Diploma in Law (GDL).

Partners 36
Assistant Solicitors 52
Total Trainees 10

Contact
Hugh MacDougald, Training Partner (020) 7593 5149
Heather Cornish (HR) (020) 7593 5077

Method of application
Online application form on website www.wslaw.co.uk

Selection procedure
Two interviews

Closing date for 2013
31 July 2011

Application
Training contracts p.a. 5
Applications p.a. 200
% interviewed p.a. 13%
Required degree grade 2:1

Withers LLP

16 Old Bailey, London EC4M 7EG
Tel: (020) 7597 6000 Fax: (020) 7329 2534
Email: jaya.louvre@withersworldwide.com
Website: www.withersworldwide.com

Partners 113
Total Staff 650
Trainees 36

Contact
Jaya Louvre
Recruitment Manager

Method of application
Application form (available online)

Selection procedure
2 interviews incl. written exercise and presentation

Closing dates for 2013
Training scheme:
31 July 2011
2011 vacation placements:
31 January 2011

Application
Training contracts p.a. 16
Applications p.a. 700
% interviewed p.a. 10%
Required grades 2:1, AAB at A-Level

Training
Salary
1st year (2010) £33,000
2nd year (2010) £35,000
Holiday entitlement 23 days
% of trainees with a non-law degree p.a. 50%

Post-qualification
Salary (2010) £53,000

Offices
London, Milan, Geneva, New York, New Haven, (Connecticut), Greenwich (USA), Hong Kong, BVI

Firm profile

Withers LLP is the first international law firm dedicated to the business, personal and philanthropic interests of successful people, their families, their businesses and their advisers.

The firm's mission is to offer a truly integrated legal service to people with sophisticated global wealth, management and business needs.

Main areas of work

The wealth of today's private client has increased in multiples and many are institutions in their own right. Withers has been able to respond to these changing legal needs and offers integrated solutions to the international legal and tax needs of its clients. The firm has unparalleled expertise in commercial and tax law, trusts, estate planning, litigation, charities, employment, family law and other legal issues facing high net worth individuals.

Withers' reputation in commercial law along with its status as the largest Private Client Team in Europe and leading Family Team sets it apart from other City firms.

International exposure at Withers does not mean working in one of the firm's foreign offices, (although trainees can do seats abroad). Much of the work undertaken in London crosses numerous jurisdictions. Currently the firm acts for around a quarter of The Sunday Times Rich List and a significant number of the US 'Forbes' and Asian 'Hurun' Rich Lists.

Trainee profile

Each year the firm looks for a diverse mix of trainees who are excited by the prospect of working with leaders in their field. Trainees must have an excellent academic background and great attention to detail. Team players with leadership potential are of interest to the firm, as is an international outlook and foreign language skills.

Training environment

Trainees spend six months in four different departments. Working in a team with a Partner and an Assistant Solicitor provides autonomy, responsibility and fast development. Buddy and mentor systems as well as on the job training ensure Trainees are fully supported from the outset.

Application

Apply online by 31 July 2011 to begin training in August 2013. Interviews take place between April and September.

Vacation scheme

The firm runs two week long placements at easter and over the summer in London and during the summer in Milan. Apply online by 31 January 2011 for places in 2011. Interviews take place between January and March.

Sponsorship

Fees plus £5,000 maintenance for both the PgDL or CPE and/or LPC are paid.

withers LLP

- **Dress to impress:** You'd be surprised at just how many complaints we heard from recruiters in 2010 about poorly turned-out interviewees. Guys in cardies or just looking grubby; girls in sky-high shoes they couldn't walk in, and/or the shortest of skirts (and, yes, some revealed their underwear). Get your mum to check you over before you leave the house.

The Bar

Barcode	678
A career at the Bar	679
The Inns of Court	684
Practice areas at the Bar	686
Chambers Reports	694

Barcode

Don't let the often curious terms used at the Bar confuse or intimidate you!

Bar Council – the General Council of the Bar, to give it its full title, is the Bar's representative body. It can be found clashing regularly with the Ministry of Justice.

Bar Standards Board – or BSB, is the Bar's regulatory body.

Barrister – a member of the Bar of England and Wales.

Bench – the judiciary.

Bencher – a senior member of an Inn of Court. Usually silks and judges, known as Masters of the Bench.

Brief – the documents setting out case instructions.

BPTC – the Bar Professional Training Course. Successful completion entitles you to call yourself a barrister in non-legal circumstances (ie dinner parties) but does not give you rights of audience.

BPTC Online – the application system through which applications to Bar school must be made.

Cab-rank rule – self-employed barristers cannot refuse instructions if they have the time and experience to undertake the case. You cannot refuse to represent someone because you find their opinions or actions objectionable.

Call – the ceremony whereby you become a barrister.

Chambers – a group of barristers in independent practice who have joined together to share the costs of practising. Chambers is also the name used for a judge's private office.

Circuit – the courts of England and Wales are divided into six circuits: North Eastern, Northern, Midland & Oxford, South Eastern, Western and Wales & Chester circuits.

Clerk – administrator/manager in chambers who organises work for barristers and payment of fees, etc.

Counsel – a barrister.

Cracked trial – a case that is concluded without a trial. This will be because the defendant offers an acceptable plea or the prosecution offers no evidence. Cracked and ineffective trials (where there is a lack of court time or the defendant or a witness does not attend) frustrate the Bench and are considered a waste of money.

Devilling – (paid) work done by a junior member of chambers for a more senior member.

Employed Bar – some barristers do not engage in private practice at chambers, but are employed full-time by a company or public body.

First and second six – pupillages are divided into two six-month periods. Most chambers now only offer 12-month pupillages; however, it is still possible to undertake the two sixes at different sets.

FRU – the Free Representation Unit. Any budding barrister should consider membership of this organisation. For more details go to our website.

Independent Bar – the collective name for barristers who practise on a self-employed basis.

Inns of Court – ancient institutions that alone have the power to 'make' barristers. There was a time when there was a proliferation of them but now there are only four: Gray's Inn, Inner Temple, Lincoln's Inn and Middle Temple.

Junior – a barrister not yet appointed silk. Note: older juniors are known as senior juniors.

Junior brief – a case on which a junior is led by a senior. Such cases are too much work for one barrister alone and may involve a lot of research or run for a long time. Ordinarily, junior counsel will not conduct advocacy.

Keeping term – eating the dinners in hall required to be eligible for call to the Bar.

Mess – the hierarchical groups of four in which students sit during dining sessions. 'Mixed messes' means that barristers and masters sit with students.

Mini-pupillage – a short period of work experience spent in chambers.

Moot – a legal debate in which students act as claimants or respondents in an appeal court (ie the Court of Appeal or Supreme Court). Typically, there will be two students on each team, acting as either senior or junior.

Pupillage – the year of training undertaken after Bar school and before tenancy.

Pupillage Portal – the online application system for pupillage.

Pupilmaster – a senior barrister with whom a pupil sits and who teaches the pupil. The Bar Council is encouraging the term pupil supervisor.

QC – one of Her Majesty's Counsel, formerly appointed by the Lord Chancellor. The system fell into disuse in 2004 and has now been revived with a new, more open appointments system. In the reign of a male monarch, the term is KC (King's Counsel).

Set – as in a 'set of chambers'.

Silk – a QC, so named because of their silk robes.

Supervisor – the new name for a pupilmaster.

Tenant/tenancy – permission from chambers to join their set and work with them. A 'squatter' is someone who is permitted to use chambers' premises, but is not actually a member of the set. A 'door tenant' is someone who is affiliated with the set, but does not conduct business from chambers' premises.

A career at the Bar

Being a barrister is, to quote one sage QC, 'quite simply, the best job in the world'. True, the Bar is a highly competitive world in which the hours can be punishing and the work arduous, but the equation of excitement, advocacy, extraordinary experiences, a sense of personal fulfilment and kudos is unique.

Essential Bar stats: a harsh reality

Small wonder then that becoming a barrister is so deeply competitive. The statistics are sobering: the number of candidates starting the Bar Vocational Course (as it was known until 2010) rose from 1,407 in 2000/01 to 1,749 in 2008/09, while the total number of 'first-six' pupillages available fell from 695 to 463 in the same period. Hoping to address this over-subscription by raising admission standards for the new Bar Professional Training Course (BPTC), the Bar Standards Board has given legs to some of the recommendations of *The Wood Report*. An aptitude test, for example, is being piloted in 2011 to establish applicants' suitability for the BPTC. The hard fact is that roughly only one in four who commence the course gain pupillage and even fewer achieve the ultimate goal of tenancy. These odds will probably discourage the casual applicant, but the average would-be barrister is made of stern stuff and usually has a deep-seated commitment to this branch of the profession.

Will you make it?

So, we've established your vocational drive, but what else helps you make the grade? This is a hard one. Meet enough pupils and barristers and you can see what makes someone successful. The fact that you're gobby/argumentative/confident doesn't mean you'll make it, nor is success guaranteed by superstar academic results and an ability to complete the *Times* crossword in three minutes. Ask a chambers recruiter to define the qualities they look for and they will speak in fairly general terms (academic credentials, people skills, analytical skills, commitment, passion, an ability to express ideas) with the vague caveat that 'you know a good one when you see one'. Perhaps it's best to say that those who thrive at the Bar are people who offer the right traits for their chosen area of practice. Crime is all about guts, personality, advocacy ability and being to-the-point, down-to-earth and capable of assimilating and recalling facts easily. It's not necessary to be a genius. Commercial practice is a more sophisticated game. Intelligence, an analytical mind, excellence on paper, commercial acumen and an easy manner with business clients are a must, and specialisms like tax attract true brainboxes. While advocacy is still important in commercial practice, deriving pleasure from crafting a masterpiece of written advice or explaining a phenomenally complex legal argument succinctly is arguably even more so. By reading the **Chambers Reports** and **Practice Areas at the Bar** you will understand more about the skills required in the various specialist areas of practices.

Is the cost of training prohibitive?

The GDL conversion course is quite expensive and the BPTC is painfully expensive, so you need to be fairly confident about your prospects of succeeding at the Bar. Many criminal or general common law sets pay their pupils the bare minimum award of £833.33 per month (as prescribed by the Bar Council). Some commercial sets make large pupillage awards available, ensuring that they are in line with the salaries of trainee solicitors at big City solicitors firms; they will even advance funds for the BPTC year. Unless you've a source of cash, getting through law school and pupillage is a pricey business most commonly funded through bank or parental loans. Read the Funding section on page 77 for more ideas. Of all the potential sponsors out there, the four Inns of Court have the deepest pockets and they make more than £4.5m available each year to students. See page 684 for more on the Inns.

Huge debts aren't so much of a problem if you'll soon be earning a fat income, but the common perception that all barristers are loaded isn't quite right. Those determined to serve their community will find the public funding of civil, family and criminal cases is in the midst of a rationalisation by the Legal Services Commission (LSC). Go to our website if you want to read more about the state of Legal Aid in the UK. Despite this gloomy prognosis, it is worth remembering that privately paying clients still need legal advice and commercial sets continue to thrive. There's no question that tenancy at one of the best commercial sets pays very well indeed: some Comm Bar stars earn well over £1m a year, while pupils who make it to tenancy in good-quality sets can outstrip the salaries of their solicitor peers immediately.

Do remember that within each area of practice at the Bar there are a few Premier League sets and many others in lower divisions: the difference in earnings between the top and the bottom is substantial.

Get Bar ready

If you're still at university there's plenty you can do to prepare yourself for a shot at the Bar. If there is anything a little *outré* about your CV – you're mature or you have poor A levels, for instance – getting a First is the best idea. Applicants with 2:1s are two a penny and a 2:2 will scupper your chances unless you can evidence some truly remarkable alternative qualities. In general, chambers are more interested in your undergraduate performance than what you can muster up on the BPTC, but frankly you should try to get the best grades at every stage. As for postgraduate degrees – a master's from a very good university, either in the UK or abroad – it must be your choice whether to undertake one or not. All we can say is that many of the Bar's most successful candidates have such a qualification, though by no means all of them. A master's degree is no silver bullet.

The best way to demonstrate commitment to the Bar is to undertake mini-pupillages – that's barristerspeak for work experience. Whether assessed or unassessed, minis all involve observing barristers in chambers and probably also in court, although the degree of involvement varies hugely from one set to another. A good mini will see you sit in on a pre-trial conference (with the client's permission) and be included in discussions about the law. Don't become fixed on the idea of spending a whole week in chambers as you may find it easier, more economical and just as beneficial to get a couple of days here and there. Assessed minis have an added element of paperwork or grading through oral discussion. A typical scenario will see mini-pupils given a set of papers to analyse before producing a piece of written work, which may then be discussed with a supervisor. Some sets only conduct assessed minis or make them a formal part of the recruitment process, but the average set recognises that would-be pupils can't go everywhere and during our travels around the Bar this year we met many pupils who hadn't done a mini at their own set.

A mini-pupillage is an important point of contact with a set and an opportunity to show your mettle and create a good impression for a later application. It's also CV and interview fodder: take notes, don't be afraid to ask questions at appropriate moments and be sure to reflect on what was good and bad about your experiences. Recruiters tell us that candidates who simply list or describe legal work experience fall down in comparison with those who can articulate what they've learned from shadowing practitioners.

Not all sets offer mini-pupillages, and some will only take students in the final year of academic legal studies (be it degree or GDL), so start off by checking their websites carefully for how and when to apply. In general you should aim for as many as it takes you to decide which areas of practice interest you. Gaining pupillage may be a strictly fair process these days, but personal contacts can still help in obtaining a mini. Apply to an Inn of Court to be assigned a sponsor, or if you've started dining at your Inn then start schmoozing. There are more networking tips on our website.

Stand out from the crowd

The Bar Standards Board prescribes that BPTC students must undertake a certain amount of pro bono work. To ensure that you do land something that interests you and adds real weight to a pupillage application form, it is a good idea to investigate the options as soon as possible. You should also heed the advice of the QC who said: 'Do everything you can.' Get involved with every debating and mooting opportunity that crops up, enter mock trial competitions at law school and keep an eye out for essay competitions. The scholarships offered by the Inns are not just a way of funding your education: don't underestimate the capacity of a major prize or award to mark you out from other well-qualified candidates.

Through the Portal

Unless taking time out from academia, most LLB candidates start to make pupillage applications during their final undergraduate year, although in an attempt to snap up the best candidates some of the top commercial sets encourage students to apply in their penultimate year. In general, however, a large number of pupillage offers tend to be made to students following the completion of the BPTC. In 2009, the Bar Council brought in a new pupillage application system called Pupillage Portal, which lets users tailor their applications for each of the sets they apply to. The maximum number of sets users can apply to through the Portal is 12 and the Pupillage Portal operates just once a year. Though participation is voluntary for chambers, if they run their own separate application schemes they must still advertise all vacancies on the Portal website www.pupillages.com and in the *Pupillages Handbook*, which is published in March each year to coincide with the National Pupillage Fair in London.

The Portal is reasonably easy to use, though drama can be avoided if you fill out all the required details in a word document and then paste it into the required fields. In general, the fields in which you write are generously sized, with a maximum of around 350 words allowed for your perfect answers to questions like 'Why do you want to be a barrister?' and 'What areas of law interest you?' You also have 300 words for a 'covering letter' and a further 500 to discuss any further experiences you feel are relevant. Additionally, sets are now able to add a unique tailor-made question to the form. This year we heard

'Which book do you most resemble?' was popular. Do bear in mind that chambers' recruiters can feel quite worn down by excessively long forms, so try to find the right balance between detailed and snappy answers, and definitely leave out that one time you went to band camp.

Students can be alerted by e-mail or SMS with the results of their applications, and remember, when you do get good news you have at least two weeks to make a decision. It's important to remember that if you withdraw from the Portal you cannot reapply in the same year, so save yourself the grief and do your research thoroughly before selecting your 12 sets.

It is possible to use the Portal to make a single 'clearing' application. This facility is also used by those who were unsuccessful with all of their 12 first-round applications. The Portal clearing phase allows sets with unfilled vacancies to scout for suitable candidates. It is for the sets to make the first move and applicants are advised not to approach them directly. In making a clearing application it's best to keep your parameters as wide as possible to retain your appeal to a broad range of sets. Your application will be accessible to all chambers participating in the clearing process. As of 2010, clearing applications could be made between March and mid-September, and October was the month when chambers could view them and make their approaches.

Beyond the Portal

A good number of sets recruit pupils outside the Portal machinery because they don't like its format or timetable and feel their interests will be better served by other means. The application method at each non-Portal set will be different; however, all must still advertise vacancies on www.pupillages.com. Some choose to mirror the Portal timetable in their own application procedures, but many don't and this can bring its own problems. The 'exploding offer' phenomenon is a real difficulty: what do you do if a non-Portal set makes you an attractive offer before your 12 Portal applications play out? The decision here must be yours. The good news is that non-Portal sets are generally very good at laying out the specifics of their application process on their websites.

Interviews: getting them right

So you've got an interview – well done. Dress neatly and discreetly with hair tidy, teeth flossed, tie sober, jacket done up. Most chambers will be grading you on standard criteria that include everything from intellect to personality, and many publish their guidelines online.

You can expect your first interview to involve a discussion of the hottest topics in your prospective practice area and some investigation into you and your application form. Remember: you'll face a panel that wants you to stand out. Naturally you should read *The Times'* law supplement every Thursday (you can get it e-mailed), keep your subscription to *Counsel* up to date and maybe even set the Pupillage Portal website as your homepage. Preparation for interviews should consist of more than boning up on the law; now more than ever it's also important to be clued-up on current affairs. Finally, think about what isn't on your CV and how you can account for disappointing grades or anything that is missing.

For second interviews expect a larger panel made up of a broader cross-section of people from chambers. While the format of the interviews may vary between sets, the panel will always want to assess the depth of your legal knowledge, your advocacy potential and your strength of character. Weaknesses on your CV will be sniffed out and pursued with tenacity. Don't let them push you around; if you can support your position then stick to it. Resolve is just as necessary for a career at the Bar as receptivity; recruiters want to know that you can fight your corner. As one observed: "*It is amazing how many people can't stand up for themselves, which is all you want to see.*"

Criminal and mixed sets will commonly give you an advocacy exercise, such as a bail application or a plea in mitigation (their basic structures will fit on a post-it, so why not note them down and keep with you at all times). Most sets, if not all, will pose a legal problem, although the amount of preparation time you are given can range from ten minutes to a week. If you know that this is going to happen then do take an appropriate practitioner's text unless you know that one will be made available to you. That said, chambers generally aren't looking for faultless knowledge of substantive law, but they are trying to get an insight into how your mind works. As one seasoned interviewer explained: "*We are more interested in seeing how a candidate approaches a problem than whether or not they get the right answer.*" Of course, other recruiters may not be so forgiving! A second interview is often the time when an ethics question may raise its head. You can prepare by reading the Bar's Code of Conduct, which is available on the Bar Council's website.

Of course, to all rules there are exceptions, but these days sets are pretty good about detailing their procedures online, so with the right research you shouldn't be in for any shocks.

Try, try and try again?

What if you still don't have pupillage by the time you have finished the BPTC? Rather than seeing an enforced year out as a grim prospect, view it as a time to improve your CV and become more marketable. If you are interested in a specialist area of practice consider a master's degree. If the thought of another year in education brings you out in a cold sweat then seek out some useful practical experience. The most obvious answer is to apply for paralegalling and outdoor clerking jobs at solicitors' firms. Although these positions are rarer than hens' teeth, right now, the work you do as a paralegal should teach you how cases actually work and how solicitors – your future clients – operate. As a clerk you will be in court all the time taking notes. This will give you insight into the procedures and politics of trials. The year might also be spent with an organisation that works in an area related to your legal interest. We have interviewed several lawyers who secured pupillages following a period with a company, charity or not-for-profit organisation.

Pupillage

If you do gain a pupillage, congratulations! Now the hard work really starts. How the pupillage year is divided varies from set to set, but no matter how many pupil supervisors are allotted, the broad division is between the first, non-practising six months and the second, when pupils are permitted to be on their feet in court. During the first six, pupils are tethered to their supervisor, shadowing them at court, conferences and in chambers. They will also likely draft pleadings, advices and skeletons or do research for the matters their supervisor is working on. The nature of the second six will depend on the specific area of practice. At a busy criminal set it can mean court every day, and many civil or commercial sets specialising in areas like employment, PI, construction or insurance will send their pupils out up to three times a week. Some big commercial or Chancery sets actively prefer to keep pupils in chambers throughout the year, either for the purposes of assessment or because of the nature of the work means pupils are simply too inexperienced.

Tenancy

Tenancy is the prize at the end of the year-long interview that is pupillage. Effectively, an offer of tenancy is an invitation from a set to take a space in their chambers as a self-employed practitioner, sharing the services of the clerking and administrative teams. How many tenants a set takes on post-pupillage is usually as dependent on the amount of space and work available in chambers as on the quality of the candidates. If you are curious about a set's growth, check to see how many new tenants have joined in recent years by viewing the list of members on its website and compare that against the number of pupillages offered in the same period.

Usually tenancies are awarded after a vote of all members of chambers, following recommendations from a tenancy committee, clerks and possibly also instructing solicitors. Decisions are commonly made in the July of the pupillage year, allowing unsuccessful pupils time to cast around for other tenancy offers or a 'third six' elsewhere. There is evidence to suggest that civil and commercial sets have higher pupil-to-tenant conversion rates than criminal sets. Certainly, it is quite usual for a 12-month criminal pupillage to be followed by a third or subsequent six somewhere other than at a pupil's first set. However, plenty of commercial pupils do also find themselves looking for a third six. The general rule is that if a third six is not successful, it is perhaps time to look outside the Bar. It's been reasonably common for pupils to move to solicitors' firms, although since September 2010 the option of swiftly re-qualifying as a solicitor by taking the Qualified Lawyers Transfer Test (QLTT) is no longer available. That said, the regulatory barriers that prevented barristers from becoming law firm partners have now been lifted by the Legal Services Act.

And finally...

Few readers will have changed their minds about a career at the Bar after reading these pages. If there's one thing wannabe-barristers have in common it is a firm belief that they are one of the lucky ones who will succeed.

	99-00	00-01	01-02	02-03	03-04	04-05	05-06	06-07	07-08	08-09	09-10
BVC applicants	2,370	2,252	2,119	2,067	2,570	2,883	2,917	2,870	2,864	2,540	2,657
BVC enrolments	1,490	1,407	1,386	1,332	1,406	1,665	1,745	1,932	1,837	1,749	1,793
Students passing the BVC	1,201	1,081	1,188	1,121	1,251	1,392	1,480	1,560	1,720	1,330	n/a
First-six pupils	681	695	812	586	518	571	515	527	561	463	342 (1)
Second-six pupils	704	700	724	702	557	598	567	563	554	515	460 (1)
Pupils awarded tenancy	511	535	541	698	601	544	531	499	494	497	261 (2)

Certain figures were unavailable from the Bar Council at the time of going to press. The BVC was replaced by the Bar Professional Training Course in 2010.
(1) Figures from period 1st October 2009-16th July 2010 (2) Figures from period 1st October 2009-11th December 2009

- **Wise words from a QC:**
  "People will look at our website and see 60-something mostly white faces, mainly from Oxbridge, and think 'I don't stand a chance because I'm not like them'. The message I'd love to get across is: yes you do, we'll give you the same crack of the whip that everyone else gets." The posh boys might get better preparation from their tutors but if you have real talent you shouldn't be afraid to give it a shot – no matter what your background.

The Inns of Court

The four Inns of Court appear as oases of calm amid the hustle and bustle of London's legal heartland. Named Lincoln's Inn, Inner Temple, Middle Temple and Gray's Inn, they have many similarities with Oxbridge colleges, not least their libraries, chapels, halls and ancient traditions.

The Inns provide teaching, guidance, scholarships, a social network for members and a calm environment in which to work. Stroll through the Inns and you can practically breathe history. Out in their gardens you can relax with a drink from an on-site bar or play croquet; inside you're surrounded by imposing oil paintings, the austere expressions of past grandees, judges, heads of state and prime ministers gazing out from the wood panelling.

The Inns are the only institutions with the power to 'call' a person to the Bar. Indeed, students must join one of the four Inns before starting their BPTC and, since membership is for life, it's a decision worth mulling over. Although all four provide similar services and facilities, they each have a different flavour and atmosphere, if only due to their differing sizes. Such things are hard to describe, of course, so before picking one take any available opportunity to visit the Inns to see which one most appeals. This is easily done – just call up and ask for a tour. The Inns also produce a wealth of promotional materials/application guides/newsletters all packed with information – soak it up.

At the latest, you'll need to join an Inn before starting the BPTC, but it's a good idea to consider which one much earlier because between them they've got more than £4m to give out in scholarships for GDL and BPTC students as well as pupils. The deadlines for scholarship applications are usually in the calendar year before the course begins, so mark your diary once you have perused the detailed information on the Inns' websites or in their hard-copy brochures.

Getting a scholarship is competitive. Applicants face panels of current members (sometimes including judges) who will examine academic records and set challenges to determine on-the-spot presentation and advocacy skills. Achievements such as 'overcoming hardship' are sometimes also considered, as are extra-curricular activities like sporting or musical ability. The top scholarships are the prestigious 'named' scholarships. These can be worth in the region of £15,000. There are also a huge number of smaller awards.

It's advisable to get mini-pupillages and/or other work experience and internships under your belt, especially as there are additional funds to help facilitate these. Check out the Inns' websites or brochures for more information. For students living away from London, there are funds available to help cover transport costs to visit the Inns, and money is available to cover the cost of 'qualifying sessions'. Some of these 'qualifying sessions' are educational, others are purely designed to help students socialise, network and absorb the customs of the Bar. Sessions range from tradition-laden dinners in the Inns' halls to debates, seminars, advocacy weekends or more informal knees-ups in the gardens. During one visit we saw pinball machines being set up by people who would later be dressed as Elvis. Twelve qualifying sessions must be attended if you are to be 'called to the Bar'.

Once a member, a student can be mentored by a practitioner in their chosen field, and there are marshalling schemes whereby students can shadow a judge for a week, observing cases and discussing them at the end of the day. There are educational workshops to polish advocacy skills and seminars discussing areas of law or courtroom technique. Then there are a range of societies for things like drama, music and mooting/debating. All Inns offer mooting at internal, inter-Inn or national level, which we fully recommend you get involved with.

Although this all sounds very exciting, don't get carried away. Ensure that you have this mantra in mind at all times: Securing a Pupillage is Extremely Hard. A BPTC provider is unlikely to turn you away if you've got the cash to spend, but you cannot make your Lord Chief Justice fantasy come true just by completing the course. Even with a much sought-after scholarship, the road to becoming a barrister is neither cheap nor simple. Do remember that the Inns can help you to improve your chances of gaining pupillage, so become adept at networking, study extremely hard and moot, moot, moot.

	Lincoln's Inn	Inner Temple	Middle Temple	Gray's Inn
Contact	Tel: 020 7405 1393 www.lincolnsinn.org.uk	Tel: 020 7797 8250 www.innertemple.org.uk	Tel: 020 7427 4800 www.middletemple.org.uk	Tel: 020 7458 7900 www.graysinn.info
Architecture	The Old Hall was built in 1490 and the larger Great Hall in 1845, the same year as the library. The Stone Buildings are Regency. The largest Inn, it covers 11 acres.	12th-century Temple Church stands opposite the modern Hall built after the original was destroyed in WWII.	Grand. Smoking rooms decked out in oak, Van Dyck paintings and the largest private collection of silver (after the Royal Family's). Ornate carvings in the splendid Elizabethan Hall which is tucked down an intricate maze of alleys and narrow streets.	Suffered serious war damage and is largely a 1950s red-brick creation, albeit with its ancient Hall and Chapel intact. Disabled access has recently been improved.
Gardens	Always open, the gardens are especially popular at lunchtimes.	Well kept and stretching down to the Thames. Croquet, chess and giant Connect Four may be played.	Small and award-winning and handy for the bar.	Famous walks good for nearby City Law School students. Restaurant in gardens during summer.
Style	Friendly, international and large.	Sociable, progressive and switched on.	Musical, arty and very sociable. Christmas revels are notorious.	Traditional and, thanks to its smaller size, offers a personal touch.
Gastronomy	Meals in Hall are subsidised for students.	Lunch served every day. Subsidies for students.	Fairly priced, good-quality lunch served daily.	Lunch served in Hall every day. Subsidised rates for students.
Accommodation	14 flats available for students and 3 are let to pupils. All on-site.	Not for students.	13 subsidised single rooms for scholars in Clapham.	Not for students.
Bar	The stylish Members' Common Room has a restaurant and a terrace bar.	The Pegasus Bar has a terraced open-air area. Good for people watching but not a place to go incognito.	Modern bar conveniently located beneath the library and opens onto the lawns. Good for intimate chats in winter.	A walkway between the Hall and the South Square buildings is being rebuilt to house a bar.
Old Members	John Donne Lord Hailsham LC Lord Denning MR Muhammad Ali Jinnah H. Rider Haggard Wilkie Collins Some 16 British Prime Ministers	Dr Ivy Williams (first woman called to Bar) Bram Stoker Judge Jeffreys of 'Bloody Assizes' M K Gandhi Lord Falconer of Thoroton	Sir Walter Raleigh William Blackstone Charles Dickens William Makepeace Thackeray	Sir Francis Bacon Thomas Cromwell Dame Rose Heibrom (the first female QC, the first female Old Bailey judge and the first female treasurer at an Inn)
Points of Interest	Together with the Royal Navy, Lincoln's Inn takes the Loyal Toast seated. This commemorates a meal with King Charles II when the entire company got too drunk to stand. Inn offers subsidised trips to the Hague, Luxembourg & Strasbourg.	Temple Church includes part of Knights Templar's round church, which was modelled on the Church of the Holy Sepulchre in Jerusalem and used as a film set in *The Da Vinci Code*.	Shakespeare's *Twelfth Night* first performed here. 2008 was the 400th anniversary of the Temple's Charter which granted the freehold of the land to Inner and Middle Temple. Hall has a table from the Golden Hind. Every new barrister signs their name on it.	Shakespeare's *Comedy of Errors* first performed here. Been law teaching on the site of Gray's Inn since the reign of Edward III. The ornate carved screen in the Hall is made from an Armada ship.
Scholarship Interview Process	Panel interview. No set question beforehand. Expect chat about preferred areas of practice and items of legal interest in the news. Scholarship awarded solely on merit then weighted according to financial means.	20-minute interview. GDL scholars entitled to automatic funding for BPTC, but can apply for higher award. Merit and academic excellence prioritised, but all awards (save for the top ones) means tested.	Every applicant interviewed. 15 minute panel interview tests on-the-spot presentation skills.	Shortlisted applicants interviewed by a three-person panel looking for an ability to think on one's feet rather than legal knowledge. Extra-curricular achievements taken into consideration - eg music, sport or overcoming adversity.
Scholarship Money	A total of almost £1.5m available each year through over 160 scholarships. BPTC: up to 70 scholarships of between £6,000 and £17,000 and up to 40 bursaries of up to £3,000 each.	A total of £1.26m available. GDL: 5 major scholarships and various awards totaling £181,500. BPTC: 7 major grants (of between £15k and £20k), and awards totalling £1m.	A total of around £991,000 available. A fund of £820,000 for BPTC scholarships and awards. A fund of £100,000 for GDL scholarships and awards. Another fund for accommodation and overseas scholarships amounting to £71,000 in 2009	A total of over £795,000 available. GDL: around 16 awards of between c.£5,000, and £9,000. BPTC: around 56 awards of between £4,000 and £17,000 each. Various overseas scholarships and misc awards, eg £10k Hebe Plunkett award for disabled.

Practice areas at the Bar

Use these practice area summaries to help you work out which you want to try.

The Chancery Bar in a nutshell

The Chancery Bar is tricky to define. The High Court has three divisions: Family, Queen's Bench (QBD) and Chancery, with cases allocated to and heard by the most appropriate division based on their subject matter. But what makes a case suitable for the Chancery Division? Historically it has been the venue for cases with an emphasis on legal principles, foremost among them the concept of equity. Put another way, Chancery work is epitomised by legal reasoning. Cases are generally categorised as either 'traditional' Chancery (trusts, probate, real property, charities and mortgages) or 'commercial' Chancery (company law, shareholder cases, partnership, banking, pensions, financial services, insolvency, professional negligence, tax, media and IP). Most Chancery sets will undertake both types of work, albeit with varying emphases. However, the distinction between Chancery practice and the work of the Commercial Bar (which has historically been dealt with in the QBD) is less apparent than it once was. Barristers at commercial sets can frequently be found on Chancery cases and vice versa, though some areas, such as tax and IP, require specialisation.

The realities of the job

- This is an area for those who love the law and love to grapple with its most complex aspects. It's all about the application of long-standing legal principles to modern-day situations.
- Barristers must be masters of communication and very practical in the legal solutions they offer to clients. Complex and puzzling cases take significant unravelling and the legal arguments/principles must be explained coherently to the solicitor and the lay client. Suave and sophisticated presentation when before a judge is also vital.
- Advocacy is important, but the majority of time is spent in chambers perusing papers, considering arguments, drafting pleadings, skeletons and advices, or conducting settlement negotiations.
- Some instructions fly into chambers, need immediate attention and then disappear just as quickly. Others can rumble on for years.
- Variety is a key attraction. Traditional work can involve human interest, for example wills and inheritance cause all sorts of ructions among families. Commercial Chancery practitioners deal with the blood-on-the-boardroom-table disputes or bust-ups between co-writers of million-selling songs.
- Schedules aren't set by last-minute briefs for next-day court appearances, so barristers need self-discipline and good time management skills.
- The early years of practice feature low-value cases like straightforward possession proceedings in the county court, winding-up applications in the Companies Court and appearances before the bankruptcy registrars. More prominent sets will involve baby barristers as second or third junior on larger, more complex cases.

Current issues

- The Chancery Bar continues to attract not only high-value, complex domestic cases, but also an increasing number of offshore and cross-border instructions. They might involve Russian and Eastern European business affairs or massive offshore trusts.
- The scope of the Chancery Division means that practitioners get involved in some enormous commercial and public law matters.
- A good example of a large Chancery Division case is that brought by the developers of London's Chelsea Barracks site against the Qatari investors who pulled out of funding the redevelopment after Prince Charles criticised its design.

Some tips

- An excellent academic record is essential. Most pupils in leading sets have a First-class degree. You should enjoy the analytical process involved in constructing arguments and evaluating the answers to problems. If you're not a natural essay writer, you're unlikely to be a natural-born Chancery practitioner.
- Don't wander into this area by accident. Are you actually interested in equity, trusts, company law, insolvency, IP or tax?
- Though not an accurate portrayal of modern practice, Dickens' *Bleak House* is the ultimate Chancery saga.

Read our Chambers Reports on...

2 Temple Gardens	Four New Square
3 Verulam Buildings	Henderson Chambers
3-4 South Square	Maitland Chambers
7 King's Bench Walk	One Essex Court
Blackstone Chambers	Pump Court Tax Chambers
Crown Office Chambers	Serle Court

The Commercial Bar

In a nutshell

The Commercial Bar handles a variety of business disputes. In its purest definition a commercial case is one heard by the Commercial Court or a county court business court. A broader and more realistic definition includes matters dealt with by both the Queen's Bench and Chancery Divisions of the High Court, and the Technology and Construction Court (TCC). The Commercial Bar deals with disputes in all manner of industries from construction, shipping and insurance to banking, entertainment and manufacturing.Almost all disputes are contract and/or tort claims, and the Commercial Bar remains rooted in common law. That said, domestic and European legislation is increasingly important and commercial barristers' incomes now reflect the popularity of the English courts with overseas litigants. Cross-border issues including competition law, international public and trade law and conflicts of law are all growing in prominence. Alternative methods of dispute resolution – usually arbitration or mediation – are also popular because of the increased likelihood of preserving commercial relationships that would otherwise be destroyed by the litigation process.

The realities of the job

- Barristers steer solicitors and lay clients through the litigation process and advise on strategy, for example how clients can position themselves through witness statements, pleadings and pre-trial 'interlocutory' skirmishes.
- Advocacy is key but as so much of it is paper-based, written skills are just as important as oral skills.
- Commercial cases can be very fact-heavy and the evidence for a winning argument can be buried in a room full of papers. Barristers have to work closely with instructing solicitors to manage documentation.
- Not all commercial pupils will take on their own caseload in the second six. At first, new juniors commonly handle small cases including common law matters like personal injury, employment cases, possession proceedings and winding-up or bankruptcy applications.
- New juniors gain exposure to larger cases by assisting senior colleagues. As a 'second junior' they assist the 'first junior' and QC by carrying out research and preparing first drafts. This provides the opportunity to pick up tips on cross-examining witnesses and how best to present arguments.
- In time, a junior's caseload increases in value and complexity. Most commercial barristers specialise by building up expertise on cases within a particular industry sector.
- Developing a practice means working long hours, often under pressure. Your service standards must be impeccable and your style user-friendly, no matter how late or disorganised the solicitor's instruction. In a good set you can make an exceedingly good living.

Current issues

- In the past couple of years the commercial litigation market has picked up, not least because of fallout from the credit crunch. There has been an increase in the number of disputes across the board, but most especially in relation to insurance, professional negligence and financial institutions. Third-party funding of litigation, and costs risk-sharing arrangements are now becoming more prevalent.
- One of the biggest cases of the last few years was a \$100m compensation claim by 30,000 people from Côte d'Ivoire against oil trader Trafigura over injuries caused by toxic waste dumping in 2006. In the financial sector, big investment banks like Raiffeisen, RBS and Barclays have been fighting cases over the purportedly misleading sale of financial products.
- The trend for increased mediation and arbitration continues. One effect of this is that only the big, multi-issue cases tend to reach court, as there are so many other opportunities for dealing with smaller, less complex cases.

Some tips

- Competition for pupillage at the Commercial Bar is fierce. A First-class degree is commonplace and you'll need impressive references.
- Don't underestimate the value of non-legal work experience; commercial exposure of any kind is going to help you understand the client's perspective and motivations.
- Bear a set's specialities in mind when deciding where to accept pupillage – shipping is very different to employment for example.

Read our Chambers Reports on...

2 Temple Gardens	Four New Square
3 Verulam Buildings	Henderson Chambers
3-4 South Square	Maitland Chambers
7 King's Bench Walk	One Essex Court
Blackstone Chambers	Pump Court Tax Chambers
Crown Office Chambers	Serle Court

The Common Law Bar

In a nutshell

English common law derives from the precedents set by judicial decisions rather than the contents of statutes. Most common law cases turn on principles of tort and contract and are dealt with in the Queen's Bench Division (QBD) of the High Court and the county courts. At the edges, common law practice blurs into both Chancery and commercial practice, yet the work undertaken in common law sets is broader still, and one of the most appealing things about a career at one of these sets is the variety of instructions available.

Employment and personal injury are the bread and butter at the junior end, and such matters are interspersed with licensing, clinical negligence, landlord and tenant issues, the winding-up of companies and bankruptcy applications, as well as small commercial and contractual disputes. Some sets will even extend their remit to inquests and criminal cases.

The realities of the job

- Barristers tend to engage with a full range of cases throughout their careers, but there is an opportunity to begin to specialise at between five and ten years' call. Although you can express an interest in receiving certain work from the clerks, most sets expect their juniors to be common law generalists.
- Advocacy is plentiful. Juniors can expect to be in court three days per week and second-six pupils often have their own cases. Small beginnings such as 'noting briefs' (where you attend court simply in order to report back on the proceedings) and masters' and district judges' appointments lead to lower-value 'fast-track' personal injury trials then longer, higher-value, 'multi-track' trials and employment tribunals.
- Outside court, the job involves research, an assessment of the merits of a case and meetings with solicitors and lay clients. The barrister will also be asked to draft statements of claim, defences and opinions.
- Dealing with the volume and variety of cases requires a good grasp of the law and the procedural rules of the court, as well as an easy facility for assimilating the facts of each case.
- Interpersonal skills are important. A client who has never been to court before will be very nervous and needs to be put at ease.
- At the junior end, work comes in at short notice, so having to digest a file of documents quickly is commonplace.
- Acting as a junior on more complex cases allows a younger barrister to observe senior lawyers in court.

Current issues

- The trend for mediation and arbitration of disputes, and the trend for solicitors to undertake more advocacy themselves, have to some extent reduced work at the junior end. However, while solicitor advocates frequently take on directions hearings, they are still rarely seen at trial.
- Conditional fee agreements – especially for PI claims – have definitely affected barristers' remuneration. Ongoing changes to the public funding of legal services are also having an impact. On a more positive note, the growth of third-party funding of cases and increased use of risk-sharing arrangements by solicitors may lead to an increase in the volume of work for barristers.
- Britons have become increasingly litigious over the past few decades. Personal injury and clinical negligence claims (often against the NHS) are on the rise. Individuals are increasingly aware of the ever-expanding protections afforded by health and safety regulation and professional codes of conduct. The result: more litigation.

Some tips

- Though there are a lot of common law sets, pupillages and tenancies don't grow on trees. You'll have to impress to get a foot in the door and then make your mark to secure your next set of instructions.
- If you want to specialise, thoroughly research the sets you apply to – many want their juniors to retain a broad practice many years into tenancy, while others do allow some space to carve out a niche.

Read our Chambers Reports on...

2 Temple Gardens	Four New Square
3 Verulam Buildings	Maitland Chambers
3-4 South Square	Old Square Chambers
7 King's Bench Walk	One Essex Court
Cloisters	Serle Court
Crown Office Chambers	Thirty Nine Essex Street

The Criminal Bar

In a nutshell

Barristers are instructed by solicitors to provide advocacy or advice for individuals being prosecuted in cases brought before the UK's criminal courts. Lesser offences like driving charges, possession of drugs or benefit fraud are listed in the magistrates' courts, where solicitor advocates are increasingly active. More serious charges such as fraud, supplying drugs or murder go to the Crown Courts, which are essentially still the domain of barristers. Complex cases may reach the Court of Appeal or Supreme Court. See the diagram of courts on page 101. A criminal set's caseload incorporates everything from theft, fraud, drugs and driving offences to assaults of varying degree of severity and murder.

The realities of the job

- Criminal barristers need a sense of theatre and dramatic timing, but good oratory skills are only half the story. Tactical sense and great time management are important.
- The barrister must be able to inspire confidence in clients from any kind of background.
- Some clients can be tricky, unpleasant or scary characters. Some will have pretty unfortunate lives, others will be addicted to alcohol or drugs, have poor home lives and little education.
- Barristers often handle several cases a day, frequently at different courts. Some of them will be poorly prepared by instructing solicitors. It is common to take on additional cases at short notice and to have to cope with missing defendants and witnesses. Stamina and adaptability are consequently a must.
- Sustained success rests on effective case preparation and an awareness of evolving law and sentencing policies.
- Pupils cut their teeth on motoring offences, committals and directions hearings in the magistrates' courts. By the end of pupillage they should expect to be instructed in their own right and make it into the Crown Court.
- Juniors quickly see the full gamut of cases. Trials start small – offences such as common assault – and move onto ABH, robbery and possession of drugs with intent to supply.

Current issues

- To save costs, the Crown Prosecution Service has increasingly brought a significant proportion of advocacy in-house. The CPS wants many of its lawyers to develop to become Senior Crown Advocates and handle contested trials in the Crown Court. Whether a happy equilibrium between the Bar and CPS prosecutors will be reached remains to be seen, but the move has reduced the work available at the Bar's junior end.
- Legal Aid cutbacks and reforms are also hitting the number of available criminal instructions and remuneration. This is the major issue for all those practising at the Criminal Bar. Cuts will remove at least £325m from Legal Aid's £2.2bn budget. A fair chunk of that is due to come from the fees paid to barristers. If you're willing to accept the likelihood of more limited financial rewards, the Legal Aid Criminal Bar should still prove irresistible. Read more on our website.
- Partially as a consequence of Legal Aid cutbacks, many top-end criminal sets are branching out into regulatory, VAT tribunal and professional discipline work.
- Private paying criminal practice is as healthy as ever.
- The 2010 Bribery Act has seen UK laws brought in line with an OECD Bribery Convention. It widens the definition of bribery and applies to the activities of UK-based companies anywhere in the world.

Some tips

- Mini-pupillage experience and plenty of mooting and debating are required before you can look like a serious applicant.
- Some top sets will want to see your Pupillage Portal practice area choices restricted to crime and crime/mixed civil.
- The Criminal Bar tends to provide more pupillages than other areas, but these don't necessarily translate into tenancies because the market is so competitive. Third and fourth sixes are not uncommon.
- There are many ways of getting exposure to the criminal justice system. See page 33 for tips on useful voluntary opportunities.

Read our Chambers Reports on...

2 Bedford Row

The Employment Bar

In a nutshell

The Employment Bar deals with any and every sort of claim arising from the relations or breakdown of relations between employees and employers. Disputes are generally resolved at or before reaching an Employment Tribunal, which deals with cases relating to redundancy; unfair dismissal; discrimination on the grounds of gender, sexual orientation, race, religion or age; workplace harassment; contract claims; and whistle-blowing. In most cases a Tribunal will consist of an Employment Judge sitting with two 'wing members', one from a Trades Union and one from a Business background. Appeals are heard by the Employment Appeal Tribunal (EAT) and high-value claims and applications for injunctions to prevent the breach of restrictive covenants or use of trade secrets are usually dealt with in the county courts or the High Court.

Accessibility is a key aim of the employment tribunal system, legal representation is not required, and many more cases proceed to a full hearing than in other areas of civil law. One reason for this is that awards of costs against unsuccessful parties are rare. Such is the emphasis on user-friendliness that employment claims can even be issued online. Claimants will often represent themselves, meaning a barrister acting for a respondent company faces a lay opponent. Nonetheless, many cases are so complex, or worth so much money, that both parties seek specialist legal representation from solicitors and barristers.

The realities of the job

- Most advocacy takes place in employment tribunals or the EAT, where the atmosphere and proceedings are less formal. Hearings are conducted with everyone sitting down and barristers do not wear wigs. The emphasis is on oral advocacy, with witness statements generally read aloud.
- Tribunals follow the basic pattern of examination in chief, cross-examination and closing submissions; however barristers and have to modify their style, especially when appearing against someone who is unrepresented.
- A corporate respondent might pay for a QC, while the applicant's pocket may only stretch to a junior. Large-scale equal pay or City 'team move' cases run much like other high-end civil litigation. Solicitor advocates feature prominently in Tribunals.
- Employment specialists need great people skills. Clients frequently become emotional or stressed, and the trend for respondent companies to name an individual (say a manager) as co-respondent means there may be several individuals in the room with complex personal and professional issues at stake.
- Most juniors also undertake civil or commercial cases, some criminal matters. Few juniors act only for applicants or only for respondents.
- UK employment legislation mirrors EU law and changes with great rapidity. Cases are regularly stayed while others with similar points are heard on appeal.

Current issues

- The Tribunals are overflowing with work following the economic downturn, which has led to long delays in proceedings. There is ample work for juniors on 'fixed fee' arrangements, especially for insurers or large employers.
- The Equality Act 2010 could lead to an upturn in discrimination cases.
- Layoffs and bonus disputes resulting from the economic downturn are a key source of claims. Bonus disputes, in particular in the financial sector, are a hotly debated topic, as are 'team-moves'. Equal pay cases are another important area.
- The headline-grabbing 2010 British Airways strikes created a flurry of work for a number of sets. Future private and public sector restructurings (like the part-privatisation of the Royal Mail) could lead to further strike disputes.

Some tips

- Get involved with the Free Representation Unit. FRU employment law opportunities are varied and invaluable.
- If you find FRU oversubscribed, try actively seeking out other legal advice centre experience.
- Practically any kind of job will give you first-hand experience of being an employee. Not to be underestimated, especially when you consider that as a barrister you will be self-employed.
- High-profile cases are regularly reported in the press, so there's no excuse for not keeping abreast of the area.

Read our Chambers Reports on...

Blackstone Chambers
Cloisters
Littleton Chambers

The Family Bar

In a nutshell

Family law barristers deal with the array of cases arising from marital, civil union or cohabitation breakdown and related issues concerning children. Simple cases are heard in the county courts, while complex or high-value cases are listed in the Family Division of the High Court. Emphasising the importance of this area, UK government stats reveal that around half of divorcing couples have at least one child aged under 16, and together their divorces affect nearly 150,000 children a year. Consequently, a huge amount of court time is allotted to divorce, separation, adoption, child residence and contact orders, financial provision and domestic violence.

The realities of the job

- Financial cases and public and private law children's work each offer their own unique challenges.
- Emotional resilience is required, as is a capacity for empathy, as the work involves asking clients for intimate details of their private life and breaking devastating news to the emotionally fragile. Private law children's cases can sometimes involve serious allegations between parents and require the input of child psychologists. The public law counterpart (care proceedings between local authorities and parents) invariably includes detailed and potentially testing medical evidence.
- For many clients, involvement with the courts is out of the ordinary and they will rely heavily on their counsel to guide them through the process. The law can never fix emotional problems relating to marital breakdown or child issues, but it can palliate a situation.
- The job calls for communication, tact and maturity. Cases have a significant impact on the lives they involve, so finding the most appropriate course of action for each client is important. The best advocates are those who can differentiate between a case and client requiring a bullish approach and those crying out for settlement and concessions to be made.
- Where possible, mediation is used to resolve disputes in a more efficient and less unsettling fashion, requiring a different approach to litigation.
- Teamwork is crucial. As the barrister is the link between the client, the judge, solicitors and social workers, it is important to win the trust and confidence of all parties.
- The legislation affecting this area is comprehensive, and there's a large body of case law. Keeping abreast of developments is necessary because the job is more about negotiating general principles than adhering strictly to precedents.
- Finance-oriented barristers need an understanding of pensions and shares and a good grounding in the basics of trusts and property.
- The early years of practice involve a lot of private law children work (disputes between parents), small financial cases and injunctions in situations of domestic violence.

Current issues

- A few years ago barristers believed that mediation and an increase in solicitor advocates would mean a downturn in work for juniors. Yet, with the exception of child cases, in which solicitors have always been encouraged to do their own advocacy, the volume of instructions appears to have continued largely unabated. This is despite the fact that 2008 saw divorce rates fall to the lowest levels since 1979.
- Big divorces are big news. The wealth and assets involved in cases such as that of Boris Berezovsky and his wife Galina far outstrip the reasonable needs of the parties, but precedents for huge payouts have been established and such cases draw significant attention, with the media often being used strategically.
- Cases involving the division of assets/child law issues following the breakdown of a civil partnership are beginning to appear.
- Pre-nuptial agreements were big news in 2010. A Supreme Court ruling in *Radmacher v Granatino* is expected to clarify the status of pre-nups under English law.
- Ongoing reform of the Legal Aid system is hitting the Family Bar hard.

Some tips

- The Family Bar is quite small and competition for pupillage is intense. Think about how you can evidence your interest in family law. See our **Pro Bono and Volunteering** section on page 33.
- Younger pupils might find it daunting to advise on mortgages, marriages and children when they've never experienced any of these things personally. Arguably those embarking on a second career, or who have delayed a year or two and acquired other life experiences, may have an advantage.
- Check the work orientation of a set before applying for pupillage, particularly if you don't want to narrow your options too early. For example, some sets specialise only in the financial aspects of divorce.

Public law at the Bar

In a nutshell

Centred on the Administrative Court, public law relates to the principles governing the exercise of power by public bodies. Those which most often appear as respondents in the High Court include government departments, local authorities, the prison service and NHS trusts. Often the headline cases are challenges to central or local government policies. Other big-ticket work comes from public inquires. However, for all the (in)famous cases reported in the media, there are hundreds of public bodies taking daily decisions that affect just about everybody in the country. It is decisions like these – on immigration, welfare, planning applications or a child's school allocation – which provide most work for private practitioners.

The most important process in public practice is judicial review: the Administrative Court may order that any decision made unlawfully be overturned or reconsidered. Nowadays – much to the dismay of the *Daily Mail* – decisions are often reviewed on the basis of the Human Rights Act 1998 (HRA). Human rights issues continue to be a major source of work for the Public Law Bar.

Many barristers also have practices in areas which dovetail with their public law practice. Criminal barristers will, for example, frequently handle issues relating to prisoners or breaches of procedure by police, whereas commercial barristers may handle judicial review of decisions made by the Department of Business, Innovation and Skills. Equally, barristers who do not profess to specialise in public law may undertake some judicial review work.

The realities of the job

- The Administrative Court is extremely busy, so an efficient style of advocacy is vital. Barristers need to cut straight to the chase and succinctly deliver pertinent information, case law or statutory regulations.
- Barristers need a genuine interest in the legislative process and the fundamental laws by which we live.
- A real interest in academic law is a prerequisite. Complex arguments are more common than precise answers.
- While legal intellect is vital, frequently real world, emotive issues demand a practical outlook and an ability to stand back from the issue in question.
- Junior barristers often hone their nascent advocacy skills at the permissions stage of judicial review in short 30-minute hearings.

Current issues

- The Planning Act 2008 introduced a new system for decisions on applications to build nationally significant infrastructure projects (NSIPs) in England and Wales.
- The relentless reforms to legal aid funding will affect public law cases and the livelihoods of barristers.
- The coalition government plans to extend the scope of the Freedom of Information Act. This will mean that pressure groups, the media and individuals will be able to scrutinise the actions, plans and success of public bodies closer than ever before.
- Prior to the 2010 election, the Conservatives mooted a Freedom Bill and replacing the HRA with a 'British Bill of Rights.' While this issue has been put on hold by the coalition government, the future of the HRA – and UK human rights law – remains unclear.
- There are an increasing number of coroners' inquests, with prison and military deaths dominating the field.

Some tips

- Having the highest possible academic credentials is a given when applying to a public law set but many candidates will *also* have significant hands-on experience or related further academic study.
- The competition for public practice pupillage is exceptionally fierce, as public law and human rights are fields beloved by law students. A strong interest in current affairs is essential.
- Public international law is more popular still – just think of the numbers undertaking postgraduate studies in this area – but it's an incredibly small field with few openings. Moreover, it's dominated by sitting or ex-professors at top universities, alongside Foreign Office veterans and the occasional very senior barrister.
- If administrative and constitutional law were not your favourite subjects then you might want to consider a little rethink before choosing public law.
- As a rewarding alternative, there are opportunities available within the Government Legal Services.
- An interest in current affairs and knowledge of the latest headline cases are essential.

Read our Chambers Reports on...

2 Bedford Row	Crown Office Chambers
2 Temple Gardens	Four New Square
4-5 Gray's Inn Square	Henderson Chambers
Blackstone Chambers	Old Square Chambers

Shipping & International Trade at the Bar

In a nutshell

This is such a well-defined specialism at the Commercial Bar it requires its own summary. Shipping and trade work mostly centres upon contract and tort; indeed English case law is awash with examples from the world of shipping. Barristers handle disputes arising from or concerning the carriage of goods or people by sea, air and land, plus all aspects of the financing, construction, use, insurance and decommissioning of the vessels, planes, trains and other vehicles that carry them. There is often a complex international element to such cases, drawing in multiple parties – for example a wrecked vessel might be Greek-owned, Pakistani-crewed, Russian-captained, last serviced in Singapore, carrying forestry products from Indonesia to Denmark, insured in London and chartered by a French company – but English courts are very often the preferred forum for the resolution of such matters, not least because of the worldwide significance of the London insurance market. Trade disputes are often resolved through arbitration conducted in various locations, Paris and London being among the most important.

'Wet' cases deal with problems at sea, while 'dry' cases relate to disputes in port or concerns over the manufacture and financing of vessels. The Bar also has a number of aviation, road haulage and rail specialists, and the sets that dominate these areas also tend to be able to offer commodities trading experts.

The realities of the job

- Cases are fact-heavy and paper-heavy. To develop the best arguments for a case, barristers need an organised mind and a willingness to immerse themselves in the documentary evidence. This can be time-consuming and exhausting.
- There are opportunities for international travel.
- Cases can run on for years and involve large teams of lawyers, both solicitors and barristers. Young barristers work their way up from second or third junior to leader over a number of years. New juniors do get to run their own smaller cases, eg charter party and bills of lading disputes.
- The world of shipping and trade has its own language and customs.
- Solicitor clients will usually work at one of the established shipping firms, but lay clients will be a mixed bag of financiers, shipowners, operators, traders and charterers, protecting and indemnity associations (P&I clubs), salvors and underwriters.

Current issues

- There is a general downturn in cargo claims due to the increased safety of ships and the success of various conventions such as the International Safety Management Code.
- P&I clubs in particular continue to be increasingly watchful of costs. This has sparked the recent development of instructing barristers directly, cutting out the solicitor middleman.
- Clients are further trying to save money by embracing mediation, although gloomier economic conditions always see a rise in cases going to court.
- The recession has had a particular effect on 'dry' shipping. A ship takes a long time to build. Shipyards are churning out vessels ordered in the economic boom times, which no one wanted once the recession hit. The result: disputes.
- Piracy is on the rise, and it's now affecting waters that have ordinarily been considered safe. A good case in point is the Maltese-flagged 'Arctic Sea', which was hijacked in the Baltic Sea in August 2009 as it transported timber from Finland to Algeria.
- In Spring 2010 the UN Security Council urged for the creation of an international tribunal for prosecuting pirates. Funded by international donors, a court to try suspected pirates operating in the Gulf of Aden has since opened in the Kenyan port of Mombasa.

Some tips

- The leading sets are easy to identify. A mini-pupillage with one or more of them will greatly enhance your understanding and chances.
- Despite the prominence of English law, the work calls for an international perspective and an appreciation of international laws. This can be developed within a first or masters' degree and on the BPTC.

Read our Chambers Reports on...

7 King's Bench Walk Quadrant Chambers

Chambers Reports: Introduction

Making an informed choice about where to apply for pupillage isn't easy. Having established the practice area in which you want to specialise, you then need to select your dozen Pupillage Portal scheme sets and consider how many other sets outside the scheme you will apply to. How do you know where you'll fit in and whether a set will be interested in you?

These days the majority of chambers' websites deliver all the pertinent information – not just about their size, nature of work and location, but also about the nature of pupillage and mini-pupillage. Many even carry their full pupillage policy documentation online. Internet surfing can only take you so far though, and there is no substitute for seeing life inside a set during a mini-pupillage. Because it is impossible to do minis at every set, we've done some of the hard work for you.

Since the summer of 2003, we have been calling in on various chambers, taking time to speak with pupils, juniors, QCs, clerks and chief execs. The task is a big one so we visit each of our chosen chambers every other year and refresh the existing Chambers Report for the intervening years. This year's roll call of 23 sets includes 14 new features and nine reprinted from our 2010 edition. We have tried to visit as many different types of set as possible to give a good sense of the range of areas of practice available. Our visits took us from the grandeur of the Chancery Bar to the more modest surroundings of sets conducting a significant amount of publicly funded work. There should be something to suit most tastes, be they commercial, common law, criminal, IP, tax, or otherwise.

The sets covered this year are all in London, where the majority of chambers (and pupillages) are based, but in your wider research remember that there are some excellent chambers in the regions, mostly in the larger cities of Leeds, Liverpool, Manchester, Birmingham and Bristol. The wild card in our pack is the Government Legal Service, which although not a set operating out of chambers, still offers what we regard as a cracking pupillage. What we have deliberately avoided is poor-quality sets and we make no excuses for our decision to only review highly regarded organisations. Bear in mind, however, that our selected sets are not the only ones in the Premier League in each practice area. Given the time we would visit many others.

Whichever chambers you do choose, be reassured that the prime aim of recruiters is to find talented applicants and then to persuade them to accept an offer. They do not expect ready-formed barristers to turn up at their door for interview and they gladly make allowances for candidates' lack of knowledge or experience on specific subjects. Much has been said and written about how awful pupillage interviews can be, and how pupillage itself amounts to little more than a year of pain and humiliation. From what we can tell, in an increasingly modern, business-oriented profession that is taking greater notice of what constitutes good HR practice, this is not the norm. Sure, interviews can be challenging, but they are for the most part designed to get the best out of candidates. As for pupillage, it is in the best interests of any set that it should provide a useful and rewarding experience for pupils.

Of course, that still doesn't make it a walk in the park for a pupil. The itinerary for our visits included conversations with members of the pupillage committee, pupilmasters or supervisors, the senior clerk, junior tenants and, most crucially, current pupils. The aim was not merely to get the low-down on pupillage at each set but also to learn something about each chambers' persona and to pick up tips for applicants. To this end we drank endless cups of tea, selflessly munched our way through kilos of biscuits and took numerous guided tours, checking out artwork and libraries along the way. If we've communicated the qualities that make each set unique then we've done our job and it's over to you to make your choices.

Set	Location	Head of Chambers	QCs/Juniors
Atkin Chambers	London	Nicholas Dennys QC	14/23
2 Bedford Row*	London	William Clegg QC	19/52
Blackstone Chambers	London	Mill QC/Beazley QC	34/50
Cloisters	London	Robin Allen QC	5/42
Crown Office Chambers	London	Andrew Bartlett QC	14/75
One Essex Court	London	Lord Grabiner QC	24/48
39 Essex Street*	London, Manchester	Richard Wilmot-Smith QC	26/60
Government Legal Service*	London	N/a	464
4-5 Gray's Inn Square*	London	Straker QC/Griffiths QC	15/39
Henderson Chambers*	London	Charles Gibson QC	9/34
Keating Chambers*	London	John Marrin QC	20/31
7 King's Bench Walk*	London	Gavin Kealey QC	20/27
Littleton Chambers*	London	Clarke QC/Freedman QC	12/37
Maitland Chambers	London	Michael Driscoll QC	18/48
Four New Square*	London	Jeremy Stuart-Smith QC	19/51
Old Square Chambers*	London, Bristol	Cooksley QC/McNeil QC	8/55
Pump Court Tax Chambers*	London	Andrew Thornhill QC	10/20
Quadrant Chambers*	London	Persey QC/Rainey QC	12/38
Serle Court	London	Alan Boyle QC	15/36
3/4 South Square*	London	Trower QC/Moss QC/Dicker QC	19/29
2 Temple Gardens*	London	Benjamin Browne QC	10/39
3 Verulam Buildings	London	Ali Malek QC	18/45
Wilberforce Chambers	London	John Martin QC	22/27

* Sets visited in 2010

Atkin Chambers

The facts

Location: Gray's Inn, London
Number of QCs/Juniors: 14/23 (8 women)
Applications: 112
Apply through Pupillage Portal
Pupils per year: Up to 3
Seats: 2x3 and 1x6 months
Pupillage Award: £47,500 (can advance £10,000 for BPTC)

Chambers and Partners' Construction Set of the Year 2010

Atkin Chambers is a construction set. No, wait! Keep reading! If the image that springs to mind is all hard hats and builders' bums, you're way off the mark.

No restaurants for the wicked

Just listen to the testimony of a junior in the second year of practice. "*I've had a banking law case where we've been looking to recover some money from a bank that we say was paid wrongfully, a case where we've been looking to resist electricity companies that are coming against the owner of a tiny little restaurant up in North London, and another where a couple have had an acrimonious split. The girlfriend has sued the boyfriend for 30 grand that she says she lent him, and he's counterclaimed a £7,000 holiday that she paid for on his credit card. I was like: 'I thought this was a construction set!'*"

So you see, 'construction' is a useful label to tag onto Atkin for the purposes of things like *Chambers UK* rankings (where it comes in Band 1, naturally), but it's not as easy to define as you might think. "*The solicitors who instruct us know that, but students often see these categories as quite hard and fast.*" Atkin's official remit in fact covers energy, professional negligence, IT and more besides. When you've discounted its technical facets, IT law has more in common with construction than you might think. Be it an office block or a computer, "*it's all about building something. As far as the law is concerned, it's the same thing – contract and tort.*" In fact, many of the really important cases in contract and tort came from construction law. Perhaps a better description for the set is the one a pupilmaster gave us: "*We are commercial coming from the niche.*"

We're not saying that Atkin isn't still heavily invested in 'classic' construction cases – you'll often see its members in the Technology and Construction Court (TCC) acting on high-profile matters. Recently almost all members of chambers have been involved in disputes arising out of the design and construction of Wembley Stadium. International arbitration is another hugely important area of work for chambers, with barristers regularly flying out to everywhere from Scotland to Siberia. Many instructions come from the Middle East, India and East Asia and the word from the set is that it is "*punching above its weight getting into China, although it's still tough.*" As if to emphasise Atkin's success in this field, it was the first chambers to receive the prestigious Queen's Award for Enterprise in the International Trade category.

Knowing me, knowing you

Atkin normally takes three pupils per year, but the patter of tiny feet in its corridors was conspicuous by its absence in 2008/09. The candidates it wanted accepted offers elsewhere – mostly at the magic circle commercial sets – and chambers decided that it was better to take no one on at all rather than to offer pupillage just for the sake of it. On discovering this, we asked what Atkin has to offer that the magic circle doesn't. "*Firstly, a specialisation, which I think will become increasingly important with the changes in the legal profession and the way barristers and solicitors work,*" replied a member of the pupillage committee, Fiona Parkin. "*It seems to me that the only way the Bar is going to survive is by offering real pockets of specialisation and that's what we provide. Secondly, we are smaller and so you know people – not just to say hello to:*

Chambers UK rankings

Construction	International Arbitration
Energy & Natural Resources	Professional Negligence
Information Technology	

you genuinely know everyone that you work with really quite well. I think that makes for a fantastic working environment." In 2009/10 the set hosted three pupils, although none were taken on as tenants. The set subsequently took on a third sixer.

Academic excellence is a given to get in here, but of the 12 juniors under ten years' call, five are non-Oxbridge and several don't have First-class degrees, so there's no snobbery. Since we're quoting facts and figures: two of the 12 are from an ethnic minority background and three are female. Ten of them read law at undergraduate level. The further up the set you go, the less diverse it gets: of the 26 senior juniors and QCs one is from an ethnic minority background and five are women.

About 20 people get invited to interview with the Pupillage Committee, usually consisting of six barristers from all levels of seniority. Although it might seem that way, "*it's not meant to be a daunting experience.*" The interview is designed to spot those with an agile mind and is divided into three parts. The first part is "*an opportunity to ask questions about them and why they want to come to this chambers – it's amazing how many people haven't thought about that.*" The second part is a legal problem, usually based in contract and tort. That takes about 15 minutes, then there's a discussion on a topical question that poses a moral dilemma – the right to die, for instance.

Constructive witticism

Pupillage is structured to gradually increase in difficulty as the year goes on. "*You do feel a real sense of progression.*" In the first three months you can expect to see "*a good cross-section of smaller cases with all the basic stuff.*" In this first six, pupils generally won't work for anyone apart from their supervisors, although "*if someone is going to the House of Lords or the Court of Appeal, we try to get them along to that as well.*" By the end of the first six, it's expected that they will have "*a decent grasp of what the issues are*" and be able to start producing work of value (ie something the pupilmaster will actually be able to use). Almost everything pupils do is 'live' with the exception of two assessed written exercises during the first six. If there are problems, "*we won't let them fester;*" chambers tries to get right on top of any niggles before they worsen, which is perhaps why the six-month break option in the pupillage is almost never utilised.

In the second six, it's rare for pupils to develop much of a caseload. Chambers feels that it's more important to learn the job properly; "*there's quite a lot to pick up,*" after all. Atkin does provide advocacy training, however, and there are three advocacy exercises during the year. The first is pupil v pupil, but by the third go they'll be arguing before a big cheese, usually a former member of chambers, possibly even a real High Court judge, "*which is exciting and terrifying in equal measure.*"

The second six brings written exercises. The first is what chambers calls 'panel work'. "*You're given just over five weeks to do six different pieces for six different members of chambers.*" There's just one deadline for all of them, "*so it's up to you to manage your time. You have to make a judgement and think, 'This piece will take four days, this one will take a week' and so on. It's good because it's actually very indicative of how your practice will be.*" Normal pupillage hours are more like 9am to 6pm, but during this period "*you will be working quite late and you will be working weekends.*" Finally, there's The Test, which is a "*quite complex*" fictitious set of instructions. Pupils have a week to produce written advice and a set of pleadings, and essentially "*it's their opportunity to showcase what they've learnt.*"

The tenancy decision is taken shortly afterwards and, in "*an attempt to get into a subjective process as much objectivity as possible,*" the assessed work is the key factor. Pupilmasters produce reports, but these are of lesser importance. The personality of pupils isn't completely disregarded when the decision is taken – they have to be able to "*fly the flag*" and not be a complete embarrassment to the set – but chambers recognises that "*some clients want academic barristers, some want duff-'em-up types and some want people they can go down the pub with.*" You'll find all three breeds here.

With plenty of "*real characters*" among the senior members, it's perhaps not surprising that juniors are exposed to "*some of the funniest conversations I've ever heard*" at tea (every day, 4pm). The youngest members of the set are clearly quite close and will go out for drinks on Friday evenings.

And finally...

From *"piddling little disputes that can be nonetheless quite complex and cutting-edge"* to massive international arbitrations that will make your fortune, the experience that Atkin offers can be as varied as any mainstream commercial set.

2 Bedford Row

The facts

Location: Bedford Row, London
Number of QCs/Juniors: 19/52 (15 women)
Applications: 475
Apply through Pupillage Portal
Pupils per year: 4
Seats: 2x6 months
Pupillage award: £22,000 (no advance)

Right at the pinnacle of the Criminal Bar, 2BR demands candidates *"with common sense and their heads screwed on."*

This top-ranked set has been involved with many of the nation's most prominent criminal cases.

Crime pays

2 Bedford Row's reputation was originally built around the practice of its founder William Clegg, and it has now become one of the hottest names at the Criminal Bar. Members of the set have defended hammer killer Levi Bellfield; five murder suspects in the Stephen Lawrence case; Jill Dando's alleged killer Barry George; and the police officers who shot Jean Charles de Menezes. *"It's really the best criminal set if you want to work at the top of the field,"* a junior enthused. Members also acted for Munir Hussain, the businessman jailed after he fought armed robbers in his home with a cricket bat, and helped Greenpeace activists arrested after a protest at the Kingsnorth power station in Kent. This was the first time climate change considerations were successfully brought into the defence in a criminal case. The set has also been involved in Russian mafia murder cases and the defence of a 14-year-old boy charged with sexually assaulting his younger brothers and sister.

A reflection of the economy as much as anything else, fraud defence is an area chambers is *"really heading into more."* 2BR was involved in one of 2009's biggest political scandals, acting for Ian Clement, former deputy mayor of London, over his fraudulent expense claims. As you can tell from this rundown of cases, the set is primarily engaged in defence work, although there is also prosecution work on behalf of the CPS. Senior clerk John Grimmer made another timely point: *"Publicly funded cases account for a little over half of our work now, and we have recognised that we want to be innovative and change our practice areas before we are forced to."*

On this very issue, pupillage committee chair Sandesh Singh told us about the rise in regulatory instructions. Currently around 20% of the set's instructions relate to regulatory matters (mostly health-related), but the aim is to achieve a 50/50 balance between these and criminal instructions. *"There's sports law, medical law, General Dental Council and General Optical Council work,"* explained a pupil. *"It's good that the set has a plan B."* Health and safety defence work has so far included representing a company in the Buncefield oil refinery explosion case and defending a firearms instructor who accidentally shot someone during a training exercise. Members also undertake prosecution work for the Department for Transport and the Trading Standards Authority.

More than academics

From the 450-500 or so pupillage applications received each year, between 80 and 100 result in an invitation to a *"probing but informal"* first interview. *"The first round includes a general chat about your CV and then a legal/political question."* The next stage sees 15 candidates attend a longer second interview, which includes an advocacy exercise (usually a plea in mitigation) and a number of questions on a legal issue. Recruiters are looking for three main things: a dedication to the Criminal Bar; real-life advocacy experience, *"like working for FRU, tribunal experience via the College of Law, or even taking up your neighbour's cause in a legal battle;"* and, thirdly, *"life experience – our members include a former copper, a tabloid jour-*

Chambers UK rankings

Crime	Health & Safety
Fraud	Professional Discipline

nalist and two lads from the army." Doing a 2BR mini-pupillage is "*useful, but by no means essential*" for a realistic shot at pupillage.

Having a first-class degree from a first-class university "*is not really something we're bothered about – academic background doesn't matter,*" insited Sandesh Singh. "*We don't have a '2:1 and above' policy; we sometimes take on people with a 2:2 if they are fabulous in other ways.*" The statistics bear out Singh's claim: only a quarter of 2BR's members are Oxbridge alumni, against an average of over 70% at the sets featured in this guide. So what qualities do you need to have? "*Applicants should be hard-working, intelligent, personable and good at dealing with people. You shouldn't apply if you're shy of hard work or are precious about certain things. You have to be prepared to suddenly get a train to Liverpool or the Isle of Wight.*"

Basement fundamentals

To discover more about the set's pupillage, we were led down to its basement library, where pupils keep their nose to the grindstone. Pupillage is a tough game at 2 Bedford Row: the recruitment committee admits that its recruits "*get worked pretty bloody hard.*" Pupils have two pupilmasters in each six. "*One is more senior* [over 14 years' call] *and one more junior* [8 to 14 years] *so that you get some heavy stuff and then some knock-about one to two-week trials in the Crown Court.*" Pupils spend slightly more than half of their time with the more junior supervisor, "*getting to know the nuts and bolts of the Crown Court.*" Around 50% of pupils' work is crime-related, with fraud and regulatory making up the remainder. "*A typical day in your first six is spent going to court with your junior pupilmaster; then another member will set you paperwork for later on.*"

The second six brings "*a change of pace.*" Pupils commonly put in 12-hour days. After "*court in the morning, having picked up the papers the night before,*" it's not uncommon to then spend evenings on research tasks, either for themselves or their pupilmaster. It's the real thing from the start – "*I had a trial on my first day,*" a pupil proudly recalled. "*It was in the Magistrates' Court on a racially aggravated assault. I was terrified, but then I realised I was actually really well prepared.*" During pupillage, "*you mainly work in the Magistrates' Court and the Crown Court... and you get to do a bit of everything.*" After one or two years of tenancy, you're "*predominantly in the Crown Court,*" doing anything from "*five-week complex trials to high-street punch-ups and murders.*"

Gaining tenancy is "*necessarily political,*" but members claim it's "*less so here than elsewhere, and more based on ability.*" The pupillage committee assures us that the tenancy decision is merit-based: "*It just depends on how good they are because there is an increasing amount of work for people at the bottom end.*" In 2010, one of four pupils was granted tenancy. Five elements are officially taken into account: an interview with the tenancy committee to discuss "*a load of difficult* [ethical and legal] *questions;*" two to three pieces of written work; references from solicitors and judges; confidential comments from other members of chambers; and pupilmasters' reports. The set also presents pupils with "*daunting*" advocacy exercises, "*which are becoming more and more important.*" Most exercises take place in chambers, but one is "*a mock trial in a real courtroom, where members attend and play witnesses. It's seriously high pressure and you have to present your case in front of a retired judge.*"

In practice, "*a lot depends on who you've impressed,*" a pupil revealed; "*the juniors, the seniors, the clerks – it's absolutely vital to impress the clerks.*" A junior agreed: "*Pupillage is competitive, but it's not hard to get to know as many people as possible and work for them.*" John Grimmer told us just how important it is for pupils to have the right attitude: "*We expect that they will pass through the clerks' room and have a rapport with us. I'm looking for people who I will be able to sell; people with common sense and their head screwed on.*"

Chambers' social life centres on a pub on Sandland Street. "*You'll regularly walk past the Old Nick and see your pupilmaster, and he'll ask you to come in for a pint.*" As well as a favourite pub, members share one or two other things in common – an appetite for hard work and a commitment to the independent Criminal Bar. "*We don't drink as much as we used to in this set any more,*" one tenant said wistfully, "*but everyone still has a sense of humour.*"

And finally...

The recruiters at 2 Bedford Row value talent and hard graft in equal measure. This set should be viewed as the best of the best if you're thinking about criminal and fraud practice, especially if you want to also work in the regulatory sphere.

Blackstone Chambers

The facts

Location: Temple, London
Number of QCs/Juniors: 34/50 (22 women)
Applications: 300
Apply through Pupillage Portal
Pupils per year: 4-5
Seats: 4x3 months
Pupillage Award: £52,500 (can advance £15,000 for BPTC)

At the apex of public, commercial and employment law, Blackstone is a top set full of top talent.

Jack-of-all-trades and master of, well, all of them, Blackstone Chambers is in a really positive phase.

Considerable economic stress in this period in history

Unusually, we conducted our interviews with members of Blackstone in the open air. Sitting on the set's roof terrace on a blazing hot summer's day, with views of Parliament to the left, St Paul's to the right and a wide blue sky overhead, it was hard not to come away wanting to write an equally sunny and positive feature. Fortunately, chambers' recent history is as glorious as was the weather. It has succeeded at everything it has set its hand to: top-tier rankings in *Chambers UK* for an impressive eight practice areas pay testament to that. Now, we said Blackstone was a jack-of-all-trades, but that's not quite true – it doesn't want to spread itself too thin. The best way to view the set is as a three-legged stool, with commercial, employment and public law all of roughly equal importance. "*We want to ensure there is a proper spread of work across all practice areas,*" says chambers director Julia Hornor.

The high-profile cases Blackstone has been involved in are numerous, so we'll just mention one from each of its three main areas. A darling of the Bar, Dinah Rose QC acted on *R (Binyam Mohamed) v Secretary of State for Foreign and Commonwealth Affairs*, seeking disclosure of information regarding the torture of a British resident held in Guantanamo Bay. Other members of Blackstone advised the BBC on its rights and liabilities during the Jonathan Ross/Russell Brand affair, while on the employment side, barristers have successfully defended a couple of law firms in age discrimination cases brought by former partners.

Despite the economic downturn, or perhaps because of it, chambers remains very busy. "*Because of the areas we deal with, and because of the spread that we have, we can shift our balance a little bit as the market demands. Public law is unlikely to disappear and we do an awful lot of regulatory and financial services work. I think we had seven members on the Northern Rock litigation.*" The set has expanded in a number of areas, hiring barristers throughout 2009 and 2010.

Go away or we shall taunt you a second time

At the first interview, prospective pupils rock up to Blackstone about 20 minutes early and select one of half a dozen topical subjects on which they will then be grilled. "*Mine was at about the time of the Big Brother racism furore,*" says one pupil, "*and the question I chose was about whether Ofcom should require broadcasters to censor live television.*" Expect a pretty tough ride at this stage and be sure to keep your head. "*You start talking and think you are rolling along nicely, and then all of a sudden you are being cross-examined by seven people.*" Often one member in particular will really lay into you, "*but it's a different person every time. When I arrived here, I couldn't believe how nice the woman who had been heckling me was!*" Coming away from this encounter feeling "*brutalised*" doesn't necessarily mean you're out of the running.

The next stage is a week-long (and potentially partly funded) assessed mini-pupillage, which includes two days devoted to a piece of set work, plus a look at the live

Chambers UK rankings

Administrative & Public Law	Fraud
Civil Liberties	Immigration
Commercial Dispute Resolution	Media & Entertainment
	Professional Discipline
Competition/European Law	Public International Law
Employment	Public Procurement
Environment	Sports Law
Financial Services	Telecommunications

matters the pupil supervisors have on their desks. There's also a trip to court to see advocates in action. Particularly impressive mini-pupils "*are not necessarily the ones who know masses of law, but those who are able to engage with, and talk with clarity about, whatever problem they are presented with.*" Second interviews don't take place until quite late in the summer. By this point, about 15 candidates remain, and "*they mainly want to talk about what you saw in your mini-pupillage and how you felt about it. They are basically trying to assess how keen you are on chambers and whether if they make an offer you're going to accept it.*" Oxford and Cambridge grads naturally do well, but it's worth noting that a recent pupil not only didn't go to Oxbridge but doesn't have a degree at all. A Certificate of Academic Standing from the Bar Council, plus a glittering previous career with a news agency, was intellectual qualification enough for Blackstone.

A mandate from the masses, not some farcical aquatic ceremony

It's chambers' policy that pupils spend one seat with someone who does a lot of employment law, and one with someone who does a lot of public law. The remaining two seats had been, for one junior, mostly commercial. "*I had to read through a film script to work out which bits were actually the property of the scriptwriter. That was quite fun.*" He also got involved with the Formula 1 'Spygate' case for McLaren. "*That was not only high-profile but a really interesting bit of law.*"

"*Perhaps more is expected from you later on,*" but first-seat work won't be essentially any different from fourth-seat work. For one supervisor at least, "*every last bit of it is live, in the sense that I'm hoping that work product from pupils will be useful to me. Inevitably some of it is low-grade stuff, working out how to present a case. I aim for them to do a draft pleading, or a skeleton argument, or an opinion before I have to, so if they come up with something good I can then incorporate it.*" One pupil found it "*very encouraging*" that a paragraph she had written went out largely unchanged her second week. Pupils also go along to conferences with clients and see the strategy side of cases.

Chambers runs "*a very detailed advocacy programme,*" and pupils will "*probably do a FRU case or two*" in order to get some experience, but they won't be in court all the time. For juniors, however, it's a different story. "*In terms of getting advocacy experience early on, there's nothing like employment law. You simply don't get that in commercial practice,*" says a junior. Blackstone is keen to ensure that all junior tenants undertake plenty of court work, "*so they get used to cross-examining witnesses and standing in front of any type of judge. That is what will give them the edge in later years.*" Chambers is most definitely "*looking for advocates*" and not "*shrinking violet eggheads.*"

Over the course of the year there are six written exercises and seven advocacy training sessions (of which only the post Christmas ones are assessed). When it comes to deciding tenancy, "*by far the most important views are those of the pupilmasters,*" but having said that, Blackstone is "*a true democracy. I've always been of the view that the closest comparison with chambers is the anarcho-syndicalist collective in Monty Python. It truly is one person, one vote and each person can vote as they see fit.*" In practice, however, it's unheard of for chambers to go against the views of four unanimous pupilmasters. In 2010, all four pupils were happy to accept tenancy offers.

We dance when we are able

Friday night drinks take place whenever there are mini-pupils in chambers (ie most of the summer) "*and even at other times, three Fridays out of four either someone will be having drinks in their room or everyone will go to the Edgar Wallace.*" Friday fish-and-chip lunches at the Inner Temple are also a tradition.

Blackstone has "*no platonic ideal of a barrister*" and members say that the set is "*remarkably happy considering how diverse we are in terms of personalities. Politically we range from Marxists to some people who are pretty conservative, both big C and small. We've had people stand for Parliament for all three major parties.*"

And finally...

If you want further proof of how settled chambers is, take a look at the number of QCs it has. Many of them turned down appointments to the Bench to stay in practice. *"No one ever leaves this place."*

Cloisters

The facts

Location: Temple, London

Number of QCs/Juniors: 5/42 (19 women)

Applications: 327

Apply through Pupillage Portal

Pupils per year: 2

Seats: 4x3 months

Pupillage Award: £35,000 (can advance £7,500 for BPTC)

Head of chambers Robin Allen QC says: *"You should come here if you want to be a fearless lawyer."*

Employment, PI and clin neg specialist Cloisters attracts those with a keen interest in the rights of the individual.

Neither tarnished nor afraid

Cloisters' practice has changed quite considerably since it came into existence in the early 1950s. Originally focusing mainly on criminal law, its civil practice gradually grew, especially in the fields of employment, personal injury and clinical negligence. Its founding members were fairly left-wing, and in the old days it "*invariably*" acted for claimants. In fact, senior clerk Glenn Hudson says that once upon a time 90% of its work came from just one firm, Thompsons (the country's largest PI specialist). Chambers' caseload is now far more balanced with instructions coming from hundreds of solicitors. Instructions on the employment side are now an even mix of respondent and claimant matters, while PI and clin neg still retain a strong claimant slant. Approximately 65% of the work that comes to chambers is employment, commercial and regulatory law, 20% is PI and 15% clin neg.

Some time ago, the criminal barristers decided to go their separate ways, mainly to Charter Chambers and Tooks Chambers. Combined with the increase in respondent work, this saw the set drift towards the centre politically, but that doesn't mean it has ditched its original ideals. In a recent talk to some of its interns (what Cloisters now calls mini-pupils in a valiant attempt to sound modern and with-it), head of chambers Robin Allen QC said: "*You should come here if you want to be a fearless lawyer.*" "*That might sound a bit overblown,*" says Anna Beale, a member of the pupillage committee, "*but I think it's probably true. We have a reputation for doing those cutting-edge cases, generally for claimants, and there is a defining feeling that we are all here because we broadly believe in the same things that chambers believes in.*" One of those cutting-edge cases is *Abbott & Others v South Tyneside MBC*, in which the Employment Appeal Tribunal ruled that 300 low-paid male workers were discriminated against after they failed in a claim over bonuses, while a group of low-paid women with a similar claim succeeded. In another matter, Cloisters is acting for an Orthodox Jewish couple who claim that an automatic security light in their communal accommodation forces them to break their Sabbath rules.

Chambers wants to be regarded as the best in the business for the work that it currently does. It also plans to "*see if we can pick up some of the public law work that we were once so well known for. Ten years ago we were the number-one public law set, ahead of all the others, but with people getting* [judicial] *appointments and retiring, that work has dropped away.*"

Suit you?

Each CV received by chambers gets marked out of 20 by two members. The first ten points are for academic ability (for example, we're told a 2:1 plus a relevant Master's would score 6.5). Two extra points are available here for demonstrating outstanding academic ability (coming top in your year, that sort of thing). The second ten points are more subjective and are awarded for various different qualities. These are: 'soft' communication skills (having worked in a customer service industry, say a supermarket, would help); advocacy (ie formal presentation skills – ex-teachers or actors would probably score well for this); initiative and independence (are you suited to a self-employed career, can you juggle lots of tasks?) and

Chambers UK rankings

Clinical Negligence	Personal Injury
Employment	

commitment to the law (past work experience and so on). A final mark is available for "*suitability for Cloisters:*" do you have an interest in the rights of the individual? Get yourself some experience with FRU, we say.

Around 60 people are invited to a first interview. In previous years Cloisters posed a contract and tort-type problem of the type you might find in an exam. Finding that "*a bit too focused on strict legal knowledge,*" it changed things this year. "*We gave them a slightly altered and fictionalised real case and asked them to summarise the main points and challenge the decision.*" Roughly 15 people get through to second interview stage, at which applicants tackle another problem question, "*sometimes related to our practice areas but not always.*" As the question is posed seven days in advance, be prepared for some thorough questioning. Finally, there's a discussion on a topical subject: whether Dwain Chambers should be allowed to compete in the Olympics came up in 2008.

Off the wall

The first six is spent sitting with your supervisor and going to court with them. The second six is when things get really juicy. "*You can expect to be in court with your own cases fairly regularly*" right from the off, and with work still being set by your supervisor, plus a series of assessed exercises to handle, it's fair to say there's "*quite a lot to juggle in the second six.*" Those assessed exercises are vital as the tenancy decision is heavily based on them. In fact, very little weight is given to the reports of the four supervisors – odd, we thought – but Cloisters insists that this method is fairer and that they are trying to move away from "*the old school where everyone just votes on whether they like you or not.*" There are four assessments. The first is a drafting exercise, the second "*an advice with a whole list of things that no one person would ever need to know to research,*" the third is advocacy, and the whole thing concludes with an interview in front of five or six members of chambers who "*all pile in.*" By this point, pupils are probably going to have to work reasonably late to fit everything in. "*I generally leave between 7.30pm and 9.30pm, and am doing weekend work as well – although I'm good about making sure I take one day off a week,*" said a pupil with the second assessment coming up. The hours are much less onerous at the start of pupillage. So is it oral or written skills that count most? The answer depends on what you eventually specialise in. An employment barrister will be in court or tribunal on a weekly basis; a PI specialist on the other hand may find that 80-90% of the time is spent drafting papers and advices.

A word on pro bono. Each barrister does at least five days of pro bono work per year, either at a legal advice centre or for clients who just miss out on legal aid. "*People spend a lot of their effort and time on cases that are very poorly paid, if at all,*" said one pupil. Chambers takes pride in accepting "*cases that are a bit off the wall.*" One such was the lotto rapist case, which Cloisters' Paul Spencer handled on a pro bono basis. It went right up to the House of Lords, and he managed to get the law changed for the benefit of his client, the rapist's victim.

Cloisters but not cloistered

As you might imagine, we get fed a lot of PR at the *Student Guide*, so it was refreshing to find Cloisters relatively free of marketing spin. We notice that the submissions it sends to *Chambers UK* (in which sets try and persuade us why they should be ranked) are some of the most polite we've ever seen, and you might notice that the profiles of members on the website are listed in egalitarian alphabetical order rather than QCs first. The photo of junior Sally Cowen seems to have been taken in a car park. We're not complaining – we think it's terrific that there's a lack of PR BS. During our visit, clerks acknowledged that there are areas in which chambers hasn't done quite as well as it would have liked. They freely admit that "*all chambers are going through the downturn in the work* [available to] *the Bar.*" And, shock-horror: "*All chambers have internal politics,*" and it's no different here.

One year we dubbed Cloisters 'Bolly Chambers' because of the quantity of champagne that was consumed. Even in these straitened times members "*do like having an excuse to go out together.*" Says a clerk: "*We've lost a couple of people to sets that are very much 'heads down and work' in atmosphere, and privately they have said that's what they miss. It's those little things that you take for granted until you've moved on.*" Juniors share rooms, so there's always someone to bounce ideas off, and if you want proof that Cloisters is a party set, one of the current pupils had come to their first interview straight from Glastonbury. "*They said, 'You've clearly been doing too many of these interviews because you've lost your voice...'*"

And finally...

Cloisters has come a long way from the left-wing, claimant-only set it started out as and new tenants will doubtless see the set evolve further. In 2010, one of the two pupils was taken on as a tenant, while the other remained for a third six.

Crown Office Chambers

The facts

Location: Temple, London
Number of QCs/Juniors: 14/75 (18 women)
Applications: 130
Outside Pupillage Portal Scheme
Pupils per year: Up to 3
Seats: 2x3 + 1x6 months
Pupillage Award: £42,500 (can advance £15,000 for BPTC)

Senior clerk Julian Campbell describes this as *"a forward-thinking traditional set."*

Crown Office Chambers is the largest common law set at the Bar. Its strong backbone of insurance expertise crosses several fields of practice.

Alien ants

2010 marks Crown Office Chambers' tenth anniversary, the set having been formed in 2000 through the merger of One Paper Buildings and 2 Crown Office Row. These were two premier insurance sets and "*the watchwords were strength in depth.*" It was felt that since they had such similar practice area footprints, their union would create a 'superset' better able to withstand the slings and arrows of legal fortune. Chambers can look back and say the merger was a good move. Clerks tell us that "*turnover has increased year on year*" (up 15% in 2008/09), and that "*the business of chambers has picked up*" because "*there are enough people specialising in each of our chosen areas that we can offer our clients a range of barristers. If there's a case that requires four or five barristers of different levels, we have the skills all in one chambers.*"

COC doesn't focus on one specific area of practice. Instead, it has identified a number of key sectors in which it is capable. Broadly, these are: construction, insurance, professional negligence, personal injury, health and safety, product liability and clinical negligence. The ambition is simple: "*within five years to have doubled our turnover in all of those.*" The set can justifiably claim to have strength in each of these areas, but looking through the *Chambers UK* rankings over the past few years, we notice that a couple of areas in particular have come to the fore.

The first is personal injury. By the sheer number of instructions received, this is COC's biggest area of work. The set sits in *Chambers UK*'s top tier and has a particularly good reputation for industrial disease cases. Members have acted on deafness claims brought by ex-employees of the former vehicle manufacturer British Leyland, and the employers' liability 'Trigger' litigation, which will determine whether employers or insurers should pay for many of the asbestos claims of the past 50 years. Other PI cases of note include one in which a claimant was attacked by a herd of cows while crossing a field in the Lake District, suffering serious injuries. There was a footpath across the field but it was unmarked, and a claim was brought against the farmer in negligence and under the Animals Act. Another was US rock band Alien Ant Farm's $40m claim against a coach operator, one of the largest PI claims in UK history.

With "*fewer but bigger cases*" than PI, construction is the second area to which we draw your attention. Despite COC having fewer members working in this area than Keating and Atkin, our *Chambers UK* colleagues describe it as a 'thoroughly viable alternative' to those specialist construction sets. The star here is Roger ter Haar QC, who has been working on a couple of arbitrations pertaining to a £200m claim arising out of a telecommunications project on the London Underground and a $50m claim against a state-owned Bulgarian company on behalf of an Arab contractor. And yet even members this senior won't specialise too much. In addition to having built a crack reputation for construction cases, Mr ter Haar is ranked by *Chambers UK* in several other areas.

Chambers UK rankings

Clinical Negligence	Personal Injury
Construction	Product Liability
Health & Safety	Professional Negligence

Martian melodies

There doesn't seem to be much we can tell you about COC's application form that it doesn't tell you itself. You can find the form on its website and you'll see that intellect, work style, people skills, communication, self-awareness, commitment and motivation are what you'll be judged on. Chambers operates outside the Pupillage Portal scheme and wants to see something more than "*generic*" answers.

The same goes for the interview process. About 20 people are invited to a first-round interview, and about ten make it to a second, where a typically atypical question might be 'Explain an iPod to a Martian'. It should be obvious from this that oral skills are highly prized. A junior told us: "*I wanted to be a barrister because I wanted to be in court. Now, I know people who want to be barristers because they want to advise on complicated points of law. There are chambers that do one and chambers that do the other.*" COC places emphasis on advocacy, for the early years at least. Said one source: "*Our most junior tenant is in court three or four times a week,*" further honing skills that she had begun to develop in her second six. So, "*if you don't have the ability to be an effective advocate this would not be the chambers for you.*"

"*That doesn't mean there isn't any research or writing bits of advice, because there's that as well.*" Plenty of it by all accounts. Recruits spend the year with four pupilmasters, and in every seat there are two fixed, written assessments, set and marked by a relevant specialist. An assessed advocacy course begins after Christmas, and COC tells us it is looking for a general upward trajectory in the quality of pupils' advocacy skills, rather than stellar performance after stellar performance. Everyone shares the same pupilmasters to ensure fairness of assessment, and these supervisors are selected to give pupils exposure to pretty much all chambers' practice areas. The idea being that it's unwise to put "*all your eggs in one basket.*" Pupils are also encouraged to work for other members of chambers, getting to know more of them by doing so. The tenancy decision is made in July and based partly on the results of the assessments and partly on comments from other members of chambers, but mainly on reports given by pupilmasters. In 2009, the set's sole second-six pupil was offered tenancy, while in 2010 all three pupils were successful.

Back to the future

"*I would describe this as a forward-thinking traditional set,*" says senior clerk Julian Campbell. We asked for clarification of this apparent contradiction in terms. "*We're not a set that would dispense with the Bar's traditions – we like them – but behind the scenes it is run in a very businesslike way.*" An executive committee is the driving force these days: "*It's not practical when you are this size to have all decisions taken by a plenary chambers meeting,*" says a junior. "*That was what happened when I started out, and the meetings would be interminable. People would go on at great length about how much they agreed with each other! The executive committee has made it more efficient.*" One recent decision of note is an "*affiliation*" with Edinburgh's Compass Chambers. It's the first such tie-up between an English and a Scottish set, and the thinking is that it will help improve the service to insurance industry clients wherever cross-border claims are involved. A business mindset is also reflected in the fact that chambers "*doesn't tolerate second-rate practice, and members are even bearded from time to time. Of course they are self-employed people, but they very much run under a Crown Office Chambers banner, and there is a certain level of expectation because of that.*"

We think chambers' large size really is its defining feature. It has made the push towards a more necessary corporate structure; it has made it possible to carry out a broad range of practice, and it naturally dictates the culture of the place. Members admit that "*to a certain extent you lose the family atmosphere*" of a smaller set, but then knowing what some families are like, is that such a disadvantage? You might not know everyone at COC, but its size does ensure "*there will always be a critical mass of people at about your level doing your thing.*" Equally, there's the space to avoid people you don't get on with. We sense that COC is a broad church with room for both pockets of the old school and the new breed of barrister. Speaking of bonding, bar a couple of the marketing events, pupils are invited to all social functions, from chambers drinks on Thursdays or Fridays to the annual Christmas jolly.

And finally...

Bigger is better for COC. Its six diverse areas of practice give it a solid foundation to withstand whatever the economy and the changing professional environment might throw at it.

One Essex Court

The facts

Location: Temple, London
Number of QCs/Juniors: 24/48 (12 women)
Applications: c. 200
Apply through Pupillage Portal
Pupils per year: 4-5
Seats: 2x3 and 1x6 months
Pupillage Award: £60,000 + earnings (can advance £20,000 for BPTC)

Chambers and Partners' Commercial Litigation Set of the Year 2010

An elite but straightforward set, One Essex Court takes pride in being *"not a formal, suit-wearing place – quite the reverse in fact."*

Rebels with a cause

The name One Essex Court was first heard in the narrow alleyways and leafy squares of the Temple in 1966, when a group of four barristers and a clerk broke away from a set in Mitre Court. "*Some of them were Catholic, some were Jewish, and in those days the Bar was a lot more English and Establishment. These were people who weren't going to get a place at the leading sets of the time, so they started their own chambers.*"

Current members ascribe OEC's subsequent phenomenal success to the ethos of "*meritocracy*" that was present right from the beginning. It's now a part of the magic circle of commercial sets, although this wasn't cause for boasting during the course of our interviews with members, clerks and pupils – in fact as far as we can remember, the words 'magic circle' didn't crop up once. But nonetheless you'll see chambers at the forefront of all kinds of big commercial disputes, including the Buncefield and Northern Rock litigations and the bank charges test case. Members have also acted on cases such as *Esure v Direct Line* (in an IP kerfuffle over a mouse-on-wheels logo), *Chelsea FC v FC Lyn Oslo* (a spat over the signing of John Obi Mikel) and *Cable & Wireless v Ofcom* (for eight fixed-line operators in an appeal relating to mobile phone termination charges). While other chambers tend to have certain specialist areas, OEC remains very much a set of generalist practitioners.

Senior clerk Darren Burrows is following in the footsteps of two legends in their own lifetimes, Robert Ralphs and Paul Shrubsall, who were instrumental in bringing clerking into the modern era. Since Shrubsall's retirement in 2008 no sweeping reforms have been made, but chambers is increasingly looking to market itself to clients outside the UK. "*That isn't something we've pursued heavily in the past, but we now have good client bases in the Caribbean and the Far East.*" Competition and EU-related work is another growing market that it wants to capitalise on. "*It's a developing area, and one that students are interested in.*" A high demand from solicitors for junior counsel has resulted in chambers "*talking to a number of firms*" about farming juniors out to them for periods of two or three months – "*a mini-secondment if you like.*"

Sanity not vanity

The selection process for pupils begins not with the Pupillage Portal, but "*by going to student law fairs and encouraging people of talent to apply.*" At £60,000, the sum chambers pays pupils is one of the highest at the Bar, "*so that no one can say, I didn't apply because I couldn't afford to.*" More people want to do mini-pupillages than there are places available, so chambers doesn't insist that you do one. "*If we did, middle class kids with pushy parents who know how to work the system would have a massive advantage.*"

Three members of the pupillage committee read every application. Said one: "*I used to ask myself, 'Is this person cleverer than I am?' If they were, they got an interview. But these days that's virtually everyone, so I have to be a little more critical.*" Academic achievement is "*a necessary but not a sufficient requirement.*" As a junior

Chambers UK rankings

Banking & Finance	Fraud
Commercial Dispute Resolution	Intellectual Property
Competition/European Law	International Arbitration
Energy & Natural Resources	Professional Negligence

pointed out: "*My pupilmaster told me 80 Oxbridge Firsts apply each year, and we only interview 40 people!*" So something extra is required, and that something is inevitably subjective. "*Personally, I don't give a toss whether someone's travelled or not – that isn't difficult these days,*" says a QC. "*There was one applicant though, who'd travelled in the second half of his gap year because he had gone door-to-door selling paintbrushes in the first half. I thought that was bloody impressive. It takes more persuasive skill to sell paintbrushes than you'll need with a commercial court judge. They have to listen to you whether they like it or not. A bloke on the doorstep can just tell you to f*** off.*"

The pupillage interview consists of a legal problem and a brief chat. Applicants get an hour and a copy of *Chitty on Contracts* to prepare for the problem, to which "*there is no right answer, but we are expecting them to at least see what the issues are.*" How interviewees react to further probing is important. "*We asked a question to one guy and he said: 'That's a very good point, but I'll come back to it later,' which was quite a ballsy thing to do. Of course if he hadn't come back to it, that's just dodging the question and he'd have failed. But he did, and that's good organisation.*" The purpose of the chat is essentially "*to ensure that they're not completely mad.*" As long as you're not round the bend, out to lunch, barking, barmy or generally bonkers, you'll be fine. If you are any of these things, there may still be space for you somewhere at the Bar, but you'll have to be exceptionally brilliant for clients to put up with you. Speaking of which, senior clerks are also present at the interview stage to give their opinion on "*whether the applicant is saleable in the market.*" This is a commercial operation, after all.

What the chat is not about is finding out: "*Are they One Of Us?*" Eton-educated members rub shoulders quite happily with those from bog-standard comprehensives (as David Blunkett so charmingly put it), of which there are plenty, including "*one guy whose father runs a market stall in Leicester.*" Three of the four 2008/09 pupils were women, one was non-Oxbridge and one was from an ethnic minority background, although it's fair to say that OEC, like the rest of the Bar, is still predominantly male and white.

Smash and grab

Pupils essentially "*live the daily practice life*" of their pupilmasters, whose styles differ. Some will deal with one case at a time; others will juggle as many matters as they can. Some will regularly leave at 6.30pm; others will stay until 8pm. There is no obligation to work particularly long hours most of the time, but "*if the pressure is on it's good to see that you are committed.*" As a junior told us: "*The occasional late night isn't going to do you any harm. You may even find yourself coming in on a weekend once or twice because you want to be in control. But no one will demand that you do that.*" If you need to leave at 5pm to pick your kids up, that's fine too. During pupillage, everything is live. "*There's nothing you do that's just an exercise. You're never just rehashing some old silk's case that he thinks he really should have won and wants every pupil to re-perform it for him. Everything is going to be used.*" In the second six, pupils will be in court relatively frequently with their own caseload of "*what we call the Robert Ralphs £50 specials*" – road traffic smashes and the like. However, since "*at the junior end most of what we do is written,*" oral and drafting skills are equally important.

After six months the head of the pupillage committee gives pupils "*a fairly candid view*" of whether they are in the running for tenancy. Those who aren't occasionally decide to seek their fortune elsewhere, but are more than welcome to stay for the second six. Obviously it's not an ideal scenario, but it's not the end of the world if you "*stuff up something massively. If the rest of your work is excellent and you're clearly cut out for the Bar, there would be no point throwing you away because of one mistake.*" The whole of chambers votes on tenancy and it's necessary for 75% of the members to be in favour for a motion to be carried. OEC has an excellent record for keeping its pupils: three out of four were kept on in 2009 and all four took up tenancy in 2010.

While not an obligation, pupils are "*almost expected to be the mainstay*" of Friday night drinks. It's generally "*not heavy on work chat. Lord Grabiner will stick his head in every now and then, and when he's there everything's a little more focused on the great man. He'll give us a bit of wisdom and say hello before he heads off for his weekend.*" Pupils are invited to all chambers' events, including the summer party and *The Times* Law Awards (which it sponsors) to make them feel part of the "*OEC family.*"

And finally...

At OEC there is ample proof that brilliance doesn't have to come with a side order of arrogance.

Thirty Nine Essex Street

The facts

Location: Temple, London; Manchester

Number of QCs/Juniors: 26/60 (22 women)

Applications: 350-400

Apply through Pupillage Portal

Pupils per year: 3-4

Seats: 4x3 months

Pupillage award: £40,000 (can advance £8,000 for BPTC)

An expanding set with a wide range of work. Candidates need to get their business heads on to make a decent impression here.

This commercial and common law set exudes an air of bustling confidence. Its tidy and meticulously designed interior reflects a progressive but controlled approach to business development.

Expansive horizons

This set believes big is beautiful. Over the past decade, 39 Essex Street has ballooned from around 30 to over 85 members. "*We have a strategy which includes expansion up to a figure of around 100 barristers at the moment,*" said chambers director Michael Meeson. "*All our practices are growing and we need more personnel. Our expansion is dictated by the needs of each practice area.*" Chambers recently spilled over into an annexe and opened a sub-office in Manchester; it also has plans for a small base in Dubai. Total billing was up 16% in 2009 and annual turnover is now around £30m.

Why is the set doing so well? "*Firstly, the art of advocacy is more in fashion than it ever was. Because of the recession, more cases are going all the way,*" Meeson explained. "*Secondly, you've got to keep your name out there and we have just rebranded.*" The set's brochures and website now show the number 39 cropping up in a variety of odd places, as if it's starring in a cross between *Where's Wally* and *Sesame Street*. The interior of its Victorian premises has also been redesigned in corporate purple and clean white, with minimalist seascapes adorning the walls.

Apart from size and ambition, another key attraction of 39 is the broad scope of its work – *Chambers UK* ranks it in over a dozen practice areas. Instructions are grouped into four main areas: common law; environmental and planning; commercial/construction; and public law. The set's old core of common law PI, professional negligence and clin neg work is "*robust and healthy,*" while "*purely commercial disputes are ever increasing, here and overseas.*" Members were involved in the Trafigura toxic waste case, as well as a dispute over the construction of the Nelson Mandela Bay Stadium for the 2010 World Cup.

Many public law instructions come from the Treasury Solicitor's department. Members also act for the Home Office on immigration, mental health and prison matters, while other clients include the MoJ, the Foreign Office, NHS trusts and local authorities. Away from the public sector, the set recently defended BT in a £4m claim by Tiscali over breaches of consumer protection regulations and was involved in a dispute over the building of a block of flats in Hong Kong. One of the specialities of the environmental and planning group is nuclear power, "*which is good for us as we're about to enter a new era of building nuclear power stations in this country.*"

Four slices of the pie

Chambers is characterised by a well-structured pupillage. "*It's a pretty tight regime,*" one pupil told us. They went on to add that this all reflects the fact that the set is "*becoming ever more like a business.*" Pupils complete four 'seats': one in each of the set's four core areas, so "*two are public and two are private law-related.*" This means pupils benefit from an "*incredibly broad*" experience. "*At the moment,*" said one, "*I'm in a public law seat, representing the government on prisons issues. A few*

Chambers UK rankings

Administrative & Public Law	Immigration
Civil Liberties	Local Government
Clinical Negligence	Personal Injury
Construction	Product Liability
Costs Litigation	Professional Discipline
Environment	Professional Negligence
	Tax

weeks ago I was working for a construction company whose building fell over. Those two areas require very different styles of writing and a different approach."

Seats last two or three months, and pupils sit with their supervisors, who are "*scrupulously fair.*" For example, the set has a rule that members always pay when out for lunch with a pupil, and "*pupils' hours are controlled; they're 9am to 6pm.*" In the first six, pupils are "*thrown right in*" with extensive shadowing and drafting practice. "*I worked on the big challenge to the third runway at Heathrow,*" said one; "*my supervisor got me to do a huge piece of drafting – it was in the papers and everything!*" Some supervisors hand out 'dead cases' for pupils to go over, but concrete research tasks for live matters are more common. The hours may lengthen in the second six "*when you start getting your own cases,*" typically small claims, road traffic accidents and some contractual matters.

Supervisors ensure that pupils don't become overloaded with tasks for other members. "*Most of your work is just for your supervisor; everything else has to go through them.*" The large size of the set means it's impossible to impress (or even know) absolutely everyone, so pupils can at least escape the pressure of having to get their face known in all corners of chambers. There's no need to pick a specialism as a pupil, but by the time they are three or four years' call, juniors will have built up a practice around one of the set's main pillars. "*To say I specialise is too strong,*" one told us, "*but 30 to 40% of my work is on environment and planning, 30 to 40% is general commercial and the rest is PI and some RTA claims.*" They continued: "*The clerks are responsive to what you want to do and try to steer that work towards you.*"

39 steps

Pupils receive regular assessment and feedback by way of "*half-term and half-time reports.*" They are tested on oral advocacy skills in in front of a silk who plays the part of a judge, and an audience of tenants. Meanwhile, a 'shadow pupillage panel' ensures they complete written work "*for two or three top members of chambers with complicated practices.*" These exercises influence the tenancy decision, but it's the pupil supervisors who really hold the keys to chambers. "*Supervisors will get together and discuss pupils' performance*" and then advise the tenancy committee accordingly. "*There's no secretive cabal,*" pupils told us; "*you just need to do good work and not worry about sucking up to people.*" We're assured that "*extremely high*" objective standards determine who secures tenancy. "*It's made painfully clear to the pupils again and again that we are not in competition: there is room and work for all of us.*" In 2010, two pupils were offered tenancy and a third was set to finish their pupillage after we went to press.

Winning a pupillage in the first place is a tough affair, with two rounds of interviews and a "*mind-bendingly difficult*" problem question. Michael Meeson says candidates "*need to be interesting and have done other things.*" Go to our website to find out more.

What's in a number?

With the aim of integrating them, "*a month in, the pupils go bowling with the clerks and some junior tenants, just to loosen things up.*" The pupils themselves sometimes get quite close. One was somewhat embarrassed to tell us: "*We meet every day for coffee before work and 80% of days for lunch and sometimes for drinks after work too!*" Chambers hosts drinks evenings and in-house lunches on alternate weeks, and pupils make good use of both. A junior confirmed that there are no social obligations once you're a member, but while you're a pupil "*it's difficult for people to get an impression of you if they don't meet you at drinks.*"

When they first arrive, pupils certainly notice the set's size: "*The clerks' room is massive and a bit intimidating,*" whispered one, and yet barristers and pupils evidently have a lot of respect for the clerking team – one pupil even described clerking head David Barnes as "*an absolute hero.*" Although the set's management is committed to a businesslike approach, this doesn't translate into a hard-nosed, overly commercial culture, and we learned that barristers can "*focus on work, not the business side of things.*"

And finally...

'What's in a number?' asks this set's publicity material. When it comes to the number 39 we'd say there's quite a lot for a wannabe barrister to consider.

Government Legal Service (GLS)

The facts

Location: London
Number of barristers: 464 (265 women)
Applications: 2,500 (barristers + solicitors)
Outside Pupillage Portal
Pupils per year: 10
Seats: 2x6 or 3x4 months
Pupillage award: £23,280-£25,600 + BPTC fees and a maintenance grant of £5,435-£7,625

An attractive alternative to the independent Bar, the GLS offers a varied pupillage and the chance to work on headline cases.

The GLS's 450 or so barristers assist a single client: the government. Involving advice on legislation and policy, as well as litigation and advocacy, the GLS offers a unique pupillage.

Joined at the hip

From the Department for Work and Pensions (DWP) and the Ministry of Justice (MoJ) to Her Majesty's Revenue and Customs (HMRC) and the Home Office, over 30 government departments employ lawyers. The work they do varies widely, as you can read in the feature on the GLS's solicitors' training contract on page 294. Our Bar-bound sources this year had been involved with benefit fraud, MPs' expenses, the implementation of the 2010 Equality Act and health secretary Andrew Lansley's proposed restructuring of the NHS. The concept of public service tends to be what drives people here. "*I didn't want to work in the private sector, making money for a law firm,*" one current pupil told us. "*I did consider the independent Bar, but I decided the GLS was the most attractive way forward. It offers a huge variety of work, which is of national importance and influences the law of the land.*"

Aspiring government barristers apply via the same process as trainee solicitors and simply tick a box on the application form to indicate their preferred direction. For more on the application process visit our website. But, 'we'll let you into a little secret,' says the GLS's own homepage. 'Once qualified, we tend not to distinguish between barristers and solicitors. They're all 'lawyers' in our eyes and both groups perform similar work.' So why does the GLS recruit both? It's chiefly to "*offer something to both sides of the profession,*" although departments do clearly value barristers' advocacy skills.

The structure of a GLS pupillage is necessarily different to that of a training contract. Pupils are assigned to a 'home department', and over half are based at the Treasury Solicitor's Department (TSol). Pupils complete either two six-month seats or three four-months seats. After their year of pupillage, barristers spend two years as 'legal officers' before stepping up the pay scale to become Grade 7 government lawyers. In their first year as a legal officer, barristers usually complete two six-month seats to mirror the experience of their trainee solicitor counterparts.

In TSol, dedicated supervisors monitor the work given to pupils. Elsewhere, pupils are more of an integral part of each team. The GLS "*puts a lot of effort into training and training sessions,*" and supervisors in all departments provide frequent feedback. "*Your bread-and-butter work is your own caseload,*" one source said; "*they expect you to hit the ground running.*" Another pupil added: "*From the second day I started doing work which would go out to clients.*" Within their teams, pupils are treated just like qualified junior lawyers: "*I'm dealing with case management discussions over the phone, giving advice to clients and drafting witness statements. You certainly don't spend your first two years here photocopying and sitting in on meetings.*"

One seat is usually spent with barristers in chambers. This is chiefly to satisfy BSB regulations, though the insights gained while at the independent Bar are immensely useful. "*Because your first permanent position within TSol is likely to be in litigation, you will spend a lot of time instructing barristers' chambers*" and it helps to know the ins and outs of how chambers operate.

Bish bash mish mash

TSol provides legal representation – mostly on litigation matters – to other government departments (lawyers always refer to these departments and the policymakers they advise as "*clients*"). You might find yourself working on "*high-profile sex and race discrimination cases,*" unfair dismissals or harassment cases for the Ministry of Defence. Alas, pupils don't have "*top secret*" security clearance, although plenty of the work is classed as confidential. "*Sometimes you work on things which are in the paper weeks later, and you finally get to mention you worked on that case.*" TSol sees mostly defendant work, while DWP lawyers are involved with prosecuting benefit fraudsters, and those at HMRC prosecute over tax evasion. One source explained how bringing tax prosecutions is not optional for the government: "*We don't have the scope to decide we won't pester you for that £7,000 of VAT, even if it costs £8,000 to litigate, as often much will depend on the outcome of a lead case.*" The government doesn't usually settle out of court, so lawyers play an important role in "*facilitating the case through the litigation process... dealing with any applications along the way, taking it to a tribunal and instructing counsel.*"

Besides litigation, advice on policy implementation is the second core strand of work. One pupil summed up their role in simple terms: "*A government department turns a policy the electorate has voted for into something that can actually happen. When it does that, it needs lawyers to tell it what it can and can't do. So, a lot of the questions you get from clients are, 'Can I do this?' You tell them if they can, and help them solve any problems.*" For example, lawyers working on the restructuring of the NHS are "*looking at every reference to a Primary Care Trust or a Strategic Health Authority in legislation to make sure that when they are abolished they will be accounted for somehow.*" Across departments, lawyers advise on issues like the employment of civil servants, the release of information under the Freedom of Information Act and the impact of European legislation on government contracts. Advisory seats are varied to say the least: "*One day I might be advising on space satellites, the next on the appointment of bishops by the Prime Minister.*"

A third type of duty is the creation of new legislation: "*Sometimes you help draft statutory instruments, where you bring in a new law. You get to see your own writing on the statute books!*" A small strand of their overall remit, helping draft bills and statutory instruments is perhaps the most complex work pupils do and "*it requires a fair amount of training.*"

Advocating change

So why choose the GLS over the glamour of swanning around as a barrister in private practice? Our interviewees mentioned variety of work, high levels of responsibility, work-life balance, job security and flexibility as advantages. "*Having job security and knowing you can take holiday when you want means a lot,*" commented one pupil. There are some other important differences: government lawyers earn less than many in private practice, they remain generalists throughout their career and most importantly do far less advocacy than their peers. "*Don't apply to the GLS if in your heart of hearts what you really want to do is advocacy,*" one source advised. On our website you can read more about the differences pupils saw between private practice and life in government. You'll also find a feature detailing the intricacies of the GLS's recruitment procedure.

The GLS's meritocratic application process attracts highly motivated individuals. "*Some people are very driven and committed to going the extra mile for the government.*" TSol and other departmental legal teams are not hard-nosed places though. "*I think there's a very informal and welcoming environment,*" said one pupil; "*I count some people here as my good friends.*" Another source commented that the independent Bar was "*nowhere near as diverse as we are here.*"

And finally...

Despite the threat of government cuts, the GLS will still recruit in 2011. That's very good news as it offers a pupillage that immerses people into valuable and interesting areas of legal practice.

4-5 Gray's Inn Square

The facts

Location: Gray's Inn, London

Number of QCs/Juniors: 15/39 (10 women)

Applications: 300

Apply through Pupillage Portal

Pupils per year: Up to 3

Seats: 4x3 months

Pupillage award: £39,000 (can advance some for BPTC)

If you consider high-end public law *"the sexy stuff"* then 4-5 Gray's Inn Square could prove irresistible.

This set is brimming with expertise in several areas of public law and is a serious force when it comes to planning. Its commercial practice group is building up.

No bugs on us

4-5 Gray's Inn Square was dealt a significant blow at the turn of the millennium, when seven members defected to Matrix Chambers. Then another eight members departed following a mooted merger with Monckton. Like the Y2K bug, however, that difficult episode can be consigned to the annals of early noughties history. The set has moved on, and in 2009/10 recorded its best-ever financial performance.

A history of steady year-on-year pupil recruitment and smart lateral hires at junior and senior levels, has clearly reaped rewards. Recently, for example, chambers scooped Richard Clayton QC (current Chair of the Constitutional and Administrative Law Bar Association). Growth has rendered the set's name somewhat misleading, as it has already extended into numbers 2 and 6 Gray's Inn Square to accommodate all its new arrivals.

Core strength

Chief among the set's core strengths is public law. In terms of the volume of instructions, this makes up the bulk of chambers' work, a fact that is especially apparent at the junior end. The barristers here are highly regarded for respondent matters, and count a multitude of local authorities, various central government departments and regulators as key clients. For example, the set has 11 barristers on the prestigious Attorney General's Panels of Counsel. Headline matters include the Baha Musa Inquiry, representing three soldiers during investigations into the abuse of civilian detainees in Iraq, and acting for the probation service, defending Boy George's challenge to its decision to refuse permission for him to appear on *Celebrity Big Brother*.

The set has strengthened its applicant practice and regularly receives instructions from leading firms and NGOs like Fisher Meredith and The Public Law Project. Cases include appearing for an asylum seeker in a test case concerning the scope of Article 6 of the ECHR – one of the final cases to be heard by the House of Lords and one of the first on which the new Supreme Court delivered judgment. As a pupil put it, the set is a great place to be doing "*the sexy stuff.*"

The public work dovetails nicely with the set's planning practice, an area in which members represent local and central government bodies as well as private developers. Although the flow of planning instructions was hurt by the recession, it remains 4-5 Gray's Inn Square's biggest money-spinner, with environmental law a corollary practice. Recent highlights include representing East Sussex County Council on a highly controversial compulsory purchase order issued over a site within an Area of Outstanding Natural Beauty, and representing Maidstone Borough Council during an inquiry into proposals for a 112 hectare international freight terminal. The third central pillar of the set's work is its commercial practice, which again overlaps with public and planning issues. Pupils will undertake a commercial 'seat' during their year in chambers, and they quickly learn that the set handles some high-end matters.

Chambers UK rankings

Administrative & Public Law	Local Government
Education	Planning
Environment	Professional Discipline

Laws, damned laws and statistics

Chambers is proud of its approach to recruiting. The process of picking pupils is a finely honed one, and its hit-rate in terms of identifying individuals of the calibre required for tenancy is excellent. As our source on the pupillage committee said: "*Statistically, you will probably get a tenancy.*" Indeed, in 2010 both pupils gained tenancy, while all three did in 2009. In fact, only one person hasn't made the grade in the last eight years.

Pupils sit with either three or four supervisors to ensure exposure to the full breadth of chambers' practice. As one member of the pupillage committee put it: "*It's not random at all. Every pupil sees every aspect of chambers.*" That means the first three supervisors will, as a rule, specialise in one of the three core practices: public, planning and commercial, although the work rarely divides that neatly.

Pupils spend a good deal of time with their supervisors, and for the first three months the "*official rule is you're not supposed to do work for anyone else.*" Unofficially, bits and pieces from other members might find their way to the pupil. Throughout the year, the bulk of a pupil's work is research and drafting for their supervisor, or devilling for other members of chambers. There are also opportunities for short secondments, whereby pupils might spend one or two days a week with major clients like Ofgem, the Financial Ombudsman Service or a local authority. The pupils we spoke to had not yet undertaken any advocacy of their own, having just entered their second six; not a great surprise, given the nature of the set's work. That said, there is scope for pupils to appear in winding-up applications and do bits and pieces at county court hearings and employment tribunals.

Ahead of the tenancy decision, pupils undergo three advocacy assessments that are similar in structure to the second stage of the pupillage application. More important still are the reports submitted to the tenancy committee by pupil supervisors. "*Those reports carry the most weight,*" said one pupil, but supervisors are also good about "*setting pupils up to work with others. That means a lot of people see the work you do,*" which is potentially useful if you need a few more votes in the summer. For full information on how to navigate the pupillage application process go to our website.

While undoubtedly hard work, baby juniors and current pupils were clear that pupillage isn't the overwhelming experience that it's often portrayed as. One said: "*The refrain has always been, 'We don't care how good the work is, we just want to see you improve,' and I think that's true.*" There's a fair bit of responsibility to shoulder, and in this sense pupils are "*treated more like juniors.*" Yet it's good to hear that "*it's not really a highly pressurised environment.*" This culture is reflected in the pupils' typical working day. Although there might be the occasional "*crazy week*" involving 11pm finishes, as a rule pupils are in at 8.30am and out by 6.30pm. "*People don't like you working late or at the weekends, and they will tell you that.*"

No BS

4-5 Gray's Inn Square is a set in the old sense – an association of individuals rather than a distinct commercial entity. One tenant remarked on how "*there's definitely no single culture*" and that seems a fair conclusion. Certainly, there are traditional elements: there's a quiet, studious air as smartly dressed men and women purposefully pace the carpeted floors, along corridors lined on both sides with leather-bound books. Pupils are expected to be "*in suits, shaven, with an ironed shirt.*" And yet one suggested that the suits and boots we saw on our visit might not be entirely representative of all members. "*There are those who wear waistcoats with watches on chains and those who come into work in jeans every day.*"

It's not just a set that looks traditional. Beyond aesthetics, it is quite traditional in the sense that it has avoided some of the less attractive elements of modern business models. One barrister remarked that 4-5 Gray's Inn Square doesn't indulge in "*general corporate BS: there are no marketing executives or anything like that. The best way we can market ourselves is through doing good work.*" It's not a place where you'll find barristers "*reaching out*" to "*touch base*" on an issue "*going forward*" before "*close of play.*" None of this should be taken as stuffiness or fustiness: our sources were absolutely convinced otherwise. Clerks and barristers refer to each other by first name, rather than surname or 'sir'. Juniors tend to socialise together at lunchtime and have annual drinks with pupils. There's a sports day in the summer at the country home of a senior member, and staff and members occasionally pop into The Bunghole pub in the evening.

And finally...

Handsomely paid, prestigious and with terrific tenancy possibilities, 4-5 Gray's Inn Square should be a key target for the publicly minded.

Henderson Chambers

The facts

Location: Temple, London
Number of QCs/Juniors: 9/34 (8 women)
Applications: 200+
Apply through Pupillage Portal
Pupils per year: 2
Seats: 4x3 months
Pupillage award: £42,500 (can advance a sum for BPTC)

Chambers and Partners' Health & Safety Set of the Year 2010

This classic common law set is big on health and safety, product liability, consumer law and employment.

Regulation, regulation, regulation

Firmly anchored in the brickwork of its Inn, Henderson can be viewed as a typical Temple set. A somewhat shabby entrance (a rebuild is underway) leads to wood-panelled rooms with dusty books on the shelves, high-backed leather chairs and views across the sweeping lawns of Inner Temple Gardens. "*The standards and behaviour expected here are relatively traditional, but it's definitely a forward-looking place,*" a source said. Too right: don't confuse stuffy rooms with stuffy people. We visited on the day of the Apple iPad launch and Henderson already had one proudly on display in its lobby. "*It's from one of our American clients,*" a junior informed us. "*We got it in yesterday and we were told it was one of the first ones in the country.*" One member was even responsible for the world's first court order served via Twitter.

Henderson has built up specialisations in a number of areas. "*We've really made inroads in the last five to eight years into core areas like product liability and health and safety, and new ones like consumer finance law,*" entrepreneurial chief clerk John White told us. Other (overlapping) specialisms include property, employment, environment and local government. White said Henderson has built on its common law base and "*tactically*" capitalised on the fact that "*the regulatory and disciplinary side of things is much more important now than in the past.*" White and the other clerks are the motor under Henderson's bonnet: "*They are excellent at marketing chambers and bringing in new work,*" one loyal member explained.

Among Henderson's specialisms, "*product liability is the major focus, from drug trial work to industry faults.*" Barristers chiefly act for the defence – eg representing BP in a claim by over 100 Colombians regarding oil pipeline damages – but there are also claimant cases. On the health and safety side, chambers is involved in public inquiries, representing Network Rail in the Potters Bar and Lambrigg rail disaster inquests. Fans of PI and disease litigation have been kept busy with the Buncefield litigation and the atomic veterans case (where Henderson acted for the MoD). Members also helped a Manchester United youth player win £4.5m in compensation after a nasty tackle from an opponent ended his career, and some have also worked on a case involving "*a load of exploding cars.*" Consumer protection work matters include trading standards and food safety, and the set represented food producers over the mass product recall related to Sudan Red colouring.

Top to bottom

With all this top work on offer, don't expect to get into Henderson without doing your homework properly. For both interview rounds you'll be asked to prepare a legal problem question and during the two interviews you'll need to "*control your nerves and articulate and think at the same time.*" Head to the *Student Guide* website for our in-depth report on the application process. You'll also be able to read about Henderson's enthusiasm for third sixers.

Although recruiters want you to "*communicate enthusiasm about the right areas of law,*" John White told us he "*doesn't expect someone at that stage in their life to know what they want to do. I would much rather have someone who is open to all sorts of things.*" For Henderson, talent

Chambers UK rankings

Consumer Law	Professional Discipline
Health & Safety	Public Procurement
Information Technology	
Product Liability	Real Estate Litigation

is more important than experience. Pupils' and baby juniors' work is broad: they assist more senior members on big public inquiries, "*huge drug cases*" and group litigation, as well as getting their own smaller employment, property and PI cases. "*There is a deliberate attempt to keep what people at the junior end do general,*" we're told. Tenants begin to specialise after about five years' call, most often in product liability or health and safety.

There is "*a steady stream of employment work for juniors, lots of which comes down from Eversheds.*" Barristers appear for both claimants and respondents. "*Supervisors are very trusting about giving you complex work to do, rather than drip-feeding you less interesting stuff,*" a pupil revealed. Half way through the year, all pupils spend four weeks in the Brussels office of US legal giant McDermott Will & Emery, where they get a taste of commercial and European law with the two QCs who are partners there.

The set has recently introduced a four by three-month seat system. Pupils have four supervisors, who are at least seven years' call (but usually more experienced). "*In the first few months you only work for your supervisor.*" After that there's more devilling work, especially in the second six. "*I spent a lot of my second six getting through the list of members to work with,*" a baby junior told us. Starting with "*one or two*" court appearances a week, work is ramped up until pupils are on their feet "*every other day.*" As one summarised: "*My time in the second six is two-thirds written work for other people and one-third my own court work.*"

Pupil assessment is pretty rigorous ("*we have a lever-arch file for each candidate*") but it's not a case of all or nothing. "*You're not judged in the first couple of months,*" recruiters insist; "*we're not expecting the world of our pupils.*" Despite this, "*there will be critical written feedback on any piece of work you do.*" Supervisors also submit an appraisal form to the recruitment committee at the time when the tenancy decision is made. There are two or three practical advocacy exercises for which pupils are given a brief to prepare and then have to "*respond on the hoof to arguments.*" In the end they'll be performing in front of a master, but luckily "*not everything depends on these exercises.*" Most weight is put on reviews by pupil supervisors, and clerks' views are taken into account as well. "*The pupillage committee wants you to be able to show that you can work at a reasonably high level with consistency and stamina, and that you have an ability to get on with people.*" The set took on its sole pupil as a tenant in 2010.

Knock-out punch

Henderson's digs were undergoing a long (and overrunning) refurb when we visited in summer 2010. The plan was to retain the traditional look but make the entrance look a little less like a run-down Victorian primary school. "*By the time you publish it should be all spick and span and looking fantastic,*" John White assured us. Most tenants share a room, which means you "*overhear people's phone calls and can chat a lot about your cases.*"

Henderson "*encourages individuality and putting your views clearly.*" It's an "*extremely collaborative,*" "*sociable*" and perhaps somewhat eccentric place. Head of chambers Charles Gibson has an electric drum kit in his room and "*loads of other tenants have musical instruments.*" Gibson is also a keen amateur boxer: "*He's known as 'No Excuses' Gibson in the East End.*" No word of a lie, guv'ner! Dynamic senior clerk John White is held in close affection by Henderson's members. "*Events aren't stilted here and chambers isn't a horribly well-behaved place,*" said a source. We certainly picked up on chambers' warm and informal culture during our visit.

Members like to go out for lunch in Middle Temple Hall and there's an annual Christmas party, which last year involved "*some pretty outrageous carol singing.*" A Henderson week is finished off with Friday drinks: "*At 5pm the ring-around starts from Lauren on reception.*" For pupils, drinks are "*definitely good for getting to know people,*" but they're more about socialising than schmoozing. Indulging in a drop of wine ourselves at the end of our visit, we chatted about Chelsea restaurants full of red corduroy, how you never drink rosé in the winter and the story of an old lady rolling her Nissan Micra in Eastbourne.

And finally...

Henderson's pupillage is much broader than its health and safety and product liability specialisms suggest. The set's traditional fixtures and fittings disguise a contemporary wit and flair.

Keating Chambers

The facts

Location: Temple, London
Number of QCs/Juniors: 20/31 (14 women)
Applications: 130
Apply through Pupillage Portal
Pupils per year: Up to 4
Seats: 4x3 months
Pupillage award: £50,000 (can advance £15,000 for BPTC)

A perfect pick for construction law, Keating is also a good choice for contract and tort aficionados.

Keating's long-established supremacy at the Construction Bar makes it a go-to set for the biggest domestic and international construction disputes.

The home of construction

The universal view of Keating is that it wrote the book on construction. Well, actually, it did. *Keating on Construction Contracts*, first authored by Donald Keating in 1955 and now in its eighth edition, is recognised as the construction bible. To this day, tenants continue to contribute towards what one member described as "*a signature of our set.*"

In fact, Keating Chambers first began to specialise in the field of construction as recently as the early 1980s, during Donald's tenure as its head. In the context of the Bar, where chambers and Inns are saturated in history and tradition, and things move v-e-r-y s-l-o-w-l-y, its ascent was actually fairly rapid. Refusing to rest on its laurels, in May 2010 Keating appointed a new director of clerking, the highly regarded Paul Cooklin (previously of top insolvency set 3-4 South Square) to help grow its practice even further.

The nature of Keating's clients and sheer size and scale of the cases it handles are a testament to the set's reputation. It was involved in *Multiplex Construction v CBUK*, a dispute arising out of the construction of the new Wembley Stadium and described by *The Lawyer* as one of the top ten trials of 2008. Keating continues to act for Multiplex Construction in a claim against consultancy firm Mott MacDonald on another matter related to the Home of Football: a professional negligence claim relating to the steelwork design, valued at £250m. The set is also active overseas. In 2010, Keating barristers helped arbitrate disputes in Poland, Denmark, Dubai, Kazakhstan, South Africa, Iran and Singapore to name but a few. One matter was an arbitration concerning a road-building contract between a Japanese company and the government of Tanzania.

If reading about Keating's distinctly specialist work in what might be viewed (uncharitably) as a less-than-glamorous industry has you reaching to turn the page, there are two reasons to pause before doing so. Firstly, it's worth bearing in mind that a variety of work exists within the construction bracket: professional negligence, energy and procurement issues, for example. Secondly, only a handful of the set's practitioners come from technical backgrounds, which is reflective of its approach to recruitment. "*The message from us is that no technical knowledge is required. As long as you are interested in commercial work the rest will follow,*" a member of the pupillage committee explained.

In many respects, construction is a perfect area for candidates with a love of commercial law. If the combination of "*complicated law and complicated facts*" excites you, and contract and tort were your favourite subjects, then Keating should be somewhere near the top of your list. Additionally, the pupillage award of £50,000 (right up there with many of the general commercial chambers) should provide additional motivation to help you harness your inner engineer.

Pupillage: the nuts and bolts

If illustrated in pie chart format, Keating's practice would look "*like one big fat cherry pie*" of construction. "*The content of work is pretty standard across the board,*"

Chambers UK rankings

Construction	International Arbitration
Energy & Natural Resources	Professional Negligence

which means that rather than exposing pupils to different work, instead the set "*tries to give pupils a spread of seniority and style.*"

Over the year, pupils sit with four supervisors. During the first six months they shadow them at client conferences, mediations and court appearances. The remaining time is spent researching and drafting particulars of claim, replies, defences and advices, often in parallel with the pupil supervisor. "*It's basically loads of drafting all the time.*" However, pupils are encouraged to solicit work from other members. "*I've knocked on doors at the suggestion of my pupil supervisor, and since then I've worked for around 15 or 20 other members of chambers,*" said one.

It's not exactly a gentle introduction – "*they don't ease you in: all of the work is complex*" – but naturally allowances are made early on and "*expectations of supervisors change over the twelve months. There's definitely an informal grace period of sorts. Although the first three months count, if you're getting something wrong you'll be forgiven.*" A recruitment source explained that it is important that pupils are given that time to adapt before "*emerging chrysalis-like at some stage.*"

The beginning of the second six marks a shift in focus for pupils. While drafting continues to be a major part of the training, they will find themselves on their feet between one and three times a week. It tends to be "*slow at first but then really picks up.*" Second-six advocacy is often entirely unrelated to construction or technology matters. The emphasis is on blooding pupils with any court work that's available, to furnish them with invaluable experience. Pupils take on directions hearings, RTAs – useful for gaining cross-examination experience – and infant settlement hearings, which one described as "*a bit like delivering a bunch of flowers. It's basically an administrative thing saying, 'Have this huge cheque.'*"

Alongside the court experience, there are three assessed advocacy exercises throughout the year. Pupils are required to draft skeleton arguments, which are submitted beforehand. Our sources this year didn't appear too nervous about an exercise that fell on the same day as our visit, but the tests are certainly thorough: "*The first was an adjudication. It lasted around three hours.*" As well as the advocacy exercises, each pupil supervisor writes a report that is given considerable weight in the tenancy decision. The other members of chambers for whom pupils have worked are also required to fill out "*pro forma feedback sheets,*" which are then taken into consideration before the decision is made in early July.

There's no doubt that a pupillage at Keating is hard work. Although the set does its best to ensure plain sailing for pupils, inevitably the hours are fairly long and the work demanding. Sources reported only the occasional very late night and infrequent weekend work. "*I've only once been given work on a Friday due for a Monday. And they were apologetic about the whole thing,*" said one. In many respects, that's down to the pupils' own work ethic. "*It's very stressful but almost entirely self-imposed. You do bust your balls,*" particularly because "*as a pupil you don't want to turn down work.*"

Keating and drinking

Keating is modern, commercial and unfussy, neither "*an ivory tower*" nor "*a gentleman's club.*" As a business that recognises the importance of client relationships, it makes an effort to recruit candidates with the requisite soft skills. "*We don't take particularly well to eccentrics – those people who are incredibly bright but can't boil a kettle. We like people who can communicate well with others.*" This suits the set's clientele, which is weighted more towards contractors than the companies commissioning construction projects.

Keating's social scene seems in rude health, especially at the junior end. There are periodic drinks evenings in chambers, which are apparently "*increasingly frequent as the excuses get thinner.*" There are also annual Christmas and summer garden parties, which we were assured were a fixture long before other chambers jumped on the bandwagon. Pupils and juniors have a table in Middle Temple Hall for lunch – "*good if you don't fancy getting a sandwich on Fleet Street on your own*" – and members will "*get fish and chips on a Friday and go out for a drink after work.*" Legendary barristers' haunt Daly's Wine Bar is popular and, thankfully, given the prices in that establishment, "*there's a strict rule that pupils don't pay, so you'd be foolish not to go.*" Alternatively, there's often a chambers table at the Edgar Wallace, which translates into "*a lovely big group of people with pints*" spilling out on to the pavement when the weather permits.

And finally...

The fact that Keating is so down to earth is surprising given its pedigree but apt given its fondness for foundations. In 2010, none of the four pupils were taken on as tenants.

7 King's Bench Walk

The facts

Location: Temple, London

Number of QCs/Juniors: 20/27 (10 women)

Applications: 150

Apply through Pupillage Portal

Pupils per year: Up to 4, usually 2-3

Seats: 4 in the first 9 months

Pupillage award: £45,000 (can advance £10,000 for BPTC)

Chambers and Partners' Insurance Set of the Year 2010

Modest in size but massive in intellect, 7KBW is a renowned commercial set that relishes the rigour of its practice.

Shipshape

7 King's Bench Walk is an address of note for enthusiasts of legal history. Barristers' chambers have existed on the site since the 16th century in one form or another, and some real legal heavyweights have graced the corridors. Thomas Wilde, later Lord Chancellor Truro, was resident in 1820, when he successfully defended the life and honour of the wife of George IV and notorious adulteress, Caroline of Brunswick. In the mid-1800s, Lord Halsbury and Sir Harry Bodkin Poland (of the Brides in the Bath trial) worked out of 7KBW.

Today's set can trace its roots directly to a merger of two established commercial chambers – 7KBW and 3 Pump Court. The latter counted law students' favourite and king of the straight-shooting judgment, Lord Denning, as a tenant. Impressively, the set has maintained a tradition of sending its stars to the Bench. What's more, they haven't done too badly when they got there: Lords Goff, Hobhouse and Mance are all examples of alumni who have found their way to the highest echelons of the judiciary.

Now, 7KBW is renowned for its insurance and reinsurance work, central tenets of any commercial practice, and in 2010 won Chambers and Partners' Insurance Set of the Year, just as it did in 2009, 2008 and 2007. Comprising roughly half of the set's practice, one pupil described insurance as "*fancy contract law.*" It's certainly big business: Lord Collins described it as the UK's largest invisible export after banking. Recently, 7KBW's team of Jonathan Gaisman QC and Siobán Healy QC successfully represented claimants in a trial concerning the liability of Total and Chevron/Texaco for the £1bn worth of damage caused by the explosion at the Buncefield oil depot in 2005. The star quality of 7KBW tenants is even more apparent once the dream team of Lord Grabiner QC, Jonathan Sumption QC and Gordon Pollock QC, representing the opposition, is taken into consideration.

Alongside insurance and reinsurance, 7KBW's main practice is shipping. Juniors in particular spend a good deal of their time on matters maritime. While it might sound narrow in focus, shipping law is anything but niche, covering a broad range of topics and drawing on various strands of the law.

Brilliant minds

The focus on insurance and shipping makes pupillage at 7KBW especially challenging. "*The learning curve is necessarily steep*" because "*you need to get on top of the new law and impress people.*" And remember, pupils are "*likely to be starting from a position with no background in shipping or insurance,*" which essentially means "*learning a new language.*" Although the pressure is fairly intense, the pupils we spoke to seemed to be coping. Partly, that's because they came to 7KBW to be pushed intellectually. "*It has a reputation for being academic and I was drawn to that,*" said one pupil, adding: "*You do need to love reading stuff to be here. I like being able to sit in the library and read Chitty for five hours.*" Another reflected: "*You have to be happy sitting in silence and thinking. 90% of the time you are using your brain to full capacity. It's exhausting but rewarding.*"

Chambers UK rankings

Commercial Dispute Resolution	International Arbitration
	Professional Negligence
Insurance	Shipping

We wouldn't dream of telling our readers not to apply to a set; however, before sticking 7KBW down on your Pupillage Portal form, we would urge a visit to chambers' website to check out the calibre of the junior tenants taken. By way of example, of the last five tenants taken on, all had studied law at degree level, all were Oxbridge alumni, all had First-class degrees, and each had a list of prizes as long as your arm. One member of the pupillage committee described the phenomenon as "*a bit frightening,*" but the set unashamedly says that "*what we do is an academic area of law, so we're looking for academic excellence.*"

If you are an academic superstar, make it past the single-stage, legal problem-based interview and receive an offer of pupillage, what can you expect? Up until Christmas, pupils sit with one supervisor. This is a time to get their heads down and bone up on the basics of shipping and insurance, and supervisors are "*more tolerant of mistakes*" during this period. The work itself is often opinion or pleading-based, with pupils spending much of their time drafting notes and skeletons. Tasks can be dense in both law and fact, and pupils spoke of hours sat thinking: "*Oh my God, this is unanswerable,*" but usually resolving the issue with "*a light bulb moment where you realise you will be able to find an answer.*" One aspiring tenant reminisced about "*six days analysing the meaning of one word.*"

After Christmas, pupils sit with another two supervisors before the tenancy decision in late June or early July. During this time, they are encouraged to do work for other members of chambers, including senior silks, in order to "*get as much diversity of work as possible*" and ensure their face and work product are known before the tenancy committee makes its collective mind up. Due to the complexity of the matters undertaken by the set, during the second six "*there's very little opportunity to be on your feet.*" Pupils warned us: "*Don't come here expecting advocacy; you won't see it for a long time.*" However, there are two assessed advocacy exercises during the pupillage year and they typically have a cerebral twist. "*It was the sort of problem you could look at for days and still keep coming up with new points. They want to see you think on your feet.*" In 2010, 7KBW offered tenancy to one of its four pupils.

Serious, not stuffy

It's not a huge surprise that 7KBW has a reputation as a serious and scholarly place, albeit great fun for those looking for an academic and intellectual playground. The set is rightly proud of its long and eminent history and doesn't want to lose its "*sense of tradition.*" Certainly the rabbit warren of a building lends weight to this idea. And yet, while our sources admitted: "*We don't go out of our way to cultivate a corporate image,*" pupils and tenants refuted any suggestion that the set was stuffy. One pupil commented on how "*bookishness and Oxbridge don't equal old school and formal.*" Instead, "*people know your name and juniors get on really well.*" It's common to find juniors lunching together or having "*drinks in the clerks' room on a Friday night.*" In general though, pupils were grateful that the set avoids too much "*enforced fun.*"

And finally...

Academic credentials are of the utmost importance here. Your brain will need to be as sharp as a cutlass and clear as a sea breeze.

Littleton Chambers

The facts

Location: Inner Temple, London
Number of QCs/Juniors: 12/37 (10 women)
Applications: 150
Apply through Pupillage Portal
Pupils per year: 2
Seats: 3x4 months
Pupillage award: £45,000 (can advance £10,000 for BPTC)

Since 2006, Littleton has offered tenancy to all nine of its pupils.

A progressive, businesslike set, Littleton is a big name in employment, commercial litigation and professional negligence.

Littleton: because they're worth it

Littleton Chambers has long been part of the vanguard for modernisation of the Bar. In the early 1990s it was one of the first to appoint a CEO. Current incumbent Gerard Hickie, with chambers since 2007, is from a distinctly non-legal background, having spent 20 years in general commercial management. In fact, Hickie joined chambers from beauty behemoth L'Oréal and holds both a degree in engineering and an MBA – no classics or jurisprudence scholar he. Unsurprisingly, Littleton is now a set that's increasingly involved in events and marketing, and the tenants we spoke to were appreciative: "*It's of value to know that you're joining a set that is prepared to go to the effort of branding and marketing.*" It's particularly important for juniors who haven't yet had the time to develop their own reputation and rely on the standing of the set as a whole for work. Littleton continues to push forward, and in recent years a new IT system, new clerks, a series of lateral hires and LUMU – the Littleton Urgent Mediation Unit – have all been established as chambers looks to grow its size and revenue.

The majority of Littleton's work is in the employment field. The set's members are actively involved in equal pay disputes (a growing employment sub-practice), as well as discrimination cases of all types, industrial disputes, litigation regarding fiduciary duties, and the proliferation of employment litigation concerning doctors and teachers. Littleton was also involved in the biggest industrial relations bun fight of 2010: David Reade QC acted for BA in one of its cases over the legality of its cabin crew's strikes. Employment matters tend to be a major part of all juniors' practices until the fourth or fifth year, when some will inevitably choose to specialise exclusively in commercial work.

Commercial disputes represent another major chunk of Littleton's business. It has an established reputation for commercial litigation, much of it with an international flavour such as the recent appearance by members in a complex Russian multibillion-dollar fraud. Other notable work has seen members active in minority shareholder actions and multimillion-pound misfeasance claims by liquidators. Littleton is also well regarded for its professional negligence practice.

Not so mini-pupillage

When it comes to recruiting, Littleton is determined to bag excellent candidates and its extremely thorough application process is a testament to that fact. Each year the set receives around 150 applications through the Pupillage Portal. A points system determines the 40 to 50 candidates who make it to the next stage, and the focus is at this point primarily on academic achievement. If you look at the most recent tenants, you'll understand that academic achievement is less a smattering of A*s at GCSE and more a double first at Cambridge (plus an LLM from Harvard). As one recruitment source put it: "*We wouldn't want to give the impression that there is a substitute for a strong academic background.*"

Candidates who make it through to the second round are given a legal problem – "*designed to look at their capacity*

Chambers UK rankings

Employment

for legal thinking and argument" – in advance of a half-hour interview, which focuses pretty much exclusively on that question. Between 15 and 25 people make it through this stage and are invited to undertake a mini-pupillage at the set. "*We're selling ourselves, too; lots of these people will get more than one offer.*" During the week, candidates will complete a written exercise, usually an opinion. Finally, between six and ten lucky applicants make it to the final interview, which again features a problem question set beforehand and a "*reasonably friendly*" grilling.

Pupillage itself is structured into three seats of four months, with the tenancy decision coming shortly after the move to the final seat. The work is "*mainly employment-related*" during the first six months, although there is an effort to ensure "*contrast in practice between the first and second pupil supervisors.*" Pupils undertake all the mainstays of a first six at a civil set: drafting research notes and skeleton arguments, and filling in claim forms. To some extent pupils are eased in gently and supervisors "*don't expect too much of you at first.*" Indeed, the first six months as a whole is, in the grand scheme of a notoriously stressful year, rather relaxed. "*The first six months were completely manageable. For the first four months I rarely finished past six,*" said a pupil. A tenant agreed: "*It's in no one's interest that pupils work evenings and weekends.*"

The second six is all about getting pupils on their feet. "*There's a strong emphasis on oral advocacy,*" noted one tenant. A member of the pupillage committee put it more bluntly: "*Don't apply if you're not genuinely interested in advocacy. Employment law gives you a great chance to get on your feet very early.*" Pupils can expect to handle smaller matters such as case management, procedural discussions, pre-hearing reviews and one-day cases. Certainly the pressure rises in the second six. "*It's hard work at a high tempo. No question.*" Alongside the everyday work, pupils undergo a total of six assessments – three written and three advocacy-based. The written assessments are "*benchmarked against performances in previous years,*" while the advocacy was described as "*terrifying and quite complicated.*" Normally the set looks to recruit two pupils, but in 2009 it only took one, who was then awarded tenancy in 2010.

Progressive not pompous

One of the first things we noticed while visiting Littleton was just how friendly it was at the bottom end. A junior tenant who had come to the set following a pupillage elsewhere commented: "*It has a reputation for being a friendly place.*" A pupil agreed: "*There's a sense of unity. We're here as a team.*" A third source said: "*It's a collegiate atmosphere. We seem to get along better than other sets.*" While "*not a place for big organised social occasions,*" Littleton is "*generally perceived to be quite an outgoing sort of set.*" Juniors will often eat lunch together, either in the gardens during the summer months or in one of the meeting rooms. In the evenings they will "*go for a drink probably once a week,*" with the occasional big night out. "*I've ended up in a karaoke bar with my supervisor at 4am,*" confided one pupil sheepishly.

It's no surprise then that "*everyone is very down to earth*" and "*there's no room for stuffiness.*" According to pupils, that makes it "*an easy place to get along.*" While undoubtedly packed full of razor-sharp minds working on big-ticket matters, Littleton lacks the air of scholarly detachment so often a part of the culture at leading sets. Nor does it have the feel of an old boys club. "*It's a pretty progressive set,*" suggested a tenant, and a pupil offered themselves as an example of that ethos, saying: "*I'm not a typical barrister. I went to a state school and I have a modest background, but I felt like I fitted in. It's not a typical public schoolboy set.*" The atmosphere in chambers is partly a product of the work – "*try going to an employment tribunal sounding like a pompous barrister and see what happens!*"

And finally...

A stellar reputation, excellent mix of work and open culture make Littleton a must for intellectuals who fancy getting to their feet early.

Maitland Chambers

The facts

Location: Lincoln's Inn, London
Number of QCs/Juniors: 18/48 (11 women)
Applications: 150+
Outside Pupillage Portal scheme
Pupils per year: 2 or 3
Seats: 1x3 months then 4x2 months
Pupillage Award: £60,000 (can advance £20,000 for BPTC)

Maitland is thinking about how it can pitch itself at some of the new universities and says it is *"keen to try and establish links with ethnic student lawyers' associations."*

"If you get an offer from Maitland you're not going to say no to it." Not some Corleone-style threat, but a pupil's acknowledgement of this set's position at the top of the tree.

An offer you can't refuse

Realistically who's going to say no to a Maitland pupillage offer when there's so much to be gained? For commercial Chancery practice (as opposed to traditional Chancery matters) it sits at the top of the rankings in *Chambers UK*. That state of affairs has endured pretty much since Maitland was created in 2001, when 13 Old Square and 7 Stone Buildings joined forces. Maitland is also renowned for its property expertise, an area of practice that was bolstered in a second merger in 2004, when the members of 9 Old Square also came on board. At the time, the mergers were seen as "*bold*" – tie-ups between established sets can be a tricky business, especially if there are cultural differences – but they seem to have paid off. "*When I came in seven years ago I could tell to an extent who came from where,*" a clerk told us, "*but now it's really impossible to tell.*" It was probably a wise move to shuffle the members around between the three legacy buildings so that everyone mixed in together.

Chambers receives instructions from around the world and has forged some strong links with offshore tax havens in the Caribbean, the Channel Islands and the Isle of Man. Meanwhile a number of indirect tax law specialists regularly act for Her Majesty's Revenue & Customs. Recent cases of note include Michael Driscoll QC and Ciaran Keller's victory in the Supreme Court on behalf of Star Energy in a landmark case concerning trespass by oil pipelines at depth. Others involve disputes stemming from the credit crunch such as Lehman Brothers and Northern Rock, and acting for one of the campaigners in the Parliament Square protest. Finally, it might not be typical of instructions received by the set, but we note with interest that one member of chambers advised the producer of *Monty Python and the Holy Grail* in his dispute with the Pythons over royalties and acted on disclosure applications in connection with litigation between the members of Busted.

Bildungsroman

"*From day one you will be keeping up with your supervisor's work.*" Don't panic: chambers recognises what a huge step up from law school pupillage is, and for the first three months pupils sit with one supervisor as they find their feet. From January, they move every two months in order to see a variety of practices. Pupils see quite a difference in the way supervisors do things. "*Some will give you work that's separate from what they are doing, and will talk through it with you, but it's never sent out or used in court. With others, it's a much more collaborative process where they get a live bit of work and give it to you for three days, then go over it and possibly use it.*"

While pupils are unlikely to get on their feet in court, there are five advocacy training exercises that begin after Christmas, gradually increasing in difficulty. The first looks at "*the kind of thing that a junior might be doing in a County Court fairly early on in practice,*" while the last might be "*a full-blown contested freezing order application in a commercial context; something that may well be*

Chambers UK rankings

Agriculture & Rural Affairs	Fraud
Chancery	Partnership
Charities	Professional Negligence
Commercial Dispute Resolution	Real Estate Litigation
Company	Restructuring/Insolvency

done by a QC." In one recent exercise, pupils were pitted against each other: "*It was an application to adjourn a trial. We had to prepare for the applicant's side and the respondent's side.*" Pupils insisted that this was the only time they had felt themselves to be in direct competition with each other, "*and even then, the person playing the judge was giving us a pretty hard time, so I was more concentrating on him.*"

Pupillage here is more a "*personal journey*" than a battle royale, and with the amount of work that chambers is currently receiving, there is room for every pupil who comes up to scratch. In 2009 and 2010 all pupils were offered tenancy. When it comes to that decision, performance in the advocacy exercises may be taken into consideration if the pupillage committee is unsure of someone. However, the collective judgement of supervisors over the course of nine months is viewed as a "*pretty reliable way of working out if someone is up to it or not.*" Therefore, "*the dominant factor*" in the tenancy decision "*is what the pupil supervisors collectively have made of you.*"

Listen and learn

Chambers has recently added "*a couple of slightly more interesting questions*" to its application form. This is an attempt to allow applicants the chance to differentiate themselves, so use that opportunity to the full. Around 30 or 40 go through to a first-round interview, which is less law-centred and more designed to test "*the sort of person they are, because at the end of the day this job is not just about having a decent brain but being able to inspire confidence in clients.*" From there, around 15 progress to "*a slightly more intensive and slightly more legally focused*" second-round interview. How to do well? "*It's a combination of being intelligent and being able to distil things to a key point and communicate that point effectively. If you can do that you'll really impress us.*" GDL students are at no disadvantage and the majority of younger members of Maitland did not read law at undergraduate level (we note a number of classicists in the ranks).

Chambers worries about recruiting from a wider background. "*People will look at our website and see 60-odd mostly white faces, mainly from Oxbridge, and think, 'I don't stand a chance because I'm not like them',*" said a member of the pupillage committee. "*The message I'd love to get across is: yes you do, we'll give you the same crack of the whip that everyone else gets.*" To its credit Maitland is thinking about how it can pitch itself at some of the new universities and says it is "*keen to try and establish links with ethnic student lawyers' associations.*"

Formal afternoon tea takes place daily, and pupils' attendance depends on whether their supervisor goes or not – "*some do, some don't.*" Barristers tend to use tea as a sounding board for ideas on their cases, "*which* [for a pupil] *is very useful. You might get someone very junior talking about a type of small-scale case that we haven't been exposed to so much since all our supervisors are between ten and 15 years' call.*" It's for this reason that pupils don't chat much at tea, but they are not alone in this: "*There are plenty of people who have been at chambers for ten years or more who come just to listen.*" Work is less often the topic of conversation at chambers drinks every Thursday night. Pupils almost always attend this event as it's a good way to meet members and staff.

And finally...

This weighty set does it all – from disputed wills and personal taxation problems to massive pensions disputes, property litigation, fraud and major commercial spats. Make it here and you're made, full stop.

DROIT

Four New Square

The facts

Location: Lincoln's Inn, London
Number of QCs/Juniors: 19/51 (18 women)
Applications: 78
Apply through Pupillage Portal
Pupils per year: 2
Seats: 2x3 + 1x6 months
Pupillage award: £60,000 (can advance £15,000 for BPTC)

Chambers and Partners' Professional Negligence Set of the Year 2010

The traditional environs of Lincoln's Inn disguise Four New Square's *"modern"* and *"business-like"* corporate outlook.

New by name, new by nature

Walk through the door of Four New Square and you're confronted with big modern canvases on the walls, a flat-screen TV showing *Sky News*, large designer leather and chrome chairs and the set's name emblazoned in large letters on the wall. Four New Square's swanky premises could pass for a West End PR agency, and it's only the copy of *The Lawyer* on a side table that suggests otherwise. 4NS is "*a well-oiled machine*" that "*treads a good line between modern and traditional.*" Pushing for more, we learned that 'tradition' doesn't stretch much further than "*people dressing quite smartly.*" Beyond that, everything from the multicoloured conference room chairs to the work-life policies are fully contemporary. "*This isn't a wood-panelled, 'let me put my slippers on and get these dusty books off the shelf' place,*" said pupillage committee chair Alex Hall Taylor.

4NS's aim to become more of a "*corporate entity*" means that Hall Taylor was happy to talk about the set's turnover surpassing £20m, and senior clerk Lizzy Wiseman told us we should expect it to become a general commercial set within a few years. For the moment though, it doesn't mind being labelled as top of the class for its professional negligence work. Dozens of accountants, actuaries, tax advisers, insurers, barristers and solicitors call on 4NS to defend them against fraud and negligence claims. Mountains of professional negligence litigation doesn't equal a monotonous pupillage though. "*Prof neg is the headline but there are a lot of sub-categories and we're also involved with commercial and insurance work,*" a pupil explained.

Professional negligence has led chambers into a number of other logically connected areas, such as construction, financial services regulation and healthcare. For example, it is acting for 555 claimants in a £50m-plus investment fraud claim. Among the set's other headline work is the litigation following the massive Buncefield oil depot explosion and the atomic veterans litigation brought by servicemen exposed to radiation during MoD tests in the 1950s.

Clone wars

4NS offers unassessed mini-pupillages. It's a good way of getting to know chambers and its character, and our junior sources reckon it's important to try and get on one. "*It's ridiculous to expect to impress people at interview if you don't know anything about the set. You can't just repeat the website back at them.*" If a mini isn't possible, then you can also meet 4NS members at careers fairs, Inn dinners or through personal contacts – "*the more people you meet, the better.*"

4NS was one of the few chambers to include a set-specific question for Pupillage Portal applications in 2010. This meant the number of applications dropped to 78, as a surprising number of applicants didn't bother answering the extra question. About half of all applicants were invited to a 15-minute first interview to discuss their CV. Half of those progressed to a second-round interview that looked more at legal knowledge and candidates' ability to formulate an argument. Here's a typical question: "*If scientists came to you and said they had the technology to clone humans, what legislation, if any, would you introduce?*" Finally, applicants

Chambers UK rankings

Construction	Professional Discipline
Costs Litigation	Professional Negligence
Product Liability	

attend a "*one-day mini,*" which involves shadowing a silk and preparing a brief. Alex Hall Taylor explained that 4NS is looking for four main criteria: "*Intellectual ability, which carries the most weight; potential as an advocate, which can be shown by having done mooting but also comes across at interview; dedication and motivation; and personal qualities.*" Talking the talk is key. "*Some super-bright people just don't have the presentation skills in terms of oral argument.*" If you're one of the many who thinks they have this quality, you'll also need to come across as "*self-aware, confident but not arrogant, trustworthy and persuasive.*"

Pupil power

During each of their three seats, pupils share a room with their supervisor (usually around ten to 15 years' call). At first they're likely to get a few "*dead*" cases. "*My supervisor would take an old case off the shelf, pull out her opinion, ask me to work it out and then we'd compare notes,*" said one source. Though this is "*useful at the time,*" pupils are happy to move on to exclusively shadowing their supervisors and handling "*discrete tasks*" on live cases, such as working on "*tricky disclosure points or cross-examinations.*" In their second six, pupils take on their own cases including "*possession hearings, mortgages and other small claims, contract disputes and RTAs*" where there's "*not too much money involved.*" In an attempt to keep the workload manageable, pupils do just one or "*occasionally two*" hearings a week.

It would be an understatement to say pupils are thoroughly assessed. "*There's no point making pupillage a warm, cuddly experience,*" says Wiseman. "*Being a barrister takes a lot of hard work.*" Gaining tenancy is based on "*objective standards*" and merit; "*if you're good enough, you get in.*" There are set-piece writing tasks and "*every other piece of work is marked against an A-to-E scale.*" The tenancy assessment is based on the same criteria as pupillage applications. Having a "*strong personality*" is definitely key; "*there aren't any shrinking violets here, but we're not too gung-ho or overbearing either.*" Oral presentation skills are tested via two tough mooting exercises. Pupils receive a lot of support to help improve their skills, but if they're not up to scratch by the end of the year, they will politely be shown the door. Chambers now aims to recruit two new tenants each year, so if its own pupils aren't up to scratch an external candidate will be invited in for a third six. In 2010, neither 4NS pupil gained tenancy.

Horsing around

Pupils and juniors get to know a fair number of the members through devilling and chambers breakfasts. These fortnightly eats are "*just there for socialising*" and are especially useful given the growing size of the set (which now has two annexes). "*When you walk past someone in the corridor, it's not awkward because you've often just been talking over a bagel.*" Regular chambers drinks, silks' parties and a family-friendly summer bash get pupils and QCs chinking glasses. It's no surprise that one pupil commented: "*There are definitely people here with idiosyncrasies, although that's not to be confused with egos!*" There are "*plenty of young tenants*" and "*the culture is very friendly,*" although "*there is the hierarchy you'd expect.*" At the summer party the hierarchy breaks down a little, as everyone joins in some none-too-serious sporting events. You're not expected to let the senior members win: "*One junior who had just qualified tackled a QC quite hard.*" During office hours, 4NS's two horses – Blunham Hill and Joe Twist – will cause a "*wave of excitement*" from time to time. "*Every now and then 15 members of chambers will run down to the bookies.*" You may have read in the press about 4NS facing a race discrimination claim from one of its members in 2010 (the story even got into the *Daily Mail*). The claim was dismissed by the Employment Tribunal.

And finally...

Get to know this set and its prof neg work before you apply is our advice. At the same time, keep your eyes peeled for possible future expansion into new practice areas.

- **Make full use of sets' websites:** Take note of the identity of any clients mentioned and check which recent cases a set is most proud of. These things will help you at interview. If you get wind of who will be on the interview panel do your homework on them before you submit yourself to a grilling.

Old Square Chambers

The facts

Location: Bedford Row, London; Bristol

Number of QCs/Juniors: 8/55 (21 women)

Applications: c.200

Apply through Pupillage Portal

Pupils per year: 2

Seats: 4x3 months

Pupillage award: £35,000 (can advance £10,000 for BPTC)

From headline-hitting industrial action to rail crash inquests, Old Square Chambers works on matters of critical national importance.

Neither old nor square, Old Square Chambers has a contemporary and businesslike feel to it.

Hendy-work

Old Square Chambers has its origins in claimant personal injury and employment instructions, often acting for employees and unions. "*Traditionally we were more of a trade union set,*" said pupillage committee head Ben Cooper, "*but that hasn't been the case for at least ten years.*" Senior clerk Will Meade added: "*Employment work is now 75 to 80% respondent-based, but the majority of PI work is still claimant.*" Even so, "*vestiges*" of the set's heritage remain: top silk John Hendy and his team acted for the Unite union on the BA cabin crew strike in 2010. "*Everyone gathered around the TV in the clerks' room to watch Hendy win in the Appeal Court and see one of our juniors get interviewed on Sky,*" a pupil enthusiastically recalled. Hendy also acted for the Communication Workers Union during the 2009 Royal Mail strike and is standing counsel to half a dozen other unions.

Industrial action is just a small part of OSC's work, "*although there may be more industrial action cases, given government spending cuts.*" The bulk of work is employment-related: equal pay claims, disciplinary actions, unfair dismissals – you name it. The set also acts for employers such as BT, Siemens, Ford, Jaguar and Citi. Personal injury is another OSC flagship practice: members fought a group action against Corby Council over toxic materials in the atmosphere. The set has also been involved in corporate manslaughter, health and safety, environmental, prison deaths and rail crash cases. Members have represented claimants in both the Potters Bar rail crash inquest and the inquest into the Camberwell flats fire. Understandably, there are close ties with solicitors' firms with insurance and PI specialisms, such as Irwin Mitchell, Leigh Day & Co and Beachcroft. Professional discipline instructions have been on the rise recently: members represent the General Medical Council, as well as defendant doctors and solicitors. On the environmental side, members were active on a claim against Thames Water over unpleasant odours and mosquitoes near a sewage plant.

All this work takes place in chambers' impressive premises on Bedford Row, where a hand-carved 18th century staircase and impressive fresco of a nobleman on horseback complement a glass-ceilinged clerks' room. The building had a genuinely soothing effect on us during our visit and put us more in mind of a boutique hotel than a workplace. The set also has a small Bristol annexe.

Passionate

Successful applicants go through two rounds of interviews. The first is a "*relatively short*" 20-minute interview. "*Ten minutes of that is a general interview on your CV and ten minutes is a statutory interpretation problem, which you are handed half an hour before the interview,*" Ben Cooper explained. The second interview is "*quite tough: you'll be asked to discuss more detailed scenarios and an ethical issue, such as, 'What if a witness turns up and changes their evidence?'*" In both interviews and on the initial application, the pupillage committee is looking for "*academic ability, written skills, potential as an advocate and an interest in our areas of work.*" Besides academics, people skills are most important: "*Some people*

Chambers UK rankings

Employment	Personal Injury
Environment	Product Liability
Health & Safety	

can get tongue-tied and bemused: in this chambers we're not paper-based, so we're looking for people who can make one-on-one connections." All manner of things can make your CV stand out, including "*mooting, debating, having been a manager or having given presentations.*" Having notched up mini-pupillages, "*either with us or with sets that do similar work,*" is an advantage.

"*They don't look favourably on people with a rose-tinted view of the Bar,*" one junior said, "*but you do need to have a passion for what we do.*" A commitment to legal challenges of institutional decisions, and the impact law can have on society are central to the set's philosophy. "*They asked me what things on my CV I was passionate about,*" a pupil recalled. Recruitment numbers are determined by business needs, but possibly more so by OSC's cultural ethos. "*It's all about quality and not quantity,*" explained senior clerk Will Meade. "*We could take on ten members right now, given that the work is there. But you have to build it up gradually to make sure that everyone has been brought up the Old Square way.*"

Pupils sit with four supervisors for three months each. The four 'seats' "*reflect the set's PI and employment work,*" although you can focus more on one or the other, or take a seat focusing on professional discipline or environmental law. "*It's good to move around because you start afresh and have to make a new impact on a room of people,*" said a pupil. "*In the first three months I just did work for my supervisor and people in my room, while in the second three months I did work for my supervisor and all the other members.*" Even QCs ask pupils to carry out small tasks, which means "*you feel like you have a little stake in what's going on.*" In their second six, pupils are quick off the mark with their own cases. These include "*a lot of RTAs and infant approvals, where you have to gain court approval for the money children get* [by way of settlement]." Pupils go to court three times a week and there are "*really good clerks who make sure you stick to that.*"

Trial and retribution

Pupil assessment is "*a very structured process.*" All work is graded on a one-to-five scale, "*one being dreadful, five being outstanding.*" Although a pupil we spoke to modestly denied they knew quite how they were viewed, a junior told us that during pupillage "*you know where you are at during the year.*" There are formal assessments at the end of every seat "*to spread the stress throughout the year!*" Pupils are given a set of papers and asked to produce a written advice and court submissions. "*We then ask them to do a submission as if they are in front of a judge,*" Ben Cooper explained.

It's important to "*get your face known and have a width of experience*" as "*you need to show you have aptitude in all areas of chambers' work.*" The tenancy decision is based on a variety of feedback. Our sources were happy to give us an approximate view of how much various factors affect the pupillage decision. Feedback from supervisors and formal assessment each account for around 25 to 30% of the decision; feedback from other members accounts for 20%; while feedback from instructing solicitors and clerks ("*who look more at the commercial aspect of things*") contributes around the 20% mark. "*You can't afford to jettison any of those areas of assessment,*" a pupil told us. We reckon that if you keep an eye on those areas, fit into OSC's culture and show talent, modesty and a sense of humour, you'll do well. "*The goal is always that if someone is good enough we should take them, unless there is a business concern that work might be too scarce,*" Ben Cooper said. In 2010 both pupils gained tenancy.

On the pitch

When we visited OSC we were struck by the informality of chambers and its members. We were greeted by not one, but two barristers in T-shirts and casual trousers and pupils spoke of a distinctly relaxed environment. There are "*spontaneous*" drinks events every few weeks and some members will also just "*grab people for drinks on a Friday,*" which is more common now than in years past. Lectures from tenants followed by drinks are one way the set is upping its profile: "*Everyone has a commitment to marketing, but you have to hope your liver can take it!*" Events range from the classy (one swanky event was like "*chambers by Condé Nast*") to the down-to-earth: "*Last Friday we went to watch a World Cup match with our solicitors.*" The clerks seem to know how to enjoy themselves: "*There's a football table in the clerks' room... they all play real football, too, and one of the barristers joins them.*"

And finally...

OSC works in some fascinating areas and will be ideal for those with well-developed interpersonal skills and passion for the law.

Pump Court Tax Chambers

The facts

Location: Bedford Row, London

Number of QCs/juniors: 10/20 (6 women)

Applications: 70+

Outside Pupillage Portal Scheme

Pupils per year: 2-3

Seats: 3 core supervisors

Pupillage Award: £40,000 (can advance £8,000 for BPTC)

Chambers and Partners' Tax Set of the Year 2010

Pump Court Tax Chambers is a pre-eminent specialist set consistently ranked as a leader in its field.

Love it or hate it

Tax. It's the Marmite of law. Undoubtedly, many readers will have turned the page the moment their eyes rested on that three-letter word. Frankly, all the better for those of you who're still reading: Pump Court Tax Chambers is a set right at the top of its game, practising varied and challenging work, promising phenomenal compensation, and yet remaining something of a secret among students.

Still unconvinced? Here's the hard sell on tax law. At PCTC, tax work is broadly divided into three categories: direct tax, which covers income tax, capital gains tax and the like (taxes you've heard of, in other words); indirect tax, which includes VAT and customs duties; and personal tax, which often involves trusts, inheritance tax and the occasional great estate. It's not just advisory work either, as HMRC's uncompromising stance on tax evasion makes litigation common. In other words, it's varied: tax work can involve trusts, equity, European law, contract and tort, and requires commercial nous and good soft skills. What's more, tax law changes dramatically on a yearly basis, so "*it's about constantly adapting and re-learning.*" Anyone worried that barristers here are little more than accountants should take note: "*It's got absolutely nothing to do with numbers. You can be pretty numerically illiterate and that's not a problem.*" For a more in-depth analysis of what tax law entails, see page 129.

If tax appeals, then PCTC doesn't need a hard sell. As the quality of its recent work demonstrates, it's a leader in its field. In the corporate arena, members appeared on both sides in test cases (FII GLO and Thin Cap) over the taxation of foreign dividends, a good indication of the set's traditional strength in representing the taxpayer. More recently it has become a go-to set for HMRC itself. In indirect tax matters, members have been involved in the most important VAT case of the recent past: *Marks & Spencer v HMRC*. David Milne QC was successful for Marks & Sparks in the House of Lords in a case with huge implications for the collection of VAT in the UK. Finally, the set continues to be involved in ground-breaking cases on private client matters: *Trustees of Nelson Dance's Settlement v HMRC* is one case that has rewritten the book on business property relief.

Now 30 members strong, PCTC expanded in late 2008 into neighbouring property on Bedford Row and has already filled that space. As the set continues to thrive, there's even talk of entirely new, City-based digs within the next few years.

Not rocket science, but taxing

So, presuming you have now managed to tap into your inner tax lawyer, what structure does a pupillage here take? The answer is a fairly flexible one, although there are some running themes. There's an initial three-month stint with a first pupil supervisor. That acts as a kind of "*bedding-down period up until Christmas,*" which pupils were grateful for, especially those who hadn't studied tax law before. During that time, work is geared towards private client matters and headline taxes: income, inheritance and capital gains – "*not simple, but not rocket science like derivatives. It's a foundation in reasonably*

Chambers UK rankings

Tax

accessible taxes." The private client side is lively too: "*There are family stories and bust-ups to keep you entertained*."

For the first three months, supervisors "*are obviously interested in what you produce but won't be too harsh. You're learning*." Don't mistake that for an easy ride. "*The pace at which you learn is very fast*" and the work is "*very law-heavy; there's no doubt about that*." Serious brainwork is required, even at this early stage, especially as "*none of it is 'dummy work'. It's all live, and if it's good enough to go out, it will*." However, pupils felt like they were progressing, rather than "*banging* [their] *head against a brick wall*." Of the work itself, "*a significant portion is opinion-based*," although pupils will also "*draft skeletons, work on company reconstructions, draft notes on legal points and write first drafts of lists of issues*."

As you may have guessed, this isn't a pupillage for those desperate to be on their feet. While pupils will attend court with supervisors, and "*there's an unwritten rule that whenever a member goes to the Supreme Court, they take a pupil*," they "*don't get up on their hind legs*" during the second six at all, except during assessed advocacy exercises.

Pupils generally go on to sit with another two supervisors. Interestingly, at some stage during the year, they will sit with a number of senior members – a sort of 'silk seat'. Pupils admitted that "*when sitting with silks there's pressure because you're only with them for a short period and you want to make a good impression*." Otherwise, while pupillage is inevitably a stressful time, the set does its best to ensure that pupils are not under undue pressure. "*It's a fairly steady workload with occasional pinch points few and far between*." Unfortunately neither of the two pupils gained tenancy in 2010.

How do you impress?

Generally, just over 70 applicants submit a CV and covering letter to PCTC and 20 make it to the first interview. At the CV stage, chambers looks for "*a strong academic record*" combined with a "*short but interesting covering letter demonstrating independent thought*." At no stage should candidates "*trot out clichés*."

At the first interview, a question is set and candidates are given time beforehand and statutory extracts to help them respond. The question may or may not relate to tax, but either way "*it is completely self-contained: no prior experience of tax is necessary. It's about statutory interpretation and then application of that interpretation*." A recruitment source revealed that the question "*normally has some ambiguity*." A discussion of the set question takes around 15 minutes of the half-hour interview, with an initial ten minutes of "*general 'why the Tax Bar?' questions*" and a final five minutes for candidates' questions.

At the second interview, between five and eight people "*to whom we could realistically make an offer*" are invited back for a written exercise. The assessment lasts eight hours, can be done at home or at chambers, and is "*blind marked and looked at by everyone who took part in the first interview*." The set generally aims to recruit two pupils and, if there is still nothing to separate the candidates, may invite them back in for a further assessment. In 2009, that took the form of a discussion of a recent Court of Appeal case.

Elevenses

If you felt the need to pigeonhole PCTC then certainly "*the buildings and decor are quite traditional*," but the set is run as a commercial enterprise. It does retain, albeit in a slightly updated form, some of the Bar's traditional rituals. Rather than afternoon tea, each morning at 11am there's chambers coffee. Don't let the pastries persuade you that it's a strictly social occasion: "*It's a chance to see everyone, but it's also a brain trust*." Expect to see some heavyweight silks mooting points of law or "*general discussion of legal issues and ideas*" alongside friendly chitchat. That might sound a tad intimidating, and pupils confessed that "*if it's more of a social-type gathering, you're much more free to contribute. If it's about legal issues, you probably don't have as much to say*."

Chambers hosts the occasional evening for its rotating artist-in-residence and throws Christmas and summer parties, including a weekend in Bristol last year in a senior member's Clifton residence. Those at the junior end often lunch together, "*normally in Gray's Inn Hall, but sometimes just popping out for pizza*." On Friday night they may head to the Old Vic with the clerks. On the whole though it's a set where "*people tend to go home once they've finished their work*."

And finally...

If you're a tax enthusiast, or just looking for an intellectually rigorous pupillage, this prestigious set, bizarrely, attracts just 70 or so applications each year. Why not be one of them?

Quadrant Chambers

The facts

Location: Fleet Street, London
Number of QCs/Juniors: 12/38 (8 women)
Applications: 84
Outside Pupillage Portal scheme
Pupils per year: up to 3
Seats: 4x3 months
Pupillage award: £55,000 (can advance up to £7,500 for BPTC)

A new management team is pushing this set forwards, and not only in its established areas of practice.

Still successfully focused on its aviation, shipping and general commercial practice, Quadrant Chambers is keen to straddle the divide between the contemporary and the traditional.

The shipping forecast

The members of Quadrant Chambers are rightly proud of its "*showcase*" premises on Fleet Street. Indeed, one member told us they "*felt a bit shabby*" when the set first moved into its sleek new home. Four buildings (apparently including an ancient brothel, a one-time tea house and a former branch of Lloyd's bank) were knocked into one, each retaining a separate style, so stuccoed Regency era ceilings and wrought-iron Victorian banisters complement glass-and-steel walkways. Senior clerk Gary Ventura told us the building is intended to represent a mix of "*the traditional and the contemporary.*" The set appointed a CEO in 2009, who now co-runs chambers with the senior clerk and two heads of chambers. "*He came from outside the legal profession with experience in management consulting and opened up chambers' eyes to a better approach to interacting with clients,*" Ventura said. The four head honchos are now "*under the same wrapper*" and involved in all areas of management and "*promoting chambers to the marketplace.*"

"*We're pre-eminent in shipping and aviation,*" explained Ventura, "*and we're continuing to develop international arbitration, energy, insurance and reinsurance, commodities and banking and finance.*" It's a broad remit but somehow all connected. "*The shipping market is buoyant at the moment,*" Ventura added (with a straight face, take note). Why? "*It's all because of the recession,*" explained a junior. "*We're extremely busy on the international contractual side as everyone is trying to get out of contracts which they signed up to in the good times – for instance to build ships.*"

While the volume of non-shipping and aviation instructions is expected to grow, Ventura notes that "*shipping accounts for probably a little over half of the practice at the moment and I can't see that falling below 50%.*" Members have been involved in litigation concerning the wreck of the 'MSC Napoli' off the Cornish Coast, the collapse of a drilling rig in the Bay of Bengal, a crashed high-speed ferry and unneeded ships built by the Chinese. In the world of aviation, they have worked on the independent review of the 2006 Nimrod crash in Afghanistan. The nature of shipping and aviation means that "*almost all the work is international*" and chambers' links to Hong Kong and Singapore are particularly strong. In a rare non-commercial, non-shipping piece of work, one tenant has been acting for a pretender to the throne of Romania.

Apply without?

If you want a slice of all this, take note that applications to Quadrant are made outside the Pupillage Portal. "*Firstly, so as not to be part of a giant bureaucracy, and secondly to snap up the best applicants,*" explained new pupillage committee head Tom Macey-Dare. Around 35 applicants are invited to complete a test set of papers. They are sent a brief and given a few days to write and return an opinion. "*It's on an area of law we do; the last one was a sale of goods problem,*" said Macey-Dare. When we asked what

Chambers UK rankings

Aviation	Travel
Shipping	

would get you through the first cull, we were told: "*A First! And that's only partly in jest. We're not impressed if you've done hundreds of Duke of Edinburgh's Awards – we want gently rounded personalities but a good degree from a good university is key.*" You will need to have some legal knowledge to complete the written assessment brief (although six months on the GDL and a common-sense approach will get you a long way).

Those who get past the first round are asked to perform in a 45-minute interview in front of a panel of senior juniors. The panel reads first-round test papers and quizzes candidates on them, as well as on another legal problem and an ethical question. Although Macey-Dare told us: "*Personality and the gift of the gab are not what we're looking for,*" you'll need to be able to "*give sensible and clever answers and have a nice manner so that judges and tribunals will warm to you.*" The pupillage committee regrets that it is difficult to tell someone's aptitude for the Bar from a CV, although detailing mooting experience and mini-pupillages is important. A mini at Quadrant is not a necessity: "*Mini-pupillages show your commitment to the Bar, but if you do ten that ceases to impress. Three is a decent number.*"

Hold onto your luggage

During the year, pupils sit with four supervisors and over time are "*given more and more responsibility.*" As with many commercial sets, you shouldn't expect advocacy experience until after pupillage. "*Once the decision is made, you're immediately on your feet.*" The mainstay of pupillage is "*increasing amounts of drafting,*" and while shadowing on big 'wet' and 'dry' shipping cases you might end up like the pupil who "*got to tell my friends I was working on piracy law.*" Pupils' experiences reflect the work of chambers as a whole: tenants mostly have broad practices until their call is into double figures. Specialisation is possible from a few years in, but not obligatory and never exclusive.

Ongoing feedback throughout the year is "*very specific about what you are doing well and what you are doing badly.*" Practice makes perfect: "*There's a lot of room in the first three months to grow and learn – you're not expected to be the finished product when you turn up.*" You are expected to do well in several formal oral advocacy exercises in front of silks and opposite another pupil. The exercises exist in part to grant pupils valuable advocacy experience and in part for assessment purposes. Supervisors assess work very closely: "*You do undertake work for other members of chambers, but most is for supervisors: it's not essential to get to know other members to gain tenancy.*" Supervisors have a massive stake in the tenancy decision: "*After all, you can't glean very much from just one piece of work for a silk,*" a member of the pupillage committee stressed.

New tenants are assigned a mentor for their first six months and often share a room with them. Mentors are there to "*ask the stupid questions of*" when juniors are first coping with their own files. Small cases such as "*people being bumped off their flights and lost luggage claims*" see them in court about once a week, while taking the junior role on cases like "*a dispute over the ownership of an aircraft*" takes up much of the remaining time.

Ship ship, hurrah

Quadrant's roomy and spacious building – which is "*a bit like an M.C. Escher painting*" – allows members to opt for their own room after six months of tenancy. You might expect this to lead to an insular culture but we're assured of the set's sociable nature. "*People wedge their doors open... and you could easily spend your whole day chatting,*" said a tenant, although another added: "*There are some quiet corners.*" There's no real Quadrant type, but "*everyone is fairly irreverent and there's plenty of humorous banter.*" Daly's Wine Bar on Essex Street is a popular Friday haunt: "*Normally some of the Quaddies will have taken over the corner and will stop anyone trying to catch the 6.31 from Waterloo.*"

And finally...

This lively commercial set is well worth considering. *"You start not knowing anything and then the support and structure kick in, so there's no reason to be afraid when you see it's a shipping set."*

Serle Court

The facts

Location: Lincoln's Inn, London
Number of QCs/Juniors: 15/36 (7 women)
Applications: 120+
Outside Pupillage Portal scheme
Pupils per year: 1 or 2
Seats: 4x3 months
Pupillage Award: £60,000 (can advance £20,000 for BPTC)

"When meeting with solicitors, my supervisor will always ask if I have anything to add – which is a little thing, but important."

Top commercial Chancery set Serle Court offers a wide range of work in relaxed surroundings.

Roman's army

Serle Court was formed in 2000 through a merger between the Chancery barristers of 13 Old Square and the commercial barristers of 1 Hare Court. The product is a set with strength in a sweep of practice areas. A clerk tells us that "*at the moment, offshore trusts work, lots of fraud work, company insolvency and property are the areas we get most enquiries about. But then sports law and all these other little cases come in as well.*"

This summary tallies well with the set's rankings in *Chambers UK*. Members are acting on one of the biggest shipping fraud cases currently ongoing, *Fiona Trust v Privalov*. It's a long story, but is essentially a matter brought by the operators of two Russian tanker fleets alleging misappropriation, conspiracy, fraud and bribery against their former president and various other individuals and companies. Keeping it Russo-related, we're told that things are busy in the oligarchy market at the moment, and Roman Abramovich has briefed new head of chambers Alan Boyle QC in fraud matters. Serle Court is ahead of the game in the offshore trusts field: many sets are only just starting to look abroad for work but this one already possesses a number of barristers who often appear in Jersey, the Cayman Islands and elsewhere. As for those other little cases, well, there are plenty of quirky ones to talk about, from the matter of the Jersey accountant claiming to be an illegitimate son of Princess Margaret, to the curious case of the Bishop of Portsmouth, the convent school and the Benedictine nun.

Bacon's buddies

Ye olde lawyer Sir Francis Bacon said that 'reading maketh a full man, conference a ready man, and writing an exact man'. Nowhere does this apply more than in the incredibly complex field of Chancery law and, taking Sir Francis' counsel to heart, pupillage consists of a mix of the three – reading in the form of research, conference in the form of contact with other barristers and solicitors, and writing in the form of drafting.

The proportion of each during the course of the four three-month seats depends largely on the pupilmaster's practice. "*My first supervisor was working on two very big fraud cases,*" said a pupil. That involved researching "*quite a lot of interesting law – jurisdictional questions and the like*" and drafting skeleton arguments and bits of witness statements. By contrast, "*in the second three months I had a supervisor who seemed to have a new set of papers every day. That meant I got a much more regular stream of little things coming in, like contractual disputes and land law.*" As you can see, pupils get exposure to the full breadth of chambers' practice, from commercial and traditional Chancery to property, IP and more. As for conferencing: "*My supervisor has been very good about recognising that I'm there, and when meeting with solicitors he'll always ask if I have anything to add – which is a little thing, but important.*" Being farmed out to several members of chambers is also commonplace. "*It's mostly quite interesting stuff, although occasionally it's one of those negative questions that pupils have to prove: can you go off and prove that there isn't anything on this subject? You'll come back having found nothing*

Chambers UK rankings

Banking & Finance	Fraud
Chancery	Partnership
Commercial Dispute Resolution	Professional Negligence
	Real Estate Litigation
Company	Restructuring/Insolvency

and inevitably some document will have been hidden behind the filing cabinet all along," joked a pupil.

What you won't get is any guarantee of your own caseload. Chambers' attitude to training is simple: "*They're here for a year as a pupil*" and that time is better spent getting to grips with more complex law than going off to court to deal with road traffic accident claims. Although a junior said that "*in practice you tend to get a bit of advocacy*" during the summer after tenancy has been offered, clerks and pupilmasters alike played down the chances of court time. However, a pupil told us that much of the work he had done for supervisors was "*essentially live, which is good for motivational reasons.*" Feedback was described as satisfactory, coming in "*traditional primary school red pen.*" Perhaps the only time it doesn't work quite so well "*is when you do tasks for other members of chambers. You will get an e-mail back saying, 'Thanks very much, very useful,' but that's usually about it.*"

Working hours for pupils are officially 9am to 6pm. It's fair to say that these normally stretch to a little longer than this, but not extortionately so. "*It's very civilised,*" said a pupil; "*I've certainly not been kept hanging around or given unreasonable amounts of work, and there's no doubt that I've been going home well before my supervisors.*"

Stars of the Bar at the bar in the Stars

When chambers moved in to its current premises at 6 New Square, everyone looked forward to coming together under one roof. Best-laid plans being what they are, within a short period of time they ran out of space. Fortunately for would-be tenants the purchase of an annexe has added extra lebensraum, even if it's a little less glamorous than the main building: "*The rooms don't overlook Lincoln's Inn and you're above Wetherspoons.*" Perhaps unsurprisingly, there's a concentration of younger barristers in the annexe, making it, in the words of a pupil, "*the relaxed end of an already relaxed set of chambers.*"

That's definitely Serle Court's style and has been for some time. "*We feel that we have a slightly more relaxed approach to the formalities of life at the Bar,*" says a pupilmaster. "*Ten years ago I think there was clear blue water between us and the rest, although I get the impression that others are catching on now and taking steps to become less stuffy.*" Pupils are actively encouraged to be seen – and heard – at morning coffee or afternoon tea, although "*you might not necessarily wish to hold forth: there are certainly elements of tact involved!*" The Seven Stars is inexplicably more popular than Wetherspoons for an after-work drink, and you'll regularly find "*the usual suspects*" there. There are also football, softball and cricket teams. But, "*whether you're the type of person who likes to socialise over a cup of coffee in the morning, a cup of tea in the afternoon, a glass of wine in the evening, or on the football pitch,*" it's important to meet other members of chambers as, though the ultimate tenancy decision is made by the pupillage committee (as advised by the pupilmasters), a good word from the rest can't hurt. Serle Court has offered tenancy to most of its pupils in the past ten years, although none were taken on in 2010. Income in the early months of tenancy is usually slow but at least £100K is guaranteed in the first two years.

So who does the set want to recruit as a pupil? Aside from social skills, academic results are hugely important for two reasons. Commercial Chancery is one of the most factually complex areas of the Bar and very intellectually demanding. Secondly, quite simply, chambers now gets about as many people with First-class degrees applying as there are first-interview places and, "*if you're trying to do it fairly, it's very hard to turn away someone with a First in favour of someone with a 2:1.*" It does sometimes happen in exceptional circumstances. Otherwise, we sense there's no specific type. The pupils at the time of our visit were a 20-something law graduate and a 30-something with a PhD in 16th century music.

And finally...

"*Everyone seems happy, and there's a lot of work coming in,*" says a junior. "*I genuinely think Serle Court is a very dynamic place to be at the moment.*" Nice place, very busy. What more is there to say?

3-4 South Square

The facts

Location: Gray's Inn, London
Number of QCs/Juniors: 19/27 (9 women)
Applications: 100
Outside Pupillage Portal scheme
Pupils per year: 2
Seats: 6x6 weeks
Pupillage award: £60,000 (can advance up to £18,000 for BPTC)

Chambers and Partners' Insolvency/Corporate Restructuring Set of the Year 2010

3-4 South Square has been involved in *"pretty much every large insolvency there has been"* – Lloyd's syndicates, Barings, Enron, Parmalat, MyTravel, Metronet, Nortel, Lehman Brothers...

City slickers

...Northern Rock, Swissair, Bradford & Bingley, Kaupthing, Landsbanki, Woolworths, Madoff Securities, Borders. Insolvency has always been 3-4 South Square's hot ticket, and in times such as these it's doing better than ever. Some 60-70% of chambers' work is insolvency law-specific, while of the remainder, a junior suggested, "*everything is in some way insolvency or restructuring-related.*" Banking and financial services is a particular specialisation. The set has advised Abbey, Credit Suisse and NatWest, as well as The Bank of England, the FSA and the Treasury.

The Insolvency Act and Companies Act of 2006 are two of the longest statutes on the books, so this set isn't for those who shy away from reading black letter law. Insolvency and restructuring cases are complex and tend to take in many different areas of law, hence members also find their work necessarily involves company law, EU law, property, personal insolvency, fraud, professional negligence, tort and public law. "*Insolvency is a context in which law happens; it's not an area of law unto itself,*" a pupil explained. "*This means that during insolvency procedures, a lot of legal questions get asked which might not otherwise be asked.*" Pupillage committee member Marcus Haywood summed up chambers' ethos: "*What differentiates us from other sets is providing real commercial solutions, not just what is right or wrong in law.*" Charismatic senior practice manager Paul Cooklin left 3-4 South Square for Keating Chambers in May 2010, leaving it temporarily in what was described to us as "*an interregnum.*" It has taken this as an opportunity for a strategic review of its management structure.

To do well here you need to have discipline, "*an eye for detail*" and "*patience.*" This last quality is particularly important because "*work is always very paper-heavy and you have to go through a lot of documentation.*" But don't mistake sharp intellect for ponderous philosophising: "*If you just want to wear a three-piece suit and tell anecdotes about maxims of equity this isn't the place for you,*" a pupil warned, another adding that chambers has "*a highly commercial environment where you work 11-hour days and you need to be on standby at the weekends.*" According to a seasoned junior, the nature of the work also requires that you're "*pretty numerate and have a genuine understanding of how City finance works.*"

Scribblers not quibblers

A pupil's work will reflect that of the set as a whole, as "*you do whatever your pupilmaster is instructed on.*" Pupillage exposes the new recruit to six supervisors (chosen from those over 12 years' call), which provides them with a "*broad spectrum*" of work. "*In the first few weeks I was given some difficult work to test me,*" a pupil told us; "*you're put in at the deep end because that's where you'll end up.*" Pupils have lately been tested on very topical matters. "*A lot of it has related to the Lehman Brothers insolvency or the Icelandic banks, but I've also done non-*

Chambers UK rankings

Banking & Finance	Company
Chancery	Restructuring/Insolvency

insolvency cases on things like fraud and misrepresentation."

"*Some supervisors are in court more and some have more paperwork,*" a pupil explained. The size of cases means pupils can't expect to have their own files, and shouldn't expect to be in court all the time. "*While shadowing my master, I've been to court a handful of times,*" one said. "*You don't get the opportunity to be on your feet in your second seat, but then you don't go to the Commercial Bar expecting that.*" As a pupil put it: "*I'd rather do something legally interesting than be on my feet all the time on things which are really barely law-related.*" So if advocacy is not the be-all and end-all, what is? Simple: drafting skills are valued as among the most important at 3-4 South Square.

The big-shot corporate insolvency cases that chambers works on often involve multinational companies and/or foreign jurisdictions. It has recently worked on cases with links to Poland, Russia, Slovakia, Switzerland, Germany, Jersey, the Cayman Islands, Singapore and Dubai. To assist its business, the set has associate members based in Australia, Germany, Hong Kong, Scotland, Singapore, South Africa, Trinidad & Tobago and the USA.

Tenancy = tenacity

To be successful, pupils say you have to "*work hard, get things right and be nice.*" Easy! Pupils usually don't complete formal written assessments, but "*all of your written work is assessed and taken into account.*" "*Each master, and all those who the pupil has done work for, provide a report,*" Marcus Haywood explained as he took us through the factors on which tenancy decisions are based. Gaining tenancy is a meritocratic yet unpredictable affair: in the past chambers has sometimes taken on all pupils, sometimes none. The latter is "*pretty rare,*" according to Haywood, and both pupils made the grade in 2010.

The set has an "*ambitious, dynamic and hard-working*" character and what one pupil described as "*pretty brutal*" hours. We get the impression you have to be quite a tough cookie to succeed here. Long hours means "*there aren't regular chambers drinks,*" but you can expect lunches in Gray's Inn Hall. When they do get together – for instance to welcome new pupils – the barristers get on well. "*They're the sort of people I would hang out with socially,*" said a pupil.

Going bust

Want in? Applicants face two rounds of interviews. The first explores a candidate's interests and motivations for joining the Bar, and poses a problem question related to insolvency law or finance. "*It requires no prior knowledge of the area,*" recruiters insist; "*we're not expecting people to know the world, but if you do start claiming expertise in something, then you have to know your stuff.*" A second interview – in front of a seven-member panel including QCs – focuses on a legal/ethical problem such as, 'What you would do if you found an obscure House of Lords decision which really helped your opponent?' Before the interview, learn about what the set does by "*reading about commercial cases in the newspaper or looking at our online Digest.*" According to a recruiter, getting in and getting on are "*not so much a question of whether someone is 'commercially aware', but whether they take a common-sense approach.*"

Chambers offers both assessed and un-assessed mini-pupillages. Try and get on one if you can; otherwise your work experience with another set or a law firm will also be viewed positively. Doing an insolvency or company law elective during your BPTC or BCL could be useful, but it's not a prerequisite. Previous career experience and/or impressive degrees are de rigueur here. As a point of interest, the two pupils who finished in 2010 both had BCLs.

"*Some people might say insolvency is innately depressing,*" a source admitted, "*but it's just something that happens in this world.*" This set's work is intellectually but not necessarily emotionally draining, so you could say that "*the stresses are the hours and the difficulty of the work.*" You need to have a tranquil and serious personality to work here as "*there are some quite jumpy people among the clients, and you have to be a calm influence and a safe pair of hands.*"

And finally...

"*Sometimes it's like doing the Times crossword,*" said a fan of the intellectually challenging work on offer. How appropriate then that one QC compiles crosswords for *The Spectator*.

2 Temple Gardens

The facts

Location: Middle Temple, London
Number of QCs/Juniors: 10/39 (20 women)
Applications: 200-250
Apply through Pupillage Portal
Pupils per year: Up to 3
Seats: 4x3 months
Pupillage award: £60,000 (can advance £22,500 for BPTC)

With an incredibly broad practice and attractive pupillage package, 2TG is a great place for the open-minded.

This civil set is a jack-of-all-trades, but it manages to master them too. It's an attractive proposition for those with an open mind.

Contemporitional? Tradiporary?

Founded shortly after WWII, 2TG is positioned at the River Thames end of the Temple, so has picturesque views of the river. Its premises mix the contemporary with a sense of history: for every bleak, modern landscape canvas on its white walls, there is a beautifully ornate original marble fireplace. In part, this is thanks to the building's Grade 1 listing, but you can't help thinking 2TG rather likes it that way. While the set holds an impressive number of seminars during term time to network and create new business opportunities, every Wednesday it simultaneously continues the old tradition of chambers tea. This is a set that synthesises new and old patterns of behaviour and it emphatically doesn't have the corporate feel of some of the flashier "*über-modern commercial sets.*"

Who burnt all the pies?

Since the 1960s, 2TG has been a purely civil set, but underneath that civil umbrella is an incredibly broad range of practices. It is particularly highly regarded for its clinical negligence and personal injury defence, which one source estimated accounts for between 30 and 40% of chambers' income. Recently, tenants have been involved in high-value claims involving severe brain injuries, as well as complex asbestos exposure cases. Over the past few years, 2TG has expanded into claimant work, partly to offer a fuller service, but also as a reaction to "*insurers squeezing and squeezing the legal profession while keeping their rates the same.*" Claimant work accounts for only around 10% of the PI and clin neg practice, but it is of an admirable quality. Members have represented claimants in the Atomic Test Veterans case against the MoD, arising out of government testing in the 1950s.

Professional discipline and professional negligence are areas of strength, and the set even publishes its own professional negligence journal. A popular choice for professional indemnity insurers, 2TG defends members of a variety of professions but in particular receives a large volume of instructions in cases of alleged insurance brokers' negligence. Recent high-profile matters include a £100m+ case following a fire at a Primark warehouse in Leicester that ruined half of the budget clothing brand's national stock, and a multimillion-pound claim brought against insurance brokers by the owners of a pie factory that burned down.

Alongside the set's historic strengths, a commercial practice has grown steadily over the past 12 to 15 years, incorporating insurance and reinsurance, banking and finance, construction, commercial fraud and private international law. 2TG's barristers have been involved in a derivatives dispute against RBS involving claims of alleged mis-selling and breach of FSA rules in relation to foreign exchange swap products. There was also a claim by an art dealer over the sale of forged works of fine art and antique furniture. Meanwhile, a burgeoning employment practice is making its presence felt and the set is also aiming to win more media and entertainment instructions.

Chambers UK rankings

Clinical Negligence	Professional Discipline
Personal Injury	Professional Negligence

Odds on

Over the past five years, 90% of pupils have been taken on as tenants, and in 2010 all three were offered tenancy. "*There's no prescribed number of tenancies available for pupils. Pupillage is an incredibly tense and hard experience, but taking away the competition element helps,*" a senior source explained. Those retention rates are a testament both to the unique and thorough recruitment process (see below), and also to the quality of training.

Pupils complete four three-month seats with no prescribed route or order, but "*the seats aren't hit or miss. We try and make sure that pupils see a practice with a high paper turnover – like smaller PI claims – as well as more specialist areas.*" The first three months are spent with a supervisor, "*working on cases in tandem.*" One pupil recalled the experience: "*We would each write the same defence, then we would sit down together and compare the two.*" While not exactly a gentle introduction, it helps to build confidence in drafting and "*by the second seat you feel very prepared.*" Although the approach might vary slightly between pupil supervisors, in the second seat pupils are "*given the papers first. You produce a draft, the supervisor would do his and then you get feedback.*" Recalling the process, a junior tenant reminisced: "*As you progress, little bits of your draft start to creep in to the final documents. It's very satisfying.*"

Once the second six is underway, so is the advocacy element of pupillage. In some civil sets, particularly those with a commercial emphasis, pupils spend very little time on their feet. By contrast, 2TG has them in court as soon and as often as possible. Pupils can expect three appointments a week for small and Fast Track claims, charging orders and infant settlements. This last type of hearing is a common way of breaking in pupils, who consequently become "*experts on Part 21 of the White Book.*" Pupils can also expect to travel. "*You get to see all sorts of glamorous places,*" laughed a baby junior recounting a second-six outing to Dartford.

The tenancy decision is made in early July, but it doesn't come out of the blue. A recruitment source explained: "*It's an ongoing decision. At the end of each seat, the pupil supervisor writes a detailed report. Reports are also written by any tenants for whom pupils have worked in the previous three months.*" The reports lead to an evaluation in which the pupil, the head of the pupillage committee and the pupil supervisor sit down together to discuss the past three months. "*Pupils are told where they have done well, and where they have done less well, and they are then given appropriate targets. It's incredibly structured.*" The system helps pupils to progress and ensures that the ultimate tenancy decision won't be a complete shock. "*Pupillage is hard work, and anyone who tells you otherwise isn't doing it right,*" a source stressed. That may be so, but the lack of competition between pupils and the detailed feedback system do take the sharp edges off.

Taking the cake

According to our sources, "*the thing that defines this set is that there's no standing on ceremony. Your pupil supervisor is as likely to make you a cup of tea as you are to make them one.*" A junior member reported being able "*to talk to the head of chambers as easily as anyone else,*" while another source confirmed: "*It's fine to chat to the big silks.*"

A running theme among our interviewees was the diversity of personalities across 2TG. According to a pupil, "*the set does such a wide range of work, it allows many different types of people to thrive*" and this makes chambers "*extremely inclusive.*" Indeed, there are weekly get-togethers for members and pupils, including tea every Wednesday – "*quite a few people get cakes from Paul* [an upmarket patisserie nearby, not a live-in pastry chef] *but a lot of people bake, too.*" A weekly drinks evening is also "*well attended,*" and from time to time there will be special events – "*if there's a fantastic success in a case then we might have a party.*"

Members describe the set as "*progressive: it's not the sort of place where people get here in the morning, shut their doors and then don't interact for the rest of the day.*" Certainly at the junior end we sensed there is excellent peer support. One pupil told us: "*Juniors are exceptionally friendly,*" and a recent tenant confirmed "*a great sense of camaraderie – we always have a table in Middle Temple Hall for lunch, which is great if you're at a loose end.*" This is the kind of set where "*if people see your light on at 10 pm, they will pop their head in and see if you fancy nipping to the pub for last orders.*"

And finally...

With a practice as wide as it is well regarded, plentiful advocacy opportunities, an enviable track record of awarding tenancy, and generous earnings, civil sorts could do a lot worse than 2TG.

3 Verulam Buildings

The facts

Location: Gray's Inn, London

Number of QCs/Juniors: 18/45 (12 women)

Applications: 150

Apply through Pupillage Portal

Pupils per year: 3-4

Seats: 4x3 months

Pupillage Award: £60,000 (can advance £20,000 for BPTC)

Brilliant in banking and finance, and impatient to reach hallowed 'magic circle' status, 3VB is a good choice for the commercially minded.

"I don't think we're the sort of chambers that looks back." We concur: 3VB is a set with the future on its mind.

Banking on success

Previously we, among others, have described 3 Verulam Buildings as 'knocking on the door of the magic circle'. Unsurprisingly, 3VB's members feel it is past knocking and is now over the threshold, muddying the carpet and stealing the silver. Or, to put it in the more diplomatic terms of a QC: "*If there is a magic circle we're in it. Our closest competitors in terms of the work we do are Fountain Chambers and One Essex Court, and those are who we come up against most often in court.*" What's more, he says, "*we have more juniors in the commercial litigation tables of Chambers UK than any other set – and bear in mind that they are the people who are pupil supervisors.*" This is undeniable, and a real pool of talent at junior silk and senior junior level means that the future of the set looks bright indeed. Perhaps the concept of the magic circle is a red herring. As our colleagues on *Chambers UK* see it, 3VB is an excellent banking and finance set constantly extending its tentacles into new areas of the commercial law market. We say, forget the talk of circles, magic or otherwise: smart applicants will know that 3VB's pool of talent will be in full bloom once they are juniors. "*That's very exciting because it means the work that people at the bottom of chambers will get led on is only going to get better.*"

This set is undeniably brilliant in the field of banking and finance disputes. And heck, what an area to excel in right now! 3VB had six members acting for various parties in the recent bank charges litigation, and there have been all manner of instructions relating to the collapse of Lehman Brothers, the failure of the Icelandic banks, problems in the derivatives markets and government-funded rescues all over the world. The set does seem to get its fair share of whatever is blowing through the English courts – it was also extremely active on a number of large insurance/reinsurance disputes that arose from 9/11 and the Equitable Life debacle.

An extensive revamp a couple of years ago makes the moniker 3 Verulam Buildings a bit of a misnomer. Chambers now occupies numbers 1, 2, 4 and 5 as well. "*I suspect we've probably got the best accommodation at the Bar now,*" asserts senior practice manager Nick Hill. Certainly, many sets would envy the fact that not only is everyone at 3VB under one roof, but there is still plenty of room to expand.

Skeleton key

As it isn't the sort of set that has grown through mergers or repeated lateral hires, recruiting the right pupils is very important and consequently chambers has put some serious thought into the interview process. The 40 or so applicants who get invited to a first interview can expect a general chat about their CV, their decision to come to the Bar and a current "*legal-ish*" topic (in past years it has concerned the anonymity of witnesses in criminal trials and the extra-territoriality of bribery legislation). Around half will make it through to a second-round interview, which involves the oral argument of a legal problem. "*They make their points and we heckle a bit.*" Hmm, a bit? "*To a realistic degree! We let everyone get well into their stride before we ask any questions and it's always done in a polite way, but it's a thorough testing of abilities and aptitude.*" The problem is

Chambers UK rankings

Banking & Finance	Insurance
Commercial Dispute Resolution	Media & Entertainment
Financial Services	Professional Negligence
Fraud	Restructuring/Insolvency
Information Technology	Telecommunications

sent to interviewees a week in advance. As still happens at some places, 3VB used to spring it on people half an hour beforehand but decided that was *"unrealistic and unfair."* In another recent innovation at the 'legal problem' stage, chambers also asks for a short skeleton argument to be submitted beforehand. *"We think that's been a distinct improvement... previously we were sometimes rather easily beguiled by people who could talk a good talk, but when it got to pupillage couldn't write a good write."* The skeleton is 900 words long, but we've heard reports that this *"doesn't stop some people submitting it single-spaced in the smallest possible font."*

While a mini-pupillage isn't required, chambers does like to see everyone it invites to second interview for at least a day or two at some point before it makes offers. Those who have made it through the process in recent years include not only 'straight through from Oxbridge' types but also a glut of people from Commonwealth universities, former actuaries and lecturers, someone who ran his own business and the former head of Insurance and Prudential Policy at the Financial Services Authority. *"Age or previous career is no boundary."* Nor is a non-law degree, although as a Pupillage Portal member 3VB feels that the sets outside that system try to nab the best GDL students early.

Me and my shadow

Pupils sit with four supervisors for three months each in order to see a range of work and types of people. They are also encouraged to work for other members of chambers. The tasks pupils are given are a mix of supervisors' current work and past cases. There are also *"shadow supervisors."* These are barristers in their first five years of practice who, as well as adding an extra level of pastoral care, *"keep an eye out for pieces of work that it would be useful to show to pupils."* Four or five advocacy exercises are scheduled for the year. *"We do take notice of how they perform in these, but it's mainly educational – so long as they don't make the same mistake in two exercises."* A pupil confirmed that this attitude doesn't just apply to the advocacy exercises: *"You're not supposed to make the same mistake twice... but they are very forgiving of the first mistake."* Chambers *"doesn't kick people out"* after completion of the first six, although if pupils don't look like they're making headway by that stage it's suggested that it might be in their best interests to look elsewhere. In the second six *"the expectations go up,"* work gets more complex, *"the feedback points get finer and more nuanced"* and pupils start to receive their own instructions. *"They definitely make sure you get something, although it's not like a criminal set where you will be constantly in court."* Chambers has the space to offer tenancy to everyone who comes up to scratch: two out of three pupils took up tenancy in 2009 and all three were kept on in 2010.

A formal afternoon tea isn't quite 3VB's style, but there is a common room that people flit in and out of throughout the day. Also worthy of note are a summer party, an annual dinner and various drinks evenings. Silk parties are de rigueur: *"One of the barristers just made silk so he had a bit of a do."* Pupils won't actually see much of each other during the day, but do meet up to socialise after office hours.

And finally...

Modern and forward-thinking, 3 Verulam Buildings is a choice pick by anyone's standards.

Wilberforce Chambers

The facts

Location: Lincoln's Inn, London
Number of QCs/Juniors: 22/28 (10 women)
Applications: c. 75-100
Outside Pupillage Portal scheme
Pupils per year: 2
Seats: 6x2 months
Pupillage Award: £48,000 (can advance £16,000 for BPTC)

The collapse of Lehman Brothers and Bear Stearns led to some meaty instructions during and in the aftermath of the global financial crisis.

Back in the 1980s, this set was one of the first to recognise the importance of branding. Accordingly, it renamed itself after one of its most distinguished members, Lord Wilberforce, great-great-grandson of William Wilberforce. It has been growing in size and reputation ever since.

Wilberforce be with you

Wilberforce is a leader among Chancery sets. For 'traditional' Chancery cases it stands alone in the top tier in *Chambers UK*. Possibly its best-known recent success was the headline-making divorce case of *Charman v Charman*, in which members represented the wife of a fabulously wealthy insurance magnate. Private clients are just one part of the story though. As one of the new breed of Chancery sets, Wilberforce's reach is wide in the commercial sphere, both in relation to Chancery Division cases and those headed for the Queen's Bench Division of the High Court. It is undisputed top dog for pensions matters, and a team including seven QCs recently represented seven of the nine parties in the Pilots National Pension Fund litigation, the largest pensions case of the year.

The set also has a fine reputation for property litigation, professional negligence, fraud, IP and more. In a much-publicised IP case, for example, members represented Lucasfilm, suing one Andrew Ainsworth for copyright infringement. Mr Ainsworth had made some of the original Imperial Stormtrooper helmets and armour for the first Star Wars film and had started to sell life-sized replicas. Meanwhile, Ian Croxford QC acted for the Ritz Hotel Group during the inquest into the death of Diana, Princess of Wales, while the collapse of Lehman Brothers and Bear Stearns led to some meaty instructions during the early weeks of the financial crisis in 2008. Other subjects recently touched on by members include feuding oligarchs, the collapse of offshore hedge funds and corruption in the former Zambian government. It's quite a mix.

Analyse this

Now around 50 barristers strong, chambers operates from three buildings on New Square and is actively looking for new premises. Said a source: "*Being under one roof is desirable in itself and will also help to make the set more collegiate.*" Although nothing had been decided by the time we went to press, a couple of options were being examined, so this is no idle speculation.

At the same time, the aim is to grow "*a little bit more,*" and the pupillage scheme is certainly going to be a part of this process. Wilberforce has a large number of QCs and "*the ratio of silks to juniors has become somewhat skewed.*" Chambers takes two pupils a year with a view to offering two tenancies if the candidates are of a sufficiently high calibre to be taken on.

So how are you likely to fare if you put yourself up for consideration? Academic ability is "*a starting point,*" of course, but we also hear from the pupillage committee that it "*doesn't insist on people having a First.*" While this might sound like good news for those who missed out on top grades, be aware that the majority of pupils – and members – do have Firsts. At interview, we're told: "*It's the way in which applicants analyse the set legal problem, and how they put forward their answers, that is crucial.*" Our source on the pupillage committee continued: "*It's very interesting that people who have only just started studying law often do better than some who've been doing law for years but who can prove completely inadequate at doing what a barrister really has to do – legal analysis at*

Chambers UK rankings

Chancery	Fraud
Charities	Pensions
Commercial Dispute Resolution	Professional Negligence
Company	Real Estate Litigation

very short notice." The trend for GDL students to perform better at interview is not unique to this set – many of the commercial and Chancery chambers we visit note the same thing. "*Common sense*" and "*a practical working knowledge of the real world*" are highly desired qualities and it is possible that GDL students, with that extra time behind them, are more likely to display these traits. Interestingly, when we asked if personality was another contributing factor we were told in no uncertain terms: "*No. We have set criteria based on what makes a good barrister, not on who's going to be nice to go to lunch with.*" This strict hiring policy, with its emphasis on fairness, has resulted in an "*eclectic*" mix of tenants. "*We get quiet ones, we get assertive ones. We get people from all walks of life. The only things they have in common are excellent academic results and a high intellect.*" All that said, an analysis of the membership of Wilberforce suggests that unless you have Oxbridge on your CV you're unlikely to make it through the recruitment process.

Tea and tenancy

"*This pupillage would suit someone who wanted a broad experience of Chancery work.*" Pupils will experience most areas of the set's business over the course of the year by sitting with six supervisors for two months at a time. Each seat naturally offers the chance to develop different skills; for example, "*somebody in the property stream will be in court a lot more than in the private client stream where there is more drafting.*" A pupil's day will tend to mirror their supervisor's. "*Mostly I'll be writing an opinion or doing a statement of case at the same time as my supervisor is doing the same thing live. That keeps the work I'm doing relevant,*" explained the pupil we spoke to. Opportunities for advocacy during the pupillage year are fairly limited. At the end of each seat supervisors prepare a short report bearing a number of criteria in mind – "*was he sufficiently analytical, was he thorough in his research and so on.*" This is "*not done on a strict numbers system*" but is simply a guideline.

People "*do generally reserve judgement on pupils until it's time for the tenancy decision to be made,*" recognising that a pupil in his (or her) first two months is very different from the same pupil six months later. Wilberforce's policy is to offer tenancy to every pupil who meets its exacting standards. "*Other chambers may not want to take two on at once, or say they don't have enough room, but it's our clear policy that we will take pupils on if we consider them to be good enough.*" The set's sole pupil wasn't taken on in 2009, although it did seek out and take on a third six pupil in order to sustain its growth trajectory. Both pupils were offered tenancy in 2010.

"*There isn't the 4 o'clock 'pens down' for tea*" that you might experience at some other sets. Instead chambers drinks take place on a Friday evening and there are also bi-weekly lunches and client events. Plus, said our pupil, "*I have been out with some of the juniors a few times and they are all very nice to me!*" Essentially, "*you can have as much of a social life as you want.*"

And finally...

Wilberforce is looking for the brightest and best so you'll need the analytical skills of Sherlock Holmes and a brain like The Mekon's. We suspect the silver tongue of Barack Obama wouldn't go amiss either.

- **General advice for life:** Carpe diem; neither a borrower nor a lender be; carpe noctem; never play cards with anyone called Doc; brevity is the soul of wit; never believe mirrors or newspapers; DON'T PANIC; if it looks too good to be true, it probably is; courtesy costs nothing; if it ain't broke, don't fix it; faint heart ne'er won fair lady; to err is human, to forgive divine; before you judge someone, walk a mile in their shoes – then you're a mile ahead and you've also got their shoes.

A-Z of Barristers

Atkin Chambers

1 Atkin Building, Gray's Inn, London, WC1R 5AT
Tel: (020) 7404 0102 Fax: (020) 7405 7456
Email: clerks@atkinchambers.com
Website: www.atkinchambers.com

No of Silks 14
No of Juniors 23
No of Pupils Up to 3

Contact
Mr Andrew Burrows
Email: pupillage@atkinchambers.com

Method of application
Pupillage: Pupillage Portal
Mini-pupillage: CV and covering letter to contact during March 2011

Pupillages (p.a.)
Up to 3 funded

Income
(2011/12) expected to be £47,500

Tenancies
Three in the last three years

Chambers profile

Atkin Chambers was the first set to specialise in the law relating to domestic and international construction and engineering projects. It has a significant and growing international practice at all levels of seniority. Chambers success in this area has been recognised by the grant of the Queen's Award for Enterprise 2005 in the category of International Trade.

Type of work undertaken

Atkin Chambers is a leader in its field: technology and construction law. Members of Chambers have been involved in many of the largest high-profile domestic and international disputes in the fields of construction, technology, power, energy, computers and telecommunications of recent years, both in court and in international and domestic arbitration. Members of Chambers are regular participants as advocates and advisers in all forms of alternative dispute resolution.

Pupil profile

Applicants for pupillage should have a first-class degree or a good 2:1 degree. Postgraduate qualifications are viewed favourably but are not essential. Applications from non-law graduates are welcome. Atkin Chambers is committed to applying equal opportunities good practice.

Pupillage

Atkin Chambers takes recruitment to pupillage and tenancy extremely seriously. The pupillage award (anticipated to be £47,500 for 2011/12 – equivalent to the sums paid by other much larger sets of chambers) reflects this.

The Pupillage year is structured to provide all of the Bar Council's training requirements and the additional training Chambers considers is necessary for successful entry into high-quality commercial work of its practice. Atkin Chambers provides its own advocacy training and assessment in addition to that provided by the Inns.

Full and up-to date details of the structure and goals of Atkin Chambers' pupillage training programme may be reviewed on the website.

Mini-pupillages

Six mini-pupillages are offered each year. Mini-pupillages will be offered to candidates who have achieved or have clear potential to achieve the academic standards required for pupillage. Whilst all applications received will be given consideration, applicants are invited to apply by letter with CV during March 2011.

Sponsorship & awards

Up to three fully funded pupilages of £47,500 per pupil for 12 months are available. Funding for the BVC year by way of drawdown is available.

2 Bedford Row (William Clegg QC)

2 Bedford Row, London, WC1R 4BU
Tel: (020) 7440 8888 Fax: (020) 7242 1738
Email: clerks@2bedfordrow.co.uk
Website: www.2bedfordrow.co.uk

Chambers profile

Widely regarded as one of the leading crime sets in the UK, 2 Bedford Row continues to excel in the fields of crime, fraud and regulatory law. Chambers has been described by "*Chambers UK* " 2008 as a "number-one criminal set" and in 2010 by Chambers and Partners as having "enormously talented lawyers with approachable outlooks".

Type of work undertaken

Chambers has a broad-based criminal practice and its members have appeared in some of the most high-profile criminal cases of recent years (R v Barry George, R v Levi Bellfield, R v Mark Dixie). In addition, members of Chambers have particular experience in the fields of confiscation/restraint, health and safety, financial services law, sports law, professional regulation/discipline and inquests. Members are frequently instructed to appear before regulatory bodies such as the GMC, the FA, the VAT tribunal and the Police Disciplinary Tribunal.

Pupil profile

Chambers recruits candidates from all backgrounds who display the highest intellectual ability, excellent advocacy skills, sound judgement and a real commitment to criminal law and its related fields. Candidates will also be well-rounded individuals who are able to communicate effectively with a wide variety of people.

Pupillage

Chambers offers up to four 12-month pupillages each year. Each pupil will have two pupil supervisors in their first six and a different two in their second six. This ensures that pupils are provided with a thorough grounding in all aspects of Chambers' practice. Chambers also provides structured advocacy training throughout the pupillage year and will pay for pupils to attend the 'Advice to Counsel' and 'Forensic Accountancy' courses.

Mini-pupillages

Chambers welcomes applications for mini-pupillage. Please see the website for details.

Funding

Chambers provides a grant of £12,000 to each pupil, paid monthly throughout the year and, in addition, guaranteed earnings of £10,000 in second six.

No of Silks 21
No of Juniors 56
No of Pupils 4

Graduate recruitment contact
Stephen Vullo
020 7440 8888

Method of application
Pupillage Portal

Pupillages (p.a.)
12 months 4
Tenancies offered according to ability

Blackstone Chambers (I Mill QC and T Beazley QC)

Blackstone House, Temple, London EC4Y 9BW DX: 281
Tel: (020) 7583 1770 Fax: (020) 7822 7350
Email: pupillage@blackstonechambers.com
Website: www.blackstonechambers.com

No of Silks 34
No of Juniors 50
No of Pupils 4 (current)

Contact
Miss Julia Hornor
Chambers Director

Method of application
Pupillage Portal

Pupillages (p.a.)
12 months 4-5
Required degree grade
Minimum 2:1
(law or non-law)

Income
Award £52,500
Earnings not included

Tenancies
Junior tenancies offered
in last 3 years: 92%
No of tenants of 5 years
call or under: 13

Chambers profile

Blackstone Chambers occupies large and modern premises in the Temple.

Type of work undertaken

Chambers' formidable strengths lie in its principal areas of practice: commercial, employment and EU, public law, human rights and public international law. Commercial law includes financial/business law, international trade, conflicts, sport, media and entertainment, intellectual property and professional negligence. All aspects of employment law, including discrimination, are covered by Chambers' extensive employment law practice. Public law incorporates judicial review, acting both for and against central and local government agencies and other regulatory authorities, all areas affected by the impact of human rights and other aspects of administrative law. EU permeates practices across the board. Chambers recognises the increasingly important role which mediation has to play in dispute resolution. Seven members are CEDR accredited mediators.

Pupil profile

Chambers looks for articulate and intelligent applicants who are able to work well under pressure and demonstrate high intellectual ability. Successful candidates usually have at least a 2:1 honours degree, although not necessarily in law.

Pupillage

Chambers offers four (or exceptionally five) 12-month pupillages to those wishing to practise full-time at the Bar, normally commencing in October each year. Pupillage is divided into four sections and every effort is made to ensure that pupils receive a broad training. The environment is a friendly one; pupils attend an induction week introducing them to Chambers' working environment. Chambers prefers to recruit new tenants from pupils wherever possible. Chambers subscribes to Pupillage Portal; applications should be made for the summer season.

Mini-pupillages

Assessed mini-pupillages are available and are an important part of the application procedure. Applications for mini-pupillages must be made by 30 April; earlier applications are strongly advised and are preferred in the year before pupillage commences.

Funding

Awards of £52,500 per annum are available. The pupillage committee has a discretion to consider applications for up to £15,000 of the pupillage award to be advanced during the BTPC year. Since Chambers insists on an accessed mini-pupillage as part of the overall application procedure, financial assistance is offered either in respect of out of pocket travelling or accommodation expenses incurred in attending the mini-pupillage, up to a maximum of £200 per pupil.

Cloisters

Cloisters, 1 Pump Court, Temple, London, EC4Y 7AA
Tel: (020) 7827 4000 Fax: (020) 7827 4100
Email: clerks@cloisters.com
Website: www.cloisters.com

No of Silks 5
No of Juniors 43
No of Pupils 2

Contact
pupillage@cloisters.com

Method of application
Pupillage Portal

Pupillages (p.a.)
2 for 12 months

Chambers profile

Cloisters is a leading set with particular expertise in employment, equality, discrimination and human rights, personal injury and clinical negligence, media and sport, and public and regulatory law. Cloisters is known for its legal excellence, approachability, superb customer service and cost-effectiveness. It recruits only barristers who can offer these qualities.

Type of work undertaken

Cloisters acts for both claimants and respondents in all its practice areas.

Employment and discrimination: Cloisters continues to be at the forefront of this type of law. Recent high-profile cases include: Ahsan v Watt (HL) – issue estoppel in tribunals, liability of political parties for discrimination; Cadman v Health & Safety Executive (ECJ) – length of service pay increments; Coleman v Attridge (ECJ) – discrimination by association.

Personal injury: Cloisters' personal injury team continues to appear in landmark cases and highly complex cases involving large sums. One of their specialisms is in cases involving occupational stress or bullying at work, which contain elements of both personal injury and employment law. Recent high-profile cases include: A v Hoare (the Lotto Rapist) (HL) – limitation periods; Sarwar v (1) Ali (2) MIB – highest-ever gross award in a personal injury case of £9.5m; Majrowski v Guy's and St. Thomas' NHS Trust (HL) – employers' vicarious liability for harassment by employees to other employees at work.

Clinical negligence: In 2007 members of the PI and clinical negligence team and their instructing solicitors secured more than £100m for claimants. The set has the knowledge and experience to handle the full spectrum of work, right up to the multimillion-pound catastrophic claims, and regularly appears on such instructions. They handle a full range of cases, including cases worth more than £10m. Recent major cases include: H v Powys Health Board – highest-ever clinical negligence award of £10.7m.

Sport: Cloisters' sport practitioners handle disciplinary regulations, consultative work, litigation, non-professional sporting activity cases and matters arising from sports and entertainment cases, such as employment or contractual issues. For example, Cloisters has acted for Dwayne Chambers, Sam Allardyce, Status Quo and Frank Warren, among others.

Pupil profile

Chambers welcomes applications from outstanding candidates from all backgrounds and academic disciplines, including lawyers coming late to the Bar.

Pupillage

Chambers offers two 12-month pupillages to those wishing to practise full-time at the Bar, normally commencing in October each year. Each pupil is supervised and the supervisor changes every three months to show the pupil different areas of practice. Second six pupils will be allocated work by clerks subject to availability of work and pupil ability.

Internship programme

Cloisters offers 12 one-week internship placements each year. All applicants must have completed at least their first year at university in any subject. The internships are unfunded, but we may pay travel costs in the event that an internee is asked to travel to court outside of London. Internship is not assessed and is not a requirement for applications for pupillage.

Funding

Cloisters offers two funded pupillages each year. Each pupil will receive an award (currently £35,000 per year). Pupils can also ask for an advance.

Crown Office Chambers

Head of Chambers: Andrew Bartlett QC
2 Crown Office Row, Temple, London, EC4Y 7HJ
Tel: (020) 7797 8100 Fax: (020) 7797 8101
Email: mail@crownofficechambers.com
Website: www.crownofficechambers.com

Chambers profile

Crown Office Chambers is one of the foremost sets of chambers specialising in civil common law work. The majority of members undertake at least some personal injury work, and some practise solely in that area. Chambers has an established reputation in other areas including construction, professional negligence, commercial contracts, insurance and product liability. It is not a 'pure commercial' set, and pupils will see a range of work during pupillage.

Pupil profile

Members pride themselves on their professionalism, an astute and business-orientated awareness of the practical needs of solicitors and lay clients, combined with an approachable and unstuffy attitude to their work. Chambers looks for the same in its pupils, all of whom are regarded as having strong tenancy potential. Pupils are expected to display the motivation, dedication and intelligence which are the hallmarks of a first-class barrister. Academically, they should have a first or upper second-class honours degree (not necessarily in law), a flair for oral and written advocacy, and a strong and committed work ethic.

Pupillage

Pupils rotate through three pupil supervisors during the course of the year. In their second six, pupils are briefed to attend County Court hearings on their own, probably at least two or three times per week. Generally these will be small personal injury cases. Pupils receive regular feedback on their work from pupil supervisors and other members of chambers. They also undertake a series of advocacy exercises in front of a panel of four members of chambers and receive extensive feedback after each exercise. There are also two assessed written exercises during the course of pupillage. Tenancy decisions are made in early July.

Mini-pupillage

Limited number of mini-pupillages in selected weeks throughout the year. Online application form downloadable from Chambers website.

No of Silks 14
No of Juniors 70
No of Pupils 3

Contact
David Myhill

Method of application
Online application form, downloadable from chambers website

Pupillages (p.a.)
Up to three per year, 12 months
£42,500 plus earnings

Tenancies
No of tenancies offered in last 3 years: 6

CROWN OFFICE CHAMBERS

One Essex Court

Chambers of Lord Grabiner QC, One Essex Court, Temple, London, EC4Y 9AR
Tel: (020) 7583 2000 Fax: (020) 7583 0118
Email: clerks@oeclaw.co.uk Website: www.oeclaw.co.uk

No of Silks 24
No of Juniors 44
No of Pupils 4

Contact
Joanne Huxley, Secretary to the Pupillage Committee

Method of application
Pupillage Portal

Pupillages (p.a.)
4 12-month
Required degree grade
Minimum 2:1
(law or non-law)

Income
Award £60,000

Chambers profile

One Essex Court is a pre-eminent set of barristers' chambers, specialising in commercial litigation. Members provide specialist advice and advocacy services worldwide, which include all areas of dispute resolution, litigation and arbitration.

Type of work undertaken

Chambers' work embraces all aspects of domestic and international trade, commerce and finance. Members of Chambers are recognised specialists in the many diverse fields characterised as commercial disputes, also regularly accepting nominations as arbitrators, mediators and experts. Chambers' work includes, but is not limited to: arbitration, banking and finance, civil fraud, commercial litigation, company and insolvency, competition and EU, energy (oil, gas and utilities), financial services, insurance, IP, professional negligence and revenue law.

Pupil profile

Chambers has for many years maintained a policy of active recruitment and expansion and only offers pupillage to those who are thought capable of becoming tenants. Provided a candidate is proven to have the requisite ability, no distinction is drawn between candidates who do and those who do not have a law degree. Pupils at One Essex Court do not compete against one another for a predetermined maximum intake.

Pupillage

Four guaranteed 12-month pupillages are offered per year, each with substantial funding. From the beginning, pupils assist pupil supervisors with their papers, do legal research, draft opinions, pleadings and skeleton arguments. There are substantial opportunities for advocacy in the second six months of pupillage. Chambers subscribes to Pupillage Portal.

Mini-pupillage

Mini-pupillages last for either one or two days. They are not assessed. A mini-pupillage is not a pre-requisite for pupillage although it is encouraged as it can provide a good opportunity both to see how Chambers works and to meet members of Chambers. Please visit Chambers' website for the application process and deadlines.

Funding

Chambers offers each pupil £60,000, supplemented by earnings in the second six. It is understood that this is amongst the highest, if not the highest, remuneration package available to pupils. An advance of the Award is available, upon request, during a prospective pupil's Bar Vocational Course ("BVC") year.

ONE ESSEX COURT

Thirty Nine Essex Street

39 Essex Street, London, WC2R 3AT
Tel: 020 7832 1111 Fax: 020 7353 3978
Email: clerks@39essex.com Website: www.39essex.com
82 Kings Street, Manchester, M2 4WQ
Tel: 0161 870 0333 Fax: 020 7353 3978
Email: clerks@39essex.com Website: www.39essex.com

Chambers profile

Thirty Nine Essex Street is a long-established civil set. It currently has 84 members, including 26 QCs. Chambers has several members on each of the Attorney General's A, B and C Panels for civil litigation. Chambers prides itself on its friendly and professional atmosphere. It was described by *Chambers UK 2010* as 'Home to some "extraordinarily bright people"'. Chambers is fully networked and its clerking and administrative services are of a high standard. Chambers works very hard but it also has extensive social, sporting and professional activities.

Type of work undertaken

Commercial law: commercial regulation; construction and engineering; corporate restructuring; costs; employment; insurance and reinsurance; media, entertainment and sports; oil, gas and utilities; project finance.

Common law: clinical negligence; health and safety; insurance; material loss claims; personal injury; product liability; professional negligence; sports injuries; toxic torts.

Environmental and Planning: compulsory purchase; contaminated land; environmental civil liability; environmental regulation; international environmental law; licensing; marine environment; planning; nuisance; rating.

Public law: central and local government (including education, housing, immigration, prisons and VAT); European law; human rights; judicial review; mental health and community care; parliamentary and public affairs.

Regulatory and Disciplinary: medical; legal; social care and education; financial services; broadcasting, communications and media; sport; transport; health and safety; building and housing; local government standards; licensing.

Pupillage

Chambers takes up to three 12-month pupils a year. During the pupillage year, each pupil will be rotated among four pupil supervisors, covering a broad range of Chambers' work. The pupils will also do a number of assessed pieces of written work for other members of Chambers. There is an in-house advocacy course. Pupils work only 9.00 am to 6.00 pm, Monday to Friday.

Chambers is a member of Pupillage Portal. Applicants should consult the Pupillage Portal timetable.

Mini-pupillage

Mini-pupillage is an important part of Chambers' selection process. It is encouraged that anyone who wishes to apply for pupillage at 39 Essex Street apply for mini-pupillage. Due to the limited number of places available, not all applicants will be successful. Applicants should be in their final year before undertaking the BVC, save in exceptional circumstances. Applications are made between 1 September and 30 November. Selection takes place between 1 December and 14 December. The deadline for acceptance of offers is mid-January. Mini-pupillages take place between mid-January and July.

Funding

Each 12-month pupillage comes with an award, currently £40,000. Of this, up to £8,000 may be drawn down during the year before pupillage commences. Awards and offers are all conditional upon passing the BVC.

No of Silks 26
No of Juniors 58
No of Pupils up to 3

Contact
Pupillage - Charles Cory-Wright QC & Marion Smith
clerks@39essex.com
020 7832 1111

Method of application
Pupillage Portal

Pupillages (p.a.)
Up to three

ThirtyNine ESSEX STREET

4-5 Gray's Inn Square

Gray's Inn, London, WC1 R 5AH
Tel: (020) 7404 5252 Fax: (020) 7242 7803
Email: clerks@4-5.co.uk
Website: www.4-5.co.uk

Pupillges funded 2
Tenants 56
Tenancies in last 3 years 8

Method of application
Pupillage Portal. Candidates should see Chambers' website for full information

Pupillages (p.a.)
Up to two 12-month pupillages

Annexes
None

Chambers profile

4-5 Gray's Inn Square is a leading set of chambers specialising in a wide range of work, including in particular public law and judicial review, planning and environmental law, commercial law, employment and human rights. A distinctive feature of Chambers is the large number of barristers who practise at the intersection of these various specialisms. Chambers believe its strong reputation owes a lot to this unusual diversity. Chambers is a large set, comprising 56 (15 QCs and 41 junior tenants), and takes a modern and innovative approach to the changing market for legal services. It has well-established links with the academic world and has a number of leading lawyers and academics among its associate tenants. It is fully committed to the Bar's responsibilities as a profession and members of Chambers frequently undertake work in a pro bono capacity. Chambers prides itself on being not only a high-quality set, but a friendly one.

Type of work undertaken

General public law (including judicial review applications for and against local government and human rights challenges); planning and environmental law (including inquiries, statutory appeals and judicial review applications) on behalf of developers and planning authorities, and all aspects of domestic and EU environmental law; employment law (including unfair dismissal, sex, race, disability and other prohibited discrimination and trade union law); commercial law (including fraud, banking, shipping, regulatory work, insurance and reinsurance); professional negligence (including actions involving property, education and solicitors); education (including human rights and discrimination, special educational needs, admissions, exclusions and transport).

Pupil profile

Chambers has a rigorous selection procedure for pupillage. To obtain a first interview, candidates must show first-class academic ability (though not necessarily a first-class degree) and strong evidence of advocacy potential. Successful interview candidates will be expected to demonstrate exceptional legal problem-solving and advocacy ability.

Pupillage

Pupils will receive a thorough training in the full range of Chambers' work during their pupillage. During the pupillage, pupils will generally be assigned to three or four different members of Chambers (pupil supervisors) to ensure they see the full range of work in which Chambers specialises. There may be some opportunity for pupils to gain advocacy experience by appearing in employment tribunals or in court. To gain additional advocacy experience pupils may take cases for the Free Representation Unit, which can be done both prior to and during pupillage. Chambers pays for all new tenants to attend the annual Advanced International Advocacy Course at Keble College in Oxford.

Mini-pupillages

Chambers welcomes applications for mini-pupillages. The deadlines for mini-pupillage applications and details of Chambers' annual open day can be found on our website.

Funding

Chambers normally offers up to two 12-month pupillages, each carrying an award of a minimum of £37,000 (2010 figure) with the possibility to draw down up to £10,000 in the BVC year at Chambers' discretion.

4-5 Gray's Inn Square

Henderson Chambers

2 Harcourt Buildings, Temple, London EC4Y 9DB
Tel: (020) 7583 9020
Fax: (020) 7583 2686
Email: clerks@hendersonchambers.co.uk
Website: www.hendersonchambers.co.uk

Chambers profile

Henderson Chambers is a leading civil common law/commercial chambers. Chambers has acknowledged expertise in all of its principal areas of practice, and members of Chambers and its pupils are frequently involved in high-profile commercial and common law litigation.

Type of work undertaken

Chambers has unrivalled expertise in product liability (which covers a wide range of commercial work including sale of goods and insurance disputes, multi-party pharmaceutical and medical device claims and regulatory and enforcement proceedings) and is consistently rated as the leading set of chambers in this area. Henderson Chambers is also widely recognised for the excellence of its health and safety work.

Members are also noted for their expertise and experience in areas including: employment law, regulatory and disciplinary proceedings, public law and judicial review, personal injury, property law, and technology and construction.

Pupil profile

Chambers looks for individuals who can demonstrate a first-class intellect whether via the traditional route of an outstanding higher education record or via proof of success in other professions, in business or in employment. Henderson Chambers is friendly and sociable, and expects candidates to be able to show how they have both worked hard and played hard.

Pupillage

Pupillages are for 12 months, usually with four different pupil supervisors for three months each. Pupils have the opportunity to spend four weeks in Brussels at McDermott Will & Emery in order to experience European practice at first hand. Pupils will attend court regularly during their second six months.

Mini-pupillage

Chambers offers unassessed mini-pupillages. Applications are by way of a CV and covering letter, which should be addressed to Richard Roberts.

Funding

Chambers offers a maximum of three, and usually two, funded 12-month pupillages with minimum remuneration of £42,500. This consists of an award of £35,000 and guaranteed earnings of £7,500 during the second six months.

No of Silks 8
No of Juniors 32
No of Pupils 2

Contact
Hannah Wilson
pupillages@hendersonchambers.co.uk

Method of application
Pupillage Portal

Pupillages (p.a.)
1-3 (usually 2) 12 month pupillages offered.
Remuneration for pupillage: £42,500 for 12 months (£35,000 award, £7,500 guaranteed earnings)

Tenancies
5 in the last 3 years.

Keating Chambers

15 Essex Street, London, WC2R 3AA
Tel: (020) 7544 2600
Fax: (020) 7544 2700

No of Silks 20
No of Juniors 31
No of Pupils currently 4

Contact
ebrowne@keatingchambers.com

Method of application
Pupillage Portal

Pupillages (p.a.)
Pupillages (p.a.): 4x12-month pupillages available

Tenancies
3 offered in last 3 years.

Chambers profile

Keating Chambers is a leading commercial set specialising in construction, technology and related professional negligence disputes. Disputes often relate to high-profile projects in the UK and overseas and typically involve complex issues in the law of tort, contract and restitution. Chambers is based in modern premises outside the Temple. In their first years of practice, tenants can expect earnings equivalent to those in other top sets of commercial chambers.

Type of work undertaken

Chambers is involved in disputes of all shapes and sizes: from residential building works to multimillion-pound projects for the construction of airports, dams, power stations and bridges. Chambers has been instructed on projects such as Wembley Stadium, the "Gherkin", the Millennium Bridge, the London Eye and the Channel Tunnel. Much of Chambers' work now also includes developing areas such as IT, telecommunications and energy. Chambers acts as advocates in litigation and arbitration throughout the UK and internationally. Some are frequently appointed as mediators, arbitrators, and adjudicators.

Chambers' area of practice is dynamic and challenging. As leaders in the field Chambers is often in cases that are reported in the law reports. Chambers regularly publishes books, articles and journals.

Pupil profile

No specialist or technical knowledge of construction or engineering is required. A thorough understanding of principles of contract and tort law is essential. Criteria are listed on the website.

Pupillage

Pupils are allocated four supervisors over the course of the year ensuring that each pupil sees a variety of work of differing levels of complexity within Chambers. Comprehensive training is provided including a programme of advocacy exercises and provision for attendance at specialist seminars and lectures. For more details, see our website.

Mini-pupillages

Chambers offers up to ten funded mini-pupillages lasting one week and 25 unfunded mini-pupillages lasting three days. For further details, see website.

Funding

Awards of up to £50,000 are available. Of this, an advance of £15,000 is available during the Bar Professional Training Course.

7 King's Bench Walk

7 King's Bench Walk, Temple, London, EC4Y 7DS
Tel: (020) 7910 8300 Fax: (020) 7910 8464
Website: www.7kbw.co.uk

No of Silks 20
No of Juniors 27
No of Pupils up to 4

Contact
Emma Hilliard (pupillage secretary)
Pupillage@7kbw.co.uk

Method of application
Pupillage Portal

Pupillages (p.a.)
Up to 4 12-month pupillages offered.
Required degree grade Minimum 2:1 (law or non-law)
Remuneration for pupillage: at least £45,000

Tenancies
Junior tenancies offered in last 3 years: 4
No of tenants of 5 years call or under: 7

Chambers profile

7 King's Bench Walk is a leading commercial set of Chambers, with a reputation for excellence and intellectual rigour. The Legal 500 describes it as "One of the Bar's true elite".

Type of work undertaken

Chambers is at the forefront of commercial litigation, specialising in particular in the fields of insurance and reinsurance, shipping, international trade, professional negligence and private international law. Most of its work has an international dimension. Members regularly appear in the High Court (particularly the Commercial Court), the Court of Appeal and the Supreme Court, as well as in arbitrations in London and overseas.

Pupil profile

Applicants must have at least a good 2:1, coupled with lively intelligence and strong advocacy skills (both oral and in writing). Chambers encourages applications from all outstanding candidates no matter what their background or academic discipline.

Pupillage

Chambers offers up to four (but typically two or three) 12 month pupillages each year. Pupils will sit with four pupillage supervisors prior to the tenancy decision in July. Pupils will assist their pupil supervisors with their work, and accompany them to hearings. Pupils will, particularly after completion of the first three months of pupillage, also do work for other members of Chambers.

Mini-pupillage

Mini-pupillages are unassessed, and last three days. They are offered in three separate periods throughout the year: 1 June to 30 September (excluding August), 1 October to 31 January and 1 February to 31 May. Applications for mini-pupillages during these periods must be received by 31 March, 31 July, and 30 November respectively. Application by way of a CV and covering letter should be made to the Secretary to the Mini-Pupillage Committee. Further details of how to apply may be found on Chambers' website.

Funding

A pupillage award of at least £45,000 will be available for the 2012/13 and 2013/2014 years, of which up to £10,000 may be drawn down during the BVC.

7KBW
BARRISTERS

Littleton Chambers

3 King's Bench Walk North, Temple, London, EC4Y 7HR
Tel: (020) 7797 8600 Fax: (020) 7797 8699
Email: clerks@littletonchambers.co.uk
Website: www.littletonchambers.co.uk

No of Silks 12
No of Juniors 38
No of Pupils currently 1

Contact
Samantha Higgins, Chambers Administrator

Method of application
Pupillage Portal

Pupillages (p.a.)
Pupillages (p.a.): 12 month 2 required degree level 2:1 (law or non-law)

Tenancies
£45,000

Chambers profile

Littleton Chambers is acknowledged as being a top class set in each of its main practice areas. Its success is based upon both the desire to maintain high professional standards and a willingness to embrace change. It prides itself on the skills of its tenants, not only as advocates and advisers on the law, but also for their analytical and practical skills.

Type of work undertaken

Littleton Chambers specialises in commercial litigation, employment law, professional negligence, sports law, mediation and arbitration.

Pupil profile

Chambers takes a considerable amount of care in choosing its pupils and prefers to recruit its tenants from persons who have completed a full 12 months of pupillage with Chambers. Chambers endeavours to take on pupils who not only have good academic skills, but who also show flair for advocacy and the ability to understand practical commercial issues.

Pupillage

Chambers generally offers pupillage to two people each year.

During your 12 month pupillage you will have the benefit of three pupil supervisors in succession. Your pupil supervisors will provide support and guidance to you throughout your pupillage, ensuring that you understand not only the nuts and bolts of a barrister's work, but also the ethical constraints which are such a distinctive feature of Chambers' professional life.

After six months pupillage, you will be entitled to take on your own work. Typically, pupils in Littleton Chambers have been briefed once or twice a week. Your pupil supervisor will provide assistance in the preparation of these briefs to ensure that your client receives the best possible service from you.

Mini-pupillage

Assessed mini-pupillage forms part of the pupillage application process. Mini-pupillages are not offered outside of this process.

Funding

Each pupillage is funded (currently £45,000 per year) and, if necessary, it is possible to draw down some of this funding during the year of Bar Finals.

Maitland Chambers

7 Stone Buildings, Lincoln's Inn, London WC2A 3SZ
Tel: (020) 7406 1200 Fax: (020) 7406 1300
Email: clerks@maitlandchambers.com
Website: www.maitlandchambers.com

Chambers profile

Chambers UK has rated Maitland as the pre-eminent commercial chancery litigation set every year since 2001.

Type of work undertaken

Maitland is instructed on a very wide range of cases – from major international litigation to county court disputes. Much of the work is done in London, though the set frequently advises and appears for clients in other parts of the United Kingdom and abroad. Barristers are recommended as leaders in their field in commercial chancery, company, charities, insolvency, media and entertainment, traditional chancery, property litigation, partnership, pensions, banking, energy, tax, agriculture and professional negligence.

Pupil profile

Academically, Maitland looks for a first or upper second. Pupils must have a sense of commercial practicality, be stimulated by the challenge of advocacy and have an aptitude for and general enjoyment of complex legal argument.

Pupillage

Maitland offers up to three pupillages, all of which are funded. All pupils in chambers are regarded as potential tenants.

Pupils spend their first two to three months in Chambers with one pupil supervisor, in order that the pupil can find his or her feet and establish a point of contact which will last throughout the pupil's time in chambers. For the balance of the pupillage year, each pupil will sit with different pupil supervisors, usually for two months at a time. The set believes that it is important for pupils to see all of the different kinds of work done in Chambers so that they can be sure that the Chancery Bar suits them; it also gives different members of Chambers the opportunity to assess them. As each member of Chambers has a distinctive method of working, dividing the pupillage up in this way helps in developing a pupil's individual approach to work at the Bar.

The set provides in-house advocacy exercises for pupils during their pupillage. These take the form of mock hearings with senior members of Chambers acting as the tribunal. They, together with other members of Chambers provide detailed feedback after each exercise. These exercises are both part of the assessment process, and help develop court skills.

Mini-pupillages

Applications are considered twice a year with a deadline of 30 April for the period June to November, and 15 November for December to May. Applications should be made with a covering letter and CV (listing undergraduate grades) to the Pupillage Secretary.

Funding

Chambers offers up to three 12-month pupillages, all of which are funded (£60,000 for pupils starting in October 2011). Up to £20,000 of the award may be drawn down in advance during BPTC year or to pay BPTC fees.

No of Silks 18
No of Juniors 48
No of Pupils up to 3

Contact
Valerie Piper
(Pupillage Secretary)
pupillage
@maitlandchambers.com

Method of application
See Chambers website from January 2011. Application deadline for pupillage in 2012-13 is 1 February 2011

Pupillages (p.a.)
Up to 3 funded

Income
£60,000 p.a.

Tenancies
6 in last 3 years

Four New Square

Four New Square, Lincoln's Inn, London, WC2A 3RJ
Tel: (020) 7822 2000 Fax: (020) 7822 2001
Website: www.4newsquare.com

No of Silks 20
No of Juniors 51
No of Pupils 2

Contact
Georgie Ruane
Tel: (020) 7822 2000
Email:
pupillage@4newsquare.com

Method of application
Online: www.4newsquare.com

Pupillages (p.a.)
Up to 2

Chambers profile

Four New Square is a leading commercial and civil set of barristers comprising 70 members, of whom 19 are Queen's Counsel. Chambers acts as specialist advocates and advisers in a wide range of civil disputes and as expert advisers in non-contentious matters. Chambers has a particularly high reputation in the field of professional liability. The leading practitioners' work on the subject, 'Jackson & Powell on Professional Negligence', was written by Rupert Jackson QC (now Lord Justice Jackson) and John L Powell QC, and continues to be written and edited by members of Chambers.

Type of work undertaken

Professional liability, product liability, chancery and commercial law, construction and engineering, insurance and reinsurance, financial services and banking.

Pupil profile

Chambers does not stream its pupils. Each has an equal prospect of securing a tenancy. Selection criteria: evidence of intellectual ability; potential as an advocate; personal qualities such as self-reliance, integrity, reliability and the ability to work effectively with colleagues and clients; motivation. Equal opportunities: Chambers observes a policy of equal opportunities in accordance with the Bar Code of Conduct. All applicants are required to complete the Bar Council Equality Code questionnaire. This is used for monitoring purposes only.

Pupillage

The first six months: You will go to court and attend conferences with your pupil supervisor. You will also assist your pupil supervisor with their written work: carrying out written advisory and drafting work on their current papers and undertaking detailed research on the law. The second six months: During your second six months, as well as continuing with work for your pupil supervisor, you will take on an increasing amount of your own court work. Chambers places a strong emphasis on advocacy and supports its pupils in gaining valuable practical experience. You can expect to be in court on your own about once a week up to the tenancy decision and potentially on a more regular basis thereafter. You will be expected to complete three assessed pieces of work for members of Chambers who are not your pupil supervisors. Advocacy: You will also take part in a assessed moot. Workshop training sessions are run to help you prepare for the moots. Environment: Chambers aims to provide a friendly and sociable atmosphere. Pupils are included in Chambers' social events throughout the year.

Mini-pupillages

Chambers also offers mini-pupillages. Applications may be made at any time of the year. Mini –pupillages are for two days and are granted after a review of an application form by two members of Chambers. Chambers will pay expenses of £50.

Funding

Chambers offers up two 12-month pupillages with awards of £60,000, comprising a £50,000 award (of which £5,000 is paid immediately upon acceptance of the offer and a further £15,000 can be drawn down during the BVC year) and guaranteed earnings in the second six months of £10,000. Pupils are allowed to keep any earnings from their second six months, including any earned in excess of the £10,000 guarantee.

FOUR NEW SQUARE

Old Square Chambers

10-11 Bedford Row, London, WC1R 4BU D: 1046 Chancery Lane
Tel: (020) 7269 0300 Fax: (020) 7405 1384
Email: clerks@oldsquare.co.uk
Website: www.oldsquare.co.uk

No of Silks 10
No of Juniors 57
No of Pupils 2

Contact
Ben Cooper
Felicity Schneider

Method of application
Pupillage Portal

Pupillages (p.a.)
2 12-month pupillages

Income
£35,000 (£25,000 award plus £10,000 guaranteed earnings)
Plus additional earnings

Tenancies
5 in last 3 years

Annexes
Bristol

Chambers profile

Old Square Chambers is recognised as a premier set in its core specialist areas of employment and discrimination, personal injury and environmental law. Chambers' defining quality is excellence, both in the specialist legal expertise it has to offer and in the customer service which it provides. Members and staff have a reputation for being approachable and unstuffy. Many members hold part-time judicial positions, sit on specialist panels, act as mediators, and edit or contribute to leading practitioner texts.

Type of work undertaken

Chambers' strength lies in the depth of experience and expertise in its core practice areas. The Employment and Discrimination Group is widely regarded as one of the foremost in the UK. Work is in all aspects of employment and discrimination law. Clients range from individual employees and directors to major trade unions, private and public sector organisations. Personal injury work covers all aspects of this wide-ranging and complex field, from employers' liability and road traffic claims to high-value head, brain and spinal injury cases, with particular expertise in disaster litigation and multi-party actions. In environmental law, Chambers has been at the forefront of developing litigation in the area of toxic torts. Members appear in high-profile multi-party claims arising from pollution of various kinds. Alongside its core areas Chambers also has expertise in professional discipline, clinical negligence, product liability, public inquiries, health and safety and ADR.

Pupil profile

Chambers assesses candidates on intellectual ability (usually a first or upper second degree will be required), potential as an advocate, interest in Chambers' fields of practice, ability to cope with hard work and pressure and interpersonal skills.

Mini-pupillages

Chambers runs a programme of mini-pupillages during the summer. Applications should be made through Chambers' website.

Funding

The current award is £35,000 (£25,000 award plus £10,000 guaranteed earnings). Pupils keep additional earnings from their second six.

OLD SQUARE CHAMBERS

Pump Court Tax Chambers

16 Bedford Row, London, WC1R 4EF
Tel: (0207) 414 8080 Fax: (0207) 414 8099
Email: clerks@pumptax.com
Website: www.pumptax.com

No of Silks 10
No of Juniors 20
No of Pupils 2-3 in any given year

Contact
Jonathan Bremner
pupils@pumptax.com

Method of application
CV and covering letter (non-Pupillage Portal)

Pupillages (p.a.)
Up to 3 funded

Tenancies
4 in the last 3 years

Chambers profile

Pump Court Tax Chambers is the largest specialist set practising exclusively in tax.

Type of work undertaken

All areas of tax work (both contentious and non-contentious) are covered. On the corporate side, clients typically include the 'Big 4' accountants and 'magic circle' solicitors sending a wide variety of work such as M&A, reconstructions and demergers and structured finance. Chambers' private client work comes from a broad range of sources – city solicitors, accountants, regional firms, chartered tax advisers and IFAs, who act for private individuals, trustees and landed estates. Much of Chambers' work concerns large scale litigation (especially in the field of VAT) and members of Chambers regularly appear in the Tax Tribunals, the High Court, the Court of Appeal, the Supreme Court and the ECJ.

Pupil profile

Chambers looks for applicants who are intelligent, articulate and well-motivated. Successful candidates will have at least a 2:1 honours degree (although not necessarily in law). Prior experience of studying tax law is not required.

Pupillage

Chambers offers up to three 12-month pupillages (terminable after six months by either party) to those wishing to practise full-time at the Bar. Pupillage normally commences in October each year. Pupils will have at least three pupil supervisors and will also sit with other members of Chambers so as to receive a broad training in all aspects of the work of Chambers.

Mini-pupillages

The programme runs throughout the year. Applications should be made via email to pupils@pumptax.com with accompanying CV and marked for the attention of the Pupillage Secretary.

Funding

Awards of up to £20,000 per six months (£40,000pa) are available. The pupillage committee has discretion to consider applications for up to £8,000 of the pupillage award to be advanced during the BVC year.

Quadrant Chambers (Lionel Persey QC & Simon Rainey QC)

Quadrant House, 10 Fleet Street, London EC4Y 1AU
Tel: (020) 7583 4444 Fax: (020) 7583 4455
Email: pupillage@quadrantchambers.com
Website: www.quadrantchambers.com

Chambers profile

Quadrant Chambers is a leading set of barristers specialising in commercial law. Members of chambers act as advocates in court, arbitrations and inquiries, and advise clients from around the world, in a wide range of industry areas. Many also act as arbitrators and mediators. A number have dual qualifications in other jurisdictions including New York, California, Hong Kong, BVI, Greece, Germany, Australia and South Africa. Former members of Chambers have gone on to chair high profile public enquiries and to sit as judges in the Commercial Court, Admiralty Court, European Court of First Instance (EGC), Court of Appeal, House of Lords, and UK Supreme Court.

Type of work undertaken

Members of Chambers undertake all types of commercial law, including banking and finance, shipping, energy, aviation, insurance and reinsurance, commodities, international trade, sports and media. Over 70% of Chambers' work involves international clients.

Pupil profile

Quadrant Chambers seeks high calibre candidates with good academic qualifications (at least a 2.1 degree) who exhibit excellent analytical abilities and outstanding written and oral communication skills.

Pupillage

Quadrant Chambers offer a maximum of three funded pupillages of 12 months duration (reviewable at six months). During their first six months, pupils sit with two pupil supervisors for three months each, and are exposed to a wide range of high quality commercial work. Successful pupils are likely to be offered a tenancy during their second six months. Further information can be found on the website.

Quadrant Chambers will be holding an open day on Wednesday 8th December 2010 designed for those in the second year of their university degree or above. The open day will provide those interested in pursuing a career at the commercial bar with an opportunity to meet members of Chambers, learn about life as a barrister and see how Chambers works. During the day, members of chambers will give talks about life as a commercial barrister, and a senior Silk will hold an advocacy workshop. Places are limited. Please visit the website for details on how to apply. Quadrant Chambers is not a member of Pupillage Portal. Please consult the Chambers website for application timetable.

Mini pupillages

Mini pupillages are encouraged to enable potential pupils to experience the work of Quadrant Chambers before committing themselves to an application for full pupillage. Please refer to the Chambers website for more details.

Funding

Awards of £55,000 p.a. are available for each pupillage, part of which may be advanced during the BPTC year, at the Pupillage Committee's discretion.

No of Silks 12
No of Juniors 37

Contact
Secretary to Pupillage Committee

Method of application
Chambers' application form

Pupillages (p.a.)
1st 6 months 3
2nd 6 months 3
12 months
(Reviewed at 6 months)
Required degree
Good 2:1+

Income
1st 6 months
£22,500
2nd 6 months
£22,500
Earnings not included

Tenancies
Current tenants who served pupillage in Chambers 29
Junior tenancies offered in last 3 years 6
No of tenants of 5 years call or under 7

Serle Court

Serle Court, 6 New Square, Lincoln's Inn, London WC2A 3QS
Tel: (020) 7242 6105 Fax: (020) 7405 4004
Email: pupillage@serlecourt.co.uk
Website: www.serlecourt.co.uk

No of Silks 15
No of Juniors 36
No of Pupils 2

Contact
Kathryn Barry
Tel (020) 7242 6105

Method of application
Chambers application form, available from website or Chambers. Not a member of Pupillage Portal.

Pupillages
Two 12-month pupillages

Tenancies
Up to 2 per annum

Chambers profile

'Forward thinking Serle Court is an approachable, commercially aware set'. 'Widely admired by many, Serle Court has a host of excellent advocates' *Legal 500*. 'Able to field true specialists in most areas relating to chancery and commercial work' and 'no other set boasts quite so unstuffy an attitude' *Chambers UK*. Serle Court is one of the leading commercial chancery sets with 51 barristers including 14 silks. Widely recognised as a leading set, Chambers is recommended in 21 different areas of practice by the legal directories. Chambers has a stimulating and inclusive work environment and a forward looking approach.

Type of work undertaken

Litigation, arbitration, mediation and advisory services across the full range of chancery and commercial practice areas including: administrative and public law, banking, civil fraud, commercial litigation, company, financial services, human rights, insolvency, insurance and reinsurance, intellectual property, partnership, professional negligence, property, sports, entertainment and media, trusts and probate.

Pupil profile

Candidates are well-rounded people, from any background. Chambers looks for highly motivated individuals with outstanding intellectual ability, combined with a practical approach, sound judgement, an ability to develop good client relationships and the potential to become excellent advocates. Serle Court has a reputation for 'consistent high quality' and for having 'responsive and able team members' and seeks the same qualities in pupils. Chambers generally requires a degree classification of a good 2:1 as a minimum. Serle Court is committed to equality and diversity and encourages and welcomes applications from women, people of minority ethnic origin and people with disabilities, as well as candidates from other groups which are under represented in the legal sector.

Pupillage

Pupils sit with different pupil supervisors in order to experience a broad range of work. Two pupils are recruited each year and Chambers offers: an excellent preparation for successful practice; a genuinely friendly and supportive environment; the opportunity to learn from some of the leading barristers in their field; a real prospect of tenancy.

Mini-pupillages

About 30 available each year. Apply online at www.serlecourt.co.uk.

Funding

Serle Court offers awards of £60,000 for 12 months, of which up to £20,000 can be drawn down during the BPTC year. It also provides an income guarantee worth up to £100,000 over the first two years of practice.

3-4 South Square

3-4 South Square, Gray's Inn, London WC1R 5HP
Tel: (020) 7696 9900 Fax: (020) 7696 9911
Email: pupillage@southsquare.com
Website: www.southsquare.com

No of Silks 19
No of Juniors 25
No of Pupils 2

Contact
Pupillage Secretary
Tel (020) 7696 9900

Method of application
CV with covering letter

Pupillages (p.a.)
Up to two 12-month pupillages offered each year

Chambers profile

Chambers is an established successful commercial set, involved in high-profile international and domestic commercial litigation and advice. Members of Chambers have been centrally involved in some of the most important commercial cases of the last decade including Barings, BCCI, Maxwell, Enron, Marconi, Lehman Brothers, Northern Rock and Kaupthing.

Type of work undertaken

3-4 South Square has a pre-eminent reputation in insolvency and restructuring law and specialist expertise in banking, financial services, company law, professional negligence, domestic and international arbitration, mediation, European Union Law, insurance/reinsurance law and general commercial litigation.

Pupil profile

Chambers seeks to recruit the highest calibre of candidates who must be prepared to commit themselves to establishing a successful practice and maintaining Chambers' position at the forefront of the modern Commercial Bar. The minimum academic qualification is a 2:1 degree.

Pupillage

Pupils are welcomed into all areas of Chambers' life and are provided with an organised programme designed to train and equip them for practice in a dynamic and challenging environment. Pupils sit with a number of pupil supervisors for periods of six to eight weeks and the set looks to recruit at least one tenant every year from its pupils.

Mini-pupillages

Chambers also offers funded and unfunded mini-pupillages – please see the set's website for further details.

Sponsorship & awards

Currently £60,000 per annum (reviewable annually).

2 Temple Gardens (Chambers of Benjamin Browne QC)

2 Temple Gardens, London, EC4Y 9AY DX: 134 Chancery Lane
Tel: (020) 7822 1200 Fax: (020) 7822 1300
Email: clerks@2tg.co.uk
Website: www.2tg.co.uk

No of Silks 9
No of Juniors 43
No of Pupils 2

Contact
Leanne McCabe
Pupillage Administrator

Method of application
Pupillage Portal (Summer)

Pupillages (p.a.)
Up to three 12-month pupillages
Award 2011: £60,000

Chambers profile

2tg is regarded as one of the leading commercial and civil law barristers' chambers. The firm specialises in professional negligence, insurance and personal injury and also has significant practices in banking, employment, technology, construction and clinical negligence, alongside strength in private international law.

Pupil profile

Academically, you will need at least a good 2:1 degree to be considered. The firm looks for applicants who work well in teams and have the ability to get on with solicitors, clients and other members of Chambers.

Pupillage

Chambers offers one of the most generously funded, well-structured and enjoyable pupillages at the Bar. It takes pupillage very seriously and aims to recruit the best applicants, and to ensure that its pupils have an excellent foundation from which to start a successful career at the Bar.

Pupils have three different pupil supervisors during pupillage, and will also do work for other members of Chambers. The aim is for pupils to experience as much of Chambers' work as possible during their pupillage year.

Mini-pupillages

Chambers welcomes 'mini-pupils'. Generally applicants will only be considered after their first year of a law degree or during CPE. Mini-pupillages are a good way to experience life at 2tg first hand. Normally they last for one week. However, two or three day mini-pupillages can be arranged. Chambers aims to provide you with a wide range of work during the week. It offers an assessment at the completion of your mini-pupillage and encourages you to give feedback too. Chambers also offers help with reasonable expenses (up to £50).

Mini-pupillages are usually unfunded but a few funded mini-pupillages (maximum £250 per person) are also available.

Funding

Chambers offers up to three 12-month pupillages, all of which are funded. Its pupillage award for 2011 was £60,000. Please see our website www.2tg.co.uk for details of the award for 2012.

2tg Two Temple Gardens

3 Verulam Buildings (Ali Malek QC)

3 Verulam Buildings, Gray's Inn, London WC1R 5NT DX: LDE 331
Tel: (020) 7831 8441 Fax: (020) 7831 8479
Email: chambers@3vb.com
Website: www.3vb.com

No of Silks 19
No of Juniors 42
No of Pupils 3

Contact
Mr Adam Kramer (Pupillage)
Mr James MacDonald (Mini-Pupillage)

Method of application
OLPAS (Pupillage); CV & covering letter (Mini-pupillage)

Pupillages (p.a.)
12 months: 3
Required degree grade 2:1

Income
In excess of £42,500 plus any earnings

Tenancies
Current tenants who served pupillage in Chambers: Approx 41
Junior tenancies offered in last 3 years: 5
No of tenants of 5 years call or under: 11

Chambers profile

Sitting comfortably and spaciously in a newly refurbished and expanded row of buildings in Gray's Inn, 3VB is one of the largest and most highly regarded commercial sets, its members being involved in many of the leading cases, recent examples including the test case on overdraft charges, the $700m Springwell professional negligence litigation, the $600m Honeywell dispute, Rosemary Nelson enquiry, and the substantial Langbar National Grid and Central Bank of Ecuador fraud disputes.

Type of work undertaken

3VB's 17 silks and 42 juniors lead the field in banking and financial services, and are also among the top practitioners in the fields of professional negligence, civil fraud, insurance, arbitration, and company and insolvency. Chambers also has significant expertise in IT and telecommunications, energy, construction, and media and entertainment.

Pupil profile

Commercial practice is intellectually demanding and 3VB seeks the brightest and the best. The typical successful applicant will have a first or upper second class degree (not necessarily in law) from a good university, with good mooting experience and proven experience of the commercial bar (generally through mini-pupillages with us or elsewhere). Many have a Master's degree or other legal or commercial experience.

Pupillage

Chambers seeks to recruit three 12-month pupils each year through the OLPAS process. Chambers is committed to recruiting new tenants from its pupils whenever it can. Although tenancy is offered to all pupils who make the grade, on average two out of three pupils are successful in any one year.

Mini-pupillages

Three-day mini-pupillages are an important part of Chambers' selection procedure and it is strongly encouraged that prospective applicants for pupillage apply for a mini-pupillage (e-mail James MacDonald at minipupillage@3vb.com, attaching a detailed CV).

Funding

For the year 2012/2013, the annual award will be at least £60,000, up to £20,000 of which may be drawn during the BVC year.

Wilberforce Chambers

8 New Square, Lincoln's Inn, London WC2A 3QP
Tel: (020) 7306 0102 Fax: (020) 7306 0095
Email: pupillage@wilberforce.co.uk Website: www.wilberforce.co.uk

No of Silks	22
No of Juniors	27
Method of application	Chambers application form available from website
Pupillages (p.a.)	2 x 12 months
Mini-pupillages	Total of 28 places
Award	£48,000 (2012)
Minimum qualification	2:1 degree
Tenancies in last 3 years	4

Chambers profile

Wilberforce Chambers is a leading commercial chancery set of Chambers and is involved in some of the most commercially important and cutting-edge litigation and advisory work undertaken by the Bar today. Members are recognised by the key legal directories as leaders in their fields. Instructions come from top UK and international law firms, providing a complex and rewarding range of work for international companies, financial institutions, well-known names, sports and media organisations, pension funds, commercial landlords and tenants, and private individuals. Clients demand high intellectual performance and client-care standards but in return the reward is a successful and fulfilling career at the Bar. Chambers has grown in size in recent years but retains a united and friendly 'family' atmosphere.

Type of work undertaken

All aspects of traditional and modern chancery work including property, pensions, private client, trust and taxation, professional negligence, general commercial litigation, banking, company, financial services, intellectual property and information technology, sports and media and charities.

Pupil profile

Chambers looks to offer two 12-month pupillages. You should possess high intellectual ability, excellent communication skills and a strong motivation to do commercial chancery work. You need to be mature and confident, have the ability to work with others and analyse legal problems clearly, demonstrating commercial and practical good sense. Chambers looks for people who have real potential to join as tenants at the end of their pupillage. Wilberforce takes great care in its selection process and puts effort into providing an excellent pupillage. There is a minimum requirement of a 2:1 degree in law or another subject, and Wilberforce has a track record of taking on CPE students.

Pupillage

Chambers operates a well-structured pupillage programme aimed at providing you with a broad experience of commercial chancery practice under several pupil supervisors with whom you will be able to develop your skills. Wilberforce aims to reach a decision about tenancy after approximately 9-10 months, but all pupils are entitled to stay for the remainder of their pupillage on a full pupillage award.

Mini-pupillages

Wilberforce encourages potential candidates for pupillage to undertake a mini-pupillage in order to learn how Chambers operates, to meet its members and to see the type of work that they do, but a mini-pupillage is not a prerequisite for pupillage. Wilberforce runs three separate mini-pupillage weeks (two in December and one in July). Please visit the website for an application form and for further information.

Funding

Wilberforce offers a generous and competitive pupillage award which is reviewed annually with the intention that it should be in line with the highest awards available. The award is £48,000 for 12 months and is paid in monthly instalments. A proportion of the award (up to £16,000) can be drawn down during the BVC year.

WILBERFORCE CHAMBERS

Contacts

The Law Society
113 Chancery Lane,
London WC2A 1PL
Tel: 020 7242 1222
E-mail: contact@lawsociety.org.uk
www.lawsociety.org.uk

Solicitors Regulation Authority
Tel: 0870 606 2555
E-mail: contactcentre@sra.org.uk
www.sra.org.uk

Junior Lawyers Division
The Law Society,
113 Chancery Lane,
London WC2A 1PL
Helpline: 08000 856 131
E-mail:
juniorlawyers@lawsociety.org.uk
www.juniorlawyers.lawsociety.org.uk

The Bar Council
289-293 High Holborn,
London WC1V 7HZ
Tel: 020 7242 0082
www.barcouncil.org.uk

Bar Standards Board
289-293 High Holborn
London WC1V 7HZ
Tel: 020 7611 1444
www.barstandardsboard.org.uk

Gray's Inn, Education Department
8 South Square, Gray's Inn,
London WC1R 5ET
Tel: 020 7458 7900
E-mail: quinn.clarke@graysinn.org.uk
www.graysinn.info

Inner Temple, Education & Training Department
Treasury Building, Inner Temple,
London EC4Y 7HL
Tel: 020 7797 8208
E-mail: ffulton@innertemple.org.uk
www.innertemple.org.uk

Lincoln's Inn, Students' Department
Treasury Office, Lincoln's Inn,
London WC2A 3TL
Tel: 020 7405 1393
www.lincolnsinn.org.uk

Middle Temple, Students' Department
Treasury Office, Middle Temple Lane,
London EC4Y 9AT
Tel: 020 7427 4800
E-mail: members@middletemple.co.uk
www.middletemple.org.uk

The Institute of Legal Executives
Kempston Manor, Kempston,
Bedfordshire MK42 7AB
Tel: 01234 841000
E-mail: info@ilex.org.uk
www.ilex.org.uk

The National Association of Licensed Paralegals
3.08 Canterbury Court,
Kennington Business Park,
1-3 Brixton Road,
London SW9 6DE
Tel: 020 3176 0900
E-mail: info@nationalparalegals.co.uk
www.nationalparalegals.com

Crown Prosecution Service
Rose Court,
2 Southwark Bridge,
London SE1 9HS
Tel: 020 3357 0000
E-mail: recruitment@cps.gsi.gov.uk
www.cps.gov.uk

Citizens Advice Bureau
Head Office, Myddelton House,
115-123 Pentonville Road,
London N1 9LZ
Tel: 020 7833 2181
Volunteer Hotline: 08451 264264
www.citizensadvice.org.uk

The Law Centres Federation
22 Tudor Street
London EC4Y 0AY
E-mail: info@lawcentres.org.uk
www.lawcentres.org.uk

Free Representation Unit
6th Floor, 289-293 High Holborn,
London WC1V 7HZ
Tel: 020 7611 9555
E-mail:
admin@freerepresentationunit.org.uk
www.thefru.org.uk

The Bar Lesbian & Gay Group
E-mail: contactus@blagg.org
www.blagg.org

Lesbian & Gay Lawyers Association
c/o Alternative Family Law,
3 Southwark Street,
London SE1 1RQ
Tel: 020 7407 4007
E-mail: andrea@lagla.org
www.lagla.org.uk

Interlaw Diversity Forum (LGBT)
Email:
daniel.winterfield@simmons-simmons.com
www.interlawdiversityforum.org

LawWorks
National Pro Bono Centre,
48 Chancery Lane,
London WCA2 1JF
Tel: 020 7092 3940
www.lawworks.org.uk

The Society of Asian Lawyers
c/o Ingram Winter Green Solicitors,
Bedford House, 21A John St,
London WC1N 2BF
E-mail: info@societyofasianlawyers.org
www.societyofasianlawyers.org

Society of Black Lawyers
www.blacklawyer.org

The Association of Muslim Lawyers
E-mail: info@aml.org.uk
www.aml.org.uk

The Association of Women Barristers
E-mail: chambers@187fleetstreet.com
www.womenbarristers.co.uk

The Group for Solicitors with Disabilities
c/o Judith McDermott,
The Law Society, 113 Chancery Lane,
London WC2A 1PL
Tel: 020 7320 5793
E-mail:
Judith.McDermott@lawsociety.org.uk
www.gsdnet.org.uk

LPC/CPE Central Applications Board
PO Box 84, Guildford,
Surrey GU3 1YX
Tel: 01483 301282
www.lawcabs.ac.uk

Pupillage Portal
E-mail: enquiries@Pupillageportal.com
www.pupillages.com
c/o The General Council of the Bar,
289-293 High Holborn,
London WC1V 7HZ
Tel: 020 7242 0082

Career Development Loans
Tel: (freephone) 0800 585505
www.direct.gov.uk